International Marketing

Eighth Edition

International Marketing

E i g h t h   E d i t i o n

VERN TERPSTRA

University of Michigan

RAVI SARATHY

Northeastern University

The Dryden Press
Harcourt College Publishers
Fort Worth   Philadelphia   San Diego   New York   Orlando   Austin   San Antonio
Toronto   Montreal   London   Sydney   Tokyo

Publisher   Mike Roche
Acquisitions Editor   Bill Schoof
Market Strategist   Lisé Johnson
Developmental Editor   Jana Pitts
Project Editor   Laura Miley
Art Director   Scott Baker
Production Manager   James McDonald

Cover credit: Corbis Images Inc.

ISBN: 0-03-021112-3
Library of Congress Catalog Card Number: 99-074020

Address for Domestic Orders
The Dryden Press, 6277 Sea Harbor Drive, Orlando, FL 32887-6777
800-782-4479

Address for International Orders
International Customer Service
The Dryden Press, 6277 Sea Harbor Drive, Orlando, FL 32887-6777
407-345-3800
(fax) 407-345-4060
(e-mail) hbintl@harcourtbrace.com

Address for Editorial Correspondence
The Dryden Press, 301 Commerce Street, Suite 3700, Fort Worth, TX 76102

Web Site Address
http://www.harcourtcollege.com

THE DRYDEN PRESS, DRYDEN, and the DP LOGO are registered trademarks of Harcourt, Inc.

Printed in the United States of America

9 0 1 2 3 4 5 6 7 8   043   9 8 7 6 5 4 3 2 1

The Dryden Press
Harcourt College Publishers

To Bonnie—**VT**

To my wife and children: Beth and Rahul, Leela, and Meera—**RS**

The Dryden Press Series in Marketing

Preface

International marketing has become a necessary way of life for firms that wish to survive and grow in the dynamic world economy of the new millennium. New markets are opening and old markets are evolving. New competitors are appearing and old competitors are growing through alliances, acquisitions, and mergers. The global village is becoming a global marketplace. To paraphrase the poet, "No company is an island unto itself." This continuing globalization has forced both businesses and business schools to become more sophisticated about international marketing. *International Marketing* has evolved accordingly.

The eighth edition reflects recent developments in the world economy and their implications for international marketing. It continues to address the challenges and opportunities facing both small exporters as well as large multinationals. This text has been used around the world and has been translated into Chinese; there are new editions of it in Taiwan and Indonesia. The authors each have very broad international experience. Between them they have taught on every continent.

CHANGES TO THIS EDITION

All of the chapters and tables have been revised and updated. New examples are given in each chapter to illustrate current practice and problems. The hundreds of examples range from Avon, Amway, AT&T to Wal-Mart, Xerox, Yamaha, and Zenith. New Global Marketing boxes are added to provide more extensive illustrations than the shorter, in-text examples. There is coverage of such new issues and challenges as the Euro in the EU, a new chapter dedicated to the Internet, and the Big Emerging Economies (BEMs). There are also cases dealing with the environment, ethics, and the international marketing of cigarettes.

Overall, we have included expansive references to current international marketing literature to help advanced students and practitioners pursue in greater depth areas of particular interest to them. Supporting these new directions are several cases, notably:

- Agro Industria Exportadora, exporting agricultural products from Mexico.

- Indorayon, about the international marketing of wood pulp and refined wood pulp products from Indonesia.

- North American Watch Corporation, covering the development of an extensive watch product line ranging from luxury to low-end watches designed to address distinct market segments.

- Gucci, describing the growing role of luxury-goods marketing in global markets.

- The Indian automobile industry, about the spate of multinational foreign direct investment in an emerging market of great future promise but with a near-term threat of overproduction and saturation.

- Sony, in 1996, an update of an earlier Sony case and analyzing the implications of both the line of business and cultural shifts in strategic focus at the well-known Japanese electronics and entertainment multinational.

- Enron in India, about the risks inherent in multibillion-dollar, private-sector participation in electricity infrastructure construction.

INSTRUCTIONAL RESOURCE PACKAGE

The learning supplements provided with this edition of *International Marketing* have been updated and revised to provide instructors with effective and valuable teaching tools. The following ancillaries are available to adopters of the textbook.

Instructor's Manual

This comprehensive and valuable teaching aid combines the Instructor's manual which contains chapter summaries, chapter learning objectives, lecture illustrations, questions and answers, case teaching notes, transparency masters, and transparency teaching notes with a comprehensive test bank for instructors to draw from. The instructor's manual has been rigorously revised in this edition to provide professors with a thorough and up-to-date teaching tool.

Testing Resources

This valuable resource provides testing items for instructors' reference and use. The new edition of the test bank has undergone substantial changes. Approximately one-half the questions have been edited or rewritten. The test bank contains over 1,300 multiple-choice, true/false, short-answer, and extended-essay questions varying in difficulty. The test items are also available in a computerized format, allowing instructors to select problems at random by level of difficulty or type, to customize or add test questions, and to scramble questions in order to create up to 99 versions of the same test. DOS, Mac, or Windows formats are provided. The RequestTest phone-in testing service is also available to all adopters. Individual tests can be ordered by question number via fax, mail, phone, or e-mail with a 48-hour turnaround period. Finally, The Dryden Press is able to provide instructors with software for installing their own online testing program that allows tests to be administered over a computer network or via individual terminals. This program allows instructors to grade tests and store test results with greater flexibility and convenience.

Video Package

The video package has been prepared to provide a relevant and interesting visual teaching tool for the classroom. Video segments on the European Union and its struggle to develop into a global village and Pier 1 and its innovative relationships with the Third World represent just a couple of the video cases that support this package.

The Dryden Press may provide complimentary instructional aids and supplements or supplement packages to those adopters qualified under our adoption policy. Please contact your sales representative for more information. If as an adopter or potential user you receive supplements you do not need, please return them to your sales representative or send them to: Attn: Returns Department, Troy Warehouse, 465 South Lincoln Drive, Troy, MO 63379.

ACKNOWLEDGMENTS

Like earlier ones, this edition has benefited from the contributions of many people. We thank the hundreds of American, Asian, European, and Latin American executives we have worked with consulting, researching, and at seminars over the years. They have given us many practical insights and examples. Our students, both in the United States and abroad, also have challenged and stimulated us to sharpen our analyses.

Many faculty colleagues gave us cases, materials, and constructive suggestions through the editions. We gratefully acknowledge some of them: Robert Ballinger, Siena College; Andrew C. Gross, Cleveland State University; Donald G. Halper, University of the Pacific; Basil Janavaras, Mankato State University; A. H. Kizilbash, Northern Illinois University; J. Alex Murray, Wilfrid Laurier University; Philip J. Rosson, Dalhousie University; John K. Ryans, Jr., Kent State University; Dharma de Silva, Wichita State University; Steve Walsh, SUNY-Oneonta; John A. Weber, University of Notre Dame; Attila Yaprak, Wayne State University; P. Everett Fergusson, Iona College; Allan P. Miller, Towson University; Sheb True, Loyola Marymount University, Los Angeles; and Arturo Vasquez, Florida International University.

We also thank Professor Farok Contractor of Rutgers University for permission to include the Metro Corporation case in this edition.

We want to thank the ninety-five professors who responded to the market survey questionnaire with many helpful comments and suggestions for this edition.

Special thanks goes to Thomas Lloyd of Westmoreland Community College for his superb revision of the instructor's manual, test bank, and transparency masters.

We wish to thank our book team at The Dryden Press—Bill Schoof, Senior Acquisitions Editor; Rebecca Linnenburger and Jana Pitts, Developmental Editors; James McDonald, Production Manager; Laura Miley, Project Editor; Linda Blundell, Permissions Editor; Scott Baker, Senior Art Director; and Lisé Johnson, Executive Market Strategist for their commitment to excellence. Finally, we always welcome comments and suggestions from users of this edition, as it is through such feedback that we can continue to provide an up-to-date and useful product.

Vern Terpstra
Ravi Sarathy
July 1999

Brief Contents

Contents

THE INTERNATIONAL ENVIRONMENT

In Part 1 we look at the world environment in which the international marketer must operate. The economic, political, and cultural dimensions of the world's markets form a complex mosaic that constrains the practice of international marketing.

◆ ◆ ◆

Introduction

The Concept of Global Marketing

Chapter 1

Learning Objectives

International marketing has become more important to companies around the world for three reasons: Foreign markets constitute an increasing portion of the total world market, foreign competitors are increasing their market share in one another's markets, and foreign markets can be essential sources of low-cost products, technology, and capital. In a word, the United States and other major economies are now more interdependent with world markets.

The main goals of this chapter are to

1.   Show how the United States and other nations are more interdependent with the world economy.

2.   Distinguish between international marketing and marketing in the domestic context.

3.   Show the varieties of ways in which a firm may practice international marketing through the examples of firms such as Nintendo and Walt Disney.

4.   Describe how large U.S. multinationals increasingly market overseas through foreign subsidiaries as well as through exports.

5.   Emphasize that global marketing is a matter of perspective in which firms consider the whole world as their market.

"The world is too much with us," said Wordsworth. In a different sense, that could be the complaint of many domestic firms that see themselves threatened by imported goods. Import competition has been increasing. For example, imports were only 1 percent of U.S. gross domestic product (GDP) in 1954; they were 6 percent of GDP in 1964, 10 percent in 1984, 9.4 percent in 1991, and 11.9 percent in 1997. Exports and imports, as a proportion of GDP, have been increasing in similar fashion in most of the world's major economies. This book deals with the significance of this international interdependence for the business firm.

As data in Table 1–1 indicate, U.S. imports have been steadily growing, contributing to a worsening balance of trade. Although U.S. interdependence with the world economy is still less than that of many other nations included in Table 1–1, it is likely to increase. Many more U.S. firms, whether they like it or not, will be forced to become part of world markets and global competition. Meanwhile, other nations such as South Korea and Germany have had open economies for some time. Their firms are more accustomed to selling in international markets. Hence, U.S. firms have some catching up to do to compete effectively and gain market share in world markets.

International marketing is best explained by first briefly reviewing marketing in a domestic context. Although **marketing** can be defined in several ways, in this book we define it broadly as the collection of activities undertaken by the firm to relate profitably to its market. The firm's ultimate success depends primarily on how well it performs in the marketplace. This requires knowledge of the market. Therefore, the first task of the firm is to study its prospective buyers. Who are they? Where are they? What factors are important in their purchase (or nonpurchase) of our product? The second task of the firm is to develop the products or services that satisfy customer needs and wants. The third is to set prices and terms on these products that appear reasonable to buyers while returning a fair profit. The fourth task is distributing the products so that they are conveniently available to buyers. As its fifth task, the firm must inform the market about its wares; it must use marketing communications to get buyers interested. With the advent of the Internet, distance-mediated communication, sale and service become important even as they are facilitated.

Furthermore, the firm's marketing responsibility does not end with the sale. There is an implied warranty of satisfaction with the product; thus, the firm must often reassure the buyer, and, in many cases, perform after-sale service. In addition, firms must monitor the marketing activity of their domestic and international competitors and develop appropriate long-term marketing strategies and competitive responses. **Marketing management,** therefore, is the planning and coordinating of all of these activities in order to achieve a successfully integrated marketing program.

INTERNATIONAL MARKETING: A CLOSER LOOK

The activities just described—market research, product development, pricing, distribution, and promotion—together constitute the essence of marketing. What then is international marketing? **International marketing** *consists of finding and satisfying global customer needs better than the competition, both domestic and international, and of co-ordinating marketing activities within the constraints of the global environment.* Table 1–2 examines this definition in greater detail and breaks down the main components of international marketing into five objectives: finding and satisfying global customer needs better than the competition does, both domestic and international, and coordinating marketing activities within the constraints of the global environment.

Identifying Global Customer Needs

Customer needs can be identified by carrying out international marketing research. Such research helps the firm to understand customer needs in different markets and whether they are different from those of the customers that it currently serves.

| TABLE 1-1 | International Trade Profiles, Selected Countries ($ Billions) |

Year	Exports	Imports	Gross Domestic Product	Comments
United States				Major U.S. trading partners: Japan, Canada, Mexico and EU; major exports: capital goods and industrial supplies; major imports: capital goods, industrial supplies, consumer goods, and automobiles.
1996	$614	$803	$7,636	
1994	508.	682.	6,734.	
1992	440.	537.	6,020.	
Japan				Major trading partner: U.S.; major exports: automobiles; major imports: minerals and fuels.
1996	400	317	4,620.0	
1994	375.7	233.3	4,598.0	
1992	260.6	156.3	3,653.5	
Germany				Major trading partners: EU, U.S., and Japan; major exports: machinery and vehicles, major imports: vehicles, aircraft, and chemicals.
1996	519	448	2,361	
1994	261.1	232.7	2,054	
1992	275.6	262.1	1,807.7	
South Korea				Major trading partners: U.S. and Japan; major exports: semiconductors; major imports: machinery and transport equipment.
1996	128	144	485	
1994	120.00	127.8	381.3	
1992	98.2	104.8	308.2	
Brazil				Major trading partners: Latin America, U.S., and Europe; major exports: metallurgical products; major imports: raw materials.
1996	48	53	684	
1994	43.5	33.20	588.1	
1992	36.1	20.6	409.2	

Sources: *Economist Intelligence Unit*, Country Reports, various issues.

A U.S. company seeking to sell washing machines in Europe must know that Europeans often wash their clothes with hot water at a temperature of 60° centigrade, whereas in the United States most washing is done at lower temperatures. Companies also need to analyze market segments across countries in order to position their products appropriately for entry into international markets.

Satisfying Global Customers

If needs differ across countries and regions, a company must consider how to adapt its products and the various elements of the marketing mix to best satisfy customers around the world. If prices must be lowered, the company must consider how to design a product to lower manufacturing costs and decide whether to manufacture the product in a particular country to achieve lower manufacturing costs. A well-articulated distribution and logistics system is needed to make goods and services available at the point of sale in sufficient quantities. Firms also need to develop global customer databases and information systems to understand and respond to customer needs and purchasing decisions.

Being Better Than the Competition

Firms must contend with both domestic and global competitors. Global competitors could include large multinationals and state-owned enterprises that might not be profit oriented, as well as small local firms. Long-term success comes in part from assessing,

TABLE 1-2	International Marketing: The Essentials
Objective	*Corresponding Action*
Finding global customer needs.	■ Carrying out international marketing research and analyzing market segments; seeking to understand similarities and differences in customer groups across countries.
Satisfying global customers.	■ Adapting products, services, and elements of the marketing mix to satisfy different customer needs across countries and regions.
	■ Including in manufacturing and technology decisions the implications of costs and prices, development of global customer information databases, and distribution channel and logistics information.
Being better than the competition.	■ Assessing, monitoring, and responding to global competition by offering better *value;* developing superior brand image and product positioning; broader product range; low prices; high quality; good performance, and superior distribution, advertising, and service.
	■ Recognizing that competitors can include state-owned enterprises, other multinationals, and domestic firms, with different goals, such as market share over profits.
Coordinating marketing activities.	■ Coordinating and integrating marketing strategies and implementing them across countries, regions, and the global market, which involves centralization, delegation, standardization, and local responsiveness.
Recognizing the constraints of the global environment.	■ Recognizing that the global environment includes: —Complex variation due to governmental, protectionist, and industrial policies. —Cultural and economic differences. —Marketing infrastructure differences. —Financial constraints due to exchange-rate variation and differences in inflation rates.

monitoring, and responding to actions by global competitors, especially through understanding the competitive and comparative advantages enjoyed by competitors.

Coordinating Marketing Activities

International marketing creates a new level of complexity because firms must coordinate their marketing activities across countries. This can involve staffing and allocating responsibilities across marketing units in different countries and deciding which decisions to decentralize or to control from headquarters, whether to develop standardized campaigns and plans, and how much local responsiveness is appropriate.

Recognizing the Constraints of the Global Environment

As firms attempt to market in the international arena, they must cope with cultural and economic differences that exist in the marketing infrastructure, such as the structure and sophistication of the distribution system, the financial constraints imposed by exchange-rate changes and varying inflation rates, and the impact of government policies, especially protectionist and other policies that may unfairly benefit competitors and create difficulties in market entry. We discuss each of these issues in greater detail in the course of this book.

At its simplest, international marketing involves exporting products to a few countries. A firm becomes more of an international marketer as it increases its direct involvement in overseas markets by participating in pricing, promotion, after-sale service, and ultimately, manufacturing.

The company may begin manufacturing overseas to lower its costs in order to be able to match the lower prices of strong international competition. Sometimes it might manufacture and sell in the same market. However, a firm may not find it feasible to go alone into foreign markets. In this case, its international marketing endeavor becomes more complex as it joins with a partner that has specialized knowledge of a specific foreign market and its customers or, perhaps, good contacts in the local government. The partner may be needed to share risk and contribute capital, products, or a distribution channel. Sometimes the local government may prohibit the foreign company from operating in its country unless it has a local partner.

Companies unwilling to commit capital and management time to marketing in foreign countries might be happy to settle for less risk, less involvement, and lower returns by licensing their product or technology to a foreign company. The goal is still to earn profits from foreign demand, but the approach is indirect. Management is saying: "We'll take fewer headaches in return for lower profits."

Some firms find that the only way to match foreign competition in their home market is to sell foreign products imported either from factories established and operated overseas or from independent manufacturers overseas who make products according to designs and specifications provided by the home company.

Foreign customers can force a company to change the ways it does business. A foreign buyer may insist that the selling firm accept payment in kind: orange juice or wine or chickens in return for machinery. If the firm accepts the offer, it then finds itself peddling orange juice and chickens around the world, a consequence of the growing trend toward countertrade in international marketing.

Thus, international marketing can include activities such as:

Exporting.
Overseas manufacturing.
Working with local partners (joint ventures).
Licensing and franchising overseas.
Importing, sometimes from overseas subcontractors.
Countertrade.

INTERNATIONAL MARKETING MANAGEMENT

The complexity of international marketing is largely due to two factors: global competition and the global environment. Competitors with different strengths now come from all over the world. Likewise, the global environment presents a bewildering variation in national governments, culture, and income levels. As a result, domestic marketing management is often portrayed as the task of responding to the uncontrollable factors in the firm's environment while manipulating the controllable factors. International marketing management has the same task but with the critical distinction that both the "uncontrollables" and the "controllables" are different internationally. Thus, price, product, channels of distribution, and promotion vary across, say, France, Brazil, India, and the United States.

An added dimension of international marketing management is the coordination and integration of the firm's many national marketing programs into an effective multinational program. Indeed, a principal rationale of multinational business operations, as opposed to the alternative of independent national companies, is that the division of labor and the transfer of know-how in international operations enable the whole to be greater than the sum of its parts.

A practical result of these differences is that an international marketing manager requires a competence broader than that of domestic marketing managers or managers of marketing in a specific foreign country. Failure to recognize this may account for the fact that a majority of the blunders committed by American firms abroad are in the field of marketing.

In other words, the international marketing manager has a dual responsibility: **foreign marketing** (marketing within foreign countries) and **global marketing** (coordinating marketing in multiple markets in the face of global competition). These two aspects of global marketing management are discussed further in Chapter 6 and are illustrated throughout Part 2.

It is interesting to consider what international marketing managers think are the most important aspects of their duties and responsibilities. Professor Kashani at IMD, Switzerland, conducted a survey of marketing and general managers.[1] The sample was predominantly European (72 percent) and split among industrial products (45 percent), consumer goods, (21 percent), pharmaceuticals (14 percent), and services (20 percent). Their main concerns are spelled out in Table 1–3.

THE GLOBAL MARKETPLACE

Let us consider some examples of companies operating in the global marketplace to get a sense of the range of activities that constitute international marketing. It is helpful to see how different companies make decisions regarding their products, prices charged, distribution channels, countries sold to, and partners chosen, all in order to increase sales and profits.

Nintendo in America

Is there a teenager in America who has not played a Nintendo game? This 100-year-old Japanese company of the same name that originally sold playing cards began marketing the Nintendo game machine as "Famicom," a family computer, in Japan in 1983. The company test-marketed its computer in New York in 1984. By 1991 it had achieved a greater penetration with its product than that had by any other home computer or personal computer (PC): 30 million Nintendo machines had been sold to U.S. consumers.

The Nintendo machine is simple and is designed to be hooked up to the home TV set. The company calls it a "game" rather than a "computer" so as not to intimidate families. The first Nintendo machines did not have a keyboard, had no functions other than to play games, and were sold through toy stores, priced at just under $100 retail.

The United States had been through one video game craze with the Atari just a few years earlier, with the market peaking at $3.2 billion in 1983. Therefore, Nintendo carefully controlled the availability of games for its machines. It designed the Nintendo machine with a proprietary chip so that the game software cartridges would play on the Nintendo only if they had a complementary, compatible chip— one that only Nintendo could insert. Therefore, anyone who wanted to sell a game for Nintendo use had to license the game software to Nintendo, which then manufactured the cartridge.

Nintendo's licensing agreements also required that the software developers not sell the same game to other video game manufacturers. Such control enabled Nintendo to keep the games scarce and relatively high priced at $40 a cartridge. It prevented a proliferation of shallow and repetitive games, which it saw as the cause of the fading of the Atari-led video game boom in 1983.

As a result, Nintendo's U.S. sales increased from $800 million in 1987 to $1.7 billion in 1988, $2.5 billion in 1989, and $3.3 billion in 1990 before falling to $2.8 billion in 1991, with a U.S. market share of nearly 80 percent. Nintendo was able to capture one of every five dollars spent on toys in the United States.

Since Nintendo sold about 6 to 12 games for each machine, it was slow to introduce a technologically more advanced game machine. Meanwhile, its competitor Sega had been unable to dent Nintendo's hold on the marketplace. Hence, Sega introduced a 16-bit system called "Genesis" in 1991, about a year before Nintendo did. Sega also introduced a new CD-ROM add-on for Genesis, well ahead of Nintendo's plans to launch a similar system. However, Sega did not achieve much success until it introduced a new game, Sonic the Hedgehog, which was wildly attractive to young game players.

TABLE 1–3	The Major Concerns of Marketing Managers
1. Developing new products.	The pace of innovation is so high that every firm must be capable of launching new products in a timely fashion; time to market is a critical variable in determining competitive advantage.
2. Developing relationships with suppliers, distributors, even customers.	Complexity of technology and markets demands that companies develop long-term partnership relations with key suppliers to jointly develop products and processes; with distributors to launch detailed marketing campaigns in many countries; and with customers to learn about the utility of their products in use and cooperatively develop product modifications and new products.
3. Fewer but stronger global competitors.	The resource and scale needs of global markets are leading to mergers and acquisitions and greater concentration, resulting in fewer but larger competitors with greater resources and abilities to implement global strategies over a longer time horizon; this places pressure on firms to grow themselves, to seek alliances, and to constantly scout for partners or acquisition candidates; the alternative is to be swallowed up.
4. Enhanced price competition.	The faster commoditization of products, coupled with scale economies from being global, results in severe price competition; firms must either reduce costs themselves to withstand lower prices or innovate constantly to compete with differentiated products rather than price.
5. Greater regional integration and government regulations.	The European Union, NAFTA, and the ASEAN block are examples of the growing impact of regionalization on international marketing. Government regulations affecting international market entry such as local content laws and nontariff barriers are also important influences on strategy.
6. Developing a marketing culture.	Stressing that listening to the customer is paramount, that enhancing and using communication capabilities are essential to successful international marketing, and that beyond the customer are other important constituencies, such as the environmental lobby; and listening to their voices is much a part of the marketing function.

Source: K. Kashani, "Marketing Futures: Priorities for a Turbulent Environment," *Long-Range Planning* 28, no.4, (1995): 87–98.

Nintendo then developed a 16-bit "Super Family Computer" as its next-generation product. Because Sega had introduced its machine first, and had enjoyed some time in the marketplace free from Nintendo's competing 16-bit machine, Sega and Nintendo split the emerging market for 16-bit systems, with each firm having sold between 5 million and 6 million new systems by 1992. As with the earlier generation of systems, seeding the market with the 16-bit systems fueled the sale of a large number of relatively high-priced games (about $40 to $50 each). The intense competition led both Sega and Nintendo to cut prices on their 16-bit systems from about $200 to around $100 by year-end 1992.

Competitive pressure is typical for profitable industries: Nintendo in 1990 earned profits of $350 million on sales of $2.5 billion. Such profits attract competition, and Nintendo, therefore, later found it difficult to maintain its 80 percent share of the market. Yet Nintendo has been remarkably successful in holding a commanding share of the game computer market and in developing a strong brand image. Nintendo's success is due to its vision in seeing that middle-class families in the advanced nations worldwide were ready for an unintimidating family computer.[2]

Once Sega had begun chipping away at Nintendo's monopoly with its 16-bit Sega Genesis, Sony decided to enter the market with an even more advanced technology machine, the Sony PlayStation, which uses 32-bit graphics and plays games from a CD-ROM. These two features allow for more complex and faster games with breathtaking graphics, colors, and sound. Sega also launched a 32-bit CD-ROM–based game machine, and Nintendo seemed to be left behind, particularly as Nintendo's machines were still the older 16-bit–based technology, and it did not have plans to launch a CD-ROM–based game machine. Instead, it entered into a partnership with Silicon Graphics of the United States, a manufacturer of advanced computers used in industry for engineering and video applications. This partnership was to launch a 64-bit game machine, but still cartridge-based.

By acting as a gatekeeper, deciding which games would be manufactured on a cartridge for use with its machines, Nintendo was able to charge approximately 20 percent of the retail price as its fee. Not wanting to give up this lucrative practice, it eschewed the CD-ROM–based approach, which would have meant opening up access to its audience to third-party games from independent suppliers. Instead, it hoped that its advanced technology partnership would allow it to create fast real-time 3-D graphics, allowing it to retain its lead in the marketplace. Again, because Nintendo was slow to introduce a newer technology machine, Sony was able to gain considerable market share with its Sony PlayStation. By the end of 1998, there were over 500 games available for the PlayStation as compared to less than 100 for the N64, and Sony had about a two to one lead in market share over Nintendo. Sega had almost no sales as its machine was seen as less worthy by game players.

As PCs gain market share in Japan, the threat exists that games will be played on multipurpose PCs rather than on dedicated game machines. These technological uncertainties coupled with Sony's strong performance with the PlayStation, and Sega's planned introduction of a 128-bit game machine, will affect the continued ability of Nintendo to command the market profitably.

The game machine business is a fascinating example of how technology and marketing can interact in forming a profitable worldwide consumer-oriented industry and how environmental change can threaten market leadership. While competition and technological change challenge Nintendo in the dedicated game machine market, it has some strong weapons with which to counterattack: notably, its large installed base of users who continue to seek games for the machines they already own; a loyal group of customers who are satisfied Nintendo users and see no reason to switch; and its decade-long domination and swelling cash hoard, which allow it to cut prices and spend heavily on Research and Development to keep up with competitors' moves and technological change.[3]

Disney with a Foreign Accent

With characters such as Mickey Mouse that have been known all over the world from movies and cartoons shown for 50 years, Tokyo Disneyland was a logical creation. It began in 1983 as a joint venture between Mitsui Real Estate Development Co. and Keisei Railway Co. Walt Disney Co., however, has no ownership share; it designed the amusement park and supplies its managerial expertise, receiving in return royalties of 10 percent of gate and 5 percent of concessions.

Disney then began expanding into Europe. Construction of Disneyland Paris began in the summer of 1989, 20 miles east of Paris, at a cost of $2.8 billion for its first phase. The Paris location was chosen in part because 109 million people live within a six-hour drive. A high-speed train enables visitors from Paris to reach the park in 30 minutes. Unlike its stake in Tokyo Disneyland, Disney owns 49 percent, the maximum permitted by the French government. Disney began by promoting the Disney characters with corporate partners. Renault saluted Mickey Mouse in its Champs-Elysées showrooms, and Banque Nationale de Paris featured Mickey in promotions. Disney started a Disney Channel on European television in a joint venture with media entrepreneur Rupert Murdoch and aired Disney entertainment specials in Europe. Disney adapted the park to European tastes. "Fantasyland" focuses on the Grimm Brothers' fairy tales and Lewis Carroll's *Alice in Wonderland*. A "Discoveryland" exhibit draws attention to European thinkers such as Jules Verne, Leonardo da Vinci, and H. G. Wells. Signs are in multiple languages, and employees are expected to speak at least two languages.

In its first year of operations, attendance at Disneyland Paris was about 20 percent lower than targeted. High European admission prices, about 30 percent higher than at Disney World in Orlando, recession in Europe, and roads blocked by protesting farmers have been cited as some reasons for lower-than-planned attendance. Disney also encountered some labor problems because French workers were less willing to comply with stringent Disney standards pertaining to dress, hairstyle, and general appearance.

Disneyland Paris opened to high hopes in April 1992, but incurred continual losses for the next three years prior to registering a minuscule profit of 2 million French francs before extraordinary gains on a debt restructuring.

Why did this park perform poorly when Disneyland operations in the United States and Japan were such successes? Reasons include: (1) location—a 30-minute train ride from Paris with little else in the area to hold tourists' interest; (2) high prices; (3) a limited number of rides allowing tourists to see all of Euro Disneyland in a day and providing them little incentive to stay overnight at Disney-owned hotels; and (4) a European recession that cut down the number of visitors (attendance dropped from around 9.8 million in the first year to 8.8 million in 1993 to 1994, and about 9 million in its third year of operations). Competitors also emerged, such as Blackpool Pleasure Beach, Tivoli Gardens in Copenhagen, and Anheuser-Busch's Port Aventura in the sunnier climate near Barcelona, Spain.[4] For all these reasons, the highly leveraged amusement park, with over $3.4 billion in debt, incurred over $750 million in losses its first three years and was forced to restructure its operations. (See Figure 1–1.) Disney had spent heavily on creating a hotel complex around the park outside of Paris. However, since the park was only a short train ride away from the center of Paris, many tourists avoided staying at park hotels, instead opting to combine a day trip to the park with a hotel stay in Paris. This is quite unlike Orlando, where Disney is the major attraction, and tourists, principally Americans, seem to enjoy structuring their holidays around entertainment provided by Disney.

Disneyland's management postponed a second phase of expansion in which a second park similar to MGM Studios in Florida was to be built. They lowered admission prices by 20 percent, reduced hotel rates, and cut costs, including reducing employment from 17,000 workers initially to about 12,000, of which 4,000 are seasonal workers. Disney, the parent company, agreed to forego its royalty fees on ticket and merchandise sales until 1998, as did the banks, who agreed to defer interest and principal payments until 1998. These charges together are estimated to add up to FFr 700 million a year. Dropping them temporarily allowed the renamed Disneyland Paris to record a profit of FFr 170 million for the three months ended June 1995, and allowed it to nearly break even in the fiscal year ended September 1995. Disney management also added a new ride, Space Mountain, to attract teenagers, and obtained new equity from Prince Al-Walid bin Talal of Saudi Arabia, who contributed $430 million in equity, and who would end up owning about 20 percent of the restructured operations. The company's stock price, which was offered initially at 72 francs and reached a high of over 150 francs, dropped to about 7 francs when the operation seemed in danger of bankruptcy before recovering to about 15 francs in mid-1998. Disneyland Paris continues to be mildly profitable but faces high interest charges once the banks begin demanding interest on the restructured debt, and it may be a long while before it becomes an economically attractive investment.

Some critics have claimed that Disney can never be a success in Europe because of the cultural differences between the Disney approach to amusement parks and European consumers' expectations. What is clear is that even the best-run companies can face problems in transplanting their entertainment formulas to overseas locations.[5]

Table 1–4 compares attendance and spending-per-person figures during the first four years of operation for each of the three theme parks.

Spending figures are not strictly comparable as the Paris park opened in 1991, while the Tokyo park opened in 1983, and the U.S. park in the 1960s. What is apparent is that the Paris park has not been able to attract the same number of visi-

FIGURE 1–1   **Annual Attendance for Amusement Parks in Western Europe**

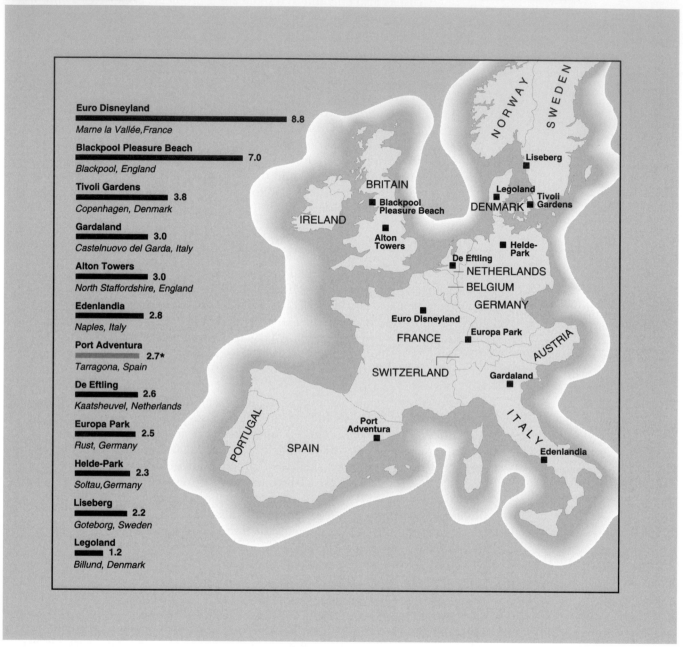

Source: *The New York Times,* August 23, 1995, C-19.

tors as the other two parks, with a shortfall of about 2 million visitors a year. This shortfall spells the difference between profit and loss and explains why the Paris park has been beset by financial difficulties.

You See the Nicest People on Japanese Motorbikes

The Japanese have long appreciated that international marketing can be profitable. In 1960 Japanese motorcycles were almost unknown in the United States, but Japan was already the biggest producer of motorcycles in the world. Its small (125cc) bikes were made for narrow and crowded streets and were affordable given Japan's low purchasing power. In the United States, motorcycles meant Harley-Davidson

| TABLE 1-4 | Attendance and Spending at Disney's Major Theme Parks |

	Disney World (United States)		Tokyo Disneyland (Japan)		Disneyland Paris (France)	
Year	Attendance (Thousands)	Spending per person	Attendance (Thousands)	Spending per person	Attendance (Thousands)	Spending per person
1	10,700	$13.08	5,683	$25.00	8,670	$85.00
2	11,600	14.78	10,151	25.52	9,800	68.70
3	10,000	18.68	10,700	25.34	8,800	53.30
4	12,500	18.90	10,950	30.00	9,000	NA

hogs ridden by the "Wild Ones," made famous by Marlon Brando—definitely not what the boy next door would ride. Japan set out to convince Americans to buy small 125cc motorcycles instead.

Beginning in 1960, Honda and then Yamaha and Suzuki began marketing motorcycles in California. Honda's ad, "You meet the nicest people on a Honda," was designed to change the image of motorcycles in general. Producing about 90 percent of the world's motorcycles, Japan enjoyed economies of scale that allowed it to price bikes at around $250, low enough to attract many new buyers who had never owned a motorcycle before. In addition, California was relatively close to Japan, and its citizens had a reputation for being willing to try new ideas and fads.

As sales mounted, the Japanese expanded distribution gradually across the United States, ploughing back profits into distribution and advertising. They also began producing and marketing larger motorcycles, convincing many of their customers to trade up to more powerful models. By 1966 Japanese manufacturers had about 85 percent of the U.S. market and were beginning to go after Harley-Davidson, with large bikes of 750cc and up. They also introduced new models of motorcycles, off-road bikes, and combination bikes for touring. In 1983 Harley-Davidson had to ask the U.S. government for protection as it tried to recover from years of losses and lost market share brought on by the inexorable march of Japanese motorcycles. What is astonishing is that Japan began marketing these bikes to the United States in 1960, at a time when few American companies took Japanese firms seriously as competitors.[6] Large numbers of Americans were converted into buyers of small motorcycles, a market segment that had not previously existed.

Profiting from the Newly Rich

Succeeding in international marketing has much to do with forming and understanding consumer tastes in different countries. Dickson Poon of Hong Kong has made himself a fortune estimated at $1 billion by selling luxury brand-name goods to the newly rich from Japan and the fast-growing countries of Southeast Asia, namely, Hong Kong, Malaysia, Singapore, South Korea, and Taiwan. While working as an apprentice in Geneva at Chopard, a jeweler and maker of fine watches, Poon absorbed the ambience of high-fashion, high-price retailing. Stores were understated, refined, luxurious, and there was no hard sell. He took this style back to Hong Kong, opening a European-type store with fine interiors in Hong Kong's most upscale shopping center. He emphasized attentive service and carefully selected merchandise, concentrating on brands such as Chopard, Rolex, Hermes, and Audemars Piguet. The concept worked, and he next obtained the Charles Jourdan fashion franchise, adding names such as Polo/Ralph Lauren and Guy Laroche, and obtaining, in some cases, licensing rights to manufacture and distribute franchise products in the Far East or even, occasionally, worldwide. His signature is an elegant shop in a prime location; he now

Dolls for Chinese Children

China has over 1 billion people, of whom about one-third are between 3 and 16 years of age, totaling about 375 million. Because population-control practices in China typically restrict families to one child each, parents and grandparents lavish much love and attention on the only child. Among other things, this means that they are willing to splurge on toys. Anthony Chirico, who founded Nanuet Entertainment, had been selling to China such U.S. TV shows as "G.I. Joe" and "Teenage Mutant Ninja Turtles." He saw a potential opportunity to increase his markets in China by selling Western toys there, and he teamed up with a client who had been marketing the Robotech line of plastic figures in the United States. Chinese children have traditionally played with toys made of wood and metal, and the newer colorful plastic figures priced between $1.60 and $30, Chirico speculated, might be attractive to them and their families.

The U.S. toy introduction was accompanied by an 85-episode cartoon series. Chirico began by licensing the TV cartoon show for nominal fees and by persuading the Chinese TV stations to allow his company to insert TV commercials for Robotech toys in the middle of programs. (Chirico also

operates over 70 such stores. But his winning insight is the appeal of famous brand names to newly rich customers. About one-third of Dickson's sales are to traveling Japanese businesspeople and tourists. In November 1987 he purchased S. T. DuPont, which makes luxury lighters and pens. His aim was to use the DuPont name to introduce new lines of menswear, luggage, and watches. His business is vanity, making a profit from it wherever it can be found.[7]

The Asian economic crisis that began in June 1997 hurt retail sales all across Asia and Dickson Poon was no exception. Sales dropped sharply as the newly rich lost their assets in the stock market and were threatened with job losses and recession. Even so, Dickson Poon continued to expand in Asia, developing larger stores, focusing on major brands such as Tommy Hilfiger and Ferrari and selling off a portion of his ownership in major European luxury goods firms such as Austin Nichols (UK) and DuPont (France). These equity sales allowed him to raise capital for further expansion in Asia at a time when the economy is reeling and competitors are running for cover. What he is banking on is the long-term continued growth of Asia as the recession winds down and incomes start rising again and new fortunes are made.

Korean Furs (for Less)

Similar thinking drives the world's largest fur manufacturer, Jindo Fur Company of South Korea. Jindo's goal is to develop a chain of stores selling furs worldwide. It targets the low end of the market—furs selling under $2,000. This figure was chosen because approximately 60 percent of all fur sales are at or below this price. In order to sell profitably at this price, Jindo uses Korean labor and vertical integration. It buys pelts at auctions in North America, Scandinavia, and Russia. Jindo then treats and assembles the pelts in its Seoul factories before selling them in its worldwide outlets. There are 45 Jindo fur salons, located in South Korea, Hong Kong, Europe, North America, Hawaii, and Guam. Although tropical islands might seem like odd locations, Jindo markets furs to tourists on vacation.[8]

Jindo began its worldwide marketing by selling in duty-free shops to Japanese tourists and advertising in in-flight magazines. As Dickson Poon also discovered, its discounted prices were appealing to Japanese tourists when compared with the high prices charged at home. Recently a joint venture, Jindorus, was established

had to overcome the Chinese preference for showing commercials in 5-minute blocks at the end of programs.) These negotiations took three years. The programs also were dubbed into Mandarin Chinese and were attractive to Chinese stations because their themes, family values, and world cooperation against aliens are not in conflict with Chinese values. A Hong Kong–based toy company supervised production of the toys in China and also distributed them. Chirico was able to convince the Chinese TV stations to start showing the Robotech cartoon series shortly after the toys went on sale in department stores.

The toys were first introduced into Shanghai and Guangdong, the most prosperous areas of China, and then into other provinces. As kids in Guangdong became exposed to Hong Kong TV, however, their tastes evolved to the likes of Batman. As a result, Robotech toys began to sell better in the distant provinces in northeast China, where newer fads like Batman had yet to catch on.

Chinese parents' preoccupation with their sole children is not limited to buying them toys. Chinese parents play English-language tapes to their unborn child, hoping to give the child a head start. Later, the child might hear Tang dynasty poetry, music, and the Roman alphabet and numbers, which could provide Western marketers new global marketing angles.

Sources: Andrew Tanzer, "China's Dolls," *Forbes*, December 21, 1992; and "Study This, Baby: Chinese Fetuses Bear Heavy Course Loads," *The Wall Street Journal*, February 8, 1994.

with Interlink of Russia. The first store was opened in the Intourist Hotel in Moscow, with additional stores to be opened as the Russian economy improves. Jindo sees a huge untapped market potential for furs, but attention to both costs and global marketing expansion is essential to its long-term success.

Where the Buyers Are

Sometimes foreign markets may be the only markets in which a company's products can be sold. Take water desalination, for instance. About two-thirds of the world's water desalination plants used to convert saltwater into fresh water are in Saudi Arabia. These plants use considerable energy and are expensive to run. Saudi Arabia has plentiful energy and high incomes, and it is a country where saltwater is plentiful, while fresh water is scarce. Ionics, Inc., of Watertown, Massachusetts, has built its business around water desalination, with considerable sales coming from North Africa and the Middle East.

Where the Ideas Are

Overseas markets can also be a source of new product ideas. Environmentalists in the United States and Europe have been pushing for cleaner, less-polluting electric cars to replace gasoline-powered vehicles in order to reduce dependence on imported oil. California has even mandated that 2 percent of cars sold in 1998 and after be emission-free. The practical problem is that electric-car batteries retain only enough energy to be driven about 60 miles before requiring a recharge. A battery that promises extended ranges—180 to 250 miles—and that can be recharged in minutes rather than hours is understandably generating much excitement. Its producer is an Israeli company, Electric Fuel Corp.

Electric Fuel is running a two-year field test in Germany with the German phone and postal services, car companies Mercedes-Benz and Opel, and Siemens. If the tests are successful, about 40,000 phone and postal services delivery vehicles could switch over to electric batteries. What's more, recharging is quickly accomplished by removing spent fuel cassettes and replacing them with new ones, the used fuel cells being reprocessed chemically at regeneration plants. These batteries are also safe;

GLOBAL MARKETING

Exporting Lumber to Japan

In the depths of the recession in 1981, Webco Lumber of Oregon watched its sales drop 80 percent from the 1979 peak, and over half of its employees were laid off or had left. Webco decided to look for some Japanese business. Participating in a two-week trade mission to Japan, led by Oregon's Department for Economic Development, it met with 60 Japanese companies. The trip cost $5,000. Barbara Webb, president, told the treasurer, Ronald Webb, "I don't think we can afford not to go."

Within six weeks of the trip to Japan, several Japanese companies sent representatives to the Webco sawmill. They were careful buyers, with exacting standards. They wanted hemlock, white fir, and Douglas fir grown in the Cascade range, harvested from the western slopes between altitudes of 2,000 and 4,500 feet. Such trees grow more slowly, leading to a tighter ring count and a more attractive grain. Twenty rings an inch is considered ideal by Japanese buyers, and eight rings are the minimum accepted. The Japanese use a traditional post-and-beam method of construction, which takes longer to build and is perhaps less strong than the interlocking frame of hidden two-by-fours that the United States uses, but requiring 20 percent less wood. More wood is thus left exposed, in accordance with the Japanese

Electric Fuel's zinc-air batteries, for example, operate at ambient temperatures and use a combination of zinc, zinc oxide, and air, instead of dangerous molten chemicals used in batteries from other developmental efforts.[9]

How the World Would Like to Smell

Gillette wanted to create an "intentionally global" fragrance—that is, a line of deodorants, shaving gels, aftershave, and related products that would appeal to men both in the United States and Europe. However, Carl Klumpp, Gillette's chief perfumer, knew that European men were heavier users of fragrances, starting with shower gel, then deodorant body spray, and perhaps finishing off with eau de toilette. American men own cologne and aftershave but don't wear them routinely—"less than one-quarter had a killer cologne for attracting women" and most felt that the subject was too personal to discuss with friends.[10] Klumpp, who might begin the day spending 30 minutes smelling different substances for practice, decided on a citrusy chypre family of fragrances for starters; then he asked four of the world's major fragrance supply houses to come up with a formula with his preferred smell. After much testing, Gillette launched the Cool Wave line of deodorants in 1992. It and the similarly conceived and launched Wild Rain line were enormous successes in both the United States and Europe. And while Klumpp swears by his nose, he also uses a gas chromatograph to analyze the aroma molecules in different substances, making it easier to combine fragrances and copy specific smells.

RISKS AND DIFFERENCES OF FOREIGN MARKETS: RUSSIA

Getting the product to the consumer can be quite a feat in emerging markets. Ben & Jerry's, the manufacturers of super-premium ice cream in unusual flavors, began a 70 percent joint venture with the company Iceverks, manufacturing and selling ice cream in Karelia, Russia, 700 miles north of Moscow. The companies deliberately waited two years before expanding into Moscow, as they did not want quality to suffer because of poor logistics and supply problems: There were shortages of refrigerated trucks, which had to be imported. Franchisees lacked freezers, and Iceverks had to sell or lease equipment to them so that ice cream could be kept frozen. Franchisees and their employees

appreciation for attractive wood grain. Hence, Webco had to be more careful in harvesting lumber that was meant for sale to the Japanese.

The Japanese use different sizes of wood, too. The American mill would have to change its sawmill setup and also its woodcutting process in the forest, where trees are "bucked" to the appropriate length. The Japanese buyer is also insistent on exact sizes, whereas in the United States sawmills cut large volumes that produce minor variations in standard sizes.

When Webco began cutting its first major Japanese order, a Japanese representative was on hand, and he would periodically stop the cutting to measure the dimensions. An order that would normally be cut in one and a half days took twice as long. Webco found that all of its Japanese customers insisted on watching their orders being cut, so it actually converted one of its buildings into a guesthouse for these buyers. While the unfamiliar sizes took longer to cut, the volume of Japanese orders enabled the mill to grow again and begin rehiring workers.

The Japanese buyers wanted high quality and a long-term relationship, extending even after the U.S. industry recovered and sales could be diverted back to U.S. buyers. In the past, U.S. mills had used export orders as a way of sopping up excess capacity, dropping them as soon as U.S. business became available again. Webco has not followed that pattern. The company's export business from Japan, says Barbara Webb, "is the only reason we are alive."

Source: "Small Sawmill Survives by Setting Its Blades for Exports to Japan," *The Wall Street Journal,* May 7, 1982.

had to be taught to be polite to customers and to restock inventory before completely running out of certain flavors. Franchisees themselves were selected based on personal contacts and trust: Iceverks chose a small Moscow distributor, Vessco, because key managers at the two companies had been classmates. Despite these efforts, continued Russian economic difficulties made profitable operation a distant dream, leading Ben & Jerry's to restructure their Russian venture and consider U.S. expansion instead.

A somewhat different tack was taken by Mary Kay in selling cosmetics in Russia. With economic liberalization, Russian women began to seek Western cosmetics. At the same time, several Russian state-owned enterprises privatized, and Russian women were often likely to get laid off in the downsizing. These women were seeking new jobs and stable income sources. Mary Kay thus found a ready-made environment for its products—reasonably priced American cosmetics—as well as for its sales approach of multilayered marketing. Relying on women acting as independent representatives, buying cosmetics for themselves at 40 percent off retail and then selling them in small groups of friends and acquaintances, Mary Kay found Russian women avid to take on the job of selling its products, particularly because a Mary Kay representative could earn $300 to $400 a month compared to an average salary for Russian women of a little over $100 a month. Mary Kay has had to train its representatives, of course, with more experienced representatives training new recruits in areas such as the quality and use of products, looking well groomed, being polite and complimentary to all potential clients, and even basic bookkeeping. Representatives from more distant locales face further difficulties, having to come to Moscow to replenish their cosmetics supplies. Mary Kay expects to have around 17,000 reps in Russia by the end of 1995, 60 percent of whom are full-time, and the company expects sales there of $36 million. Barring political stumbles, economic growth and a large population make Russia a promising market for consumer products such as cosmetics and ice cream.[11]

Grohe Faucets: When Exports and a Strong Currency Do Not Mix

Grohe is Germany's market leader in kitchen and bathroom faucets, exporting about two-thirds of its output. However, its U.S. sales are only about 5 percent of its total. One problem is that Grohe concentrates on European design faucets that are solid brass, a segment that is only 2 percent of the U.S. market. Grohe also manufactures mainly in Germany, where high wages translate to higher-cost products. The appreciating mark makes the company's products more expensive, giving an advantage to Italian competitors, for example. Pricing its goods in dollars to make them more attractive compared to the competition means reducing the sales price in marks. Grohe can reduce the strong D-mark's impact by buying materials overseas; for example, it buys one-third of its brass abroad. It has also diversified by acquiring German faucet maker Rost, whose faucets address different segments—commercial, industrial, and institutional markets. A longer-term solution might be to move some production out of Germany and to acquire U.S. plumbing fixture companies and smaller faucet companies in lower-wage countries such as Portugal.[12]

Piracy Lives On!

William Tay, owner of the *Hye Mieko,* saw his ship leave Singapore, headed for Cambodia with photographic supplies and general cargo. He lost contact with the ship when it was about 180 nautical miles from Cambodia. Having had another ship hijacked earlier and $2 million of cargo stolen, he hired a Lear jet to search for his ship. Searching in international waters off the coast of China, he found it 60 miles from Vietnam. The ship, which seemed to have a naval vessel in its wake, did not respond to signals, so Tay took some pictures and flew to Shanwei, 120 kilometers from Hong Kong, where the ship was expected to land. The hope was that the Chinese authorities would help recover the ship and its cargo. China launched a campaign against sea pirates and in 1994 alone investigated 209 cases of piracy, recovering 22 ships.[13]

Learning from the Examples

As our examples show, several reasons exist to market products internationally:

1. The most obvious reason is the market potential of world markets. Firms such as Nintendo, Disney, the Japanese motorcycle industry, and Jindo Furs have all benefited from exploiting foreign market potential.

2. Geographic diversification is another reason. Webco Lumber is a firm whose long-run prospects are brighter for having diversified internationally. (See "Global Marketing," "Exporting Lumber to Japan.")

3. Using up excess production capacity and taking advantage of a low-cost position due to experience-curve economies and economies of scale are other reasons. The Japanese motorcycle industry's thrust into the United States was aided greatly by its superior low-cost position.

4. A product can be near the end of its life cycle in the domestic market while beginning to generate growth abroad. Dickson Poon's export of brand-name luxury goods marketing to the Far East is an example of taking advantage of the general rise in conspicuous consumption that accompanies prosperity. Selling Robotech toys to China is an example of responding to lagging product cycles in developing countries.

5. Sometimes overseas markets can be the source of new products and ideas. Companies in foreign markets can become joint-venture partners, providing capital and market access.

6. Tested market entry methods can work in emerging markets such as Russia, as shown by Mary Kay. Emerging markets, however, require patience and sometimes innovative market entry modes as in the case of

Ben & Jerry's in Russia. International marketing can bring risks, expected ones as in the case of international currency risk for Grohe, but also unexpected ones such as piracy in the China Sea.

7. One of the most difficult aspects of international marketing is developing products with universal appeal, as illustrated by Gillette with its fragrances. Lego is faced with trying to make its bricks appealing to children in the Far East in the face of competition from video games. In addition, success in one country does not always translate to success everywhere, as shown by Disney's woes with Disneyland Paris.

8. Any successful international marketing effort will attract competition. Nintendo has seen its 90 percent video-game market share erode as competitors innovate with new products, price cutting, alliances, and persistence.

THE U.S. FIRM IN THE GLOBAL MARKETPLACE

Although the global market is attractive, U.S. firms have been slow to take advantage of it. The United States has always been one of the world's largest markets. It is also a self-contained, continent-sized market. For about 20 years after World War II, little foreign competition existed in the United States, but now foreign firms from all over the world vie for a piece of the U.S. market. At the same time, other countries have grown so fast and become so prosperous that their markets have become more attractive than the U.S. market. Examples include the fax machine, which initially grew rapidly in Japan, and only subsequently became popular in the United States as the Japanese market was reaching saturation. Likewise, the market for railroad cars now is small in the United States as compared to Europe, where train transportation is more popular. Also, the building of nuclear power plants in the United States has become strictly regulated, even though foreign countries readily accept them as a source of energy. Ignoring foreign markets and foreign competition has two dangers for U.S. companies: losing market share at home and not profiting from higher growth in overseas markets.

Export Sales and Sales from Foreign Subsidiaries

Larger U.S. firms have generally been able to participate in global marketing due to their superior financial and managerial resources. Table 1–5 lists U.S. companies with the largest **foreign sales from their overseas operations.** Firms such as Mobil (foreign revenues of $60 billion), Texaco ($59 billion), and Procter & Gamble ($36 billion) have insignificant exports compared to revenues earned by their subsidiaries located in other countries.

For almost every company on the list, it is more efficient to sell from their foreign manufacturing subsidiaries than through exports. It may even be that exports have no chance, either being too high priced in relation to local competition or being kept out by government barriers. Most of the firms on the list could not maintain their market share in foreign markets without establishing a foreign subsidiary.

The question of how much a firm should obtain from foreign revenues and how much it should export is unresolved. Is it better to be a Ford, with foreign revenues five times that of exports, or an IBM, with foreign revenues nine times that of exports, than to be a Boeing, which gets most of its overseas sales through exports from the United States? As we shall see later in this book, as market conditions and the product life cycle change, companies may find that effective selling overseas requires foreign subsidiaries and that such foreign subsidiary sales may replace exports.

TABLE 1-5	Foreign Sales of U.S. Multinational Corporations, 1997		
	Foreign Sales ($ billions)	*Total Sales ($ billions)*	*Foreign Sales (as a percent of total sales)*
Exxon	92.5	120.3	77
General Motors	51.0	178.2	29
Mobil	35.6	60.0	59
IBM	45.8	78.5	58
Ford	47.0	145.3	32
Texaco	33.3	59.8	56
Citicorp	21.6	34.7	62
Chevron	23.1	48.8	47
Philip Morris	20.0	56.1	35
Procter & Gamble	17.5	35.8	49
DuPont	16.3	39.7	41
Hewlett-Packard	23.8	42.9	56
GE	27.0	90.9	30
Intel	14.0	25.1	56
Compaq	11.2	24.6	45
Boeing	11.8	21.9	54
American International Group	16.5	30.6	54
Coca-Cola	12.4	18.8	66
Dow Chemical	11.3	20.0	56
Motorola	13.5	29.8	46
Xerox	12.4	21.6	57
United Technologies	10.1	24.7	41
Digital Equipment	8.7	13.0	66
Pepsi-Cola	7.0	20.9	34
Johnson & Johnson	10.9	22.6	48
ITT	4.1	8.8	47
3M	7.8	15.1	52
AT&T	7.3	75.1	10

Source: *Forbes,* July 27, 1998.

Importance of Foreign Direct Investment (FDI)

Companies can generate international sales from exporting or by selling goods made by their subsidiaries in foreign countries. Over time, exports tend to be replaced by sales from foreign subsidiaries for a variety of reasons: It is cheaper to sell goods made in a foreign country because tariffs and transportation costs are avoided; making goods in a foreign market slips by government protectionism and barriers to trade; and goods and services can be more easily adapted to the tastes of foreign consumers. Finally, exchange-rate effects can be avoided because goods are produced and sold under the same currency regime.

It is instructive to consider recent trends in foreign direct investment. The United Nations Conference on Trade and Development's (UNCTAD) 1994 *World Investment Report* notes that trade within a firm, between a firm's subsidiaries in several countries, was *$1.6 trillion in 1993,* or about one-third of total world trade. A U.S. Bureau of Economic Analysis (BEA) study also underlined the importance of trade by subsidiaries of multinationals.[14] The BEA reported that for the United States in 1993, 30 percent of exports were made by American firms and by subsidiaries of foreign multinationals, sending goods to their affiliates overseas. On the import side, about 37 percent of imports were from related companies of multinationals with operations in the United States. Moreover, U.S. multinationals earned $62 billion on sales made by their foreign subsidiaries. Thus, the magnitude and growth of foreign direct investment is just as significant in international marketing as are exports and imports from the parent country. The UNCTAD report notes that the 250,000 foreign affiliates of 40,000 multinational corporations had sales revenues of $5 trillion, or about three times the export-import transactions between such subsidiaries.

The total stock of FDI around the world was about $2.4 trillion in 1994, with the United States accounting for about $610 billion of that investment, or about one-fourth. Of the total stock of FDI in the world, roughly $580 billion has been invested in developing countries, and this figure has been growing rapidly; 37 percent of new FDI in 1994 went to developing countries as compared to 17.5 percent in 1988.

The United States is the single biggest recipient of FDI, with inward FDI stock of $504 billion. Other countries that have attracted large amounts of FDI include the United Kingdom—$214 billion—and France, Germany, Spain, and Canada, each of which has received FDI in excess of $100 billion. Inward FDI is mainly a function of the attractiveness of the country as a production site and as a local market. Surprisingly, Japan has received very little FDI, less than $20 billion. Japan's large continuing trade surplus coupled with its low levels of inward FDI means that Japanese companies face very little challenge for market share from their foreign competitors. This is a tremendous competitive advantage because they can use their domination of, and profits from, the Japanese market to fund and subsidize entry into foreign markets. Japan, however, has been quite aggressive in investing in FDI overseas and was the leading source of outward FDI between 1988 and 1990. This may have been an attempt to avoid the effects of a strengthening yen and to deflect trade pressures caused by a rising trade surplus. Since 1991, the United States has been the leading foreign investor, investing $69 billion overseas in 1993 alone.

Among developing countries, China, Singapore, Indonesia, Mexico, and Brazil have received the largest amounts of FDI, with their stock of inward FDI exceeding $40 billion each. China has been an attractive market in recent years because it has liberalized its economy and welcomed foreign capital. What the overall picture of FDI suggests is a simple but fundamental lesson: A company that is serious about international marketing must inevitably move to investing in key markets. This is borne out by the fact that FDI from developing countries is on the rise. Their share of outward FDI flows increased to 16 percent in 1997, from about 7 percent in 1989. Cemex's $2 billion investment in acquiring two of Spain's largest cement companies to become a leading player in Europe's cement market is only one example of the growing trend toward FDI by all of the world's leading multinationals, whether from the advanced nations or from the emerging market countries.[15]

INTERNATIONAL MARKETING: THE TRADE BARRIER OF THE MIND

As its trade deficit shows, the United States lags behind other nations in the general level of international trade activity. Then how does a U.S. firm approach overseas markets? In most cases, reluctantly.

As Kenneth Butterworth, chairman of Loctite Corp., puts it, "The problem really lies in the mind. That is the greatest trade barrier in America."[16] In other words, long insularity and overdependence on the American market have made American firms unsure about their ability to capture markets overseas. Culture, language, and environmental differences are sometimes intimidating. Firms from other countries, however, have certainly overcome such differences. And many U.S. companies are following

Lego and Strategic Adaptation

Lego comes from the Danish words "leg godt," or "play nicely." Lego toys seem out of place in today's world of video games like "Mortal Kombat," where putting together colorful little plastic bricks to build castles appears childish. But Lego, founded in 1949, thrives, perhaps because young children like to put bricks together to make pirate ships, bridges, and fortresses, which they can then take apart or use in imaginary games. Parents also like to buy Legos, finding them wholesome and something they might have played with when they were children. In fact, Lego found that about 13 percent of Lego sets in the Netherlands were bought for use by adults! About 80 percent of all children who play with Legos are boys, and Lego has been experimenting with pastel colors and themes that might appeal more to girls, such as dollhouses and nurseries. (See the Web site at **http://www.lego.com/scala/**) The newer Mindstorm line incorporates motors and batteries so that Lego creations can be programmed and made to spring into action.

Lego, which is a privately owned and secretive company, is enormously profitable. Its Danish-registered companies alone show profits after taxes of around $70 million on sales of about $900 million. Lego has another 23 companies regis-

suit. Loctite Corp., for example, insists on looking like a local firm, rarely posting U.S. executives overseas permanently. Over half of its employees are not from the United States, and most of its top managers have foreign executive experience, which has taught them the value of persistence and patience in approaching foreign markets.

Due to continued U.S. trade deficits, small and medium-sized businesses are being urged, both at the federal and state levels, to export. They can get help by signing up on trade missions sponsored by the U.S. Department of Commerce and other organizations. Export finance is available to carry export receivables for longer periods and to offer favorable interest-rate financing. The larger number of foreigners and immigrants hired by these companies helps them learn about opportunities in foreign markets, as well as efficient ways to approach these markets. A weaker dollar also makes exporting easier. From its peak in 1985, the dollar declined by 60 percent in 1995 against currencies such as the yen, the German mark, and the Swiss franc, before appreciating once again through 1997. Dollar depreciation makes U.S. products more competitive and allows U.S. firms to raise prices while offering goods and services priced lower than those of foreign competitors.

Ultimately, international marketing is a matter of perspective. The term *global marketing*[17] best captures this perspective of the world as the market, with individual countries being submarkets. For those who hold such a view, the distinction between domestic and international marketing disappears, and the focus is on market opportunities, wherever they may be.

THE APPROACH OF THIS BOOK

The sources of the differences between international and domestic marketing are to be found not in the functions themselves but in the parameters that determine how the functions are performed. Therefore, students of international marketing should be able to identify the relevant parameters and understand how they affect the marketing program. This book assumes that readers have that ability from their background in other marketing courses. Part 1 discusses the world environment in which international marketing is practiced. Part 2 analyzes the management of marketing in this multinational context. Part 3 deals with planning and coordinating the international marketing program.

tered outside Denmark, about which information is scant. However, Lego is finding that markets in Europe and the United States are mature. Sales grew in real terms by 2 percent in Germany, while dropping by 8 percent in the United States in 1994. A lower-priced U.S. competitor, K'nex, in partnership with Hasbro, has been gaining share. Lego has naturally turned to the East, with sales in Japan growing 14 percent and in Korea 50 percent (though from a small base). As families in India and China reach the middle class, Lego hopes they, too, will buy Lego bricks for their kids. Counterfeiting is a problem, though, because the bricks are easy to copy, and lower prices appeal to the generally lower-income consumers in Asia.

Lego's Legoland theme park near its Billund, Denmark, headquarters was opened in 1968 and attracts a million visitors a year. The park features miniature versions of famous landmarks such as the Statue of Liberty, as well as animals and rides all built from Lego bricks. More recently, Lego has begun building a theme park near Windsor Castle in London, called Legoland Windsor, which is entirely made of Lego bricks with one attraction being the heart of Paris. It is aimed at children 2 to 13 years old and stresses that learning is fun. For example, guests "ride" in cars built out of Lego bricks and focus on learning responsible driving. A similar theme park is scheduled to open in 1999 in California.

Source: C. Darwent, "Lego's Billion-Dollar Brickworks," *Management Today*, September 1995; "Lego Interlocks Toy Bricks, Theme Parks," *The Wall Street Journal*, December 27, 1994; "Playing Well with Others/ MIT's Media Lab; Interview" *Technology Review*, May 15, 1998; and Greg Johnson, "Legoland Contented to Build Slowly; New Theme Park Not Billing Itself as Rival to Bigger Neighbors," *Los Angeles Times*, December 17, 1998.

Part 1: International Environment (Chapters 1–5)

In domestic business studies, consideration of the environment plays a critical though somewhat unrecognized role in the behavior of the firm. A number of "environmental" courses in the curriculum deal with topics such as business and society, business and government, business conditions, and business law. In the functional courses, too, much attention is paid to the external environment of the firm. In marketing, for example, there will be discussions of buyer behavior, demographic trends, competition, laws regulating pricing or promotion, developments in retailing, and so on. Part 1 of this text attempts to cover the same ground for international marketing.

Part 2: International Marketing Management (Chapters 6–16)

The various functions of marketing as they are performed in the international environment are discussed in Part 2. An examination of the problems peculiar to international marketing should help to broaden the student's understanding of marketing in general as well. The foreign environment dealt with in Part 1 will then be seen to be the key variable in international marketing. In addition, Part 2 stresses the importance of an overall marketing strategy to shape and guide the formulation and implementation of specific international marketing tasks.

Part 3: Coordinating International Marketing (Chapters 17–19)

A second critical international aspect of marketing management, considered in Part 3, is the task of integrating and coordinating many individual national marketing programs into an effective multinational operation. A large part of our discussion centers on international marketing by manufacturers. However, the specific international marketing problems of service industries are covered in Chapter 16. We discuss and illustrate with many examples the large multinational firms' marketing practices. By this we do not mean to exclude small firms. Much of the discussion applies equally as well to small firms as to large ones. Many of the problems peculiar to small firms in international marketing are covered in the discussion of exporting throughout the chapters in Part 2. Another major influence is the spread of the Internet and of global computer networks, linking firms with their customers and far-flung operations of a firm with all of its internal divisions. A separate chapter focuses on how the Internet is changing customer-firm relationships and how the Internet and global networks may be used to communicate with customers, learn from them, and market to them. Such global networks also facilitate communication within the globally dispersed mulitnational firm, a possibility that enhances its international marketing capabilities.

SUMMARY

As foreign economies continue to grow and account for a larger portion of the total world market, and as foreign competitors actively seek market share in the United States, many U.S. firms are being forced into some degree of international marketing. This may extend to foreign manufacturing, carrying out joint ventures with local partners, licensing, importing, and taking part in countertrade transactions. The varied strengths of foreign competitors and the ramifications of dealing with different national governments and economic and cultural differences in foreign markets contribute to the complexity of international marketing.

Companies compete globally because (1) strong market potential exists overseas, (2) selling internationally allows them to enhance their long-run profitability, (3) low-cost production and quality are critical to successfully competing in global markets, and (4) they can achieve success by carefully choosing certain market segments, as witnessed by Dickson Poon's success in profitably marketing luxury goods to the growing numbers of newly rich in the Far East.

Large U.S. multinationals are more likely to get more of their foreign revenues from sales of their foreign subsidiaries than through exports. This can be a key element of strategic success in international marketing. More important, though, is a global marketing perspective of the world as one market, with individual countries treated as submarkets and the focus on exploiting market opportunities wherever they may occur.

QUESTIONS

1.1 What is international marketing, and how does it differ from domestic marketing?

1.2 Why is international marketing important to most U.S. firms?

1.3 Consider the examples described in the section "The Global Marketplace." Compare and contrast the international marketing actions of these firms. Focus on their choices in the areas of products, market segments, the sequential choice of countries to sell to, pricing, and the use of licensing and joint ventures.

1.4 Why did Webco decide to export lumber to Japan? How did Japanese buyers differ from U.S. buyers?

1.5 How do large U.S. multinationals compete in the global marketplace? Why do most of them sell more from their foreign subsidiaries than through exports?

1.6 "The greatest trade barrier to exporting lies in the mind." Explain.

1.7 "Global marketing is a shift in perspective." Explain.

1.8 Choose a prominent, publicly held company in your city and find out what its total foreign revenues have been for the past five years. Also study the comments about international markets made by the chair of the company in its annual report. How important is international marketing to this firm?

ENDNOTES

1 K. Kashani, "Marketing Futures: Priorities for a Turbulent Environment," *Long-Range Planning* 28, no. 4 (1995): 87–98.

2 "Just Like the Computer Games It Sells, Nintendo Defies Persistent Challengers," *The Wall Street Journal*, June 27, 1989; and "Atari Tests Technology's Antitrust Aspect," *The Wall Street Journal*, December 14, 1988.

3 See *Computer Gaming*, Johnny Wilson, "Bad Moon Rising: A Primer on PC Game Industry Myopia," January 1999; "Nintendo Unveils 64-bit Game Player in Bid to Top Sony, Sega CD Machines," *The Wall Street Journal*, November 27, 1995; "Older Machines Win Video-Game Crowd," *The Wall Street Journal*, December 26, 1995; "3-D Video Games: The Next

Generation," *Business Week,* October 16, 1995; "Nightmare in the Fun House," *Financial World,* February 21, 1995; and "Sega," *Business Week,* February 21, 1994.

4. "Step Right Up, Monsieur," *The New York Times,* August 23, 1995.

5. See "Euro Disney's Fiscal Loss to Spur Study of Woes by U.S. Concern," *The Wall Street Journal,* July 9, 1993; "Euro Disney's Loss Narrowed in Fiscal 1994," *The Wall Street Journal,* November 4, 1994; "Euro Disney's Prince Charming?" *Business Week,* June 13, 1994; "A Faint Squeak from Euro-Mickey," *The Economist,* July 29, 1995; and "Euro Disney Posts First Annual Profit," *The Wall Street Journal,* November 16, 1995.

6. See *Strategy Alternatives for the British Motorcycle Industry* (London: Her Majesty's Stationery Office, 1975); and *Note on the Motorcycle—1975,* Harvard Business School, Case #578-210.

7. Andrew Tanzer, "Keep the Calculators out of Sight," *Forbes,* March 20, 1989; and Louise Lucas, "Dickson Concepts Faces Loss As Recession Bites," *Financial Times,* December 11, 1998.

8. "Jindo to Set Its Export Goal," *Korea Economic Daily,* December 8, 1994.

9. "Electric Fuel of Israel Poised to Draw Two More European Concerns to Project," *The Wall Street Journal,* May 30, 1995.

10. "Thank Carl Klumpp for the Swell Smell of Right Guard," *The Wall Street Journal,* May 11, 1995.

11. "For Mary Kay Sales Reps in Russia, Hottest Shade Is the Color of Money," *The Wall Street Journal,* August 30, 1995; and "Ben & Jerry's Is Trying to Smooth out Distribution in Russia as It Expands," September 19, 1995.

12. "Faucet Maker Hoping to Tap Fresh Markets," *The Wall Street Journal.*

13. "Owner Hires Plane for Search and Spots Vessel," *The Straits Times* (Singapore), June 27, 1995.

14. Bureau of Economic Analysis, "An Ownership-Based Disaggregation of the U.S. Current Account, 1982–93," *Survey of Current Business,* October 1995.

15. See *The Wall Street Journal,* "U.S. Companies Again Hold Wide Lead over Rivals in Direct Investing Abroad," December 6, 1995; and "Developing World Gets More Investment," December 15, 1995. Also, "Helping Handouts," *The Economist,* 73, and "Foreign Investment" (tables), December 16, 1995, 97; "Investing Abroad" (tables), December 23, 1995; and "Trade Statistics: Not by the Book," December 9, 1995.

16. "You Don't Have to Be a Giant to Score Overseas," *Business Week,* April 13, 1987.

17. Gerald Hampton and E. Buske, "The Global Marketing Perspective" in *Advances in International Marketing,* vol. 2, ed. Tamer S. Cavusgil (Greenwich, CT: JAI Press, 1987).

FURTHER READINGS

Boddewyn, Jean. "Comparative Marketing: The First Twenty-five Years." *Journal of International Business Studies* 12 (Spring–Summer 1981).

Cateora, Philip and John L. Graham. *International Marketing.* 10th ed. Homewood, IL: Irwin, 1998.

Czinkota, M. R., and I. Ronkainen. *International Marketing.* 5th ed. Fort Worth: Dryden, 1998.

Hampton, Gerald, and E. Buske. "The Global Marketing Perspective" in *Advances in International Marketing,* vol. 2, ed. Tamer S. Cavusgil. Greenwich, CT: JAI Press, 1987.

Jain, Subhash. *International Marketing Management.* 5th ed. Boston, MA: South-Western Publishing, 1995.

Jeannet, Jean-Pierre, and Hubert Hennessey. *International Marketing Management.* 3d ed. Boston, MA: Houghton Mifflin, 1995.

Kashani, K. "Marketing Futures: Priorities for a Turbulent Environment." *Long-Range Planning* 28, no. 4, 1995: 87–98.

Kaynak, Erdener, ed. *Global Perspectives in Marketing.* New York: Praeger, 1985.

Onkvisit, Sak, and J. Shaw. *International Marketing.* 3rd ed. New York: Macmillan, 1996.

Ricks, David. *Big Business Blunders: Mistakes in Multinational Marketing.* Homewood, IL: Irwin, 1983.

Shanklin, William L., and David A Griffith, "Crafting Strategies for Global Marketing in the New Millenium," *Business Horizons,* September–October 1996, p. 11–16.

Terpstra, Vern. "The Evolution of International Marketing." *International Marketing Review* 4 (Summer 1987).

Agro Industria Exportadora S.A. (AI)

AI was founded in 1973. Its original owners were from Zamora and Michoacan, in Mexico, and they planned to buy agricultural produce and process it for sale, using labor-intensive processes. AI's operations, employing as many as 450 people, lasted until 1982. During this early period, the founding partners invited Mr. Gonzalez, from Guadalajara, to join the company as a manager. Over time he received an ownership interest, and in 1978 he decided to buy out the original owners, a process that was completed in 1982. At this point, however, the Mexican economy was in a parlous state, with the peso being heavily devalued after a long period of being tied to the dollar at a fixed parity of 12.5 per dollar. The difficult economic situation led Mr. Gonzalez to cease operations.

However, given Mexico's potential in agriculture and agribusiness, the International Finance Corp. (IFC), which is a division of the World Bank, decided to make agribusiness investments in Mexico. IFC invited a Mexican national, Mr. Ojeda, who was also a director of Banamex, to become involved in such a venture. He in turn contacted Mr. Gonzalez to restart operations, with a greater focus on exporting.

The reborn company slowly found its feet and, in 1986, Mr. Ojeda quit Banamex to become a partner in the company, with additional capital investment from the venture capital arm of Banamex. The company decided to focus on exporting frozen vegetables and sought another partner, Mr. Polari, a big grower of vegetables. Mr. Polari's association with the company lasted three years, until 1989, when he sold his share in the company. By then, AI had its ownership divided as follows: Mr. Gonzalez held 25 percent, Mr. Ojeda had 35 percent, with the balance held by an investor from Mexico City. IFC, which had held an ownership stake in the company during its difficult years, sold out, as is its custom once the company seemed to be on an even keel and did not require continued IFC capital or support.

Initially, the company had canned Anaheim chilies for export to the United States. Once the United States opened its market to the import of *fresh* Mexican chilies, however, prices shot up and selling canned chilies was no longer viable. Hence, AI had to find another product line for its canning plant, which had started initial operations in 1987.

Mr. Gonzalez had been invited to Japan and in scouting business opportunities there noticed that the Japanese were heavy users of grapefruit segments, in jellies, cakes, pies, and so on. He returned to Mexico thinking that this represented a potential opportunity for AI. However, some practical problems immediately arose. Whereas chilies are high in acidity, fruit is generally low in acid and high in sugar content. As a result, cans are liable to explode easily. Hence, AI had to experiment with new canning methods and processes. However, Japanese canning technology as applied to grapefruit was not useful to AI because of differences in weather, altitude (Guadalajara is about 3,000 feet above sea level), and humidity. Further, fresh fruit is soft and has a different texture from frozen produce. Therefore, AI had to adapt its production processes. Its initial exports to Japan were of poor quality, and shipments suffered from spoilage. Consequently, AI had to request time from its Japanese clients to solve its production problems.

In 1990, AI decided to change over to using imported U.S. cans. The cans needed a special enamel coating to accommodate citrus products. Further, the Mexican cans oxidized easily, even before use, and were not of uniform quality, as different kinds of steel imported from Spain, Venezuela, and so on were used in production. Consequently, AI decided to import cans from Florida, even though this meant paying for transporting empty cans that were being shipped to the AI plants. But the U.S. cans were of superior quality, and soon AI stopped experiencing problems with exploding cans and other problems of uneven quality. AI had learned that the Japanese were continually seeking quality improvements, and at continually lower prices.

At first, AI exported on an exclusive basis to Marubeni Corp. However, when Marubeni began lowering the quantities it purchased, AI began to seek additional Japanese distributors, including additional Japanese trading companies Mitsui and Toshoku. Because AI had established a good name in Japan, it had actually been approached by Marubeni about becoming a distributor. AI's competition came from Mexico, Israel, and South Africa. AI had the best quality (or so it claimed), though its prices were slightly higher. AI felt that it was too difficult to sell directly to the final Japanese consumer firms, who numbered about 50 in all: major grocery chains, food processors, and others.

AI typically processed the fruit in Mexico, packed it in cans without labels, and used a Mexican shipping line for transportation to Japan. It shipped about one container every 10 days to Japan, with the final customer price about double the FOB Manzanillo price.

A critical point in export success is the quality of the raw material, that is, the produce. AI took care in its purchasing. Japanese customers wanted the grapefruit segments to be all of the same size. Hence, AI had two people permanently stationed at the growers' sites, where they made commitments to purchase fruit at the bloom stage, picking producers based on taste, freshness, and fruit size. Once fruits were ready to pick, picking was done every day, with AI's two people on flat-out supervision. Once the fruit was received, it was graded by size, with the smaller units sold off to juice firms. Only fruit of the requisite size was exported to Japan. On average, for fruit with a value of 100 pesos, transportation costs added another 120 pesos. Imported cans were stored in-bond, to avoid duties, since the cans were destined for re-export. Most of the fruit exports to Japan were in #10 cans, containing 2 kilograms of product and 1 kilogram of syrup. As is to be expected, AI faced seasonal cycles and had to develop multiple fruit lines to keep themselves busy year round. For example, in the 1992 fiscal year, AI exported:

Grapefruit	August–December	1.575 million pounds
Valenciana oranges	January–March	1.470 million pounds
Lemons	May–August	.4 million "cell sacks" (that is, lemon juice in lemon-like containers)

AI felt that it had to pick produce lines for its plant that were not chosen by its competitors. Its most recent produce addition is strawberries, with a target of 7 million pounds annually. To enter this line, AI made an agreement with Congeladora de Samora, whereby it took over operations of their factory in return for a 50–50 split of the profits. Strawberries are generally sold in 30-pound plastic pails, in Pure-Pak cartons, or in 425-pound drums for use by jam manufacturers.

Foreign Markets

AI has a U.S. food broker, World Food Sales, which it owns. World Food's sales director was a former partner of AI in its earlier incarnation, and has over 30 years of experience in frozen produce. AI pays a 6 percent sales commission to World Food. World Food also represents other Mexican food produce companies, such as growers of broccoli and cauliflower. Sometimes the U.S. broker served as an alternative export conduit to Japan, enabling AI to export incremental quantities if demand from its (then) exclusive distribution arrangement in Japan was low. As part of operating procedures, all sales are made on letters of credit, and quotes to all international customers are priced in U.S. dollars.

In addition to Japan and the United States, AI also sells to Europe, principally to Germany. Like Japan, Germany requires quality and is willing to pay a higher price if necessary. Mr. Gonzalez' wife is German and was instrumental in helping break into the German market, achieved gradually by repeated visits to the World Food Fair, held every third year in Cologne, Germany. German exports are to IC Frozen Foods, the German distributor, who also exports to Sweden and Denmark, where it has representatives.

The United Kingdom is a more difficult market, as lower-quality, highly discounted products compete with AI's produce. AI has also considered Korea as a market though a 1991 visit indicated that while AI quality was considered superior, its prices were held to be high.

New Directions

AI's goal is to diversify its export markets. In 1990, its export sales were 70 percent to the United States and Canada, 25 percent to Japan, and 5 percent to Europe. In 1992, the respective percentages were 60, 30, and 10. For 1993, targeted percentages were 50, 40, and 10. AI notes that each market has peculiarities and presents a different set of challenges. For the U.S. market, AI is experimenting with new lines such as broccoli, cauliflower, romanesco (a hybrid of cauliflower and broccoli), Brussels sprouts, and cucumbers, both pickled and fresh. Cucumbers represent its latest success, which it buys from 92 growers who devote 205 hectares to the crop, with total exports being 4.4 million pounds. AI is renting a plant to process cucumbers. It houses three grading machines, where the cucumbers are first sorted by size. They are then hydrocooled, loaded onto 40-ton trailers in green plastic bags, along with 2 tons of ice, and then exported at a temperature of 38 degrees to the United States, with more ice added after crossing the border. The cucumbers continue on to Colorado, where they are washed, packed, and sold as fresh produce. The entire cycle averages 17 hours from receipt of cucumbers to the crossing of the border, with a total elapsed time of 24 hours to Colorado. The central and critical element is freshness.

Role of Logistics

Logistics are extremely important. AI uses the Mexican carrier Aguilas de Oro with a handoff at the border to Middleton Trucking, which has a fleet of 110 trucks. The crossing point is Laredo, Texas, which is extremely hot. Therefore, the produce has a high risk of perishability. Success is partly a matter of minimizing transportation costs. In July and August, at the height of the cucumber-pickling season, trucking rates are seasonally low due to excess capacity, and AI is able to negotiate rates averaging one cent per pound for ordinary cargo to Laredo, and 2 cents for cooled cargo—a saving of almost 33 percent over normal tariffs. AI negotiated directly with trucking companies such as Middleton, choosing Middleton over competitive bids from Freymiller and Prime.

Another bottleneck is the availability of containers, and major clients such as Vlasic guarantee the availability of containers at the border. In general, it is important to first arrange the U.S. transportation leg with Middleton before closing the link by entering into a contract with its Mexican partner. An alternative is to sell cucumbers in a brine solution for pickling, with the cucumbers in brine sent to the United States for further processing: washing, slicing, and then sale to clients such as McDonald's or to major pickling companies such as Vlasic Foods. AI cucumber sales reached 2.75 million pounds of brine pickles in 1992.

For shipment to Europe, the company contracts for a certain number of containers each month to transport its products, currently 10 to 12 containers a month, on terms typically set out separately as FOB plant, plus freight, in-bond expenses, transloading and ocean freight. For 1993, shipping estimates were at 150 containers of produce, split 70 percent broccoli and 30 percent romanesco, which is gaining a market. Three hundred tons of romanesco were shipped in 1992, with an estimated 1,000 tons to be shipped in 1993. Romanesco is costlier to grow, however, with a pound of seed costing $2,500 versus $200 for a pound of broccoli seed. AI buys the seed and provides it to the better growers who are more likely to grow a crop from the expensive seed.

Costs and Regulations

AI's food processing is labor intensive though seasonal. For example, the grapefruit segment preparation requires an assembly line of about 2,250 women who cut, peel, segment, and can the grapefruit. A key is intelligent buying of raw materials, signing contracts with growers in advance, and never growing one's own produce. For 1992, AI sales were $16 million, yielding a profit of $1.5 million. For 1993 estimates were for sales of $27 million, with a net profit target of about 8.5 percent.

As a Mexican company, capitalization is also critical, especially in export markets where working capital requirements are higher. To enable AI to take a longer-term perspective on export markets, AI's partners contributed an additional $1.5 million in capital in order to reduce borrowing costs (over 30 percent on an annual basis on peso-denominated debt in Mexico).

A complication is divergent agricultural standards in different export markets. Regulations differ across countries about permissible levels of chemical additives and fertilizers.

Hence, the two supervisors assigned to grower relations must monitor the farming process. AI often deliberately supplies chemicals and fertilizers to facilitate certification of additive levels in the export produce. In addition, AI will carry out the necessary inspections prior to export, as in the case of strawberries destined for the U.S. market, where permissible chemical parts per million have been lowered from .5 to .05.

Duties are a concern, as most advanced nations protect agricultural products. For example, duties on vegetables to the United States have averaged 17 percent, on strawberries 14 percent, and on average, about 13 percent of shipment value. With the passage of NAFTA, these tariffs will be lowered but will not disappear. In comparison, Central America enjoys duty-free access to Europe and the United States, a considerable advantage over AI produce. Similarly, in Japan, there is a 17 percent duty on products in a sugarcane-based syrup, but syrup with a corn base can enter duty free. At the same time, quality standards are such that exports to Japan must meet higher quality standards than exports for the market in the United States.

The Future

AI is serious about expanding its export business. Its owners believe that in international business, once they make a deal, they must honor it. In one case, they bought lemons out of season at six times the regular price, and air-freighted the cellsack product in order to meet a commitment to a customer. The customer's satisfaction led to a large order the next year. The partners are convinced that AI can only succeed by building up long-term relationships in export markets. Timely delivery is also a must, given the perishable and seasonal nature of the products. Third, there is no question that AI must deliver the best-quality products, both to win customers and to get repeat orders.

Questions

1. How did AI first enter export markets? What factors enabled it to compete in the U.S. market?
2. How did AI enter the Japanese market? What were the challenges in exporting to Japan?
3. Trace the evolution of AI's expansion in international markets, in terms of product lines and geographic market scope.
4. Would you consider that AI has been successful in entering international markets? What are the factors critical to AI's success?
5. What are the challenges facing AI as it seeks to continue expanding internationally? Do you have any recommendations for AI in terms of products, markets, and the way it conducts international business?

Source: Case prepared by Professor Ravi Sarathy, Northeastern University, for use in class discussion. © 1996, all rights reserved.

Commodore International

Product Line

Commodore's product line consists of three distinct lines: the C64/128 home computer, the IBM PC-compatible, and the Amiga professional line, the newest. The Amiga line represents the "new" Commodore, and the company's future depends on how well Amiga does in global markets. Table 1 summarizes the sales of each of these product lines.

The Amiga Line   This is Commodore's flagship line and its most innovative product. The city of Atlanta used Amigas in preparing its winning proposal to bring the Olympic games to the city. The proposal allowed Olympic committee members to see how the Olympic games and facilities might look in Atlanta.

The Amiga is a multimedia computer intended for use in applications requiring intensive use of video, graphics, and sound. As of June 1992, 3.7 million Amigas had been sold, with unit sales up 26 percent in fiscal 1990 and 38 percent in fiscal 1991. Amiga revenues increased at a slower rate, 11 percent in 1990 and 23 percent in fiscal 1991.

The IBM-Compatible Personal Computer Line

Based on the MS-DOS operating system, these are lower-priced IBM clones meant for use in homes and businesses and in laptop models. These IBM-compatible clones have a negligible market position in the United States but are strong in Europe. They accounted for 24 percent of worldwide sales in 1992 as against 20 percent in 1988, and 10 percent each in 1987 and 1986.

Commodore International is a pioneer in home computers. Over 12 million of its C64/128 model had been sold by June 1992, making it one of the most widely distributed, inexpensive home computers. Despite its penetration into the home market, Commodore does not have a significant position in the U.S. computer industry; less than 10 percent of its total sales come from North America, which includes the United States and Canada.

As Table 2 reports, Commodore's market share in Europe has been increasing. It is number two in the PC (personal computer) business in Europe, behind IBM but ahead of Compaq. It is particularly strong in Germany, where it is number one in the home computer market. In Germany, its computers have been sold to major corporations such as BMW and Thyssen, as well as to the German government, army, and national railway.

TABLE 1

Revenues from Commodore's Product Lines[a]

IBM-compatible	24	28	29	24	20	10	10
C64/128	13	16	18	31	39	70	80

[a]Figures represent the percentage of total worldwide sales.

Its Amiga 2000 was used to help position the launch of the Ariane 3 rocket, which carried two commercial satellites into orbit. Commodore has a strong brand image in Germany, having sponsored the popular Bayern München soccer team for many years; this has helped it in selling Commodore computers to Germany's 60,000 sports clubs. Similarly, it has supported soccer teams and Olympic athletes in the United Kingdom, and sponsored the sailboat *Commodore Rucanor* in an around-the-world race. However, its total worldwide sales grew little from 1986 to 1992. Commodore has been experiencing falling sales in the United States, unlike its growth in Europe.

The C64/128 Line   This mature home computer line accounted for 13 percent of sales in 1992 as against 31 percent of revenues in 1989, and 80 percent of sales in 1986. Although sales have declined from 1 million units in 1988 and 1989 to 700,000 in 1990, 800,000 in 1991, and 650,000 in 1992, 12 million units had been sold by 1992. Over 10,000 software packages are available for the C64/128 line, making it an affordable and versatile entry-level home computer. Commodore uses promotions that bundle new software packages, such as a Terminator II, with the computer. Potential new markets for this mature line could open up in Germany and Eastern European countries.

The CDTV Line   This is Commodore's newest product, which is aimed at consumer and professional markets. Commodore's CDTV packages a CD-ROM drive with an Amiga computer that can be attached to a TV set and controlled by an infrared remote device or a keyboard. When attached to computers, CD-ROM devices can store enormous quantities (about 600 megabytes) of data, including text, graphics, full-motion video and animation, and sound files. CD-ROMs can bring multimedia to users, whether it be high-tech encyclopedias, auto-repair manuals, or interactive games. Other companies such as Sony and Philips have also entered this new market segment. Commodore has entered into an agreement with a Japanese consortium to develop applications and promote this product, which is still early in the product life cycle stage, in Japan.

Case prepared by Ravi Sarathy for use in classroom discussion. ©1993, all rights reserved. Please do not quote without permission.
Sources: Commodore International Annual Reports, 1989 to 1992; "Lost Opportunity," *Forbes*, November 13, 1989; and "Commodore Turns to Advertising in Attempt to Improve U.S. Sales," *The Wall Street Journal*, October 12, 1989.

TABLE 2						
Commodore International Sales Distribution by Geographical Area (Year Ended June 30)						
Europe[a]	88	84	75	69	67	63	51
Asia/Australia[a]	4	5	7	7	7	5	4
Total sales (millions of dollars)	$911	$1,047	$887	$940	$871	$807	$889

[a]Figures represent the percentage of total worldwide sales.

The Amiga Line

Commodore is staking its future on the Amiga line, which has interesting competitive advantages in its niche of graphics-intensive computing. The Amiga can capture video images from a videotape or a camcorder and overlay text, graphics, and sound, which can then be recorded on a laserdisk or videotape. The Amiga is aimed at professional customer segments because it offers strong applications in the development of both training and business presentations.

Operating Systems   Amiga computers use an operating system called Amiga Dos, which is different from MS-DOS used on IBM-compatibles. Thus, because software written in MS-DOS cannot run on Amigas, software developers may be reluctant to commit scarce resources to writing programs for the Amiga unless there is reason to believe that Amigas will sell well. Amiga has attempted to overcome this problem by creating an add-on circuit board that allows the Amiga to act as an IBM clone and to read software and files created for MS-DOS use. Because there are so many more MS-DOS machines sold worldwide, it is more attractive for developers to produce software for them.

This is not the case in Europe, however, because MS-DOS is less well established there, especially in the home market. In Europe, an array of incompatible computers, each with its own operating system and installed base, is the norm. As a result, Commodore actually may have encountered low resistance to purchasing Amiga products.

Amiga 2000 and 2500   These models are meant for users who need to make multimedia presentations. The user can interface headings, charts, graphs, and animation with videotape presentations. This makes the Amiga useful for interactive training and education presentations that combine computers and videotape sequences.

Amiga 3000 and the 3000 UX   These are powerful machines intended for use in science, business, and engineering, where quick graphic application and the Unix operating system are needed, as in CAD/CAM applications. The machine is also used in medicine, which requires sharp color graphics for diagnostics and research. The Neurosurgical University Clinic in Vienna uses the Amiga to detect medical anomalies. These machines form an integral part of a system used for four-dimensional ultrasonic imaging at the Imperial College of Science in the United Kingdom. Physicians use the Amiga with thermographic photography to diagnose illness and determine whether patients are healing properly. Surgeons use the Amiga's graphic capabilities to locate brain cancer within one millimeter of its true position. In plastic surgery, the Amiga can be used to digitize a patient's portrait on the screen and to display a variety of possible alterations prior to actual surgery.

A recent prize-winning application using an Amiga was developed by the U.K. National Computing Centre with the Scottish Police College. In the United Kingdom, unruly soccer crowds sometimes cause riots. With four Amiga 2000 workstations and an Amiga 3000 as a central controller, a simulation system teaches police cadets crowd-control techniques. Each workstation shows a different view of the crowd inside and outside a soccer stadium. The system's sound capability allowed radio messages from various police officers to be recorded and stored for replay during the simulation and debriefing. As incidents occurred, each police cadet had to decide what to do. Different simulated events tested a cadet's decision-making and communication abilities.

The Amiga is also invaluable to professional musicians. Music teachers and students, musicians interested in electronic and synthesized music, and composers and songwriters can use the Amiga with music software and appropriate interfaces to compose, store, and revise musical compositions.

Amiga 3000s are the heart of the "Touch Toronto" system of kiosks found in hotel lobbies, shopping malls, and airports. The system gives users screen access to Toronto shopping, restaurant, and entertainment information. After users pick a restaurant by area of city, type of food, and price range, for example, they can call up a map to find out how to get to the restaurant from the kiosk location and even make reservations or pick up discount coupons. Similar Amiga-based kiosks have been developed in Boston and Stockholm. Printemps, a large Paris department store, uses them to help customers select wedding gifts.

Amiga 500 and 600   The lower-priced Amiga 500 and 600 offer home computer users advanced graphics and allow them to script, edit, and add animated effects to create their own home movies and video productions. These Amigas can also be used to compose music and work out musical arrangements.

Entrenched Competition Commodore Amigas must compete against the more established Apple and IBM brand names. Commodore must decide whether to concentrate on specific vertical customer segments such as the music studios and video production houses and the corporate training market or to target the general-purpose education market. This last market is large and therefore attracts other powerful competitors such as Apple and IBM.

Amigas seem to be achieving reasonable market penetration. One million Amigas had been sold by mid-1989, 2 million by December 1990, 3 million by December 1991, and 3.7 million by June 1992.

Commodore's Challenges

Commodore faces many challenges. One is finding adequate U.S. distribution channels to reach home and business consumers. The major U.S. computer store chains have already committed to lines such as IBM, Apple, Compaq, and Hewlett-Packard. At one time, Commodore sold the C64/128 line through general retailers such as Toys 'R Us. With discount pricing, it undercut traditional computer retail channels. As a result, computer retailers are somewhat unenthusiastic about Commodore products. Commodore has been selling directly to academic institutions, faculty, and students, offering large discounts in attempting to grab the market of future multimedia computer users for its Amigas. In contrast to the U.S. situation, Commodore has good distribution in Europe through office products dealers, mass distribution channels, and even direct sales.

Image Commodore has been known in the United States as the manufacturer of the C64 machine intended for use with game software. Commodore has to overcome this image in order to be taken seriously by the business and professional markets, although video experts clearly regard the Amiga as an ideal choice for multimedia production. Looking to its long-term U.S. image, Commodore initiated a $15 million U.S. advertising campaign focused on the theme "Amiga: The Computer for the Creative Mind." These ads featured a teenage expert named Stevie, who is approached by Tommy Lasorda asking for advice on the Dodgers' team lineup, and Astronaut Buzz Aldrin, who wants to talk to Stevie about plans for a new space station. Of course, obtaining the advice involves using the Amiga computer.

Foreign Exchange Fluctuations in foreign exchange also affect Commodore earnings. Because it is a U.S. corporation, its financial data are reported in dollars. But because the bulk of its sales and profits come from Europe, strong European currencies translate into increased dollar sales and earnings. For example, in 1992 its European sales would have been $25 million higher, when translated into U.S. dollars, if European exchange rates had remained stable. That is, Commodore's sales reported in U.S. dollars are affected by whether the European currencies are strengthening or weakening.

Manufacturing Operations Commodore has manufacturing operations in Germany and the Philippines. It also has a semiconductor facility in the United States, where it makes a proprietary chip that is combined with the Motorola 68000 chip (the same chip used in the Apple Macintosh) to provide the Amiga with its superior graphics processing capabilities.

The European Focus Commodore has been concentrating on growth in Europe. Over the years, it has opened new sales subsidiaries in Spain and Portugal, has restructured operations in the United Kingdom and Germany, and has recruited new managers for sales subsidiaries in Scandinavia, Australia, Benelux, Switzerland, Italy, and Germany (its largest market). However, Commodore needs to increase U.S. sales in order to become a global marketer.

Commodore is at a crossroads in its development. It has developed an advanced graphics computer and must decide how to market it successfully around the world in a timely fashion. It must decide whether to re-emphasize its U.S. market and, if so, how to gain market share in the United States. It has to decide which products to emphasize in which countries and how to take advantage of its European strength to gain market share in the United States and the Far East.

Questions

1. Why does Commodore obtain over 90 percent of its sales from outside the United States? Is Commodore in a healthy position?

2. How has Commodore been able to be successful in Europe? Has its European success shaped its product development, choice of customer segments to target, manufacturing decisions, and other aspects of the company's operations?

3. Should it try to increase its U.S. sales relative to worldwide sales? How could it go about increasing U.S. sales?

4. What are some of the major challenges confronting Commodore management? Does the fact that Commodore is a multinational company give it an advantage in facing these challenges?

5. What aspects of Commodore are worth imitating by other U.S. companies interested in international marketing?

Chapter

2

Economic Environment

The World Economy

When a firm leaves its home market to market internationally, it must deal with the challenges of the larger, more complex world economy. Here we introduce the various dimensions of that environment.

The main goals of this chapter are to

1. Present an overview of world trade—the economic linkages between nations.

2. Explain the usefulness of data on the balance of payments, the record of international economic transactions.

3. Discuss commercial policy, that is, how nations regulate their trade, and how it constrains the international marketer.

4. Describe how WTO and UNCTAD influence trade, offering both promise and threat to a firm.

5. Explore the developments in Eastern Europe that present both challenges and opportunities to Western firms, and the attempts at regional economic integration.

6. Discuss the international financial system and the factors affecting the pricing and financial side of international marketing.

7. Discuss the role of the United States in the world economy and how the home country affects a firm's international marketing.

Marketing is an economic activity affected by the economic environment in which it is conducted. International marketing has a twofold economic environment: (1) the global, or world, economy, and (2) the economy of individual countries. This chapter will discuss the international economy, and Chapter 3 will consider the relevant dimensions of foreign economies.

It is reasonable to speak of the "world economy" because the nations of the world do relate to each other economically. Nations, of course, also relate to each other politically, diplomatically, militarily, and culturally. Many of these other elements of international relations are intertwined with economic considerations. For example, Marco Polo's travels and the Crusades had significant economic impact. The great voyages of discovery and the building of colonial empires were motivated by economic as well as political aspirations. More recently, economic considerations have played a role in regional cooperative movements such as the **European Union (EU).** International economic concerns are also frequent items on the agenda of the United Nations and its affiliated agencies.

The existence of this world economy is critical for the business firm. Because nations do relate to each other economically, international business operations are possible. Today, in fact, international marketers are major participants in international economic relations. For that reason, it is necessary to examine the world economy to see how it aids and constrains international marketing. We begin by considering international trade, a major element in international economic relations. Figure 2–1 illustrates how the international environment influences the firm's international marketing.

NATION TRADES WITH NATION

Although our primary concern is international marketing rather than international trade, a brief survey of international trade will prove useful. Trading between groups has been going on since the beginning of recorded history. Much early trade was economically motivated and conducted through barter or commercial transactions. However, a large part of the exchange of goods historically occurred through military conquest: "To the victor belong the spoils." The predominant pattern of international trade today is the voluntary exchange of goods and services.

FIGURE 2–1   **The International Environment of Marketing**

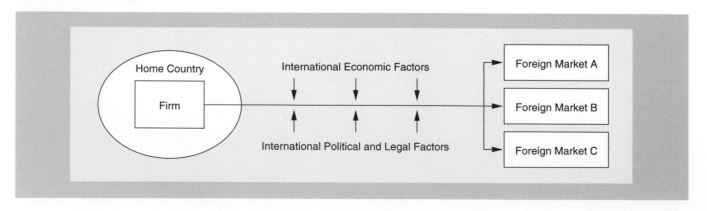

A Picture of World Trade

Global Volume

The volume of world trade in 1998 was about $6.6 trillion, a figure larger than the gross national product (GNP) of every nation in the world except the United States and four times the GNP of Latin America. This is one indication of international trade's importance as part of world economic activity. Not only is it large in volume, but it is also one of the fastest-growing areas of economic activity. Since World War II, the volume of world trade has risen faster than most other indicators of economic activity. In fact, it has increased twice as fast as world GNP.

Internationalism is increasing as a way of life. Both nations and firms must consider its significance for their own well-being. Nations moving in the direction of trade expansion can raise their standard of living. Nations moving in the direction of trade restriction can enhance their political separation and isolation, but at the expense of economic progress. Firms, like nations, must recognize that they are in the world marketplace both in considering opportunities for growth and in facing new competition. The isolationist position today is difficult to maintain for firms as well as for nations. One can't just say "Stop the world—I want to get off."

Foreign Trade of Individual Nations

Let us consider the importance of foreign trade to individual nations. In the United States, exports and imports of goods and services were $1.9 trillion, or over 25 percent of GNP in 1997. This percentage is twice as high as it was 20 years earlier. Yet even this doesn't adequately measure the importance of foreign trade to the U.S. economy. For one thing, exports in some lines are much higher percentages of output, over 50 percent in some cases. Some major U.S. exports in 1997 were capital goods, $253 billion; industrial supplies and materials, $148 billion; automotive, $60 billion; and other consumer goods, $70 billion.

Conversely, imports account for a large part of U.S. supplies in many categories—100 percent for coffee, crude rubber, diamonds, some minerals, and bananas, for example. Major import categories in 1997 were the same as for exports: capital goods, $229 billion; industrial supplies and materials, $204 billion; consumer goods, $171 billion; automotive, $130 billion. Clearly, some industries are much more trade dependent than others.

Some nations are also much more dependent on trade than others. The United States is the world's leading importer and exporter, but such trade is only a little over 25 percent of its GNP. The figures are much higher for other developed countries, for example, 55 percent for Germany, 106 percent for the Netherlands, and 120 percent for Belgium. Put another way, Belgium imports about $20,000 per capita, but the United States imports about $5,000 per capita. Most less developed countries have low figures because they lack foreign exchange.

The export involvement of the nation influences that of the firm. It is not surprising, therefore, that firms from heavy exporting countries tend to be more internationally oriented than those from other countries. For example, the average U.S. manufacturer is less apt to be an exporter than is the average Belgian or Dutch firm.

Foreign Trade of Individual Firms

Foreign trade is just as important to the firm as it is to the nation. In fact, much of international marketing involves international trade—the cross-border movement of goods and services. In relation to this subject, "Global Marketing" shows how one company, Ford, tied together fifteen different countries around the world to present a Ford Escort.

GLOBAL MARKETING

Component Network for Ford Escort—Europe

1. *United Kingdom*—Carburetor, rocker arm, clutch, ignition, exhaust, oil pump, distributor, cylinder bolt, cylinder head, flywheel ring gear, heater, speedometer, battery, rear wheel spindle, intake manifold, fuel tank, switches, lamp, front disk, steering wheel, steering column, glass, weatherstrips, locks.

2. *France*—Alternator, cylinder head, master cylinder, brakes, underbody coating, weatherstrips, clutch release bearings, steering shaft and joints, seat pads and frames, transmission cases, clutch cases, tires, suspension bushes, ventilation units, heater, hose clamps, sealers, hardware.

3. *Germany*—Locks, pistons, exhaust, ignition, switches, front disk, distributor, weatherstrips, rocker arm, speedometer, fuel tank, cylinder bolt, cylinder head gasket, front wheel knuckles, rear window spindle, transmission cases, clutch, steering column, battery, glass.

4. *Sweden*—Hose clamps, cylinder bolt, exhaust down pipes, pressings, hardware.

5. *Netherlands*—Tires, paints, hardware.

6. *Belgium*—Tires, tubes, seat pads, brakes, trim.

7. *Norway*—Exhaust flanges, tires.

8. *Denmark*—Fan belt.

9. *Austria*—Tires, radiator and heater hoses.

10. *Switzerland*—Underbody coating, speedometer gears.

11. *Italy*—Cylinder head, carburetor, glass, lamps, defroster grills.

12. *Spain*—Wiring harness, radiator and heater hoses, fork clutch release, air filter, battery, mirrors.

13. *Canada*—Glass, radio.

14. *United States*—EGR valves, wheel nuts, hydraulic tappet, glass.

15. *Japan*—Starter, alternator, cone and roller bearings, windscreen washer pump.

Composition of World Trade

A study of the commodity composition of world trade gives further insight into international economic relations. Considering just four commodity categories—food, fuel, other primary commodities, and manufactured goods—we see long-run shifts in market share.

The shares of both food products and other primary commodities have declined 50 percent in the past three decades. The share of fuel has fluctuated but has not increased as the power of OPEC has waned. Each group has a trade share of about 10 percent or less, leaving manufacturers as the only growth area in merchandise trade, accounting for about 75 percent of all nonservice trade. This is up from just over 50 percent 30 years earlier.

The developing countries as commodity producers are very unhappy about this situation. The drop in their share of international trade roughly parallels the drop in the proportion of primary materials exported to total exports. Several reasons exist for these changing market shares. One is the development of synthetics and other substitutes for primary products. Another is growing agricultural self-sufficiency in the industrialized countries.

A third reason is the growth of manufacturing in total world output. Countries with falling market shares consequently need to change their product line, that is, to industrialize. This does not mean dropping existing primary exports but rather adding manufactured exports, which is just what most less developed countries are trying to do.

An important omission in our discussion of the composition of world trade has been services (advertising, banking, communications, insurance, transportation, etc.). This is a growth area of world trade and one of special interest to U.S. firms, which often have a comparative advantage in those businesses. Trade in services is

GLOBAL MARKETING

Services Also Travel Abroad

Many major accounting firms, advertising agencies, banks, construction firms, consulting firms, and other service organizations are active international marketers. The number of service industries is very large and, with modern technology and increasing globalization, more and more services are entering international trade.

Bangalore, India, is the Silicon Valley of India. In the mid-80s, Texas Instruments (TI) set up a large software programming operation in Bangalore. The success of this operation encouraged over 30 other companies to set up software "factories" in Bangalore, including IBM and Motorola. Indian-owned software companies also exist (such as Infosys), which sell their programs abroad. General Electric and Siemens are among Infosys's international customers.

On the other side of the world, in Ireland, software consultants in Quarterdeck's Dublin office answer phone inquiries routed from the United States. Meanwhile, in Jamaica, clerks in Montego Bay handle hotel reservations called in from toll-free numbers in the States. Starbucks has gone from Seattle to Britain, Japan, Malaysia, New Zealand, and Singapore.

over one-fourth the size of merchandise trade. Unfortunately, data on trade in services are much harder to come by than data on merchandise trade, but we do know that as of 1998, the United States was the leading exporter and importer of services, just as it was for merchandise trade.

For international firms, a detailed study of the composition of world trade reveals what is being traded as well as who is buying and selling. Trend analysis shows which products are growing and which are fading, indicating opportunities available to the firm. The interest of less developed countries in industrialization may also create investment opportunities for the firm in manufacturing or processing. Ventures such as these could help less developed countries increase manufactured exports by adding items to their export line or by refining or processing their primary commodities.

Patterns of World Trade

Who are the major players—and winners—in the game of international trade? Table 2–1 identifies them, showing that the industrial countries supply two-thirds of all exports, finding good external markets for their factories. They also buy two-thirds of all imports, thus raising their standard of living.

Although large in number and in population, the developing countries, including OPEC, supply only about 32 percent of world exports and take about 30 percent of world imports—about the total of the three leading countries combined (the United States, Germany, and Japan). With over half the world's population, the developing countries of Asia have only 18 percent of world exports.

Because of their small share of exports and imports, the developing countries receive a significantly smaller contribution of international trade to their income and standard of living than do the industrial countries. The exceptions to this

TABLE 2–1	World Trade Shares, 1997		
		World Exports—Merchandise	
		Billions of Dollars	*Percent*
By Economic Category			
Developed Countries		$3,594	68%
Developing Countries		1,701	32
Total		$5,295	100%
By Geographic Region			
Western Europe		$2,269	43%
Asia (excluding Japan)		959	18
North America		904	17
Latin America		280	5
Central and Eastern Europe		179	3
Mid East		163	3
Africa		120	2
Leading Countries			
United States		$689	12.6%
Germany		512	9.4
Japan		421	7.7

Source: *WTO Focus* (Geneva: World Trade Organization, March 1998), 3, 6.

gloomy Third World picture are the **newly industrializing countries (NICs),** which have gained significant shares of trade in recent years. Major members of this group include Hong Kong, Singapore, South Korea, Taiwan, and now China.

The overall picture of world-trade patterns provides necessary background for understanding world trade. However, it is often more important to the individual firm to identify the trading patterns of the particular nations it is dealing with. Table 2–2 shows the major trading partners of the United States. To complement this information, a firm might use a product breakdown by country to provide a more complete profile of a nation's trade.

Similar tables can be prepared for most countries and are useful when the firm is considering where to locate. These facts provide clues to the reasons for a particular country's trade patterns. The statement that most trade is with industrial countries is borne out by the figures for the United States, but the importance of other factors becomes evident as well. For example, the role of Canada and Mexico as trading partners of the United States cannot be explained very well in terms of their size or degree of industrialization. **Geographic proximity** is an important consideration. Countries that are neighbors are better trading partners, other things being equal, than those distant from each other. The lower transport costs are accompanied by greater familiarity and ease of communication and control.

The **political influences** on trade can also be revealed in such a table. For example, although Cuba is also a close neighbor of the United States, practically no trade exists between the two countries. The point here is that an analysis of trade patterns both on an aggregate and on a national basis can be useful to the firm in planning its global marketing and logistics systems. Examination of the causes of trade patterns suggests possible approaches either to adapting to the patterns or to modifying them.

International Trade Theory

In domestic marketing, much emphasis is placed on the analysis of buyer behavior and motivation. For the international marketer, a knowledge of the basic causes and nature of international trade is important. It is easier for a firm to work with

TABLE 2-2	Major Trading Partners of the United States		
Major Customers	*Billions of Dollars*	*Major Suppliers*	*Billions of Dollars*
Canada	$152	Canada	$168
Mexico	71	Japan	121
Japan	66	Mexico	86
United Kingdom	36	China	63
South Korea	25	Germany	43
Germany	25	United Kingdom	33
Taiwan	20	Taiwan	33
Netherlands	20	South Korea	23
Singapore	18	France	21
France	16	Singapore	20

Source: U.S. Department of Commerce, 1998.

the underlying economic forces than against them. To work with them, however, the firm must understand them.

Essentially, international trade theory seeks the answers to a few basic questions: Why do nations trade? What goods do they trade? Nations trade for economic, political, and cultural reasons, but the principal economic basis for international trade is difference in price; that is, a nation can buy some goods more cheaply from other nations than it can make them itself. In a sense, the nation faces the same "make-or-buy" decision as does the firm. Just as most firms do not go for complete vertical integration but buy many materials and supplies from outside firms, so most nations decide against complete self-sufficiency (or **autarky**) in favor of buying cheaper goods from other countries.

An example given by Adam Smith helps illustrate this: In discussing the advantages to England in trading manufactured goods for Portugal's wine, he noted that grapes could be grown "under glass" (in greenhouses) in England but that to do so would lead to England's having both less wine and fewer manufacturers than if it specialized in manufacturers. In fact, Smith's major conclusion was that the wealth of nations derived from the division of labor and specialization. Applied to the international picture, this means trade rather than self-sufficiency.

Comparative Advantage

It has been said that price differences are the immediate basis of international trade. The firm that decides whether to make or buy also considers price as a principal variable. But why do nations have different prices on goods? Prices differ because countries producing these goods have different costs. And why do countries have different costs? The Swedish economist Bertil Ohlin came up with an explanation generally held to be valid: Different countries have dissimilar prices and costs on goods because different goods require a different mix of factors in their production and because countries differ in their supply of these factors. Thus, in Smith's example, Portugal's wine would be cheaper than wine made in England because Portugal has a relatively better endowment of wine-making factors (for example, land and climate) than does England.

What we have been discussing is the principle of **comparative advantage,** namely, that a country tends to produce and export those goods in which it has the greater comparative advantage (or the least comparative disadvantage) and import those goods in which it has the least comparative advantage (or the greatest comparative disadvantage). On this basis, it is possible to predict what goods a nation will export and import. As Smith suggested, the nation maximizes its supply of goods by concentrating production where it is most efficient, and trading some of these products for imported products where it is least efficient. An examination of the exports and imports of most nations tends to support this theory.

Product Life Cycle

A recent refinement in trade theory is related to the **product life cycle,** which in marketing refers to the consumption pattern for a product. When applied to international trade theory, it refers primarily to international trade and production patterns. According to this concept, many products go through a trade cycle wherein one nation is initially an exporter, then loses its export markets, and finally may become an importer of the product. Empirical studies have demonstrated the validity of the model for some kinds of manufactured goods.[1]

Outlined below are the four phases in the production and trade cycle, with the United States as an example. We'll assume a U.S. firm has come up with a high-tech product. (See also Chapter 9.)

Phase 1. U.S. export strength is evident.
Phase 2. Foreign production starts.
Phase 3. Foreign production becomes competitive in export markets.
Phase 4. Import competition begins.

In Phase 1, product innovation is likely to be related to the needs of the home market. The firm usually serves its home market first. The new product is produced in the home market because, as the firm moves down the production learning curve, it needs to communicate with both suppliers and customers. As it begins to fill home-market needs, the firm begins to export the new product, seizing on its first-mover advantages. (We assume the U.S. firm is exporting to Europe.)

In Phase 2, importing countries gain familiarity with the new product. Gradually, producers in wealthy countries begin producing the product for their own markets. (Most product innovations begin in one rich country and then move to other rich countries.) Foreign production will reduce the exports of the innovating firm. (We assume that the U.S. firm's exports to Europe are replaced by production within Europe.)

In Phase 3, foreign firms gain production experience and move down the cost curve. If they have lower costs than the innovating firm, which is frequently the case, they export to third-country markets, replacing the innovator's exports there. (We assume that European firms are now exporting to Latin America, taking away the U.S. firm's export markets there.)

In Phase 4, the foreign producers now have sufficient production experience and economies of scale to allow them to export back to the innovator's home country. (We will assume the European producers have now taken away the home market of the original U.S. innovator.)

In Phase 1 the product is "new." In Phase 2 it is "maturing." In Phases 3 and 4 it is "standardized." The product may become so standardized by Phase 4 that it almost becomes a commodity. Textiles in general are an example of a product in Phase 4. Products in Phase 4 may be produced in less developed countries for export to the developed countries. This modification of the theory of comparative advantage provides further insight into patterns of international trade and production and helps the international company plan logistics, such as when it will need to produce—or source—abroad.

Balance of Payments

In the study of international trade, the principal source of information is the **balance-of-payments** statement of the trading nations. These are summary statements of all the economic transactions between one country and all other countries over a period of time, usually one year.

In governmental reporting, the balance of payments is often broken down into a current account and one or more capital accounts. The current account is a record of all the goods and services the nation exchanged with other nations. The capital account includes international financial transactions, such as private foreign investment and government borrowing, lending, or payments. The international marketer usually is more interested in the details of current account transactions, that is, the nature of the goods being traded and their origin and destination. The *World Trade Annual* contains an international summary based on United Nations data.

Marketing Decisions

The balance of payments is an indicator of the international economic health of a country. Its data help government policymakers plan monetary, fiscal, foreign exchange, and commercial policies. Such data can also provide information for decisions in international marketing. In our discussion of international trade, we presented tables containing information useful in international marketing decisions; these tables are drawn from balance-of-payments data. Two important decisions for a firm are the choice of location of supply for foreign markets and the selection of markets to sell to. Balance-of-payments analysis can show which nations are importers and exporters of the products in question. The firm can thus identify its own best import and export targets, that is, countries to sell to and countries to supply from. Longitudinal analysis of the balance of payments can help to track the international product life cycle.

When the firm is considering foreign market opportunities, it finds a country's import statistics for its products to be a preliminary indicator of market potential. Furthermore, the firm can get an indication of the competition in these countries by noting the nations supplying the products in question. The statistics sometimes even permit identification of low-price supplying nations and high-price (high-quality?) suppliers. Please note, though, that the use of balance-of-payments data requires that a period of several years be considered to get an idea of trends.

Data in Table 2–3 are taken from the *World Trade Annual,* a comprehensive five-volume publication detailing exports and imports by Standard International Trade Classification (SITC) category. Only very partial data are given for illustrative purposes.

Page 42 shows a partial list of some of the major importing countries for dental instruments and the countries that supplied them. Page 43 shows a similar list of the exporters and the markets to which they exported. Analysis of this kind of data from countries' balance of payments permits helpful competitive analysis.

Financial Considerations

Up to now, we have considered primarily the current account in the balance of payments, especially the movement of goods reflected in that account. A look at the capital account is also useful. A nation's international solvency can be evaluated by checking its capital account over several years. If the nation is steadily losing its gold and foreign exchange reserves, there is a strong likelihood of a currency devaluation or some kind of exchange control, meaning that the government restricts the amount of money sent out of the country as well as the uses to which it can be put. With exchange control, the firm may have difficulty getting foreign exchange to repatriate profits or even to import its products. If the firm is importing products that are not considered necessary, the scarce foreign exchange will go instead to goods on which the nation places a higher priority.

TABLE 2–3   **Example of Import/Export Statistics from Balance-of-Payments Data**

SITC Number / Importer / Provenance	Quantity Unit		Value Thousands of U.S. Dollars
872.01 Dental Instruments			
Canada ....Tot			3709
USA			3156
Austria			97
Germany			356
Sweden			72
USA ....Tot			6397
Brazil			127
Japan			1910
Austria			1336
Denmark			929
Germany			262
Ireland			211
Italy			56
Sweden			1009
United Kingdom			76
Switzerland			427
Israel ....Tot			1075
USA			203
Japan			517
Finland			71
France			160
Japan ....Tot	W	12	3626
USA	W	3	410
France	W		138
Germany	W	5	2053
Switzerland	W	2	945
Austria ....Tot	W	606	10335
USA	W	2	104
Denmark	W	5	721
Finland	W	4	397
France	W	1	55
Germany	W	147	4560
Italy	W	446	4158
Sweden	W		77
Switzerland	W	1	218
Belgium-Lux ....Tot	W	48	3291
USA	W	8	388
Japan	W	4	189
Denmark	W	4	376
Finland	W	2	89
France	W	2	344
Germany	W	10	936
Italy	W	17	798
Switzerland	W		75
Denmark ....Tot	W	30	3104
Japan	W	1	181
Finland	W	7	551
Germany	W	5	548
Italy	W	13	422
Sweden	W	3	175
Switzerland	W	1	1143
Finland ....Tot	W	9	734
Denmark	W	7	466
Switzerland	W		70
France ....Tot	W	67	4248
USA	W	13	609
Turkey	W	22	128
Belgium-Lux	W		141
Denmark	W	5	494
Finland	W	2	119
Germany	W	7	657
Italy	W	15	1444
Spain	W	1	54
Sweden	W	1	309
Switzerland	W	1	207
Areas Nes	W		66
Germany ....Tot	W	238	13942
USA	W	8	819
Israel	W	1	53
Japan	W	8	945
Austria	W	7	767
Denmark	W	4	369
872.01 Dental Instruments (Cont.)			
Germany (continued)			
Finland	W	13	947
Italy	W	172	6406
Sweden	W	1	97
Switzerland	W	18	3195
Slovakia	W	4	154
Greece ....Tot	W	7	349
Germany	W		76
Italy	W	3	117
Ireland ....Tot	W	1	82
Switzerland	W		54
	W	64	9208
Italy ....Tot	W		
USA	W	3	408
Japan	W	1	128
Austria	W		55
Denmark	W	1	80
Finland	W	3	335
Germany	W	50	7099
Sweden	W	1	371
Switzerland	W	2	618
Netherlands ....Tot	W	45	4361
USA	W	2	107
Belgium-Lux	W	1	79
Germany	W	29	2686
Italy	W	10	843
Sweden	W	2	520
Switzerland	W		51
Portugal ....Tot	W	27	1321
Italy	W	25	1183
Spain ....Tot	W	194	6655
USA	W	6	233
France	W	16	182
Germany	W	59	2617
Italy	W	91	2816
Portugal	W	14	157
Sweden	W	1	510
Untd Kingdom	W	3	67
Sweden ....Tot	W	67	22621
USA	W	1	86
Denmark	W	9	13694
Finland	W	2	212
Germany	W	53	8048
Italy	W		138
Switzerland	W	1	214
Untd Kingdom ....Tot	W	66	3807
USA	W	1	129
Finland	W	10	449
Germany	W	10	849
Italy	W	42	1654
Sweden	W	1	207
Switzerland	W	1	191
Hungary	W		198
Iceland ....Tot	W	1	146
Norway ....Tot	W	54	5847
Denmark	W	10	1048
Finland	W	20	1570
Germany	W	21	2779
Sweden	W	2	295
Switzerland	W		68
Switzerland ....Tot	W	42	5838
Denmark	W	1	136
Germany	W	29	4584
Italy	W	11	701
Sweden	W		148
Untd Kingdom	W		105
Australia ....Tot			226
Germany			54
New Zealand ....Tot			92
USA			50

SITC Number / Exporter / Destination	Quantity Unit	Value Thousands of U.S. Dollars

872.01 Dental Instruments

Exporter / Destination	W	Qty	Value
USA (continued)			
Qatar			55
Saudi Arabia			274
Untd Arab Em			104
Turkey			84
China			436
Hong Kong			822
Korea Rep.			691
Malaysia			619
Oth. Asia Nes			632
India			217
Singapore			562
Thailand			1203
Austria			119
Belgium-Lux			842
Finland			167
France			2096
Germany			9547
Greece			94
Italy			4415
Netherlands			1756
Spain			933
Sweden			95
Untd Kingdom			950
Norway			57
Switzerland			448
Hungary			52
Poland			137
Latvia			79
Lithuania			1398
Russian Fed			968
Ukraine			109
Australia			2916
New Zealand			154
Israel ....Tot			676
USA			169
Germany			323
Japan ....Tot	W	9	1800
USA	W	6	823
Colombia	W		51
Hong Kong	W		56
Korea Rep.	W		302
India	W		130
France	W	1	140
Italy	W		61
Austria ....Tot	W	36	4087
Germany	W	1	472
Italy	W	3	410
Switzerland	W	2	116
Czech Rep	W	4	262
Hungary	W	1	72
Russian Fed	W	14	2141
Croatia	W	4	88
Slovenia	W	5	364
Belgium-Lux ....Tot	W	6	844
Finland	W		87
France	W	1	84
Netherlands	W	4	478
Denmark ....Tot	W	147	12523
Japan	W	2	173
Austria	W	11	957
Belgium-Lux	W	10	792
Finland	W	5	404
France	W	30	2482
Germany	W	25	2106
Italy	W	12	997
Netherlands	W	14	1182
Portugal	W	2	144
Spain	W	1	93
Sweden	W	15	1212
Norway	W	13	1286
Switzerland	W	2	411
Russian Fed	W	1	73
Finland ....Tot	W	349	23984
USA	W	3	170
Israel	W	3	150
Japan	W	6	503
Turkey	W	2	104
China	W	74	4103
Korea Rep.	W	13	342
Oth. Asia Nes	W	4	133
Singapore	W	2	116
Thailand	W	21	1025
Austria	W	4	451

872.01 Dental Instruments (Cont.)

Exporter / Destination	W	Qty	Value
Finland (continued)			
Belgium-Lux	W	5	383
Denmark	W	5	498
France	W	22	2023
Germany	W	49	3423
Greece	W	2	113
Italy	W	17	1323
Netherlands	W	5	448
Portugal	W	2	177
Spain	W	4	300
Sweden	W	21	1973
Untd Kingdom	W	9	911
Norway	W	14	1951
Switzerland	W	1	129
Czech Rep	W	4	413
Hungary	W	1	56
Poland	W	5	180
Slovakia	W	1	57
Belarus	W	2	118
Estonia	W	17	868
Latvia	W	2	88
Lithuania	W	2	116
Russian Fed	W	20	1323
Ukraine	W	2	90
Australia	W	2	195
France ....Tot	W	30	1449
Morocco	W	5	315
Guinea	W	2	99
Canada	W		148
Untd Arab Em	W	1	85
Korea Rep.	W	1	67
Germany	W	5	252
Russian Fed	W	1	104
Germany ....Tot	W	1094	129355
S. Afr. Cust. U	W	7	877
Algeria	W		131
Libya	W	2	241
Morocco	W	1	78
Tunisia	W	1	54
Egypt	W	4	286
Angola	W		71
Ethiopia	W	4	412
Ghana	W		134
Canada	W	4	427
USA	W	31	3247
Argentina	W	1	111
Brazil	W	8	1333
Israel	W	5	310
Japan	W	76	11889
Cyprus	W	1	95
Jordan	W	1	68
Kuwait	W		71
Lebanon	W	1	86
Saudi Arabia	W	11	1303
Untd Arab Em	W	2	260
Turkey	W	1	112
China	W	3	450
Hong Kong	W	7	881
Indonesia	W	2	368
Korea D P RP	W		58
Korea Rep.	W	13	1533
Malaysia	W	6	794
Oth. Asia Nes	W	10	811
Pakistan	W	1	68
India	W	5	605
Singapore	W	30	2067
Thailand	W	5	834
Kazakstan	W	1	74
Austria	W	60	8801
Belgium-Lux	W	42	4274
Denmark	W	15	2109
Finland	W	3	881
France	W	163	18224
Greece	W	31	2196
Ireland	W	1	143
Italy	W	90	9389
Netherlands	W	72	9317
Portugal	W	9	759
Spain	W	79	6294
Sweden	W	26	3203
Untd Kingdom	W	54	6329
Norway	W	12	1495
Switzerland	W	54	8509
Albania	W	4	208
Bulgaria	W	4	377
Czech Rep	W	4	550
Hungary	W	8	562

W = weight in metric tons
Source: *World Trade Annual 1995*, vol. 4 (New York: Walker and Company, 1997), 179, 551.

The firm's pricing policies, too, are affected by the balance-of-payments problems of the host country. If the firm cannot repatriate profits from a country, it tries to use its transfer pricing to minimize the profits earned in that country, gaining its profits elsewhere where it can repatriate them. If the exporting firm fears devaluation of a currency, it hesitates to quote prices in that currency, preferring to give terms in its home currency or another "safe" currency. Thus, for both international marketing and international finance, the balance of payments is an important information source.

Commercial Policy

One reason international trade is different from domestic trade is that it is carried on between different political units, each one a sovereign nation exercising control over its own trade. Although all nations control their foreign trade, they vary in the degree of such control. Each nation invariably establishes laws that favor its nationals and discriminate against traders from other countries. This means, for example, that a U.S. firm trying to sell in the French market faces certain handicaps deriving from the French government's control over its trade. These handicaps to the U.S. firm are in addition to any disadvantages resulting from distance or cultural differences. By the same token, the French firm trying to sell in the United States faces similar restrictions when competing with U.S. firms selling in their home market.

Commercial policy is the term used to refer to government regulations bearing on foreign trade. The principal tools of commercial policy are tariffs, quotas, exchange control, and administrative regulation (the "invisible tariff"). Each of these will be discussed in turn as it relates to the task of the international marketer.

Tariffs

A **tariff** is a tax on products imported from other countries. The tax may be levied on the quantity—such as 10 cents per pound, gallon, or yard—or on the value of the imported goods—such as 10 or 20 percent *ad valorem*. A tariff levied on quantity is called a *specific duty* and is used especially for primary commodities. Ad valorem duties are generally levied on manufactured products.

Governments may have two purposes in imposing tariffs: They may wish to earn revenue and/or make foreign goods more expensive in order to protect national producers. When the United States was a new nation, most government revenues came from tariffs. Many less developed countries today earn a large amount of their revenue from tariffs because they are among the easiest taxes to collect. Today, however, the protective purpose generally prevails. One could argue that with a tariff, a country penalizes its consumers by making them pay higher prices on imported goods; it penalizes its producers that import raw materials or components. The rationale is that a policy that is too liberal with imports may hurt employment in that country's own industries.

Tariffs affect pricing, product, and distribution policies of the international marketer as well as foreign investment decisions. If the firm is supplying a market by exports, the tariff increases the price of its product and reduces competitiveness in that market. This necessitates a price structure that minimizes the tariff barrier. A greater emphasis on marginal cost pricing could result. This examination of price is accompanied by a review of other aspects of the firm's approach to the market. The product may be modified or stripped down to lower the price or to get a more favorable tariff classification. For example, watches could be taxed either as timepieces at one rate or as jewelry at a higher rate. The manufacturer might be able to adapt its product to meet the lower tariff.

Another way the manufacturer can minimize the tariff burden is to ship products completely knocked down (CKD) for assembly in the local market. The tariff on unassembled products or ingredients is usually lower than that on completely finished goods. The importing country employs a tariff differential to promote local employment. This establishment of local assembly operations is a form of the phenomenon known as a **tariff factory,** the term used when the primary reason a local plant exists is to get behind the tariff barrier to protect markets that a firm can no longer serve with direct exports. Taken to the extreme, the phenomenon would result in complete local production rather than just assembly.

In some circumstances, the firm may seek to turn the tariff to its own advantage. Assume that the host country is exerting pressure for local manufacture that will be noncompetitive with existing sources. The firm might acquiesce on the condition that the plant it sets up be protected by tariffs imposed against more efficient outside suppliers. It would seek this protection as an "infant industry" against mature companies abroad. Thus, if the firm becomes a local company it may benefit from the tariff protection.

Quotas

Quantitative restrictions, or **quotas,** are barriers to imports. They set absolute limits on the amount of goods that may enter the country. An import quota can be a more serious restriction than a tariff because the firm has less flexibility in responding to it. Price or product modifications do not get around quotas the way they might get around tariffs. The government's goal in establishing quotas on imports is obviously not revenue. It gets none. Its goal is rather the conservation of scarce foreign exchange and/or the protection of local production in the product lines affected. About the only response the firm can make to a quota is to assure itself a share of the quota or to set up local production if the market size warrants it. Since the latter is in accord with the wishes of government, the firm might be regarded favorably for taking such action.

The Japanese auto companies in the United States illustrate problems firms can have with quotas. For many years, the United States had a "voluntary" quota on Japanese car imports. Japanese producers responded in two ways: (1) They exported more expensive cars with higher margins, thereby earning high profits. (2) They also built assembly plants in the United States as the long-run solution to quota constraints.

In 1989, the U.S. Customs Service ruled that the Suzuki Samurai and most small vans would be classified as "trucks" subject to a 25 percent tariff rather than as "cars," subject to a 2.5 percent duty. The positive side of the ruling was that this would allow more "car" imports by the Japanese (to replace the vehicles reclassified as trucks). American auto firms applauded the decision but the Japanese (and European) producers complained.

Exchange Control

The most complete tool for regulation of foreign trade is **exchange control,** a government monopoly of all dealings in foreign exchange. Exchange control means that foreign exchange is scarce and that the government is rationing it out according to its own priorities. A national company earning foreign exchange from its exports must sell this foreign exchange to the control agency, usually the central bank. In turn, a company wishing to buy goods from abroad must buy its foreign exchange from the control agency.

Firms in the country have to be on the government's favored list to get exchange for imported supplies. Alternatively, they may try to develop local suppliers, running the risk of higher costs and indifferent quality control. The firms exporting to that nation must also be on the government's favored list. Otherwise, they will lose their market if importers can get no foreign exchange to pay them. Generally, exchange-control countries favor the import of capital goods and necessary consumer goods but not luxuries. While the definition of "luxuries" varies from country to country, it usually includes cars, appliances, and cosmetics. If the exporter does lose its market through exchange control, about the only option is to produce within the country if the market is large enough for this to be profitable.

Another implication for the firm when foreign exchange is limited is that the government is unlikely to give priority to a company's profit remittances as a way of using the country's scarce foreign earnings. In this situation, the firm tries to use transfer pricing to get earnings out of the host country or to avoid accumulating earnings there. It accomplishes this by charging high transfer prices on supplies sold to the subsidiary and low transfer prices on goods sold by that subsidiary to affiliates of the company in other markets. The firm's ability to do this depends on the plan's acceptance by tax officials of the country.

For international executives in exchange-control countries, dealing with the government exchange authorities is a major preoccupation and problem—and never more so than in Venezuela, where, in 1989, the government issued arrest warrants for 47 executives of multinational companies for abuses in dealing with the government foreign exchange office. All charged professed innocence, and many left the country.

Invisible Tariff and Other Government Barriers

There are other government barriers to international trade that are hard to classify—for example, administrative protection, the invisible tariff, or **nontariff barriers (NTBs).** As traditional trade barriers have declined since World War II, the NTBs have taken on added significance. They include such things as customs documentation requirements, marks of origin, food and drug laws, labeling laws, anti-dumping laws, "buy national" policies, and so on. Because these barriers are so diverse, their impact cannot be covered in a brief discussion. Their implications will be discussed in Part 2. For the present, it is sufficient to note that they can affect many elements of marketing strategy. See "Global Marketing," "The Anti-Dumping Weapon of the Steel Industry."

OTHER DIMENSIONS AND INSTITUTIONS IN THE WORLD ECONOMY

GATT–WTO

Because each nation is sovereign in determining its own commercial policy, the danger is that arbitrary national actions will minimize international trade. This was the situation in the 1930s when international trade was at a low ebb and each nation tried to maintain domestic employment while restricting imports that might help foreign rather than domestic employment. The bankruptcy of these "beggar my neighbor" policies was evident in the worldwide depression to which they contributed. This unhappy experience led the major trading nations to seek better solutions after World War II. One outcome of their efforts was the **General Agreement on Tariffs and Trade (GATT),** now called the **World Trade Organization (WTO).**

Although GATT's initial membership consisted of only 23 countries, these included the major trading nations of the Western world. Today, WTO is more than ever the world's trading club, accounting for over 90 percent of world trade. It has about 130 members, with more wanting to join, notably China. GATT–WTO has certainly contributed to the expansion of world trade. Since 1947, it has sponsored eight major multilateral tariff negotiations, the latest being the Uruguay Round, which lasted from 1986 to 1993. As a result of these conferences, the tariff rates for tens of thousands of items have been reduced, and a high proportion of world trade has seen an easing of restrictions.

Providing a framework for multilateral trade negotiations is a primary reason for WTO's existence, but there are other WTO principles that further trade expansion. One is the principle of **nondiscrimination.** Each contracting party must grant

GLOBAL MARKETING

The Anti-Dumping Weapon of the Steel Industry

Anti-dumping laws are meant to prevent foreign firms from selling into the U.S. market at "unfairly low prices" and harming American competitors. In the past two decades the U.S. steel industry accounted for almost 50 percent of all the complaints filed before the U.S. International Trade Commission (ITC). They have lost more than half of these cases.

The steel industry has found that it is not necessary to win the case before the ITC to be a winner. The director of the American Institute for International Steel explains, "You can use the trade laws to affect supply in the marketplace. Whenever the market goes soft, the steel industry will file."

When the market is weak and the industry files a case, it takes months to go through a four-step legal process. If the industry wins the first round, showing a "reasonable indication" of harm from imports, preliminary duties are placed on the imports and importers must post a bond to cover them. If the importers finally win the case months later, the duty is not paid and the bond is lifted. In the meantime, while the case is unwinding, the U.S. steelmakers have been able to raise prices and increase their sales because of the deterrent effect of the anti-dumping complaint on imports. One study showed that the average petitioner between 1980 and 1992 showed a $46 million increase in market value as a result of filing an anti-dumping petition.

Sources: *The Wall Street Journal,* March 27, 1998. A1; "Creating Barriers for Foreign Competitors: Anti-dumping" Sarah Marsh, *Strategic Management Journal,* volume 19, 25 (1998).

all others the same rate of import duty; that is, a tariff concession granted to one trading partner must be extended to all WTO members under the most-favored-nation clause (MFN).

Another WTO principle is the concept of **consultation.** When trade disagreements arise, WTO provides a forum for consultation. In such an atmosphere, disagreeing members are more likely to compromise than to resort to arbitrary trade-restricting actions. All in all, world-trade cooperation since World War II has led to a much better trading policy than the world might have expected. GATT–WTO has been a major contributor to this.

Some indication of the scope of WTO's activities in this area can be seen in "Global Marketing," "Some WTO Committees and Working Groups." Economic troubles are making further contributions from WTO very difficult. Unemployment in the industrialized nations, large trade deficits in the United States, and heavy debt in many developing countries are causing nations to give more attention to national concerns than to international cooperation.

UNCTAD

Although GATT–WTO has been an important force in world-trade expansion, benefits have not been distributed equally. The less developed countries have been dissatisfied with trade arrangements because their share of world trade has been declining, and the prices of their raw material exports compare unfavorably with the prices of their manufactured goods imports. Though many of these countries are members of WTO, they felt that GATT did more to further trade in goods of industrialized nations than it did to promote their own primary products. It is true that tariff reductions have been far more important to manufactured goods than to primary products. The result of these countries' dissatisfaction was the formation of the **United Nations Conference on Trade and Development (UNCTAD)** in 1964. UNCTAD is a permanent organ of the United Nations General Assembly and counts over 160 member countries.

The goal of UNCTAD is to further the development of emerging nations—by trade as well as by other means. Under GATT, trade expanded, especially in manufactured goods, creating a growing trade gap between industrial and developing

GLOBAL MARKETING

 Some WTO Committees and Working Groups

MEETINGS (November)

3–4	Working Group on Transparency in Government Procurement
3–5	Committee on Regional Trade Agreements
5–7	WP on Preshipment Inspection
7	Council for Trade in Goods
10	Cttee. on Trade in Civil Aircraft Cttee. on BOP Restrictions
10–12	Textiles Monitoring Body
11	Council for Trade in Services
12–13	Cttee. on Tech. Barriers to Trade
13	Council for Trade in Goods
14	Cttee. on Trade in Financial Serv.
17	Cttee. on Government Procurement Cttee. on Trade and Development
17–21	Council for TRIPS
18	Dispute Settlement Body
19	Council for Trade in Goods
20–21	Committee on Agriculture
21	Committee on Rules of Origin
24–26	Cttee. on Trade and Environment
25–26	Trade Policy Review: EC
26	Working Party on GATS Rules
27–28	WG on the Interaction between Trade and Competition Policy

Source: *WTO Focus,* September 1997, 8.

countries. UNCTAD seeks to improve the prices of primary goods exports through commodity agreements. If the commodity-producing countries could get together to control supply, this would mean higher prices and higher returns.

UNCTAD also worked to establish a tariff preference system favoring the export of manufactured goods from less developed countries. Since these countries have not been able to export commodities in a quantity sufficient to maintain their share of trade, they want to expand in the growth area of world trade: industrial exports. They believe they might achieve this if manufactured goods coming from developing countries faced lower tariffs than the same goods coming from developed countries.

UNCTAD has made modest progress. One achievement is its own formation, a new club for world trade matters that is a lobbying group for developing-country interests. Tanzanian leader Julius Nyerere called it "the labor union of the developing countries." Through UNCTAD, developing countries have also received preferential tariff treatment from the EU, Japan, and the United States, as they requested. Overall, UNCTAD has focused world attention on the trade needs of developing countries and has given them a more coherent voice. UNCTAD's committees and studies have also made for a more informed dialog.

WTO, UNCTAD, and the Firm

WTO's success in reducing barriers to trade has meant that a firm's global logistics can be more efficient. Further, the firm, through its subsidiaries in various markets, can help protect its interest in trade matters through discussions with governments in advance of trade negotiations. In the United States, for example, a committee holds hearings at which business representatives can present their international

**Eastern Europe:
Commerce Opens for BISNI**

The Commerce Department, recognizing the pote
portance of the Eastern European market, has opene
ness Information Service for the Newly Independe
(BISNIS). It is a one-stop shop for U.S. firms inte
doing business in these countries.

BISNIS has established a network that provides t
with continuous updates on business opportunities a

Source: Department of Commerce, 1998.

These s
nese Econo
Africa, Sout
Given t
ing its expo
has been es
develop a b
cial Center.
stronger co
gic industri
technologie
nologies (ir
energy tech

Regional

Another m
ings. The E
only one of
the same re
litical ties b
us here. **Re**
tions to atta
military fiel
There a
must give u
hope the be
economic ir
get larger re
other objec
seeks a stro
The re
economies

trading problems. These problems are noted for consideration in WTO negotiations. Firms in the EU usually work with trade associations that channel industry views to the EU negotiators. Brazil also looks to trade associations for industry views.

UNCTAD can have a more direct impact on the firm than WTO. International firms can play a major role relating to the tariff preferences granted by the industrialized nations. Developing countries have limited experience in exporting manufactured goods. Elimination of tariffs by itself is not sufficient to help them. Here the multinational firm can be a decisive factor. If the firm combines its know-how and resources with those of the host country, it could offer competitive exports. Included in the firm's resources is its global distribution network, which could be the critical factor in gaining foreign market access. Also, the firm supplies the foreign marketing know-how lacked by most developing-country producers. For example, if Ford had the choice of importing engines from its plant in Britain or its plant in Brazil, it might choose Brazil if engines from Brazil had a zero tariff and engines from Europe faced a 15 percent duty.

A complementarity of interest may exist between the less developed countries and international firms in the question of preferences. On the one hand, the marriage of these interests could help nations achieve their industrialization and balance-of-payments goals; on the other, multinational companies could expand their international markets and participate more actively in the growth of the less developed nations, which have a majority of the world's population.

The New Eastern Europe

One of the major developments in recent history was the fall of the Berlin Wall and the decline of the Communist-bloc monolith. Today more than 20 independent states were formerly members of the Communist bloc dominated by the Soviet Union. The breakdown and fragmentation of this Communist monolith reduced the threat of war between East and West and significantly improved economic relations between the two groups. Each side considered the other to be the enemy until about 1990; today they share generally friendly relations. The Western nations are even contributing financial assistance to Eastern European nations.

During the Cold War, many government restrictions existed on trade between East and West. One of the major sources of regulations on the Western side was NATO. During the last years of the Cold War, each side shipped only about $60 billion of goods annually to the other—very small volume given the size of each group. Today, with these restrictions being relaxed and with the Eastern countries moving toward a freer market economy, the volume of trade could rise dramatically.

The countries of Eastern Europe provide a very attractive potential market for Western firms. For one thing, they have a population of about 400 million, which is more than that of all of Western Europe. Second, they have some familiarity with and a desire for Western goods and a Western standard of living—and they are closer to reaching it than markets in the Third World. As a result, Western firms from many countries and many industries are either participating in Eastern Europe markets or are considering doing so. A brief profile is given in Table 2–4.

It should be noted that the GNP figures for the former USSR countries would be very much higher if they were on a purchasing power parity basis instead of on a dollar exchange-rate basis.

Although the market potential looks attractive, many potential problems in Eastern Europe should cause Western firms to proceed cautiously. After years of Communist rule, Eastern European countries need to establish a legal system that can deal properly with a market economy and property rights. In addition, they lack hard currencies and stable monetary systems. After decades of a command economy, people and institutions lack a commercial or market mentality. Problems in adjusting to a market economy have caused political instability. The Russian crisis of

TABLE 2–4	Central Europe and	

	Population (Millions)
Central Europe	
Albania	3.3
Bulgaria	8.4
Czech Republic	10.3
Hungary	10.2
Poland	38.6
Romania	22.6
Slovak Republic	5.3
Former USSR	
Armenia	3.8
Azerbaijan	7.6
Belorussia	10.3
Estonia	1.5
Georgia	5.4
Kazakstan	16.5
Kyrgyzstan	4.6
Latvia	2.5
Lithuania	3.7
Moldova	4.3
Russia	147.7
Tajikistan	5.9
Turkmenistan	4.6
Ukraine	50.7
Uzbekistan	23.2

Source: *1998 World Bank Atlas* (Washington, DC: World Bank, 1998)

TABLE 2–5	Big Emerging Markets

Big Emerging Markets	1997 Total Imports (billions of dollars)
Chinese Economic Area (China, Hong Kong, Taiwan)	$464
ASEAN[a]	354
India	41
South Korea	145
Mexico	113
Argentina	31
Brazil	66
South Africa	26
Poland	42
Turkey	47
Total	1,329

Source: Calculated from *International Financial Statistics,* August 1998.
[a]ASEAN—Brunei, Burma, Indonesia, Laos, Malaysia, Philippines, Singapore, Thailand, Vietnam.

their protective walls and are forced to change in a more competitive direction. Furthermore, the group of countries together may be able to afford an industry too large for any individual member country. Thus, industrialization can be aided by regional integration. All this could mean greater wealth, progress, and self-sufficiency for the region. Various forms and degrees of economic integration are possible.

Free-Trade Area

Although all regional groupings have economic goals, the various groups differ in organization and motivation. There are three basic kinds of organization for economic integration. The simplest is a **free-trade area,** in which the member countries agree to have free movement of goods among themselves; that is, no tariffs or quotas are imposed against goods coming from other members. The European Free Trade Association (EFTA) was a major example. Composed of Austria, Britain, Switzerland, and the Scandinavian countries, EFTA achieved an industrial free-trade area in 1967. EFTA, however, lost most of its membership when Britain and Denmark joined the EU in 1973, followed by Austria, Finland, and Sweden in 1994. The remaining members continue EFTA as an industrial free-trade area, although agricultural products are still subject to restrictions. In any case, EFTA and the EU have been joined in a giant industrial free-trade area since 1977, joining most of Western Europe together for trade in manufactured goods.

In the 1960s, the Latin Americans responded to European integration moves by forming regional groupings of their own. In Central America, they formed the Central American Common Market; in South America, they formed the Latin American Free Trade Area; the Andean countries broke away from LAFTA to form the Andean Common Market. Unfortunately, none of these groups has made rapid progress. In the early 1990s, the Southern Cone countries (Argentina, Brazil, Paraguay, Uruguay) formed Mercosur, which has made rapid progress. It is now the most successful and promising regional grouping apart from the EU.

During the Vietnam War, a number of Southeast Asian nations formed ASEAN (Association of Southeast Asian Nations). ASEAN had political overtones as well as economic goals, but it made only modest progress at economic integration over the next two decades. In 1998, however, the leaders reaffirmed their

TABLE 2-6	Some Principal Regional Economic Groupings

Group Name	Members
ANCOM: Andean Common Market	Bolivia, Colombia, Ecuador, Peru, Venezuela
ASEAN: Association of Southeast Asian Nations	Brunei, Burma (Myanmar), Indonesia, Malaysia, Philippines, Singapore, Thailand, Vietnam, Laos.
CACM: Central American Common Market	Costa Rica, El Salvador, Guatemala, Honduras, Nicaragua
ECOWAS: Economic Community of West African States	Benin, Burkina Faso, Cape Verde, Ivory Coast, the Gambia, Ghana, Guinea, Liberia, Mali, Mauritania, Niger, Nigeria, Senegal, Sierra Leone, Togo
EU: European Union	Austria, Belgium, Denmark, Finland, France, Germany, Greece, Ireland, Italy, Luxembourg, Netherlands, Portugal, Spain, Sweden, United Kingdom
Mercosur	Argentina, Brazil, Paraguay, Uruguay (Bolivia and Chile have observer status)
NAFTA: North American Free Trade Area	Canada, Mexico, United States

commitment to achieve an Asian Free Trade Area (AFTA) by 2003. The Asian troubles may affect this.

The United States is a member of two free-trade areas, one with Israel and one with Canada and Mexico in NAFTA. NAFTA is very important because it creates a free-trade area of 360 million consumers—as large as the EU-EFTA grouping. As with any regional grouping, NAFTA has encountered some rough spots, but its importance can be seen in the fact that the three member countries are each other's largest customers and suppliers.

There was discussion during the Clinton administration of forming a free trade area of all the Americas, North and South. Though there is interest from most countries in the Americas, it is still just an idea on the horizon.

Customs Union

Though similar to a free-trade area in that it has no tariffs on trade among members, a **customs union** has the more ambitious requirement that members also have a uniform tariff on trade with nonmembers. Thus, a customs union is like a single nation, not only in internal trade, but also in presenting a united front to the rest of the world with its common external tariff. A customs union is more difficult to achieve than a free-trade area because each member must yield its sovereignty in commercial policy matters, not just with member nations but with the whole world. Its advantage lies in making the economic integration stronger and avoiding the administrative problems of a free-trade area. For example, in a free-trade area, imports of a particular good would always enter the member country with the lowest tariff on that good, regardless of the country of destination. To avoid this perversion of trade patterns, special regulations are necessary.

The leading example of a customs union is the EU. Although the EU is often referred to as the *Common Market*, it is more accurately described as a customs union. In July 1968, the EU achieved a full customs union, a goal toward which member nations had been working since January 1, 1958. Though this is a slower timetable than that of EFTA, it represents a much more ambitious endeavor because it includes not only a free-trade area among members but also a common external tariff. In addition, it covers agricultural products, which were omitted by EFTA.

Common Market

A true **common market** includes a customs union but goes significantly beyond it because it seeks to standardize or harmonize all government regulations affecting trade. These include all aspects of government policy that pertain to business—for example, corporation and excise taxes, labor laws, fringe benefits and social security programs, incorporation laws, and antitrust laws. In such an economic union, business and trade decisions would be unaffected by the national laws of different members because they would be uniform. The United States is the closest example of a common market. Even here, however, the example is not perfect, because different states do have different laws and taxes pertaining to business. U.S. business decisions, therefore, are somewhat influenced by differing state laws.

The EU is the best contemporary example of a common market in formation. It always had the goal of achieving such status, but what it achieved earlier was actually a customs union with a few extra dimensions. What was exciting about 1992 was the member states undertaking 300 new directives to reach a true common market by harmonizing the different national regulations in 12 member countries. Even though this goal was not reached fully by 1992, great strides toward market integration were made. The fact that 300 directives were still necessary 30 years after forming the EU shows how difficult and complex it is to form a true common market.

The Single Market continues in Europe with two major new steps. One is the monetary union with the Euro as the new single currency for most member countries. The second is the coming addition of five new members from Central Europe. However, given the fact that the EU members have multiple languages, as well as diverse cultures, histories, and legal systems, it is not surprising that they continue to have trouble emulating the common market environment of the much more homogeneous United States.

Other Groupings

A number of examples exist of looser forms of economic cooperation. Many of these are of interest because they can affect the operations of the firm. Many nations of Africa are associate members of the EU and enjoy preferential entry of their goods into EU countries. EU producers in turn have an advantage over non-EU producers in selling to the associated states. Turkey is also an associate member of the EU. Israel signed an agreement in 1970.

The appearance of regional economic groupings is a promising development both for the regions and for multinational firms. The unfortunate reality is that except for the EU and Mercosur, these groupings have made very little progress. (See "Global Marketing," "Mercosur Marches On.")

While NAFTA has its problems, it should be a solid performer. Efforts elsewhere have done little, though ASEAN and Mercosur hold promise for the future. Where integration is successful, it offers great opportunities for firms that can operate within the group, but also great challenges for those that are on the outside. Firms should monitor their development.

Regionalism and the Multinational Company

The rise of regional groupings means that fewer but larger economic entities are gradually replacing the multitude of national markets. When a firm is considering an investment decision, the relevant market area may include up to 15 countries rather than just one national market. For example, the "United States of Europe" was one expression used to describe the new Europe. Much of the U.S. investment in Western Europe in the 1960s, and again in the 1980s, was a result of the larger market offered by the EU. In the 1980s the Japanese matched U.S. investments in the EU.

The firm's logistics will be modified by regional groupings. There will be pressures to supply from within a region rather than to export to it. The firm will have the added incentive of the larger market, but it will be pressured to get behind the external tariff to compete with local producers. At the same time, these local producers will become stronger competitors due to economies of scale in the larger

GLOBAL MARKETING

Mercosur Marches On

Mercosur is one of the brightest stars in the economic integration league. The group (Argentina, Brazil, Paraguay, and Uruguay) numbers over 200 million people and accounts for well over half of all Latin American GNP. Associate members Bolivia and Chile increase that share even more. The group has made serious moves toward a customs union and is even negotiating a free trade accord with the European Union.

The performance and promise of Mercosur have caught the eye of multinationals who have initiated or expanded their activities there. Bayer, Eli Lilly, Electrolux AB, and General Electric are examples. The automakers, however, are leading the way. Citroen, Peugeot, Renault, and Volkswagen are all adjusting and expanding there. Fiat put $1.6 billion of new money into Brazil and Argentina and will have a new model designed especially for Mercosur.

General Motors returns to Argentina with a new car and truck assembly plant costing over $1 billion. Ford also is investing over $1 billion in Argentina to modernize and add capacity. It will produce the Escort there, as well as a new compact pick-up truck. Chrysler, a newcomer, will invest about $100 million to produce all-terrain vehicles and assemble the Jeep Grand Cherokee. Toyota is putting another $100 million to expand its Mercosur operations. These expressions of confidence from the multinationals will help assure the success of Mercosur.

market, the alliances they are forming, and the stronger competition in the free-trade area. A firm's operations within a regional group will tend to be more uniform and self-contained than they would be in ungrouped national markets.

The firm's marketing program will be modified. As the differences in markets diminish, greater uniformity will occur in marketing to the member countries. The firm will gain economies of scale in product development, pricing, distribution, and promotion. For example, as member nations harmonize their food, drug, and labeling laws, the firm can eliminate product and packaging differences that were required by different national laws. Similar modifications will occur in the other functional areas. The following examples illustrate how firms have adapted to take advantage of the new market realities created by regional groupings.

A manufacturer of home-care products closed down eight national production sources in Europe soon after its common market was formed. The firm concentrated its continental European production in the Netherlands to gain economies of scale possible within the free-trade area. To further facilitate and benefit from centralized production, the firm standardized its package sizes and designs, including color, even though copy was continued in different national languages.

As another example, Eversharp was challenging Gillette's strong position in razor blades in Latin America. Gillette had plants in Argentina, Brazil, Mexico, and Colombia. Eversharp chose to begin production in Venezuela, where it could purchase a local blade manufacturer. There it could protect the local market while gaining entry into third markets in LAFTA. One of Eversharp's managers in Venezuela acted as LAFTA coordinator to search out opportunities for further concessions in LAFTA markets. With the help of the Venezuelan government, happy to see its exports expand, this effort paid off. Two of Gillette's protected markets, Mexico and Colombia, were opened to Eversharp through the LAFTA negotiation process.

International Financial System

A major goal of business is to make a profit, so firms pay close attention to financial matters. International companies must be even more concerned with financial matters than national firms are because they must deal with many currencies and many national financial markets where conditions differ from one to the other. Marketing across national boundaries involves financial considerations, which we will discuss here.

Exchange Rate Instability

The international payments system is the financial side of international trade. A special dimension is the fact that transactions occur in many different currencies. Dealing with multiple currencies is not a serious problem in itself. The difficulty arises because currencies frequently change in value vis-à-vis each other, and in unpredictable ways. Since 1973 the major currencies have been floating, often in a volatile manner.

The exchange rate is the domestic price of a foreign currency. For the United States, this means that there is a dollar rate, or price, for the British pound, the Swiss franc, and the Brazilian real, as well as every other currency. If one country changes the value of its currency, firms selling to or from that country may find that the altered exchange rate is sufficient to wipe out their profit, or, on the brighter side, give them a windfall gain. In any case, they must be alert for currency variations in order to optimize their financial performance. (See "Global Marketing," "Facing the Mexican Peso Crisis.")

In the days of the gold standard, exchange rates did not change in value. The stability and certainty of the international gold standard came to an end, however, with the advent of World War I. The international financial system of the 1930s had no certainty, stability, or accepted rules. Instead, there were frequent and arbitrary changes in exchange rates. This chaotic and uncertain situation contributed to the decline in international trade during that period. The worldwide Depression of the 30s was reinforced by the added risks in international finance.

In 1944, some of the allied nations met at Bretton Woods to design a better international economic system for the postwar world. One element of this system dealt with international trade and left us with WTO. Another element, concerned with the need for international capital, led to the formation of the World Bank. A third aspect involving the international monetary system resulted in the establishment of the International Monetary Fund (IMF).

International Monetary Fund (IMF)

The Bretton Woods international monetary system was an attempt to avoid the uncertainty of the 1930s and to regain some of the stability of exchange rates that existed under the gold standard. Countries that joined the **International Monetary Fund (IMF)** were required to establish a par value for their currency (in terms of the U.S. dollar) and maintain it within plus or minus 1 percent of that value. Up to 1970, the Bretton Woods system of stable "pegged" rates worked reasonably well, although numerous devaluations occurred during that period. The increased confidence in the international monetary system contributed to the great surge in international trade since World War II.

In the late 1960s and early 1970s, there existed very large funds in the hands of corporations, banks, and others with international dealings. This made it increasingly difficult for central banks to defend the par value of their currency. The holders of funds tended to move them out of currencies they considered weak, and into currencies they considered strong.

GLOBAL MARKETING

Facing the Mexican Peso Crisis

The promise of NAFTA for American marketers was improved access to the large and growing Mexican market. A major stumbling block to this access occurred in 1994–95 when the peso lost half of its value vis-à-vis the dollar. American firms marketing in Mexico had to devise a variety of crisis strategies to deal with this challenge. Some examples:

Apple Computer. Instead of a large rise in sales of imported PCs, Apple saw sales decline. It continued advertising, eased credit for dealers, and held seminars to create demand.

Ford. Postponed new import model; shifted production of some models to Mexico.

Kraft Foods. Most of Kraft's local products are made in Mexico except for cereals, in which it competes with Kellogg's local production. Kraft sacrificed margins to stay in the market.

Maybelline. With imported products, Maybelline cut margins and offered free in-store makeovers. Triple-digit interest rates caused retailers not to carry inventory so Maybelline had to deliver more frequently.

Nabisco. Shifted to local production. Mexican-made Oreos cost about half their U.S.-made counterparts.

Procter & Gamble. Adopted strategy of import substitution and export expansion.

Wal-Mart. More local products on the shelves.

McDonald's. Offered a free burger with its McTrio Grande.

Such strategies are relevant for the Asian crisis of the late 1990s.

Source: *Business Week,* May 15, 1995, 82, 83; *Business Latin America,* June 26, 1995, 1.

Those who were moving funds called the action prudent management because they were protecting their assets. Others called the same activity speculation. In any case, the results were the same. Central banks had fewer resources than those who were moving funds and had to give up the struggle to maintain the par value of their currencies. As a result, since 1973, the major industrialized countries have let their currencies "float," that is, fluctuate daily according to the forces of supply and demand. Thus, the international marketer today must contend with exchange rates that are continually moving targets, a complication for international pricing and logistics. (These implications will be covered in Chapters 14 and 15.)

The Bretton Woods system of pegged exchange rates is dead. However, the IMF did not die, nor did it fade away. It now has a more nebulous role, however, in a world of floating exchange rates. Even so, the IMF is a help to international marketing. It still lends money to countries with problems, enabling them to continue their international trade—and making them better customers. The IMF also continues to provide a forum for international monetary cooperation that lessens the chances of nations taking arbitrary actions against others, as occurred in the 1930s. More recently, the IMF played a critical role in solving Mexico's problems in 1994, and in the Asian and Russian crises of the late 1990s.

World Bank

The **International Bank for Reconstruction and Development (IBRD, or World Bank)** is another institution conceived at Bretton Woods. It also has an impact on the world economy in which international business operates. Whereas the IMF is concerned with the provision of short-term liquidity, the World Bank supplies long-term capital to aid economic development. The World Bank is parent to the International Development Association (IDA), created for the purpose of giving "soft" loans to the least developed countries, that is, long-term loans at very low interest rates. Lending by these two groups supports all aspects of development, including infrastructure, industrial, agricultural, educational, tourist, and population-control projects.

World Bank activities have improved the international economic environment and aided international business. The supply of capital has meant a higher level of economic activity and, therefore, better markets. For example, many firms are suppliers to projects in developing countries for which the World Bank and IDA lend billions of dollars. This often opens up new import markets that might have been impossible to enter had the World Bank not given assistance to the country. Many firms find profitable contracts in projects financed by the World Bank.

The United States in the World Economy

Although the international environment of the firm is important, the global influence of its home base cannot be ignored. In ways varying from country to country, the home government affects the international operations of the firm, both positively and negatively. A Swedish or Dutch multinational company operates under a set of advantages and constraints different from those that affect a U.S. firm or a Japanese firm or a firm from one of the former colonial powers, England or France. Since most of the readers of this book are U.S. residents, we will examine the advantages and constraints peculiar to a U.S. multinational company. The pattern can be applied to international firms domiciled in other nations.

One impact on the firm's international operations is its home government's policies toward such business. Most governments encourage exports. U.S. government assistance is through the information and promotional services of the Department of Commerce. Furthermore, the Export-Import Bank helps finance American exports, and there is a government-assisted program of export credit insurance and political-risk insurance.

The U.S. foreign aid program has helped U.S. companies export to markets that otherwise would have been closed because of their lack of foreign exchange. If the foreign aid programs have a favorable effect on recipient nations' attitudes toward the United States, this will improve the environment for the firms. A critical determinant of the firm's ability to export is, of course, the resource endowment of its home country. Furthermore, the business environment at home may have taught the firm skills that aid its performance abroad.

Other U.S. policies relate to international business. The government has encouraged investment in less developed countries by its investment-guarantee program. Government tax policy is favorable to business in foreign countries. Firms do not pay U.S. tax on foreign earnings until they are remitted back to the United States. In effect, while this money is being used abroad, it is an interest-free loan from the U.S. Treasury.

The government's commercial policy can help or hinder the firm internationally. A free-trading posture makes it easier for the firm than a protectionist policy because the latter stimulates retaliation in foreign markets. The firm is often able to influence its nation's commercial policy through representation to the appropriate government bodies.

Other government actions and national achievements can affect the firm internationally. U.S. antitrust policy has constrained U.S. companies abroad. American technological and space achievements aid U.S. companies in sales of high-technology products. In part, these technological advances are supported by government funds for research and development. On the other hand, foreign dissatisfaction with the U.S. role in the world can threaten foreign operations of U.S. firms. Dissatisfaction over some U.S. action may lead to a march on the U.S. Embassy abroad—or the local Goodyear plant or Coca-Cola bottler located there.

For example, when the United States sanctioned India for its nuclear tests in 1998, Coke and Pepsi trucks were destroyed in India's streets.

The size and wealth of the U.S. economy are a source of both envy and resentment. They affect the image of U.S. companies abroad—they are often considered to have an unfair advantage over local companies. The United States is the world's leading exporter and importer. This lends weight to U.S. commercial policy negotiations, which is favorable to the foreign sales by U.S. firms. Since the U.S. market is so attractive, other countries must open up their markets if they wish to sell to the United States. In all these ways, a company's nationality affects its international marketing.

SUMMARY

International trade, the economic link between nations, is one of the largest and fastest-growing aspects of the world economy. A study of the subject should include the composition of trade—that is, the shifting shares of manufactured goods versus various other commodities—and the patterns of trade, both globally and for individual countries, to help a firm's international logistics planning.

The theory of international trade helps in understanding a nation's comparative advantage and is useful for locating supply or production sources. The international product life cycle theory can help the firm know when to source, or produce, abroad.

The balance of payments is a summary statement of a nation's economic transactions that can be analyzed to determine market potential and competition in a country.

All countries have regulations on their international trade (commercial policy), usually to protect employment in home industries. Tariffs and quotas are the major tools used by industrial countries to control their trade. These affect the firm's pricing, product, and logistics decisions. Exchange control is a more comprehensive and rigid form of trade control.

WTO, as the world's trading club, works to liberalize the exchange of goods and services between countries. To the degree it is successful, it facilitates the firm's international marketing. UNCTAD is the lobby for developing countries' interests in trade. Its efforts, too, can affect the firm's international marketing and influence the firm's logistics.

After the decline of Communism and the fragmentation of the Communist bloc, the countries of Eastern Europe offer a large potential market. Some economic, cultural, legal, and political problems may need to be solved before that potential is realized, however. Other big new markets are also emerging—BEMs.

In the growing interdependence of the world economy, nations are finding it desirable to have some economic integration with their neighbors. This offers more resources, larger markets, and economies of scale to help them compete in the competitive world economy. The EU is the major successful integration story. Efforts elsewhere have made little progress, although NAFTA and Mercosur are bright spots. Where integration is successful, it offers opportunities for those firms that can operate inside the group, but also challenges for those on the outside.

The major world currencies have been floating since 1973. The resulting instability and uncertainty disrupt the sourcing patterns and the pricing of the international firm. The IMF, though no longer able to maintain stable currencies, is still a force for moderation and stability in international finance. By lending to deficit countries, IMF helps to keep their markets viable and open to the international marketer. The World Bank, through its development loans, provides resources to help poorer countries strengthen their economies and become more prosperous, and thus more attractive markets for the international firm. World Bank projects themselves can provide attractive marketing opportunities.

A firm's home country is an important determinant of its international marketing success. U.S. regulations, for example, can limit a firm's international marketing, but the government also supports international business by making available information, insurance, financing, and other kinds of assistance. Moreover, the large, competitive U.S. domestic market is a good training ground for international marketing. The U.S. image in the world, however, can be an advantage or disadvantage for the firm's international marketing.

QUESTIONS

2.1 What can be learned from studying the composition and patterns of world trade?

2.2 How can an understanding of international trade theory help the international marketer?

2.3 What is a balance of payments? Of what use is it to international marketing?

2.4 How can an exporter respond to a new tariff imposed on its product? To a quota?

2.5 What are the implications of exchange control to the international marketer?

2.6 What is WTO, and what does it do for the environment of international marketing?

2.7 Under UNCTAD pressure, preferential treatment has been granted to many

developing countries. What might this mean for the multinational firm?

2.8 What problems/opportunities are posed for the firm by the new Eastern Europe?

2.9 Why might a U.S. exporter feel threatened by the formation of regional economic groupings? How might the firm react?

2.10 How might a firm react to the appearance of the new big emerging markets (BEMs)?

2.11 What might Europe of the Euro mean for U.S. firms already operating in the EU?

2.12 How can the IMF be considered a friend of the international marketer?

2.13 What are the potential benefits of World Bank activity for international marketing?

ENDNOTES

[1] Louis T. Wells, Jr., "A Product Life Cycle for International Trade?" *Journal of Marketing* (July 1968): 1–6.

FURTHER READINGS

Garten, Jeffrey E. *The Big Emerging Markets and How They Will Change Our Lives.* New York: Basic Books, 1997.

Brouthers, Keith, Lance Brouthers, and George Nakos. "Entering Central and Eastern Europe: Risks and Cultural Barriers." *Thunderbird International Business Review* (September 1998): 485–504.

For further discussion of international economic questions and institutions, see standard texts in the field, such as the following:

Yarbrough, Beth, and Robert Yarbrough. *The World Economy,* 4th ed. Fort Worth, TX: Dryden Press, 1997.

DATA SOURCES

World Development Indicators. Washington, DC: World Bank (annual).

International Financial Statistics. Washington, DC: International Monetary Fund (monthly).

Survey of Current Business. Washington, DC: U.S. Department of Commerce (monthly).

United Nations. *Statistical Yearbook.* New York: United Nations (annual).

United Nations. *Yearbook of International Trade Statistics.* New York: United Nations (annual).

World Trade Annual. New York: United Nations (annual).

Foreign Exchange Rates

Country	Currency (per U.S. Dollar, September 21, 1998)	Rate
Argentina	Peso	.9900
Brazil	Real	1.1814
Britain	Pound	.5951
Canada	Dollar	1.5277
China	Renminbi	8.2784
India	Rupee	42.5050
Indonesia	Rupiah	11,150.0000
Japan	Yen	134.4700
Mexico	Peso	10.1700
Philippines	Peso	44.7900
Russia	Ruble	16.3820
South Africa	Rand	6.1425
South Korea	Won	1,392.5000
Switzerland	Franc	1.3905
Turkey	Lira	275,010.0000

Questions

1. Find the latest quotations for these currencies. (*The Wall Street Journal* is a convenient source.)
2. Calculate the approximate changes in the value of these currencies. Show the increase or decrease vis-à-vis the U.S. dollar.
3. Why have these changes occurred? (Give a general explanation.)
4. What are some of the implications for international marketing of changing exchange rates?

U.S. Pharmaceuticals, Inc. (A)

U.S. Pharmaceuticals (USP) is a U.S. firm with about 30 percent of its sales outside the United States. USP concentrates on the ethical drug business but has diversified into animal health products, cosmetics, and some patent medicines.

These other lines account for about one-fourth of USP's $800 million sales.

USP's international business is conducted in some 70 countries, mostly through distributors in those markets. In six countries, however, it has manufacturing or compounding operations. (*Compounding* refers to the local mixing, assembling, and packaging of critical ingredients shipped from the United States.) USP's only Latin American manufacturing/compounding operations are in Latinia, a country with a population of about 30 million. Some products are shipped from Latinia to other Latin American markets.

USP's Latinian plant is operated by the pharmaceutical division. It is engaged in the production and especially the compounding of USP's ethical drug line. It does no work for other USP divisions (cosmetics, proprietary medicines, and animal health). All the other divisions, which also sell in Latinia, export their finished products from plants in the United States. The Latinian plant employs 330 people, of whom only two are North Americans—the general manager, Tom Hawley, and the director of quality control, Frixos Massialas.

USP's cosmetics and toiletries business accounts for $150 million in sales and is handled by a separate division—Cosmetics and Toiletries. The division sells in only 38 of USP's 70 foreign markets. One of the division's better foreign markets is Latinia, where it has sales of over $8 million and an acceptable market position. Cosmetics and Toiletries has a marketing subsidiary in Latinia to handle its business there. Jim Richardson, an American, heads the subsidiary. The rest of the staff are Latinians.

Jim Richardson was very disturbed by the latest news received from the Latinian Ministry of International Trade. Tariffs were being increased on many "nonessential products" because of the balance-of-payments pressures the country had been experiencing for the past year and a half. For USP's Cosmetics and Toiletries, specifically, this meant a rise in the tariffs it pays from 20 percent to 50 percent ad valorem. The 20 percent duty had posed no particular problem for Cosmetics and Toiletries because of the prestige of the imported product and the consumer franchise it had established, Richardson explained. He believed, however, that the 50 percent duty was probably an insurmountable barrier.

Cosmetics and Toiletries' competition in Latinia was about evenly divided between local firms and other international companies from Europe and North America. Jim believed that local firms, which had about 40 percent of the market, stood to benefit greatly from the tariff increase unless the international firms could find a satisfactory response. When Jim received the news of the tariff increase, which was to be imposed the first of October—one week away—he called a meeting to consider what Cosmetics and Toiletries could do. Deborah Neale, manager, Cosmetics Marketing, and Emilio Illanes, manager, Toiletries Marketing, met with Jim to discuss the situation.

Several different courses of action were proposed at the hastily called meeting. Deborah suggested, "We could continue importing, pay the high duty, and change the positioning strategy to appeal to a high-price, premium market." Another idea was to import the primary ingredients and assemble (compound) and package them in Latinia. (Duties on the imported ingredients ranged between 10 percent and 35 percent ad valorem.) Emilio suggested asking Cosmetics and Toiletries in the United States for a lower price on the products shipped to Latinia so that the duty would have a lesser impact on the final price in the local market. Jim mentioned the alternative that none of them wanted to think about. "If we can't compete at those high prices, we may have to give up the market."

Questions

1. Evaluate the alternatives that were brought up at the meeting.
2. Are there any other possible courses of action?
3. Propose and defend a course of action.
4. How would your response differ if, instead of a tariff increase, Latinia had imposed a quota cutting the imports of these products by 75 percent?

Economic Environment

The Foreign Economies

Learning Objectives

A firm wishing to market abroad must select target markets from the 200 or so countries in the world economy. Toward that end, the firm wants some idea about the size of the market in various countries to help it establish its potential markets and priorities abroad. It also wants to know about the nature of these markets to determine the kind of marketing task it will face there.

The main goals of this chapter are to

1. Explore how information on population size, density, and distribution helps give an initial idea of market size.

2. Explore how information on income, both national income and per capita income, can further identify potential markets.

3. Describe what constitutes the nation's physical endowment, and explain how it gives clues to the nature of a firm's market and marketing task.

4. Explain how the nature of economic activity in a country can suggest how a firm's marketing will fit in.

5. Examine the effects of the infrastructure of a country (transportation, communication, etc.) on a firm's marketing there.

6. Demonstrate why the degree of urbanization is a useful indicator both of market potential and the marketing task in a country.

The second dimension of the economic environment of international marketing includes the **domestic economy** of every nation in which the firm is selling. Thus, the international marketer faces the traditional task of economic analysis, but in a context that may include 100 countries or more. This chapter addresses the economic dimensions of individual world markets. The investigation will be directed toward answering two broad questions: (1) How big is the market? and (2) What is the market like? Answers to the first question help determine the firm's market potential and priorities abroad. Answers to the second question help determine the nature of the marketing task.

SIZE OF THE MARKET

The firm's concern in examining world markets is the potential they offer for its products. The international marketer must determine market size not only for present markets but also for potential markets. This helps allocate effort among present markets and determine which markets to enter next. **Market size** for any given product is a function of particular variables, and its determination requires an ad hoc analysis. However, certain general indicators are relevant for many goods. We will see how world markets are described by the following general indicators: (1) population—growth rates and distribution, and (2) income—distribution, income per capita, and gross national product.

Possible markets are numerous. The *United Nations Statistical Yearbook* lists data for over 200 political entities. Of course, many of these are very small. UN membership itself counts about 185 countries. On a more practical level, the World Bank counts 133 countries with a population of over 1 million. The number of these nations that are worthwhile markets varies according to the firm's situation. However, many companies sell in over 100 markets. Singer and Komatsu, for example, sell in over 150 countries.

Population

It takes people to make a market and, other things being equal, the larger the population in a country, the better the market. Of course, other things are never equal, so population figures in themselves are not usually a sufficient guide to market size. Nevertheless, the consumption of many products is correlated with population figures. For many "necessary" goods, such as ethical drugs, health care items, some food products, and educational supplies, population figures may be a good first indicator of market potential. For other products that are low in price or meet particular needs, population also may be a useful market indicator. Products in these latter categories include soft drinks, ballpoint pens, bicycles, and sewing machines.

Population figures are one of the first considerations in analyzing foreign economies. One striking fact is the tremendous differences in size of the nations of the world. The largest nation in the world has about 10,000 times the population of the smallest countries. Well over half the people of the world live in the ten countries that have populations of more than 100 million. On the other hand, two-thirds of the countries have populations of less than 10 million, and about 60 have fewer than 1 million people. (See "Global Marketing," "Whirlpool Discovers China.")

The marketer is concerned primarily with individual markets, but regional patterns can also be important for regional logistics. For example, Asia contains six of the ten most populous markets. By contrast, Africa, the Middle East, and Latin America are rather thinly populated. Nigeria is the only populous African nation, with 115 million people. Turkey is the largest Mideast market with 63 million people. Latin America has only two relatively populous countries: Brazil with 161 million and Mexico with 93 million. Europe, much smaller in land area but more densely populated, has four countries with populations over 57 million. (See Table 3–1.)

TABLE 3-1	The World's Most Populous Nations				

Country	Population (millions)	Country	Population (millions)
1. China	1,215	14. Philippines	72
2. India	945	15. Turkey	63
3. United States	265	16. Iran	63
4. Indonesia	197	17. Thailand	60
5. Brazil	161	18. Egypt	59
6. Russia	148	19. United Kingdom	59
7. Pakistan	133	20. France	58
8. Japan	126	21. Ethiopia	58
9. Bangladesh	122	22. Italy	57
10. Nigeria	115	23. Ukraine	51
11. Mexico	93	24. South Korea	46
12. Germany	82	25. Myanmar	46
13. Vietnam	75	26. Congo, Democratic Republic	45

Source: *1998 World Bank Atlas* (Washington, DC: World Bank), 24, 25.

Population Growth Rates

The international marketer must be concerned with population trends as well as the current population in a market. This is because many marketing decisions will be affected by future developments. Although most countries experience some population growth, many countries in Western Europe have reached a stationary population.

The World Bank projects the high-income countries' population will grow at only 0.3 percent annually to 2010. At the other extreme, the low-income countries are expected to grow at 2.2 percent yearly. China and India are expected to grow at a slower rate but will still add over 300 million to their combined populations. Of a total world population of about 7.5 billion in 2010, the high-income countries will account for less than 1 billion.[1]

These differential population growth rates can affect the firm's long-run evaluation of markets. Markets must be evaluated on an individual basis, but an overview is useful and is given in Table 3–2. The data in the table reflect the strong correlation between level of economic development and population growth. The rich countries have stable populations; the poorer countries are growing rapidly. This fact illustrates another World Bank finding: Affluence is the most powerful contraceptive.

Distribution of Population

Understanding population figures involves more than counting heads. It makes a difference what kind of heads one is counting. The population figures should be classified—by age group, sex, education, or occupation, for example—in ways that show the relevant segments of the market. Religious, tribal, educational, and other attributes will be discussed in Chapter 4. Here we consider such population characteristics as age and density.

Age. People in different stages of life have different needs and present different marketing opportunities. In the U.S. market, many firms recognize different market segments related to age groupings. Each country has a somewhat different profile as to age groupings. Generally, however, there are two major patterns, one for the developing countries and one for the industrialized countries. The developing

Whirlpool Discovers China

With over one-fifth of the world's population within its borders, China has intrigued international marketers for years. The deterrent to entry has been the political-legal uncertainty prevailing there. Nevertheless, its growing economy and giant population have prompted many multinationals to take the plunge.

Whirlpool was a relative latecomer to China, but in the mid-1990s, it established four joint ventures for producing refrigerators, washing machines, microwave ovens, and air conditioners. The company expects the China market to equal that of North America in 10 years.

To help overcome its lack of experience in China, Whirlpool hired as president of its China operations a Mr. Chu, an overseas Chinese. Mr. Chu was born in Guangdong, but his family moved to Hong Kong, where he grew up. He has a college degree from the United States and spent 15 years working with foreign firms wanting to enter China.

As a further precaution, the company hired an expert in *feng shui* (good fortune) to advise on the construction of a training center at Hong Kong headquarters "to accommodate our Chinese colleagues who would be visiting." The *feng shui* consultant approved the layout but warned that the points on the building's gables would bring ill fortune. Whirlpool had them rounded off with spheres.

countries are experiencing population growth and have relatively short life expectancies. This means that about 40 percent of their population is in the inactive, dependent 0–14 age group and just over half in the productive 15–64 age group. Contrast that with the rich industrialized countries, which have only 20 percent in the dependent 0–14 group versus two-thirds in the 15–64 group and over one-eighth in the over-65 category. This "senior" category is a very important market in the high-income countries, but also in China, which has well over 100 million citizens in that group.

Density. The concentration of population is important to the marketer in evaluating distribution and communication problems. The United States, for example, had a population density of 29 persons per square kilometer in 1998. This is only about one-fifteenth of the population density of the Netherlands. Even with a modern transportation network, distribution costs in the United States are likely to be higher than in the Netherlands. Promotion is also facilitated where population is concentrated.

Other things being equal, the marketer prefers to operate in markets with concentrated populations. There is a great difference in population density among nations and regions of the world. On a regional basis, population densities range from less than 5 persons per square kilometer in Oceania to about 120 per square kilometer in Asia.

Regional figures on population density give generally good clues as to the densities of countries within the region. Occasionally, however, there are some extremes around the regional average. For example, in Southeast Asia the range is from 20 persons per square kilometer in Laos to 930 in Bangladesh. In Europe, the range is from 14 in Norway to 460 in the Netherlands.[2] Nevertheless, in evaluating a particular country, a firm is interested in the figures not only for that country but also for a potential regional market that could be served by common production facilities.

Even when the density figure for a given country is used, careful interpretation is necessary. For example, Egypt is listed as having about 58 persons per square kilometer. That is very misleading because Egypt's population is among

TABLE 3-2	**Population Growth Rates, 1980–1996**	
Economic Grouping	*Population Growth Rate (%)*	*Population 1996 (Millions)*
Low-income Countries (63)	2.6%	3,236
India	2.0	945
China	1.3	1,215
Middle-Income Countries (94)	1.7	1,599
High-Income Countries	0.7	919
World	1.7	5,754

Source: *World Development Report 1998* (Washington, DC: World Bank, 1998), 42–44.

the world's most concentrated, almost entirely located along the Nile River. The rest of the country is desert. Canada provides a similar example with a density of three persons per square kilometer but with most of the population concentrated in a narrow band along the U.S. border, leaving the major portion of the land-mass unoccupied. In such cases, the population is very much more concentrated and reachable than the statistics indicate. (See "Global Marketing," "Population Growth: Promise or Peril?")

Income

Markets require not only people but people with money. Therefore, it is necessary to examine various income measures in a country to go along with a population analysis. We will look at three aspects of income in foreign markets: the distribution of income among the population, the usefulness of per capita income figures, and gross national product.

Distribution of Income

One way of understanding the size of a market is to look at the distribution of income within it. **Per capita income figures** are averages and are meaningful, especially if most people of the country are near the average. Frequently, however, this is not the case. Few nations have a very equal distribution of income among their people, but the high-income economies are somewhat better than the other country categories. In the United States, of course, marketers are very attentive to differences in income levels if their product is at all income sensitive.

Most countries have an uneven distribution of income. An extreme example is Brazil, where the lowest 20 percent of the population receives just over 2 percent of the income and the highest 20 percent receives over 65 percent. The industrial countries are not exactly egalitarian either. In those rich markets, the share of the lowest 20 percent ranges from under 5 to about 9 percent.

The more skewed the distribution of income, the less meaningful the per capita income figure is. When most people are below the per capita income figure and there is a small wealthy group above it, the country has a **bimodal income distribution** but no middle class.[3]

A bimodal income distribution means that the marketer must analyze not a single economy but a dual economy. The poor group must be studied separately from the wealthy group. One might find, for example, that the two groups are not different segments of the same market but are actually different markets. Brazil, India, and Mexico are examples of countries with sizable groups of affluent consumers alongside a majority of the population living in poverty. Italy is an example of a European country with a dual economy, that is, the impoverished South versus

Population Growth: Promise or Peril?

The birth of a baby is usually a joyous event for the family involved. Economists and others react in different ways to the birth of hundreds of millions of babies each year, depending on where they are born. In the rich industrial countries, most of which are experiencing little or no population growth, economists perceive new births as adding buoyancy to the economy and new workers for tomorrow.

The vast majority of the new births each year, however, occur in the developing countries where different conditions apply. Two groups of countries are leading the population explosion. One is the Muslim nations, such as Bangladesh, Iran, Iraq, and Yemen, which are expected to double or triple their populations by 2025. Similar growth is expected in many sub-Saharan African nations, such as Ethiopia, Kenya, and Tanzania. By itself, India is predicted to grow from 850 million people in 1990 to 1,350 million in 2025. In these developing areas, economists take a different view of population growth.

The World Bank is concerned that aid to developing countries will be wasted if a country's population grows

the affluent North. For many products, the affluent groups in these countries can be considered as strong a potential market as similar groups in North America.

Per Capita Income

The statistic most frequently used to describe a country economically is its **per capita income.** This figure is used as a shorthand expression for a country's level of economic development. Partial justification for using this figure in evaluating a foreign economy lies in the fact that it is commonly available and widely accepted. A more pertinent justification is that it is, in fact, a good indicator of the size or quality of a market.

The per capita income figures vary widely among the countries of the world. Figures for 1998 show Mozambique at $90 per capita and Switzerland at $44,320 as the extreme cases. The World Bank finds over 50 percent of the world's population living in countries with an average per capita income of only $490. That is less than 2 percent of the $25,870 average for the high-income countries. If markets are people with money, these figures show a grim picture of many world markets. Five-sixths of the world's population has less than one-fourth of the world's GNP according to the data in Table 3–3.

Table 3–3 is a summary of the data for all of the countries tracked by the World Bank. The table in "Global Marketing" shows the actual economic groupings used by the World Bank in its analyses. The bank reports provide a good starting point for foreign market studies. Because per capita income figures are relied on so extensively, however, the following words of caution are in order.

Purchasing Power Not Reflected. Per capita income comparisons are expressed in a common currency—usually U.S. dollars—through an exchange-rate conversion. The dollar figure for a country is derived by dividing its per capita income figure in national currency by its rate of exchange against the dollar. The resulting dollar statistic for a country's per capita income is accurate only if the exchange rate reflects the relative domestic purchasing power of the two currencies. There is often reason for doubting that it does.

The **exchange rate** is the price of one currency in terms of another. The supply and demand determinants of that price are the demand for and supply of foreign exchange, or a country's imports and exports—plus speculative demand. A coun-

more rapidly than its economy. Bank president Barber Conable said that "societies in which population is growing so fast must accept that many, perhaps most, of these new lives will be miserable, malnourished, and brief." In 1990, the World Bank allocated $1 billion to population control programs.

At the Environmental Summit Rio in 1992, many observers noted that failure to address the population issue would nullify any progress made on other issues. Noel Brown, a director of the UN Environmental Program, said, "We already have a full occupancy planet." Numerous environmental problems are linked to population. For exam-ple, today, 80 percent of deforestation results from population. Some say that the world has already exceeded the saturation point in its ability to process many wastes. However, the Vatican and fundamentalist Muslim countries are against population planning programs. This makes them a hard sell for the World Bank (and kept them out of the Rio summit).

The international marketer, like the World Bank, must observe and evaluate population growth on a country-by-country basis.

Source: All figures from the World Bank.

try's external supply and demand have quite a different character from supply and demand within the country. Thus, it is not surprising that the external value of a currency (the exchange rate) may be different from the domestic value of that currency. Furthermore, speculation can further pull a currency away from its "true" value. Table 3–4 on page 71 illustrates some differences between the exchange-rate value of a currency and its real purchasing power. In every case, the real purchasing power is more than three times the exchange-rate value. These great differences are found especially in developing countries.

The limitations of an exchange rate in indicating relative purchasing power can be illustrated further. Take the experience of tourists, who soon learn that their own currency does not have an "average" value in terms of their consumption in any given foreign country. Instead, they observe that some prices appear high; others low. In other words, the value of their own currency there depends on what they buy with it.

If they wish to live in the same style abroad as at home, their expenses probably will be higher than if they live like the residents of the host country. For example, the price of white bread in Germany is twice as much as it is in France. Of course, the Germans do not consume as much white bread as the French. This indicates another aspect of prices and purchasing power—that is, people tend to consume more of the things that are inexpensive in their country. However, the exchange rate reflects the *international* goods and services of a country, and not its *domestic* consumption.

A further example is the case of exchange-rate changes, as with a devaluation or currency appreciation. Britain devalued its currency by 14.3 percent in November 1967. This certainly did not mean that the British market for any given product was down 14 percent the day after the devaluation. Yet this is what is implied with the use of per capita income figures derived from an exchange-rate conversion. A more extreme example involves Japan. In 1985 the Japanese yen was 240 to the U.S. dollar. In 1988 the yen was 120 to the dollar. This meant that, in dollar terms, the Japanese market was twice as large in 1988 as in 1985. This was obviously not true in real terms, as American marketers to Japan learned. Their sales to Japan rose only modestly. It is precisely because of the inadequacies of per capita income figures expressed in U.S. dollars that the World Bank has worked so hard to determine true purchasing power.

TABLE 3–3	Per Capita Income			
Country Category	Number of Countries	GNP (Billions of U.S. Dollars)	Population (Millions)	Income Per Capita (U.S. Dollars)
Low-Income	63	$ 1,597	3,236	$ 490
Lower-Middle Income	63	1,963	1,125	1,740
Upper-Middle Income	31	2,178	473	4,600
High-Income	53	23,772	919	25,870
World	210	29,510	5,754	5,130

Source: *1998 World Bank Atlas* (Washington, DC: World Bank, 1998), 38.

Lack of Comparability. Another limitation to the use of per capita income figures is that there is a twofold lack of comparability. First, many goods entering into the national income totals of the developed economies are only partially in the money economy in less developed countries. A large part of a North American's budget, for example, goes for food, clothing, and shelter. In many less developed nations, these items may be largely self-provided and therefore not reflected in national income totals.

Second, many goods that figure in the national income of developed nations do not figure in the national incomes of poorer countries. For example, a significant amount of U.S. national income is derived from such items as snow removal, heating buildings and homes, pollution control, military and space expenditures, agricultural support programs, and winter vacations in Florida or other warmer states. Many less developed nations are in tropical areas, and their citizens are not necessarily poorer for not having the above-mentioned items of consumption. However, their national income figure is lower because of the absence of these items. The author spent eight years in a rural area of Congo. Although not living entirely in the African manner, he found his food, clothing, and housing expenses to be a fraction of those he incurred living in the northern part of the United States. This meant that a given income went much further for consumption of these basic items.

Sales Not Related to Per Capita Income. A third limitation to using per capita income figures to indicate market potential is that the sales of many goods show little correlation with per capita income. Many consumer goods sales correlate more closely with population or household figures than with per capita income. Some examples might be Coca-Cola, ballpoint pens, bicycles, sewing machines, and transistor radios. Industrial goods and capital equipment sales generally correlate better with the industrial structure or total national income than with per capita income. For example, the airport and office buildings in Kinshasa, Congo, are equipped in much the same way similar places in New York City are. Extractive or manufacturing industries tend to use similar equipment wherever they are located. Where governments run health and education programs, per capita income is not necessarily a useful guide to the national potential in goods supplied to the health and education industries.

Uneven Income Distribution. Finally, per capita figures are less meaningful if there is great unevenness of income distribution in the country. This has already been discussed.

TABLE 3-4	Per Capita Income Measured Two Ways		
Country	According to Exchange-Rate Conversion	According to Purchasing Power	Multiplier[a]
Mozambique	80	500	6.3
Ethiopia	100	500	5.0
Congo, Democratic Republic	130	790	6.1
Bangladesh	260	1,010	3.9
Vietnam	290	1,570	5.4
Mongolia	360	1,820	5.1
Ghana	360	1,790	5.0
India	380	1,580	4.2
Nicaragua	380	1,760	4.6
China	750	3,330	4.4
Bolivia	830	2,860	3.4
Colombia	2,140	6,720	3.1

[a] Column 2 divided by column 1.
Source: Calculated from *1998 World Bank Atlas* (Washington, DC: World Bank, 1998), 42, 43.

Gross National Product (GNP)

Another useful way to evaluate foreign markets is to compare their gross national products. **Gross national product (GNP)** measures the total domestic and foreign value added claimed by residents. **Gross domestic product (GDP)** is GNP less net factor income from abroad. For certain goods, total GNP is a better indicator of market potential than is per capita income. Where this is true, it is useful to rank countries by GNP. Table 3–5 lists the economies with a GNP of at least $100 billion in 1998. The fact that only 31 nations qualify for this list gives another insight into the poverty in the world and the limitations of most economies.

It is helpful to contrast the GNP approach to measuring market potential with the per capita income approach. For example, Iceland's per capita income in 1996 was $26,580 and India's was $380—both on an exchange-rate basis. Judging from these figures, Iceland is more than 60 times as attractive economically as India. However, India's GNP was 50 times as large as that of Iceland and its population over 1,000 times as large. This is an extreme example, but it illustrates the need for proper comparisons.

At this point, we should balance our criticism of the per capita income approach. For goods that require high consumer income, it may be true that a small country like Belgium (about 10 million people) is a better market than India, even though Belgium's GNP is less than that of India. For example, in 1998, Belgium had more cars and personal computers than India. On the other hand, India consumed four to six times as many trucks and buses and tons of cement and steel. Obviously, the relevant income figure for evaluating a market depends largely on the product involved.

NATURE OF THE ECONOMY

In addition to their size and market potential, foreign economies have other characteristics that affect a marketing program, including those produced by the nation's physical endowment, the nature of its economic activity, its infrastructure, and its degree of urbanization.

GLOBAL MARKETING

World Bank Economic Groups

Low-Income
Per Capita $490

Afghanistan
Angola
Armenia
Azerbaijan
Bangladesh

Benin
Bhutan
Bosnia and Herzegovina
Burkina Faso
Burundi

Cambodia
Cameroon
Central African Republic
Chad
China

Comoros
Congo, Democratic Republic
Congo, Republic
Côte d'Ivoire
Equatorial Guinea

Eritrea
Ethiopia
Gambia, The
Ghana
Guinea

Guinea-Bissau
Guyana
Haiti
Honduras
India

Kenya
Kyrgyz Republic
Lao PDR
Lesotho
Liberia

Madagascar
Malawi
Mali
Mauritania
Moldova

Mongolia
Mozambique
Myanmar
Nepal
Nicaragua

Niger
Nigeria
Pakistan
Rwanda
São Tomé and Principe

Senegal
Sierra Leone
Somalia
Sri Lanka
Sudan

Tajikistan
Tanzania
Togo
Uganda
Vietnam

Yemen, Republic
Zambia
Zimbabwe

Lower-Middle Income
Per Capita $1,740

Albania
Algeria
Belarus
Belize
Bolivia

Botswana
Bulgaria
Cape Verde
Colombia
Costa Rica

Cuba
Djibouti
Dominica
Dominican Republic
Ecuador

Egypt, Arab Republic
El Salvador
Estonia
Fiji
Georgia

Grenada
Guatemala
Indonesia
Iran, Islamic Republic
Iraq

Jamaica
Jordan
Kazakhstan
Kiribati
Korea, Democratic Republic

Latvia
Lebanon
Lithuania
Macedonia, FYR
Maldives

Marshall Islands
Micronesia, Fed. Sts.
Morocco
Namibia
Panama

Papua New Guinea
Paraguay

Peru
Philippines
Romania

Russian Federation
Samoa
Solomon Islands
St. Vincent and the Grenadines
Suriname

Swaziland
Syrian Arab Republic
Thailand
Tonga
Tunisia

Turkey
Turkmenistan
Ukraine
Uzbekistan
Vanuatu

Venezuela
West Bank and Gaza
Yugoslavia, FR
(Serbia/Montenegro)

Upper-Middle Income
Per Capita $4,600

American Samoa
Antigua and Barbuda
Argentina
Bahrain
Barbados

Brazil
Chile
Croatia
Czech Republic
Gabon

Guadeloupe
Hungary
Isle of Man
Libya
Malaysia

Malta
Mauritius
Mayotte
Mexico
Oman

Palau
Poland
Puerto Rico
Saudi Arabia
Seychelles

Slovak Republic
Slovenia
South Africa
St. Kitts and Nevis
St. Lucia

Trinidad and Tobago
Uruguay

High Income
Per Capita $25,870

Andorra
Aruba
Australia
Austria
Bahamas, The

Belgium
Bermuda
Brunel
Canada
Cayman Islands

Channel Islands
Cyprus
Denmark
Faeroe Islands
Finland

France
French Guiana
French Polynesia
Germany
Greece

Greenland
Guam
Hong Kong, China
Iceland
Ireland

Israel
Italy
Japan
Korea, Republic
Kuwait

Liechtenstein
Luxembourg
Macao
Martinique
Monaco

Netherlands
Netherlands Antilles
New Caledonia
New Zealand
Northern Mariana Islands

Norway
Portugal
Qatar
Réunion
Singapore

Spain
Sweden
Switzerland
United Arab Emirates
United Kingdom

United States
Virgin Islands (U.S.)

Source: *World Development Indicators 1998* (Washington, DC: World Bank, 1998), 1.

TABLE 3-5	Countries with Gross National Product over $100 Billion (1998)		
Country	*Billions of U.S. Dollars*	*Country*	*Billions of U.S. Dollars*
1. United States	$7,434	17. Switzerland	$ 314
2. Japan	5,149	18. Argentina	295
3. Germany	2,365	19. Belgium	269
4. France	1,534	20. Sweden	227
5. United Kingdom	1,152	21. Austria	227
6. Italy	1,140	22. Indonesia	213
7. China	906	23. Turkey	178
8. Brazil	710	24. Thailand	177
9. Canada	570	25. Denmark	169
10. Spain	563	26. Norway	152
11. South Korea	483	27. South Africa	132
12. Netherlands	403	28. Poland	125
13. Australia	368	29. Greece	120
14. India	358	30. Finland	119
15. Russia	356	31. Portugal	101
16. Mexico	342		

Source: *1998 World Bank Atlas* (Washington, DC: The World Bank, 1998), 42, 43.

Physical Endowment

Natural Resources

A nation's **natural resources** include its actual and potential forms of wealth supplied by nature—for example, minerals and waterpower—as well as its land area, topography, and climate. The international marketer needs to understand the economic geography of a nation in relation to the marketing task there. Land area as such is not very important, except as it figures in population density and distribution problems. However, local natural resources can be important to the international marketer in evaluating a country as a source of raw materials for local production.

Merck, for example, built a compounding plant in India and received the Indian government's permission to ship key ingredients from the United States. This permission was later withdrawn, and Merck had to locate a new raw-material source in India to keep the plant operating.

Another reason for exploring the country's resource base is to evaluate its future economic prospects. Some countries that today have relatively weak markets might develop more rapidly than others because of their richer resource endowment. New technologies or discoveries can revolutionize a nation's economic prospects. Oil changed the outlook for Libya and Nigeria, for example.

By the same token, technological change can also impoverish an economy that is largely dependent on just one export commodity. For example, the development of rayon, nylon, and synthetic rubber did great damage to the countries exporting silk and natural rubber. What would be the impact on Brazil if a good synthetic coffee were developed? A glance through the maps in any good atlas will give a picture of how the various natural resources are distributed among the nations of the world.

Topography

The surface features of a country's land, including rivers, lakes, forests, deserts, and mountains are its **topography.** These features interest the international marketer for they indicate possible physical distribution problems.

Flat country generally means easy transportation by road or rail. Mountains are always a barrier that raises transportation costs. Mountains also may divide a nation into two or more distinct markets. For example, the Andes Mountains divide many South American countries into entirely separate areas. Although these areas are united politically, the marketer often finds that culturally and economically they are separate markets. Deserts and tropical forests also separate markets and make transportation difficult. The international marketer analyzes the topography, population, and transportation situation to anticipate marketing and logistical problems.

Navigable rivers are desirable because they enable economical transportation. The Mississippi River and the St. Lawrence Seaway are North American examples. In Europe, river and canal transportation are more important than anywhere else. Even landlocked Switzerland can ship by river barge to Atlantic ports. The accessibility of a market should also be determined by its ports and harbors—contact with sea transportation.

Landlocked countries such as Bolivia, Zambia, and Zimbabwe are more costly to reach than neighboring countries with seaports. These countries have transportation problems other than cost if there are political differences with the neighbors whose seaports and railroads they must use. Finally, the existence of lakes, seashores, rivers, and mountains can indicate particular marketing opportunities. Suppliers to the tourist, recreation, and sporting industries find markets in countries endowed with places for boating, skiing, and similar recreational activities.

Climate

Another dimension of a nation's physical endowment is its **climate,** which includes not only the temperature range, but also wind, rain, snow, dryness, and humidity. The United States is very large and has great climatic variations within its borders. Most nations are smaller and have more uniform climatic patterns. Climate is an important determinant of the firm's product offerings. An obvious example is the heater or air conditioner in an automobile. However, climate also affects a whole range of consumer goods from food to clothing and from housing to recreational supplies. Even medical needs in the tropics are different from those in temperate zones.

Extremes of climate may dictate modifications in product, packaging, or distribution. For example, electric equipment and many packaged goods need special protection in hot, humid climates. There is great international variation in climate; for example, India has 13 inches of rainfall in July, Guinea has 51 inches, and New York City has 4 inches.

Climate may have another, more subtle effect on the nature of the market. Although insufficient evidence exists to prove cause and effect, most of the less developed countries are tropical or subtropical. Tropical countries generally have low per capita incomes and a high percentage of the population in agriculture. Gunnar Myrdal's gloomy conclusions as to Asia's prospects for development were based in part on his evaluation of the adverse effects of climate.[4] The marketing manager needs to be aware of climate to the extent that it affects people as consumers or workers.

Nature of Economic Activity

Rostow's View

The stages of economic growth described by economist Walt Rostow provide a useful description of foreign economies.[5] According to Rostow, all the nations of the world are in one of the following levels of economic development: (1) the traditional society, (2) the preconditions for takeoff, (3) the takeoff, (4) the drive to maturity, and (5) the age of high mass consumption. Each level represents a different type of economy, that is, differing production and marketing systems. The marketing opportunities and problems encountered by the international firm vary according to the host country's stage of economic growth.

Although Rostow's classification was developed from the viewpoint of the economist, a similar type of analysis may be useful to the international marketer. In Chapter 7 we suggest how international marketers might develop a classification system to meet their own needs. Here we look at various aspects within foreign economies that affect the marketing task.

Farm or Factory?

One way to determine the kind of market a country offers is to look at the origin of its national product. Is the economy agricultural or industrial? What is the nature of its agricultural, manufacturing, and service industries? Such an analysis is especially useful to industrial marketers. However, even consumer goods marketers find that consumer demands and mentality are related to the nature of economic activities in the country. For example, there are invariably differences in the consumption patterns of the farmer compared with those of a factory worker.

Table 3–6 shows some of the international variation in patterns of economic activity. There is a very strong inverse correlation between the size of a nation's agricultural sector and its level of development and income. The poorer the country, the more it depends on agriculture—and the less income it generates in manufacturing industry. It is understandable why the poorer countries are striving to industrialize. This kind of data is useful for marketing because the nature of the market and the marketing task follow the nature of the economy.

Input-Output Tables

Although it is useful to analyze an economy in terms of its agricultural and industrial sectors, frequently it is desirable to make a more detailed examination. Such sources as the *United Nations Statistical Yearbook* show national production in a wide range of products and commodities. Industrial marketers are especially concerned with the industrial structure of an economy. A firm that sells to particular industries must know which economies contain those industries as well as the industries' sizes. Even beyond this, the firm would like to know the technology used in its client industries. For example, many nations have textile industries, but not all use the same combinations of materials, labor, and equipment. The economist would say they do not all have the same production function.

If the firm can construct **input-output tables** for its industry for relevant markets, it can gain a better idea of how its supplies or equipment fit in with the industrial structure in given markets. Such tables are often used in U.S. marketing, and their use is increasing in international marketing. Although their construction can be difficult, the technique is worth mastering. As our data improve, economic analysis through input-output tables is becoming more common.[6]

Infrastructure of the Nation

A manufacturing firm generally divides its activities into two major categories: production and marketing. These operations depend on supporting facilities and services outside the firm. These external facilities and services are called the **infrastructure** of an economy. They include paved roads, railroads, energy supplies, and other communication and transport services. The commercial and financial infrastructure includes such things as advertising agencies and media, distributive organizations, marketing research companies, and credit and banking facilities. The more adequate these services in a country, the better the firm can perform its production and marketing tasks there. Where these facilities and services are not adequate, the firm must adapt its operations, or perhaps avoid the market altogether.

| TABLE 3-6 | Share of Agriculture in Gross Domestic Product, 1998 | | |

Countries	Agriculture Share of GDP (Percent)	Per Capita Income (U.S. Dollars)	Population (Millions)
Low-Income	34%	$ 490	3,236
India	28	380	945
China	21	750	1,215
Lower-Middle Income	12	1,740	1,125
Upper-Middle Income	9	4,600	473
High-Income	3	25,870	919

Source: *World Development Indicators 1998* (Washington, DC: World Bank, 1998), 12–14, 180–182.

When considering the potential profitability of operations in a given country, the international marketer must evaluate the infrastructure constraints as well as the market potential. As might be expected, tremendous variation exists internationally. Generally, the higher the level of economic development, the better the infrastructure. Table 3–7 gives some indication of the variation in energy services available.

Energy

The statistics on energy production per capita serve as a guide to both market potential and the adequacy of the local infrastructure. Marketers of electrical machinery and equipment and consumer durables are concerned about the extent of electrification throughout the market. In countries with low energy consumption, the marketer will find that power is available only in the cities, not in the villages or countryside, where most of the population may live. Energy production is also closely related to the overall industrialization of an economy and thus is correlated to the market for industrial goods there. Finally, energy production per capita is probably the best single indicator as to the adequacy of a country's overall infrastructure.

Transportation

The importance of transportation for business operations needs no elaboration. Transportation capabilities, infrastructure, and modes vary significantly from country to country depending on the topography and level of economic development. The share of road, rail, river, and air transport varies by country but the World Bank has no good comparable data. For information here the firm needs local sources in the market. It can also consult with transportation companies. One good example is given in "Global Marketing," "Avon in the Amazon."

Communications

In addition to being able to move its goods, a firm must be able to communicate with its various audiences, especially workers, suppliers, and customers. Communications with those outside the firm depend on the communications infrastructure of the country. Intracompany communications between subsidiaries or with headquarters depend equally on local facilities. Table 3–8 shows the distribution and availability of several communications media in the major regions of the world.

In general, variations in communications infrastructure follow variations in the level of economic development. Thus, Japan and the countries of Western Europe

TABLE 3-7	**Energy Consumption Per Capita**		

Region and Country	Kilowatt Hours (Per Capita)	Region and Country	Kilowatt Hours (Per Capita)
Canada	15,147	Asia	
United States	11,571	China	637
Western Europe		India	339
Austria	5,800	Indonesia	263
France	5,892	Japan	6,937
Germany	5,525	Pakistan	304
Italy	4,163	Thailand	1,199
Spain	3,594		
United Kingdom	5,081		
Latin America		Africa	
Argentina	1,519	Algeria	513
Brazil	1,610	Congo, Rep.	207
Chile	1,698	Egypt	896
Colombia	948	Kenya	123
Mexico	1,305	Nigeria	85
Peru	525	South Africa	3,874

Source: *World Development Report 1998/99* (Washington, DC: World Bank, 1998), 224, 225.

are well supplied with all kinds of media, whereas the developing countries in Africa, Asia, and Latin America are weak in all the media, except perhaps for radio.

A more complete and detailed listing of countries in the manner of Table 3–8 would benefit the international manager in two ways. First, it would aid analysis of the communication and promotional possibilities in foreign markets. Second, it would help to locate marketing subsidiaries or regional headquarters where good internal and international communication facilities exist.

Commercial Infrastructure

Equally as important to the firm as the transportation, communication, and energy capabilities of a nation is its **commercial infrastructure.** By this is meant the availability and quality of such supporting services as banks and financial institutions, advertising agencies, distribution channels, and marketing research organizations. Firms accustomed to strong supporting services at home often find great differences in foreign markets. Wherever the commercial infrastructure is weak, the firm must make adjustments in its operations, which affect costs and effectiveness.

No comparable table on commercial infrastructure is available, and data in this area are more difficult to find. Nevertheless, a firm can get reasonably good information on the commercial infrastructure of a country. The best sources are commercial attachés in embassies, and domestic service organizations with foreign operations, for example, banks, accounting firms, and advertising agencies.

Urbanization

One of the most significant characteristics of an economy is the extent to which it is urbanized—the degree of **urbanization.** Numerous cultural and economic differences exist between people in cities and those in villages or rural areas. These differences are reflected in the attitudes of the people. Modern transportation and communica-

GLOBAL MARKETING

Avon in the Amazon

The Avon lady usually rings telephones and doorbells and travels city streets. The infrastructure in the Amazon would not seem conducive to selling Avon. Phone and doorbell and paved street are not found in the Amazon. In fact, it is uncommon to see doors on the stickframe houses. Yet Avon has over 40,000 representatives selling in the Amazon, and does over $70 million worth of business there.

Making their way across rivers, down dusty roads, up hills, and through swamps, the Avon women in the Amazon, nonetheless, reach gold miners, prostitutes, farmers, and others trying to scratch out a living. They travel on foot, in canoes, on riverboats, and on small aircraft. Because their customers live in places with no banks, no infrastructure, and no major employers, payments are made through barter. How are they paid? In chickens, eggs, gold, fruit, vegetables, or services.

Source: *Los Angeles Times*, September 12, 1994, B1; *Business Latin America*, February 20, 1995, 6.

---

tion have greatly reduced the differences between urban and rural populations in the United States, but in much of the world the urban-rural differences persist. Because these differences are important determinants of consumer behavior, the international marketer needs to be aware of the situation particular to each market.

Farm versus City

Several reasons exist for the contrasting behavior of urban and rural populations. Urbanites tend to be dependent for all their material needs, whereas rural dwellers often supply much of their food, clothing, and shelter through their own efforts. City dwellers must meet their needs through money payments to others. Cities are centers of industry and commerce. Because city dwellers deal in a commercial-industrial framework, they become more sophisticated consumers than rural dwellers, who are often unaware of the technical and economic complexities of modern society. Hill and Still found that products aimed at rural markets in developing countries required more adaptation than products sold in urban markets.[7]

Cities are the places in an economy where communications media are most developed; information contributes to the city dweller's sophistication. Cities also offer more possibilities for formal and informal education, which affect the literacy, skills, and attitudes of their inhabitants. Urbanites, therefore, tend to be less conservative and tradition-oriented than rural dwellers. There is a stronger demonstration effect of new products and consumption patterns in urban areas, which leads to stronger markets there.

The international marketer must study the relation of urbanization to the consumption of the firm's product. For some products in some countries, urban and rural populations are distinct segments; in other cases, there is no difference; in yet others, the firm may decide that urban areas provide the only feasible market. Several factors may favor the urban markets: income and consumption patterns, distribution facilities, and communications possibilities. Cities such as Bangkok, Istanbul, and Jakarta, for example, have a highly disproportionate share of their countries' consumption of many consumer goods.

Table 3–9 shows the degree of urbanization for the World Bank economic groupings. Looking at the averages for the four groupings, we see a strong correlation between degree of urbanization and the level of economic development. Looking at some of the country figures within each economic group, we see some wide deviations from the group average. Urbanization is an important indicator of the attractiveness of a

TABLE 3-8	Distribution of Communications Media			
	Telephones per 100 Population	*Newspaper Copies per 1,000 Population*	*TVs per 1,000 Population*	*Radios per 1,000 Population*
United States	63	228	776	2,122
Western Europe				
France	56	237	579	891
Germany	49	317	550	935
Italy	43	105	436	802
Spain	39	104	490	312
United Kingdom	50	351	612	1,429
Latin America				
Argentina	16	138	347	673
Brazil	7	45	278	393
Colombia	10	64	188	178
Mexico	10	113	192	256
Venezuela	11	215	180	443
Asia				
India	1	n.a.	61	81
Indonesia	2	20	147	148
Japan	49	576	619	912
Philippines	2	65	121	144
Thailand	6	48	221	190
Africa, Central Europe, Mideast				
Egypt	5	64	126	307
Hungary	19	228	441	625
Israel	42	281	295	478
Poland	15	141	408	441
South Africa	9	33	101	314
Turkey	21	44	240	162

n.a. not available
Source: *Statistical Abstract of the United States 1997* (Washington, DC: Bureau of the Census, 1997), 842.

market. For example, the United States has a very large land area with a low population density. Because three-fourths of the population is urban, however, distribution and communications are relatively easy and efficient. The other highly urbanized nations provide similarly attractive markets from this point of view.

The developing countries are generally much less urbanized, especially the low-income nations. Combined with low incomes in these regions, the lack of urbanization makes these markets unattractive to many consumer goods marketers. Not only are these poor markets small but they are difficult to reach when most of the population is rural. Thus, the degree of urbanization is an indicator of both the size of the market and the nature of the marketing task. Though this kind of data is especially significant for consumer goods marketers, even industrial goods firms find a correlation between their market potential and urbanization. Because urbanization is increasing, the marketer needs up-to-date figures.

TABLE 3-9	Urban Population as a Percent of Total Population		

Economic Group	Country	Average for Economic Group
Low-Income		29%
Rwanda	6%	
China	31	
Egypt	45	
Lower-Middle-Income		56
Indonesia	36	
Algeria	56	
Russia	76	
Upper-Middle-Income		73
Malaysia	54	
Mexico	74	
Argentina	88	
High-Income		78
Austria	64	
United States	76	
Canada	77	
United Kingdom	89	

Source: *World Development Indicators 1998* (Washington, DC: World Bank, 1998), 154–156.

Other Characteristics of Foreign Economies

Our survey of foreign economies has been introductory rather than exhaustive. It should be helpful, however, in giving the market analyst a feel for the relevant dimensions of national economies. Before concluding this chapter, we look briefly at a few other characteristics of foreign economies that can be important in operations there.

Inflation

Each country has its own monetary system and monetary policy—except for the 11 European countries in the Euro group. The result is differing financial environments and rates of inflation among countries. Of all the nations analyzed by the World Bank, less than one-half had single-digit annual inflation rates for the period 1990–1996. That means the others had more serious challenges with double- or triple-digit rates, or worse.

There are some interesting regional patterns in the inflation picture. The United States and Canada had low inflation during this period, as did Western Europe—which facilitated transition to the Euro. Latin America was generally in the low double digits (Bolivia at 11 percent) except Brazil with 675 percent. The six large Asian nations with almost 3 billion people all had low rates, Japan, 1 percent to China, 12 percent. Africa, for the most part, had moderate inflation with Cameroon at only 6 percent. Two egregious exceptions were Angola at 1,103 percent and Congo Democratic Republic at 2,747 percent. The "leaders" in the inflation race, unfortunately, were the states of the former Soviet Union, ranging from the Kyrgyz Republic at 256 percent to Russia at 349 percent to Georgia at 2,279 percent.

It might be noted that inflation means a further complication for operating in foreign markets. High rates of inflation complicate cost control and pricing. Differential rates of inflation also influence how the firm moves funds and goods among its various markets. The marketing implications of inflation are discussed in Chapter 15.

Role of Government

The business environment and the nature of business operations in an economy are very dependent on the role government plays in that economy. If government has strong Socialist leanings, it may restrict the sectors of the economy where private companies may be engaged. Where international companies are allowed to operate, governments have regulations restricting their operations.

In a number of countries, international companies may have the government as a partner in a joint venture. This is especially true in less developed countries that lack a strong private sector to provide the capital. Such a partnership provides its own constraints on the international company.

Foreign Investment in the Economy

When contemplating operations in a foreign economy, the international marketer is interested to know what other international firms are operating there. This information gives clues as to the government's attitude toward foreign companies. It helps to determine something about the competitive environment the firm will encounter.

That a country has few or no international companies operating in it could indicate a good opportunity for one to enter—or it could indicate that the environment is inhospitable. Conversely, an economy that has many international companies operating in it indicates an open market but one that may be very competitive. A distinction must be made, of course, between extractive industries and manufacturing or marketing subsidiaries. Extractive industries go into a country for raw-material supply rather than for marketing reasons.

Table 3–10 presents the number of U.S. companies with investments in selected markets. (Unfortunately data are not available for other investing countries.) The figures are for two base years, 1975 and 1996, so trends can be identified. Canada is given as a basis for comparison. The companies include extractive and service industries as well as manufacturing. Though the data do not reveal the size of the investment in each country, they do indicate generally how U.S. firms evaluated the different markets. Canada and Western Europe remain the most popular markets, but there has been a leveling off or even retrenchment in many places.

Latin America is the next most popular area for U.S. investors, led by Brazil and Mexico. NAFTA should enhance Mexico's share, and regional agreements in Latin America will maintain that continent's attractiveness. Asia is more distant, but rapid economic growth drew American firms until the Asian crisis caused a pause. China has become the major investment partner in Asia, in spite of continuing uncertainty. Africa is still a relatively unknown continent for U.S. firms, except for the "new" South Africa, which is again proving attractive for international marketers.

The reader can go through Table 3–10 and evaluate personally the role of geography, politics, and economics in determining the patterns of U.S. foreign investment. The international marketer must be alert for trends. In some nations, there may be a leveling off, or even a decrease, in foreign investment. Bosnia and Iraq are extreme examples. It is also possible to identify growing economies with relatively stable political environments and an absence of strongly negative attitudes toward foreign investors. Such a table needs to be kept up to date because changes in the investment climate can occur rapidly. For example, liberalization in Eastern Europe is changing the figures there.

| TABLE 3-10 | U.S. Firms Operating in Selected Foreign Countries, 1975 and 1996 |

	Number of Firms, 1975	Number of Firms, 1996
Canada	1,560	1,188
Africa		
Egypt	56	78 ✓
Ghana	19	13
Kenya	72	36
Nigeria	51	52 ✓
South Africa	314	115
Zambia	11	19 ✓
Asia		
India	261	176
Indonesia	73	131 ✓
Philippines	193	160
Sri Lanka	15	18 ✓
Taiwan	130	221 ✓
Thailand	150	150 ✓
Latin America		
Argentina	233	176
Brazil	478	407
Chile	116	126 ✓
Colombia	233	132
Mexico	876	560
Peru	221	81
Western Europe		
France	726	726 ✓
Germany	1,100	836
Italy	541	462
Netherlands	707	460
Norway	77	120 ✓
Spain	349	351

Source: *Directory of American Firms Operating in Foreign Countries*, 8th, 14th eds. (New York: Uniworld Business Publications, 1975, 1996).

SUMMARY

The two main areas of investigation for a company evaluating a foreign market are (1) the size of the market and (2) the nature of the economy. Population is one of the primary indicators of market size. Two-thirds of the countries have less than 10 million people and represent small markets, especially compared to the United States. Growth rates vary widely and are generally inversely correlated with the attractiveness of a market. The marketer is concerned about the distribution of the population among different age groups with different purchasing power and consumption patterns. Population density is important for evaluating distribution and communication problems.

Markets are "people with money," so income figures on a country are necessary for market evaluation. One dimension is the distribution of income among the members of a society. Countries with a bimodal distribution of income represent dual economies with two major market segments, generally one rich and one poor. Countries with a more even distribution of income or a large middle class represent more of a mass market.

Per capita income is the most widely used indicator of market potential. Figures vary widely, with the poorest countries reporting less than 1 percent of the per capita income of the richest countries. World Bank studies show that these figures are often inaccurate, however. Actual purchasing power in many poor countries is three to eight times as high as that indicated by the per capita income figure expressed in dollars. Per capita income figures are a useful indicator of potential for some consumer goods but misleading for others and for industrial goods.

Total GNP gives an idea of the total size of a country's market and is a helpful indicator of potential for some kinds of products. The range of GNP figures between the largest and smallest economies is over 10,000 to 1.

A country's physical endowment affects the nature of its economy. Its natural resources are one indicator of its economic potential and raw material availability. Its topography helps determine physical distribution problems and market accessibility. Its climate influences the kind of products offered and the kind of packaging needed.

Countries can be grouped according to the nature of their economies or level of economic development, as Rostow has done. Such groupings can be a useful form of segmentation for international marketers. Also, their economies can be divided into agricultural, manufacturing, and service sectors for better analysis. Input-output analysis can be a powerful tool for industrial marketers.

A firm's ability to operate in a country depends on the supporting facilities and services available, collectively called its infrastructure. The transportation and communication facilities in a country affect its ability to get its goods to consumers and to communicate with customers, suppliers, and the home office. Energy availability affects the kinds of products that can be sold to consumer and industrial markets. The country's commercial infrastructure (ad agencies, wholesalers, etc.) constrains the firm's marketing task and capability there.

Generally, major differences exist between urban consumers and rural consumers. Countries differ greatly in their degree of urbanization, with the number of city dwellers declining with the level of economic development. The marketing task varies between the city and the countryside.

Inflation complicates the marketing task, and its incidence varies, generally being much higher in developing countries. The role of government as regulator, customer, and partner is another variable affecting the firm's marketing in a country.

QUESTIONS

3.1 Discuss the use of population size as an indicator of market potential.

3.2 What is the significance of a nation's population growth rate for the international marketer?

3.3 Why is the international marketer interested in the age distribution of the population in a market?

3.4 What is the dual economy phenomenon, and what does it mean for international marketing?

3.5 Discuss the limitations of per capita income in evaluating market potential.

3.6 In evaluating markets, what kind of firms might prefer per capita income figures? GNP figures?

3.7 What is the value of knowing about a country's natural resource base?

3.8 What can topography tell the international marketer about a foreign market?

3.9 Discuss the role of climate in international market analysis.

3.10 Marketing opportunities and problems in a country vary according to its level of economic development. Discuss.

3.11 What marketing differences might be encountered in an agricultural versus an industrialized country?

3.12 Discuss a nation's infrastructure as a constraint on marketing there.

3.13 How does the degree of urbanization in a country affect a firm's marketing?

ENDNOTES

[1] *World Development Indicators 1998* (Washington, DC: World Bank, 1998), 190, 191.

[2] Ibid.

[3] Ibid., 198, 199.

[4] Gunnar Myrdal, *Asian Drama* (New York: The Twentieth Century Fund, 1968).

[5] W. W. Rostow, *The Stages of Economic Growth* (New York: Cambridge University Press, 1960).

[6] Input-output tables give a detailed picture of the industrial structure of an economy, showing the interconnections between the various sectors. The input-output matrix shows what each industry bought from every other industry in a given year. For a discussion of input-output analysis, see Wassily Leontief, *Input-Output Economics* (New York: Oxford University Press, 1966).

[7] John S. Hill and Richard R. Still, "Effects of Urbanization on Multinational Product Planning," *Columbia Journal of World Business* (Summer 1984), 62–67.

FURTHER READINGS

Leontief, Wassily. *Input-Output Economics.* New York: Oxford University Press, 1966.

Rostow, W. W. *The Stages of Economic Growth,* 2d ed. Cambridge: The University Press, 1971.

DATA SOURCES

Europa Yearbook. London: Europa Publications, Ltd., annual.

United Nations. *United Nations Demographic Yearbook.* New York: United Nations, annual.

United Nations. *United Nations Statistical Yearbook.* New York: United Nations, annual.

U.S. Bureau of the Census. *Statistical Abstract of the United States.* Washington, DC: U.S. Government Printing Office, annual.

World Bank Atlas. Washington, DC: World Bank, biannual.

World Development Report. Washington, DC: World Bank, annual.

American Mining Machinery, Inc.

American Mining Machinery (AMM) is a specialized producer of equipment for the extractive industries. Its machines tend to be large and expensive, each averaging over $150,000. AMM was founded in 1902 by Edward Bednar, an inventive mining engineer, with backing from a few wealthy investors. Bednar ran the company quite successfully and quite autocratically, until his retirement at age 75 in 1948. His son, Harry Bednar, succeeded him as president and continued his father's management style, which could be described as anti-union paternalism.

Both Bednars were skilled engineers and designers with an intuitive rather than professional approach to the actual administration of the business. They were rather casual about such matters as financial controls and market planning. Nevertheless, AMM sales had risen to $190 million by the time Harry Bednar retired in 1986. At this time, the board of directors succeeded in getting a nonfamily professional manager appointed as president. With the help of an executive search firm, they chose Michael Luce, 41, who had been division manager with a capital equipment firm in Cleveland. Luce had an engineering degree as well as an M.B.A. and was much more oriented to management than to technical areas.

At the end of 1991, the board of directors reviewed the five years of Luce's presidency. Though sales had risen only to $208 million, this was attributed to conditions in the industry during this period. On the other hand, the board was very pleased with the increased profitability of AMM. The controls and procedures initiated by Luce had caused net profits to rise from 3 percent to 6 percent of sales, which meant a handsome return on investment.

The board was now considering Luce's proposal to expand AMM's operations outside the United States. The strong feelings and prejudices of the Bednar family had confined AMM's operations to the United States. Luce argued that there was a bigger potential market for AMM in the mining industries outside the United States than inside and that the company could no longer let personal political feelings hinder its growth.

Questions

1. What are the 25 countries with the largest production in the extractive industry?
2. What 10 countries would you recommend to AMM for further investigation as target markets? Explain and defend your choices in terms of estimated market size and any other variables you consider relevant (economic, political, or other).

Source: *Industrial Commodity Statistics Yearbook*

Medical Specialties, Inc.

Medical Specialties, Inc. (MSI) is a U.S. firm founded in 1955 by a small group of medical and scientific research professionals. The firm is unusual in that its product line is aimed at two specific but unrelated markets: prenatal and postnatal care and geriatric medicine. The firm has grown steadily, and sales now are almost $200 million.

Janice R. Becker, M.D., president of MSI, recently has been thinking about foreign markets for the firm's products.

The question was on the agenda at the last meeting of the board of directors (none of whom has had international experience save for some overseas military service). The board was interested but cautious. Members suggested that Becker begin to investigate possible markets in Western Europe as being closest to MSI's U.S. experience. They were also influenced by all the talk they had heard about Europe and the Euro. (The firm is already selling in Canada.)

Becker met with Ben Markowitz, MSI's marketing vice-president. After some discussion, they agreed on a list of factors they believed would be useful as a preliminary screening device for Western European markets. These variables were population, per capita income, birthrates, infant mortality rates, life expectancy, and ratio of physicians to population.

Questions

1. Prepare a table showing the scoring of the European countries on these variables. Your list should have the 15

EU countries plus the major EFTA countries (Norway and Switzerland). You may wish to add a few others.
2. What 10 countries do you believe are the best initial target markets? Explain and defend your choices.
3. What other information would you like on these countries?

Source: *United Nations Demographic Yearbook* and *World Development Report* (annual).

CASE 3.3

Unicola

Unicola is a medium-size beverage and snack food company based in the United States. Annual sales are $450 million. The firm has developed some special enriched beverage and snack foods that offer high nutritional value as well as convenience and refreshment. Unicola is interested in foreign markets for these new products. (Its present business is confined to the United States and Canada.) The company believes that these products should not be promoted as "health foods" but as traditional soft drinks and snacks because consumers do not like to buy products just because "they are good for you."

In view of the importance of promotion to the successful introduction of these products, George Horton, Unicola advertising manager, has been looking at promotional possibilities in various foreign markets of interest. One of these areas is Southeast Asia. His preliminary screening includes four variables: (1) newspaper circulation per capita, (2) radio receivers per capita, (3) television receivers per capita, (4) population. The markets being investigated have already been screened on the basis of political criteria. After the political screening, the following Southeast Asian nations remain on the list for a further screening on the basis of promotional possibilities: Bangladesh, Hong Kong, India, Indonesia, Malaysia, Pakistan, Philippines, Singapore, South Korea, Sri Lanka, Taiwan, Thailand, and Vietnam.

Questions

1. Prepare a table showing the scoring for these 13 countries on the four criteria suggested.
2. Which five countries would you choose as offering the best possibilities for promoting Unicola's products? Explain and defend your choices.
3. What other information would you need on these countries? How would you get it?

Source: *United Nations Statistical Yearbook, Statistical Abstract of the United States.*

Cultural Environment

The People of the World

Economic factors are important in determining a consumer's ability to purchase a product. Whether a purchase actually occurs, however, depends largely on cultural factors. Therefore, to understand markets abroad, the marketer must have an appreciation for the cultural environment of buyer behavior. In this chapter we look at the major ingredients of that cultural environment.

The main goals of this chapter are to

1.   Show how a country's material culture determines whether a firm's products fit in with a culture's way of life and what adaptation may be necessary.

2.   Explain the role of a culture's language in shaping the marketing task.

3.   Explore the subject of a society's aesthetics—its sense of beauty, proportion, and appropriateness—in connection with a firm's products and its communications.

4.   Describe the way that the local educational system can help or hinder a firm's marketing and staffing situation.

5.   Discuss the effect of a country's religious situation on consumer behavior.

6.   Distinguish among different values and attitudes that influence purchasing decisions.

7.   Explain how the social organization in a given country (family, age group, class, etc.) affects consumer behavior.

Marketing has always been recognized as an economic activity involving the exchange of goods and services. Only in recent years, however, have sociocultural influences been identified as determinants of marketing behavior, revealing marketing as a cultural as well as economic phenomenon. Because our understanding of marketing is culture bound, we must acquire a knowledge of diverse cultural environments in order to achieve successful international marketing. We must, so to speak, remove our culturally tinted glasses to study foreign markets.

The growing use of anthropology, sociology, and psychology in marketing is explicit recognition of the noneconomic bases of marketing behavior. We now know that it is not enough to say that consumption is a function of income. Consumption is a function of many other cultural influences as well. Furthermore, only noneconomic factors can explain the different patterns of consumption of two individuals with identical incomes—or, by analogy, of two different countries with similar per capita incomes.

A review of consumer durables ownership in EU countries with similar income levels shows the importance of nonincome factors in determining consumption behavior. For automatic washing machines the range is from 72 percent in Sweden to 96 percent in Italy; for dishwashers, from 11 percent in the Netherlands and Spain to 34 percent in Germany; for clothes dryers, from 5 percent in Spain to 39 percent in Belgium; for microwave ovens, from 6 percent in Italy to 37 percent in Sweden; for vacuum cleaners, from 56 percent in Italy to 98 percent in the Netherlands. It is remarkable that the same countries (Italy, Netherlands, Sweden) can be at the high-penetration level for some appliances and at the low-penetration level for others. Only cultural difference can account for these variations.

WHAT IS CULTURE?

Culture is too complex to define in simple terms. It seems that each anthropologist has a definition. Certain agreed-on fundamentals, however, appear in this definition by Hoebel: "Culture is the integrated sum total of learned behavioral traits that are shared by members of a society."[1] One fundamental is that **culture** is a total pattern of behavior that is consistent and compatible in its components. It is not a collection of random behaviors, but behaviors that are related and integrated. A second fundamental is that culture is learned behavior. It is not biologically transmitted. It depends on environment, not heredity. It can be called the man-made part of our environment. The third fundamental is that culture is behavior that is shared by a group of people, a society. It can be considered as the distinctive way of life of a people. We will look at the elements of culture after we consider the role of cultural analysis in U.S. marketing.

Cultural Analysis in U.S. Marketing

In approaching the cultural environment of international marketing, it is revealing to see how cultural analysis is used in U.S. marketing. If we scan textbooks in marketing, we see that none is without one or more chapters on the contributions of the behavioral sciences to marketing. In addition to chapters on consumer behavior, concepts derived from the behavioral sciences occur in chapters on marketing research, promotion, and pricing. Even the product is defined in terms of psychic as well as physical utility. For example, the marketing manager is supposed to be familiar with the following concepts: (1) reference groups, (2) social class, (3) consumption systems, (4) family structure and decision making, (5) adoption-diffusion, (6) market segmentation, and (7) consumer behavior.

Another evidence of the role of cultural analysis in U.S. marketing is the number of persons trained in anthropology or sociology who are working in marketing. Major companies employ such people. Others work in advertising agencies or consulting

GLOBAL MARKETING

Culture Shapes Foreign Marketing

International marketers all have stories to tell of their adventures—and misadventures—in foreign market cultures. These cultural constraints can affect all aspects of the marketing program. A couple of examples:

Cosmetics. Maybelline and Max Factor add brighter colors to their lipstick and makeup for Latin America. Vidal Sassoon adds more conditioner and a pine aroma to some shampoos in the Far East. Amway's skin-care line in Japan has less lather,

and Amway removes the pork proteins found in some of its products for Muslim markets, such as Malaysia.

Promotion. Hollywood has found the best way to promote its movies in Asia is to use popular local musicians. When Warner Bros. released "Lethal Weapon 4" in Hong Kong, its major promotion was a music video with a very popular heavy-metal band. Though music didn't relate to the film, scenes from the film were interspersed on the video. The song became the movie's "Asian theme song."

In Taiwan, a leading female singer made a music video based on "The English Patient." The studios usually don't even have to pay the local artists because both parties benefit.

---

firms. University consultants to industry today come not only from schools of business and engineering but also from departments of anthropology and sociology. Considering that most U.S. marketers are born and bred in the U.S. culture, such attention to cultural analysis is notable. How much more important is such analysis in foreign markets, where the international marketer generally knows little about the local culture. (See "Global Marketing," "Culture Shapes Foreign Marketing.")

Elements of Culture

Varying definitions exist of the elements of culture, including one that counts 73 "cultural universals." We use a simpler list covering eight major areas: (1) technology and material culture, (2) language, (3) aesthetics, (4) education, (5) religion, (6) attitudes and values, (7) social organization, and (8) political life. (We reserve the political aspect of culture for Chapter 5.) Our discussion of culture is not definitive and perhaps would not satisfy the anthropologist. Nonetheless, it should contribute to an understanding of the cultural environment as it affects the firm's foreign marketing. A broad definition of culture would include economics as well; however, the subjects are often treated separately, as we have done here.

MATERIAL CULTURE

Technology and Material Culture

Material culture includes the tools and artifacts—the material or physical things—in a society, excluding those physical things found in nature unless they undergo some technological procedure. For example, a tree per se is not part of a culture, but the Christmas tree is, and so is an orchard. **Technology** refers to the techniques or methods of making and using those things. Technology and material culture are related to the way a society organizes its economic activities. The term *technology gap* refers to differences in two societies' ability to create, design, and use things.

When we refer to industrialized nations, developing nations, the nuclear age, or the space age, we're referring to different technologies and material cultures. We can also speak of societies being in the age of the automobile, the bicycle, or foot transportation. Or in the age of the computer, the abacus, or pencil-and-paper calculation. The relationships between technology, material culture, and the other aspects of life are profound but not easily recognized because we are the products of our own culture. It is primarily as we travel abroad that we perceive such relationships.

When discussing this topic, Karl Marx went so far as to say that the economic organization of a society shapes and determines its political, legal, and social organization. That is the essence of his economic determinism, his materialistic interpretation of history. Few today would take such a strong position, but we can recognize many examples of the impact of our tools, techniques, and economic organization on the nature of life in our society. For example, our behavior as workers and consumers is greatly influenced by our technology and material culture.

The way we work, and how effectively we work, is determined in large part by our technology and material culture. Henry Ford's assembly line revolutionized U.S. productivity and ultimately our standard of living. The U.S. farmers' use of equipment and technology has made them the world's most productive agriculturalists. Ironically, agriculture is one of the most capital-intensive and technology-intensive industries in the United States. The R&D is not done by the farmer, however, but by land-grant universities, equipment manufacturers, and seed and chemical companies. The computer, as one of our newest artifacts, affects the way we work, the kind of work we can do, and even where we work. If we consider the nature of the factory and agricultural methods and the role of the computer in an African nation, we can see technology and material culture as a constraint on work and productivity in a culture.

The way we consume and what we consume are also heavily influenced by our technology and material culture. For example, the car has helped to create the suburbs with their accompanying lifestyle and consumption patterns. The car has also shaped dating behavior. Television has a wide-ranging impact on consumer and voter behavior. The microwave oven influences not only the preparation of food but also the nature of the food consumed. Considering artifacts such as the Sony Walkman or the cellular telephone, one can imagine further ramifications of each new product on the life of the consumer. Knowing the impact of these products in the U.S. culture, one can conjecture how consumer behavior might be different in countries with much lighter penetration of such products. For example, the number of persons per car ranges from 1.9 in the United States to 12 in Mexico, 250 in India, 500 in China, 1,000 in Uganda and Vietnam, and 2,500 in Bangladesh.[2]

Material Culture as a Constraint

Managers need insight into how material culture in foreign markets affects their operations there. In manufacturing, foreign production by the firm may represent an attempt to introduce a new material culture into the host economy. This is usually the case when the firm builds a plant in a less developed country. The firm generally checks carefully on the necessary economic prerequisites for such a plant: for example, raw-material supply, power, transportation, and financing. Frequently overlooked, however, are the other cultural preconditions for the plant.

Prior to making foreign production decisions, the firm must evaluate the material culture in the host country. One aspect is the economic infrastructure, that is, transportation, power, communications. Other questions are these: Do production processes need to be adapted to fit the local economy? Will the plant be more labor intensive than plants at home? The manager discovers that production of the same goods may require a different production function in different countries.

Material Culture and Marketing

It is equally important for marketers to understand the material culture in foreign markets. For example, the industrial marketer finds it useful to obtain input-output tables for these markets. Where tables can be even partially designed, the firm has a better idea of how its products relate to the material culture and industrial structure of the country. Such information helps identify customers and usage patterns.

In the giant, diversified economy of the United States, almost any industrial good can find a market. Going down the scale of development, however, industrial goods marketers find increasingly limited markets in which they can sell only part of their product line, or perhaps not any of it. The better the picture of the material culture in world markets, the better able the firm is to identify the best prospects. The prospects in countries where the principal agricultural implement is the machete differ from those in which it is the tractor.

In the early 1970s, General Motors created a "basic transportation vehicle" (BTV) for Third World markets. It was an innovative attempt to respond to markets with a very different technology and material culture. Ford developed a similar vehicle, called the "Model T for Asia." After being marketed in a number of Third World countries for several years, both products eventually failed.

In 1988, Toyota introduced its own version, the "Toyota utility vehicle" (TUV). In two years, the Kijang version, a 62-horsepower model, had 20 percent of the market in Indonesia. Offered as either pickup or van, the Kijang starts at one-third the price of a Toyota Corolla.

Consumer goods marketers are also concerned with the material culture in foreign markets. Such simple considerations as electrical voltages and use of the metric system must be taken into account. Product adaptations may also be necessitated by the material culture of the family. Does the family have a car to transport purchases? Does the family have a stove to prepare foods, or a refrigerator to store them? If electrical power is not available, electrical appliances will not be marketable unless they can be battery powered. To those who wash clothes by a stream or lake, detergents or packaged soaps are not useful; they provide a market for only bar soaps.

Other parts of the marketing program are also influenced by the material culture. The promotional program, for example, is constrained by the kinds of media available. The advertiser wants to know the availability of television, radio, magazines, and newspapers. How good is the reproduction process in newspapers and magazines? Are there advertising and research agencies to support the advertising program? The size of retail outlets affects the use of point-of-purchase displays. The nature of travel and the highway system affects the use of outdoor advertising.

Modifications in distribution may be necessary. These changes must be made on the basis of the alternatives offered by the country's commercial infrastructure. What wholesale and retail patterns exist? What warehouse or storage facilities are available? Is refrigerated storage possible? What is the nature of the transport system—road, rail, river, or air—and what area does it cover? Firms that use direct channels in the United States, with large-scale retailers and chain-store operations, may have to use indirect channels with a multitude of small independent retailers. These small retailers may be relatively inaccessible if they are widely dispersed and transportation is inadequate. Chapter 11 discusses these issues.

If local storage facilities are insufficient, the firm may have to supply its own or provide special packaging to offer extra protection. Whereas highways and railroads are most important in moving goods in the United States, river transport is a major means in some countries. And in others, air is the principal means. Thus, in numerous ways, management is concerned with the material culture in foreign markets. (See "Global Marketing," "Material Culture Matters.")

Imperialism?

Perhaps the most subtle role of international marketing is that of agent of cultural change. When the firm introduces new products into the market, it is, in effect, seeking to change the country's material culture. The change may be modest—a new food product—or it may be more dramatic—a machine that revolutionizes

Material Culture Matters

In Asia, Häagen-Daz quality requirements preclude it from making ice cream there. Instead, the ice cream is shipped from California and carefully monitored throughout the trip. In China, Häagen-Daz even shipped its own refrigerated trucks to ensure a safe continuous cold-chain from airport to storage to display case. Retailers are encouraged to take special Häagen-Daz refrigerators that defrost less often.

Mexico offers American marketers a growing market. Its material culture offers challenges also. Because the mail system is not reliable, companies usually must present their bills in person. Only nine phone lines exist per 100 people, and phone lines still get crossed occasionally. Only about one-third of the roads are paved, posing logistics problems. The new toll roads are excellent but expensive—the round trip between Mexico City and Acapulco costs $150 for a car and much more for a truck.

agricultural or industrial technology in the host country. The product of the international firm is alien in the sense that it did not originate in the host country. The firm must consider carefully the legitimacy of its role as an agent of change. It must be sure that changes it introduces are in accordance with the interests of the host country. The people may resent the firm's products as a form of "Americanization," "westernization," or "imperialism"; along this line, someone coined the term *Cocacolanization* in regard to U.S. business abroad.

In Canada, foreign sources—especially American—account for 95 percent of movies shown and 83 percent of magazines sold, as well as books and records.[3] Partly because of this, there is a Ministry of Canadian Heritage whose director is pushing legislation to limit the share of U.S. movies and magazines. There are also regulations requiring TV stations to offer 60 percent "Canadian content" and radio stations to have 35 percent "Canadian content" in their popular music broadcast.

LANGUAGE

Language is the most obvious difference between cultures. Inextricably linked with all other aspects of a culture, language reflects the nature and values of that culture. For example, the English language has a rich vocabulary for commercial and industrial activities, reflecting the nature of the English and U.S. societies. Many less industrialized societies have only limited vocabularies for those activities but richer vocabularies for matters important to their culture.

An Indian civil servant, Nabagopal Das, commented on the important role of the English language in India's development. He said it would be a serious error for India to replace English with Hindi or other Indian languages because none of them gives adequate expression to the modern commercial or technical activities necessary for India's development. On the other hand, these other languages are more than adequate, indeed rich, for describing the traditional culture. Similarly, Eskimo has many words to describe snow, whereas English has one general term. This is reasonable because the difference in forms of snow plays a vital role in the lives of Eskimos. The kinds of activities they can engage in depend on the specific snow conditions. Of course, in the United States, the subculture of skiers has a richer vocabulary for snow than that of the nonskiers.

Because language is such an obvious cultural difference, everyone recognizes that it must be dealt with. It is said that anyone planning a career in international business should learn a foreign language. Certainly, if a career is going to be importantly involved with a particular country, learning that language will be very useful. However, learning German or Japanese is not a great help to those whose careers do not involve Germany or Japan. Because it is usually impossible to predict to which countries a career will lead, it is best to study a language with large international use. Americans are fortunate in having English as their mother tongue, for English comes close to being a world language for international dealings. Table 4–1 shows the number of speakers of the major world languages. The figures for English are misleading because, for almost every country, English is the first choice as a second language. Over 80 percent of the home pages on the global Internet are in English. In the European Parliament, 11 languages are spoken, but the European Central Bank uses just one—English.

Language as a Cultural Mirror

A country's language is the key to its culture. Thus, if one is to work extensively with any one culture, it is imperative to learn the language. Learning a language well means learning the culture because the words of the language are merely concepts reflecting the culture. For the firm to communicate well with political leaders, employees, suppliers, and customers, it must assimilate this one aspect of culture more than any other.

Study of the language situation within foreign markets can yield useful information about them. The number of languages in a country is a case in point. In a real sense, a language defines a culture; thus, if a country has several spoken languages, it has several cultures. Belgium has two national languages, French in the South and Flemish in the North. This linguistic division goes back to the days of Julius Caesar, but even today political and social differences exist between the two language groups.

Canada's situation is similar to Belgium's, with both French and English languages and cultural groups. Many African and Asian nations have a far larger number of languages and cultural groups. Africa has one-tenth of the world's population but one-third of its languages. To communicate in this diversity, *lingua francas* have been chosen for communication between the groups. These are language bridges, usually the language spoken by the largest or most powerful group. In the former Soviet Union, it was Russian; in India, it is Hindi; in many countries it is the colonial language.

Congo serves as an example of this situation in many Third World countries. Separate tribal languages are spoken by the numerous tribes living there. Four African lingua francas partially link four regions of Congo, but the only national language is again a European one—French. Such situations present real obstacles to learning the "language of the people." The usual approach in these situations is to rely on the European language and the lingua francas for business and marketing communications. Unfortunately, these are not the mother tongue of most nationals.

Diversity: Linguistic and Social

Other problems accompany language diversity within a nation. Many tribal languages are not written. All intertribal communications are in the lingua franca, which is a written language. However, because the lingua franca is not everyone's native tongue, it does not communicate as well as the parties' native languages. The European languages used in former colonies have the virtue of covering a wide territory. However, they are foreign to the culture and spoken by only a small part of the population.

Language differences within a country may indicate social as well as communication problems. In both Canada and Belgium, the two linguistic groups have

TABLE 4–1	Major World Languages		
Language	*Speakers (Millions)*	*Language*	*Speakers (Millions)*
Mandarin	1,025	Bengali	207
English	497	Portuguese	187
Hindi	476	Malay Indonesian	170
Spanish	409	French	127
Russian	279	Japanese	126
Arabic	235	German	126

Source: *World Almanac 1998* (Mahwah, NJ: K111 Reference Corp., 1998), 444.

occasionally clashed to the point of violence. Angola, Nigeria, and India are examples of less developed countries where linguistic groups have also engaged in hostilities.

The United States is not exactly a linguistic melting pot either, as Table 4–2 shows. Spanish accounts for over half of all the foreign-language speakers, of course, but even several of the other groups provide segmentation for marketing and media purposes. While the United States is more homogeneous than the EU, the melting pot is not complete.

Even in China where 1 billion "speak Mandarin," more than 10 sociolinguistic groups exist. Among the Han Chinese, many Sinitic sublanguages and dialects exist, whose speakers are often unable to understand each other. These linguistic variations are related to cultural differences.

Many former colonies have some linguistic unity in the language of the former colonial power, but even this is threatened in some countries. For example, in India, Hindi is an official language along with English. Hindi has the advantage of being an Indian language but the drawback of belonging to just one segment of India's population. When it was declared an official language, riots broke out by the other language groups.

It is said that a language defines a cultural group—that nothing distinguishes one culture from another more than language. But what does it mean when the same language is used in different countries? French, for example, is the mother tongue not only for the French but also for many Belgians and Swiss. Spanish plays a similar role in Latin America. The anthropologist, however, stresses the *spoken* language as the cultural distinction. The spoken language changes much more quickly than the written and reflects the culture more directly. Although England, the United States, and Ireland use the same written English, they speak somewhat different "dialects." These three cultures are separate yet related, just as are the Spanish-speaking cultures of Latin America.

Even where a common language is spoken, different words are occasionally used as well as different pronunciations. In Latin America, for example, the word for tire is not the same in all the Spanish-speaking countries. In England, they say "lorry," "petrol," and "biscuits," but in the United States, we say "truck," "gasoline," and "cookies." It should be noted, incidentally, that even within one country—for example, the United States, where almost all speak "American" English—there are different cultural groups, or subcultures, among which the spoken language varies. Table 4–2 gives some indication of these cultural groups.

| TABLE 4-2 | Top 25 Languages, Other Than English, Spoken at Home by Americans |

#	Language Used at Home	Total Speakers over 5 Years Old (Thousands)	#	Language Used at Home	Total Speakers over 5 Years Old (Thousands)
1.	Spanish	17,339	14.	Hindi, Urdu related	331
2.	French	1,703	15.	Russian	242
3.	German	1,547	16.	Yiddish	213
4.	Italian	1,309	17.	Thai	206
5.	Chinese	1,249	18.	Persian	202
6.	Tagalog	843	19.	French Creole	188
7.	Polish	723	20.	Armenian	150
8.	Korean	626	21.	Navajo	149
9.	Vietnamese	507	22.	Hungarian	148
10.	Portuguese	430	23.	Hebrew	144
11.	Japanese	428	24.	Dutch	143
12.	Greek	388	25.	Mon-Khmer	127
13.	Arabic	355			

Source: Bureau of the Census, U.S. Dept. of Commerce.

Language as a Problem

In advertising, branding, packaging, personal selling, and marketing research, marketing is highly dependent on communication. If management is not speaking the same language as its various audiences, it is not going to enjoy much success. In each of its foreign markets, the company must communicate with several audiences: its workers, managers, customers, suppliers, and the government. Each of these audiences may have a distinctive communication style within the language common to all. The number of language areas the firm operates in approximates the number of countries it is selling in. Any advantage gained by the fact that one language may be used in more than one country is partly offset by the fact that in many countries, more than one language is necessary.

When Lotus was planning to introduce *Lotus 1-2-3* into Japan, it formed a development team. The team expected to work three months in Japan modifying the input and output routines. The job lasted 18 months! The Japanese write in four alphabets, and Kanji, used for business correspondence, is almost incompatible with keyboard entry. *Lotus 1-2-3* had to speak Kanji. The solution was to work with a Japanese software company. (See "Global Marketing," "English in Japan.")

Language diversity in world markets could be an insuperable problem if managers had to master the languages of all their markets. Fortunately, that is not the case. It is true that, to be effective, any person assigned to a foreign operation for a period of a year or more should learn the local language. However, cultural bridges are available in many markets. For example, in countries where the firm is operating through a distributor, the distributor may act as the bridge between the firm and its local market. In advertising, the firm can rely on a local advertising agency. Agency personnel, like the distributor, probably speak the advertising manager's language—especially if the firm communicates principally in English. For example, the Dutch firm Philips uses English as the official company language, even though it is domiciled in the Netherlands. Because of its widespread operations, it finds

GLOBAL MARKETING

English in Japan

One thing the Japanese import steadily from the United States is the English language. Examples are "besuboru"— "baseball," "akshon puran"—"action plan," and "sekshuaru harasumento"—"sexual harassment."

English is also used for local marketing purposes—by the Japanese. As one copywriter noted, "It's not important whether the writing makes sense. The main purpose of the English is to be 'with it.' I don't expect people to *read* it."

A coffee marketer says "using English gives products a stylish image in Japan." Its coffee package says "Ease Your Bosoms." "This coffee has carefully selected high-quality beans and roasted by our all the experience." A company spokesperson explained that its "coffee is so relaxing, it takes a load off your chest."

A ski jacket emphasizes long-term relationships—in English. "Let's go skiing since 1886." A sports bag notes "a drop of sweat is the precious gift for your guts."

In southeast Asia, Japanese managers use English almost 60 percent of the time.

Source: *Detroit News,* February 25, 1992; *The Wall Street Journal,* May 20, 1992.

English the most useful language for all its markets. In the Chrysler-Daimler Benz merger, American English was made the corporate language.

In countries where the firm has subsidiaries, the language requirement becomes greater. The firm then has more direct communication with its audiences. Even here, however, the burden is lessened because among its national managers, the firm can usually count people of the "third culture." This expression is used to describe nationals who have become so familiar with another culture that they become a bridge between the two. This is the best solution to both the language gap and the culture gap.

We have suggested that there are ways to circumvent the language problem. However, we hasten to add that language is a critical factor. It is the key to understanding and communicating with the local cultures around the world. The international firm does need language capabilities, not only among its distributors and other collaborators but also among its own personnel. A United Kingdom study showed that a third of small exporting companies lost opportunities because of linguistic problems.[4]

Canada provides an illustration of a situation requiring linguistic sensitivity by the international firm. In labor negotiations in Quebec, General Motors helped underwrite the cost of an interpreter to provide documentation in both French and English. GM agreed to recognize the French-language version of the contract as official. Other guidelines recommended to alleviate tension between the two groups were (1) bilingual labeling and advertising; (2) bilingual annual reports and press releases (French in Quebec), and (3) bilingual executives for operations in Quebec.

AESTHETICS

Aesthetics refers to the ideas in a culture concerning beauty and good taste, as expressed in the arts—music, art, drama, and dance—and the appreciation of color and form. International differences abound in aesthetics, but they tend to be regional rather than national. For example, Kabuki theater is exclusively Japanese, but Western theater includes at least all of Western Europe plus the United States and Canada in its audience.

Musical tastes, too, tend to be regional rather than national. In the West, many countries enjoy the same classical and popular music. In fact, with modern communications, popular music has become truly international. Nevertheless, there are obvious differences between Western music and that of the Middle East, Africa, or India. Likewise, the dance styles of African tribal groups or the Balinese are quite removed from Western dance styles. The beauty of India's Taj Mahal is different from that of Notre Dame in Paris or the Lever Building in New York.

Design

The aesthetics of a culture probably do not have a major impact on economic activities. In aesthetics, however, lie some implications for international business. For example, in the design of its plant, product, or package, the firm should be sensitive to local aesthetic preferences. This may run counter to the desire for international uniformity, but the firm must be aware of the positive and negative aspects of its designs.

A historical example of lack of cultural sensitivity is illustrated by early Christian missionaries from Western nations who were often guilty of architectural "imperialism." The Christian churches built in many non-Western nations usually reflected Western rather than indigenous architectural ideas. This was not done with malicious intent but because the missionaries were culture bound in their aesthetics; that is, they had their own ideas about what a church should look like.

The U.S. government faces a similar problem in designing its embassies. The U.S. Embassy in India received praise both for its beauty as a building and for the way it blended in with Indian architecture. The U.S. Embassy in London, however, has received more than its share of criticism for various things, including the size of the sculpted American eagle on top of the building. Some Britons also took exception to the architecture of the London Hilton. For the firm, the best policy is to design and decorate its buildings and commercial vehicles to reflect local aesthetic preferences. In its thousands of outlets abroad, McDonald's has learned to adapt its facilities to local tastes.

Color

The significance of different colors can also vary from culture to culture. In the United States, for instance, we use colors to identify emotional reactions; we "see red," we are "green with envy," or we "feel blue." Black signifies mourning in Western countries, whereas white is often the color of mourning in Eastern nations. Green is popular in Muslim countries, while red and black are negative in several African countries. Certain colors have particular meanings because of religious, patriotic, or aesthetic reasons. The marketer needs to know the significance of colors in a culture in planning products, packages, and advertising. For any market, the right choice of colors will be related to the aesthetic sense of the *buyer's* culture rather than that of the *marketer's* culture. Generally, the colors of the country's flag are safe colors. Japan has a Study Group for Colors in Public Places. It wages war on "color pollution." Its mission is "to seek out better uses for color, to raise the issue of colors."

Music

There are also cultural differences in music. An understanding of these differences is critical in creating advertising messages that use music. The music of nonliterate cultures is generally functional, or has significance in the people's daily lives, whereas the music of literate cultures tends to be separate from the people's other concerns. For example, a Western student has to learn to "understand" a Beethoven symphony, but aborigines assimilate musical culture as an integral part of their existence. Ethnomusicologist William Malm says that understanding the symbolism in different kinds of music requires considerable cultural conditioning. Therefore, homogeneity in music throughout world cultures is not possible.[5] One implication for the firm is that wherever it uses music, generally it had best use that of the local culture. A contrary example is Pepsi's use of a Michael Jackson commercial in many countries, including Japan and Russia.

Paul Anka provides an example of the value of "going native" in music and language. Anka has recorded 10 albums that have sold, collectively, 10 million copies, none of which has been heard in the United States. The secret is that the songs in the albums were sung in Japanese, German, French, Spanish, and Italian—songs that Anka composed strictly for those countries in a style indigenous to their musical cultures.

Anka isn't fluent in those languages. He worked for months in each country with local musicians on music and lyrics that would appeal to each nation. He sang in the local language phonetically. Anka said, "As far as my income is concerned, I could live off the rest of the world and never play the U.S. again. They love you when you record in their language."[6]

Brand Names

The choice of brand names is also affected by aesthetics. Frequently, the best brand name is one in the local language, pleasing to local taste. This leads to a multiplicity of brand names, which some firms try to avoid by searching out a nonsense word that is pronounceable everywhere but has no specific meaning anywhere: *Kodak* is a famous example. In other cases, local identification is important enough that firms seek local brand names. For example, Procter & Gamble has 20 different brand names for its detergents in foreign markets.

The aesthetics of a culture influence a firm's marketing there, often in ways that marketers are unaware of until they have made mistakes. The firm needs local inputs to avoid ineffective or damaging use of aesthetics. These inputs may be from local marketing research, local nationals working for the firm, and a local advertising agency or distributor.

EDUCATION

In the United States, education usually means formal training in school. In this sense, the aborigines in Australia or the Pygmies in Africa are not educated; that is, they have never been to school. However, this formal definition is too restrictive. **Education** includes the process of transmitting skills, ideas, and attitudes, as well as training in particular disciplines. Even so-called "primitive" peoples have been educated in this broader sense. For example, the Bushmen of South Africa are well educated for the culture in which they live.

One function of education is the transmission of the existing culture and traditions to the new generation. This is as true among the people of the United States as among the aborigines of Australia. However, education can also be used for cultural change. The promotion of a Communist culture in China was a notable example, but this, too, is an aspect of education in most nations. For example, in India educational campaigns are carried on to improve agriculture and to quell the population explosion. In Britain, business schools were established to improve the performance of the economy.

International Differences in Education

In looking at education in foreign markets, the observer is limited primarily to information about the formal process, that is, education in schools. This is the only area for which the United Nations Educational and Social Council (UNESCO) and others have been able to gather data. Literacy rates are also used to describe educational achievement. (See Table 4–3.)

			GNP Per
Illiteracy Rate[a]	Number of Countries	Population (Millions)	Capita (U.S. Dollars)
60 percent or more	23	427	$ 310
40–59 percent	22	1,322	460
20–39 percent	24	1,558	700
5–19 percent	30	814	3,150
Less than 5 percent	25	806	23,050

TABLE 4–3   **Literacy and Development**

[a]For ages 15 and older.
Source: *World Bank Atlas 1995* (Washington, DC: World Bank, 1995), 15.

The education information available on world markets refers primarily to national enrollments in the various levels of education—primary, secondary, and college or university. This information can give the international marketer insight into the sophistication of consumers in different countries. One can also observe a strong correlation between educational attainment and economic development.

Because only quantitative data are available, there is a danger that the qualitative aspects of education might be overlooked. Furthermore, in addition to the limitations inherent in international statistics, the problem exists of interpreting them in terms of business needs. For example, the firm's needs for technicians, marketing personnel, managers, distributors, and salesforces must be met largely from the educated population in the local economy. In hiring people, the firm is concerned not only with the level but also with the nature of their education.

Training in law, literature, or political science is probably not the most suitable education for business needs. Yet in many nations, such studies are emphasized almost to the exclusion of others more relevant to commercial and economic growth. Too often, primary education is preparation for secondary, secondary education is preparation for university, and university education is not designed to meet the needs of the economy. University education in many nations is largely preparation for the traditional prestige occupations. Although a nation needs lawyers and philosophers, it also needs agricultural experts, engineers, managers, and technicians. The degree to which the educational system provides for these needs is a critical determinant of the nation's ability to develop economically.

Education and International Marketing

The international marketer must be something of an educator also. The products and techniques the firm brings into a market are generally new to that market. The firm must educate consumers about their uses and benefits. Although the firm does not use the formal educational system, its success is constrained by that system because the firm's ability to communicate depends in part on the educational level of its market.

The international marketer is further concerned about the educational situation because it is a key determinant of the nature of the consumer market and the kinds of marketing personnel available. Some implications are the following:

1. If consumers are largely illiterate, advertising programs and package labels need to be adapted.

2. If girls and women are largely excluded from formal education, marketing programs must differ from those aimed at the U.S. homemaker.

3. Conducting marketing research can be difficult, both in communicating with consumers and in getting qualified researchers.

4. Products that are complex or need written instructions may need to be modified to meet the educational levels of the market.

5. Cooperation from the distribution channel depends partly on the educational attainments of members in the channel.

6. The quality of marketing support services, such as advertising agencies, depends on how well the educational system prepares people for such occupations.

RELIGION

In this chapter we are concerned with the cultural environment of business. We have already seen several aspects. The material culture, language, and aesthetics are, in effect, outward manifestations of a culture. If we are to get a full understanding of a culture, however, we must gain a familiarity with the internal, or mental, behavior that gives rise to the external manifestations. Generally, it is the **religion** of a culture that provides the best insights into this behavior. Therefore, although the international company is primarily interested in knowing *how* people behave as consumers or workers, management's task will be aided by an understanding of *why* people behave as they do.

Numerous religions exist in the world; here we will discuss briefly animism, Hinduism, Buddhism, Islam, the Japanese situation, and Christianity. We selected these on the basis of their importance in terms of numbers of adherents and their impact on the economic behavior of their followers. These religions account for over three-fourths of the world's population. Estimates by researchers in 1995 gave the following numbers for the major religions for the year 2000: animism, 240 million; Buddhism, 360 million; Christianity, 2,000 million; Hinduism, 860 million; Islam, 1,200 million.

Animism or Nonliterate Religion

Animism is the term used to describe the religion of aboriginal peoples. It is often defined as spirit worship, as distinguished from the worship of God or gods. Animistic beliefs have been found in all parts of the world. With the exception of revealed religion, some form of animism has preceded all historical religions. In many less developed parts of the world today, animistic ideas affect behavior.

Magic, a key element of animism, is the attempt to achieve results through the manipulation of the spirit world. It represents an unscientific approach to the physical world. When cause-and-effect relationships are not known, magic is given credit for the results. The same attitude prevails toward many modern-day products and techniques.

For example, during the author's years in Congo, he had an opportunity to see reactions to European products and practices that were often based on a magical interpretation. As one instance, a number of Africans affected the wearing of glasses, believing the glasses would enhance the intelligence of the wearer. Some consumer goods marketers in Africa have not hesitated to imply that their products have magical qualities. Of course, the same is occasionally true of marketers on U.S. TV.

Other aspects of animism include ancestor worship, taboos, and fatalism. All of these tend to promote a traditionalist, status quo, backward-looking society. Because such societies are more interested in protecting their traditions than in accepting change, marketers face problems when working with them. Marketers' success in bringing change depends on how well they understand and relate to the culture and its animistic foundation.

Hinduism

There are over 800 million Hindus in the world, most of them in India. In a broad sense, about 90 percent of India's population is Hindu, but in the sense of strict adherence to the tenets of Hinduism, the number of followers is smaller. It is a common dictum that Hinduism is not a religion but a way of life. Its origins go back to about 1500 B.C. It is an ethnic, noncreedal religion. A Hindu is born, not made, so Americans cannot become Hindus, although they can become Buddhists, for example. Modern Hinduism is a combination of ancient philosophies and customs, animistic beliefs, legends, and more recently, Western influences, including Christianity. A strength of Hinduism has been its ability to absorb ideas from outside; Hinduism tends to assimilate rather than to exclude.

Because Hinduism is an ethnic religion, many of its doctrines apply only to the Indian situation. However, they are key in understanding India. One important Hindu practice is the caste system. Each member of a particular caste has a specific occupational and social role, which is hereditary. Marriage is forbidden outside of the caste. Although efforts have been made to weaken this system, it still has a strong hold. Discrimination based on caste is forbidden by the Indian constitution, but such deep-rooted customs do not disappear with the passage of a new law. The caste system is aimed at preserving the status quo in society.

Another element, and a strength of Hinduism, is *baradari,* or the "joint family." After marriage, the bride goes to the groom's home. After several marriages in the family, there is a large joint family for which the father or grandfather is chief authority. In turn, the older women have power over the younger. The elders advise and consent in family council. The Indian grows up thinking and acting in terms of the joint family. If a member goes abroad to a university, the joint family may raise the funds. In turn, that member is expected to remember the family if he or she is successful. *Baradari* is aimed at preserving the family.

Veneration of the cow is perhaps the best-known Hindu custom; Gandhi himself called this the distinguishing mark of the Hindu. Hindu worship of the cow involves not only protecting it; eating the products of the cow is also considered a means for purification. Another element of traditional Hinduism is the restriction of women, following the belief that to be born a woman is a sign of sin in a former life. Marriages are arranged by relatives. Although a man may remarry if widowed, a woman may not. This attitude toward women makes it all the more remarkable that India placed a woman, Indira Gandhi, in its highest office.

Nirvana is another important concept, one that Hinduism shares with Buddhism. It will be discussed in the following section.

Buddhism

Buddhism springs from Hinduism and dates from about 600 B.C. Buddhism has approximately 350 million followers, mostly in South and East Asia from India to Japan. There are, however, small Buddhist societies in Europe and America. Buddhism is, to some extent, a reformation of Hinduism. It did not abolish caste but declared that Buddhists were released from caste restrictions. This openness to all classes and both sexes was one reason for Buddhism's growth. While accepting the philosophical insights of Hinduism, Buddhism tried to avoid its dogma and ceremony, stressing tolerance and spiritual equality.

At the heart of Buddhism are the Four Noble Truths:

1. The Noble Truth of Suffering states that suffering is omnipresent and part of the very nature of life.

2. The Noble Truth of the Cause of Suffering cites the cause to be desire, that is, desire for possessions and selfish enjoyment of any kind.

3. The Noble Truth of the Cessation of Suffering states that suffering ceases when desire ceases.

4. The Noble Truth of the Eight-Fold Path that leads to the Cessation of Suffering offers the means to achieve cessation of desire. This is also known as the Middle Way because it avoids the two extremes of self-indulgence and self-mortification. The eight-fold path includes (1) the right views, (2) the right desires, (3) the right speech, (4) the right conduct, (5) the right occupation, (6) the right effort, (7) the right awareness, and (8) the right contemplation. This path, though simple to state, is a demanding ethical system. Nirvana is the reward for those who are able to stay on the path throughout their lifetime or, more probably, lifetimes.

Nirvana is the ultimate goal of the Hindu and Buddhist. It represents the extinction of all cravings and the final release from suffering. To the extent that such an ideal reflects the thinking of the mass of the people, the society's values would be considered antithetical to such goals as acquisition, achievement, or affluence. This is an obvious constraint on marketing. Of course, not all Buddhists are so world-denying.

Islam

Islam dates from the seventh century A.D. It has over 1 billion adherents, mostly in Africa and Asia. The bulk of the world of Islam is found from the Atlantic across the northern half of Africa, the Middle East, and across Asia to the Philippines. Islam is usually associated with Arabs and the Mideast, but non-Arab Muslims outnumber Arab Muslims by almost three to one. The nations with the largest Muslim populations are all outside the Mideast. Bangladesh, India, Indonesia, and Pakistan all have over 100 million Muslims. Although there are two major groups in Islam (Sunni, 90 percent, and Shia, 10 percent), there is enough similarity between them on economic issues to permit identification of the following elements of interest to us.

Muslim theology, *Tawhid*, defines all that one should believe, whereas the law, *Shari'a*, prescribes everything one should do. The Koran (*Qur'an*) is accepted as the ultimate guide. Anything not mentioned in the Koran is likely to be rejected by the faithful. Introducing new products and techniques can be difficult in such an environment. An important element of Muslim belief is that everything that happens, good or evil, proceeds directly from the Divine Will and is already irrevocably recorded on the Preserved Tablet. This fatalistic belief tends to restrict attempts to bring about change in Muslim countries; to attempt change may be a rejection of what Allah has ordained. The name Islam is the infinitive of the Arabic verb *to submit*. Muslim is the present participle of the same verb, that is, a Muslim is one submitting to the will of Allah.

The Five Pillars of Islam, or the duties of a Muslim, include (1) the recital of the creed, (2) prayer, (3) fasting, (4) almsgiving, and (5) the pilgrimage. The creed is brief: There is no God but God, and Mohammed is the Prophet of God. The Muslim must pray five times daily at stated hours. During the month of Ramadan, Muslims are required to fast from dawn to sunset—no food, no drink, no smoking. Because the Muslim year is lunar, Ramadan sometimes falls in midsummer when the long days and intense heat make abstinence a severe test. The fast is meant to develop both self-control and sympathy for the poor. During Ramadan, work output falls off markedly, which is probably attributable as much to the Muslim's loss of sleep (from the many late-night feasts and celebrations) as to the rigors of fasting. The average family actually spends much more on the food consumed at night during Ramadan than on the food consumed by day in the other months. Other spending rises also. One Egyptian writer claimed that spending during Ramadan equalled six months of normal spending corresponding to Christmas spending in the United States.[7]

By almsgiving the Muslim shares with the poor. It is an individual responsibility, and there are both required alms (*zakat*) and freewill gifts. The pilgrimage to Mecca is a well-known aspect of Islam. The thousands who gather in Mecca each year return home with a greater sense of the international solidarity of Islam. Spending for the pilgrimage is a special form of consumption and affects other consumption also.

Muslims are not allowed to consume pork or alcohol. There is also a prohibition against usury, although this is often ignored in modern business practice. The role of women is quite restricted in Muslim nations, but very conservative Pakistan elected a woman, Benazir Bhutto, as prime minister. Some marketing implications of Islam are noted in Table 4–4.

Japan: Shinto, Buddhist, and Confucianist

Japan is a homogeneous culture with a composite religious tradition. The original national religion is Shinto, "the way of the gods." In the seventh century, however, Japan fell heavily under the influence of China and imported an eclectic Buddhism mingled with Confucianism. In 604, Prince Shotoku issued a moral code based on the teachings of both Confucius and Gautama Buddha. Its 17 articles still form the basis of Japanese behavior. The adoption of the religions from China was only after the authorities decided they would not conflict with Shinto. Traditional Shinto contains elements of ancestor and nature worship; state or modern Shinto added political and patriotic elements. Government figures count 107 million followers of Shinto and 93 million Buddhists, a tremendous overlap.

Among the more important aspects of modern Shinto are (1) reverence for the divine origin of the Japanese people and (2) reverence for the Japanese nation and the imperial family as head of that nation. We use the term *modern* Shinto because when the imperial powers were restored in 1868, state Shinto became a patriotic cult, whereas sectarian Shinto was purely religious. Of course, sectarian Shinto, through ancestor worship, also affects Japanese attitudes. In many houses, there is a god-shelf (*Kamidana*) in which the spirits of the family ancestors are thought to dwell and watch over the affairs of the family. Reverence is paid to them, and the sense of the ancestors' spirit is a bulwark of the family's authority over the individual. (See "Global Marketing," "Shinto in Japan.")

The impact of modern Shinto on Japanese life is reflected in an aggressive patriotism. The mobilization of the Japanese of World War II and their behavior during the war are examples. One longtime observer said, "Nationalism is the Japanese religion." More recently, the economic performance of Japan is due, in part at least, to the patriotic attitude of those working in the economic enterprise. The family spirit carried over to the firm, which has meant greater cooperation and productivity. Some Eastern religions seek virtue through passivity. Shinto, by contrast, stresses the search for progress through creative activity. Japan's economic performance clearly seems to follow the Shinto path. The aggressive Japanese attitude is reflected in the company song of Kyoto Ceramics, a Japanese firm.

> As the sun rises brilliantly in the sky,
> Revealing the size of the mountain, the market,
> Oh, this is our goal.
> With the highest degree of mission in our heart, we serve our industry
> Meeting the strictest degree of customer requirement.
> We are the leader in this industry and our future path
> Is ever so bright and satisfying.

TABLE 4-4	Islam and Marketing

Islamic Element	Marketing Implication
1. Daily prayers	Consider when planning sales calls, work schedules, customer traffic, and so forth.
2. Prohibition against usury (charging interest)	Avoid direct use of credit as marketing tool.
3. Zakat (compulsory almsgiving)	Use "excessive" profits for charitable purposes.
4. Religious holidays (example— end of Ramadan)	A major selling time for food, clothing, and gifts.
5. Public separation of sexes	Access female consumers by saleswomen, catalogs, home demonstrations, and women's shops.

Source: Mushtaq Luqmani, Zahir A. Quraeshi, and Linda Deline, "Marketing in Islamic Countries," *MSU Business Topics* (Summer 1980): 20, 21.

Christianity

Since most readers of this book are likely to be from countries where Christianity is the dominant religion, little time need be spent describing it. What concerns us here is the impact of the different Christian religious groups (Roman Catholic and Protestant) on economic attitudes and behavior. Two studies have dealt with this subject: Max Weber's *The Protestant Ethic and the Spirit of Capitalism* and R. H. Tawney's *Religion and the Rise of Capitalism.* The Eastern Orthodox churches are not discussed here, but their impact on economic attitudes is similar to that of Catholicism.

Roman Catholic Christianity traditionally has emphasized the Church and the sacraments as the principal elements of religion and the way to God. The Church and its priests are intermediaries between God and human beings, and apart from the Church there is no salvation. Another element is the distinction between the members of religious orders and the laity, with different standards of conduct applied to each. An implicit difference exists between the secular and the religious life.

The Protestant Reformation, especially Calvinism, made some critical changes in emphasis but retained agreement with Catholicism on most traditional Christian doctrine. The Protestants, however, stressed that the Church, its sacraments, and its clergy were not essential to salvation: "Salvation is by faith alone." The result of this was a downgrading of the role of the Church and a consequent upgrading of the role of the individual. Salvation became more an individual matter.

Another change by the reformers was the elimination of the distinction between secular and religious life. Luther said all of life was a *Beruf,* a "calling," and even the performance of tasks considered to be secular was a religious obligation. Calvin carried this further and emphasized the need to glorify God through one's calling. Whereas works were necessary to salvation in Catholicism, works were evidence of salvation in Calvinism.

Hard work was enjoined to glorify God; achievement was the evidence of hard work; and thrift was necessary because the produced wealth was not to be used selfishly. Accumulation of wealth, capital formation, and the desire for greater production became Christian duty. The Protestant Reformation thus led to greater emphasis on individualism and action (hard work) as contrasted with the more ritualistic and contemplative approach of Catholicism.

Although it is useful to recognize the separate thrust of Roman Catholic and Protestant Christianity, it is also important to note the various roles Christianity in general plays in different nations. Some nations reflect varying mixtures of Catholic and Protestant, and the resulting ethic may be some combination of both doctrines. Of course, it is true for Christians, as with Buddhists, Hindus, or Muslims, that there are wide variations in the degree to which the adherents follow the teachings. In all groups, there are segments ranging from fundamentalist to conservative to casual.

GLOBAL MARKETING

Shinto in Japan

The hold of tradition in Japan is vividly apparent in religion. Most shops have, tucked away somewhere, a shrine to a deity whose customary symbol is a pair of foxes. Japanese companies generally choose a patron god or goddess. These deities are part of Japan's own native folk religion, Shinto.

Jan Swyngedouw, a Belgian professor of Japanese culture and religion at Nanzan University in Japan, points out that Japan is the only industrialized country in the world with its own native religion still intact. As a national religion unique to Japan, Shinto helps knit the nation together and separate the Japanese from outsiders.

Unlike Western religions, Shinto has no scriptures or commandments. It does have customary practices, including ancestor worship adopted from Confucianism. And it has a body of traditional myths, passed on from one generation to the next. The priests do not preach. They tend their shrines and offer quiet places for reflection and prayer, as well as for weddings and elaborate baby-blessing ceremonies.

Shinto coexists with Buddhism, and a Japanese can embrace both. Many a Japanese has been married at a Shinto shrine and buried with a Buddhist ceremony. But despite this tolerance of diverse religious traditions, Christianity has never taken hold in Japan. Swyngedouw has an explanation. "The Japanese," he says, "are already saved. They are a sacred race. It is understood, in the traditions of Shinto, that they descend from God."

These beliefs, he adds, do involve a danger of ultranationalism. On the positive side, they contribute to a sense of unity of purpose. This spills into the workplace. Over the past several decades, the Japanese have extended their religious feelings to the company, according to Swyngedouw. The transfer can take place because of the sense of sacredness the Japanese feel toward their country, its development, and its place in the world. This devotion, he says, is sometimes called the religion of being Japanese.

Source: Carla Rapoport, "Understanding How Japan Works," *Fortune* 120, no. 13 (Fall 1989):18. © 1989 The Time Inc. Magazine Company. All rights reserved.

Religion and the Economy

In our discussion of the various religions, we suggested some economic implications that we elaborate on here. Religion has a major impact on attitudes toward economic matters. In the section "Attitudes and Values," we discuss the different attitudes religion may inspire. Besides attitudes, however, religion may affect the economy more directly as in the following.

1. Religious holidays vary greatly among countries, not only from Christian to Muslim, but even from one Christian country to another. In general, Sundays are a religious holiday where Christianity is an important religion. In the Muslim world, however, the entire month of Ramadan is a religious holiday for practical purposes. The firm must see that local work schedules and marketing programs are related to local holidays, just as American firms plan for a big season at Christmas.

2. Consumption patterns may be affected by religious requirements or taboos. Fish on Friday for Catholics used to be a classic example. Taboos against beef for Hindus or pork for Muslims and Jews are other examples. The Muslim prohibition against alcohol has been a boon to companies like Coca-Cola. Stroh's and some other brewers sell a nonalcoholic beer in Saudi Arabia. On the other hand, dairy products find favor among Hindus, many of whom are also vegetarian.

3. The economic role of women varies from culture to culture, and religious beliefs are an important cause. Women may be restricted in their capacity as consumers, as workers, or as respondents in a marketing study. These

differences can require major adjustments in the approach of a management conditioned in the U.S. market.

Procter & Gamble's products are mainly used by women. When the company wanted to conduct a focus group in Saudi Arabia, however, it could not induce women to participate. Instead, it used the husbands and brothers of the women for the focus group.

4. The caste system restricts participation in the economy. The company feels the effects not only in its staffing practices (especially the salesforce) but also in its distribution and promotional programs, because it must deal with the market segments set up by the caste system.

5. The Hindu joint family has economic effects. Nepotism is characteristic of the family business. Staffing is based on considerations of family rank more than on other criteria. Furthermore, consumer decision making and consumption in the joint family may differ from those in the U.S. family, requiring an adapted marketing strategy. Pooled income in the joint family may lead to different purchase patterns.

6. Religious institutions themselves can play a role in economic matters. The Church, or any organized religious group, can often block the introduction of new products or techniques if it sees the innovation as a threat. On the other hand, the same product or technique can be more effectively introduced if the religious organization sees it as a benefit. The United States has seen the growing role of religious groups. "Global Marketing" gives some examples from other countries.

7. Finally, religious divisions in a country can pose problems for management. The firm may find that it is dealing with different markets. In Northern Ireland there is strong Catholic-Protestant hostility. In India, Muslim-Hindu clashes led to the formation of the separate Muslim state of Pakistan, but the problem is not settled yet. In the Netherlands major Catholic and Protestant groups have their own political parties and newspapers. Such religious divisions can cause difficulty in staffing an operation or in distributing and promoting a product. Religious differences may indicate market segments that require separate marketing strategies and media.

Clearly, the international firm must be sensitive to religious differences in its foreign markets and willing to make adaptations. To cite one example, the firm that is building a plant abroad might plan the date and method of opening and dedicating it to reflect the local religious situation. A firm's advertising, packaging, and personal selling practices especially need to take local religious sensitivities into account.

ATTITUDES AND VALUES

Our attitudes and values help determine what we think is right or appropriate, what is important, and what is desirable. Some relate to marketing, and these are the ones we will look at here. We must consider attitudes and values because, as someone said, "People act on them." Douglas North, the Nobel Prize–winning economist said, "People act on the basis of ideologies and religious views."

Marketing Activities

Ever since Aristotle, selling activities have failed to gain high social approval. The degree of disapproval, however, varies from country to country. In countries where marketing is rated very low, marketing activities are likely to be neglected and un-

GLOBAL MARKETING

Marketers Get Religion

Religion has a way of getting marketers' attention. Some examples follow:

London. A World Cup soccer promotion became an embarrassment for McDonald's. The chain printed a Koran scripture on throwaway bags. Islamic officials said the sacred words from the flag of the Saudi World Cup team should not be crumpled up and thrown away. The words were: "There is no God but Allah, and Mohammed is his Prophet."

Malaysia. Citicorp and other Western banks opened Islamic banking branches here. A Malaysian bank offers an interest-free VISA card. It charges a fee as a percent of customer annual spending.

India. McDonald's operates here without Big Macs. Deferring to the Hindu prohibition against beef consumption, they serve chicken and fish—and vegetable burgers. The first McDonald's without beef.

Mideast. Multinationals adapt the verbal and visual cues in their ads to Muslim sensitivities.

Paris, Jakarta. Chanel, the French fashion house, apologized to the Muslim world, saying it unwittingly put verses from the Koran on dresses in its Paris show, including some fairly revealing models. After a Muslim group in Jakarta protested, Chanel destroyed the dresses with the offending designs, along with the negatives of the photos made of the garments.

derdeveloped. Capable, talented people are not drawn into business. Often, marketing activities are left to a special class, or perhaps to expatriates. One is reminded of the medieval banking role filled by Jews, or the merchant role of the Chinese in Southeast Asia. In any case, the international firm can have problems with personnel, distribution channels, and other aspects of its marketing program, depending on a country's attitude toward business. There is a brighter side to this picture, however. Because marketing is well developed in the United States, the U.S. firm abroad may have an advantage in marketing.

Wealth, Material Gain, and Acquisition

The United States has been called the "affluent society," the "achieving society," and the "acquisitive society." These somewhat synonymous expressions reflect motivating values in our society. In the United States, wealth and acquisition are often considered the signs of success and achievement and are given social approval. In a Buddhist or Hindu society where nirvana or "wantlessness" is an ideal, people may not be so motivated to produce and consume. Marketers obviously prefer to operate in an acquisitive society. However, as a result of the revolution of rising expectations around the world, national differences in attitudes toward acquisition seem to be lessening. For example, Buddhist Thailand is proving a good market for many consumer goods firms.

Change

When a company enters a foreign market, it brings change by introducing new ways of doing things and new products. North Americans in general accept change. The word *new* has a favorable connotation and facilitates change when used to describe techniques and products. Many societies are more tradition-oriented, however, revering their ancestors and traditional ways of consuming.

The marketer as an agent of change has a different task in such traditional societies. Rather than emphasizing what is new and different about the product, the marketer might relate it to traditional values, perhaps noting that it is a better way of solving a consumer problem. In seeking acceptance of its new product, the firm might try to get at least a negative clearance—that is, no objection—

from local religious leaders or other opinion leaders. Any product must first meet a market need. Beyond that, however, the product must also fit in with the overall value system to be accepted.

Campbell met this kind of obstacle when it was introducing its canned soups into Italy. In conducting marketing research, it received an overwhelmingly negative response to the question "Would you marry a user of prepared soups?" Campbell had to adjust its marketing accordingly.

Risk Taking

Consumers take risks when they try a new product. Will it do what they expect it to do? Will it prejudice their standing or image with their peers? Intermediaries handling the untried product may also face risks beyond those associated with their regular line. In a conservative society, there is a greater reluctance to take such risks. Therefore, the marketer must seek to reduce the risk involved in trying a new product as perceived by customers or distributors. In part, this can be accomplished through education; guarantees, consignment selling, or other marketing techniques can also be used.

Consumer Behavior

The attitudes we have been discussing are relevant to understanding consumer behavior in the markets of the world. International managers must have such an understanding to develop effective marketing programs. Because of the impossibility of gaining intimate knowledge of a great number of markets, they must rely on help from others in addition to company research. Those who may assist in understanding local attitudes and behavior include personnel in the firm's subsidiary, the distributor, and the advertising agency. Although the firm is interested in changing attitudes, most generally it has to adapt to them. As Confucius said, "It is easier to move mountains than to change the minds of men."

Social Organization

Kinship

Social organization refers to the way people relate to other people. This differs somewhat from society to society. The primary kind of social organization is based on kinship. In the United States, the key unit is the family, which traditionally included only the father and mother and the unmarried children in the household. Of course, the definition is changing, as is reflected in each census. The family unit elsewhere is often larger, including more relatives. The large joint family of Hinduism was discussed previously. In many other less developed nations, there is also a large extended family. Those who call themselves brothers in Congo, for example, include those whom we call cousins and uncles.

The extended family in developing countries fulfills several social and economic roles. It does not necessarily depend on a specific religious sanction, as does the *baradari* of Hinduism. The extended family provides mutual protection, psychological support, and economic insurance or social security for its members. In a world of tribal warfare and primitive agriculture, this support was invaluable. The extended family, still significant in many parts of the world, means that consumption decision making takes place in a larger unit and in different ways. Pooled resources, for instance, may allow larger purchases. (For this reason, per capita income may be a misleading guide to market potential.) The marketer may find it difficult to determine the relevant consuming unit for some goods. Is it a household or family? How many members are there? As Table 4–5 demonstrates, the size of households varies greatly around the world.

TABLE 4–5	Average Number of Occupants per Household			
United States	2.62		Mexico	4.64
Canada	2.67		India	4.86
Germany	2.88		Nigeria	5.01
Japan	3.00		Pakistan	6.76

Source: *International Marketing Data and Statistics,* 1998 (London: Euromonitor, 1998), 395.

Common Territory

In the United States, **common territory** can be the neighborhood, the suburb, or the city. In many countries of Asia and Africa, it is the tribal grouping. The tribe is often the largest effective unit in many countries because the various tribes do not voluntarily recognize the central government. Colonialism tried to gather diverse tribes into a single nation. Unfortunately, nationalism has not generally replaced tribalism. Tribalism, or ethnic divisions, often leads to bloody conflict, shown by such examples as Angola, Congo, Kosovo, Rwanda, and Pakistan. Even in Europe, the Scots and the Welsh are not happy about being under British rule. For the marketer, these groupings based on common territory might be a clue to market segmentation in many countries.

Special-Interest Group

A third kind of social grouping, the **special-interest group** or association, may be religious, occupational, recreational, or political. Special-interest groups can also be useful in identifying different market segments. For example, in the United States, the Sierra Club, the National Organization for Women (NOW), and the National Rifle Association (NRA) represent market segments for some firms.

Other Kinds of Social Organization

Some kinds of social organization cut across the three categories above. One is **caste** or **class groupings.** These may be detailed and rigid, as in the Hindu caste system, or they may be more loose and flexible, as in U.S. social classes. The United States has a relatively open society, but there is still concern about social standing and status symbols. While social class is more important and more rigid in many other countries, each country has its own social and ethnic groupings which are important for its society and its economy. These groupings usually mean that some groups are discriminated against and others are favored. The firm needs to know this social organization because it will affect its marketing program. Different groups may require different marketing strategies.

Another kind of grouping, based on age, occurs especially in the affluent industrialized nations. We recognize both the "senior citizen" and the teenage subcultures. Senior citizens usually live as separate economic units with their own needs and motivations. They are a major market segment in the industrialized countries. And although teenagers do not commonly live apart from their families, they nonetheless compose a significant economic force to be reckoned with. See "Global Marketing," "Are Teens the First Truly Global Consumers?"

As noted in our discussion of the extended family, there is much less separation between age groups in less developed areas. Generally strong family integration occurs at all age levels, as well as a preponderant influence of age and seniority, in

GLOBAL MARKETING

Are Teens the First Truly Global Consumers?

International marketers are getting excited about a new global market—the world's teenagers. They are becoming more numerous, more prosperous, and more alike. BSB, the American ad agency, videotaped teens' bedrooms in cities around the world, such as Des Moines, Los Angeles, Jakarta, Mexico City, Paris, Santiago, Singapore, and Tokyo. They found an amazing similarity of contents: Nikes and Reeboks, Levis, Sega and Nintendo, NBA jackets, and rugged shoes from Timberland or Doc Martens.

Another U.S. agency, DMB&B, studied the cultural attitudes and consumer behavior of 6,500 teenagers in 26 countries. Results showed teens around the world living very parallel lives. Some of the forces at work include the media, with

American movies, TV shows, and especially MTV playing a big role. (MTV in Europe alone has 200 advertisers.) Global events like the Olympics and World Cup are important too. Another factor is the shopping environment. From South Africa to Europe to the Far East, the malls all look alike. To some extent this is an Americanization of consumer behavior. When asked what country had the most influence on fashion and culture, the United States was named by 87 percent of teens in Latin America, 80 percent of Europeans, and 80 percent of those in the Far East.

These are indeed promising developments for international consumer goods marketers. Caution is necessary, however, before firms implement a one-size-fits-all strategy. Many seasoned observers note that cultural differences persist. It is still difficult to speak with one voice throughout the world. Perhaps that is why Coca-Cola prudently began its own multiyear study called "The Global Teenager" to guide it in marketing to this group.

contrast to the youth motif prevalent in the United States. Of course, Generation X and the baby boomers are important age groupings in the United States.

A final aspect of social organization concerns the role of women in the economy. Women seldom enjoy parity with men as participants in the economy, and their participation declines as one goes down the scale of economic development. The extent to which they participate in the money economy affects their role as consumers and consumption influencers. Even developed countries exhibit differences in attitude toward female employment. For example, there are some significant differences in female employment between the United States, several European countries, and Japan. These differences are reflected both in household income levels and consumption patterns.

In spite of the constraints we have noted, the economic role of women is undergoing notable change in many countries. One piece of evidence is that U.S. and European multinationals (but not Japanese) have successfully employed women managers on assignments in such unlikely places as Brazil and Saudi Arabia. Other evidence is provided by the Women in Management program at the American University in Cairo. Egyptian companies have more female middle-level managers than many Western firms. The affluence of many Muslim OPEC nations has led to more education and power for Arab women, who have been among the most restricted. In Kuwait, for example, women not only own boutiques but also serve as presidents of companies and even as corporate chairpersons.

Cultural Variables and Marketing Management

Culture is an integrated pattern of behavior shared by people in a society. We have looked at several dimensions of culture. The importance of these cultural variables to firms marketing internationally is that what they are *able* to do in marketing to a particular society and what they *want* to do is shaped by these variables. In other words, international marketing is a function of culture. Table 4–6 is a matrix repre-

| TABLE 4-6 | Cultural Variables and Marketing |

| | Marketing Functions | | | | | |
Cultural Variables	Product	Promotion	Price	Distribution	Marketing Research	Strategy Formulation
Technology and material culture						
Language						
Aesthetics						
Education						
Religion						
Attitudes, values						
Social organization						
Politics-Law						

senting the interrelationships between cultural variables and international marketing functions.

SUMMARY

Culture is an integrated pattern of behavior and the distinctive way of life of a people. The various dimensions of culture influence a firm's marketing.

Worker behavior and consumer behavior in a country are shaped by its technology and material culture. The kinds of products a firm can sell and its distribution and promotional programs are constrained by the country's infrastructure. This includes not only the country's transportation and communications systems but also such things as the availability of media and advertising agencies.

Communication is a major part of the marketing task, so the firm must communicate in the languages of its markets. This may require adaptation in packaging and labeling, advertising and personal selling, and marketing research. Fortunately, national employees, distributors, and advertising agencies help with the language problem.

Each society has its own ideas about beauty and good taste—its own aesthetics. In the design and color of its products and packaging, its advertising and selection of music and brand names, the firm must try to appeal to those tastes.

Differences in literacy and consumer skills, as a result of a country's educational system, determine what kinds of adjustments in products and in marketing communications are necessary. The quality of marketing support services (advertising, marketing research) in a country is also affected by the output of the educational system there.

Religion is a major determinant of attitudes and behavior in a society. Each country has its own religious profile, but such major world religions as animism, Buddhism, Hinduism, Christianity, and Islam cover 80 percent of the world's population. Each of these religions has its own particular impact on the attitudes and behavior of consumers who follow the religion. For example, the traditional animist might be reluctant to accept new products. The devout Buddhist who is seeking an absence of desire, or a state of wantlessness, is not a strong potential consumer. Other religious impacts on marketing include religious holidays and product taboos, the role of women in the economy and society, and the caste system. Finally, religious divisions in a country may indicate market segments that require different marketing programs and salesforces. Japan's composite religious tradition has also affected the economy of that country.

Attitudes and values greatly affect consumer behavior. Attitudes toward wealth and acquisition, toward change, and toward risk taking are especially important for the international marketer who may be introducing innovation to a society in the form of new products—and even new lifestyles.

Social organization refers to the way people relate to each other and to the various groups and divisions in a society. The size and nature of the family, tribalism and ethnic divisions, and different roles for women or age groups (such as senior citizens), all may influence a marketing program.

QUESTIONS

4.1 What is culture?

4.2 Give examples of cultural concepts used in U.S. marketing.

4.3 How can a nation's technology and material culture affect a firm's marketing in that country?

4.4 Discuss the role of the international marketer as an agent of cultural change. Is this role legitimate?

4.5 Why are international marketers interested in the linguistic situation in their markets?

4.6 How can the international firm deal with the language challenges in its foreign markets?

4.7 How can the aesthetic ideas and values of a society influence the firm's marketing there?

4.8 How is international marketing constrained by the educational level in a market?

4.9 What, if anything, does a country's religious situation have to do with a firm's marketing there?

4.10 Discuss the marketing implications of the following religious phenomena: (a) religious holidays, (b) taboos, (c) religious institutions (church and clergy), (d) nirvana.

4.11 Identify some constraints in marketing to a traditional Muslim society.

4.12 What is the marketing significance of these aspects of social organization: (a) the extended family, (b) tribalism, (c) the role of women in the economy?

4.13 Convenience Foods Corp. has asked you to do a cultural analysis of a South American country where it is considering operations. How would you go about this task?

ENDNOTES

1 Adamson Hoebel, *Man, Culture and Society* (New York: Oxford University Press, 1960), 168.

2 *International Marketing Data and Statistics,* 1998, 115.

3 *The Wall Street Journal,* September 24, 1998, B1.

4 *Financial Times,* April 4, 1995, 11.

5 Interview at the University of Michigan with William Malm, September 20, 1992.

6 *Detroit News,* "Hollywood," UPI, May 18, 1981.

7 *International Herald Tribune,* May 8, 1989, 1.

FURTHER READINGS

Barkema, Harry, and Frank Vermeulen. "What Culture Differences Are Detrimental for Joint Ventures." *Journal of International Business Studies* 28, no. 4 (1997): 845–864.

Carey, George, Xiaoyon Zhao, Joan Chiaramonte, and David Eden. "Is There One Global Village for Our Future Generation?" *Marketing and Research Today* (February 1997): 12–16.

Kamela, Naoki, and Jeremiah Sullivan. "English as the Lingua Franca of the Far East." *Multinational Business Review* (Spring 1996): 52–62.

Nakata, Cheryl, and K. Sivakumar. "National Culture and New Product Development." *Journal of Marketing* (January 1996): 61–72.

Newman, Karen, and Stanley Nollen. "The Fit between Management Practices and National Culture." *Journal of International Business Studies* 27, no. 4 (1996): 753–779.

Terpstra, Vern, and Kenneth David. *The Cultural Environment of International Business,* 3d ed. Cincinnati: SouthWestern, 1991.

Bottled Spirits

The Hopi are the westernmost tribe of Pueblo Indians, located in northeastern Arizona. There are less than 10,000 of them. They typically live in terraced pueblo structures of stone and adobe and are clustered into a number of small, independent towns. Like all Pueblo Indians, the Hopi are peaceful, monogamous, diligent, self-controlled, and very religious.

The most conservative tribe in the Southwest, the Hopi want no tourists to photograph, sketch, or record their dances. They do, however, allow visitors to observe their ceremonies, where they may watch masked Kachina dancers impersonate Hopi gods. The Hopi also invite tourists into their homes to buy Kachina dolls or Hopi pottery.

Kachinas are the Hopi Indians' holy spirits. They are sometimes personified by masked dancers and sometimes represented by wooden dolls. There are roughly 250 different Kachinas. Although the Hopi will sell Kachina dolls to tourists, they are sensitive to how others may use the Kachina costume or idea. For example, in 1987 Miss New Mexico won the costume competition in the Miss USA competition wearing a Kachina costume. Hopi religious leaders complained that that use was sacrilegious.

In another incident, the Hopi protested when Kentucky's Ezra Brooks distillery began marketing its bourbon in bottles shaped like Kachina dolls. The Brooks distillery had planned to distribute as a Christmas promotion 5,000 of the Kachina doll bottles in Arizona and the Southwest. It had already shipped 2,000 bottles when the Hopi complaint reached it.

Reflecting the Hopis' anger, tribal chairperson Clarence Hamilton asked, "How would a Catholic feel about putting whiskey in a statue of Mary?" The Hopi not only complained but they also asked for the help of Senator Barry Goldwater of Arizona, a noted collector of Kachina dolls—but not the whiskey-bottle variety.

Questions

1. What should the distillery do? What courses of action are open to it?
2. Propose and defend your solution to this problem.
3. Could this problem have been avoided? How?

Foremost Dairy in Thailand

Foremost Foods Company is the world's largest processor of whey-based products, including lactose and high-protein items. Foremost International, the international arm of Foremost Foods, has operations in 16 countries, including Guam, Indonesia, Taiwan, El Salvador, Guatemala, Saudi Arabia, and Iran.

Foremost Foods produces and markets several proprietary grocery-shelf items and is a leading processor and distributor of dairy products, principally in the western United States. According to its annual report, the company's long-term objective in the food industry is to be an aggressive, profitable, multinational marketer of a broad line of nutritious food products to the consumer. In keeping with these goals, it entered Thailand in 1956. By 1990, Foremost sales in Thailand were over $30 million.

When Foremost and three local partners set up their first dairy products processing plant in Thailand in 1956, they were starting from scratch in a market where milk and ice cream were virtually unknown commodities. Hence, the first problem was how to make people aware of dairy products, their many uses, and the sanitary measures necessary to keep them fresh. In cooperation with the Thai government, company representatives were sent into schools to give talks on sanitation and nutrition, at the same time supplying the schools with dairy products for the students. The program was a huge success, and a demand was created.

Next came the tricky question of refrigeration. How was the corner grocer to keep milk from souring and ice cream from melting? The answer was to supply every one of the tiny retail outlets—"mom and pop" groceries and restaurants—with a freezer, either through leasing, or more often, under the terms of a conditional sales contract. If the contracts were met, the freezers were sold to the stores for one U.S. dollar. The initial capital outlay was sizeable, running into hundreds of thousands of dollars, and the accompanying headaches were many (e.g., keeping stores from unplugging the freezers at night to save electricity and preventing their use for other products), but the effort eventually worked.

From the beginning, Foremost has tailored operations to the local Thai scene. Products find their way to market via crude water transportation and brightly colored company trucks. They are sold either from pushcarts, from company retail outlets, or through traditional channels (e.g., wholesalers).

The pushcarts, also brightly decorated in the local style with dragons and brilliant umbrellas, are supplied by the company and operated by independent retailers. These sidewalk salespeople come to a company-owned depot every morning to pick up their pushcarts and their day's supply of milk and ice cream. At the end of the day, they return and pay for the amount sold, with a profit margin for themselves, of course. That margin approximates 20 percent, but the sidewalk salespeople can, and do, set their own retail price.

The company-owned retail outlets are modern soda fountains dispensing such U.S. favorites as the chocolate sundae and vanilla milkshake. The company builds the store, supplies the equipment, and hires and trains local people to manage the operation, to cook, and to wait on customers.

The category accounting for the biggest chunk of total sales (almost 80 percent of which are in the Bangkok area) is composed of wholesalers, small stores, restaurants, hotels, and schools. A Thai salesperson (Foremost normally has only one expatriate in Bangkok, the general manager) usually is assigned a territory and given responsibility for one category of outlet, such as all corner grocery stores, and another salesperson handles all the schools.

To train its salesforce, Foremost first taught trainees basic English, and expatriate instructors learned basic Thai. With such a minimal bilingual communications channel established, the sales-force-to-be was taught about dairy products. The last part of the program consisted of sales techniques, for which key Thai staff were sent to the United States for training, while several Americans went to Thailand to instruct the local salesforce.

The patient cultural bridge building has paid off well. Foremost already has replaced the original plant with a larger, more modern one. More meaningful still for the long pull, a very strong brand identification was created. Today *Foremost* and *milk* are all but synonymous in Thailand.

Question

1. Identify and outline in detail the marketing program of Foremost Dairy in Thailand as depicted here. For each element in that marketing program, identify the particular factor in the Thai environment that gave rise to the marketing approach used.

An American Firm Wins Big in Japan

AFLAC became the official name of the American Family Life Assurance Company in 1992. AFLAC entered the Japanese market in 1975. It soon became one of the most successful foreign companies in any industry operating in Japan. By 1982, 1 in 20 Japanese households was an AFLAC policyholder. By 1988 the ratio was 1 in 6, and by 1995 about 1 in 4

Japanese households had an AFLAC policy. About 30 million Japanese are insured by the company. AFLAC had become the fourth largest insurance company in Japan, and Japanese revenues in 1995 were $4 billion. The only foreign company with greater revenues in Japan was Coca-Cola.

Founded in the United States in 1955, AFLAC specializes in cancer insurance (about 90 percent of its policies are in this field). Although AFLAC was the second foreign insurance company to enter the Japanese market, it was the first company, either Japanese or foreign, to introduce a policy for cancer protection in Japan. Two Japanese firms also issued independent health insurance coverage, but they had a much smaller number of policies outstanding.

Cancer insurance is a controversial product in the United States (it is banned in four states) because consumer advocates argue that disease-specific policies are an inefficient, costly form of coverage. Attitudes in Japan are somewhat different. When AFLAC hired Nomura Research to see what its customers wanted, the answer was higher coverage. On the government side, company president John Amos had developed very good relations with the powerful Japanese bureaucracy. Indeed, in 1988 John Amos was named by *Forbes* magazine as the insurance industry's most innovative executive for his success in penetrating the Japanese market. Because of differences between the U.S. and Japanese markets, AFLAC is in the unusual position of obtaining almost three-quarters of its total revenue from Japan versus only about one-quarter from the United States.

Japan is one of the largest insurance markets in the world. About 90 percent of Japanese households carry life insurance with a relative contract value much higher than in either Europe or the United States. Japan also has rather comprehensive national health insurance, so private company plans supplement the government program in such areas as private rooms, costly major disease, and lost income. AFLAC's cancer insurance sales grew rapidly, in part because cancer is the major cause of death in Japan, and it is usually associated with very costly treatment and long stays in the hospital. Thus, the Japanese perceive cancer as the most threatening and the most expensive disease they can encounter, and they want to provide for it as best they can.

Most Japanese insurance companies use homemakers as a part-time salesforce for door-to-door sales. Amos came up with another idea—use retired Japanese workers to sell to their former colleagues. "Their retirement benefits weren't good enough to last them forever, so AFLAC became a little like their social security," he recalled. AFLAC employed about 10,500 sales agents.

Japanese corporations agreed to encourage their workers to buy the insurance and to deduct the premiums from the monthly paychecks. Retired executives from each corporation are often enlisted to do the actual selling. Over 17,000 such payroll groups have been established. Over 92 percent of the corporations listed on the Tokyo Stock Exchange use AFLAC's payroll deduction plan, although less than half of their employees subscribe to it. Even Nippon Life and Dai-Ichi Mutual Life, two of Japan's largest life insurance companies, offer AFLAC's cancer policies to their employees.

Another part of AFLAC's approach is "bank set sales." This is a program whereby a bank automatically deducts the annual premium from the accumulated interest on a policyholder's savings account and transfers it to AFLAC's account. Some 250 banks were participating in this program, serving about 500,000 policyholders. The Japanese have a very favorable attitude toward saving, and this program appeals to their orientation toward saving plus their strong desire for insurance coverage. Because the banks enjoy a strong reputation, AFLAC's insurance program gains further credibility by this association with them.

AFLAC has not relied on advertising in Japan, depending instead on its strong sales network and full-time salesforce. Because the company innovated cancer insurance and because of its different marketing approach, however, it received a lot of publicity in the various media.

In 1994, AFLAC expanded its product line with "Super Care," a policy for nursing-home care, and "Super Cancer," an upgrade on its original policy. Super Cancer allows for a cash payment when cancer is first diagnosed. Nursing-home costs are another major concern in Japan because the population has a very long life expectancy.

One indicator of the company's success is a first-year renewal rate of 90 percent—and 94 percent after the second year. Both of these figures are higher than in either the Japanese or U.S. life insurance industries. AFLAC views these figures as corroboration of its product and marketing program.

Question

1. Describe AFLAC's marketing program in Japan—product policy, pricing, promotion, and distribution. Explain how this marketing program relates to the Japanese culture and economy and why it is so successful.

The Political-Legal Environment

Learning Objectives

The political environment of international marketing has three dimensions: the host-country, the home-country, and the international environments. The many laws affecting international marketing fall into three categories: U.S. law, international law, and foreign law.

The main goals of this chapter are to

1.   Identify the areas of the host-country environment that a firm must understand, including that country's national interests, such as sovereignty, security, and prestige, as well as the controls it uses to achieve those goals, in order to assess political risk.

2.   Describe how a firm is involved in international relationships and discuss the consequences.

3.   Identify the areas of the home-country environment that affect a firm's international marketing.

4.   Explain how U.S. export controls, antitrust law, and tax law affect the feasibility and profitability of a U.S. firm's international marketing.

5.   Discuss the effect of international organizations such as the IMF and the WTO and of regional groups such as the European Union on the international legal environment.

6.   Describe how treaties between the United States and other countries can facilitate U.S. firms' marketing in those countries.

7.   Describe the international conventions on patents and trademarks that help a firm protect itself against piracy.

8.   Identify the different types of foreign laws that affect the four P's of marketing.

The politics and the laws of a nation obviously influence the practice of international marketing. This chapter examines the nature of the political-legal environment and its impact on international marketing.

THE POLITICAL ENVIRONMENT

The **political environment** of international marketing includes any national or international political factor that can affect its operations. A factor is political when it derives from the government sector. The political environment comprises three dimensions: the host-country environment, the international environment, and the home-country environment. Surveys have shown that dealing with problems in the political arena is the number one challenge facing international managers and occupies more of their time than any other management function. Yet international managers' concerns are different from those of the political scientist. Managers are concerned primarily about political risk—the possibility of any government action adversely (or favorably) affecting their operations.

Host-Country Political Environment

By definition, the international firm is a guest, a foreigner in all of its markets abroad. Therefore, international managers are especially concerned with nationalism and dealings with governments in host countries.

Host-Country National Interests

One way to get a feeling for the situation in a foreign market is to see how compatible the firm's activities are with the interests of the host country. Although each country has its own set of national goals, most countries also share many common objectives. *Nationalism* and *patriotism* refer to citizens' feelings about their country and its interests. Such feelings exist in every country. The celebration of a major holiday in recognition of the country's birthday and its achievement of independence or nationhood reinforces the sense of national identity and nationalism.

All countries wish to maintain and enhance their national sovereignty. Foreign firms, individually or collectively, may be perceived as a threat to that sovereignty. The larger and more numerous the foreign firms, the more likely they are to be perceived as a threat—or at least an irritant. In times of turmoil, foreign firms—or foreign embassies—may be targets.

Countries wish to protect their national security. Although the foreign firm is not a military threat as such, it may be considered as potentially prejudicial to national security. Governments generally prohibit foreign firms from involvement in "sensitive" industries, such as defense, communications, and perhaps energy and natural resources. For example, when Libya nationalized the service stations of foreign oil companies, the reason given was that this commodity is too important to be in the hands of foreigners. If the firm is from a country deemed unfriendly to the host country, it may have difficulty operating or even be denied admission.

Countries are also concerned about their national prestige. They establish national airlines and try to send winning teams to the Olympics as ways of gaining international recognition. Economically, they may foster certain industries for the same reason. Foreign firms may be prevented from entering those industries or from acquiring a national firm in a certain industry. Many countries seek "national solutions" to help troubled companies to retain what are perceived to be national champions. International firms need to be sensitive to these issues and to be careful not to be too "foreign." This includes advertising and branding policies as well as ownership and staffing. Establishing local R&D would be perceived favorably in this context.

All countries want to enhance economic welfare. Generally, this means increasing employment and income in the country. Foreign firms contribute to this by the employment they generate. They can contribute further by using local suppliers and having local content in their products. They can contribute further still by exporting from the country and generating foreign exchange. They can contribute in a different way by supplying products, services, and/or training that enhances productivity.

Host-Country Controls

Host countries don't depend entirely on the goodwill of the foreign firm to help them achieve their national goals. To try to ensure desirable behavior by foreign firms—and to prevent undesirable behavior—governments use a variety of tools. We note some of these controls here.

1. *Entry restrictions.* If allowed to enter the country, the firm may be restricted as to the industries it may enter. It may be prohibited from acquiring a national firm. It may not be allowed 100 percent ownership but may be required to enter a joint venture with a national firm. It may be restricted as to the products it sells. For example, the Indian government decided that soap and matches could be made by cottage industry. This naturally affected the operations of Unilever and Swedish Match in India.

2. *Price controls.* Once in the country, the foreign firm may encounter a variety of restrictions. One of the most common is price controls, which in inflationary economies can severely limit profitability. Gerber left Venezuela because a decade of price controls prevented a profitable operation. Other regulations may affect advertising or other marketing practices of the firm.

3. *Quotas and tariffs.* The country's quotas and tariffs may limit the firm's ability to import equipment, components, and products, forcing a higher level of local procurement than it may want.

4. *Exchange control.* Many countries run chronic deficits in their balance of payments and are short of foreign exchange. They ration its use according to their priorities. Foreign firms may be low on that priority list and have difficulty getting foreign exchange for needed imports or profit repatriation.

5. *Expropriation.* Defined as official seizure of foreign property, expropriation is the ultimate tool for controlling foreign firms. This drastic action is fortunately occurring less often as developing countries begin to see foreign direct investment as desirable. From a peak of 83 cases in 1975, the number declined as the 1980s progressed, with only one case in 1985. It is a rare phenomenon in the '90s.

Venezuela was generally considered a low-risk political environment until 1989, when the country began investigating corruption in the official foreign-exchange institution Recadi. It said foreign firms were involved and issued arrest warrants for 47 foreign executives. Companies under scrutiny included General Motors, Toyota, Johnson & Johnson, Bristol Myers, and Goodyear. Dozens of executives left the country. Cornelius Koreman, president of Ford Venezuela, said, "It is the first time in my career I've had someone try to arrest me for doing nothing."[1] He had to operate out of company headquarters in Dearborn, Michigan. In an unrelated case, a Caracas judge ordered the arrest of the Venezuelan presidents of Procter & Gamble and Colgate-Palmolive for alleged misleading advertising of their products.

Political-Risk Assessment

The Venezuelan example shows the importance of continuous monitoring of host-country political environments because they can change rapidly. The Asian miracle becomes the Asian crisis, for example. Political risk can be a challenge not only to the firm, but also to its employees. (See "Global Marketing," "Kidnapping as a Political Risk: A Japanese Example.")

The firm must develop political and diplomatic skills in-house but will probably also use consultants with expertise on particular countries. Commercial services available are useful for providing continuing input. Some firms provide evaluations as to the political risk of specific countries. These services are moderate in cost—up to a few thousand dollars a year, depending on coverage. Various firms use different methods and come up with somewhat different country ratings as to political risk, although many are quite comparable. Table 5–1 indicates one firm's country risk service.

In its own study of the political environment, the firm can include a preliminary analysis of its political vulnerability in a particular host country. Elements in such an analysis include external and company factors.

External Factors

1. *The firm's home country.* Other things being equal, a firm has a better reception in a country that has good relations with its own.

2. *Product or industry.* Sensitivity of the industry is an important consideration. Generally, raw materials, public utilities, communications, pharmaceuticals, and defense-related products are most sensitive.

3. *Size and location of operations.* The larger the foreign firm, the more threatening it is perceived to be. This is especially true if the firm has large facilities and is located in a prominent urban area, such as the capital. This serves as a constant reminder of the foreign presence.

4. *Visibility of the firm.* The greater the visibility of the foreign firm, the greater its vulnerability. Visibility is a function of several things. Two are the size and location of the firm's operations in the country. Another is the nature of its products. Consumer goods are more visible than industrial goods. Finished goods are more visible than components or inputs that are hidden in the final product. Heavy advertisers are more visible than nonadvertisers. International brands are more provocative than localized brands.

5. *Host-country political situation.* The political situation can affect the firm. The country's political risk should be evaluated.

Company Factors

1. *Company behavior.* Each firm develops some record of corporate citizenship based on its practices. Some firms are more sensitive and responsive to the situation in the host country than others. Goodwill in this area is a valuable asset.

2. *Contributions of the firm to the host country.* Many of these are quite objective and quantifiable. How much employment has been generated? How much

GLOBAL MARKETING

Kidnapping as a Political Risk: A Japanese Example

Kidnappings of Japanese Company Officials and Others, 1978–1998

Country	Company/Occupation	Days in Captivity
El Salvador	Manager, Toray Industries affiliate	Killed
El Salvador	Manager, Toray Industries	114
Iraq	Two engineers with ties to electronics companies	150
Philippines	Manager, Mitsui	137
Laos	Manager, Mitsui	8
Philippines	Aid worker	65
Pakistan	Three students	45
Colombia	Two engineers for Toshiba	111
Colombia	Electronics company operator	22
Panama	Employee of Citizen Watch Co. affiliate	Killed
Mexico	Employee of Yamaha Motor affiliate	A few hours
Mexico	President, Sanyo Electric Mexican unit	9

Source: Japan Overseas Enterprises Association.

tax has been paid? How many exports has the firm generated? What new resources or skills has the firm brought in?

3. *Localization of operations.* Generally, the more localized the firm's operations, the more acceptable it is to the host country. There are several dimensions to localization, including having local equity, hiring local managers and technical staff, using local content in the products, including local suppliers of goods and services, and developing local products and local brand names.

4. *Subsidiary dependence.* This factor is somewhat in contradiction to the preceding point. The more the firm's local operation depends on the parent company, the less vulnerable it is. If it cannot function as a separate, self-contained unit but is dependent on the parent for critical resources and/or for markets, it will be seen as a less rewarding takeover target.

Political monitoring and analysis are continuing tasks for the firm. The information that these analyses provide must be used to manage the firm's political relations. Table 5–2 suggests some approaches to managing host-country relations, both before and after entering the country.

TABLE 5–1   **The EIU Quarterly Risk Ratings Review**

Overall Country Risk Rating	*Specific Investment Risk Ratings*
This rating assesses the overall risk of investment in the country. **Political risk**—measuring political stability and the effectiveness of the politcal system. **Economic policy risk**—measuring the quality and consistency of economic policy management and performance. **Economic structure risk**—measuring economic variables central to solvency. **Liquidity risk**—measuring the stability of the country's funding base and the risk of imbalances between its resources and obligations.	The subcategory scores are also used to compile three separate ratings that measure the risk of specific investments. **Currency risk rating**—assessing the risk of a devaluation against the U.S. dollar of 20 percent or more. **Sovereign debt risk rating**—assessing the risk of a build-up in arrears of sovereign debt. **Banking risk rating**—assessing the risk of a build-up in arrears on foreign currency debt by the country's private banking institutions.

Source: Economist Intelligence Unit, 1998.

International Political Environment

The international political environment involves political relations between two or more countries. This is in contrast to our previous concern for what happens only *within* a given foreign country. The international firm almost inevitably becomes somewhat involved with the host country's international relations, no matter how neutral it may try to be. It does so, first, because it is a foreigner from a specific home country and, second, because its operations in a country are frequently related to operations in other countries, either on the supply or demand side or both.

One aspect of a country's international relations is its relationship with the firm's home country. U.S. firms abroad are affected by the host nation's attitude toward the United States. When the host nation dislikes any aspect of U.S. policy, it may be the U.S. firm that is bombed or boycotted along with the U.S. Information Service office. English or French firms operating in the former colonies of those countries are affected by that relationship, favorably or otherwise. In 1998, U.S. sanctions on India because of nuclear tests led to Coca-Cola and Pepsi trucks being destroyed by mobs in New Delhi.

A second critical element affecting the political environment is the host-country's relations with other nations. If a country is a member of a regional group, such as the EU or ASEAN, that fact influences the firm's evaluation of the country. If a nation has particular friends or enemies among other nations, the firm must modify its international logistics to comply with how that market is supplied and to whom it can sell. For example, the United States limits trade with various countries. Arab nations have boycotted companies dealing with Israel.

Another clue to a nation's behavior is its membership in international organizations. We mentioned regional groupings, but other international organizations also affect a member's behavior. Members of NATO, for example, accept a military agreement that could restrict their military or political action. Membership in WTO reduces the likelihood that a country will impose new trade barriers. Membership in the IMF or the World Bank also puts constraints on the country's behavior. Many other international agreements impose rules on their members. These agreements may affect patents, communication, transportation, and other items of interest to the international marketer. As a rule, the more international organizations a country belongs to, the more regulations it accepts, and the more dependable is its behavior.

TABLE 5-2	Managing Host-Country Relations

Pre-Entry Planning

1. Avoid threatening countries.
2. Negotiate with host government.
3. Buy insurance—OPIC, MIGA (Overseas Private Investment Corp., Multilateral Investment Guarantee Agency).
4. Adjust entry method.

Post-Entry Operations

1. Have a monitoring system.
2. Develop corporate communications program.
3. Develop local stakeholders (employees, suppliers, customers).
4. Have appropriate national executives and advisory board.
5. Change operations over time as perceived host-country cost-benefit ratio changes. Examples: new products and processes, more local equity and management, new exports, local R&D.
6. Have contingency plans.

Home-Country Political Environment

The firm's home-country political environment can constrain its international operations as well as its domestic operations. It can limit the countries that the international firm may enter. The United States, for example, prohibits U.S. firms from dealing with Cambodia, Cuba, Libya, and North Korea. It has special restrictions on trade with Iran and Iraq. (See "Global Marketing," "U.S. Government: Friend or Foe?") The United States also can limit the products its firms can sell abroad under its strategic technology controls. That power is even occasionally exercised against foreign firms, such as Toshiba, which was penalized for selling to the Russians technology that allowed their submarines to move more quietly.

The best-known example of the home-country political environment affecting international operations used to be South Africa. Home-country political pressures induced more than 200 American firms to leave that country altogether. After U.S. companies left South Africa, the Germans and the Japanese remained as the major foreign presence. German firms did not face the same political pressures at home that U.S. firms had. However, the Japanese government was embarrassed when Japan became South Africa's leading trading partner. As a result, some Japanese companies reduced their South African activity. Matsushita closed an office there; Sanyo and Nissan reduced their exports to South Africa; NEC and Pioneer Electronics agreed to suspend exports.

A more recent example occured when pressure from American human rights groups induced some American firms to leave Myanmar. Pepsico, for example, pulled out of a joint venture, even though it had 85 percent of the soft drinks market there.

One challenge facing multinationals is that they truly have a triple-threat political environment. Even if the home country and the host country give them no problems, they can face threats in third markets. Firms that do not have problems with their home government or the host government, for example, can be bothered or boycotted in third countries. Nestlé's problems with its infant formula controversy were most serious, for example, not at home, in Switzerland, or in African host countries, but in a third market—the United States. Table 5–3 gives an indication of U.S. political concerns as they apply to U.S. exports.

GLOBAL MARKETING

U.S. Government: Friend or Foe?

When American firms evaluate opportunities abroad, they must consider not only the market and the competition. One of the major actors to be considered is the U.S. government and its potential role. This role can either be supportive of, or in opposition to, the firm's goals.

On the helpful side, for example, the Clinton administration played an influential role in helping Boeing win a $5.2 billion order from Saudi Arabia over Airbus. On the opposing side, Conoco lost a $1 billion Iranian oil deal when the White House announced a complete ban on American firms helping Iran. Conoco's three years of negotiation had led to the first U.S. company development contract in Iran since 1979.

Unfortunately for the Clinton administration and American firms, no other country supported the American embargo. This meant that Iran wasn't hurt by the ban, but foreign competitors gained at the expense of U.S. firms. The U.S. oil industry was the biggest loser, including producers, contractors, and equipment suppliers. Losses were estimated at over $4 billion. Consumer goods exporters' losses were significant also but much smaller. To add insult to injury, however, the ban opened the market for their international competitors.

THE LEGAL ENVIRONMENT

In addition to the political environment in a nation, the **legal environment**—that is, the nation's laws and regulations pertaining to business—also influences the operations of a foreign firm. A firm must know the legal environment in each market because these laws constitute the "rules of the game." At the same time, the firm must know the political environment because it determines how the laws are enforced and indicates the direction of new legislation. The legal environment of international marketing is complicated, having three dimensions. For a U.S. firm, these are (1) U.S. laws, (2) international law, and (3) domestic laws in each of the firm's foreign markets.

U.S. Law and International Marketing

U.S. marketers are familiar with domestic regulations affecting marketing, such as the Pure Food and Drug Act and the Robinson-Patman Act. These are not the U.S. laws that affect international marketing, however. Numerous other laws are relevant for international marketing and relate to exporting, antitrust, and organization and ownership arrangements.

Export Controls

Like other countries, the United States has a variety of controls on export trade, but it has more than most countries. Since these are continually evolving with the political climate, we will not give precise details but merely an indication of the kinds of controls used. One kind of control pertains to *country destinations*. There are absolute prohibitions or severe restrictions on exports to several countries, such as Cuba, Iraq, Libya, North Korea, and the Sudan. A few years earlier, China and Vietnam were on that list but Libya was not. The ban also prohibits the sale of components that go into a foreign firm's products that are destined for one of the prohibited markets.

For example, before the United States began trading with China, the French wanted to sell planes to that country. However, the inertial guidance system for this aircraft was supplied by General Electric, which was forbidden by the U.S. government to sell this key component to the French for this purpose. This type of conflict can be avoided only if the U.S. firm has less than 50 percent ownership of the firm supplying the parts.

Another U.S. export control relates to the nature of the products exported. Many products are exported without restriction under the monitoring eye of the Department of Commerce. These are usually goods easily obtainable elsewhere and not considered significant for national security. For products having national security or foreign policy significance, however, tighter controls, or even prohibitions, exist. Examples are terrorism equipment, missile technology, and nuclear technology. Others relate to foreign policy concerns such as regional stability. (See Table 5–3.) These controls can hurt the firm in two ways. One is administrative time and expense. About 35,000 export licenses are issued by the United States annually. Another is lost sales. David Richardson estimates that these controls cost U.S. companies about $24 billion in lost sales a year.[2] Foreign buyers may switch suppliers because of such controls.

These controls are imposed to protect U.S. security and foreign policy interests. Violation can bring severe punishment. In 1995, two technology company CEOs were convicted of illegally exporting equipment for making missiles. Penalties were: fines of $250,000 each; up to five years in prison; a $1 million fine for each company. These controls can be a serious constraint on both product line and market selection for some international marketers. The long arm of U.S. law reaches even to operations and firms outside the United States, as the following examples show.

The German subsidiary of Digital Equipment Corp. was fined $1.5 million for allowing sophisticated computers to be shipped to the former Soviet Union. ASEA, the Swedish firm, was fined $440,000 for allowing the illegal transfer of U.S.–made computers to Russia. L. M. Ericsson, another Swedish firm, was assessed a $3.1 million fine for allowing the shipment of a sensitive air traffic control device there.

Another restriction on the freedom to export is in pricing. Although the marketer would like to base export prices on supply and demand and company considerations, the Internal Revenue Service (IRS) can also influence the price. For example, the IRS has a say in transfer prices on exports to foreign affiliates of U.S. companies. On such exports, the exporter might wish a low transfer price as a way of aiding the subsidiary, of gaining income in a lower tax jurisdiction. However, the IRS does not allow unduly low transfer prices because they lower the firm's U.S. profits and therefore lower the firm's U.S. income taxes.

Antitrust Controls

It might seem strange that U.S. antitrust laws would affect the *foreign* business activities of U.S. companies. However, that is a fact of life. The opinion of the U.S. Justice Department is that even if an act is committed abroad, it falls within the jurisdiction of U.S. courts *if the act produces consequences within the United States.* Many activities of U.S. business abroad have some repercussions on the U.S. domestic market. The question arises primarily in three situations: (1) when a U.S. firm acquires a foreign firm, (2) when it engages in a joint venture with a foreign firm, or (3) when it makes some overseas marketing agreement with another firm.

When a U.S. firm expands abroad by acquiring a foreign company, the Justice Department is concerned about the possible impact on competition in the United States. It may take action under Section 7 of the Clayton Act, which prohibits certain corporate amalgamations that could reduce competition. Action is more probable if the acquired firm were in the same product line as the U.S. company.

Remington Arms Company tried to acquire Sweden's AB Norma Projektilfabrik. Norma was attractive because Sweden had a free-trade agreement with the EU on industrial products. Remington hoped to use Norma to get a foothold in the EU, where high tariffs were pricing Remington out of the market. The Justice Department, however, ruled that acquiring Norma would allow Remington to increase its U.S. market share because Norma was selling 10 percent of its output in the United States. Remington gave up in the face of the challenge.

TABLE 5–3	**U.S. Government Departments and Agencies with Export Control Responsibilities**

1. Department of Commerce
2. Department of State
3. Department of Treasury
4. Arms Control and Disarmament Agency
5. Nuclear Regulatory Commission
6. Department of Energy
7. Department of Defense
8. Department of the Interior
9. Drug Enforcement Administration
10. Food and Drug Administration
11. Patent and Trademark Office

Source: Bureau of Export Administration, Department of Commerce, February, 1999.

Joint venturing with foreign firms either in the United States or abroad can lead to government intervention similar to that in the preceding example. The reasoning by the government is the same—competition in the U.S. market will be reduced by a particular marriage of a U.S. and foreign firm. For example, Chrysler asked the government to challenge GM's venture with Toyota to operate a California auto plant known as NUMMI.

General Electric and Hitachi sought to form a joint venture in the United States to produce televisions. GE wanted to bolster its relatively weak position and Hitachi wanted to increase its small 2 percent market share. The Justice Department challenged the venture, stating, "Our investigation has led us to conclude that this venture would eliminate potential competition between GE and Hitachi in the manufacture and sale of television sets. It would create the third or fourth largest producer in an already concentrated industry. We are not persuaded that the venture is needed to maintain the viability of either party."

We have seen how U.S. laws can reach foreign countries and touch the international marketing of U.S.—and foreign—firms. Obviously, these laws also affect the international marketing by foreign firms in the United States. An example is given.

Panasonic: New York Attorney General Robert Abrams charged Panasonic with threatening to cut supplies to retailers unless they raised prices 5 to 10 percent. Panasonic president Imura allegedly pressured retailers personally. According to Abrams, among the many retailers that complied, at least partly, were Circuit City Stores, Dayton Hudson Corp., and Kmart. Abrams called the case "the largest vertical price-fixing scheme in the nation's history." Panasonic eventually agreed to pay rebates of $17 to $45 to more than 700,000 consumers, resulting in payment of more than $16 million.[3]

In the late '90s, U.S. antitrust authorities began increasingly to target foreign cartels, with one-third of their cases against foreign companies and fines totaling over $200 million annually. There was also increasing cooperation with competition authorities in the EU and Japan.

Organization and Ownership Arrangements

The organization of a firm can be influenced by specific laws that are designed to promote foreign trade. The general, more restrictive laws may, indeed, allow certain exceptions to firms meeting specified conditions.

Webb-Pomerene Associations. The **Webb-Pomerene,** or **Export Trade, Act** deliberately permits the cooperation of competing firms in export trade. This 1918 act specifically excludes from antitrust prosecution the cooperation of competitive firms in the development of foreign markets; that is, firms that compete domestically can collaborate in exporting. The law was passed following a study by the Federal Trade Commission, which noted, "If Americans are to enter the markets of the world on more nearly equal terms with their organized competitors and their organized customers, and if small American producers and manufacturers are to engage in trade on profitable terms, they must be free to unite their efforts."[4]

The commission's intent was that U.S. exporters be given countervailing power to enable them to compete against foreign oligopolies or cartels and to prevent foreign monopsonists from playing off one exporter against another. It was expected that this policy would be helpful to small firms that could combine and gain economies of scale in export. Actually, some very large American firms such as the major film producers, cigarette makers, and chemical companies, set up Webb-Pomerene Associations.

Foreign Sales Corporation (FSC). Most governments use the power of taxation to encourage or discourage different kinds of activity. Members of the EU remit value-added taxes on exports, permitting lower costs and encouraging exports. The United States does not have value-added taxes, so it has sought other tax devices to encourage exports. The effort in operation today is the **foreign sales corporation,** or **FSC**, invented by Congress in 1984. A FSC is a sales company set up in a foreign country or U.S. possession that can obtain a tax exemption on a portion of export earnings. Because the costs of establishing a FSC might discourage small firms, the law allows a FSC to be shared by up to 25 exporters. Several states (Delaware, Illinois, Michigan, New York, and Virginia) were organizing shared FSCs to spur their medium- and small-size firms into exporting.

The details of these arrangements for gaining tax benefits in exporting are not important here. What is significant is the potential impact of home-country tax law on the firm's method of organizing for exports. Countries want to expand exports, and tax incentives seem to offer the strongest motivation to firms for doing so. If the firm's goal is profits, management must consider tax laws in organizing its international marketing activity. The firm's choice of a country to supply international markets depends in part on the export incentives offered by different countries.

Export Trading Company (ETC) Act. In 1982 President Reagan signed the Export Trading Company Act. This was another effort by the United States to aid exports. An **export trading company (ETC)** is supposed to emulate Japanese trading companies' export success. To get the size and sophistication needed for this, the legislation permitted banks to invest in ETCs and eased antitrust restrictions on export activities. It was hoped that this freer environment would encourage the participation of large U.S. banks and corporations with international experience, as well as aid small firms that could collaborate in the ETC and enjoy financial strength and economies of scale.

Although ETCs may offer promise for the future, they have achieved only limited success. The Department of Commerce has issued approximately 170 certificates for corporate ETCs, mainly to small companies, including many export management companies converting to ETC status. Sears started an ETC but discontinued it after a few years because it was unprofitable. Likewise, GE created and then closed one. The failure of these two powerful, promising ETC candidates is a bad omen for the future of the ETC. Some giant banks, such as Chase Manhattan and the Bank of America, have experienced very modest performance in ETC arrangements. The export business of U.S. ETCs has been very limited, achieving only a small portion of the success obtained by Japanese trading companies.

Other Controls

Examples of other controls include the U.S. laws against bribery by U.S. firms and against support of Arab boycotts.

Foreign Corrupt Practices Act. In the 1970s the practice by U.S. firms to bribe foreign officials received much publicity. Although bribery has been a longstanding practice by firms in all countries, the publicity created a scandal in the United States. The most sensational cases involved United Brands and the president of Honduras, and Lockheed and the Japanese prime minister. As a result of the public outcry in 1977, the U.S. government passed the Foreign Corrupt Practices Act to prohibit U.S. firms from engaging in these types of practices abroad.

Elimination of such payoffs is certainly desirable. The problem for U.S. firms was that their competitors from Japan and Western Europe were not forbidden to use bribes. U.S. firms complained that the act put them at a serious competitive disadvantage because bribery has often been the most effective form of persuasion in business and government markets abroad. Fortunately, in 1997, the 29 OECD member countries—and five others—signed a Convention of Bribery of Foreign Public Officials. The parties are obligated to criminalize such bribery. Time will tell how this works out. (Bribery as promotion is discussed in Chapter 13.)

Anti-Arab Boycott Rules. The conflict between Israel and the Arab states has influenced U.S. control over the international marketing of U.S. firms. The oil wealth of the Arab states has given them power that they use in several ways. One way is to try to force companies that sell to their now-rich markets not to have any dealings with Israel. In other words, the Arabs boycott firms that sell to Israel. Because the Arab markets are collectively much larger than the Israeli market, many firms are tempted to drop the Israeli market and sell to the Arabs. This is counter to U.S. foreign policy, however, so the government has legislation to prevent U.S. firms from cooperating with the Arab boycott. Research by James Hines shows that this antiboycott legislation significantly reduces American firms participation in the boycott of Israel.[5]

The application of the U.S. antiboycott rules can be costly. Consider the case of Sara Lee. Although Sara Lee had been active in Israel and had been blacklisted by the Arab League, when the company attempted to protect its L'eggs trademark in Kuwait, it divulged certain information that had been prohibited by the U.S. government. As a result, the Commerce Department's Office of Antiboycott Compliance fined Sara Lee $2.35 million. The company appealed those charges. The most famous case involving the antiboycott rules, however, was Baxter International. (See "Global Marketing," "Baxter's Boycott Caper.")

International Law and International Marketing

No international lawmaking body corresponds to the legislatures of sovereign nations. What then is **international law?** For our present discussion, we define it as the collection of treaties, conventions, and agreements between nations that have, more or less, the force of law. International law in this sense is quite different from national laws that have international implications, such as the U.S. antitrust laws. The international extension of U.S. law is on a unilateral basis. International law involves some mutuality, with two or more countries participating in the drafting and execution of laws or agreements.

Our discussion of the impact of international law begins with those international agreements having a general effect on international business and then addresses those dealing with more specific marketing questions. Then we look at the legal implications of regional groupings.

FCN and Tax Treaties

The United States has signed **treaties of friendship, commerce, and navigation (FCN)** with many countries. FCN treaties cover commercial relations between two nations. They commonly identify the nature of the rights of U.S. companies to do

GLOBAL MARKETING

Baxter's Boycott Caper

In May 1993, Baxter International pleaded guilty to cooperating with the Arab boycott of Israel and paid fines of $6.5 million. The history follows.

In 1971, Baxter built a plant in Israel. Soon after that, Baxter was placed on the Arab League blacklist, cutting its Mideast business. In 1985, Baxter bought American Hospital Supply (AHS). Soon after, AHS business in the Mideast faded away.

Also in the mid-'80s, Baxter wanted to enter a profitable joint venture with Nestlé. Nestlé, however, insisted Baxter had to be off the blacklist or its own Mideast business would be hurt. In 1986, Baxter began investigating the building of a plant in Syria. This was later dropped because of complaints by Jewish groups in the United States.

In the late '80s, Baxter did three things: It sold its Israeli plant, offered discounted hospital supplies to Syria, and wrote a letter to the Arab League promising not to make new investments in Israel or sell new technology to Israel. (All these actions were illegal under the U.S. law against cooperation with the Arab League's boycott of Israel.)

In 1989, Baxter was removed from the Arab League blacklist. In the early '90s, however, Baxter's actions were revealed, largely through the efforts of a former employee. This led to the 1993 judgment. Collateral damage included debarment from Pentagon procurement; loss of some U.S. hospital business; complaints from major stockholder groups; and great public relations damage.

business in those nations with which the United States has such a treaty, and vice versa. FCN treaties usually guarantee "national treatment" to the foreign subsidiary; that is, it will not be discriminated against by the nation's laws or judiciary.

Of a similar type are the tax treaties that the United States has signed with a number of nations. The purpose of such treaties is to avoid double taxation; that is, if a company has paid income tax on its operations in a treaty nation, the United States will tax the firm's income only to the extent that the foreign tax rate is less than the U.S. rate. Thus, if the corporate income tax rates are equal in the two countries, there is no tax to pay in the United States on income earned in the other country. Obviously, tax treaty nations are, other things being equal, better places for a subsidiary than countries that do not have such a treaty. Most Western industrialized nations have treaties similar to these of the United States.

IMF and WTO

While the International Monetary Fund (IMF) and the World Trade Organization (WTO) were discussed in Chapter 2, here we merely note that both agreements are part of the limited body of effective international law. Both agreements identify acceptable and nonacceptable behavior for member nations. Their effectiveness lies in their power to apply sanctions. The IMF can withhold its services from members who act "illegally," that is, contrary to the agreement. WTO allows injured nations to retaliate against members who have broken its rules.

International marketers are interested in both IMF and WTO because of a shared concern in the maintenance of a stable environment conducive to international trade. These firms are concerned about the IMF's ability to reduce restrictions on international finance, and they support WTO's efforts to free the international movement of goods. For an idea of how nations use the WTO in trade disagreements, see "Global Marketing," "WTO Dispute Settlement—Active Panels—1998."

The legal reach of WTO and the IMF does not extend to the international marketer's behavior but rather to the behavior of the nations within which the firm is

GLOBAL MARKETING

 **WTO Dispute Settlement-
Active Panels—1998**

Complainant	Subject of the complaint	Complainant	Subject of the complaint
United States	Japan—Measures affecting consumer photographic film and paper.	Canada	Australia—Measures affecting the importation of salmon.
India, Malaysia, Pakistan, Thailand	United States—Import prohibition of certain shrimp and shrimp products.	Japan, EC, United States	Indonesia—Certain measures affecting the automobile industry.
United States	EC, UK, Ireland—Customs classification of certain computer equipment.	Brazil	EC—Measures affecting importation of certain poultry products.
Mexico	Guatemala—Anti-dumping investigation regarding imports of Portland cement from Mexico.	United States	Australia—Subsidies provided to producers and exporters of automotive leather.

marketing. The environment for international marketing is more dependable and less capricious because of these two organizations.

UNCITRAL: A Step Ahead

The United Nations established a Commission on International Trade Law (UNCITRAL) with a goal to promote a uniform commercial code for the whole world. The commission works with government and private groups, such as the International Chamber of Commerce. Its first output (in 1983) was the Convention on Contracts for the International Sale of Goods. The convention is somewhat similar to Article 2 of the Uniform Commercial Code of the United States. Its purpose is to bridge the communications gap between countries having different legal systems as well as minimize contract disputes and facilitate the task of selling goods between countries. In the 1990s, UNCITRAL is working on a Model Law on Procurement, International Commercial Arbitration, and Electronic Commerce.

ISO

Numerous other international organizations have a semilegal influence on international marketing. One group of special interest is the International Standards Organization (ISO). Industry groups in most of the major industrial countries participate in the work of ISO.

Differing national standards are a major hindrance to international trade. To overcome such obstacles, ISO has been working, through its technical committees, to develop uniform international standards. But standardization is a slow task because changing national standards often hurts vested interests. In this area, multinational companies and their subsidiaries can have a voice in determining the standards for tomorrow. Each national subsidiary of the company can present its views, perhaps joining forces with its national trade association, to the relevant ISO body

Complainant	Subject of the complaint	Complainant	Subject of the complaint
EC, United States	Korea—Taxes on alcoholic beverages.	United States	India—Quantitative restrictions of imports of agricultural, textile, and industrial products.
European Communities	India—Patent protection for pharmaceutical and agricultural chemical products.	United States	Japan—Measures affecting agricultural products.
European Communities	Argentina—Measures affecting textiles and clothing.	New Zealand	EC—Measures affecting butter products.
EC	Chile—Taxes on alcoholic beverages.	Korea	United States—Anti-dumping on DRAMS of one megabyte or above from Korea.

Source: WTO, 1998.

in that country. Thus, when international negotiations are held, the company can be sure that its viewpoint is presented. Perhaps because the export market is relatively small compared to the domestic market, U.S. industries have been less active in ISO than other exporting nations. This lack of interest may be costly in the long run; the United States may find itself closed out of many markets. For example, Western Hemisphere standards for television sets are different from those set by the International Telecommunications Union (ITU). This difference has cost U.S. manufacturers lost sales to areas with other standards, namely, Africa, Asia, and Europe.

Patent Protection Systems
Many firms have patented products to sell. When selling outside their home market, they want to protect their patent right. Generally, patents must be registered separately in each country where the firm wants protection. This can be a time-consuming and expensive process. For example, it is estimated that 10 percent of the development costs of Hovercraft was spent on securing patents around the world. Individual national registration is also expensive for nations because each goes through a similar search and evaluation procedure, duplicating the efforts of other countries.

In one two-year period, three American drug companies—Squibb, Merck, and Upjohn—filed 349 international patents at a cost of $30 million or about $85,000 per patent. Consider the cost for Borg-Warner, an industrial marketer, which has 15 patent attorneys who at any time are considering up to 400 "disclosures." B-W typically applies for between 100 and 150 patents each year, 80 percent of which are approved. The company holds over 1,500 patents in the United States and over 3,000 abroad.

The purpose of patent protection is to prevent others from selling the patented product wherever the patent is registered. This element of monopoly protection allows higher prices and encourages R&D activity by the firm. Because of the expense and inconvenience of patenting in multiple countries, various efforts have been made to develop a multilateral approach to patenting. The main feature of these is a simplified application system, which can be a major convenience for firms desiring protection in many countries, although individual national filing fees generally still must be paid. The benefit is the elimination of duplicative procedures. Developing countries will tend to accept the preliminary search and evaluation findings of the industrialized countries. The importance of protection can be seen in "Global Marketing," "Pirates Still at Large."

Several bodies are leading this effort. The most significant is the Paris Union (officially, the International Convention for the Protection of Industrial Property). This organization represents 94 countries. The Inter-American Convention represents Latin America plus the United States.

The EU has a European Patent Office (EPO) but its approach is far from a Single Market success. The EPO grants a bundle of national patents, all different in scope and conditions. There must be a full translation of the filing for each state where protection is sought. A 150-page filing for all EPO states would cost $270,000 for translation, plus lawyers' fees and national filing costs. The *total* cost of a patent application in Japan is $19,000 and only $7,000 in the United States.

Because the vast majority of patents originate in the industrialized countries, the less developed nations argue that, for them, patents mean high prices for products, import monopolies rather than local manufacturing, and high royalty payments for the use of patents. These nations are expected to attempt to change the patent system to give them less expensive access to technology through UNCTAD and the World Intellectual Property Organization (WIPO), a UN agency.

WIPO has been given centralized administration over various unions (Paris, Madrid, etc.). The developing countries in WIPO are trying to move to decisions by majority, which would give them effective control over future developments—and less protection to patent holders.

Trademark Conventions

Trademarks are another form of intellectual property. Like patents, trademarks or brands must go through a national registration process to be protected; registration is less time-consuming and costly, though. There are two major international trademark conventions. One is the Paris Union, which also covers patents. The Paris Union allows a six-month protection period in the case of trademarks, as contrasted with a one-year period for patents. That is, registration of a trademark in one member country gives the firm six months in which to register in any other member countries before it loses its protection in those countries.

The second major convention is the Madrid Arrangement for International Registration of Trademarks, which has 26 members, mostly in Europe, although China has also joined. The United States is not a member, although a U.S. firm's subsidiary in a member country can qualify for benefits under the Madrid Arrangement. The advantage of the Madrid Arrangement is that it permits a registration in just one member country to qualify as registration in all other member countries, with appropriate payments.

A third convention, and a major one, is the new EU Community Trademark—a significant advance in Europe. It allows for one registration and payment instead of 15—true one-stop shopping.

In addition, the former French colonies have their own multinational arrangement, and an Inter-American Convention for Trademark Protection gives coverage to countries in the Western Hemisphere similar to that given by the Paris Union. The most interesting question in brand and trademark protection concerns the countries that are not members of one of these arrangements. (See the U.S. Pharmaceuticals case at the end of this chapter.)

GLOBAL MARKETING

Pirates Still at Large

Piracy costs producers untold billions of dollars every year and the numbers are not going down. It is a global phenomenon, serious even in the United States with strong laws and producer associations. The piracy *rate,* however, is much higher in the rest of the world.

Hungary. Western producers formed a Brand Protection Association but Russian, Ukrainian, and Chinese mafia assure that firms like Levi-Strauss and Nike are plagued with low-cost imitations.

Philippines. Over 80 percent of software is pirated and even government offices use illegally copied software.

Mexico. A week after Windows 98 came out in the States, it sold for less than one-fourth its U.S. price in Mexico City. Top hotels at Mexican resorts steal cable TV programming and even advertise the service. The problem is similar in other Latin American countries. In spite of their patent laws, firms like Nike and Guess are losers, as well as software firms. Most of the goods come from Asia.

China and Hong Kong. Both have made serious efforts to fight piracy—with little effect. An estimated 95 percent of all software in China is pirated. Movies like *Titanic* are available on disc for about $3 as soon as they hit movie screens in the United States. Windows 98 is also $3. Firms such as Heinz and Procter & Gamble are also pirated.

Conflict over trademark or brand-name protection can lead to costly, acrimonious legal battles. One case that was neither costly nor acrimonious, however, involved General Motors' choice of a name for a sporty new Chevrolet—the Beretta. The 463-year-old Italian weapons maker with the same name brought suit in New York against GM, but a settlement was reached rather quickly. GM gave $500,000 to the Beretta Foundation for Cancer Research and got the right to use the name. GM executive Roger Smith also gave President Pier Giuseppe Beretta a Beretta GTU coupe and received from Beretta a rifle and a shotgun.

Regional Groupings and International Law

As we learned in Chapter 2, many nations have felt the need for larger market groupings to accelerate their economic growth. Such regional groupings have developed on all continents. What each grouping has found, however, is that economic integration alone is not sufficient without some international legal agreement. Initially, this takes the form of the treaty that establishes the regional grouping. Inevitably, however, as integration proceeds, further legal agreements are necessary. In this way, the body of international (regional) law grows. Because these groupings are primarily *economic* alliances, the international law that develops relates primarily to economic and business questions. Therefore, regional groupings provide a development of international law of interest to multinational companies.

The EU Example.   The basic law of the EU is the Rome Treaty. Under this international law, the member countries succeeded in forming a customs union and harmonizing certain economic regulations. By 1985, however, the attainment of a true common market was still a long way off. Under Jacques Delors, a new initiative was launched. The Single European Act identified further measures needed to create a common market. It was adopted by the member governments at the end of 1985 and specified 1992 as the target date.

The single market measures are being gradually adopted by the member states but, as of 1998, almost one-fifth had yet to be implemented in all 15 member states. The impact of the Euro will bring new dimensions. Business and marketing in the EU will largely be governed by these new international laws rather than by national laws of the member countries. An example of the bite of the European law was when fines of $117 million were levied against 16 steel firms for price fixing.

Reinforcing the strength of international law in the EU is the European Court of Justice, which is much more effective in dealing with supranational legal questions than the famous World Court in The Hague.

Experience Elsewhere. The EU has made by far the most progress of all the regional groupings. This is true especially in the area of regional law. The Central American Common Market made great strides in its early years but has been stagnant since 1969 because of disagreements between members. The Andean Common Market also started off reasonably well in its early years but then became less effective. Advances seem to come slowly after an initial burst of activity.

Mercosur is one of the newest regional groupings but it has made dramatic progress in its early years. It made association agreements with Bolivia and Chile and was negotiating a potential free trade agreement with the EU. There was even discussion of a common currency for Mercosur, like the Euro in the EU. In Asia, the ASEAN group has made only halting steps toward freer trade and harmonization of laws. The Asian crisis hit them heavily of course.

The World of International Law

The body of international law is small compared to domestic law. Nevertheless, we have seen examples of international law and the ways it can impinge on international marketing. Furthermore, international law, whether regional or global, is the growth area in the legal environment of international marketing.

Because agreement is easier to obtain with a small number of countries, regional law grows faster than does other international law. International law generally facilitates international trade. If a change in law is unfavorable, however, firms will want to be informed about the change in order to optimize performance within the new constraints.

Two other areas of international law need scrutiny by international marketers. One is the codes of conduct developed by international groups such as UNCTAD and the OECD. Although these codes for multinational firms are not true international law, in a practical sense they become the norms by which nations, labor unions, and other critics judge the multinational. As an illustration, the World Health Organization (WHO) passed a code of conduct for the marketing of infant formula that for all intents and purposes serves as international law on the subject.

The second development affecting the internationalization of law is the increasing cooperation between countries in legal matters. As one example, Britain and the United States have a treaty spelling out situations in which judgments of the courts of one country will be enforced in those of the other. Most commercial disputes will be covered. Broader than that treaty is the informal cooperation between regulators in different countries. Regulators visit various countries and exchange information in formulating new regulations concerning business. In the antitrust area, there have been exchanges of personnel between the United States and the EU.

Legal cooperation exists among the industrialized countries. Developing countries work together in UNCTAD and WIPO where mechanisms exist for the exchange of information on the multinationals. The rapid transplantation of regulatory initiatives from one country to another means that companies can no longer deal with regulations on an individual country basis but must devise coordinated strategies.

Foreign Laws and International Marketing

U.S. laws play a ubiquitous role in U.S. business practice. The laws of other nations play a similar role regarding the activities of business within their boundaries. The importance of foreign laws to the marketer lies primarily in domestic marketing in each foreign market. Problems arise from the fact that the laws in each market tend to be somewhat different from those in every other market.

Differing Legal Systems

Before considering national peculiarities in marketing law, we look briefly at the basic legal systems that underlie individual national law. Most countries derive their legal system from either the common law or the civil or code law traditions. **Common law** is English in origin and is found in the United States and other countries (about 26) that have had a strong English influence, usually a previous colonial tie. Common law is tradition oriented; that is, the interpretation of what the law means on a given subject is heavily influenced by previous court decisions as well as by usage and custom. If there is no specific legal precedent or statute, common law requires a court decision. To understand the law in a common law country, one must study the previous court decisions in matters of similar circumstance, as well as the statutes.

Civil or **code law** is based on an extensive and, presumably, comprehensive set of laws organized by subject matter into a code. The intention in civil law countries is to spell out the law on all possible legal questions rather than to rely on precedent or court interpretation. The "letter of the law" is very important in code law countries. However, this need to be all-inclusive may lead to some rather general and elastic provisions, permitting an application to many facts and circumstances. Because code law countries do not rely on previous court decisions, various applications of the same law may yield different interpretations. This can lead to some uncertainty for the marketer.

Code law is a legacy of Roman law. It is predominant in Europe and in nations of the world that have not had close ties with England. Thus, code law nations are more numerous than common law nations. Many civil code systems are influenced by the French, German, or Spanish systems because of previous colonial or other relationships. For example, the German code has had influence on the Teutonic and Scandinavian countries. There are about 70 civil law countries.

Islamic law represents the third major legal system. About 27 countries follow Islamic law in varying degrees, usually mixed with civil, common, and/or indigenous law. The Islamic resurgence in recent years has led many countries to give Islamic law, Shari'a, a more prominent role. Shari'a governs all aspects of life in areas where it is the dominant legal system, as in Saudi Arabia. Rules not defined by Shari'a are left to decision by government regulations and Islamic judges. Although it has harsh penalties for adultery and theft, Islamic law is not dramatically different from other legal systems insofar as business is concerned. In Saudi Arabia, for example, the Committee for Settlement of Commercial Disputes operates in a manner that would not be uncongenial to a Westerner.

The differences among legal systems are important to the international marketer. Because the legal systems of no two countries are exactly the same, each market must be studied individually and appropriate local legal advice sought when necessary. The following merely alerts the marketer to some of the variations in legal systems abroad.

Foreign Laws and the Marketing Mix

One familiar with marketing regulation in the United States will not be surprised at the range of laws affecting marketing in other nations, although one may be surprised at the lack of such regulation in some less developed countries. We will not catalog foreign laws but rather show how they influence the four P's of marketing—that is, product, price, place (distribution), and promotion. The treatment is brief

GLOBAL MARKETING

Disney As Cop

Walt Disney Co. is a major international marketer. Because of the success of its movies and its theme parks near Paris and Tokyo, the use of Disney characters on products is very popular, but Mickey Mouse and his friends have become the target of counterfeiters in many countries. To fight this, Disney has its own licensing operations abroad. The Disney office in Singapore licenses manufacturers in Indonesia, Malaysia, Singapore, Thailand, and Brunei so that Disney characters can be found on apparel, toys, stationery, gifts, home furnishings, music, books, computer software, and personal care products.

Legitimate sales in the Asian region were $30 million in 1990, but Brandt Handley, regional director, estimated that counterfeit sales were much higher. The worst offenders operated in Thailand and Indonesia from which they supplied other countries. In 1989, Disney began a crackdown on counterfeiters. It hired a legal firm, a public relations company,

and a team of private investigators in Thailand. The group identified the offenders, and in some cases, put undercover operatives in target factories. Police then raided the factories.

Disney's lawyers allowed the offenders to make out-of-court settlements, with a 90 percent success rate. The public relations firm publicized the enforcement campaign to deter others. Disney took similar action in Singapore, where it raided five major retailers selling mainly imported counterfeit products. Disney again reached out-of-court settlements, with damages paid by the offenders, who made public apologies in the newspapers.

Handley had some suggestions for fighting the counterfeiters.

1. Take the initiative. The government probably won't.
2. Have an organized program with legal, public relations, and investigative teams.
3. Be persistent. The problem won't go away.
4. Focus on the big players and rely on publicity to scare off the smaller players.
5. Consider licensing the violators and turn them into legitimate revenue sources.

Source: *Business Asia,* September 23, 1991, 329.

and suggestive of the problem areas. A more extensive study is in order when considering a specific market. For example, Japan has 10,942 laws to regulate business.

Product. If we consider **product** as everything the consumer receives when making a purchase, the international marketer will find many regulations affecting the product. The physical and chemical aspects of the product are affected by laws designed to protect national consumers with respect to its purity, safety, or performance. As the thalidomide tragedy showed, nations differ as to the strictness of their controls. The Food and Drug Administration had not cleared the drug for sale in the United States, but many deformed babies were born in Europe, where it was legal.

In a similar vein, European manufacturers were disturbed by U.S. safety requirements for automobiles, which had to be modified to meet the needs of one market. Because the U.S. market is large, the adaptation was not so serious as meeting the peculiar requirements of a small market. Nevertheless, Jaguar temporarily stopped selling sedans in the United States in 1968 because of U.S. safety requirements. This highlights what frequently appears to be the protectionist use of these laws. Although consumers should be protected, different safety requirements are not necessary for the consumers of every country. By maintaining different standards, nations seem to be saying that consumers in other countries are not being adequately protected. One reason nations often persist in particular legal requirements is that they protect their own producers. For example, Britain kept French milk out by requiring it to be sold in pints rather than metric measures. German noise standards kept British lawnmowers off German lawns.

Fortunately, in the late 90s, the United States and the EU drafted an agreement to accept each others standards for a wide range of products. This Mutual Recognition Agreement will save millions of dollars on both sides of the Atlantic.

Automobiles were not included and the U.S. Food and Drug Administration retained its control over pharmaceuticals.

China now has a product liability law to protect Chinese consumers. Some, unfortunately, have used it to target foreign companies. Procter & Gamble was sued by a woman who said its shampoo had melted her hair. It turned out the shampoo was counterfeit.

Labeling is subject to more legal requirements than the package. Labeling items covered include (1) the name of the product, (2) the name of the producer or distributor, (3) a description of the ingredients or use of the product, (4) the weight, either net or gross, and (5) the country of origin. As to warranty, the marketer has relative freedom to formulate a warranty in all countries.

Brand names and trademarks also face different national requirements. Most of the larger nations are members of the Paris Union or some other trademark convention. That ensures a measure of international uniformity. However, differences exist between code law countries (ownership by **priority in registration** of a brand) and common law countries (ownership by **priority in use**) in their treatment of the brand or trademark.

Foreign tobacco companies faced a challenge along this line in Japan. Japan Tobacco, Inc. (JTI), a government monopoly, had 98 percent of cigarette sales, and foreign firms faced many restrictions. Negotiations between the U.S. and Japanese governments in 1985 liberalized the cigarette market somewhat. Then foreign companies were disturbed to find that JTI had applied for trademark rights for 50 foreign brand names of cigarettes not yet sold in Japan. In Japan, brand ownership is by priority in registration. Kinya Kitsukawa, marketing manager of JTI, said, "This isn't cheating. Anyone can apply for trademarks. Maybe the foreign companies were idle or lazy in not protecting their brands."[6]

Pricing. Price controls are pervasive in the world economy. **Resale-price maintenance (RPM)** is a common law relating to pricing. Many nations have some legal provisions for RPM, but with numerous variations. Another variable is the fact that some countries allow price agreements among competitors.

Some form of government price control is another law in a majority of nations. The price controls may be economywide or limited to certain sectors. For example, France has had a number of economywide price freezes. At the other extreme, Japan controls the price on only one commodity—rice. Generally, price controls are limited to "essential" goods, such as foodstuffs. The pharmaceutical industry is one of the most frequently controlled. Control here sometimes takes the form of controlling profit margins.

For example, at one time Ghana set manufacturers' margins at between 25 and 40 percent, depending on the industry. Argentina allowed a standard 11 percent "profit" on pharmaceuticals, whereas Belgium fixed maximum prices and both wholesale and retail margins on pharmaceuticals. Germany did not set margins but had an obligatory price register with both prices and margins for public scrutiny. In 1998, China introduced price controls on pharmaceuticals, cutting the prices of imported and joint venture produced drugs by over 20 percent. The pricing formula restricted profit margins.

Distribution. Distribution is an area with relatively few constraints on the international marketer. The firm has a high degree of freedom in choosing distribution channels from among those available in the market. Of course, one cannot choose channels that are not available. For example, France had a specific prohibition against door-to-door selling, but the Singer Company received a special exemption from this law. One major question is the legality of exclusive distribution. Fortunately, this option is allowed in most markets. In fact, the strongest legal constraint does not apply to firms managing their own distribution in foreign markets but rather to exporters who are selling through distributors or agents.

Careful selection of an agent or distributor is critical in two ways. First, the quality of the distributor helps determine the firm's success in the market. Second, the contract with the distributor may commit the exporter to a marriage that is difficult and costly to terminate. The challenge for the exporter is to be aware of national laws concerning distributor contracts in order to avoid potential problems. It is much easier to enter an agency agreement than to end one. See "Global Marketing," "In Ecuador, Breaking Up Is Hard to Do."

Promotion. Advertising is one of the more controversial elements of marketing and is subject to more control than some of the others. Most nations have some law regulating advertising, and advertising groups in many nations have self-regulatory codes. (New Zealand has no fewer than 33 laws relating to advertising.) Advertising regulation takes several forms. One pertains to the message and its truthfulness. In Germany, for example, it is difficult to use comparative advertising and the words *better* or *best*. In Argentina, advertising for pharmaceuticals must have the prior approval of the Ministry of Public Health. Even China brought foreign firms to court over their advertising claims under its new law.

Another form of restriction relates to control over the advertising of certain products. For example, Britain allows no cigarette or liquor advertising on television. Finland is more restrictive and allows no newspaper or television advertising of political organizations, religious messages, alcohol, undertakers, diet drugs, immoral literature, or intimate preparations. Another restriction is through the taxation of advertising. For example, Peru once implemented an 8 percent tax on outdoor advertising; Spain taxed cinema advertising.

Sales promotion techniques encounter greater restriction in some markets than in the United States. There is often no constraint on contests, deals, premiums, and other sales promotion gimmicks in the United States. The situation is quite different in other countries. As a general rule, participation in contests must not be predicated on purchase of the product. Premiums may be restricted as to size, value, and nature. A premium may be limited to a certain fraction of the value of the purchase and might be required to relate to the product it promotes; that is, steak knives could not be used as a premium with soap, or a towel with a food product. Free introductory samples may be restricted to one-time use of the product rather than a week's supply. In the infant formula controversy, sampling was completely forbidden. Variations are great, but in most cases the U.S. marketer is more limited in host countries than at home.

Enforcement of the Laws

The firm needs to know how foreign laws will affect its operations in a market. For this it is not sufficient to know only the laws; one must also know how the laws are enforced. Most nations have laws that have been forgotten and are not enforced. Others may be enforced haphazardly, and still others may be strictly enforced.

An important aspect of enforcement is the degree of impartiality of justice. Does a foreign subsidiary have as good a standing before the law as a strictly national company? Courts have been known to favor national firms over foreign subsidiaries. In such cases, biased enforcement makes it one law for the foreigner and another for the national. Knowledge of such discrimination is helpful in evaluating the legal climate.

The Firm in the International Legal Environment

Whose Law? Whose Courts?

Domestic laws govern marketing within a country. Questions of the appropriate law and the appropriate courts may arise, however, in cases involving international marketing. As noted, few international laws apply to international marketing disputes. Nor is there an international court in which to try them, except for the European Court of Justice for the EU.

GLOBAL MARKETING

In Ecuador, Breaking Up Is Hard to Do

In 1976, the outgoing military regime in Ecuador passed the Dealers Act. It allows for damages to be paid to Ecuadorian businesses when a foreign company ends a distribution agreement, even if done in accordance with the original contract.

During the 90s, several American firms were penalized under the act. Some examples: Proctor & Gamble, $45 million; Colgate, $40 million; DuPont, $12 million; UPS, $2.3 million. In P&G's case, the company claimed that the charges were equal to 100 years of net income. All the companies were refusing to pay and were fighting in the courts—and appealing to the U.S. government.

The courts response in the UPS case was to order an auction of the UPS trademark name. It was bought by UPS's former partner who tried to sell it back to UPS.

The U.S. government was investigating the companies' complaints and considering economic sanctions against Ecuador. Also, potential foreign investors were being frightened away by these cases so Ecuador's President Alarcon introduced legislation to try to overturn the law.

Source: *The Wall Street Journal*, August 26, 1997, A6.

When commercial disputes arise between principals of two different nations, each would probably prefer to have the matter judged in its own national courts under its own laws. By the time the dispute has arisen, however, the question of jurisdiction has usually already been settled by one means or another. One way to decide the issue beforehand is by inserting a *jurisdictional clause* into the contract. Then when the contract is signed, each party agrees that the laws of a particular nation, or state in the case of the United States, governs.

If the parties do not have prior agreement as to jurisdiction, the courts in which the appeal is made decide the issue. One alternative is to apply the laws of the nation in which the contract was signed. Another is to use the laws of the country where contract performance occurs. In one of these ways, then, the issue of which nation's laws shall govern is already out of the company's hands when a dispute arises. Most companies prefer to make that decision themselves and therefore insert a jurisdictional clause into the contract, choosing the more favorable jurisdiction. Of course, the choice of jurisdiction must be acceptable to both parties.

The decision as to which nation's courts will try the case depends on who is suing whom. The issue of which courts have jurisdiction is separate from the issue of which nation's laws are applied. Suits are brought in the courts of the country of the person being sued. For example, a U.S. company might sue a French firm in France. This kind of event leads not infrequently to the situation in which a court in one country may try a case according to the laws of another country; that is, a French court may apply the laws of New York State. This could happen if the parties had included a jurisdictional clause stating that the laws of New York State would govern; it could also happen if the French court decided that the laws of New York State were applicable for one of the other reasons mentioned.

Some U.S. courts have a particularly long international reach. The California Supreme Court ruled that a Taiwanese tire maker, Cheng Shin, could sue a Japanese tire valve maker, Asahi, in a California court, even though Asahi does no business in California. In a motorcycle accident, the driver was killed when his tire burst. The family sued Cheng Shin, who settled out of court. He decided Asahi should share the cost and brought suit in California with the approval of the California Supreme Court. The implications of this global reach were so threatening to foreign firms that when Asahi appealed to the U.S. Supreme Court, it was joined in its appeal by the Confederation of British Industry and even the U.S. Chamber of Commerce in London.

Arbitration or Litigation?

The international marketer must be knowledgeable about laws and contracts. Contracts identify two things: (1) the responsibilities of each party, and (2) the legal recourse to obtain satisfaction. Actually, however, international marketers consider litigation a last resort and prefer to settle disputes in some other way. For several reasons, litigation is considered a poor way of settling disputes with foreign parties. Litigation usually involves long delays, during which inventories may be tied up and trade halted. Further, it is costly, not only in money but also in customer goodwill and public relations. Firms also frequently fear discrimination in a foreign court. Litigation is thus seen as an unattractive alternative, to be used only if all else fails.

More peaceful ways to settle international commercial disputes are offered by conciliation, mediation, and arbitration. Conciliation and mediation are informal attempts to bring the parties to an agreement. They are attractive, voluntary approaches to the settlement of disputes. If they fail, however, stronger measures such as arbitration or litigation are needed. Because of the drawbacks of litigation, arbitration is used extensively in international commerce.

In fact, litigation costs are so high in the United States that they even got the attention of Congress. Firms did not wait for Washington, however. Each year over 40,000 civil cases that formerly would have gone to court are now settled out of court with savings estimated at $200 million. For example, Motorola's 100 lawyers are charged with seeking every alternative to a court trial. Since the program began, the company's litigation costs have been reduced by 75 percent.

Arbitration generally overcomes the disadvantages of litigation. Decisions tend to be faster and cheaper. Arbitration is less damaging to goodwill because of the secrecy of the proceedings and their less hostile nature. This means that the climate for conciliation is better so that almost one-third of the cases are settled in direct talks before the judgment stage is reached. Decisions are more equitable and informed because of the expertise of the arbitrators, who are not judges but people with practical experience. Arbitration allows business to continue while the dispute is being settled. It neutralizes the differences between different legal systems because decisions are not based on points of law but rather on practical considerations of equity. Each party also has the satisfaction of avoiding the courts of the adversary's country.

In an increasing number of countries, arbitration awards have the status and enforceability of court decisions. This was ensured for the United States when the Supreme Court in 1974 upheld the primacy of arbitration. Deciding against Alberto-Culver, the Court said that the parties must submit to the agreed-upon arbitration and may not bring suit in U.S. courts. This was reaffirmed strongly in 1981 when the Court upheld President Carter's deal with Iran whereby private U.S. claims against Iran were to be settled by international arbitration rather than by U.S. courts. The fact that such foes as Iran and the United States agreed to this was a significant development in international law.

The arbitration procedure is relatively simple and straightforward. If the firms wish to settle disputes by arbitration, they include an arbitration clause in the contract. A common form is the one suggested by the American Arbitration Association:

> Any controversy or claim arising out of or relating to this contract, or the breach thereof, shall be settled by arbitration in accordance with the Rules of the American Arbitration Association, and judgment upon the award rendered by the Arbitrator(s) may be entered in any Court having jurisdiction thereof.

Because of its advantages, arbitration is increasingly popular for settlement of commercial disputes. Two developments support this trend. One is from UNCITRAL, which has formulated a model law on arbitration. This law, because of its multinational source, could lead to a leveling of national arbitration rules into a single global standard. The second development is the increase in the number of centers for hearing arbitration. The International Chamber of Commerce (ICC) in Paris is a leading center, but in recent years New York, London, Geneva, Stockholm, and other European cities have become more important, in addition to such nontraditional locations as Bermuda, Hong Kong, and Kuala Lumpur.

China created its own arbitration tribunal in 1989, and Beijing is now the busiest arbitration center in the world. Even with its problems, foreign firms find the tribunal far superior to going into a Chinese court. The World Bank's International Center for the Settlement of Investment Disputes (ICSID) also hears arbitration disputes; it is especially useful when a government is a party in a commercial dispute.

We've stressed the advantages of arbitration over litigation. Although it is very important, arbitration should not be considered a panacea. It does cost time and money. Cases can take as long as two years, and the average cost is over $100,000. (Rates vary according to the sum in dispute.) Nevertheless, if disagreements do arise, it is a much preferred alternative. The ICC says that only 8 percent of its decisions have been challenged.

The following landmark case illustrates the usefulness of arbitration: In 1983, IBM sued Fujitsu for stealing software used in its mainframe computers. After four years of very expensive legal battles, the issue was still unresolved. In December 1986, the two companies gave the case to two arbitrators from the American Arbitration Association and agreed to dispense with all the legal machinery. In September 1987, the arbitrators came up with a solution acceptable to both parties.

This landmark case showed the inability of the traditional legal system to handle complex disputes over new technology. The two arbitrators even received powers over future software relations between IBM and Fujitsu.

The Marketer Is Not a Lawyer

What are the implications of all of the legal parameters discussed in this chapter for the international marketer? Even lawyers generally do not have detailed knowledge concerning all the domestic, international, and foreign legal aspects involved in international marketing. Although the international marketer cannot know all the relevant laws, it is essential to know which decisions are affected by the laws. A firm can call in legal counsel when special expertise is needed. Legal counsel in this case includes not only the domestic legal staff but also legal representation from the firm's foreign markets.

The firm's need for legal expertise is related to its international involvement. If the firm only exports or licenses, its legal needs are fewer than if it has foreign subsidiaries and joint ventures. Where it operates through licenses or distributors, these parties relieve the firm of some of its legal burden. If it has subsidiaries, however, it needs local legal counsel.

With the growth of international business and the proliferation of national and international regulation, the international legal function is becoming more complex. Firms will need an international legal staff at headquarters, and local lawyers in foreign subsidiaries. In host countries, the task will be largely decentralized because of local peculiarities. However, some coordination and exchange of experience will be necessary to optimize performance of the firm's international legal function.

SUMMARY

The host country's behavior is guided by its national interests, such as security, sovereignty, prestige, and economic welfare. To achieve its goals, it uses a variety of controls over the firm, such as entry restrictions, price controls, quotas and tariffs, exchange control, and even expropriation. These national interests and controls constitute the political environment of an international firm.

The firm needs to evaluate the host-country environment and assess its own political risk there. Then it needs a plan for managing host-country relations, both before and after entering the country.

The international firm often gets involved in international relations, usually against its will. It needs to know how a given host country relates to its own country and to other nations as well. Also, the firm's home country may restrict its international marketing activities. The United States, for example, is especially attentive to these issues.

Many U.S. laws affect U.S. firms' international marketing, relating to regulation of exports and the antitrust implications of overseas ventures as well as special organizational formats to help U.S. firms market abroad, such as Webb-Pomerene Associations, foreign sales corporations (FSCs), and export trading companies (ETCs).

Still other U.S. laws concern the behavior of U.S. firms abroad. The Foreign Corrupt Practices Act prohibits bribery, and antiboycott provisions are meant to prevent U.S. firms from cooperating with the Arab boycott of Israel.

Treaties of friendship, commerce, and navigation (FCNs) ensure that U.S. firms will not receive discriminatory treatment in a foreign legal system. UNCITRAL's Convention for the International Sale of Goods smooths the international selling task. IMF and WTO, each in its own way, help to create an environment more favorable to international marketing. ISO is creating standards for international products that the firm must incorporate into its product planning.

International patent conventions help international firms protect their most valuable intellectual property.

Regional economic groupings, especially the EU, are writing new multicountry laws covering many aspects of business. These facilitate international marketing in the region.

Each foreign country has its own legal system, which is shaped by the common law, code law, or Muslim law tradition. These foreign laws affect all aspects of product policy, including the physical product itself, the package and label, the brand name, and the use of warranty.

Pricing and promotion programs are generally more strictly regulated in foreign markets than in the United States.

In cases of legal disagreements, each party usually prefers its own country's courts. A jurisdictional clause should be included in an international marketing contract in case a problem arises. However, rather than litigate in a foreign court, many international firms prefer to settle differences by arbitration. This is often more efficient and equitable and less damaging to continuing relations.

QUESTIONS

5.1 Explain the threefold political environment of international marketing.

5.2 Discuss the various kinds of host-country controls over the international firm.

5.3 How might a firm analyze its own political vulnerability in a particular host country?

5.4 What can a firm do to help manage its host-country relations?

5.5 Identify the elements of the international political environment.

5.6 Explain the foreign policy concerns in U.S. export controls.

5.7 Discuss the various aspects of international marketing that can be affected by U.S. laws.

5.8 Discuss the ambivalent attitude of the U.S. government toward antitrust in international business.

5.9 Give examples of the kinds of international laws that can influence the firm's international marketing.

5.10 Explain the firm's concerns relating to international patent and trademark law.

5.11 Discuss the influence of regional groupings—especially the European Union—on the development of international law.

5.12 Show how foreign laws can affect the four P's of marketing.

5.13 Why is arbitration preferred to litigation?

ENDNOTES

[1] *Daily Journal* (Caracas, Venezuela), May 17, 1990, 1.

[2] *Fortune,* October 3, 1994, 29.

[3] *The Wall Street Journal,* January 19, 1989, B1.

[4] Federal Trade Commission, *Report on Cooperation in American Export Trade,* Part 1, 1916, 8.

[5] "American Paricipation in International Boycotts," NBER Paper 6116, July, 1997.

[6] *The Wall Street Journal,* March 7, 1986, 20.

FURTHER READINGS

Antitrust Guide to International Operations. Washington, DC: U.S. Government Printing Office, 1988.

Hildebrand, Doris. "Legal Aspects of Euromarketing." *European Journal of Marketing* 28, no. 7 (1994): 44–54.

Keillor, Bruce D., Gregory Boller, and O. C. Femell. "Firm Political Behavior in the Global Marketplace." *Journal of Business Research* 40 (1997): 113–126.

Kennedy, Charles. *Political Risk Management.* Westport, CT: Quorum Books, 1987.

Minor, Michael S. "The Demise of Expropriation." *Journal of International Business Studies* 25, no. 1 (1994): 177–188.

Nill, Alexander, and Clifford Schultz II. "The Scourge of Global Counterfeiting." *Business Horizons,* November, 1996: 37–45.

Sood, James. "An International Patent Protection System." *Thunderbird International Business Review,* March, 1998: 165–179.

Sorachek, Bernard. *International Business Law.* Princeton, NJ: Darwin Press, 1994.

The Political-Legal Environment of Cigarette Marketing

Ever since the U.S. Surgeon General's report about the dangers of smoking, cigarette marketing has become a controversial activity. This hasn't hurt the profits of the manufacturers, however. A Paine-Webber analyst noted that Philip Morris cigarette shipments were growing at almost 5 percent a year (over 7 percent overseas). He concluded, "Cigarettes are a global growth business. Marlboro, the number one brand, does a nifty $13 billion per year."

The controversy and ethical questions surrounding tobacco affect firms related to the industry as well as the cigarette manufacturers themselves. For example, Elizabeth Bramwell, manager of Gabelli Growth Fund, won't buy tobacco stocks because she doesn't feel comfortable with the product. Yielding to shareholder pressure and the threat of legal liability, Kimberly Clark spun off its $400 million tobacco-related paper business. Its stock rose over 3 percent on the news. Ad agencies are wary of tobacco accounts which used to be plums.

One agency executive said, "It's unfair to accept an account for which you can't promise your best. Many in the agency feel strongly about tobacco." The manager at another agency said, "We work for wine, beer, and spirits clients, but tobacco crosses the line." Nevertheless, cigarettes continue as a global business. We will review the situation facing cigarette marketers in different parts of the world market.

The U.S. Situation

"Surgeon General's Warning: Smoking causes lung cancer, heart disease, emphysema, and may complicate pregnancy." This warning, or a similar one, required in print ads and on cigarette packages, illustrates the industry's problem. The health dangers of their product have forced the manufacturers into a decades-long battle with a variety of critics and challenges. This battle continued into the 90s.

Package warnings and advertising restrictions were the earliest regulations the companies had to face. Losing the electronic media forced manufacturers to become more broad-gauge and innovative in their promotion. One popular medium was billboards and scoreboards in sports stadiums. In 1992, however, the San Diego Padres decided to remove the Marlboro Man from the biggest billboard in Jack Murphy Stadium. This action was part of a larger movement by antismoking activists to take away this medium from the tobacco firms. Other stadiums followed suit: the Seattle Kingdome, Oakland Coliseum, Minnesota's Metrodome, Houston's As-

trodome, and Baltimore's new stadium. The critics next target: Racing car events.

Joe Camel was an effort by RJR to improve the image of its sagging Camel brand. Joe was a sunglasses-clad, bulbous-nosed cartoon camel. He appeared in an array of macho gear and was meant to appeal to younger males who had been deserting the Camel brand. The campaign was successful. Camel's share of the 18-to-24-year-old segment jumped from 4.4 percent to 7.9 percent. A study by the American Medical Association found that Joe Camel appealed far more to children than to adults. The Centers for Disease Control found that the number of teens smoking went up from about 25 percent when the Joe Camel campaign began to about 37 percent in 1998. The Surgeon General, Antonia Novello, asked RJR to cancel its campaign voluntarily. Even *Advertising Age* ran an editorial titled "Old Joe must go."

Lawsuits were another challenge facing the industry. Over 350 suits have been filed by people claiming injury or death from cigarette smoking. Only about 20 of these ever made it to a jury, and only two ever received a jury award. However, in the late 90s a $368 billion settlement was almost passed in Congress and when that failed, the top tobacco firms agreed on a $206 billion payment to the various States participating in the agreement. In addition, the companies agreed to another $1.7 billion to fund antismoking campaigns and to start a foundation to reduce smoking among youths. Not surprisingly, the tobacco lawsuits have gone global—from Brazil to Canada to Europe, Israel, and Japan. These have been encouraged by the $200 billion settlement also.

On another front, the state of Massachusetts put on the November 1992 ballot a proposal to increase the tax on cigarettes from 26 cents to 51 cents. To combat it, the tobacco companies formed a group called Citizens against Unfair Taxation (with no identification of an industry association). (The industry had defeated a similar proposal in Montana in 1991.) The antismoking forces (including the American Cancer Society) were outspent 10 to 1. This time, however, the proposal passed. In 1998, California raised the cigarette tax by 50 cents a package.

Also in 1992, the Minnesota Department of Health began a series of ads accusing cigarette companies of exploiting women. "We want to make women mad at the cigarette companies,"[1] said Lyle Wedemeyer, director of the agency preparing the ads. Reports from the Office of the Surgeon General noted that since 1987, lung cancer surpassed breast cancer as the leading cancer killer of women. Also, pregnant women who smoke have babies that are shorter and lighter than babies of nonsmokers. Minnesota is one of 17 states that received federal money to reach less educated and lower-income groups with antismoking messages.

Other challenges for the tobacco companies in the 90s were the continuing reports on smoking and health. The Environmental Protection Agency confirmed the danger of secondary smoke, especially for children. Studies by the American Medical Association concluded that cataracts, the leading cause of blindness, affect 3 million Americans and that 20 percent of them are caused by smoking. The Food and Drug Administration (FDA) sought permission to regulate cigarettes as they do drugs. FDA Commissioner David Kessler said, "If we could affect the smoking habits of just one generation, we could radically reduce the incidence of smoking-related death and disease. Nicotine addiction begins when most users are teenagers, so let's call this what it really is: a pediatric disease."[2]

The harshest attack came from the American Medical Association (AMA) in 1995. It called tobacco "a drug delivery vehicle" and called for FDA regulation. After analyses of tobacco industry internal documents, the AMA charged that these "show us how this industry has spread confusion by suppressing, manipulating, and distorting the scientific record." Dr. Glantz, one of the researchers, claimed, "The documents show that by the 1960's, B&W [Brown & Williamson] and B.A.T. [British American Tobacco] had proved in their own labs that cigarette tar causes cancer in animals. In addition, by the early 1960s, their scientists were acting on the assumption that nicotine is addictive."[3]

Perhaps because of all these challenges, unit volume of U.S. cigarette sales declined 2 to 3 percent a year during the 1980s; this decline in volume was offset by increased prices. The industry was continuing the battle and spending $4 billion on advertising, promotions, and sponsorships in the United States. The industry also began a strong marketing drive abroad where about 75 percent of all cigarettes are sold. Almost three-quarters of Philip Morris' cigarette sales are from foreign markets.

Western Europe

The European Union passed a ban on both tobacco advertising and sponsorship. In 1992, France passed a law requiring that restaurants, factories, offices, and other public spaces set aside separate areas for smokers. Italy proposed even stronger legislation—a ban on smoking in public places and on public transport. Both countries fine violators. With some time lag, it appears that Western Europe is following the U.S. pattern of restrictions.

The cigarette companies are putting great efforts into their European marketing. Their European promotional budgets are the same as in the United States, about $4 billion. As part of its effort, and to combat the French blackout of all cigarette ads, Philip Morris established a Marlboro-Classic clothing line and Marlboro Travel Services. Ads for both businesses feature the Marlboro Man—sans cigarette. More than 900 stores in Europe stock the Marlboro line. The travel business promotes trips to the U.S. West in states such as Colorado and Wyoming. It operates through some 5,000 French travel agencies.

Eastern Europe

The breakdown of the Communist bloc and Eastern Europeans' move toward market economies have attracted many consumer goods marketers from the West—especially tobacco companies. With a population and smoking propensity larger than that in Western Europe, Eastern Europe is a market to be seized. For example, Hungarians smoke more cigarettes per capita than any other group except the Japanese. Some Russian industrial centers experienced riots because of cigarette shortages.

When the (then) Soviet Union announced a "cigarette famine" in 1990 because of production inadequacies, Philip Morris and RJR Nabisco said they would ship 34 billion cigarettes to the country. In Czechoslovakia, Philip Morris paid $430 million to buy the national cigarette company, Tabak. It became by far the largest U.S. investor in the country. U.S. and European tobacco companies have been quick to invest across Eastern Europe from (former) East Germany to Russia to Kazakstan.

Health issues are of less concern in Eastern Europe. Zdensk Kucera, director of the National Health Center in Prague, said, "There is a sort of ecological fatalism here. People say 'The air and water are so polluted and the food is so contaminated that it's stupid to worry about my lifestyle.'" A Western tobacco executive noted that "there is little awareness of health and environmental problems in Hungary. We have about 10 years of an open playing field."[4] Nevertheless, television and radio advertising of cigarettes is banned in most Eastern European countries. U.S. companies promote their brands with colorful store displays, banners, and sponsorship of sporting events.

Hungary presented an interesting situation. In 1992, Western tobacco companies were openly defying cigarette advertising laws. The government conceded that the laws were vague and needed changing. Nevertheless, the Consumer Protection Agency ordered the removal at retail outlets of table umbrellas, light boxes, and window decals advertising such brands as Camel and Marlboro. The marketing director of British American Tobacco (BAT) said, "We're ignoring the removal orders."[5] Philip Morris, RJR, and BAT formed an association to lobby lawmakers for a more liberal, voluntary advertising code.

The agency also ordered removal of the trolley signs for Camel boots that showed the Camel icon. The trolley cars looked like a Camel cigarette package. RJR said these ads weren't for cigarettes but for footwear. The agency ruled that since most Hungarians don't understand the word "boots" in English, the sign indirectly advertises cigarettes.

The newest marketing and public relations effort by the tobacco companies in Eastern Europe has been to give money to a wide variety of public and charitable causes: hospitals, schools, scholarships, orphanages, senior citizens, and even police and fire brigades. Philip Morris gave Christmas presents to a homeless shelter in Budapest. A company spokesman noted that "people had tears in their eyes when they saw the presents, and they knew they came from Philip Morris."[6]

Asia

With well over one-half of the world's population, Asia is a giant cigarette market. Chinese smoke one-third of the world's cigarettes and one study indicated that one in three young men in China will eventually die from tobacco-related illness.[7] Indeed, the world's largest tobacco company is Chinese; it has a monopoly in that country. Many other Asian countries have had national monopolies with barriers against outside producers. This led U.S. tobacco companies to bring action against Japan, Korea, Taiwan, and Thailand under Section 301 of the 1974 Trade Act. Section 301 condones U.S. retaliation against countries that do not allow U.S. exporters to "participate in their economies on the basis of nondiscrimination and fair treatment."

The Cigarette Exporters Association enlisted the U.S. trade representative to fight for the opening of these markets. Sometimes the association was supported by senators from tobacco states, including Senators Helms and McConnell, who wrote letters to the various governments. Other senators have opposed this action. Senator Ted Kennedy complained that the "United States has become an accomplice in the industry's abuse policy by threatening trade sanctions against countries that restrict access to U.S. cigarettes."[8] U.S. pressure has been resisted by the national monopolies and occasionally by other nationalistic interests. At a demonstration before the U.S. Embassy in Bangkok, leaflets saying, "If smokers have to die, they should die with Thai tobacco" were distributed by local activists.

Several Asian countries restrict cigarette advertising, even China. China also requires warning labels on packages. Promotional restrictions, but especially discriminatory treatment, have kept the foreign market share low in most Asian markets, except for Hong Kong, where U.S. firms have 80 percent of the market, as compared to only 5 percent in Korea.

Because of ad restrictions, U.S. firms use point-of-sale posters, such as those for "Kent" holidays and pictures of the Marlboro Man (without the name); they also sponsor sporting or cultural events, such as the Salem concert with Cyndi Lauper and Tina Turner. Cigarette firms also moved to Macao television when Hong Kong banned cigarette ads on TV. Macao obligingly increased its signal for transmission to the Hong Kong audience.

In Asia, the antismoking movement is relatively new but is being aided by groups from outside, such as the American Cancer Society. In 1991, a 14-nation group of antismoking organizations met in Hong Kong to map out a four-year strategy. The group, the Asian Consultancy on Tobacco Control, formed a computer network to gather news on U.S. tobacco company activities. The group's strategy is to train activists to combat smoking in the region. The tobacco companies also united in opposition to their critics, forming the Asia Tobacco Coalition.

As the antitobacco movement grew in Asia, new restrictive measures were introduced in many countries. In 1995, South Korea banned cigarette vending machines from public places, primarily to prevent teenagers from easy access to cigarettes. Hong Kong, Malaysia, South Korea, Taiwan, and Thailand all banned the selling of cigarettes to anyone under 18. Thailand introduced the impotence argument and requires all packs to carry this warning: "Cigarette smoking causes sexual impotence." This idea had been noted in American urologists' offices for nearly two decades. The theme was also picked up in a California anitsmoking ad campaign. The strictest country was Singapore, which not only bans all tobacco advertising, but makes it a crime for minors to possess cigarettes.

Antismoking groups received support in 1992 from a powerful new voice, the World Bank. Faced with the costs to Third World countries—one estimate suggested that 7 million people there will die yearly from smoke-related ailments by 2025—the Bank adopted its own antismoking policy. To discourage tobacco use, the World Bank will not lend money for tobacco-related activities. It will also allow governments to exclude cigarette imports from required agreements to liberalize trade.

The World Health Organization noted that tobacco-related illness would be the leading cause of death by 2020 and that 500 million would die from it by 2025. In light of this, Bro Brundtland, the new head of WHO in 1998, declared a new front in the fight against tobacco. She wants to focus WHO's efforts on the developing countries, like the World Bank.

Questions

1. Identify in some detail the legal, political, and other challenges facing cigarette marketers in the United States and abroad.

2. Identify the various interest groups, organizations, and institutions the companies must consider as they market cigarettes.

3. Identify in detail the marketing and other strategies and tactics cigarette companies are using to meet these challenges. Can you suggest any other approaches?

4. Apart from the legal and political dimensions, do you see any ethical dimensions to these issues? If so, what questions would you raise and how would you respond to them?

Endnotes

1 *The Wall Street Journal,* September 4, 1992, B9.
2 *The Wall Street Journal,* July 13, 1995, A3.
3 *The Wall Street Journal,* July 14, 1995, B5.
4 *The Wall Street Journal,* December 28, 1992, B1.
5 *Ibid.*
6 *Financial Times,* November 20, 1998, 5.
7 *The Economist,* May 16, 1992, 24.
8 *The Wall Street Journal,* November 10, 1998, 81.

CASE 5.2

U.S. Pharmaceuticals, Inc. (B)

U.S. Pharmaceuticals (USP) is a U.S. firm with about 30 percent of its sales outside the United States. USP concentrates on the ethical drug business but has diversified into animal health products, cosmetics, and some patent medicines. These other lines account for about one-fourth of USP's $800 million sales.

USP's international business is conducted in some 70 countries, mostly through distributors in those markets. In six countries, however, USP has manufacturing or compounding operations. (Compounding refers to the local mixing, assembling, and packaging of critical ingredients shipped from the United States.) USP's only Latin American manufacturing/compounding operations are in Latinia, a country with a population of about 30 million. Some products are shipped from Latinia to other Latin American markets.

USP has run into a problem in Latinia recently with its newest drug, Corolane 2. This drug is effective in treating certain intestinal diseases and infections. The drug has been under development for several years. Three years ago, when it showed considerable promise in the extensive testing process, USP registered the name Corolane 2 in the United States and several other major world markets. Last year, USP introduced Corolane 2 in the United States and several large foreign markets. Its early promise was confirmed by its quick acceptance by the medical profession in these countries.

Because of Corolane 2's initial success, USP plans to introduce it in all of its foreign markets. It planned both to manufacture and to market the drug in Latinia. A problem arose, however, because Jorge Rodriguez, a Latinian citizen, had already registered local rights to the name Corolane 2. Though a questionable procedure, this is perfectly legal, for Latinia is a code law country that gives exclusive rights to trade names according to priority in registration rather than to priority in use, which is the basis for exclusive rights in the United States. Furthermore, Latinia is one of several countries around the world that is not a member of the international patent and trademark agreements.

The problem for USP was that it could not sell Corolane 2 under that name in Latinia because Rodriguez owned the rights to it. Of course, Rodriguez was quite willing to sell his rights to the Corolane 2 name for $20,000.

Registering foreign brand names was Rodriguez's way of supporting himself. He made a good living by subscribing to foreign trade and technical publications (especially in the medical field) and registering all the new names he found. Not all of these names would be exploited in Latinia, but enough of them were to make it profitable for him. Corolane 2 was a typical case. Early in its development process there were journal articles telling of successful tests and applica-

tions. As soon as the name Corolane 2 was mentioned in one of these articles, Rodriguez registered it in Latinia. It turned out that he beat USP lawyers to the registration by just two weeks.

USP had encountered problems like this before in Latinia and some other countries. It conducted R&D on many projects, most of which did not reach the market. Some company officials believed it was not profitable to register every new product name in every market.

Questions

1. Identify and evaluate the alternatives open to USP in Latinia.
2. What variables are important in this decision?
3. How could this kind of problem be avoided?

PART TWO

INTERNATIONAL MARKETING MANAGEMENT

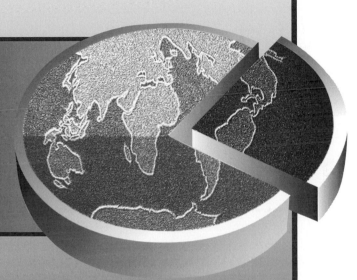

In Part 1 we examined the environmental variables that shape the management of international marketing. In Part 2 we consider the strategies and individual elements of the marketing plan that can lead to successful international marketing, given those environmental constraints. We discuss typical marketing decisions and problems faced, highlighting those intrinsic to the international arena. A chapter on the international marketing of services is included.

◆   ◆   ◆

Global Marketing Strategy

Learning Objectives

This chapter explains how a company can formulate international marketing strategy. Once a carefully thought-out strategy is in place, effective and consistent actions can be taken in the various areas of the marketing mix.

The main goals of this chapter are to

1. Describe the process of formulating global marketing strategy that is consistent with, and integrated with, the firm's overall global strategy.

2. Delineate the steps involved in arriving at a global strategy.

3. Explain how global strategy relates to the product line and to individual country markets. We discuss the basic question of adaptation versus standardization of the marketing mix for the various country markets, pointing out why some adaptation may be necessary.

4. Describe how firms compete in the global marketplace. We show how firms configure and coordinate the value-added chain to obtain a global competitive advantage.

5. Detail the effects on strategy formulation of corporate goals such as a short-term orientation or the pursuit of market share. We highlight basic strategies based on being a low-cost producer or competing with differentiated products and show how this influences the choice of strategies for international marketing.

6. Discuss government influences and the impact of major trends such as European integration in 1992 and the creation of the Euro and the emergence of the triad economies of Europe, Japan, and the United States. Throughout the chapter, we use company examples to illustrate the concepts being discussed.

7. Discuss the global automobile and personal computer (PC) industries in some detail to provide a better understanding of how global strategy unfolds.

To formulate market strategy, the marketer must consider the existence of global markets for the firm and competitors who think and act globally. Worldwide competition is intense enough that firms must plan on obtaining significant market positions in *all* major developed country markets, where technology has become so widely diffused that "all developed countries are equally capable of doing everything, doing it equally well and doing it equally fast."[1] Widespread availability of information and volatile currencies pose additional challenges to the firm seeking leadership in a global industry.

A **global industry** can be defined as an industry in which a firm's competitive position in one country is affected by its position in other countries and vice versa. "If no one challenges a global competitor in its home market, the competitor faces a reduced level of rivalry; its profitability rises and the day when it can attack the home markets of its rivals is hastened."[2]

George S. Yip has developed an interesting framework for analyzing a company's global strategies.[3] He begins with environmental factors that lead an industry to become global. Terming them *industry globalization drivers,* he includes (1) market factors, (2) cost factors, (3) competitive moves, and (4) other environmental factors.

In response to these environmental changes pushing a firm to develop global strategies, a firm can adopt a variety of strategic approaches, which Yip terms *global strategy levers.* These include:

Participating in significant major markets.
Offering a range of mostly standardized products worldwide.
Configuring value-added activities across countries, based on country comparative advantage.
Developing global marketing strategies.
Developing a program of competitive moves integrated across countries.

MARKETING AND ITS LINKS TO GLOBAL STRATEGY

Marketing does not take place in isolation but is inextricably linked to a firm's overall strategy. International marketing is likewise linked to its global strategy. Takeuchi and Porter use the term *linkage* to describe how technology development and manufacturing can make global marketing more effective and further enhance global competitive advantage.[4]

Table 6–1 summarizes the linkages between global marketing strategy and overall corporate strategy in the areas of technology, global logistics, manufacturing, finance, organization structure, competitive response, personnel, and government relations. Thus, a firm cannot cut prices to match its global competitors unless its global manufacturing policies allow it to manufacture at low cost. Similarly, a global hedging policy is needed if a company wants to prevent local prices from going up or down because of currency fluctuations. And unless the company has a policy of transferring experienced personnel to new markets, it cannot expect to benefit from their accumulated expertise.

Domestic marketing seeks to obtain and keep customers in the home market; likewise, *the goal of international marketing is to create and retain customers in global markets.* The customers may themselves be global in character, or they may be limited to individual national markets. The added complexity is that the firm faces global competitors.

GLOBAL STRATEGY: A FRAMEWORK

Firm-level global strategies cut across product lines. For example, global management of international financial flows can match cash inflows and outflows in a spe-

| TABLE 6-1 | Linkages between Global Corporate Strategy and Global Marketing Strategy |

Strategy Area	Examples of Linkage
Technology	Worldwide patents allow foreign marketing from a protected position; the firm does not have to fear price-based competition.
Global Logistics	Developing a worldwide logistics network allows the firm to promise speedy delivery, attracting clients with just-in-time inventory systems.
Manufacturing	Multiple, geographically dispersed manufacturing sites allow the firm to effect least-cost sourcing and to cut prices in order to gain market share.
Finance	Centralized global hedging and swaps permit production line management to set prices in terms of local currencies without having to worry about exchange-rate fluctuations.
Organization Structure	A decentralized or matrix organization supervised by headquarters executives with extensive international line experience allows for balancing of local responsiveness and global integration.
Competitive Response	The company may form strategic alliances to respond to market forces such as 1992's Single Europe and retaliate against a competitor's encroachment into one's domestic market by price-cutting and new-product introductions to dent the competitor's cash flow in its critical home market. (See "Global Marketing," "Competitiveness in the Global Automobile Industry.")
Personnel	Transfer of experienced personnel into new markets permits transfer of know-how and helps achieve standardization and expertise in implementation.
Government Relations	The company may pool country-risk analysis and expertise across product lines and across countries, and transfer government relations know-how to critical markets.

cific currency and integrate cash needs for specific currencies across product lines. If a company has several product lines in Japan, it can aggregate the surplus or deficit cash flow produced by each product line; it thus has a total deficit or surplus position in yen that must be financed and hedged. This procedure can reduce spending on hedging and reduce the firm's overall exchange-rate risk. If the firm has organizationally distinct product-line divisions, however, deliberate planning is needed to achieve such integration of foreign-exchange management.

Similarly, a multinational firm selling several distinct product lines within a country can gain economies of scale by performing a basic analysis of that country market's cultural, political, and economic structure before considering competition and demand profiles for individual product lines.

Another major firmwide influence that cuts across product lines is management attitude. Management attitudes that lead to focusing on the domestic market and/or on a few foreign markets without regard to global markets and competition hinder the formulation of global actions. The lack of global vision is one reason that a firm's global strategies may be inadequate and even why it has not formulated a global strategy.

The consequences of management attitudes can be seen in the attempts of family-led European corporations to adjust to the Single Market. Many such family corporations were led by CEOs who grew up during World War II and conceived of Europe as a series of nations that had once been at war. It was difficult for such executives to abandon nationalistic thinking and formulate pan-European strategies, although the younger generation, their sons and daughters, have less difficulty in this regard.

Global Strategy and the Product Line

Figure 6-1 sets out the framework for developing product-line global strategy. The three basic influences are the global environment, the industry, and the firm itself. In analyzing the firm, we evaluate its **competitive advantage;** that is, why the firm

GLOBAL MARKETING

China: The Market at the End of the Rainbow.

There are over 1.2 billion people in China, and incomes have been doubling every seven years since 1980. This means that growing numbers of Chinese citizens can afford to buy goods and services: prepared foods, clothes, motorcycles, refrigerators, insurance, and vacations. Take orange juice, for instance. China is among the world's leading producers of oranges, but the Chinese drink little orange juice. Generally, it is drunk by adults at banquets and by children. Seagram's Tropicana division is one of North America's largest orange juice producers, owning large orange plantations in Florida and deriving nearly half its sales from the United States. Because China looked like a huge market, Tropicana decided to enter the orange juice market there. Initially, it imported juice and concentrate, resulting in a luxury drink consumed mostly by foreigners. After much searching, it decided to set up an orange juice plant in southwestern China, near

Zhongxian, high above the Yangtse river, in the region where the Three Gorges Dam is being built. But farmers had treated oranges as a low-cost side-crop, with trees left to grow on their own, without fertilizer or irrigation. Tropicana wanted to get the farmers to plant over 1 million new trees using seeds provided by Tropicana. These trees needed to be watered and fertilized and nurtured to yield sufficient quantities of high-grade orange juice. But the trees would not yield fruit for several years, raising the question of whether farmers would be willing to spend money today in the hopes of good returns after several years. The region is remote and Tropicana and its Chinese partner, the Chongqing Three Gorges Group, would have to overcome poor infrastructure and a lack of roads in getting their juice to the major markets, towns far to the east such as Shanghai and Beijing and Hong Kong. But Seagram is convinced that its $55 million investment will pay off if one looks beyond Asian turmoil to a China 20 years hence, a China likely to be far more prosperous, with fast highways and even higher incomes.

China is equally attractive to overseas Chinese, such as the Wei brothers from Taiwan. Their firm, Ting Hsin Interna-

should be able to make a profit in its chosen line of activity in the face of competition and why customers should buy its product or service, preferring it to that of the competition. Competitive advantage can come from many sources: a firm's proprietary technology, its superior manufacturing, its skills in marketing or in managing global financial flows, and its overall management talent and organizational capabilities. These sources of competitive advantage compose the firm's **value-added chain.** It is through carrying out these activities that the firm provides value to the product. The firm is able to attract customers because of its superiority over its competitors in one or more elements of the value-added chain. That is, the firm attracts customers because of its superior technology, manufacturing, or marketing.

The second factor to consider in attempting to formulate a strategy for competitive advantage involves several global environmental influences. Most important is the global competition that the firm faces. Then, host-government actions, which vary from country to country and can affect the firm's freedom to carry out its strategy, must be considered. Also important are the firm's customers, the reason for its being. Careful customer analysis is absolutely critical to developing competitive advantage. Last, suppliers and their influence over the firm are relevant to strategy formulation.

Carpano et al. studied the relationships among strategies, environments, and firm performance, using data on 75 firms in global and multidomestic industries.[5] They found that no one strategy was always superior, suggesting that the environment in which the firm finds itself dictates the appropriate strategy. Thus mass-market standardized strategies are more effective in global industries than in multidomestic industries. One could use Yip's globalization drivers to determine

tional Group, owns the largest market share in China's instant noodle market. They have created a national brand, their logo a pot-bellied chef, Master Kang or Kang Shi Fu. A growing number of working couples made instant noodles a popular product. Initially, their instant noodles were priced 50 percent higher than local Chinese brands. They decided to sell the noodle packages shrink-wrapped together with styrofoam bowls, banking on a Chinese need to be able to eat clean food when they traveled: "When do I eat and will it be clean?" Since hot water is easily found in a tea drinking population, the noodles with a bowl could tap into a large market served only by expensive Japanese imports. When the Wei brothers saw that the product was successful, they expanded rapidly since the product was easy to copy and they wanted to cut production costs quickly, ahead of their imitators. Their Chinese roots allowed them to develop a large variety of noodles that catered to Chinese tastes while they were able to project a higher-quality image because they could be seen as a foreign product, as they featured Taiwanese-style soup noodles. The four brothers control and run the company, splitting responsibilities for areas such as operations, finance,

business relations, and marketing. A key tactic is their use of large numbers of sales agents who visit wholesalers across China on a regular basis. On these visits, the agents gather market information and learn about competitors' moves such as promotional discounts. Ting Hsin advertises extensively on TV, a relatively new medium in China, while constantly testing new flavors and launching them, such as chili noodles for the Sichuan palate, pork-free noodles for Muslim populations in western China, and smaller snack packages for children. While also testing new lines such as biscuits and fried chicken outlets, noodles account for 80 percent of their sales and remain the product line that will determine their continuing success.

China's stunning growth has created large domestic enterprises that are beginning to look outward, even as their markets are being populated by foreign firms. The Haier is China's leading manufacturer of white goods, products such as refrigerators, washing machines, air conditioners, and other home appliances. To compete with foreign firms' products in China, firms such as Haier know that they need to offer superior technology, durability, and quality, all at a

whether an industry is becoming global; and if it is still in the multidomestic stage, strategies adapted to each country market might result in better performance.

The third major influence is the industry to which the product line belongs. Basic industry analysis is necessary to establish its stage of growth, future prospects, and barriers to entry. A fundamental tool is the international product life cycle, which may be at different stages in different national markets. This life cycle is useful in forecasting demand and selecting potential markets for future entry.

The rayon industry manufactures rayon fiber used to make yarn, then cloth, and finally, garments. As the garment industry concentrates in the low-wage countries of the Far East, in China, India, Sri Lanka, and others, rayon manufacturers are motivated to locate their rayon factories near their customers, the garment-producing companies. Thus, rayon factories are being increasingly located in the Far East, even though they are capital intensive and seem anomalous in low wage countries. The Indorayon factory, described in a subsequent case, is an example of how industry attractiveness can vary over time across countries.

Product-Line Strategy for Individual Country Markets

After the firm has developed an initial strategy, it must begin to consider individual markets. Although global marketing involves considering all of a firm's markets with regard to their interdependence, a decision must be made about whether strategy will be the same in all of its markets or whether aspects of strategy, including global marketing strategy, will be adapted to fit individual countries. In part, this depends on the goals set for a product line within a particular

competitive price. This means lowering costs with scale economies, efficiency in managing inventories, and a carefully planned sales campaign. Haier began with technology and specialized equipment for refrigerators obtained from Germany. Later, it procured industrial freezer technology from Italy, air conditioners through a joint venture with Mitsubishi, and Freon-free refrigerators from the U. S. Environmental Protection Agency. But it also set aside 4 percent of an estimated $750 million in revenues for in-house R&D, planning to raise this to 8 percent as finances permitted. This allows it to invent its own new technology products, such as Big Prince, an environmentally friendly and energy saving refrigerator. It rewarded employees for individual excellence, promoting them, a practice at odds with the traditional state-owned company mentality of paying everyone equally regardless of performance. In a departure from surly treatment of customers by state-owned monopoly sales outlets, Haier emphasized service and listening to the customer, with a toll-free hot line, guarantee of delivery or repair of its appliances within 24 hours, a serious undertaking in a country as far-flung as China; and continuously adding and altering prod-ucts to satisfy customers, such as a miniwashing machine that washes a small number of items, but is compact and cheap, fits into small flats, and requires little water, a feature important in a country where water supply interruptions are frequent and running water supply still scarce.

One of its slogans says: "Never Say No to the Market." Haier is now beginning to take its products overseas, with a factory in Indonesia, another planned to start up in the Philippines, with additional overseas manufacturing planned for other Asian and Latin American countries. President Zhang Ruimin notes, "To build a name brand, you can't just stay in China. Haier has to combat the perception that goods made in China are of low quality, a challenge it faced in Germany by placing two refrigerators with their identifying marks removed before German retailers, one the Haier product, and asking retailers to identify the Chinese import; this test allowed them to get large orders. Haier's long-term goal is to get one-third of production, each devoted to domestic sales, exports, and goods manufactured in overseas plants. It is doing all it can to fulfil its other slogan, "Haier- Tomorrow's Global Brand Name."

Sources: *The Wall Street Journal,* "Tea and Tropicana: Seagram Wants Juice to Be Chinese Staple," January 2, 1998; "Coals to Newcastle, Ice to Eskimos; now, Noodles to the Chinese," *The Wall Street Journal,* November 17, 1997; and, "Would America Buy a Refrigerator Labeled Made in Qingdao?" *The Wall Street Journal,* September 17, 1997.

country market. In some markets, the firm may seek market share, planning to obtain profits after market share has been established. In other cases, the goal may be to challenge strong global competitors as a means of preserving competitive balance across countries. In still other markets, the firm may simply want to establish a small market presence and wait for the day when the market becomes more attractive. In some more mature markets, the firm may actively seek profits and set up return-on-investment targets. The goals set for each country and for the product line as a whole determine which strategies are selected. As part of setting strategy, firms must choose which country markets to enter. The goals a firm sets for a market partly determine whether it will enter a particular country market.

Next, the firm must analyze whether it must change its marketing policies in a specific market because of government restrictions, competitive pressures, or differences in customer needs that may arise from economic and cultural differences. This choice between standardizing policies across markets or adapting them and becoming locally responsive is fundamental to international marketing. Not all aspects of global strategy need to be adapted for each market. Local responsiveness can vary across the marketing mix, with perhaps promotion and distribution tailored to individual national markets while the same basic product and price strategies are used for all markets.

The interaction between product-line goals and environmental analysis affects strategies in a variety of areas, including technology, manufacturing, marketing, customer service, competitive policy, and managing government relations. As described in Table 6–1, linkages exist between marketing strategy and strategy in

GLOBAL MARKETING

Competitiveness in the Global Automobile Industry

In attempting to compete in the global automobile industry, a firm is constrained by its cost to produce a car, the time it takes to design a new model, and the relative quality that it is able to achieve in building a car. Thus, when an auto firm is considering its global marketing strategy, it must consider whether changes in other aspects of its strategy are necessary in order to provide greater freedom in formulating a responsive global marketing strategy. Consider the following comparison of the global auto industry.

Automobile Industry Comparisons across Regions (1989 Averages)

	Japan	*United States*	*Europe*
Hours to Manufacture a Car	16.8	25.1	36.2
Quality, Calculated as Defects per 100 Cars	60.0	82.0	97.0
Factory Space Necessary to Manufacture a Car (sq. ft. per car per year)	5.7	7.8	7.8
Percent of Work Force in Teams	69.3	17.3	.6
Suggestions per Employee per Year	61.6	.4	.4
Hours Spent Training New Workers	380.0	46.0	173.0
Percent of Welding Automated	86.0	76.0	77.0
Percent of Painting Automated	55.0	34.0	38.0

other areas. Explicit consideration of these linkages leads to a more integrated strategy and thus more successful international marketing.

In addition, the interdependence of many national markets must be considered: When do changes in one market dictate changes in marketing strategy in other markets? A firm may develop standardized global policies for a product line in some aspects of strategy, such as making anti-lock brakes standard on all cars it sells, but in the area of technology, for example, it may adopt a regional policy covering a group of countries, such as including GPS-based navigational systems on all luxury cars sold in the countries of the European Union. In other areas, such as advertising and promotion, it may adopt national policies.

Although it is difficult to categorize strategies, in essence they all purport to find out what customers around the world want and then to satisfy these desires better than the competition. The basic strategy thrust is either (1) becoming the lowest-cost producer and competing on the basis of low prices, (2) providing a differentiated product and competing on the basis of providing unique value to the customer, or (3) avoiding competition and seeking government help to operate in protected markets.

Finally, strategies must be implemented if they are to be of use. How well they are implemented depends on organization structure and personnel assigned to a given country. Once implementation has begun, feedback of results is essential to monitor the plan and decide when and how it should be changed.

Cavusgil and Zou examined the link between strategy and performance for a sample of 79 firms across 16 industries involved directly in 202 export ventures.[6] They analyzed firms along several dimensions, including export marketing strategy,

The data in the table indicate clearly that decisions on how to organize factories and how to train and treat workers, plus the emphasis on quality, result in giving Japanese car producers great freedom in marketing their cars; their overall strategy allows them to market new models quickly, to promise and deliver high quality, and to reduce costs in manufacturing, allowing low prices if necessary. The point is that global marketing strategy cannot be separated from overall global strategy; they work hand in glove and allow corporations to be more responsive, more market oriented.

Of course, auto manufacturers around the world have been responding to Japan's lead in manufacturing efficiency. Over time, they have cut manufacturing costs, and the competitiveness game has now shifted to design parameters, including the time and cost to develop and launch new car models. While Ford may have spent $6.6 billion to launch its "world car" Mondeo, the trend is to spend less and take less time to develop. Ford has created five car-design centers scattered around the world, each one focusing on a specific car segment (i.e., minivans, compact cars, etc.). Standardizing components so that they can be used across different vehicles is another thrust. An example is Ford's goal of reducing its types of vehicle platforms—chassis—from 25 to 16 by the year 2000 so that switching models on the assembly line is easier and faster. Car manufacturers are also seeking to get their suppliers to cut costs, with Ford's goal being a 20 percent price cut by suppliers by the year 2000.

While developing global strategy, individual car markets such as the United States are of paramount importance. Poor performance in the critical U.S. market, which accounts for a third of Nissan sales, resulted in losses at Nissan headquarters, forcing it to request a Japanese government loan of 100 billion yen to help it recover. Its mistakes in the United States included a car product line that was not as appealing; its Altima was seen as too small compared to Honda's Accord and the Toyota Camry; it manufactured too many cars in its U.S. plants, forcing it to offer substantial rebates to get rid of inventory, causing a "rebate habit," in which U.S. consumers waited for Nissan to offer rebates before buying its cars. It also offered its cars at low monthly lease payments, based on an inflated residual value, in order to stimulate sales; this resulted in further losses when the cars came off lease and were sold off through dealer auctions. Nissan's recovery will depend on whether it can make Nissan cars that the public wants, with advertising that stresses the car's features and value, such as an ad extolling the Maxima's engine as one of the 10 best in America.

Sources: "The Endless Road: Survey of the Car Industry," *The Economist,* October 17, 1992; "Ford Fights Its Costs," *The Economist,* October 14, 1995; and "Nissan's Motor Crisis Was Made in the USA," *The Wall Street Journal,* November 25, 1998.

firm characteristics, product characteristics, industry characteristics, and export market characteristics. They found that firms achieved better export performance when management was internationally competent, was committed to the export venture, adapted the product to meet export customer requirements, and provided strong support to their foreign distributors and/or subsidiaries.

Egelhoff raises the point that performance may be affected by how well the strategy is implemented rather than by how brilliant or unique the strategy as formulated is.[7] He studied Japanese semiconductor firms and, over the time frame that he examined, he suggested that their superior performance was due to better strategy implementation of rather ordinary strategies. Of course, more recent evidence suggests that Japanese semiconductor firms concentrating on high-volume memory chips have been beset by Korean competition, while U.S. firms have prospered by moving into high-margin specialized microprocessor chips for graphics, telecommunications, and multimedia applications. The difficulty with relating strategy to performance, therefore, may partly lie in the time frame over which results are evaluated.

Competitive Advantage

As Figure 6–1 shows, competitive advantage provides the basis for choosing a strategy. Competitive advantage is achieved by matching a firm's capabilities with the chain of value-added activities. That is, a product line or service emerges following the completion of a series of activities such as technology development, manufac-

FIGURE 6-1   **Global Strategy at the Firm**

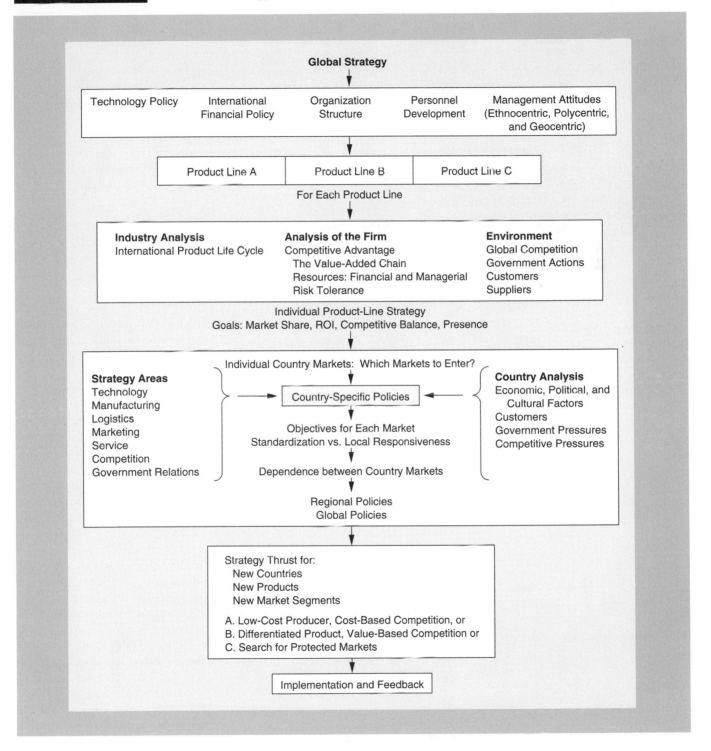

turing, logistics, marketing, and after-sales service. A firm with a competitive advantage in one or more activities that constitute the value-added chain is able to make a long-term profit by specializing in those activities. Table 6–2 illustrates the application of the value-added chain to a hypothetical global firm.

| TABLE 6-2 | The Firm and the Global Value-Added Chain |

Countries/ Markets	Technology	Purchasing	Manufacturing	Logistics	Marketing	Service
United States	X		X	X	X	X
Europe			X	X	X	X
Japan	X			X	X	X
Southeast Asia		X	X		X	X
LDCs					X	X
Eastern Europe					X	
Others						

LDCs = less developed countries.
X = firm carries out the value-added activity in that country.
Note: The above represents a hypothetical firm's choices about countries and value-added activities, that is, configuration and coordination.

The Basic Questions: Which Activities and Where?

In a global industry, the firm must decide not only which value-added activities it will carry out itself but also where (in which countries) such activities will be carried out. Thus, two decisions are being made:

1. The firm decides which activities it will specialize in and which activities it will subcontract, thus adopting a make-or-buy decision on each of the activities that constitute the value-added chain; for example, a firm in the running-shoe business might decide to develop a new type of running shoe in-house in its own laboratories, using its own equipment and scientists; then, it might provide product specifications and ask another company to manufacture the product; after receiving delivery of the shoes, the firm might carry out its own marketing campaign in major markets around the world. Thus it controls the technology and marketing activities while subcontracting the manufacturing value-added activity.

2. The firm must also decide where it will carry out the value-added activities it has chosen; here, principles of comparative advantage come into play in deciding which activities are most appropriately carried out in which countries. A country typically has a comparative advantage in activities that use large amounts of its abundant factor of production. For example, a country with large quantities of abundant unskilled labor might be an appropriate site for manufacture of products that use unskilled labor, such as garments or shoes.

Going back to our example of the running shoe company, suppose that the company had decided to let another independent company manufacture running shoes based on its technology and design. With the addition of the country factory, the company could decide not to subcontract the manufacturing of shoes but instead manufacture them itself in another (low-wage) country by making an investment and managing a running-shoe factory. The company could add manufacturing to its value-added chain by carrying out the activity in a different country. Moreover, if it decides to continue to subcontract the manufacturing, it must decide which country's manufacturers to use as a source of supply. In choosing between competing subcontractors in different countries, the company will consider

GLOBAL MARKETING

Marzotto's Global Growth

Marzotto Spa is a 100-year old major Italian textile and clothing company that did 90 percent of its manufacturing in Italy. Because high Italian labor costs made it difficult for Marzotto to compete in export markets, it acquired, in a bold move, a 63.7 percent stake in the German menswear company Hugo Boss in December 1991 for $165 million. The Boss acquisition offered two benefits: its German and U.S. factories have allowed Marzotto to diversify its manufacturing base and to reduce its dependence on the Italian economy and the Italian wage and inflation rates. At the same time, Boss has a strong image and market share overseas, which will allow Marzotto to reduce Italian sales to 45 percent of total sales as compared to 70 percent in 1991.

Combining Boss and Marzotto also means buying raw materials and other factor inputs jointly, exchanging manufacturing technology and trading managerial know-how by rotating managers between the Marzotto and Boss operations. The company has also acquired a controlling stake in a Czech fabric company. One result has been steadily improving financial performance. As can be seen, sales and profitability have improved, with profits growing faster, though they are still only about 1 percent of sales. Shifting production to Central Europe and the United States has helped cost competitiveness and marketing, as has a weak lira. Future plans include beginning to manufacture in Mexico for the U.S. market.

The Hugo Boss unit decided to launch two new brands under the Hugo Boss umbrella: the Hugo line of casual clothes in unusual colors designed to attract stylish, young urban shoppers, and the Baldessarini line, using costly fabrics and Italian styling to attract an older, more affluent clientele. These new lines are sold through separate stores, and while cannibalization of the original Hugo Boss line is a danger, the goal is to make the Boss name generic for fine men's clothing the way the Levi's name is synonymous with jeans.

By 1995, over two-thirds of Marzotto's sales came from outside Italy. Marzotto's moves demonstrate how marketing and bringing value to the customer depend partly on management and manufacturing decisions, including Marzotto's long-range plan to diversify out of Italy.

Sources: "Italy's Marzotto Bets on Global Growth," *The Wall Street Journal,* November 30, 1992; "International Company News: Recovery for Italian Clothing Group," *Financial Times,* April 24, 1995; and "Focus at Hugo Boss Shifts from Germany," *The Wall Street Journal Europe,* June 29, 1995.

the factors of low delivery cost, quality, timely delivery, and low risk of interruptions of supply.

Companies within the same industry can take different approaches to the value-added chain. Kogut cites the examples of Panasonic and Radio Shack in the consumer electronics industry.[8] Another example of the configuration of the value-chain is provided by the relationship between Pitney Bowes (PB) and Matsushita, which is set out in Figure 6–2. PB has long dominated the postage-meter business in the United States, a business that requires its salesforce and engineers to visit its customers' premises for service and annual testing of postage-meter equipment. Its competitive advantage stems from its extensive field salesforce, its corporate image built up over several decades, and its vast, installed customer base of both large and small corporations. However, the postage-meter business is a mature one, faced with competition from E-mail, the fax machine, and express-mail services. Hence, PB decided to branch out into the production of high-end fax machines with specialized features likely to appeal to corporate users: incoming and outbound message encryption; fax server capability to store, redirect, and forward faxes to mailboxes; fax broadcast capability, unattended communication with customers whereby they can retrieve information, such as downloading shipment status, from corporate databases; as well as high-quality, high-speed, high-volume laser printing of images and complex graphics.

PB still needed to offer reliability and fast service, however. Its business solution was to develop a partnership with Matsushita, under which PB would derive the product specifications from its interaction with its customer base. Matsushita

FIGURE 6-2   **Pitney Bowes, Matsushita, and the Value Chain**

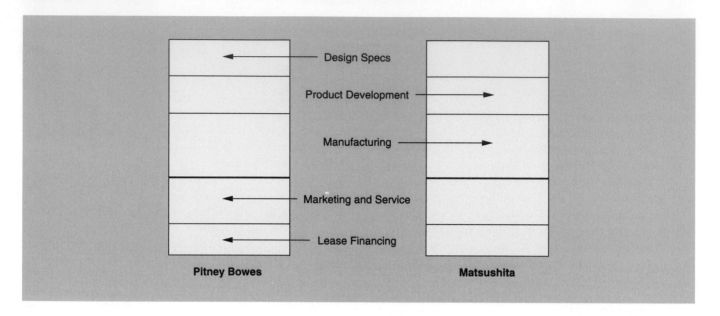

would carry out product development and manufacturing, and PB would market the products as well as arrange for lease financing, a principal component of corporate sales. Figure 6–2 summarizes the configuration of the value chain between PB and Matsushita.

To summarize, making decisions about a firm's choices within the value-added chain is not a one-time exercise. The firm must constantly assess the shifting nature of comparative advantages across countries and its own competitive advantage when compared to that of its competitors. A firm can stay globally competitive only if it conducts such constant re-examination and then changes its global strategy as needed.

Environmental Change and Value-Added Choices

Comparative advantage can shift over time as economies grow and acquire technology, capital, and skilled labor. Companies must change their value-added configuration to accommodate such shifts. If wage costs are important to the firm's competitive advantage and wages rise in its present manufacturing location, it must consider whether to shift manufacturing to another, lower-cost location, as discussed in the following example.

Micromotors are used in products such as cameras, hair dryers, cordless tools, and in cars to run adjustable mirrors, central door locks, and fuel injection systems. Hong Kong's Johnson Electric Ltd. is the world's second largest producer of micromotors. Because wages in Hong Kong rose at a rate of 15 to 20 percent a year, Johnson subcontracted its labor-intensive processes to factories in China, where wages are a fifth of those in Hong Kong. Johnson supplies equipment, technology, and components; and Chinese partners provide land, labor, and the factory building. Johnson ships components by truck in the morning and receives subassemblies back by evening, with final assembly and quality control performed in Hong Kong. Such subcontracting has allowed Johnson to increase output by 60 percent while reducing the number of employees in Hong Kong. Johnson has invested in automated equipment in Hong Kong. It works closely with customers such as Black & Decker, Kodak, and Sunbeam to design specialized value-added motors. As Johnson grows, it continues to stress quality. The China connection allows it to use low costs in competing with Mabuchi Motor, the Japanese company that is the global industry leader.[9]

Configuration and Coordination of the Value-Added Chain

Combining value-added chain analysis with the complexities of global markets requires that firms make decisions about both configuration and coordination.[10] **Configuration** refers to the decision about where a firm's value-added activities are carried out. Once the activities have been spread out (configured) in different countries, the firm must coordinate them to manage them effectively. Configuration decisions can result in a company having a presence in more than one national market. We can distinguish between a global perspective, a multidomestic perspective, and a (domestic) market-extension perspective.[11]

The **market-extension** idea, which is typically the way in which a small firm becomes involved in international marketing, represents an unplanned and short-term exploitation of foreign markets while the domestic market remains the focus of the company. Products developed for the home market are sold in one or more overseas markets to obtain incremental revenue, with little planning of the role of foreign markets in the firm's overall strategy.

A **multidomestic** perspective represents a careful consideration of foreign markets but with a clearly separate orientation toward each country market. That is, the firm approaches each market on its own terms, and little effort is made to capitalize on interdependencies between various markets. Such an approach may be consistent with the nature of consumers and line of business.

An example is Fidelity's entry into the Japanese money management market. The Japanese save a considerable portion of their income—around 20 percent—which represents a rich pool of funds to be tapped by financial service firms such as banks, insurance companies, money management firms, and mutual funds. However, Japanese pension fund regulations had prevented foreign money management firms from access to this pool of funds, and foreign mutual funds were prohibited from marketing their foreign funds to the Japanese. They were required to set up separate mutual funds to be marketed in Japan, which prevented them from relying on and advertising their past performance.

Recent changes in Japanese government regulations have opened up the pension fund management market to foreign firms, and foreign mutual funds can now market funds in Japan without having to set up new Japanese units. Only about 3 percent of Japanese household financial assets are in mutual funds, as compared to 6 percent in the United States, and U.S. firms such as Fidelity hope that marketing a standardized product that has been time-tested in the United States will help them win significant market share in Japan. Another factor likely to influence Japanese investors is that Japanese financial markets have performed poorly over the 1990–1998 period—Japanese investors may be looking to U.S. funds for superior returns. Of course, a strong yen and exchange-rate volatility can affect the returns from foreign investments, and such volatility is a factor that firms like Fidelity and Merrill Lynch will have to manage if they are to retain Japanese accounts.[12]

Fidelity thus obtains economies of scale by realizing that its research on U.S. companies can be sold to both American and Japanese customers. Scale economies could also be obtained, for example, by combining product development for several markets, by developing a regional or global brand, by running common advertising themes, or by centralized manufacturing for sale to several markets. A multidomestic perspective is generally appropriate for industries with low economies of scale and major differences in customer profiles across national markets. Sometimes governments may force a company to adopt a narrow single-country approach, deliberately encouraging such local responsiveness, particularly in critical industries such as telecommunications and software. In such cases, corporate strategy might accommodate government pressures. In return, it might negotiate for favors such as protection against foreign competition and fiscal incentives. However, if competitors are acting globally, a fragmented nationally responsive strategy will be less successful in the long term.

A **global perspective** is one in which the firm directs special attention to the interdependence among national markets and competitors' actions in those markets when formulating its own strategic plans. Such an approach can lead to economies of scale in technology development, manufacturing, and marketing and in making the appropriate competitive responses.

In the early 1960s, Komatsu was a small manufacturer of a narrow line of earth-moving equipment of indifferent quality, selling mainly in a protected Japanese market. When Caterpillar sought to enter the Japanese market through a joint venture with Mitsubishi, Komatsu quickly signed technology licensing agreements with U.S. firms to upgrade its products. Next, Komatsu launched an internal program, first to match Caterpillar in quality and then to reduce costs. Komatsu's corporate slogan became "Encircle Caterpillar."

Komatsu began to sell its products extensively in neighboring Asian countries and to the Middle East and Third World countries, where much infrastructure development was taking place. It next embarked on a factory automation program and a new-product development program. It also set up dealer networks in Europe and the United States. By 1980 it had begun to capture market share in the United States. When the dollar began gaining value, Komatsu cut prices and was able to increase its U.S. market share to about 25 percent by 1984 while Caterpillar experienced losses. In 20 years, Komatsu had become number two in the world in earth-moving equipment, the result of a carefully balanced global strategy with equal attention given to (1) configuration of value-added activities across global markets and (2) coordination of these growing and far-flung activities.[13]

It is unrealistic to discuss global marketing strategy without considering the extent of international business development within the firm. That is, firms pass through stages of internationalization: A company must first decide whether to sell internationally, and if it does, which markets to enter, how to be competitive in the global arena, and which mode of entry to adopt for a particular market. In the next stage, the firm must consider multiple international markets, having to choose between consolidating its market position in foreign country markets where it already has a presence or extending its sales and marketing reach to additional countries. In the third stage, the firm becomes truly global when it is established in several countries and faces the task of developing synergies across markets in marketing, manufacturing, R&D, and service and begins to evolve organization structures to coordinate marketing decisions and aspects of the marketing mix across countries. Figure 6–3 presents this contingency approach to developing global marketing strategy and can be considered as an overlay to Figure 6–1; depending on the international sophistication and development of the firm, different aspects of strategy should be emphasized.[14]

WHY SHOULD FIRMS THINK GLOBALLY?

Reasons to plan for global markets and to compete on a global basis can be summarized as follows:

Markets.
Technology, especially patents.
Production resources.
Competition.
Customers.
Governments.
The time factor: speed of response.

FIGURE 6-3   **Phases in Global Marketing Evolution**

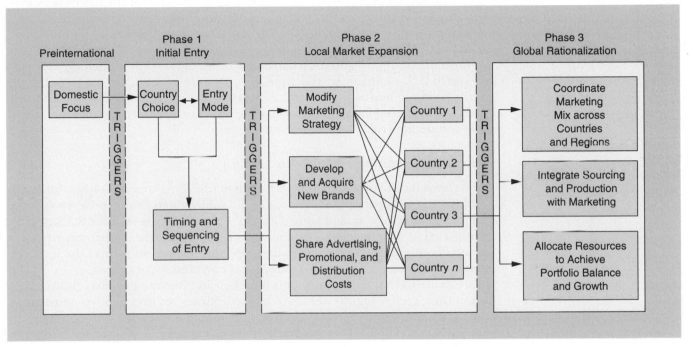

Source: Susan P. Douglas and C. Samuel Craig, "Evolution of Global Marketing Strategy," *Columbia Journal of World Business* Volume 24, no. 3 (Fall 1989). Copyright 1989. Used with permission.

Global Markets

Markets are one reason a firm should think globally. A global orientation could exploit major markets around the world. Post–World War II economic development created three areas of roughly equal economic size: United States-Canada, Europe, and Japan with its neighboring countries.

Each of these blocs represents roughly one-third of the world market, so a company that sells only in the United States is ignoring roughly two-thirds of the potential world market.[15] Further, as markets grow more alike, especially in the developed countries, additional sales in Europe and Japan can be gained with a product that may have been initially designed for the U.S. market.

What we are really saying is that there is a convergence of national markets, with European, Japanese, and U.S. markets for certain products displaying similar profiles. Hence, selling simultaneously to all of these markets could maximize sales, especially if the company has introduced its products ahead of competition. Overhead costs can be spread out over a larger volume base, allowing a lower price to be charged. If sales volume in the United States has already exceeded the breakeven point, R&D and other fixed costs have been amortized. In this case, the firm can capture a larger market share in overseas markets by charging lower prices, because product-development costs have been recovered.

Most multinationals that market globally depend on certain critical markets for a stable source of profits and cash flow, usually their home market and some other markets in which they have been long established. To have a global orientation requires a firm to look beyond its familiar markets and to recognize the need for a market presence in all major national markets in order to protect the firm's position in the critical markets.

Certain markets are highly innovative "lead" markets,[16] and a presence in them helps firms refine their products and services and learn lessons that can be transferred to other markets. Innovative ideas are not all that abundant, so being able to leverage new ideas across markets gives the global company an advantage over its national or regional competitors. As an example of the use of lead markets, large Japanese manufacturers and trading companies have made sizable equity investments in start-up, high-technology U.S. companies in California's Silicon Valley. Aside from an ownership share, they generally obtain exclusive product-distribution rights for Japan and access to advanced technology. Although the small U.S. company benefits from the possibility of selling to the large but difficult Japanese market, the Japanese firm can license the technology and begin manufacturing in Japan, thus readying itself for the product cycle stage when low-cost competitors can gain a competitive edge.

Global Technology Markets

One characteristic of lead markets is their function as a showcase for new technologies. Technology is a critical element of the value-added chain and a resource, as are raw materials or skilled labor. Certainly, technology is an essential factor for firms seeking to compete in world markets using a differentiated-product strategy thrust. Technology is expensive to develop, but patents can protect the firm's investment, allowing it to recoup development costs and make a profit.

U.S. firms that export products based on intellectual property rights suffer when their technological rights are pirated. Piracy reduces exports and also reduces domestic sales when imports based on pirated intellectual property enter the United States. The U.S. International Trade Commission has estimated such combined losses total nearly 2 percent of these high-technology firms' exports.[17]

Global Production Resources

Production resources are another reason to think globally. Global sourcing of raw materials and scarce commodities can result in their timely delivery and reduced cost. A global strategy also allows firms to plan manufacturing configuration across countries to take advantage of the availability of another resource—labor, whether it be cheap unskilled labor or high-quality, technically skilled, and expensive labor (such as large pools of trained scientists).

Global Competition

A global competitor that is strong and unchallenged in its home market can undercut its competitors in their strong markets by deliberately channeling resources into these markets. Such a competitor buys market share with price cuts and by accepting low profits or even losses for a while. Such threats can be countered only by similar tactics from a similar global position. Such an exchange of threats, or **cross-patrolling,** helps maintain the balance of power while firms go about further strengthening their competitive advantages. A global presence helps firms plan for both offensive and defensive strategic responses, as circumstances warrant.

Game theory can be useful in developing strategic competitive responses in international marketing by developing both competitive and cooperative strategies.[18] To do so, firms need to develop a schematic map of all the major global competitors and their interdependencies. Then, the firm must identify how game players add value, the rules and tactics each player follows, and the scope of these tactics before attempting strategy changes.

Time-Based Global Competition

Time is becoming an important factor in global competition. Speedy introduction of new products and rapid response to competitive actions are essential to maintain competitive strength. The ability to respond speedily is heightened when a firm has a global presence because it can draw on resources, ideas, and personnel from a variety of national markets.

Honda exemplifies such behavior; when faced with stiff competition from Yamaha in motorcycles, it responded by introducing 113 new models in just 18 months, equal to changing its entire product line twice over.[19] These rapid model changes had several consequences:

- Motorcycles came to be judged on fashion, with consumers expecting newness and freshness.

- Honda brought technology to the forefront, with four-valve engines, composite materials, direct drive, and other features.

- Although the number of new-product introductions forced Honda's sales and service networks to work overtime, its bewildering variety of models left Yamaha in the dust with over 12 months' inventory at one point. As Stalk put it, "Variety had won the war."[20]

How was Honda able to introduce over 100 models in 18 months? By managing time well, using flexible manufacturing and rapid-response systems, and stepping up the pace of innovation. Why does time-based competition work? Customers are willing to pay high prices for new products introduced in a timely fashion. Even small innovations introduced frequently can be appealing to consumers and aid in sharpening product differentiation. If the customers are themselves using just-in-time techniques, they are willing to pay more for timely delivery. Another reason is that a firm capable of speedy product development, manufacturing, and delivery can reduce costs by saving on inventory (particularly work in progress) and working capital. Time-based competition asks how quickly the product can be made for a given quality and price. Stalk believes that Japanese companies compete on the basis of time: The firm that can implement new-product introductions faster, manufacture a variety of products efficiently, move swiftly to sales and distribution, and do all of this faster than competition gains competitive advantage.[21]

Global Customers

Customers also play a role in influencing the firm's global orientation. As customers themselves become global, their first impulse is to continue to do business with established suppliers. Banking on this tendency, Recruit Co., a Tokyo computer service company that found that U.S. computer service firms did not offer extra capabilities to handle Japanese-language computing, set up an office in New York City. Large Japanese banks such as Dai-Ichi Kangyo that were expanding into the United States had to have this capability, so Recruit moved into the United States to retain such clients.

Similarly, Hitachi Ltd. had sold few of its large mainframe computers in the United States; but when its Japanese customers started building factories and opening offices here, Hitachi expanded its U.S. presence to maintain its relationships with those clients. Hitachi plans to use its U.S. operations to win business from new Japanese clients such as the Japanese auto parts makers who themselves followed the Japanese auto firms, and firms such as Nomura Securities, which has been expanding its U.S. brokerage operations. To serve a potentially larger market, Hitachi expanded product development and marketing in the United States, creating new software and augmenting consulting operations for Japanese clients.

Even IBM Japan moved Japanese marketing and system engineers to the United States once it realized that its Japanese clients wanted IBM Japanese-made equipment and familiar faces.[22] Such relationship building is particularly important in industrial marketing. But similar motivations can be found in consumer-oriented companies; for example, *The Wall Street Journal* began marketing a European edition partly because of the growing number of American managers in Europe. (Another factor was that European demand for American business news and stock quotes was growing.)

Government Actions

Government actions can be a very important influence on global strategy. For example, governments can strengthen competitive advantage by subsidizing national firms. Such support can be most helpful in the early stages of the development of an industry, reducing risk and augmenting scarce resources.

Subsidies estimated at about $25 billion since the inception of Airbus in 1972 have allowed it to offer a family of new commercial jet aircraft.[23] Without them, Airbus would have been unable to fund the development of its three new models, the A320, the A330, and the A340. Internal cash flow would have been inadequate because Airbus has not made a profit in all its years of existence.

Governments may also participate directly in competition through **state-owned enterprises (SOEs).** Such enterprises do not have to worry about profits because they are backed by the deep pockets of the national treasury. SOEs often have objectives such as maintaining employment and earning foreign exchange, which may lead to behavior quite at odds with profit-maximizing behavior. Private firms competing against such government-owned enterprises must worry about maintaining long-term profitability. In competing with Airbus, for instance, Boeing must maintain profits high enough so that it can set aside the $5 billion or more to develop next-generation aircraft following the successful launch of the 777.

Government influence can be felt in other ways. An example is South Korea's dominance of their domestic car industry.[24] Imports account for a small share of the South Korean car market while the South Koreans have been attacking European and U.S. markets. Daewoo began selling cars in the United Kingdom by setting up its own network of Daewoo Motor Show sales centers, offering customers a three-year free warranty, transparent pricing, and membership in the Royal Automobile Club. Daewoo also set up advanced technology research centers in Europe, acquiring 65 percent of the Austrian company Steyr-Daimler-Puch AG.[25] Korean government tariffs of 8 percent (down from 10 percent) are one reason for the low import market share in Korea. Nontariff barriers are a more important reason. Foreign cars had to undergo 38 car-safety tests, such as steering and fuel-leak tests, with the Korean government refusing to accept test results from the exporting country markets.

Higher taxes on cars with big engines (typical of U.S. cars), special excise taxes of 25 percent, lower drivers' license fees for drivers of small cars, and slow customs-approval procedures for entry of imported cars into South Korea are other barriers. As a result, a Ford Mercury Sable with a sticker price of $18,000 ends up costing $40,000. A Korean preference for domestically made cars, the scale economies and cost advantages of Korean car manufacturers whose combined output was around 3.5 million cars in 1995, and a generalized (95 percent) preference for small cars are other reasons for the imports' poor performance. Ultimately, lowering import car prices, providing better service, doing some domestic manufacturing of after-sales service parts in joint ventures, and better distribution are likely to help foreign-car manufacturers win market share in South Korea. Pressure from their own governments might also help. It is clear that government help can be a major factor in overseas market penetration.

CORPORATE GOALS AND GLOBAL STRATEGY

Global strategy differs among multinational firms according to whether:

- The dominant orientation is short term or long term.
- Profits and return on investment are willingly sacrificed in return for higher market share.
- Global or national competitive position is more important in determining competitive strategy and response.

◆ Time, as mentioned earlier, is a key goal, with corporations giving strategic priority to the timely formulation and implementation of strategy.

Modes of Global Competition

Are there some standard approaches to global competition? In a broad sense, the following are such approaches: competing (1) based on low costs, (2) with differentiated products, and (3) by seeking protected markets.

Competing as a Low-Cost Producer

If a firm can produce its product or service at a lower cost than competitors can, yet achieve comparable quality, it can lower its prices and still make an adequate profit. Or it can charge the same prices as its competitors and make higher profits because its costs are lower.

Low-cost production is typically linked to high-volume production. Economies of scale reduce costs, and learning and experience curve factors also lead to cost reduction. **Learning curve economies** result from workers becoming more productive as they work at a job longer and learn from mistakes. Similarly, **experience-curve economies** result from learning to manage a line of business better. As accumulated production grows, the company learns to manage its machines better, reduces overhead, and typically finds that average cost per unit declines with each doubling of accumulated volume of production. Low cost and high market share are closely linked because the large market share allows for large-volume production.

Competing with Differentiated Products

Some firms rely on attracting customers with products that their competitors do not have. Such **differentiated products** may have superior design or better performance, better quality and reliability, or more durability, or they may be backed by better service or may simply appeal more to the consumer for aesthetic and psychological reasons. Examples abound: Caterpillar Co., when initially faced with competition from Komatsu, said that its prices, which were 10 to 15 percent higher than Komatsu's, reflected the higher quality and value offered. When a luxury automobile such as BMW or Mercedes-Benz sells for over $80,000, the price reflects superior engineering, performance, and also a certain cachet. The buyers are willing to pay extra for the prestige a luxury automobile seems to confer.

Firms that compete on this basis must monitor world markets to ensure that the features differentiating their product have not been copied by competitors. They must constantly work on new features because what is a differentiated product today will soon become a commodity. The global competitor must constantly stay ahead of the pack or the basis of its competitive advantage disappears. Once the product has become a commodity, the lowest-cost competitor will win out.

Competing by Seeking Protected Markets

We mentioned earlier that government is a key factor affecting global competition. One mode of competition, therefore, is to rely on government protection against foreign competition. Such protection buys time by holding the efficient competitor at bay until the firm can lower its costs or develop a differentiated product. If it fails in these attempts, it can at least make profits until the foreign competitor figures out a way to evade the protectionist barrier, perhaps by setting up manufacturing and sales facilities within the protected sales market. Once that happens, of course, the inefficient, protected firm disappears.

We mentioned Airbus earlier as a firm receiving government subsidies and protection. After being in operation for 18 years, Airbus finally launched a commercially successful product, the A320, which has received enough orders to take it beyond the breakeven point. Airbus seems to have used protection wisely to develop a family of competitive aircraft. In 1992, the U.S. and European governments agreed that subsidies for new aircraft development should not exceed 30 percent of producer costs. However, it is difficult to monitor implementation of such accords.

Where Do Global Competitors Come From?

New firms are constantly augmenting the pool of potential competitors. They do so through market extension, extension of product lines into new market segments, and forward or backward integration by suppliers. Competitors often emerge from their domestic markets to begin challenging established firms in major foreign markets. Komatsu began emerging as a global competitor in just such a fashion. Firms from countries such as South Korea have begun competing in industries such as consumer electronics, where such companies as Samsung, Gold Star, and the Lucky Group have gained market share in color televisions, VCRs, and personal computers, as well as in semiconductors. In this case, market extension forms the basis for the entry of new competitors. The South Korean companies have extended their reach to global markets after solidifying their position at home.

Firms may also diversify into new-product markets to emerge as potent competitors. Examples abound in the biotechnology area, which is rich in small R&D–oriented start-up companies. It takes years to complete the research and to shepherd new drug applications through the U.S. Food and Drug Administration process to the point of approval, after which an approved drug may be marketed as a high-priced pharmaceutical. Large companies such as Hoffman-La Roche have their own R&D labs but are aware that their global marketing clout can easily meet the competition of new drugs not developed in-house. At the same time, the fear exists that innovative new drugs will be developed by one of the start-up biotechnology research outfits. Hence, Hoffman purchased a significant ownership stake in Genentech, one of the first major biotechnology start-ups and signed a marketing agreement with Amgen, paying handsomely for the right to market Amgen's bacteria-fighting G-CSF drug over the initial 10 years of the drug's introduction.[26]

Existing competitors may also extend their product lines to enter new market segments. Japanese auto firms in the United States have followed such a policy. Honda was the first, with the high-priced Acura being a product for the luxury car segment in the United States. Honda's action was promptly followed by Nissan and Toyota, with their Infiniti and Lexus lines. Such product extension moves by the Japanese auto industry affect the market share of Cadillac and Lincoln, as well as Mercedes, Volvo, Saab, and BMW.

Finally, competition can also develop from forward or backward integration by suppliers. This is happening in semiconductors, with manufacturers of memory chips and microprocessors deciding to incorporate their semiconductor components into board-level and systems products, thus selling complete systems as opposed to components. Such moves not only create competition for the firm but also affect its logistics position by creating uncertainty of supply. When shortages of critical components develop, will the supplier prefer to feed its own manufacturing lines?

Assessing Global Competition

Global strategy must include careful study of sources of competition and the likely responses of individual competitors in global markets. Such an analysis usually begins with an assessment of a competitor's strengths and weaknesses, its goals, and how it should respond to the firm's actions. Much depends on the balance of competitive power, that is, whether the competitor is a leader in a particular product/market area. The same firm may hold a dominant market position in one national market and play catch-up in another. And within the same country/market, the firm may be a leader in one product line and hold a minor market share in another product line. Thus, how a firm reacts depends on its market position, whether it is a market leader, whether it seeks to challenge the market leader, or whether it is a follower, holding a small market position and using niche strategies to hold on to its market share.

GLOBAL MARKETING

Whirlpool in Europe

For most of its existence, Whirlpool was a U.S.–based manufacturer headquartered in rural Benton Harbor, Michigan, and focused mainly on selling to the U.S. market. Whirlpool acquired KitchenAid to enter the premium market and Roper to have an entry in the value-oriented segment. However, Whirlpool saw little market share growth and slim margins in the U.S. market because of intense competition and growing concentration. The formation of a Single Europe gave Whirlpool the impetus to consider expanding into the European market, with Asia as its second priority. Europe was attractive both for its consumer income levels and market size. It was also attractive because it had many small manufacturers, and the fragmented European industry would likely begin consolidating in a fashion similar to the United States. Whirlpool reasoned that its experience in the consolidating U.S. market would help it be a winner in Europe. It

also felt that it was essential to be an "insider" in Europe, with established distribution and local-market knowledge. Because a new, independent venture would be costly and take too long, Whirlpool began to look for a partner with the following parameters:

- ◆ Strength in three core product areas: laundry, refrigeration, and cooking appliances.

- ◆ A strong presence across major European markets; Philips was the second largest manufacturer in Europe.

- ◆ A strong brand image across all segments; Philips had four brands (Philips, Bauknecht, Ignis, and Laden), all of which had a reputation for quality.

- ◆ Technological capabilities; Philips was strong in no-frost capability, insulation, and built-in appliances.

- ◆ Cultural fit with Whirlpool managerial philosophy and practices.

Based on the above factors, in 1989, Whirlpool initiated a joint venture with the Dutch Philips company. In 1991 it acquired

---

A special place is held in global competition by **national champions**—firms that have dominant positions in their national markets and often receive government support. In the European auto industry, Fiat in Italy and Peugeot and Renault in France enjoy such a position, with their dominant market share in their home markets partly attributable to regulations that restrict Japanese auto imports. Similar national champions can be found in the computer industry, where firms such as Olivetti in Italy and France's Bull dominate their home markets but have low market share across Europe when compared to U.S. computer firms with a pan-European presence. With continuing European integration, the position of these nationally dominant firms is less secure as it becomes harder for the national governments to justify favored treatment of national companies in unifying Europe.

Impact of Government Actions on Strategy

Sometimes national governments come to the aid of their national champion firms, especially in industries in which a national presence is deemed important. Thomson, the French state-owned electronics company, is in such a position. Its sales are about equally divided between defense products and consumer electronics—it is the world's fourth largest manufacturer of television sets and VCRs. When defense spending began to decline, it pursued diversification into semiconductor manufacturing, an industry dominated by Japanese and U.S. industry. It merged its semiconductor operations with SGS of Italy and is working on an EU-funded microchip research program in collaboration with Siemens and Philips. French government support is an essential element of the strategy to challenge Japanese firms in semiconductors, televisions, and VCRs.[27]

the firm from Philips, instantly transforming itself into a company that was rapidly globalizing. A plus was that Philips had a strong international presence, with worldwide operations and sales, including an agreement with China.

Whirlpool was then faced with the challenge of integrating European operations into a global framework. Whirlpool CEO David Whitwam has described the need to unify two "parochial margin-driven" companies into "customer-focused organizations."

Whirlpool saw a competitive advantage in understanding how customers viewed the product, seeing products such as the microwave and the kitchen range as part of appliances helping in better food preparation. From its usability lab in Italy, Whirlpool learned that consumers wanted a microwave to brown food, which led to the introduction of the best-selling VIP Crisp model. Whirlpool's challenge was to take the best practices wherever they arose and integrate them across its worldwide organization. As an example, it took the European Philips' focus on ISO 9000 quality processes and integrated them with the U.S. focus on the Baldrige awards, together with ideas from other Whirlpool units from around the world. It then created a set of quality standards titled the "Whirlpool Excellence System."

In part, this meant developing common technology and manufacturing processes, and then allowing regional manufacturing and marketing organizations to adapt product features and dimensions to local needs. An example is the formation of cross-border product development teams. For example, the CFC-free refrigerator developed with insulation technology from Europe, compressor technology from

Much of what we have said about global strategy formulation assumes free markets. Government intervention in international business is quite common, however, and firms must temper their global strategies to accommodate government actions that serve to fragment a global outlook. Doz and Prahalad describe the juggling act that corporations must engage in to handle the conflicting demands of global integration and national responsiveness.[28] Changes in product and process technology, economies of scale, national factor cost advantages, and global distribution all require a global stance. Yet political processes and the interventionist policies of governments require firms to modify their global integration policies and accommodate government demands. That is, the underlying thrust is still global strategy, but temporary and shifting local accommodations are necessary to continue to do business.

An example is Nissan in Europe, which faces problems due to protectionist pressures from European governments. Japanese automakers voluntarily agreed to restrict their European exports, with an import ceiling in the United Kingdom of about 11 percent of the total market, and an even lower 3 percent share of the French market. In response, Nissan opened a small factory in Northern England, producing about 50,000 cars a year, with some of the output being exported to other European countries. Local content is about 70 percent; that is, the value-added chain in Britain accounts for about 70 percent of the car's value. France would not accept exports of these cars from Britain as European products, however, classifying them instead as Japanese autos subject to the 3 percent ceiling. An industry association headed by Umberto Agnelli of Fiat suggested that autos should have at least 80 percent local content to be classified as European.

France's two manufacturers, Renault and Peugeot, account for 23 percent of the market, and about one job in 10 in France still relies, either directly or indirectly, on the auto industry. This may explain French opposition to the Nissan imports from Britain. Imported Japanese parts used in engine assembly in Britain are being replaced with British-made parts. Nissan could obtain higher economies of scale if complete engines were imported from Japan because volume in a Japanese

Brazil, and manufacturing and design expertise from the United States.

The fundamental change was in organizational culture, convincing employees that they needed to learn to think global. Above all, Whirlpool did not want to impose U.S. values or approaches on its worldwide organization. Whitwam commented that Whirlpool must avoid "the temptation to build Rome in a day . . . You may own the land but not the builders." This involved a several-stage process. In Asia, for example, the local unit first learned about local consumers and built up local sales and overall capabilities. Then, it built a regional distribution system centered around three regional offices: one for Singapore and Southeast Asia, another for greater China, and a third for Japan. This was followed by a design, engineering, and development center in

Singapore, to eventually extend to a manufacturing center in Asia.

At the same time, Whirlpool did rationalize and unify European and U.S. operations and developed pan-European design teams that worked with U.S. designers on products sharing common platforms. This allowed distinct products such as the high-end Bauknecht, the broad-based Whirlpool brand, and the utilitarian Ignis to all share a common interior, saving costs. By 1996 Whirlpool expected 85 percent of its European appliances to share a common platform. Other rationalization moves include reducing European warehouses from 36 to 8, developing integrated regional European companies, cutting the number of Philips' suppliers by half, and rebranding products so that former Philips brand products are all sold under the Whirlpool name.

Sources: Regina Fazio Maruca, "The Right Way to Go Global: An Interview with Whirlpool CEO David Whitwam," *Harvard Business Review,* March–April 1994, 134–145; "Call It Worldpool," *Business Week,* November 28, 1994; and David Whitwam, "Whirlpool's Approach to the New Europe," *Journal of European Business,* September/October 1990, 5–8.

plant would be higher. The sacrifice of cost economies, however, is the price in terms of national responsiveness that Nissan is paying for freedom of access to the European market.[29]

GLOBAL MARKETING STRATEGIES

Clearly we cannot separate global marketing strategy from overall corporate strategy. Decisions about technology, new-product development, and manufacturing inevitably affect marketing decisions and marketing success. Thus, a corporate strategy focused on time-based competition and speedy innovation requires that the marketing division plan for continued new-product introduction and relay feedback on customer information to the product-development department to help speed the innovation process. If a firm decides to focus on being the lowest-cost producer, low selling price becomes an essential element of the global marketing mix.

Impact of Differences among National Markets

Keeping in mind the linkages between a firm's overall global strategy and global marketing strategy, a decision must be made between standardization versus adaptation to local markets. Management complexity is reduced with a completely standardized marketing mix applied without change to all national markets. Usually some local adaptations are necessary, however, to accommodate differences in consumer tastes, income levels, government regulations, and differences in distribution channels and structure of competition.

In trying to decide what degree of adaptation is appropriate, the firm must consider the factors that distinguish different national markets:

◆ Buyer profiles differ across countries; taste, income, culture, and buying decision processes are different.

♦ The marketing infrastructure differs from country to country; different kinds of media are available in different countries, and differences exist in what products and messages are acceptable in advertising.

♦ Variations in countries' transportation and communications systems affect marketing approaches such as the use of mail order. Different legal provisions may govern conditions of sale.

♦ Distribution systems differ in the number of layers and in ease of access, and differences in the physical environment of various national markets may dictate changes in product design and sale.

Szymanski and his coauthors used the Yip framework of globalization drivers and strategy levers to formulate a model linking standardization to business performance, that is, to market share and profitability. (This model is described in Figure 6–4.) Their research covered U.S., U.K., Canadian, and European markets. They found that "businesses may be better off standardizing their strategic resource mix to capture the benefits purported to be associated with a standardized approach to serving multiple markets";[30] they also found that "offering a broad product line and selling high-quality products with high levels of customer service seem to be especially conducive to superior market share performance."[31] They found, too, marketing communications (advertising, promotion, etc.) crucial to capturing market share, creating brand loyalty, and lowering susceptibility to price promotions by competitors.

Some Adaptation Is Necessary

The real question is not whether to adapt but how much to adapt. Some elements of the marketing mix are more likely to be standardized than others. The basic product itself probably needs to be standardized in order to permit economies of scale in manufacture. Firms are also likely to standardize brand names and the basic advertising message. Adaptation is more likely in areas such as packaging, pricing, sales promotion and media decisions, distribution channels, and after-sales service. Although management is motivated to standardize in order to reduce costs and management complexity, satisfying consumers in different markets and responding to competition should be the main criteria. Government restrictions could also circumscribe the degree of standardization possible.

The Global Marketing System

Doz and Prahalad stress the importance of managing the global marketing system.[32] They focus on managing net prices in the various markets in order to control global cash flow. The global marketing system, in their view, has three components:

1. Presence in multiple markets in order to take advantage of their differences—that is, use high prices and cash flow in markets where the firm is dominant and competition weak in order to subsidize market penetration by charging lower prices in other markets. (Of course, this assumes that leakage of low-priced products back into the high-priced markets is not a danger.)

2. Global brand presence and strong distribution to help achieve target prices in various markets.

3. Deployment of extended product lines and product families across countries to gain economies of scope and greater competitive strength and allow opportunities for cross-subsidization across businesses and across national markets.

| FIGURE 6–4 | Globalization Drivers, Strategy Levers, and Business Performance |

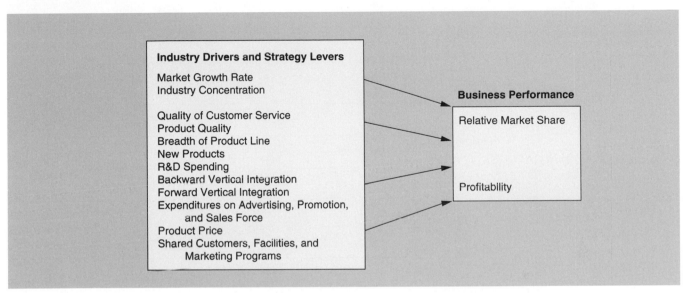

Source: Figure 2 in D. Szymanski, S. G. Bharadwaj, and P. R. Varadarajan, "Standardization versus Adaptation of International Marketing Strategy," *Journal of Marketing 57* (October 1993), 4.

Coordinating the Global Marketing System

As mentioned earlier, coordination of global marketing activities is as essential as configuring marketing activities across national markets. Table 6–3 summarizes some of the various coordination issues, highlighting the adaptation-standardization dichotomy for various elements that enter into formulating a global marketing strategy. Such coordination can take place in the following ways:[33]

1. *Using similar methods to carry out marketing activities across countries.* Avon Products' use of door-to-door sales of cosmetics in different markets or some companies' use of similar standards for warranty and after-sales service across countries are examples of such an approach.

2. *Transferring marketing know-how and experience from one country to another.* This is particularly true in transferring information gained in lead markets to other countries.

3. *Sequencing marketing programs* so that successful elements are gradually introduced into different markets, often in conjunction with evolution of the product life cycle there.

4. *Integrating efforts across countries* so that international clients with operations in many countries can be offered the same service in each country. For example, a client may wish to use the same computer equipment or software at all of its international subsidiaries. Closing such a sale might require coordination of the sales effort in key markets where the largest subsidiaries are located; a clincher might be offering worldwide service with a response time of 48 hours maximum.

TARGETING INDIVIDUAL COUNTRY MARKETS

Because management must determine the sequence in which various global markets should be entered, an essential ingredient of global marketing is to assess their

TABLE 6–3	**Global Marketing Strategy Choices**

	Total Standardization			*Complete Adaptation*
New-Product Development/ Product Line	X			
Marketing Mix				
Product Positioning				X
Market Segmentation		X		
Brand Policy	X			
Packaging				X
Advertising and Promotion		X		
Distribution Channels				X
Pricing			X	
Customer Service		X		
Country Markets				
Market 1	X			
Market 2		X		
.				
.				
.				
Market *n*				X

X = a hypothetical firm's choice.
Source: Adapted from John Quelch and E. Hoff, "Customizing Global Marketing," *Harvard Business Review,* May–June 1986.

attractiveness. Criteria include current size and growth prospects, the product life cycle stage in that market, level of competition, similarity to existing markets, and the extent of government restrictions.

Corporate Goals and Choice of Markets

The firm's objectives help decide which markets are attractive, as shown in Table 6–4. Three kinds of objectives are apparent:

- ◆ Short-term and long-term returns on investment in the form of profits and cash flow.

- ◆ Market-share objectives, partly aimed at maintaining competitive balance and serving to provide credibility in exchanging threats with key global competitors.

- ◆ Entry into lead markets, with learning objectives paramount, at least initially (a special case might be that of protected markets, but even here, entry is based on either attractive economic returns or the impact on a global competitor of gaining market share in the protected market).

Firms primarily interested in profits seek high-growth markets where they encounter less competition, obtain higher margins, and may consider early entry into protected markets.

Firms that are aggressively challenging their competitors prioritize markets based on growth characteristics and market share held by key competitors. They enter markets that offer a chance of achieving reasonable market share, which can then be used as a deterrent in cross-patrolling (exchange of threat) with key global competitors.

| TABLE 6–4 | Market Characteristics and Corporate Objectives |

Market Characteristics	Goal			
	Competitive Response/ Retaliation	Cash Flow/ Profits	Market Share	Lead Market Entry
Size/Market Potential				
Growth Prospects				
Margins				
Product Life Cycle Stage				
Similarity to Existing Markets				
Level of Competition				
Basis of Competition: Value-Added Chain Emphasis				
Government Attitudes				

Firms seeking to establish a presence in lead markets choose markets based on the growth prospects and product life cycle stage but give little attention to competitors' market share or their own profit and market-share prospects.

Last, firms seeking to enter protected markets first evaluate the likelihood of establishing cordial relations and favorable treatment from local government.

A firm may have different objectives for different markets. Typically, it seeks strong profits and cash flow from one or two critical markets, including its home market. It might adopt market-share and competitive-balance objectives for emerging markets where the competition is strong. Simultaneously, it might seek protected markets in large developing countries. Firms find it easier to develop an integrated global strategy, however, by consciously tailoring objectives to country market characteristics. Risk perception and risk balancing play a considerable part in foreign market entry strategies. Brouthers suggests an integrated approach to risk management, wherein balancing high- and low-risk areas such as political and financial risk is appropriate.[34]

Market Positioning in the Triad Economies

In considering which national markets to enter, most firms seek to balance their market position in three major regional markets: North America, consisting of the United States, Canadian, and Mexican markets; Europe, variously called the Single Market and the European Union, even Euroland; and the Japan/Southeast Asia market, consisting of the rich high-income Japanese market and the fast-growing, though recently stalled, neighboring countries of Taiwan, Hong Kong, South Korea, Singapore, Thailand, and Malaysia. These market regions are sometimes referred to as the **triad economies.** If and when oil prices recover, the OPEC countries will constitute another significant bloc of markets. The former Communist nations of East Europe represent another group of markets with possible future potential as they adopt free-market approaches to economic growth. The developing countries of the world, including those large self-contained markets of India, Brazil, and China, and the smaller nations ranging from low-income to poor to extremely poor, also must be considered.

Certain nations and industries manifest a pattern in their expansion into foreign markets. For example, U.S. companies typically begin overseas expansion by branching into Canada, the United Kingdom, and then Europe. Studies of Japanese

GLOBAL MARKETING

Philips and the Value Chain

Figure 1 summarizes the value chain as seen by Philips for the media and multimedia business in which it specializes. Philips divides its business into the following major value-added activities:

1. *Content* is the creative portion of the media business, such as writing a book or composing a song, or writing the software for a new video game. Philips seeks to create such creative content through music (its Polygram division) and movies, videos, and interactive software.
2. *Packaging* refers to assembling content and marketing the package. Examples would be a book or magazine publisher, a broadcaster, a music company. Philips participates in this niche, including the provision of video production equipment.

3. *Distribution* is delivering the package to end users, through TV and cable TV networks, newspapers, retailers, and software companies. Philips is a major distributor of video and telecommunications equipment and distributes music, movies, and cable programs. It owns video rental chains and is involved in developing interactive channels.
4. *User Access* relates to equipment that consumers use to view or access content, including consumer electronics equipment such as TVs and VCRs, as well as new products such as multimedia Internet PCs and PDAs—personal digital assistants. Philips provides a wide range of such equipment. It also provides professional audio and video equipment.
5. *Users* are the people and audiences who use the content: consumers at home, professionals who consume business information, the medical establishment, and educational institutions. Philips markets to all of these groups.

companies show some distinct patterns of overseas market expansion.[35] Japanese typically begin with establishing themselves in the domestic Japanese market. Then one pattern of expansion is to refine international strategies in the developing countries neighboring Japan before moving into advanced developed-country markets such as the United States; such a pattern has marked Japanese expansion in steel, petrochemicals, autos, watches, consumer electronics, and cameras. A slightly different pattern emerges in high-technology industries, such as computers, in which Japan expanded into markets similar to the United States, such as Australia, before entering U.S. and European markets.

Equally significant was the manner in which Japanese companies built a marketing network in foreign markets. Initially, they used independent distributors, such as regional wholesale jewelers in the United States to sell watches. Next, after sales had reached a reasonable level, they began establishing their own branches and sales companies, taking control of local advertising, promotion, and after-sales service. Subsequent steps included local production in developing and developed countries and eventual establishment of a globally integrated manufacturing and sales network.

Responding to Regional Integration

Changing economic and political circumstances within a country can affect a firm's global strategies. The creation of the Single Europe in 1992, the U.S.-Canada Free Trade Agreement, and the North American Free Trade Agreement (NAFTA) rep-

Thus, Philips is along the entire continuum of value creation in the media industry, from hardware to creative content. The company considers this an appropriate response to the growing emergence of media and the rapid acceptance of multimedia by both business and industry.

FIGURE 1   **Philips and the Value Chain**

CONTENT	PACKAGING	DISTRIBUTION	USER ACCESS	USERS
Books	Publishers	TV Broadcast	Set-top Device	Professional Consumer
Newspaper	TV/Cable Networks	Cable	Multimedia PC	Home Consumer
Magazines	Film Studios	Telephone	Personal Digital Assistants	Industry
Software	Software	Satellite	Video and Game Players	Hospitals
Filmed Entertainment	Music Publishing	Manufacturing	Television	Schools
Recorded Music		Delivery		
On-line Business Information		Retailers		

Source: Philips *1994 Annual Report*, pp. 6–7.

---

resent three examples. All three are attempts at regional integration that reduce barriers between markets within the region, leading to market growth.

European Union and the Creation of the Euro

Companies responded to European plans for a single market in a variety of ways; by taking over other companies with significant market share and brand presence in major European markets; by establishing manufacturing facilities and sales subsidiaries in the EU; and by integrating Europe into their global plans, such as developing products in Europe for the global market. The Euro makes for greater pan-European competition and requires firms to rethink European pricing and hedging strategies; cross-country comparison shopping becomes easier, facilitating cross-border pan-European direct marketing, with prices quoted in Euro across Euroland; and the Euro with a common monetary policy will provide impetus to common VAT tax rates and other forms of fiscal harmonization.

Acquiring firms with a dominant market position in a national market allows the acquiring company to expand sales into neighboring countries, capitalizing on and extending brand presence across national borders. It takes time to develop such brand presence and to develop distribution channels in the various European countries. Saving time while pre-empting the competition is perhaps the most significant reason for such acquisitions. European union has added pressure on firms to establish a significant pan-European brand presence before the competition does so. Sometimes this requires developing manufacturing facilities across Europe, striking strategic alliances, or acquiring key firms in European nations where the firm has a weak market presence.

U.S.–Canada Free Trade Agreement

Reactions to this alliance have been similar, with the lowering of tariffs leading to a reshuffling of manufacturing activities. Large-volume manufacturing is being concentrated in the United States, with more specialized low-to-medium volume production being shifted to Canadian factories; again, firms hope to achieve cost reductions that could be used to lower prices and increase sales in both the United States and Canada.[36]

Marketing to Japan

The Japanese market is considered difficult to break into. It is a highly competitive one, usually requiring considerable adaptation, which is easier with well-informed local operations handling Japanese market research and advertising. Japanese distribution can be Byzantine. Although it takes time to establish adequate control of distribution channels, the effort can be well worthwhile.[37]

As Japan's wealth grows, the large-car segment has become the fastest-growing part of the automobile market. Imported cars have obtained reasonable levels of market penetration, obtaining 25 to 33 percent of the large-car segment of the market since 1987. West German manufacturers accounted for over 70 percent of all Japanese car imports. How West German car manufacturers have gone about winning sales in Japan is instructive:[38]

- Both BMW and Mercedes-Benz have set up their own independent dealer networks in Japan, replacing their former reliance on Japanese importers.

- They have used financing as a marketing tool, offering low interest rates and long repayment periods. One result is that monthly payments on the costly imports are about the same as on domestic cars.

- Targeted and heavy advertising is used. Mercedes advertises mainly in the economic daily newspaper, *Nihon Keizai,* thus reaching about 50 percent of its customers. BMW advertises weekly with 60-second spots on prime-time television. Advertising stresses the BMW corporate image because Japanese buyers seem swayed more by the reputation of the company than by product-specific features.

- Price stability is also used. Despite a falling yen, both BMW and Mercedes have kept yen prices constant.

Of course, neither German auto manufacturer faced Japanese competition. Now that Toyota, Nissan, and Honda have all introduced upscale models such as the Lexus, Infiniti, and Acura, maintaining market share may be more difficult for them.

Strategy in the Global Automobile Industry

How are the world's automakers responding to the globalization of the auto industry?

Ford

Ford's goal is to become the number one car manufacturer worldwide, pushing out General Motors. Ford has raised its market share significantly in the United States, from 21 percent in 1985 to 26.5 percent in 1998 (each percentage point of U.S. market share is about $2.5 billion in sales), while GM's share fell to 30 percent. The question is, Does increasing market share, which means increased sales, also mean greater profits? For example, Ford's Taurus became the best-selling car in the United States, edging out the Honda Accord. But 59 percent of Taurus sales were to auto rental and other corporate fleet customers versus just 5 percent fleet sales for Honda. Fleet owners replace their cars frequently, leading to possible repeat sales. However, this, in turn, creates a glut of relatively new used cars, that may be more attractive to the individual customers than high-priced new cars. Additionally, fleet purchasers, who buy in volume, have the clout to demand large price discounts and attractive financing, cutting into automakers' profits. Consequently, GM has cut back fleet sales to 29 percent from 31.5 percent.

Ford's chairman, Alex Trotman, has defined true auto industry leadership as consisting of leadership in market share plus product quality, customer satisfaction, return on investment, and employee morale.[39] Other key aspects of Ford's overall strategy include:

Increased manufacturing capacity to meet increased demand as it materializes; Ford achieved this by restructuring its factories rather than building new ones. That is, it invested $674 million to add an assembly line to build the Explorer sport-utility vehicle at its existing St. Louis minivan plant.

Globally focused new product development such as the $6 billion effort to develop a world car—the Mondeo family of compact cars designed for both Europe and the North American market. Ford's new car models are to be built on the same "platform," using common engines and parts to reduce product development costs and speed up the pace of new product introduction.

Marketing innovations such as two-year auto leases with low up-front payments.

Cost cutting such as freezing most costs at 1995 levels for four years and eliminating bureaucracy and redundancy, especially in new product development.

Enhanced motivation by requiring the top 80 officers at Ford to own shares equal in value to their annual salary and by possibly extending this requirement to its top 350 managers.

No company, including Ford, can develop a global strategy without thinking of its position in the key developing markets of Asia, notably India and China. The United States and Japan are slow-growing markets, and Europe is slow growing and crowded with the six major manufacturers: Ford, GM-Opel, Renault, Peugeot, Volkswagen, and Fiat, each with 10 to 14 percent of the market.

The promise of future growth lies in Asia and Latin America. Japanese auto companies control about 90 percent of the Southeast Asian auto market, with one out of four cars sold being a Toyota. Ford has drawn on its 25 percent ownership of Mazda to develop factories in Thailand, Malaysia, and Indonesia. At the same time, it has attempted to solidify its own brand name, developing a series of joint ventures with well-connected government-owned companies in China. Such essential long-term moves do raise concerns about risk and possible harm to profits in the short run.[40]

Toyota

How does Toyota's global strategy compare to Ford's? Toyota, like all Japanese manufacturers, has been able to export more competitively because of a weak yen, which has dropped in value against the dollar from a low of 80 yen to an average of 125 yen over the 1985–1998 period. Toyota, which dominates the Japanese market with a 40 percent market share, gets about half of its total sales from Japan, and a weak Japanese economy has cut into its Japanese sales. One problem is that its manufacturing is concentrated in Japan. Its new president, Hiroshi Okuda, who comes with considerable overseas experience, has plans to build one-third of its cars overseas by the year 2000.[41] Toyota's culture is a feudal one, however, with a seniority-based system causing managers to take 35 years to reach top management levels. The Toyota family still dominates the company and may not want to close plants in Japan while simultaneously expanding overseas. However, Toyota is still the benchmark against which all car companies compare themselves and has been improving its efficiency in order to be competitive even with a strong yen.

Toyota was able to develop a new minivan in just 19 months—8 months less than the average in-house developmental time of 27 months. A four-month design process, followed by a 15-month period to move from concept approval to production allowed Toyota to challenge competitive minivans models in high demand, in this case, Chrysler's Voyager minivan. The shorter design time allows Toyota to respond to consumer tastes before they change and also reduces overall fixed costs of product development thereby lowering prices and enhancing profitability. Toyota was able to reduce its time to production by limiting design changes and reducing the number of internal reviews during the development process. Further, Toyota used two design groups to compete against each other to produce rival designs and it integrated computer-aided design and engineering systems so that design changes automatically updated other systems such as parts lists and equipment.[42]

GM and Global Product Development Efforts

In developing a global strategy, carmakers come up squarely against differences in cultures and customers. Most of the world's consumers worry about fuel prices and want fuel-efficient cars. Smaller cars are welcome as being fuel-efficient and more suitable for narrower roads and country lanes, congested downtown spaces, and even the smaller driveways and parking garages underneath apartment buildings. The United States, on the other hand, enjoys some of the world's lowest fuel prices. Vast open spaces and multilane highways, urban spaces and cities that favor automobile traffic to pedestrian traffic, and a working population that is willing to commute 45 minutes to an hour to work all make for a U.S. market demanding large, fast cars that are less fuel efficient. Designing a world car then is a constant process of compromise between the values of the United States and the rest of the world.

GM's approach to designing world cars is a case study in balancing such tensions. As its Cadillac luxury car division loses sales in the United States—younger affluent buyers preferring European and Japanese models such as BMW, Mercedes-Benz, Acura, Lexus, and Infiniti—GM has turned to its German Opel division for a new luxury model that will attract younger customers to its Cadillac brand. Opel's Omega became the basis of the Cadillac Catera, but importing a car made in Germany when the deutsche mark is strong means that GM will make little profit on the car. Yet GM needs a European design car to retain market share, and using an existing Opel model allowed Catera development costs to be cut to about $100 million. A brand new car, on the other hand, might have cost over $1 billion.

Similarly, GM's Saturn will develop a new model, based on the Opel Vectra, to compete against the Honda Accord and the Toyota Camry. The model will be manufactured in the United States but will still use a costly Opel engine and need to be redesigned to use plastic doors and fenders, a feature common to other Saturns. Buyers like the plastic because it is resistant to dents and scratches.

The Opel Vectra has also provided about 25 percent of the design of Saab's new 900 model (Saab is 50 percent owned by GM); U.S. designers and engineers are the source of GM's new front-wheel-drive minivan line intended both for the European and U.S. markets. With minivans, the issue is size. Narrower minivans are better for narrow European roads, but U.S. consumers perceive them as somewhat small.[43]

Another crucial aspect of global strategy to market automobiles is the poor showing of U.S. auto companies in Japan. The United States' 3 percent market share in Japan is about what Japan's share of the U.S. market was in the early 1970s. To increase market shares in Japan, the Big Three U.S. auto manufacturers plan to offer right-hand drive cars, increase the number of dealers in Japan, and import cars from Europe as well as from the United States. [44]

GM and the Czech Republic

The counterpart to global strategy is implementation and adaptation in individual markets. An example comes from GM's move in the Czech Republic, a market that is dominated by cars produced by the local Skoda Company. Skoda's locally manufactured compact cars have long dominated the Czech market; the company sold 95,000 cars in 1992 out of a total market of about 120,000 cars. Its low manufacturing costs and basic design mean that even the cheapest imported car costs several thousand dollars more than the Skoda Felicia. While foreign cars captured about one-third of the market in 1994, they were mostly higher-priced cars.

Following 1992, rising local wages and a drop in tariffs on imported cars, together with an appreciation of the Czech koruna (partly tied to a strong deutsche mark) led to higher prices for Skoda's compact cars. This gave GM's Opel division the opening to grab market share in the Czech Republic. GM began importing cars from its Spanish factory, aided by a weak peseta. Moreover, it imported a redesigned Corsa Eco, a stripped-down hatchback with two doors and no radio or power steering. Dealer margins were cut. These actions together allowed Opel to price its Eco at about $8,700, just $500 above Skoda's cheapest car. As a result, GM sold 600 cars in one month, seven times the usual sales level. In an immediate reaction, Ford, Seat, and Fiat all cut their prices, making the Czech market more competitive at the low end. Skoda in turn expanded capacity and increased exports, focusing on Germany and the United Kingdom.[45]

Summary: Overall Strategy Issues in the Global Automobile Industry

Based on the above brief examples, the following steps may be necessary to develop a global market position in automobiles:

1. Developing the right car for a market in a timely fashion.

2. Cutting costs by designing cars that need fewer parts and fewer labor hours to produce and by developing long-term supplier partnerships to improve quality and reduce costs over the model life.

3. Attaining national and regional market balance by defending and maintaining market share in the major markets of Japan, the United States, and Europe. For U.S. car companies, market share in Japan has to be increased. In Europe, with trade barriers falling by the year 2000, a shakeout is likely because there are far too many manufacturers for a relatively stagnant market. The emerging markets of Asia and Latin America are the areas of future growth, and here government regulations, alliances with local firms, and risk management are keys to long-term success.

4. Achieving financial strength and improving cash flow management are important in what is a cyclical business. Toyota holds an unbelievably strong position with a cash hoard of over $50 billion.

5. Diversifying, as Honda did with its strong motorcycle business, and as GM did with the integration of Hughes' electronics and EDS' computer systems.

6. Overcoming government barriers to trade that prevent strong competitors from developing market share around the world. The United States and Japan have long been at odds over U.S. access to the Japanese car market; the Europeans have also shut out Japanese competitors, although this barrier is scheduled to fall in the year 2000. A threat on the horizon is South Korea, which will achieve a domestic production capacity of around 5 million units by 1998 while having a domestic market of only 2 million units.

The Global PC Market[46]

The U.S. market has embraced PCs in no uncertain fashion, spurring on innovative PC manufacturers and retailers. The 1990s saw PC demand begin to boom in Europe and Asia, and by 1995, the European home-PC market was about 10.5 million units and $22 billion in sales, as compared to the U.S. market of 9.5 million units and $16 billion in sales (see the table that follows). Moreover, the lower penetration rates of PCs in households meant that much of future PC demand growth would come from Europe and Asia. While 39 percent of U.S. households have PCs, Germany has 30 percent; United Kingdom, 25 percent; France, 22 percent; and Japan, 21 percent.

Much of the growing PC demand is for multimedia computers, with demand rising as prices fall below $1,000. U.S.-made software is also available in multiple languages. U.S. manufacturers such as Compaq that are seeking to target the Asian market (where home PC sales exceeded business sales for the first time in 1995) have focused on six issues:

1. *Building brand image, and emotion-based advertising campaigns,* on the basis that PCs are becoming a home appliance. Brands do matter in the U.S. PC business. An October 1995 survey showed that customers were willing to pay a premium for branded PCs from IBM, Compaq, H-P, Dell, and Apple. Brands may matter because of technological insecurity on the part of the customer and because PCs are becoming commodities insofar as their circuitry and components are concerned. The "Intel inside" campaign is an appeal to customers to seek branded components over and above the PC brand itself.

2. *Multiple retail distribution points.* For example, Packard Bell started selling its computers at Tower Records in Singapore during the Christmas season. While major U.S. manufacturers such as Dell and Gateway have become industry leaders using the direct sales mail-order channel, there are cultural barriers in using such channels in overseas markets. Customers may be reluctant to commit significant financial resources to buying a computer sight unseen. Hence it might be necessary for a manufacturer to have retail showrooms.

3. *Developing support and service networks.* While many customers are familiar with computers at their office, they may need help setting up a home computer. Internet-based access to hot lines that have the ability to do remote diagnostics via modem and then download new software "fixes" are a recent innovation, as is the use of a nationwide network of third-party maintenance and service agents.

4. *PC designs.* Some are made to fit in with living room decor, such as Acer's emerald green home PCs or a combined TV/computer. Apple's new Imac is another example of innovative design that boosts sales.

5. *Overseas manufacturing capacity.* Developing a significant foreign market share requires building overseas, cost-competitive manufacturing capacity responsive to local needs. For the U.S. industry as a whole, foreign PC sales are about half of total sales, with the added attraction of higher margins on overseas sales.

6. *A stage-by-stage Asian market penetration.* For example Dell's approach focused first on Japan and Australia, then on Hong Kong, Singapore, and Malaysia.

Forecasted Home PC Sales, 1995–2000

	PCs Sold (Millions)	Sales ($ Billions)
1995		
Europe and Asia	10.5	$22
United States	9.5	16
2000		
Europe and Asia	25.0	48
United States	16.0	27

Other Asian markets are to follow. Forecasting Asian markets to account for 30 percent of global PC sales in the year 2000, future stages include a planned manufacturing facility in Penang, Malaysia, and service centers across Asia prior to intensified direct selling campaigns.

In this context, it is interesting to consider why Japanese firms have traditionally lagged behind the United States in gaining market share in the global PC industry. Their relative failure might have been due to several factors, including a small, domestic Japanese market whose growth was stunted by competing proprietary standards; U.S. manufacturers' scale economies and access to low-cost components produced in the Far East; and mail-order firms such as Dell dominating the price-conscious end of the market, leaving little room for the Japanese to follow their traditional strategy of first winning market share at the low end. U.S. firms also had entrenched advantages of strong brand images, nationwide service networks, control of distribution channels—particularly retail shelf space—and large discounts and subsidies to the retail channel to promote product and train customers. U.S. firms were also able to listen to and learn from their large customer base, leading to a rapid rate of product innovation—a moving target that was difficult for the Japanese to focus on.

The U.S. market is a market where selling to the home is dominated by a few superstore retailers such as CompUSA, and obtaining shelf space may be the crucial factor in success in the home PC market. Hitachi's strategy to enter the U.S. market is worth noting:

◆ As PCs are becoming a commodity business, scale and low cost matter.

◆ 500,000 units represents minimum break-even scale for Hitachi.

◆ This requires that Hitachi grab significant share in the fast-growing Japanese market, which would provide a base from which to attack the U.S. market.

◆ In the United States, the best segments to be targeted would be high-end notebooks and servers for PC-based networks. While the home market is growing fast, it offers lower margins and is a highly competitive business with distribution channels clogged with product from the established market shareholders. Hence, a strategy of selling higher-margin, business-oriented PCs, servers, and notebooks allows some cross-subsidization to build market share in the home PC business where initial losses are likely.

◆ Building U.S. market share might require subsidizing the PC business with profits from manufacturing memory chips.

◆ Building a profitable business might take several years; hence, financial strength to withstand subpar performance is necessary.

GLOBAL MARKETING

Apple and the PC Industry

Apple has long distinguished itself in the personal computer world by making and selling computers based on a proprietary operating system standard: Until 1995 it was unwilling to license its operating system to other manufacturers seeking to manufacture Apple-compatible clones. Because it had no clone competitors to innovate hardware and software advances, it had to spend more on research and development to keep up with developments in the industry. Research and development costs must be spread over the unit volume of Apple computers sold, and because Apple held less than 10 percent of the total personal computer market as of 1995, its unit R&D cost was high.

Apple's early technological lead of a graphical operating system, its suitability for desktop publishing, use of images, and digital video production and editing allowed it to charge premium prices. But as the Intel/Windows standard began catching up and offering roughly comparable performance at lower prices, Apple found it hard to convince customers to pay high prices for the privilege of using the Mac standard.

Outside the United States, a key element of Apple's strategy was its penetration of the Japanese market. The Japanese were slower to adopt the PC compared to the U.S. market, and major manufacturers such as NEC had developed their own distinct and incompatible proprietary standards. Hence, Apple's Mac standard was not a disadvantage in Japan, as the IBM PC standard was not yet established. Moreover, Apple's graphical interface had been adapted to the Japanese *kanji* alphabet, making it more appealing to Japanese users. A brand image–oriented marketing campaign allowed Apple to increase its share of the Japanese market from 2 percent in 1990 to 15 percent in 1994 and earn gross margins of nearly 50 percent.

1995 saw a major change in Apple's Japanese fortunes as Windows became more established and Japanese manufacturers began adopting the Windows standard. Fujitsu launched a major PC price war, seeking to boost its market share from 9 percent in 1994 to one-third of the market by 1997. As a result, Apple's market share growth in Japan was

♦ Decentralized U.S.-based management with control over design and manufacturing, principally assembly of imported components, could be essential to long-term success in the U.S. market.

♦ Acquisitions of smaller U.S. PC firms may be crucial to developing U.S. market presence. Success may stem from a volume-based strategy that follows from a simple premise: Today's value-added products are tomorrow's commodity products. Technological changes can also threaten PCs, with manufacturers who guess wrong on the technological preferences of home-computer buyers likely to be ignored in the marketplace. Home PC buyers bought the Pentium-based advanced PCs in larger numbers than businesses, and a leading company such as Packard Bell lost sales and market share when it introduced 75MHz-Pentium PCs only to find that home buyers wanted the faster 100-MHz PCs. Another threat comes in the form of networked PCs, costing under $500 and connecting to the Internet. These PCs have specialized video and audio capabilities and allow the user to utilize software, computing power, and storage from the Internet.[47]

SUMMARY

Most companies are being forced into marketing their products or services globally because (1) demand for their products is global and (2) they face global competition.

Global marketing strategy must form part of, and be consistent with, a firm's overall global strategy. Linkages exist between the two in areas such as technology, manufacturing, organization structure, and finance.

halted, and margins dropped sharply, down to 20 percent. Since Japan accounted for a fifth of Apple's sales, this hurt Apple's overall performance. The company could no longer count on Japanese profits to provide a cushion against the effects of a more competitive U.S. market. Declining profits and market share in its two key markets meant that Apple had to rethink its strategy for the personal computer market.

Apple's Strategic Problems

For Apple to recover market share in global markets, solutions to several issues must be considered:

Apple's research and development costs as a percentage of sales are high in relation to the Wintel standard. For example, Compaq's research and development costs are 4 percent lower than Apple's.

Apple incurs high marketing costs, about 15 percent of sales, to push and sustain the Apple brand; PC manufacturers' marketing costs are around 10 to 11 percent.

Differentiation is being reduced as Microsoft's Windows 95 becomes as easy to use as the Apple operating system.

Competition is increasing in Japan, a key, high-profit Apple market. As a result, margins are falling.

Apple has been forced to cut prices in the United States and elsewhere to compete against Wintel, cutting margins despite higher costs. As a result, its gross margins declined from 28 percent in the quarter ended December 1994 to about 18 percent for the December 1995 quarter.

Once customers are lost to the Wintel standard they do not come back, because of lower prices and the investment in software and in learning. They also become accustomed to the multiplicity of vendors from whom they can buy products and software as needed.

Further, Apple is weak in the business market, a higher-end market segment with greater likelihood of repeat purchases and product upgrading.

Apple has experienced shortages of units in the retail channel at crucial selling seasons because it has underestimated demand.

Apple has had to contend with shortages and late deliveries of critical, specialized components unique to Apple

Formulating global strategy begins with corporate strategies that cut across product lines. Then product-line strategies are formed, influenced by the industry, the firm's competitive advantage, and its value-added chain. Other important influences are the environment, competition, government actions, and the firm's customers and suppliers.

Next, the firm sets product-line strategy for individual markets. It also considers whether to standardize policies across markets or adapt them to individual markets.

Basic strategies are to become the lowest-cost producer, provide a differentiated product, or seek government protection against foreign competition. Configuration and coordination decisions follow. In configuring value-added activities, companies typically choose between market extension, a multidomestic perspective, and a global perspective.

Some of the variables to be considered in adopting a global perspective include differences in global markets, customers, and competition; different host-government policies, technology, and production resources; and the time factor.

The government's policies can influence strategy by keeping foreign competition out and by subsidizing the global strategies of national champion firms.

A company may be willing to sacrifice short-term profits for higher market share, or it may place priority on its competitive position worldwide rather than in specific national markets. This suggests that a portfolio approach to individual national markets may be shortsighted, causing a firm to cede competitive position to other multinationals with longer-term orientations.

Global competitors emerge by (1) diversifying out of national markets that they dominate, (2) diversifying into new products, or (3) extending their product lines into new product segments. Suppliers are another source of competition.

Macs. Component manufacturers were stretched because PC demand was growing at over 20 percent in 1995, and high demand in the Windows PC market (90 percent of the total market) was more attractive than for the Apple standard, which requires product modification and involves smaller volumes. As a result, Apple could not get components on time, and had to wait as long as 18 weeks for specialized ASICs (application specific integrated circuits). This hamstrung its attempts to expand production to keep pace with sales.

As Apple's decline gathered steam, Apple went through two CEOs before calling back founder Steve Jobs as its new temporary CEO, while he still held a major ownership stake

and management interest in Pixar, a state-of-the-art film animation company. Jobs spun off several Apple products such as Newton, its handheld palmtop organizer, and concentrated on a newly designed Apple Mac that would parallel the performance of the IBM PC compatible world. His bold new design, transparent housing, green-gray color, and overall radically innovative look, coupled with a competitive price won back many Apple fans, with Apple becoming the best-selling personal computer in late 1998. Whether this represents the first step on the comeback trail is hard to predict, but Apple's initial recovery owed a great deal to customer-oriented product innovation, to competitive matching, and to original product design, in its aesthetic sense.

Sources: See "Apple Is Facing Widespread Shortages of Its Products," *The Wall Street Journal,* August 11, 1995; "Apple Likely Loss May Spur Cutbacks, Merger," December 18, 1995; and "Apple Is Getting Battered in Japan, Too," December 18, 1995.

Factors leading to adaptation in global marketing strategy include differences in customers; marketing infrastructure; legal, transportation, and communication systems; and distribution channels. In general, national markets are sufficiently different that adaptation in some elements of the marketing mix is necessary.

Another component of a global marketing system is market position: Should the company aim to sell the same product to different segments in the various country markets or sell to the same segment in each country with some product adaptation?

Coordinating the global marketing system is a complex task. Some common methods include using similar marketing approaches across countries, transferring marketing know-how and experience, sequencing marketing programs across countries, and integrating approaches to multinational clients.

Management must decide which countries to target. Factors relevant to this decision include the market size and growth, the product life cycle stage in that market, the level of competition, the similarity to markets already served, and the influence of government restrictions. In general, multinationals seek market position in all three of the triad economy regions: the United States, Europe, and Japan.

Another challenge is to respond to regional integration, such as the creation of Europe's Single Market. Alliances and acquisitions are two common approaches. The key goals are to obtain distribution and brand presence in a timely manner across Europe.

Another marketing challenge is selling to Japan. The critical issues are providing quality, overcoming the Japanese preference for domestic products, and working with complex distribution systems.

The unfolding of global strategy can be seen in examples from the automobile and PC industries.

QUESTIONS

6.1   Why must companies think globally?

6.2   What is a global industry?

6.3   How is marketing strategy linked to global strategy?

6.4   What are some factors that affect global strategy at the level of the firm?

6.5   How can management attitudes affect global strategy?

6.6 What are some factors that influence global strategy at the product-line level?

6.7 What is the value-added chain? How is it relevant to a firm in formulating a global strategy?

6.8 What are some goals that a firm might set for itself in individual country markets?

6.9 What are the basic strategies open to a firm in the global marketplace?

6.10 What does "configuring the value-added chain" mean? How do firms differ in their perspective on configuring the value-added chain in different countries?

6.11 What are some factors that lead a firm to think globally?

6.12 What is a "lead" market? Why is it important?

6.13 Give an example of how time and speed of response affect global competition.

6.14 Why is it dangerous to adopt a portfolio approach in international marketing?

6.15 How can government policies affect a firm's ability to compete globally?

6.16 Explain why standardization versus adaptation is a fundamental issue in international marketing.

6.17 Highlight the key issues in coordinating the global marketing system.

6.18 How would a firm target individual country markets?

6.19 How does European Union and the Euro affect a firm's global marketing strategy in Europe? Why have firms reacted by acquiring and merging with other European firms?

6.20 Discuss global competition and marketing strategy in the personal computer industry worldwide, and in the global auto industry.

ENDNOTES

1. Peter Drucker, "The Transnational Economy," *The Wall Street Journal,* August 25, 1987.

2. Gary Hamel and C. K. Prahalad, "Do You Really Have a Global Strategy?" *Harvard Business Review,* July–August 1985.

3. George S. Yip, "Global Strategy . . . in a World of Nations," *Sloan Management Review* (Fall 1989): 29–41; and "Industry Drivers of Global Strategy and Organization," *The International Executive,* September/October 1994, 529–556.

4. Hirotaka Takeuchi and M. Porter, "Three Roles of International Marketing in Global Strategy," Chapter 4 in *Competition in Global Industries,* ed. M. Porter (Boston: Harvard Business School Press, 1986).

5. Claudio Carpano, James J. Chrisman, and Kendall Roth, "International Strategy and Environment: An Assessment of the Performance Relationship" (Survey of U.S.–owned multinationals), *Journal of International Business Studies* 25, no. 3 (1994): 639–656.

6. S. Tamer Cavusgil and Shaoming Zou, "Marketing Strategy-Performance Relationship: An Investigation of the Empirical Link in Export Market Ventures," *Journal of Marketing* 58 (January 1994): 1–21.

7. William G. Egelhoff, "Great Strategy or Great Strategy Implementation—Two Ways of Competing in Global Markets" (Illustrated by U.S. and Japanese semiconductor firms), *Sloan Management Review* 34 (Winter 1993): 37–50.

8. Bruce Kogut, "Designing Global Strategies: Comparative and Competitive Value-Added Chains," *Sloan Management Review,* (Summer 1985), 15–27.

9. "Small Motors, Big Profits," *Forbes,* July 11, 1988.

10. M. Porter, "Competing in Global Industries: A Conceptual Framework," Chapter 1 in *Competition in Global Industries,* ed. M. Porter (Boston: Harvard Business School Press, 1986).

11. See Thomas Hout, M. E. Porter, and E. Rudden, "How Global Companies Win Out," *Harvard Business Review,* September–October 1982.

12. "Tired of Poor Returns, Many Japanese Send Their Savings Abroad," *The Wall Street Journal,* December 26, 1995.

13. *Komatsu Ltd.,* Harvard Business School Case Services #9-385-277.

14. Susan P. Douglas and C. Samuel Craig, "Evolution of Global Marketing Strategy: Scale, Scope, and Synergy," *Columbia Journal of World Business* 24, no. 3 (Fall 1989).

15. Kenichi Ohmae, *Triad Power: The Coming Shape of Global Competition* (New York: Free Press, 1985).

16. Jean-Pierre Jeannet and H. Hennessey, *International Marketing Management* (Boston: Houghton-Mifflin, 1988), Chapter 8, 259.

17 U.S. International Trade Commission, "Foreign Protection of Intellectual Property Rights and the Effect on U.S. Industry and Trade," *Report to the U.S. Trade Representative,* Investigation No. 332-245, Publication 2065, February 1988.

18 Adam M. Brandenburger and Barry J. Nalebuff, "The Right Game: Use Game Theory to Shape Strategy," *Harvard Business Review,* July/August 1995, 57–71.

19 George Stalk, "Time—The Next Source of Competitive Advantage," *Harvard Business Review* 66, no. 4 (July–August 1988).

20 Ibid., 45.

21 See also Joseph L. Bower and Thomas Hout, "Fast-Cycle Capability for Competitive Power," *Harvard Business Review* 66, no. 6 (November–December 1988).

22 "Japanese Computer Firms See a Market in Domestic Customers' U.S. Operations," *The Wall Street Journal,* May 4, 1988.

23 "All Shapes and Sizes: A Survey of the Civil Aerospace Industry," *The Economist,* September 3, 1988.

24 "S. Korean Cars: Foreign Devils," *The Economist,* October 21, 1995.

25 "Now Detroit's Artillery Is Trained on Seoul," *Business Week,* September 25, 1995; and "Rivals' Concern Deepens as S. Korea Drives into the European Auto Market," *The Wall Street Journal,* October 23, 1995.

26 "Biotech Goes Glitzy," *The Economist,* August 29, 1992.

27 "Thomson: Battling On," *The Economist,* July 15, 1989.

28 Yves Doz and C. K. Prahalad, *The Multinational Mission* (New York: Free Press, 1987).

29 "When Made-in-Europe Isn't," *The Economist,* October 8, 1988.

30 D. Szymanski, S. G. Bharadwaj, and P. R. Varadarajan, "Standardization versus Adaptation of International Marketing Strategy," *Journal of Marketing* 57 (October 1993): 11.

31 Ibid., 13.

32 Yves Doz and C. K. Prahalad, "The Dynamics of Global Competition," in *The Multinational Mission* (New York: Free Press, 1987), 47–48.

33 Takeuchi and Porter, "Three Roles of International Marketing in Global Strategy."

34 Keith Brouthers, "The Influence of International Risk on Entry Mode Strategy in the Computer Software Industry," *Management International Review* 35, no. 1 (1995): 7–28.

35 Somkid Jatuspritak, Liam Fahey, and Philip Kotler, "Strategic Global Marketing: Lessons from the Japanese," *Columbia Journal of World Business* 2, no. 1 (Spring 1985): 47–53.

36 "Getting Ready for the Great North American Shakeout," *Business Week,* April 4, 1988.

37 "Ways into Fortress Japan," *The Economist,* October 22, 1988.

38 "Foreign Business in Japan: Drive on, Fritz," *The Economist,* October 22, 1988.

39 "Alex Trotman's Goal: To Make Ford No. 1 in World Auto Sales," *The Wall Street Journal,* July 18, 1995.

40 "Ford Opens Throttle," *Business Week,* September 18, 1995.

41 "Toyota Names a Chief Likely to Shake up Global Auto Business," *The Wall Street Journal,* August 11, 1995.

42 "Japanese Car Makers Speed up Car Making," *The Wall Street Journal,* December 29, 1995.

43 "Can Opel Deliver the 'World Cars' GM Needs?" *Business Week,* December 4, 1995.

44 "U.S. Auto Makers Revamp Lineups, Strategies to Expand in Japanese Market," *The Wall Street Journal,* October 25, 1995.

45 "GM's Opel Dents Czech Auto Market," *The Wall Street Journal,* November 9, 1995.

46 This section draws on a variety of sources: "Personal Computers: The End of Good Times?" *The Economist,* December 9, 1995; "Dell Computer," *Financial World,* October 24, 1995; and *The Wall Street Journal:* "PC Shipments in the U.S. Top Estimates," December 18, 1995; "Compaq Maintains Hold on PC Market," August 8, 1995; "Japan's PC Firms Boot Up to Invade U.S.," November 3, 1995; "Computer 2000 Aims to Expand," November 6, 1995; and "Marketing Plays a Bigger Role in Distinguishing PCs," October 16, 1995.

47 "Will Your Next Computer Be a Tin Can and a Wire?" *The Economist,* October 14, 1995.

FURTHER READINGS

Brandenburger, Adam M., and Barry J. Nalebuff. "The Right Game: Use Game Theory to Shape Strategy." *Harvard Business Review,* July/August 1995, 57–71.

Brouthers, Keith. "The Influence of International Risk on Entry Mode Strategy in the Computer Software Industry." *Management International Review* 35, no. 1 (1995): 7–28.

Cavusgil, S. Tamer, and Shaoming Zou. "Marketing Strategy-Performance Relationship: An Investigation of the Empirical Link in Export Market Ventures." *Journal of Marketing* 58 (January 1994): 1–21.

Dertouzos, Michael, Richard Lester, Robert Solow, et al. *Made in America.* Cambridge, MA: MIT Press, 1989.

Douglas, Susan, and Dong Kee Rhee. "Examining Generic Competitive Strategy Types in U.S. and European Markets." *Journal of International Business Studies* 20 (Fall 1989): 437–463.

Doz, Yves, and C. K. Prahalad. *The Multinational Mission.* New York: Free Press, 1987.

Egelhoff, William G. "Great Strategy or Great Strategy Implementation—Two Ways of Competing in Global Markets" (illustrated by U.S. and Japanese semiconductor firms). *Sloan Management Review* 34 (Winter 1993): 37–50.

Ghoshal, Sumantra. "Global Strategy: An Organizing Framework." *Strategic Management Journal,* September–October 1987, 425–440.

Hamel, Gary, and C. K. Prahalad. "Do You Really Have a Global Strategy?" *Harvard Business Review,* July–August 1985.

Hampton, Gerald M., and Erwin Buske. "The Global Marketing Perspective." In *Advances in International Marketing,* vol. 2, ed. S. Tamer Cavusgil. Greenwich, CT: JAI Press, 1987.

Hout, Thomas, M. E. Porter, and E. Rudden. "How Global Companies Win Out." *Harvard Business Review,* September–October 1982.

Kogut, Bruce. "Designing Global Strategies: Comparative and Competitive Value-Added Chains." *Sloan Management Review,* Summer 1985, 15–27.

Ohmae, Kenichi. *Triad Power: The Coming Shape of Global Competition.* New York: Free Press, 1985.

Porter, M., ed. *Competition in Global Industries.* Boston: Harvard Business School Press, 1986, especially Chapter 1, "Competing in Global Industries: A Conceptual Framework."

Quelch, John A., and Edward J. Hoff. "Customizing Global Marketing." *Harvard Business Review,* May–June 1986.

Stalk, George. "Time—The Next Source of Competitive Advantage." *Harvard Business Review,* July–August 1988.

Szymanski, D., S. G. Bharadwaj, and P. R. Varadarajan. "Standardization versus Adaptation of International Marketing Strategy." *Journal of Marketing* 57 (October 1993): 1–17.

Takeuchi, Hirotaka, and M. Porter. "Three Roles of International Marketing in Global Strategy." In *Competition in Global Industries,* ed. M. Porter. Boston: Harvard Business School Press, 1986.

Windmere Corporation

Windmere Corporation, headquartered in Miami Lakes, Florida, sells a variety of hair, beauty, and personal care products to consumers and to the professional (barber shop and beauty salon) market. It celebrated its 25th year in business in 1988. Windmere is one of the largest U.S. suppliers of curling irons and curling brushes and is a leading seller of hand-held hair dryers, instant hair setters, and lighted cosmetic mirrors. It introduced its first 1,000-watt hair dryer in 1973. Its current product line includes the Crimper, an appliance that adds texture and volume to hair with a permanent wave effect; kitchen appliances such as toasters and fans; air fresheners; and the Clothes Shaver, which is designed to remove lint and fuzz from woolen, linen, and other garments. Table 1 summarizes Windmere's major product lines.

TABLE 1	Windmere's Major Product Lines

Personal Care Products

Hair dryers; Clothes Shaver fabric lint and fuzz remover, and electric shavers; health and beauty aids; lighted makeup mirrors; combs and brushes; cosmetics; Plac Trac plaque remover; and shower massagers.

Professional Sales Products

Professional hair styling tools, nail care accessories, combs, and brushes.

Home Electrical Appliances

Ceiling and table fans, heaters; manufacturing subcontracted toasters, blenders, and hand mixers.

Environmental Products

Air filtration and air cleaning devices and fragrance-added air fresheners.

Lodging Industry

Hotel amenities, such as wall-mounted hair dryers and lighted mirrors.

Windmere Production Policies

Most of these products are manufactured in Hong Kong and China by the Durable Electrical Metal Factory Ltd., an 80 percent owned manufacturing operation. Windmere first subcontracted with Durable in 1972 and acquired a 50 percent joint interest in it in the late 1970s. Windmere chose Durable as its local joint venture partner because it had the contacts and expertise in the People's Republic of China (PRC). Windmere faced production constraints in Hong Kong with labor shortages and rising wage rates. Therefore, in 1981, Durable expanded capacity by setting up a factory in mainland China.

In January 1989, Windmere bought out a portion of its joint venture partner's interest in Durable to become an 80 percent owner of the Durable facilities in Hong Kong and mainland China.

The Durable factory is vertically integrated, manufacturing its own tools, dies, and injection molding equipment. Besides manufacturing components, it also carries out quality testing and assembly. Advantages to owning production facilities in China include the following:

◆ The ability to maintain a continuous flow of new products with innovative designs that lower costs of production.

◆ Provision of tooling for new products at low cost.

◆ Reduction of the lag between product innovation and market launch.

♦ Flexible production scheduling to be able to accelerate or reduce production of product items based on sales performance, thus reducing inventory buildup and risk of inventory obsolescence.

♦ Control over quality during every phase of manufacturing to meet the rigorous standards of the U.S. market.

Durable is one of the largest low-cost producers of small appliances in the Far East. Of a total of 1.7 million square feet of factory space, 1.5 million feet are located in the PRC, where about 80 percent of Windmere's products are manufactured. The rest of the factory space is in Hong Kong. Of approximately 12,000 employees, 10,000 are in mainland China, which makes Windmere one of China's largest foreign employers.

The Durable factory facilities are expanded and upgraded constantly. For example, Durable's capabilities have been expanded to include motor manufacturing, electroplating, anodizing, spray painting, and powder coating. The bulk of Durable's sales go to Windmere. Durable also manufactures new products such as toasters, blenders, hand mixers, air cleaners, soft contact lens cleaners, waffle irons, heaters, and other home appliances for third parties, such as Sunbeam, Waring, Rival, Krupps, Bausch & Lomb, and Trion. These third-party sales allow existing capacity to be utilized to a great degree, leading to increased recovery of fixed costs. The decision to seek third-party business was first made in 1985 when excess capacity developed because Windmere reduced its purchases from Durable because of poor sales in the United States.

Table 2 summarizes the role of the Durable plant in Windmere's operations through 1988, just before Windmere acquired control of Durable. Windmere's share of profits in 1988 from its Durable manufacturing plant was about $5.7 million. Over the years, it accumulated earnings of $67 million from its foreign operations, on which no taxes were paid because the profits had not been repatriated to the United States, but were used to reinvest in expanding foreign operations.

Table 3 summarizes Durable's in-house and third-party sales for the period 1989–1991.

Windmere's banner year in 1988, when Durable dramatically increased its sales to Windmere and to third parties, was instrumental in Windmere's decision to acquire 80 percent control of the Durable facility. Expansion at Durable increased its break-even sales level in 1989 to $130 million. Windmere's acquiring control of Durable coincided with a period of reduced sales at Windmere due to a weak U.S. retail environment. The reduced utilization of the Durable manufacturing capacity meant that Windmere's gross margins were negatively affected by underabsorbed overhead in manufacturing. Windmere had to restructure its Durable operations and reduce capacity to cut the break-even amount to below $100 million by the end of 1990. Such restructuring extended to appointing Sam Yung, a Hong Kong manager with 20 years of manufacturing experience, as the executive director at Durable.

Implications of Manufacturing in the PRC

The Durable manufacturing facility is located in Bao An county, in Guangdong province, about 1,200 miles south of Beijing. It supplies 85 to 90 percent of Windmere's products. Building on its expertise in China, Windmere has begun helping other companies that want to develop manufacturing operations in China. It helped an embroidery manufacturer set up factories in Hong Kong and China in return for a percentage of profits of the venture. It plans to develop its consulting expertise in this area.

However, investing in expanding manufacturing operations in China increases Windmere's fixed costs. Capacity must be utilized, which means that Windmere must continue to sell the output of the Durable factory. As Tables 2 and 3 show, Durable's output fell in 1985 and then again between 1989 and 1991. Because the Chinese and Hong Kong factories are distant from the principal market, the United States, Windmere must cope with inventory shortages in the United States by shipping products air freight, which adds to total delivery costs. The additional time needed to move goods from the Far East factories to the United States means that additional inventories must be maintained, resulting in higher working capital and carrying costs. At the end of December 1991, the combined inventories of Windmere and Durable totaled $69 million, compared to a total cost of goods sold for the year of $104 million.

U.S. government attitudes toward China also affect Windmere. On June 4, 1989, the Chinese army moved against students demonstrating in Tiananmen Square. Investors began to worry about the safety of investments in mainland China. Production declined in Windmere's Chinese factories, and its stock price fell from a high of $27 to below $10. Several U.S. representatives and senators began to question the granting of most-favored-nation status to China. In July 1992, Congress approved a bill that would have linked the continuation of China's most-favored-nation status to human rights in China. President Bush vetoed the legislation, but if such legislation were to pass, elimination of most-favored-nation status for goods coming from China could result in high tariffs, making Windmere's Chinese imports into the United States uncompetitive.

TABLE 2	Durable Manufacturing Company Profile (Millions of Dollars)			
	Total Sales[a]	*Durable Sales (In-House)*	*Percent Manufactured in the People's Republic of China*	*Number of Employees*
1988	$181.1	$100	83%	12,000
1987	71.5	55	80	7,500
1986	35.3	28	50	6,000
1985	26.4	17	—	—
1984	46.2	33	—	—

[a]Includes intercompany sales to Windmere.

In 1991 the U.S. trade representative's office began investigating China's trade practices and its inadequate protection of intellectual property. If the negotiations and discussions with China on these topics are not resolved to U.S. satisfaction, Chinese imports could face higher tariffs.

Efforts to Expand Sales

Because of the fixed costs of the PRC facility, Windmere must continue to expand its U.S. sales to continue using its factories in China effectively. It has focused on developing a family of brand names in addition to private branding and OEM (original equipment manufacturer) business, as well as developing additional product lines to push through its distribution channels.

Windmere has concentrated on developing brand identities for each of its major product lines. It has tried to develop its flagship consumer products Windmere brand name

TABLE 3	Durable Manufacturing Company Sales, 1989–1991 (Millions of Dollars)	
	In-House	*Third Party*
1989	$75	$40
1990	69	28
1991	63	25

with a national TV campaign around the theme, "It doesn't cost a fortune to look like a million." Its professional salon products from the Belson products division are marketed under the Salon Designs, Pro Star, and Premiere brand names; professional nail care such as the European Secrets line and brushes and combs are marketed under the Comare brand name. Cosmetics are sold through the Jerome Alexander name, and lodging industry amenities are differentiated with the Jerdon name. This has enabled Windmere to gain large national retail clients such as Wal-Mart, Eckerd Drug, Service Merchandise, Kmart, Target, Caldor, and Lechmere.

New Products

Windmere has upgraded mature products such as the hair dryer with a hands-free design and by adding an appliance leakage circuit interrupter (ALCI), which protects against electric shock, meeting new safety standards. Windmere also introduced shock protector plugs that incorporate ground fault circuit interrupters that protect against electrical surges. This allows consumers to convert ordinary electrical appliances to shockproof appliances; such plugs represent an entry into the home-improvement industry. Windmere manufactures its own ALCIs and can thus obtain slightly lower costs.

Windmere's new-product introductions have included the Clothes Shaver and the Crimper. Its new EnviroResearch line of air filtration appliances includes technology for dispensing fragrances without using aerosol sprays or powders.

Windmere has also branched out into selling fans, humidifiers, heaters, and other seasonal products through a 50 percent owned joint venture with Paragon Sales; this joint-venture sales company is now one of the three largest distributors of

TABLE 4	Windmere Corporation Revenue Breakdown by Geographic Region (Millions of Dollars)				
	Total Sales	*U.S. Sales*	*International Sales*	*Gross Margins (Percent)*	*Net Income*
1991	$141.6	$ 82.4	$59.2	26.6%	$−9.5
1990	154.8	84.1	70.8	29.5	−3.7
1989	178.7	96.8	81.9	30.6	7.7
1988	193.3	145.0	48.3	41.1	32.6
1987	145.2	113.3	32.0	40.0	11.9
1986	95.3	79.1	16.2	39.6	5.2
1985	91.0	74.9	16.1	38.4	−4.3
1984	91.0	76.3	12.4	39.6	5.9
1983	73.6	66.1	6.5	41.6	7.3

electric oscillating fans in the United States. (Windmere previously distributed Australian-made Mistral fans on an exclusive basis before selling oscillating fans under the Windmere brand name.) The fans are manufactured at the Durable factory.

Windmere has attempted to develop new market segments by combining its lighted makeup mirrors with a wall-mounted hair dryer and by directly marketing these appliance amenities to hotel chains such as Sheraton and Radisson.

Windmere formerly sold to the professional barber and beauty trade through a chain of 151 Save-Way beauty supply stores, concentrated principally in the Southeast United States: Florida to Virginia and west to Alabama. It sold the Save-Way beauty supply line of business for approximately $24 million in 1989.

At one point, Windmere licensed the Ronson brand name and sold rotary-head electric shavers purchased from a Japanese supplier. The market leader was Norelco, which sells products manufactured by Philips of the Netherlands. Norelco promptly accused Windmere of patent violations and initially won the case on grounds of unintentional patent infringement. As a result, Windmere wrote off $1.4 million in inventory and tooling and decided to abandon the rotary electric shaver market. However, it appealed the judgment and Philips was subsequently found guilty of monopolizing the market. Windmere was awarded damages and re-entered the shaver market. Philips in turn has appealed and the matter is still in the courts.

In addition, in October 1990, Lasko Metal Products, one of Windmere's competitors, petitioned the U.S. International Trade Commission (USITC) to impose antidumping coun-

tervailing duties on fans imported from China. Windmere imports such fans through its Paragon 50 percent joint venture. In October 1991, the USITC ruled that dumping was taking place but that Windmere fans imported through the joint venture were not being dumped and hence did not have to pay the higher anti-dumping duties.

Windmere's International Marketing Focus

Windmere's international sales occur in Canada, Europe, Latin America, and the Far East (see Table 4). Products are supplied in foreign markets through a company-owned trading company based in Hong Kong and Canadian and Dutch subsidiaries. Windmere closed Hairflayre, its joint-venture subsidiary in the United Kingdom, due to poor results, choosing to use established independent distributors instead. Windmere adapted products for the United Kingdom and European markets, including a European-style variable temperature hair dryer and a mini dual-voltage hair dryer for worldwide travel. Windmere also has selected distributors for Far Eastern markets, particularly in China, Taiwan, and Korea. It uses independent distributors to penetrate new markets in Japan and Australia.

Recent Windmere Actions

1991 after-tax losses were $9.5 million, greater than 1990 losses of $3.7 million. Slow-selling inventories had to be written off due to obsolescence, and several customer bankruptcies led to bad debt write-offs in the United States. To improve finances, Windmere repatriated approximately $7.8 million of foreign earnings, offsetting these against U.S. losses to produce no significant tax liability.

Windmere has achieved success in the past by relying on Chinese labor, paid 30 cents an hour. Will this be a strategy for continued success in the future, or is Windmere on shaky ground in continuing to base its international business around manufacturing in China for sale to the United States and other international markets?

Questions

1. Has Windmere been successful? What are the elements of Windmere's international strategy?
2. What choices has Windmere made with regard to value added? How has it configured the value-added chain? Why?

3. Analyze Windmere's strategy in terms of comparative and competitive advantage. Do you see any weaknesses in its strategy choices?
4. What are the risks to Windmere of manufacturing in China? What other risks does Windmere face?
5. Analyze Windmere's product line. Are these differentiated products? What is your estimate of the demand for such products over the next three to five years in the United States, Europe, Japan, and the Far East? Could competition easily arise in these product lines?
6. What do you recommend that Windmere do over the next two to three years? For the longer term?

Case prepared by Professor Ravi Sarathy for use in class discussion. ©1993. All rights reserved.
Sources: Windmere Corporation Annual Reports 1987–1993; "Windmere Tries to Comb Out the Kinks," *Business Week,* July 24, 1989; and "U.S. Importers Aren't Jumping Ship—Yet," *Business Week,* June 26, 1989.

C A S E   6 . 2

A. L. Labs, Inc.

A. L. Labs manufactures and distributes generic pharmaceuticals and animal feed. The U.S. unit is majority owned and controlled by its Norwegian parent, A. L. Oslo; 1988 was the first year that U.S. sales accounted for more than 50 percent of total (worldwide) sales.

Animal-Feed Segment

A. L. Labs began operating in the United States by selling animal-feed additives. Patent protection on bacitracin had expired, and the Norwegian parent company developed a biologically stable and effective product branded as BMD, sold as an antibiotic mixed into feed to aid in animal growth and to prevent disease. Major U.S. markets were the broiler and swine industries. Since it left no residue in animal tissue and thus was not ingested by humans, BMD easily met the human safety standards of the U.S. Food and Drug Administration (FDA) and was able to boast an advantage over the penicillin, tetracycline, and sulfa products already on the market. Another ad-

vantage to BMD is that bacteria do not build up resistance to it as they do to penicillin and tetracycline. Sales of BMD and other bacitracin antibiotic products accounted for 16, 21, 24, and 25 percent of total company sales in 1988, 1987, 1986, and 1985, respectively.

New manufacturing processes helped raise quality and reduce production costs. In the United States, enhanced technical service marketing focused on educating potential users about the product's advantages. The company carried out a constant round of controlled animal tests to establish the optimal relationship between amounts of BMD used in its various formulations and animal weight gain. Such studies helped convince farmers that BMD in the most economic doses would work with a variety of modern animal-feed rations. Promotion of new potential applications led to rapid acceptance of BMD in the United States. It has achieved considerable penetration in the poultry market, and promotional efforts gradually raised penetration in the swine industry from 20 percent a few years ago to around 35 percent in 1988. It has continued to grow in recent years.

In 1982 A. L. Labs began manufacturing BMD in a U.S. plant in Chicago Heights, purchasing fermentation cultures from A. L. Oslo as well as paying annual royalties (of 2.5 percent on sales) in return for the license from the parent company to produce BMD in the United States; capacity has been expanded several times. By 1987, capacity limits had once again been reached at the Chicago Heights plant, and additional purchases of BMD from Norway were being made while plant expansion was being considered. Because the Danish krone had appreciated against the U.S. dollar, production costs had also increased, for imported BMD was more expensive than that produced in U.S. plants. In the years 1985 through 1988, A. L. Labs' purchases from its parent totaled $7 million, $9.3 million, $8 million, and $9 million, respectively, and license fees paid to the parent for the same period were $.6 million, $.8 million, $1 million, and $1.1 million, respectively. But such foreign sourcing is partly due to having a foreign parent company with a global manufacturing capability including factories in Copenhagen and Jakarta, Indonesia, as well as in the United States (in Chicago Heights, Baltimore, and Niagara Falls).

Subsequent to the success of BMD, new products introduced for the animal-feed market included Vitamin D3, a life-essential nutrient required by livestock and poultry for proper growth and health. Animals normally produce D3 when in contact with direct sunlight. But because commercial farming of livestock and poultry is done indoors in artificial light, D3 must be provided as a micronutrient feed additive. A. L. Labs' premium brand called ColorGuard Vitamin D3 is a brilliant blue, permitting visual verification that it has been mixed in the feed. Another new product is Solutracin, a water-soluble concentrated form of BMD for treatment of poultry diseases. Plans are to extend the use of BMD to the cattle market and to improve the efficiency of marketing to animal-feed markets to take advantage of the growing consolidation of farms and the trend to large farms.

Table 1 provides information on the proportion of revenues derived at A. L. Labs from each of its three major product segments, as well as from overseas sales. As can be seen, the company has gradually increased the proportion of its business derived from the United States; at the same time, it has diversified away from animal feed so that its principal product line now is pharmaceuticals, specifically generic pharmaceuticals.

Generic Pharmaceutical Segment

By 1985 A. L. Labs had begun focusing on the distribution of generic pharmaceuticals and increasing its presence in U.S. markets. This shift was based on the satisfactory results from acquiring Dumex Ltd., headquartered in Copenhagen, Denmark. Dumex functions partly as a European development division, building on known pharmaceuticals and formulat-

ing and shepherding new drug applications through the approval process in Europe. Dumex also can obtain Danish government funding for new drug projects.

For example, Dumex obtained a grant to work with physicians in developing a treatment for a skin disorder, acne rosacea, that is generally treated with antibiotics, which may lead to undesirable side effects and resistance problems. Metronidazole, a generic antibacterial drug, was combined with Decubal, an existing Dumex skin cream. The result was a new drug, Elyzol, which has already received approval in Sweden and Denmark and captured a dominant market share. The drug is now being registered in other European countries and will soon be in the United States; clearly, there are opportunities for cross-fertilization of new drug discoveries between Europe and the United States. Dumex relied on sales reps to sell in Europe; but as new branded products have been created, it has taken more control of its sales, creating three new sales organizations alone in 1988 in West Germany, Switzerland, and Portugal.

Hence, in 1986 A. L. Labs acquired ParMed, a distributor of generic pharmaceuticals. Along with telemarketing to pharmacies, the company used an in-house magazine, *The Prescription,* to provide information about new generic pharmaceuticals and their profit potential (equal, the company claims, to that of branded drugs). ParMed helps independent pharmacists cope with the mandate to prescribe generics for Medicare-paid prescriptions. A side benefit for A. L. Labs is that telemarketing selling techniques perfected at ParMed can be tried out in foreign markets.

Diversification into Liquid Pharmaceuticals

In 1987, in A. L. Labs' biggest move, it acquired Barre Labs for almost $100 million. Barre began operations in 1923 and, concentrating on liquid generic pharmaceuticals, attained a strong position in cough and cold remedies, which typically have higher sales in the winter months. Taste, texture, appearance, and fragrance are all important in manufacturing liquid versions of drugs. The total market in 1988 was $150 million, with only about 12 percent of all approved liquid drugs having a generic counterpart, compared to 24 percent of generic capsules and tablets. Of course, profit margins on generic drugs are lower and fall as more manufacturers begin making a particular one and as the major drug companies cut prices on their branded products once the period of patent protection expires.

Liquid pharmaceuticals are particularly important in the over-65 (geriatric) market and in pediatric markets (particularly children under 6). Senior citizens, who use two to three

TABLE 1	A. L. Labs Revenues						
	1991	*1990*	*1989*	*1988*	*1987*	*1986*	*1985*
Sales by Segment (millions of dollars)							
Animal Health	$ 73	$ 63	$ 57	$ 51	$46	$39	$32
Pharmaceuticals	184	177	166	149	85	58	50
Human Nutrition	38	34	43	36	27	26	25
Sales by Geographic Region (millions of dollars)							
U.S. Sales	$172	$159	$156	$132	$73	$47	$29
Percentage of Total Sales	58%	58%	58%	55%	46%	38%	30%
Foreign Sales	$123	$116	$110	$108	$87	$78	$69
Percentage of Total Sales	42%	42%	42%	45%	54%	62%	70%
Assets by Geographic Region (millions of dollars)							
U.S. Assets	$239	$218	$192	$155.3	$40.1	$20.6	NA
Foreign Assets	120	110	98	95.5	79.4	71.7	NA

times the pharmaceuticals that other segments of the population do, prefer liquid pharmaceuticals. And the senior citizen group is a growing segment.

The increased concentration on generic pharmaceuticals also seems appropriate given passage of the Medicare Catastrophe Coverage Act of 1988, which mandated that U.S. pharmacies must dispense generic drugs when filling Medicare patients' prescriptions unless a physician specifies otherwise. A. L. Labs expected generics to capture 22 percent of a $1.8 billion total liquid pharmaceutical market in the United States in 1995. Barre's current 40 percent market share should therefore increase.

The objectives of the Barre acquisition were to (1) give A. L. Labs a strong position in selling to the geriatric market, the largest consumer of liquid pharmaceuticals; (2) increase its presence in the U.S. market; and (3) reduce the preponderance of foreign sales and thus the volatility resulting from rapidly changing exchange rates of European currencies vis-à-vis the dollar.

Barre's position in liquid pharmaceuticals has been described by I. Roy Cohen, CEO, as the "wings of the business"; he says that A. L. Labs deliberately chose the liquid drug market over pills and capsules to avoid competition. Barre plans to diversify into ointments, aerosols, and injectables. A part of its strategy is to concentrate on "unit-of-use," that is, exact quantities of liquid drugs in prescription-sized tamper-resistant containers. Many pharmacists use gallon jugs of liquid pharmaceuticals, pouring out quantities needed for each prescription. Barre plans to stress the potential liability problems that this might create.

Barre was purchased from Revco Labs, which had gone private in a leveraged buyout and was raising capital by shedding what it thought were peripheral business lines. A. L. Labs plans to sell more Barre products to large drugstore chains, a plan that Revco as a major chain could not as easily carry out. Barre Labs also provides products that can be introduced into Europe, complementing new products supplied by Dumex and A. L. Oslo.

Human Nutrition: A Candidate for Divestment?

The third major line of business is human nutrition. A. L. Labs' human nutrition products consist principally of formulated powdered milk products developed by Dumex and sold mainly in the Far East in Malaysia, Singapore, and Thailand and in the Middle East, as well as through the P. T. Dumex subsidiary in Indonesia and its licensees. Dumex receives royalties from a license granted to two subsidiaries of the East Asiatic Company of Denmark (EAC), located in Malaysia and Thailand. Dumex sales of human nutrition milk products in 1988, 1987, 1986, and 1985 to the two subsidiaries of EAC totaled $29.7 million, $22.7 million, $23.2 million, and $18 million, respectively.

Dumex recently granted an option to EAC to acquire the Dumex trademark in 1995, while preserving the flow of royalties from Dumex sales in the Far East for the next 10 years. Although competition is heavy in this line of business, Dumex has the advantage of an established brand name. It obtains raw materials by buying bulk powdered milk supplies from the New Zealand Dairy Board for processing and sale as formulated milk products in the Far East. This line of business has exhibited slow growth, with demand fluctuating, as in Nigeria, where an oil-related recession reduced demand considerably.

A. L. Labs most recent initiative is a new treatment for gum disease that the company is developing in Europe. Work on this periodontal gel began in 1989, initiating a long series of tests necessary to obtain European approvals. Similar studies were begun in the United States as the company began to see successful results from its European tests. A. L. Labs sees this approach as an interesting model for new pharmaceutical drug development—new ideas are first tried out in Europe, and then "bridged" into the United States, if appropriate.

In conjunction with its animal feed business, the company expanded into the fish vaccine business by acquiring a U.S. company that provides aquatic animal health products, including its bacterins for farmed fish worldwide from its federally licensed U.S. facility. It also introduced its BMD product line into Mexico to take advantage of increased commercial farming there.

Overall, A. L. Labs has managed to achieve sales growth without sacrificing profits. Table 2 summarizes sales and net income after taxes at A. L. Labs during the period of 1983 through 1992. Of course, past sales and profit success are no guarantee of continued prosperity, and A. L. Labs is constantly reassessing its plans for the future.

Questions

1. What are the benefits to A. L. Labs of having a foreign parent? How has this affected its choice of strategy in international marketing?
2. Trace the evolution of A. L. Labs' product and geographic area strategy. What are the strengths

TABLE 2	A. L. Labs: Sales and Profits (Millions of Dollars)	

	Total Sales	Net Income
1992[a]	$211.8	$16.20
1991	295.0	5.10
1990	275.5	14.10
1989	266.3	11.80
1988	236.5	8.75
1987	159.0	6.60
1986	123.6	5.50
1985	96.8	5.50
1984	88.4	4.31
1983	47.6	1.61

[a]Estimated after divestment of human nutrition line.

of the approach adopted? And what, in your opinion, are the flaws in its approach to global markets?
3. Most U.S. companies attempt to increase their foreign sales. A. L. Labs has been successful in decreasing foreign sales as a percent of total sales to the point at which U.S. sales now account for 58 percent of total sales. Why has A. L. Labs chosen to implement such a strategy?
4. Why has A. L. Labs positioned itself so that generic pharmaceuticals have become its largest product line?

Case prepared by Professor Ravi Sarathy for use in classroom discussion. All rights reserved.
Source: A. L. Labs Prospectus, June 30, 1988; Annual Reports 1987 and 1988.

CASE 6.3

Indorayon

Indorayon produces paper pulp and dissolving pulp used in manufacturing rayon in N. Sumatra, Indonesia. It has access to low-cost Indonesian labor and to its abundant tropical

forests as sources of wood for its pulp factories. It employs 2,612 people: 866 in the pulp mill, 763 in the rayon fiber plant and 971 in logging and planting. It began operations in 1989, recently expanding its pulp mill and starting up a new rayon fiber plant. Sukanto Tanoto is the founder and President Commissioner. He is also head of the family conglomerate, the April Group, of which Indorayon is a part. He owns 68 percent of its share capital, with his brother, Polar Yanto

Tanoto, who serves as president director of the company, owning an additional 5.8 percent.

Paper Pulp Market

Paper pulp is a commodity product. As a commodity, world prices are determined by supply and demand. Softwood and hardwood are the two main categories of trees used in the production of paper pulp. Pine trees, a main ingredient of softwood pulp, are used in the production of lower-quality paper products (tissue, newsprint, paper hygiene products). Eucalyptus trees, which yield hardwood pulp, are used in the production of higher-quality paper products (stationery, printing paper). Trees mature faster in tropical climates, allowing their conversion into paper pulp earlier. Because of Indonesia's optimal climatic conditions, the eucalyptus growing cycle is about twice as fast as that of hardwood trees in North America, about eight years versus 15 to 20.

Wood is the primary raw material used in the production of paper pulp. When logs arrive at the mill, they are first debarked, then cut into wood chips. Conveyor belts take the chips to large steel digestor tanks, where they are mixed with a variety of chemicals and heated under pressure, producing cellulose fibers. This is the point where the pulp would be sold to be made into paper.

This is a global industry with principal competitors located in North America, Japan, South America, and Europe. Prices are set in relation to the U.S. Southern Bleached Softwood and Hardwood Kraft Pulp index. Paper pulp prices are cyclical, with peaks every five to seven years. Pulp prices have been declining in the last three years due to the emergence of new pulp producers and the world economic recession. (See Figure 1.) For example, from 1989 to 1993, prices declined from US$713 to US$382 per ton of pulp. (See Table 1 and Table 2.)

The paper pulp market is highly competitive. Price is a main competitive factor, with service and reliability less important. Indorayon is a relatively small company in a global industry. Competitors are anticipating new pulp mills even within Indonesia. In fact, a fellow member of the RGM Group, P. T. Riau Andalan Pulp and Paper, is slated to open a new pulp production plant by 1995. Selling on the local market, it will be in direct competition with Indorayon.

Indorayon Production Costs

Wood is the chief component in pulp production costs. Average production costs are $251 per ton. Plant capacity is 240,000 tons per year. (See Table 3.) To meet this capacity, the mill requires 1.2 million cubic meters of wood, or 38,000 hectares of forest a year. Logging and transportation fees are

TABLE 1	Pulp Production	
Region	*Produce*	*Consume*
North America	50%	43%
Europe	20	23
Asia	16	20

$94 per ton. This includes delivery of wood to the pulp mill, government concession and royalty fees, labor costs for logging, and provisions for replanting.

The company has a highly integrated production process, recycling new materials to derive its own energy. Lignin is a by-product of the wood-chip heating process. It in turn is used to fire the generators that generate plant electricity and produce the steam that runs the pulp dryers. Ninety-five percent of the chemicals used in the paper pulp process are recycled. Sodium sulfate, a by-product of rayon production, is recycled from the pulp production process.

Other production costs include equipment and labor. Indonesian labor is among the most cheaply priced in Asia; the nonsalaried nursery and logging workers are paid $2 per day (Rp. 4,000). The mill is equipped primarily with modern competitive pulp mill technology from Europe. Total capital investment figures were almost $500 million by June 1993. (See Table 4 and Table 5.)

Markets

Indonesia is a large world market, with a total population of over 186 million. Only China, India, and the United States rank higher. Although it has the lowest per capita consumption of printing and writing paper (7.7 kilograms per person in 1991), the country's paper production increased 23.8 percent annually between 1985 and 1992. Other expanding economies of Asia are geographically distant from the world's principal pulp producers. (See Table 6.) Indorayon is strategically placed to supply this burgeoning Asian market; it is closer to the Korean and Japanese markets than to those in Northern Europe and North America. The factory is located in Porsea near Lake Toba in North Sumatra. The pulp is shipped to the Port of Belawan, located across the Strait of Malacca from Singapore. Logging and transportation fees are $94 per ton. From the port, the pulp is shipped to both the domestic and worldwide export markets. Indorayon had 56 customers in 1992, but is dependent on two key customers. These Indonesian companies account for 24.7 percent of Indorayon's net operating revenues. (See Table 6 and Figure 2.)

TABLE 2	Average Pulp Prices Paid by Customers[a]					
	Year Ended December 31				*Six Months Ended June 30*	
	1989	*1990*	*1991*	*1992*	*1992*	*1993*
Blended average	$713	$615	$504	$473	$474	$382
Softwood-export	710	613	524	475	460	378
Softwood-domestic	731	634	518	486	461	356
Hardwood-export	—	539	452	469	498	382
Hardwood-domestic	—	589	475	504	476	393

[a]Prices do not include prices for unbleached paper pulp, which are lower than prices for bleached paper pulp.
Source: *Indorayon Prospectus,* October 7, 1993, 22.

| FIGURE 1 | Historical Prices for Bleached Kraft Market Pulp Delivered in the United States |

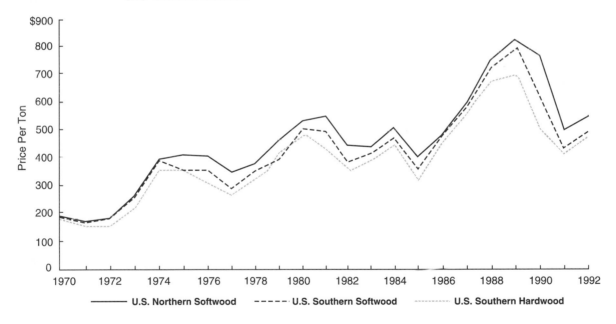

—— U.S. Northern Softwood   ----- U.S. Southern Softwood   ·········· U.S. Southern Hardwood

Source: *Indorayon Prospectus,* October 7, 1993, 36.

The company's 1992 export sales were 63.2 percent of tons sold, and domestic sales were 36.8 percent of tons sold. Export sales are made in dollars; domestic sales are made in the rupiah equivalent of the dollar price. For the last 25 years, foreign investment in Indonesia has been $63 billion and Indonesian investment, $105 billion.

Diversification

Recently Indorayon began investing in a rayon production facility. A total of $500 million was invested in both the paper pulp mill expansion and the rayon fiber plant. Rayon sells for $1,850 per ton versus $385 per ton for paper pulp. From 1989 to 1992, Indonesia's textile and garment exports grew from

TABLE 3	**Pulp Production and Sales**					
		Year Ended December 31			**Six Months Ended June 30**	
	1989[a]	*1990*	*1991*	*1992*	*1992*	*1993*
Production (thousands of tons)						
Softwood pulp	117.8	127.8	101.2	95.0	49.9	28.3
Hardwood pulp	—	23.2	49.6	86.8	42.1	60.3
Total	117.8	151.0	150.8	181.8	92.0	88.6
Sales (thousands of tons)						
Softwood pulp	91.8	161.2	102.1	89.6	49.7	36.4
Hardwood pulp	—	22.5	50.0	81.1	39.1	65.4
Total	91.8	183.7	152.1	170.7	88.8	101.8
Sales (billions of Rupiah)						
Softwood pulp	Rp.97.9	Rp.178.6	Rp.104.1	Rp.83.5	Rp.46.1	Rp.31.3
Hardwood pulp	—	23.4	43.0	79.6	38.4	49.5
Total	Rp.97.9	Rp.202.0	Rp.147.1	Rp.163.1	Rp.84.5	Rp.80.8

[a]The Company commenced commercial production of paper pulp in 1989, and the 1989 sales amounts include some unbleached pulp produced on a trial basis prior to the commencement of commercial operations, which are not reflected in 1989 production amounts. Other periods include insignificant amounts of unbleached paper pulp.
Source: *Indorayon Prospectus,* October 7, 1993, 22.

$1.8 billion to $4.3 billion. At 2.4 kilograms per person, Indonesia's per capita textile consumption was appreciably lower than Singapore's 9.5 kilograms and the United States' 20 kilograms. The company plans on concentrating its rayon dissolving pulp sales in the growing Southeast Asian export market. In addition, the United States and the European Union are attractive markets because rayon yarn and rayon garments are not subject to their import quotas.

The company's existing pulp mill already contains the equipment that produces dissolving pulp, the principal raw material for rayon production. The rayon dissolving pulp facility offers Indorayon the flexibility of responding to changing market demand. Depending upon the relative prices of pulp and rayon, the company can decide whether to make pulp or redirect the dissolving pulp to the rayon facility. The pulp mill has been expanded to allow for fast switching between production of hardwood and softwood products. The production process is not disrupted; all that it requires is changing the type of wood fed into the mill. The first rayon production line was up and running in July 1993, and the second was due to commence in October 1993. The rayon fiber plant lines have a combined capacity of 60,000 tons of dissolving pulp. Additionally, the plant is close to the market where most of the garment and textile industries of the world are located. Indorayon is optimistic that rayon pulp sales will contribute significantly to its net operating revenues.

Indonesia's rayon market is served by two main competitors, Lenzing Indonesia and Indo Bharat. These two companies together produce more than 175,000 tons of rayon fiber, and total production of rayon fiber is expected to reach about 300,000 tons by the year 2000, about 20 percent greater than projected domestic demand. The balance would have to be exported to the yarn manufacturers, textile producers, and garment factories in neighboring countries such as China, Vietnam, India, Sri Lanka, and others.

Government Reliance

Indorayon relies primarily on government concessions for its wood supply. A small percentage is leased from residents. Softwood tree concessions of 86,000 hectares (1 hectare = 2.471 acres) are to be used until 2004. The government stipulates replanting of logged areas, but no logging of replanted trees is allowed. The company had logged 7.24 percent of the softwood concession by June 1993. The hardwood tree concession of 269,060 hectares expires in 2035. (The logging and subsequent replanting of hardwood reflects better hardwood prices in recent years; hardwood yields 20 percent more pulp

TABLE 4	Financials: Summary Financial and Statistical Information		

	Year Ended December 31		
	1990	1991	1992
	Rp.	Rp. *(Rp. in billions and US$ in millions)*	Rp.
Income Statement Data			
Net Operating Revenues	201.9	147.1	163.0
Gross Profit	118.0	62.3	73.4
Operating Profit	97.5	38.6	41.9
Interest Income	13.4	29.4	44.3
Interest Expense	21.7	5.7	16.8
Other Income (Expense) excluding net interest	11.1	(3.8)	9.4
Deferred tax (benefit)	9.2	(0.8)	(1.4)
Net Profit	91.1	59.3	80.2
Balance Sheet Data			
Working Capital	91.4	104.7	10.9
Property, Plant and Equipment—Net	444.9	569.5	988.2
Total Assets	615.8	790.7	1,515.9
Total Debt	62.4	209.7	461.7
Shareholders' Equity	510.6	545.6	625.8
Other Financial Data			
Depreciation and Amortization	22.1	23.4	25.6
Capital Expenditures	46.9	159.9	449.5
EBITDA	144.1	87.6	120.8
Ratio of Earnings to Fixed Charges	5.6x	5.1x	2.6x
Ratio of EBITDA to Interest Expenses and Bank Financing Charges	6.6x	15.4x	7.2x
Operating Profit as a Percentage of Net Operating Revenues	48.3%	26.2%	25.6%
Gross Profit as a Percentage of Net Operating Revenues	58.4%	42.4%	45.0%
Statistical Data			
Softwood Pulp Sales (tons in thousands)	161.2	102.1	89.6
Hardwood Pulp Sales (tons in thousands)	22.5	50.0	81.1
Blended Average Pulp Sales Price (US$)	615.0	504.0	473.0

per ton of timber than softwood.) For each hectare cleared, the company plants 1,600 eucalyptus trees, or 16 trees for every one harvested. The company had logged 1.71 percent of this concession by June 1993.

The government can change its concession fees at any time. If the government were to revoke its concessions, this would have adverse effects on material cost. The company must submit annual and 15-year logging plans for approval.

Environmental Issues

The government concessions are regulated by the Ministry of Forestry, which has strict environmental guidelines. If a

TABLE 4 — Financials: Summary Financial and Statistical Information

Pro Forma Year Ended December 31, 1992	Six Months Ended June 30		Pro Forma Six Months Ended June 30, 1993
	1992	1993	
US$	Rp.	Rp.	US$
78.1	84.5	80.8	38.7
35.1	38.1	29.3	14.0
20.0	23.1	13.6	6.5
21.2	16.7	36.6	17.5
17.1	1.9	13.3	10.9
4.5	1.6	5.3	2.5
(0.7)	(0.7)	(0.6)	(0.3)
29.3	40.2	42.8	15.9
90.7	143.3	(13.2)	79.2
473.2	618.5	1,030.4	493.5
815.0	885.2	1,500.9	807.8
310.1	254.6	516.5	336.3
299.7	585.9	636.2	304.7
12.8	12.5	12.4	6.3
215.3	59.5	48.7	23.3
57.8	53.9	67.7	32.4
1.7x	4.0x	2.5x	1.7x
3.4x	28.4x	5.1x	3.0x
25.6%	27.3%	16.8%	16.8%
45.0%	45.1%	36.3%	36.3%
	49.7	36.4	
	39.1	65.4	
	474.0	382.0	

company does not comply with the guidelines, it runs the risk of heavy fines and even retraction of its licenses and concessions. In response to Indonesia's Environmental Impact Management Agency regulations, Indorayon imposes its own strict standards on its effluent- and pollution-control systems. The company meets biological-oxygen-demand (BOD) levels of 51mpl and produces elemental chlorine-free pulp, which is environmentally superior to chlorine-bleached pulp. The company meets not only Indonesian standards but world paper-pulp production standards as well. The company is able to recycle al-

TABLE 5	Average Pulp Production Costs

	Year Ended December 31, 1992	Six Months Ended June 30, 1993
	(Rp. Thousands)	
Average Pulp Production Costs per Ton		
Wood[a]	Rp. 190.8	Rp. 184.6
Chemicals	47.6	40.6
Energy	75.0	74.0
Other Materials	67.9	64.2
Labor (pulp mill)	35.2	38.1
Administration	8.9	17.3
Depreciation	84.2	92.2
Total Average Cost per Ton (Rp.)	Rp. 509.6	Rp. 511.0
Total Average Cost per Ton (US$)[b]	US$251.0	US$246.0

[a]These costs do not reflect the effect of the increase in concession fees payable to the Government which became effective in June 1993. If such fee rates had been in effect beginning on January 1, 1992, the Company's wood cost per ton for the year ended December 31, 1992, and for the six months ended June 30, 1993, would have increased by Rp. 8,251 and Rp. 6,455, respectively. These costs also exclude indirect overhead costs associated with work performed on immature plantations that the Company expects to benefit future periods.

[b]The US$ average cost per ton is calculated by dividing the total average cost per ton in Rupiah by the average of the Dollar-to-Rupiah exchange rate at the beginning and the end of the period.

TABLE 6	World Markets

	Year Ended December 31								Six Months Ended June 30, 1993	
	1989		1990		1991		1992			
Region	Tons	%	Tons	%	Tons	%	Tons	%	Tons	%
	(Tons in Thousands)									
Indonesia	14.5	15.8	73.2	39.8	59.0	38.9	62.8	36.8	28.6	28.0
South Korea, Japan, and Taiwan	37.4	40.8	35.7	19.4	45.2	29.7	42.7	25.0	30.5	30.0
Other ASEAN countries[a]	12.7	13.8	12.6	6.8	12.1	8.0	20.2	11.8	24.8	24.4
Pakistan	1.3	1.4	—	—	4.6	3.0	13.0	7.6	5.9	5.8
India, Bangladesh, and Sri Lanka	8.9	9.7	9.5	5.2	11.0	7.2	14.8	8.7	9.7	9.5
People's Republic of China and Vietnam	5.5	6.0	7.2	3.9	2.0	1.3	7.5	4.4	1.3	1.3
Middle East	8.0	8.7	35.0	19.1	18.0	11.8	8.1	4.7	—	—
Europe	2.7	2.9	9.3	5.1	0.2	0.1	—	—	—	—
Other	0.8	0.9	1.2	0.7	—	—	1.6	1.0	1.0	1.0
Total	91.8	100.0	183.7	100.0	152.1	100.0	170.7	100.0	101.8	100.0

[a]Consists of Malaysia, Thailand, Singapore, Brunei, and the Philippines.

FIGURE 2

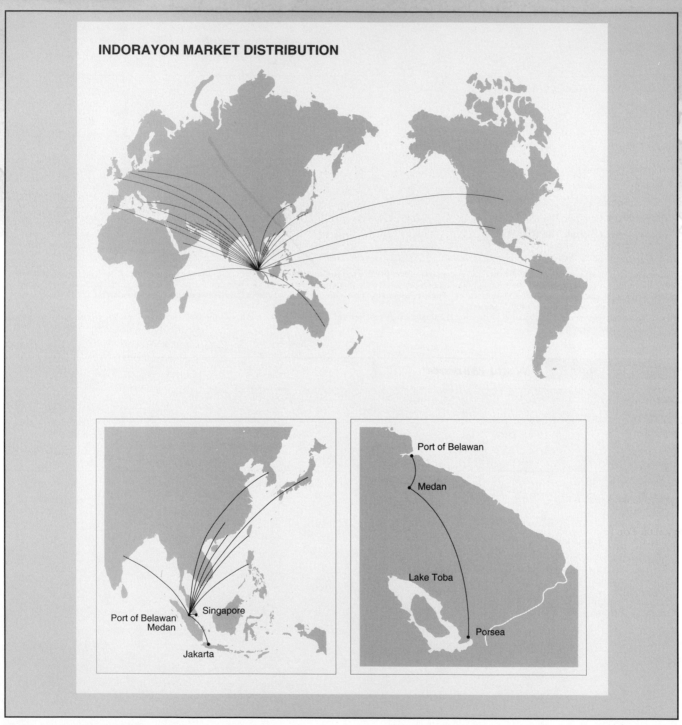

INDORAYON MARKET DISTRIBUTION

TABLE 7	Company Board of Commissioners		
Name	*Position*	*Country*	*Distinctions*
Sukanto Tanoto	President Commissioner Founder of RGM Group	Indonesia	Advanced management courses at Stanford and Harvard Universities
Wahyudi Prakarsa	Commissioner of the Company	Indonesia	Director, Masters in Management Program, University of Indonesia; MBA, University of Wisconsin; Ph.D., Accountancy, University of Missouri
Ian Dicker	Commissioner of the Company	Australia	Business Consultant; former Managing Director, Ansell Int'l; MBA and B.A., Commerce, University of Melbourne
R. Hikmat Kartadjoemena	Commissioner of the Company	Indonesia	Director of Pacific Bank; former Chief Representative and Country Manager for Chemical Bank; former Manager of Unibank

most 95 percent of its by-products for its energy needs. The new plant increases this environmental ability of Indorayon.

Management

Please see details of the management structure in Tables 7–9.

The Asian economic crisis and political turmoil caused considerable disruption of operations, creating losses and a cash flow constraint. Since Suharto stepped down from power, environmental activists have shut down Indorayon operations for weeks on end. "Shut Indorayon or War" says a banner that hangs across the main road to the mill. With Suharto gone, companies like Indorayon have to deal with an ever-changing coalition of local leaders and environmental pressure groups. Local communities want some of the revenues that Indorayon earns, where formerly most of the proceeds were shared with the central Government in Jakarta. For Indorayon, the pulp mill's closure has reduced cash flow by $27 million. After incurring net losses of 444 billion rupiah ($40 million) in 1997, the recent forced closure has placed the company in danger of defaulting on $270 million of bonds. When the original Indorayon facilities were built in 1988, the facility for waste-water treatment was an unlined holding pond that eventually collapsed in 1994, sending thousands of gallons of untreated waste into the local river system. Indorayon then built a new and modern $10 million treatment facility, but the seeds of distrust were sown. Environmentalists also blame Indorayon for Lake Toba's falling water level, saying that Indorayon's plan-

tation trees are mostly eucalyptus, which suck out more water from the ground than the tropical hardwoods native to the area. Part of the problem may lie in the fact that the initial Indorayon pulp factory, spewing strange-smelling smoke, was put down in the middle of the native Batak farming community without consulting local leaders. Though Indorayon has a 20-member community-outreach team, not a single member is from the Batak group, a culture of fiery personalities and tribal rivalries.[1]

Indorayon must now decide how best to plan its future operations to ensure survival past the crisis and then renew its growth.

---

[1]Dan Murphy, "It's the People's Will", *Far Eastern Economic Review,* November 12, 1998.
Case prepared by Professor Ravi Sarathy, with the research assistance of Heidi Hample, for use in class discussion. ©1996. All rights reserved.

TABLE 8	Company Board of Directors		
Name	*Position*	*Country*	*Distinctions*
Polar Yanto Tanoto	President Director	Indonesia	Chairman of the Indonesian Wood Panel Association
Per Reidar Haugen	Director, COO	Sweden	Thirty years experience in pulp and paper industries; former General Manager of Mondi Paper Co.; MS, University of Maine; Ph.D., University of Manchester
Semion Tarigan	Director	Indonesia	Member, Technical Faculty, University of Sumatra, Utara

TABLE 9	Company Executive Officers		
Name	*Position*	*Country*	*Distinctions*
Brett Hutton	General Manager, Finance	Australia	Over 23 years experience in finance; former CEO, Whitakers, Ltd. (Australian publicly listed forest products co.); economics degree, University of West Australia
Hannu Thomasfolk	General Manager, Pulp Mill	Sweden	Eighteen years experience in paper and pulp industry; graduate, Royal Institute of Technology in Stockholm; former General Manager & Managing Director of Utansjo Bruk AB
Raymond Walsh	Production Manager, Pulp Mill	Canada	Over 28 years experience in paper and pulp industry; former Pulp Mill Manager, Mondi Paper Co.; graduate, Fort William Collegiate Institute, Ontario, Canada
K. G. Bapat	Production Manager, Rayon Fiber Plant	India	Over 25 years experience in rayon fiber production; former Deputy Production Manager of Grasin Industries Ltd.; Chemical Engineering degree, University of Nagpur, India
Pekka Kahkonen	Maintenance Manager	Indonesia	Over 20 years experience in pulp and paper industry; former Technical Manager of Anpro Pointo OY; degree in Mechanical Engineering, Kotka Technical College
S. N. Khanna	General Manager, Rayon Fiber Sales	India	Over 17 years marketing experience; former Marketing Manager for Thai Rayon Co. Ltd.; MBA, University of Poona, India
Gunawan Wanamarta	General Manager, Pulp Sales	Indonesia	Former Indonesian Marketing Manager for Monsanto Co.; Ph.D., Agriculture, Michigan State University

Chapter 7

International Marketing Intelligence

Learning Objectives

When a firm initially considers marketing to the world, it finds world markets to be "foreign" in several senses: They are located outside the firm's home country; they have different languages, currencies, and customs; and they are unfamiliar to management. Lack of knowledge of world markets is thus the first barrier to overcome in marketing internationally. Marketing decisions cannot be made intelligently without knowing the environment. For this reason, our study of international marketing management begins with the nature and scope of international marketing intelligence.

The main goals of this chapter are to

1.   Review the range of tasks involved in international marketing research. We outline typical problems encountered in conducting research overseas and ways to solve such problems.

2.   Present techniques for conducting research, including analysis of demand, regression analysis, and cluster analysis.

3.   Discuss the screening of international markets and give an example indicating the typical steps involved.

4.   Explain how to evaluate information collected through international marketing research.

5.   Discuss the role of models in marketing research and present detailed models for deciding the mode of market entry, analyzing cross-cultural, household purchasing behavior, the effects of religiosity on consumption, and the impact of country-of-origin effects.

BREADTH OF THE TASK

International marketing intelligence is more comprehensive than domestic marketing research. Although all of the firm's domestic marketing research studies have potential for international application, they are not sufficient to provide all the information necessary to make sound international marketing decisions. The firm needs an information system not only to identify and measure market potential in foreign markets but also to take into account the many cultural, political, and macroeconomic variables that are ignored or assumed to be constant in domestic studies.

One group of specifically international parameters affecting marketing decisions includes the economic factors considered in Chapter 2. A second group encompasses the political-legal aspects of international relations, as discussed in Chapter 5. A third element is the analysis of competition. Although the firm must analyze the competitive situation in each market, this kind of analysis alone is not sufficient. Because competition in many industries is now international, the study of the competitive situation must also be multinational. It cannot be limited to studies of individual markets.

Finally, international comparative studies are an additional dimension of analysis. As can be seen, the distinctiveness of international marketing intelligence arises from the fact that the firm is operating within a number of foreign environments. These differences necessitate not only the adaptation of domestic techniques but also the development of new methods of analysis. The scope of the international researcher's task is apparent in the following notice:

> The International Division is seeking a research analyst to work on broad scope individual projects relating to . . . international economic and marketing research. . . . *The general subjects which will be researched are economic statistics, sales and marketing forecasts, distribution methodology, market planning on existing and new products,* and related subjects which would have an impact on aggregate marketing plans for given geographical areas. . . . Because of the scope of the projects, it is necessary to have a much broader familiarity with economic and marketing subjects than may be normally required for a marketing research professional. [Emphasis added.]

The small international marketing firm has information needs similar to those of the large firm. However, it must rely more on others for its international information needs—its distributors, licensees, or joint-venture partners, for example. Or it may choose to market through another firm that has superior knowledge of foreign markets.

WHAT INFORMATION IS NEEDED?

We assume that the firm has already decided to go international. Its next decision, then, is which world markets to enter. Since the firm cannot usually sell to all world markets, it must find a way of ranking them according to their attractiveness. This requires an investigation of their market potential and the local competitive situation. Once the firm has identified desirable target markets, it must decide how to serve those markets—by exporting, licensing, or local production, for example.

Once a decision has been made to market in a particular country, standard marketing questions arise, such as product decisions, pricing decisions, or channel decisions. These decisions can be further broken down until eventually a very specific local issue is reached—the kind of package and label that should be used for the firm's floor wax in the Philippines, for example. The information needed to make these decisions is frequently provided by marketing research (see Table 7–1).

TABLE 7-1	Information for Marketing Decisions

Marketing Decision	Intelligence Needed
1. Go international or remain a domestic marketer?	1. Assessment of global market demand and firm's potential share in it, in view of local and international competition and compared to domestic opportunities
2. Which markets to enter?	2. A ranking of world markets according to market potential, local competition, and the political situation
3. How to enter target markets?	3. Size of market, international trade barriers, transport costs, local competition, government requirements, and political stability
4. How to market in target markets?	4. For each market: buyer behavior, competitive practice, distribution channels, promotional media and practice, company experience there and in other markets

THE INFORMATION PROVIDED BY MARKETING RESEARCH

What information should international marketing research provide? Obtaining information about consumer behavior and product-related information come to mind as typical marketing research objectives, but the objectives of international marketing research should be broader. Table 7–2 summarizes the principal tasks of global marketing research.

The fact of being in a global market means that the firm must seek information to help it to understand the country and regional environment, as well as the consumer and the product. The firm must assess the global competitors that it will face in order to compete better with them. Only then does information about the industry and the product make sense, and better research and decisions on the marketing mix can result.

Marketing Environment

Research should emphasize gathering information about the country and region of interest and evaluating comparative information across countries. Both political and economic information are relevant. The *political dimension of information gathering* includes data on the following:

1. *Political structure and ideology.* What does the political leadership of the country seek? What roles do major institutions such as business, labor, the educational sector, and religion play in shaping national goals?

2. *National objectives.* What are the country's goals for the defense sector, its fiscal, monetary, and investment policy; and the foreign trade sector? What are its industrial and technology policies for sunrise or burgeoning industries and its social policy (for example, how do they affect income distribution and conspicuous consumption)? Is autonomy a goal, does the nation seek to reduce import dependence, and is developing national champions in industries considered critical?

3. The *economic dimension of information gathering* is more familiar. It includes obtaining data on economic performance, covering indicators such as GNP, per capita income levels and growth rates, stage of the business cycle, balance of trade and balance of payments, productivity, labor costs and capital availability, capacity utilization, inflation rates, savings and investment, employment levels, educational attainment, population

TABLE 7–2	The Task of Global Marketing Research: What Should It Determine?

The Marketing Environment	*The Competition*	*The Product*	*Marketing Mix*	*Firm-Specific Historical Data*
Political context: leaders, national goals, ideology, key institutions	Relative market shares	Analysis of users	Channels of distribution: evolution and performance	Sales trends by product and product-line, sales-force, and customer
Economic growth prospects, business cycle stage	New product moves	Who are the end-user industries?	Relative pricing, elasticities, and tactics	Trends by country and region
Per capita income levels, purchasing power	Pricing and cost structure	Industrial and consumer buyers	Advertising and promotion: choices and impacts on customers	Contribution margins
End-user industry growth trends	Image and brand reputation	Characteristics: Size, age, sex, segment growth rates	Service quality, perceptions, and relative positioning	Marketing mix used, marketing response functions across countries and regions
Government: legislation, regulation, standards, barriers to trade	Quality: Its attributes and positioning relative to competitors	Purchasing power and intentions	Logistics networks, configuration, and change	
	Competitor's strengths; favorite tactics and strategies	Customer response to new products, price, promotion		
		Switching behavior		
		Role of credit and purchasing		
		Future needs		
		Impact of cultural differences		

Analyzing the Findings: Answering Questions from the Market Research Information

- Which markets are attractive in the short and long run?
- How do we attract customers?
- What do customers think of our product and that of competition?
- What do we do about competition? Cooperate or compete? With whom?
- What new products should we introduce?

- What should the price be?
- Which distribution channels should we use?
- How much advertising and promotion is necessary?
- Which countries should we target next?
- How should we overcome barriers to entry?

demographics, age distribution, public health, and income distribution. Marketing infrastructure is also of interest, including the structure of wholesaling and retailing, laws concerning pricing and promotion, the physical distribution infrastructure, and the extent of development of consumer protection. All of these help determine the attractiveness of the market, as well as obstacles to entry and marketing of goods and services as well as the long-term profit potential.

4. *Government regulation* is another area for market research, particularly with regard to product and safety standards, barriers to entry (affecting foreign companies and their products), and controls over managerial and marketing autonomy. Does the government implement industrial policies that benefit domestic companies and industries at the expense of foreign firms?

Competition

Assessing foreign competitors involves developing additional levels of understanding since foreign competitors may have distinct and different objectives that shape their strategy and tactics. They may also possess hidden resources and strengths that are culture specific and not apparent to the outside firm. For example, close family and other ties may exist between a competitor's top management and influential individuals in government and the political arena. In conducting such assessment, the firm must first investigate the assumptions it holds about its foreign competitors regarding their objectives and capabilities; then it can assess potential strategies and make plans in terms of which new markets to enter, what modes of entry to take, how vulnerable it will be, and the expected strength of reaction by competition to its moves in that market. Essentially, the firm must be able to anticipate how its foreign competitors might act or react and to use such information to prepare contingency plans for quick response as appropriate.

Users of the Product

The firm must understand users, both of its product and those of its competitors. A paramount consideration is documenting and understanding cultural differences as they affect customer needs, products demanded, and purchasing behavior. Analysis and market research can focus on end-user industry categories and, if relevant, on unique characteristics of consumers. Information to help in *segmentation* should be gathered, using parameters such as age, sex, size, income levels, growth rates of consumption, regional differences, purchasing power, influence over purchasing and purchasing intentions, and the role of credit granting in purchasing behavior. Another major area of research is *product benchmarking* or quality comparisons, which makes objective comparisons of a firm's products and its competitors' products; this can be used to understand product positioning issues by competitors within an industry, as well as positioning across countries, customer response to new product introductions, and the potential for customers' purchasing the firm's own brands instead of competitors' brands. Finally, research should identify market trends for the medium and long term, rather than solely providing information for decision making on immediate marketing plans and actions.

Marketing Mix

As we shall see later, a company can standardize or adapt its product as well as its marketing mix to different country markets. Hence, it is also necessary to research marketing mix choice in international markets. The following are areas that should be investigated:

1. *Distribution channels*—Their evolution and the firm's comparative performance in different channels and those of its competitors.

2. *Comparative pricing strategies and tactics*—The price positioning by all competitors, price elasticities, and customer response to differential pricing behavior.

3. *Advertising and promotion*—The range of choices available, the differences in the allocation of promotion expenditures, the delineation of the advertising response function in different markets, and the comparison of competitor choices in advertising and promotion.

4. *Media research*—Useful in determining where to advertise in order to reach target audiences. Major market research firms such as A. C. Nielsen and the Kantar Group (part of WPP) provide media research and media measurement services.

5. *Service quality issues*—Relative to positioning by competitors' and customers' reactions to higher levels of service.

6. *Logistics of network capabilities*—Delivery and stockout performance and the use of information systems to improve delivery and customer service. This

relatively new area of marketing concern results from increased emphasis on just-in-time inventory systems and customer-direct delivery, bypassing retail inventories. Other key research issues are comparative performance of competitors and customer requirements.[1]

FIRM-SPECIFIC HISTORICAL DATA

Forgotten in marketing research is the role of a firm's internal information system in providing data for marketing decisions. Marketing research often can be facilitated by setting up the required database outline and implementing internal data collection; this is particularly necessary for international markets since much information that could be generated within the firm is ignored or lost. Useful data could include sales history by product and product line, by customer and salesforce, by distribution channel, within a country and across countries; analysis of such historic data for trends across countries and regions; derivation and analysis of contribution by product, product line, customer, and region; and development of market response functions across countries to permit comparison of past marketing mix decisions and to suggest future mix decisions that may differ from country to country, within a country, or across regions.

Once marketing research has been completed, the information that it generates must be analyzed so that questions about future marketing plans and actions can be answered. Major questions that are relevant in international marketing fall into two categories: *market and competition* decisions and *product and marketing mix* decisions. In regard to market and competition, the firm should mainly be concerned with three issues:

1. Understanding how customers rate it in comparison to the competition.

2. Determining its chances to attract customers.

3. Deciding whether to compete or cooperate with the competition.

As to product and marketing mix, the firm should look at several factors:

1. Choosing which products to introduce, which distribution channels to use, and how to advertise and promote the product.

2. Identifying barriers to attractive markets and finding ways to overcome them.

Marketing research can also play a role in helping formulate global strategy. While strategy sets a path for how a firm should interact with its customers, competition, and environment, market research can help by providing information and analyses on environmental trends; changes in competitive behavior and government regulation; and shifting consumer tastes. In other words, market research can provide strategic information by focusing on futures research and scenario development. Market researchers who pride themselves on quantitative modeling and statistical rigor might disdain this "soft" world, leaving it to megatrend visionaries such as Naisbitt. However, market research can resolve strategic planning issues such as:[2]

1. Determining the firm's mission, scope, and long-range objectives.

2. Anticipating environmental changes and their effects, and the resulting opportunities and threats they pose.

3. Understanding the firm's capabilities versus the strengths and weaknesses of competitors.

The above ideas are a far cry from information gathering about consumer responses to new products, prices, and advertising. Yet just as good information is necessary for tactical marketing, so, too, is good information needed to develop and assess long-range plans.

Problems in International Marketing Research

Because of its complexity, international marketing may encounter difficulties that are uncommon in domestic marketing research. One problem is that intelligence must be gathered for many markets—over 100 countries in some cases—and each country poses a unique challenge. A second problem is the frequent absence of secondary data (data from published and third-party sources). A third problem is the frequent difficulty in gathering primary data (data gathered firsthand through interviews and field research).

Problem of Numerous Markets

Multiplying the number of countries in a research project multiplies the costs and problems involved, although not in a linear manner. Because markets are not identical from one country to another, the research manager must be alert to the various errors that can arise in replicating a study multinationally. Mayer identifies five kinds of errors to look for in multinational research:[3]

1. *Definition error,* caused by the way the problem is defined in each country.

2. *Instrument error,* which arises from the questionnaire and the interviewer.

3. *Frame error,* which occurs when sampling frames are available from different sources in different countries.

4. *Selection error,* which results from the way the actual sample is selected from the frame.

5. *Nonresponse error,* which results when different cultural patterns of nonresponse are obtained. For example, in one five-country study, the response rate ranged from 17 percent to 41 percent. Furthermore, in one country, women composed 64 percent of the respondents, but in another country men represented 80 percent of the respondents.

Problems with Secondary Data

Secondary data for market analysis are less available and less reliable for many foreign markets and low per capita income countries tend to have weaker statistical sources than those with higher per capita income. Secondary sources of information are relatively cheap to acquire, however, and can help prevent a firm from making major mistakes in its international marketing. Major steps in using secondary data include:[4]

1. Determining research objectives.

2. Clarifying what information is needed.

3. Identifying where such secondary information can be found.

4. Deciding whether the information source is reliable (who put out the information and whether there is a hidden agenda).

5. Assessing the quality of data (accuracy, timeliness, representativeness) and the compatibility of data from different sources.

6. Interpreting and analyzing the information.

7. Drawing conclusions and then relating them to the marketing problem at hand to see if conclusions suggest courses of action or backup planned decisions or actions.

The use of probability sampling is necessarily limited where the nature of the relevant universe cannot be reliably determined. Quota sampling is limited for the same reason, so the most frequently employed technique is the convenience sample. This is defensible primarily because of a lack of alternatives.

Comparing Several Markets. When data for several markets are compiled, the researcher may find that many gaps exist. For example, current data on number of automobile registrations may only be available for a few countries in the group of interest. Data quality may vary and the estimates may not be reliable. The underlying definitions may not be the same, with some countries excluding light trucks from automobile registrations while others include them. Many countries lack specialized firms that develop industry data for specific industries such as automobiles or air conditioners.

Table 7–3 shows the top 10 market research firms. In 1996, the top 25 global market research firms had revenues of $6 billion and 50,000 employees; 45 percent of their sales were derived from outside their home country. For comparison purposes, only 9 of the top 50 firms did any international business in 1989—a clear indication that international marketing research is on the rise, a consequence of the growing importance of global markets. These firms perform a variety of marketing research services, such as

- Forming consumer panels to use as focus groups and to monitor purchasing behavior.
- Providing media measurement services to audit use and relate expenditures to sales.
- Measuring audiences for media such as TV and radio.
- Providing sales and market share for a number of firms in specific industries, notably the pharmaceutical and health care industries, computers, and electronics.
- Performing multicultural consumer research.
- Collecting data on how marketing communication affects brands.
- Doing brand equity studies.

Problems with Primary Data

Much of marketing research involves getting information from people about their perceptions concerning a company's products, brands, prices, or promotion. People differ from country to country, in their income levels, culture, attitudes, and understanding of business issues, including specific items on surveys and questionnaires. Hence, personal interviews require skilled interviewers. Telephone surveys may work poorly and give biased results in countries with low rates of telephone penetration, such as in most of Africa and in countries such as China and India. The use of mall-intercept techniques to obtain personal interviews may give erroneous results because malls are not as widespread in many countries, even in Europe, and the subgroup of people visiting a mall may be unrepresentative of the broader audience. Mail surveys require a developed postal system, good mailing

| TABLE 7-3 | Top 10 Market Research Firms: A Profile |

Firm	Home Country	Number of Countries with Operations	Number of Employees	Revenues ($ Million)	Percent sales outside Home Country
A. C. Nielsen	United States	45	18,000	1,359	79
Cognizant	United States	62	7,100	1,224	49
Kantar Grp.	United Kingdom	19	2,824	473	60
Information Resources	United States	17	3,900	406	15
G & K AG	Germany	31	2,920	318	45
Sofres Grp.	France	19	2,771	276	55
Infratest Burke	Germany	11	780	168	36
IPSOS	France	11	1,120	161	61
Arbitron	United States	1	530	153	0
PMSI/Source Informatics	United States	8	950	152	29

Source: *Marketing News,* August 18, 1997; Honomichl Global 25: Top 25 global marketing/ad/opinion research firms profiled.

lists, and an educated population. Accurate and complete street addresses are necessary to give representative samples for mail questionnaires. If mail and telephone surveys are not practical, the researcher is left with personal interviewing as an alternative. With a largely rural population in the poorer countries, the problem then becomes one of physically reaching the people. Poor roads and lack of regular public transportation may make interviewing them economically unfeasible. In tropical areas, many roads are impassable during the rainy season. Surveys may be limited primarily to urban areas.

In addition, the environment may favor distinct research methodologies; such as instruments with a diversity of questions; the use of physical stimuli, such as the product, an advertisement, or a jingle; the control of the data-collection environment, including using simulations or tests of products in use; other criteria such as the perceived anonymity of the respondent. The sensitivity of the information requested, the experience of personnel conducting the survey, and the quality of the data desired will also suggest specific research approaches. Respondents may feel social pressure to respond with answers they perceive to be "socially correct." Speed, cost, and controlling for bias also affect the choice of technique.

Languages

Language, discussed at length in Chapter 4, is the initial cultural difference that comes to mind when one thinks of foreign markets. At the minimum, the language difference poses problems of communication; solutions to these problems may be expensive. First, the research design and specifications must be translated twice, first (in the case of a U.S. firm) from English into the language of each country where the study is to be conducted. Then, on completion of the study, the results must be translated back into English. More important than translation expense is the communication problem, also discussed in Chapter 4. Even business respondents may have difficulty if they are asked in their native language about stock turnover or other business concepts that they are unaccustomed to using.

Social Organization

Much of marketing research involves gaining insights into the buyer's decision process. Such research is predicated on the assumption that the decision makers and influencers have been identified. In foreign markets, the researcher usually finds that the social organization is different enough that it is necessary to identify anew the decision makers and influencers. (This subject, including the varying roles of women, is discussed in Chapter 4.) Differences in social organization affect the industrial market as well as the consumer market. The nature of the decision-making structure in foreign companies is possibly different from that in U.S. companies, due to the greater importance of family business in other countries and a greater general stress on relationships.

Obtaining Responses

Respondents and businesspeople may be reluctant to participate in marketing research for various reasons. Respondents may suspect the questioner of being a government tax representative rather than a legitimate market researcher, or they may be reluctant to respond for fear of giving information to competitors. The idea of businesspeople giving information to anyone, whether the government or an individual, is not well accepted in many countries. In addition, one of the researcher's greatest problems is trying to demonstrate the value of the research to the respondent personally. Unless this can be done, little will be accomplished with many business respondents.

Consumers, too, may be reluctant to respond to marketing research inquiries. This may be in part the result of a general unwillingness to talk to strangers. Foreign respondents are often more reluctant to discuss personal consumption habits and preferences than are Americans. In contrast to the reluctant respondent is the cooperative respondent who feels obliged to give responses that will please the interviewer rather than state true opinions or feelings. In some cultures this is a form of politeness, but it obviously does not contribute to effective research.

Reluctant or polite responses are not the only barriers. Occasionally, the respondent is not able to answer meaningfully. For example, illiteracy is a barrier when written material is used. This problem can be avoided by using oral interviews. Even when the interview is oral, however, a communication problem that could be called "technical illiteracy" may arise; that is, the terms or concepts used might be unfamiliar to respondents, even though phrased in their native language. They may not understand the questions and thus be unable to answer. Or they may answer without understanding, giving a useless response.

Quite apart from the terms used, respondents may be unable to cooperate effectively because they are asked to think in a way foreign to their normal thought patterns. They are being asked to react analytically rather than intuitively. Whatever the particular cause of the inability to respond, it is basically a translation problem. The research designer must be able to translate not only the words but also the concepts. The cultural gap must be bridged by the research designer.

Researching Hispanic Consumers. International marketing research invariably comes up against cultural differences that affect the use and efficacy of standard Western methods and may lead to erroneous interpretation of findings because of cultural misunderstandings. Professionals must then turn for help to experts who can help bridge cultural gaps. These issues are addressed in a recent book on doing research on Hispanic populations in the United States and elsewhere.[5] The book first addresses the question of who Hispanics in the United States are, summarizing demographic census results, describing their various countries of origin, and identifying basic Hispanic values such as the importance of family, the importance of feeling empathy for others, views of prescribed gender roles, and time orientation.

While Hispanics may be broadly alike, researchers need to bear in mind differences among Hispanic subgroups of Cuban, Mexican, Puerto Rican, and Central American origin, and how these differences affect how they are identified in conducting research. Misidentification and mislabeling can affect response rate and willingness to participate, replicability, and the generalizability of studies. Other pertinent issues include how to gain access to survey participants, how to enhance completion of survey instruments, and how to get beyond socially desirable responses. Such cultural differences require that standard, culturally appropriate instruments be adapted. Questionnaire translation is equally important because often there is no one correct way to translate an English word into Spanish or some other language, and multiple attempts at validation with different native speakers may be necessary.

Another study of Hispanic consumer behavior asserts that immigrant Mexicans have to learn to consume, and in doing so, combine consumption patterns learned from being Mexican with consumption patterns learned from American society. Eventual consumption patterns, therefore, are likely to be a hybrid of Mexican and U.S. consumption values.[6] As an example, the study cites the initial unwillingness of Mexicans to buy frozen produce or meat, based on the custom of buying it fresh and on a daily basis.

The international marketer's job is made easier when concepts and measurement instruments have been developed and validated across several cultures. While anthropologists have a long history of instrument adaptation, similar efforts are at a rudimentary stage in marketing. An example of such a direction is the concept of consumer ethnocentrism and an associated scale, CETSCALE. Tested and proven to be reliable across four countries, which are one another's major trading partners,[7] CETSCALE may be expected to be applied to other countries in the future.

Convergence of Consumer Behavior across Countries

Just as one might expect significant divergence among consumers because of cultural and religious differences, a growing convergence of consumer behavior is occurring across countries caused by multinational media and the standardized global marketing strategies of multinationals. For example, a 1995 study from Roper Starch Worldwide (see Table 7–4) suggests that four broad types of consumers exist—types generalizable to 1.97 billion consumers worldwide.[8] In the same vein, a Gallup poll conducted in the major cities of Argentina, Brazil, Chile, Colombia, and Mexico divides consumers into eight segments across countries, based on questions about income, education, occupation, type of home, and ownership of automobiles and durable goods.[9] The survey excluded low-income workers (about 17 percent of the working population) and ignored rural markets. Based on its sample of 17,564 people, Gallup divided Latin American consumers into eight categories:

Emerging professional elite: 14%	Progressive upper-middle class: 13%
Traditional elite: 11%	Self-made middle class: 11%
Skilled middle class: 9%	Industrial working class: 14%
Self-skilled lower middle class: 13%	Struggling working class: 15%

Improvisation

Some improvisation is probably used in all marketing research, but a higher degree is needed in international markets. **Improvisation** may be loosely defined as unconventional ways of getting the desired market information and/or finding proxy variables when data are not available on the primary variables.[10]

TABLE 7–4	Roper Starch's Four Major Types of Consumers Worldwide			
Consumer Type	*Percent of Global Sample*	*Percent of U.S. Sample*	*Major Features of Group*	*Sample Comment*
Deal makers: Negotiate and haggle before buying	29%	37%	Well-educated group with average levels of affluence and employment, found predominantly in the United States and in developing countries, where bargaining in open air bazaars is part of the shopping tradition and "half the fun."	"I feel really satisfied with myself, even excited, when I get a really good deal."
Price seekers: Interested primarily in obtaining the product at a low price	27	36	Found mainly in the United States and in markets such as Europe and Japan, where discount retailing is not widespread; includes a high proportion of retirees, the lowest education levels, an average level of affluence, and a female skew.	
Brand loyalists	23	17	Least affluent group, mostly male, median age 36, with average levels of education and employment.	"Once I find a brand that satisfies me, I usually don't experiment with new ones."
Luxury innovators: Seek new, prestigious brands	21	11	Most educated and affluent group, mostly male, median age 32, with the highest proportion of executives and professionals.	

Results are based on feedback from 37,743 respondents from 40 countries.
Source: Roper Starch Worldwide 1995 Global Consumer Trends Surveys, March/April 1995, as summarized in "Portrait of the World," *Marketing News,* August 28, 1995, 20–21.

One such approach is the use of national consumption statistics, by volume or units, for various items. Such statistics filter out exchange-rate anomalies that arise in the use of currency-based economic indicators. Examples of such information include the number, in units, of radios, televisions, and VCRs used; life expectancy at age one; the number of hospital beds available and doctors per 100,000 people; consumption of various food items on a per capita basis; the per capita availability of goods such as telephones, cars, and motorcycles; the number of airline and train revenue passenger miles sold per year; the consumption of electricity and steel; and the average number of years of schooling completed by the population. All such indicators are generally available for a variety of countries and can be used to group countries and can be correlated with market-size information.

New Services to Aid the International Firm

As international business continues to grow, more and more international marketing research services are available to aid firms. Existing international marketing research organizations are expanding into more countries with more services, and new organizations are entering the field. It is not possible to catalog all of these but an example is International Information Services Ltd. (IIS), a global product pick-up service for consumer packaged goods manufacturers. It has 400 clients in over 30 countries, including Coca-Cola, General Foods, J. Walter Thompson, and Unilever. Each day supermarkets in 120 countries are "raided" by IIS shoppers buying products or searching for information needed by clients. They provide samples of competitive products, client products for monitoring of quality, and/or information on competing brands (ingredients, varieties, sizes, prices, etc.).[11]

Learning by Doing

If the costs of primary marketing research are too great, another way to evaluate a market is by becoming an exporter. After a year or two of export experience, the firm will know more about actual market behavior than could be learned from a preliminary market study. If the market proves difficult or unprofitable, the firm can withdraw without major losses. If the market proves attractive, the firm might consider a heavier commitment in the country.

OTHER RESEARCH TECHNIQUES TO USE IN DEVELOPING COUNTRIES

Moyer has suggested four techniques that are relevant for researching small, lower income markets:[12] analysis of demand patterns, multiple-factor indexes, estimation by analogy, and regression analysis.

Analysis of Demand Patterns

Countries at different levels of per capita income have diverse patterns of consumption and production. (This commonplace observation is illustrated in Figure 7–1.) The importance of this statement lies in the fact that the researcher can usually get data at this macro level for most countries. This simple technique, known as the multiple-factor index approach, thus allows insights into the consumption-production profiles of many countries. Though relatively crude, it gives a clue both to a country's present position and the direction it is going. This in turn helps the firm identify possibilities for export or local production in that market.

Multiple-Factor Indexes

A multiple-factor index measures market potential indirectly, using as proxies a number of variables that intuition or statistical analysis reveal to be closely correlated with the potential market for the product in question. For example, a manufacturer of modular housing may look at these factors:

♦ The rate of household formation.

♦ Population demographics to gauge the percentage of the population in the age bracket from 20 to 30 years, a prime household forming segment.

♦ Income-level segments with some minimum per capital household income such as $2,000 per year being used to gauge purchasing power.

Smoothing out these numbers over several time periods and relating them to historic house sales and new housing construction may provide useful estimates of potential market size.

Estimation by Analogy

For countries with limited data, estimating market potential can be a precarious exercise. Given the absence of hard data, one technique—estimation by analogy—can be helpful in getting a better feel for market potential in such countries. This estimation is done in two ways: (1) through cross-section comparisons and (2) through the displacement of a time series in time.

The **cross-section comparison approach** involves taking the known market size of a product in one country and relating it to some economic indicator, such as disposable personal income, to derive a ratio. This ratio (of product consumption to disposable personal income in our illustration) is then applied to another country where disposable personal income is known in order to derive the market potential for the product in that country.

The **time-series approach** estimates the demand in the second country by assuming that it has the same level of consumption that the first country had at the same level of development (or per capita income). This technique assumes that

FIGURE 7-1   **Typical Patterns of Growth in Manufacturing Industries**

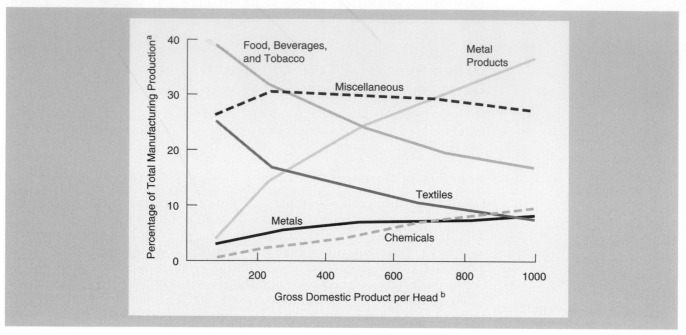

[a]Based on time-series analysis for selected years, 1899–1957, for 7 to 10 countries depending on commodity.
[b]Dollars at 1955 prices.

product usage moves through a cycle, with the product being consumed in small quantities (or not at all) when countries are underdeveloped and in increasing amounts with economic growth. Thus, looking at meat and egg consumption in Taiwan in the late 60s and early 70s can allow a rough estimation of demand for meat and eggs in mainland China in the 90s, with Chinese incomes being at about the levels prevalent in Taiwan in the early 70s.

Both approaches have limitations. The cross-section method assumes a linear consumption function. Both assume comparable consumption patterns among countries. When these assumptions are not true, the comparisons are misleading. When more sophisticated techniques are not feasible, however, estimation by analogy is a useful first step.

Using Long-Term Trend Data to Estimate Market Size

The parcel tanker industry provides an example of how long-term trend data can be used to estimate market size. Parcel tankers (as distinct from oil tankers) are used to transport bulk liquids such as chemicals. Freight rates can vary depending on demand and supply. In 1995, rates were about $60 per ton, compared to around $48 per ton in 1994. Operating leverage is high in the industry. A $1 increase in the freight rate, for example, can mean an additional $11 million in operating profit for a major parcel tanker company such as Stolt-Nielsen, a Norwegian tanker company that transports, stores, and distributes bulk liquids. Such tankers are usually chartered for long periods, and as charters end and new charter periods are negotiated, charter rates can be increased depending on the prevailing demand-supply patterns.

For a company such as Stolt, forecasting demand and supply is important in determining both what charter rates might be like in the future, as well as whether to order new tankers to be built. This decision is important because, depending on shipyard backlog, tankers must be ordered to precise design specifications and then built, with delivery from time of order stretching out to as long as two years. Figure 7–2 sets out trend data on parcel tanker demand and supply, in thousands of metric tons, for the period 1969 to 1998. Several factors go into compiling such data, especially the forecasts for the near-term future period, 1995 to 2000. Demand figures are derived from estimating the rate at which worldwide transportation of chemicals is growing, which in turn is related to GDP growth, particularly in Southeast Asia; demand is growing at 5 to 7 percent a year. Then, on the supply side, the existing number of tankers available is known, and to that is added the number of new tankers being built and the rate of scrappage. That is, old, obsolete tankers nearing the end of their seaworthy days and posing environmental hazards because of leakage problems will be taken out of service, thus reducing the total supply. All of these factors are used to derive the supply and demand figures shown in Figure 7–2.

As can be seen, demand will outstrip supply over the next few years by almost one million metric tons, suggesting that freight rates will rise sharply and that several new tanker orders will be placed. To the extent that a company such as Stolt-Nielsen is armed with such information earlier than its competitors, it can charge higher rates and lease its tankers on spot rates rather than on long-term charters, thus increasing its profits. It can also order new tankers earlier, thus being able to increase its capacity in a timely fashion, taking advantage of healthy demand conditions. By placing orders early, it can also be more sure of getting its tankers delivered on time (a latecomer may find that the shipyards are too busy, that delivery is far off, and that by the time delivery occurs, demand and supply may once more have moved into balance, reducing rates once again.)

Based on the demand and supply projections, Stolt-Nielsen has ordered 10 new parcel tankers for delivery over the next three years. It took delivery of a 37,000-ton, all-stainless-steel chemical tanker from Danyard in Denmark, and will be getting six more from the same yard, as well as three others of similar design from a shipyard in France. Stolt might scrap some older tankers during the same time frame. In addition, the company is expanding into Asia by establishing special tank container cleaning and repair facilities and developing bulk chemical storage locations in Japan, Korea, Taiwan, mainland China, and Singapore.[13] The researcher should, however, keep in mind that as global economic conditions change, such forecasts need to be updated. For example, during the 1997–98 period, the Asian economies fell into a recession, and their demand for basic products such as chemicals dropped sharply, affecting world demand for tankers to transport chemicals. At the same time, shipyards in countries such as Korea, China, and Japan attempted to preserve jobs by cutting ship prices, leading to a shift of demand for ships to these countries and creating the possibility of overbuying currently—in essence "borrowing" from future demand, with the possibility of limiting future demand. These new developments might change the forecasted demand supply imbalance shown in Figure 7–2.

Regression Analysis

Regression analysis provides a quantitative technique to sharpen estimates derived by the estimation-by-analogy method just discussed. Cross-section studies using regression analysis benefit from existing predictable demand patterns for many products in countries at different stages of growth. The researcher studies the relationship between gross economic indicators and demand for a specific product for countries with both kinds of data. The relationship derived can then be transferred to those countries that have only the gross economic data but not the product-consumption data.

Moyer's use of this is presented in Table 7–5. The equation used here was the simple regression $y = a + bx$, where y is the amount of product in use per thousand of population and x is per capita GNP.

FIGURE 7–2 Parcel Tanker Supply and Demand Balance (1969–1998)

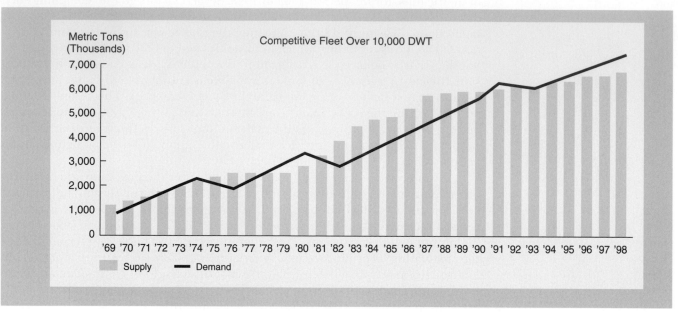

Source: "Investing in Neglected Stocks," *Wall Street Transcript,* July 31, 1995, 119, 364.

The regression results in Table 7–5 suggest that an increase of $100 in per capita GNP would result, on the average, in an increase of 10 automobiles, 10 refrigerators, 9 washing machines, 7 TV sets, and 27 radios per 1,000 population. Construction of such a table relevant to the products of a specific firm can be very useful. The model can use additional independent variables beyond GNP per capita. For example, airlines forecast air traffic growth with two factors, per capita GNP growth and the yield in cents per mile ("yield" is the air fare for a route divided into the distance, or number of miles on that route). Over long periods, this regression model has proved reasonably accurate, with air traffic growing as incomes grow and dropping as fares rise.

There are limitations to using regression, however. For example, as a product approaches saturation levels, the rate of consumption declines, requiring a different equation to explain the relationship. Nevertheless, regression analysis can provide useful insights.

Comparative Analysis

Comparative analysis[14] is an attempt to organize information and experience to maximize their usefulness. In international marketing, this means that the company gathers and organizes its intelligence from all its global operations to see what new insights can be gained.

Grouping or classifying objects is an important step in understanding markets. Competing products can be grouped together to understand the different segments that are being targeted. Consumers can be grouped to assess customer segments. And countries can be grouped to determine which markets are similar to one another. In this way, a generic strategy can be prepared for the countries belonging to a group rather than approaching each country individually. Moreover, groups of countries can be compared in evaluating market performance. One of the difficulties of comparative market performance assessment is that markets are different, so the comparison may be unfair. Performing comparisons only on countries that are similar enough to belong to a group mitigates this problem.

| TABLE 7–5 | Regression in Product in Use per 1,000 Population on per Capita Gross National Product | | |

Product	Number of Observations	Regression Equation	Unadjusted R^2
Autos	37	$-21.071 + 0.101x$	0.759
Radio sets	42	$8.325 + 0.275x$	0.784
TV sets	31	$-16.501 + 0.074x$	0.503
Refrigerators	24	$-21.330 + 0.102x$	0.743
Washing machines	22	$-15.623 + 0.094x$	0.736

Source: Reed Moyer, "International Market Analysis," *Journal of Marketing Research,* November 1968, 358.

Cluster Analysis

The approaches used to develop a short list of potential markets include comparative analysis of countries using macroeconomic and consumption data. Cluster analysis is a favored technique of identifying similar markets. The goal here is to ensure that the countries with the greatest potential make it to the short list for further investigation.

The mathematical techniques of cluster analysis were used by Sethi to develop seven distinct groups of countries. To develop these distinct groups, Sethi first used four sets of variables for each of the countries to be analyzed:[15]

1. *Production and transportation variables,* measured by items such as air passenger and cargo traffic, electricity usage, number of large cities, and population.

2. *Consumption variables,* based on income and GNP per capita, the number of cars, televisions, hospital beds, radios, and telephones per capita, and educational levels of the population.

3. *Trade data,* derived from import and export figures.

4. *Health and education variables,* using data such as life expectancy, school enrollment, and doctors per capita.

Once "scores" for these four variables are developed for each country, the countries themselves are grouped into seven distinct groups. The implication is that if similarity of countries within the groups is sufficiently strong that similar marketing strategies can be used for all countries within a group.

Similar cluster analysis techniques are used by Economist Intelligence Unit (EIU) to group markets based on the opportunities they offer (Figure 7–3). EIU's indexes cover market size, market growth rates, and market intensity (which measures the relative concentration of wealth and purchasing power in those countries). For example, the market-size index is derived from data on population, consumption statistics, steel consumption, cement and electricity production, and ownership of telephones, cars, and televisions. Note the similarity of the variables used at EIU to those used by Sethi in his analysis.

Clustering Countries by Product Diffusion Patterns

A problem with clustering countries on the basis of macroeconomic variables is that the resulting segments may not be helpful to international marketers because

FIGURE 7-3   **EIU Market Indexes: Size, Growth, and Intensity of 20 Largest Markets**

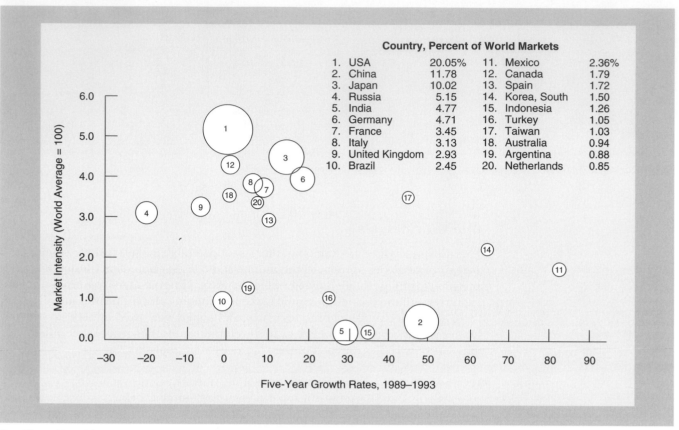

Country, Percent of World Markets			
1. USA	20.05%	11. Mexico	2.36%
2. China	11.78	12. Canada	1.79
3. Japan	10.02	13. Spain	1.72
4. Russia	5.15	14. Korea, South	1.50
5. India	4.77	15. Indonesia	1.26
6. Germany	4.71	16. Turkey	1.05
7. France	3.45	17. Taiwan	1.03
8. Italy	3.13	18. Australia	0.94
9. United Kingdom	2.93	19. Argentina	0.88
10. Brazil	2.45	20. Netherlands	0.85

Note: The position of the center of each circle shows the intensity of the market (when measured against the vertical axis) and its cumulative growth over the 1989–1993 period (when measured against the horizontal axis). The size of the circle indicates the relative size of the market as a percentage of the total world market.
Source: Economist Intelligence Unit (EIU), as reported in *Cross-border Monitor,* August 30, 1995, 12.

acceptance and diffusion of new products may vary within the proposed segments. An alternative is to segment countries based on how similar they are in the rate at which new products are adopted (the product diffusion rate). (See Table 7–6 for a comparison of these approaches.) If such segments could be derived, managers could use information from the **lead market,** about variables such as growth in market size, when sales reach a peak, to make inferences on the same variables for **lagging markets.** This allows a country to belong to more than one segment at the same time. For example, the United States could be in the leading markets segment for a product such as advanced personal computers, while lagging in the use of products such as smart cards or high-speed trains.

Macroeconomic data such as the standard of living are, of course, important in explaining the readiness of a country market to accept innovation; in addition, a diffusion-based segmentation approach uses data about factors such as lifestyle (use of phones per capita, for example), and cosmopolitanism (tourist expenditures and receipts). A recent research study looked at the relationship between such country-level variables and sales growth over a 14-year period for three consumer durables—color TV sets, VCRs, and CD players—for 12 advanced industrial nations from Europe, as well as Japan and the United States.[16]

The study showed that segments based on product adoption rates did not agree with segments derived from broad macroeconomic data alone, suggesting that countries that look similar from a broad macroeconomic perspective may differ in the rate at which they are willing to adopt and buy new products. Cultural factors such as language and religion, which were not specifically included in the study, may play

TABLE 7–6	Two Approaches to Country Segmentation in International Marketing
Segmentation Using Macroeconomic Data	**Segmentation Using Product Diffusion Approaches**
Production and transportation variables; personal consumption data; trade data; and health and education statistics	Long-term time series data on product sales; traditional macroeconomic data (shown in previous column); and lifestyle data, indicators of cosmopolitanism

an important role in explaining differences in the product diffusion rate. In addition, other recent studies have noted the importance of culture, mobility, and sex roles as important factors in explaining differences in product adoption rates.[17]

Screening Potential International Markets

Another marketing research screening technique useful to derive a short list of key country markets is described here, as applied to the market for kidney dialysis equipment.[18] The first step is to determine which countries can afford such medical equipment. The high cost of kidney dialysis equipment and necessary supplies and personnel limits the market to wealthy countries. Hence, a first screen might be based on the wealth of a country, measured by the following:

1. A total GDP of over $15 billion.

2. GDP per capita of at least $1,500.

This screen alone reduces the number of potential markets to 28 countries outside North America.

Next, the markets must have specialized hospitals and doctors who can competently administer dialysis treatment. In addition, the treatment is expensive and requires a certain level of government support and subsidy, or the market for private patients alone would be too small to justify attempts at market penetration. Thus, a second screen would include other criteria:

1. No more than 200 people per hospital bed.

2. No more than 1,000 people per doctor.

3. Government health care expenditures of at least $100 million.

4. Government health care expenditures of at least $20 per capita.

This calculation then results in a set of 19 countries as potential markets.

A third screen analyzes the markets in terms of the current market for dialysis equipment. Two factors are used:

1. At least 1,000 deaths per year due to kidney-related causes. A lower number might indicate that the market for dialysis equipment is already being well served by competition.

2. At least 40 percent growth in the number of patients being treated with dialysis equipment.

This results in just three markets being considered: Italy, Greece, and Spain.

A fourth screen consists of carefully evaluating the three countries in terms of existing competition, political risk, and other factors. Management subjectivity can enter here because some managerial judgment is required in evaluating the strength of competition and political risk. Management may well decide to enter more than one of the three markets identified thus far. It may also go back to the third screening step and reduce the required rate of growth to, say, 30 percent, in order to add some additional potential markets.

Once a short list of potential markets has been made up, individual markets must be studied more carefully. At this point, information can be obtained from the Department of Commerce's Comparison Shopping Service (CSS). A CSS survey covers a product in a particular country market, indicating the product's overall marketability, chief competitors, comparative prices, customary entry, distribution, and promotion practices, trade barriers, and the degree to which the company's product competes. About 50 key countries are covered by this low-cost and timely service.

Gap Analysis

The goal of gap analysis is to analyze the difference ("gap") between estimated total market potential and a company's sales.[19] The gap can be divided into four categories:

1. *Usage gap.* The usage gap refers to total industry sales being less than the estimated total market potential. Such gaps may have their explanation either in estimation errors or in unpredictable changes in consumer tastes and behavior, such as, for example, eggs being less in demand than expected. In the United States, such a usage gap would probably be traced to health-related concerns.

2. *Competitive gap.* Competitive gap refers to existing market share compared with expected market share; analysis is needed to indicate why market-share shifts have taken place and what is needed to regain market share from competitors.

3. *Product-line gap.* Product-line gap arises because a company does not have a full product line compared to its competitors; thus, it loses sales. An example might be in the computer industry, where a part of the product line is small, portable laptop computers. To the extent that Dell was late in marketing or did not have a laptop computer available, its market share was less than it would have been if it had fielded a full product line. Toshiba faced the opposite problem, offering only laptops in the U.S. market and losing corporate sales because the clients wanted to buy both laptops and PC servers and desktops from the same company.

4. *Distribution gap.* A company with a distribution gap is failing to target part of the market because of a lack of distribution facilities or agents. Closing such a gap would require that the firm extend distribution and product availability to cover all regions and segments of the market.

Input-Output Tables

Input-output tables, discussed in Chapter 3, provide an analytical tool of great value in studying demand in foreign markets. They are becoming increasingly available for many more countries, particularly for the advanced industrialized nations and the newly industrializing countries such as Brazil, Taiwan, and India. They are useful both for industrial product analysis and for the analysis of market demand for intermediate components and materials. Input-output tables give specific attention to how production functions vary among nations and thus allow the researcher to adjust market forecasts to account for such country differences.

Information Sought by Marketing Research Professionals

The journal *Marketing News* surveyed marketing professionals to ascertain the types of decisions most requiring quantitative market research. Four areas were highlighted:

1. Information in making new product development decisions: 21 percent.

2. Pricing decisions: 16 percent.

3. Setting and allocating sales efforts: 5 percent.

4. Market segmentation: 3 percent.

In terms of information actually gathered by market research, 19 percent of the professionals surveyed obtained quantitative data on market size, 14 percent on pricing trends, 12 percent on overall market trends, 11 percent on segment size, 7 percent on competitor information, and 6 percent on information about competitors. This survey's suggestion that approximately four of five marketing professionals see little need for quantitative market research data about marketing issues or decisions is remarkable.[20]

A more recent survey of 166 American and 37 Japanese market research firms has shown that marketing research practices are surprisingly similar in the two countries.[21] Japanese firms conduct more research projects focusing on marketing information system design, import and export strategy development, and forecasting. Given the much greater role of exports in Japanese international business strategy, such an export focus seems warranted. More Japanese research is done on distribution channel issues, perhaps because Japanese distribution is convoluted, inefficient, and more complex, with many more intermediaries between customer and firm. Japanese firms also seem to contract out sales research studies, usually done in-house by U.S. firms, to firms with greater access to databases and the ability to store data, resulting in studies characterized by greater confidentiality and privacy.

GOING BEYOND MARKET DEMAND: COST AND TECHNOLOGY TRENDS

Market research focuses mainly on market potential and consumer behavior. In international marketing, research into cost and technology trends is also essential. In addition, if the firm considers establishing a sales subsidiary, warehouses, service centers, and manufacturing operations, political risk analysis is necessary to assess whether it will be able to stay in the market for some length of time.

Cost trends shed light on relative cost competitiveness. For example, raw materials or components may be available from certain sources at lower cost than from others. Similarly, information about substituting newer low-cost materials—such as plastics for metal—and redesigning products to use fewer parts is relevant to a cost research study.

Technology trends reveal the future direction of new products and ultimately affect sales and market share. Such research generally focuses on markets in which technological innovations are first presented. It aims to establish directions that the industry is likely to take and the relative position of key competitors in key technologies. For example, an innovation in the computer industry is the growing use of specialized machines as file servers in a network. How soon such machines will become standard, how fast the current customer base will demand such file servers, and how quickly competition will introduce such machines are questions that research into technology trends attempts to solve.

GLOBAL MARKETING

Where Are All the Young 'Uns?

The United States is a mature $5 trillion economy. An estimated 40 million children under the age of 10 live in the United States, and their parents are fairly indulgent, spending about $225 per child, on average. Even so, the U.S. toy market has been fairly stagnant, with 1990 sales of about $9 billion, not much higher than 1986 sales of $8.8 billion. Major U.S. toy companies such as Mattel, Hasbro, and Tyco must therefore look to overseas markets to obtain higher rates of growth. Where should they turn?

Estimates of the numbers of children (in millions) under age 10 in 1990 are as follows:

China	275
India	240
Southeast Asia	120
South America	115
Europe	70
Russia	50
Japan	15

Foreigners spend far less on their children's toys, however. Even in affluent Europe, average per child spending is approximately $100. Therefore, overseas growth requires motivating

INFORMATION SOURCES FOR INTERNATIONAL MARKETING

Generally speaking, three basic sources of foreign market information exist: (1) secondary sources or published information, (2) knowledgeable individuals within the domestic market, and (3) empirical research in foreign markets.

U.S. Government Department of Commerce

The Department of Commerce is the chief government source of foreign market information, and it actively seeks to aid U.S. firms in selling abroad. The umbrella organization for this purpose in the Department of Commerce is the International Trade Administration (ITA). It manages the U.S. Commercial Service, a network of district offices in major cities around the country. These offices offer personal consultation to U.S. firms interested in doing business internationally.

Another service of ITA is the publication of information on many topics of interest to the international marketer. *Business America,* its biweekly magazine, is an excellent source of trade leads and information on developments in world trade. *Overseas Business Reports* is a regular series on most major markets of the world. Information covered in these reports includes economic and marketing data on each country, guidelines on how to do business there, copyright and trademark laws, and business and import regulations. In addition to international market information, the Department of Commerce offers specific guidance in locating customers, agents, or licensees in foreign markets (see Table 7–7).

The Department of Commerce aids provide a good starting point for much foreign marketing research. First, they cover a wide range of subject matter as well as countries, and second, all this material and assistance are available at very modest cost. The latest useful product is the National Trade Data Bank information on CD-ROM. (See "Global Marketing," "The National Trade Data Bank: Marketing Information for Exporters.")

parents to spend more on toys for their children and focusing on markets where there are large numbers of children and a growing disposable income.

Tastes in toys may also be affected by culture; hence, in order to capitalize on what at first blush looks to be a beckoning worldwide market, careful research is needed on who buys toys, what sorts of toys are likely to sell, and what is the best mode of entry.

Major toy manufacturers are indeed targeting toy markets in emerging nations. China's toy market is forecasted to grow from about $1 billion in 1994 to around $12 billion by the year 2007. Western toy firms have begun establishing joint ventures in China to manufacture toys and are attempting to sell up to 30 percent of the manufactured toys within

the Chinese market. Since the toy industry thrives on innovation, it is relatively open to new ideas, thus providing a point of entry to small, new companies from countries such as Taiwan and Hong Kong. Toy manufacturers are strategizing to decide which categories of toys may sell best in these emerging nations, from categories as disparate as male action figures, plush toys, large dolls, fashion dolls, toys with electronic chips, and board games. For small companies, licensing new toy ideas might be preferable to wrestling with local distribution arrangements and negotiating merchandising programs and tie-ins with complementary firms such as fast food and photo-finishing outlets.

Sources: David Mehegan, "A Cure for Toy Troubles," *The Boston Globe*, December 2, 1990; "Breakfast Seminar: Strategies for Growth," *Playthings*, May 1994.

Other Government Departments

Other government departments also provide information on international trade matters. Among these are the Agency for International Development, the Federal Trade Commission, the Department of Agriculture, and the International Trade Commission. The Department of Labor publishes a periodical titled *Labor Developments Abroad*. These examples merely indicate the extent of the U.S. government's interest in foreign countries and the way its information services can benefit the international marketer.

Other Governments

Many foreign governments have a large amount of data on their own economies, much of which is available from the country's embassy or consulate. In some cases, information can be obtained from a distributor or a subsidiary within the country. If the country is seeking to attract foreign investment, its information services are likely to be especially good. It probably has a development office in the United States, such as the Indian Investment Center in New York City. Many countries have Web sites maintained by their foreign investment bureaus, the central bank, and other major trade organizations, such as JETRO, the Japan Trade Research Organization, in the case of Japan.

International Organizations

Chief among international organizations, of course, is the United Nations and its affiliated organizations. There is no doubt about its major role in gathering and disseminating information about all aspects of the world economy. Its economic commissions conduct numerous studies and issue regular publications such as the *Economic Survey of Europe* and the *Economic Survey of Latin America*. The *United Nations Statistical Yearbook* is an invaluable source of data on over 200 countries.

The National Trade Data Bank: Marketing Information for Exporters

The Department of Commerce's National Trade Data Bank (NTDB) supplies data monthly on CD-ROM; monthly updates include the full text of thousands of documents useful in international marketing. Major data sources contained on the CD-ROM include *Annual Industrial Outlook* and the *World Factbook,* containing country profiles; marketing research reports on specific products, industries, and countries; economic statistics for foreign countries, including interest and exchange rates, labor costs and rates, export and import statistics, and foreign investment figures. The *Foreign Trader's Index* contains lists of organizations in foreign countries, their product line interests, and how they might help U.S. exporters.

For example, a company interested in considering industrial food service equipment for hotels, restaurants, hospitals, company cafeterias, and so on might begin the search on CD-ROM with the keyword *industry* and then request *marketing research reports* from the next menu; then information about a particular *country* could be requested. From the list of countries, the company could pick *India,* which would bring up a list of nearly 100 marketing research reports available for India. Selecting *restaurant catering equipment* from the list would give the full text of a study by U.S. foreign commercial service personnel in Delhi, providing information on size of the market, sales in recent years, U.S. market share, principal competitors, upcoming trade shows if any, major customers, and other useful information.

Another search, say, of the market for notebook computers in Australia might yield a research report prepared by the U.S. embassy in Australia. The report could show that imports account for nearly all of the notebook computers sold in Australia and that the Australian market is growing at 38 percent a year. U.S. competitors have a one-third market share but face stiff competition from Japan, Taiwan, and Hong Kong. The market leader is Toshiba.

The NTDB service is relatively inexpensive, at $35 for a single copy of the NTDB CD-ROM or $360 for an annual subscription from the U.S. Department of Commerce, National Trade Data Bank, Office of Business Analysis, Room 4885, HCHB, Washington, DC 20230. The information can be printed out, copied to disk, and read into other software packages such as Excel, or word-processing packages. It is a useful and essential first step for any company beginning its marketing research into foreign markets.

Source: Melissa Malhame, "The National Trade Data Bank: A Valuable Resource for Exporters," *Business America,* April 1991.

Many UN agencies are relatively unknown to the public, but they are doing work that is important to international corporations. For example, manufacturers of pharmaceuticals, foodstuffs, and hospital equipment must be up-to-date on the activities of the World Health Organization. Personnel managers in international companies need to be informed about the publications and services of ILO (International Labor Organization). Companies producing foodstuffs, fertilizers, or farm equipment are interested in the activities of the Food and Agriculture Organization (FAO). In fact, FAO has established the Industry Cooperation Program to promote closer relations with industry. Some of the international companies belonging to the program are General Foods, H. J. Heinz, Merck, Union Carbide, Nestlé, Massey-Ferguson, Unilever, and Shell.

Other international organizations also provide useful information. The Organization for Economic Cooperation and Development (OECD) is the most active. Its bimonthly *General Statistics* gives the major economic indicators for the member countries (the industrialized countries of the West). The OECD also publishes studies on many other topics of interest to the international marketer and now sells subscriptions to its valuable economic data.

Other regional organizations supply information on their regions. The European Union (EU), for example, is especially useful for information on developments affecting that area. A number of U.S. companies have located their European headquarters in Brussels partly to be near its power center. The EU also has an information center in Washington, D.C., and in New York City.

In addition, the International Monetary Fund issues the monthly *International Financial Statistics,* while the World Trade Organization (WTO) publishes world trade data. Also highly useful is the World Bank, with its annual *World Development Report.*

On-Line Databases

Secondary data-collection efforts can be pursued on-line, using the Internet and commercial-service provider access to a wealth of databases. For example, the Economic Bulletin Board (EBB) of the U.S. Department of Commerce can be accessed from a variety of on-line services, allowing users to examine a host of economic data and market research reports prepared by U.S. government agencies. Nearly every major government organization maintains a Web page allowing users to access published reports by each of these agencies. A brief example using the ABI/Inform database illustrates the potential of this medium. Suppose that a researcher is interested in gathering secondary data on the vacation market in Bermuda. Using Boolean logic after logging on to ABI/Inform, available through Dialog or the Lexis/Nexis database, the researcher can issue a query such as "Bermuda and (cruise or vacation or travel) and 199*." Such a query would bring up data sources relating to vacations, cruises, or travel, all linked to Bermuda since 1990.

Access to such on-line databases is not cheap, but with practice and advance formulation of a search strategy, including a careful delineation of key search terms, researchers can quickly put together a vast set of material from diverse sources pertinent to the research question at hand.[22] Aside from the standard sources such as Dow Jones, Lexis/Nexis, and the Internet, researchers can consult database directories such as *Computer-Readable Databases,* from Gale Research, Detroit, and *Data Base Directory* from Knowledge Industry Publications, White Plains, New York.

Other Sources of Information

Many industries have their own trade associations that serve as clearinghouses for information related to international business. For example, the Aerospace Industries Association in Washington, D.C., prepares an annual report including information on the international business performance of the industry, international business prospects for the coming year, international business historic time series, and relevant government legislation and industry events. It also serves as a lobbying agency for the industry. Similar organizations exist for nearly every major industry, such as telecommunications, the semiconductor industry, machine tools, the software industry, and so on.

Beyond a narrow, single-industry focus are national associations such as the Chamber of Commerce and the National Foreign Trade Council, composed primarily of larger, U.S.–based firms. Similar organizations exist in other countries such as the Keidanren in Japan, and their newsletters and libraries serve as important repositories of relevant secondary information. Individual states and cities also have foreign-trade associations and agencies, such as Massport in Boston, Massachusetts, which often leads trade missions to foreign markets and serves as a rallying point for international business initiatives at the state level. A strong point of such associations is the self-help feature, in that their members are often businesspeople with international business experience who can help their colleagues with specific details of international business in a specific country.

In addition, advertising agencies, banks, airlines, express package services, shipping organizations, freight forwarders, and the major accounting and management consulting firms are also useful sources of international business information. As business has expanded abroad, these groups have followed their clients. Many can offer services abroad that are as good as those they offer at

TABLE 7–7	**Department of Commerce Aid to Foreign Market Research**

A quick, easy way to match your international business requirements to the programs, services, and publications described in this guide.

IF YOU ARE SEEKING INFORMATION OR ASSISTANCE REGARDING ⟶ *USE* ⬇	*Potential Markets*	*Market Research*	*Direct Sales Leads*	*Agents/ Distributors*	*Licenses*
U.S. and Foreign Commercial Service	•	•	•		•
District Export Councils					
Trade Opportunities Program			•	•	•
Agent/Distributor Service				•	
Overseas Business Reports	•	•			
Foreign Economic Trends	•	•			
Small Business Administration		•			
International Chambers of Commerce					
Export Statistics Profiles	•	•			
Export Information System Data Reports	•	•			
Annual Worldwide Industry Reviews	•	•			
International Market Research	•	•			
Country Market Surveys	•	•			
Custom Statistical Service	•	•			
Product Market Profile	•	•			
Market Share Reports	•	•			
Country Market Profiles	•	•			
Country Trade Statistics	•	•			
Background Notes		•			
International Economic Indicators	•	•			
World Traders Data Reports					
Commercial News USA	•		•	•	
Export-Import Bank					
Export Mailing List Service	•	•	•	•	
Commerce Trade Shows	•	•	•	•	•
Commerce Trade Missions	•	•	•	•	•
Export Development Offices		•			
Catalog Exhibitions			•		
Major Projects Program					
Overseas Private Investment Corporation					
Private Export Funding Corporation					
Foreign Sales Corporation					
Commerce Business Daily	•		•		
Free Ports and Free Trade Zones					

Source: *A Basic Guide to Exporting* (Washington, DC: U.S. Department of Commerce, 1986).

home. Foreign market intelligence is not limited to U.S. firms; more and more, local organizations in the major industrial countries compete with the U.S. consulting and research groups. Besides the general market research groups, such specialized market information services as A. C. Nielsen are operating in major world markets. Other examples include bank newsletters and periodic reports such as the accounting firms' information guides to taxation and doing business in a variety of overseas markets.

Credit Analysis	Financial Assistance	Risk Insurance	Tax Incentives	Export Counseling	Export Regulations	Overseas Contracts	Marketing Strategies	Trade Complaints
				•	•		•	•
				•				
						•		
	•			•				
					•			
•								
	•							
•							•	
•							•	
						•		
•			•					
	•							
	•			•				

As international business expands, the researcher can expect foreign market information services to grow along with it. There are more than 1,100 market research agencies in 60 different countries.[23]

A basic reference book is the *Glossary of Marketing Research*, published by the European organization ESOMAR.[24] The book's main feature is an alphabetical list of marketing research terms in English and in several other languages—French, German, Italian, Spanish, and Dutch—with indexes that allow cross-referencing.

The Company's In-House Expertise

Companies frequently forget their own in-house expertise. Over the years, a company can build up databases and informed personnel with field experience who may return from foreign assignments and move on to other domestic postings. Any company could benefit from developing a systematic framework for inventorying the overseas knowledge and experience of its personnel in a centralized database so that they can access "the wealth" when projects require a certain kind of knowledge, an in-house *Knowledge Intranet*. Failure to utilize such expertise is exacerbated as a company grows and develops multiple regional and national units, each with its own staff, projects, and historical databases. Of course, personnel turnover is another way to lose accumulated knowledge and expertise, as the tacit knowledge embedded in key personnel is lost when they leave the company, without attempts having been made to transform their knowledge into explicit knowledge that can be stored and accessed through corporate intranets.

Related parties such as suppliers, distributors, and even major customers can be another source of information for a company's secondary data gathering. Developing detailed plans under which a company's distributors are asked to provide headquarters with systematically gathered information about a product market in their territory can substantially enhance a firm's international market information. Such data may extend to pricing policies of competitors, new product introductions, brand image, customer satisfaction, and market growth rates.

Information for Sale

Many of the previous information sources are either free or offered at nominal cost. In the case of governments, the information service is subsidized. In the other cases, the supply of information is incidental to the main business of the supplier. Domestic examples of such organizations are A. C. Nielsen, Ward's (automotive reports), and Dodge (construction reports). Such organizations have extensive international coverage. (See Table 7–3.)

One important source on foreign business is found in the numerous directories of foreign firms in manufacturing, retailing, and other lines of business. Some cover just one country, but others are international in coverage. There are even guides to these directories so that it is possible to locate all those relevant to a particular need. An example is *Trade Directories of the World,* a loose-leaf volume by Croner Publications.

A number of companies publish information about international trade. Dun and Bradstreet is one of the companies actively providing international financial and marketing information to those who buy its services, including banks and manufacturers. Among its important publications are *International Market Guide, Continental Europe,* and *International Market Guide, Latin America.*

Two widely used services have an entirely international focus. The Economist Intelligence Unit (EIU), which is associated with *The Economist* magazine, is one. EIU services include quarterly reports on economic and political matters for most countries of the world, as well as regular reports on marketing in Europe and other special topics. EIU also conducts specialized market studies for individual firms, but in this capacity it competes with other consulting firms.

The other widely used information service is Business International (BI), since merged with the EIU. With correspondents in all parts of the world, BI publishes weekly newsletters on developments affecting international business as well as on companies' international experiences and problems. The weekly letters specialize by area on Europe, Asia, China, Latin America, and Eastern Europe. Other BI publications include investing, licensing, and trading conditions (in over 50 countries) and financing foreign operations, annual services with loose-leaf supplements.

MARKETING RESEARCH MODELS

Modeling Consumer Behavior

Why U.S. Buyers Buy Japanese Cars

Market research professionals often seek to model consumer behavior in the international marketplace. One model attempts to explain why U.S. households buy Japanese cars.[25] Developed by Dardis and Soberon-Ferrer, it hypothesizes that buying Japanese cars is affected by household characteristics that, in turn, determine the weight given to different product attributes, leading eventually to the decision to buy or not buy a Japanese car. Specifically, the variables used to profile *household characteristics* include income, age, sex, marital status, race, education of the head of the household, geographic location within the United States, and a variable labeled "the origin of disposed stock," meaning, whether a previous car sold (if any) was of Japanese or other origin (i.e., whether that household had previously owned a Japanese car).

In a similar fashion, *product attributes* modeled included variables that primarily capture automobile quality: cost of repair, frequency of repair, operating efficiency (miles per gallon), weight (a means of gauging comfort and safety), the depreciation rate (a reflection of the resale value of the car), and finally, the purchase price of the car, which is held constant to isolate the effect of the quality variables.

It is important to marketers to develop a model on which to base their data collection and analysis efforts. The model can be modified to include additional variables such as social class, religion, and occupation. The bottom line is that an explicit model allows a directed research effort to gather and analyze data, which permits validation and modification of the model. For example, the Dardis and Soberon-Ferrer model showed that lowering the depreciation rate of the car by 1 percent a year increased the probability of buying a Japanese car from 22 to 26 percent. Similarly, lowering the fuel economy (miles per gallon) by 10 percent dropped the probability of buying a Japanese car from 22 percent to 14 percent.

The implications for marketing strategy are clear. For a U.S. company trying to catch up to the perception of Japanese cars, several methods exist to lower the probability that a household will buy a Japanese car: Rather than rely on vague appeals to buy American, companies should improve U.S. cars so that they depreciate slower, cost less to own and operate, and require repair less frequently. Significantly, the proposed model, when applied to past car-purchasing decisions, was able to correctly predict whether households would buy a Japanese or non-Japanese car 96 percent of the time.

Household Buying Behavior

A Study from Saudi Arabia

For many products, buying decisions are made jointly, by households, by husbands and wives, and in some cases, by children. Products such as houses, automobiles, furniture, and consumer durables such as refrigerators and stoves would fall in this category. Understanding whether households in different countries approach major purchasing decisions differently is critical in making international marketing decisions about product positioning, advertising appeals, direct-mail and telemarketing campaigns, and building loyalty. Marketers are interested in who makes the buying decisions in a family, and the relative influence during critical steps such as whether to buy, when to buy, where to buy, and how much to pay. Several competing theories exist to explain family purchasing behavior:

1. *Culture-defined behavior,* whereby cultural norms prescribe which spouse has more power in influencing purchase decisions.

2. *Resource contribution–based power,* whereby the spouse who contributes more resources (e.g., income, status, education, etc.) is more powerful in influencing decisions.

3. *Relative involvement,* whereby the spouse who has the greater interest and involvement in a product or service will have more influence over its purchase. Countries and societies can be categorized[26] as: (1) patriarchies; (2) modified patriarchies, consisting of modernizing nations that were patriarchies in the recent past; (3) transitional egalitarian, with movement toward equality of influence within the family, and greater weight being given to education, occupation, and income; and (4) egalitarian, with strong norms about equality of husbands and wives and power sharing. Household purchasing behavior can be expected to differ across these different kinds of societies.

A study on family purchasing behavior in Saudi Arabia showed how role behaviors of husbands and wives can significantly differ across countries.[27] Limited to a sample of 249 upscale, married Saudi women, the study is interesting as a study of family purchasing behavior in a developing country. It found that (1) husbands dominate consumer decision making in Saudi Arabia, as is the case in many developing countries; (2) husbands are dominant in deciding on buying a car and on "where to buy," except in the case of women's clothing; (3) in many cases, Saudi wives who work and/or are more educated, have more influence over purchasing decisions. Overall, husbands dominate purchase decisions in what is a predominantly patriarchal Saudi society.

Country-of-Origin Effects

An important variable affecting consumer purchase in international marketing is the country of origin (CO). There are many products where the CO is important to consumers, such as perfumes, cars, high-fashion clothes, consumer electronics, and software; for all these products country-specific stereotypes exist, with certain countries being associated positively with certain products. Examples are French perfumes and German cars. For such products, knowing the CO affects how consumers evaluate a product. In many cases, the country of manufacture (COM) is also relevant (e.g., in India, consumers often want to look inside TV sets to see where components have been manufactured). Figure 7–4 presents a conceptual scheme showing how CO and COM affect purchasing behavior, product-line decisions, and profitability.

As can be seen from Figure 7–4, once consumers are aware of CO, their familiarity with the brand, level of involvement in the purchase decision, and existing preference for domestic products become relevant, as do product- and market-level influences, such as the type of product and brand image. In industrial product buying, "rational" purchasing might be more prevalent, and thus greater credence might be given to country-of-manufacture effects; product attributes might be relevant, such as quality, performance, design, aesthetics, price, and prestige. A powerful brand image may be associated with a company and may overcome the origin of manufacture area. The reputation of the dealer or intermediary may muffle or enhance CO or COM effect, and truth-in-labeling requirements as well as demand conditions can mediate the effect of CO.

Environmental influences also come into play, including the existence of global markets (when CO may become less important); level of economic development of the countries from which products come; and political, social, and cultural influences favoring certain nations. Together these influences result in a country-stereotyping effect and ultimately affect the purchase decision.

FIGURE 7–4   **A Conceptual Framework for Assessing the Country-of-Origin Influence**

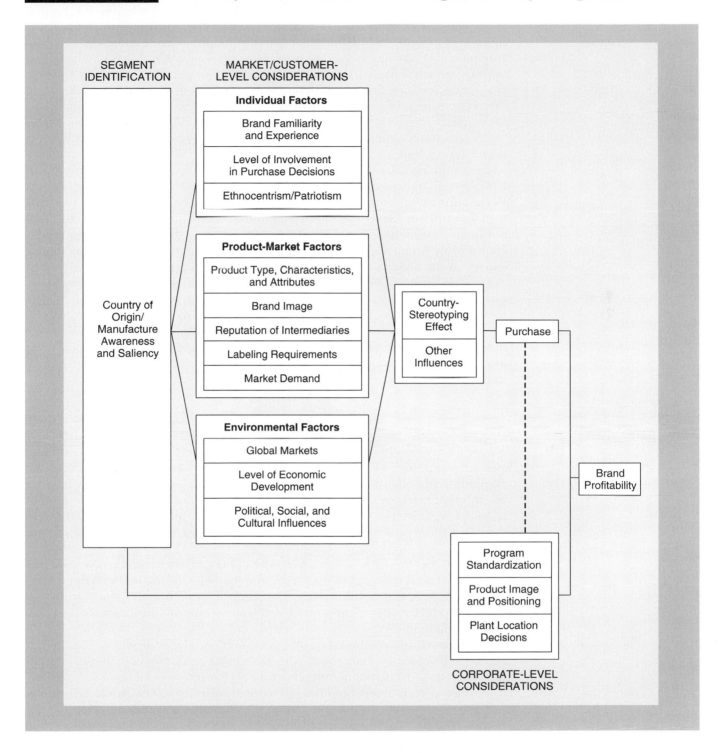

What does this mean for the firm? CO and COM effects have implications for standardization of marketing programs (whether to source from one or more locations, how to adapt), for positioning the product, selecting the image in advertising, and even plant location decisions, all other things being equal. Together, these disparate decisions affect overall brand profitability.[28]

Religiosity and Consumer Behavior

Cultures differ in many ways, with a central difference being religion. It is natural to ask whether religion affects consumer behavior. For example, are devoutly religious people different from more secular people when it comes to enjoying shopping and buying a large variety of material goods? What sorts of advertising appeals are more likely to resonate with a religious person? In order to answer such questions, one first has to define religiosity and then attempt to relate it to different aspects of marketing and consumer behavior. Table 7–8 summarizes these ideas.

A recent study attempted to trace the effects of religiosity on consumption behavior for a sample of Japanese and U.S. consumers.[29] The study found that consumer shopping behavior did not seem significantly different between devout and casually religious Japanese individuals. However, in the United States, devout Protestants were "more economic," buying products on sale, shopping in stores with lower prices, being open to buying foreign-made goods, believing that there was little relation between price and quality, tending to not believe advertising claims while preferring subtle and informative advertisements. Differences also existed at the national level, with Japanese shoppers preferring to buy domestically made products, visiting many stores to find the right brand, enjoying shopping, and preferring stores with better service. As an exploratory study, with a total sample of under 250 drawn from just two cities, Tokyo and Washington, D.C., and with none of the respondents having progressed beyond a high school education, we cannot generalize from this study. It is useful in suggesting directions for international marketing research, particularly when marketing to countries with distinct religious systems such as India, the Middle East, Japan, and China.

SUMMARY

International marketing research is complex primarily because of the difficulty of gathering information about multiple, different foreign environments. The first step is to determine what information to gather. Other problem areas include the availability and quality of primary and secondary data, the comparability of data on different markets, and hindrances in gathering information about areas such as social organization and culture. Although new services are available to help deal with these problems, improvisation and learning from experience are still important.

Techniques for market research in developing countries include analysis of demand patterns, the use of multiple-regression models, estimation by analogy, comparative analysis, and cluster analysis. Gap analysis, input-output tables, estimation of cost and technology trends, and clustering by product diffusion patterns are other useful tools.

The information gathered through research must be evaluated for quality, accuracy, and relevance. Data should be gathered at local, regional, and headquarters levels; a more difficult question is where such efforts should be supervised.

Information sources about foreign markets include the U.S. government, particularly the Department of Commerce, international organizations such as the United Nations, the OECD, and the World Bank, industry and business associations, consulting houses, and on-line databases. A resource often ignored is information scattered within the company and derived from the company's own experience in various markets.

Models are an essential part of market research. The model explaining why U.S. consumers buy Japanese cars is illustrative of such an approach, as are other consumer behavior models, household buying behavior models, and models of country-of-origin effects.

TABLE 7-8	Linkage of Religion and Consumer Behavior

Variables Measuring the Importance of Religion to Consumers	*Aspects of Consumer Behavior Likely to Be Affected by Religiosity*
• Belief in religion • Religious practice (e. g., church attendance) • Moral consequences of being religious • Religious socialization, in the family, at schools • Self-described level of religiosity • Consequences of religion for society	• Owning (many) material possessions • Enjoyment of shopping • Consumption versus thrift • Paying more for quality or brand names • Status deriving from buying higher-priced goods • Searching for bargains • Reaction to advertising appeals (based on sex, power, glamour, speed, social acceptance) • Religion-based prohibitions and sanctioned behavior (e. g., avoiding alcohol, being charitable) • Importance of longer product warranties and guarantees, service • Country-of-origin and country-of-manufacture effects

QUESTIONS

7.1 "International marketing intelligence is more comprehensive than domestic marketing research." Discuss.

7.2 Can domestic marketing research techniques be used in researching foreign markets? Explain.

7.3 Why is it often more difficult to get responses to marketing research in other countries than it is in the United States?

7.4 Explain how the economic and commercial infrastructure in a country can affect the marketing research task there.

7.5 Define the "data problems" in international marketing research.

7.6 How can international marketing researchers deal with the problems encountered in their task?

7.7 How can international marketers prepare a comparative analysis of their foreign markets?

7.8 How might comparative analysis and groupings of foreign markets aid in solving international marketing research problems?

7.9 Discuss the U.S. government as an information source for markets abroad.

7.10 Name some of the business and trade associations that provide assistance to the international marketing researcher. Explore the kinds of information provided by one such association in your town.

7.11 Identify firms in your own community and determine what kinds of foreign marketing assistance are available to them locally or within the state.

7.12 Suggest criteria for evaluating information in international marketing research.

7.13 How should the firm decide whether to gather its own intelligence or to buy it outside?

7.14 Why is screening foreign markets important? Explain how screening was used in identifying key markets for kidney dialysis equipment (see discussion in "Screening Potential International Markets").

7.15 How can models be used in international marketing research? Discuss the information gathering implications of models encompassing (a) buying foreign cars, (b) household buying behavior, (c) country of origin and manufacture, and (d) religiosity.

ENDNOTES

1 John H. Roberts and James M. Lattin, "Review of Research and Prospects for Future Insights," *Journal of Marketing Research,* 34, (August 1997): 406–410.

2 See Figure 4 in N. Zabriskie and A. B. Huellmantel, "Marketing Research as a Strategic Tool," *Long Range Planning* 27, no. 1 (1994): 107–118.

3 Charles S. Mayer, "Multinational Marketing Research," *European Research* 6 (March 1978): 77–83.

4 M. R. Czinkota and I. A. Ronkainen, "Using Secondary Sources of Research: Market Research for Your Export Operations," *International Trade Forum,* July 1994.

5 Gerardo Marin and Barbara V. Marin, *Research with Hispanic Populations* (Newbury Park, CA: Sage Publications, 1991).

6 Lisa Peñaloza, "Atravesando Fronteras/Border Crossings: A Critical Ethnographic Exploration of the Consumer Acculturation of Mexican Immigrants," *Journal of Consumer Research* 21 (June 1994): 32–54.

7 R. Netemeyer, S. Durvasula, and D. R. Lichtenstein, "A Cross-National Assessment of the Reliability and Validity of CETSCALE," *Journal of Marketing Research* 28 (August 1991).

8 "Portrait of the World," *Marketing News,* August 28, 1995, 20–21.

9 "Gallup Offers New Take on Latin America," *Advertising Age,* November 13, 1995.

10 M. Antonio, "Forecasting at Procter and Gamble in Italy," *Journal of Business Forecasting,* 16 (Summer 1997): 19–20.

11 *Marketing News,* March 1, 1985, 19.

12 Reed Moyer, "International Market Analysis," *Journal of Marketing Research,* November 1968, 353–360.

13 "Asian Business Strategies—Stolt-Nielsen S.A.," *Japan Chemical Week,* July 27, 1995, 3.

14 Bertil Liander, Vern Terpstra, M. Y. Yoshino, and Aziz A. Sherbini, *Comparative Analysis for International Marketing* (Boston: Allyn & Bacon, 1967).

15 S. Prakash Sethi, "Comparative Cluster Analysis for World Markets," *Journal of Marketing Research,* August 1971.

16 K. Helsen, K. Jedidi, and W. S. DeSarbo, "A New Approach to Country Segmentation Utilizing Multinational Diffusion Patterns," *Journal of Marketing* 57 (October 1993): 60–71.

17 See H. Gatignon, J. Eliashberg, and T. S. Robertson, "Determinants of Diffusion Patterns: A Cross-Country Analysis," *Marketing Science* 8 (Summer 1989): 231–247; and H. Takada and D. Jain, "Cross-National Analysis of Diffusion of Consumer Durable Goods in Pacific Rim Countries," *Journal of Marketing* 55 (April 1991): 48–54.

18 J. Jeannet and H. Hennessey, *Global Marketing Strategies,* 3rd ed. (Boston: Houghton-Mifflin, 1995).

19 J. A. Weber, "Comparing Growth Opportunities in the International Marketplace," *Management International Review* 1 (1979).

20 *Marketing News,* January 7, 1991.

21 E. Naumann, D. W. Jackson, and W. G. Wolfe, "Examining the Practices of U.S. and Japanese Market Research Firms," *California Management Review* 36, no. 4 (Summer 1994).

22 Katherine S. Chiang, "How to Find Online Information," *American Demographics,* September 1993, 52–55.

23 J. Heilbrunn, ed., *AMA Marketing Encyclopedia,* American Marketing Association, 1995.

24 Jan van Rees, ed. *Glossary of Marketing Research* (Amsterdam: European Society for Opinion and Marketing Research [ESOMAR] 1989).

25 Rachel Dardis and H. Soberon-Ferrer, "Consumer Preferences for Japanese Automobiles," *Journal of Consumer Affairs* 28, no. 1 (Summer 1994): 107–129.

26 Robert T. Green, J. P. Leonardi, J. L. Chandon, I. Cunningham, B. Verhage, and A. Strazzieri, "Societal Development and Family Purchasing Roles: A Cross-National Study," *Journal of Consumer Research* 9 (March 1983): 436–442. And, R. Hyman, "Marital Power and the Theory of Resources in Cross-Cultural Context," *Journal of Comparative Family Studies,* 1972, 50–67.

27 Ugur Yavas, E. Babakus, and N. Delener, "Family Purchasing Roles in Saudi Arabia: Perspectives from Saudi Wives," *Journal of Business Research* 31 (1994): 75–86.

28 Saeed Samiee, "Customer Evaluation of Products in a Global Market," *Journal of International Business Studies* 25, no. 3 (3rd Quarter 1994): 579–604.

29 James Sood and Yukio Nasu, "Religiosity and Nationality: An Exploratory Study of Their Effect on Consumer Behavior in Japan and the U.S.," *Journal of Business Research* 34 (1995): 1–9

FURTHER READINGS

Bergstrom, Gary L., and Mark England. "International Country Selection Strategies." *Columbia Journal of World Business* 17, no. 1 (Summer 1982).

Cavusgil, S. Tamer. "Guidelines for Export Market Research." *Business Horizons,* November–December 1985.

Chiang, Katherine S. "How to Find Online Information." *American Demographics,* September 1993, 52–55.

Czinkota, M. R., and I. A. Ronkainen. "Using Secondary Sources of Research: Market Research for Your Export Operations." *International Trade Forum,* July 1994.

Dardis, Rachel, and H. Soberon-Ferrer. "Consumer Preferences for Japanese Automobiles." *Journal of Consumer Affairs* 28, no. 1 (Summer 1994): 107–129.

Day, Ellen, R. J. Fox, and S. M. Huszagh. "Segmenting the Global Market for Industrial Goods: Issues and Implications." *International Marketing Review* 5, no. 3 (Autumn 1988).

Douglas, Susan P., and Samuel Craig. *International Marketing Research.* Englewood Cliffs, NJ: Prentice-Hall, 1983.

Goodnow, James D. "Developments in International Mode of Entry Analysis." *International Marketing Review* 2, no. 3 (Autumn 1985).

Helsen, K., K. Jedidi, and W. S. DeSarbo. "A New Approach to Country Segmentation Utilizing Multinational Diffusion Patterns." *Journal of Marketing* 57 (October 1993): 60–71.

Jeannet, Jean-Pierre, and H. Hennessey. *International Marketing Management.* Boston: Houghton-Mifflin, 1995, 147–150.

Johansson, Johnny K., and I. Nonaka. "Market Research the Japanese Way." *Harvard Business Review* 65, no. 3 (May–June 1987).

Liander, Bertil, Vern Terpstra, M. Y. Yoshino, and A. Sherbini. *Comparative Analysis for International Marketing.* Boston: Allyn & Bacon, 1967.

Marin, Gerardo, and Barbara V. Marin. *Research with Hispanic Populations.* Newbury Park, CA: Sage Publications, 1991.

Malhotra, Naresh K. *Marketing Research: An Applied Orientation.* Englewood Cliffs, NJ: Prentice-Hall, 1993.

Moyer, Reed. "International Market Analysis." *Journal of Marketing Research,* November 1968.

Naumann, E., D. W. Jackson, and W. G. Wolfe. "Examining the Practices of U.S. and Japanese Market Research Firms." *California Management Review* 36, no. 4 (Summer 1994).

Netemeyer, R., S. Durvasula, and D. R. Lichtenstein. "A Cross-National Assessment of the Reliability and Validity of CETSCALE." *Journal of Marketing Research* 28 (August 1991).

Parameswaran, Ravi, and Attila Yaprak. "A Cross-National Comparison of Consumer Research Measures." *Journal of International Business Studies* (Spring 1987).

Penaloza, Lisa. "Atravesando Fronteras/ Border Crossings: A Critical Ethnographic Exploration of the Consumer Acculturation of Mexican Immigrants." *Journal of Consumer Research* 21 (June 1994): 32–54.

Samiee, Saeed. "Customer Evaluation of Products in a Global Market." *Journal of International Business Studies* 25, no. 3 (1994): 579–604.

Sekaran, Uma. "Methodological and Theoretical Issues and Advancements in Cross-Cultural Research." *Journal of International Business Studies,* Fall 1983.

Sethi, S. Prakash. "Comparative Cluster Analysis for World Markets." *Journal of Marketing Research,* August 1971.

Sood, James, and Yukio Nasu. "Religiosity and Nationality: An Exploratory Study of Their Effect on Consumer Behavior in Japan and the U.S." *Journal of Business Research* 34 (1995): 1–9.

van Rees, Jan, ed. *Glossary of Marketing Research.* Amsterdam: European Society for Opinion and Marketing Research (ESOMAR), 1989.

Weber, J. A. "Comparing Growth Opportunities in the International Marketplace." *Management International Review* 1 (1979).

World Bank. *World Development Report.* New York: Oxford University Press. Published annually.

Yavas, Ugur, E. Babakus, and N. Delener. "Family Purchasing Roles in Saudi Arabia: Perspectives from Saudi Wives." *Journal of Business Research* 31 (1994): 75–86.

Zabriskie, N., and A. B. Huellmantel. "Marketing Research as a Strategic Tool." *Long Range Planning* 27, no. 1 (1994): 107–118.

CASE 7.1

The Indian Automobile Industry, 1995*

Two-lane blacktops called national highways. Where buses list dangerously to one side because of riders hanging onto the doors, yet stop right on the highway to pick up more passengers. Where traffic might slow down behind herds of cows and sheep, quite normal, and sometimes behind a farmer driving a flock of ducks home. Where a cordoned-off area of the highway, blocked by paving stones, is given over to drying wheat and other grains. Where the only way to pass is to swing over into the opposite lane against ongoing traffic. When a truck or bus bears down on one, the driver of a mere car has no option but to swerve over onto the dirt shoulder, threatening the vendor of sweets or the squatting villagers exchanging gossip. A fast foreign car can rarely strut its stuff as it crawls along at 30 or 40 miles an hour behind ancient trucks belching black smoke and camel caravans or elephants carrying grass.

Could such a market attract the world's premier car companies? Table 1 lists recent foreign automobile company investments in India.

Does this spate of foreign investment into India's auto industry make sense? As Figure 1 shows, total motor vehicle sales (new vehicle registrations) were about 260,000 units in 1994, with car sales being about 230,000 (see Figure 2). Figure 1 shows a forecast of new-vehicle registration rising to around 400,000 units by the year 2000; a year later, this forecast has risen to nearly 575,000 units (see Figure 2). Interestingly, luxury cars are forecast to account for an increasing proportion of total car sales. Total production should reach 1 million units by 2000. India, of course, is not the only emerging market receiving attention from multinational car manufacturers.

Manufacturers such as Fiat envision building a mass-market global car with a global network of component manufacturing and assembly plants, allowing for parts and subassemblies interchange, lowering costs through economies of scale and reducing risks through geographical production and market diversification. Fiat has launched a Project 178,

---

| TABLE 1 | Foreign Automobile Investment in India |

Foreign Investor	Local Partner	Detail of Proposed Investment
Suzuki	Maruti Udyog	First foreign joint venture set up in 1983; produces three small car models, a van, and a utility vehicle; production around 200,000 units a year; the basic Maruti 800 costs about $6000; has 75% share of the car market.
Peugeot	Premier Auto, Bombay	$200 million project to build 15,000 Peugeot 309 cars annually; to rise to 20,000 by the year 2000; estimated car price over $12,000.
Fiat	Premier Auto, Bombay	License the Fiat Uno, to be produced locally and priced at about $8,000.
GM (Opel Germany)	Hindustan Motors	Manufacture up to 20,000 Opel Astras a year, beginning in 1995; these would be larger sedans.
Mitsubishi	Hindustan Motors	Mitsubishi to buy 10 percent equity, and build facility to manufacture 10,000 Lancers annually, rising to as much as 100,000 eventually.
Daimler-Benz	Tata Engineering	Assemble 2,000 E-series Mercedes Benz cars, to be priced at $58,000 (2 million Rupees); a 51-49 joint venture with assembly near Pune using used equipment imported from Germany as part of Benz's equity contribution.
Daewoo (South Korea)	DCM Group	Build 25,000 Cielo cars starting late 1995, with goal of 100,000 cars a year, priced at about $14,000, to compete with Maruti's similarly priced Esteem.
Honda	SriRam Industrial Group-SIEL	$280 million, 60-40 joint venture near Delhi, to produce 10,000 1.3- to 1.5-liter engine cars initially, growing to about 30,000 units in three years; estimated market size for this segment around 150,000 cars by the year 2000.
BMW	Hero Motors	Assemble upscale BMW cars.
Ford	Mahindra & Mahindra	$800 million in a 50-50 joint venture to build midsize cars—Escorts and Fiestas—priced at around $13,000, with production capacity of around 100,000 units annually.

FIGURE 1   Indian Automobile Market, Production and Sales Forecasts, and Vehicles on the Road

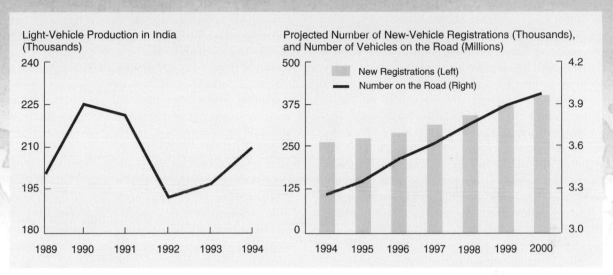

Source: Light-vehicle production figures from the Indian Ministry of Finance, Center for Monitoring the Indian Economy. Projected registrations and numbers of vehicles from the Economist Intelligence Unit. Cited in *The Wall Street Journal*, October 21, 1994.

FIGURE 2   Forecasted Demand and Sales, Luxury and Standard Cars, 1985 to 2000

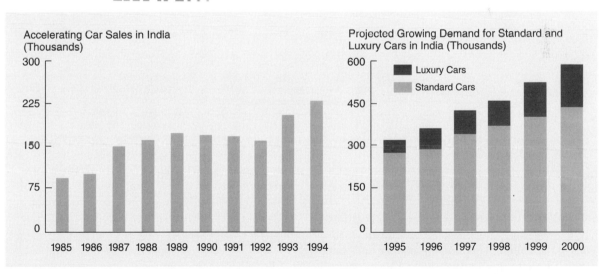

Source: The Association of Indian Automobile Manufacturers, and the National Council of Applied Economic Research. Cited in *The Wall Street Journal*, October 11, 1995.

under which suppliers in Brazil, for example, would be able to supply exactly the same part to a factory in India as it would to a neighboring plant.[1] The 178 is a family of cars based on a modified Uno platform—both three- and five-door hatchbacks, four-door sedan, wagon, pick-up, and van. Project 178 purchasing chief Fabrizio Ceccarini says, "We want to be able to build the same car in any country to the same level of quality and are asking our suppliers to ensure that we can do that. They must be able to meet our cost and quality criteria and be able to supply a part anywhere in the world."

The Indian government had formerly frowned on developing a domestic car industry, forcing out both Ford and GM in the 1950s. A Socialist government thought that cars were wasteful and preferred direct investment in building public transportation systems. However, after 40 years of indifferent economic progress, during which India saw many of its Asian neighbors prosper, including its one-time nemesis, China, the government decided to begin promoting private enterprise. It liberalized the entry of foreign auto companies into India, lowered tariffs and taxes, and made financing available for new-car purchases. Car manufacturing has a broad multiplier effect on the economy, creating several more jobs in parts manufacturing and support industries such as car dealerships, repair, and aftermarket parts supply and retailing. India is also a reasonably stable democracy, forecasted to grow nearly 6 percent a year over the next decade, with a population of about 850 million people. India is still poor, however, with per capita income of less than $1,000 annually even after adjustments for differences in purchasing power. However, the distribution of income is skewed. Economists estimate that about 600,000 households in India have an annual income in excess of $30,000; given low Indian wages, such that a chauffeur costs only $80 a month and a two-bedroom apartment might rent for about $130, a $30,000 income has much greater purchasing power, perhaps equal to an income three times as high in the United States. Thus, there is more disposable income to spend on luxury goods. Satellite TV brings home messages about Western brands and conspicuous consumption.

It is striking then to note that most foreign auto investment into India is aimed at producing "luxury" cars priced at two to three times the basic Maruti 800, which costs about 200,000 rupees, approximately $6,000. Maruti currently has over 75 percent of the market and has been manufacturing cars since 1983. Maruti 800 purchasers must wait six months to receive a car as there is a backlog. But most new foreign entrants prefer to tackle the upper-income segment in India. How much room is there for expensive cars? Are foreign auto companies misguided in ignoring India's mass market?

*Case prepared by Prof. Ravi Sarathy, Northeastern University, for use in class discussion. © 1995. All rights reserved.
Sources: "Auto Makers Hurry to Get a Piece of India's Market," *The Wall Street Journal,* October 21, 1994; "Foreign Cars Risk a Wrong Turn in India," Oct. 21, 1994, and "In India, Luxury Is within Reach of Many," October 17, 1995; *Business Asia,* September 25, 1995, and September 12, 1994; and *Automotive News,* November 27, 1995.

CASE 7.2

Whirlpool: The European Market*

Whirlpool is a major U.S.–based appliance manufacturer. It moved aggressively into Europe when it purchased a 53 percent interest in the Philips major home appliance line of business. In 1990 it bought out the remaining 47 percent, thus obtaining a wholly owned home appliance subsidiary in Europe. However, Europe experienced a recession shortly thereafter, and European operating margins have been disappointing, at 3.3 percent in 1991, about 4 percent below comparable U.S. levels. Table 1 presents recent Whirlpool sales and operating profits.

To improve its European business, Whirlpool needs to gather additional information about the European home appliance market. Table 2 summarizes market share for Whirlpool and its major competitors in 1990, which is a useful starting point. What else is needed to develop appropriate and comprehensive plans for European marketing?

The Wish List

The following represents a sample "wish list" of information that managers would find useful in preparing European marketing plans. It is based on information typically gathered in the United States.

1. *The European economy.* The end of the recession in Europe will stimulate economic activity in many fields including the market for home appliances. Within

TABLE 1

**Whirlpool Corporation Revenues
(Millions of Dollars)**

	1991	*1990*	*1989*
Revenues			
North America	$4,236	$4,165	$4,116
Europe	2,540	2,456	2,169
Operating Profits			
North America	326	277	311
Europe	83	73	101

TABLE 2

**1990 Market Share in Europe
by Competitor (Percent)**

Electrolux	19%
Bosch-Siemens	13
Whirlpool	10
Miele	7
Temfa	6
AEG	5
Merloni	4
General Domestic	4
Candy	4
Other	28

Europe, the macroeconomic growth rates in the European countries vary; beyond the Single European Market, growth rates in the East European countries and the EFTA countries are also important.

2. *Housing starts.* In the U.S. market, information on housing starts is useful in predicting the demand for major home appliances. However, given the large base of installed appliances in the United States, only about 25 percent of appliances are sold directly to builders.

3. *Replacement demand.* Approximately 75 percent of U.S. sales are through the retail channel and primarily represent replacement sales; brand loyalty is an important consideration in determining whether a company such as Whirlpool can increase its sales by taking away customers from competitors. Differing from appliance to appliance, the length of the replacement cycle also affects when and how often the appliance is replaced.

4. *Appliance-specific information.* Major home appliances include clothes washers and dryers, refrigerators, dishwashers, and kitchen ranges (stoves). This category includes microwave ovens, the last major new home appliance introduced. On the horizon is the microwave clothes dryer. For each appliance, product considerations affect market size, competition, market share, and profits. Table 3 summarizes the relative penetration rates for major household appliances in Europe and the United States. The market for each major appliance could be growing at different rates. Each appliance has its own price points, representing high-, medium-, and low-priced appliances. Understanding how prices are evolving in a segment of the appliance market is useful. Different competitors have different strengths in each of these major home appliances, and profit margins can be significantly different from appliance to appliance. Cost structure can also differ for each appliance, although in general, home appliances are raw materials and parts intensive. About 70 percent of cost of goods sold is in materials: steel, plastics, motors, timers, and so on; another 10 percent is in labor, and the rest is in fixed overhead costs.

5. *Distribution channels.* In the United States, retail sales are split evenly between Sears (33 percent), major national and regional dealers (33 percent), and smaller local shops (the remaining 33 percent). In the United States, there is a move to free retail dealers from having to carry inventories. Instead, the retailer relays the order to the company, which ships it directly within a few days. Whirlpool is experimenting with a Quality Express program that would supply customers directly within 48 hours. When such an innovation was tried by Shaw Industries in the carpet business, low inventory cut-to-order retailers took 50 percent of the distribution channel. The advantages to the manufacturer are higher margins, more information about customer preferences, and the possibility of stealing competitors' customers.

6. *Competition.* The European industry is fragmented, as indicated in Table 3.

TABLE 3

Market Penetration by Type of Appliance (Percent)

	Europe	*United States*
Dishwashers	25%	54%
Dryers	18	66
Kitchen Ranges	92	107
Washers	88	75
Refrigerators	97	100

Understanding competitors' plans in areas such as price setting, cost structure, and plans for product introduction is important. Competitors in financial difficulties, experiencing problems with quality or with dealer networks, who are dumping a product on the market, represent both a threat and an opportunity, which is relevant to setting short-term marketing responses and long-term marketing plans. Acquisitions and consolidations continue to be important in Europe, and such information can help Whirlpool grow by "buying" market share through acquiring competitors that may have specific strengths such as a strong local brand or significant market share in one or two European countries.

Opportunities in Europe

European markets have the potential to grow faster than those in the United States, mainly because the level of penetration of some major appliances such as dishwashers and dryers is far lower than in the United States (see Table 3). There may also be opportunities for trading up as European incomes grow, houses become more spacious and energy efficient, and multiple features and ease of use become driving considerations in replacement purchase decisions.

However, the European market differs from the U.S. market. Design differences exist between European countries, and the features that make a model a top-selling item in one country may leave customers in another country quite indifferent. There are currently local brands specific to each country; pan-European advertising is in its early stages. Whirlpool faces the special problem of ensuring that current Philips brand users switch to Whirlpool brand appliances at the end of the decade when its rights to the Philips brand name end. Whirlpool's competition may not be the same company in all European country markets. Whirlpool needs to design and carry out marketing research that can provide the information necessary for it to compete successfully in the more competitive European Union.

Questions

1. What market research information does Whirlpool typically gather in the U.S. market?
2. Should Whirlpool be gathering the same information for Europe?
3. Design a marketing research plan for the European major home appliance market. Specifically, how should Whirlpool identify differences between European countries that are germane to product design and marketing mix choices?
4. Try to obtain some information you listed in your answer to question 3. What are the difficulties in gathering information about the European market?
5. Looking beyond Europe, for what other countries or regions should Whirlpool be gathering information? Why? How should it go about gathering such information?
6. Recently, European consumers have become concerned with environmental matters, giving rise to "green" parties and "green" products. Is this relevant to marketing home appliances? If so, how should Whirlpool incorporate such environmental considerations in its marketing research?

---

* Case prepared by Professor Ravi Sarathy for use in classroom discussion. All rights reserved.
Sources: Whirlpool Corporation Annual reports; Kidder Peabody company report; *Whirlpool Corporation,* by David Dwyer, September 1992.

International Product Policy

The Basic Product and Its Attributes

Learning Objectives

International marketing involves satisfying consumer needs in foreign markets. The question often asked is, "Can I sell my product in international markets?" A better question would be, "What products should I be selling in international markets?" International product policy should be the cornerstone around which other aspects of the global marketing mix are designed and integrated.

The main goals of this chapter are to

1.   Delineate the influences that lead a company to standardize or adapt its products.

2.   Discuss the product attributes that are considered in addition to the basic product itself in formulating international product policy.

3.   Examine approaches to market segmentation in foreign markets and to franchising as a mode of entry.

A central issue in approaching global markets is whether products sold in the home market should be adapted or standardized for international markets. This raises the question of whether a company can successfully design and market a global product. Other issues have to do with standardizing or adapting product features, such as packaging and labeling, brands and trademarks, and warranty and service policies.

In Chapter 9, we consider complementary aspects of international product policy: (1) the selection and management of the international product line and (2) product planning and development in international business.

WHAT TO SELL ABROAD: PRODUCT POLICY FOR INTERNATIONAL MARKETS

The easiest course for a firm just beginning to go international is to sell products designed for the home market as is in foreign markets. As the firm meets with success in foreign markets, it begins to consider choosing between the two extremes of (1) adapting to the point of creating an entirely new product and (2) keeping the product exactly the same.

Swatch: An Example of Successful Global Standardization

Standardization is more appropriate, of course, when customers are similar overseas, and such standardization can apply to services as well as to products. An interesting example is the Swatch watch collection made by the Swiss company SMH. Cheap, and mass-produced in Switzerland, they are plastic fashion items selling for about $40 all over the world. The product concept involves manufacturing and marketing a striking, low-cost, high-quality watch. The watch is designed to appeal to the low-end segment of the market accounting for 450 million units out of a total market of 500 million. SMH decided to enter this segment where Swiss companies had zero market share, making and selling an "emotional" product that would allow the wearer to convey an image, to make a fashion statement.

Two Swatch collections are launched each year for a total of 140 models. A team of 20 or so designers from Europe, America, Japan, Australia, and elsewhere develops designs that are then culled and presented to a management committee, which selects the items for each season's line. These watches have become collectors' items and are cheap enough that an individual can own several Swatches—in fact, the average customer in Italy owns six watches. Having established a brand name and an image, Swatch launched a joint venture with VW to make a minicar with replaceable panels that permit an ever-changing appearance. It later switched partners, working with Daimler Chrysler. The two-seat Smart, as the Swatchmobile has been dubbed, was launched in October 1998 in Europe, through a limited number of dealers, scattered across Europe. The Smart is an ultralight highly fuel efficient two-seater, with plastic doors, hood and trunk. These lightweight materials allow fuel efficiency to reach nearly 60 miles per gallon (about 4.8 liters per 100 kilometers). It takes under 5 hours to assemble a Smart, because only a quarter of the Smart's value is added in the assembly stage. The Smart's suppliers provide entire subsystems as modules, even installing the module—be it the door, front end or dashboard—in addition to being given development responsibility for their subsystem. Thus, Daimler becomes a coordinator of a factory. The Smart is being marketed as the ideal city car for old European cities with narrow streets and relatively compact city centers.[1]

ADAPTATION VERSUS STANDARDIZATION OF THE PRODUCT

Table 8–1 summarizes the main factors that influence a firm to pursue standardization or adaptation strategies when introducing products into new international mar-

| TABLE 8-1 | Factors Favoring Product Standardization versus Adaptation |

Standardization	Adaptation
High costs of adaptation	Differences in technical standards
Primarily industrial products	Primarily consumer and personal-use products
Convergence and similar tastes in diverse country markets	Variations in consumer needs
Predominant use in urban environments	Variations in conditions of use
Marketing to predominantly similar countries (i.e., the triad economies)	Variations in ability to buy—differences in income levels
Centralized management of international operations when mode of entry is mainly exports	Fragmentation, with independent national subsidiaries
Strong country-of-origin image and effect	Strong cultural differences, language, etc., affecting purchase and use
Scale economies in production, marketing, and R&D	Local environment–induced adaptation: differences in raw material available, government-required standards and regulations
Standardized products marketed by competitors	Adaptation strategy successfully used by competitors

kets. The goals of reducing costs and complexity lead companies to consider standardization, while a customer orientation sways them toward product adaptation.

Factors Encouraging Standardization

The attractions of standardization are obvious. It can result in lower costs and economies of scale in manufacturing, product development, and marketing. Managerial complexity is reduced, and export marketing is facilitated when the same product is exported to several countries.

High Costs of Adaptation

Low-volume markets and the specific nature of the adaptation contemplated can contribute to an increase in overall manufacturing costs that make it difficult to sell the product at a reasonable price (that covers costs) and yet be attractive enough to garner market share and ultimately render profits. In the case of washing machines and dryers, Whirlpool found that the colder Scandinavian countries required more powerful heating elements to dry clothes completely as opposed to Italy where it was common to hang clothes out to dry, especially in good weather. Adding a different drying module made the dryers less competitive especially when European economies experienced a slowdown in their economic growth.

Industrial Products

Products in which technical specifications are critical tend to be uniform internationally. Differences significant in international business are "people differences," that is, cultural differences. In general, then, industrial goods are more standardized than consumer goods. Even when industrial goods are modified, the changes are likely to be minor—an adaptation of the electric voltage or the use of metric measures. Of course, differences may be forced on the company by distinct and different national standards in areas such as environmental protection.

Convergence and Similar Tastes in Diverse Country Markets

As countries obtain similar income levels and develop economically at the same pace, their consumption patterns are likely to converge. Europe is a good example of this trend, with the creation of the European Union and the Euro creating a single large market with growing similarity of tastes and incomes. This allows firms to sell a product that is standardized for much of Europe. To succeed, of course, the standardized product must offer value beyond that available from competition.

Levitt sees globalization as succeeding because of the appeal of lower prices coupled with world-standard technology, quality, and service, all of which persuade consumers to drop local preferences.

> Global competition spells the end of domestic territoriality: When a global producer offers his lower costs internationally, his patronage expands exponentially. He not only reaches into distant markets, but also attracts customers who previously held to local preferences and now capitulate to the attractions of lesser prices.[2]

Washing machines in Europe.   An example of such behavior comes again from the washing machine industry in Europe. Marketing research conducted by Hoover, a major producer of washing machines, showed that consumers from the various European countries had distinct preferences. With regard to dimensions, Italians wanted a shorter machine, while most others wanted a 34-inch height; France, Italy, and Britain opted for a narrow machine, but West Germany and Sweden wanted a wide machine, as well as stainless steel drums; the others were content with enamel drums. Britain wanted a top-loading feature, but the others preferred front-loading washing machines. With regard to washing machine capacity, Italians wanted 4 kilos, Britain and France 5 kilos, and West Germany and Sweden expressed a need for 6 kilos. Spin speed ranged from a preference for 60 rpm in France to medium speed (400 rpm) in Italy to high speed (700 to 850 rpm) in Britain, Sweden, and Germany. Britain and Sweden did not want a water-heating module in the washing machine (because homes in these countries have central hot water), but Italy, Germany, and France did want such a feature. France and Britain preferred an agitator washing action; the others wanted a tumble washing action. Each country also had a distinct preference with regard to external styling: British respondents wanted an inconspicuous appearance, Italians wanted brightly colored machines, the Germans wanted an indestructible appearance, the French opted for elegance, and the swedes preferred a "strong" appearance.[3] Implementing changes to the machine produced in England to satisfy national preferences, however, would have increased cost by about $18 per unit, as well as the requirements of additional capital investment.

Research also showed that both the heavily promoted top-of-the-line German washing machine and the cheap Italian machine at half the price were best sellers. In fact, the Italian machine was selling well even to the German market. Levitt inferred from this that an aggressively promoted low-priced washing machine with standard features would be the correct product choice. He notes, "Two things clearly influenced customers to buy: low price regardless of feature preferences, and heavy promotion regardless of price." That is, the low price is capable of convincing customers to accept the absence of certain features. Low price alone is not enough, however. Aggressive promotion, quality, and service are equally important ingredients of the marketing mix.

Hoover's experience with washing machines suggests that standardization can work as part of a well-thought-out marketing mix. It probably works better with products that do not directly influence a consumer's well-being. That is, products such as clothing, food items, cosmetics, and footwear may be less amenable to standardization than industrial products and machines of various sorts. As the example of food in Japan shows, food products are a class for which standardization may be foolhardy. (See "Global Marketing," "Food Products for the Japanese Market.")

An opposite and extreme reaction to standardization is the concept of mass customization. The idea here is to make individually customized products at the low cost of standardized, mass-produced goods. This can be accomplished through modularity, with different processes and tasks coming together in a dynamic, changing fashion to accommodate the needs of different customers. The organization, therefore, is constantly developing new products. Companies such as Toyota are at the forefront of this mass customization drive, evolving from the continuous improvement approach typical of Japanese organizations. Mass customization also requires organizational changes, flexible and quick response teams, as well as information systems and computer networks to bring together product design teams to fit changing customer demands and to monitor progress toward meeting customers' needs.[4] This philosophy is captured in Nissan's motto for the year 2000: "Five A's—any volume, anytime, anybody, anywhere, anything."

Predominant Use in Urban Environments

An intriguing study by Hill and Still showed that products targeted to urban markets in developing countries required only minimal changes from those marketed in developed countries. Products targeted to semi-urban markets required more changes, and products targeted for national markets in developing countries needed even further adaptation to accommodate the requirements of the poorer, more culturally diverse population. These three levels of product adaptation were found through study of 61 subsidiaries operating in 22 less developed countries.[5] This suggests that urban environments are similar across countries and products such as compact cars designed to be used primarily in large cities could be standardized across groups of countries that share similar levels of income and economic development.

Marketing to Predominantly Similar Countries

As suggested in Chapter 7, cluster analysis reveals groups of countries that are similar on a number of dimensions. Using the results of such cluster analysis, firms can market standardized products within such groups of similar countries. The dimensions to group countries will vary depending on the product, and could include variables such as income, language, degree of urbanization, phone penetration, and so on.

Centralized Management and Operating via Exports

If a firm markets overseas principally through exports, it is likely to sell standardized products. Given the costs of adaptation, such firms might choose export markets that are more likely to accept standardized products. Exporters from India, for example, selected foreign markets for which little or no product adaptation was needed.[6]

Country-of-Origin Effects

Items considered to be typical U.S. products might advantageously retain their U.S. character in foreign markets. Wrigley's chewing gum, Coca-Cola, and Levi's are examples, as are French products such as perfumes or fashion women's clothing. Electronic products, cameras, and small cars seem to benefit from a Japanese home country image. In such cases, firms may experience real gains from selling the standardized product as sold in their home markets.

Economies of Scale in Production

Standardizing a product at a production site allows the firm to gain scale economies in manufacturing. As the company multiplies production facilities around the world, this advantage decreases. Similarly, as the optimum size of plant becomes a smaller proportion of world demand, pressure toward product uniformity decreases.

Economies in Research and Development

If the firm offers the identical product around the world, it gets more mileage out of its R&D efforts. Less research needs to be directed toward the individual desires of national markets, allowing effort to be focused on developing the next-generation product. Standardized products thus yield an advantage in product-development costs and may shorten the time to develop new products.

Economies in Marketing

Even when marketing is done on a national basis, economies of scale are possible with standardized products. Although sales literature, sales-force training, and advertising may vary somewhat from country to country, they will be much more similar when the product is uniform than when it must be adapted for each national market. Service requirements and parts inventories are easier with a standardized product. When a promotional carryover from one market to another occurs because of common language and media spillover, it is not a wasted carryover but an extra return on the advertising.

Factors Encouraging Adaptation

The greatest argument for adapting products is that by doing so the firm can realize higher profits. Modifying products for national or regional markets may raise revenues by more than the costs of adaptation. Specific factors encouraging product adaptation include:

Differences in Technical Standards

Firms must meet technical standards in order to sell in different national markets. For example, agricultural products sold into the U.S. must meet guidelines for maximum levels of chemical additives and fertilizers used in growing such products. In Europe, there are restrictions on the sale of beef from cows treated with growth hormones.

Consumer and Personal Use Products

Products sold to consumers and for personal use are likely to meet with market success when adapted to local markets. Products such as food, clothing, and entertainment cater to highly individual tastes and hence must adapt to the differing needs of local populations. For example, Coca-Cola found itself losing market share in Japan to companies marketing a variety of new soft drinks: sugarless blended Asian teas, fermented milk drinks, fruit-flavored noncarbonated drinks with less sugar. Rather than stick with its cola soft drinks, it began imitating its Japanese competitors, offering its own version of Asian tea, under the brand name Sokenbicha; its fermented milk drink called Lactia to compete against Calpis's Calpis Water brand. Consequently, Coca-Cola's newer drinks outsold traditional cola drinks by a three-to-two margin. Coca-Cola was able to push its late entry competing drinks in Japan because it controlled over 40 percent of Japan's vending machines, which can be found on nearly every street corner and train platform in Japan. It could stock its drinks in these vending machines, bypass Japan's inefficient and tightly controlled traditional hierarchical distribution system, and use its advertising and marketing clout to win back younger customers who had been forsaking cola drinks for the newer variety of drinks.[7]

Variation in Consumer Needs and Differing Use Conditions

Although a given product fulfills a similar functional need in various countries, the conditions under which the product is used may vary greatly from country to country. Climate, for instance, has an effect on products sensitive to temperature or humidity, making it necessary to modify these products for tropical or arctic markets. Consider, for example, the differences in oil drilling in the Sahara compared with offshore drilling in Alaska. Another factor is the difference in the skill level of users, especially between consumers in industrialized nations and those in less developed countries. In regard to cars, trucks, and tires, differing road and traffic conditions may require product changes.

Variations in national habits of wearing and washing clothes may necessitate different kinds of washing machines or soaps and detergents, for example. In some countries, clothes are worn a longer time between washings than they are in the United States. Thus, a different washing process is needed. In some European countries, boiling water is used for washing, so the washing machine must have a special heater built in. In many countries, washing is done with tap water, in a bucket, or by a stream, not within some closed machine or container. Therefore, Procter & Gamble and Unilever sell soap or detergent bars in those markets.

The importance of use conditions is apparent for European car manufacturers. An American family may own multiple cars—a minivan for weekend family trips and a small car for the daily commute to work. Both the United States and Japan have speed limits so that cars typically travel at 55 to 75 miles per hour on highways. Europe's laws are different, however, with speeds allowed in excess of 100 miles per hour, for example, on German highways. A single car is owned but is commonly used for multiple purposes. Moreover, buyers of small cars are demanding luxury features traditionally more common on bigger cars. In response, manufacturers intending to sell cars in Europe are trying to develop products for what they perceive to be distinct segments. Ford envisions four segments: *traditionalists,* who look for wood and leather in their cars; *environmentalists* or *"life survivors,"* who seek the cheapest options; and *adventurers,* who like cars and pick them to match their self-images. Other companies such as VW, Peugeot, and BMW rely on a corporate brand image, as their studies seem to show that buyers of their "brand" of cars are loyal repeat buyers. All the branding and niche adaptation may not be enough, however, in a market where production exceeds demand by about 2 million cars, and new competition in the shape of Korean imports is expected.[8]

Variations in Ability to Buy—Differing Income Levels

The income per capita of the world's nations ranges from over $40,000 to under $300. This affects not only the demand for consumer durables but also for inexpensive consumer products. Product features may have to be adapted to make the product affordable at lower income levels. In Western countries with high incomes, bicycles are leisure products and consumers look for advanced features such as lightweight alloys, a large number of gears, detachable wheels, and so forth, all of which add to the cost of the bicycle, with the average price hovering around $400 for a higher-end bicycle. In contrast, bicycles are used as basic transportation in countries such as China and are heavy, rugged machines with an average selling price of under $50. Similarly, developing countries can best afford small cars selling from less than $10,000 with a desirable price point perhaps being as low as under $5,000. Yet major auto firms such as GM have launched their automobile ventures in countries such as China, selling luxury sedans, Buicks that will sell for around $40,000, limiting the size of the market and pushing back payback periods to as long as 15 years.[9]

Fragmented Independent National Subsidiaries

Some firms have foreign operations that predate World War II. Because of the economic nationalism prevailing at that time, these subsidiaries were largely self-contained national operations. Many of them developed products for their markets without regard to international product uniformity within the company. These subsidiaries have grown accustomed to their independence and may press to be allowed to develop their own national products, even when it might be desirable to standardize product development. Some multinationals may deliberately follow a policy of considerable decentralization as a fundamental aspect of their overall strategy. In such cases, product adaptation is likely to be the norm.

When Ford sought to develop its world car, the Focus, it had to merge product development units in North America and Europe, a reorganization that required decisions at the highest levels in order to convince fiercely independent national teams to begin cooperating and shed some of their autonomy.[10]

The firm that has production facilities in several countries can adapt products more easily than does the firm that must rely on exports from domestic plants.

National subsidiaries also can exert pressure on the parent firm to localize products. Because they are interested in profits, they seek the product that will sell best in their market; and because they want to prevent having their functions taken over by a headquarters office, they try to be as "national" as possible.

The Impact of Cultural Differences

Cultural differences affect tastes, the acceptance of products, and consumption habits. Food is an area in which cultural differences dominate. Introducing food products into foreign markets when the food itself is unknown to the population can be challenging. Of course, over the past four decades, U.S. consumers have embraced Chinese and Thai foods and Mexican hot sauces, so gradually refining consumer tastes is a possibility. Such a challenge faces Ocean Spray, a marketing cooperative that has begun marketing cranberry fruit–based drinks in world markets. Since cranberry juice has an unusual, almost astringent, aftertaste, Ocean Spray has to follow a patient strategy of giving away free samples and letting consumers taste the juice. In the United Kingdom, for example, it began mixing cranberry with black currant juice. It has also publicized the cranberry's health benefits based on a Harvard University study indicating that cranberry juice helps fight urinary tract infections. Additionally, it has used influential opinion shapers such as Australian chef Iain Hewitson to cook on TV with cranberry sauce as a means of convincing customers to try and to repeatedly use cranberry juice and other products.[11]

Environmentally Induced Adaptation: The Influence of Governments

Nations may forbid certain goods to be imported or manufactured in their country. Conversely, they may require that the product be manufactured locally, not imported. Demands for local production or a high degree of "local content" in the product often lead the international firm to modify it. Governments' taxation policies can affect the nature of the products offered in their markets, a notable example being the European tax on car and engine size that has been a predominant influence on car design there.

Product adaptations may be required by local market regulations. Islam, for example, prohibits the consumption of alcohol. European and U.S. firms have been attempting to sell nonalcoholic beer in the Middle East, targeting Saudi Arabia, a hot, dry, desert country. While Western nonalcoholic beer typically contains about 0.5 percent alcohol, nonalcoholic beer sold in Saudi Arabia must be totally alcohol-free; this requires reformulation and special manufacturing. To avoid using the word *beer*, the drink is called a malt beverage and cannot be advertised, so marketers must rely on in-store promotions and contests. The target market segment is younger Saudis who have traveled and perhaps lived abroad. Growth is strong, however, at double digits over the past three years, and though the current market is small, at 250,000 barrels, it is a potential future market that attracts Western firms.[12]

Government regulations on products, packaging, and labeling are an important cause of product variation among countries, especially in foods and drugs. Italy, for example, allows only spaghetti made from durum wheat to be called *pasta*. Government specifications affect some industrial goods, too: Trucks, tractors, and tires often must meet different government specifications in different markets.

The rise of regional groupings provides a modifying influence, but the differences do not disappear rapidly as long as national producers find government regulations such an effective form of protection against foreign firms.

Corporate Strategy and Competitive Actions

A different approach to the standardization versus adaptation debate is to consider successful firms to understand what they did and how their success was related to their strategic choices. A study of exporters from Central America, for example, noted that firms that relied on low costs and standardized products met with initial success but were often overwhelmed when even lower-cost competition emerged from countries such as China, with their low wages and much larger scales of production. Such small firms from developing countries were more likely to succeed if they chose niche segments and developed quality products for this segment while continuing to reduce costs.[13]

Another study looked specifically at what determined product adaptation and promotion adaptation in export operations, considering variables such as packaging, labeling, product positioning, and the promotional approach.[14] The researchers suggest that company characteristics, product and industry characteristics, and specific features of the export market will all determine the extent of product and promotion adaptation. This approach is set out in Figure 8–1.

Adaptation in an Industrial Product Setting

Adaptation need not be restricted to consumer products. *Lotus 1-2-3,* the formerly best-selling spreadsheet software package, underwent a major revision to serve the needs of the Japanese market. The adaptation took two years and involved a Japanese software developer as a partner. Major changes included the following:

◆ Translation of all text (menus, help screens, documentation, etc., into Japanese).

◆ Incorporation of the latest techniques for entering the more than 7,000 Japanese characters from a normal-size keyboard (kana-to-kanji conversion); this feature was licensed from the Japanese partner.

◆ Addition of a sort field for phonetic sorting (based on the pronunciation of kanji).

◆ Addition of a Japanese data format, counting from the start of the emperor's reign (Lotus was told politely not even to think of incorporating a provision for entering a new emperor's name; culturally, one could not question the emperor's immortality).

◆ New graph types commonly used by Japanese business, including "radar" charts and "high-low-open-close" charts; graphs could also be printed directly from within the program, unlike in the U.S. version.

◆ New functions specifically used by Japanese business and analysts (in quality control, for instance).

◆ The option of disabling the beep that usually sounds when an inappropriate character is typed. Desks are close together in offices, and the Japanese might not want their mistakes to be broadcast within hearing range of their officemates.

◆ Capability of supporting several Japanese PC operating systems used on Japanese computers such as the NEC9800, the Toshiba J-3100, and the Fujitsu FM-R personal computer, in addition to the IBM 5500 family. (These are distinct from MS/DOS, which is customary on the IBM-PC.)

Lotus indicated that it practically rebuilt its software from the ground up. The result was that the Japanese version was given a special Nikkei International Award for Creative Excellence, Lotus being the only international company to receive such an award in 1986. More practically, the Japanese version of *Lotus* immediately became the best-selling business software product after its introduction in 1986.[15] It is clear that adaptation was crucial to Japanese success.

PRINCIPLES FOR PRODUCT ADAPTATION

From the foregoing examples, variables that tend to foster product adaptation can be summarized as follows:

FIGURE 8-1   **A Testable Framework of Product and Promotion Adaptation**

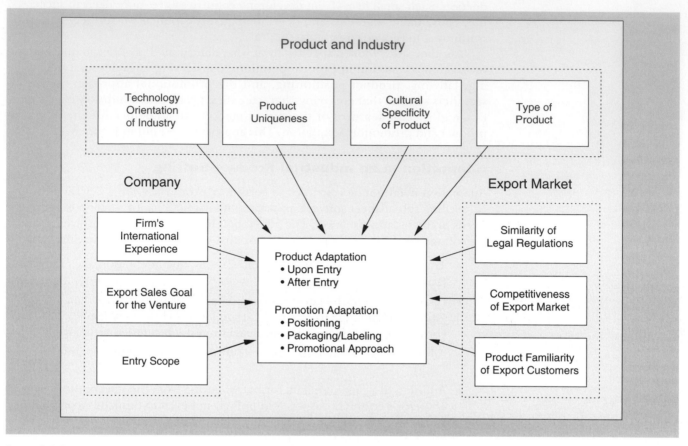

Source: S. T. Cavusgil, Shaoming Zou, and G. M. Naidu, "Product and Promotion Adaptation in Export Ventures: An Empirical Investigation," *Journal of International Business Studies* 24, no. 3, (1993), 485.

1. Most important are variations in customer needs, conditions of use, and ability to buy; this can influence adaptation in the basic product, its attributes and features, as well as in ancillary areas such as packaging.

2. Next in importance are market idiosyncrasies, such as different technical standards; a similar thrust toward adaptation is created by the existence of different languages, as illustrated in the *Lotus* software adaptation for the Japanese market.

3. If competition has introduced adapted products that are well received, a similar response might be tactically correct.

4. If the costs of adaptation are not high, adaptation is more likely. Thus, because of its high R&D costs, a high-tech product will be adapted less than another type of product.

5. Local production parameters, such as available raw materials, skill level of labor force, and nature of equipment, might force adaptation.

6. Government regulations leading to differences in standards might also force product adaptation; thus, cars imported into the United States must meet this country's emission controls. Some Volkswagen Beetles manufactured in Mexico cannot be imported into the United States for this reason.

GLOBAL MARKETING

Food Products for the Japanese Market

BSN, the French food company, is famous for its Danone brand yogurt. Since yogurt consumption per person in Japan was only a tenth of French consumption, BSN viewed the Japanese market as having considerable untapped potential. Japan had many yogurt companies, but they made and sold yogurt drinks, with solid yogurt products only a quarter of the market. BSN conducted a six-month study with yogurt flown in from France. Then it introduced flavored yogurt to Japan, allying with Ajinomoto, a large food company, in a joint venture. Actual sales were only a fifth of forecasts, however, and after eight years, BSN had not reached a break-even point.

One problem was that the Japanese did not have clear preferences for Western foods. Hence, they bought what was heavily promoted. When Danone was no longer heavily promoted, they moved to other products, or back to drinking Japanese yogurts. Thus, while BSN thought that it was introducing a healthy food, the Japanese consumers were using Danone products as a substitute for yogurt drinks. Understanding its competition better helped BSN compete slowly against the established Japanese yogurt manufacturers, Meiji

Milk, Yakult, and Morinaga Milk. With a 10 percent market share, it faces a long, slow haul to profits.

The breakfast cereal market in Japan presents an interesting contrast. The Japanese consume an average of only half a box a year compared to the U.S. average of 15 boxes a year. Until recently, breakfast cereals were considered a children's snack, and supermarkets stocked a few boxes next to the section with cookies and potato chips to attract children. But sales suddenly increased, up 60 percent in 1988 to $142 million (the U.S. market, in contrast, is about $5 billion). Kellogg has been in Japan for 27 years and has a 70 percent share of the market.

New competition has emerged, such as Nestlé, and the Japanese Cisco Co. now has 17 brands to Kellogg's 13. As the health-conscious Japanese are beginning to eat cereal for breakfast instead of rice and miso soup, new cereals are being introduced that contain bran, granola, whole rice, and even vegetables, sometimes in one-cup portions to allow customers to try new products. One such product, Kellogg's "Genmai Flakes," is made from ground whole rice (instead of corn) and is the second-best selling cereal after Corn Flakes. Nestlé's best-selling Vegetable Time is a salty corn-flake cereal with vegetable powder, in three colors: green for spinach, orange for carrot, and yellow for pumpkin.

As these two examples show, adaptation is more likely to lead to success when selling food products in Japan.

Sources: "A Hard Lesson to Swallow," *Financial Times,* July 14, 1988; and "Japanese Are Snapping Up Cereals as Market Crackles with Entries," *The Wall Street Journal,* July 13, 1989.

---

7. Cultural preferences are an important reason for adaptation, especially in personal-use products such as clothing or food and in products or services for which design and taste are prominent.

PRODUCT ATTRIBUTES IN INTERNATIONAL MARKETS

Product policy goes beyond the product itself—attributes such as brands and trademarks, country of origin, packaging and labeling, and warranty and service policies represent key decision areas.

Brands and Trademarks

A major focus in international marketing is protecting the company's brands and trademarks. Another is deciding whether there should be one international brand or different national brands for a given product. Another question regards the role of private branding in international marketing (covered in a subsequent section). If the company uses its own brands, it may want to use multiple brands in the same market to target different customer segments (though this results in higher cost). The main question is whether to promote local country-specific brands or to establish global and regional brands with appeal across countries.[16] Table 8–2 sets out the major branding choices in international marketing and summarizes their advantages and disadvantages.

TABLE 8-2	A Perspective on Branding

Advantages	Disadvantages
No Brand	
Lower production cost	Severe price competition
Lower marketing cost	Lack of market identity
Lower legal cost	
Flexible quality and quantity control	
Branding	
Better identification and awareness	Higher production cost
Better chance for product differentiation	Higher marketing cost
Possible brand loyalty	Higher legal cost
Possible premium pricing	
Private Brand	
Better margins for dealers	Severe price competition
Possibility of larger market share	Lack of market identity
No promotional problems	
Manufacturer's Brand	
Better price due to more price inelasticity	Difficulty for small manufacturer
Retention of brand loyalty	with unknown brand or identity
Better bargaining power	Brand promotion required
Better control of distribution	
Multiple Brands (in One Market)	
Market segmented for varying needs	Higher marketing cost
Competitive spirit created	Higher inventory cost
Negative connotation of existing brand avoided	Loss of economies of scale
More retail shelf space gained	
Existing brand's image not damaged	

Global Brands

Building a global brand is inherent in using a standardized product. Its success depends on a growing convergence of consumer tastes and the coordination of global advertising and promotion. Also important is the development of communications media with multinational reach, such as the simultaneous transmission around the world of the Summer Olympics. In such cases, because the same transmission is received around the world, firms benefit if the brands featured in the transmission are familiar to the world audience.

The advantages of global branding include economies of scale in advertising. The uniform image can appeal to globe-trotting consumers. Global brands are also important in securing access to distribution channels. In cases in which shelf space is at a premium, as with food products, a company has to convince retailers to carry its products rather than those of competitors. Having a global brand may help persuade them because, from the retailers' standpoint, a global brand is less likely to languish on the shelves.

In developing global brands, the marketing manager has to decide what brand image to project across markets. For example, Reebok blends lifestyle and athletic prowess in its U.S. ads, while its European image is focused mainly on athletics. To learn more about brand image, Roth examined the links between a country mar-

| TABLE 8-2 | A Perspective on Branding (continued) |

Advantages	Disadvantages
Single Brand (in One Market)	
Marketing efficiency	Market homogeneity assumed
More focused marketing permitted	Existing brand's image hurt when trading up/down
Brand confusion eliminated	Limited shelf space
Advantage for product with good reputation (halo effect)	
Local Brands	
Meaningful names	Higher marketing cost
Local identification	Higher inventory cost
Avoidance of taxation on international brand	Loss of economies of scale
Quick market penetration by acquiring local brand	Diffused image
Variations of quantity and quality across markets allowed	
Worldwide Brand	
Maximum marketing efficiency	Market homogeneity assumed
Reduction of advertising costs	Problems with black and grey markets
Elimination of brand confusion	Possibility of negative connotation
Advantage for culture-free product	Quality and quantity consistency required
Advantage for prestigious product	LDCs' opposition and resentment
Easy identification/recognition for international travellers	Legal complications
Uniform worldwide image	

Source: Sak Onkvisit and John J. Shaw, "The International Dimension of Branding," *International Marketing Review* 6, no. 3 (1989), Table 1, 24.

ket's cultural and socioeconomic factors, and the nature of brand image chosen, whether functional or sensory.[17] He then related these choices to product performance in that market, after adjusting for the firm's experience with the market, the nature of competition, and the choices made by the firm across the marketing mix. He found that in countries such as China, France, and Belgium, where the degree of separation between high- and low-power-status individuals is high, brand images should stress social and sensory needs. Similarly, in countries where individualism is low, as in much of Asia, brand images that stress group membership and affiliation are likely to be more successful.

Landor Associates in association with Louis Harris Associates had been conducting "image power" surveys for over a decade. Image power is a way to measure a brand's strength, developed by combining five separate elements:

- Share of mind (awareness and familiarity)
- Share of heart (high regard)
- Value (value for money)
- Momentum (potential for future growth or success)
- Singularity (business choice)

An Image Power Index of 100 represents perfect brand strength (100 percent share of mind, share of heart, value, momentum, and singularity), whereas an Image Power Index of zero represents no brand strength (0% share of mind, share of heart, value, momentum, and singularity).

Table 8–3 reports the results of a recent Image Power survey.

Gillette: Building and Maintaining Product and Brand Leadership

An example of the power of building and investing in a brand is provided by Gillette's launch of the Sensor razor and blades. With the advent of the cheap disposable razor, the shaving device business seemed to have become a commodity business driven by low price and intensive distribution. Gillette initially went along with this trend, reduced advertising spending, and saw its gross margins decline. Then, with the invention of the Sensor razor, key Gillette executives decided that the company needed to spend heavily across the world, both in the United States and Europe, to build up the Gillette corporate brand name and position the Sensor as a premium-priced product.

Since customers using the new Gillette Sensor would perhaps spend only an additional $10 per year than if they had used disposable razors, it would not weigh heavily on their pock-

etbooks. By switching customers to the Sensor line, however, Gillette could profit from the 90 percent gross margins on the recurring volume sales of blades to Sensor razor users. To implement its strategy, Gillette combined its European and North American organizations so that they would follow a unified brand promotion and premium-price strategy. After spending $200 million on research and development and over $100 million a year in advertising on the Sensor, Gillette began obtaining annual sales of $390 million. Gillette's Sensor became one of the most successful new product introductions ever, getting 42 percent of the combined market for nondisposable razors.[18]

All new products become mature and Gillette's Sensor was no exception. Gillette's natural response was to launch another new shaving innovation, its Mach 3 razor. This product took six years to develop, with Gillette spending $750 million on product development, and another $300 million on first-year advertising and marketing costs. Why did the Mach3 cost over a billion dollars to develop? One reason is that it used a three-blade razor to provide a close, smooth shave. It featured a new blade alignment, with each blade positioned

Table 8–3 is only about U.S. firms, and focuses solely on industrial marketing, which is why familiar names such as Coca-Cola, Daimler-Benz, Gillette, and Sony do not appear on this list. Different companies would appear on the list depending on the nature of the survey and in which countries the surveys are done, but such surveys are helpful in understanding the power of brands and in determining the value of brands—brand equity. For instance, a survey of Latin American brands shows brands from companies such as Bimbo (Mexico, bread and snacks), Brahma (Brazil, beer) and Maseca (Mexico, tortillas and corn flour) as having high recognition and sustainability. ("Staying Power," *Business Latin America,* November 23, 1998). A Gallup survey in China found the most popular brands to be Coca-Cola, Head and Shoulders, Honda, Mercedes-Benz and Pepsi-Cola, followed by Philips, Motorola, Daihatsu, Playboy, and Star TV. (Gallup China survey, *Business China,* November 10, 1997, p. 11).

BRANDING

A brand, once developed and recognized, can have a long life: Major brands such as Lipton, Ivory, Gillette, and Coca-Cola have been popular for over 70 years. A big question then is how to build up brand recognition in international markets. Brands can be built up through advertising, but advertising merely builds on the brand's foundation, which rests on (a) quality, (b) innovation, (c) superior service, (d) customer satisfaction, and (e) value. In consumer products, brand personality is also relevant: namely, how a brand creates and reinforces buyer's self-image in products such as designer clothing brands, cars, shoes, and so on. The return to the firm is brand loyalty and repeat purchases and a loyal customer; since acquir-

progressively closer to the face to reduce irritation while shaving closer. Gillette suggests that the new angle of the cartridge to the razor handle makes shaving more like using a paintbrush. The cartridge in which the three blades were enclosed had a pivot point at the bottom to increase the cartridge's stability, and tiny fins at the bottom edge of the cartridge that always touched the skin first, freeing hairs from their follicles and helping reduce irritation while shaving closer. The cartridges were redesigned to be loaded with a snap-in single point docking system so that shavers would not be able to load the cartridge upside down, a problem with older razors.

Closer shaves mean sharper blades, which could lead to exceedingly thin edges, which could wear out quickly. Hence, Gillette chose an untested technology, namely, to coat the blade edges with a carbon layer, developing its own 60-foot-long $20 million new machines to deposit carbon inside a vaccum chamber along the blade edges. Robotic arms shuffle 12,000 blades at a time into these deposition machines, with a planned volume of 3.6 billion blades annually. Gillette also had to design continuous assembly machinery, like those used in soft drink bottling plants, each costing $15 million, to assemble the Mach3 cartridges. In its Boston factory, six such machines can assemble 600 cartridges a minute, allowing costs to fall through economies of scale and making the new technology affordable.

The new Mach3 product is priced at 35 percent premium to the SensorExcel cartridges, Gillette's former top of the line product. To reduce sticker shock, the Mach3 cartridges would be sold in packs of 4 and 8, in contrast to the 5 and 10 cartridge sizes for the Sensor. The added cost per person could be $7 to $18, depending on whether the blades were changed weekly or less often. The Mach3 costs 50 percent more to make than the Sensor product line, and the large investment means that Gillette must achieve high volume sales faster in order to obtain reasonable payback periods. Hence, Gillette aims to sell the Mach3 in over a 100 countries within 18 months of U.S. launch, a major undertaking. Blades account for about half of its profits and command a two-thirds global market share. The new Mach3 launch is critical to Gillette's continued success in the shaving marketplace.

Sources: "The Best a Plan Can Get," *The Economist,* August 15, 1992; and "How Gillette Is Honing Its Edge," *Business Week,* September 28, 1992. "Gillette Finally Reveals Its Vision of the Future and It Has 3 Blades," *The Wall Street Journal,* April 14, 1998; and "How Gillette Brought Its Mach3 to Market," *The Wall Street Journal,* April 15, 1998.

---

ing customers is costly, loyal customers who buy regularly are valuable to a firm. Furthermore, brands provide customers with a guarantee of value and quality, making the customer's choice easier; it frees them from the confusion and message fatigue endemic to a competitive marketplace; brands become a short cut to consumption, allowing the customer to make safe choices, secure that satisfaction and value will result if the brand is purchased. Conversely, breaking this compact with the customer can quickly result in a brand's decline. Brands allow a firm to charge premium prices, and the profits from premium pricing, coupled with steady market share and repeat purchases, result in measurable cash flow, which is at the heart of brand equity calculations.

Creative approaches to building brand recognition are helpful. A distributor of British skiwear, Nevica USA, offered photographers free skiwear and a fee each time one of their photographs was published in a ski magazine showing Nevica-clad skiers. Similarly, Franklin Sports Industries built name recognition by giving away batting gloves to baseball players. Because the Franklin name appeared in large letters on the back of these gloves, they were prominently visible whenever TV cameras focused on a batter. When photographs of batters appeared in newspapers or on the cover of magazines such as *Sports Illustrated,* the Franklin name was generally visible.[19]

Brand Extensions

Brand extension allows a firm with an existing presence in overseas markets to quickly establish its new products. Using a well-known brand name with a reputation for quality can extend an aura of high quality to the new product. Brand extension can allow the new product to be introduced with lower advertising expenditures. The comfort

| TABLE 8–3 | Landor Associates U.S. Business-to-Business Image Power Survey, 1998 |

	Image Power Rank		*Image Power Rank*
Microsoft	84	U.S. Postal Service	41
UPS	72	Hewlett Packard	40
VISA	72	Delta Airlines	39
AT&T	71	Compaq	37
Fed Ex	67	Dell Computer	36
Xerox	64	Chase	36
IBM	57	MCI	36
Master Card	53	Southwest Airlines	36
American Express	51	Citibank	34
Hertz	47	American Airlines	33
Canon	47	Novell	33
Marriott Hotels	45	Budget Rent a Car	32
Anderson Consulting	44	Allstate Insurance	32
State Farm Insurance	44	Pitney Bowes	32
Avis	42	Holiday Inn	31

Source: Landor Associates Web site: **http://www.andor.com/American/Home/News/index.html.**

level and familiarity associated with a well-known brand can motivate customers to try the new product rather than a competitor's product. Brand extensions can include launching the same product in a different form, adding the brand name to related products often used together ("companion" products), building on the company image and expertise, and communicating unique or designer attributes. However, there are dangers: The original brand and product can be damaged by extending the brand image to undesirable products and settings. There must be a fit, some complementarity, between the original product and the proposed product/brand extension.[20]

Hewlett-Packard (H-P), for example, was successful in extending its brand image to the home PC market. It first obtained a foothold in this segment by selling ink-jet printers, which were cheap and allowed low-cost color printing that appealed to home PC customers with children. It helped that the Japanese firms who dominated the previous generation of dot-matrix printers stayed with them for too long, which slowed down their entry into the ink-jet market because of H-Ps strong patent position. With its strong brand association in the home PC segment due to its printer sales, H-P was able to launch multimedia PCs intended primarily for the home market. It was able to get retail shelf space because it already supplied retailers large numbers of ink-jet printers. This allowed for bundling together PCs with printers. Finally, H-P's size and extended product range plus high margins from ink-jet cartridge sales meant that H-P could undercut home PC prices and even accept losses in the interest of building long-term market share.[21]

Mattel, the owner of the successful Barbie doll line, has been increasing Barbie doll sales by developing a collector's line that is high priced and aimed at adults who may have owned Barbie dolls as children. Mattel is also continually introducing new Barbie dolls, such as a Barbie doll teacher, along with a related full line of accessories such as a blackboard, schoolroom, and Barbie's ubiquitous dresses.

Movie tie-ins are also a popular mode of enhancing sales for Mattel, as sales get a boost from manufacturing dolls tied to Disney films like *Pocahontas, The Lion King,* and *Beauty and the Beast.*[22]

Brand Protection: When and Where?

Protecting a brand in international markets can begin with registering them in the countries of interest with the appropriate authorities. Blanket registration in all countries might be wise if the costs of registration, which may amount to a significant sum, are within the budgetary capabilities of the firm. Smaller firms may wish to be more selective.

Brand protection can come about through use of the brand name in common-law countries, or through legal registration of the brand name in code-law countries. However, use should follow registration and vice versa. While the firm must incur registration costs—primarily legal fees and administrative payments—use costs are higher, involving the import of material quantities of a product and the development of distribution channels and marketing campaigns. Less than diligent registration and use of a brand name or trademark may result in a firm's having to buy back the rights to its name at a possibly inflated sum, depending on the emerging market potential in the country.

A related problem is imitation brands: local brands are introduced that are reasonably close facsimiles of the international brand, such as a "Coalgate" brand competing with the better-known international brand Colgate. Another related problem is the nature of local reaction to well-known international brands. Phonetic equivalents of English-language brands may not translate well into a foreign language, possibly resulting in an undesirable meaning. An example is the U.S. candy bar Snickers, which is too close to the commonly used British "knickers," ladies' undergarments. A third problem might be that the English brand name may be too close to an existing brand name in the local language. For example, "Sears," when spoken by a Castilian Spanish speaker, sounds remarkably similar to "Seat," the Spanish automobile company. The solution was to use the full Sears Roebuck name to avoid confusion. Sometimes the brand name may be changed to make it easier for the native tongue. Ocean Spray cranberries, for example, when translated into Chinese characters that sound out as "Hoshien Pei," has the added advantage of meaning healthy refreshment. Matsushita, when first entering the U.S. market, could not use its National brand because it was already taken, and because the Japanese parent company's name was deemed difficult for U.S. consumers to say. A new brand name, Panasonic, was generated and promoted.

Product Piracy and Counterfeiting

As more trade becomes technology intensive, intellectual property protection is essential to maintaining competitive advantage. Firms spend large amounts of money creating technology through R&D. It takes investment in people—programmers and musicians and directors and actors—to produce software, a best-selling record, or a successful film. Pharmaceutical companies can easily spend $100 million over 10 years to develop a new pharmaceutical drug. Patent copyright law protects such investments.

Different nations have different regulations on what can be protected, the extent of protection, and the period of protection. Developing nations need technology and are unwilling to pay large royalties to multinationals, but the triad economies increasingly depend on technology-based exports. Even within the developed nations, major differences exist in how technology is protected. A celebrated instance is the end of copyright protection in Japan for the Beatles' *Sergeant Pepper* album. Japanese law limits copyright protection for record companies to 20 years. Hence, in 1987, when the copyright expired, a Japanese compact disk manufacturer introduced nine discount-priced collections of Beatles songs. In another example, a branch of Marubeni Corp., a giant trading company, was able to buy master tapes and issue recordings of jazz classics by artists such as Miles Davis, John Coltrane, and Nat King Cole. In contrast, the U.S. copyright law provides 75 years of protection to producers, performers, and record companies.[23]

GLOBAL MARKETING

Protecting Brand Names and Trademarks

Timberland is a U.S. company with a reputation for making rugged, outdoor-use footwear and clothing. Its logo is a tree, and its name and logo have developed a strong image connoting high quality and durability. It began registering its name and logo around the world and found that a Brazilian company, Samello, was using the Timberland name on its own products. Timberland sued to prohibit Samello's use of its name. However, it is normally difficult to win such suits, and Timberland's lawyers chose an unusual approach; instead of requesting that the product name be protected, they argued that Timberland was the actual name of the company, and hence, as a trade name, it was protected even without registration. Timberland won the court case, but an appeal is making its way through the Brazilian legal system.

Another problem in Brazil arose when Timberland contracted with a Brazilian firm to manufacture shoes. The contract stated that the order was not final until samples had been inspected and approved. Timberland canceled the order because the samples were not sized properly; it then found that the Brazilian subcontractor had already made over 5,000 pairs of shoes with the Timberland logo. The Brazilian company was given permission to sell the shoes in the United States provided that Timberland's name and logo were removed. Shortly thereafter, Timberland found these shoes on sale in the United States at a deep discount but with the tree logo intact. Timberland's reputation for quality had been affected by the sale of substandard shoes, an action that could destroy the carefully built brand image and company reputation.

To avoid such problems, Timberland's lawyer, Ethan Horwitz, with the law firm of Darby & Darby, recommends that firms register their trademarks wherever they manufacture, even if the country is used only as an export platform;

Protecting Brand Names

Marlboro is a global brand. The Marlboro man never speaks, but the image of the U.S. cowboy in a red flannel shirt has universal appeal. Marlboro accounts for over one-quarter of Philip Morris's cigarette revenues, nearly 300 billion cigarettes a year. It is a quintessential U.S. product, perhaps because of Hollywood's westerns seen the world over. The value of this brand alone to Philip Morris has been estimated at $10 billion.[24]

Undercutting such a brand presence could destroy Philip Morris's ability to maintain its competitive edge. Yet recent EU legislation does have such a negative impact. As one of its Single Market policies, the EU is harmonizing advertising. As part of such rules, cigarette print and poster ads (the only form of advertising open to cigarette manufacturers) are restricted to presentation of the cigarette packaging and information about tar and nicotine content, with health warnings to take up between 10 and 20 percent of the ad space. Such a restriction prevents companies from using familiar images such as the Marlboro man and the Virginia Slims woman.

Because prices are largely determined by excise taxes, creative advertising is the major approach to discriminating between brands. The EU legislation takes away a significant competitive edge enjoyed by Marlboro. Tobacco companies, however, have few hopes of lobbying against such restrictions because the EU bases its regulations on the fact that tobacco products kill 440,000 people every year in its member countries.[25]

From the manufacturer's standpoint, the lack of protection can result in sales lost to the imitators, who are seen as competing unfairly. The reduced sales and cash flow in turn reduce investment in innovation. Consumers may ultimately suffer from a lack of new high-technology and innovative products. Countries dependent on technology, such as the United States, will see their exports decrease, and job losses can result in the affected industries. Overseas, U.S. firms will lose sales to foreign companies that can copy technology or brand names or copyrighted material

apply for a trademark in countries that the firm expects will be good markets over the next 10 years; and trademark and aggressively protect trademarks through lawsuits in countries where piracy and counterfeiting are rampant.

The fear of losing rights to brands is not an idle one. South Africa's supreme court ruled that McDonald's did not own the rights to its trademark in South Africa because it had not used its name there in the previous five years. McDonald's had registered its name in South Africa and renewed its rights but had not opened operations there because of apartheid sanctions (which were lifted in 1991). The judge also decided that McDonald's trademark was not well-known among South Africa's majority black population and, therefore, two small South African companies that wanted to open their own McDonald's restaurants in Durban and Johannesburg were free to do so. McDonald's is, of course, appealing the ruling.

A similar problem faced Grand Met, which marketed Smirnoff vodka worldwide, selling 5 million cases and spending $10 million annually in promoting the brand. Its right to the Smirnoff name came under attack in Russia from Boris Smirnoff, a descendant of Pyotr Smirnoff, who founded the Smirnoff vodka business over 100 years ago. With the Bolshevik Revolution the Smirnoffs lost their business, as did most holders of private property. Grand Met's Heublein division acquired the rights to the Smirnoff name in the 1930s from one of Pyotr's sons, Vladimir. A lawsuit by Boris Smirnoff claimed that Vladimir had no right to sell the name. In December 1995 the Russian Patent Office Chamber of Appeals did invalidate Heublein's trademarks. Aside from whether the Russian contention has merit, Grand Met has pointed out that it has spent millions over the past 50 years building up the value of the Smirnoff brand, and that when Heublein acquired the name, total U.S. sales were only about 5,000 cases. Grand Met estimated the brand's value to be about $1.4 billion, and the brand's value could diminish if Grand Met could not claim to be the "Official Purveyor to the Russian Imperial Court."

Sources: "U.S. MNC Wins Some Rounds against Trademark Pirates," *Business International,* June 8, 1992; "Hunting the Big Mac in Africa," *The Economist,* November 11, 1995; and "Who Owns the Smirnoff Name?" *Business Week,* January 15, 1996.

with impunity. In the short run, foreign industry and foreign consumers are the beneficiaries.[26] Overall, world welfare is likely to decline over time unless regulations allow a fair return to investments in technology and product differentiation.

PRIVATE BRANDING

In **private branding,** which is common in consumer goods marketing, the manufacturer cedes control over marketing to the retailer or distributor. That is, the manufacturer supplies goods, but the retailer sells these goods under its own brand names. Thus, a marketer such as Spiegel might order quantities of dresses, linens, towels, lamps, and accessories, all to be sold under the Spiegel catalog brand name. Indeed, Spiegel has increased the proportion of private-label apparel that it sells to about 60 percent of total garment sales. Most of its purchases are from Far East clothing subcontractors. The original manufacturer's identity is lost, and its margins tend to be lower on private-brand sales.

Private branding provides a quick and relatively low-cost approach to penetrating foreign markets, though the seller fails to establish any relationship with the ultimate buyer and hence has little control over the marketing relationship. The manufacturer has no say on the prices charged and receives little direct feedback from the market. Nor can service and after-sales support be used as a means of forging long-term ties with the ultimate buyer. However, private branding is a useful means of test-marketing products in markets whose potential is likely to grow in the future. Positioning is also important in selling such private brands. Low prices alone are not enough because profitability is restricted due to lower profit margins. The goal is to match branded product quality as well as offer prices that are sufficiently below that of branded products to convince considerable numbers of customers to switch to the private label. For manufacturers who supply firms such as Spiegel, careful sourcing is necessary to lower procurement costs without diminishing quality, while also meeting delivery deadlines and supplying the contracted for quantities.[27]

When product specifications are provided by a buyer such as Spiegel, which has a database of 6.4 million active catalog customers,[28] private-brand sales become a window on an emerging market and allow the manufacturer to better position itself for future direct entry. Spiegel benefits from its name becoming a well-known brand.

However, such private-label experience may not easily transfer across national markets. For example, Sainsbury, Britain's largest supermarket operator, has been successful in the United Kingdom in selling private-label products such as smoked salmon and its own brand of champagne. When it expanded into the United States, it decided not to push its private-label approach until it learned how private-label products in these product categories are evaluated by U.S. consumers.

An interesting trend is the proliferation of private brands in supermarkets and chain stores in Europe. The German low-price food chain, Aldi, sells mostly its own private brand of food products. It contracts the manufacturing of basic products such as flour, rice, and noodles and aims for margins of about 12.5 percent, lower than the 16 percent margin typical in French hypermarkets or the 25 percent margin of British supermarkets. At the same time, Aldi concentrates on quality equivalent to brand-name products but at a lower price. As neighborhood shops disappear across Europe and more customers shop at chain stores and hypermarkets, such private branding could increase.

How serious is the threat to established brands from private labels? Private-label sales are increasing in importance, accounting for about 15 percent of U.S. supermarket sales, more so in recession years. The proportion is considerably higher in Europe, where large grocery and supermarket chains such as the previously mentioned Sainsbury and Tesco dominate and accordingly provide more shelf space to their in-house private brands. Sainsbury, for example, had Cott Corporation manufacture their Classic Cola and was able to capture 15 percent of the U.K. cola market, accounting for 65 percent of cola sales within Sainsbury.

Private labels have increased in prominence because their quality has gone up. Premium private labels have emerged, such as Loblaw's President's Choice line of over 1,500 grocery items. With private labels available for a wide variety of goods, consumers may be more willing to buy them over higher-priced national brands. As such European retailers begin to expand into the United States, private-label merchandise could increase in importance there.

Store brands and private labels are more of a threat when the national brands do not command high market shares uniformly across a national market. In such cases, efficient retailers can win market share for their private label or store brands, depending on:[29]

◆ The demographics of their local markets.
◆ Scale and scope economies of the retailer.
◆ Retailer pricing, promotion and assortment (product range) tactics.
◆ Retailer expertise in the category (frozen foods, soft drinks, etc.).
◆ Extent of competition in the local retail sector.
◆ Extent of competition from all brands in the category.
◆ National brand manufacturers promotion and advertising strategies.

Manufacturers of branded goods have fought back, however, with several tactics:[30]

Convincing retailers of the greater overall profitability of carrying branded goods—greater turnover and more repeat buying make up for lower retailer margins.
Reducing the price gap between the national brand and the private label, while realizing that some premium is necessary to pay for brand advertising and for the greater reassurance of quality and performance that a brand conveys.

Combining brand marketing with complementary sales promotions and enhanced channel relationships.

Continuing to improve the brand so that it offers value commensurate with pricing; in other words, manufacturers continuing to invest in and build up brand equity.

PRIVATE BRANDS AND ORIGINAL EQUIPMENT MANUFACTURER (OEM) SALES

OEM contracts are related to brand strategies, especially in the marketing of components and subassemblies. Without OEM contracts, manufacturers of airbags, such as TRW or Morton International, would face the task of convincing individual automobile buyers to install their airbag as standard equipment on cars manufactured without an OEM contract. In the international arena, this would mean these manufacturers would compete against other manufacturers of airbags. Instead, under an OEM contract, the sale is made to the auto manufacturer, and the final consumer buys the airbags as part of the auto and does not specify the make of airbag he or she prefers.

OEM deals are an industrial marketing task, and the selling cycle may be long, entailing careful assessment by several executives and engineers. When the sale is made, however, it is for large volumes, and repeat business is likely as long as price, delivery, and quality standards are satisfactory. OEM sales generally involve direct selling to and close involvement with the buyers, often to the extent of redesigning products or adding features for large-volume customers. There is also a risk factor: If such a customer decides to switch suppliers, the loss of volume might result in unabsorbed overhead and excess capacity.

OEM sales are indirect means of penetrating different segments of a market, whether domestic or foreign. Tandy Corporation, the operator of 4,800 Radio Shack computer stores in the United States, agreed to manufacture 16- and 32-bit portable computers for Matsushita, which would sell them in the United States under its Panasonic brand name. Matsushita's aim was to circumvent the 100 percent punitive tariffs imposed by the U.S. government on these imports. Tandy was happy to enhance its reputation for quality and low-cost manufacturing by being associated with the Panasonic label. At the same time, it obtains preferential access to and low prices in buying Matsushita's memory chips—an item periodically in short supply. Furthermore, Matsushita is selling the computers purchased from Tandy through office products retailers—a large corporate segment to which Radio Shack has had difficulty in selling.

Thus, the OEM sale to Matsushita allows Tandy to (indirectly) penetrate the Fortune 500 segment while selling to individuals and small businesses through the Radio Shack chain. Long term, the alliance will also help Tandy in developing products for the Japanese market.[31]

The Japanese have been very successful international marketers in recent years, and private branding has played a role in their success. Mitsubishi was an unknown factor in automobiles. By marketing initially under the Chrysler name, it was able to get quickly established in the U.S. market. Japanese producers led by Sony and Matsushita were marketing 80 percent of their videotape recorders under private brands, two of the leading ones being RCA and Zenith. Hitachi supplied large computers to Olivetti, BASF, and National Advanced Systems for sale under their names.

The newest firms using private branding to break into foreign markets are manufacturers from the "Four Tigers"—Hong Kong, Korea, Singapore, and Taiwan. They use the brands of their customers to make up for the lack of consumer recognition and acceptance of their own company names. Their customers include such established names as Mattel and IBM in addition to such prominent retailers as Kmart, Lord and Taylor, Nieman-Marcus, J.C. Penney, and Sears. Partly because of the fear that brand owners may seek lower-cost suppliers, leaving the original producer without a market, firms such as Tatung, Samsung, Lucky-Goldstar, and Hyundai have begun to promote their own brand names.

Another situation may confront the smaller firm if it wishes to market abroad through an export management company (see Chapter 10) rather than through its own export department. The export management company may want its own brand on the goods to achieve greater control and protection in market development. If the manufacturer accedes, the producing firm is giving up developing a market for itself. This can hurt the firm later if it wants to go more directly into foreign markets.

COUNTRY-OF-ORIGIN EFFECT

Numerous studies have shown that consumers evaluate a product not only by its appearance and physical characteristics but also by the country in which it was produced. This is the **country-of-origin effect.** Certain countries have a good image for certain kinds of products—Germany for cars, France for women's fashion, and Britain for men's fashion. If a firm is producing a product in a country that does not have a favorable image for that product, it may have a hard task marketing it. (See Chapter 7 for a model to measure the country-of-origin effect.)

Some products are binational in origin, such as the Honda Civic made in the United States. How do consumers rate such products? That is, which country of origin do they give more weight to? A study of color TVs and subcompact autos with binational origins found that both the source country and brand name affect perception of quality, although source country seems more important than the brand name. Further, the country of origin does not influence the consumer's perception of all attributes of the product in the same way. German products, for example, were rated high on quality but low on economy. The country effect may carry across product categories so that a product from Germany may be regarded as being of high quality whether it is a car or a toaster.[32]

PRODUCT STANDARDS

Product standards in different markets determine whether a foreign product needs to be adapted to conform to the local standard before being sold. Standards can either be technical standards or government-mandated ones. Technical standards are enforced by the market in the sense that the best technical standards receive the approval of customers in the form of their purchases, and, over time, the industry settles on a certain standard. An example would be the worldwide acceptance of the Intel chips and the Microsoft Windows operating system software as standards for the IBM-compatible PC market. Apple's Mac system has been an opposing standard and has gradually lost global market share, falling to below 5 percent of the market, as the Wintel standard took hold. Its nonstandard equipment was particularly harmful in the business environment where most companies opted for the Wintel standard, for cost and compatibility reasons. However, consumers care more about ease of use and Apple was able to recover some ground with its iMac introduction, because consumers were attracted to its unusual design as well as its integrated system approach and its relatively lower price; Apple was able to make inroads with a segment of the market that valued design and ease of use and were less price conscious.

The power of adhering to a global standard is discernible in Japan where PC manufacturers have gradually coalesced around the IBM PC and Wintel standard. This stance has isolated NEC, which was the market share leader with 53 percent of the market in 1992, but with its own proprietary NEC PC-98 standard that is not sold outside of Japan and is incompatible with the IBM PC standard. As major Japanese companies such as Hitachi and Fujitsu began to make IBM-compatible PCs and sell them to their established mainframe customer base, NEC saw its market share erode.[33]

Differences in product standards can act as trade barriers, with governments enacting such standards in the public interest. In some cases it is conceivable that the market would stop buying goods of dubious quality, making government regulation and passage of standards unnecessary. Other regulations such as those ensuring that children's toys are not dangerous and clothes not flammable may be justified because consumer preferences and incomes vary, and richer countries may want to spend more of their incomes on assuring themselves of higher levels of safety or environmental cleanliness.[34]

In another example, the EU raised antipollution standards for small-car engines, making such cars more expensive. The new standards impact heavily on manufacturers such as Peugeot and Renault, for which small cars are about one-third of total output. The same standards benefit German automakers, who already met stricter German antipollution standards. Hence, they gain on competition, as do the U.S. companies such as Ford and General Motors. The new standards also create increased demand for catalytic converters and fuel injection systems, which are needed to control emissions to meet the new standards.

Often government standards can become a means of keeping out foreign competition. With new pharmaceuticals, Japan demands that tests be conducted in Japan before marketing approval is received. The fact that U.S. companies have already met rigorous U.S. FDA standards is not sufficient. One consequence is that U.S. pharmaceutical companies must spend additional time and money getting Japanese approvals, which acts as an impediment to entering the Japanese market. Such regulations also give the Japanese competitors additional time to study new products from overseas and develop a response.

In many Third World markets, the process of setting standards is just beginning. These countries often lack technical expertise and the financial resources to do an adequate job on their own. Therefore, they often turn to authorities from Europe, Japan, and the United States. Industries from the United States would certainly gain from helping in this process so that sales of U.S.–made products would be facilitated.

For example, the Saudi Arabian Standards Organization (SASO) has been receiving help from experts from Japan, the United Kingdom, France, and West Germany in updating product standards for more than 42,000 products. The standards being developed seem to favor manufacturers from those countries. Once Saudi standards are set, they are likely to be copied by smaller neighboring countries such as Bahrain, Kuwait, and the United Arab Emirates, all oil-producing countries with rising incomes.

The Saudi example is not unique. Brazil received a gift of several volumes of literature on German product standards in Portuguese, and European interests have helped India build a $16 million laboratory to certify that Indian electronic components meet European standards. The hope is that the labs will help India meet European standards and thus increase its exports to Europe; then it might use its hard currency earnings to import European telecommunication products. Japan has initiated a training program for standards personnel from 28 developing countries and sends out Japanese standards experts to provide training in developing countries.

Although U.S. products may be safe and technically excellent, it is not enough that they meet Underwriters Laboratories (UL) standards alone. Unless U.S. firms as a group can influence other nations to accept UL standards as their own, they will probably lose some markets to foreign competitors that have become more adept at influencing and adhering to different national standards. Another way that standards can serve to exclude foreign products is the cumbersome certification requirements that some countries enforce, raising costs prohibitively.

Sometimes companies can take advantage of the fact that standards have yet to coalesce in key markets. Summit Technology is a small manufacturer of laser systems used in eye surgery. It makes excimer lasers, which emit light in the deep ultraviolet range and allow shallow and precise cuts to be made, permitting removal of tissue as thin as one-third the thickness of human hair. Summit submitted to tests in the United States in order to receive FDA approval, which can take several years. In the meantime, Summit was able to sell 90 such excimer laser systems in Europe, Japan, and Korea. These sales were instrumental in generating cash flow so that Summit could survive the slow process of obtaining FDA approval.[35]

PRODUCT POLICY AND INTERNATIONAL COMPETITION

Part of a product development and launch campaign is the strategic marketing investment made to ensure that the product captures market share in the long term. That is, new products need strategic nurturing over time if they are to wrest market share from the existing product leaders. An example is Glaxo, which launched its anti-ulcer drug Zantac when SmithKline's Tagamet had a near monopoly in the marketplace. A carefully targeted marketing campaign over six years, however, allowed Glaxo to get 50 percent of the market. Glaxo's objective for its marketing investment was to achieve sustainable market share. It needed to identify customers for Zantac and to ensure their retention so that sales recur while customer acquisition costs are reduced.

For companies playing catch-up as Glaxo did against an entrenched competitor, this means identifying a group of the competitor's customers who are ready to switch, and who could generate high levels of sales and profits. Such customers might be less sensitive to price and more concerned with service and product innovativeness. A third element is seeking customers who are "share determiners," such as medical residents who were the key to allowing Glaxo to win long-term market share. The stage of the product cycle also matters.

RTE-ASEA was a late entrant to the electrical transformer market and won market share by targeting GE and Westinghouse customers who were considering switching. It won over a portion of this segment over time while making sure that the issues preoccupying potential "switchables" among its own customer base were attended to so that they became loyal customers.[36]

CUSTOMER SATISFACTION AND LOYALTY

Understanding why customers switch is an integral part of formulating a marketing plan, particularly in competitive markets at later stages of the product cycle. Satisfied customers are generally loyal customers, providing the firm with significantly greater volumes of business; however, a loyal customer may be so because of other factors such as monopoly conditions among suppliers, high switching costs, and loyalty-promotion programs such as frequent-flyer plans. Such customers might desert if they could. To complicate matters, not every customer will experience the same level of satisfaction even though the product and service they receive are identical. Hence, great importance is attached to understanding what makes customers truly satisfied and highly loyal. Customer satisfaction results from several conditions:

1. Basic product attributes meet customer expectations.

2. Customer support services increase product effectiveness and enhance ease of use.

3. Prompt and satisfactory procedures exist for dealing with customer dissatisfaction.

4. Unusual service appears to customize the product or service for the customer.

Horst Schulze, president of Ritz-Carlton Hotels, summarizes: "Unless customers are excited about what you are doing, you have to improve."[37]

Changes in the customer base can force a company to change its product strategy. Coats Viyella, the British textile conglomerate, had long run its business by relying on the manufacturing scale and breadth of its product line to attract and keep its customers, which it saw as being various retail chains. However, as the retail industry consolidated, chains such as Marks & Spencer began to acquire more power and could choose their suppliers. In response, Coats Viyella narrowed its business to five core product lines: clothing, home furnishings such as bed linen, yarn, fashion retailing, and precision engineering products that grew out of Coats' own manufacturing heritage. In addition, Coats began acquiring firms such as Tootal with factories all over the Far East and began shifting labor-intensive manufacturing (such as zipper production) to lower-wage countries such as Morocco. It also developed EDI—Electronic Data Interchange—to speed up supplies to major customers such as Marks & Spencer, allowing it to receive instructions on product colors and styles and then to supply such orders in two weeks. A similar setup links Coats' Jaeger retailer and other chains to the factory, improving distribution while reducing unsold inventory. However, EDI raises the possibility of factories in the Far East directly linked to Western retailers, raising the question of what useful purpose an intermediary Western owner serves. The long-term answer may lie in quality and design capabilities exceeding that of Far Eastern suppliers.[38]

MODE OF ENTRY AND NEW-PRODUCT SUCCESS

The success of the international marketing of a product or service is partly influenced by how a firm chooses to enter the market, whether directly or indirectly, and whether through overseas manufacturing, licensing, the use of distributors, and so on. Three sets of variables influence the company's decision about how to carry out its international marketing.[39]

1. *Global strategic variables,* which include the level of global concentration, global synergies between national market entry and market shares, and the global strategic motivations of the firm and its competitors.

2. *Transaction-specific variables,* that is, the importance of proprietary knowledge within the firm that is relevant to successful overseas market entry, as well as whether such knowledge is implicit, unwritten, and tacit, so that it cannot be easily transferred in arms-length negotiations to independent parties.

3. *Environmental variables,* specific to each country, such as country risk, cultural distance, and unfamiliarity associated with each location; the forecasted distribution and uncertainty of demand from each market location; and the intensity of competition at each site; all of these together affect the desirability of adopting entry modes that involve the firm more closely with the market. Figure 8–2 summarizes these associations.

An example of such an integrated approach to market entry is provided by P&G, whose efforts in China led to its becoming the largest consumer products company there with $500 million in annual sales and half of the shampoo market. P&G began in 1988 with its Head and Shoulders shampoo, using advertising to draw attention to dandruff in a country of black-haired people and followed it with intensive distribution; it then rolled out two additional brands, Rejoice and Pantene, also with anti-dandruff formulas, and despite a 300 percent price premium to local brands, it was able to capture 57 percent market share in three major cities. P&G's goal was to be number one from the start, gradually introducing other P&G products after shampoo and detergent had established themselves. P&G used several tactics:

1. It spent more on TV advertising than any other company in China.

2. It brought in over 100 American expatriate managers to implement and train local managers in American marketing techniques.

3. It obtained total retail coverage by developing detailed maps of 228 major Chinese cities and by visiting nearly every small retail mom-and-pop

FIGURE 8-2   **An Eclectic Framework of the Entry Mode Choice**

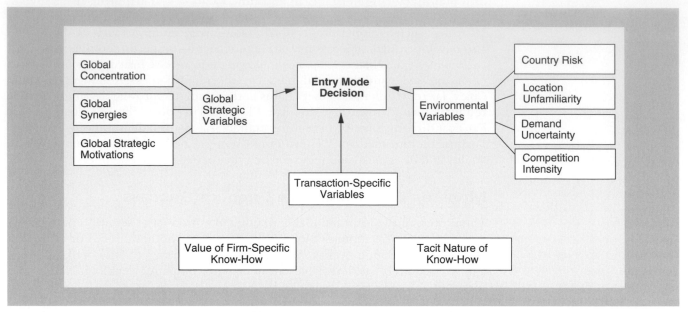

Source: W. Chan Kim and Peter Hwang, "Global Strategy and Multinationals' Entry Mode Choice," *Journal of International Business Studies* 23, no 1 (1992): 33.

shop and bigger department stores, getting them to stock P&G products.

4. It handed out free sample-size P&G detergent with every washing-machine sale and sold detergent in smaller-sized packages.

5. It offered incentives to distributors for early payment and cut off those who would not pay within 40 days.

6. It acquired three of China's major detergent manufacturers and two of the top Chinese brands.

P&G showed conclusively that a coordinated marketing campaign can establish Western brands in China, that it is a fast-growing mass market, and that no major brand—be it cognac or soap or computers—can afford to be out of the Chinese market.[40]

The importance of overall strategic objectives in affecting international marketing in individual countries is borne out by examining the different approaches used by American and Japanese firms in the United Kingdom. A research study by Peter Doyle and his colleagues[41] examined several issues:

1. Were Japanese firms more interested in long-term market share gains?

2. Did U.S. and U.K. firms focus more on short-term profit performance?

3. Did Japanese firms adapt their strategies more closely to the needs of the U.K. market?

4. Did local market needs or different management functions determine the shape of local organization structures?

Based on the study, Doyle and his coauthors imply that adaptation at the local market level is needed—"an ethnocentric export-based model of trade, rather than the geocentric global competitiveness (model)." The strong Japanese yen may have played a part in forcing the Japanese to become more local market–oriented; but this focus helped create flexible local organization with a clear mission to dominate the local market.

IKEA: Integrated Strategy for New-Product Launch across Multiple Markets

An example of adapting various facets of marketing strategy to export markets in the manner outlined above by Doyle can be seen in IKEA's approach to the U.S. market. IKEA pioneered the idea of low-cost, ready-to-assemble furniture in Sweden at a time when furniture was high-priced, made to order, and distributed through small retailers specializing in furniture. IKEA's Scandinavian design and low prices appealed to young couples and families with children. IKEA grew rapidly and gradually extended across Europe. It found success by emphasizing its Scandinavian origins, while persuading customers of its quality, yet acknowledging its unorthodox self-service approach to selling furniture. It also began sourcing its furniture from Eastern Europe to assure itself of low production costs. However, it was slow to expand in the United States, knowing that the United States had often been the stumbling block for other successful European retailers. When it did open in the United States, it realized that some adaptation would be necessary:

1. It had to adapt its furniture to larger American physiques; for example, Americans found its beds too narrow.

2. It had to specify product dimensions in inches rather than the metric system.

3. It had to develop "suites" of furniture to cater to the American penchant for buying furniture as a group, for the bedroom or dining room, living room, kitchen, and so on.

4. It had to redesign its furniture for U.S. use patterns, for example, deeper cabinets to hold larger dinner plates and larger glasses as Americans preferred to drink water with lots of ice in it, necessitating larger containers.

5. Because long queues and out-of-stock items led to disgruntled customers, IKEA upgraded its point-of-sale systems and added more check-out stations to speed up customer processing. It also increased local manufacture to prevent inventory shortages caused by a lengthy supply chain.

6. Appreciation of the Swedish kroner and other European currencies made its imported furniture more expensive and at odds with its marketing message of selling affordable furniture. Again, the solution was to increase its sourcing of locally made furniture, working with and developing U.S. suppliers to the point where they accounted for 45 percent of products sold at U.S. IKEA stores, from 15 percent formerly.

7. It also had to match U.S. customer service expectations by accepting a more generous product returns policy than in Europe and by offering next-day delivery to attract customers who did not want to cart their own furniture, a key aspect of the IKEA model in Europe.

With these modifications, IKEA expanded the number of U.S. stores and was able to increase North American sales.[42] Figure 8–3 summarizes how the various interlinked aspects of IKEA strategy contributed to its overall distinctive competence and market success.

FIGURE 8-3   **IKEA: Linking Competencies and Customers**

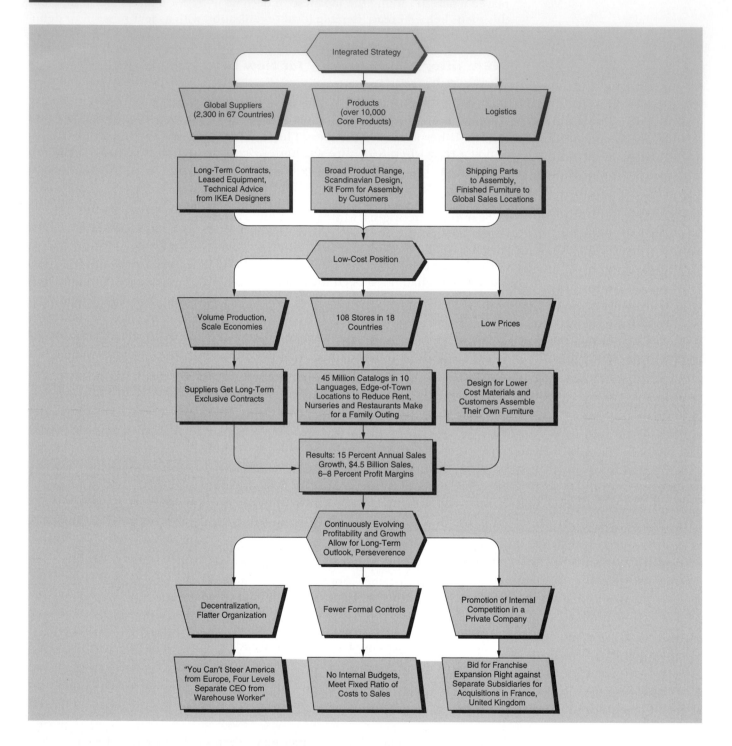

PACKAGING AND LABELING

Packaging

Packaging is very much part of a product's attributes, and companies expend considerable effort in developing packaging that is recognizable and distinctive as well as functional. Examples of factors that require packaging adaptation:

1. Changes in climate across countries, requiring more protective packaging against extremes of cold and heat.

2. Lengthy and difficult transportation and logistics networks, requiring that packaging protect goods against breakage and damage.

3. Lengthy periods on shelves at retailers before final sale, again requiring that packaging be protective and maintain freshness.

4. Varying sizes of packaging, with smaller-sized packages required in lower-income countries because they may be more affordable; smaller size may also be more common in countries where more frequent shopping trips are made and shoppers may carry their purchases on foot back to their dwellings.

5. Differences in packaging forms because of consumer preferences: for example, whether toothpaste is sold in squeeze tubes or upright cans, and whether glass containers or cardboard boxes are used for dispensing fruit juices and drinks.

6. Some standardization of packaging used to help the product be recognizable, such as Kodak's familiar yellow boxes.

7. Growing environmental consciousness on the part of consumers attempting to persuade firms to ensure that their packaging materials are biodegradable and/or recyclable and cause the least harm to the environment; an example is the growing use of slim cardboard packs to sell CDs instead of bulkier plastic boxes. Packaging adds bulk to a product and takes up more space during shipment. It might be more economical to ship the products in bulk and package them inside the destination markets. Whether this is feasible will depend on the capabilities of the domestic packaging industry, particularly in terms of quality, use of advanced technology packaging and printing processes, cost and timely delivery, and availability of quality materials.

Labeling

Primary considerations in labeling are providing information to the consumers and the use of multiple languages. Regulations in many countries require that detailed product composition and nutritional information be provided, as well as warning messages in the case of products that may be harmful or hazardous. Firms may also want to provide instructions for proper product use, in which case readability and the quality of communication matter. Merely translating text from the home country's language may not be sufficient. Country regulations may also require that information be presented in all of a country's or region's official languages. In Europe, this means compressing information in microscopic-sized fonts on the exterior of the package, or including a text insert with detailed information and instructions inside the package. This is necessary for products such as consumer electronics devices, tools, pharmaceuticals, and food products because the manufacturer desires to communicate detailed information such as how to set up equipment, energy consumption levels, recommended dosages, and recipes. These language complexities motivate manufacturers to use icons, diagrams, and cartoons to instruct consumers in the use of their products. Such pictorial descriptions transcend language and make it easier to introduce products into new markets.

GLOBAL MARKETING

Establishing New-Product Standards

Technologically impeccable products such as the Betamax VCR, the minidisc, and the digital compact cassette have received little consumer support and led to disappointing sales. Perhaps in response, consumer electronics firms, initially in opposing camps, led by Sony and Toshiba, buried their differences and opted for a common standard for a new compact disc product, the digital video disc, or DVD. The DVD would be compatible with existing CD-ROMs and music CDs and store about 4.7 gigabytes of information, enough for the average full-length Hollywood movie. The movies would be stored in a digital format, raising fears of unauthorized transmission and piracy over the Internet. Encryption devices could be developed, and the attraction of the new DVD format is that movie studios could repackage and sell films from

their libraries akin to what happened with recorded music, when buyers replaced their record libraries with new CDs. The DVD is also attractive to video game and multimedia educational training-material developers, who can combine more moving images with other content in a computer readable format.

A similar move to developing universal standards is seen on the Internet, where firms such as Netscape are giving away their Netscape Internet browsers for the World Wide Web in order to establish it as the universal standard. Their intent is to profit from selling ancillary software for companies who wish to set up Internet servers and home pages to conduct electronic commerce with their clientele. On the horizon is another such incipient standard—Java from Sun Microsystems—which allows the computer user connected to the Internet to use software stored somewhere on the network and thus "hollow out his own computer." This renders its power and speed secondary to the breadth of programs and information available on the network.

Sources: "Disk Standard Will Shake Up Video Market," *The Wall Street Journal,* September 18, 1995; and George Gilder, "The Coming Software Shift," *Forbes ASAP,* August 28, 1995, 147–162.

WARRANTY AND SERVICE POLICIES

Customers buying products are buying utility, function, and performance as much as image and status. In the case of products with a clear function or utility such as washing machines, hair dryers, hiking boots, and cars, customers want reassurances that the product will work as promised. Firms entering international markets are faced with the choice of standardizing their warranty policies, that is, offering the same warranty worldwide, or adapting it to change warranty terms for specific countries or regions, on the basis of various factors such as use conditions, government regulations, price and cost of delivering warranty service, and so on. A related question is that of matching or exceeding competition, that is, using warranties as a differentiating factor in gaining market share against competition and using warranties to overcome other product attributes that may hinder international market share achievement such as a negative country-of-origin effect.

Standardization

Warranty standardization is encouraged by several conditions:

1. The presence of multinational customers who might not accept a lower standard of warranties than that which they receive in other, perhaps more advanced, industrial markets.

2. Goods purchased on one market but used elsewhere: for example, cars, which may be purchased in Germany and driven across Europe; different levels of warranty in different European countries might antagonize customers and cause them to switch brands.

3. Products affecting human health and safety, such as aircraft, pharmaceutical drugs, and food products, for which, for ethical reasons, the firm cannot justify offering a lower level of warranty in certain markets.

4. When the firm offers standardized products worldwide, warranty standardization is likely to follow.

Localization

Warranties may be adapted to different local markets in several cases:

1. Competition is weak and firms do not feel pressure to incur additional costs that a standardized warranty policy might entail. This is likely in near-monopoly markets. Examples of this involve travel policies and denied-boarding compensation to passengers on foreign routes with little competition.

2. When multiple sources of production exist, differing quality levels may make offering uniform warranties difficult. This reflects a weak response to a flaw in a firm's sourcing policies, however.

3. Differing use conditions may cause a product to fail sooner, and warranties may be adapted to make allowances for such use. For example, warranties differ for cars used as taxicabs rather than used as private vehicles.

4. A lack of an international service network can make meeting warranty promises difficult. Again, cutting warranties in such a case would be an inadequate response. The correct approach would be to build up service capabilities worldwide so that uniform warranty policies could be offered and met.

5. Stronger warranties may be offered in markets in which a firm is new as a means of overcoming customer unfamiliarity with the product and as a means of building an installed base and market share against entrenched incumbents. Such higher warranty levels would typically revert to the worldwide norm after an introductory period.

After-Sales Service

While warranties represent the front end of a marketing bargain with the customer, following up on and delivering on the implied warranty promise is facilitated by the company's after-sales service network; thus, there must be a strong level of consistency between a company's warranty policies and its worldwide after-sales service network. Building such a network requires choosing locations from which to offer service, investing in physical facilities, equipment and parts, staffing and training of qualified service technicians, and a logistics and information network to keep track of service performance and customer complaints so that they are handled in a satisfactory manner.

Providing and proving the existence of a service capability may make the difference in winning new clients in overseas markets in industrial product settings. Customers justifiably worry about committing resources and critical portions of their firm's processes to products from a distant supplier with an unproven record in the marketplace. Companies such as Caterpillar have built up a strong international market position on the basis of a promise to deliver service parts within 48 hours to anywhere in the world, a promise which is much appreciated by users of expensive earth-moving equipment, for whom equipment failure might mean late completion of a project with serious negative financial consequences.

Firms have to decide whether to offer the international service capability themselves or offer it through their distributors and agents or contract it to independent third parties. A central issue here is goal congruence: Are distributors interested in investing the necessary capital in building up a strong service network, or are they mainly interested in short-term sales gains before moving on to the next hot product? Given distributor capital shortages and a lower commitment to long-term market share, firms may have to offer both financial and technical support to their distributors to ensure a high level of service capability. This could include carrying a supply of parts to ship to distributors as needed and offering extensive training to a distributor's service personnel on an ongoing basis at the firm's own expense. This raises practical questions such as where to conduct the training, how often to conduct it, how to ensure effective training, what language to offer the training in, whether to use on-line, computer-based support to service personnel in distant locations, and whether to offer incentives to enhance motivation and quality of the service personnel.

Offering efficient service does not mean maintaining multiple service sites in every major market and city, however. Using operations research techniques and modeling the demand for services, multinational firms can develop optimal configurations of parts depots, service centers, and levels of staff so that targeted service efficiency levels can be met for minimum investment while maintaining high levels of customer satisfaction. An interesting development is the offering of graded service plans to customers, whereby clients can choose the level of service they want, with higher charges accompanying higher levels of service. This is illustrated by the computer software business, where basic service might mean a few free hours followed by a per-minute charge for phone consultation to a blanket lump-sum, fee-based, year-round, on-site service for all of a firm's users and all of its installed base of computers. The difficulty is to strike a balance between offering the requisite level of service to stay competitive and keep customers and offering higher levels of fee-based service for customers who use a product or service more intensively and see economic value in paying for premium service.

SEGMENTATION ACROSS NATIONAL MARKETS

Marketing managers also decide, based on a product's attributes, which segments of the market they will target. Will segmentation decisions made for the domestic market be carried over to foreign markets? The firm also has to decide whether to standardize the positioning or image of a product across countries. Does it want to sell to the same customer segment across countries, or does it want to sell the same (standardized) product but to different segments in various countries (because a standardized product may appeal to different segments in different countries)?

Canon's positioning of the AE-1 camera (an affordable electronic auto-exposure single-lens reflex camera) during its global introduction illustrates this concept. Although the AE-1 was targeted to replacement buyers in Japan, it was intended for upscale first-time buyers in the United States and for older, technologically knowledgeable buyers in West Germany. The differences in segments targeted dictated accompanying changes in other elements of the marketing mix. (See Table 8–4.)

ALTERNATIVES TO DIRECT ENTRY: FRANCHISING ABROAD

Companies need not sell their product overseas in order to exploit market potential. Franchising, licensing, and other indirect modes of entry are feasible approaches to obtaining profits and market share abroad.

U.S. franchising is becoming increasingly important to foreign companies. Franchising in the United States is, of course, regulated by law, and foreign firms must abide by these laws. Since U.S. laws require elaborate disclosure and registra-

TABLE 8–4	Diverse Segment Positioning of Canon's AE-1 Camera		
Marketing Activities	*Japan*	*United States*	*Europe*
Target audience	Replacement buyers among young people	First-time buyers of SLR cameras who can be converted from box cameras to SLR	Replacement buyers who can be converted from old-fashioned cameras to SLR
Advertising message	"Continuous-shooting SLR": single-lens reflex that allows sequences of two frames per second	"So advanced, it's simple": Using sports celebrities to show the camera's ability to meet the challenge of fast-paced sport action and its suitability for nonprofessional photographers	No catch-phrase used in Europe: ads stress technological superiority resulting from use of microprocessor in the central processing unit or "brain" of the camera as well as speed and ease of use
Advertising media	Newspaper, television, magazine	Even split between television and newspaper/magazine: also official sponsor of Winter Olympics Games, Avon Tennis Championship, Professional Golfers Association, etc.: very substantial increase in promotional budget	Magazines, billboards, cinemas, bus/trains: substantial increase in promotional budget
Distribution	Specialty stores	Use AE-1 as means of shifting distribution from specialty stores to mass merchandisers: extensive dealer promotions and dealer training programs	Multiunit specialty chains: some dealer promotions
Price	Retail list price of 85,000 yen (with 50 Fl.4 lens and case) or U.S. $290 at time of introduction	Determined locally; retail list price of $430 at time of introduction and actual selling price of below $300	Differ from country to country

Source: H. Takeuchi and M. Porter, "Three Roles of International Marketing in Global Strategy," in *Competition in Global Industries,* ed. M. Porter (Boston: Harvard Business School Press, 1986), 140.

tion and make it difficult to take away a franchise once it is granted, foreign firms may prefer to test their concepts through company-owned stores. If it begins franchising, the firm's capital, commitment, and cultural knowledge must make its concepts work in the U.S. market.[43]

The supervision of foreign franchisees is problematic, and requires a local management base that becomes economical only after a minimum number of outlets has been reached—about 50 in a market such as the United Kingdom. One solution is to use local partners in setting up a master franchise licensee and use this as a base to sublicense individual franchises. American International Group (AIG), a U.S. insurance company, has followed this approach by obtaining a master franchise for selected foreign markets and using its network of contacts in the East Asian markets to find local partners.[44] If necessary, it can also act as a venture capitalist, providing funding for interesting franchise concepts.

One danger in using master franchising agreements is that choosing the wrong company to receive the master franchise can destroy an entire market for the franchising company. Great care must be taken because the master franchisee will be a key partner in adapting the franchise product, obtaining government approvals, and negotiating with the informal network of suppliers and competitors. The importance of taking care in choosing the master franchisee can be seen in the contrasting results obtained by Kentucky Fried Chicken (KFC) and McDonald's in Hong Kong. KFC entered the Hong Kong market in 1973, opening 11 stores in the first year. Its local partner helped it secure chicken from China. High prices, poor locations, and quality

GLOBAL MARKETING

Franchising

Chi-Chi's, a U.S.–based operator of Mexican restaurants, developed eight overseas outlets between 1989 and 1992. Europe seemed a logical target region, and the first overseas restaurant opened in 1989 in Luxembourg. A Chi-Chi's employee from Luxembourg and his family, who were in the restaurant business, organized a master franchise group and began taking the Chi-Chi's concept overseas.

Luxembourg proved to be a good choice because of its central location and large numbers of visiting businesspeople to the point that the restaurant is being expanded from 108 to 180 seats. Next, Chi-Chi's opened a franchised restaurant in Kuwait. The company was approached by a Kuwaiti, but was reluctant to deal because Kuwait seemed to be an unlikely location. A Chi-Chi's executive visited Kuwait, however, and came back impressed with the professionalism of the prospective Kuwaiti partner. The company decided to go ahead because it had a quality partner.

Next, Chi-Chi's moved into Germany, its original choice as the market for initial entry. It chose a master franchisee for the state of Hesse and later granted rights for three other states in Germany. Five units were opened and four more were under construction. Most recently, the Luxembourg franchisee obtained the rights to Belgium, opening a restaurant just outside Brussels that seats nearly 375 people. Brussels is also the base of Chi-Chi's international operations.

On average, the European units appear to generate more revenues, perhaps because menu prices are higher and Europeans customarily drink more beer and wine with their meals. The U.S. distribution center supplies tableware and uniforms; fresh food is purchased locally. European operations look different, operating in existing buildings without the Mexican facade customary in the United States, although the internal atmosphere is preserved by having franchisees choose from

---

problems (an unappealing taste), however, led KFC to close its stores within two years. It subsequently re-entered the market in 1985.

Meanwhile, McDonald's chose a master franchisee in 1973, opened one store in 1975, and added a second store a year later. By 1988, McDonald's had 30 stores in Hong Kong and over 50 by the mid-90s. Its success was due to an outstanding choice of partner and its willingness to adapt the franchise concept. In Hong Kong, McDonald's changed its name to mean "at your service" in Chinese. Although franchising is partly a service concept, many of the principles governing product and marketing mix adaptation apply equally as well.

International franchising is often a result of demand pull. That is, a successful U.S. experience with a particular franchise concept attracts the interest of foreign entrepreneurs who seek foreign franchise rights. Foreign expansion can be enormously rewarding. Foreign operations accounted for 57 percent of its revenues and nearly 59 percent of pretax profits. However, caution in expansion is advised, as overseas failure may cast a long shadow and may stunt further foreign expansion. McDonald's has operations in 104 nations, but its major expansion is targeted at countries such as Brazil and China, where incomes and cultural tastes do not easily support consumption of McDonald's foods. In Brazil, eating breakfast at home is an ingrained habit. As crisis swept Asia and South America in 1997–98, affordability became an issue, with a typical Brazilian greasy-spoon meal costing half what a Big Mac costs.[45]

Table 8–5 summarizes the international expansion of U.S. franchisors. U.S. restaurant chains are the most active in franchising overseas, with the largest overseas franchising markets being Japan, Europe, Canada, Mexico, and Brazil.

Some of the major difficulties in developing international franchising are outlined in Table 8–6.[46]

one of five standard designs. The Kuwait franchise, for example, does not have a cantina bar area. All menu choices at international operations are all-Mexican, without the bow to items such as steak and hamburgers, which were added to U.S. franchise menus.

Key issues are control and providing uniform quality. Chi-Chi's does this by sending two company executives who stay with a new franchise and supervise the physical environment and food specifications, leaving only when the franchise is operating smoothly and to Chi-Chi's satisfaction. Subsequently, Chi-Chi's sends quality inspectors to check on performance standards. It plans to expand into the Far East. Terry Smith, president of Chi-Chi International, observes, "The right people—people who believe in the concept—are more important than a country's demographics."

It would be difficult to extend franchise operations to Eastern Europe because that area has a recent history of treating customers and consumers with disdain. Another problem is finding entrepreneurs because a whole generation grew up

working for the state and were not rewarded for performance. Franchising can overcome part of this problem because a complete solution is taught to the franchisee. Other obstacles to franchising in Eastern Europe exist:

1. Finding the appropriate partner, especially if capital is needed.
2. Lack of clear-cut provisions for protecting intellectual property, trademarks, and so on.
3. Difficulties in financing and in repatriating profits in hard currency.
4. Infrastructure difficulties including primitive distribution systems, difficulties in procuring quality supplies locally, and obtaining clear title to real estate.

Despite these difficulties, attractive franchise opportunities exist in areas such as hotels, fast food, clothing and shoes, and business services such as accounting and software.

Sources: "Fast Food Franchisor Writes Recipe for Expansion into Overseas Markets," *Business International,* September 7, 1992; and "Early Bird Franchisors Try East European Markets," *Business International,* September 21, 1992.

SUMMARY

In deciding what products the company should sell overseas, the basic question is whether to standardize or adapt the products for foreign markets.

Factors encouraging standardization include economies of scale in manufacturing, R&D, and marketing; preserving the country-of-origin image; and serving globe-trotting customers.

Factors encouraging adaptation include greater profit potential, differing-use conditions, income levels, and consumer tastes, local market laws, operating plants in many countries, consumer profiles, and competition. Adaptation is more likely if the costs are low and do not force the company to raise prices.

Consumer tastes are converging in the developed nations of the world, leading to greater acceptance of a standardized product in such countries. The washing-machine industry example shows how careful standardization of product features and some elements of the marketing mix can be a successful strategy.

An important decision area in international markets is brand policy. The major choice is whether to opt for local brands or global brands. Global brands are consistent with a standardization approach to world markets.

Issues important to brand policy in international markets include protecting against brand piracy, paying attention to the cultural connotations of brand names, and dealing with government regulation in the area of brands and trademarks.

Another decision is whether to use private branding. Although it may facilitate sales, the company has little contact with the ultimate consumer and learns little about changes at the consumer level. Original Equipment Manufacturer (OEM) sales are similar to private branding.

The country of origin of a product affects how it is perceived and accepted in foreign markets, and both technical and government-mandated standards affect a company's ability to market products in various foreign markets. When product

TABLE 8–5	**Survey of U.S. Franchisors with International Operations (By Business Category and Number of Foreign Establishments, 1994)**[a]

Category	U.S. Franchisors with International Operations		U.S. Franchisors' Foreign Establishments	
	Number	*Percent*	*Number*	*Percent*
Restaurants	41	22.5%	4,221	31.3%
Business aids/services	17	9.3	302	2.2
Retailing, nonfood	15	8.2	392	2.9
Educational products/services	14	7.7	1,837	13.6
Automotive products/services	14	7.7	1,775	13.1
Construction/home improvement	14	7.7	555	4.1
Cleaning services	12	6.6	1,932	14.3
Personal care services	11	6.0	680	5.0
Printing/signs	8	4.4	582	4.3
Auto/truck rental	6	3.3	401	3.0
Postal/shipping	5	2.8	125	0.9
Travel services	4	2.2	346	2.6
Recreation	3	1.7	56	0.4
Laundry/dry cleaning	3	1.7	50	0.4
Retail food, nonconvenience	2	1.1	9	0.1
Hotels/motels	1	0.6	12	0.1
Rental equipment	1	0.6	2	0.0
Other	11	6.0	229	1.7
Total	182	100.0%	13,506	100.0%

[a]Data reflect responses to a survey conducted by the periodical *Global Franchise*.
Note: Totals may not add due to rounding.
Source: Compiled by USITC staff from *Global Franchise*, "1994 International Franchise Directory" (Second Quarter 1994), 52–66. In U.S. International Trade Commission, *Industry and Trade Summary: Franchising*, USITC Pub. 2921 (September 1995).

standards are set by consumer acceptance in the marketplace, a company can benefit immensely when its standard becomes the global standard like the Windows operating system did in the PC market.

New product introductions by international competition can force reexamination of a company's product introduction policies. Relevant factors include building customer loyalty to retain customers; revisiting the chosen mode of market entry based on strategic, environmental, and transaction specific variables; and focusing on long-term goals.

Packaging adaptation may be necessary to protect the product because of differences in climate or a longer-than-average time spent in the distribution channel. It may also be necessary to meet the package-size preference of local consumers as well as cultural preferences regarding color, style, and materials.

Labeling may have to be adapted because of language differences, the need to inform consumers, and government requirements. Multilingual labels are one solution.

Warranties are standardized when possible. Multinational customers, "tourist" goods, competitive pressures, the nature of the product itself, and common sources of production are factors leading to standardization. However, cost savings, competitive actions, and the lack of even quality in the global service network may lead the firm to offer different warranties in different countries.

For certain products, it is imperative that worldwide after-sales service be offered. Service training, the use of third parties such as distributors, and maintaining satisfied customers are some of the major factors to keep in mind.

TABLE 8-6	Issues in International Franchising
Laws and government regulations	Most countries are catching up to U.S. levels of required disclosure;[47] for example, it took several years of litigation for the European Court of Justice to decide that a noncompetition agreement within a franchise agreement did not constitute anticompetitive behavior.[48]
Antitrust laws	Affect franchisors' rights to control elements such as sourcing, quality, control over product mix, restrictions on geographic expansion, prices, confidentiality of information, and noncompete provisions.
Strength of intellectual property protection	Affect the ability of franchisors to maintain exclusivity and control over franchisee operations; see the earlier discussion on the problems of McDonald's in South Africa.
Dispute resolution and settlement mechanisms	Most franchise agreements are with individuals; contract enforceability becomes important to ensuring the franchise system's integrity.
Availability of financing	Local financing may be limited, as banks may be unfamiliar with franchising and unwilling to lend to franchisees.
Taxation of franchisee payments	Taxes may be higher depending on whether the initial fee is immediately expensed or amortized over time.
Franchising in multiple countries	Franchisors may have to adopt different accounting practices, operational procedures, and business establishment forms to minimize local taxation. Moreover, geographic distance can make franchisor management supervision and communication difficult.
Level of economic development	Affects per capita purchasing power and local citizenry's ability to afford a franchise's products or services. Other economic factors such as inflation rates and high real estate costs are also pertinent.
Infrastructure bottlenecks	For example, electricity shortages may interrupt continued operations and levels of service; poor roads may make timely delivery of supplies problematic.
Cultural differences	Affects acceptance of the franchise concept and its standards and parameters; franchise adaptation cuts at the heart of the franchise concept, which is built on standardization; adaptation can raise legitimate concerns about preserving quality and the franchise's overall reputation. Also impacts other areas, for example, training programs may have to be modified.

Another interesting decision is whether to sell to the same segment in different foreign markets. This depends on product characteristics. A standardized product may require that the company target different segments in different countries.

Franchising is a popular way to enter foreign markets. Cultural issues affect whether the franchise concept needs adaptation. The master franchise concept, which needs a strong local partner, is another useful approach to serving culturally distinct markets.

QUESTIONS

8.1 What does selling a standardized product in global markets imply?

8.2 In what ways might a product be adapted for global markets?

8.3 What factors encourage global standardization of a product?

8.4 What factors encourage firms to adapt their product for foreign markets?

8.5 Are consumer tastes converging around the world? If so, what is the implication of this trend for international marketing?

8.6 Discuss the washing-machine example cited in the text in terms of the standardization versus adaptation debate.

8.7 What are some approaches to brand policy in international markets?

8.8 Should a firm have one brand worldwide? Would your answer differ among products, such as perfumes, photographic film, credit cards, and computers?

8.9 Why are trademark and brand piracy important? How can a firm protect itself against such actions?

8.10 What are the pros and cons of private branding in international markets?

8.11 What are OEM sales? How can they be used to increase foreign market penetration?

8.12 What is the importance of "country of origin" in international product marketing?

8.13 How do product standards affect international marketing? What can the firm do with respect to standards to bolster its foreign market position?

8.14 Discuss the promotional and protective aspects of packaging in international markets.

8.15 Evaluate the international labeling situation facing (1) a pharmaceutical firm and (2) a razor blade manufacturer.

8.16 What are the considerations involved in establishing a warranty policy for international markets?

8.17 Is offering worldwide service essential to international marketing?

8.18 Industrial Controls Corp. began exporting to Europe and Latin America two years ago. Now service problems are beginning to hurt its reputation and threaten future sales. What might the company do to improve its situation?

8.19 How does the existence of different customer segments overseas affect international marketing?

8.20 Discuss how Canon positioned its AE-1 camera worldwide in the face of divergent customer segments.

8.21 How is franchising relevant to international marketing? What are some issues in franchising abroad?

ENDNOTES

1 William Taylor, "Message and Muscle, An Interview with Swatch Titan Nicolas Hayek," *Harvard Business Review,* March–April 1993, 98–110; and, "Can Daimler's Tiny *Swatchmobile* Sweep Europe?", *The Wall Street Journal,* October 2, 1998.

2 T. Levitt, "The Globalization of Markets," *Harvard Business Review,* May–June 1983.

3 See Levitt, "Globalization of Markets," Exhibit 1.

4 B. Joseph Pine II, B. Victor, and A. C. Boynton, "Making Mass Customization Work," *Harvard Business Review,* September–October 1993, 108–119.

5 John S. Hill and Richard R. Still, "Effects of Urbanization on Multinational Product Planning," *Columbia Journal of World Business,* Summer 1984, 62–67.

6 Madhav P. Kacker, "Export-Oriented Product Adaptation," *Management International Review* 6, no. 1 (1975): 61.

7 "For Coca-Cola in Japan, Things Go Better with Milk," *The Wall Street Journal,* January 20, 1997.

8 "When Horrid for Car Makers Is Smashing for Customers," *The Economist,* September 30, 1995.

9 "Would They Really Rather Have a Buick?" *The Wall Street Journal,* December 16, 1998.

10 "Ford Hopes Its New Focus Will Be On A Global Best-Seller," *The Wall Street Journal,* October 8, 1998.

11 "Unknown Fruit Takes on Unfamiliar Markets," *The Wall Street Journal,* November 9, 1995.

12 "Nonalcoholic Beer Hits the Spot in Mideast," *The Wall Street Journal,* December 6, 1995.

13 Luis V. Dominguez and C. Sequeira, "Determinants of LDC Exporters' Performance: A Cross-National Study," *Journal of International Business Studies* 24, no. 1 (1993): 19–40.

14 S. T. Cavusgil, Shaoming Zou, and G. M. Naidu, "Product and Promotion Adaptation in Export Ventures: An Empirical Investigation," *Journal of International Business Studies* 24, no. 3 (1993): 479–506.

15 See "Lotus Announces #1 Ranking and Design Award for Its Japanese Version of 1-2-3," and "Lotus Announces Shipment of Release 2J, A Japanese Version of 1-2-3," Lotus Development Corporation News Releases, February 24, 1987, and September 10, 1986.

16 For a detailed treatment, see Sak Onkvisit and John J. Shaw, "The International Dimensions of Branding: Strategic Considerations and Decisions," *International Marketing Review* 6, no. 3 (1989).

17 Martin S. Roth, "The Effects of Culture and Socioeconomics on the Performance of Global Brand Image Strategies," *Journal of Marketing Research,* May 1995, 163–175.

18 "The Best a Plan Can Get," *The Economist,* August 15, 1992; and "How Gillette Is Honing Its Edge," *Business Week,* September 28, 1992.

19 "Name of the Game: Brand Awareness," *The Wall Street Journal,* February 14, 1991.

20 David Aaker, "Brand Extensions: The Good, the Bad, and the Ugly," *Sloan Management Review,* Summer 1990, 47–56.

21 "Hewlett-Packard: Big, Boring and Booming," *The Economist,* May 6, 1995.

22 "America's Toy Industry," *The Economist,* December 16, 1995.

[23] "A Cruel Cut for Sergeant Pepper," *Business Week,* June 22, 1987.

[24] "Here's One Tough Cowboy," *Forbes,* February 9, 1987.

[25] "EC May Chase Tobacco Symbols like Marlboro Man into Sunset," *The Wall Street Journal,* October 10, 1989.

[26] See Steven Globerman, "Addressing International Product Piracy," *Journal of International Business Studies* 19, no. 3 (Fall 1988); Richard S. Higgins and Paul Rubin, "Counterfeit Goods," *Journal of Law and Economics,* October 1986; and M. Harvey and I. Ronkainen, "International Counterfeiters: Marketing Success without Cost or Risk," *Columbia Journal of World Business* (Fall 1985).

[27] "Europeans Witness Proliferation of Private Labels," *The Wall Street Journal,* October 20, 1992.

[28] "Spiegel Resumes Strategy of Focusing on Goods Made under Private Labels," *The Wall Street Journal,* July 13, 1988.

[29] Sanjay K. Dhar and Stephen Hoch, "Why Store Brand Penetration varies by Retailer," *Marketing Science,* Fall 1997.

[30] S. Hoch and S. Bannerji, "When Do Private Labels Succeed?" *Sloan Management Review,* Summer 1993, 57–67; John Quelch and D. Harding, "Brands versus Private Labels: Fighting to Win," *Harvard Business Review,* January–February 1996, 99–109; and "The Private Label Hoax," *Financial World,* October 10, 1995.

[31] "Tandy Corp. Fights Hard to Shake Radio Shack Image," *The Wall Street Journal,* December 8, 1988.

[32] Some interesting studies on the country-of-origin phenomenon include C. Min Han and Vern Terpstra, "Country-of-Origin Effects for Uni-national and Bi-national Products," *Journal of International Business Studies* 19, no. 2 (Summer 1988); Warren J. Bilkey and Erik Nes, "Country-of-Origin Effects on Product Evaluations," *Journal of International Business Studies* 13, no. 2 (Spring–Summer 1982); and Johny K. Johansson and Hans B. Thorelli, "International Product Positioning," *Journal of International Business Studies* 16, no. 3 (Fall 1985).

[33] "Japan's PC Market Bows to U.S. Makers as NEC Stronghold Continues to Loosen," *The Wall Street Journal,* February 14, 1995; and "NEC Stands Alone as Fujitsu Adopts IBM PC Standard," *The Wall Street Journal,* October 19, 1993.

[34] Alan Sykes, *Product Standards for Internationally Integrated Goods Markets* (Washington, DC: Brookings Institute, 1995).

[35] "Summit Technology: European Sales Boost Growth," *Boston Globe,* April 1, 1991.

[36] A. J. Slywotzky and Benson Shapiro, "Leveraging to Beat the Odds: The New Marketing Mind-Set," *Harvard Business Review,* September–October 1993, 97–107.

[37] T. O. Jones and W. Earl Sasser Jr., "Why Satisfied Customers Defect," *Harvard Business Review* (November–December 1995), 88–99.

[38] "'Coats Viyella' Concentrating the Mind," *The Economist,* February 18, 1995.

[39] W. Chan Kim and Peter Hwang, "Global Strategy and Multinationals' Entry Mode Choice," *Journal of International Business Studies* 23, no. 1 (1992): 29–53.

[40] "P & G Viewed China as a National Market and Is Conquering It," *The Wall Street Journal,* September 12, 1995.

[41] Peter Doyle, J. Saunders, and V. Wong, "Competition in Global Markets: A Case Study of American and Japanese Competition in the British Market," *Journal of International Business Studies* 23, no. 3 (1992): 419–442.

[42] "Furnishing the World," *The Economist,* November 19, 1994.

[43] "U.S. Franchising Grows Attractive to Foreign Firms," *The Wall Street Journal,* December 22, 1988.

[44] See "For U.S. Franchisers, a Common Tongue Isn't a Guarantee of Success in the U.K.," *The Wall Street Journal,* August 16, 1988; "U.S. Fast-Food Franchises Go East in American International Venture," *The Wall Street Journal,* November 15, 1988; and "Why You Won't Find Any Egg McMuffins for Breakfast in Brazil," *The Wall Street Journal,* October 23, 1997.

[45] U.S. International Trade Commission, *Industry and Trade Summary: Franchising,* USITC Pub. 2921 (September 1995), Washington, DC: USITC.

[46] Yanos Gramatidis and D. Campbell, eds. *International Franchising: An In-depth Treatment of Business and Legal Techniques* (Boston: Kluwer Publishing, 1991). "Private Labels," *The Wall Street Journal,* October 20, 1992.

[47] See P. Zeidman and M. Avner, "Franchising in Eastern Europe and the Soviet Union," *DePaul Business Law Journal* 3 (Spring 1991); and *Global Franchising Alert,* December 1994, on "Mexican Franchise Regulation, and Self-Regulation by Franchising Associations in South Africa and Italy."

[48] Jean-Eric de Cockborne, "The New EEC Block Exemption Regulation on Franchising," *Fordham International Law Journal* 12 (1989).

FURTHER READINGS

Bilkey, Warren J., and Erik Nes. "Country-of-Origin Effects on Product Evaluations." *Journal of International Business Studies* 13, no. 2 (Spring–Summer 1982).

Cavusgil, S. T., Shaoming Zou, and G. M. Naidu. "Product and Promotion Adaptation in Export Ventures: An Empirical Investigation." *Journal of International Business Studies* 24, no. 3 (1993): 479–506.

Christopher, R., R. Lancione, and J. Gattorna. "Managing International Customer Service." *International Marketing Review,* Spring 1985.

Dominguez, Luis V., and C. Sequeira. "Determinants of LDC Exporters' Performance: A Cross-National Study." *Journal of International Business Studies* 24, no. 1 (1993): 19–40.

Doyle, Peter, J. Saunders, and V. Wong. "Competition in Global Markets: A Case Study of American and Japanese Competition in the British Market." *Journal of International Business Studies* 23, no. 3 (1992): 419–442.

Globerman, Steven. "Addressing International Product Piracy." *Journal of International Business Studies* 19, no. 3 (Fall 1988).

Gramatidis, Yanos, and D. Campbell, eds. *International Franchising: An In-depth Treatment of Business and Legal Techniques.* (Boston: Kluwer Publishing, 1991).

Han, C. Min, and Vern Terpstra. "Country-of-Origin Effects for Uni-national and Bi-national Products." *Journal of International Business Studies* 19, no. 2 (Summer 1988).

Hill, John S., and Richard R. Still. "Adapting Products to LDC Tastes." *Harvard Business Review,* March–April 1984.

Hoch, S., and S. Bannerji. "When Do Private Labels Succeed?" *Sloan Management Review* (Summer 1993), 57–67.

Jones, T. O., and W. Earl Sasser, Jr. "Why Satisfied Customers Defect." *Harvard Business Review,* November– December 1995, 88–99.

Kim, W. Chan, and Peter Hwang. "Global Strategy and Multinationals' Entry Mode Choice." *Journal of International Business Studies* 23, no. 1 (1992): 29–53.

Levitt, T. "The Globalization of Markets." *Harvard Business Review,* May–June 1983.

Onkvisit, Sak, and John J. Shaw. "The International Dimensions of Branding: Strategic Considerations and Decisions." *International Marketing Review* 6, no. 3 (1989).

Pine II, B. Joseph, B. Victor, and A. C. Boynton. "Making Mass Customization Work." *Harvard Business Review,* September–October 1993, 108–119.

Quelch, John, and D. Harding. "Brands versus Private Labels: Fighting to Win." *Harvard Business Review,* January–February 1996, 99–109.

Roth, Martin S. "The Effects of Culture and Socioeconomics on the Performance of Global Brand Image Strategies." *Journal of Marketing Research,* May 1995, 163–175.

Slywotzky, A. J., and Benson Shapiro. "Leveraging to Beat the Odds: The New Marketing Mind-Set." *Harvard Business Review,* September–October 1993, 97–107.

Still, Richard R., and John S. Hill. "Multinational Product Planning: A Meta-Market Analysis." *International Marketing Review,* Spring 1985.

Sykes, Alan. *Product Standards for Internationally Integrated Goods Markets.* Washington, DC: Brookings Institute, 1995.

Taylor, William. "Message and Muscle, An Interview with Swatch Titan Nicolas Hayek." *Harvard Business Review,* March–April 1993, 98–110.

Walters, Peter G. P. "International Marketing Policy: A Discussion of the Standardization Construct and Its Relevance for Corporate Policy." *Journal of International Business Studies* 17, no. 2 (Summer 1986).

Wind, Yoram. "The Myth of Globalization." *Journal of Marketing,* Spring 1986.

Wind, Yoram, and Susan P. Douglas. "International Portfolio Analysis and Strategy: The Challenge of the 80s." *Journal of International Business Studies* 12, no. 3 (Fall 1981).

IKEA*

IKEA, founded in 1953, designs and sells inexpensive furniture and accessories. It operates its no-frills furniture stores in 45 countries, and its sales have increased at a 33 percent annual growth rate, exceeding $6 billion in 1992, as compared to $2.1 billion in sales in fiscal 1987. IKEA's concept is straightforward: On the marketing side, sell inexpensive, ready-to-assemble furniture that is well made to customers who are willing to carry it away themselves; on the manufacturing side, design the furniture and then subcontract manufacturing to low-cost sources around the world that can produce high-quality products. As the furniture itself is sold in kit form, the pieces actually are made in different locations, with IKEA purchasing from the manufacturers with the lowest prices.

IKEA's furniture comes boxed and must be assembled at home. The boxed kits must be picked up by the customer after purchase from the adjacent self-service warehouse and taken home. It tends to locate near freeway exits and outside cities, where space is available at low rates. This allows the firm to provide ample parking space, and customers can easily get in and out of the store without encountering traffic jams. IKEA also cooperates with local car-rental companies to help customers rent small trucks to transport their orders.

The furniture design is Scandinavian modern, built mainly of pine, with textiles in pastel colors. The international product line is less varied than that sold within the home markets of Scandinavia. IKEA's market is the "young of all ages." It has a flair for marketing to young couples with children: Its warehouses are festively decorated, provide day care for children, and feature inexpensive restaurants specializing in Swedish meatballs. The focus on child care and the in-store restaurants aim to keep people in the stores until they buy something, preventing their exit because of bored and unmanageable children or the desire to get a meal.

The emphasis is on low-priced furniture, priced 30 to 50 percent below the fully assembled furniture of the competition. Prices vary for the same basic product from market to market, but not greatly.

IKEA's founder, Ingvar Kamprad, grew up on a farm in southern Sweden and began a business selling flower seeds and ballpoint pens through mail-order catalogs. He insists that employees be "cost-conscious to the point of stinginess." He has written: "Too many new and beautifully designed products can be afforded by only a small group of better-off people. We have decided to side with the many."

IKEA has always been innovative in selling furniture. When it entered Sweden in the early 1950s, furniture retailers were small firms, purchasing furniture to customer specifications and placing an order with the manufacturer only after receiving a commitment from the customer. Furniture was expensive and bought in sets, such as a dining room suite, and credit was an important sales tool. IKEA entered into this market with large showrooms outside cities, the option to buy one piece of furniture at a time, self-service for cash, and low prices.

In 1973 IKEA entered Switzerland with its first store near Zurich. It had to decide whether to rely on the IKEA company name to position itself as a Scandinavian furniture company (in which case, it might be confused with Danish furniture) or to identify IKEA as a distinctive Swedish company. IKEA knew that it would have to address Swiss concerns (for the Swiss were perceived to be a conservative group) about a Swedish company and its way of selling furniture.

IKEA prepared a set of ads that deliberately brought up typical conservative Swiss opinions of and reactions to IKEA (see Table 1). These ads consisted of letters sent by a conservative Herr Bunzli to IKEA saying what he thinks of the company's ideas and way of selling furniture in Switzerland. The aim of the campaign was to joke about the old-fashioned values of the Swiss and appeal to those who would like to change. The ads exemplify IKEA's philosophy, which is to take advantage of being an unknown foreigner and use advertising that is attention getting and provocative. Managers in all countries are required to follow this advertising strategy, though they can use local agencies, following guidelines from headquarters.

The first year IKEA was in Switzerland, 650,000 people visited its stores. The next year, IKEA entered the huge West German market and subsequently France, drawing on its experiences with the German- and French-speaking parts of Switzerland.

IKEA has a special organization structure dedicated to smooth and speedy entry into foreign markets. This foreign-expansion group has several key subunits: a European deco-manager; a manager of construction; and a first-year group, whose responsibility is to create and manage new overseas outlets during the first year. The construction manager selects a site and supervises the creation of the new store, overseeing inventories and installation of fixtures, communications networks, and so on. The first-year manager oversees hiring, reassignment of experienced employees from other IKEA locations, training, advertising campaigns, and deciding on the

TABLE 1	**Themes in IKEA's Swiss Advertising Campaign**
Theme of IKEA's Sales Approach	*Message: Joke about Swiss Conservatism*
No delivery by IKEA	The Swiss will not transport and assemble furniture themselves even if the price is low.
Purchaser assembles the furniture.	What a stupid idea. You can't make us Swiss do that.
IKEA makes pine furniture.	We don't use pine: we aren't Swedish.
The Swiss need status furniture.	Swedes, go home.
IKEA does make quality furniture.	Only Swiss-made goods can be high quality.

Source: Adapted from Rita Martenson, "Cross-Cultural Similarities and Differences in Multinational Retailing."

"assortment" of product line to be carried. Furniture is typically ordered from a central warehouse in Sweden and starts arriving three months before opening day.

Planning of a new outlet begins about 10 months before opening day. Since IKEA has expanded rapidly, the first-year group cannot spend a whole year nurturing new outlets as originally envisioned. Training has to be speeded up to allow local management to take over sooner. Staff begin working about two months before opening day to familiarize themselves completely with IKEA's mode of operations and product line to ensure a smooth opening. Advertising begins at about the same time. The staff generally takes a trip to IKEA's outlets in Scandinavia, culminating in a press conference the day before store inauguration.

IKEA Enters the United States

Already established, with nine stores in Canada, the United States seemed the next logical market. California was its first pick, with Boston the second choice. Executives who set out to study the California market encountered some obstacles, however. California has unique standards for upholstered furniture that would have raised costs by 15 percent. Its system of unitary taxation by which it taxed California's "share" of IKEA's worldwide income was unpalatable.

Boston was attractive because of its huge itinerant student and yuppie populations. Government regulations and lack of responsiveness on the part of state officials, however, led the company to establish its first warehouse and retail operation in suburban Philadelphia instead.

Philadelphia made special efforts to help IKEA. Why? Jobs and tax revenues. Through the Greater Philadelphia International Network, a small-business–backed office that tries to attract foreign investment, IKEA officials were introduced to bankers and real estate brokers, given a helicopter tour of the city, and invited to cocktail parties every evening of their three-day stay.

Location, of course, is critical to this kind of company. The Philadelphia market area, which includes Delaware and southern New Jersey, had large numbers of young middle-income families and relatively inexpensive commercial real estate. The Network helped IKEA find space in a mall next to a turnpike exit in the suburb of Plymouth Meeting. "Pennsylvania Turnpike, Exit 25" is the sort of address it seeks. (Forty percent of its customers were likely to be from out of state.)

The store attracted 130,000 customers during its inauguration in June 1985 and averages 30,000 a week. IKEA has shifted its North American headquarters from Vancouver to Philadelphia. It opened a second store in the Virginia suburb of Dale City, near Washington, D.C., in the spring of 1986, where weekend crowds are averaging 15,000. Together, the two stores had total sales of $77 million in 1987, and IKEA admits that it underestimated the market by 50 percent. Severe inventory shortages have consequently developed. Future expansion sites included Baltimore; Pittsburgh; and Newark, New Jersey. The plan was to have several stores served by a major central warehouse.

IKEA clearly focuses on customer value. It is constantly concerned with two questions: How can the product be improved? How can we become a better place to work? The company expects all its employees to be thrifty, and even the head of its North American operations flies economy class to Scandinavia. The point is that anything that does not add customer value is to be avoided.

Recently, IKEA has expanded its operations, arranging to build a chain of budget-priced hotels across the United States and Canada under the Swedish Inn name. The chain will appeal to the same clientele that buys IKEA furniture and will be publicized in the stores, with discounts offered to IKEA customers. Further savings are expected to come from furnishing the hotels with IKEA furniture products.

IKEA's Imitators

Success breeds imitation. A California company, Stor, plans to open 30 stores similar to IKEA on the West Coast, including toy-filled day-care rooms. The knock-down kit idea has spread to other market niches. Bush Industries, another furniture company, has grown from $14 million sales in 1982 to $93 million in 1987 by manufacturing and selling kit furniture for electronic products: furniture to house and display audio and video products, VCRs, and personal computers and printers. By 1987 Bush was selling 115 different furniture models ranging in price from $20 to $500, in 6,000 stores such as Sears and Best Products. Other U.S. manufacturers competing with Bush include Tandy Corp's O'Sullivan Industries and Sauder Woodworking.

Paul Bush, president, notes that ready-to-assemble (RTA) furniture is perhaps 40 percent of the furniture market in Europe, but only about $2 billion in sales in the United States; dealers dislike it. Bush was able to sell its furniture by going through new channels such as electronic retailers, mail-order office supply houses, catalog stores, and the audio, video, and microwave departments of big stores such as Sears and J. C. Penney.

Bush has adapted the idea of RTA furniture to U.S. needs. It must be easy to assemble, and precision fit is important, because the user, who will assemble it, will not be satisfied with less than perfect fit. Bush pioneered soft forms, with smooth, curved edges. Oak furniture is traditional in the United States, conveying a solid heavy feel, darker in tone than pine, which is light and feels insubstantial. Hence, Bush introduced oak RTA by combining oak solids with oak veneers. The lower price and immediate delivery have gradually increased the share of RTA in the U.S. market; in fall of 1987 Bush introduced RTA bedroom furniture in oak.

Questions

1. Analyze IKEA's international expansion. Why was it successful?

2. To what extent does its product line need to be adapted to foreign markets?

3. Did IKEA have to adapt other aspects of the marketing mix when entering foreign markets?

4. Prepare a time chart showing how IKEA proceeds in opening a new international store.

5. How did IKEA enter the United States? Why did it choose Pennsylvania?

6. How might IKEA's success have stimulated the ready-to-assemble (RTA) market in the United States?

7. How did Bush adapt RTA furniture to fit U.S. market needs? Does the success of Bush Industries represent a niche that IKEA should consider expanding into?

* Case prepared by Ravi Sarathy for use in classroom discussion. All rights reserved.
Sources: Rita Martenson, "Is Standardization of Marketing Feasible in Culture-Bound Industries? A European Case Study," *International Market Review,* Autumn 1987; "How a Major Swedish Retailer Chose a Beachhead in the U.S." *The Wall Street Journal,* April 7, 1987; Peter Fuhrman, "The Workers' Friend," *Forbes,* March 21, 1988; and James Cook, "A Better Mousetrap," *Forbes,* March 7, 1988.

CASE 8.2

Domino's Pizza in Japan

When Michael Jackson was in Tokyo and wanted a snack between concerts, he called on Domino's Pizza for a vegetable special with no cheese—and within 30 minutes it was ready, served piping hot in his dressing room. All of Tokyo seems to like Domino's pizza: the busy homemaker faced with hungry kids and no time to make dinner, the office worker with her friends over for an evening of chat and music. As always, the Japanese love the service: one phone call and, 30 minutes later, pizza delivered to the home.

Domino's Pizza International (DPI)

Domino's first foreign venture was in Canada. Company officials viewed this as the logical first step toward globalization because of Canada's proximity to the United States, both geographically and culturally. In Canada the corporate-owned and the franchised stores were both moderately successful. Again following the logic of cultural and language similarity,

Domino's entered the Australian market. Rather rapidly during the middle and late 1980s, Domino's entered a total of 16 foreign markets from China to Hong Kong to Honduras to Western Europe.

Domino's Pizza to Japan

When Domino's Pizza was considering entry into the Japanese market, it could count on no cultural or linguistic similarity to help its analysis. Therefore, it hired a consultant, who expressed the following concerns: The Japanese do not eat much cheese; fast-food restaurants are not considered desirable employers; the Japanese are not entrepreneurial; real estate is very expensive; and banks do not like to lend to small businesses. On the other hand, Japan does have a high population density, high per capita income, substantial westernization, and wide acceptance of the delivery concept. The consultant concluded that Japan was not ready for a pizza delivery service.

Higa-San Meets Tom Monaghan

Y. Higa, a Japanese businessman, and Domino's founder Tom Monaghan did not accept the consultant's recommendation. At first Higa was uncertain about the wisdom of a tie-up between the food business and Higa Corp., originally a Japanese trading company dealing in lumber and medical equipment. However, when he visited Monaghan in 1984 at Domino's Ann Arbor headquarters, he was impressed by several things: the rapid growth of Domino's in the United States and abroad, the fact that this growth had allowed Monaghan to buy the Detroit Tigers baseball team for $53 million, and Monaghan's enthusiastic description of Domino's operating methods.

Higa decided he wanted to bring the Domino's concept and operating method to Japan. Higa felt that the "secret ingredient" he could bring to the deal was his knowledge and feel for the marketplace, the culture, and the people. He thought that with more Japanese women working and coming home tired, home delivery of food would work.

Also, more Japanese were traveling abroad and developing a taste for new foods. The previous success of McDonald's and the eventual success of Kentucky Fried Chicken was a good omen, too.

Higa's undergraduate degree from Wharton and his M.B.A. from Columbia helped him to have a good feel for U.S. operations. Furthermore, there was some relevant experience in the Higa family. His father, Yetsuo Higa, helped bring Pepsi Cola to Japan in the 1950s, and his brother-in-law, Shin Ohkawara, was president of Kentucky Fried Chicken Japan Ltd. Higa made an agreement with Domino's, giving him the exclusive right to develop and franchise stores in Japan.

Domino's Pizza in Japan

The first Domino's Pizza opened in Tokyo's Azabu district in 1985. Azabu is a trendy, westernized district. From that start, Domino's Pizza of Japan became the company's most successful foreign operation. Royalty income per store was almost twice as high as that in Britain, the second-best foreign market in terms of royalty income. By 1989 there were 54 Domino's Pizza outlets in Japan, and sales in 1988 reached $43 million. By starting with the innovators and westernized Japanese in the Azabu district, Domino's found a group ready to consume home-delivered pizza. These consumption leaders also influenced other segments of the population, increasing Domino's popularity in Tokyo.

The pizza is sold by Y. Higa Corporation, Domino's licensee for Japan. Home delivery itself is familiar to the Japanese, accounting for a large share of the estimated 12 trillion yen in annual restaurant sales. The problem in a city as crowded as Tokyo is how to get the pizza to the house fast and still hot.

Higa wanted to copy Domino's U.S. promise of a guaranteed delivery by car in 30 minutes or your money back. Japanese cities are crowded, however, and finding an address in Japan is quite difficult. Streets are not straight, are not named, and houses are numbered according to when they were built; it is possible for two houses built at about the same time to have the same number. Population density is also much greater in Japanese cities as compared to U.S. cities; a Japanese store might have 14 times as many people in its territory in Tokyo, when compared to the number of people in an average territory that a U.S. pizza store might serve. On top of these differences, the horrendous traffic in Tokyo almost guaranteed that the 30-minute delivery promise would be impossible to meet, especially since each order is made up fresh after the phone call.

The solution was to design special three-wheeled Honda scooters that could maneuver easily in Tokyo's traffic. Painted with Domino's red, white, and blue logo (a moving Domino billboard), the scooters have sloping windscreens and protective roofs. The pizzas cost from $7 to $23, and a refund of about $5 is given if the delivery does not arrive in the trademark 30 minutes—Domino's version of just-in-time logistics. (These figures are at average 1989 exchange rates.)

The original fleet of five scooters was inadequate to meet the demand, so five more were added the second week of operation, five more the third week, until the original store had 25 three-wheelers. Each store now may have up to 20 three-wheelers.

The scooter driver is the delivery person, often a part-timer and a college student earning extra money. The driver wears a distinctive uniform, different from other Japanese delivery people, who usually come in a white smock.

The full-color menu is on expensive coated paper, unlike the usual paper flyers. Customers are impressed and hold on to their menus, which are left in their mailboxes by part-time workers.

Domino's Japanese locations do not provide on-premises restaurant service. If you want pizza, you have to order it and wait to eat it at home. Real estate is expensive in Tokyo and hard to find, and such a policy allows Domino's outlets to be located in small spaces.

There are no franchisees. Higa owns and operates all the shops and buys fresh ingredients from a sister company (owned by another member of the Higa family), which are then cooked into pizzas immediately from scratch, beginning with tossing the dough. As one might expect, extensive training in the art of pizza making is provided by a Domino's University.

Domino's strives for international uniformity of both product and operating methods. The pizza dough, cheese, and sauce are as uniform as possible internationally. Toppings, however, may vary. In Japan, pepperoni is the most popular, but tuna and corn are offered, too. Each store is limited to a total of 12 varieties.

Each store pays 3 percent of sales into a promotional fund. Door hangings and direct mail, including the fancy menu, are used for advertising rather than TV or radio.

A Success Story?

Domino's Pizza International (DPI) is pleased with its decision to enter the Japanese market and with its Japanese employees. "They do exactly what you tell them." Diligent, hard-working, and team-oriented, they follow the rules to the letter, allowing Domino's system to operate at its most efficient.

Higa gives some of the credit to DPI for sending one of its most experienced veterans for an extended time in Japan to help establish the operation. And, of course, the company set up a Domino's University for local training.

Questions

1. In Japan, Domino's is marketing both a product and a service. Review Domino's Japanese marketing program in detail. For each item in the program, identify how it was standardized internationally or adapted to the Japanese market.
2. Explain why this standardization or adaptation was used.
3. Identify and explain all the factors that appear to have contributed to Domino's success in Japan, in spite of the consultant's recommendation against the operation.

International Product Policy

New-Product Development and Product-Line Policies

Chapter 9

Learning Objectives

In Chapter 8, we discussed how a firm's basic product fits into global markets. We considered product features such as packaging, labeling, brand name, and warranties and how these may change as they encounter global markets. This chapter considers additional aspects of product policy surrounding new-product development and product-line policies.

The main goals of this chapter are to

1. Discuss diverse approaches to product development for international markets.

2. Consider how technology-intensive industries approach global product development.

3. Discuss Japanese views and examples of international product development.

4. Understand how policies on conducting global R&D and global acquisitions and divestitures contribute to global product development.

5. Analyze the role of benchmarking and quality improvements in developing world-class products.

NEW-PRODUCT DEVELOPMENT

New-product development for multiple international markets is based on two major ideas: understanding consumer needs in different countries and building on the firm's relationship with such customers; second, drawing on both the firm's knowledge base and assets to develop products that can satisfy global markets.

Importance of Consumer Needs

Consumer needs are the starting point for product development, whether for domestic or global markets. Take pianos, for instance. A great many pianos are gathering dust in living rooms around the world—40 million of them by one estimate. Yamaha, with 40 percent of the global market and facing declining demand, had to rethink customer needs. It chose to retrofit pianos (for about $2,500) with a computer board that can capture music from the piano as it is played; the piano can then be used as a playback instrument. It can even play back performances by great piano artists. The piano is linked to a computer that "reads" disks of piano music and then causes the piano to play the music back. This is the player piano concept all over again, with disks substituting for paper rolls.[1] What was a dead business is being revived by creating a value-added product in response to consumer needs.

Products for Foreign Markets: A Conceptual Framework

In addition to consumer needs, conditions of use and ability to buy the product form a framework for decisions on new-product development for foreign markets. The strategy may be product extension, with or without significant product adaptation, new products for specific foreign markets, or design of a global product for all markets. In using this framework, the development process encompasses the product itself as well as the communication about the product (that is, advertising) and so on. Table 9–1 summarizes the implications of this concept.

When consumer needs and conditions of use are not taken into account, failure is the result. Heinz Co., attracted by the size of the Brazilian market, set up a joint venture with Citrosuco, an orange juice exporter, to launch its first product, Frutsi, a fruit drink that had been successful in Venezuela and Mexico. Every street corner in Brazil, however, has a little store selling freshly squeezed orange juice at low prices. Although Heinz could keep pure fruit juice content at 10 percent in most countries, Brazilian regulations set a minimum of 30 percent. This raised prices and made Frutsi uncompetitive with the fresh-squeezed variety. To complicate matters, the additional fruit juice shortened shelf life, necessitating new packaging.

To penetrate the market, Heinz gave cases of Frutsi to retailers on consignment, to be paid for after the product was sold. This led to overstocking and many cases of spoiled product had to be returned (brownouts and electric supply interruptions are common in Brazil, and the hot climate hastened product deterioration when refrigeration failed). Then Heinz spent $200,000 on TV advertising featuring a robot character that wasn't considered friendly enough. Although a name change to Suco da Monica, based on a popular Brazilian cartoon character, helped sales, Heinz decided to pull out. All three of the factors in Table 9–1—customer need, ability to buy, and conditions of use—were unfavorable to Heinz in Brazil.[2]

Adoption and Diffusion of New Products

New-product introduction entails adoption and diffusion (use). There are five stages: *awareness, interest (knowledge), evaluation (of information, to decide whether to try or not to try), trial, and finally adoption (continuing use).*[3] **Awareness** is the stage of communicating the existence of the new product or innovation to potential adopters/consumers. The second stage of deepening **interest** is related to obtaining detailed knowledge about the new product or innovation. Next, consumers

TABLE 9-1			Market Characteristics and Product-Line Strategies
If:			**Then:**
Customer Need	**Conditions of Use**	**Ability to Buy**	**Product-Line Strategy**
Same	Same	Exists	Product and Communications Extension
Different	Same	Exists	Product Extension and Communications Adaptation
Same	Different	Exists	Product Adaptation and Communications Extension
Different	Different	Exists	Product and Communications Adaptation (with new products in the future)
Same	Not Applicable	Low to None	New Product and Communications

Source: Warren J. Keegan, "Multinational Product Planning: Strategic Alternatives," *Journal of Marketing,* January 1969.

must **evaluate** the knowledge gathered to decide whether to break old habits and take the risk of trying the new product. The **trial** phase is when the new product is actually being used for the first time. Last, consumers assess their experience from first use and decide whether to continue using the product—**adoption.**

Mirroring the stages by which consumers decide to adopt new products are the stages of decision making that firms go through in introducing the products. First there is idea or **concept generation,** then **screening** of (several) competing new-product ideas, and then **evaluation** of a short list of such ideas in view of consumer needs, costs of production, current revenues, and competitive actions. Next, the firm enters the **prototype** stage, in which trial runs of the new product are made. After ascertaining product viability and quality from an engineering and production standpoint, the firm then moves to **product testing** in the marketplace. If testing is successful, the product is **launched** into the wider market, perhaps with additional modifications based on results from the testing phase. Results from the product launch are then evaluated, and the product is kept on the market, completing market entry. Competition is a complicating factor, since retaliatory moves by competitors may hinder an accurate assessment of market acceptance. Success breeds imitation, so rarely does a new product have the market to itself unless protected by strong patents and copyrights (as in the case of new pharmaceutical drugs).

Product Development

Interface of Customer Needs and the Company's Knowledge Base
One conception of new-product development in rapidly changing environments sees new products as the outcome of a meeting of "relationships and knowledge."[4] Every company has a relationship with its existing customer base. Companies also possess knowledge, skills, resources, and competencies. This can be technology, accumulated experience, business processes, and methodologies. Companies wanting to create new products or services can ask themselves how their customers are going about creating value and assess whether their competencies allow them to develop products that can be inputs to the customer's own new value-creating business directions. Companies must, therefore, constantly increase their knowledge base and their competencies. If this process results in knowledge exceeding customer requirements, they can go further afield in search of new customers and new markets.

Core Competence, Product Platforms, and Product Families
Meyer and Utterback[5] extend the relationship between a company's core competencies and new products to suggest that effective product development has

distinct layers, with a bedrock of **core competencies,** upon which are first built **product platforms,** then product families marketed to customers. The concept of a product family built on a platform rising out of core competencies suggests a clear product-development path for next-generation products, while stressing both new-product compatibility with the product family and the constant need for innovation and strengthening of the underlying core competencies. The diagram in Figure 9–1 illustrates the product platform concept.

Two French Examples. The connection between a firm's knowledge and competencies on the one hand, and relationships with existing customers on the other, is illustrated in the history and growth of two of France's largest companies, Générale des Eaux and Lyonnaise des Eaux. These companies started in the mid-1800s providing water and sewer services to French cities. Over time they expanded by providing additional services required by cities: railroads, canals, electricity generation and supply, and all manner of public infrastructure. The companies have benefited by a unique French law of "concessions" that grants private companies the right to provide public infrastructure projects for a fixed term—30 to 60 years, say—during which they can make a profit. What is interesting about these two companies is that they have grown by seeing themselves as managers of cities.

Providing public services at a profit is a tricky and complex business, perhaps even a thankless task, and the success of these two firms lies in their ability to provide "the financial, social, legal, managerial, and technical engineering" that allows public infrastructure projects to be efficient and profitable. What is also interesting is that as cities evolve, these firms are able to provide new services. For example, they have branched out into waste-management services, and provide electricity to 10 percent of Paris by generating electricity from incinerating the garbage collected. They have adopted environmentally safe technologies and have expanded overseas, managing water distribution networks and waste-water treatment in 50 cities on six continents, including many small cities in the United States. Their product development strategy is summed up in the view of a Générale executive, "Our people have no a priori right to say no to a client request. If one of the companies in the group cannot produce what the client wants, then we will create a company that can."[6]

Compression and Experiential Strategies

Eisenhart and Tabrizi looked at 72 product-development projects from 36 Asian, U.S., and European firms operating in the fast-paced, global computer industry.[7] They contrasted two different approaches:

1. *The "compression" strategy,* which assumes that the steps to develop new products are known, and that rapid product development is crucial and can be speeded up by using methods such as planning, the use of CAD, supplier involvement, powerful project leaders, and multifunctional teams.

2. *The "experiential" strategy,* which is based on the notion that new-product development is an uncertain process and what matters is creativity, a process relying on factors such as real-time experience, flexibility, and improvisation.

They argued that both perspectives, compression and experiential strategies, are necessary for successful product development.

A different approach to product development suggests postponing product definition as long as possible. By delaying product specifications until close to product launch, the firm can take advantage of the latest developments in core technologies and consumer preferences.[8]

FIGURE 9–1   **A Framework to Integrate Markets, Platforms, and Competencies**

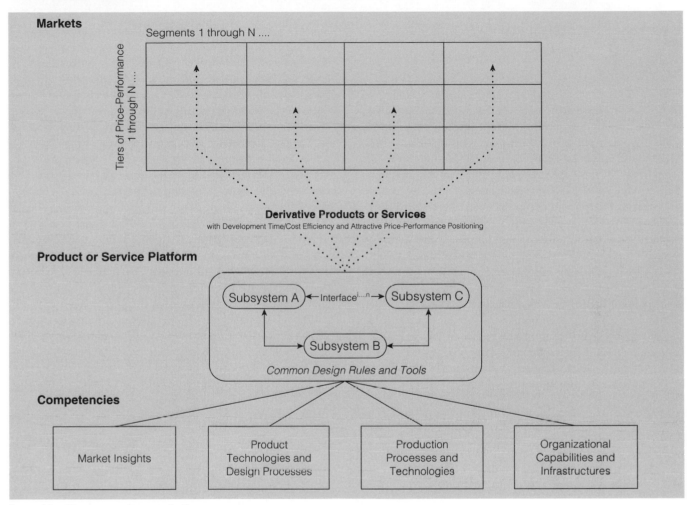

Source: Marc Meyer, personal communication.

Sensory Segmentation

Another approach to international product development is an approach called *sensory segmentation,* which divides customers according to their response to sensory product characteristics. Such cross-country segments allow the development of a limited range of products within a product line to satisfy a large number of product needs across countries. This approach is most useful in consumer product development as illustrated by the following example.

A multinational marketer of various fruit-flavored sodas in over 50 countries found that the sheer number of flavors led to problems in sourcing, quality control, variable acceptance criteria, and, consequently, lower product-line profitability. The company characterized sensory perceptions along the following dimensions: flavor type, flavor level, color, use of a sweetener, acidity, and cloud. The company had to choose sensory variables that could be controlled through changes in the product formulation and in the manufacturing process so that the company could respond to consumer preferences with product modifications or new products. Products were chosen or specially blended to conform to the different sensory packages desired. When tested against competitors' products in different countries, analysis of consumer panel preferences yielded three sensory segments: "low-impact" seekers who wanted mild products; "medium-impact" seekers; and "high-impact" seekers

GLOBAL MARKETING

Can Rain Forests Help Develop New Products?

Folk remedies exist the world over. Native plants have given the Western world several important medicines. Foxglove yields digitalis, used in heart medicine. Garlic can lower cholesterol. Oranges can help fight colds. The bark of the Pacific yew tree yields taxol, which can help fight cancer. About one-quarter of all medicines come from plants.

Shaman Pharmaceutical, Inc., a small company, was established in 1989. Its new-product strategy was based on studying how indigenous civilizations in rain forests around the world used tropical plants in treating disease and illness. For thousands of years, these native peoples had used the plants and herbs around them to treat sick people. Shaman believed that the process of finding new pharmaceuticals could be speeded up by making use of the wisdom of traditional cultures. To do this, Shaman employed ethnobotanists and doctors. Ethnobotanists, who study how different cultures use plants, and doctors, who verify which illnesses are being treated, could together identify tropical plants worthy of further study.

Shaman's doctors and botanists worked with local medicine providers to screen tropical plants and systematically investigate the rain forests for potential new drugs. Shaman then used biotechnology to isolate and extract the active compounds in these tropical plants for further study. The compounds were then shepherded through the new-drug investigation process mandated by the FDA and other national regulatory agencies.

In order to bring effective new drugs to market in a timely fashion, Shaman focused on certain common diseases such as respiratory viral infections that affect children. It is estimated that about 20 to 40 percent of the world's population suffers from flu and other respiratory infections. From its plant studies, Shaman isolated an antiviral compound, termed SP-303, and began testing this drug under FDA guidelines. A similar approach was used for compounds for possible treatment of fungal infections, particularly in AIDS patients. In all, Shaman collected over 400 plants and began closely investigating about half of them to develop antiviral, antifungal, and analgesic drugs. Shaman also developed partnerships with larger and well-funded companies such as Lilly and Merck and signed an agreement with an Italian firm, Inverni della Beffa SpA, for commercial manufacture under license of its SP-303 compound.

Sources: Shaman Pharmaceutical initial public offering prospectus, January 27, 1993, and "Shaman's IPO Success Sets Example for Biotech Firms," *The Wall Street Journal,* January 28, 1993.

---

who wanted robust products with the sweetest taste and the darkest color. Developing products to meet the needs of each sensory segment across countries allowed the company to reduce the number of products marketed internationally while still meeting the needs of large numbers of customers in each country.[9]

Technology Upheavals: The Silicon Graphics Approach

Companies in high-technology industries face the certainty that current generation technology will become obsolete. Their dilemma is balancing incremental improvements to the current technology-based product line versus focusing on the next-generation technology that will make their current products obsolete and dramatically reduce their sales. Companies can't really avoid the next-generation technology because their competitors will innovate and inevitably cause their current markets to vanish. Hence, the challenge is how to manage new-technology product development. Ed McCracken, President of Silicon Graphics (SG), sees the company's job as producing chaos by being an innovation leader, deliberately upsetting the applecart. Otherwise, a company's mature-technology products will become commodities, and with shrinking margins the company will not be able to spend on R&D and on learning about changing customer needs. McCracken even suggests that long-term planning is dangerous in such industries, that reducing product-development time allows Silicon Graphics to start a new-product-development initiative later, and factor in the latest customer perceptions and wants. SG's approach is based on six fundamentals:[10]

1. *Form product-development teams focused on specific customer segments* based on their needs and then let the engineers design new products in cooperation with customers. Market research is useless in such a context; instead, the best technology and R&D staff must work with far-sighted, "lighthouse" customers to sense and respond to paradigm shifts, such as a shift to three-dimensional images and digital video in desktop computing. SG machines are heavily used by movie-makers for such things as special effects, animation, and morphing. SG engineers benefit as movie-makers push systems to their limits and learn from movie-makers' criticism. This pushes SG to "stay on the leading edge."

    Another example of an SG "lighthouse" customer is Nissan. When asked how SG's computers could serve Nissan better, a senior Nissan engineer explained how a machine could store a complicated database to allow Nissan engineers to examine the interactions of machine part changes with all other parts of the subsystem. This would allow Nissan to speed up its own product development. While such a machine would have to be 10 times faster than anything SG had to offer, it provided them with a new product direction to pursue.

2. *If new products cannibalize existing products that are still growing, so be it.* The paralysis caused by fear of cannibalization of existing product lines can be deadly to long-term growth.

3. *Use new technology and capabilities to address high-end frontier customers* in a rapidly changing technology environment, and use older technology to develop cheaper, low-end, mass-market products. SG deliberately stays out of product lines with gross margins less than 50 percent, however, because such products would not fit in with its insistence on pushing the technology frontier.

4. *To create chaos, build on core capabilities,* defined as:

    ◆ Microprocessors that include three-dimensional graphics along with audio and video processing.

    ◆ Intuitive interfaces, requiring less customer training on advanced systems; this allows SG to charge lower prices and move the technology into higher-volume markets.

    ◆ Symmetric multiprocessing, allowing SG supercomputers to use micro-processor arrays to manipulate vast volumes of graphics data at high speeds.

    ◆ Shared architecture and operating system across all SG machines; proprietary but open architecture allows a company to set technical standards for an entire industry and consolidate its market share.[11]

    ◆ Bright technological people; as a technology company, SG's fortunes are determined by its people. The technical merits of ideas rather than hierarchy or status should determine new-product directions.

5. *Alliances are essential* to SG's pace of innovation. It has alliances with Time-Warner in the set-top interactive TV controllers, and with Nintendo in developing an advanced-generation videogame machine using SG's graphics strengths. While SG designs its own advanced graphics microprocessors, it does not feel the need to manufacture them, turning to third-party silicon foundries such as Solectron.

Similarly, it relies on third-party software developers to develop innovative applications for its advanced-capability computers.

6. *Financial targets provide control over the new-product development process,* such as insisting on gross margins of 50 percent, R&D at 12 percent of sales, and 15 percent growth in sales per employee.

Vision in Product-Line Development: Sandoz and Nutrition

Sandoz, a Swiss pharmaceutical company, merged with Ciba to form one of the world's largest drug companies, Novartis. Prior to this merger, Sandoz diversified out of the drug business by buying the U.S. baby-food company, Gerber, for $3.7 billion. One might question such a diversification on the grounds that margins are lower in the nutrition food business than in pharmaceuticals. Sandoz Chairman Marc Moret, however, offered some interesting insights into why Sandoz acquired Gerber Foods, noting that nutrition and pharmaceutical products are both appropriate and complementary products for a health care company: "Our vision of nutrition is one of a continuum from diet and medical nutrition to treating highly complex diseases with innovative compounds." Nutrition contributes to health, and by acquiring Gerber, Sandoz could provide both nutrition products and drugs. Gerber possesses databases and research facilities oriented to infants and young children, while Sandoz's drug-development experience can help Gerber develop medically nutritional products, particularly for an aging population. Sandoz is a leading distributor of nutrition products to nursing homes in the United States, and Sandoz can develop baby-food markets in emerging developing nations. Such complementarity provides some balance to the income stream from pharmaceuticals, which is beset by growing health care regulation and cost- and price-reduction pressures.[12]

However, such diversification can reduce the overall profitability of the firm, because the high-profit pharmaceutical sector may be offset by slower growing and lower profit more competitive segments. Johnson & Johnson (J&J) faced exactly this problem, when its pharmaceutical division took a large write-off because several of its new experimental drugs were rejected during the FDA approval process. At the same time, its medical device business lost market share to coronary stent competitors who quickly launched superior second-generation devices used in heart surgery. Simultaneously, J&J found that it had to introduce its new cholesterol-lowering margarine as a food product rather than as a dietary supplement, reducing profit potential in its consumer product sector, built around famous brands such as Tylenol, Neutrogena, and Band-Aids. J&J had to consider whether it would be better off splitting itself into three separate companies so that the long-term profit potential of each division would be more apparent, while losing the possible risk-reduction benefits of conglomerate type diversification.[13]

Swiss Investing in U.S. Biotech Firms. Swiss pharmaceutical companies have also been buying stakes in U.S. biotechnology companies to ensure a stream of new pharmaceutical products. A technological revolution has hit pharmaceutical drug development, and the former emphasis on synthesizing new compounds in labs and then testing for human efficacy is being replaced by using biotechnology processes and genetic engineering to develop or imitate disease-fighting substances in the human body. For example, researchers are beginning to agree that cancers, whether genetically inherited or episodic, are caused by gene breakdown; certain genes function as green and red lights, starting and stopping cell growth, and impairment of these functions causes uncontrolled growth and cancerous cell mutations.[14]

Swiss pharmaceutical companies have responded to this trend by buying controlling stakes in U.S. biotech companies for two main reasons: First, the United States is rich in small biotech start-ups that require capital and a hands-off atmosphere in which to do research; second, Switzerland is hedged in by environmental legislation that displays a fear of genetic engineering. Switzerland has repeatedly tried to ban the use of genetically modified animals for new drug-testing purposes, a cornerstone of biotech research. Furthermore, it is a small country with a few large companies that dominate the industry, and scientists are unlikely to take risks in such an environment or to find the free-wheeling culture required for breakthrough work typical of start-up U.S. biotech firms. Finally, Switzerland has a strong currency, a low cost of capital, and concentrated shareholdings so that Swiss firms can afford to take the long-term view without pressure from institutional money managers seeking short-term share-price rises. For these reasons, Swiss firms have spent over $7 billion investing in over 100 U.S. companies, in major U.S. research institutions such as the Dana Farber Cancer Institute in Boston or the Scripps Research Institute in LaJolla, California, and in setting up U.S. venture-capital firms investing in start-up biotech companies.[15]

What is interesting is that Swiss companies are spending about half their R&D budget on research conducted outside their firms, primarily investing in U.S. companies. While U.S. pharmaceutical firms such as Merck are also investing in biotech start-ups, they have also diversified by buying pharmacy distribution companies such as Medco Containment Systems that dispenses pharmaceuticals on behalf of health care payers. Merck hopes to use such information to sell more of its own pharmaceuticals over prescriptions for rivals' drugs, while also meeting the payor's requirement for cost control. Merck's stance seems to be that margins on drugs will decline because of health care cost-cutting and that Merck's future lies as much in gaining market share and selling more of its own drugs, whether proprietary or generic. The biotech industry presents a clear example of how differing vision among competitors within a global industry can lead to different paths for product-line development.

A Step-Wise Approach

As the costs of developing new products go up, projects are screened several times in order to ensure that only viable projects receive continued funding. The outline of a biotech company's multiple-stage approach to new-product development is summarized below.[16] (The company manufactures biotech materials and equipment for use by researchers and testing labs.) The company's Project Approval Team—PAT—is composed of the heads of manufacturing, quality assurance, finance, R&D, and marketing, with two additional rotating members from R&D and marketing. PAT evaluates projects in several phases:

1. *Idea generation* begins with pilot funding for a project generated by any R&D scientist. The results of the initial investigation are documented in an idea-evaluation report and screened by the PAT co-chairs, usually from marketing and R&D. If deemed promising, the idea is investigated further with additional funding, and then another report is generated with a proposal suggesting a feasibility study and possible product development. This report is screened by PAT.

2. *The feasibility study,* resulting in product definition, includes specifications, market potential, and return on investment estimates. It is reviewed by PAT.

3. *Product development* includes a specifications stage establishing components used, packaging, fitness testing, and hazard and stability evaluation. Cost estimates and sales forecasts are used to refine rates-of-return calculations, and test marketing is conducted. If PAT approval is positive at this stage, *final optimization* begins, with an initial batch made, and attention to documentation, quality-assurance specs, regulatory compliance, and final

design. Marketing is called in to develop product promotion and advertising.

4. *Product launch* occurs as the product is handed off to the operating divisions.

It is interesting to observe the evaluation criteria used by PAT:

- ◆ Potential for patent-protected market position
- ◆ Long-term market potential, and long-term impact on the company
- ◆ Possibility of alliances and external funding
- ◆ Estimated financial returns
- ◆ Fit with company's core competencies and with manufacturing, marketing, and distribution capabilities
- ◆ Probability of technical success

While the model described above represents the needs of product development in a technology-intensive industry, widely relevant are several of the concerns, including the balancing of technological, financial, and marketing issues.

JAPANESE APPROACHES

It is interesting to study the new-product development process in Japan, given its industries' capture of significant market share in global markets. We consider two examples, from the automobile and copier industries.

Japanese New-Car Development

Broadly speaking, American cars might be seen as providing comfortable transportation, while German cars provide speed, and Japanese cars have traditionally offered quality, reliability, and value for money. Major Japanese producers have approached this task by conceiving of new-car development as a series of important steps. The first is developing the product concept. The Japanese car companies begin with the premise that customers want more original products, but cars have different levels of meaning for different people. The focus is therefore on expanding the minds of designers. With a product concept established, the companies turn to specific R&D projects in areas such as new materials and processes; then comes market analysis, including consideration of investment needs, competition, and profit analysis; then, production planning and supplier choice; and finally, planning marketing strategy and product launch. Table 9–2 summarizes how Japan's major auto manufacturers approach these critical steps.[17]

Canon and the Personal Copier

Canon had successfully introduced the AE-1 camera, the world's first electronic automatic SLR camera. The copier division wanted to emulate the camera division with an equally stunning new product. Moreover, profits were too dependent on cameras, and Canon wanted to diversify. Therefore, Canon decided that its goal would be to develop a copier for offices with fewer than five employees that did not then use copiers. There were 4.1 million such offices in Japan in 1979, employing 8.7 million people. Under existing technology, however, the cheapest copier would cost more than 500,000 yen ($2,500), would need service by professional engineers, and was costly because it was sold through dealers and the manufacturer's direct sales force. For these three reasons, copiers were too expensive for the small-firm market.

TABLE 9-2	Japanese Company Approaches to New-Car Development

Product Concept Customers want more original products, but cars have different levels of meaning for different customers. The focus is, therefore, on expanding the minds of designers.	**Nissan:** Concept of cars as the "production of a mobile life stage" and "presentation of new life space." **Toyota:** Targeted a car concept, the Lexus, for a segment of the U.S. car-buying public characterized as a 43-year-old male living in Los Angeles with $100,000 income. To satisfy such a customer, Toyota conceived three design goals: a maximum speed of 250 km. per hour, fuel economy of more than 22.5 mpg, and the quietest car in production. **Honda:** The Civic was based on a "man maximum, machine minimum" principle, so that there would be more space for passengers. Of course, the Civic also pioneered a revolutionary clean-engine technology.
R&D Broadly focused on new materials, processes, increased use of electronics	**Nissan:** Focus on "development of the world's best suspension." **Toyota:** Lexus concentrated on aluminum and composite material engines and electronic controls for air intake and exhaust. **Honda:** Civic's clean engine was developed through teams of researchers submitting different solutions to the same problem.
Product Design Multiple parameters: performance, comfort, fuel efficiency, safety, environmental controls, differential national regulations; differing consumer tastes and segments, computer-aided design (CAD), with shared designs across models, links to computer-aided manufacturing (CAM)	**Nissan:** Three segments/divisions: full-size, compact, and subcompact; merit system to promote younger workers in product development. **Toyota:** New-product development committee to replace the chief examiner system; two committee chairs, a design engineer at the development stage, and a production engineer at the product preparation stage. **Honda:** The Civic: employees given responsibility and project management focuses on teamwork; use of guest engineers at product development stage to bring in ideas from different company cultures.

Source: T. Sasaki, "How the Japanese Accelerated New Car Development," *Long-Range Planning* 24, no. 1 (1991): 15–25.

With this in mind, Canon came up with its *Personal Copier Product Concept:*[18]

Goal: A copier priced under $1,000 (200,000 yen).

Issues: Defining target market segment, quality level required for personal use maintenance, target price and cost, size and weight, and new functions to be added.

Product concept: Compact, light-weight, price less than 200,000 yen ($1,000), maintenance through exchange of disposable parts, and added functions for ease of use and versatility.

Approach: While incorporating cost and reliability issues, study disposable photoreceptors, development apparatus, instant toner fuser, and new materials and components. Study other electronic consumer products such as fans and TVs to learn about cost versus reliability. Obtain compactness through outer structural design using foam plastics, piston-motion mechanism using mechanical clutch, and small diameter (60-mm) photoreceptor drum.

Organization structure: Task Force X for prototype model, and engineering model inspired by Team X for AE-1 camera. The composition of this task force is shown in Figure 9–2.

Slogan: "Let's make the AE-1 of copiers."

Canon attributed its success in developing the personal copier, to several reasons:

1. Senior management's vision of an under-$1,000, maintenance-free copier.

2. Companywide cooperation as exemplified by the setting up of Task Force X (illustrated in Figure 9–2).

3. Use of young engineers, average age 27.

4.   Designation of a product champion, Hiroshi Tanaka (Director of Reprographics Products Development Center), who acted as a bridge between top management and young engineers.

5.   Balancing of cost versus reliability, leading to invention of cartridge-based technologies.

6   A well-structured development process, allowing chronology of product concept to sales launch to be completed within three years.

Additional factors specific to Japanese product development are discussed by Harryson in a comparison of Sony and Canon. Factors such as job rotation of engineers, the direct transfer of R&D teams to production as their product reaches commercialization, and the role of center of excellence are all noted as pertinent.[19]

Supplier Relationships

Supplier relationships are a critical element of Japanese approaches to new-product development. Japanese companies such as Toyota or Nissan make complex products requiring mass production, assembly, and integration of several subsystems and thousands of parts. Typically they (1) work with few suppliers; (2) develop long-term partnerships with them; (3) require continuous improvement from suppliers in quality, speed, and time to supply, and the lowering of price and number of parts; and (4) most importantly, involve a limited number of key suppliers early on in designing and developing new products. The apex companies such as Toyota have several tiers of suppliers and deal directly only with tier-one suppliers, who in turn work with the next tier, and so forth.[20]

Not all suppliers are capable of being full-fledged partners, because they may lack the necessary people skills, technology, prototype-building ability, and knowledge base. Hence, some first-tier companies may not be equal partners, but instead have considerable responsibility for developing a complex assembly to meet specifications as set by the customer. Others, with lesser skills, may simply execute instructions from clients, even building commodity parts on a per-order basis. A supplier firm cannot be a partner to every client, and it may be better off being simply an order taker and supplier for some clients.

An example of the supplier partner approach to new-product development comes from Nippondenso, a major supplier of parts to the global auto industry. Toyota is one of its principal customers, and in developing a new line of alternators, the company used several years of basic research and a survey of customer preferences on size and performance. Different alternator housing types, wire specifications, regulators, and terminals added up to 700 variations from which the customer could choose. Once chosen, Nippondenso would work with the customer to customize certain product aspects such as where the alternator mounts would be located. In this way, Nippondenso took over the entire alternator research and product development function, supplying Toyota and other major auto manufacturers on a global basis.

Role of Global Sourcing

If low-cost, timely development, and high-quality, state-of-the-art components are desired, global sourcing is often a necessary step. Kotabe and others[21] have interesting insights into the strategic role of offshore sourcing by multinationals. They point out that a firm that shifts from supplying a market through exports to supplying that market through a manufacturing plant in that country also has to rethink its component sourcing decisions. New choices must be made because of tariffs, transportation costs, lower costs from local sources of supply, and overall greater familiarity with new local-supplier capabilities. Several variables affect the sourcing decision:

FIGURE 9-2   **Canon's New Personal Copier: Organization of Task Force X**

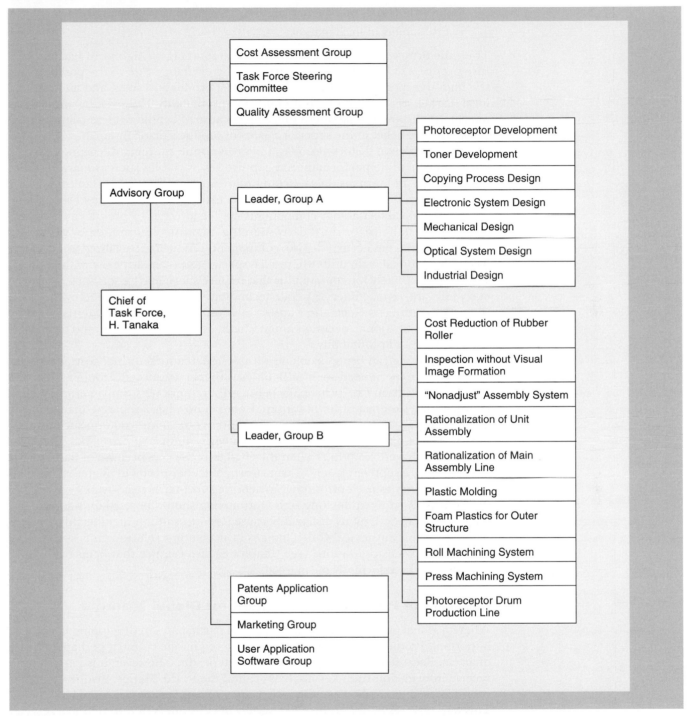

Source: Teruo Yamanouchi, "Breakthrough: The Development of the Canon Personal Copier," *Long-Range Planning* 22, no. 5 (1989).

- ◆ Tariff and nontariff barriers
- ◆ Nationality of the parent multinational
- ◆ Stage of the product in the product life cycle
- ◆ Exchange rate

- ◆ Transportation cost
- ◆ Production costs
- ◆ Growth in sales in local market
- ◆ Profitability in local market

Thus, the firm will be motivated to begin local sourcing by high tariff barriers; mature products or components; an appreciating exchange rate in the parent country; high transportation costs; low local-market production costs; and an attractive local market, as reflected in growth rates and profitability. However, Japanese firms may be predisposed to Japanese sourcing because of supplier infrastructure, relationships, and belief in the superior quality of products made in Japan.

Environmental factors also play a key role in the sourcing decision, affecting global product-line performance as captured by variables such as market share, sales growth, and returns on sales and on investments. The important mediating environmental factors are product and process innovation and asset specificity: That is, advanced technology components may be affected by product and process innovations; in-house or third-party sourcing might be determined by where the most innovation has occurred. Also, components requiring specialized assets might have to be sourced from units where such specific assets already exist, with in-house sourcing more likely for components that require specialized assets such as proprietary software, or machinery. Overall, technology intensity—measured by the levels of R&D spending—affects the transfer of equipment and components between units of a multinational, decisions about whether to source offshore, and ultimately, market share and profitability.

Outsourcing can bring problems with design, manufacturing, costs, and quality. Compaq experienced such difficulties with its outsourced supplier of laptop PCs, Japan's Citizen Co., principally because there were no Compaq employees in charge of the Compaq order at Citizen. Compaq now has a separate management group to supervise its outsourcing and requires control information such as daily quality data and the output from product integrity audits. Similarly, U.S. and Japanese car firms were both hurt when they had to recall cars because of flaws in seat belts made by a supplier, Japan's Takata Corp. A deeper problem might be the company's tendency to use outsourcing to achieve short-term cost savings—a strategy that is actually costly in the long run. Outsourcing should be used only as part of a long-term strategy. Unions dislike it because it reduces union membership and undermines their authority, while changes in marketing relationships such as the move to "mass customization" (see Chapter 8) also require that firms bring back in-house what was formerly outsourced.[22]

Location of Product Development for Global Markets

Where a global product is developed and who participates in developing it are both important. Product development may be centered in one country, perhaps at headquarters. Because the product is to be a global product, however, it is important to receive information from key markets around the world. Hence, involving foreign subsidiaries at the early stage of product concept development is crucial to success. This way, features of importance to a variety of consumers in different markets can be considered.[23] Firms must recognize, however, that development teams tend to "own" products and are reluctant to accept designs from other teams even when these designs originate within the company. In theory, it appears sound to assign central responsibility for designing a particular product to a particular team in a particular country, the assumption being that this team's design will then be adopted globally. Organizational conflicts can undermine this plan, however, and a company may be forced to compromise and accept two versions of what was meant to be a global product.

Benefits of Decentralized Product Development

Companies with well-established foreign subsidiaries usually encounter demands for increased local autonomy. This may be reinforced by the nationalistic feelings of subsidiary personnel, most of whom are probably citizens of the local country. Participation in such a fundamental corporate activity as development of new products is one of the most forceful ways of showing that one has "a piece of the action." In this situation, the firm must weigh the payoff in improved morale against any loss of efficiency in product development.

In industries in which product development is very slow and costly, companies may be forced to go outside for new products. The pharmaceutical industry provides a good illustration. Although most firms in the industry are research-intensive, none can have a very complete product line from internal research only. It takes too many years and too much money to bring a new drug to market. In this industry, therefore, we see a fourfold approach to product development:

1. Internal R&D

2. Acquisition of firms with new products

3. Licensing a new product from the firm that developed it for markets where that firm is not represented

4. Joint venturing with a firm that has complementary products

Unilever is one international company that deliberately seeks the advantages of international research development. The company has development activities in four European countries as well as close liaison with its associated companies in the United States and India. As one vice-chairman put it, "By locating research and development activities in a number of countries, an international company can take advantage of its unique ability to do research in a variety of national environments. . . . The probability of success is increased if there is good liaison between the laboratories. . . . There is a greater chance of sparking off new ideas."

Local Market Needs

Another encouragement to decentralized product development is local market need. Some products require continuous local testing during the development process if they are being designed primarily to meet market specifications (tastes, use conditions, and so on) rather than technological standards. Development close to the market is practical because these use conditions usually cannot be simulated in the firm's domestic laboratories. According to this reasoning, one would expect to find consumer goods developed locally more often than industrial goods. Furthermore, when demand for a product is limited to one market, it is usually developed in that market.

Other Local Market Considerations

Perishability raises the question of the adequacy of the local transportation infrastructure and of the ability of local distribution channels to store and display the product effectively until sale. Lack of refrigerated trucks, freezers at supermarkets, and cold-storage warehouses, as well as electricity supply brownouts, are common problems restricting the sale of products such as ice cream or frozen fish and meat in developing countries.

Local markets may also differ on the strength of a local consumer movement and the degree of product liability that the international marketer must bear in that market. While local laws may permit reduced product liability when compared to the home market, companies seeking a global image will set an internal standard that will apply to all country markets. Such conflicts are particularly apparent in products such as cigarettes, toys, pharmaceuticals, and consumer appliances. Of course, it is also possible that excessively onerous product liability in markets such as the United States may deter firms from manufacturing and selling in the market. An example comes from the general aviation industry, in which makers of small four-seat-and-under aircraft have all but left the U.S. market because of product liability laws that place the manufacturer at risk even after a decade of product sale and use. Legislation has found fault with manufacturers even in the face of irresponsible user behavior.

Given the importance of local market considerations, firms often use bidirectional approaches, whereby both local market and headquarters issues and personnel help shape new-product development. The outline of such a concurrent bottom-up and top-down process is described in Table 9–3.

Cooperation in Developing Products

As the costs of developing new products rise and diverse technologies are needed, consortium approaches have increased appeal. The consortium partners typically have complementary assets in design or technology, and the alliance is initiated to develop new products more speedily (see "Global Marketing," "Developing Multiple New High-Technology Products: Sony's Approach"). IBM and Toshiba, for example, began collaborating in the design of lightweight computer screen displays used in laptop computers because they had complementary technologies. Small color screens that use low energy are essential for the next generation of laptops. IBM joined Toshiba in order to learn from Toshiba's expertise in manufacturing and uses these color screens in its laptop computers.[24]

Creating a Common Standard

Collaboration can also result in a common standard being adopted. Palmtop devices are widely used by executives to keep track of appointments, phone numbers, for notetaking, and so forth. These devices need to be compatible across manufacturers and with other devices such as desktop and laptop computers, cellular phones, and the Internet. Hence, manufacturers are trying to coalesce around common standards with groups of manufacturers attempting to establish their standards as the world standard. Microsoft, a relative latecomer to this product area, is trying to establish its Windows CE standard against more established standards set by firms such as 3Com and Psion.[25]

Strategic Fit

A joint venture between Johnson & Johnson and Merck was set up to develop and market over-the-counter versions of prescription drugs. They were developing a compound called Pepcid, based on an antiulcer drug. They acquired the over-the-counter drug business of ICI, the British multinational,[26] whose sales were about $125 million annually, of which $90 million was from Mylanta antacid, one of the top 25 U.S. over-the-counter drugs. While the approval process to market Pepcid as a nonprescription drug was expected to take three to four years, the agreement with ICI gave the joint venture a product to sell in the meantime.

National Consortia

Governments have formed national consortia to develop new products in the face of global competition. Examples of this are the organizations Sematech and Microelectronics and Computer Consortium (MCC), created as consortia of U.S. companies in the semiconductor and semiconductor production equipment fields, to pool knowledge, share financial risk, and create common standards on which to

TABLE 9-3	Concurrent Headquarters and Local Market Influences on Product Development

Headquarters Influences	*Local Market Influences*
—Recognition by HQ marketing unit of the need for a new or modified product	—Suggestion by local manager of customer need for a new or modified product
—Initiation at HQ of product development process, including lab tests, cost and market (sales) analysis	—Suggestion by preliminary market analysis of further development
—Test marketing in local market	—Contact with HQ to receive information on and permission to develop modified or adapted version of existing product
—Local market product launch	—Ensuing development, with help of HQ labs as necessary
	—Test marketing to decide whether to go ahead
	—Approval from HQ for new product launch, with standards for quality, brands, and packaging

basc product development. These initiatives were taken in response to the growing Japanese domination of these product areas.

Incremental Innovation

Much of new-product development consists of small but steady improvements to existing products. This is especially true of industrial products. As product use increases, customer feedback provides suggestions for additional features that should be incorporated. Similar competitive products provide another source of ideas. Periodic evaluation of one's product in relation to those of the competition can result in the development of a checklist of areas to determine where competitors' products have an advantage. This activity is essential to keeping and gaining market share. By the same token, incremental innovations based on information from existing customers and focus groups allow a company to keep one step ahead of competition, continually providing differentiated products for a higher price rather than being forced to compete on a lowest-cost basis.

An example of such an approach is Mitsubishi Electric's changes to its line of residential air conditioners.[27] Between 1979 and 1985, Mitsubishi first introduced integrated circuits to control the air conditioning cycle. Then it replaced the integrated circuits with microprocessors. Moreover, it made the product easier to install and more reliable. Specifically, it made several changes:

1. It used quick-connect, precharged freon lines that clicked together to replace the older version of freon lines that had to be cut to length from copper tubing, bent, soldered together, purged, and then filled with freon. This older fabrication process was costly, requiring skilled labor and creating the possibility of a higher defect rate than the new process.

2. It used simpler wiring, a two-wire connection with neutral polarity, to replace the older model, which used six color-coded wires. Because the product was easier to install, the new air conditioner could be sold through mass-market outlets, and local contractors could install it more easily.

3. In 1982 it introduced a high-efficiency rotary compressor to replace the obsolete reciprocating compressor. The condensing unit was designed with louvered and inner fin tubes for better heat transfer, all of which made the air conditioner more energy efficient.

GLOBAL MARKETING

Developing Multiple New High-Technology Products: Sony's Approach

Developing new high technology is always risky. With new technologies, the market has not yet anointed a particular technological approach as the one best suited for meeting customer needs. Short product cycles raise the possibility that despite solving technology problems, the firm introducing the new product may not generate sufficient sales to justify investments in developing the product. Sony, as one of the world's leading high-technology developers, seems to be relatively insulated from such problems. It has succeeded by following an interesting and cautious approach to develop new high-technology products in areas complementary to its main areas of interest and expertise.

Sony's approach is to form alliances with small new companies whose technologies can complement Sony's in-house technologies and whose focus is on end-users and industries not served by Sony. Examples abound:

1. In the optical-drive market, Sony worked with Pinnacle Micro, Inc., to sell a rewritable optical disk drive.
2. To develop a high-definition TV camera, Sony collaborated with Panavision, whose expertise in lenses complemented Sony's video electronics.
3. In the video-conferencing market, Sony has a cooperative arrangement with Compression Labs, whereby Sony specializes in image-quality improvement and Compression Labs contributes technology to compress images for telephone transmission.
4. In the computer data-storage device area, Sony supplied an 8 mm. tape drive that is a central component for Exabyte Corp.'s 8 mm. tape storage system.
5. In the interactive TV market, Sony formed an alliance with Microsoft to jointly develop set-top boxes for controlling interactive TV services.

Of course, such alliances don't occur overnight; Sony may work with small companies as distributors or suppliers before moving to a collaborative effort involving sharing of proprietary information and information about markets. It uses such an approach principally for products that it does not see as vital to its future; this approach allows Sony to determine whether new markets are emerging without heavy commitment of time or capital. At the heart of these arrangements, however, is trust: Sony and its partners must be willing to work together, sharing critical information.

Sources: "Sony Adopts Strategy to Broaden Ties with Small Firms," *The Wall Street Journal,* February 28, 1991; "Sony Heads Down the Info Highway and Decides Not to Go It Alone," *The Wall Street Journal,* April 14, 1995.

---

4. In 1983 it added sensors and more computing power, resulting in further energy efficiency gains.

5. In 1984 it added an inverter, with additional electronic controls, which afforded greater control over the speed of the electric motor, again increasing the unit's efficiency.

Thus, through a series of small steps, Mitsubishi was able to offer customers a technologically advanced product that also saved energy.

Although R&D is necessary to create new products, converting research into commercially viable products is not a trivial task. For this reason, product testing is crucial to the product-development process.

Product Testing

As part of the development process, the product must be tested under realistic use conditions. Another reason for testing in a number of markets is to meet national requirements on product specifications and performance. For example, in the case of food products, drugs, and electrical or transportation equipment, some local testing may be necessary to receive government authorization to sell. In the case of pharmaceuticals, there is often a special factor. Obtaining the U.S. FDA approval of new drugs is a very time-consuming process. Drug manufacturers often test and certify their drugs in other markets and begin marketing there before getting final approval in the United States, thus expediting international introduction of the product.

Finally, local product testing may be advisable for promotional reasons. Although the firm must test its own products vigorously, there may be advantages in having local testing done outside the firm. It may improve the firm's local public relations by using national testing organizations. Such certification may be valuable to an international firm in its efforts to demonstrate adaptation to local market conditions.

As an example, Abbott Laboratories develops its new drug products and then sends them to universities and hospitals around the world for testing. Findings are reported in various national medical journals. These actions have the dual advantages of extensive international testing under different conditions plus publicity value when findings are reported.

ROLE OF ACQUISITIONS AND DIVESTMENTS

As market environment and customer preferences both change, firms are constantly faced with a choice: Evolve the product line to stay abreast of customer needs and address competitiveness issues to maintain market share in a changed industry environment; or divest product lines, either because industry conditions have diminished the product's attractiveness, or because changes in the customer base and their preferences make the company's current products less satisfactory. The following examples of corporate divestment and acquisition strategies to reformulate the product line are instructive of the considerations going into making such decisions.

L'Oreal's Entry into U.S. Mass-Cosmetics Market

L'Oreal, whose worldwide sales were almost $10 billion in 1994, launched a bid to acquire the U.S. cosmetics company Maybelline, whose annual sales were $350 million, offering roughly one and a half times sales plus acquisition of another $150 million in debt. Maybelline's main products are mascara, eye shadow, and lipstick, sold primarily through drugstores and other mass-market outlets. As a smaller company in a segment dominated by larger companies such as Procter & Gamble (Cover Girl, Max Factor) and Revlon, Maybelline had found it difficult to match the advertising and promotional expenditures of the larger companies. Its new makeup brand for older women, Revitalizing, had performed below expectations in competition with Revlon's "Age Defying" brand. With a deep-pocketed parent such as L'Oreal, however, Maybelline could match advertising spending by Revlon and get better access to shelf space in drugstores and other outlets.

L'Oreal, in return, gets additional mass-market products to add to its own line and thus be able to offer a wider product range to drugstores. The new lines also help balance its upscale brands such as Ralph Lauren, Armani, and Lancôme cosmetics, providing greater diversification across segments. Furthermore, L'Oreal may be able to learn from Maybelline's experience in marketing to ethnic groups, such as its "Shades of You" brand for African-American women. In addition, L'Oreal's international distribution channels can push more Maybelline product in overseas markets. In Europe L'Oreal needs such lower-priced products to compete against P&G and Unilever, which are pushing into European markets with mass-market brands. Maybelline appears to be a logical progression to L'Oreal's previous moves of reacquiring its U.S. licensee Cosmair in 1993 and the German Jade Kosmetik line in October 1995. L'Oreal had traditionally focused on France and the European market. The pressures of globalization require that L'Oreal become a major player in the United States and Japan, the world's two largest cosmetics markets. Shiseido is dominant in Japan, and L'Oreal planned a 60 percent owned joint venture in Japan with its second largest cosmetic company, Kose Corp. As an American brand, Maybelline might appeal to Japanese consumers who are becoming more cost-conscious after several years of economic recession. While the acquisition is pricey, launching a new brand is both costly and risky. By buying Maybelline, therefore, L'Oreal can be sure of controlling a well-established brand.[28]

Given Maybelline's attractiveness, it is not surprising that the German company Benckiser began trying to outbid L'Oreal and buy Maybelline for itself. Benckiser is a strong, 170-year-old German detergent business that had decided to diversify into cosmetics. By acquiring the low-priced fragrance line, Coty, in 1992, Benckiser obtained a 31 percent share of the U.S. mass-fragrance market. The cosmetics division grew to the point that by 1994 it accounted for about 45 percent of sales, with the rest being detergents. Acquiring Maybelline would give Benckiser an additional product line for the mass market and reduce seasonal dependence on fragrance sales, which occur primarily in the Christmas season. It would also increase its U.S. sales to the point that they nearly equaled EU sales, and give it scale economies in competing against giant firms such as P&G or Unilever.[29]

Acquisitions to Extend Geographic Reach

Sometimes acquisitions are a necessary step in expanding market share in key regional and national markets to permit viable competition against the market leader. A case in point is Kimberley-Clark (K-C) and Procter & Gamble (P&G), two fierce leading competitors in the tissue products industry—including diapers and facial tissues. K-C and P&G have comparable market shares in the U.S. diaper market, with K-C's Huggies brand having 40 percent to P&G's 36 percent for Pampers and Luvs brands. P&G dominated the European market, however, with 68 percent of the U.K. market and over 50 percent of the French market. Hence K-C spent $7.3 billion to acquire Scott Paper in order to double its European market share and become a more viable competitor to P&G. Scott has a strong market presence in southern Europe, in countries such as Spain and Italy, and the acquisition gives K-C the possibility of positioning brands in different segments of the market. For example, it could now position its own Kleenex brand as a high-end facial tissue and Scott's ScotTissue and Viva paper towels as value brands.[30]

Reshuffling Beverages for Pet Foods at Quaker Oats

Sometimes divestment occurs because of the perceived superior profitability of one product line over another. Quaker Oats' strategy shift led it to concentrate on healthy foods, grain-based products, and "good-for-you" beverages. In implementing this strategy, it purchased Snapple, a beverage company, for over $1.7 billion, incurring high levels of debt. It then proceeded to get rid of its pet-food line, selling its European pet-food operations with $800 million in sales to the British Dalgety PLC. Quaker also sold the U.S. pet-food operations with sales of $540 million to H. J. Heinz Co., which allowed Heinz to become number two in the U.S. industry behind Ralston Purina's 25 percent market share. Similarly, Dalgety obtained the number two market position in Europe just behind Mars Inc., with each having around 12 percent of the European market. Clearly, Quaker perceives profits and performance from the beverage industry to be superior, while both Heinz and Dalgety felt that increased volume and scale would help improve their performance in the pet-food industry.[31] For Quaker, the Snapple acquisition led to large losses, forcing Quaker to sell off the Snapple line to a management buyout firm at a huge loss. Shuffling product portfolios is ultimately a bet on management's foresight and abilities in managing new product lines.

PRODUCT-LINE DIVERSIFICATION

Disregarding the Rules

Management theorists such as Meyer and Utterback (cited earlier in this chapter) have suggested for some time that product-line diversification should relate to the firm's unique competitive advantages, its core competencies. Firms in Southeast Asia do not seem to be guided by such principles in their product-line expansion, however. An example comes from President Enterprises (PEC) of Taiwan. PEC is a highly vertically integrated food company that not only manufactures products such as instant noodles, yogurt, and beverages but also sells them through its own distributors and retailers. As a Chinese firm, it may have a better understanding of its Chinese customers' food tastes, and has been able to develop some premium brands. What is intriguing, however, is the close relationship between its product-line expansion and the increases in purchasing power of its Taiwanese customer base. It is interesting to consider how a brand's personality can change as the brand moves from country to country. Brand personality can include facets such as sincerity, excitement, competence, sophistication, and ruggedness, each of which can have differential appeal to customers in countries as diverse as China and the United States.[32]

Figure 9–3 demonstrates how PEC has branched out from basic products such as vegetable oil and flour into instant noodles as Taiwanese GDP per capita climbed, and then opened convenience stores to cater to harried working couples. PEC's latest diversification occurred with its entry into finance and insurance services.[33]

PEC uses alliances with companies such as Japan's Kikkoman and PepsiCo to enter product lines such as soy sauce and snack foods and to open Kentucky Fried Chicken fast-food restaurants. It sees its future growth coming from mainland China, and it has begun selling its instant noodles there, adapting them to different regional tastes.

A similar approach to diversification guides the activities of the Thailand-based Charoen Popkhand (CP) Group in China. It sees that its 12 years of experience in China and its network of contacts with Chinese state officials are critical to its future. Hence, it has formed alliances with other firms to bring in product-based expertise: with Honda for motorcycle technology, with Heineken for beer brewing, with NYNEX for telephone projects. Once a source of product-specific technology is obtained, CP Group brings in experienced Chinese managers from its operations around Asia and brings in as local partners high-level officials from the local municipal governments. Thus CP's formula for product expansion is based on its Chinese experience and contacts, as well as a patient long-term view of opportunities in China. The actual product-specific competence seems secondary.[34]

The question arises, How can firms from Southeast Asia disregard factors such as core competence in expanding willy-nilly? The answer may lie in two areas: one, that competition is still stunted in these regions, and large well-established firms have an edge in entering new industries. As economic development proceeds, a shakeout might occur, at which point companies may have to focus their strategies more closely and follow their core competencies. The second explanation is that knowledge of Chinese culture and contacts within China, managerial talent, and access to capital are the scarce factors, and companies such as PEC and CP Group have both. They possess experienced managers who can use cash flow from profitable Taiwanese and South Asian operations to fund their rapid product line and geographic expansion. As Chinese, they have family and clan connections across Southeast Asia. Such competencies might be part of the tacit knowledge base on which firms such as PEC build their expansion. What the experience of PEC and CP Group suggests, then, is that in economies in relatively early stages of development, core competence may stem from cultural knowledge and access to scarce resources as well as from more traditional factors such as technology and brand names.

FIGURE 9–3 **A Renegade's Approach to New-Product Development: Disregarding Core Competence**

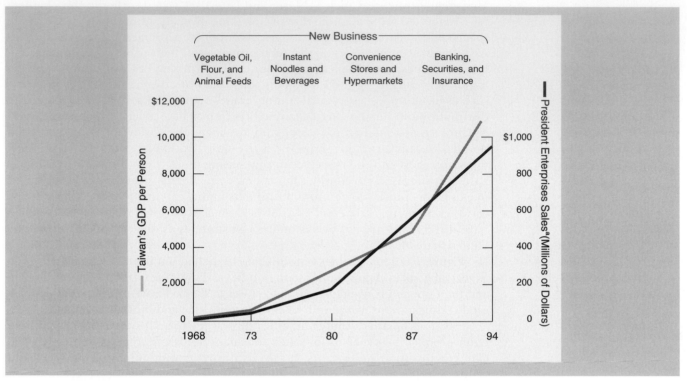

ᵃExcludes consolidated group sales
Source: Company reports cited in "How to Conquer China (and the World) with Instant Noodles," *The Economist,* June 17, 1995.

Refocusing and the Value Chain

A different approach to product-line marketing is seen in Grand Met's restructuring of its Green Giant (GG) vegetable business in the United States. Green Giant processes and sells vegetables in cans and frozen packages and was experiencing losses because of a price war in this commodity business. Grand Met decided that Green Giant's losses were caused in part by vegetable-processing plants that were idle most of the year, because canning and freezing could occur only when fresh vegetables arrived. After the processing, the canned or frozen vegetables had to be carried in inventory for long periods, another source of cash drain. Hence, Grand Met decided that GG should focus only on the marketing of processed vegetables. They accomplished this through several steps:

1. GG would supply its own strains of proprietary seeds to farmers who would grow vegetables under contract.

2. J. R. Simplot, a potato concern from Idaho, would process the vegetables.

3. United Refrigeration would freeze and store the vegetables at the same site and transport them as needed.

GG developed the same model for its canning line and was able to shut several vegetable-processing plants, diverting the savings into R&D on new frozen-food items such as "Rice Accents," a frozen mixture of rice, vegetables, and seasonings, and to enhanced marketing of the GG line. These changes allowed GG to gain a

GLOBAL MARKETING

New Product Directions at Samsung

Samsung's product diversification is a daring attempt to fundamentally change a company's entire product line. Samsung gets over half its sales ($14.6 billion) and much of its profits ($1.2 billion) from its semiconductor division, which did not exist 10 years ago. It now commands a 16 percent global market share in D-Ram memory chips. Samsung plans to use this cash flow to invest in a variety of new industries. Expecting, for example, to be a major player in the world's automobile industry, it plans to build a 100-seat jet and to buy three jet aircraft from Boeing to start an airline, and is negotiating partnerships and alliances with U.S. entertainment companies such as Disney and Dreamworks. All of these require that Samsung move out of the shelter of a protected domestic market to achieve greater market share internationally, build more complex value-added products, and focus on quality as well as quantity. It must also acquire technology as necessary (i.e., a license from Nissan to build cars), although Samsung expects to dispense with imported automobile technology within eight years. Last, it must launch a program of international acquisitions to acquire market presence, brand names, and technology.

Samsung's international market ambitions are forcing radical change on the company. Much will depend on whether semiconductor demand holds up so that cash flow is unimpaired and Samsung can continue to invest in and develop its international marketing strategy. It recently signed long-term contracts to supply semiconductors to firms such as IBM, Dell, and Sun Microsystems. The estimated peak value of such contracts is $65 billion, while total demand for D-Rams over the five-year period could total $380 billion. Few multinationals are attempting to make over their product line to such an extent, and it remains to be seen whether Samsung can pull off such a thorough restructuring in competitive global markets.

Sources: "Chairman Lee's Great Leap Forward," *The Economist,* March 25, 1995; "Korea's Samsung Plans Very Rapid Expansion into Autos, Other Lines," *The Wall Street Journal,* March 2, 1995; and "Samsung Signs Pacts to Provide Semiconductors to U.S. Concerns," *The Wall Street Journal,* December 8, 1995.

leading market share of 21 percent to number two Birds Eye in the U.S. frozen vegetable segment. In canned vegetables, GG began catching up to Del Monte with 15.4 to 16.1 percent market shares for the two companies.[35]

Product-Line Success and Downstream Value Activities

New-product development and eventual success may hinge on careful planning of downstream marketing activities. An example is the product-line evolution of Tat Konserve Sanayii, a Turkish tomato processor. Tat enjoys the comparative advantages of Turkey's soil, good growing climate, and relatively cheap labor. It exports 70 percent of its output from three factories processing 7,000 tons of raw vegetables a day. It works closely with small contract farmers to whom it provides selected seeds, fertilizer, and finance. Tat uses reverse-osmosis processing technology to retain vitamins and enzymes in the fruit. Perhaps its most important step, however, was to develop an exclusive distribution arrangement with Kagome, which controls half of the Japanese tomato paste market. Tat sold a 7 percent stake to Kagome in 1987, later raised to 15 percent. While Japan is its main market, Tat also exports to North Africa and the Middle East, and supplies the main food companies such as Nestlé in Malaysia and Unilever in Brazil. If Turkey joins the European Union (EU), Tat's access and sales to the EU could be enhanced. Tat demonstrates the importance of structuring the value chain in order to obtain success in international marketing of commodity product lines.[36]

Product-Line Extensions[37]

A review of the various corporate examples cited suggests that firms use product-line extension as a way of broadening their appeal to customers and as a means of offering additional products on domestic and international markets. Following this chapter is a case on Boeing and Airbus, which notes that product-line extensions, termed derivative aircraft, have been the mainstay of the aircraft industry over the past decade. However, product-line extensions do have a downside as well. Quelch and Kenny, for example, found that at one company "filler" products were 65 percent of the line but only 10 percent of sales. Reducing the number of such items could increase shelf space for core products in the line. Of course, the company has to plan for customers of the products to be dropped, attempting to move them to core products, perhaps through special incentives. Table 9–4 summarizes the positive and negative aspects of a policy of product-line extension.

Nintendo provides an example of extending the domestic product line to foreign markets. As noted previously, Nintendo broke into the U.S. market with a family entertainment computer that was already a best-seller in Japan and followed a similar strategy in marketing its portable Game Boy—a small hand-held version of the Nintendo computer. When the Game Boy was introduced in Japan, it sold 200,000 units in the first two weeks.[38] It was also successful in the United States.

A strong factor in product extension to foreign markets is client needs—that is, the needs of the company's home customers as those customers travel abroad. An example is provided by the credit-card business, dominated by U.S. firms. Visa had issued about 187 million cards by the end of 1988, and American Express nearly 31 million. (There are about 370 million credit cards in circulation in the United States.) In comparison, JCB Co., Japan's largest credit-card company, with 39 percent of the Japanese market, had issued 16 million cards. Only 30,000 of these cardholders are outside Japan. JCB wanted foreign cardholders to account for at least 10 percent of its total, while also increasing the number of Japanese cardholders. JCB had to convince shops around the world to accept the JCB card to meet the needs of Japanese who are traveling. Holiday Inn agreed to do so at its 1,500 hotels in 52 countries, and JCB signed agreements with U.S. ATM networks to allow JCB cardholders to use their cards at automated teller machines in the United States.

JCB has also differentiated itself from its global competitors with certain innovations. It allows cardholders to buy gift certificates that are accepted by all merchants who accept the JCB credit card. JCB gets a commission when the certificates are exchanged for goods, and it also earns interest on the "float," the funds it receives for the gift certificates but that do not have to be paid out until the certificates are actually used. JCB offers a monthly catalog of goods that cardholders can purchase, and it provides a service wherein it handles customer complaints with merchants from whom purchases were bought with JCB cards. JCB has little doubt that real growth can come only by expanding overseas.[39]

Competitive Influences on the Product Line

Competition serves as a benchmark in assessing how to satisfy customer needs worldwide. The competition's product line is particularly relevant. If a firm wants to be one of the top three or four players in an industry, it must match competitors' product lines. The powerful competitive impetus to match product lines can best be appreciated in the auto industry in the United States.

The luxury car segment can be divided into two subsegments, with GM/Cadillac and Ford/Lincoln appealing to older buyers, and the prestigious, highly engineered super-expensive European cars such as BMW and Mercedes catering to the young rich. As shown in Table 9–5, Cadillac and Lincoln dominate this segment in number of units sold. On a price basis, the U.S. luxury cars are attractively priced. It is this market that the Japanese have targeted. Their theory is that as their consumers—the owners of Sentras and Maximas and Camrys—get older, they may trade up, and the Japanese

| TABLE 9-4 | The Pros and Cons of Product-Line Extension |

Advantages	*Negative Aspects*
—Allows narrow customer segments to be satisfied; for example, offering a cereal formulated with added bran and a low-fat, healthy oil might attract health-conscious older consumers.	—Too many items in the product line muddy image, leading distribution channels to unilaterally decide which items in the product line they will stock.
—Minor product modifications to add a "new" product allow firms to claim that they are innovative and to target customers who are looking for something new.	—Reduces brand loyalty by encouraging customers to experiment and switch.
—Allows a firm to cover both high and low price points, putting out both premium-priced products and a lower-priced, bare-bones product.	—Crowds out genuine new-product ideas.
—Multiple and similar products allow excess capacity to be used without costly setup and product changeover costs.	—Cannibalizes demand from other items in the product line and does not enhance overall demand.
—Allows additional sales, at least in the short run; it is also cheaper as launching and establishing a new brand could cost as much as $30 million.	—As total products in the line grow faster than shelf space, retailers control what is displayed; disappointing performance may give impetus to a private label usurping the company's brand.
—Permits additional shelf space, which can keep out a competitor's products.	—Increased complexity leads to higher costs, stockouts at the retail level, manufacturing problems, errors in forecasting demand, material shortages, and less management and R&D attention to new-product efforts.
—Distribution channels often demand unique variations on the basic product line so that they can differentiate themselves, such as a larger package or with added features to attract customers.	—Customers and retailers may be turned off by too many product-line items and opt for brands with one or two all-purpose offerings.
—Allows response to competitive threat, for example, me-too products to match the success of Chrysler's minivan or of baking soda–based toothpaste.	

want to have cars that they can trade up to. Profit margins are higher on these cars, which is important as the yen gets stronger and the Japanese lose their competitive advantage in the economy car segment. The Japanese product-development goal is simple: to match the German cars in engineering and styling and compete on price.

The first Japanese company to follow this upscale-segment entry strategy was Honda, when it insisted that a separate Acura brand identity be established, with physically separate dealers and distinctive buildings. The Lexus and Infiniti follow the same approach, choosing from the best dealers and then requiring them to build new facilities to sell only Lexus or Infinitis. As Table 9–5 shows, the Japanese have successfully entered this market segment.[40]

Also interesting is the growth of other entrants into the luxury car segment, as the increased demand for, and higher margins in, luxury cars, coupled with the success of the Japanese, have also led other car manufacturers to launch car models for this segment. As the luxury segment gets more crowded and even mid-range cars start offering luxury features, the European manufacturers have found that they have to offer greater value and even accept lower prices set in part by the Japanese entrants such as Lexus and Infiniti. While the two traditional U.S. makers of luxury cars, Lincoln and Cadillac, have lost considerable market share, the Europeans have had to cede ground to the Japanese models, which collectively hold about one-fifth of the market.[41]

Other Influences on the Product Line

Product-line choices for individual markets are affected by additional factors, such as government regulations, the level of economic development of the market, the company's growth patterns, and the length of time the firm has been in a particular foreign market. The mode of entry into a foreign market, whether through exports or licensing or joint ventures, also plays a role.

| TABLE 9–5 | U.S. Luxury Car Market |

Make of Automobile	1985		1994	
	Units Sold	Percentage Share	Units Sold	Percentage Share
Cadillac	298,800	35.1%	210,686	20.6%
Lincoln	165,100	19.4	179,166	17.5
BMW	87,900	10.3	84,501	8.3
Mercedes	86,900	10.2	73,002	7.1
Volvo	51,600	6.1	81,788	8.0
Audi	48,000	5.7	12,575	1.2
Acura	—	—	44,711	4.4
Lexus	—	—	87,419	8.6
Infiniti	—	—	51,445	5.0
Others	113,400	13.2	195,974	19.3
Total	851,700	100.0	1,021,267	100.0

Sources: Ray Windecker, "The 100% Rule," *Ward's Automotive Industries,* October 1992, 104; and *Ward's Automotive Handbook,* 1995.

Government regulation, domestic and foreign, often affects product lines. Some governments prohibit export of certain products for national security reasons. This keeps some domestic products from being included in foreign product lines. The Export Control Act, for example, gives the U.S. president power to restrict exports to Communist countries. Such controls are being relaxed, however, with better East-West relations.

Host-country governments have shown increasing interest in the local product lines of multinationals and may bar certain products from their markets. Islamic countries, for instance, bar liquor; as a result, Anheuser-Busch has created a nonalcoholic beer for Islamic markets. Host-country pressures can also encourage firms to enter completely new product areas to please the local government. International Protein Corporation, for example, began a boat-building operation in Panama as a condition for participating in fishmeal and shrimp operations. And because of the Indian government's restrictions on foreign involvement in low-technology industries, Hindustan Lever (Unilever's Indian subsidiary) switched its emphasis from toilet articles to animal feeds and chemicals.

The level of economic development in a country also affects the choice of products to be sold there. Established firms usually have a domestic product line that ranges from mature products to advanced, higher-technology products. Firms from industrialized countries find that the choice of products from this line for foreign markets depends on the level of development of those markets. This is as true for consumer goods, such as those from CPC International or General Foods, as for industrial marketers such as Dow Chemical or General Electric.(GE) A GE executive remarked:

> We're placed to track right up the development curve with countries growing economically. Our first businesses in a country are those necessary for infrastructure building such as power generation and transmission and locomotives. As light industry starts, we can take in our small motors and other low-technology industrial products. As electrification spreads, our consumer housewares find a market. Finally, when advanced manufacturing begins, we can take in our engineering plastics and other high-technology products.

Impact of Method of Entry

The nature of the firm's involvement in foreign markets is another product-line determinant. If the firm enters a market through exports only, it theoretically has freedom to choose as many or as few products as it wants in each market. Once it establishes an export operation, however, it will feel some pressure to expand the product line to gain economies of scale; if it uses an export agent, this pressure becomes less because the intermediary can spread the cost over other products carried. "Buy national" policies, tariffs, and transport costs are other restraints on the export line.

Licensing offers less freedom in product selection. Appropriate licensees may not be available for all the products a firm wants to enter in a market; licensees may not have satisfactory technology, or the best candidates may be licensed to competitors. Even if the firm finds suitable licensees, they may be producing products that compete with those of the licensor. The product line of the licensee, therefore, can limit the product line of the licensor in that market. Occasionally, the firm can overcome such limitations by using different licensees in a country. The feasibility depends on the availability of licensees and the divisibility of the licensor's product line. If the licensor's products are competitive, the licensee would not want another firm in the country to be involved.

The joint-venture approach can restrict the firm's foreign product line, too. Most joint ventures of international firms bring together two companies, each with a particular product line, just as does licensing. If the national partner has complementary products, this confines the product-line possibilities of the international partner.

Wholly owned foreign operations offer the greatest product-line flexibility. The firm can initially produce products in its foreign plants—products deemed best suited to local market needs, use conditions, competitive situation, and purchasing power. With initial success and market evolution, additional products can be introduced and adapted for the foreign market.

Divestment within a Product Line

Divestment of specific products from the product line is another option. As the following example of Zenith's laptop computer division shows, divestment may have less to do with a product's intrinsic attractiveness than with resources and a firm's strategies.

Zenith's sale of its PC division to Bull (the French state-owned computer company) to concentrate on consumer electronics presents an interesting example of how companies can have opposite views on product diversification and divestment in international markets. Zenith Data Systems held a 28 percent, or number one, market share worldwide in the portable or laptop computer segment. The parent Zenith Corp. also owned the Zenith consumer electronics division. Zenith decided to sell off the portable computer segment to Bull for over $600 million, using the proceeds to reposition itself in the worldwide color television market. This area faced stiff competition from low-cost Far Eastern producers, prompting major U.S. producers such as GTE (Sylvania), Motorola, and GE/RCA to sell off their TV lines. Because Zenith could not afford to be in both the PC market and the television market, it opted for the TV market.

This line of business was dominated by Japanese companies, European companies such as Thomson and Philips, and South Korean companies such as Samsung and Lucky Gold Star. A major future opportunity lay in high-definition TV (HDTV), which would offer wide, sharp, cinema-like pictures and compact disk–quality sound.[42] Zenith decided to concentrate its resources on developing HDTV products for this future global market. It was one of the few U.S. companies doing so. Later, Zenith had to sell out to Korean companies due to competitive market pressures.

At the same time, even as Zenith abandoned the laptop market where it had the lead, Bull sought to enter it. Bull's market presence is mainly in the mainframe and minicomputer markets, so why did it want the Zenith PC line?

1. Bull immediately gained a commanding market share in the PC segment by taking over the Zenith computer line.

2. Zenith is strong in the United States, and the acquisition doubled Bull's U.S. revenues.

3. Zenith had significant U.S. government orders ($560 million in 1988), including an Air Force computer order, and it was a bidder in the $1 billion federal Desktop III contract. Thus, the Zenith acquisition gave Bull a strong presence in selling to the U.S. government.

4. In addition, Zenith has been developing an advanced PC as part of a consortium, using an extended industry standard architecture bus as an alternative to IBM's Micro Channel–based PS/2 computers.[43] Since Bull had already backed the IBM standard, the Zenith acquisition gave it a stake in the alternative standard being developed by IBM's competitors. In effect, the Zenith acquisition allowed Bull to hedge its bets on technical standards for advanced PCs.

Both Zenith's reason for divestment and Bull's reasons for the acquisition make sense when viewed in light of each firm's global product policies.

Firms within the same industry can thus arrive at different decisions about product diversification. Competitive behavior may lie in entering product lines in which competition is entrenched. For example, Glaxo was unrepresented in the over-the-counter (OTC) prescription drug sector. When SmithKline merged with Beecham, thus giving SmithKline an OTC capability for its Tagamet antiulcer prescription drug, Glaxo then had to match this by finding a similar OTC channel for a version of its antiulcer drug Zantac. Glaxo's defensive move was an alliance with the Swiss firm Sandoz, giving it U.S. marketing rights for a nonprescription version of Zantac.[44]

Banned at Home, Sold Abroad

Ethical considerations sometimes also affect the nature of the product line sold overseas. Cigarettes provide an example. U.S. public sentiment opposed to the spread of cigarette smoking has steadily increased to the point that smoking is banned in most public places, and growth prospects for cigarette usage in the United States are negative. At the same time, there is a huge potential for increasing the sale of tobacco products in developing countries such as China or Thailand. The U.S. government position seems contradictory; it opposes discriminatory measures taken by the Thai government that restrict the sale of tobacco products by U.S. multinationals, but it is opposed to the spread of cigarette smoking in the United States. The question relates to whether it is correct for governments and companies to promote the sale of products, such as cigarettes, in overseas markets that it restricts at home.

A similar controversy surrounds the sale of a drug that induces abortions early in pregnancy. The pill, RU486, sometimes referred to as the *morning-after pill*, is marketed by a French company, Roussel-Uclaf S.A. It is considered an inexpensive, safe, and less traumatic way to end pregnancies as opposed to surgical abortions. Although the drug had been legally approved for sale in France and China and had undergone extensive testing, the company decided against marketing it in the United States because of fear of protests from antiabortion forces.[45]

Roussel-Uclaf ultimately decided to license U.S. patent rights for RU-486 to the nonprofit Population Council, which conducted clinical trials using the drug on 2,100 women, prior to applying to the FDA for approval for widespread use in the United States. Roussel-Uclaf asked the Population Council not to use the name RU-486 for the drug but instead to use the generic name mifepristone. Once the drug received FDA approval, the council would find a manufacturer and develop a brand name. Surveys have shown that over a third of U.S. doctors who don't currently perform abortions would offer the new abortion pill to their patients. Use of the pill requires three visits to doctors, which is followed by the use of another drug, prostaglandin. As is to be expected, antiabortion activists have attempted to launch boycotts of prescription drugs from Hoechst Celanese, Hoechst Roussel, and Copley Pharmaceuticals, all units of the parent company Hoechst. They would like the U.S. license to the Population Council to be rescinded and production of the drug outside the United States stopped.

The issues here are complex and controversial, and they are increasingly important for international marketers. Governments have different product and safety standards. To what extent can firms take advantage of these differences? Their resolution depends on the informed judgment and the conscience of the decision maker. It would seem, however, that ethical and economic decisions should concur, particularly in the domain of product safety.

FOREIGN-MARKET CHOICE: MATCHING PRODUCTS TO MARKETS

Each international marketer has to decide which products to sell to which countries. Several approaches exist to making this decision:

1. Using the international product life cycle (IPLC) to identify potential markets.

2. Screening markets to extract a short list of those with the highest potential.

3. Assessing individual markets in terms of how well they meet the firm's objectives (market share, return on investment, or matching competition).

4. Conducting a competitive audit to isolate markets in which risk-return trade-offs are most attractive.

5. Deciding on realistic market-share objectives for the markets chosen.

International Product Life Cycle (IPLC)

The international product life cycle (referred to here as the IPLC) was described in Chapter 2. It comprises stages of demand growth, staggered in time across countries, representing lags in income and development of consumer demand in the various countries. Typically, demand first grows in the innovating country and in other advanced industrial nations similar to the innovating country. Only later does demand begin in the less developed countries. Production, consequently, first takes place in the innovating country, with excess production (greater than domestic demand) being exported to satisfy demand elsewhere. As the product matures and technology is diffused, production occurs in other advanced industrialized countries and then in less developed countries (see Figure 9–4).

This sequential introduction of new products means that the firm has different product lines in different markets. As noted by a Gillette executive in 1984, "Yesterday's product in the U.S. is today's product in Latin America and tomorrow's in Africa."[46]

International Trade and Production in the Product Cycle

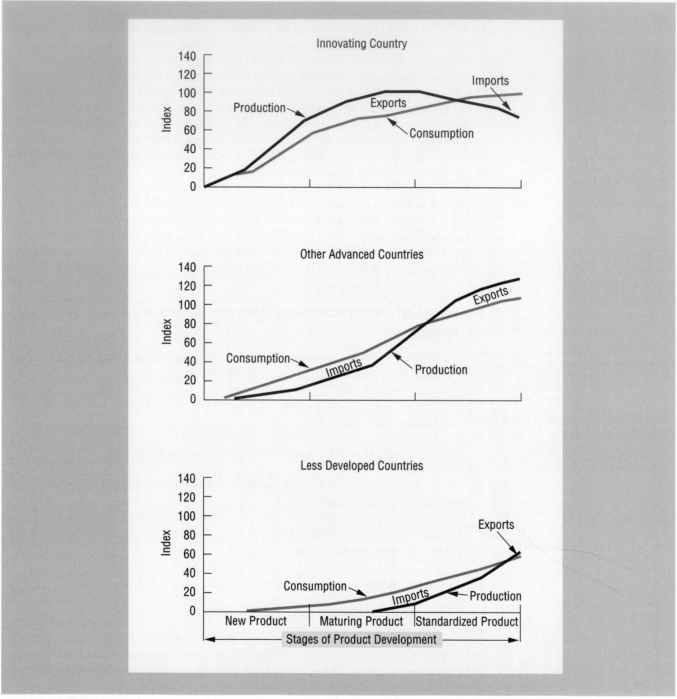

Source: Raymond Vernon and Louis T. Wells, Jr., *Manager in the International Economy,* 5th ed. (Englewood Cliffs, NJ: Prentice-Hall, 1986), 83. Reprinted by permission of Prentice-Hall, Inc.

A further implication of this life cycle is that as products become mature in the firm's home market, they may be dropped there but continue to be sold in other markets. In other words, the sequence for dropping products generally follows the same order as for adding products. This again leads to different product lines in different countries. This is a strength of the international marketing firm. It can continue to exploit its mature products, even when they are no longer sold in its home country or the other industrialized nations.

A concrete example of product life cycles is seen in Figure 9–5, which illustrates the demand curve from 1975 to 1994 for recorded music in three formats: LPs (long-playing 12-inch records), cassette tapes, and the newest mass product, compact discs (CDs). The chart clearly shows that LPs are an obsolete product with minimal sales in the 1990s, after reaching peak sales in the 1970s. LPs were replaced by CDs, a technology that offered superior sound, greater durability and smaller size. Not coincidentally, CDs sell for a higher price (between $11 and $13 each at U.S. retail channels) and provide greater margins than LPs. As the generation that purchased LPs gets older and more prosperous, they tend to replace their LP collection, often worn-out records of their favorite music as youths, with more expensive CDs. Demand thus gets a boost from replacement sales as well as from the current younger generation's buying new music on CDs.

CDs allow record companies to repackage their past hits in the form of compilations so that their library of recorded music can yield additional recurring income. Cassette tapes offer convenience and portability and are an avenue for copying music so that a CD owner can make a tape for his car stereo. As the chart shows, however, cassette tapes seem to be on the decline. The three demand curves taken together point to the inevitability of obsolescence and also point out that new formats for selling recorded music will emerge.

For the international marketer, the issues of growth and obsolescence in the U.S. market raise many interesting questions:

◆ Are LPs obsolete all over the world?

◆ When will the demand for CDs start tapering off in the advanced industrial nations, and when will demand for CDs start taking off in the poorer countries?

◆ As demand starts growing in developing countries, should manufacturing of CDs begin in these nations? Should they become export platforms for CDs sold in the advanced industrial countries?

◆ What new formats are around the corner that might replace cassette tapes and CDs in the future? Will selling digital music over the Internet replace CDs?

◆ As a purveyor of recorded music, how should a company strategize for these likely developments?

As the above questions suggest, inevitable change is permanent, and firms that perceive this and adapt their strategies to cope with it are more likely to do well in international markets.

Technology and the IPLC

Technology can compress product cycles, increasing risk and underlining the importance of maintaining product leadership through technological innovation. Ford, for example, designed a new two-liter engine with two valves per cylinder to be used as the base engine for a variety of cars built in factories around the world. The Japanese moved quickly, however, to develop and introduce a 16-valve, high-performance engine, which shortened the life of Ford's new engine to only four years, too short to recover product-development costs satisfactorily or to earn a return on investment. Yet Ford had to match its competition by introducing a 16-valve engine of its own.

Alternative technologies can also present an interesting conundrum for the IPLC. If recognized as superior in the marketplace, they can suddenly make an existing product obsolete before its life cycle has had a chance to play itself out. Consider the way the Beta-format VCR introduced by Sony lost ground when the VHS standard was adopted worldwide as the VCR diffused into global markets.

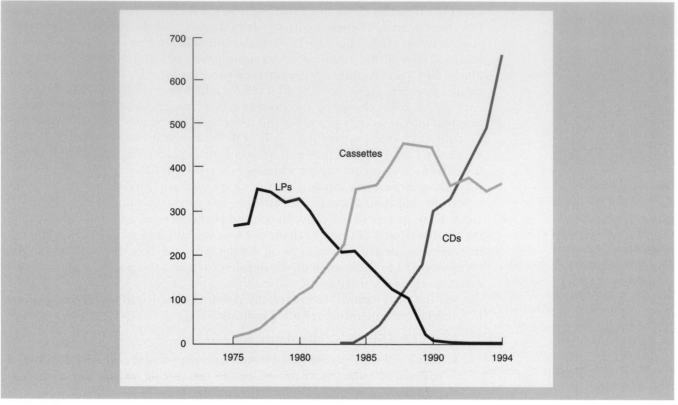

Source: *The Economist,* December 23, 1995, 78.

Even low-technology products such as toys have an IPLC. Tonka had enormous success in the United States with its Mask line of toys, which were subsequently introduced to Europe, where sales increased just at the time they began dropping in the United States. Delayed marketing and advertising, however, caused a lag in the stimulation of demand for Mask toys in Europe. The important point is that Tonka was able to generate additional sales and profits from a toy line whose product-development costs had already been amortized.

The Tonka example also suggests that if there is no lag in marketing a product in the triad economies, demand is likely to grow simultaneously in them. As multinationals move to global marketing and develop global brands, and as communications media instantaneously bring news of market developments to all of the advanced nations, corporations may not be able to delay a product introduction into some advanced countries. If they do, their competitors might steal the market. And, as the example of Ford's engine that became obsolete within four years shows, a phased introduction of a new product into advanced nations may be a luxury that companies can ill afford. Short IPLCs dictate that a firm move expeditiously to stimulate and take advantage of demand in all of the key markets of the world. If the firm lacks the cash or other resources necessary for such simultaneous market penetration, however, the logical step is for it to develop strategic alliances.

Market Potential and Market-Entry Decisions

In considering which markets to enter, a key issue is unrealized market potential. Consider the European market for credit cards as shown in Figure 9–6.

GLOBAL MARKETING

Cosmetics for the Russian Market

Russia's recent economic development has been marked by high inflation, unemployment, an underground economy, entrepreneurial start-ups, and confusion over the rules governing foreign enterprise. It is against this background that Hazel Bishop (HB) decided to sell cosmetics to Russia. HB was a well-known brand in the 1950s and 1960s; it sells medium-priced lines in the United States through outlets such as Wal-Mart and Woolworth's. Russia seemed to offer a market for mid-priced, quality Western cosmetics. Hence, HB formed a joint venture with Effect, a Ukrainian cosmetics manufacturer. HB would ship products to Effect, which would distribute these products in Russia and Ukraine.

HB and Effect used test marketing to determine the appropriate mix of products to ship. They found a ready market for basic cosmetics such as lipstick and nail polish, while less familiar products such as foundation makeup sold less well. Multiple distribution outlets were used, including special shops where purchases could be made only with hard currency, department stores, drugstores, and new shops opening up in cities. The cosmetics were displayed on open racks, allowing customers to help themselves; HB hoped that this would stimulate impulse buying. Traditionally, cosmetics were kept behind the counter or in display cases.

The U.S. products were sold without adaptation, even keeping the text on the packages in English, which served to underline the U.S. origin of the products. Wanting to establish its brand name ahead of market growth, HB launched a TV campaign inviting contestants who wanted to become HB's spokesperson for a line called "Russian Red Lipsticks" to submit entries with photographs; the winner was to be picked in a U.S.–style beauty contest.

HB eventually plans to produce the cosmetics locally after the economy becomes more stable, with a smoothly functioning supplier infrastructure for obtaining production inputs and a more productive labor force. Russian market potential is not limited to mass-market goods, however. About 10 percent of the economy can afford luxury goods, consisting of former Communist politicians who have entered business, young entrepreneurs, and those who have earned their wealth through crime and black-market activities. Eighty percent of the 5,100 Mercedes cars sold in Russia in 1994 were its top-of-the-line S-class series. As Russia continues to grow, both the mass-market and the high-end market can be lucrative segments.

Sources: "Hazel Bishop Offers Ex-USSR Different Shades of Red," *Business International,* October 12, 1992; and "Companies Tap EE Luxury Goods Market," *Business Eastern Europe,* April 18, 1994, 4.

It is apparent that credit-card usage in the United States and Canada is about 50 to 65 percent higher than in Europe. Equally interesting, debit cards are more widespread in Europe than in the United States. Debit cards essentially ask consumers to pay in advance and allow the debit card issuer the benefit of the float; they are the opposite of the unsecured credit arrangement that underlies the credit card. Credit-card issuers in the United States rely on interest rates topping 18 percent per annum to earn profits from credit-card issuance, while such an interest rate earnings channel is closed off in the case of debit cards.

Debit cards thus present a glimpse into major cultural differences in the European attitude to, and use of, credit. European merchants, for example, seem less willing to grant unsecured credit, and European consumers seem more interested in the convenience feature of cards than in their credit-extending capabilities. For the credit-card firm such as Visa or Mastercard, this issue is worth exploring in order to decide whether to focus on marketing credit or debit cards.

A second aspect of the European credit-card market is the utility of credit cards, as reflected in the number of merchants that accept such cards. Again, Europe, with the exception of Spain, is behind the United States and Canada in merchants' willingness to accept credit cards. This fact may reflect the reluctance of merchants to pay the 3 to 5 percent discount off the sale proceeds as the commission to the credit-card issuer. Or it may reflect the need to market more intensively and convince merchants that the increased volume of business that they might gain and the reduction in bad debts outweigh the commission that they may have to pay the credit-card issuer. What

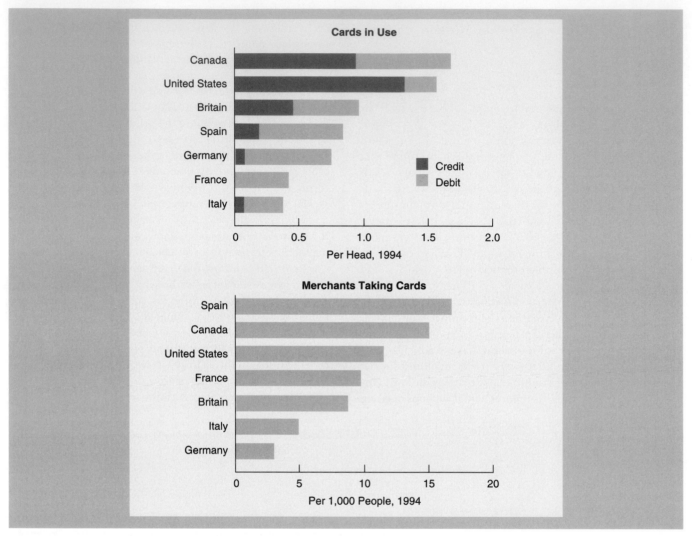

FIGURE 9-6   **The Market for Credit and Debit Cards in Select Countries**

Source: Credit Card Research Group data, appearing in *The Economist,* November 4, 1995, 115.

the data on credit-card usage suggest is that there is market potential in Europe, but that how such potential should be exploited needs additional study.

In general, companies might be better off targeting markets where significant market shares are likely to be achieved. In such fast-growing markets, new customers do not have pre-established links with suppliers that are emerging; growth makes the established competitors slack and inattentive to new entrants; and demand may exceed supply from established suppliers, leading to openings for other firms seeking entry. Ryans[47] found that firms adapting the product achieve highest market share in the introductory and growth phases of the market and less during maturity and decline phases.

The market-entry decision must weigh unrealized market potential against the strength of competition. Multinationals within an industry are all likely to have similar data, leading them to similar rankings of individual country market attractiveness. Hence, the strength of competition likely to be encountered is important. **Competitive audits** are a formal way of judging the strength of competition in markets of interest. Table 9–6 presents the basic questions that form part of a competitive audit.

TABLE 9–6	Competitive Audit of a Foreign Market

Basic Information

1.   Which competitive products are sold in country X?
2.   What are the market shares of competitive products?
3.   How do competitive products compare with our own in reputation, features, and other attributes?
4.   Which support facilities (production, warehousing, sales branches, and so on) do competitors have in country X?
5.   Which problems do competitors face?
6.   What relationships do competitors have with the local government? Do they enjoy special preferences?

Marketing Information

1.   Which distribution channels are used by competitors?
2.   How do competitors' prices compare with our own?
3.   What credit terms, commissions, and other compensation are extended by competitors to their channel members?
4.   What promotion programs are used by competitors? How successful are they?
5.   How good is competitors' post-sales service?

Market Supply Information

1.   How do competitive products get into the market?

If they are imported:

2.   Who are the importers?
3.   How do importers operate?
4.   What credit, pricing, and other terms are extended to importers by foreign suppliers?
5.   How long has each importer worked with a foreign supplier? Is he or she satisfied with the supplier?

If they are produced locally:

6.   Who are the producers?
7.   Are the producers entirely locally owned, or is there foreign participation?
8.   What advantages do local manufacturers have over importing competitors?

Source: Franklin R. Root, *Entry Strategies for International Markets* (Lexington, MA: Lexington Books, 1987), 42–44.

Results from the competitive audit can be combined with assessment of market potential to begin estimating market share likely to be achieved by the company. Then, depending on objectives, the company assesses whether a specific market represents an attractive opportunity for entry.

Government regulations and attitudes may also be factors affecting market attractiveness. Import-substituting governments often use tariffs and regulations to keep out foreign multinationals and foster the growth of domestic companies. In such instances, foreign firms must decide whether they want to participate in local markets by licensing technology to the local firm in the hope of eventually securing entry once the government liberalizes its economic policies regarding foreign multinational participation in the domestic economy. Table 9–7 presents a framework for analyzing government's role in LDCs in influencing market attractiveness. The analysis was designed to assess attractiveness for export opportunities, but it can also be used in judging market attractiveness for other modes of entry.

In sum, a firm evaluates risk, competition, probable returns, and resource commitments needed before judging whether it should enter a particular market. A checklist for screening foreign market entry might include the following:

1.   What is the product's competitive position at home? (What is transferable to overseas markets?) Is the product new?

TABLE 9-7	**Consumer Product Export Opportunities to Liberalizing LDCs: A Life-Cycle Approach**		
Stage	*Government Policies*	*Market Characteristics*	*Foreign Exporter Opportunities*
Preliberalization	▪ Encouragement of import substitution ▪ Severe restrictions on consumer imports ▪ Possible production limitations on consumer products ▪ Heavy taxation on consumption and/or higher incomes; discouragement of conspicuous consumption	▪ Sellers' market ▪ Restricted competition ▪ Pent-up consumer demand	▪ Very restricted
Liberalization	▪ Greater encouragement of free enterprise and competition ▪ Encouragement of export orientation ▪ Allowance of wider income disparities	▪ Greater availability of consumer products ▪ Wider choice of products ▪ Increased consumption of consumer products	▪ Substantially increased
Partial Retraction	▪ Re-enactment of higher tariffs and quotas and/or decreased importer access to foreign exchange ▪ Re-enactment of import substitution	▪ Slower consumption growth likely ▪ Competition from local production	▪ Curtailed or threatened ▪ Continued access via foreign investment may be possible

Source: Kate Gillespie and D. Alden, "Consumer Product Export Opportunities to Liberalizing LDC's," *Journal of International Business Studies* (Spring 1989).

2. Is there a market? What is its size? How does the product relate to consumers' needs, ability to buy, and conditions of use in that market? Is adaptation necessary in product attributes, the physical product, and its packaging?

3. Is the market growing? How attractive is it? What is the level of product saturation?

4. Is there much competition? What does the competitive audit show?

5. Will government regulations diminish chances of success?

6. Will the product require much training, after-sales service, and complementary products?

7. Is the product likely to be obsolete soon? (That is, is this type of product undergoing rapid technological change?)

8. What resources (management time, financial resources) will have to be committed to this market?

9. What are the potential returns from the market, and what is its level of risk? Where does it rank when compared with alternatives?

10. What are the objectives for this market? (Possible objectives include market share, profits, defense against a competitor, response to local government, and maintenance of a presence in lead markets.) The firm must also distinguish between strategic and short-term objectives for the market.

11. If entry into the market is through a partnership, such as a joint venture or strategic alliance, is there agreement on objectives? Is there likely to be conflict over goals?

12. How patient is the company? How long will top management be prepared to wait until success is achieved? For example, if a firm has few managers who speak Japanese and if they have little knowledge of day-to-day management problems of doing business in Japan and few personal business contacts there, then it cannot expect early success from Japanese market entry.[48]

Based on the foregoing, companies generally are selective in their foreign-market expansion. The steps outlined above should lead to a short list of potentially attractive markets, from which one or two are chosen for entry after exhaustive investigation. The process is, of course, not static. Markets discarded as being unattractive can be assessed more favorably with the passage of time and changing economic conditions. This constant revaluation of markets is seen in Coca-Cola's approach to certain foreign markets.

Coca-Cola: Rethinking Foreign-Market Entry

Coca-Cola has traditionally been content with supplying the syrup to prepare the soft drink and letting the local bottlers market the drink. As Coca-Cola grows more dependent on foreign earnings (about 80 percent of total earnings), however, and as the U.S. market becomes saturated (5 percent growth a year, whereas foreign growth is about 16 percent), managing growth in foreign markets becomes more important. It has devised several ways to tailor its strategy to match product penetration and future potential of each market:

1. *Japan.* It continues to rely on a dozen bottlers that are Japan's largest food and trading companies, such as Kirin, Mitsubishi, Mitsui, and Kikkoman. It also developed unique drink products for the Japanese palate such as milk- and yogurt-based drinks.

2   *United Kingdom.* It formed a 49 percent owned joint venture with Cadbury-Schweppes and took over bottling from franchises held by Grand Met and Beecham.

3   *France.* Coca-Cola bought back bottling rights from Pernod-Ricard, which had sold Coke in France for 40 years. Consumption in France is only 13 percent of the U.S. average of 46 gallons per person, however, and it hopes to raise consumption by controlling the marketing directly. Paris may also have an important role as the center from which to ship concentrate and cans to other parts of Europe, an important capability in the Single Market.

4. *Brazil.* In the world's third largest market for soft drinks, with a hot climate and 140 million thirsty people, Coke is being challenged by Pepsi. Pepsi had formed an alliance with Brahma, Brazil's largest beer company, and had been able to capture 25 percent of the cola market in São Paulo within

Will Chilled Food Charm U.S. Shoppers?

Marks & Spencer, the British retailing giant, pioneered the selling of fresh refrigerated foods in England. Under its St. Michael brand, it offers reasonably priced dishes such as salmon en croute with cream sauce, spaghetti carbonara, and crepes suzettes. Chilled food is not frozen food; rather, it is freshly prepared and needs to be heated or lightly cooked before serving.

Marks & Spencer planned to sell similar fresh refrigerated foods in the United States through its U.S. subsidiary's grocery stores. Bringing this concept over to the United States was not simple, however. Consider several aspects:

1. *Logistics.* Chilled foods spoil easily unless a constant temperature is maintained. Consequently, Marks & Spencer has developed close ties to farms and factories in the United Kingdom, using its own fleet of trucks, called the Cold Chain, to deliver these foods across Britain to 264 stores daily.

    The United States is much bigger, and maintaining a complex distribution system would be more difficult and costly here. Truckers would have to be aware of the nature of the foods they are delivering, and supermarkets would need to pay attention to shelf life, rotating stock more often. Moreover, the United States does not have much experience operating a smoothly functioning refrigerated trucking and warehouse system.

2. *Substitutes.* U.S. supermarkets stock other varieties of take-home and premium easy-to-prepare foods in delis, salad bars, and in-store bakeries. Wide choice in deli sections and in precooked carry-out meals make chilled foods less appealing.

3. *U.S. tastes.* U.S. food tastes may be more faddish, changing often compared with European tastes. And nutritional issues are more important here, too. Safeway,

---

a year. Because Brazil's per capita consumption is only about a quarter of U.S. consumption, there is much potential. Coca-Cola began introducing large plastic-bottle containers of Coke (2-liter bottles to Pepsi's 1.5 liters) and diet versions of Coke. Heavy investment and advertising are seen as the key to maintaining a 50 percent market share in this fast-growing market.

5. *Australia.* Coca-Cola purchased a 41 percent interest in Amatil, Australia's largest local Coke bottler. Australia has the third largest per capita consumption of Coke after the United States and Mexico, and Coca-Cola has a 53 percent market share there. It also formed a joint venture to buy out its bottler in New Zealand, a small market.

6. *India and China.* Coca-Cola's recent attention has been focused on India and China. In 1993, Coke purchased soft drink brands from Parle, India's leading soft drink manufacturer. It also entered into a joint venture for bottling and marketing with the Parle company owners. This was intended to give Coke a 60 percent market share in India and access to distribution for Coke products through Parle's 60 bottlers. Subsequently, Coke has had conflicts with its joint-venture partner over its desire to bottle Pepsi drinks in its plants.

In China, Coke has been careful to form joint ventures with state-owned bottling plants in key cities, gradually developing production capabilities and market share. Between 1985 and 1996, the share of foreign soft drink manufacturers in China grew from zero to nearly 20 percent, with Coke getting about two-thirds of that. By allying with powerful and well-connected government companies, Coke

for example, is offering take-out Chinese food in some stores. U.S. shoppers may be concerned with whether the chilled foods are low-fat or high in fiber, something that Marks & Spencer has not had to worry about with British customers.

4. *Price.* Chilled food is marketed as gourmet food and is accordingly high priced and sold to the young and affluent. This may limit its U.S. market to certain regions, such as downtown Manhattan in the state of New York.

5. *Suppliers.* In moving to the United States, Marks & Spencer will need to develop closer U.S.-based suppliers in a new food category. Will it be able to find quality suppliers as needed?

6. *Shopping habits.* The British shop every day in stores with perishables replenished every day. Refrigerated food may be less appealing to customers who prefer to shop once a week; frozen microwaveable food is much easier to store for a few days.

7. *Competition.* Other large U.S. food companies are also interested in the fresh-refrigerated food concept and are working with their own recipes. Campbell, for example, has a "Fresh Kitchen" line of refrigerated sauces, entrees, and desserts; Campbell uses a temperature-sensitive patch that turns blue if the food has not been refrigerated properly. Mary Kay Haben, a Kraft General Foods vice-president, has said, "It's an energizer to see how the chilled foods category has developed in the United Kingdom and to think about what it could be here [in the United States]." Nestlé has also entered this area, with its Carnation division selling refrigerated pastas and sauces, and its Nestlé Enterprises subsidiary test-marketing upscale entrees and salads under the "FreshNes" brand.

Sources: "Will U.S. Warm to Refrigerated Dishes?" *The Wall Street Journal,* June 18, 1989; and "Proud Sainsbury—a British Tradition," *Washington Post,* October 8, 1994.

---

obtains some insurance against a local backlash, which is inevitable as local soft drink manufacturers find their market share eroding.

Coca-Cola's current main focus is on developing countries. After having left because of Indian government controls over brand name usage, it returned to India, where soft drink consumption is growing at 20 percent a year, partly in response to Pepsi Cola's 39.9 percent share in a joint-venture, local bottling operation. Coca-Cola awarded its Coke bottling franchise in China to several government companies in order to win market share. Clearly, the company will do what it takes in each market to be successful. Thus, the fact that Coke is a global brand does not imply standardization of the entire marketing mix.[49]

GLOBAL R&D MANAGEMENT

Investing in R&D in technology-based industries is risky, as the R&D spending may not result in a commercially viable product. Typically, pharmaceutical industries, for example, spend over $300 million over a 10-year period to develop a new pharmaceutical drug, and seven of every 10 such drugs do not recover their R&D costs. In such an industry, large firms such as Ciba or Glaxo or Merck must conduct research in-house as well as buy ownership rights to R&D being carried on in small research boutiques, funding the research in return for rights to the ensuing product, if successful. In such cases, two approaches pioneered at Merck are useful:[50]

1. View the funding of R&D projects as the buying of **options,** with a small and limited downside risk (the loss of the R&D investment) being balanced by a large unlimited upside risk (if the project results in a successful blockbuster drug). That is, the company providing the funding has the right to back out of the project at any time if it deems that progress

is unsatisfactory, or, continuing funding at the next stage, to retain its rights to the fruits of the research. Using such a methodology, traditional-option pricing models can be used, with the necessary data points being (a) the total amount of investment in the R&D project; (b) the estimated value of future cash flows from the project if successful; (c) the time period over which the company (Merck) can exercise its option; (d) an internal investment hurdle rate (the cost of capital for projects of such a risk class); and (e) a variable that measures the volatility of investment in such a class of R&D projects, averaged across the company's and industry's experience over the recent past. Such analysis allows the pharmaceutical firm to determine whether the value of the option is greater than the investment to be made in the R&D project.

2. View and analyze several R&D projects as a group, subjecting them to probabilistic analysis to ascertain the range of future outcomes likely from funding one or more specific R&D projects. This approach is set out in Figure 9–7, a computer simulation model that analyzes pharmaceutical R&D projects. It uses as input estimated ranges (i.e., optimistic, average, and pessimistic numbers rather than point estimates) for a number of variables:

    a. Scientific and therapeutic effectiveness variables
    b. R&D project investments and downstream capital expenditures
    c. Profit models based on product prices and quantities, production, and selling costs
    d. Macroeconomic variables such as interest rates, inflation, and exchange rates

Using the model and the variables, the computer generates several iterations, each time drawing a number for each variable from the probabilistic distribution stored in its database. The final output is a series of probability distributions showing the range of expected outcomes. This exercise permits the firm to make better decisions about funding projects, continuing investment in projects, and deciding on the overall size of the R&D effort.

While health care reform creates uncertainty about the demand environment, the pharmaceutical industry across the United States and Europe provides sound lessons in how to innovate in an information-intensive industry whose fundamental technology is changing rapidly. Rebecca Henderson's study of U.S. and European pharmaceutical companies suggests that innovative success is due to three characteristics:[51]

1. Maintaining close ties to the scientific community at large so that the company continues to be knowledgeable about new information.

2. Betting on a wide variety and mix of projects across several technologies, disciplines, and fields.

3. Innovating in their R&D organization so that both product line and functional interests are borne in mind and balanced.

Rationale for Global R&D

Most multinationals are increasing the amount of R&D that they carry out at multiple locations around the world. One reason is that a firm's ability to innovate globally contributes to its overall international competitiveness.[52] Conducting global R&D also helps firms meet host-country national interests as it facilitates technol-

FIGURE 9–7   Merck's R&D Planning Model

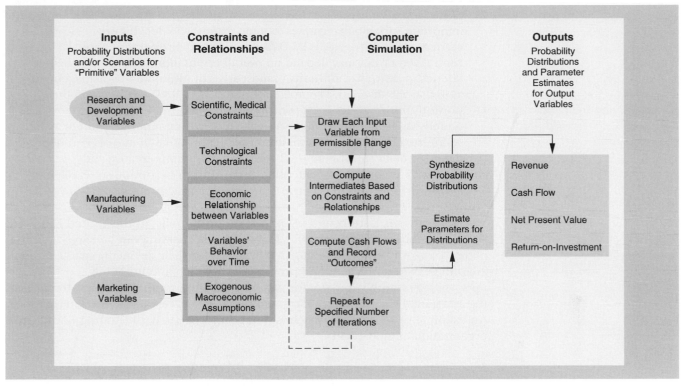

Source: Nancy Nichols, "Scientific Management at Merck," *Harvard Business Review,* January–February 1994, 95.

ogy transfer. Multinational foreign R&D is more possible because of the increased availability of skilled scientific talent and technology resources in other countries, enhanced intellectual property protection, and better communication capabilities that allow integration and supervision of a dispersed global R&D effort. Comparative advantage comes into play in the sense that different countries may have world-class capabilities. For example, top-notch scientists in specific areas of expertise might be best found in certain countries, such as the development of robotic technologies in Japan or pharmaceutical drug development in Switzerland.

Government incentives may also make it cheaper to conduct overseas R&D when specific program funding exists for technologies deemed in the national interest, such as Project Espirt to promote advanced technology computing in Europe. Availability of low-cost, high-quality research personnel, such as Russian research scientists, as well as the success of some multinationals with foreign R&D, may motivate other multinationals to attempt the same. Conducive government regulation and a hospitable climate to specific kinds of R&D may also play a part in deciding where to locate the R&D effort.

KEY ISSUES IN DEVELOPING A GLOBAL R&D CAPABILITY[53]

Linking product development for international markets with a global R&D network raises several critical issues for management:

1. *Where should the firm carry out the foreign R&D?* Relevant factors in picking overseas R&D sites include integration with existing manufacturing and sales operations; host-government regulations and requirements; and the

quality of local research infrastructure, including availability of scientists and the level and sophistication of the research efforts of local universities.

2. *How much autonomy should the firm grant the local R&D operation?* This important variable determines to some extent who decides what research is carried out at the overseas R&D facilities. Whether operations are centralized or not may depend on overall orientation of the firm, whether it tends to centralize authority in most areas of multinational management, as well as the distinctive competence of the local R&D facilities and their previous history of research contribution to the firm. Criticality of the underlying technologies being investigated, the amount of resources committed, and time pressure to complete the research may also influence the degree of centralization. Whether the research is creative and pathbreaking or more of extension and diffusion of previous research may also contribute to using central control or granting greater autonomy.

For example, a study of R&D labs of multinationals in the United Kingdom showed that most of them played a limited role in carrying out basic research, but played a major role in developing new products for their distinctive markets and in adapting existing products and processes for their markets.[54] One approach sets up specific research mandates for major overseas labs with a specific lab functioning as a global clearinghouse for the multinational's research efforts in that area. An example of such an approach is shown in Figure 9–8, illustrating Kao Corp.'s organization of global R&D.

3. *How should the firm coordinate global R&D?* A major goal of global R&D is the sharing of information. Information communication among scientists and engineers is critical to enhanced research productivity. Measures include periodic meetings and presentations, stage-gate and milestone achievement monitoring systems,[55] travel and telephone contacts, the creation of multinational project teams, job rotation across R&D labs in different countries, and a company culture that fosters open cross-national research communication. Stage-gate systems are procedures in which product development is broken up into a series of steps or stages. At the end of each stage are milestones that must be achieved in order to move on to the next stage. These function as gates: hence, the term *stage-gate system.*

Also relevant is whether a scientific culture prevails, which may cut across several national cultures, or whether local cultural norms prevail in affecting operations and effectiveness of the overseas R&D labs. Arnoud de Meyer[56] studied communication within the global R&D operations of 14 multinationals that together manage several thousand R&D employees. He summarizes communication and coordination mechanisms into several categories:

- ◆ *Socialization efforts* to create a corporationwide R&D culture, using devices such as temporary assignments in other labs; relatively constant traveling to facilitate face-to-face meetings; clear rules and procedures for matters such as documentation of work; and training programs.

- ◆ *Formal communication procedures* emphasizing meticulous reporting and documentation; databases of findings to facilitate researcher access to results in far-flung locations; and planning procedures involving researchers and managers from multiple sites.

- ◆ *Boundary-spanning roles* through the identification and use of special individuals who can facilitate transfer of information across R&D labs

FIGURE 9–8   **International R&D at Kao Corp.**

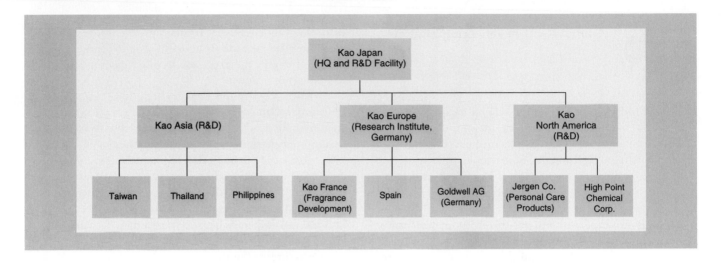

through travel, presentations, and special conferences; such individuals are relatively technologically able as well as experienced and reasonably high ranking in the hierarchy so that they can utilize informal channels and know who has information or should receive it.

◆ *Organizational structures,* including the use of central coordination staff and a network organization facilitated by electronic communication.

◆ *Electronic communication,* including the use of videoconferencing, E-mail, and shared databases. (However, de Meyer suggests that periodic face-to-face meetings are essential to supplement the use of electronic communication technologies.)

4. *Where do overseas R&D units fit into the organization structure?* Approaches include the use of matrixes, subordinating overseas R&D to headquarters R&D, and making it part of existing product-line or geographic divisions. The decisive factor should be whether the organization structure contributes to effectiveness and efficiency.

5. *What staffing and personnel issues must the firm confront?* How are people chosen for the overseas R&D labs? Who is the R&D manager? How important are criteria such as the ability to manage multicultural research professionals? Are scientific personnel chosen locally or in concert with regional and central headquarters? How are they assigned among projects to promote their own learning and growth?

As can be seen from the above discussion, many questions must be resolved in developing and managing the global R&D effort. This area is likely to increase in importance as multinationals increase their global manufacturing and marketing presence.

BENCHMARKING PRODUCTS AND PERFORMANCE

A common-sense approach to improvement is to compare one's products to those of competition, note the dimensions along which competitors' products are superior,

Global R&D in Emerging Markets

China and India can be interesting sites for locating part of a company's global R&D and product development efforts. One such company is Bio-Rad Labs, a medium-sized U.S. producer of analytical instruments, biotechnology materials and supplies, and clinical diagnostics. It has been conducting R&D and product development in China since 1986 and combines the knowledge and research abilities of Chinese scientists with its own capabilities in product development, manufacturing, and marketing. For example, since 1987 it has been marketing worldwide a DNA-cutting enzyme used in gene sequencing that was discovered by a scientist at the Shanghai Institute of Biochemistry. Its main problem is getting sufficient supplies because its agreement is to market product manufactured by the professor. In other cases it licenses the technology or product.

Critical steps in this strategy include (1) ensuring that the relevant Chinese state authorities permit the commercialization of the product; (2) maintaining close ties to Chinese hospitals, universities, labs, and state agencies so that Bio-Rad keeps abreast of the latest developments and is able to move decisively to sign up products or processes of interest; and (3) developing a salesforce that is both technically and managerially trained so that they can act as the eyes and ears of Bio-Rad and alert top management to potential licensing or marketing deals.

Once promising opportunities are identified, Bio-Rad provides funding, equipment and reagents, and additional

---

and use knowledge of these gaps to guide product improvement and future development.[57] Product line benchmarking can be divided into four main areas:[58]

Focus (market segmentation, product specifications, service levels)
Relative value (understanding end use in order to add value)
Market dominance (market share and relative return on investment)
"Looking end to end" (improving flow of information and physical product)

Benchmarking actually took root in the auto industry when U.S. automakers decided to study the manufacturing and quality-management practices of their Japanese competitors to gauge the magnitude of quality gaps and then use Japanese practices as a guideline to improve their operations and catch up to the Japanese. Motorola was another early user of benchmarking, defining it as a way for a company to compare its own products and practices against a best-in-class standard, and then use the information to improve its operations.

A recent study of the global auto industry[59] disclosed that out of 71 plants studied worldwide, Japan had five world-class plants (out of 9 studied), while France, Spain, and the United States had 3 (out of 11), 2 (out of 4) and 3 (out of 14), respectively. The United States had made enormous strides, with Japan having a 30 percent quality advantage over the United States in terms of customer complaints measured in parts per million: 193 for Japan versus 263 for the United States. The Japanese lead was attributed to manufacturing-process discipline and to supply-chain coordination. A benchmarking study on new-product development found that the most important differentiator of best practice was matching R&D to market needs, rather than speeding new products to market, which, in turn, was more important than management of R&D with constrained resources.[60]

Benchmarking in the Global Auto Industry

An example of applying benchmarking is the development of the first Ford Taurus. Ford studied competitors' products and copied what it deemed to be the best

technology to the scientist to support and speed up the research so that products can be developed rapidly. This network of trained sales people also allows Bio-Rad to sell equipment and supplies to the same research partner institutions and to modify its product line as Chinese priorities change. For example, when China began promoting the local production of semiconductors, Bio-Rad began selling quality-assurance and control equipment. Bio-Rad launched a wholly owned manufacturing operation in Beijing in 1994 to make and sell clinical diagnostic kits to hospitals across China as well as to export to other Asian countries.

India also offers low-cost but highly educated engineers and scientists and has emerged as a software development center for U.S. companies such as H-P and DEC. Many Western capital-equipment suppliers have begun to use India as a base for developing process engineering for new plants,

including Lurgi and Uhde (Germany), Inventa (Switzerland), Paul Wurth (Luxembourg), Chemtex and Bechtel (U.S.), and John Brown (U.K.). Chemtex helped Reliance India build both polyester and other acrylic yarn plants and its Bombay offices, which employ 572 people and service clients such as DuPont and Indian Organic in India and overseas. A major attraction is that salary costs are about one-tenth of Western levels. Bechtel has a similar operation that is connected by satellite link to its London offices so that design software and computer databases can be shared and close communication can be maintained. Indian government labs also offer a source of new technology, as DuPont has found working with the Indian Institute of Chemical Technology to develop petrochemicals for crop protection worldwide.

Sources: "India as an Engineering and R&D Base," *Business Asia*, April 24, 1995; and "The Business of Science," *Business China*, May 16, 1994.

features, such as seats on the Opel Senator in Europe, the Toyota Cressida's door firmness, and the Audi 5000's trunk closure. Ford first tore down their rivals' cars to the component level and studied them to determine where their rivals were superior. Then, Ford used reverse engineering to determine how to assemble the components in order to match the world-class performance of that feature in their competitors' cars.[61] The new Taurus models are being benchmarked against Chrysler's LH models, which are built in a Canadian facility, which, in turn, was benchmarked against Honda practices. At GM, the Saturn division was established after studying and incorporating the best practices of auto companies worldwide. Now Saturn has become the benchmark for other divisions within GM. When Toyota was developing the Lexus GS300, it studied the BMW 535i, which Donald W. Brown, national product manager at Toyota Motor Sales U.S.A., Inc., called "a driver's car in terms of steering response, handling, and brakes." Mercedes and BMW are still the global benchmarks against which handling and performance are measured. Toyota also studied the new Mercedes S-Class cars for their flexibility in accommodating different tastes in comfort, for example, in building an adjustable seat cushion for different drivers or adding a remote phone extension. Toyota, however, had to balance these additional features against the added weight and fuel consumption that an adjustable seat might entail or the difficulty in repairing a remote cell-phone jack without tearing down the car.

Since benchmarking can be difficult and can raise fears of competitive spying, several independent agencies have sprung up to conduct industrywide benchmarking, such as the International Benchmarking Clearinghouse, part of the American Productivity & Quality Center in Houston, Texas.

Quality as a Marketing Edge: ISO 9000

In Europe customers often ask their suppliers if they have received ISO 9000 certification. In the United States, firms who win the Baldrige Quality Awards trumpet their feat in full-page ads in the business press. The Japanese are known for their attention to quality and their insistence that suppliers reduce defective parts per million on incoming parts. In all these cases, the link between product quality and marketing is a strong one, as better quality produces results:

- Superior performance
- Reliability
- Durability
- Ease of maintenance
- Matching or exceeding competitors' product features
- Superior service: speedy, courteous, and competent after-sales service

Ultimately, superior quality can reduce a customer's life-cycle ownership costs, enhancing customer loyalty, repeat buying, and word-of-mouth advertising. Here we briefly examine ISO 9000 as a key quality standard in international marketing.

ISO 9000 subsumes a series of standards, promulgated by the International Standards Organization in Geneva, that allow the customer to specify the level of quality expected from suppliers while allowing independent third parties to certify that the required levels of quality are being achieved. The EU has mandated that certain product categories such as medical devices, telecommunications products, and construction products meet ISO 9000 guidelines. As more European customers gave preference to ISO 9000–certified suppliers, U.S. and Japanese firms also sought certification under the ISO 9000 guidelines and began to require that their suppliers also do so.

ISO 9000 has, therefore, become a de facto global standard. Firms, however, can go beyond ISO 9000 in areas such as responsiveness to customer requests (outlined in ISO 9004). It is useful to review how marketing considerations can be blended with more manufacturing-oriented quality processes.[62] ISO 9004 suggests the roles that marketing should play:

- Take the lead in establishing quality requirements for the company by determining customer needs and communicating them throughout the company.

- Translate customer needs into specifications, including performance and sensory characteristics, installation configuration, statutory and technical standards, packaging, and quality assurance.

- Set up an information system to monitor customer satisfaction and dissatisfaction and to feed back such pertinent information to facilitate design and manufacturing changes.

- Develop early warning systems to spot performance problems with new-product introductions, continuously monitor product performance against quality specifications such as reliability and safety, and track and analyze customer complaints so that corrective action can be taken in design and manufacturing.

How companies might move to obtain ISO 9000 certification is illustrated by the following example of the Foxboro Co.

Foxboro Seeks ISO 9000 Certification

The steps that Foxboro (a subsidiary of U.K.–based Siebe PLC) took to achieve ISO 9000 certification provide an overview of what a company can expect, as summarized below:[63]

1. Obtain senior management's commitment.

2. Create an ISO Steering Council, which puts in place the ISO development program, with allocation of adequate resources.

3. Educate the Steering Council on ISO 9000. They will be seen as The Experts and as the conduit for communicating ISO 9000 issues to the company. They will address questions about why ISO 9000, what is already in place in the company, and what remains to be done.

4. Evaluate and select a certification agent—either a U.S. certification agency, working with the British Standards Institute (BSI) or a European agency with U.S. offices, such as the Dutch DnV company.

5. Develop procedures for meeting ISO 9000 certification at the corporate, plant, and departmental levels.

6. Standardize and define documentation.

7. Educate all employees about ISO 9000.

8. Train internal quality-audit teams to monitor progress toward reaching certification standards and to monitor continued compliance.

9. Facilitate certification audit.

Foxboro's experience suggests that quality cannot be left to manufacturing, that marketing must work as a team with manufacturing and design and realize that marketing actions, such as salesforce behavior, promotion and advertising, and customer complaint handling all contribute to overall product quality.

SUMMARY

Three major issues for an international company are (1) deciding which new products to develop for global markets, (2) selecting the product line for individual foreign markets, and (3) deciding which foreign market to enter.

Several concepts are useful in developing new products: matching customer needs to a firm's knowledge base, basing products on core competence and common product platforms, and using both compression and experiential strategies in product development. As always, the starting point is consumer needs. Together with conditions of use and ability to buy, consumer needs indicate whether extension, adaptation, or completely new development of products and marketing mix is the appropriate strategy.

Ideas for new products should be sought in all major markets, both domestic and foreign. Distributors, licensees, joint-venture partners, and overseas subsidiary personnel are all potential sources. So are the competition, new patent filings, the plans of governments and international agencies, and the foreign buyer's consumption system.

Japanese product-development approaches offer some useful insights, particularly their use of supplier partnerships and working backward from a customer needs–based product configuration to actual product development, as illustrated by the Canon copier example.

Where the new-product development activity is located is important. Multiple sites may prevent the "not-invented-here" syndrome (in which all "foreign" ideas are rejected on the basis of not having been invented at home) from taking hold.

Fast-moving technology requires specialized product-development techniques, including a willingness to foster chaos and deliberately cannibalize one's own products, as suggested by Silicon Graphics' CEO.

R&D is typically carried out in a firm's largest markets, provided that the necessary scientific and technical personnel are available. It can be decentralized within the product line or across the product line. Sometimes basic R&D work is carried out in one or two central locations and applications of lesser import at more distant locations. R&D may be decentralized because of demands for local autonomy or in order to monitor technological developments in key lead markets. Government pressures and adaptation to the local market also influence the diffusion of R&D activity. Budgets and communication networks are tools helpful in coordinating geographically dispersed R&D labs.

New-product ideas must be screened to select the more promising ones for further development. Screening may be done successively at the national, regional, and headquarters levels. Screening criteria should include production and marketing considerations, as well as legal factors, financial returns, logistics constraints, and government views.

Foreign-market testing is another essential step. Representative markets may be used as a surrogate for testing in every potential foreign market.

Product development through consortia and strategic alliances is becoming more common. Cooperation may lead to agreement on common standards and may arise because of a strategic fit among complementary skills.

Incremental innovation—keeping ahead of competition through continuous improvements—is as important as implementing radical changes and major new-product introductions.

Product testing in foreign markets may be necessary because of different use conditions and government regulations. There are also promotional benefits from testing specifically for foreign markets.

A general question in product-line management is whether to replicate the domestic product line in foreign markets. Market similarity and similar client needs support such product-line extension. Other determinants of the product line for overseas markets include competitive response, government regulation, level of economic development of the market, the firm's growth targets, and the length of time it has been in a market.

The mode of market entry also affects product line. A joint-venture agreement, for example, may prohibit certain domestic products in a line from being introduced.

Adding and divesting products from the product line are equally important decisions. Legal considerations are involved, as well as cost, competition, market, and other financial considerations.

The use of international product life cycle (IPLC) information helps in the identification of promising foreign markets. Technology diffusion and the presence of competing technologies are important elements in assessing foreign-market potential according to the product life cycle.

Market potential must be balanced with market saturation assessment. Markets should be chosen so that significant market share gains can be achieved.

Competitive audits are important in arriving at realistic market share targets. Government policies also delineate the extent to which foreign firm participation is encouraged.

Risk, competition, probable returns, and resource commitments suggest which foreign markets the firm should enter. These factors form the basis of a suggested checklist.

Quality provides a marketer with an edge. Global benchmarking is one approach to ensuring that a new product does not fall far behind offerings from competitors. Obtaining world-class quality is an essential stage of product development, and meeting ISO 9000 certification is one way to ensure that processes to ensure quality production are in place.

QUESTIONS

9.1 Explain how consumer needs, conditions of use, and ability to buy affect new-product development.

9.2 Explain how Yamaha's attention to consumer needs enabled it to revitalize the worldwide piano market.

9.3   How are ideas diffused and new products adopted? How are these concepts relevant to new-product development in international markets?

9.4   What are some potential sources of ideas for new-product development? How can a firm obtain international inputs? Contrast the new-product possibilities of a company that only exports with those of a company that has several wholly owned foreign plants.

9.5   Where should new-product development activity be located? What are the advantages and disadvantages of decentralization?

9.6   What are some common patterns in global R&D? What pressures lead management to decentralize global R&D? How can such decentralized new-product development be coordinated and controlled?

9.7   How and where should new-product screening be done? What should be the role of the foreign subsidiary in this process?

9.8   How are marketing and production considerations used in screening new products for international markets?

9.9   Why are strategic alliances used in new-product development?

9.10 Analyze the Mitsubishi air conditioner example cited in the text as an example of incremental innovation. What are the benefits of using an incremental innovation approach?

9.11 Product testing must be done locally even if product development is centralized. Discuss.

9.12 Is market testing necessary before a firm introduces new products into foreign markets?

9.13 What are the determinants of a firm's product line in foreign markets?

9.14 How does the nature of a firm's involvement in foreign markets affect the composition of its product line? Contrast the product-line alternatives open to an exporter with those available to a licensor.

9.15 Discuss the decision to add or drop products to or from the product line in international markets. Explain how these considerations affected the divestment of the personal computer line by Zenith and its sale to Bull.

9.16 How does competition affect product-line composition? Illustrate your answer with reference to the luxury car segment in the United States.

9.17 What factors are relevant to the choice of foreign markets?

9.18 How does the use of international product life cycle (IPLC) information help screen foreign markets for possible entry?

9.19 What is a competitive audit? How can it help in choosing foreign markets for possible entry?

9.20 Analyze how and why Coca-Cola has been rethinking its foreign market entry choices.

9.21 What are the implications of ISO 9000 for a firm developing products for international markets?

9.22 How should a firm use benchmarking in developing world-class products?

ENDNOTES

1   See Kenichi Ohmae, "Getting Back to Strategy," *Harvard Business Review,* November–December 1988.

2   "Why Heinz Went Sour in Brazil," *Advertising Age,* December 5, 1988.

3   E. M. Rogers, *Diffusion of Innovation* (New York: Free Press, 1983).

4   Richard Normann and Rafael Ramirez, "From Value Chain to Value Constellation: Designing Interactive Strategy," *Harvard Business Review,* July–August 1993.

5   Marc Meyer and J. M. Utterback, "The Product Family and the Dynamics of Core Capability," *Sloan Management Review,* Spring 1993, 1–19.

6   Normann and Ramirez, 76.

7   Kathleen Eisenhardt and B. Tabrizi, "Accelerating Adaptive Processes: Product Innovation in the Global Computer Industry," *Administrative Science Quarterly* 40, no. 1 (March 1995).

8   G. Kalyanaram and V. Krishan, "Deliberate Product Definition: Customizing the Product Definition Process," *Journal of Marketing Research* 34 (May 1997): 276–285.

9   Howard R. Moskowitz and Sam Rabino, "Sensory Segmentation: An Organizing Principle for International Product Concept Generation," *Journal of Global Marketing* 8, no. 1 (1994).

10 S. Prokesch, "Mastering Chaos at the High-Tech Frontier: An Interview with

Silicon Graphics's Ed McCracken," *Harvard Business Review,* November–December 1993.

11   Charles Morris and C. H. Ferguson, "How Architecture Wins Technology Wars," *Harvard Business Review,* March–April 1993.

12   "Sandoz AG Is Foraging for Additional Food Holdings," *The Wall Street Journal,* February 21, 1995.

13   "At J&J, a Venerable Strategy Faces Questions," *The Wall Street Journal,* March 5, 1999.

14   Webster K. Cavenee and Raymond L. White, "The Genetic Basis of Cancer," *Scientific American,* March 1995, 72–79.

15   "Basel's Drug Giants Are Placing Huge Bets on U.S. Biotech Firms," *The Wall Street Journal,* November 29, 1995.

16   S. Kalagnanam and S. K. Schmidt, "Analyzing Capital Investments in New Products," *Management Accounting,* January 1996, 31–36.

17   T. Sasaki, "How the Japanese Accelerated New Car Development," *Long-Range Planning* 24, no. 1 (1991): 15–25.

18   Teruo Yamanouchi, "Breakthrough: The Development of the Canon Personal Copier," *Long-Range Planning* 22, no. 5 (1989): 11–21.

19   Sigwald J. Harryson, "How Canon and Sony Drive Product Innovation through Networking and Application-focused R&D," *Journal of Product Innovation Management* 14 (July 1997): 288–295.

20   Rajan R. Kamath and J. K. Liker, "A Second Look at Japanese Product Development," *Harvard Business Review,* November–December 1994.

21   Masaaki Kotabe and K. S. Swan, "Offshore Sourcing: Reaction, Maturation and Consolidation of U.S. Multinationals," *Journal of International Business Studies* 25, no. 1 (First Quarter 1994): 115–140; Jane Murray, M. Kotabe, and A. R. Wildt, "Strategic and Financial Performance Implications of Global Sourcing Strategy: A Contingency Analysis," *Journal of International Business Studies* 26, no. 1 (1995): 181–202; and P. Swamidass and M. Kotabe, "Component Sourcing Strategies of Multinationals: An Empirical Study of European and Japanese Multinationals," *Journal of International Business Studies* 24, no. 1 (1993): 81–99.

22   "The Outing of Outsourcing," *The Economist,* November 25, 1995, 57.

23   See H. Takeuchi and I. Nonaka, "The New New-Product Development Game," *Harvard Business Review,* January–February 1986.

24   "IBM, Toshiba to Produce Screens Jointly," *The Wall Street Journal,* August 31, 1989.

25   Ibid.

26   "Drug Firms Set Plan to Acquire Some ICI Assets," *The Wall Street Journal,* October 10, 1989.

27   George Stalk, Jr., "Time—The Next Source of Competitive Advantage," *Harvard Business Review,* July–August 1988, 49–50.

28   *The Wall Street Journal,* "L'Oreal to Buy Maybelline Inc.," December 11, 1995, and "Maybelline Provides a New Look That May Aid L'Oreal," December 12, 1995.

29   *The Wall Street Journal,* "Germany's Benckiser May Outbid L'Oreal's Offer to Buy Maybelline," January 15, 1995, and "German Firm Seeks U.S. Cosmetics Fix," January 16, 1996.

30   "Kimberley-Clark and P&G Face Global Warfare," *The Wall Street Journal,* July 18, 1995.

31   *The Wall Street Journal,* "Heinz Agrees to Acquire Quaker Oats' North American Pet-Food Operations," February 7, 1995; and "Quaker to Sell European Pet-Food Line to Dalgety of UK in $700 Million Pact," February 6, 1995.

32   Jennifer L. Aaker, "Dimensions of Brand Personality," *Journal of Marketing Research* 34 (August 1997): 347–356.

33   "How to Conquer China (and the World) with Instant Noodles," *The Economist,* June 17, 1995.

34   "CP Turns Chicken Feed into Vast Chinese Empire," *Asian Wall Street Journal,* December 8, 1993.

35   "How Grand Met Made Ailing Green Giant Jolly Again," *The Wall Street Journal,* June 6, 1995.

36   "A Canny Move by Koc," *Financial Times,* July 5, 1994.

37   John Quelch and David Kenny, "Extend Profits, Not Product Lines," *Harvard Business Review,* September–October 1994.

38   "Nintendo Goes Portable, Stores Go Gaga," *The Wall Street Journal,* October 4, 1989.

39   "Credit Card Firm a Success in Japan, Looks Overseas," *The Wall Street Journal,* July 26, 1989.

40   See "The Coming Traffic Jam in the Luxury Lane," *Business Week,* January

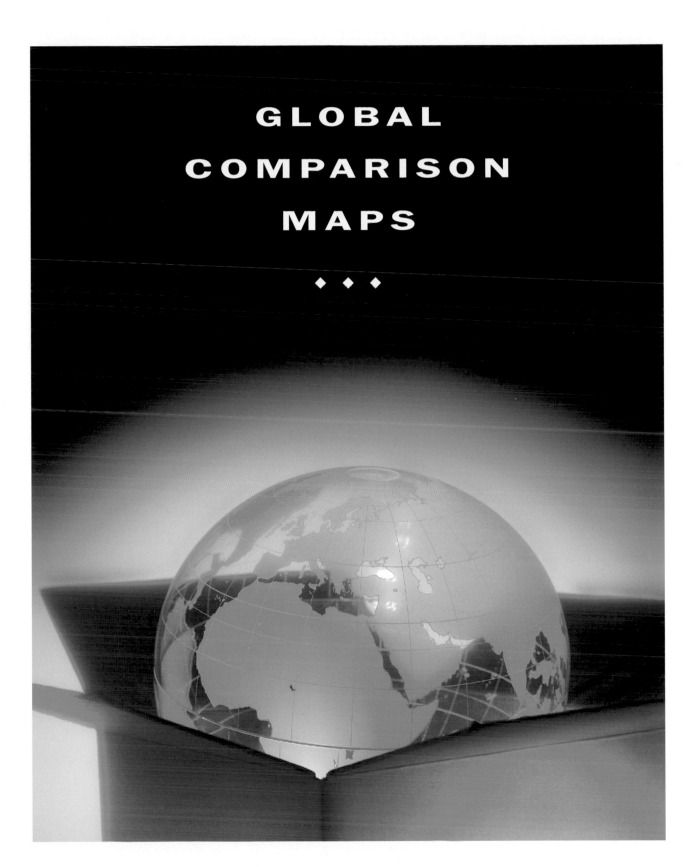

GLOBAL COMPARISON MAPS

◆ ◆ ◆

Maps

Manufacturing: A Major Factor in Gross Domestic Product

ANGUILLA
ANTIGUA & BARBUDA
BARBADOS
BELIZE
CAYMAN ISLANDS
DOMINICA
GRENADA
GUADELOUPE
MARTINIQUE
MONTSERRAT
ST. KITTS & NEVIS
ST. LUCIA
ST. VINCENT
TRINIDAD & TOBAGO
TURKS & CAICOS ISLANDS
U.K. VIRGIN IS.
U.S. VIRGIN IS.

ST. HELENA

BAHRAIN
GAMBIA
SÃO TOMÉ AND PRÍNCIPE

Source: *World Factbook*, 1997–1998

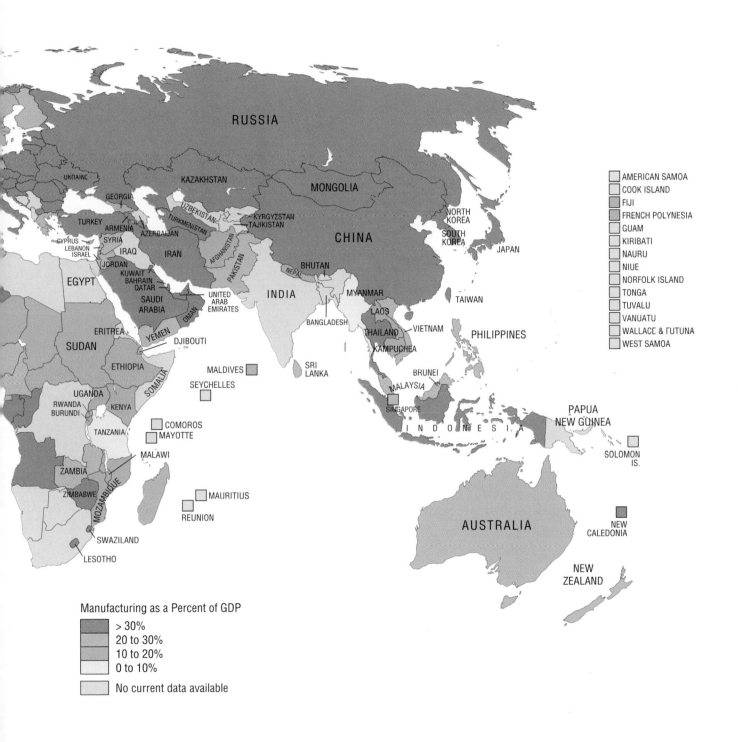

RUSSIA

UKRAINE

KAZAKHSTAN

MONGOLIA

GEORGIA

UZBEKISTAN

KYRGYZSTAN
TAJIKISTAN

NORTH
KOREA

TURKEY

ARMENIA

AZERBAIJAN

TURKMENISTAN

CHINA

SOUTH
KOREA

JAPAN

CYPRUS
LEBANON
ISRAEL

SYRIA

IRAQ

IRAN

AFGHANISTAN

JORDAN

KUWAIT
BAHRAIN
QATAR

PAKISTAN

BHUTAN

TAIWAN

NEPAL

EGYPT

SAUDI
ARABIA

OMAN

UNITED
ARAB
EMIRATES

INDIA

MYANMAR

LAOS

BANGLADESH

VIETNAM

PHILIPPINES

ERITREA

YEMEN

THAILAND

KAMPUCHEA

DJIBOUTI

SUDAN

MALDIVES

SRI
LANKA

BRUNEI

SEYCHELLES

MALAYSIA

ETHIOPIA

SOMALIA

SINGAPORE

UGANDA

KENYA

I N D O N E S I A

PAPUA
NEW GUINEA

RWANDA
BURUNDI

COMOROS

MAYOTTE

SOLOMON
IS.

TANZANIA

MALAWI

ZAMBIA

MAURITIUS

ZIMBABWE

REUNION

MOZAMBIQUE

AUSTRALIA

NEW
CALEDONIA

SWAZILAND

LESOTHO

NEW
ZEALAND

☐ AMERICAN SAMOA
☐ COOK ISLAND
☐ FIJI
☐ FRENCH POLYNESIA
☐ GUAM
☐ KIRIBATI
☐ NAURU
☐ NIUE
☐ NORFOLK ISLAND
☐ TONGA
☐ TUVALU
☐ VANUATU
☐ WALLACE & FUTUNA
☐ WEST SAMOA

Manufacturing as a Percent of GDP

☐ > 30%
☐ 20 to 30%
☐ 10 to 20%
☐ 0 to 10%

☐ No current data available

Economic Strength

Top World Economies (GDP in million dollars U.S.)

United States ($6,952,020)
Japan ($5,108,540)
Germany ($2,415,764)
France ($1,536,089)
United Kingdom ($1,105,822)
Italy ($1,086,932)
China ($697,647)
Brazil ($688,085)
Canada ($568,928)
Spain ($558,617)
South Korea ($455,476)
Netherlands ($395,900)
Australia ($348,782)
Russia ($344,711)
India ($324,082)
Iran ($310,000)
Switzerland ($300,508)
Argentina ($281,060)
Belgium ($269,081)
Taiwan ($257,000)
Mexico ($250,038)
Austria ($233,427)
Sweden ($228,679)
Indonesia ($198,079)
Denmark ($172,220)
Thailand ($167,056)
Turkey ($164,789)
Norway ($145,954)
South Africa ($136,035)
Saudi Arabia ($125,501)
Finland ($125,432)
Poland ($117,663)
Portugal ($102,337)
Israel ($91,965)
Greece ($90,550)
Malaysia ($85,311)
Singapore ($83,695)
Ukraine ($80,127)
Colombia ($76,112)

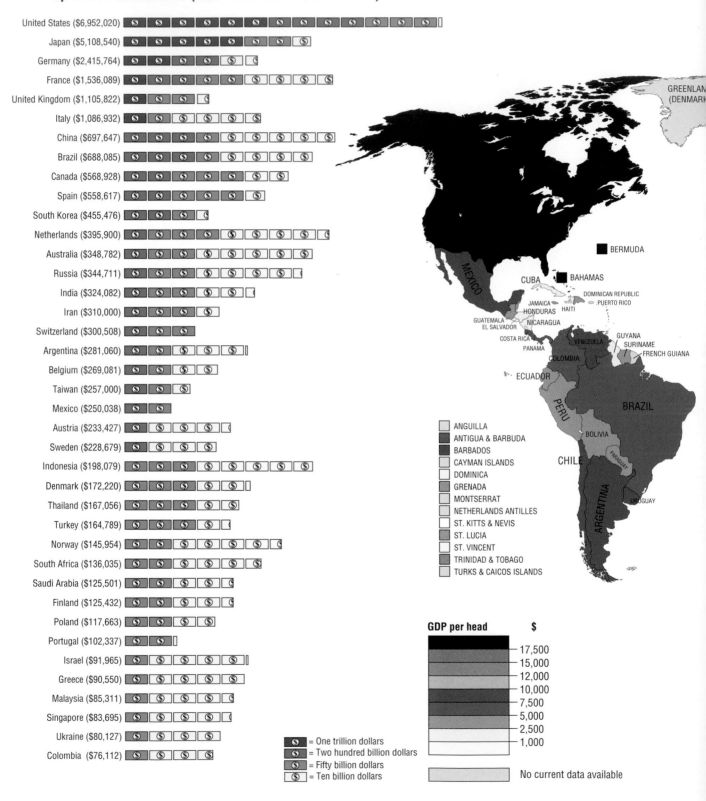

ANGUILLA
ANTIGUA & BARBUDA
BARBADOS
CAYMAN ISLANDS
DOMINICA
GRENADA
MONTSERRAT
NETHERLANDS ANTILLES
ST. KITTS & NEVIS
ST. LUCIA
ST. VINCENT
TRINIDAD & TOBAGO
TURKS & CAICOS ISLANDS

GREENLAND (DENMARK)
BERMUDA
MEXICO
CUBA
BAHAMAS
DOMINICAN REPUBLIC
JAMAICA
HONDURAS
HAITI
PUERTO RICO
GUATEMALA
EL SALVADOR
NICARAGUA
COSTA RICA
PANAMA
VENEZUELA
GUYANA
SURINAME
FRENCH GUIANA
COLOMBIA
ECUADOR
PERU
BRAZIL
BOLIVIA
CHILE
PARAGUAY
ARGENTINA
URUGUAY

$ = One trillion dollars
$ = Two hundred billion dollars
$ = Fifty billion dollars
$ = Ten billion dollars

GDP per head $
17,500
15,000
12,000
10,000
7,500
5,000
2,500
1,000

No current data available

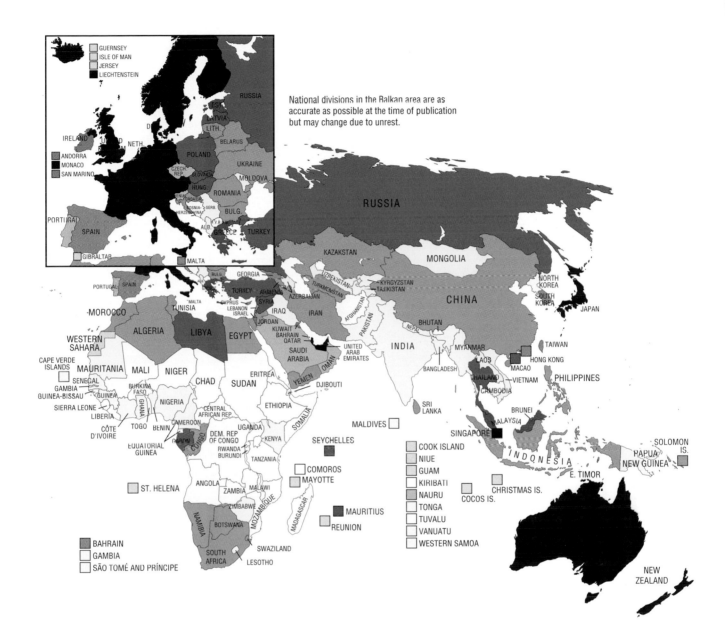

National divisions in the Balkan area are as accurate as possible at the time of publication but may change due to unrest.

Source: The *World Factbook*, 1997.

International Groupings

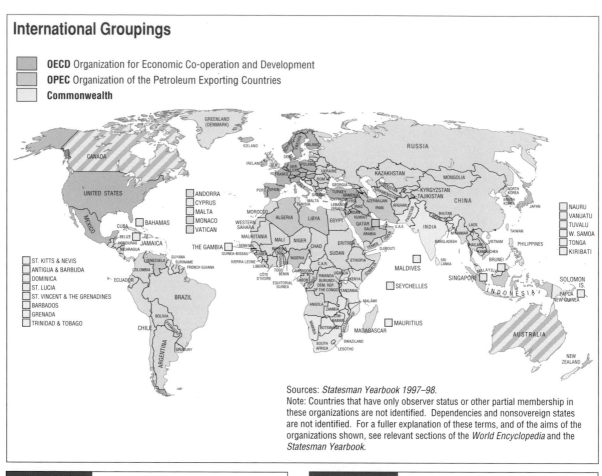

Sources: *Statesman Yearbook 1997–98*.
Note: Countries that have only observer status or other partial membership in these organizations are not identified. Dependencies and nonsovereign states are not identified. For a fuller explanation of these terms, and of the aims of the organizations shown, see relevant sections of the *World Encyclopedia* and the *Statesman Yearbook*.

MIDDLE-EAST

OAPEC Organization of Arab Petroleum Exporting Countries
Gulf Co-operation Council
The Arab League

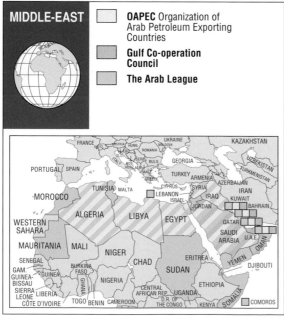

EUROPE-TRADE

EU European Union
EFTA European Free Trade Association
Association membership in EU

PACIFIC BASIN

AFTA ASEAN (Association of South East Asian Nations) Free Trade Area

MYANMAR — LAOS
THAILAND
CAMBODIA
VIETNAM
PHILIPPINES
BRUNEI
MALAYSIA
SINGAPORE
INDONESIA
PAPUA NEW GUINEA

AFRICA

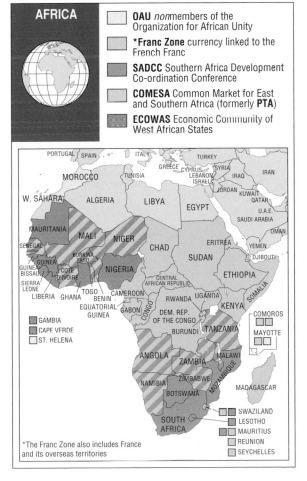

OAU *non*members of the Organization for African Unity

***Franc Zone** currency linked to the French Franc

SADCC Southern Africa Development Co-ordination Conference

COMESA Common Market for East and Southern Africa (formerly **PTA**)

ECOWAS Economic Community of West African States

PORTUGAL SPAIN ITALY TURKEY
GREECE CYPRUS SYRIA IRAN
MOROCCO TUNISIA LEBANON IRAQ
ISRAEL JORDAN KUWAIT
W. SAHARA ALGERIA LIBYA EGYPT QATAR
U.A.E.
SAUDI ARABIA
MAURITANIA OMAN
MALI NIGER
SENEGAL CHAD SUDAN ERITREA YEMEN
GUINEA BURKINA FASO DJIBOUTI
BISSAU GUINEA CENTRAL
SIERRA COTE NIGERIA AFRICAN REPUBLIC ETHIOPIA
LEONE D'IVOIRE
LIBERIA GHANA TOGO CAMEROON SOMALIA
BENIN RWANDA UGANDA
EQUATORIAL GABON KENYA
GUINEA CONGO DEM. REP. COMOROS
OF THE CONGO
BURUNDI TANZANIA MAYOTTE
GAMBIA
CAPE VERDE ANGOLA MALAWI
ST. HELENA ZAMBIA
NAMIBIA ZIMBABWE MOZAMBIQUE
BOTSWANA MADAGASCAR
SWAZILAND
SOUTH LESOTHO
AFRICA MAURITIUS
REUNION
SEYCHELLES

*The Franc Zone also includes France and its overseas territories

AMERICAS

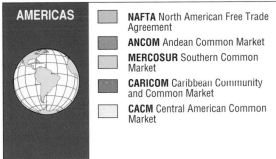

NAFTA North American Free Trade Agreement

ANCOM Andean Common Market

MERCOSUR Southern Common Market

CARICOM Caribbean Community and Common Market

CACM Central American Common Market

GREENLAND (DENMARK)

CANADA

UNITED STATES

MEXICO

BAHAMAS
CUBA
HAITI
DOMINICAN REPUBLIC
BELIZE JAMAICA
GUATEMALA NICARAGUA
EL SALVADOR
HONDURAS VENEZUELA GUYANA
COSTA RICA SURINAME
PANAMA COLOMBIA FRENCH GUIANA
ECUADOR
PERU BRAZIL
BOLIVIA
CHILE PARAGUAY
ARGENTINA URUGUAY

ST. KITTS & NEVIS
ANTIGUA & BARBUDA
MONTSERRAT
DOMINICA
ST. LUCIA
ST. VINCENT & THE GRENADINES
BARBADOS
GRENADA
TRINIDAD & TOBAGO

Services as a Portion of Gross Domestic Product

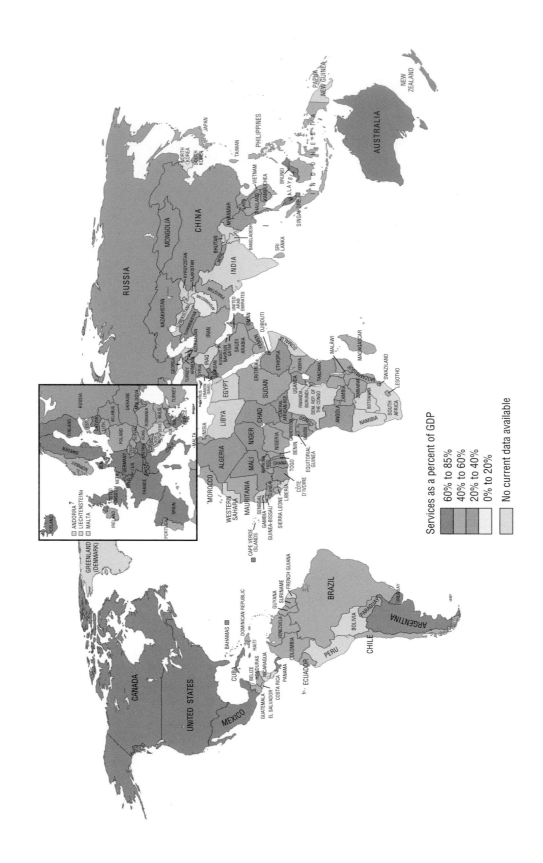

Services as a percent of GDP

- 60% to 85%
- 40% to 60%
- 20% to 40%
- 0% to 20%
- No current data available

Source: *The World Factbook 1997–98*

Religions of the World: A Part of Culture

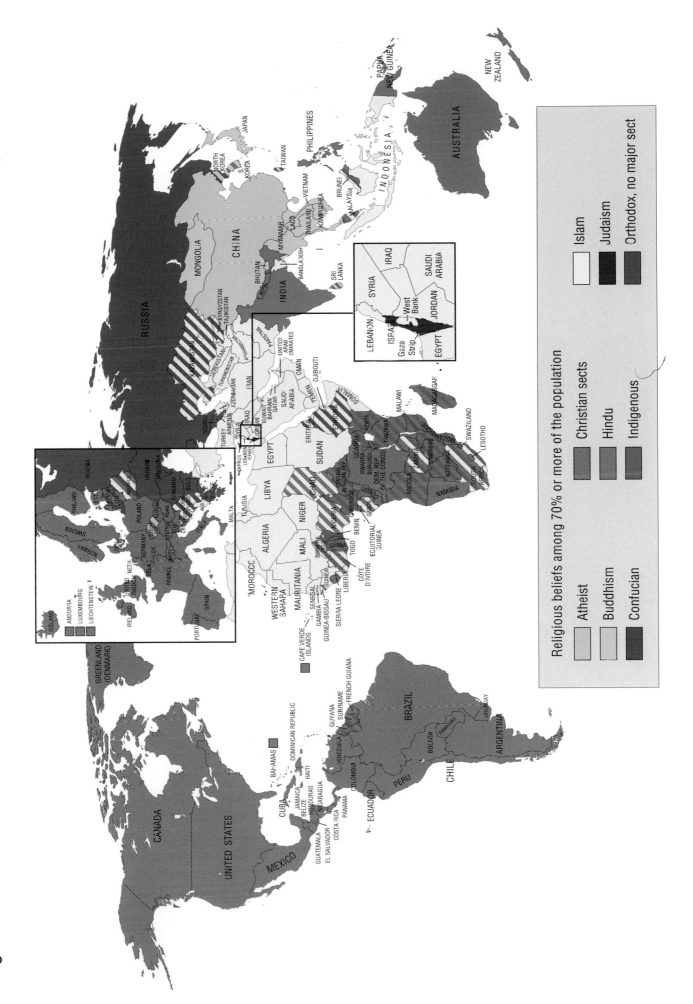

Religious beliefs among 70% or more of the population

Atheist	Christian sects
Buddhism	Hindu
Confucian	Indigenous
Islam	
Judaism	
Orthodox, no major sect	

Source: *The World Factbook 1997–98*

Emerging Economies of Central and Eastern Europe

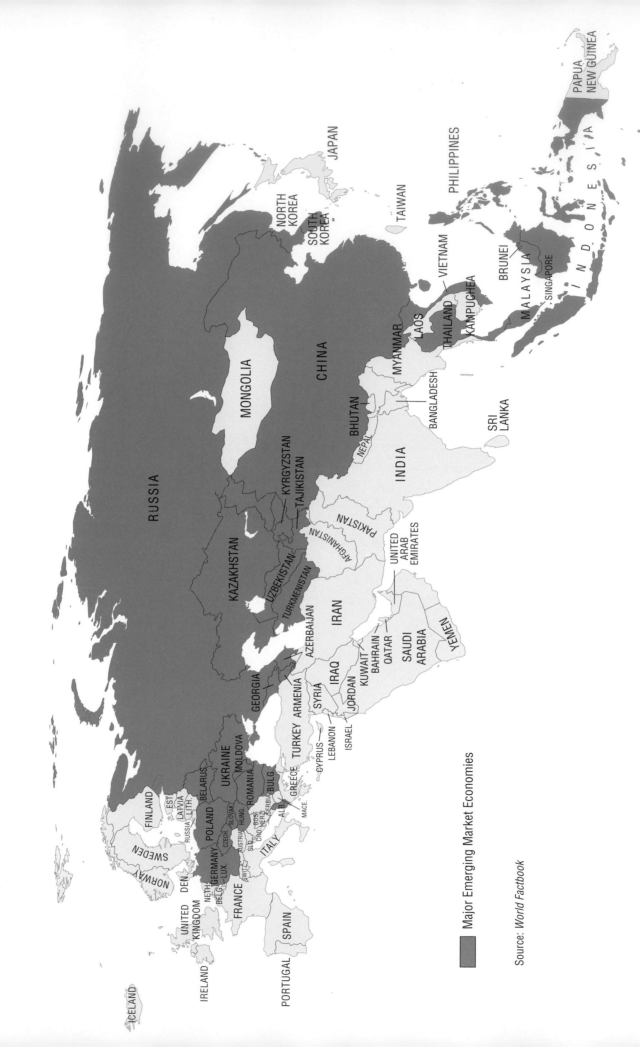

Major Emerging Market Economies

Source: *World Factbook*

Income Distribution: A Factor in Evaluating Market Potential

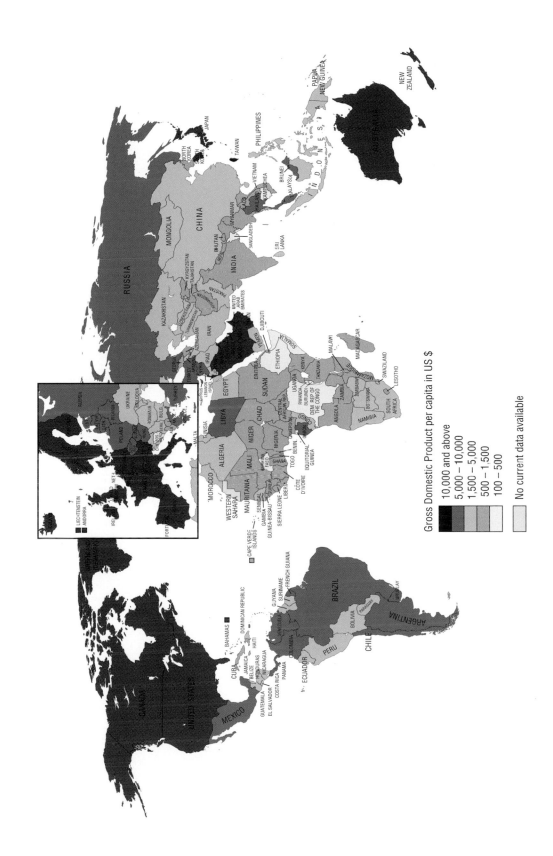

Gross Domestic Product per capita in US $

- 10,000 and above
- 5,000 – 10,000
- 1,500 – 5,000
- 500 – 1,500
- 100 – 500
- No current data available

Source: *The World Factbook 1997–98*

Inflation Rates and Interest Rates Around the World

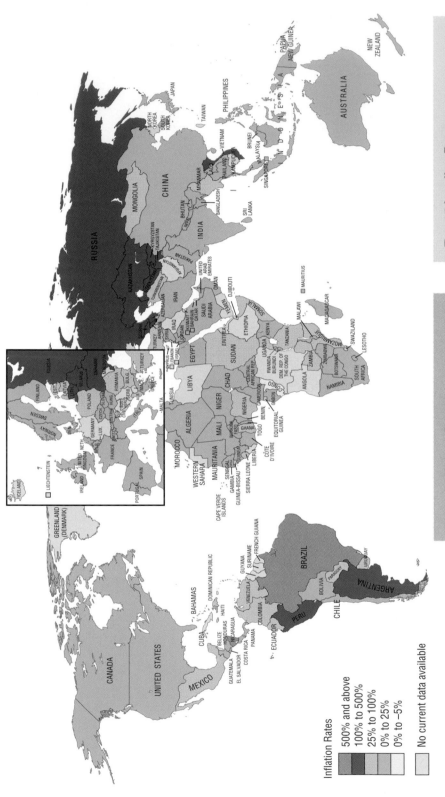

Inflation Rates

- 500% and above
- 100% to 500%
- 25% to 100%
- 0% to 25%
- 0% to –5%
- No current data available

Top 15 Inflation Rates

Nicaragua	1311.2	Belarus	136.7
Brazil	900.3	Azerbaijan	122.8
Peru	492.2	Uzbekistan	109.1
Argentina	317.2	Tajikistan	104.3
Ukraine	297.0	Vietnam	102.6
Georgia	228.3	Lithuania	102.3
Kazakhstan	150.2	Kyrgyzstan	100.9
Armenia	138.6		

Top 15 Lending Rates

Ukraine	250.3	Peru	53.6
Mongolia	233.6	Jamaica	49.5
Zambia	113.3	Venezuela	46.6
Uruguay	95.1	Ecuador	44.0
Bulgaria	64.1	Colombia	40.5
Lithuania	62.3	Slovenia	39.4
Latvia	55.9	Ethiopia	39.0
Bolivia	55.6		

Source: *World Development Report 1996*

The Cost of Living in the World's Major Business Cities

(in U.S. dollars)

■ Apartment rents
■ Public transportation
■ Food prices

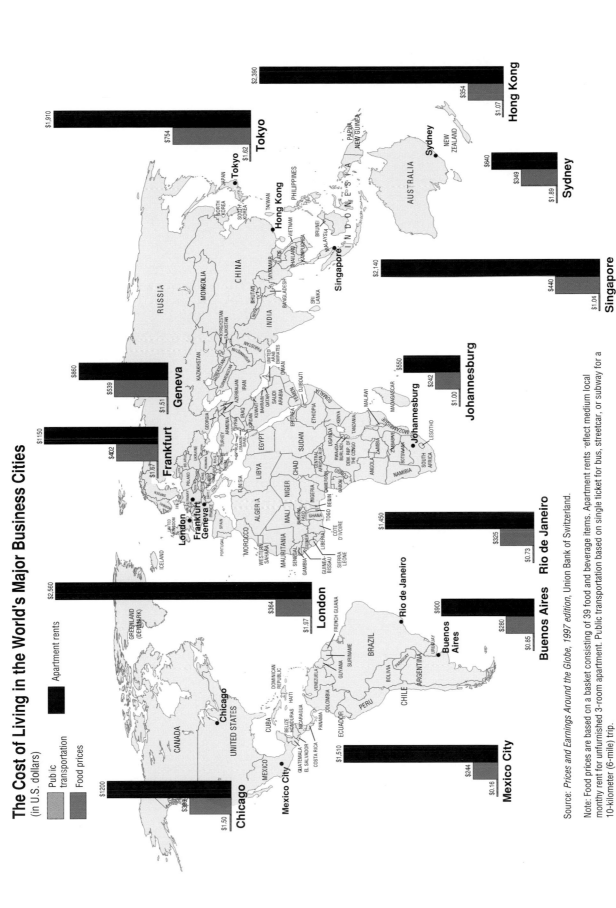

Chicago
$1200
$386
$1.50

Mexico City
$1,510
$244
$0.16

London
$2,560
$364
$1.97

Frankfurt
$1150
$402
$1.67

Geneva
$860
$539
$1.51

Tokyo
$1,910
$754
$1.62

Hong Kong
$2,390
$354
$1.07

Sydney
$640
$349
$1.89

Singapore
$2,140
$440
$1.04

Johannesburg
$550
$242
$1.00

Buenos Aires
$900
$280
$0.85

Rio de Janeiro
$1,450
$325
$0.73

Source: *Prices and Earnings Around the Globe, 1997 edition*, Union Bank of Switzerland.

Note: Food prices are based on a basket consisting of 39 food and beverage items. Apartment rents 'reflect medium local monthly rent for unfurnished 3-room apartment. Public transportation based on single ticket for bus, streetcar, or subway for a 10-kilometer (6-mile) trip.

30, 1989; and "Trying to Crack the Luxury Car Market," *The Wall Street Journal,* August 7, 1989.

41 "Luxury Cars: Revving up Quietly," *The Economist,* October 1, 1994.

42 See "Zenith's Return to Roots Is Risky Plunge," *The Wall Street Journal,* October 5, 1989; and "Super Television," *Business Week,* January 30, 1989.

43 "Bull to Acquire Zenith Data," *Electronic News,* October 9, 1989.

44 "Glaxo Plans Non-prescription Ulcer Drug for U.S., Intensifying Industry Battle," *The Wall Street Journal,* December 23, 1987.

45 "Abortion Pill Is Expected to Generate U.S. Black Market, More Controversy," *The Wall Street Journal,* October 31, 1988.

46 *Business Week,* August 31, 1984, 131.

47 Adrian B. Ryans, "Strategic Market Entry Factors and Market Share Achievement in Japan," *Journal of International Business Studies,* Fall 1988.

48 Kenichi Ohmae, "Planting for a Global Harvest," *Harvard Business Review,* July–August 1989. See also Hermann Simon, "Market Entry in Japan: Barriers, Problems and Strategies," *International Journal of Research in Marketing* 3, no. 2 (1986).

49 See "Soft Drinks Get the Hard Sell in Europe," *The Wall Street Journal,* November 21, 1988; "Foreign Fizz," *The Economist,* July 15, 1989; "Pepsi Aims to Liberate Big Market in Brazil from Coke's Domination," *The Wall Street Journal,* November 30, 1988; "France's Pernod-Ricard to Sell to Coke," *The Wall Street Journal,* May 26, 1989; and "Coca-Cola Continuing Overseas Push Plans to Acquire New Zealand Bottler," *The Wall Street Journal,* August 10, 1989.

50 Nancy Nichols, "Scientific Management at Merck," *Harvard Business Review,* January–February 1994.

51 Rebecca Henderson, "Managing Innovation in the Information Age," *Harvard Business Review,* January–February 1994.

52 L. Franko, "Global Corporate Competition: Who's Winning, Who's Losing, and the R&D Factor As One Reason Why," *Strategic Management Journal* (1989): 449–474.

53 Joseph L. C. Cheng and D. S. Bolon, "The Management of Multinational R&D," *Journal of International Business Studies* 24, no. 1 (1993): 1–18.

54 Robert Pearce and M. Papanastassiou, "R&D Networks and Innovation: Decentralized Product Development in Multinational Enterprises," *Univ. of Reading, Discussion Papers in International Investment and Business Studies* VIII, Series B, no. 204 (October 1995).

55 Robert G. Cooper, "Stage-Gate Systems: A New Tool for Managing New Products," *Business Horizons,* May–June 1990, 44–54.

56 Arnoud de Meyer, "Tech Talk: How Managers Are Stimulating Global R&D Communication," *Sloan Management Review,* Spring 1991.

57 For some background readings on benchmarking, see: Mohamed Zairi and R. Hutton, "Benchmarking: A Process-Driven Tool for Quality Improvement," *TQM Magazine* 7, no. 3 (1995): 35–40; A. S. Walleck, et al., "Benchmarking World-Class Performance," *The McKinsey Quarterly,* no. 1 (1991); and R. C. Camp, "A Bible for Benchmarking by Xerox," *Financial Executive,* July/August 1993.

58 "Benchmarking Goes Global: Chemical Companies Are Shifting Away from Cost-Cutting and Looking at Practices in Product Development and Globalization," *Chemical Marketing Reporter,* April 10, 1995.

59 "Japan Still Rules the Lean World," *Industry Week,* April 3, 1995.

60 Edward B. Roberts, "Benchmarking the Strategic Management of Technology— I," *Research-Technology Management* 38, no. 1 (January/February 1995): 44–56.

61 "The Truth Behind Benchmarking," *Ward's Auto World,* May, 1993, 41.

62 H. Michael Hayes, "ISO 9000: The New Strategic Consideration," *Business Horizons,* May–June 1994, 52–60; also see A. Faye Borthick and H. P. Roth, "Will Europeans Buy Your Company's Products?" *Management Accounting,* July 1992, 28–32.

63 "How One U.S. Firm Attained ISO 9000 Certification," *Business International,* September 28, 1992.

FURTHER READINGS

Ayal, Igal. "International Product Life Cycle: A Reassessment and Product Policy Implications." *Journal of Marketing,* Fall 1981.

Bilkey, Warren J., and Erik Nes. "Country-of-Origin Effects on Product Evaluations." *Journal of International Business Studies,* Spring–Summer 1982.

Borthick, A. Faye, and H. P. Roth. "Will Europeans Buy Your Company's Products?" *Management Accounting,* July 1992, 28–32.

Camp, R. C. "A Bible for Benchmarking by Xerox." *Financial Executive,* July–August 1993.

Cheng, Joseph L. C., and D. S. Bolon. "The Management of Multinational R&D." *Journal of International Business Studies* 24, no. 1 (1993): 1–18.

Cooper, Robert G. "Stage-Gate Systems: A New Tool for Managing New Products." *Business Horizons,* May–June 1990, 44–54.

Eisenhardt, Kathleen, and B. Tabrizi. "Accelerating Adaptive Processes: Product Innovation in the Global Computer Industry." *Administrative Science Quarterly* 40, no. 1 (March 1995).

Giddy, Ian H. "The Demise of the Product Life Cycle in International Business Theory." *Columbia Journal of World Business* (Spring 1978).

Hayes, H. Michael. "ISO 9000: The New Strategic Consideration." *Business Horizons,* May–June 1994, 52–60.

Henderson, Rebecca. "Managing Innovation in the Information Age." *Harvard Business Review,* January–February 1994.

Johansson, Johny K., S. P. Douglas, and I. Nonaka. "Assessing the Impact of Country-of-Origin on Product Evaluation: A New Methodological Perspective." *Journal of Marketing Research* 22 (November 1985).

Johansson, Johny K., and Hans B. Thorelli. "International Product Positioning." *Journal of International Business Studies* 16, no. 3 (Fall 1985).

Kalagnanam, S., and S. K. Schmidt. "Analyzing Capital Investments in New Products." *Management Accounting,* January 1996, 31–36.

Kamath, Rajan R., and J. K. Liker. "A Second Look at Japanese Product Development." *Harvard Business Review,* November–December 1994.

Keegan, Warren. "Multi-National Product Planning: Strategic Alternatives." *Journal of Marketing,* January 1969.

Keshani, Kamran. "Beware the Pitfalls of Global Marketing." *Harvard Business Review,* September–October 1989.

Kotabe, Masaaki, and K. S. Swan. "Offshore Sourcing: Reaction, Maturation, and Consolidation of U.S. Multinationals." *Journal of International Business Studies* 25, no. 1 (First Quarter 1994): 115–140.

Meyer, Marc, and J. M. Utterback. "The Product Family and the Dynamics of Core Capability." *Sloan Management Review,* Spring 1993, 1–19.

Moskowitz, Howard R., and Sam Rabino. "Sensory Segmentation: An Organizing Principle for International Product Concept Generation." *Journal of Global Marketing* 8, no. 1 (1994).

Murray, Jane, M. Kotabe, and A. R. Wildt. "Strategic and Financial Performance Implications of Global Sourcing Strategy: A Contingency Analysis." *Journal of International Business Studies* 26, no. 1 (1995): 181–202.

Nichols, Nancy. "Scientific Management at Merck." *Harvard Business Review,* January–February 1994.

Normann, Richard, and Rafael Ramirez. "From Value Chain to Value Constellation: Designing Interactive Strategy." *Harvard Business Review,* July–August 1993.

Ohmae, Kenichi. "Getting Back to Strategy." *Harvard Business Review,* November–December 1988.

Ohmae, Kenichi. "Planting for a Global Harvest." *Harvard Business Review,* July–August 1989.

Onkvisit, Sak, and John J. Shaw. "An Examination of the International Product Life Cycle and Its Application within Marketing." *Columbia Journal of World Business,* Fall 1983.

Pearce, Robert, and M. Papanastassiou. "R&D Networks and Innovation: Decentralized Product Development in Multinational Enterprises." *University of Reading, Discussion Papers in International Investment and Business Studies,* Series B, vol. VIII, no. 204 (October 1995).

Prokesch, S. "Mastering Chaos at the High-Tech Frontier: An Interview with Silicon Graphics' Ed McCracken." *Harvard Business Review,* November–December 1993.

Quelch, John, and David Kenny. "Extend Profits, Not Product Lines." *Harvard Business Review,* September–October 1994.

Roberts, Edward B. "Benchmarking the Strategic Management of Technology—I." *Research-Technology Management* 38, no. 1 (January/February 1995): 44–56.

Root, Franklin. *Entry Strategies for International Markets.* Lexington, MA: Lexington Books, 1987.

Sasaki, T. "How the Japanese Accelerated New-Car Development." *Long-Range Planning* 24, no. 1 (1991): 15–25.

Swamidass, P., and M. Kotabe. "Component Sourcing Strategies of Multinationals: An Empirical Study of European and Japanese Multinationals." *Journal of International Business Studies* 24, no. 1 (1993): 81–99.

Terpstra, Vern. "International Product Policy: The Role of Foreign R&D." *Columbia Journal of World Business,* Winter 1977, 24–32.

Walleck, A. S., et al., "Benchmarking World-Class Performance." *The McKinsey Quarterly,* no. 1 (1991).

Wind, Yoram. "The Myth of Globalization." *Journal of Marketing,* Spring 1986.

Yamanouchi, Teruo. "Breakthrough: The Development of the Canon Personal Copier." *Long-Range Planning* 22, no. 5 (1989): 11–21.

Zairi, Mohamed, and R. Hutton. "Benchmarking: A Process-Driven Tool for Quality Improvement." *TQM Magazine* 7, no. 3 (1995): 35–40.

Grand Met: The Development of World Brands

Grand Met (GM) is a British conglomerate whose lines of business include wines and spirits, beer, dog food, a chain of stores selling contact lenses and glasses, and over 1,700 retail betting shops in the United Kingdom and Ireland. GM once owned the Intercontinental chain of hotels. In 1987 its revenue totaled nearly $10 billion, divided as follows:

	Percent of Sales
Wines and Spirits	39%
Brewing and Retailing	20
Foods	16
Consumer Products	19
Hotels	6

In October 1988 the company launched a takeover bid for Pillsbury, the U.S. food products conglomerate based in Minneapolis, for $5.2 billion. The successful acquisition transformed GM into one of the world's largest food companies, ranking with Nestlé and Philip Morris. Earlier, it had announced the sale of its Intercontinental Hotel subsidiary to a Japanese group, Seibu/Saison, for $2.3 billion, thus refocusing its business and gathering resources for the Pillsbury bid.

The Pillsbury Acquisition

What does GM get by buying Pillsbury? Pillsbury is a $10 billion company, deriving 35 percent of its sales from foods. Its leading brands are Green Giant, Pillsbury, Le Sueur, Jeno's, Bumble Bee Seafood, and Häagen-Dazs. The remaining 65 percent of its sales come from its restaurants, which are Burger King, Bennigan's, and Steak & Ale. About 86 percent of Pillsbury's sales, by volume, come from products with a number one or number two market share.

GM hopes to use its retailing skills to increase Pillsbury food sales overseas, especially in Europe, where Green Giant and Haagen-Daz are already well known. It believes that what it learned in selling liquor—about appealing to the psyche of the buyers—applies equally to selling food. In marketing liquor, image matters at least as much as price.

"Do you promote microwave pizza like you do Absolut vodka? Yes. A lot of the basics are the same," claims one GM executive. Pillsbury pioneered microwave foods, and GM

plans to capitalize on these items because they are just beginning to catch on in Europe. Its strength is its ability to add value to brands by pushing them through its strong distribution networks and throwing the weight of increased advertising behind them, thus creating the required image that is viewed as so important to gaining market share. Lower costs are also achievable, as the acquisition makes GM the eighth largest international food processor. The company has always been run with few staff personnel: Ian Martin, who became Pillsbury's chairman, says, "The primacy of the line manager is one of our most fundamental beliefs." And, "The three basics are to cut costs, build brands, and develop new products—in that order." GM has a central staff in London and at U.S. headquarters in New Jersey of just 160, while Pillsbury, with half GM's revenues, had a staff of 350.

GM is also ready to drop the weak brands. After acquiring Pillsbury, it decided to sell off Bumble Bee—which falls behind Starkist (Heinz Co.) and Chicken of the Sea—and Van de Kamp—which falls behind Gorton's (General Mills) and Mrs. Paul's (Campbell Soup). These product lines might appeal to other foreign companies wanting an immediate entry into the U.S. market, as well as to U.S. competitors such as Campbell Soup and ConAgra.

The Burger King Challenge

Burger King represents the biggest challenge and gamble, however. GM is a restaurateur, owning 2,000 pubs and franchising 4,500 more pubs in the United Kingdom; it had also revived the failing chain of Berni's Steak Houses, in many cases converting them to the "Pastificio" Italian-style restaurant chains. It expanded into Germany by buying Wienerwald, a 231-store, spit-roasted chicken chain. But selling "bangers and mash" in the United Kingdom is a far cry from competing with McDonald's worldwide. There are about 240 units in the Berni chain of restaurants compared to about 5,600 Burger Kings.

Of the 5,600 Burger King stores, only about 600 are overseas; McDonald's overseas stores constitute about 25 percent of its total. The Burger King stores were unevenly managed, considered by observers to be scruffy looking at times. In fast foods, it is important to provide an identical experience from store to store, hence the need for carbon-copy consistency. Burger King franchise owners have complained of shoddy service and high prices on food supplies provided by the Pillsbury-owned subsidiary Distron. Pillsbury has had four separate advertising campaigns in four years for Burger King and spent $164 million on advertising for it, compared to $650 million spent at McDonald's. But per-store sales have actually fallen:

Burger King Store Statistics

	1988	1987
Worldwide Sales	$5.4 billion	$5.05 billion
Number of Stores	5,687	5,179
Average Store Sales, U.S.	$996,000	$1,020,000

World's Leading Liquor Concerns Based on 100 Top-Selling Brands (Millions of Cases)

Grand Metropolitan	34.8
Guinness	30.9
Seagram	22.8
Bacardi	21.8
Suntory	17.9
Allied-Lyons	17.3
Pernod-Ricard	12.5
Brown-Forman	11.3
American Brands (Jim Beam)	9.2
Pedro Domecq	7.7

Barry Gibbons, the GM executive put in charge of turning around Burger King, plans to focus on cleanliness and good service. He notes, "A bad cup of coffee at the end of a meal is just as damaging as a bad advertising campaign." He laid off about 550 management personnel, consolidating field office marketing, financial, and personnel functions at headquarters and doing away with a couple of layers of staff functions. He also began searching for a new ad agency for the $150 million plus account. Gibbons wants to attract the "snack and grazing" set, which means diversifying the menu.

He also wants routine problems handled at regional offices: "My philosophy is that if a snake walks through the door, kill it; don't call McKinsey & Co." He split up the food service subsidiary, Distron, into separate procurement and distribution operations, allowing franchisees to choose services that they needed; some 40 percent of the franchisees were already buying their supplies elsewhere. Since GM owns only 15 percent of the Burger King franchises, maintaining conformity is difficult. Communication and morale building are necessary. Accordingly, Gibbons has videotaped talks and delivered some in person to the firm's employees.

GM does have some experience with franchising through its pubs in the United Kingdom, and through the 1,300 Pearle Vision outlets that it operates in the United States. Sales increases could come from overseas expansion and from menu changes, such as providing breakfasts at Burger King.

The Alcohol Business: A Mature Product Line?

GM's liquor business is a mature business with low growth prospects. GM is the world's largest liquor-marketing concern, selling 34.8 million cases in 1987.

Liquor consumption is declining at about 2 percent annually in the developed countries. As a result, Seagram, for example, is de-emphasizing liquor and moving into other product lines such as orange juice, acquiring Tropicana Products for $1.2 billion. Seagram also moved to dominate the wine cooler business, where it has a 36 percent market share. It is refocusing its portfolio of brands, dropping poor-selling brands, such

as Calvert whiskey and gin and Wolfschmidt and Crown Russe vodkas, and aiming for a higher-priced, loftier image by concentrating on high-margin brands such as Chivas Regal. As part of this strategy, Seagram purchased Martell and Cie., the prestigious French cognac maker, by beating out GM in a bidding contest. GM ended up with a profit on its 20 percent stake in Martell and retained rights to distribute Martell in East Asia.

Acquisitions in Wines and Spirits

GM, on the other hand, increased its market share in the liquor business by acquiring Heublein for $1.2 billion in 1987 to gain control of Smirnoff vodka. The purchase was negotiated in four days, at about 11 times earnings. (In comparison, Seagram paid 38 times earnings for the French cognac company Martell.) GM acts speedily when necessary; it is a strategically opportunistic company. It has been successful in marketing original creations such as Bailey's, a milky-sweet concoction of cream and Irish whiskey—now the world's best-selling liqueur.

GM also expanded into the U.S. wine business by purchasing Almaden vineyards for $128 million. In 1989 it followed up by acquiring Christian Brothers for over $100 million. Christian Brothers controls 1,200 acres in the Napa valley, about 3 percent of the wine grape–growing area. Its Greystone cellars in St. Helena draw 400,000 visitors a year, making it California's second-largest tourist destination after Disneyland. This purchase allowed GM to become the largest owner of vineyards in the Napa valley. Christian Brothers had not been faring well, with its wine shipments declining 14 percent in 1988 and brandy shipments down 21 percent. Christian Brothers' brandy is number two in the United States; Gallo is number one.

GM clearly expects to do a better job of marketing than Christian Brothers did. Prior to the Christian Brothers acquisition, GM had 13 percent of the U.S. table wine market, and

12 percent of the spirits market. An insurance policy comes in the form of the 1,200 acres of Napa valley, a real estate position that is unique.

GM's major liquor brands include Smirnoff and Popov Vodka; J&B; Bailey's Irish Cream; Gilbey's gin and vodka; Croft sherry and port; Almaden, Inglenook, and Lancers wine; Le Piat d'Or, a table wine exported from France; Black Velvet Canadian whiskey; Dreher Brandy (Brazil); Malibu, a coconut rum; and Heublein cocktails. In addition, it is the importer of Cinzano, Absolut vodka, and Cuervo tequila.

Global Competition in Liquor: Pernod of France

As part of this acquisition strategy, GM also tried to gain control of Irish Distillers PLC, the sole maker of Irish whiskey. Its opponent was Pernod-Ricard S.A., of France. Both Pernod and GM were trying to gain control of the Irish whiskey market segment, including two of the best-known independent brands, Jameson and Bushmills. As Pernod's president, Thierry Jacquillat, has noted, "You can buy any of several bourbon whiskey companies, but there's just one Irish whiskey company."

Pernod-Ricard was formed when France's two leading makers of pastis (a strong anise-flavored aperitif) merged in 1975. Pernod is now the biggest seller of alcoholic drinks in Europe, and third largest in the world, after GM and Seagram. It bought out 18 competitors in France and abroad in recent years. Equally significantly, it has focused on soft drinks. In 1975, 75 percent of its revenues came from alcoholic drinks; by 1987, 64 percent did, and the goal is to reduce that to 50 percent. Its big seller is Orangina, a fizzy orange juice drink. Pernod also marketed Coca-Cola in France before deciding to sell the franchise back to Coca-Cola Co.

Pernod's need for Irish Distillers was perhaps greater than GM's. Pernod is not a global player and lacks international brands. Its Ricard anisette is the world's third largest-selling brand but almost unknown outside of France. "As consumers switch to international brands, domestic products such as aniseed spirits in France are in decline," notes Michelle Proud, a stock analyst at NatWest. Pernod did acquire Austin Nichols Co., the maker of Wild Turkey bourbon, in 1980. Its other well-known brands are Dubonnet aperitif and Biscuit cognac. If Pernod had failed in its acquisition bid for Irish Distillers, it could well have been bought out because it becomes harder for an independent firm with a few brands to succeed in a global marketplace dominated by global brands.

GM's reasons for wanting to buy Irish Distillers were similar to its motives in its other acquisitions: Irish Distillers had no international distribution network, and GM hoped to increase profits by marketing whiskies such as Jameson through its worldwide distribution network. "Putting another brand through its existing distribution network would cost next to nothing," is the opinion of Mary Hall, the editor of *International Drinks Bulletin* of London. GM's global presence can also filter back to the United States. For example, it test-marketed a juice drink, Aqua Libra, which is a mixture of sparkling water, passion fruit juice, and apple juice, in England. After a successful national introduction there, it began selling the drink on the U.S. East Coast.

Building a brand name from scratch is expensive, time-consuming, and risky. And well-known U.S. brands have potential to be "exported" to markets around the world. After the Pillsbury acquisition, GM would have roughly equal contributions from foods, liquor, and retailing and property. Interestingly, GM currently values its existing brands on its balance sheet at £588 million; and the Pillsbury acquisition would add to its books about $2 billion of intangible assets from Pillsbury. Thus, the acquisition cost of the Pillsbury family of brands would be about twice the value of GM's existing brands. Further, GM's brands are weak in the United States, except for Alpo, and sales of GM brands might be strengthened through the use of Pillsbury channels and with access to Pillsbury customers.

Alpo: The Pet Food Business

There is always a danger that acquisitions might draw attention away from existing lines of business, leading to their neglect. For example, GM's Alpo line of pet food is marketed as a dog food. In the United States, pet cats outnumber dogs by 58 million to 49 million, according to the Pet Food Institute. The trend is away from dogs, who need more attention, to the self-reliant cat. Hence, Alpo wanted to build cat food into about 40 percent of its business, developing a feline image without losing its "meaty, masculine" dog food image. The question was whether it should launch a national line of Alpo cat food or experiment regionally with its small Tabby line of cat food. Furthermore, Alpo is strong mainly in canned dog food, with a 24 percent market share, and sales of $439 million. Overall, though, its share is less than 8 percent. It has performed less well in new products such as dog treats and diet dog food. It spends $35 million a year in advertising, and a push into cat food would bring it into competition with Ralston-Purina, Heinz, and Carnation.

Alpo launched a $70 million promotion to sell a new line of canned and dry cat food featuring cartoon character Garfield on the package. By the end of 1989, through aggressive price cutting, it was able to get a 5 percent share of the canned cat food market and about 3 percent of the dry cat food market. Then, in February 1990, GM announced that it wanted to sell off the Alpo line, which earned about $45 million on sales of about $400 million in 1989.

An essential part of GM's product-line reshuffling was the sale of its hotel business; it used the proceeds to help pay for a portion of Pillsbury's purchase price. The question arises as to

Pet Food Market-Share Leaders, 1988

	Market Share
Ralston-Purina	28.8%
Carnation	11.8
Quaker Oats	11.6
Heinz	10.2
Kal Kan	9.4
Alpo	7.7

why Seibu/Saison wanted to buy the Intercontinental Hotels that GM wanted to get rid of. Seibu Department Stores are stylish, with high prices. Seiji Tsutsumi, the owner of the Seibu chain, expanded by guessing that the Japanese would become bigger spenders and that a segment of this market would prefer to buy one stylish but expensive suit to two lower-quality ones; and that the future of retailing in Japan would lie in selling style, not brands. Seibu/Saison became Japan's biggest retail group, with annual sales (1987) of about 3.5 trillion yen.

Tsutsumi further decided that department stores could sell one-stop consumerism. It was a short step, then, to provide travel and tourism services as part of the Seibu/Saison chain. Thus, Seibu's strategy of catering to the globe trotting Japanese customer required that it buy into an existing hotel chain, while GM perhaps saw its small stake in the hotel business as peripheral to its goal of concentrating on global brands and global marketing of these brands.

Questions

1. Outline the international marketing strategy of Grand Met (GM) as made apparent through its acquisition and divestment moves internationally.
2. How have GM's moves led to a refocusing of its product lines into three main areas: food, alcoholic beverages, and restaurants? What are the keys to success in these three product lines?
3. What strengths/weaknesses does GM have that might help and/or hinder its achievement of its international strategy?
4. What should GM do with Burger King in the United States and internationally?
5. What synergies, if any, exist between GM's liquor lines and the Pillsbury acquisition?
6. Do you agree with the decision to sell the Intercontinental Hotels chain? In what ways does this help fulfill GM's overall international strategy?
7. Is GM too thinly spread? That is, is it in too many product lines? For example, should it be getting rid of its Alpo pet food line?

Sources: "With Bid for Pillsbury, Grand Met Tries to Join Top Consumer Firms," *The Wall Street Journal*, October 5, 1988; "Pillsbury Could Be a Grand Coup for Grand Met," *Business Week*, October 17, 1988; "Pillsbury's Burger King Could Be Hard to Digest," *The Wall Street Journal*, October 6, 1988; "Brothers Who Run Japan's Seibu Empire Step up Their Rivalry," *The Wall Street Journal*, December 21, 1988; "European Liquor Giants Pursue a Jackpot," *The Wall Street Journal*, October 4, 1988; "Now Alpo Wants to Dish It Out to Kitty," *Business Week*, September 19, 1988; "U.K.'s Grand Met Says It Will Sell Alpo Subsidiary," *Business Week*, February 9, 1990; "Can a New CEO Pull Burger King Out of the Fire?" *Business Week*, May 22, 1989; "Grand Met Unit to Acquire Christian Brothers," *The Wall Street Journal*, May 17, 1989; "Pillsbury Puts 2 Seafood Lines on the Block," *The Wall Street Journal*, May 23, 1989; "Going Soft," *The Economist*, May 16, 1987; and Pillsbury Co. 1988 Annual Report and Grand Metropolitan Annual Report 1988.

CASE 9.2

Boeing & Airbus: Competing Product Lines.[1]

In 1994, Airbus received 125 aircraft orders as compared to 120 orders for Boeing, the first time in post-war history that Boeing did not have the leading market share. Airbus's market share leadership was not a temporary phenomenon; it continued to gather orders from the world's leading airlines.

In 1998, Airbus obtained orders for 556 aircraft, in comparison to Boeing's 615 aircraft. Most notably, Boeing only received orders for 14 of its 7474 aircraft, an aircraft category in which it has a monopoly and through which Boeing had earned the bulk of its profits. In 1997 Boeing incurred a pretax charge of $3 billion, owing to a merger with McDonnel-Douglas and due to problems with its production operations. However, Boeing has survived in the aircraft industry for over 60 years, with capable and experienced management that has guided it through previous recessions in a cyclical industry.

Over the past decade, Boeing has waged a continual campaign to reduce subsidies granted to Airbus, fearing that such subsidies made it difficult for it to compete with Airbus and to earn sufficient cash flow and profits to fund the development of new-generation and larger jets. Its recent performance raises an interesting question: How serious is the threat from Airbus and how should Boeing plan its international product development and marketing to continue replicating its past successes?

Boeing's major and only competitor is Airbus, McDonnell-Douglas (MD) having been acquired by Boeing. Airbus Industrie is a multinational consortium consisting of two state-owned enterprises, France's Aerospatiale (with 37.9 percent of Airbus) and Spain's CASA (4.2 percent), the semiprivate Deutsche Airbus from West Germany (37.9 percent) and the wholly private British Aerospace (20 percent), all of which receive subsidies for aircraft development and customer financing of aircraft sales.

The Commercial Jet Transport Industry

The industry has been characterized as a "Sporty Game[2]," where introducing each new aircraft involves betting the continued survival of the company. The industry is now a duopoly, with Boeing and Airbus being the only manufacturers of large civilian jets. They work hand-in-glove with three aircraft engine manufacturers, GE (and its French joint venture GE-Snecma), Pratt and Whitney (a subsidiary of United Technologies), and Rolls Royce, a British company. New airframe models typically require new engines, and development of new airframes and engines is estimated to cost about $4 billion apiece, with total investment in the aircraft exceeding $6 billion five to six years after the launch of a model. However, Airbus has been discussing the largest civilian jet ever, its A-3XX, which could cost in excess of $10 billion to develop.

New aircraft development requires long lead times and with eventual sales volume amounting to perhaps one or two aircraft a day in a good year. Planning the introduction of a new aircraft involves looking ahead about 20 years: 5 years for the planning, and a product life of 15 years or more. Hence, considerable market-forecasting abilities are required, particularly since airline demand is highly cyclical.

Once an aircraft model moves beyond development into production, the cost of production of initial batches of aircraft cost will be far higher than, say, the 300th unit manufactured, owing to learning curve driven cost reduction; hence, it is vital that the gamble represented by development of a new aircraft model be transformed into continuing sales. Yet few aircraft have yielded volume sales sufficient to generate profits to their manufacturers. The De Havilland Comet, the

pioneer jet introduced in 1952, sold only 112 units, while the Boeing 707, introduced in 1958, sold nearly 1,000 units. Given a break-even volume of about 600 units for the smaller jets,[3] Boeing has achieved profitability with its 707 (1,010 sold), 727 (1,831 sold) and 737 (4,250 sold), while the 747 with nearly 1,300 units sold is also a profit contributor given its far higher unit price of about $150–160 million and higher margins due to its monopoly position. (As a consequence, break-even volume on the 747 is lower, at about 300 units). Airbus may have reached breakeven with its A300/310 (781 ordered through 1998), though development costs of extending the product family may have raised the break-even volume significantly.

However, introducing derivatives further pushes back the payback period; as additional development costs are incurred, though, it also extends product life. Thus, a company seeking to make commercial jets must be prepared to wait 10 years or more to recover its investments, and even longer to make a profit. Price cutting by a less profit-oriented competitor will reduce margins and contribution and thus push back the break-even point further and affect the willingness of top management to approve funding for new-generation aircraft development projects. At the same time, lower prices and margins reduce cash flows and prejudice the ability of a firm to fund new-aircraft development from internal sources.

Future growth and the bulk of the market for commercial aircraft would appear to lie overseas. U.S. traffic is expected to represent only about one-third of world traffic, with Europe and Canada and the rest of the world representing another third each.[4] Foreign airlines will thus be the major customers for aircraft manufacturers, with government-owned airlines representing a significant share of the customer group. Political pressures could significantly affect a sale and hinder a private company that cannot obtain government help.

Commercial aircraft manufacturing can be highly profitable. Operating leverage beyond breakeven is high: with about 4,000 737 aircraft sold, total contribution is about $16 billion. It is the possibility of demand growth fueled by rising world incomes, trade, and airline traffic that attracts firms to this industry. If an aircraft model is successful, as in the case of the 747 where Boeing had no competition, profits can be enormous.

How Do Airlines Buy Planes?
Airlines sell perishable commodities: An empty seat is revenue that is lost for ever. Airlines would like to fly their planes with every seat sold, which means that they would like aircraft with different passenger capacities for different routes, based on traffic demand patterns. Routes can also vary in distance, with major transcontinental routes such as New York–Tokyo or London–Sydney requiring

long-range aircraft. In addition, the gradual development of international hub-and-spoke systems means that different-sized but short-range aircraft may be needed depending on passenger density within each hub-and-spoke system.

Further, the larger the plane, the heavier the engine needs to be, and matching engine thrust to aircraft size determines fuel economy and speed, which become important as more and more airlines seek nonstop flight schedules. Aging aircraft fleets are another factor, where the costs of replacing fully depreciated aircraft must be balanced against fuel and maintenance costs that are comparatively higher with the older aircraft. Environmental controls and noise abatement provisions complicate this trade-off as airline freedom to operate older noisy aircraft over crowded cities is gradually circumscribed. Technical obsolescence of the existing fleet, with improved safety arising from advanced avionics also color demand for new jet aircraft.

If existing model planes are sufficiently discounted in price and cheap fuel reduces the economic gains to be had from the more expensive new generation aircraft, airlines might prefer to buy the (cheaper) older models and hope to squeeze the manufacturers into financing the aircraft at low risk to the consumers (the airlines). Airlines buying jet aircraft are hence guided by their route structure, the balancing of fuel versus labor versus capital costs, and would probably prefer a family of aircraft (of differing ranges and passenger capacity) from one manufacturer in order to economize on flight-crew training, inventory of spare parts, spare engines, maintenance, and related expenses. But the business cycle and outlook for traffic growth influence the willingness of airlines to buy expensive new aircraft and add on large amounts of long-term debt. Therefore, offering attractive aircraft financing and flexible delivery of aircraft becomes important. As in any new product launch, firms gamble that the product will appeal to the market. The risks of being wrong are magnified in the commercial jet market because the costs of development are so high.

In sum, aircraft product offerings from the manufacturers must meet niches set by the confluence of range, passenger capacity, and engine choices desired, and with the requisite speed, fuel economy, and personnel savings—all this at a reasonable and competitive price, while also matching financing terms offered by competitors.

Airbus, McDonnell-Douglas and Boeing: Competing Product Portfolios

Airframe manufacturers work within their customers' decision calculus to design and manufacture aircraft relying on forecasts of expected modal route ranges and passenger densities, with current and proposed product offerings representing the outcome of this course of analy-

sis. Figure 1 sets out the current product portfolios of the three competing manufacturers. The launch of the newest commercial jet aircraft models, namely the A319, A320 and A321, the A330, and A340—all from Airbus; the MD-11 from McDonnell-Douglas; and the 737 derivatives, including the newest -500, -600, and -700 from Boeing, can best be understood in light of the product map represented in Figure 1, which concentrates on two dimensions: range and passenger capacity. Other factors such as speed, fuel economy, number and type of engines, number of required flight crew, aircraft reliability experience, and financing terms also influence the choice between competing aircraft. However, range and capacity are helpful in demarcating broad product segments within which the factors mentioned above can play a further role. Figure 1 includes:

Aircraft that have been recently discontinued (such as the DC-10)

Aircraft currently in service

Aircraft that have been launched and have received orders, with delivery set over the next few years (the A320, A330 and A340, the MD-11, the 737-400 and 737-500, and the 747-400 and the 777; aircraft development may be interrupted if market signals are negative, such as in the case of the MD-12 and the Boeing 7J7).

Three distinct groups emerge:

- A crowded short-haul, short-capacity segment
- A competitive medium-haul, medium-sized segment
- A long-range segment that is the object of new-product launches
- *A fourth segment* may be emerging consisting of planes with 300 to 375 seats and flying extremely long distances, comparable to the 747 but with about 15 percent fewer seats. This is the segment that has new entrants, including the MD-11, the A 300/340, and the Boeing 777.

Boeing Boeing has long been successful because of its canny product forecasting abilities. Its first product, the 707, was successful despite being several years behind the British Comet. Since then, it has offered jets to meet demand in a variety of segments:

1. The 727 and 737 for short-range small-capacity routes; these compete against new aircraft launched by competitors, the MD-80 series, and the A320 from Airbus; the 727 and 737 are the two most successful aircraft ever introduced, with respective sales of about 1,800 and 4,000 units. While the 727 has been withdrawn from production

FIGURE 1   **Boeing, Airbus, and McDonnell-Douglas Jet Aircrafts: Number of Seats and Ranges**

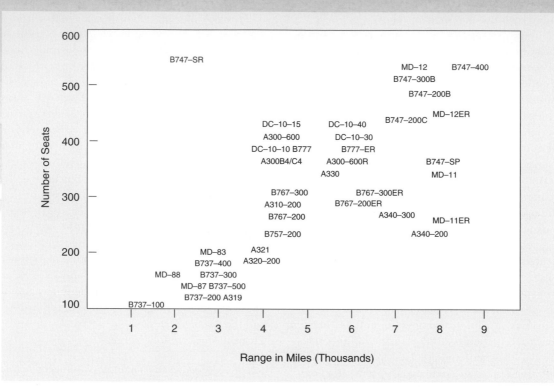

because it is an outdated design, inefficient in fuel consumption and noisy, the 737 is still in production, with several derivative model aircraft, the 737-400 and the 737-500, followed by the next-generation 737-600 and 737-700, recently introduced—all in response to competition from McDonnell-Douglas and Airbus.

2. The 747 for large-capacity long-range routes; Boeing pioneered this segment, at the insistence of Pan Am, and nearly bankrupted itself in the process; but the aircraft is high priced, currently at about $150 million each, and provides profit margins of 25 percent or more, principally because Boeing had a monopoly in this segment. The recent emergence of new offerings such as the MD11 and the A330/340 will begin to provide competition principally at the lower passenger capacity levels in this segment;

3. The 757 and 767 for medium-range medium-capacity and small-capacity long-range routes; these are new offerings from Boeing in response to the Airbus A300/310 aircraft. They are smaller in capacity than the Airbus aircraft, but are two-engine fuel-efficient aircraft, with the 767 gradually carving out a role in long-distance over-water trans-Atlantic and trans-Pacific flights.

4. And as suggested above, a possible new segment containing the Boeing 777, which itself is a competitive response to longer range Airbus 330/340 aircraft.

When the 747 was being developed, Boeing almost went bankrupt in 1969–71; aircraft development expenditures resulted in negative cash flow, and employment declined from a peak of 101,000 in 1968 to about 37,000 in 1971. Now, 25 years later, Boeing is on its fourth version of the 747, which, priced at over $150 million per plane, is a major source of earnings, while employment is at about 120,000 (end 1991).

Boeing delivered 376 aircraft in 1968, 97 in 1972, then reached a peak of 299 in 1980, but only 146 in 1984. In dollars, Boeing's revenues from commercial jets declined from $7.7 billion in 1980 to $5.4 billion in 1984. Cyclicality is a fundamental part of the industry. (See Figure 2.)

Despite these fluctuations, Boeing has consistently maintained a dominant market share, as shown in Table 1. However, Boeing's market share has dropped since 1980, particularly in segments where competition from Airbus and McDonnell-Douglas has intensified. Table 1 breaks out orders

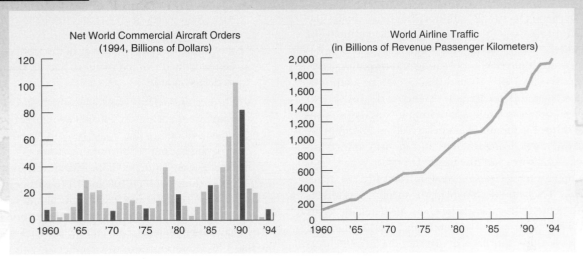

| FIGURE 2 | Relationship between Airline Traffic Growth and Demand for Aircraft |

Source: McDonnell-Douglas 1994 annual report, p. 12.

| TABLE 1 | Aircraft Orders, in Units, by Market Segments |

Aircraft Segment	1970–1980	1981–1985	1986–1989	1990–1993	Total Orders from Model Inception up to 1/31/99
Short-Range, Small-Capacity					
Boeing 727	960	50	0		1,831
Boeing 737	600	681	1,089	483	4,250
BOEING TOTAL FOR SEGMENT	1,560	731	1,089	483	6,081
McDonnell-Douglas: DC-9, MD-80 series	442	369	422		2,167
MD-90			105	123*	134
Airbus A320		90	456	124	A319, 320, and 321:
A321			54	159	1,923
Medium-Range, Medium-Capacity					
Boeing 757/767	264	117	400	514	1,830
Lockheed L-1011	166	10			—
Airbus A300/A310	268	159	208	141	781
McDonnell-Douglas: DC-10	278	19			446
Long-Range, Large-Capacity					
Boeing 747	378	124	248	242	1,287
McDonnell-Douglas: MD-11			126	52	200
Airbus A330/A340			207	41	507

*Includes both MD-80s and 90s.

by segments for each of the three manufacturers, and further tracks orders over distinct time frames.

The market segments identified are not rigid, chiefly due to the ability to vary seating capacity on a particular model of aircraft. Airlines have some flexibility to adapt capacity by offering one or multiple classes of seating and by putting seats closer together; and aircraft manufacturers can adapt airframes by stretching them, literally extending the fuselage to hold more passengers, while upgrading the engines to provide more thrust for the now-heavier aircraft and perhaps redesigning the wings, using winglets and so forth to increase aerodynamic efficiency and fuel burn.

Developing such *derivative* aircraft is less costly and therefore less risky. This approach enabled MD to launch its MD11, a derivative of the DC10, at a cost of about $500 million versus over $2.5 billion at Airbus for its competing A330/340 aircraft. Boeing has used this approach in offering the 747-400, thus trying to protect its monopoly position in the 747 segment and extending the product family, while conserving cash and reducing risk associated with developing a brand new plane.

But sticking to derivative aircraft, while safe, can allow a bolder competitor to pioneer a new aircraft model in a new segment of the market and develop a monopoly position much as Boeing did with the 747. For example, Boeing was unable to prevent Airbus from gaining a significant presence in the 150-seat segment of the market. Airbus's A320's launch success may in part be traced to Boeing product strategy of delaying the launch of a competing similar-sized new-technology aircraft, the 7J7, and ultimately canceling this project.

The 7J7 represents an interesting case of product development. Boeing decided to cancel the launch of the 7J7[5] for several reasons:

- ◆ Low fuel prices reduced the incentive to buy an expensive new technology aircraft such as the 7J7 as its promised fuel economy was less attractive economically.

- ◆ Price was a factor, as the 7J7 would compete with Boeing's own 737-400 and the A320; Boeing estimated that the 7J7 should be priced at about $27 million (1987 $), about the price at which the 737 was on offer. Airlines seemed unwilling to pay more for the new technology under existing economic conditions and did not want to commit the traditional one-third advance payment over the four-year development period.

- ◆ Airlines disagreed on the desired passenger capacity for a new aircraft, seeking somewhere between 150 and 170 seats.

- ◆ The version of the unducted fan UHB engine that GE was to provide could not accommodate a stretched version of a 170-seat jet, which would have been a likely product-development move at Boeing in the future; therefore, waiting till the UHB engine was better defined seemed prudent both to Boeing and to its customers.

- ◆ Further, as Boeing's backlog was high and employment at almost 140,000 people, scarcity of human resources that could be committed to the 7J7 program became a constraining factor.

Instead, Boeing launched a derivative version of the 737, the 737-500, seating between 100 and 125 passengers, and with a range of between 1,700 and 2,800 nautical miles. In this segment of the market, Boeing also faces competition from two other small passenger jet manufacturers, the Fokker F-100 and the Bae 146. However, these two smaller aircraft are principally intended for short-range regional airline flights. As commuter airlines become affiliates and subsidiaries of the major carriers, with their principal role being that of providing feeder traffic for longer routes, their purchases of these smaller aircraft become subject to their major airlines' partner's approval. Moreover, commuter airlines are beginning to use small jet aircraft rather than use turboprops. Boeing continues to chip away at Airbus's stronghold in this segment, with its latest derivative aircraft, the 737-600 and 737-700.

Airbus   Airbus's product strategy has been one of catching up to Boeing, with two central goals:

1. Matching Boeing's broad product range, by providing an Airbus *family* of aircraft to meet a variety of range and passenger capacity needs: single and twin-aisle aircraft for short-, medium- and long-range flights; that is, Airbus had to grow beyond its two available models (the A300 & A310) and develop aircraft that could match Boeing offerings across the entire product line.

2. At the same time, utilize advanced technology, including the so-called "fly-by-wire" avionics and more fuel-efficient engines and airframe design, thus making the Airbus offerings efficient and attractive and capable of being flown by two-man crews. (The use of advanced cockpit instrumentation in the A300 and the follow-on A310 allowed them to be certified with a minimum crew of two pilots, eliminating the need for a flight engineer and resulting in considerable personnel cost reductions.)

Airbus's initial product offerings were the A300 and the A310. The A300 was designed to meet a gap in the market for twin-engine medium-size aircraft and designed with the route needs of the major European airlines in mind. The 310 was a longer-range derivative, introduced in 1978. Both aircraft were designed to suit the needs of European airliners, whose routes did not cover long distances, but needed passenger capacities of around 250 seats: hence, the term "airbus." Cost reduction was achieved by using the same jigs and tooling and a shared assembly line for the 300/310 program, though they did not share the wing, which is one of the most expensive components of an aircraft. However, this initial narrow market focus also reduced the appeal of the Airbus aircraft to U.S. airlines, which generally fly longer routes.

Hence Airbus launched two derivatives, the long-range 310-300 with a fuel tank in the horizontal stabilizer and a stretched A300-600. With about 800 aircraft sold, these programs have barely exceeded breakeven, and a private enterprise firm would have lacked the cash flow with which to embark on further new-aircraft product development.

Yet despite disappointing A300/310 sales, Airbus moved on to the 150-seat market, with the A320, undergoing certification with fly-by-wire controls. This refers to the use of computer-based controls of the aileron, rudder, and other aircraft responses, replacing the more traditional mechanical controls. The A320 is a short-haul twin-engined aircraft, seating between 150 and 180 passengers in a single-aisle configuration, with 150 being a popular size. It is conventionally powered in that it uses tried and tested GE turbofan engines and achieves fuel economies with design innovations.

Given the lack of cash flow and profits from the A300/310 program, the A320 program was entirely dependent on government funding for its development costs. But, market prospects looked attractive because airlines would be considering replacement of the aging DC9s and 727s. Because Boeing was deep in the launch of the 757/767 model family, it would be less able to launch yet another program for a new model 150-seat aircraft.

Airbus has been successful with the A320. It had received 439 orders for the A320 by the time of its maiden flight on February 22, 1987, including 262 firm orders, 157 options, and 20 commitments. It followed up with the derivative launch of both larger and smaller versions of the A320: the A321, to carry about 180 passengers, and the A319, which would carry 124 passengers and compete directly with Boeing's newest 737-500 aircraft. The A320 and the follow-on A321 and A319 have together gathered over 1900 orders and thus become the first aircraft in the Airbus family to break even. Even more important, Boeing's derivative 737-700 is not seen by airlines as fully matching the A320s fly-by-wire and other advanced technology capabilities.

With the 150 and midsize (200–250 seats) segments covered, Airbus launched the long-range high-capacity A330/340 series, again with shared design, such as the twin-aisle cross-section of the A300/310, a variable camber high-efficiency wing and a shared new final assembly line. Its existing A300/310 aircraft needed new wings to improve range and efficiency (wings are the single most critical and expensive element of the airframe, costing perhaps one-third of the total plane cost), and adapting the same wing to the A330 and A340 could further reduce the joint-aircraft development costs.

The A330, a high-capacity medium-range jet, can carry 330 passengers with a range of about 5,500 miles; it is intended as a twin-engine replacement for wide-body trijets such as the DC-10 and the L-1011, with sufficient range to operate on transatlantic routes. The A340 is designed as a four-engine long-range aircraft with 260 to 290 passengers and will be offered in two versions: the A340-200, seating 262 and capable of flying 7,650 nautical miles, or nonstop from New York to Hong Kong, while the A340-300 is to carry 295 passengers over a distance of 6,850 nautical miles.

The A330/340 program is, of course, subsidized and represents the latest provision of subsidies that have benefited the Airbus consortium. Since Airbus does not publish its accounts, it is difficult to estimate the extent of subsidies made available to it. But Airbus began taking orders in 1972, with first deliveries in 1974; by the end of 1998, it had sold a total of about 3,200 planes. Since the break-even volume for a single model has been estimated at around 600 units, it is a certain that Airbus has recorded continual losses: Demisch[6] has estimated total subsidies to Airbus over the years of its existence at between $12 to 15 billion, including launch aid for its new models, the A320 and the A330/340 series. U.S. Treasury estimates are similar, with $10 billion having been spent by the consortium, and an additional $3.2 billion earmarked for the A330/340 programs[7].

The surety of government subsidies and the early commitment from the French government may have emboldened Airbus to gamble on obtaining enough unit volume to derive profits from new-aircraft product launches, despite the presence of Boeing and MD. Or perhaps Airbus had reasoned that its government backing could enable it to sustain losses while sapping MD's will to remain in the commercial aircraft market. Airbus's success with aircraft sales, particularly the A320, will have a direct effect on its costs and thus its competitive position. From Boeing's viewpoint, Airbus will be less inefficient than it used to be because considerable scale economies and cost reductions can be expected. Investment needs will, of course, be high, while risks will also increase due to a higher fixed-cost base.[8]

McDonnell-Douglas

(Note: Though MD is now a subsidiary of Boeing, it is useful to consider its product-development path because it had an impact on both its competitors.) MD derived most of its sales from the military and space sectors, with commercial aircraft accounting for about 25 percent of its 1994 sales of $13.2 billion. MD gradually lost ground with its short-range small-capacity jets, the MD-80 series, and decided to re-establish itself as a credible competitor by attacking Boeing's monopoly position in the long-range wide-body jet market, its 747 market, with the launch of the MD-11, a 330-seat very long-range plane and a replacement for the L-1011-500s, the DC-10-30s and the 747-SPs. The driving argument for a derivative stretched version seemed to be the airport gate shortages and airspace congestion faced by U.S. airlines. In an effort to optimize revenues in a capacity-constrained environment (airlines cannot fly as many flights as they would like), they could trade fuel economy and range for more seats, more short-range high-volume aircraft, and the stretched MD-11 version is aimed at this need, seating up to 500 passengers on short-range routes.

The MD-11, a two-man-crew operated tri-jet, was supposed to fill a void between the 747 and 767. McDonnell-Douglas planned to invest $500 million in nonrecurring costs in addition to funds from risk-sharing partners that include GE, P&W, Sperry, Rohr, Aeritalia, and CASA. By the end of 1994, MD-11 orders were under 200 planes and MD decided to write off MD-11 development costs that had earlier been capitalized on the assumption that at least 300 MD-11s would be sold. It also stopped work on an MD-12 long-range jet which would have required additional overseas partners.

Recent New-Product Developments

The B-777 Aircraft   Boeing's product-development effort during much of the 1990s was focused on developing and launching the Boeing 777 aircraft. It is designed to be the world's largest twinjet, and in its initial version will carry between 375 and 400 passengers, with a 4,200 nautical miles (NM) range, and it is positioned between the 767 and the 747, with a mid-1995 initial delivery target. The 777 would be the widest and most spacious airline in its class, with great interior flexibility. Airlines could easily add or remove and shift lavatories and galleys and change seating configuration as needed. The 777 is designed with folding wingtips, to be able to park at older airport gates without requiring expensive renovations. It is to compete with the MD-11 and the A330/340 aircraft, which have smaller passenger capacities than the 747 but somewhat similar ranges; they were introduced earlier than the 777, being first to market with a long-range but medium-capacity aircraft carrying about 350 passengers, perhaps addressing the needs of the emerging Asian airlines.

All three competitive offerings are intended to replace the aging L-1011s and the DC-10s, estimated to be a $20 billion market. United was the launch customer for the 777, buying 34 aircraft, to replace its DC-10s. The initial version could replace trijets on U.S. domestic routes and on short transcontinental routes such as New York–London, as well as on regional routes in the Far East. Compared to the A330-300, the 777 would be more fuel-efficient, and carry more passengers. A long-range version that could carry 305 to 325 passengers in three classes and fly up to 6,600 NM is planned for delivery beginning December 1996.

Cathay Pacific is typical of the airlines ordering the 777. It has several long flights from its hub in Hong Kong and has ordered both the 777 and 10 Airbus A330s. The Airbus planes will be delivered between 1995 and 1996, with the Boeing aircraft coming in between 1996 and 1998. CP's $1.7 billion Boeing order is for the longer-range 777, in a 320-passenger configuration to fly about 5,600 miles nonstop, with options on 11 more 777s. It plans to press both its suppliers to develop stretch versions, expanding seating capacity by about 20 percent. In building the 777, Boeing will use Japanese suppliers, with Mitsubishi, Kawasaki, and Fuji building about 20 percent of the airframe; Frank Schrontz, Boeing CEO, notes, "We would rather have the Japanese with us than with Airbus."

After the initial product was certified and launched, derivative 777 models with larger passenger capacity and longer range began to be developed. At the same time, Boeing began working on new-generation versions of its venerable 737 family of aircraft.

The latest airline industry response to the product positioning strategies of Boeing and Airbus is reflected in 1998 orders, summarized below:

1998 Aircraft Orders, Boeing and Airbus

Boeing	*Total: 656*	*Airbus*	*Total: 556*
717 (former MD 90)	65	A319	190
737	373	A320	195
747	14	A321	52
757	50	A300-600R	32
767	42	A330	24
777	71	A340	63
MD 80	24	—	—
MD 11	13	—	—
MD 90	4	—	—

Looking to the Future: The Global Air Traffic Environment

Oversupply of Aircraft Capacity Relative to Demand

Is there a current oversupply of planes? Between 1985 and 1990, world traffic grew at 7 percent p.a., aircraft orders rose at 30 percent p.a., and production increased at 16 percent p.a. Hence, airlines developed excess capacity, while the world economy underwent a recession which lasted through 1993. In consequence, domestic and international airlines reduced their capital spending, requesting aircraft delivery postponements; American, European, and Far Eastern airlines all implemented such budget reductions. Despite subsequent recovery, airlines have been cautious in adding capacity and ordering new aircraft, preferring to fly their planes with more passengers. (See the table that follows).

Orders as a Percent of World Fleet

	Net Orders	World Fleet	World Fleet (%)
1977	351	4,954	7.1%
1978	704	5,132	13.7
1979	579	5,468	10.6
1980	439	5,751	7.6
1981	329	6,004	5.5
1982	203	6,084	3.3
1983	221	6,237	3.5
1984	369	6,337	5.8
1985	648	6,657	9.7
1986	706	7,042	10.0
1987	601	7,422	8.1
1988	1,154	7,860	14.7
1989	1,760	8,314	21.2
1990	1,088	8,912	12.2
1991	299	9,326	3.2
1992	340	9,992	3.4
1993	81	10,514	0.8
1994	197	10,991	1.8
1995	636	11,377	5.6
1996	968	11,805	8.2
1997	1,080	12,332	8.8

Pacific-based airlines became the biggest source of aircraft orders as the major U.S. airlines were noticeably reticent in ordering new planes. Forecasts suggest that by 2015, about half of all wide-body jets will be flying Pacific routes and these routes will account for 70 percent of all wide-body seats. (The average number of seats on Pacific routes is likely to be around 350 seats.) This boom in demand for larger passenger-capacity aircraft is reflected in the fact that nearly all 777 orders come from the Pacific region; the larger stretch version of the 777 received 31 launch orders, all from Pacific airlines, with JAL and Singapore Airlines subsequently ordering another 39 planes. After zero 777 sales in 1994 and only 17 units sold in the previous two years, 1995 saw a burst of ordering by the Pacific airlines, which have been opting predominantly for the 777. In all, Boeing received orders for 92 777s in 1995. In the 150-seat market, Boeing was able to get SAS, a long-time MD customer to switch to the 737-600. In 1995, Boeing received orders for 176 of its new-generation 737 planes.

Beginning in 1997 the Asian economies underwent a recession with GDP growth stagnating or turning negative. Currency devaluation and scarce bank lending reduced the capacity of Asian airlines to order aircraft even as air traffic demand in these economies declined sharply. 747 orders were particularly affected and Boeing saw its order book shrink as airlines asked to renegotiate already placed orders. At the same time, Boeing had difficulty with its production operations, with a rapid ramp-up in capacity leading to production snafus and late completion of ordered aircraft.

Financing Difficulties

Airline financing has become harder to secure, as lenders became less willing to finance purchase of aircraft to be flown on competitive routes, though funding is still available for aircraft purchase for new routes in stable markets. Rates of traffic growth and yields are low; the reduced cash flow forces airlines and lenders to cut capital spending budgets.

Leasing of aircraft has also become more costly. Finance leases are long-term leases in which the airline obtains ownership of the aircraft at the end of the lease. Operating leases are short-term leases used by smaller airlines, with the lessor gaining depreciation benefits, lease income, and the potential profit from selling the used plane at a premium. However, such profit on sale has declined as more used planes are available on the market. With finance leases, the major players have been Japanese banks and their investors, who have retreated from the market with the decline of the Japanese capital market and the disappearance of tax shelters on leasing commercial jets, particularly the defense double-dip lease that allowed tax breaks on the finance leases to be claimed both in the United States and in Japan. Drying up of such lease financing is a factor reducing demand for new aircraft.

Upgrading Older Aircraft instead of Replacing Them Airlines are trying to cut aircraft spending by upgrading older aircraft through retrofit/hushkit attempts, thus preserving capacity without buying new aircraft. Delta retrofitted 80 of its older 727-200 and 737-300 aircraft, as did US Air & American. Delta retrofitted its youngest 727s with Honeywell's new glass cockpit avionics, and Rolls Royce Tay, 670 engines, thus reducing crew needs to two from three, saving $400,000 per year in labor and overhead. Retrofit hardware costs $15–17 million versus $30 million for a new aircraft. Such retrofitting meets noise-reduction requirements and yields 10 to 15 percent fuel savings, provided the aircraft still has 12 or more years of economic life: that is, there must be about 35,000 to 40,000 cycles still remaining on a 727 for the retrofitting to be economically viable.

When a major airline such as Delta moves ahead to upgrade older 727s, it legitimizes retrofitting as an alternative to buying in a poor economy. Of course, this will reduce demand not only of 737 and 757s, but also the MD-80 and -90 and A320/321. Such retrofitting may particularly affect the 757, which was designed as a replacement for the aging 727, to allow airlines to comply with the Noise Reduction act; however, deadlines have been eased, and the difficult financial state of airlines contributes to the reluctance to consider the newer technology 757 as an alternative. Of course, a sudden change in oil prices could make all the older aircraft fuel obsolete and possibly revive the demand for newer-technology aircraft such as the 757 and the 777. At the end of 1993 approximately 1,110 commercial jet transports out of the total world fleet of over 11,000 aircraft were in out-of-service status. By the end of 1994, that number had declined to approximately 950. Over 200 of these aircraft needed major maintenance or modification. Due to noise constraints and the inferior operating economics of older aircraft, Boeing estimated that over half of the remaining stored aircraft would not return to commercial service.

Looking to the Future: The Global Air Traffic Environment

The major industry trend is faster growth outside the United States. Table 2 summarizes global airline traffic growth trends. As in the case of many a product industry, higher rates of airline traffic growth are occurring outside the United States.

Long-Term Market Forecasts Boeing has forecast that 15,462 jet aircraft would be purchased by the year 2014, totaling $1,037 billion, based on an annual world air traffic growth rate of 5.1 percent. (See Table 3.) Airbus forecasts 14,937 aircraft orders through 2014 and plans to achieve a 35 percent global market share. Boeing received 346 aircraft or-

TABLE 2	Growth of Airline Passenger Traffic by Region

	North America	Eastern Asia/ Pacific	Europe	Latin America	Middle East	Africa
			Percentage Growth Rate:			
1976–86	7.3	9.5	6.5	8.1	11.5	8.0
1986–96	5.1	6.8	5.8	6.4	5.0	5.5
1996–2006	4.6	6.5	5.5	6.3	5.4	5.5

TABLE 3	Manufacturers' Forecasts of Aircraft Market Size, 1995–2014

Manufacturer:	*Boeing*	*Airbus*	*MD*
Global traffic growth	5.1 percent	5.1 percent	5.7 percent
Demand for aircraft, # of units	15,462	14,937	13,272
Aircraft demand, $ Billions	1,037	1,000	1,024
Aircraft in fleet:			
Beginning	10,629	8,903	9,500
End of forecast period	20,683	16,588	18,014

Source: Manufacturers' forecasts as summarized in *Airline Business,* August 1995.

ders in 1995 to Airbus's 106 and MD's 114. In dollars, Boeing's 1995 orders were worth $31.2 million, compared to $7 billion for Airbus and $4.3 billion for MD.

Boeing's 1998 forecast, for the period 1998–2017 is as follows:

Worldwide Demand for Commercial Airplanes, 1998–2017

The total market potential for new commercial airplanes is estimated at 17,650 airplanes, or an equivalent $1.25 trillion in 1997 U.S. dollars. These orders would consist of:

12,260 single-aisle airplanes

4,360 intermediate-size airplanes

1,030 747-size or larger airplanes

Boeing's foreign sales by geographic area were as follows:

TABLE 4

Boeing Commercial Aircraft Sales by Geographic Region (Dollars in Millions)

(Dollars in Millions) Year ended December 31,	1997	1996	1995
Asia, other than China	$11,437	$ 8,470	$ 7,059
China	1,265	951	754
Europe	7,237	4,198	4,087
Oceania	1,078	821	658
Africa	192	156	154
Western Hemisphere, other than the United States	228	466	734
	21,437	15,062	13,446
United States	24,363	20,391	19,514
Total sales	$45,800	$35,453	$32,960

Boeing, which gets about 75 percent of its sales from overseas is not alone in depending on exports. Airbus estimated that about 80 percent of its production was exported. This globalization of demand has led to development of a global supplier network, with about 30 percent of the 767 components originating outside the United States, and 20 percent of the 777 being produced by Japanese firms alone. Airbus similarly purchases components from over 500 U.S. firms in 34 states. Global markets have also led to attempts

by the FAA to harmonize international airworthiness standards and certification procedures.[9]

Table 5 summarizes Boeing's financial results.

Subsidies to Airbus   In the face of competition from Airbus, Boeing has sought U.S. government help in attempting to limit the product-development and export-financing subsidies given Airbus by the consortium member governments. It has attempted to prevent Airbus gains in market share, particularly with long-established Boeing customers; and it has launched new aircraft models such as the 777 and the 737-700 to compete directly against the new Airbus aircraft.

In April 1992 the EC and the United States seemed to reach agreement that government subsidies on new aircraft-development should not exceed 33 percent of the total aircraft-development cost, such subsidies presumably including low-interest loans and R&D grants. Indirect subsidies, such as spillover benefits from military contracts, were not to exceed 5 percent of the company's commercial aviation sales. Such a cap would affect aircraft developed after April 1992, such as a cogitated superjumbo (competitive with the 747 and the MD-12) from Airbus.

As the aircraft market recovers, continued government support may enable Airbus to continue to develop new aircraft models, forcing Boeing not to back down on R&D. Boeing continues to be the market share leader in the global aircraft industry, but Airbus has emerged as a viable competitor with a full product line. The global aircraft market is changing, with the Far East becoming more important. Pressures from major markets such as China to conduct more in-country manufacturing are also affecting the nature of the industry. Understanding the changing world environment and responding to these changes will determine whether Boeing can continue to dominate the global aircraft market.

Questions:

1. What are the market segments within the commercial aircraft industry? How have the three competitors approached these segments?
2. Is Boeing the strongest company in the industry, in terms of product line?
3. Compare Boeing's and Airbus's competing products.
4. Trace how Airbus has filled out its product line. Can its product introductions be seen as competitive responses to Boeing?
5. How do customers influence the aircraft product line?
6. What factors influence an airline in buying jet aircraft?
7. What should Boeing do?
8. How relevant are subsidies in this industry? How should Boeing react to Airbus subsidies in developing a new aircraft?

| TABLE 5 | The Boeing Company: Five-Year Summary (Dollars in Millions) | | | | |

	1997	*1996*	*1995*	*1994*	*1993*
Sales and other operating revenues					
Commercial aircraft	$26,929	$19,916	$17,511	$19,778	25,120
Information, space, and defense systems	18,125	14,934	14,849	14,676	14,090
Total	$45,800	$35,453	$32,960	$34,969	$39,711
Research and development expense	1,924	1,633	1,674	2,076	2,077
General and administrative expense	2,187	1,819	1,794	1,776	1,798
Additions to plant and equipment,net	1,391	971	747	883	1,349
Depreciation of plant and equipment	1,266	1,132	1,172	1,294	1,211
Employee salaries and wages	11,287	9,225	8,688	9,037	9,551
Year-end workforce	238,000	211,000	169,000	183,000	195,000
Financial position at December 31					
Total assets	$38,024	$37,880	$31,877	$32,259	$31,199
Working capital	5,111	7,783	7,490	6,299	5,108
Net plant and equipment	8,391	8,266	7,927	8,399	8,838
Cash and short-term investments	5,149	6,352	4,527	3,064	3,194
Total debt	6,854	7,489	5,401	5,247	5,840
Customer and commercial financing assets	4,600	3,888	4,212	5,408	5,534
Shareholders' equity	$12,953	$13,502	$12,527	$13,173	$11,966
Backlog:					
Commercial aircraft	$ 93,788	$ 86,151	$73,715	$68,158	$78,172
Information, space and defense systems	27,852	28,022	21,773	18,798	18,485
Total	$121,640	$114,173	$95,488	$86,956	$96,657

Boeing's aircraft backlog at the end of 1997 was $94 million.

---

9. Will there be new competitors entering this industry? Where will such competition come from? How should Boeing deal with this potential development?

10. Is U.S. government intervention necessary to enable Boeing to compete effectively in the global aircraft market?

Endnotes

1 Case prepared by Professor Ravi Sarathy, Northeastern University, for use in class discussion. ©1999, all rights reserved.

2 John Newhouse, *The Sporty Game* (New York: Knopf, 1985).

3 Assuming aircraft development costs of $3.5 billion, a sales price of $30 million and margins of about 20 percent, break-even volume is 584 units; these assumptions are for a current-generation small jet such as the A320.

4 *The Economist*, Table 2–7, 56.

5 AWST, "Boeing Delays 7J7 Program; Mid-1993 Certification Expected," August 31, 1987, 28–31.

6 Wolfgang Demisch, and Christopher Demisch, "Boeing Company Report," (New York: First Boston Co., Jan. 27, 1987), 3.

7 "U.S. Says Talks with Common Market over Airbus Subsidies Are Deadlocked," *The Wall Street Journal*, December 18, 1987.

8 AWST, "Airbus Charts Long-Term Plan for Civil Aircraft Product Line," June 1, 1987, 40.

9 See George A. Berman, *Regulatory Cooperation with Counterpart Agencies Abroad: The FAA's Aircraft Certification Experience*, prepared for the Administrative Conference of the United States, May 1991.

North American Watch Corporation (NAWC)

The goal of the North American Watch Corporation (NAWC) is to create "beautiful watches of exceptional value" for each of its chosen market segments. NAWC designs, manufactures, and distributes high- quality watches ranging from luxury to the mid-priced and moderately priced categories. NAWC was founded in 1961 by Gedalio Grinberg, the present chairman and chief executive officer. He had been the distributor of Omega watches in Cuba before he left Cuba for the United States after Castro's takeover. The company started as the exclusive importer and distributor of Piaget watches, adding the Corum line in 1967. In 1970 and 1983 NAWC acquired the Swiss manufacturers of Concord and Movado watches. In 1980 Grinberg was joined by his son, Efraim Grinberg, the present president and chief operating officer and director. While the company is publicly held, the Grinbergs, father and son, own about 40 percent of the stock and control the company, with 65 percent of the voting power (their Class A stock has supervoting rights).

Industry Overview

The watch market can be segmented along price lines. While fewer units of the more expensive watches are sold, the dollar volume of the high-priced segment makes it the largest single segment of the watch market (see Table 1). The largest watch markets are North America, Western Europe, and the Far East, accounting for 75 percent of the world watch demand. The United States is the single largest market.

TABLE 1

Worldwide Watch Market

Retail Segments	Sales (Billions of Dollars)	Sales (Millions of Units)
$400 +	$3.8	16
$80–$400	2.7	96
Less than $80	2.8	698

NAWC began in the industry by being the dealer for the high-priced Swiss watches, Piaget and Corum. Over the years NAWC has gradually added to its line of brands, first adding Concord, then Movado, and finally the Esquire line in 1993.

NAWC has gradually added new lines, with each additional line allowing NAWC to penetrate lower-priced and larger watch market segments. NAWC's goal is to sell watches in the luxury, expensive, medium-priced, and moderately priced segments. Exhibit 1 details the company's various brands, collections, and price points.

Luxury watches, generally selling for over $5,000, are made from 18K gold, platinum, and may be set with gems; they often have intricate mechanical movements and are made almost exclusively in Switzerland. NAWC distributes the Piaget and Corum brands, which account for 14 to 15 percent of NAWC sales, and compete with brands such as Rolex, Patek Philippe, and Cartier. Piaget has long been advertised as the "most expensive watch in the world." The Piaget Tanagra line consists of rounded link bracelet watches; Dancers are thinner and dressier; Gouverneurs are very traditional with mechanical movements and leather straps; and the Polo line consists of sporty watches. Corum watches are advertised as an "Investment in Time."

Expensive watches, selling for between $1,000 and $5,000, generally feature precision quartz-analog movements, may be made from gold or stainless steel, and are generally manufactured in Switzerland. NAWC's Concord competes against brands such as Omega, Breitling, Baume & Mercier, and so on. Concord is known for its ultrathin movements, advertised as "A fine line between sculpture and engineering." As part of the 1992 celebrations of the 500th anniversary of the discovery of the New World, Concord commissioned five one-of-a-kind technologically innovative watches that toured the world and were immediately sold after their introduction at an aggregate retail price of over $2 million. Concord advertises in print media across the United States, and internationally in magazines such as the Straits Times (Singapore).

Medium-priced watches, selling between $400 and $1,000, have mainly quartz-analog movements and are manufactured in Switzerland and the Far East. They are made mainly of stainless steel with a gold finish, with NAWC's Movado competing against brands such as TAG-Heuer, Raymond Weil, and Gucci. The Concord and Movado lines accounted for about 75 percent of NAWC sales, with about one-third of such sales coming from international markets. Movado is famous for its "Museum Watch" found in the permanent collection of the Museum of Modern Art in New York and at the Victoria & Albert Museum in London; it consists of a single dot at the 12 o'clock position on a numberless dial often with a black face, described as "the reduction of form to function to achieve the purest expression of time." NAWC promotes the Movado through sponsoring cultural groups such as the American Ballet Theater and the Singapore Dance Theater and has developed the Movado sports collection featuring Pete Sampras, a winner at Wimbledon and the U.S. Open tennis tournaments. Movado buys spot ads on television and advertises in international media such as *Der Spiegel* (Germany) and *Ming Pao* (Hong Kong).

Moderately priced watches, selling between $80 and $400, are manufactured primarily in the Far East; their designs may be classical or trendy, reflecting current fashion trends. NAWC's Esquire competes against Bulova, Citizen, and Seiko. Major fashion houses such as Anne Klein, Gucci, Fossil, and Guess sell watches in this segment. The Esquire line is relatively new, launched by NAWC in 1993 and accounting for about 5 percent of sales. NAWC plans to expand the Esquire line significantly and has increased the number of retail outlets selling Esquire watches from 300 to 700 in the 18 months since introduction of the line. Esquire is an outgrowth of NAWC's expertise in manufacturing watches in Switzerland and consists of several distinct lines such as a sport submersible watch, traditional-looking watches with white lacquer dials and black Roman numerals in circular or rectangular cases, watches with retro-style designs, and fashion watches with mother of pearl dials, all designed to sell between $60 and $250. Intended to appeal to a broader audience, NAWC uses TV ads for the Esquire line, as well as diverse print media such as *Newsweek, People, Sports Illustrated, Glamour,* and *Forbes.* The tag line is, "The Esquire Watch—it has your name on it."

NAWC does not compete in the mass-market segment, of which perhaps the best known is Swatch. NAWC's distinct brands are profiled in Table 2.

NAWC does all its advertising in-house, allocating to it 15 percent of sales. Advertising is targeted at the final consumer, relying heavily on magazines and other print media. Exhibit 2 summarizes sales by each of the company's major brands in the United States and overseas.

Design and Manufacturing

NAWC works closely with the Swiss Piaget and Corum companies, relaying them information on U.S. consumer tastes and changing preferences, and has helped develop and refine collections such as the Piaget Tanagra and Dancer lines. Design on the watches it manufactures are mostly conducted in-house, in facilities in Switzerland, Hong Kong, and the United States. NAWC often draws on ideas from earlier collections, such as Movado La Nouvelle inspired by a three-tier movement developed by Movado in 1911. Esquire has a separate Hong Kong facility, and NAWC works with its suppliers to develop several collections each year. Designing new and updated Movado and Concord collections can take 18 months to two years, with new models introduced annually at the International Watch

and Jewelry Trade Fair in Basel, Switzerland. New Esquire models take 6 to 8 months to develop and launch, and two collections are introduced to the trade each year, in May for the fall season and in October for spring sales.

NAWC assembles the majority of its Movado and Concord lines in Switzerland using Swiss movements, cases, bracelets, and other accessories. The assembly requires highly skilled individuals, and Swiss watch apprentices spend several years specializing in watchmaking and in a particular step such as dial and hand setting, casing, bracelet assembly, or polishing and finishing. Manufacturing managers typically have over 15 years' experience in watch assembly. Esquire watches are assembled by independent contractors in the Far East using Swiss movements and locally supplied components. Contractors are qualified by NAWC, which tests preproduction samples, conducts cross-section tests of cases and bracelets, and reviews technical drawings.

In 1991, worldwide industry production was approximately 800 million watches, worth $9.3 billion in wholesale sales. The main producing countries are Switzerland, Japan, and Hong Kong. Table 3 summarizes shipments from the three producers.

Only 5 percent of Swiss-made watches are sold in Switzerland. The Swiss watch industry is highly dependent on the export market. Swiss movements are purchased by NAWC from ETA, the largest supplier of Swiss movements in Switzerland and a subsidiary of SMH, the makers of Swatch. Aside from SMH, no other competitor makes as wide a range of watches as NAWC. Because a majority of NAWC's sales are in North America and the Far East, while a significant portion of its costs are in Swiss francs, the company is subject to the effects of exchange-rate volatility, particularly fluctuations in the value of the U.S. dollar against the Swiss franc.

Sales and Distribution

The U.S. high-quality watch market is highly competitive, seasonal, and cyclical. Exhibit 3 summarizes NAWC's financial performance for the 1989 to 1993 period. Watch sales in the United States and Canada are higher in the second half of the fiscal year, concentrating during the Christmas season. NAWC distributes Piaget and Corum watches in North America, the Caribbean and Central America, and sells the Movado, Concord, and Esquire lines (which it manufactures) worldwide. The company has begun selling Movado watches through special Movado Design Stores on Madison Avenue in New York City, and in three other U.S. locations. It has also begun using direct mail and catalog sales. Major outlets for Movado and Concord in the United States are department stores such as Macy's, Saks Fifth Avenue, Neiman-Marcus, and jewelry chains. The Esquire brand is sold principally in department stores but newer mass-

TABLE 2	NAWC's Brand Portfolio and Segmentation Strategy		
NAWC Brands and Average Price	*Product Characteristics*	*Marketing Strategy*	*Advertising and Promotion*
Luxury: Piaget and Corum; $10,000	Swiss-manufactured; NAWC sole U.S. distributor; Piaget watch case carved from a single 18K block of gold; Corum hand-crafted, custom-made Swiss-manufactured by NAWC	Enhance the company's historical prominence by strengthening its marketing and distribution of Piaget and Corum brands	Advertise in *Forbes, The Economist, New York Times, The Wall Street Journal;* sponsor equestrian events (polo), yacht races, other sports events
Expensive: Concord, $3,000–$4,000		Increase sales penetration in the medium-sized and higher segments by new collections and line extensions across price ranges building on the Concord name	Advertising stresses Concord's ultrathin quartz engineering and hand-crafted elegance; special promotions such as Mariner to coincide with discovery of New World
Medium-priced: Movado $300–$1,000	Swiss movement; manufactured in Switzerland by NAWC; appears in N.Y. Museum of Modern Art—MOMA collection	Increase scope of Movado's brand in United States and internationally by capitalizing on prestige of Movado Museum watch; attract customers from other segments	Advertise "Museum watch"; use alternative distribution channels, that is, Movado stores, mail order, and 800 numbers; sponsor artistic and cultural events; advertise on network and cable TV
Moderately priced: Esquire, $80–$400	Swiss movement; manufactured by NAWC in the Far East; styled to resemble more expensive lines	Develop significant presence in U.S. and international moderate-price segments; offer affordable quality, Swiss movement, with image and design of expensive watches	Advertise to hit broader consumer demographics, in *Esquire, Newsweek, People, Time, Sports Illustrated;* expand to *Glamour, Vogue, Vanity Fair*

market outlets are becoming important. The Piaget and Corum lines are sold only through independent jewelers. Sales are made to the trade by a direct sales force, which also sells overseas. A direct sales force of about 20 employees operates from offices in Germany, Hong Kong, Singapore, and Switzerland, with an additional 34 independent distributors for countries across Latin America, Japan, the Middle East, and European countries such as Austria, Italy, Spain, and the United Kingdom. NAWC has long-term contracts with its international distributors, requiring them to not sell competitive products, and these distributors account for a quarter of NAWC's international sales. Exhibit 4 provides an analysis of NAWC's cost structure and selling expenses and a breakdown of its sales between the U.S. and international markets.

Grinberg has noted that as the United States came out of a recession, people wanted the best value in whichever price range they decided to buy. At the same time, people were beginning to buy multiple watches as fashion statements, increasing the size of the market especially at the lower end. However,

TABLE 3		
Wholesale Watch Industry Shipments		
Source	*Billions of Dollars*	*Millions of Units*
Switzerland	$4.9	128
Japan	2.4	376
Hong Kong	0.8	164

he preferred elegant classics because more trendy, sporty looks were likely to fade. Over time he felt that people were more likely to return to "timeless elegance," such as a Corum watch made from two halves of an 18-karat gold coin, the U.S. $20 Double Eagle.

He wanted NAWC to grow by focusing on all segments. Additionally, foreign market opportunities were increasing, especially for brands such as Corum in Japan, and in countries such as Hong Kong and Indonesia. Another challenge, particularly in the United States, was obtaining representation for his watches in multiple channels, because the concept of a carriage trade was disappearing—watches were beginning to be sold in a variety of outlets ranging from posh jewelers to mass-merchandise outlets. Satisfying the ultimate customer is important, as is the need to satisfy retailers by offering quality, technology, design, and a reasonable price.

In 1993, NAWC was able to raise $35 million in new equity by selling nearly 3 million shares to the public. The capital infusion allowed it to retire high-priced junk bond debt, reduce its interest costs, and free up cash flow for reinvesting in the global watch business.

The challenges facing NAWC are to increase sales volume from its Esquire labels so as to raise overall profit margins by spreading its fixed costs over a larger base; and to reduce the cyclical nature of its business by reducing dependence on the North American market. Grinberg wondered, however, whether the market segmentation developed over years of experience in the U.S. market would have to be altered to take advantage of burgeoning opportunities in Asia and other emerging markets.

Questions

1. Analyze NAWC's portfolio of watch brands. Why does NAWC have so many different brands?
2. Does NAWC run the risk of some of its brands competing with each other? What can it do to prevent this?
3. Evaluate NAWC's use of design, manufacturing, distribution, pricing, and advertising for its various product lines and brands.
4. What are the risks that NAWC faces in U.S. markets and overseas in marketing its watches? What are the weaknesses in NAWC's domestic and international marketing strategy?
5. What recommendations do you have for NAWC to improve its overall performance?

| EXHIBIT 1 | **Company Brand Price Points** |

Brand	Selected Collections	Suggested Retail Price Range		
Piaget	Dancer	$ 2,990	to	$ 42,000
	Piaget Polo	4,990	to	60,000
	Tanagra	4,990	to	82,000
	Gouverneur	6,500	to	25,000
	High Jewelry Watches	65,000	to	2,500,000
Corum	Quadratus	1,790	to	25,000
	Admiral's Cup	2,490	to	75,000
	Gold Coin	3,900	to	37,500
	Symbiose	11,990	to	30,000
	Collector Timepieces	10,000	to	250,000
Concord	Saratoga	795	to	54,000
	Delirium	795	to	29,000
	Royal Gold	895	to	19,900
	Concord Mariner	950	to	14,950
	Super Line	30,000	to	500,000
Movado	Gentry	195	to	495
	Museum Collection	225	to	2,500
	Concerto	295	to	895
	Movado Gold	595	to	6,500
	Movado 1881 Suisse	1,390	to	15,000
	Artists Series	15,000	to	30,000
Esquire	Classic	60	to	95
	Club	75	to	185
	Fashion	75	to	195
	Sports	80	to	250

| EXHIBIT 2 | **Company Net Sales (Dollars in Thousands)** |

	Fiscal Year Ended January 31				Six Months Ended July 31			
	1992		1993		1992		1993	
Piaget and Corum	$ 18,662	14.3%	$ 20,001	14.9%	$ 7,533	14.4%	$ 7,346	13.1%
Concord and Movado								
Domestic	60,410	46.4	56,719	42.3	18,659	35.6	24,884	44.4
International	39,646	30.5	42,257	31.5	20,506	39.2	15,554	27.8
	100,056	76.9	98,976	73.8	39,165	74.8	40,438	72.2
Esquire[a]	—	—	2,798	2.1	—	—	2,504	4.5
Other[b]	11,415	8.8	12,378	9.2	5,678	10.8	5,740	10.2
Total sales	$130,133	100.0%	$134,153	100.0%	$52,376	100.0%	$56,028	100.0%

[a]The Company introduced its Esquire line in the second half of fiscal 1993.
[b]Includes sales by the Company's service and watch repair operations, sales from the Company's Movado Design Store and Movado Company Stores, and sales of Swatch watches in the Caribbean Islands (pursuant to a distribution arrangement that expired at the end of fiscal 1993).

EXHIBIT 3   Selected Data from Consolidated Financial Statements (Dollars in Thousands, Except Per Share Amounts)

	Fiscal Year Ended January 31					Six Months Ended July 31	
	1989	1990	1991	1992	1993	1992	1993
Statement of operations data:							
Net sales	$ 131,920	$ 143,416	$ 152,722	$ 130,133	$ 134,153	$ 52,376	$ 56,028
Cost of sales	70,431	68,962	75,364	62,221	68,294	27,618	28,330
Selling, general, and administrative expenses	53,332	57,070	62,617	60,395	53,331	22,917	24,455
	123,763	126,032	137,981	122,616	121,625	50,535	52,785
Operating income	8,157	17,384	14,741	7,517	12,528	1,841	3,243
Net interest expense	6,465	7,352	9,043	8,686	8,996	4,462	4,048
Income (loss) from continuing operations before income taxes	1,650	9,284	5,698	(1,169)	3,532	(2,621)	(805)
Provision for income taxes	73	2,894	1,840	1,105	207	836	275
Income (loss) from continuing operations	1,577	6,390	3,858	(2,274)	3,325	(3,457)	(1,080)
Net income (loss)	$ 268	$ 5,628	$ 15	$ (1,164)	$ 3,325	$ (3,457)	$ (1,080)
Net income (loss) per common share	$ 0.07	$ 1.58	$ —	$ (0.35)	$ 1.00	$ (1.04)	$ (0.32)
Weighted average common shares outstanding	3,701,856	3,559,234	3,346,510	3,333,654	3,333,654	3,333,654	3,333,654
Cash dividends paid per common share	$ 0.048	$ 0.048	$ 0.096	$ 0.096	$ —	$ —	$ 0.024
Selected operating data:							
Gross profit margin	46.6%	51.9%	50.7%	52.2%	49.1%	47.3%	49.4%
Income (loss) from continuing operations as a percentage of net sales	1.2%	4.5%	2.5%	(1.8)%	2.5%	(6.6)%	(1.9)%
Net income (loss) as percentage of net sales	0.2%	3.9%	0.0%	(0.9)%	2.5%	(6.6)%	(1.9)%
Balance Sheet data (end of period):							
Working capital	$ 84,411	$ 83,925	$ 108,527	$ 98,526	$ 97,958	$ 99,202	$ 94,549
Total assets	131,405	142,114	161,135	150,627	144,075	155,995	152,322
Long-term debt	49,219	44,331	61,118	64,366	64,494	64,389	64,527
Shareholders' equity	34,770	40,578	46,788	35,909	35,776	36,494	32,952

EXHIBIT 4	Statement of Operations, Percentages, and Revenue by Geographic Area

	Fiscal Year Ended January 31			Six Months Ended July 31	
	1991	1992	1993	1992	1993
Net sales	100.0%	100.0%	100.0%	100.0%	100.0%
Cost of sales	49.3	47.8	50.9	52.7	50.6
Gross profit	50.7	52.2	49.1	47.3	49.4
Selling, general, and administrative expenses	41.0	46.4	39.8	43.8	43.6
Net interest expense	6.0	6.7	6.7	8.5	7.2
Income (loss) from continuing operations before income taxes	3.7	(0.9)	2.6	(5.0)	(1.4)
Net income (loss)	0.0	(0.9)	2.5	(6.6)	(1.9)

	Revenue from Sales (Dollars in Millions)	
	Domestic	International
Fiscal 1991	$100,872	$51,850
Fiscal 1992	81,994	48,139
Fiscal 1993	81,865	52,288

Case prepared by Prof. Ravi Sarathy, Northeastern University, with the research assistance of Heidi Hample, for use in class discussion. All rights reserved, © 1996.
Sources: North American Watch Corporation Prospectus, September 1993; "North American Watch Corporation, Investor Brief," *The Wall Street Transcript,* August 8, 1994; and "Watches and Clocks," *Jewelers' Circular-Keystone,* July 1993, 649.

Distribution

Foreign-Market Entry

Once the firm has chosen target markets abroad, the question arises as to the best way to enter those markets. We consider the major entry methods and criteria for selecting them here.

The main goals of this chapter are to

1.   Explore the many types of indirect exporting possible, including export management companies, trading companies, and piggybacking.

2.   Explain how cooperation among companies wishing to export can increase effectiveness and offer cost economies.

3.   Discuss the challenges, problems, and rewards of do-it-yourself, direct exporting.

4.   Give the reasons for assembling products abroad as a way to enter the market.

5.   Discuss the advantages and disadvantages of contract manufacturing, licensing, joint ventures, and wholly owned operations as ways of entering foreign markets.

The distribution question facing the international marketer is very simple to state: How can I most profitably get my products to foreign customers? The marketer must deal with this question in two stages: (1) the firm's method of entry *into* foreign markets and (2) the selection of distribution channels *within* each of the firm's foreign markets. A subsequent management task is the coordination of global logistics. This chapter will deal with the first of these stages.

HOW TO ENTER FOREIGN MARKETS

We cannot overemphasize the importance of the choice of method of entry into foreign markets. It is one of the most critical decisions because the entry decision is a macrodecision. That is, when the firm chooses a level of involvement in foreign markets, it is also making choices about its marketing program there. For example, if the firm enters a market through a distributor or licensee, it is limiting its freedom in such areas as marketing research, product policy, pricing, and promotion. The constraining influence of the level of involvement will be a recurring theme as we discuss the firm's international marketing.

We assume the firm has decided to go abroad and that it has chosen its markets. See Chapters 6 and 7. It then faces the question of how to reach these markets. The range of alternatives is wide enough that almost any company in any product area can find some appropriate way to reach foreign markets. The nature of entry ranges from indirect exporting to wholly owned production in foreign markets (see Figure 10–1).

Before exploring these alternatives, the firm should decide what it wants from its channel to foreign markets because this will help it choose the one that best meets its needs.

Decision Criteria for Entry Method

The selection of the method of entry to foreign markets depends on some factors peculiar to the firm and its industry, for example (1) company goals regarding the volume of international business desired, geographic coverage, and the time span of foreign involvement; (2) the size of the company in sales and assets; (3) the company's product line and the nature of its products (industrial or consumer, high or low price, technological content); and (4) competition abroad. The firm must evaluate these factors for itself; we merely note them here because our decision model will not help in evaluating them—that is, a case-by-case approach is necessary.

Other criteria relate more generally to the method of entry to foreign markets and are less firm and industry specific.

Number of Markets

Companies differ as to the number of countries they want to enter. Different entry methods offer different coverage of international markets. For example, wholly owned foreign operations are not permitted in some countries; licensing may be impossible in other markets because the firm cannot find qualified licensees; or a trading company might cover certain markets very well but have no representation in other markets. To get the international market coverage it wants, the firm may have to combine different entry methods. In some markets, it may have wholly owned operations; in others, marketing subsidiaries; in yet others, local distributors. For example, DuPont has 40 countries with wholly owned or joint-venture manufacturing operations, 20 countries with marketing subsidiaries, and more than 60 countries with distributors.

Penetration within Markets

Related to the number of markets covered is the quality of coverage. An export management company might claim to give access to 60 countries. The producer

FIGURE 10–1   **Alternative Methods of Foreign Market Entry**

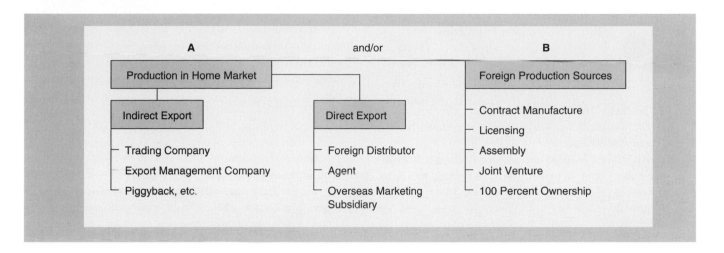

must find out if this "access" is to the whole national market or if it is limited to the capital or a few large cities.

Market Feedback

If the firm wants to know what is going on in its foreign markets, it must choose an entry method that will provide this feedback. Although in general the more direct methods of entry offer better market information, feedback depends in part on how the firm manages a particular form of market entry.

Learning by Experience

Experience is the best teacher, and the firm obtains more international marketing experience the more directly it is involved in foreign markets. The firm with international ambitions should choose an entry method to help it gain experience and realize these ambitions. The firm cannot "learn by doing" if others are doing the international marketing.

Control

Management control over foreign marketing ranges from none at all—for example, selling through a trading company—to complete control, as in a wholly owned subsidiary. The firm may want a voice in its foreign marketing, for instance, pricing and credit terms, promotion, and servicing of its products. The extent to which such control is critical to the firm bears heavily on its choice of entry method.

Incremental Marketing Costs

There are costs associated with international marketing, no matter who does it. However, the producer's incremental marketing outlays and working capital requirements vary with the directness of the channel. For example, with indirect exporting, there are practically no additional outlays by the producer.

Profit Possibilities

In evaluating the profit potential of different entry methods, the long-term sales and costs associated with each entry method must be estimated. Costs and profit margins are less important than total profit possibilities. For example, one entry method may offer a 25 percent margin on a sales volume of $2 million, but another

GLOBAL MARKETING

Entry Strategies for China

China's market offers exciting potential, but this is constrained by cultural and political peculiarities that affect the entry strategy. Some examples:

Anheuser-Busch bought a stake in Tsingtao, China's largest brewery, and is now selling Budweiser in China. Miller Brewing (U.S.) and Foster's Brewing (Australia) also bought into Chinese brewers.

British Petroleum entered an alliance with overseas Chinese in Singapore to build a terminal and distribute natural gas in Fujian province.

Ford and General Motors entered joint ventures with Chinese firms to produce light trucks for China.

Mars distributes M&Ms in China through the East Asiatic Trading Company based in Hong Kong.

Philips has one wholly owned venture and 16 joint ventures with Chinese firms covering different products in its line.

TCBY ("The Country's Best Yogurt") gave a master franchise to Hong Kong's Top Green International (TGI). Over 1,000 outlets were opened in China in the first year by TGI.

Wal-Mart formed an alliance with overseas Chinese to build superstores in China.

Warner Brothers reached an agreement with China's exclusive film-import agency to distribute Warner's films in China (dubbed in Mandarin).

Kodak in 1998 agreed to invest $1 billion in China to try to gain a dominant position there. It took over three failing state-owned film producers, which gave it more operating freedom and shorter distribution channels.

---

may offer a 17 percent margin on a sales volume of $10 million. The latter entry method probably would be more attractive.

Investment Requirements

Investment requirements are highest in wholly owned foreign operations. Plant investment, however, is not the only consideration; capital also may be required to finance inventories and to extend credit. Because the amount of capital required varies greatly by method of entry, this financial need can be an important determinant.

Administrative Requirements

The administrative burdens and costs of international marketing vary by entry method. These include documentation and red tape, as well as management time. For example, indirect exporting or licensing may involve little additional burden on management.

Personnel Requirements

Personnel needs also vary by method of entry. Generally, the more direct kinds of involvement require a number of skilled international personnel. If the firm is short of "internationalists," it is constrained in its alternatives.

Exposure to Foreign Problems

The more directly the firm is involved in foreign markets, the more management must deal with new kinds of legislation, regulation, taxes, labor problems, and other foreign-market peculiarities. If the firm is unable or unwilling to deal with those problems, it must choose an entry method that lets someone else handle them.

Flexibility

If the firm expects to be in foreign markets for the long run, some flexibility in its method of entry is important. Any entry method optimal at one point in time may be less than optimal five years later. Not only do the environment and the market change, so, too, do the company situation and goals. The firm therefore wants flexibility—the ability to change to meet new conditions. It may wish to expand to take advantage of growing markets or to contract because of adverse developments.

Although not easy to achieve, this flexibility is greater where the firm has planned for it in choosing its method of entry. For this reason, firms sometimes gain experience with limited forms of involvement before committing themselves heavily to a market.

Risk

Foreign markets are usually perceived as riskier than the domestic market. The amount of risk the firm faces is not only a function of the market itself but also of its method of involvement there. In addition to its investment, the firm risks inventories and receivables. The firm must do a risk analysis of both the market and its method of entry. Exchange-rate risk is another variable.

Risks are not only economic; there are also political risks. The firm's political vulnerability may differ from market to market (as we saw in Chapter 5). The level of involvement is one factor in that variability. Generally, the more direct and visible the entry, the more vulnerable it is politically.

A Simple Decision Model

The criteria for evaluating foreign-market entry methods can be combined in a matrix, as is done in Table 10–1. The firm finds that each of the entry methods has a different score on the different dimensions. By relating these scores to the firm's own situation and needs, management can choose the most appropriate entry strategy.

The approach illustrated by Table 10–1 seeks to answer two questions: (1) How well can the firm market through any particular entry strategy? (2) What are the costs and benefits of different entry strategies? Depending on its needs, the firm can use the matrix to select entry strategy for individual markets, for regions, or for the whole international market. The large firm could apply this approach by product line or division. The matrix is also useful for evaluating specific channel candidates in a given country. For example, a firm could modify it and use it to decide between a distributor, a licensee, and a joint-venture partner in Brazil.

Usually the decision facing a manager is to choose one entry method from among several alternatives. However, many times a firm uses a number of entry methods in combination—different entry methods for different countries or different product divisions, for example. Two company illustrations show some of the real-world complexity that we simplify in our discussion. The first involves a Honeywell division using five entry methods for world markets; in the second, General Electric uses four different entry methods in one market for different divisions.

The Aerospace and Defense Group (ADG) is a major division of Honeywell. It has five different ways of interacting with foreign markets. In order of priority, they are as follows:

1. Honeywell Control Systems' foreign subsidiaries

2. The ADG international sales force

3. Manufacturer's representatives abroad

4. Licensees abroad

5. Control Systems' foreign distributors

TABLE 10-1	**Matrix for Comparing Alternative Methods of Market Entry**

Evaluation Criteria	*Indirect Export*	*Direct Export*	*Marketing Subsidiary*	*Marketing Subsidiary— Local Assembly*	*Licensing*	*Joint Venture*	*Wholly Owned Operation*
1. Number of Markets							
2. Market Penetration							
3. Market Feedback							
4. International Marketing Learning							
5. Control							
6. Marketing Costs							
7. Profits							
8. Investment							
9. Administration							
10. Personnel							
11. Foreign Problems							
12. Flexibility							
13. Risk							

In Mexico, General Electric (GE) has four different kinds of involvement for different parts of the company. GE has wholly owned factories for several of its industrial electrical products, and it has a joint venture for major appliances. A marketing subsidiary exists for distributing imports from the United States. Finally, there are licensees for locomotives and lighting systems.

INDIRECT EXPORTING

The firm is an **indirect exporter** when its products are sold in foreign markets but no special activity for this purpose is carried on within the firm. In indirect exporting, the sale is like a domestic sale. In fact, with indirect exporting the firm is not engaging in international marketing in any real sense. Its products are carried abroad by others, and its distribution problems are similar to those in domestic sales. Although exporting this way can open up new markets quickly, the firm's control is very limited. Several methods of indirect exporting exist.

Foreign Sales through Domestic Sales Organization

A firm likes to have a buyer come to it. Occasionally, even a foreign buyer does this. Products are sold in the domestic market but used or resold abroad in several ways.

1. Foreign wholesale or retail organizations that have buying offices in the firm's home country may find the firm's product desirable for their market. For example, Macy's has buying offices in 30 countries. Wal-Mart has many also.

2. Manufacturers and firms in extractive industries often have U.S. offices to procure equipment and supplies for their foreign operations. In selling to

the U.S. firms in this category, a company would have the advantage if it is already supplying their domestic operations. Reaching the foreign firms in this group requires special marketing. For example, AGIP, the Italian Oil Company, has 20 buyers in the United States and exports over $100 million a year from the United States.

3.   A slightly different situation arises when companies with multinational operations buy equipment and supplies for them through their regular domestic purchasing. Many small industrial marketers can trace their international involvement to such a beginning. Indeed, many exporters receive their initial export orders unsolicited.

Suppose that a national company builds a plant in a foreign market. It buys a machine from its domestic supplier through the normal domestic procedure. The machine is shipped and installed in the new foreign plant. A foreign producer visits the plant and takes note of the machine. Sometime later the supplying firm receives its first foreign order. Such a sequence of events has often led to an active export involvement by the supplying firm. It has benefited from the demonstration effect and received a free introduction to the foreign market.

4.   International trading companies are very important for some markets of the world. Most large trading companies are of European or Japanese origin. In Japan, for example, some of the largest enterprises are trading companies, such as Mitsui and Mitsubishi. They handle the majority of Japanese imports. The trading companies of European origin are important primarily in trade with former European colonies, particularly Africa and Southeast Asia. For example, the United Africa Company is the largest trader in Africa. These companies all have U.S. procurement offices.

The size and market coverage of these trading companies make them attractive distributors, especially with their credit reliability. They cover their markets well and can also service the products they sell. For example, Unisys used United Africa Company for selling computers.

There is a potential drawback to the use of trading companies. They are likely to carry competing lines, and the latest product added might not receive the attention its producer desires.

The sales from these kinds of indirect exporting are as good as domestic sales, but they may be less stable. Because it is so far removed from the ultimate market, the firm has very little control. Although the firm welcomes any new sales, those arising from the sources mentioned here may prove too uncertain to be included in long-term planning. This might move the firm in the direction of more control over its foreign sales.

Export Management Companies

Another form of indirect exporting is the **export management company (EMC),** often considered as constituting the export department of the producer. That is, the producer gets the performance of an export department without establishing one. The economic advantage arises because the EMC performs this function for several firms at the same time.

Compared with the approaches above, working with an EMC generally means that the firm has closer cooperation and increased control. The EMC often uses the letterhead of the manufacturer, negotiates on the firm's behalf, and gets its approval on orders and quotations. Theoretically at least, the EMC approach to indirect exporting seems ideal for the medium-sized or small firm because the firm can overcome its limitations in size and foreign market knowledge while retaining some control.

The following list enumerates the potential advantages of using an EMC.

1. The producer gains instant foreign-market knowledge and contacts through the operations and experience of the EMC.

2. The manufacturer is spared the burden of developing in-house expertise in exporting, a significant cost saving, because the EMC's costs are spread over the sales of several manufacturers.

3. Consolidated shipments offer freight savings to the EMC's client.

4. A line of complementary products can get better foreign representation than the products of just one manufacturer.

5. Most EMCs accept foreign credit responsibility.

Evaluating the EMC. Because of their potential advantages, EMCs can be very attractive for a new exporter. Many thousand U.S. manufacturers have used the EMC for exporting to all or some of their foreign markets. In evaluating this alternative, the exporter should determine to what degree the advantages apply in its particular case. Some EMCs may be too new or too small to have adequate foreign-market knowledge and contacts. Some may handle too many lines to give proper attention to a new exporter. EMCs may represent as few as 3 or 4 clients or as many as 50. Many tend to be market specialists rather than product specialists, so product expertise may be weak, especially if they handle many lines. Their market coverage is often regional rather than global. The exporter may need more than one EMC or more than one entry method to cover all of its markets.

One advantage of the EMC is that it gives the manufacturer access to instant foreign-market knowledge and exporting know-how. This can be a potential disadvantage, however, if the producer never develops such capabilities itself. As foreign sales grow, it may become important for the firm to do its own exporting. Although initially the EMC may offer great economies, at some volume of sales it becomes more profitable for the manufacturing firm to set up its own export department. When the firm reaches this point, it wants its own foreign-market knowledge and exporting know-how.

Looking at the relationship from the EMC's viewpoint is revealing. It is often vulnerable to the extent that it does a good job. It builds up foreign markets in the manufacturer's name and with the manufacturer's brands. When the market is well secured, the manufacturer may decide to take over the exporting to this now-large foreign market. The EMC, of course, then loses a major source of revenue.

To protect themselves, many EMCs have changed the nature of their operations, using their own letterhead to establish their own identification. Instead of selling on commission, they buy for resale to control prices and terms and use their own brand name on some products. The manufacturer doesn't have as much control over the new type of EMC, but that doesn't mean that it is less effective than the more traditional type.

We noted a number of potential advantages and limitations to using an EMC. In conclusion, we suggest that most small firms should consider an EMC when evaluating export possibilities. The exporter-to-be needs to develop a list of export requirements and targets and match these against the capabilities and market coverage of various EMC candidates.

GLOBAL MARKETING

Your Friend, the Export Management Company

Forest Lumber Company (Mississippi) buys and resells all types of forest products, including lumber, logs, and flooring material. It handles all export functions, and the producers incur no costs until the product is sold.

International Trade and Marketing (ITM in Washington, D.C.) exports for 10 makers of orthopedic equipment to world markets, but focuses primarily on developed countries. ITM takes title.

Dreyfus & Associates (New York) exports for eight tool manufacturers. Dreyfus finds foreign buyers, buys the goods, ships them, extends credit, and collects payments. Dreyfus uses foreign trade shows and spends over $2,000 a month on phone calls and faxes.

International Projects (Toledo, Ohio) is a complete export manager for 16 companies making pleasure boats, hospital supplies, air conditioner repair equipment, and stationary.

Overseas Operations Inc. (California) handles builders' hardware, housing accessories, door locks, and computer software and accessories for a global market. Overseas Operations takes title but the products are shipped directly from the producer's plant with shipping arranged by Overseas Operations.

The United States has more than 2,000 export management companies. Because they provide economies of scale and other advantages in international marketing, they are a continuing factor in U.S. international trade. They are a far cry from the Japanese trading companies, but the same economic logic underlies their operations. They are not just for small companies either. More than one-third of their clients have sales over $50 million and more than one in eight has over $500 million in sales. Even General Electric used an EMC for its airport lighting division.

Cooperation in Exporting

Cooperation in exporting is another way to enter foreign markets without bearing the costs and burdens of an in-house export department. Among the forms of cooperation in exporting are Webb-Pomerene associations (mentioned in Chapter 5), export trading companies (ETCs), and piggybacking.

Webb-Pomerene Associations

Notable in that it permits competing firms to cooperate for export marketing, a **Webb-Pomerene association** can act as the exporting arm of all member companies, presenting a united front to world markets and gaining significant economies of scale. Its major functions are the following:

1. Exporting in the name of the association

2. Consolidating freight, negotiating rates, and chartering ships

3. Performing market research

4. Appointing selling agents in the United States or abroad

5. Obtaining credit information and collecting debts

6. Setting prices for export

7.   Allowing uniform contracts and terms of sale

8.   Allowing cooperative bids and sales negotiation

Firms in a Webb-Pomerene association can research foreign markets more effectively together and obtain better representation in them. By establishing one organization to replace several sellers, they may realize more stable prices, and selling costs can be reduced. Through consolidating shipments and avoiding duplicated effort, firms realize transportation savings, and a group can achieve standardization of product grading and create a stronger brand name, just as the California fruit growers did with Sunkist products. Most of the benefits derive from economies of scale and countervailing power. Flexibility is a final advantage. Many degrees of cooperation and product and market coverage are possible, so joining a Webb-Pomerene association is not an all-or-nothing affair.

With the many attractions of Webb-Pomerene associations, it is surprising that not more of them are operating. As shown in Table 10–2, there were only 15 registered as of 1998, down from 36 associations in 1981. More than 200 associations were formed under the Webb-Pomerene Act of 1918, but many never actually operated.

The majority of associations are in some kind of commodity business, as with the cotton exporters. A few commodity groups include some of the largest U.S. companies, such as the soda ash group that includes FMC, Kerr-McGee, Stauffer Chemical, and Tenneco. Other groups deal in manufactured goods or services and also include some of the larger companies in the United States. The cigarette exporters include the leading U.S. cigarette makers, and the film-exporting groups have all the major U.S. movie producers. It is interesting that there are three Webb-Pomerene associations of film producers, with generally the same membership. The three associations cover different parts of the world.

Export Trading Companies

Export trading companies (ETCs), permitted in the United States since 1982, are a U.S. attempt to emulate Japanese trading companies. An ETC acts as the export arm of a number of manufacturers. Because EMCs and Webb-Pomerene associations play a small role in exports from the United States, the government wanted a more powerful mechanism to assist U.S. exporters. ETCs allow giant U.S. corporations or banks to form a trading company with the size, resources, sophistication, and international network more comparable to that of Japanese trading companies. The advantages to an exporter are much like those offered by EMCs and Webb-Pomerene associations (foreign market knowledge, economies of scale, etc.) but to a greater degree because of the greater resources and coverage of the ETC.

Some major U.S. banks, such as Bank of America, Citicorp, and First National of Chicago, and major corporations, such as Borg-Warner, General Electric, General Motors, and Sears, formed ETCs so the outlook was promising. Unfortunately, not much developed from these undertakings. The Sears ETC folded after less than five years. General Electric had the largest ETC, but it too ended after a few years. Part of GE's problem was getting U.S. exporters to use its ETC. The results suggest that the U.S. attempt to imitate the Japanese *Sogoshosha* is a failure. There are over 100 U.S. ETCs, but they are small EMC-type firms, not the mighty trading companies envisioned. Indeed, most of these ETCs, like EMCs, have fewer than 50 employees. Examples are Ultramedic International in New Hyde Park, New York, which specializes in medical equipment and supplies for customers in Latin America, and the Meridian Group of Companies, in Los Angeles, which specializes in swimming pool equipment.

Even though ETCs have not become global giants like the Japanese *Sogoshosha*, they can be a useful form of entry to foreign markets for many U.S. exporters. Even 3M uses an ETC for some products for some markets.

| TABLE 10–2 | Webb-Pomerene Associations |

Afram Films	Paperboard Export Assoc. of the U.S.
American Cotton Exporters Assoc.	Phosphate Chemicals Export Assoc.
American Motion Picture Export Co.	Phosphate Rock Export Assoc.
American Natural Soda Ash Corp.	Sulphate of Potash Magnesia Export Assoc.
American Poultry USA, Inc.	Texas Produce Export Assoc.
American Wood Chip Export Assoc.	UAN Solutions Export Assoc.
American-European Soda Ash Shipping Assoc.	United States Cigarette Export Assoc.
Motion Picture Association	

Source: Federal Trade Commission, 1998.

Piggyback Exporting

In **piggyback exporting,** one manufacturer uses its overseas distribution to sell another company's product along with its own. Although not new—General Electric was doing it some 50 years ago—this method is becoming more important today. Two parties with different interests—the carrier and the rider—make up the piggyback operation.

The **carrier,** the firm actually doing the exporting, is usually the larger firm with established export facilities and foreign distribution. It may have several reasons for adding the product of another manufacturer. The new noncompetitive product may round out a gap in its product line, or it may mean greater economies of scale and profits in exporting. As much as one-sixth of Borg-Warner's export sales and profits came from piggybacking.

By piggybacking, companies can please foreign distributors by giving them a more complete line of products. Also, it can mean extra customer convenience by offering related products. For example, Singer sells fabrics, patterns, and sewing accessories in addition to sewing machines. Finally, firms with seasonal sales may piggyback to keep their export operation working at full capacity throughout the year. For the carrier firm, piggybacking is a sale of know-how and services rather than a sale of products.

Schick Safety Razor tried piggybacking after encountering difficulty in the German market. After dissatisfaction with a German distributor and a temporary alliance with another consumer goods company, Schick set up its own sales subsidiary in Germany, hiring an executive from Gillette. A large sales force was hired to give the necessary retail coverage. The costs of this approach would have been very high if only Schick products had been sold. Fortunately, American Cyanamid wanted a distributor for its Breck hair products. It also had its own salesforce in Germany, but it was selling industrial products. Schick became the Breck distributor for Germany. This worked so well that Schick later agreed to distribute the cosmetic products of another U.S. firm. Perhaps most important, Schick's own market share in Germany rose from 3 to 7 percent in one year. The large sales force made possible by piggybacking was a major factor in this outcome.

Piggyback Decisions: The Carrier. A firm that has a gap in its product line or excess capacity in its export operation has two options. One is to develop internally the products necessary to round out its line and fill up its exporting capacity. The other option is to acquire the necessary products outside by piggybacking (or acquisition). Piggybacking may be attractive because the firm can get the product quickly (someone already has it). It is also a low-cost way to get the product because the carrier firm does not have to invest in R&D, production facilities, or market testing for the new product. It can just pick up the product from another firm.

Piggybacking can be extremely attractive for the carrier, but some concerns exist about quality control and warranty. Will the rider maintain the quality of the products sold by another firm? This depends in part on whose brand name is on the product. If the rider's name is on the product, the quality incentive might be stronger. A second concern is continuity of supply. If the carrier develops a substantial market abroad, will the rider firm favor its own marketing needs in tight demand conditions? Each of these items should be a subject in the agreement between the two parties. If the piggybacking arrangement works out well, there is another potential advantage for the carrier. It might find that the rider is a good acquisition candidate or joint-venture partner for a stronger relationship.

The Rider.   For the rider, or company using an export company to "carry" its products to foreign markets, piggybacking is one alternative route to foreign markets. It offers established export and distribution facilities and shared expenses, benefits similar to those offered by the EMC, the ETC, or a Webb-Pomerene association. The rider must compare a piggybacking opportunity to these other alternatives as to how well each meets the needs of geographic diversification and market coverage, economies of scale in exporting, testing foreign markets, and learning international marketing. Given the growth of piggybacking in recent years, it appears that it is frequently a satisfactory answer to these needs.

Method of Operation.   Although piggyback agreements may be more flexible than agreements with export management companies or Webb-Pomerene associations, the same points must be considered for the protection of carrier and rider. Among these are terms of sale, promotional arrangements, market coverage, and provisions for termination of the agreement. The Schick-Cyanamid agreement again serves as an example. The contract provided that Schick sell Breck cosmetics in its own name, but for the account of Cyanamid; that is, the products remained Cyanamid property until sold. Schick agreed not to sell its own similar products or similar products of a third company.

The contract stipulated that Schick was to receive a higher commission during the launching period. Cyanamid was authorized to check Schick's accounts with an independent auditor and to withdraw Breck cosmetics from the market if sales were disappointing. Should Schick be taken over by a third company, Cyanamid had the right to cancel the contract.

In selling, piggybacking offers two types of arrangements: (1) The carrier sells the rider's product on a commission basis, or (2) the carrier buys the products outright, acting more like an independent distributor. The latter alternative is more common, but the appropriate choice depends on the situation of the two firms.

Branding policies are variable in piggybacking. The carrier may buy the products, put its own brand on them, and market them as its own products, as Borg-Warner does with auto replacement parts it buys from other manufacturers. More commonly, the carrier retains the brand name of the producer and the two work out promotional arrangements between them. The choice of branding is a function of the importance of brand to the product and of the degree to which the brand is well established. Borg-Warner kept the producer's name on the small appliances it bought from Hamilton Beach, the Toastmaster products of McGraw-Edison, and the garbage disposers of In-Sink-Erator Company.

The piggyback approach can be flexible also as to product coverage. The carrier may handle just one or all of the rider's products. For example, Du Pont markets its own industrial chemicals in Thailand but piggybacks its agrochemicals with Shell. WYKO, a smaller firm, sells its full line of optical testing equipment through Matsushita in Japan.

In terms of country coverage, piggybacking may offer just one market—or the whole world. For example, AT&T used Toshiba just for Japan, and Hitachi used NAS only for the U.S. market. Uniflow, a producer of ice-making and beverage-cooling equipment, had successfully exported to Europe, Africa, and Latin America but was unable to enter Japan until it piggybacked with Matsushita, just for Japan. By contrast, Champion Spark Plug offered markets throughout Southeast Asia for several Australian and European auto parts makers. Sankyo Seiki, a robotics firm, used the global coverage of IBM, as did Stratus minicomputers.

Other advantages of piggybacking can be seen in the examples of Whirlpool with Sony and IBM with Minolta: Whirlpool had been exporting appliances to a Japanese distributor for 12 years. Then it switched to piggybacking with Sony in Japan and found its sales increasing. Sony not only had good distribution and service capabilities, but also it gave more sophisticated promotion and association with the Sony reputation. For Sony, the gains came from a wider complementary product line.

Minolta began selling small copiers with the IBM brand in the United States through IBM. Although Minolta had its own U.S. distribution under its own name, IBM gave it much greater coverage of the U.S. market. The advantage to IBM was in gaining a low-priced copier without the time and expense of developing one itself.

DIRECT EXPORTING

In our discussion of indirect exporting, we examined ways of reaching foreign markets without working very hard. Indeed, in the indirect approaches, foreign sales are handled the same way as domestic sales: The producer does the international marketing only by proxy, that is, through the firm that carries its products overseas. Both the international marketing know-how and the sales achieved by these indirect approaches, however, are limited. The firm can commit itself further by direct exporting.

The difference between indirect and direct exporting is that in the latter, the manufacturer performs the export task rather than delegating it to others. In **direct exporting,** the tasks of market contact, market research, physical distribution, export documentation, pricing, and so on, all fall on the firm. Direct exporting usually results in more sales than does indirect exporting. Whether it also yields higher profits depends on whether the sales increase is greater than the increase in costs from an in-house export operation. Table 10–3 gives an overview of the export marketing task.

The choice between indirect exporting and direct exporting is analogous to the choice between selling through a manufacturer's representative or through the firm's own salesforce in domestic marketing. The advantages of directness are not only increased sales but also increased control, better market information, and development of expertise in international marketing. The costs of going direct are high because the exporter bears them alone, whereas they are shared in the indirect approaches. Although we contrast direct and indirect exporting, they are not mutually exclusive. A firm might export directly to large markets but export indirectly to smaller markets.

The Task of Export Management

To gain the benefits of direct exporting, the firm must pay the costs of performing the export management task. Depending on the size of foreign sales, export management may range from a part-time activity for one person to a large export department with a specialized staff and a full-time export manager. As an additional variation, the export department could be a part of the international division, or there could be separate export departments in the product divisions. Regardless of the volume of export sales or the organizational structure, however, export management has certain tasks. (See Table 10–3.) The first is choosing export markets.

TABLE 10-3	Outline for an Export Plan

Part I: An Export Policy Commitment Statement

Part II: The Situation/Background Analysis

- Product
- Operations
- Personnel and export organization
- Resources of the firm
- Industry structure, competition, and demand

Part III: The Marketing Component

- Identification, evaluation, and selection of target markets
- Product selection and pricing
- Distribution method
- Terms and conditions
- Internal organization and procedures
- Sales goals: Profit (loss) forecasts

Part IV: Tactics: Action Steps

- Primary target countries
- Secondary target countries
- Indirect marketing efforts

Part V: An Export Budget

- Pro forma financial statements

Part VI: An Implementation Schedule

- Follow-up
- Periodic operational/management review (measuring results against plan)

Addenda: Background Data on Target Countries and Market

- Basic market statistics: Historical and projected
- Background facts
- Competitive environment

Source: *Basic Guide to Exporting* (Washington, D.C.: U.S. Department of Commerce, 1998), 6.

Choosing Foreign Markets

In indirect exporting, foreign-market coverage is usually dictated by the company that takes the product abroad; that is, it is already selling in certain markets, and these are the ones it can offer the manufacturer. Of course, the manufacturer can add other markets by using other intermediaries that cover the additional markets wanted. By direct exporting, management can make its own selection of markets.

In theory, the firm could have the whole world as its market. In practice, it is usually limited to a part of the world's markets. For a U.S. company, U.S. restrictions on trading with certain countries might eliminate them from consideration. The firm may eliminate other markets in order to concentrate on those offering the greatest potential. Some markets may be too small; others may have too much competition; yet others may have tariff barriers or trade restrictions on the firm's products.

To choose export markets, the firm needs some analytical approach to evaluate and rank markets according to potential. Among the variables are demand, competition, and government. (The approaches and information sources needed for such an analysis were discussed in Chapter 7.)

Choosing Representatives in the Target Markets

Once the firm has selected its markets, it must have representation there. If both the markets and the firm are large enough, the firm can establish its own sales subsidiary, exporting to itself and controlling its marketing program there. The more frequent approach, especially in smaller markets, is to select local representatives to distribute the firm's products.

The firm usually has several distributor candidates in each target market, the names of which can be obtained from many different sources: the Department of Commerce, foreign business directories, commercial banks, steamship companies, airlines, and so on. After the firm obtains a list of candidates, it must secure information about each one in order to select the best. The firm needs to know their method of operation—whether they buy for their own account, whether they carry inventory, how many on their sales staff, what product lines they carry—and their effectiveness and reliability in marketing and in paying their bills.

A Dun and Bradstreet report or a Department of Commerce International Company Profile (ICP) can give information on several of these questions. For example, an ICP gives background information on the company, number of employees, sales area, products handled, reputation of company, foreign companies represented, and so on. (See Table 10–4.) These sources can be followed up with inquiries through banks, U.S. clients of the candidate, and other references to get a fuller picture. All this can be done in the home country of the exporter.

After all this information has been gathered, however, the exporter should visit the market before making the final choice. Such a visit provides a feeling for the market that written reports can't convey, but more importantly, it gives further insights on the distributor—probably the most important single factor in export performance. As noted by an international marketer at Corning Glass, "The key to export success is a strong presence in the market."[1] Furthermore, once the contract has been signed, the laws of the country may make it very difficult to break the contract and get another distributor. Finally, the choice of a distributor is important because it may play a role in the future as joint-venture partner or acquisition candidate. For example, when 3M established a marketing subsidiary in the Netherlands, it did so by acquiring its distributor there. For these reasons, the initial selection must be made very carefully.

Paying a visit to the better candidates and viewing their operations help the export manager make the best choice. Establishing personal familiarity makes future communication more meaningful. In some markets, the firm may not be able to develop a list of acceptable distributor candidates, in which case it might be happy to find even one that is being used by a competitor. (A good model is seen in "Global Marketing," "The Gold Key to Agent-Distributor Selection.")

Physical Distribution and Export Documentation

Once the firm has chosen foreign distributors, it must get the product to them. This task differs from the same task in the domestic market. Different shipping companies and modes of transportation are necessary; for example, the use of ships and airplanes is more common in exporting than in delivering goods within a country. Packaging costs for export usually are high because the distances and numerous changes in modes of transportation require that the product be handled more frequently. Of course, air shipments avoid some of these problems.

Another complication of shipping to foreign markets is export documentation. The paperwork required for exports is greater than for domestic shipping, and the importing nation requires documents of its own. The United Nations estimates that 7 percent of international trade represents documentation cost, eventually involving 40 documents and 27 parties per transaction. This is not unmanageable, however, because more than 100,000 U.S. firms are exporting. Finally, insuring shipments to foreign markets is more complicated than insuring domestic shipments.

The complications noted here, combined with firms' lack of familiarity with foreign markets, have deterred many managers from giving adequate consideration to

TABLE 10-4	**International Company Profiles**

Take the gamble out of exporting to new customers abroad by using a U.S. Department of Commerce International Company Profile (ICP). These thorough background checks on your potential client will reduce your risk and allow you to enter new business relationships with confidence.

Commercial specialists in U.S. embassies and consulates abroad will conduct an investigation for you and deliver the results in 30 to 45 days, at a very reasonable cost. Reports include up-to-date information on your potential clients, such as:

- Bank and trade references
- Principals, key officers, and managers
- Product lines
- Number of employees
- Financial data
- Sales volume
- Reputation
- Market outlook

An International Company Profile may also include information on:

- Subsidiary/parent relationships
- Recent news items about the firm
- The firm's U.S. Customers
- Operational problems
- Activities of prominent owners
- Branch locations

The commercial specialists abroad who conduct your research will also give you their recommendation on whether you should enter a business relationship with the subject firm, and, if so, on what basis. Your request is held in strict confidence—the subject firm does not know who ordered the report

Source: U.S. Dept. of Commerce, 1998.

foreign opportunities. Although paperwork and other complications involve extra work and cost, many sources of expertise are ready to help the exporter. Overseas freight forwarders are skilled in handling physical distribution and documentation; banks take care of the international financial aspects; insurance companies handle foreign shipments and can even insure credit to foreign customers. There are also companies that do export packaging.

Most exporters use some outside expertise, the amount often depending on the volume of export sales. The exporter has, in effect, a make-or-buy decision. Can we do these tasks more efficiently in-house, or should we purchase them outside? As export volume increases, the exporter tends to do more and more in-house.

Other Marketing Tasks

Additional responsibilities of export management include market intelligence, pricing, and promotion. In indirect exporting, marketing information is gathered by the firm selling abroad. The firm supplying the goods may receive little market feedback. The export manager needs continuing market information, some of which is available from domestic sources. Foreign distributors are another important source. When export volume is large enough, the export manager should visit foreign markets to keep informed. (We described the market-intelligence function more fully in Chapter 7.)

Pricing for foreign markets involves new dimensions. First, the manager must decide whether to quote in U.S. dollars or other currencies. Then it is necessary to determine whether the quote should be **F.O.B.** (free on board—plant or port of exit), **C.I.F.** (cost, insurance, freight) to foreign port, or one of several other possible quotes. Should exports be at full cost or marginal cost? How should the firm handle tariffs and other add-ons to the plant price? If promotion is needed, the export manager has responsibility for it. One may work with an export advertising agency and/or with national distributors in cooperative advertising programs. (Export pricing and promotion are discussed in detail in Chapters 12, 13, 14, and 15.)

The Gold Key to Agent-Distributor Selection

Patrick Calabrese is president of Grieve Co. of Round Lake, IL, a manufacturer of industrial ovens and furnaces. The company wanted to sell to Southeast Asia so Calabrese sought help from the Department of Commerce. First, he signed up for the Gold Key Service, which is custom-tailored for U.S. firms planning to visit a country. It includes orientation briefings, market research, introductions to potential partners, and interpreter service. Calabrese also used the Department's Agent-Distributor Service to get the names of prospective representatives, adding the names from inquiries the company had received from the region.

Calabrese then went on a five-week trip to Thailand, Malaysia, Singapore, Indonesia, and Taiwan. Commercial officers from the embassies made appointments for him and arranged for interpreters. He interviewed a total of 28 agents. While in each country, he selected an exclusive agent, then gave a training session on Grieve Co. and its products.

"I had many long days and many long nights, but I accomplished a lot," he said. "I interviewed, evaluated, selected, and trained in each country." The Gold Key Service cost Grieve Co. between $250 and $300 per day, plus the costs of an interpreter.

Source: *Business America*, July 12, 1993, 3.

Marketing through Foreign Distributors

We have noted some of the major marketing tasks the exporter must perform from its home-country base. The actual marketing to final customers abroad must be done by the firm's distributor in that market. One of the most challenging jobs for export managers is to obtain the cooperation of the independent distributor in the foreign marketing effort. Various strategies and tactics for doing so are discussed in Chapter 11.

Conclusions on Direct Exporting

Our discussion here has been primarily from the viewpoint of the firm whose only involvement is by exporting. Of course, exporting is a continuing part of a firm's international business and is done by those who also engage in licensing, joint ventures, and other kinds of involvement. We gave quite a bit of attention to direct exporting because it is the most common form of international marketing. We will not summarize that discussion. Rather, we conclude with a list in "Global Marketing," "The Ten Commandments for Exporters," which highlights many of the important issues for the direct exporter.

FOREIGN MANUFACTURING AS FOREIGN-MARKET ENTRY

So far we have assumed that the firm entering foreign markets is supplying them from domestic plants. This is implicit in any form of exporting. However, sometimes the firm may find it either impossible or undesirable to supply all foreign markets from domestic production.

Several factors may encourage, or force, the firm to produce in foreign markets if it wishes to sell in them. For example, transportation costs may render heavy or bulky products noncompetitive. Tariffs or quotas can prevent entry of an exporter's products. In many countries, government preference for national suppliers can also shut the door to goods produced outside the country. When such preferences exist, a firm that sells to governments must produce locally. Any of these conditions could force the firm to manufacture in foreign markets in order to sell there.

GLOBAL MARKETING

The Ten Commandments for Exporters

1. Get export counseling and develop a master international marketing plan.
2. Secure top management commitment to exporting.
3. Exercise sufficient care in selecting overseas distributors.
4. Don't depend only on unsolicited orders, but establish a basis for orderly export growth.
5. Don't neglect the export market when the domestic market is booming.
6. Treat international distributors on an equal basis with domestic counterparts.
7. Don't assume that domestic marketing techniques will be successful abroad.
8. Be willing to modify products to meet regulations or cultural preferences of other countries.
9. Print sales, service, and warranty messages in local languages.
10. Provide readily available servicing for your product.

Source: *Basic Guide to Exporting* (Washington, DC: U.S. Department of Commerce, 1992), 1X.

More positive factors also encourage a firm to produce abroad. Some markets, especially regional groupings such as the EU, are large enough to warrant an efficient plant size. In addition, local production allows better interaction with local needs concerning product design, delivery, and service. Sometimes foreign production costs are lower, especially when transportation and tariff savings are added. The firm might undertake foreign production to gain any of these advantages even though it has the option of serving the market, at least partly, by exports. Britain's chemical firm, ICI, gave these reasons for beginning production on the European continent:[2]

1. You are more credible to your customers if your plant is close.

2. You are more acceptable to local authorities and have more influence on them.

3. Britain is an island and is vulnerable to interruption of supplies.

4. Perhaps most important, with a local plant you force your own company to commit itself to the market.

Approaches to Foreign Manufacture: Assembly

Once the firm has decided to enter certain markets by manufacturing in them, it has several alternatives. Foreign production may range from assembly plants, contract manufacturing, licensing, or joint ventures to wholly owned plants. In each approach, foreign manufacturing is the source of the firm's product in the market, but the extent of its involvement in production and marketing varies with the approach it chooses.

In **foreign assembly,** the firm produces domestically all or most of the components or ingredients of its product and ships them to foreign markets for assembly. Assembly operations involve less than full-scale manufacturing but still require that significant value be added in the local market. Notable examples of foreign assembly are the automobile and farm equipment industries. When transportation costs on a fully assembled vehicle or piece of equipment are high, the firm might be more competitive by shipping CKD (completely knocked down), and assembling them in the market. Another reason for local assembly is the tariff barrier; many countries have much lower tariffs on unassembled equipment; by forcing local assembly, governments increase local employment.

The pharmaceutical industry also uses extensive assembly operations, although they should be called *compounding* or *mixing operations*. Again because of transportation or tariff barriers, a firm ships key ingredients to foreign markets and adds bulky liquids or other ingredients, plus the capsule and packaging, locally. In similar fashion, Coca-Cola ships its syrup to foreign markets, where local bottlers add the water and the container. These assembly or mixing plants abroad represent partial local manufacturing; they are a compromise between exports and local production.

If an assembly plant involves foreign investment, the firm must make an investment decision as well as a decision on how to enter the market. However, the investment commitment is not necessarily included in a decision to assemble abroad. The firm can assemble its products in foreign markets through licensing arrangements without making a capital outlay. For example, Jeep licensed Renault to assemble its cars in Belgium.

Company-owned assembly operations usually are combined with a company marketing subsidiary in the same market. A licensee that assembles may handle local distribution as well. For example, Renault distributed Jeep vehicles in some parts of Europe, whereas Jeep handled distribution in other European countries through its Swiss subsidiary.

Coca-Cola is usually distributed by national organizations licensed by the company. This allows the company to earn over half of its revenue abroad with a small amount of investment outside of its home market. Coca-Cola has the following division of labor with its foreign franchised bottlers: It supplies the syrup, engineering services, quality control, and marketing advice. The bottlers do everything else, including the local marketing. In the 1990s, however, both Coca-Cola and Pepsi are buying into their local bottlers and taking a much more active role in local marketing.

Contract Manufacturing

Contract manufacturing abroad is foreign manufacturing by proxy. That is, the firm's product is produced in the foreign market by another producer under contract with the firm. Because the contract covers only manufacturing, marketing is handled by the firm. Contract manufacturing is feasible when the firm can locate foreign producers with the capability of manufacturing the product in satisfactory quantity and quality. In some markets, such capability cannot be found. One enterprising manufacturer in Honduras was producing under contract for three American firms: American Home Products, Colgate, and Procter & Gamble (P&G).

Contract manufacturing may be attractive if the firm's competitive advantage lies in marketing rather than in production. For example, P&G in Italy had several products manufactured under contract, and Unilever did the same thing in Japan for some products. Both firms concentrated on marketing the products. Contract manufacturing obviates the need for plant investment, something the firm may wish to avoid if the market is politically uncertain or if the firm is short of capital.

Contract manufacturing enables the firm to avoid labor and other problems that may arise from its lack of familiarity with the country. At the same time, the firm gets the advantage of advertising its product as being locally made. This may be useful in public relations or for government procurement purposes. If a market proves too small or risky, it is easier and less costly to terminate a manufacturing contract than to shut down the firm's own plant. Other advantages include transportation savings (compared to exports), occasionally lower production costs abroad, and possible exports of components or supplies to the contract manufacturer.

Drawbacks to the contract-manufacturing approach may limit its application. For one, the manufacturing profit goes to the local firm rather than to the international firm. This is not serious if sufficient profit remains in marketing activities.

For another, finding a satisfactory manufacturer in the foreign market may be difficult. Quality control, too, is usually a greater problem when production is done by another firm.

From our discussion, the advantages of contract manufacturing appear to outweigh the drawbacks. One should not, however, underestimate the problems of locating and working with a contract manufacturer. Nevertheless, this avenue should be given serious attention when foreign investment is not feasible or desirable for the firm.

Del Monte chose contract manufacturing as a low-cost way of producing in Central America. It had been exporting there for many years and decided that the time had come for local production. Del Monte began with Del Campo, a Costa Rican producer of canned foods. Del Campo put out 20 different Del Monte products, using Del Monte recipes. The agreement was a straight price per item with Del Monte handling the distribution.

After several years, Del Monte decided it had a good local partner, so a closer relationship was worked out. Del Monte began to assist Del Campo with production and marketing, and Del Campo began to produce Del Monte products for other Central American countries. Del Monte negotiated an option to buy up to 67 percent of Del Campo's equity.

Licensing

Licensing is another way the firm can establish local production in foreign markets without capital investment. It differs from contract manufacturing in that it is usually for a longer term and involves much greater responsibilities for the national party. A **licensing agreement** is an arrangement wherein the licensor gives something of value to the licensee in exchange for certain performance and payments from the licensee. The licensor (the international company) may give the licensee (the national firm) one or more of the following things: (1) patent rights, (2) trademark rights, (3) copyrights, or (4) know-how on products or processes. Any of these may be given for use in a particular foreign market, or the licensee may have rights in several countries or on a whole continent.

In return for the use of the know-how or rights received, the licensee usually promises (1) to produce the products covered by the rights, (2) to market these products in an assigned territory, and (3) to pay the licensor some amount related to the sales volume of such products. The licensee assumes a much greater role than the contract manufacturer, taking over marketing in addition to production, and is thus the complete foreign-market presence of the international firm for the products covered.

Evaluating Licensing

Several features of licensing are attractive. First, it requires no capital and thus need not deter even small companies. Second, it is often the quickest and easiest way to enter a foreign market. Even the firm that has capital may face a slow process establishing local production and distribution. Third, the firm immediately gains local knowledge.

A fourth advantage is that many governments favor licensing over direct investment because licensing brings technology into the country with fewer strings and costs attached. Thus, licensing may gain government approval more quickly than direct investment. And from the licensor's viewpoint, there is no investment to be expropriated. Finally, the general advantages of foreign production also apply to licensing—savings in tariff and transport costs, local production where national suppliers are favored, and so on.

Philip Morris has a special reason for licensing. Because many governments have tobacco monopolies, the only way Philip Morris can get into their markets is to license a government to produce and sell its brands. Philip Morris does this in Western and Eastern European countries.

The disadvantages of licensing are less numerous, but they may carry greater weight. The chief fear about licensing is that the licensor may establish its own competitor. During the five or ten years of the licensing agreement, the licensor may transfer enough expertise that the licensee can go it alone, and thus the licensor may lose that market, and perhaps neighboring markets, to the former licensee. This is less likely where strong brands or trademarks are involved.

Westinghouse encountered this problem. In 1972 when the French company Framatome signed a licensing agreement with Westinghouse, Framatome was an insignificant factor in the market for atomic power. By 1980, however, Framatome was second only to Westinghouse, and the two parted company. An executive at Westinghouse acknowledged that Framatome had developed the capability to design around its patents, "but we'll attempt to stay six months to a year ahead of them."[3]

Another reason for hesitancy about licensing is the limited returns it provides. Although no capital outlay is necessary, the royalties and fees from licensing are not cost free to the licensor, which must invest management and engineering time. A direct investment approach to the foreign market requires greater effort and resources, but it may yield much greater profits. Licensing returns are limited primarily to a percentage of licensee sales, commonly 3 to 5 percent. Indeed, less developed countries are trying to reduce even further the royalties and fees paid to licensors. In one Korean case, the licensor and licensee agreed on a 5 percent royalty, but a government ministry adjusted it to 3.2 percent.

Yet another possible drawback is the problem of controlling the licensee. Although the contract should spell out the responsibilities of each party, misunderstandings and conflicts can arise in its implementation. Frequent areas of conflict are quality control, the marketing effort of the licensee, and interpretation of the exclusiveness and extent of territorial coverage. These problems arise partly because an agreement that met both parties' interests at the time of signing can become unsuitable to one or both as conditions change.

One U.S. equipment producer had a French licensee for over 30 years. The licensee was capable and aggressive in developing the French market, and the licensor was very satisfied. However, when the Common Market eliminated territorial restrictions between member nations, the licensor found the French licensee competing with its own subsidiaries in other member countries. The U.S. firm was unhappy but was afraid to terminate the agreement for fear the licensee would go off on its own and be an even more dangerous competitor, taking the French market with it.

Managing Licensing

Firms that are successful in licensing have developed certain techniques for minimizing the pitfalls of licensing and accentuating its potential benefits. We note some of them here.

1. Have a deliberate policy and plan for licensing; that is, give it proper attention.

2. Fix licensing responsibility in the firm by means of a licensing manager or department. Pfizer had nine licensing directors, one for each major business unit.

3. Select licensees carefully.

4. Draft a careful agreement and review it with the licensee. Some items to include are territorial coverage, duration, royalties, trade secrets, quality control, and a minimum-performance clause.

GLOBAL MARKETING

A Champion at Home and Abroad by Licensing

Champion Products, now part of Sara Lee, is a U.S. maker of athletic apparel and equipment. Champion began exporting in the late 1970s, but in the early 1980s the U.S. dollar was soaring and Champion's exports faded. It then decided that licensing offered the best chance of success in foreign markets.

In line with this new strategy, the company evaluated its overseas distributors as licensee candidates. Champion found that many handled other companies' products. It wanted licensees that would devote all their energies to Champion so it had to find many new ones, a difficult task because Champion was not well known at that time. Concurrent with its licensee search, Champion sought global protection for its brand name. It applied for registration and protection almost everywhere, which meant a heavy cost in filing and legal fees, but the company considered this a necessary investment.

Champion then set up a coordinating office in Florence, Italy, for styling, merchandising, buying, and contract manufacturing. The latter became necessary to supplement the licensee's output in some areas. The Florence office was important to Champion's success because it ensured that the goods sold by all the licensees had a consistent look.

In Europe, Champion had to innovate in distribution because its U.S. channel—campus bookstores and direct sales to athletic teams—did not exist. Therefore, the firm sold to retail sporting goods shops and department stores. This channel was so successful that it was later implemented in the United States, where it was also successful and resulted in an increase in sales of more than tenfold in only five years.

Champion also began to implement a global advertising strategy. It now requires all licensees to use the agency it selected, Rumrill-Hoyt, a Saatchi & Saatchi affiliate. This means that the campaign has the same thrust everywhere rather than being typically European or American. With this practice, the copy is translated into the appropriate local languages, but the campaign retains a unified message.

Source: *Business International,* May 4, 1992, 133–140.

5. Supply the licensee with critical ingredients.

6. Obtain equity in the licensee.

7. Limit product and territorial coverage.

8. Keep patent and trademark registration in the licensor's name.

9. Be a reasonably important part of the licensee's business. Canon deliberately chose a smaller firm for its copier licensee in India to get better performance.

International licensing can be an important part of company strategy; U.S. firms receive over $10 billion a year from licensing agreements. It should be noted that licensing income is not limited to royalties but includes such items as (1) technical assistance fees, (2) sale of materials or components to licensee, (3) lump-sum payments for transfer of rights or technology, (4) technology feedback, (5) reciprocal license rights, (6) fees for engineering services, (7) sales of machinery or equipment, and (8) management fees. The typical company receives five different types of return on its licensing agreements, but most of the income tends to be from royalties.

Juste Quimico Pharmaceutica, a Spanish pharmaceutical company, signed a contract with an Indian licensee. Because Juste will receive no know-how, royalty, or trademark fees, government approvals were not required. Juste sought its return by selling critical ingredients to the licensee and by getting better market access rather than depending on the limited royalties and technical fees allowed by the government. Juste hoped for a good foothold in the large Indian health-care market, plus exports to countries in Asia and Africa.

Licensing as a Fallback Strategy

Another way licensing can be attractive is as a fallback position when other approaches run into trouble. An exporter may find that tariffs or other trade restrictions have taken away one of its export markets. If it is not feasible or desirable for the firm to set up local production in that market, the firm could maintain a position there by licensing. In a similar vein, a firm producing in a country may find that political or economic problems have made its operation untenable. If it is unable to export to that market from another country, it could find licensing an attractive way to maintain some position in that market. In both cases, licensing could prove effective, not as a primary strategy, but as a fallback position to hold on to some share in the otherwise lost market.

A Final Example

A brief case study concludes our discussion of licensing: The Manhattan Shirt Company had licensees in over 30 countries, many of them in developing nations. These were administered by the company's International Licensing Division, whose manager spent 40 percent of his time traveling abroad. Though Manhattan shirts are a nonpatentable product, the company believed that its brand name and know-how were very licensable.

The company's method of operation is instructive. Manhattan began with a market survey. This was followed by a search for licensee candidates in the more attractive markets. The licensing manager visited all prospective licensees before making a selection. One criterion was that Manhattan shirts be an important part of the licensee's business, so that they would be given proper attention. The licensee's production people were required to come to the United States for training, and sales training was given in the licensee's country. The company preferred to limit the territory of a licensee. If a licensee was given more than one country, Manhattan liked separate performance clauses for each market.

The licensee was required to advertise. Whereas sales and production training were included in the royalty fee, advertising had to be at the expense of the licensee. Often the company took a part of the first year's royalties and rebated a portion to be used by the licensee for advertising, above the regular commitment.

Manhattan set up an exchange of information between members of its licensing "family." This was good for morale and also for the exchange of experiences. Most of the technical information came from Manhattan's domestic operations. The data were supplied to licensees at the same time they became available in the United States. Information was also exchanged during visits to the licensees; the manager believed that these periodic visits not only helped the performance of the licensees but also allowed Manhattan to control the agreement.

For quality control, the company required random samples of every licensee's production. Revenue control was maintained by traveling auditors who checked licensees' production and sales reports.

Joint Ventures in Foreign Markets

Foreign joint ventures in manufacturing have something in common with foreign licensing. Both involve foreign manufacturing and distribution by a foreign firm. The major difference is that in the joint venture, the international firm has equity and a management voice in the foreign firm. The equity share of the international company generally is between 25 and 75 percent. Instead of seeking a technical definition of a joint venture, however, we use a practical one: A **joint venture** is a foreign operation in which the international company has enough equity to have a voice in management but not enough to completely dominate the venture. Note that we consider only joint ventures between an international firm and a firm that is native to the country where the venture is located.

Contract manufacturing and licensing are joint ventures of a sort, and so is the exporter working with the foreign distributor, but in none of these relationships are the ties so strong as in the joint venture. As in the progression from going steady to being engaged to being married, each step represents a stronger tie. With the expansion of international operations, joint ventures have become increasingly important.

To Join or Not to Join

The joint-venture approach must be compared with both the lesser commitment of contract manufacturing and licensing and the greater commitment of wholly owned foreign production. Whatever benefits derive from foreign manufacture will, of course, be obtained in the joint-venture approach. As compared with a lesser commitment, joint ventures have the following advantages: (1) potentially greater returns from equity participation as opposed to royalties, (2) greater control over production and marketing, (3) better market feedback, and (4) more experience in international marketing. Disadvantages include a need for greater investment of capital and management resources, and a potentially greater risk than with a non-equity approach.

When joint ventures are compared with wholly owned foreign production, a different picture emerges: (1) A joint venture requires less capital and fewer management resources and thus is more open to smaller companies. (2) A given amount of capital can cover more countries. (3) The danger of expropriation is less when a firm has a national partner than when the international firm is sole owner. Because of this, Club Méditerranée has a policy of minority ownership in its foreign operations, or "villages." An analyst noted, "They always make sure that local interests are big enough that if Club Med is thrown out, those interests will suffer first."

Many governments prefer or even demand joint ventures because they believe that their nations get more of the profits and technological benefit if nationals have a share. Also, finding a national partner may be the only way to invest in some markets that are too competitive or crowded to admit a new operation. This latter point is important for many Japanese firms in the U.S. market. Fujitsu, Japan's largest computer manufacturer, found it almost impossible to break into the competitive U.S. market by itself. Therefore, it formed a marketing joint venture with TRW to get the marketing know-how and distribution it couldn't get alone.

Joint ventures compare unfavorably with wholly owned operations on only a few, but critical, points. The interests of one partner may conflict with those of the other. The interests of the national partner relate to the operation in the local market. The international firm's interests relate to the totality of its international operations; actions it takes to further global operations may not appear beneficial to the national partner. Some points of conflict are (1) transfer pricing, (2) earnings—pay out or plow back, and (3) product-line and market coverage of the joint venture.

Shared equity may also involve an unequal sharing of the burden. Occasionally, international companies with 50–50 joint ventures believe that they are giving more than 50 percent of the technology, management skill, and other factors that contribute to success but are receiving only half the profits. Of course, the national partner contributes local knowledge and other intangibles that may be underestimated. Nevertheless, some companies believe that the local partner gets too much of a "free ride."

The major complaint about joint ventures compared with 100 percent ownership is that it is difficult to integrate them into a synergistic international operation. When the international firm wishes to standardize product design, quality standards, or other activities, it may encounter disagreement from its national partners. Thus, when standardization, international exchange, and integration are important to the company, the joint-venture approach can be a hindrance. Conversely, when national operations have differing product lines and localized marketing—as in packaged foods—joint ventures pose less of a problem.

Strategic Considerations

Marketing considerations play a primary role when international firms evaluate the joint-venture approach. Local market knowledge is usually the foreign firm's major lack when entering a host country. Joining with a national firm may be the best way to obtain local marketing skills and contacts. The national partner can provide quick access through its existing market position. The foreign firm can effectively piggyback with its national partner.

One place where many firms feel the need for local marketing is in the difficult Japanese market. Anheuser-Busch, Campbell, Kodak, and Morton Thiokol (air bags) are examples of firms joining with Japanese partners to facilitate their entry into and penetration of the Japanese market. An unusual case occurred when Prudential Life Insurance Company joined with Sony to help it enter the Japanese life-insurance market. This illustrates again the importance of local marketing knowledge as a motivation in joint ventures.

Firms coming into the U.S. market also frequently feel the need for a U.S. marketing partner. For example, Volvo, which did its own automobile marketing in the United States, joined with General Motors for the U.S. truck market. After a lack of success in the U.S. market, Nikko Securities joined with Wells Fargo to build its U.S. business. The benefit for Wells Fargo is a better entry into Japan.

A second major consideration favoring joint-venture entry is oligopolistic competition. In industries characterized by a small number of competitors, the foreign firm may find entry barriers too high for solo entry into a market. It may need to join with a competing firm—or a firm in a complementary line—to have a viable presence in the market. For example, Bols and Heineken formed a joint venture to survive in the merging European market. Molson and Elders joined together to maintain a share of the U.S. beer market. When Coca-Cola joined with Cadbury-Schweppes in the United Kingdom, Pepsi responded by joining with three British brewers. In Brazil, Pepsi joined with Brahma, Brazil's largest brewer, to gain market share against leader Coke.

Two case histories illustrate contrasting aspects of company philosophy and practice in joint ventures. First consider this statement of the Scott Paper Company, a firm believer in joint ventures.

> Our foreign policy: Get there early and get married. Scott was an early arrival in 15 countries. And our growth overseas is as spectacular as the opportunities there. We are across the world from Europe to Latin America to Japan. Our markets there are growing faster than at home.
>
> All in all, there are some 500 million people in Scott's markets outside the United States. Which means our manufacturing and marketing facilities now can serve at least 80 percent of the Free World purchasing power. The potential is there. And so is Scott.
>
> We're there in an unusual relationship, too, as the 50-50 partner in most of our overseas affiliates. Not 51-49. 50-50. That 1 percent we don't have has yielded substantial dividends. In mutual trust. In the higher caliber of the corporate partners it has brought us in each country. In the knowledgeable people they bring us. It's a successful marriage if ever we heard of one.

Interestingly, in 1995, Kimberly-Clark acquired Scott, largely because of Scott's international presence.

The sad and costly experience of Xerox provides a second example. In its early years, Xerox Corp. experienced tremendous growth in the U.S. market. Faced with difficulty in meeting rapidly growing U.S. demand, the company believed it could not begin to tackle the rest of the world. Xerox therefore joined with the Rank Organization in the United Kingdom to form a 50-50 joint venture, Rank-Xerox (RX). Xerox gave the venture an exclusive license in perpetuity to manufacture and sell all xerographic machines outside North America.

This was a generous gift to the Rank Organization. Most of the world was its to sell Xerox machines in. As time went by, Xerox realized that it had been too generous. It had begun to expand capacity and to meet the demands of the North American market. Now it wanted the ability to sell its machines in other countries without having to share the profits with its partner. Since the markets outside North America belonged to the joint venture, Rank-Xerox, Xerox had to buy back the right to market its own products abroad.

A series of agreements over the years sought to rectify the initial error made by Xerox in giving away its world markets. In one agreement, RX sold marketing rights for Latin America in return for a 5 percent royalty on all Xerox sales and rental there—plus several million dollars of Xerox stock. Later Xerox paid Rank $12.5 million for the right to name 13 RX directors to Rank's 12. There were several other adjustments over the years as Xerox tried to extricate itself from its "original sin." Analysts estimate that the careless entry by Xerox into the RX joint venture would cost Xerox stockholders almost $300 million in its first 20 years. In 1998, Xerox bought out the RX copier share for $1.5 billion.

Strategic Alliances

Almost every entry method involves an alliance with a partner. It may be an export management company, a distributor, a licensee, or a joint-venture partner. In the 1980s, however, a new term arose to describe a different kind of international cooperative venture. **Strategic alliance** has no precise definition but covers a variety of usually nonequity contractual relationships, frequently between competitors and frequently between competitors in different countries. For example, Philips links with Siemens, Texas Instruments links with Hitachi, and General Motors links with Toyota. In these and hundreds of other examples, competitors from different countries contract together to meet a strategic need of each party. Because the relationship often does not fit the definition of a licensing arrangement or joint venture, the looser term, *strategic alliance,* is used.

Cross-border strategic alliances take many different forms. They have become the most popular method of international expansion as firms face internationalization pressures and feel the need for foreign help. The Japanese have been very active in alliance formation, but firms in any country are finding that, if they want to enter world markets, frequently the best—and sometimes the only—way is through an alliance. Examples exist in industries ranging from cars to computers to communications. For example, AT&T and Sprint are using alliances to go global, as did MCI. The airline industry has also become very active in alliances with Northwest-KLM as an early successful example.

Strategic alliances have a variety of objectives; a frequent one is market entry. Many firms find that a contractual arrangement with a foreign competitor is a better way to enter a market than the traditional distributor, licensee, or joint-venture approach. For example, Harris Corp. allied with Matsushita in Japan and Philips in Europe to distribute PACnet, a data communications product. Unisys and Hewlett-Packard both allied with Canon to distribute microcomputers in Japan. Glaxo contracted with E. Merck to market Zantac in Germany.

Why would a firm help a competitor enter its home market? The answer is that the local firm is getting a new product, one that is complementary rather

GLOBAL MARKETING

The Diaper Alliance

In the United States, Procter & Gamble and Kimberly-Clark are major competitors in disposable diapers. Overseas, however, Kimberly-Clark could not match P&G's massive presence in foreign markets. In seeking to catch up with P&G's world market for Pampers, the company decided to find a partner.

In most markets abroad, P&G's major competition is Unilever, which has an equally massive presence abroad.

Unilever, however, did not have disposable diapers. Thus, the common competitors of P&G formed a diaper alliance. Unilever could widen its product line against P&G and Kimberly-Clark could get substantial foreign market coverage to be a global diaper competitor of P&G.

In India, for example, Unilever enabled Huggies (Kimberly's diapers) to reach over 600,000 shops in 110 cities. In Brazil, one of P&G's big Pampers' markets overseas, Unilever distributed Huggies from Kimberly's Argentine plant to enable Huggies to become a significant competitor to Pampers there.

---

than directly competitive. Thus, E. Merck has many drugs but no ulcer remedy like Zantac. In effect, market-entry strategic alliances are a form of piggybacking. Stated differently, piggybacking is an early form of strategic alliance. Finally, we should note that though these alliances are called *strategic,* every entry method the firm uses should be equally strategic.

Wholly Owned Foreign Production

Wholly owned foreign production represents the greatest commitment to foreign markets. In principle, **wholly owned** means 100 percent ownership by the international firm. In practice, the firm usually achieves the same results by owning 95 percent or even less. The chief practical criterion for wholly owned ventures is not the completeness of ownership but the completeness of control by the international company.

Make or Buy?

The firm can obtain wholly owned foreign production facilities in two ways: (1) buy out a foreign producer—the acquisition route—or (2) develop its own facilities from the ground up. As a variation on the acquisition route, the firm can buy out a joint-venture partner. The acquisition route is especially popular, and it offers certain advantages.

Acquisition is a quicker way for a firm to get into a market than building its own facilities. Acquiring a going concern usually means acquiring a qualified labor force, national management, local knowledge, and contacts with local markets and government. And in some markets, acquisition may be the only way to enter if the industry has no room for a new competitor.

(AB) Electrolux is a billion-dollar Swedish firm selling consumer and industrial goods. After having left the U.S. market, it re-entered it by acquiring National Union Electric (NUE), a maker of vacuum cleaners and room air conditioners. Electrolux's rationale was as follows:

1. Complementarity of product lines and distribution channels made synergy possible.

2. It obtained immediate access to the U.S. market for many Electrolux products through NUE's network of 37,000 independent dealers.

3. NUE's product line could be carried throughout the world via Electrolux's worldwide marketing organization.

Rubbermaid was having trouble in Europe, where it had entered through a joint venture with a Dutch chemical firm. Finally, in 1998 it decided to acquire French and Polish plastics producers and the Dutch chemical firm. This gave Rubbermaid the existing products and markets of those firms, plus the ability to integrate its European marketing.

The alternative to acquisition is the establishment of a *new facility,* a method that may be desirable or necessary in certain circumstances. For example, in some markets, the firm will not be able to find a national producer willing to sell, or the government will not allow the firm to sell to the international company. In other markets, producers may be willing to sell but lack the caliber of facilities needed by the international firm.

For its part, the international firm may prefer a new facility over an acquisition. If the market has no personnel or management shortages, the firm feels less pressure for acquisition. Furthermore, if the firm builds a new plant, it can not only incorporate the latest technology and equipment, but also it can avoid the problems of trying to change the traditional practices of an established concern. A new facility means a fresh start and an opportunity for the international company to shape the local firm into its own image and requirements.

Xomox, for example, a small U.S. multinational, believes in starting foreign manufacturing entirely on its own. It believes acquisitions can lead to resentment on the part of local management and workers. Also, through going it alone, the firm can show its contributions to the local economy—jobs, exports, investments—that were not there before it came. Sara Lee also deliberately avoided an acquisition for its entry into the Polish market.

It is instructive to look at the actual entry patterns of American firms. Data from Ernst & Young showed Americans preferred acquisitions over joint ventures in Europe by 225 to 67. In Asia, by contrast, joint ventures were preferred over acquisitions by 91 to 27.[4]

Deciding on Wholly Owned Operations

Evaluation of the sole ownership approach is easier now that we have considered the other alternatives. The advantages of wholly owned ventures are few but powerful. Ownership of 100 percent means 100 percent of the profits go to the international firm, eliminating the possibility that a national partner gets a "free ride." Complete ownership also gives the firm greater experience and better market contact.

With no national partner, no inefficiencies arise from conflicts of interest. Perhaps the overriding argument for complete control, however, is the possibility of integrating various national operations into a synergistic international system. Lesser degrees of involvement are more likely to lead to suboptimization because national partners have goals that conflict with those of the international firm. This was important for Rubbermaid.

The limitations to the 100 percent ownership approach are several. For one thing, it is costly in terms of capital and management resources. The capital requirements prevent many firms from practicing a complete ownership strategy. Although large firms do not often find capital availability a constraint, they may face a shortage of management personnel.

Another drawback to 100 percent ownership is the probable negative host-government and public relations effect. Most nations believe that their participation in the venture should not be limited to supplying just labor or raw materials. Some governments go so far as to prohibit 100 percent ownership by the·

international firm and demand licensing or joint ventures instead. A further risk deriving from these national feelings is expropriation, which is more likely and more costly with wholly owned operations.

Finally, 100 percent ownership may deprive the firm of the local knowledge and contacts of a national partner. The local collaborator often serves as a buffer between the international firm and its various national audiences. This role of the national partner as a cultural bridge can be its major contribution, helping the firm to avoid mistakes in its encounters with nationals in business or government. By taking the acquisition route, the firm has more chance of getting such nationals than it does in setting up a new operation. The same applies to a wholly owned operation developed from a joint venture. With a new establishment, the firm can develop nationals who can be a culture bridge, but the process is slower.

Entering Eastern European Markets

In principle, the entry methods for Eastern European markets are the same as for other markets (for example, exporting, licensing, joint ventures, etc.). In practice, entry methods in Eastern Europe have to be customized by industry and by country. The legal, political, economic, and infrastructure situation varies by country as each country moves in its own way and at its own pace away from the previous Communist economy. Entry strategies and approaches used by firms in OECD markets need to be adapted for entry into Eastern European markets. (This is also the case for China as we saw earlier in this chapter.)

There are now over 20 separate countries in what was formerly the Soviet bloc. With a total population of well over 400 million, they represent an attractive market, but one that must now be entered on a customized country by country basis. The former government-run Foreign Trade Organizations (FTOs) that were the entry point in earlier East-West trade have collapsed in varying degrees in the different countries. For example, already by 1995, two-thirds of Russia's GDP was in the private sector. New marketing infrastructure is being formed gradually so firms must analyze and adapt to the situation in the markets they choose to enter.

Because of the unpredictably evolving situation in Eastern Europe, perhaps the best way to get a feel for it is to look at some specific examples of company entry strategies in the region.

Unilever bought a former state-owned oils plant near Prague and made it into a center for making soaps, margarine, and Pond's skin cream for the region. Whirlpool bought Tatramat, a Czech appliance producer. By upgrading the technology and forming an alliance with IKEA, Whirlpool become number one in the market. Gillette began business in Russia in a joint venture with a Russian holding company. In the late 90s, Gillette built a large new plant in St. Petersburg (next to a Coca-Cola facility) to serve the whole market.

Adidas
Adidas uses a flexible entry approach depending on the situation in each country. It has a 50 percent market share of branded sporting goods in Eastern Europe so its experience is noteworthy. Its preferred entry method is wholly owned marketing subsidiaries such as it has in the Czech Republic, Hungary, Poland, and Russia. Adidas uses a few independent distributors, as in Bulgaria and Slovenia. The company avoids distribution joint ventures in the region, but it has a few licensing agreements. Adidas feels distribution joint ventures are very problematic in Eastern Europe, but it accepts some production joint ventures there.

Sara Lee
When entering Poland, Sara Lee considered acquiring a local firm being privatized. It decided against acquisition because the firm would require fairly extensive restructuring and layoffs. Sara Lee felt this would be dangerous for both public

and labor relations. Instead, the company started an assembly operation and gradually expanded it, adding processes and products, going increasingly to a full-scale manufacturing operation.

Sara Lee didn't feel comfortable using local distributors in Poland because of credit and other risks, so the company goes straight to the retail shops. Because of its heavy advertising and high brand recognition, Sara Lee is able to get cash on delivery from 95 percent of the shops.

In Hungary, the brewing industry is owned by five foreign conglomerates. Foreign ownership was encouraged by the friendly business climate and tax holidays. This is the only industry in Hungary that is under foreign control, however, again highlighting the importance of analyzing both industry and country variables before entry.

CONCLUSIONS ON FOREIGN-MARKET ENTRY METHODS

We have discussed many methods of foreign-market entry, noting the advantages and disadvantages of each. We cannot say that there is one best way to enter a foreign market. The way best for the firm depends not only on its size, capabilities, and needs, but also on the opportunities and conditions in the target markets. The firm must analyze its own situation and consider how the variables discussed here apply. Optimal results come from a careful analysis of alternatives rather than merely responding to initiatives from outside the firm, which is the way many firms have carried on their international business.

Flexibility is an important aspect of the firm's choice of entry strategy. Rather than rigidly following a single approach, the firm may want variation, depending on conditions in different markets. Larger markets may permit more direct approaches, whereas smaller markets may be better served by less direct entry. It may be appropriate to use different entry strategies for different product lines or divisions. Flexibility over time is also a major consideration. As conditions change, the optimum strategy may change. The firm can gain only by anticipating developments and adapting to them, rather than fighting them. Finding creative answers to such developments is the key to the viability of the international firm. The following examples show how strategies change over time.

Weyerhaeuser set up its own sales offices in Europe, South America, Australia, and the Far East. This was a departure from the traditional policy of U.S. forest products companies to sell overseas only in conditions of excess supply or when overseas prices were higher than domestic. Weyerhaeuser committed to foreign markets permanently when exports topped 8 percent of company sales. By 1992, exports reached $2 billion and the company was among the top 20 exporters in the United States, the only firm in its industry in the top 50.

A large European chemical company had a five-stage strategy in its approach to foreign markets:

- ◆ *Stage 1*. Limited sales, a form of market testing, through trading companies or independent distributors that bought for their own account.

- ◆ *Stage 2*. Where markets looked promising, the company sent field representatives to aid the distributor. This was done in Nigeria and East Africa, for example.

- ◆ *Stage 3*. Where field representatives reported strong sales in a market, the company moved to establish its own sales organization.

- ◆ *Stage 4*. If the sales subsidiary developed the market to a highly profitable degree, the company considered plant investment. The first step was a compounding plant to mix and package ingredients imported from Europe. Examples of this are Brazil and Mexico.

◆ *Stage 5*. The final step is a complete manufacturing plant. Such a plant might produce only a few of the many products of the firm, depending on local raw material supply and markets. The company has such a plant in India.

Level of Involvement—A Two-Way Street

The normal progression of the firm in world markets is from exporting to heavier kinds of involvement, usually ending up with manufacturing operations abroad, as with the European chemical company just cited. Indeed, that is the history of most multinationals—a life cycle pattern of international involvement. However, just as life cycles have a decline phase, so the firm's involvement in a market may undergo retrenchment and a regression to lesser involvement. The extreme case would be when expropriation or other political action forces the firm to leave wholly owned operations and have nothing left in the country, such as in Cuba or Iran. More common is the situation when changes in a market or in the firm's position there cause a strategic reassessment. The factors that made the firm seek a certain level of involvement may have changed or the firm may not have been successful in maintaining that involvement, so the appropriate strategy is to accept a lesser involvement in the market.

It should be noted that such strategic withdrawals or retreats are not necessarily defeats. They are often merely the sensible business response to a new situation. Just as discretion may be the better part of valor in some military situations, so many strategic changes of involvement may be the most profitable response of the firm to certain problems in foreign markets. A few examples illustrate some of these situations:

1. Bulova, a strong international marketer of traditional watches, was being buffeted by the new electronic and quartz watches. Losses overseas caused Bulova to change from its own marketing subsidiaries to less expensive independent agents.

2. Unilever is one of the most powerful multinationals. In Mexico, Unilever had wholly owned production facilities for soaps and detergents. Severe competition from Colgate, Procter & Gamble, and La Corona (a Mexican firm) prevented satisfactory profits for Unilever. The company decided to sell its factory, maintain a marketing subsidiary, and contract-manufacture its product with La Corona.

3. In 1989, Maytag decided to go international. Having no experience, the easiest way was to buy Hoover Co., which had a strong appliance business in England and Australia and a modest presence on the Continent. In 1995, beset by fierce competition and a long recession in Europe, Maytag finally gave up and sold Hoover to Candy Sp A, an Italian appliance firm. Maytag said it would refocus on its core North American business.

SUMMARY

Firms with limited resources can find quick and easy entry to foreign markets through indirect exporting. They can make a domestic sale to companies with buying offices in the United States. These buyers may be foreign retail groups, foreign trade organizations, or corporations supplying foreign subsidiaries from the United States.

Export management companies (EMCs) are another form of indirect exporting, but they are specialized intermediaries who sell their export marketing services. Use of EMCs is a low-cost way to obtain an export department without setting up one in the firm. They offer instant market access as well as economies of scale by serving several producers. These miniversions of a foreign trading company are used by thousands of U.S. firms.

Another way to get economies of scale in exporting is by joining with other producers. One form of such legal cooperation is the Webb-Pomerene association, which acts as the exporting arm of members and is used primarily by agriculture and commodity groups. The new U.S. export trading companies (ETCs) offer another form of cooperation. They are meant to be more powerful than the EMCs and to emulate the Japanese trading companies, but they have had very limited success thus far. Piggybacking is a form of cooperation between two producers wherein one carries the other's product(s) to export markets. This is a popular form of exporting because the rider gets instant, inexpensive export marketing while the carrier gets a complementary product to round out its line.

Direct exporting, in which the firm does the whole exporting job in-house, is much more demanding than indirect exporting. There are greater personnel, administrative, and financial requirements. The firm itself must choose its foreign markets, find representatives in those markets, arrange the logistics, and then try to manage its foreign marketing, working through independent distributors.

When foreign production is desired, assembly in foreign markets is a compromise approach. It is a blend of exporting and local production as the firm ships from home parts or ingredients, which are then processed locally. It reduces transport and tariff costs and helps the firm respond better to local needs.

Contract manufacturing allows the firm to produce abroad without plant investment by contracting to use a local firm's production facilities. It saves on transport and tariff costs and avoids local investment and labor problems. It is useful when governments and/or customers favor local supply.

Working with a licensee avoids any major commitment to a foreign market. The local licensee produces and markets the firm's product. It gives the advantages of local supply at low cost, but a disadvantage is that it limits the control and returns of the firm. What's more, it may mean training a competitor.

Joint ventures—producing and marketing abroad with a local partner—can be an effective market entry. In addition to the advantages of local production, the firm may gain local market knowledge and contacts as well as potential conflicts. Joint venturing is more costly than other forms of entry except for wholly owned operations. Today, looser forms of partnering, called *strategic alliances,* are popular. These contractual, nonequity links may offer some of the advantages of joint venturing but with less commitment.

Wholly owned operations involve the greatest commitment to a foreign market. In return for this commitment, the firm receives complete control, greater international integration, and usually greater profits but also greater exposure to foreign problems. Wholly owned operations can start with a new establishment or by acquiring a local firm. Acquisitions are currently very popular because they allow quicker entry and an established market position. They may also be necessary in markets that have no room for completely new entrants. In Eastern Europe, entry methods usually have to be adapted to the peculiar situation in each of these emerging markets.

QUESTIONS

10.1 Explain market feedback, investment requirements, and exposure to foreign problems as variables in choosing an entry method to foreign markets.

10.2 Identify the ways to reach foreign markets by making a domestic sale.

10.3 Why do international trading companies offer the best entry to some markets?

10.4 Why might a small, new-to-export company be interested in using an export management company?

10.5 How can the carrier and the rider both benefit from a piggyback arrangement?

10.6 When a firm begins direct exporting, what tasks must it perform?

10.7 "When exporting to a market, you're only as good as your distributor there." Discuss.

10.8 What procedures should a firm follow in selecting a distributor?

10.9 What are the benefits to local manufacture as a form of market entry? What are the costs?

10.10 "Foreign assembly represents a compromise between exporting and local production." Discuss.

10.11 When is contract manufacturing desirable?

10.12 What are the pros and cons of licensing as a form of market entry?

10.13 How do successful licensors manage their licensing program?

10.14 Why is acquisition often the preferred way to establish wholly owned operations abroad?

10.15 Why may a firm's entry methods be different in Eastern Europe?

ENDNOTES

[1] Lecture at the University of Michigan, March 16, 1990.

[2] *Business Europe,* June 7, 1984, 179.

[3] Interview at Westinghouse, July 10, 1981.

[4] *Business Week,* December 19, 1994, 6.

FURTHER READINGS

Agarwal, Sanjeev. "Socio-Cultural Distance and the Choice of Joint Ventures." *Journal of International Marketing* 2, no. 2 (1994): 63–80.

Ajami, Riad, and Dara Khambata. "Global Strategic Alliances: The New Transnationals." *Journal of Global Marketing* 5, no. 2 (1992): 55–70.

Aulakh, Preet S., Tamer Cavusgil, and M. B. Sarkar. "Compensation in International Licensing Agreements." *Journal of International Business Studies* 29, 2 (1998): 409–420.

Howard, Donald G. "Export Management Companies in Global Marketing." *Journal of Global Marketing* 8, no. 1 (1994): 95–110.

Samiee, Saeed. "Exporting and the Internet." *International Marketing Review* 15, 5 (1998): 413–426.

Shama, Avraham. "Entry Strategies of U.S. Firms to Eastern European Countries." *California Management Review* 37, no. 3 (1995): 90–109.

Sengupta, Sanjit, and Monica Perry. "Antecedents of Global Strategic Alliance Formations." *Journal of International Marketing* 5, 1 (1997): 31–50.

Terpstra, Vern, and Joseph Yu. "Piggybacking: A Quick Road to Internationalization." *International Marketing Review* 7, no. 4 (1990): 52–63.

CASE 10.1

BMW: Marketing Subsidiaries in Foreign Markets

BMW is a German manufacturer of high-quality motor cars. About half of its sales are in the German market, with the other half from exports. In reappraising its marketing and distribution strategy both in Germany and abroad, the company believed that its multiple layers of distribution were causing inefficiencies in its marketing efforts.

BMW Germany

Originally, BMW had a dual distribution system in Germany. It employed a strong wholesaler system along with direct distribution by BMW to large dealers. This system seemed to work effectively because BMW's market share in Germany doubled in 10 years. However, the company found severe competitive distortions with this dual approach. For example, the wholesalers that received the same commission for wholesale transactions as for retail sales had gone into direct competition with retailers. The larger direct dealers sometimes sold more than the wholesalers but received the smaller dealer discount. The problems arising from BMW's distribution strategy caused the company to abolish its German wholesaler network. BMW expanded its direct dealer system to replace the business formerly handled by the wholesalers.

BMW Abroad

The company was planning to initiate a more direct selling method in its foreign markets as well as at home. It realized the need for care in order not to disturb existing import channels. However, the company believed that it was desirable to replace the present independent importers in foreign markets with company-owned marketing subsidiaries. The independent importers buy the cars from Germany and then resell to accredited dealers—who sell them to the public. In moving to company-owned marketing subsidiaries, BMW was following the international marketing approach of Volkswagen and Daimler-Benz (with Mercedes). One of the major arguments presented for going direct was that BMW could save the 15 percent commission the company paid to its importer distributors in foreign markets.

France

In line with its new policy of more direct distribution in foreign markets, BMW formed its first marketing subsidiary in France. BMW Import SA replaced the former independent French importer (which had been called BMW France but now was renamed SFAM France). SFAM France continued to sell BMW cars to *consumers* through its retail outlets in Paris and in the provinces. Sales to *dealers* henceforth were made only by BMW Import SA, the company's wholly owned marketing subsidiary. This seemed to be successful in France.

United States

In implementing its new direct marketing approach in the U.S. market, BMW faced two alternatives. It could either take over its present U.S. importer distributor or establish a new and separate BMW marketing subsidiary as in France. The company wondered which of these alternatives would be best for the important U.S. market. BMW had about 250 dealers in the United States.

Questions

1. Do you see any potential problems or disadvantages for BMW in going to direct distribution in foreign markets?
2. What advantages might the company realize by operating through its own marketing subsidiaries?
3. In making the decision for the U.S. market, what questions would you ask? What variables would you consider?

CASE 10.2

Metro Corporation: Technology Licensing Negotiation

The following pertains to negotiations between Metro Corporation and Impecina Construcciones S.A. of Peru, for the licensing of petroleum tank technology.

The Licensor Firm

Metro Corporation is a diversified steel rolling, fabricating, and construction company based in the Midwest that considers itself to be in a mature industry. Innovations are few and far between. With transport and tariff barriers and the support given by many governments to their own companies, exporting as a means of doing foreign business is rather limited. Similarly, given the large investment, modest return, and political sensitivity of the industry, direct foreign investment is all but a closed option. In a global strategic sense, then, Metro Corporation has far more frequently focused on licensing as a market entry method, with technologies confined to (1) processes and engineering peripheral to the basic steel-making process (e.g., mining methods, coke oven door designs, and galvanizing), and (2) applications of steel in construction and other industries (e.g., petroleum tank design, welding methods, and thermo-adhesion).

All Metro's licensing is handled by its international division, International Construction and Engineering (ICE), which is beginning to develop a reputation in Western Europe and South America as a good source for specialized construction technology.

The Proposed Licensee

Impecina, a private firm, is the largest construction company in Peru and operates throughout Latin America. Impecina has a broad range of interests including residential and commercial buildings, hydraulic works, transportation, and maritime works. Employing several thousand personnel, including engineers and technicians, its sales had doubled in the last five years. It was still primarily a Peruvian business with most turnover in Peru, but was in the process of expanding into Colombia, Argentina, Brazil, Venezuela, and also the North African Mediterranean countries. Impecina has advanced computer capacity with a large IBM and other computers at its branches. In oil-storage tanks, Impecina experience was limited to the smaller, fixed-cone roof designs under 150 feet in diameter.

The Technology

National Tank, Inc., a fabrication division of Metro, had designed a computerized design procedure for floating-roof, oil-storage tanks, which minimized the use of steel within American Petroleum Institute or any other oil industry standards. Particularly for the larger tanks, for instance 150-foot diameter and above, this would confer upon the bidding contractor a significant cost advantage. National Tank had spent one worker-year, at a direct cost of $225,000, to write the computer program alone. Patents were involved in an incidental manner only for the seals on the floating roof. Metro had not bothered to file for this patent except in the United States.

The Market

Peru's indigenous oil output is very low, but it imports and refines annually 50 million tons, mostly for domestic demand. Following the escalation of oil prices and tightening of supplies in 1973, the Peruvian government determinedly set about to formulate a program to augment Peru's oil storage capacity. Impecina's representatives, at a preliminary meeting with ICE in U.S. headquarters, said their government planned $200 million in expenditures on oil-storage facilities over the next three years (mostly in large-sized tanks). Of this, Impecina's "ambition" was to capture a one-third market share. That this appeared to be a credible target was illustrated by its existing 30 percent share of the "fixed-cone type under 150-foot diameter." Additionally, they estimated private-sector construction value over the next three years to total $40 million.

Approximately half of a storage system's construction cost goes for the tank alone, the remainder being excavation, foundation, piping, instrumentation, and other ancillary equipment, all of which Impecina's engineers were very familiar with.

Neighboring Colombia was building a 12-million-ton refinery, but the tank installation plans of other South American nations were not known, according to the Impecina representative.

Each of Impecina's competitors in Peru for this business was affiliated with a prominent company; Umbertomas with Jefferson, Inc., in the United States, Zapa with Philadelphia Iron & Steel, Cosmas with Peoria-Duluth Construction Inc., and so on. Thus association with Metro would help Impecina in bidding.

The First Meeting

National Tank Division had in the past year bid jointly with Impecina on a project in southern Peru. Though that bid was unsuccessful, Impecina had learned about Metro's computerized design capabilities and initiated a formal first

Sources: This case was prepared by Professor Farok Contractor, Rutgers University, as a basis for class discussion rather than to illustrate either effective or ineffective handling of an administrative situation. Copyright © by Farok J. Contractor. Used with permission.

round of negotiations that were to lead to a licensing agreement. The meeting took place in the United States. Two Impecina executives of subdirector rank were accompanied by a U.S. consultant. Metro was represented by the vice-president of ICE, the ICE attorney, and an executive from National Tank Division.

Minutes of this meeting show that it was exploratory. Both genuine and rhetorical questions were asked. Important information and perceptions were exchanged and the groundwork laid for concluding negotiations. Following is a bare summary of important issues gleaned from the somewhat circular discussion:

1. *Licensee Market Coverage.* Impecina tried to represent itself as essentially a Peruvian firm. It reviewed its government's expenditure plans and its hoped-for market share. Yet through the meeting, there kept cropping up the issue of the license also covering Libya, Algeria, Morocco, Colombia, Argentina, Brazil, and Venezuela.

2. *Exclusivity.* For Peru, Metro negotiators had no difficulty conceding exclusivity. They mentioned that granting exclusivity to a licensee for any territory was agreeable in principle, provided a minimum performance guarantee was given. At this, the question was deferred for future discussion. At one point, a Metro executive remarked, "We could give Impecina a nonexclusive—and, for example, we wouldn't give another (licensee) a license for one year (in those nations)," proposing the idea of a trial period for Impecina to generate business in a territory.

3. *Agreement Life.* Impecina very quickly agreed to a 10-year term, payment in U.S. dollars, and other minor issues.

4. *Trade Name.* The Impecina negotiators placed great emphasis on their ability to use the Metro name in bidding, explaining how their competition in Peru had technical collaboration with three U.S. companies (see above).

   "Did that mean Metro's National Tank Division could compete with Impecina in Peru?" they were asked rhetorically. (Actually, both sides seem to have tacitly agreed that it was not possible for Metro to do business directly in Peru.)

5. *Licensee Market Size.* Attention turned to the dollar value of the future large (floating-roof) tank market in Peru. Impecina threw out an estimate of $200 million in government expenditures and $40 million in private-sector spending, over the coming three years, of which it targeted a one-third share. Later, a lower market size estimate of $150 million (government and private), with a share of $50 million received by Impecina over three years, was arrived at (memories are not clear on how the estimates were revised). "Will Impecina guarantee us it will obtain one-third of the market?" brought the response "That's an optimistic figure that we hope we can realize." Impecina offered as evidence its existing one-third share of the "fixed roof under 150-foot" market, an impressive achievement.

6. *Product-Mix Covered by License.* It became clear that Impecina wanted floating-roof technology for all sizes, and fixed-roof over 100-foot diameter. It suggested the agreement cover tanks over 100 feet in size. "Would Impecina pay on all tanks (of any size)" to simplify royalty calculation and monitoring? After considerable discussion, Metro seems to have acceded to Impecina's proposal (to cover both types, only over 100 feet) based on consensus over three points.

   a. The competition probably does not pay (its licensors) on small tanks and therefore Impecina would be at a disadvantage if it had to pay on small tanks also.

   b. The market in floating-roof tanks was usually over 100 feet anyway.

   c. Impecina claimed that customers normally dictate the dimensions of the tanks, so Impecina cannot vary them in order to avoid paying a royalty to Metro.

7. *Compensation Formula.* Metro proposed an initial lump-sum payment (in two installments, one when the agreement is signed, the second on delivery of the computer program and designs), plus engineers and executives for bid assistance on a per diem rate, plus a royalty on successful bids based on the barrel capacity installed by Impecina. Impecina's U.S. consultant countered with the idea of royalties on a sliding scale, lower with larger-capacity tanks, indicating talk about "1 million barrel capacity tanks." The (rhetorical?) question, "What is Peru's oil capacity?" seems to have brought the discussion down to earth and veered it off on a tangent, while both sides mentally regrouped.

   On returning to this topic, Impecina executives, on being asked, ventured that as a rule of thumb, their profit markup on a turnkey job was 6 percent. (However, on excluding the more price-sensitive portions such as excavation, piping, and ancillary equipment, which typically constitute half the value, Impecina conceded that on the tank alone it might mark up as much as 12 percent, although executives kept insisting 5 to 6 percent was enough.)

Impecina executives later offered only royalties (preferably sliding) and per diem fees for bid assistance from Metro executives and engineers.

Metro countered by pointing out that per diem fees of, say, $225 plus travel costs amounted at best to recovering costs, not profit.

The compensation design question was left at this stage, deferred for later negotiation, the broad outlines having been laid. Metro's starting formal offer, which would mention specific numbers, was to be telexed to Lima in a week.

8. *The Royalty Basis.* Metro entertained the idea that Impecina engineers were very familiar with excavation, piping, wiring, and other ancillary equipment. Metro was transferring technology for the tank alone, which typically represented half of overall installed value.

9. *Government Intervention.* Toward the end of the discussions, Impecina brought up the question of the Peruvian government having to approve the agreement. This led to its retreat from the idea of a 10-year term, agreed to earlier, and Impecina then mentioned five years. No agreement was reached. (Incidentally, Peru had in the last two years passed legislation indicating a "guideline" of five years for foreign licenses.)

Internal Discussion in Metro Leading to the Formal Offer

The advantages derived by the licensee would be acquisition of floating-roof technology, time and money saved in attempting to generate the computerized design procedure in-house, somewhat of a cost and efficiency advantage in bidding on larger tanks, and finally the use of Metro's name.

1.a It was estimated that National Tank division had spent $225,000 (one workyear = two executives for six months, plus other costs) in developing the computer program. Additionally, it may cost $40,000 (three-quarters of a workyear) to convert the program into Spanish, the metric system, and adapt it to the material availability and labor cost factors peculiar to Peru. Simultaneously, there would be semiformal instruction of Impecina engineers in the use of the program, petroleum industry codes, and Metro fabrication methods. All this had to be done before the licensee would be ready for a single bid.

1.b It was visualized that Metro would then assist Impecina for two workweeks for each bid preparation, and four workweeks on successful receipt of a contract award. Additionally, if Metro's specialized construction

equipment were used, three workmonths of on-site training would be needed.

As the licensee's personnel moved along their learning curve, assistance of the type described in paragraph (1.b) would diminish until it was no longer needed after a few successful bids.

The following additional considerations went into a determination of the initial offer:

1. Metro obligations (and sunk costs) under paragraph (1.a) above were fairly determinate, whereas its obligations under (1.b) depended on the technical sophistication and absorptive capacity of the licensee's engineers, their success rate in bidding, and so on.

2. If Impecina's market estimates were used, over the next three years it would generate large-tank orders worth $50 million, on which it would make a profit of $3 million (at 6 percent on $50 million or 12 percent on half the amount).

3. The market beyond three years was an unknown.

4. Exclusive rights might be given to Impecina in Peru and Colombia, with perhaps ICE reserving the right of conversion to nonexclusive if minimum market share were not captured.

5. While Impecina's multinational expansion plans were unknown, its business in the other nations was too small to justify granting it exclusivity. It may be satisfied with a vague promise of future consideration as exclusive licensees in those territories.

6. Metro would try for an agreement term of 10 years. It was felt that Impecina computer and engineering capability was strong enough so it would not need Metro assistance after a few bids.

Surprisingly, the discussions reveal no explicit consideration given to the idea that Impecina may emerge some day as a multinational competitor.

In view of the uncertainty about how successful the licensee would actually be in securing orders, and the uncertainty surrounding the Peruvian government's attitude, a safe strategy seemed to be to try and get as large a front-end fee as possible. Almost arbitrarily, a figure of $400,000 was thrown up. (This was roughly 150 percent of the development costs plus the initial costs of transferring the technology to the licensee.) There would be sufficient margin for negotiations and to cover uncertainties. In order that the licensee's competitiveness not be diminished by the large lump-sum fee, a formula may be devised whereby the first five years' royalties could be reduced. (See below.)

The Formal Offer

The formal offer communicated in a telex a week later called for the following payment terms:

- $400,000 lump-sum fee payable in two installments.

- A 2 percent royalty on any tanks constructed of a size over 100-foot diameter, with up to one-half of royalties owed in each of the first five years reduced by an amount up to $40,000 each year, without carryovers from year to year. The royalty percentage would apply to the total contract value less excavation, foundation, dikes, piping, instrumentation, and pumps.

- Agreement life of 10 years.

- Metro to provide services to Impecina described in paragraph (1.a) above, in consideration of the lump-sum and royalty fees.

- For additional services, described in (1.b) above, Metro would provide, on request, personnel at up to $225 per day, plus travel and living costs while away from their place of business. The per diem rates would be subject to escalation based on a representative cost index. There would be a ceiling placed on the number of workdays Impecina could request in any year.

- All payments to be made in U.S. dollars, net after all local withholding, and other taxes.

- Impecina would receive exclusive rights for Peru and Colombia only, and nonexclusive rights for Morocco, Libya, Algeria, Argentina, Venezuela, Brazil, and Colombia. These could be converted to an exclusive basis on demonstration of sufficient business in the future. For Peru and Colombia, Metro reserves the right to treat the agreement as nonexclusive if Impecina fails to get at least 30 percent of installed capacity of a type covered by the agreement.

- Impecina would have the right to sublicense only to any of its controlled subsidiaries.

- Impecina would supply free of charge to ICE all improvements made by it on the technology during the term of the agreement.

- Impecina would be entitled to advertise its association with Metro in assigned territories, on prior approval of ICE as to wording, form, and content.

The Final Agreement

ICE executives report that the Peruvians "did not bat an eyelid" at their demands, and that an agreement was soon reached in a matter of weeks. The only significant change was Metro agreeing to take a lump sum of $300,000 (still a large margin over costs). In return, the provision for reducing one-half of the royalties up to $40,000 per year was dropped. The final arrangement called for a straight 2 percent royalty payment (on tank value alone, as before). Other changes were minor: Impecina to continue to receive benefit of further R&D; ICE to provide, at cost, a construction engineer if specialized welding equipment were used; the per diem fee fixed at $200 per day (indexed by an average hourly wage escalation factor used by the U.S. Department of Labor); and the $300,000 lump-sum fee to be paid in installments over the first year.

In other respects such as territory, royalty rate, exclusivity, travel allowances, and so on, the agreement conformed with Metro's initial offer.

An Upset

The Peruvian government disallowed a 10-year agreement life. By then, both parties had gone too far to want to reopen the entire negotiations and Metro appears to have resigned itself to an agreement life of five years, with a further extension of another five years subject to mutual consent. Given Impecina's in-house engineering and computer capability, extension of the agreement life was a very open question.

Questions

Analyze the negotiations from each party's perspective:

1. List what each party is offering and what it hopes to receive.

2. Identify the elements in each list that are "musts" and those on which flexibility may be shown, and state why.

3. Compute net cash flows for each party under several scenarios. For example: Licensee fails to get a single order; licensee gets one-third market share in Peru for three years, no orders thereafter, and no orders in any other nation; licensee gets one-third share in Peru for 10 years and half again as much in business in other nations; and so forth.

    In computing the licensor's cash flows, remember that, in addition to the direct costs of implementing an agreement, there are sometimes substantial indirect costs. What are they? How would you apply the licensor's development costs to this exercise?

    What do you think of the rule of thumb encountered in licensing literature that licensors should settle for roughly one-quarter to one-half of the licensee's incremental profit? Describe negotiating tactics or ploys each party used or could have used. Discuss the role of government intervention in licensing negotiations in general.

Distribution

Foreign-Market Channels and Global Logistics

Chapter 11

Learning Objectives

Once a firm has arranged for its products to be available in a foreign market, it must discover and manage the distribution channels to the final customers there. In this chapter, we consider the major elements in managing foreign channels.

The main goals of this chapter are to

1. Discuss how exporters, who market through foreign distributors, can influence distributors to be effective marketing partners.

2. Discuss the ways in which wholesalers and retailers differ internationally, requiring adjustment by the international marketer.

3. Note some major distribution trends that should be monitored by the international marketer.

4. Explore some of the questions a firm must answer in marketing through foreign channels: Should the firm duplicate its domestic approach? Should it use direct or indirect channels, selective or intensive distribution? How should it work with the channel? How can it keep distribution up-to-date?

5. Explain how a firm can discover appropriate logistics patterns within a given foreign market and between multiple markets and determine its use of facilities and technology in those markets.

The preceding chapter considered one question facing the international marketer: How do I get my products into foreign markets? We saw many alternative answers—and combinations of answers—to that question. Once the firm has chosen a strategy to get its products *into* foreign markets, its next challenge is distribution of the product *within* foreign markets. Our first topic in this chapter, therefore, is the management of foreign distribution; our second topic is the management of international logistics.

MANAGING FOREIGN DISTRIBUTION

Some firms that sell in foreign markets do not have the task of managing distribution within those markets. For them, this question was resolved when they decided on their method of entry. Firms that sell through trading companies, export management companies, or other indirect methods must accept the foreign distribution offered by these intermediaries. The same is true for those that sell through licensing and, generally, for those engaged in direct exporting. The firms having direct responsibility for their foreign-market distribution are those having marketing subsidiaries or complete manufacturing and marketing operations there. Having responsibility is different, of course, from having complete control. For example, the manager in a joint venture is constrained by the desires of the national partner. The wholly owned venture that resulted from an acquisition will also find its distribution options affected by the practices inherited from the acquired firm.

The first step in managing foreign distribution is to identify the firm's *goals* in the foreign market. The marketing program, including distribution, is a means toward achieving those goals. Then the marketer must identify the specific *tasks* to be performed by the channel in that market. What role is the channel expected to play—inventory, promotion, credit extension, physical distribution, service? Finally, the marketer must match this job description with the channel possibilities available in the market. There is seldom a perfect match between the firm's specifications and what is available in the market. Compromise is often necessary.

We begin by considering how exporters can manage foreign distribution. Although they work through independent distributors abroad, export managers can have an impact on the foreign marketing of their products.

MARKETING THROUGH DISTRIBUTORS IN FOREIGN MARKETS

Direct exporting through distributors abroad is the major form of international marketing. In every country it is the primary method of reaching foreign markets for smaller firms that lack the resources for a greater commitment. It is also an important form of international marketing for large multinationals who do not have their own marketing presence in all of their global markets—and most do not.

The firm's success in export markets depends largely on the performance of the distributors it uses there. The challenge, then, is, "How can we get the distributor to do a good job for us?" The key is to make the relationship continually rewarding to the distributor as well as to the international marketer. In addition, distributors should be carefully selected, the agreement carefully drawn up, and marketing support offered.

Initial Distributor Selection

In distributor selection, as in marriage, choosing the right partner is the major factor in success. We discussed distributor selection earlier, but we note a few other items here. First, careful specification of what is wanted from the distributor will help a firm choose the most suitable candidate. Not all candidates will match a firm's specifications equally well.

Second, the firm should evaluate the distributor's track record. Past performance is the best predictor of future behavior. This can be determined in part by talking with other clients of the distributor.

Third, the firm should try to assure that its line will be a reasonably important share of the distributor's business. The more important it is to the distributor, the better treatment its products will receive. Avery International tries to account for at least 10 percent of its distributors' business.

Distributor Agreement

The distributor agreement is a legal document that should spell out the responsibilities and interests of each party, protecting both. Careful preparation of such an agreement and reviewing it with the distributor should help to minimize later misunderstandings. Though it is a legal document, the agreement is too important to be left to the lawyers. Managers from both sides should review it and agree on its provisions. Finally, the contract should be a "living" document that can adjust to new circumstances so that the relationship can grow beyond the original agreement.

Financial and Pricing Considerations

The distributor wants to make as much money as possible and work as conveniently as possible. The firm's use of financial and pricing variables will affect the distributor's ability to reach those goals. For example, the firm must determine what *margins* or *commissions* are needed. Should the firm just match the competition, or are higher margins needed to break into the market or to overcome competitive disadvantages? Conversely, the firm may offer lower margins because of competitive strengths in its total offering—a form of nonprice competition. The same questions apply to *credit* terms. Does the firm need to be generous on credit or merely competitive?

The firm's use of *price quotations* will also have an effect. For example, the distributor would generally prefer a *C.I.F. quote* (cost, insurance, and freight) to an *F.O.B. plant quote* (free-on-board plant). The C.I.F. quote gives a clearer picture of landed cost and also means less work and responsibility for the distributor. (See Chapter 14 on pricing for more details.)

A second aspect of export pricing is *choice of currency* for the quotation. The distributor generally prefers a quote in the currency of its country rather than a quote in U.S. dollars. This facilitates accounting and eliminates foreign-exchange exposure for the distributor.

One other financial consideration is the *payment terms* used. For example, the use of open-account terms shows trust in the distributor—and saves the several hundred dollars required to open a letter of credit. The exporting firm must balance its need for financial security with its need to satisfy the distributor.

Marketing Support Considerations

A number of other considerations will encourage distributor performance. A well-established brand name and customer franchise will make the distributor's marketing task easier. Names such as Coca-Cola, IBM, Philips, and Sony mean that the product is partially presold. Heavy advertising and promotional support by the producer also make the distributor's job easier. In addition, there may be cooperative advertising with the distributor. Another kind of support is participation in *trade fairs,* preferably in cooperation with the distributors in the region.

Exporters usually will train the distributor's salesforce as a necessary aid to marketing. This would be done at the beginning of the relationship and as new products are added to the line. Distributors should be supplied on a timely basis with *product and promotional materials* from the home office. Establishing a regional warehouse (for example, for Europe or Asia) can ensure better product supply and service to the distributor.

Communications

If the distributor is to be an effective member of the firm's international network, communications are important. Telephone contact, preferably with an international 800 number, can ensure timely response to problems and opportunities. E-mail and computer links are also powerful tools. In addition, visits from the home office allow the face-to-face contact that humanizes the long-distance relationship. Corporate travelers could include the export manager, product engineer, and occasionally the CEO.

Establishing a regional headquarters allows closer contact and support of all the distributors in a region. A company newsletter can help create a corporate spirit among the "family" of distributors. Such a newsletter or magazine would include news and pictures about the distributors as well as the company.

Regional meetings of distributors can further encourage the family spirit and also provide economies of scale for training or motivation sessions. A computer link with distributors means on-line communication that can provide instant information, reduced transaction time, and fewer errors. General Motors realized these benefits when it established such a system with its European dealers. The dealers benefited from quicker, more accurate service and better availability of product and supplies. Levi Strauss implemented a similar system with major department store accounts in Europe.

Toro held its first international sales conference in Switzerland. The conference was attended by Toro distributors from 13 Western European countries who had previously attended the annual meetings in the United States but felt these meetings were not oriented to their particular needs. The face-to-face contact between Toro personnel and the European agents helped Toro gain better insights into the marketing problems of each of the countries represented. The language problem was solved by the use of simultaneous translations.

Other Considerations

Some firms use *contests* to provide excitement and motivation for distributors. Rewards for superior performance give recognition and encouragement to distant distributors. One popular reward is a *visit to the home country of the supplier.* Such visits are especially popular with Chinese partners. They usually include a home office and plant visit plus other points of tourist interest. For U.S. firms, it often means a trip to Disneyworld. Indeed, some U.S. firms hold distributor meetings in Orlando, Florida, to take advantage of that area's popularity.

Giving the distributor an *exclusive territory* means that the efforts in that market will rebound to the distributor's benefit. One further way to have leverage over the distributor is to take an *equity position* in the distributor. This gives the firm a different but useful kind of influence.

In a study by Rosson and Ford,[1] distributor performance was highest when the manufacturer-distributor relationship exhibited the following characteristics:

1. The roles and routines were not rigidly fixed but were adapted over time to changing circumstances.

2. Marketing decisions were made jointly by the manufacturer and distributor, rather than being imposed on the distributor.

3. There was a high degree of contact between distributor and manufacturer (letters, visits, phone calls).

GLOBAL MARKETING

Nike—Just Do It

Nike entered foreign markets in 1976 by using independent distributors. In the early 1980s, however, Nike began to take control of its distribution in Europe and now controls all of its distribution there. In Asia, where Nike had 40 distributors, the process of going direct began several years later, but the company now has its own marketing subsidiaries in Australia, Hong Kong, Malaysia, New Zealand, Singapore, and Taiwan. In some countries, Nike took over the distributor's operation; in others, the subsidiaries were started from scratch. In 1992, Nike's foreign sales were one-third of total sales.

Why did Nike decide to just do it—go direct rather than rely on local distributors? Neal Lauridsen, vice-president, said, "It's not that using distributors is bad, but they will put less investment into it than the manufacturer. We think we can go further, using our own people, than the distributor can. We spend 8 to 9 percent on advertising but it's like pulling teeth to get distributors to spend 4 percent. The [distributors'] salesmen aren't interested in positioning the brand on a long-term basis. They're interested in short-term sales." He noted also that distributors often handle many clients and can't devote the same attention to Nike that the company's own people can.

Going direct means more expense for Nike. For example, the company wants people to come to the United States four times a year for product training. Management believes that this investment leads to higher sales, increased customer satisfaction, better product selection, and improved service. Nike also introduced the Nike consumer hotline and increased local sponsorship of athletes.

Source: *Business Asia,* July 27, 1992, 263.

MARKETING THROUGH THE FIRM'S OWN PRESENCE

When the firm has its own staff in a market, it generally has responsibility for local distribution, but it still must deal with the existing distribution infrastructure (i.e., the wholesale, retail, and transport system), which will differ in some ways from that of the home market. The marketer must become familiar with the distribution environment in a market to be able to fashion an appropriate distribution strategy there.

Wholesaling in Foreign Markets

The wholesaling functions (gathering assortments, breaking bulk, distribution to retailers) are performed in all countries but with varying degrees of efficiency. Differences in the economy, its level of development, and its infrastructure all cause variation in the wholesaling function.

Size

One of the notable international differences in wholesaling is the size and number of wholesalers from country to country. Generally, the industrialized countries have large-scale wholesaling organizations serving a large number of retailers; the developing countries are more likely to have fragmented wholesaling—firms with a small number of employees serving a limited number of retailers. Finland and India illustrate this generalization. Finland has one of the most concentrated wholesaling operations in the world. Four groups account for most of the wholesale trade. The largest, Kesko (the Wholesale Company of Finnish Retailers), with a market share over 20 percent, services over 11,000 retailers. India, on the other hand, has thousands of stockists (like wholesalers) serving hundreds of thousands of small retailers. Because of the large number of small stockists, manufacturers frequently use agents to sell to the stockists, adding an extra step in the channel.

Unfortunately, there are many exceptions to the generalization. In other words, some industrialized countries have small-scale wholesaling much like some developing countries. Italy and Japan are examples. Because of Italy's fragmented distribution system, Procter & Gamble had to use an intermediary to reach the wholesale level, much as firms in India have to do. Japan is notorious for its fragmented distribution system, with wholesalers selling to other wholesalers. Half of Japan's wholesalers have fewer than four employees. Japan has almost as many wholesalers as the United States, with only half the population. Wholesaler sales are five times retailer sales in Japan, four times the U.S. ratio.

The size of wholesaling operations around the world has no easily determined pattern. One can find fragmented wholesaling structures in Europe as well as in Asia, Africa, and Latin America. One African country, Kenya, has some of the largest wholesalers in the world, and many former African colonies have large trading houses established during the colonial period. A Unilever subsidiary—the United Africa Company—has large-scale operations in many African countries. Given this unpredictable pattern, the marketer must evaluate each country individually.

The varied wholesaling picture in world markets presents a challenge to the international marketer. For efficient wholesalers, it presents an opportunity to internationalize. As of 1995, American wholesalers were earning over 10 percent of their revenues outside of the United States. The leading international wholesaler by far, however, is Makro, a Dutch firm. With its know-how and economies of scale compared to local wholesalers, Makro has large operations in Latin America (Argentina, Brazil, Colombia); in Eastern Europe (in Poland); and is looking for new markets.

Service

The most important difference in wholesaling abroad is in the services offered to the manufacturer. The quality of service usually relates to the size of operations. Smaller operators generally have limited capital and less know-how, as well as small staffs, and are unable to give the same service as large wholesalers.

In some markets, the manufacturer is tempted to bypass the wholesaler because of its costs or inefficiencies. Although this might lead to more efficient distribution, its feasibility needs to be carefully evaluated. Various factors, such as the power of wholesalers or the critical functions they perform, may preclude bypassing them. In Germany, for example, Kraft Foods found it would be more efficient to ship directly to the retailer. However, the wholesaler's control over the channel was strong enough to force Kraft to give it a payment, even though its services were not being used.

In Japan, international firms have encountered problems that led some of them to ship directly to larger retailers. This did not work, however, because then the wholesalers would not cover the other outlets. Some firms, such as Coca-Cola or Nestlé, have gone completely to direct sales, but the cost is high. Because many small dealers are financially weak, Japanese wholesalers extend them liberal credit, sometimes as long as 10 months. The manufacturer who wishes to go direct may have the financial burden instead of the wholesaler.

Levi Strauss worked with wholesalers in Japan for 10 years. Capitalizing on the craze for jeans, it decided to set up its own direct sales force. Levi Strauss normally demanded monthly payment, but Japanese department stores pay vendors on a six-month basis. Reconciling these differences was critical to the success of the company's new distribution system.

Our major observation about wholesaling is that in a majority of world markets it is small-scale and fragmented compared with the operations in the United States and some other industrialized countries. Where that is true, less service is offered by the wholesaler. The following problems can arise when the marketer faces a fragmented wholesaling structure.

1. Where the number of wholesalers is large, the contact and transaction costs of the manufacturer may be high. This raises the consumer price, too, further limiting market penetration.

2. Instead of providing credit to the channel, the wholesaler may be a demander of credit, placing a financial burden on the manufacturer.

3. Small wholesalers carry a narrow assortment of goods. This may force the manufacturer to omit some products from the line or seek out other wholesalers to carry them.

4. Small wholesalers give limited geographic coverage. The marketer can either forget about covering the whole national market or try to find other wholesalers for the neglected regions.

5. Small wholesalers give limited service in other ways, too. They carry less inventory. They give less effective selling and promotional efforts. They provide less market feedback to the producer.

In markets with fragmented wholesaling, the firm must resign itself to incomplete market coverage or try to overcome the weakness by a pull strategy, company distribution, or other means. (A *pull strategy* involves heavy consumer advertising to "pull" products through the channel.) When facing fragmented wholesaling in Italy, Procter & Gamble took a twofold approach. It emphasized its traditional pull strategy *and* inserted an extra level in the channel, using a master wholesaler that reached smaller wholesalers that contacted the retailers. In Japan, Procter & Gamble uses no less than 17,000 wholesalers, a great challenge in distribution management.

China is a particularly problematic market. Indeed, in China the large government-owned department stores help to fill in the wholesaling void by doing wholesaling themselves. Some Chinese department stores earn up to 70 percent of their revenues by wholesaling. Giordano and Ports International, two retailers with some success in China, do their own wholesaling, supplying their own retail outlets from their own warehouses.

Many of the considerations discussed here apply as well to industrial goods, but the producer's needs for know-how and service are greater than with consumer goods. This might keep industrial marketers out of certain countries or force them to seek other solutions. For example, Unisys is able to use United Africa Company in several African nations and piggybacks with Plessey, a British electronics firm, in Southeast Asia.

Retailing in Foreign Markets

International differences in retailing are as extensive and unpredictable as we saw in the case of wholesaling. The marketer must study retail patterns in each market. We shall note some of the major differences.

Greater Numbers, Smaller Size

The major variable in retailing in world markets is the great difference in numbers and size of retail businesses. The United States and the advanced industrial countries tend to have larger retail outlets and a smaller number per capita than the developing countries. That means they enjoy greater economies of scale and efficiency. Some industrialized countries do not have an extensive modern retail sector, however. Among them are Japan, Italy, Belgium, and France. Japan has more retailers than the United States with only half the population. In Germany, 75 percent of retailing is done by large units, whereas in Italy over 75 percent is done by small independents. Italy has four times as many retailers as Germany.

Retailers Find Foreign Markets Are Different

Land's End

The American catalog retailer opened a branch in Germany in 1996. It was surprised to be brought into court in 1998 by the German Center for Combating Unfair Competition. The problem: offering dissatisfied customers their money back—no questions asked. The Center argued that this could not be a true guarantee because if many dissatisfied customers returned their purchases, the company would go out of business.

The two giant German catalog companies, Otto Versand and Die Quelle, do not offer money-back guarantees. In addition to Land's End, many other American catalog firms are going into the EU.

Benetton

The giant Italian retailer operates in 120 countries but gets only 5 percent of its sales in the United States, the world's largest market. To improve its performance in the United States, Benetton decided to try something new—a partnership with Sears, an American retailer with an un-Benetton like image.

Sears will *design* and *market* a low-priced line of men's, women's, and children's clothing under a new brand—Benetton USA. It will be sold in 450 Sears stores. The clothing will be made in Asia.

A major reason for the lack of growth in efficient large-scale retailing in Belgium, Japan, France, and Italy is the legislation in these countries. Though France was one of the creators of the hypermarket (a giant supermarket), in 1973, France passed the *Loi Royer* regulating the establishment or expansion of retail stores. The effect of this law, and of similar laws in Belgium and Italy, is to give existing retailers a veto over the establishment of any new large-scale retailers. Naturally, these retailers don't want to see a big new competitor come in, so they don't give out many licenses. Japan has a similar law, *Daiten Ho*. France illustrates the restrictive effect of such laws. Between 1985 and 1995, France built 12,000 stores on 16 million square feet whereas the United States built 124,000 stores on 430 million square feet.

Japan's law states that no one can open a store larger than 5,382 square feet without permission from the community's store owners. Formerly it took eight to 10 years for a store to receive permission. Apart from the law there can be other problems. When the Lawson chain built a store in Shizuoka, Japanese shopkeepers beat up a construction worker. Later, they stormed the store at night, screaming at employees and intimidating customers. Late-night calls harassed the owners' families. Finally, someone dumped excrement outside the store. Under pressure from large Japanese retail groups and U.S. trade negotiators, the government set a one-year deadline for new store approvals. Changes are occurring more quickly now.

Some international differences in retailer size are reported in Table 11–1. One would expect an increase in retailer size with economic development, but, as the table indicates, some developed countries have as much small-scale retailing as the less developed countries. For example, in some European countries retailing is as fragmented as in China or Mexico. Japanese retailing is as fragmented as that in Brazil and more so than that in Venezuela. Caution is necessary when using the bare statistics from the table, however, because France and Japan also have some modern retail developments that can't be identified in such a simple listing. For example, Ito-Yokado, the operator of 7-Eleven stores in Japan, is now the owner of all of Southland Corp. (parent of 7-Eleven) and is modernizing all of 7-Eleven—in Japan, the United States, and elsewhere.

TABLE 11–1	**Size of Retailers in Selected Countries**			
Country	*Average Employment per Retailer*	*Country*	*Average Employment per Retailer*
Pakistan	1.2	Japan	4.4
Belgium	1.2	Brazil	4.5
Spain	2.1	France	4.5
Mexico	2.2	Sweden	5.3
Israel	2.3	Venezuela	7.2
China	2.4	Canada	8.6
Argentina	3.8	Ghana	10.7
United Kingdom	3.9	United States	13.3
New Zealand	4.3	Germany	13.4

Source: International Marketing Data and Statistics 1998 (London: Euromonitor Publications, 1998), 338–340.

A visit to only the capitals or largest cities of developing nations does not give a true picture of the retailing structure of the country. These cities may have department stores and supermarkets like those a tourist sees at home. Such evidence in the small, modernized sector of the economy, however, is not typical of the nation as a whole. Rather, they reflect the "dual economy" phenomenon; that is, the same country has two different economies, one of which includes the majority of the population in the villages and rural areas; the other includes the large cities where some industrialization and commercial development has taken place.

Retailing Services

Another variable in world markets involves the services provided by the retailer to the manufacturer. A producer might desire the following services from retailers: stocking, displaying, and selling the product; promoting the product (orally, by display, or by advertising); extending credit to customers; servicing the product; and gathering market information.

Carrying Inventory. Stocking products is a basic function of retailers in every country. The services offered, however, are not identical. Small retailers carry very limited inventories and may be frequently out of stock in certain items. This is lost business for the manufacturer. Limited inventory means a limited line of products. New entrants to the market can have difficulty getting their products accepted by retailers.

Because they are financially weak, small retailers may carry certain products only if they do not have to invest in them; that is, the retailer carries the inventory physically, but the wholesaler or manufacturer carries it financially. This is a problem even in Japan, where small dealers may get credit up to 10 months. Consignment sales are one possible answer to the retailers' inventory problem. A U.S. firm selling prepared foods partially dealt with the problem by changing from 48-can cases supplied in the United States to 24-can and 12-can cases distributed in other markets.

Product Display. When the package plays a role in persuading the consumer, display is important. The kind of display a product gets in a retail outlet depends on the physical facilities (space, shelves, lighting). The producer will find great international variations in these. At one extreme, an African *duka* may have less than

200 square feet of store space, no electric lighting, one door and one window, a few shelves, and one or two tables. The seller in the open market or bazaar would have equally limited facilities. Retail facilities range from these examples all the way up to the 250,000-square-foot hypermarket or large department store found in the United States or Europe.

General Foods in Brazil had to deal with "mom and pop" stores, usually with less than 200 square feet of space and almost no room for display. The customer asks for the item and the retailer gets it from under the counter. Local GF managers hoped to develop a display counter that could be suspended from the ceiling by wires. They also investigated self-dispensing units that could be nailed to the wall. The customer would take a piece of candy or gum, and gravity would replace it.

Merchandising skills correlate somewhat with the level of economic development, although many retailers in poorer countries have a flair for product display. Few firms in the United States rely on the retailers for display of their product, except for shelf space. Representatives of the manufacturer arrange the display themselves, but this is not possible in many markets because of the small size and dispersion of retail businesses and because the firm may have a narrower line there, offering too small a base over which to spread these costs.

Cooperation is also affected by the retailer's overall relations with the producer, as in the case of Kimberly-Clark. It was distributing Kotex in France through the *pharmacie,* which differs from a U.S. drugstore in that it is limited to dispensing medicines and related items. The company wanted to add supermarket outlets for Kotex, as in the United States. The supermarkets were willing to handle the product, but the *pharmaciens* were angry about the competition. As a result, they put all Kimberly-Clark products under the counter and refused to display them.

Promotion of the Product. Product display is frequently all that a manufacturer can expect. Occasionally, however, retailers might do some personal selling or advertising. This is more likely if the retailers have a favorable attitude toward the product and it is an important part of their sales. Use of point-of-purchase materials is another form of retailer promotion, but the small size of retail outlets makes most such displays impractical. Retailer product advertising is a form of promotion that also tends to be limited in most markets because of the small resources of retailers. These limitations force the manufacturer to rely on its own advertising.

Other Retailing Services. Credit extension, product service, and market information are other services a manufacturer might desire from retailers. Given the limited resources available to retailers in most countries, it is obvious that the manufacturer is more likely to be involved in extending credit than in finding retailers who can help. When product service is necessary, the retailers' ability to perform it depends on their resources and technical skills. Usually, the smaller the retailers, the less able they are to give service. The burden of assuring product service thus falls on the producer. When the manufacturer is unable to assure service, it may have to forgo entering some markets.

In Turkey at one time, about 60 percent of all farm tractors were estimated to be incapacitated. International Harvester could find only about 50 qualified mechanics in its own Turkish organization and in the government equipment centers. To maintain its franchise with the consumers and the government, International Harvester undertook an extensive training program.

Market feedback for the manufacturer is not something retailers consider their job. Only to the extent that the manufacturer has contacts with retailers can it get market information from them. In large markets, the producer often has contact with retailers or retail organizations. Furthermore, retail audit services are available in some large markets. In small markets and in rural areas, little retailer contact is practical.

Another problem may arise when the producer wants retailer cooperation for marketing or advertising testing. Retailers may be reluctant to cooperate, either because they do not understand how it can benefit them or because they are suspicious of outsiders looking at their business. Retailers in many countries are secretive about their operations and afraid of tax investigators. This secretiveness affects their relations with the producer. For example, one cosmetics firm wanted to do "before and after" retail product audits to test an advertising campaign in a Latin American country. Only after great difficulty did it finally secure the participation of enough retailers to conduct the test.

Distribution Trends in World Markets

Because most countries are experiencing economic and social change, to observe the wholesale or retail structure at just one point in time is not sufficient. Channel decisions must be based on what the structures will be like tomorrow as well as what they are today. Statistics on distribution are limited for most less developed nations, but one can still get an idea of distribution trends there. Because the nature of wholesaling and retailing is related to economic development, the marketer can follow economic growth as a rough guide to predict distribution changes.

For the international marketer, a review of the development of wholesaling and retailing in the United States is instructive. Developments elsewhere often parallel those in the United States in earlier periods. This is because those nations are experiencing economic and social changes similar to those that occurred in the United States. Another reason is that U.S. retailers have carried their techniques abroad. For example, Jewel Companies, the Chicago-based retailer, entered a joint venture with Aurrera, a Mexican retailer. At that time, Aurrera was tenth in Mexican retailing. By adopting many of Jewel's techniques, Aurrera rose to the number one position in Mexico.

Another aid to the marketer is the comparative-study approach. Studies of markets where the firm is already selling should give insights into markets with similar characteristics.

Kacker notes four major ways in which retailing technology is transferred internationally.[2]

1. *Seminars and training programs.* Programs of the American Supermarket Institute and National Cash Register Co. (NCR) played a major role in the spread of the supermarket concept.

2. *Foreign direct investment.* By establishing or acquiring stores abroad, retailers transfer know-how within their international family. Safeway, Sears, and Wal-Mart are U.S. examples. IKEA and Marks & Spencer are European examples. Wal-Mart has the Walton Institute of Retailing in Arkansas in which U.S. and non-U.S. managers are trained.

3. *Management contracts and joint ventures.* Sears has a contract with Seibu for the transfer of a total package of retail technology, including systems manuals. Printemps has a joint venture with Daiei for trademarks, merchandising, and training know-how.

4. *Franchising.* The most visible contemporary symbol of the international transfer of retailing know-how is the franchise. McDonald's and Kentucky Fried Chicken are notable U.S. examples. The Body Shop and Benetton are European examples. There is a McDonald's "Hamburger University" in Tokyo as in the United States.

We note four major distribution trends in world markets. One is the growth of large-scale retailing. A second is the continuing internationalization of retailing. Another is the growth of direct marketing. The fourth is the spread of discounting.

Larger Scale, Greater Retailer Power

In the affluent nations, distribution developments are similar to the U.S. pattern of recent decades. Of course, not all retail developments originate in the United States. The hypermarket, for example, was a French invention. The trend in the industrialized countries is toward larger units and more self-service. Almost everywhere, the number of retail outlets is dwindling, but the average size is increasing. Sweden, for example, had 30,000 food stores in 1955 but 5,000 in 1990. Inexorably, though at differing rates in different countries, the trend is the same. Everywhere, the causes of these changes are the same: (1) rising affluence, (2) increased car ownership, (3) more households with refrigerators, and (4) more wives working outside the home.

Even Japan and Italy are joining the bandwagon. Italy was experiencing a yearly 5 percent drop in the numbers. And Japan is seeing a steady drop in the number of mom-and-pop stores. Many 7-Eleven franchisees in Japan were former mom-and-pop store owners.

Even some developing nations, especially the newly industrializing countries, are seeing a growth in large-scale retailing. In Korea, the first supermarket appeared in 1971. The number increased to over 1,500 in one decade. In Hong Kong, the number of supermarkets has increased more than sixfold, while the number of traditional grocery stores declined by more than one-third. The forces behind these developments are the same as those that led to modern retailing in the United States and Europe: rising incomes, more automobiles, more working wives. Thus, the life cycle of retailing works its way around the world.

These trends mean stronger retailing and greater countervailing power vis-à-vis the manufacturer. The power of channel members is further reinforced by the growth of large-scale cooperative wholesaling, often on an international basis. For example, Spar International is a voluntary chain of several hundred wholesalers and about 40,000 retailers in 12 Western European countries. As a result of larger operations and greater power, European retailers are demanding more private (distributor) brands. These groups also bargain strongly on prices. Private brands already have a greater share in Europe than in the United States, and the EU has strengthened distributors in Europe.

Internationalization of Retailing

The continuing integration of the world economy is internationalizing not only the advertising, banking, and manufacturing industries; it is also reaching retailing. The life cycle of today's large retailers began with a store in one city. This slowly grew into a national operation and today it is going international. Retailers in the United States, Europe, and Japan are expanding their international ties, both with respect to procurement and to marketing. Macy's of New York, for example, has buying offices in over 30 countries.

Leading examples of retailing internationalists are U.S. franchisers, about 450 of them. McDonald's alone has more than 21,000 outlets in 104 countries. McDonald's has 8 percent of the restaurant business in France! The Japanese-owned Southland has over 13,000 7-Eleven outlets around the world. H&R Block and Pizza Hut each has over 2,000 outlets abroad. Amway, Avon, and Tupperware retail abroad; Goodyear, IBM, and Tandy-Radio Shack are U.S. producers that are also retailers abroad; Kmart and Sears are more traditional retailers operating internationally. Hard Rock Café is a well-known American abroad.

Internationalism is pushing even newer U.S. retailers abroad early in their life cycle. Wal-Mart has expanded rapidly into the Americas and Asia. (See "Global Marketing," "Wal-Mart Marches On.") Blockbuster Video has expanded even faster with

GLOBAL MARKETING

Wal-Mart Marches On

After becoming number one in American retailing, Wal-Mart looked abroad for further expansion. Now, for several years it has also been number one in global retailing with revenues of over $100 billion. With some 2,800 stores in the United States, Wal-Mart now has over 500 stores in nine countries around the world in Asia, Europe, and Latin America.

1992   *Puerto Rico.* Wal-Mart opened five stores here to get a feeling for operations outside the United States.

1993   *Mexico.* In a joint venture with Cifra, Mexico's largest retailer, Wal-Mart opened its first store here (now 145 stores).

1994   *Canada.* Wal-Mart acquired 122 Woolco stores to gain a large initial market position.
Thailand. In a joint venture with Charoen Pokphand (C-P), the overseas Chinese group in Thailand, Wal-Mart began operations here.
Hong Kong. Again, with C-P, Wal-Mart opened a number of Value clubs in the large apartment complexes that characterize Hong Kong. These are

small versions of Sam's Clubs to fit the Hong Kong environment.

1995   *Brazil.* The company joined with Brazil's largest discount retailer to open its first stores here.
Argentina. Wal-Mart began solo operations in this other large Mercosur market.

1996   *Indonesia.* The company makes a modest beginning here with just two stores.
China. Another modest start in this giant market with just two stores.

1997   *Germany.* Wal-Mart's first step into Europe is by acquiring 21 stores here.

1998   *South Korea.* Expanding its Asia presence, the company buys a majority interest in four stores, plus six development sites.
Germany. Wal-Mart acquires 74 more stores here.

Wal-Mart's march abroad is not an unqualified success. It separated from its partner C-P, causing some losses. It faces strong competition (e.g., Carrefour from France and the Dutch Makro) in several markets. It also finds that each market has unique characteristics requiring adaptations from its U.S. model. Still, sales are growing rapidly.

2,000 outlets abroad. Toys 'R Us is in Japan and Europe. Starbucks is in 10 Asian markets and hopes for 500 branches by 2003. It is using Britain as a base for European expansion. The Gap is in six countries. U.S. retailers make up 40 of the global 100.

U.S. retailers are not the only internationalists. Europeans own over 10 percent of the U.S. grocery business and have very important department and specialty store holdings. IKEA, the Swedish furniture retailer, and boutique retailers such as Benetton and Laura Ashley are increasingly visible in the United States. Carrefour is in Europe and the United States and is the retailing leader in Latin America. Printemps has gone from Paris to Japan, Korea, Saudi Arabia, Singapore, the United States, and Turkey. Ahold, the Dutch retailer, is in the Americas, Asia, as well as Europe.

The Japanese are relative newcomers to this internationalization of retailing, but they are getting deeply involved. Jusco has supermarkets in Hong Kong, Thailand, and Malaysia. Southeast Asia seems to be the natural zone of influence for Japanese retailers, and they have spread throughout the region. Indeed, while Japanese retailers account for one-half of all retail sales in Hong Kong, they have not limited themselves to that area. Wacoal, the lingerie firm, has boutiques in the United States. Major Japanese retailing groups such as Daiei, Seibu, and Jusco have ties with such U.S. retailers as Kmart, Kroger, Safeway, and Sears. Yaohan even has a Yaohan Plaza in London.

Some American Stores Owned by Foreigners

A&P	Gimbel's
Bonwit Teller	Grand Union
Brooks Brothers	7-Eleven
Eddie Bauer	Stop & Shop
Food Lion	Spiegel
Giant Food	Talbot's

Direct Marketing

In its various forms, direct marketing is a big international growth area. One form, *mail order,* is growing in Europe, Japan, and even in modernizing economies like Mexico. European mail-order sales have long surpassed those in the United States, and the large French and German mail-order firms have gone international. American-based firms, such as L.L. Bean, Land's End, and Eddie Bauer, sell several billion dollars a year in Japan. Along with their catalogs, they use toll-free 24-hour international phone and fax lines.

Personal selling direct to consumers continues to be important internationally. Amway, Avon, and Tupperware are famous U.S. examples abroad, but Sara Lee is also doing it in Indonesia. With its direct salesforce, Amway is the second largest foreign firm in Japan. In Brazil, Avon has 470,000 sales reps compared to the Brazilian army with 200,000 members. Electrolux, the Swedish appliance firm, has direct salesforces in 10 Asian countries from Japan to India. Because of the international success of these direct marketers, other firms have begun to piggyback with them. Some examples: Mattel uses Avon to introduce Barbie in China; in Latin America, Avon ladies sell Duracell batteries; Rubbermaid sells through Amway in Japan; Waterford Crystal uses Amway in the United States.

Telemarketing is another growth area in direct marketing. Harrod's of London has an international 800 number for U.S. customers, for example, and IBM uses it in Europe. Telemarketing has been attacked, however, by some groups in the Netherlands and Britain for invasion of privacy and high-pressure tactics. Specialized organizations have arisen to help firms with direct marketing. Usually, they are ad agencies, such as McCann Erickson and Ogilvy and Mather.

The Internet is the newest and most exciting development in direct marketing. There were an estimated 100 million users in 1997 with the number doubling each year. Some analysts project Internet sales of $300 billion entering the new millenium. This would not be new business but a switch of customers from shops and catalogs. Both retailers and manufacturers need to consider the impact of this development on their marketing strategies.

Discounting

Among other distribution trends is the increasing popularity of discount merchandising. "Discounters" here may mean anything from smaller shops to the giant warehouse clubs. Several factors have contributed to discounting's popularity, including the demise of resale price maintenance. In Japan, discount chain stores have replaced department stores as the country's largest retailers. Their share of the household products market was expected to reach 60 percent by the year 2000, eliminating more mom-and-pop stores. In Europe, discounters are also increasing market share at the expense of department stores. For example, Britain's supermarket giants, Sainsbury and Tesco, have seen their margins decline because of them.

As more and larger discount stores, mail-order operations, and retailer or wholesaler organizations are formed, pressure will be exerted on manufacturers' pricing and distribution practices. Firms that have become acquainted with these organizations in the United States should have an advantage as the same developments occur in other countries.

MARKETING THROUGH FOREIGN DISTRIBUTION CHANNELS

Having considered some of the principal constraints on distribution in foreign markets, we will now look at the strategic decisions facing the international marketer:

1. Should the firm extend its domestic distribution approach to foreign markets or adapt its distribution strategy to each national market?

2. Should the firm use direct or indirect channels in foreign markets?

3. Should the firm use selective or widespread distribution?

4. How can the firm manage the channel?

5. How can the firm keep its distribution strategy up-to-date?

International or National Patterns

The important question is not whether the firm should have uniform distribution patterns in foreign markets but which channels in each market are most profitable. A few factors may favor a standardized approach, particularly the possibility of economics of scale. Although these are not as easily attainable in distribution as in production, there may be some. For example, the international marketing manager may work more efficiently the more similar the task in different markets. Also, particularly with the continuing integration of Europe, the more similar the conditions, the more easily experience in one country can be transferred to another.

It can be argued that channels used in one market should be tried in another because they have been tested. Although success in one market does suggest trying the same thing elsewhere, it is not a sufficient reason. Market analysis should be done before deciding on local channels.

Numerous pressures deter the firm from standardized distribution. One is the distribution structure in a country, that is, the nature of wholesale and retail operations. Because distribution structure varies from country to country, the firm's alternatives also vary. Storage and transportation possibilities, plus the dispersion of the market, also help to determine channel alternatives. For example, Pepsi-Cola uses similar channels all over the world—that is, local bottler to truck driver/sales representative to retailer. However, in sparse areas, the truck driver/sales representative is too expensive and the company must find another method.

Another channel determinant is the market. Consumer income and buying habits are important considerations in deciding on distribution, as is the strength and behavior of competitors. On the one hand, competitors may force a firm to use the same channel they are using because they have educated the market to that channel; on the other, competitors may effectively preempt that channel and force the newcomer to find some other way to the market.

The initial application of Allstate Insurance in Japan was rejected. Its entry "would disrupt existing firms." In a different approach, Allstate joined with Seibu, the Japanese retailer. This gave Allstate a powerful sales channel. It also fulfilled a requirement that it "provide something new to customers"—the opportunity to buy insurance over the counter.

Finally, differences in the manufacturer's own situation might suggest channel differences from market to market. An important determinant is the firm's level of involvement in a market. Where the firm supplies a market through an importer-distributor, it has less freedom than where it has a local plant. Similarly, working through a licensee or joint venture is more restrictive of channel selection than is a wholly owned operation. Even where the level of involvement is the same in two markets, the firm's product line and sales volume may differ. The smaller the line and volume of sales, the less direct the channels the firm can afford to use.

The firm generally tries to use the same channels from market to market. Although adaptations are frequently necessary, a firm's channels will be similar around the world, especially in industrial goods. Even with consumer goods, there can be some carryover from country to country.

Direct sales has been successful for some U.S. companies entering foreign markets. When Tupperware entered Japan, the only channel it knew was parties in the home with a hostess. It used this direct channel in Japan and found it successful. Avon is another direct seller at home and abroad. In Taiwan, for example, 11,000 Avon ladies are selling to customers at home. And Amway has a force of 1.2 million direct sellers in Japan, making it the second largest foreign firm in Japan.

Another example is Shaklee Pharmaceuticals. Because vitamin pills are not "drugs" in Japan, they can be sold door-to-door. Shaklee uses that channel in the United States and entered Japan the same way. It was the only firm in that channel and became number one in vitamins. Japanese firms hesitated to follow suit for fear of offending the traditional channels in which they sold prescription drugs.

Direct versus Indirect Channels

Because direct channels are almost always more effective than indirect, firms like to be as direct as they can. The major determinant is the volume of sales attainable. Where volume is large, the firm can afford to go direct. When a U.S. firm considers foreign markets, it usually finds less possibility of going direct than in the United States. Many elements such as lower incomes, narrower product line of the firm, and fewer large-scale buying organizations combine to make most other markets smaller.

When foreign markets are small, many firms accept indirect distribution as the only feasible alternative. In India, for example, Unilever and other consumer goods companies sell through agents, who reach the stockists, who reach the retailers. Procter & Gamble in Italy used a similar three-stage channel. As we have seen, channels in Japan may be even more indirect than those in India and Italy. In these cases, fragmented wholesaling and retailing force the firm to go less direct than it would like. These conditions characterize most world markets.

Some firms, however, insist on trying for more direct distribution as the best way to get a strong market position. This is especially true of consumer durables or industrial goods producers. Goodyear established its own franchised dealers in Europe, just like those it has in the United States.

IBM has always gone direct to its customers with its large equipment. When the company began selling smaller equipment (copiers and computers) to smaller customers, it found its direct salesforce too expensive. IBM experimented with its own retail outlets, first in Europe and Argentina. When these proved successful, IBM began opening its own retail outlets in the United States.

In Japan, the Erina Company defied the conventional wisdom by going direct to consumers with its pantyhose. It developed a salesforce of about 200,000 agents (99 percent are homemakers). Because this was more efficient than traditional methods in Japan, its price was about half that of pantyhose sold in other channels, and Erina quickly got one-sixth of the market. The company then began looking for other products.

As noted above, the growth of the Internet, multimedia, and interactive TV are giving a new meaning to "direct marketing." Both manufacturers and retailers will have to follow and adapt to these developments.

Selective versus Intensive Distribution

Intensive distribution refers to the policy of selling through any retailer that wishes to handle the product. **Selective distribution** means choosing a limited number of resellers in a market area. Although a firm usually wants to make its product as widely available as possible, it may be necessary to select a limited number of distributors to make it worth their while to carry inventory and to provide service and promotion. For shopping or specialty goods, retailers may demand selective distribution, which protects their market by limiting competition. For industrial goods or consumer durables, selective distribution may be the only way to induce intermediaries to cooperate in providing service.

Marketing abroad, manufacturers usually give exclusive franchises to importers or wholesalers at the national level. However, selectivity at the retail level depends on local market conditions. With a multiplicity of small retailers, the firm might have difficulty locating those that can handle its product effectively. Low consumer mobility also limits the value of selective distribution.

In the 1980s, Benetton expanded rapidly in the United States, opening some 700 outlets. Because many of the outlets were in overlapping territories, stores began to cannibalize one another. As a result of dealer dissatisfaction, the number of Benetton outlets dropped to about 300. Benetton was forced to become more exclusive in its distribution. Of course, competition from Gap and Express took some of Benetton's clientele.

General Motors in Belgium tried to hinder the import of GM cars by anyone other than the company-owned distributor in Belgium. However, the European Commission ruled that the GM distributor charged excessive prices for inspections and conformity certificates for cars bought outside the GM channel. The commission levied a fine on GM for "abuse of a dominant position." Thus, GM was effectively prevented from having an exclusive distributorship in Belgium.

As the General Motors example suggests, governments are beginning to have a greater influence on distribution decisions. Outboard Marine in Norway tried to implement a selective distribution system, but the Norwegian courts ruled against the company, saying that this practice would reduce competition in outboard engines. The European Bureau of Consumer Unions asked the EU Commission to investigate the selective distribution practices of Grundig, Telefunken, and Saba, saying that such distribution seriously harms the interests of consumers. The Commission agreed to examine whether these practices raised prices "artificially."

In countries with very uneven income distribution, the firm might well use selective distribution if it sells only to a group above a certain income level. For consumer durables or industrial products, the distribution in smaller markets might be more selective because of the thinness of the market and its relative concentration. The channel follows the market.

Working with the Channel

When the firm sells directly to the retailer or to the consumer, the costs of direct distribution bring the benefits of control as well as the flexibility to respond to market conditions and better market feedback. When the firm cannot afford to go direct, it must deal with independent intermediaries. The problem then becomes one of getting cooperation rather than maintaining control. Although this problem is not peculiar to foreign markets, the firm's situation and market conditions will vary from country to country, making channel management a somewhat different task in each market. (See "Global Marketing," "Innovators Abroad: Clinique, McDonald's, and Procter & Gamble.")

The firm's success in a market often depends on how well independent intermediaries do their job. Thus, helping them to do their job becomes a major

Innovators Abroad: Clinique, McDonald's, and Procter & Gamble

When deciding on distribution channels abroad, firms usually have two choices: Do as they do at home or do as the locals do. Sometimes a third choice is available: innovating a new channel approach based on the enterprise of management and the peculiarities of the local situation. Three innovative companies are Clinique, McDonald's, and Procter & Gamble.

Clinique in Japan

The major channel for cosmetics sales in Japan is the small cosmetic specialty store. Shiseido, for example, sells through 25,000 such stores. A secondary channel is the department store. Most firms use both channels. Clinique entered Japan 15 years ago and promised department stores that it would sell only through them, giving them a monopoly of Clinique sales. In turn, Clinique demanded the most desirable floor space and the right to hire its own staff and dress them in white coats rather than store uniforms.

Surprisingly, this tough, abrupt approach proved successful. Major department stores accepted Clinique's demands, and it has become number one in department store cosmetics sales, although Shiseido is the leader overall. Seibu Department Store in Tokyo illustrates the situation. Clinique has eight counters, 40 consultants, and an eye-catching display. It has more space, more consultants, and more sales than any other cosmetics retailer there. Shiseido is squeezed along the side of the room along with several European brands.

responsibility of the marketer. Coca-Cola ran into trouble in Japan, a market accounting for 10 percent of company sales. Its response was to put in a new manager whose forte was dealing with franchised bottlers. He practiced this in Japan by visiting, listening to their problems, improving inventory service, and introducing better training programs.

Manufacturers have developed many techniques for encouraging cooperation from members of the channel, including offering margins, exclusive territories, a valuable franchise, advertising support and cooperative advertising, financing, sales force or service training, business advisory service, market research assistance, and missionary selling. All of these are known to students of marketing. We will discuss their international application only.

Levi Strauss provides a European example. When it found a weakness in the retail link of its channel in Europe, it decided to use more selective distribution and give more support to those retailers that were willing to emphasize Levi products. This extra support included special discounts, local advertising help, merchandising assistance, and training of retailer sales staff. Also, it began computer links with retailers.

A firm needs to be competitive on *margins* in each of its markets. Sometimes to break into a market, the firm is tempted to beat competitors' margins, a form of price cutting and the easiest form of competition to imitate. Usually the weak firm that has no other advantages will try this approach, but once the firm has made its entry, it may have difficulty adjusting its margins.

The international firm may or may not have a valuable *franchise* to offer its channel members. When the firm enters a new market, its brand is usually unknown. Intermediaries may be reluctant to carry the product unless the firm gives strong advertising support. Some larger international companies, such as Philips, Unilever, IBM, or Sony, are in a different position. Because of their size and reputation, they are usually considered desirable suppliers in any market they enter.

Strong *advertising support* makes intermediaries more cooperative. International firms have an advantage over national firms in this respect. First, they have

McDonald's in Switzerland

McDonald's has its recognizable outlets around the world, including Switzerland. It also has something new in Switzerland: its own brightly painted dining cars on Swiss trains. Two specially commissioned McDonald's dining cars, each seating 40, run on two routes, Geneva-Basel and Geneva-Brig. The menu includes Big Macs, fries, and shakes as well as a choice of beer and red or white wine. Egg McMuffins are not popular there, so diners can have a breakfast of croissant, marmalade, butter, and cheese.

Procter & Gamble in Russia

With the decline of Communism and the breakup of the Soviet Union, Eastern Europe is a potentially attractive, although problematic, market. After a search for a partner that would be relatively apolitical and that might survive the expected vicissitudes in the evolving situation, P&G chose Leningrad State University. The joint venture will initially import and distribute P&G brands from European plants. P&G may eventually use university buildings for initial local production.

the financial resources to advertise extensively; second, they have more expertise in advertising than most of their national competitors. A German competitor of Procter & Gamble noted that the company was able to enter any European country and "buy" a 15 percent market share just on the strength of its advertising. The resources and experience of the international company also help in cooperative advertising with channel members. The same financial resources make the international company more competitive in extending *credit* to the channel.

Rosenthal, the German porcelain maker, created a subsidiary called Table Top Retail. Its purpose is to support Rosenthal dealers to prevent erosion of market coverage. The company was losing some of its best dealers from a variety of forces, including retirement. The fund will keep these specialty stores in operation until new management can be found. Faced with similar problems, Grundig, the electronics firm, formed its own franchising system to maintain and support its dealer network. These moves are especially important in view of the increased competition in the Single Market.

The size and experience of multinational companies help them in other avenues of obtaining cooperation, such as *training* sales or service personnel, *business advisory service*, and *market research* assistance. A firm with operations in several countries can draw on its experience in helping any one market. It has economies of scale in training personnel or in operating a centralized training center for several countries. Most national firms cannot match these advantages. Furthermore, the international firm can give additional prestige by regional meetings with representatives from several countries.

An auto firm found a new way to train its far-flung network of dealers by leasing a plane and outfitting it as a classroom with cutaway training units of rear axles, engines, transmissions, and so on, plus movies, slides, and other visual aids. The first trip was an 18-stop swing through Central and Latin America, with four days at each stop. The six-man training team gave sessions (in Spanish) on technical and product training, as well as sales and management methods. The dealers plus their sales and service personnel were included.

A unique way the international firm can increase intermediaries' cooperation is by increasing its commitment to the local market. When the firm changes from imports to local production, it increases its involvement in the market and reassures local dealers. Its reliability and image are enhanced in the dealers' eyes, and it can give better delivery and service. Transportation, customs, inventory, and communications problems all decrease once the international firm establishes local production.

Missionary selling is a way to maintain contact with channel members and to help them sell the product. In markets with many small retailers, it is more difficult, but where the market is not too thin, missionary selling can play the same role it does in the United States. The Wrigley Company provides an illustration. As chewing gum caught on in Europe, European competitors emerged and used a low-price strategy to attack Wrigley's position. Rather than responding with price cuts, Wrigley used missionary selling to convince retailers of the greater profits they could obtain with Wrigley's well-established, strongly advertised brand. The strategy was successful in maintaining the company's position.

Keeping Channels Up-to-Date

The challenge of management is to keep on top of change. In international marketing, the problem is compounded because changes in the environment and the firm are occurring at different rates in different markets. Even if the firm had an appropriate strategy when it entered each market, this strategy is unlikely to remain the most desirable over time.

The variables affecting channels are numerous. In any market, the situation of the firm evolves. Generally, the volume of sales increases, the product line expands, and the level of involvement changes, that is, from importer-distributor to marketing subsidiary, or from licensee to joint venture, and so on. Developments in wholesaling and retailing are taking place. Technological change in distribution as well as evolution in purchasing behavior exert pressure on the firm's channels. Laws affecting distribution are being changed.

Growth of a Firm in a Market

The international firm in most of its markets is expanding. As it gets established in a market, its sales volume should increase, which will lead to expansion of the product line. At some level of sales, the firm will find it profitable to increase its involvement in that market. Where this growth occurs, the firm is able to go more direct. In fact, this is the strategy of many international companies. We saw the Nike example.

Union Carbide had been selling its consumer products in the fragmented Philippine market through one national distributor, an indirect channel. When the company expanded its involvement by building a plant in the Philippines, it wanted a more vigorous sales effort. To get this, Union Carbide established 4,000 Class A dealers who, while functioning as retailers, served primarily as wholesalers to Class B and C dealers. Then UC appointed 100 of its own salespeople to work with the Class A dealers. This system resulted in more aggressive marketing with more control.

Environmental Change: Large-Scale Retailing

Changes in the environment have a complex impact on the firm's marketing. The trends toward retail concentration and buying co-ops in Europe, for example, have a twofold impact. The concentration of the market means not only a greater possibility of direct distribution but also increased demand for private brands. The growth of mail order has the same result. The bargaining power of these large groups affects the pricing policy of the manufacturer. Even large Japanese retailers, such as Daiei and Takashimaya, buy direct from foreign producers.

The strategic response of the firm to large-scale retailing may be either direct channels or dual channels, that is, selling directly to large retail groups and indirectly to small retailers. Use of private brands might become necessary. In other cases, private branding may be the way to open up new markets. For example, some U.S. firms had been unable to enter the German market because German wholesalers were unwilling to carry their products. The wholesalers' associations in Germany often have been strong enough to prevent the manufacturer from bypassing them. German manufacturers have agreed to this restriction on the condition that the wholesalers in turn act as a sort of buffer against foreign firms' coming in. The rise of large retail groups buying directly opens the way for non-German firms to break into the market, although perhaps with private branding. Kodak expanded its market share in Japan by private branding for a large Japanese retailer.

Large-scale retailing organizations have caused manufacturers to make still other adaptations. The situation in the United Kingdom, which is a leader in European distribution trends, can be taken as an example. Manufacturers have increased their promotional activities to the large retailers, using missionary selling with them, but at the same time they have reduced their efforts with smaller retailers. Even as they sell more directly to large retailers, they leave small independent retailers to be serviced by wholesalers; this is, in effect, a dual-channel strategy. This strategy is used not only by a food company such as Heinz, but also by a consumer durables firm such as Philips. For example, when Heinz found that fewer than 300 buying points controlled over 80 percent of the market for its products, it stopped deliveries to the small independent retailers, leaving them to wholesalers.

Other Changes

The firm must monitor other developments affecting distribution. In some markets, rising wages are drawing people out of low-wage retailing. More self-service retailing is one result. Such a situation caused Nissan in Japan to change its distribution channel. The company was sending sales representatives door to door, but the diminishing availability of labor for this kind of retailing caused the company to consider switching to U.S.-style automobile showrooms.

Technological developments, such as the *cold chain*—meaning the availability of refrigeration in warehouses, trucks, and retail outlets—in Europe and Japan, will enlarge product-line possibilities. Unilever found the major deterrent to growth to be the retail link of the cold chain. Many retailers could not afford the freezer unit. Unilever helped retailers finance a frozen-food unit in the expectation that the growth in the company's frozen-food sales would be enough to cover financing costs.

Managing distribution often requires changing the channel when conditions change; for example, the firm may add a new channel or type of outlet. After World War II, the leading U.S. producer of ice cream faced a dilemma. Its traditional outlets were drugstores, but the new supermarkets were beginning to sell ice cream. Because adding supermarket outlets would irritate the members of the existing channel, the company decided to stay with its traditional channel. Eventually, of course, supermarkets became the overwhelming favorite outlet for ice cream. This is the kind of challenge facing firms in many markets. Multinational operating experience helps answer such questions in individual markets. Although the firm may reap ill will from existing channels, it also may gain goodwill and a strong place in the new outlet by being the first to change.

Hans Guldenberg has analyzed the impact of the Single Market on retailing and distribution in Europe as follows:[3]

1. Retailers will become even larger and more powerful with continuing concentration and integration.

2. Private brands will increase further and there will be retailer Eurobrands.

3. Retailer power will mean lower supplier (manufacturer) margins.

4. Logistics, including warehouse and production locations, must adjust for the integrated market and retailer concentration.

5. Mail order will continue to grow and become international. For example, La Redoute in France and Quelle and Otto in Germany have gone European with their mail-order operation.

6. Greater price uniformity will occur in Europe with the Euro. This means less pricing freedom for manufacturers.

LOGISTICS FOR INTERNATIONAL MARKETING

Up to this point, we have been discussing distribution from the viewpoint of the financial and ownership flows of goods, touching only incidentally on the physical movement of goods, what is usually called *physical distribution*. A somewhat broader term—*logistics*—has become popular and can be defined as including those activities involved with the choice of the number and location of facilities to be used and the materials or product to be stored or transported from suppliers to customers in all the firm's markets.

The important point about logistics is that it is much more than transportation or the mere physical movement of goods. International logistics decisions affect the number and location of production and storage facilities, production schedules, inventory management, and even the firm's level of involvement in foreign markets. According to Davies, export logistics differs from domestic in several ways:

1. Documentation for an international sale (a) costs more, (b) involves more parties, (c) has a higher penalty for error, and (d) requires more data.

2. The average export order is much larger than a domestic sale, requiring more rigorous credit checks of foreign buyers.

3. There is a new intermediary in export sales—the international freight forwarder.[4]

Physical distribution problems can limit market opportunities on the supply side as severely as low incomes do on the demand side. By the same token, improvements in logistics can open up new markets. Logistics management can offer the international marketer two ways for increasing profits: cost reduction and market expansion.

Logistics within the Foreign Market

In each market where the firm has a subsidiary, it must seek to optimize its physical distribution. In countries where it is represented by distributors or licensees, it has only a limited role in local logistics. Its approach abroad can vary according to the size of the market, the way the market is supplied, the degree of urbanization, the topography, and the transportation and storage facilities.

Congo provides an illustration of physical distribution problems within a national market. Imported goods destined for the eastern part of Congo take the following path: (1) Ocean shipping arrives inland on the Congo River at Matadi, where it is unloaded and put on a train. (2) The train goes to Kinshasa, the capital, bypassing the falls between Matadi and the capital. (3) At Kinshasa, the goods are put on a boat for a 1,000-mile river trip to Kisangani, where the river again is unnavigable. (4) There, the goods are put on a train for Kindu. (5) At Kindu, goods are transshipped by truck. It is not hard to imagine, therefore, that for many goods, physical distribution costs constitute the largest element in the price. This is reinforced by inadequate storage facilities and adverse climatic conditions causing damage and loss en route. The rebel fighting in Eastern Congo, of course, completely disrupted all logistics there.

We discussed in Chapter 3 how nations differ in transportation and communications infrastructure. Developing nations generally have a weak infrastructure and this, combined with poorer markets, forces logistic adjustments by the firm. (See "Global Marketing," "Trouble on the NAFTA Highway.") At one time, PepsiCo acquired a Mexican company whose "fleet" was 37 bicycles. Over the years, PepsiCo expanded the operation and now covers Mexico with over 7,000 vehicles. Even in industrialized countries, a fragmented wholesale-retail structure can lead to distribution inefficiencies, as we have seen. Because of the difficulty of covering the whole Japanese market, for example, many firms limit their initial efforts to just the Tokyo and Osaka metropolitan areas. On the other hand, Coca-Cola felt it was necessary to cover the whole Japanese market, so the company circumvented the existing multitiered wholesale system by franchising 54 bottlers who distribute from 500 warehouses on 8,500 trucks.

We also saw that topography is one aspect of a nation's physical endowment. The existence of rivers, deserts, mountains, or tropical forests can pose opportunities or challenges to physical distribution. Some Latin American countries, for example, are divided into almost inaccessible regions by the Andes Mountains. Because these are not affluent markets, some firms do not even try to cover the whole country but content themselves with reaching major urban areas. Bata Shoe Company in Peru is one of the rare firms that does more business in the rural areas than in the major cities. To cover these areas, Bata uses air, truck, rail, and occasionally mule or launch to reach distant outlets. In Europe, inland waterways can have the opposite effect, tying several nations together for the physical movement of goods.

Multimarket Logistics

If there were one world market, the logistics problems of international marketing would be basically the same as those in the domestic market. The world, however, is not one market but a collection of individual national markets, each under the control of a sovereign government. Governments have various methods of separating their markets from others, for example:

1. Tariff barriers

2. Import quotas and licenses

3. Local content laws

4. National currencies, monetary systems, and exchange control

5. Differing tax systems and rates

6. Differing transportation policies

7. Differing laws on products (food, drug, labeling, safety)

Trouble on the NAFTA Highway

NAFTA has greatly expanded trade between the United States and Mexico, and 90 percent of such trade is carried by truck. A serious problem with this traffic is the frequency of hijackings on Mexican highways. In one year alone, there were well over 300 hijackings, and hundreds of millions of dollars worth of goods were lost.

Sears de Mexico has beefed up security and hired a former FBI agent as security chief. Sears has 47 stores in Mexico, and in one year suffered 49 hijackings. In one week, Sears lost three trucks to bandits posing as police.

Some insurers have doubled their rates, while others are hesitating to write Mexican policies. Sears and Levi Strauss lead a corporate security lobby to meet with government officials to seek a solution to this challenge to NAFTA.

United Parcel Service (UPS) faced a different problem. Mexico did not allow UPS to use trucks bigger than four tons, which made UPS deliveries inefficient. As a result, UPS stopped overland deliveries while keeping its air service.

The United States, in turn, cancelled plans to open U.S. highways to Mexican trucks. The reason given was too many Mexican trucks were unfit for U.S. roads. In both countries, of course, domestic carrier firms were lobbying for protection.

Because the world is made up of national markets, logistics management must adapt to, or overcome, the barriers in order to achieve, as nearly as possible, an integrated world market in its own physical distribution. The goal is not merely reduction of costs but greater sales. Sales will increase if logistics improvements lead to improvements in the customer service level. The appropriate customer service level varies among countries because of competition and customer expectations. (**Customer service level** refers to delivery times, availability of parts and service, and other elements required to meet customer needs and desires.)

The firm's ability to develop a logistics system is affected by its level of involvement. Where the firm has wholly owned subsidiaries, it has the most control of the customer service level; joint ventures offer less control, and licensee and distributor markets offer the least control. This is one reason many firms prefer wholly owned ventures.

If the firm had a choice, the favored logistics arrangement would be to concentrate production at home and export to world markets. This allows economies of scale in production and eliminates many international business problems, such as dealing with foreign labor or governments or operating in an unknown environment. The Japanese had success with this approach. Several factors work against it, however: (1) transportation costs, (2) trade barriers, (3) foreign exchange risk, (4) customer service needs, and (5) political resistance. These factors often force a firm to choose a deeper commitment to the foreign market.

For example, the Japanese built auto plants in the United States and Europe because of protectionist pressures. U.S. firms expanded production in Europe also because of protectionist fears. Coca-Cola built a concentrate plant in India because of trade restrictions; and Wacoal, a Japanese lingerie firm, built a factory in Puerto Rico to avoid U.S. tariffs. In each case, it was an involuntary change from exporting from home.

The Dynamic Environment

Designing a logistics system for international markets is a continuing task. Almost every parameter of the system is subject to change. Not only are markets and competition dynamic but also transportation is in continuous evolution. We cannot assume that current transportation achievements represent the end of technological change. Rather, continuing improvements are probable, opening up new logistics possibilities.

Government barriers also change, not always for the worse. Tariff barriers have been reduced in recent decades through GATT negotiations. Other trade restrictions have been lessened because of GATT, IMF, and similar organizations. The formation of regional groupings has had a favorable effect, allowing greater rationalization of the firm's logistics, at least on a regional basis.

Mercosur, NAFTA, and the Single Market in Europe are continuing dynamic developments. Other developments include government changes in import quotas and local-content requirements. Also, many nations require exports from the foreign firms in their country. Changing international relations (e.g., Arab-Israel or East-West) also affect physical distribution.

Another favorable development is the opening up of large new markets in such places as Eastern Europe, China, and Vietnam. These markets pose large logistics challenges, however, because of their inadequate infrastructure. Weaknesses include roads, railroads, warehouses, and distribution organizations, plus other problems. In Russia, for example, security is a serious problem. Colgate has its own warehouses in Moscow with security guards 24 hours a day, seven days a week. When shipping by truck, an armed escort follows. When shipping by rail, Colgate has an armed guard inside the locked car.

The Flexible Response

Considering the dynamic nature of the international logistics environment, the marketer might conclude that there is no definitive solution. This conclusion is a useful guideline if it helps avoid large investments aimed at a definitive answer. The firm might better seek ad hoc, temporizing solutions that meet present constraints. These can then be changed as the situation changes without major new investment. Although perhaps representing second-best answers at any given time, in the long run they may add up to the best feasible solution.

Although a firm can make major investments in facilities on the basis of a currently ideal system, as changes occur in technology, the political situation, or its own goals, the firm may have to make costly adjustments. Ideally, the firm should make investments in such a way that they can be adjusted to a variety of possible future environments. The manager must keep all options open insofar as possible. Contingency planning must be an inherent part of the *modus operandi*.

MANAGEMENT OF INTERNATIONAL LOGISTICS

Physical distribution is a major cost in international marketing, and profits can be increased through cost reductions in the movement of goods. Profits can be increased further if sales rise because of an improvement in customer service. For these reasons, logistics deserves close attention. We consider the principal elements in the management of international logistics, as well as the need for international coordination.

Facilities and Technology

The facilities available in international logistics include (1) service organizations such as transportation companies and freight forwarders, (2) institutions such as free-trade zones and public warehouses, and (3) modern hardware such as computers, the telex, containerization, and jumbo jet planes.

Freight Forwarder
Foreign freight forwarders are specialists in both transportation and documentation for international shipments. The full-service foreign freight forwarder

can relieve the producer of most of the burdens of distribution across national borders. They handle all the documentation and provide information on shipping and foreign import regulations. They arrange both for shipment and insurance and consolidate shipments for lower costs. Because of their expertise in this technical area, they are used by a majority of companies to take care of overseas shipment. Their efficiency makes them valuable to both large and small companies.

Free-Trade Zones (FTZs)

Aware of the problems posed by their barriers to trade, some 50 nations have established over 500 free-trade zones, free ports, bonded warehouses, and similar devices to overcome some of the self-created problems. There are over 300 foreign-trade zones in the United States. These facilities are usually government owned and are supervised by customs officials. They permit the firm to bring merchandise into the country without paying duties as long as it remains in the zone or bonded warehouse. Many allow processing, assembly, sorting, and repacking within the zone. Countries provide these zones because they gain employment that would normally be driven away by their trade barriers.

Potential Advantages. Free-trade zones offer several advantages:

1. They permit economies of bulk shipping to a country without the burden of custom duties. Duties need to be paid only when the goods are released on a small-lot basis from the zone.

2. They permit manufacturers to carry a local inventory at less cost than in facilities they own because in their own facilities they must pay the duty as soon as the goods enter the country. If duties are high, the financial burden is significant.

    Bausch & Lomb, Inc., leased 500 square meters in the public bonded warehouses at Netherlands' Schipol Airport and shipped merchandise there at bulk rates from the United States. The company used Schipol as its European distribution center. It realized big savings by concentrating European inventories at one spot, yet it provided two-day delivery in Europe. This system also permitted its distributors and agents to reduce their own inventories, thereby improving distributor relations.

3. U.S. FTZs offer the same advantages as others and are used by U.S. and foreign firms, though more by the latter. Among the major U.S. users are General Motors and Ford, with over 10 zones each.

    One advantage for firms is that they can import ingredients or components into the zone without paying the U.S. duty on them. After assembly, the complete product can be shipped into the U.S. market at the lower rate applying to the finished good. Thus, AOC, a Taiwanese TV producer, shipped tubes and components into a U.S. zone without paying the 22 percent U.S. duty on them. After assembly, it shipped them out at the lower 11 percent duty on complete sets.

4. The ability to engage in local processing, assembly, and repacking can mean savings to the firm. It can ship to the market in bulk or CKD for advantageous freight rates. Then it can process, assemble, or repack for local distribution. In addition, the local labor costs may be less than at home. Mercosur's growth has caused FTZs to boom in that region, but the Dominican Republic has 42 zones—the most of any Latin American country.

A variation on free-trade zones allows a company to have all or part of its own plant declared a free-trade zone (FTZ) or bonded warehouse. The advantages are the same but it is even more convenient for the firm. Honda's motorcycle plant in Ohio and Olivetti's Pennsylvania typewriter plant are located in free-trade zones. In a similar manner, Brazil permitted Caterpillar to have an on-site free zone. The savings are significant for Caterpillar because duties on its imports average 50 percent and goods have to be financed for about one year. Because such zones attract or keep companies in a country, they are a growing development. Olivetti, for example, had been threatening to leave the U.S. market until it received a free-trade zone. Firms from over 20 countries are operating in U.S. FTZs.

Evaluation of Free Zones. The firm should consider foreign-trade zones to see if their advantages apply to its own situation. Their usefulness depends on duty rates. Since free zones are primarily aimed at overcoming tariff barriers, they are less important for products with low duties. Furthermore, the economies of bulk shipments and the use of low-cost local labor are benefits that can be obtained apart from the use of free zones.

The logistics planner must decide in which markets free zones can play a useful role. Each zone must be individually evaluated, because not all deliver the promised advantages. A review of Latin American free zones found some that were excellent and some that were unsatisfactory. Other benefits are that they minimize the investment needs of the firm and have built-in flexibility. If they do not work out well, other alternatives can be tried, and the firm has lost little.

Modern Technology

Supertankers, containerization, jumbo jets, and computers all are the result of modern technology, and they all affect the costs of moving goods in international marketing. Physical distribution is dependent on the state of the art in transportation and storage. Therefore, the logistics planner must make sure that the distribution system reflects the economies possible with modern technology.

In view of increased European integration, Philips spent heavily on superautomated Eurodistribution centers for each product division. Comprehensive computer systems run the entire operation on an ordering-to-forwarding basis.

Computers and communications are other aspects of modern technology that aid international logistics. They permit speedy information flow for prompt response. With almost instant communication, the firm's markets and supply sources around the world can be made part of the same physical distribution network. Communications is as much a part of logistics as the movement of goods. The varied roles of modern technology can be illustrated best by an example.

The Limited is a U.S. retail chain with 3,200 outlets and different kinds of stores: The Limited, Express, and Victoria's Secret. Part of its success may result from its mastery of modern technology in international logistics. As the following steps indicate, The Limited has been able to raise its customer-service level and gain significant competitive advantage by aggressive logistics management.

1. From point-of-sale computers in all its stores, daily sales reports flow back to company headquarters in Columbus, Ohio.

2. To restock its best sellers, The Limited sends production orders by satellite to plants in the United States, Hong Kong, South Korea, Singapore, and Sri Lanka.

3. When the goods are finished, they are flown back to Columbus on a chartered 747 that makes four flights weekly.

4. At its automated distribution center in Columbus, apparel is sorted, priced, and shipped within 48 hours.

5. Trucks and planes carry the goods from Columbus to the 3,200 stores.

6. Within 40 days of the order, the apparel is on sale. Most competitors order six months or more in advance.

This example demonstrates not only the role of modern technology but also how logistics is a total system, integrating production, distribution, and communications as complementary parts of international marketing.

Coordination of International Logistics

In international marketing, logistics almost inevitably involves more than one country. This means that some coordination is necessary. Some ITT Europe companies lost major orders because their distribution costs were too high. The company studied the problem and found some interesting results. Managers perceived their distribution costs to be about 1 to 1.5 percent. In reality, they were at least 6 percent, or over $700 million for ITT Europe. A reporting and cost-control system was installed, leading to significant savings in all aspects of physical distribution, from deliveries by suppliers, warehousing, and transportation to designing a new cardboard box for shipping. We next discuss the coordination of international logistics.

For One Market

Within each market, physical distribution is handled primarily by the subsidiary or distributor there. However, corporate headquarters should provide assistance in planning local physical distribution. It can contribute ideas and analytical techniques, such as distribution cost analysis so that the best technology is available in each market. Furthermore, some governments may require that the firm balance each dollar of imports with a dollar of export. Obviously, the local subsidiary cannot solve this problem on its own.

To improve its customer-service level in North America, BMW established three parts distribution centers for its 420 auto dealers and 290 motorcycle dealers. By calling the nearest center, dealers can hook into BMW's inventory network.

For Regional Markets

Operations within regional groupings also need coordination. As these groups achieve economic integration, a subsidiary or distributor in one member country cannot be considered merely a national operation. It becomes part of the larger regional market. For example, in the EU, physical distribution must be organized on an EU-wide basis. In Mercosur, there is increasing rationalization of both production and logistics.

As expected, the Single Market in the EU is encouraging manufacturers to rationalize and centralize their logistics. One result is a reduction in the number of warehouses used. Whirlpool went from 30 warehouses to 8 regional centers; Bosch from 36 to 10; and Eaton from 5 to 2. 3M claimed savings of $80 million a year by reducing the number of warehouses and reorganizing and centralizing its logistics.

SKF, the Swedish firm, is the world's largest producer of ball bearings. SKF chose Singapore as its sales, service, and distribution center for Southeast Asia. Singapore was chosen because it has excellent shipping and air-freight services, and it offered a free port, enabling the company to avoid tariffs and sales taxes on transshipments.

International Logistics at General Motors

General Motors (GM) markets products in a variety of ways to more than 175 countries around the world. The methods of serving these markets range from local GM manufacturing subsidiaries to licensing assembly operations to direct exporting (generally to smaller markets). The focus here is GM's exporting structure.

International Export Sales

International Export Sales (IES) is the unit established by GM to coordinate its global exports. The IES staff essentially does everything short of manufacturing the vehicles it exports. In some instances, it oversees the modification of products for overseas markets.

IES ships GM's products either as completely knocked down (CKD) kits or as fully assembled single unit packs (SUP). These go to a network of international dealers several hundred strong. The vehicles come from any one of GM's global operations, including partner operations, such as GM do Brazil, Opel in Germany, Holden in Australia, and Suzuki and Isuzu in Japan, as well as Chevrolet, Pontiac, Buick, Oldsmobile, Cadillac, and GMC Truck in North America. Which products go where is determined by market conditions and demand. For example, many developing countries need commercial vehicles—and the cheapest ones available—before passenger cars. In these cases, light commercial vehicles from Isuzu rather than from GMC Truck may be exported because the Isuzu vehicles are usually cheaper.

IES manages GM's worldwide distribution through 11 regional offices around the world and the headquarters office in Detroit. The latter handles exports to the Caribbean, Latin America, Kuwait, and China. The regional offices located in Oslo, Vienna, Ruesselsheim, Biel, Luton, Rome, San Juan, Jeddah, Dubai, Melbourne, and Tokyo handle exports to the rest of the world. These offices also support local dealers with marketing assistance.

Source: Company sources.

For International Markets

Firms that have many markets and supply sources need overall coordination for optimum integration of supply and demand. The firm wants each plant to operate at an efficient level as well as to have adequate inventories and customer service in each market. Such coordination is possible only on a centralized basis.

Centralized control of exports is one way to achieve coordination. One office, not necessarily at company headquarters, coordinates all export orders and assigns production sources for the order. Eaton, for example, produces in 43 countries. All products are exported to more than 100 countries through a marketing organization based in Switzerland.

Centralized control of exports is often tied in with regional distribution centers where inventories are held for faster local delivery. For example, Caterpillar has a parts depot in the Far East from which it ships inventory and provides services to dealers and customers in 19 Asian countries. Texas Instruments (TI) stocks materials in 16 major market areas. It uses a computer-teletype-telephone hookup with this global system. With appropriate planning, distributors and licensees can be included in the integrated logistics program. Automatic Radio International has accomplished this successfully with 160 distributors and licensees in 80 countries.

The firm can ensure integrated international logistics under various arrangements, but some centralized control will be necessary if the overall corporate interests are to be satisfied. In review, the benefit of efficient international logistics planning should be increased profits produced by (1) more stable production levels at plants in different countries, (2) lower-cost distribution, resulting in part from the possibility of combining small orders into container or planeload lots (for example, Squibb does this by using five major exporting points with intermediate break-bulk points around the globe), and (3) better customer-service levels in international markets.

In one year, Dow Chemical Company processed 25,000 foreign orders and made 12,000 export shipments. Ocean freight costs came to $12 million. Dow handled these shipments from its Midland, Michigan, headquarters through its International Distribution and Traffic Department, which had 55 employees. Dow had overseas manufacturing in 20 locations, and bulk terminals or package storage facilities in more than 35 locations.

One of the projects of the department was the preparation of price lists enabling sales representatives to quote a price on any chemical in more than 100 markets. Information necessary for these lists included insurance and freight costs, consular fees, and duties. Since some of these are constantly changing, maintaining a currently valid list is difficult. Computerizing helped here, and updated computer lists are available to sales representatives in each country.

One reason freight rates were changing was that the department was bargaining with over 30 steamship conferences on rates and classifications on its chemicals. By getting one chemical, Dowpon, reclassified, Dow cut its freight rate from $64 to $42 per long ton. This opened new markets by making it competitive with a similar German product.

Because of the importance of volume shipping of bulky chemicals, the firm operated three vessels under long-term contract. This was in addition to its regular spot- and medium-term charter arrangements. Dow's engineers also collaborated with marine engineers on the design of specialized vessels so that shipments could be made in bulk to overseas terminals.

Although Dow did its own logistics planning, it did use the service of freight forwarders—two on the Gulf Coast, one each on the East Coast, West Coast, and Great Lakes. One exception to the centralized physical distribution management at Dow was the European market. As its manufacturing and marketing operations grew in Europe, Dow found that decentralization was appropriate for control of shipments within Europe.

SUMMARY

Exporters can influence foreign distributors' marketing in several ways. The first step is careful distributor selection. This requires a job specification and evaluation of the distributor's track record according to the exporter's criteria. A second step is writing the distributor agreement to recognize the interests of both parties. A third step is making suitable financial arrangements. The exporter must choose margins, price quotes, the currency, and payment terms to satisfy both parties. A fourth ingredient is marketing support, which may include a strong brand, advertising support, distributor salesforce training, supplying promotional materials, and establishing a regional warehouse. A fifth dimension is communication, which may include an 800 telephone number, computer links, visits, a regional headquarters, and a company newsletter. Some other potential motivators include contests, rewards for good performance, an exclusive territory, and taking equity in the distributor.

Wholesalers around the world differ greatly in size and capability. Wholesaling efficiency generally rises with the level of economic development, but there are many exceptions to that trend. When wholesaling is fragmented and small scale, it constrains the local marketing of the firm by increasing transaction costs and credit requirements and by limiting the product line and geographic coverage and services offered.

Retailing shows great international variation, with a majority of countries having large numbers of small retailers. In such markets, the firm may find it difficult to secure retailer cooperation in carrying inventory, displaying the product, promoting the product, and giving market feedback.

The international marketer must monitor distribution trends. As economies develop, their distribution structures change as wholesaling and retailing become modernized and the channel members become more powerful. The internationalization of retailing is predicted to continue, with U.S., European, and Japanese retailers spreading their wings abroad. Direct marketing remains important and mail-order and telemarketing are growing. Discounting and retail price competition are spreading to more countries. Marketing via the Web is the most dynamic development to watch.

A firm would like to use the same channels in every market, but exact duplication is never possible. Differing wholesale and retail structures and consumer income and buying behavior force adjustments. Also, the manufacturer's own situation varies from market to market.

While the firm would also like to go as direct as possible to its customers, in foreign markets that is usually less feasible than at home because of smaller markets and fragmented channels.

In deciding on selective or intensive distribution coverage, the firm may find that its wishes are overruled by political or economic conditions.

In working with the channel abroad, the firm may be able to employ the techniques learned at home (e.g., margins, advertising, financing, training, advisory services, market research assistance, and missionary selling).

The firm must keep its channels up to date as its sales and product line grow. It must learn to respond to powerful retailers who demand private brands and price cuts.

In each foreign market, the firm must analyze the logistics environment and infrastructure to design an appropriate physical distribution system. In addition, the firm must try to link its many foreign markets into an effective global network. This network should be flexible enough to adapt to its dynamic environment where government, competitive, and technological parameters are changing.

In managing its international logistics, the firm uses such facilities as the foreign freight forwarder and free-trade zones where they can increase efficiency. Modern technology can be a big help in managing international logistics. The firm needs to coordinate its international physical distribution to gain the necessary efficiencies to be competitive.

QUESTIONS

11.1 Discuss the financial and pricing techniques for motivating foreign distributors.

11.2 Discuss the various ways of communicating with foreign distributors.

11.3 What are some of the international differences in wholesaling?

11.4 What problems arise when the firm faces fragmented wholesaling in a country?

11.5 Many markets have relatively large numbers of small retailers. How does this constrain the local marketing of the international firm?

11.6 What services would the manufacturer like to receive from the retailer?

11.7 What are the ways in which retailing know-how is transferred internationally?

11.8 Discuss the implications for the international marketer of the trend toward larger-scale retailing.

11.9 Discuss current distribution trends in world markets.

11.10 Why do U.S. firms tend to have somewhat different distribution channels abroad?

11.11 Identify some of the ways a manufacturer can work with the distribution channel abroad.

11.12 What has been the impact of the Single Market on retailing in the European Union?

11.13 How do export logistics differ from logistics in domestic marketing?

11.14 What are the advantages offered by using the foreign freight forwarder?

11.15 Discuss the potential benefits of using free-trade zones.

ENDNOTES

[1] Philip J. Rosson and I. David Ford, "Manufacturer-Distributor Relations and Export Performance," *Journal of International Business Studies,* Fall 1982, 52–72.

[2] Madhav Kacker, "International Flow of Retailing Know-how," *Journal of Retailing,* Spring 1988, 41–67.

[3] *Management Europe,* February 13, 1989, 13–16.

[4] G. J. Davies, "The International Logistics Concept," *The International Journal of Physical Distribution* 17, no. 2 (1987): 20–27.

FURTHER READINGS

Colla, Enrico. "Discount Development in France." *Journal of Marketing Management* 10 (1994): 645–654.

Hamill, Jim. "The Internet and International Marketing." *International Marketing Review* 14, no. 5 (1997): 300–323.

Mathur, Lynette Knowles, and Riad Ajami. "The Role of Foreign Trade Zones in U.S. Exporting." *Multinational Business Review,* Spring 1995, 18–26.

Robles, Fernando, and Syed H. Akhter. "International Catalog Mix Adaptation." *Journal of Global Marketing* 11, no. 2 (1997): 65–91.

Schary, Philip B., and Tage Skjott-Larsen. *Managing the Global Supply Chain.* Copenhagen, Denmark: Handelshofskolens Forlag, 1995.

Sternquist, Brenda. *International Retailing.* New York, NY: Fairchild Books, 1998.

General Mills Looks Abroad

In 1989, General Mills was a $6 billion company operating almost exclusively in North America, although it had a modest snack-food business in the Benelux countries and France. Management decided that the firm could not afford to ignore the potential in the rest of the world, especially in the growing, integrating markets of Western Europe. It began to consider how General Mills might enter the global market.

In its major cereals business, General Mills had to face the powerful overseas presence of Kellogg. Kellogg was not only number one in the United States but also in the rest of the world—its cereal brands are sold in over 130 countries. Kellogg initially had gone abroad in the 1920s to Britain and then to the European continent in the 1950s. With six plants in Europe and several in other parts of the world, Kellogg had about half the European market and earned over one-third of its profits outside the United States.

General Mills focused the most management attention on the European market for several reasons. It was the most affluent large market after North America, and European integration promised a more homogeneous marketing environment and a better logistics situation. Dietary habits, though diverse, seemed open to increased cereal consumption, especially considering Kellogg's success. The British consumed 13.3 pounds of cereal per person per year versus 10.1 pounds per person in the United States. In other markets, however, cereal consumption was much lower. In France, for example, it was only 1.8 pounds per person. The European average was 3 pounds per person, but it was growing rapidly in some markets.

Management of General Mills considered the increasing role of supermarkets in Europe as another favorable factor because they offered a good merchandising environment for cereals. Finally, the spread of commercial TV in Europe was a strong plus for a product that can use that medium effectively.

The decision that General Mills should enter the European market was made. Next the way to do this had to be determined.

Exporting cereals to Europe was not feasible because of transportation costs and tariffs. Some form of local production was necessary to enter the market. One possibility was licensing, but it would leave General Mills rather remote and uninvolved in a critical growth area for the company.

Establishing its own plants in Europe, as Kellogg and other competitors had done, was determined to offer General Mills the most control and the most experience. Bruce Atwater, chairman, knew that setting up a manufacturing base and distribution system from scratch would be costly and time-consuming and that it would delay entry further. The decision was made, therefore, to look for a partner in Europe that was already established in the cereal and food market.

Quaker, the U.S. cereal company, had been selling cold cereal in Europe since the 1950s and was number two behind Kellogg. It was well positioned to grow with the market. For these reasons, General Mills approached Quaker about a joint venture in cereals in Europe. The match seemed to offer advantages to both parties, but Quaker rejected it.

In looking for other alternatives, General Mills began conversations with Nestlé. Atwater already knew Helmut Maucher, Nestlé chairman, through their service on the international council of J.P. Morgan. Nestlé was a minor factor in the European cereal market but was a major factor in the European food market generally, with many factories and extensive distribution. As a food supplier to EuroDisneyland, Nestlé controlled the right to use Disney characters on its products throughout Europe and the Middle East.

The discussions with Nestlé went very well. In less than one month, a 50-50 joint venture called Cereal Partners Worldwide was formed. As the name indicates, the venture covered not only Europe but also the rest of the world except North America. The agreement had an immediate competitive effect: The number three firm in the British market, Ranks Hovis McDougall, decided to leave the cereal business and sold out to Cereal Partners. That gave the joint venture an instant 15 percent of the $1 billion British market. Elsewhere in Europe, General Mills products with the Nestlé name as family brand had achieved $250 million in sales by 1992.

In August 1992, General Mills took another step toward broader participation in world markets. It formed a second joint venture in snack foods for Europe with PepsiCo (General Mills has 40 percent and PepsiCo 60 percent). Both firms were already in the snack-food business in Europe, but PepsiCo's business was only in Britain, Spain, Portugal, and Greece, whereas General Mills was in France and Benelux. Their combined volume in Europe was about $640 million, making them equal to Britain's United Biscuits Holding PLC as the largest players in Europe's fragmented $25 billion market. In addition to their geographic diversity, the two firms differed in the kinds of snack foods they were selling, with PepsiCo strongest in the chip market.

In just three years, General Mills made giant steps toward becoming a global marketing company. In both cases, the entry method chosen was a joint venture with a firm in a related field. In each case, the partner firm was not only larger than General Mills, but also had much greater investment and experience in all world markets outside North America.

Questions

1. Evaluate the Cereal Partners Worldwide venture from General Mills' viewpoint.
   a. What benefits is the company seeking/obtaining from the joint venture?
   b. What problems might arise, now or in the future, in this venture?

2. Evaluate the same joint venture from Nestlé's viewpoint.
   a. What are the benefits for Nestlé?
   b. What problems could arise?

3. Evaluate the snack-food venture from General Mills' viewpoint.
   a. What are the benefits?
   b. What are the potential problems?

4. Evaluate the snack-food venture from PepsiCo's viewpoint.
   a. What are the benefits?
   b. What are the potential problems?

5. What other alternatives could General Mills consider in expanding its presence in world markets outside North America?

Sources: *Fortune,* June 3, 1992, 175–178; *Advertising Age,* July 30, 1992, S1; *Business Week,* August 24, 1992, 50, 51.

C A S E 1 1 . 2

Protective Devices Division

My name is Steve Ball. This story is true, but all the names in it have been changed. My job was assistant marketing manager of the Protective Devices Division of Electronic Systems, Inc. (ESI), an electronics manufacturer whose major markets were in the aerospace industry. Protective Devices Division (PDD) was an acquisition in a fairly unrelated business, the intrusion-alarm industry.

ESI's products were custom engineered and required an electronics engineer to sell them. In contrast, PDD's products were sold in a commercial market. Although PDD's products were electronic, its customers were fairly unsophisticated in electronics. Thus, PDD's markets were quite unlike any with which its parent corporation, ESI, had any experience.

ESI's sales were in the $80 million range, and PDD's were in the $4 million range. PDD had about 75 employees.

My story begins one sunny, hot day in August when I was on vacation. The phone rang. My general manager, Andy Smith (see Figure 1), was on the phone.

"Steve, this is Andy. Is your passport up-to-date?"

"Yes it is, Andy."

"Good, something has come up here. I won't be able to take that European trip I had planned, so I want you to go in my place. Is that okay with you?"

"Oh sure, Andy, I'll start planning for it right away."

When I hung up, I really had mixed feelings. It would be fun to go to Europe again. The itinerary included Germany, France, Sweden, and England. It would be in September, so the weather should be pleasant. But I also knew that now I would have to negotiate with our French distributor's manager, who was really upset with us. I'd hoped that since Andy got us in this mess, he would have the "pleasure" of dealing with Monsieur Dupuis. Also I wondered why Andy skipped my immediate boss, Tom Daniels.

Background

Two years before, I had convinced Andy that we should exhibit at the Security Equipment Trade Show sponsored by the U.S. Department of Commerce at the U.S. Trade Center in Milan, Italy. At that time, we had not exported any products. I had recently joined PDD after having been employed by a competitor in the alarm-manufacturing business in international marketing.

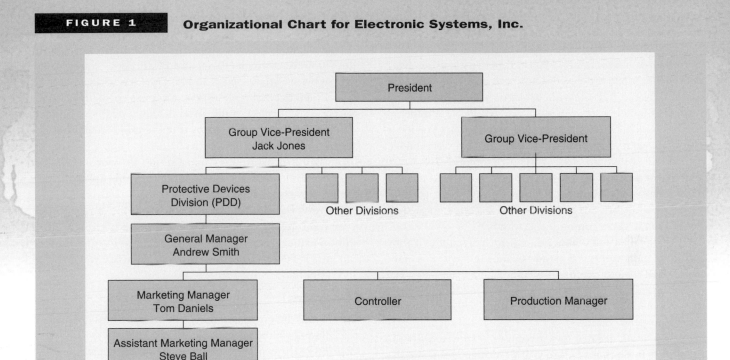

FIGURE 1   **Organizational Chart for Electronic Systems, Inc.**

Although we did not find a distributor in Italy, we did obtain a good lead in France. I visited our prospective distributor, Systemes de Securité (SDS), which placed a substantial trial order for ultrasonic intrusion-detection systems. SDS asked for the usual exclusive agreement to market our products in France. Because ESI's corporate policy did not permit exclusive distributorships, I was not able to accede to its request. However, I tried to resolve this difficulty by promising to refer any inquiries to SDS that we received from France. This I did on a number of occasions. SDS was pleased with our equipment and reordered several times.

Eventually we became so comfortable with SDS that we no longer required our sight drafts to be secured by SDS's letters of credit. By the next year, SDS was our third largest customer, following two of the largest intrusion-alarm installation companies in the United States.

About a year and a half after appointing SDS, the Telex rattled with a message from Paris. It was from another potential distributor that wished to import our products into France. In fact, it was sending a Bob Peters over to visit us in a week. I wanted to refer Peters to SDS but was overruled by Andy Smith.

"Remember, Steve, ESI's group vice-president, Jack Jones, was really adamant. He said there would be no exclusive distributorships and that means we have to talk to Bob Peters."

"Well, Andy, I can tell you right now. The SDS people are going to be very upset if they see us 'going behind their back.'"

"Oh heck, Steve, if they like our products, they'll continue to buy. Don't worry about it. We'll work something out."

Bob Peters visited the next week. He was an expatriate American who had lived in Paris for a number of years. He represented some wealthy businessmen who wanted to enter the alarm business. He claimed that the French market "had not yet been scratched." Bob made a good impression on everyone at PDD, even me. He placed a fairly significant initial order for some $8,000. At this time, SDS was purchasing about $100,000 of our products annually. Peters placed a couple of follow-up orders over the next several months.

Although I later tried to get SDS to serve Peters' company, I could reach no satisfactory conclusion with SDS, and

Peters continued to order directly from PDD. Meanwhile, our relations with SDS deteriorated.

First, SDS fell behind in paying its sight drafts. Second, it complained that some new PDD microwave intrusion-detection systems it had ordered did not work properly. In fact, the new system did "false-alarm." (It signaled the police that a protected building was being burglarized, but when the police responded, no evidence was found to indicate that a burglary had taken place. A few such occurrences are acceptable, but our new system was doing this much too often.)

At this time, we were no longer sure that SDS would continue to be a good distributor. Maybe Peters' group would be better, we thought. At least, it was easier to communicate with Peters than it was to communicate with SDS.

We then learned that another Security Equipment Show was to be held at the U.S. Trade Center in Paris. It seemed like a good idea to exhibit at this show to attract sales leads for our French distributor. Also, we could resolve the French distributor problem and perhaps find distributors for the other European countries.

Andy Smith decided to represent us in Paris, to visit ESI's subsidiary in England and to visit a German and a Swedish prospect. Although disappointed that I was not to make this trip, I also was gleeful that Andy would "have to work something out" with SDS.

The European Trip

This brings my story up to the point where the phone rang during my vacation. I went to Europe as requested. First, I vis-ited a German prospect near Frankfurt. Then, I took the Trans-European Express to Paris. Upon arrival, I attempted to contact Monsieur Dupuis. He was "not available." Bob Peters, however, welcomed me, and I was taken around to see the sights of Paris by Peters and his French associates.

I then made sure that the exhibit was correctly installed at the U.S. Trade Center. After I had repeatedly phoned Dupuis' office, he showed up at the exhibition without notice. He was furious.

"Ball, you assured me that I would be your French distributor. But you have been dealing with this upstart Peters behind my back."

"Now wait a minute, Monsieur Dupuis," I responded, "We did refer Peters to you, but you chose not to deal with him. Furthermore, SDS has been delinquent in paying for about $50,000 on orders we shipped. What are you going to do about that?"

Questions

1. Detail the origin and nature of the problems PDD is having with its French distributor.
2. From the exporter's viewpoint, what are the arguments for and against exclusive distributorship in foreign markets?
3. What can Ball and PDD do now?

Source: This case was prepared by Robert M. Balinger of Siena College, based on a personal experience. Used by permission.

International Promotion

Advertising

Learning Objectives

Advertising is a major form of promotion in international as well as domestic marketing. In this chapter, we examine the parameters of an effective international advertising program, including the subjects of international constraints, agency selection, the message and the media, the budget, and ways of evaluating, organizing for, and sharing the advertising effort.

The main goals of this chapter are to

1. Discuss how languages, regulations, and infrastructure modify the advertising task.

2. Identify the criteria used for agency selection and explain the growing role for international agencies.

3. Discuss the role of language, media, market segments, and new-product introductions in the international advertising message.

4. Show how media diversity and media developments affect the options available in a market.

5. Describe the techniques available and appropriate for setting the ad budget in foreign markets.

6. Discuss the difficulties in evaluating advertising in foreign markets.

7. Describe the different ways of organizing for international advertising—that is, the degree of centralization, decentralization, or compromise that is most effective.

8. Identify the advantages and problems of cooperative advertising.

Promotion is the most visible as well as the most culture bound of the marketing functions. In the other functions, the firm relates to the market in a quieter, more passive way. With the promotional function, the firm is standing up and speaking out, wanting to be seen and heard. We define **promotion** as communication by the firm with its various audiences, with a view to informing and influencing them.

The subject of Chapters 12 and 13 is not really international promotion, but rather promotion in international marketing. Because relatively little promotion is truly international, we are concerned primarily with the management of promotion in a number of nations. The international aspect is the coordination of the various national activities to make up the integrated international program. Promotion in international marketing plays the same role it does in domestic operations, that is, communication with the firm's audiences to achieve certain goals. Variations from country to country occur, however, in all three dimensions: means of communication, audience, and even company goals.

Promotion is aimed at selling products and enhancing the image of the company. We have seen, however, that the situation of the company and its product line often are not the same from one country to another. Therefore, the promotional task is not exactly the same in every market either. Another dimension is nationality; that is, the firm must decide whether to present itself as a local, foreign, or multinational company.

In Chapters 12 and 13, we examine the various elements of promotion. We discuss the following topics: advertising, personal selling, sales promotion, the marketing mix, special forms of promotion, and public relations. We will give a picture of the state of the art in these areas and highlight problems and decisions facing the international marketer. Our examination begins with advertising; in Chapter 13 we will discuss the other elements of international promotion.

Advertising is the paid communication of company messages through impersonal media. The messages may be audio, as in radio; visual, as in billboards or magazines; or audiovisual, as in television or cinema advertising. Advertising everywhere is used to achieve various marketing goals, which include paving the way for the sales force, gaining distribution, selling products, improving brand image, and so on. In every country, advertising is just one element of the marketing mix. Its role will depend on the other elements of the mix in that country.

Because only the practice, not the principles, of advertising varies internationally, we will not discuss principles. We begin our discussion of advertising in the international company with a review of the environmental constraints, after which we consider the advertising decisions facing the international marketing manager.

CONSTRAINTS ON INTERNATIONAL ADVERTISING

The international advertising program of a company is determined by two sets of constraints, one posed by the internal situation of the company and the other by the international environment. We look first at important elements of the international environment. Figure 12–1 illustrates some of the constraints on international marketing communication.

Languages: The Tower of Babel

We discussed language in Chapter 4; here we examine its significance for international advertising. Construction of the biblical tower of Babel stopped when the workers could no longer communicate with each other. The manager of international advertising may feel a similar constraint when facing the diversity of languages in world markets. Although some languages are used in more than one country, there are many more languages than countries. The international adver-

| FIGURE 12-1 | **Constraints on International Marketing Communication** |

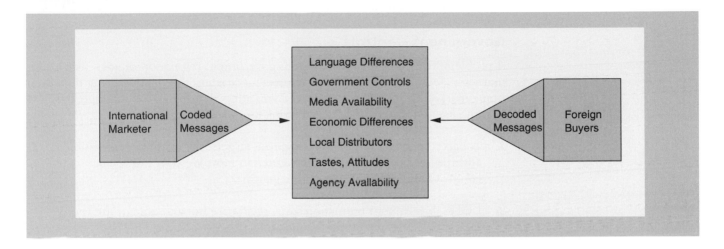

tiser does not have to know all the languages of all markets, but the firm's advertising must communicate in these languages. Even in the few cases where the product and its advertising appeals are universal, the language will not be.

Technical accuracy or perfect translations are not sufficient; persuasive messages must speak the "language of the heart," and for this, intimate local knowledge is required. Local help is of two kinds: national personnel in countries where the firm has subsidiaries, and the advertising agency located in the market. In either case, the company gets the benefit of employees in whose language the company wants to advertise. In other markets, the firm may rely on its distributor for advertising.

Role of Advertising in Society

Another constraint on the international advertiser is the different role of advertising in each country. Over half of the world's ad expenditures were once in the United States. Since 1988, however, ad outlays abroad have surpassed those in the United States. While the United States still leads all countries in *relative* advertising expenditures, ad outlays in many overseas markets are growing much faster than in the United States. For example, Spain, Korea, Taiwan, and Thailand have had advertising growth rates of 15 percent or more per year. Advertising in China grew at over 50 percent per year in the 1990s.

The level of economic development is only one factor in advertising spending. Regulations on advertising and media, as well as other cultural factors, are also important. Colombia spends twice as much (relative to GDP) as most of its Latin American neighbors. Switzerland spends four times as much per capita as its neighbor Italy.

Media Availability

Some of the media used by advertisers in the United States may not be available abroad. Two factors are at work here. One is government regulation, which may limit commercials on radio or TV. Another variable is the communications infrastructure. For example, newspaper availability ranges from 1 daily paper per 2 persons in Japan and 1 per 4 persons in the United States to a range of 1 to between 10 and 20 in Latin America, and extreme cases such as 1 to 200 persons in such countries as Bangladesh and most of Africa.

As another example, TV set ownership ranges from more than 1 set per 2 persons in the United States, Japan and much of Western Europe to 1 to 30 in India, 1 to 200 in Bangladesh and 1 to 500 in some African countries.

Government Controls

A problem for marketers everywhere is government regulation of advertising. U.S. marketers will often find foreign countries more restrictive of advertising than their home market. Government regulations can affect the media, the message, the budget, and agency ownership. The following are specific limitations.

1. Tobacco, alcohol, and drugs are special targets. For example, cigarette advertising is partially or totally banned in most Western European countries and even in India and Argentina.

2. Due to government regulation some media are not available or are very limited for commercial use.

3. Advertising messages have a variety of restrictions. Forty countries regulate the languages that can be used. Many countries have limits on comparative advertising, and about 25 countries require preclearance of certain commercials.

4. The ad budget can draw government attention. India attacked the ad budgets of foreign tire companies there, and Britain made a similar attack on the ad budgets of Unilever and Procter & Gamble, which were considered too large. Developing countries are concerned about the ad budgets of drug firms.

5. Some countries restrict ownership of ad agencies. Boddewyn found that 17 countries allowed only minority foreign ownership, and Indonesia, Nigeria, and Pakistan allowed none at all.[1]

Apart from government controls, other groups can effectively restrict firms' advertising. See "Global Marketing," "Potholes and Pitfalls in International Advertising."

Competition

The competitive situation is another variable. In some markets, an international company competes against other international companies. In others, the competition is purely national. Sound advertising strategy in one market is not necessarily sound in another market with a different situation. Furthermore, the approach of the international company provokes different reactions. In some countries, the international company causes national competitors to follow its course of action. For example, Procter & Gamble's entry into Western Europe caused national competitors to increase their advertising. During the Russian crisis, local firms changed their appeals, emphasizing the cheapness of their products. Western firms reduced their ad budgets, not wanting to devalue their brand.

Agency Availability

Another constraint on the international advertiser is the availability of ad agencies in different countries. Some countries have only one agency, for example, Bermuda, Iceland, Mozambique, and Syria. A number of countries have only two agencies, for example, Bolivia, Bulgaria, Ghana, Ivory Coast, Jordan, Morocco,

GLOBAL MARKETING

Potholes and Pitfalls in International Advertising

Advertisers like to find the most appropriate message for the local situation in each of their markets. Occasionally, an inadequate reading of the local situation can cause serious problems. Sometimes, also, an ad that is acceptable in the local market can lead to trouble elsewhere.

In introducing a new Golf into France, Volkswagen ran a campaign that included a parody of Christ's last supper. After Catholic authorities brought a lawsuit, VW and its agency (DDB Needham) dropped the campaign and gave a donation to a Catholic charity.

Cosmopolitan magazine used billboards for its launch into Hungary. They showed a woman's naked torso with a man's hands cupping her breasts from behind. "A *Cosmopolitan* reader's favorite bra" was the slogan. Soon most of the ads in Budapest were covered with black paint. The Consumer Protection Authority imposed fines on billboard owners and Grey, the ad agency.

Coca-Cola India withdrew a TV ad after a 10-year-old Calcutta boy died after leaping from a tall building, allegedly imitating the commercial that showed a youth bungee-jumping off a cliff to steal a bottle from a moving truck.

A Budweiser ad in Britain was emphasizing its American roots. It showed a bar full of American Indians drinking Bud. The campaign was very successful in Britain, but raised criticism in the United States from Indian advocacy groups who said it was insensitive to the problem of alcoholism among American Indians.

Leo Burnett Bangkok prepared an ad for a Thai potato chip company. It included a depiction of Hitler (as a bad guy) and ran on Thai TV until Israeli diplomats complained. The agency apologized.

Namibia, Nigeria, and Zambia. Frequently, the two agencies are affiliates of the large international agencies, so the service may be better than the numbers would suggest. At the other extreme are the United States and the United Kingdom, with over 500 agencies each. The quality of agency service in a country corresponds roughly to its economic development and the size of its economy. Thus, India, a poor nation in per capita income, has several good agencies because its total market is large. J. Walter Thompson has over 500 employees in its several offices there. In China, an explosion of advertising and agencies has resulted in about 170 joint ventures between local and foreign agencies.

ADVERTISING DECISIONS FACING THE INTERNATIONAL MARKETER

The international advertiser must ensure appropriate campaigns for each market and also try to get coordination among the various national programs. We will examine seven decision areas in international advertising: (1) selecting the agency (or agencies), (2) choosing the message, (3) selecting the media, (4) determining the budget, (5) evaluating advertising effectiveness, (6) organizing for advertising, and (7) deciding whether to engage in cooperative advertising abroad.

Selecting the Agency

Many marketing functions are performed within the company. With advertising, the firm almost always relies on expertise from the advertising agency. Agency selection is usually the first advertising decision the marketer has to make. Two major alternatives are open: (1) an international agency with domestic and overseas offices or (2) local agencies in each national market. Modifications of these alternatives are often available.

Selection Criteria

Naturally, the firm should choose the agency or agencies that will best help it achieve its goals. Because this criterion is not easy to determine, it is helpful to identify subsidiary criteria that can aid in the choice. First, the agency alternatives should be identified. For example: What agencies are located in each market? Which are pre-empted by competitors? Second, each agency should be evaluated using the following criteria.

Market Coverage. Does the particular agency or package of agencies cover all the relevant markets?

Quality of Coverage. How good a job does this package of agencies do in each market?

Market Research, Public Relations, and Other Marketing Services. If the firm needs these services, in addition to advertising, how do the different agencies compare on their offerings?

Relative Roles of Company Advertising Department and Agency. Some firms have a large staff that does much of the work of preparing advertising campaigns. These firms require less of an agency than do companies that rely on it for almost everything relating to advertising. Thus, a weak company advertising department needs a strong agency.

Communication and Control. If the firm wants frequent communication with agencies in foreign markets, it is inclined to hire the domestic agency that has overseas offices. The internal communications system of this agency network would facilitate communication for the international marketer.

International Coordination. Does the firm wish to have advertising tailor-made to each market? Or does it desire coordination of national advertising with that done in other markets? One of the major differences among agency groups is their ability to aid in international coordination.

Size of Company's International Business. The smaller the firm's international advertising expenditures, the less there is to be divided among different agencies. The firm's advertising volume may determine agency choice to ensure some minimum level of service. A small volume multiplied by a number of markets could interest an international agency even if it is of no interest to an agency in any one market.

Image. Does the firm want a national or international image? If it wants local identification, it might choose a local agency rather than an international one. That used to be the practice of IBM.

Company Organization. Companies that are very decentralized, with national profit centers, might wish to leave agency selection to the local subsidiary. S. C. Johnson does this.

Level of Involvement. In joint-venture arrangements, the international firm shares decision making. The national partner may have experience with a national agency, which could be the decisive factor. In licensing agreements, advertising is largely in the hands of the licensee. Selling through distributors also reduces the control of the international company. Generally, international marketers can choose only the agencies for the advertising paid for by their firms. Where the firm has a cooperative program with its distributors, it may have some voice in agency selection.

GLOBAL MARKETING

Advertising Agencies: Marriage, Divorce, Living Together

Increasing globalization and competition are forcing agencies to find innovative ways to survive and grow. Some examples.

■ *Marriage.* Chiat/Day was fired by Reebok as its U.S. agency. A major reason was its lack of a global network. Result: Chiat/Day marries (merges with) TBWA, part of the Omnicom group. TBWA has offices in 32 countries. Chiat/Day, creative shop, becomes part of an international group.

■ *Divorce.* Some advertisers feel the giant agencies have become too bureaucratic and rigid. As a result, many giant agencies have "divorced" part of their operations and set up new shops to cater to major clients. Examples: Saatchi & Saatchi spins off Team One for Lexus; Lintas spins off L-2 for IBM-PC; DDB Needham divorces Berlin Wright Cameron to try to keep the Volkswagen account.

■ *Living Together.* Nike appointed *both* McCann-Erickson and Wieden & Kennedy to handle its advertising in Japan. This alliance is not a marriage/merger and no equity has been exchanged. They are just living together. McCann is considering similar alliances elsewhere. A new lifestyle in the ad industry?

Trend toward International Agencies

Increasingly, choices are being made in favor of agencies with offices abroad. Many U.S. firms believe that an international agency yields cost savings because it avoids duplication of the creative activity involved in preparing campaigns and facilitates communication with the agency's foreign branches. Where centralized control is desired, it is facilitated by dealing with one agency with a similar international organization.

When companies want to present a united front to the world, the task is easier if the firm uses the same agency everywhere. For example, when the Kodak Instamatic was introduced globally at the same time it was introduced in the United States, some of Kodak's foreign subsidiaries switched to the local office of J. Walter Thompson. Thompson's U.S. account executive for Kodak was coordinating global advertising for the introduction. The choice of an international agency is especially common in industrial marketing, where the appeals are more common from country to country and budgets are generally smaller. Consider these examples:

◆ American Express uses Ogilvy & Mather to coordinate its domestic and international advertising in all its markets.

◆ AMF was dealing with 18 different agencies internationally. When it switched to one international agency, it found its corporate awareness improved considerably.

◆ 3M chose Grey Advertising, with 278 offices in 70 countries, to handle its advertising previously covered by 25 separate agencies worldwide.

◆ IBM consolidated its $500 million of worldwide advertising at Ogilvy & Mather, replacing 40 different agencies around the world.

Some consumer goods marketers, too, find that the same basic appeals can be used everywhere and, therefore, an international agency can be chosen.

◆ Levi Strauss tries for similarity of appeals abroad and uses McCann-Erickson in the majority of its foreign markets.

◆ For Philip Morris, Leo Burnett Co. developed the famous Marlboro theme for the U.S. market. As Marlboro went international, Leo Burnett was given foreign markets as well.

◆ Pepsi-Cola believes in global appeals and relies on BBDO as its international agency to achieve the coordinating in world markets.

◆ Guinness also chose to consolidate its global advertising for the Johnny Walker brands with Leo Burnett.

The world's top 20 agencies are listed in Table 12–1. They are all internationalists, though the Japanese agencies are somewhat limited internationally. Fifteen of the 20 are U.S. based. The U.S. dominance reflects its history as home to the first internationalists. Agencies went abroad to follow their clients who were going international. Their great expansion came in the last three decades. In 1927, there were only four U.S. agencies abroad, with a total of 21 offices. Today there are over 100, with over 2,000 offices. The top U.S. agencies are listed in Table 12–2; each is an international firm, and foreign billings represent over half of their total business. In terms of share of business abroad, McCann and Ogilvy & Mather are the leaders, each earning 70 percent of total income outside the United States.

The initial leadership of the U.S. agencies is being challenged. Agencies abroad have also gone international to serve the global interests of their clients. Alliances, acquisitions, and mergers continue as agencies try to survive and serve their clients in the world marketplace. Publicis recently acquired the Hal Riney agency to expand its U.S. presence.

The relentless growth of the multinational agencies puts pressure on those agencies that serve only one market. For example, mid-sized British agencies faced tough choices in planning for an integrated European market after 1992. They either had to forge a European network or had to sell out to one if they wanted to keep their clients who would be operating in that market. The same integration pressures of NAFTA led U.S. agencies to acquire a number of Canadian agencies. Misfortunes have befallen single-country agencies that have multinational clients. Volkswagen advertising in the United States, for example, was handled very successfully by Doyle Dane Bernbach. When this U.S. agency opened an office in Germany, Volkswagen dropped its national agency and gave the account in Germany to the German office of Doyle Dane Bernbach (now DDB Needham).

In many instances, an international agency covering foreign markets for a firm has obtained its domestic advertising as well. For example, Leo Burnett won the international account for Seven-Up in 1980 and in 1985 was awarded the U.S. account also. The giant Coca-Cola account, once held by the D'Arcy agency, was lost to McCann-Erickson in the United States after McCann got its foot in the door abroad. Thereafter, D'Arcy, too, moved into foreign markets. These examples reflect the firms' desire for coordination and convenience in their advertising programs.

The dominance of the international agencies is shown again in Table 12–3. Some indication of their global spread is given by their market positions. For example, of the 25 markets noted in the table, McCann, Ogilvy & Mather, and Young & Rubicam are in the top five in 13, 15, and 16 markets respectively. We must add a word of caution here lest we paint a one-sided picture, however. One study showed that of U.S. brands sold abroad, only one-third were handled by the same agency both at home and abroad.[2] That is gradually changing but the internationals have not yet conquered the world.

The Local Agency Survives

National agencies are a continuing alternative for the international marketer for several reasons. Although international agencies offer multimarket coverage, their networks are not always of even quality. Their offices in some markets might be very strong, whereas in others they might be only average. If the firm needs high-

TABLE 12–1	World's Top Ad Agencies

Rank	Agency	Gross Income (Millions of Dollars)	Rank	Agency	Gross Income (Millions of Dollars)
1.	Dentsu—Tokyo	$1,929.0	11.	Foote, Cone & Belding—Chicago	767.9
2.	McCann-Erickson Worldwide—New York	1,299.0	12.	Young & Rubicam—New York	707.3
3.	J. Walter Thompson—New York	1,073.0	13.	Saatchi & Saatchi—London	685.2
4.	BBDO Worldwide—New York	925.2	14.	Publicis Communication—Paris	676.8
5.	Hakuhodo—Tokyo	897.7	15.	Bates Worldwide—New York	611.0
6.	Leo Burnett—Chicago	866.3	16.	Ammirati Puris Lintas—New York	606.2
7.	DDB Needham Worldwide—New York	848.3	17.	D'Arcy, Masius Benton & Bowles—New York	524.7
8.	Grey Advertising—New York	841.8	18.	TBWA International—New York	366.2
9.	Euro RSCG—Paris	823.8	19.	Lowe & Partners Worldwide—New York	326.0
10.	Ogilvy & Mather Worldwide—New York	793.0	20.	Bozell Worldwide—New York	314.3

Source: *Advertising Age*, April 21, 1997, S24.

quality advertising in all of its markets, it might decide to use the best local agency in each market even if it does not belong to an international family.

Also, if a firm does not require coordination of its advertising in different markets, it has less need to employ an international agency. The coordination provided by international agencies is not always effective, either.

Other reasons for choosing local agencies include the desire for local image and the desire to give national subsidiaries responsibility for their own promotion. As one vice-president for European operations told the author: "Our gains from improved morale and performance from giving them this responsibility far outweigh any loss of efficiency from not requiring international coordination."

Of the several reasons for choosing national agencies, most of those we have discussed have been negative, in the sense that they are based on weaknesses in, or a lack of need for, the international agency approach. A more positive reason is the special quality a national agency has to offer. Although it is not uncommon for some of the best agencies in a market to be offices of an international group, in some cases the best agency for a firm is an independent national agency—just as some small but creative shops in the United States can exist with the giants of the industry. Sometimes their very independence and lack of size give them a flair and flexibility that may be just what the firm needs in that market. Some of the most successful campaigns are carried out by such agencies, and that is a major reason for the firm to consider them. We provide some examples here.

♦ When looking for a new creative approach to the United States, Perrier chose the small Hal Riney agency rather than one of the internationals. GM also chose Hal Riney for its Saturn car.

♦ Surprisingly, Volkswagen dropped DDB Needham for its U.S. ad business and gave the account to the small Arnold Fortuna agency in Boston.

♦ Coca-Cola provided another surprise by taking its Diet Coke account from giant Lintas and giving it to CAA, Michael Ovitz's Hollywood talent agency.

PepsiCo is a company that uses U.S. international agencies in many markets. When it moved into Japan, however, PepsiCo chose a Japanese agency rather than a U.S. affiliate. The executive explained, "We were moving into a very complex

TABLE 12–2		Leading U.S. Consolidated Agencies	

Rank	Agency	Worldwide Gross Income (Millions of Dollars)	U.S. Gross Income (Millions of Dollars)
1.	McCann-Erickson Worldwide	$1,386.1	$416.8
2.	BBDO Worldwide	1,280.2	534.8
3.	Young & Rubicam	1,271.2	535.3
4.	DDB Needham Worldwide	1,266.1	593.5
5.	J. Walter Thompson Co.	1,119.1	421.3
6.	Ogilvy & Mather Worldwide	986.5	303.7
7.	Grey Advertising	935.5	417.8
8.	Leo Burnett Co.	866.3	393.7
9.	Foote, Cone & Belding	798.9	347.0
10.	Ammirati Puris Lintas	775.4	294.5

Source: Calculated from *Advertising Age,* April 2, 1997, S38.

market. We wanted a large Japanese agency that knew its way around the key media. The American affiliates just weren't big enough, *at that time,* to do the job."

We should note one more reason local agencies may survive in some countries—nationalism. Many countries resent the role played by foreign firms in their economy and restrict them in various ways. These restrictions often apply to ad agencies, too. In the Philippines, for example, national agencies pressured the government to ban foreign ad agencies. They claimed that the industry would become dominated by the multinationals and that although they were able to handle local campaigns, the internationals' affiliates would win the major accounts because of their global ties with multinational clients. Along with a dozen other countries, the Philippines allows only minority foreign ownership of agencies. Indonesia, Nigeria, and Pakistan allow no foreign ownership at all. Such protectionism is one barrier to the growth of the multinational agencies.

Having made an appropriate bow to the independent national agencies, we again note the persistent trend toward the selection of international agencies by international companies. Although there will always be room for a certain number of quality independent agencies in each market, their relative importance is likely to decline.

Future Developments

As the advertising industry evolves, certain trends should continue:

1. Further industry consolidation through mergers and acquisitions.

2. Even greater internationalization, including more ties among U.S., Canadian, and Mexican agencies under NAFTA, more European networks by agencies there, and more foreign involvement in U.S. agencies.

3. A continuing shift by advertisers to international agencies, which will increase market share.

4. Expanded geographic coverage by the multinationals. The former Communist countries of Eastern Europe are opening up to Western

TABLE 12-3   **Global Networks of Leading U.S. Ad Agencies: Rankings in Various Markets**

Country	Young & Rubicam	J. Walter Thompson	McCann-Erickson	Ogilvy & Mather	Leo Burnett	DDB Needham	BBDO	Lintas	Foote, Cone & Belding	Grey Advertising
Argentina	3	2	5	10	9	—	6	14	4	7
Australia	3	6	5	18	7	4	2	8	11	10
Austria	13	10	9	5	—	19	7	4	8	10
Brazil	3	4	1	6	16	19	8	10	18	13
Canada	4	12	2	5	7	10	3	20	6	9
Chile	3	6	2	—	4	10	1	5	13	9
Finland	13	12	2	11	—	4	9	8	5	1
France	7	17	4	5	11	3	6	8	12	10
Germany`	6	7	9	5	12	11	1	4	3	2
Great Britain	4	1	6	3	15	11	10	13	24	8
Greece	11	1	6	3	8	5	2	4	9	19
Hong Kong	2	4	9	1	3	5	13	18	14	8
India	9	1	10	3	15	4	8	2	5	6
Italy	2	6	4	12	10	14	13	9	8	7
Japan	13	15	6	28	19	35	—	34	29	27
Malaysia	2	6	4	12	10	14	13	8	14	7
Mexico	2	3	1	7	4	16	6	9	13	10
Netherlands	2	7	9	5	14	6	1	8	4	10
Singapore	1	6	4	3	8	11	9	18	—	14
South Africa	4	11	6	1	5	—	12	9	3	10
Spain	10	8	3	1	19	11	5	15	16	4
Sweden	1	15	3	9	10	8	5	7	12	2
Switzerland	1	13	6	8	14	3	—	10	5	11
Thailand	6	3	8	2	5	17	10	1	4	14
Venezuela	5	2	4	1	3	15	6	—	10	11

— means that the agency does not do business in that country.
Source: Calculated from *Advertising Age*, April 21, 1997, S26–S39.

multinational agencies, and China now has many. The Global Village in advertising is coming.

5. Even fuller service from full-service internationals. In addition to advertising, they are acquiring capabilities in public relations, sales promotion, direct marketing, the Internet, and other marketing services.

6. The Internet will play an increasingly important role but the size and nature of that role is still being determined.

7. Drastic erosion of the exclusive commission payment system. Already by 1998, less than one-third of contracts were on a commission payment only. The rest were mostly on a fee basis with some on a combination fee plus commission basis.

Colgate, Ford, Procter & Gamble, and Unilever are among the major international advertisers leading the way to new payment forms.

Choosing the Advertising Message

A major decision for the international marketer is whether the firm should use national or international advertising appeals—a localized or standardized approach. The goal in either case is to fit the market. Although people's basic needs and desires are the same around the world, the way these desires are satisfied may vary from country to country. Because it is impossible to know each market intimately, help must be obtained from the local subsidiary or distributor and the local advertising agency. The firm may, in fact, completely decentralize responsibility so that each national operation prepares its own advertising.

Localized or Standardized?

In the preparation of advertising campaigns in the international company, arguments usually exist for both a national approach and an international approach. The arguments reflect the self-interested evaluations of the parties involved as well as the objective factors in the situation. In general, two groups tend to be biased in favor of a separate national approach: the management of the local subsidiary and the independent local agency. In each case, the argument depends in large part on the special local knowledge they contribute. The more practical it is for the international firm to treat its international market as it does its other markets, the smaller the role for the local subsidiary and the independent local agency. Because of this vulnerability, management of both the local subsidiary and the agency tend to be defensive about the uniqueness of the market and the need for special approaches there. Both will argue in terms of objective factors, but their position is influenced by their perceived vulnerability.

Subjective factors influence the other side of the argument also. The international agency and the international advertising manager naturally tend to favor an international approach. For example, assume that the international agency makes its bid for the company's business in competition with a national agency. The international agency's competitive advantage may well lie in its internationalism and its ability to coordinate advertising. Therefore, it argues on the basis of its strong points and their appropriateness to the company's need, suggesting the international approach as the best solution as well as the one it is best equipped to provide.

The international manager also has some bias toward an international approach. If each of the firm's markets is unique, thus requiring a national approach by those located there, the need for an international manager is diminished. Another element that sometimes enters in here is the desire of top management to have "one name, one image, worldwide." When executives travel abroad, many like to see the same company advertising as they go from market to market.

The decision on international uniformity in advertising is affected by the human and organizational elements discussed above. However, it should also rest on objective data. Ultimately, the needs of the market should determine the approach used. The international marketer should choose the approach that is the most profitable in terms of sales and costs.

By way of clarification, we use the words *localized* and *standardized* to refer to the two extremes of the international advertising spectrum. Completely localized advertising has only accidental similarity with that done in other countries. Completely standardized advertising is identical in all markets. Neither extreme is usually practiced. The issue for the firm is the degree to which it should move toward one or the other end of the spectrum.

Market Considerations

Several factors influence the ability of the firm to use similar appeals from market to market.

Buyer's Consumption System. The role that the firm's product plays in the buyer's consumption system is one factor. If the product is used in the same way and meets the same needs from country to country, similar appeals are more feasible. The international success of Coca-Cola, which takes a standardized approach in its advertising appeals, suggests that the product meets similar consumer desires everywhere. This is probably true for some other low-priced consumer goods, a famous example of which is Esso gasoline as promoted by Esso's "tiger" campaign. With small modifications and language changes, this campaign traveled all around the world. We provide some examples of the slogan in different languages.

- Put a tiger in your tank.
- Putt en tiger på tanken.
- Ponga un tigre en su tanque.
- Kom en tiger i tanken.
- Metti un tigre nel motore.
- Tu den tiger in den tank.
- Pankaa tiikeri tankum.
- Mettez un tigre dans votre moteur.

Another consideration is the similarity of buying motives from country to country. The same product may be purchased for a mixture of functional, convenience, and status reasons, but with a different combination of motivations in each country. The more alike buying motives are, the more desirable the use of common appeals. This is often the case with industrial goods but is less common with consumer goods. Procter & Gamble found with its fluoride toothpaste that decay prevention was an important motive in Denmark, Germany, and the Netherlands. In England, France, and Italy, however, cosmetic considerations were more important.

General Electric used an international approach with its industrial goods but a national approach with its consumer durables. The automobile market offers conflicting examples. Volvo emphasized economy, durability, and safety in both Sweden and the United States, whereas it stressed status and leisure in France, performance in Germany, and safety in Switzerland (scene of many fatal accidents). On the other hand, BMW tried to maintain a uniform international image.

Language. Another market factor is language overlap from market to market. One world language would obviously facilitate uniform international advertising. Fortunately for those who use the English language, English is gradually coming to fill that role. Of course, the present role of English does not yet permit international campaigns in English, except in the case of some industrial goods or goods that appeal to some international jet set.

Although language overlap among countries is not sufficient to permit global campaigns, a few multilanguage areas do facilitate multinational advertising on a less-than-global basis. Minor examples are found in Europe, where the German language covers Austria and most of Switzerland in addition to Germany, and the French language covers parts of Belgium, Switzerland, Luxembourg, and Monaco, as well as France. More important examples are the following: (1) the English-speaking world, covering up to 600 million people in dozens of nations; (2) the French-speaking world, including the former French colonies (including Quebec) in addition to the European countries mentioned above; and (3) the Spanish-speaking world, including most of the Americas south of the United States. (New York City is a local example of a sizable Spanish-language market.) Even though not all residents of these areas are fluent in the dominant language, its role is large enough to facilitate the internationalization of advertising there.

Two examples illustrate the practical importance of language overlap: Unilever introduced its Radion detergent into Germany with a heavy ad campaign. Because several German media overlap into Austria, Austrian consumers sought Radion in Austrian stores. Because Radion had not yet been introduced into Austria, Unilever lost the benefit of the free advertising carryover.

As another example, Anheuser-Busch, a heavy advertiser of Budweiser beer in the United States, began marketing "Bud" in Canada, hoping for a 1 to 2 percent market share. It was pleasantly surprised to gain almost 8 percent of the market in a few months. One reason was the big carryover of U.S. TV commercials for "Bud" into the Canadian market.

A Note on Translations. Language diversity does not, by itself, prevent the use of international appeals. If a translation is the only adaptation needed in an advertising message, it does not modify the similarity of the appeal. The humorous examples of translation errors—for example, *corpse* for *body*—are recounted frequently because they make interesting copy but statistically they are not significant.

David Kerr of Kenyon & Eckhardt gave some guidelines for translation. He suggests that the English language to be used in international campaigns should be of the 5th- or 6th-grade vocabulary level and contain no slang or idioms. Furthermore, copy should be short because other languages invariably take more time or space to say the same thing the English copy says. The growing use of visual presentation—pictures and illustrations—minimizes the need for translation. Thus, more and more European and Japanese advertisements are purely visual, showing something, evoking a mood, and citing the company name. Such simple illustrations also avoid part of the problem of illiteracy in poorer nations.

While visuals are one way to avoid translation problems, they can have translation problems of their own. For example, AT&T ran an international campaign using the thumbs-up illustration. To the Russians and the Poles, the illustration had a negative meaning, instead of the positive one intended, because the palm of the hand was showing. With the help of YAR Communications, the thumbs-up illustration was retained, but with the back of the hand showing. YAR is one of the few agencies that specializes in translating cultural images, not just dialogue, to avoid such problems.

International Market Segments. Another factor is the existence of international market segments; that is, certain markets within a nation often have counterparts in a number of other nations. In many ways, these markets resemble their counterparts in other countries more than they do other markets in their own country. The international jet set is one example. The youth market is another, and probably includes two segments: the adolescent group and the college-age group. The concerns of college students on all continents seem remarkably similar. Such similarities among age groups can provide a truly international market. There are numerous examples of successful appeals to these national market segments that together constitute an international market for a product. American Express uses Ogilvy & Mather to carry its campaigns to its market segment in over 30 countries.

Levi Strauss & Company has found an international market segment for its Levis. The company prepares its international advertising by beginning with its U.S. ads. One purpose of the advertising campaigns abroad is to achieve a similarity of image from country to country. Company sales seem to attest to the correctness of this approach. Overseas sales rose 500 percent in five years. As someone has said, the groups who buy Levis do speak a common language—the language of youth.

Similarly, Young & Rubicam was able to develop an international campaign for Oil of Olay. The commercials featured women from various countries, all of whom "share the secret of Olay." Though ages, incomes, and languages varied, they found groups of women everywhere concerned about wrinkles.

GLOBAL MARKETING

Celebrities as International Marketers

Celebrities have long been seen in commercials in the United States, but they are being seen increasingly in markets abroad. Who is used and how they are used depends on the cultural situation in each country, as well as the marketing situation of the firm.

Some examples:

Japan   Charles Bronson was the pioneer, appearing in ads for Japanese toiletries. Next was Farah Fawcett promoting Camellia diamonds. Madonna was a smash success in a Mitsubishi ad for VCRs. Bruce Willis appeared in jewelry ads, and Daniel Day-Lewis for face cream. After the success of *Titanic,* Leo Di Caprio appeared in a commercial for Orico, a credit-card company.

Korea   Samsung, in its corporate image advertising theme, "World Best," used all of the following:

Alexander Graham Bell, Charles Lindbergh, Neil Armstrong, Franklin D. Roosevelt, and Margaret Thatcher.

Hyundai Electronics used Alvin Toffler in its corporate image campaign, "New Frontier." Daewoo Motors used Carl Bernstein, the Pulitzer Prize winning journalist of Watergate reporting fame.

Singapore   At a time when some Americans don't know who Fran Tarkenton is, he is doing commercials in Singapore.

Russia   When Russian rock singer Nicolay Rostorguyev had a big hit, RJ Reynolds began using him to promote Peter I cigarettes. L'Oreal has a billboard campaign with Claudia Schiffer, and Golden Lady (stockings) had Kim Basinger in TV spots. Hollywood stars are popular, but Panasonic had to drop Olympic Champion Carl Lewis from its promotions because of Russia's racial prejudice. Nike also used Michael Jordan in a much smaller way in Russian ads.

A final market consideration is the gradual development of the world or regional consumer. What we already see in certain market segments will gradually expand to broader segments of the world's population. Advances in communications, transportation, and production lead to an international democratizing of consumption. People will not be alike, but market segments will become more international in scope, making possible greater use of similar appeals in advertising. The European Single Market is accelerating the emergence of the European consumer. In the United States, marketers speak of market segments on a national basis. They usually do not separate Michigan consumers from Maine or Missouri consumers. The United States, in a sense, is merely the first and most successful of the regional groupings. We already see advertising campaigns coordinated for groupings of countries. Such industrial marketers as Bayer, IBM, and Sulzer organize one campaign for a group of industrialized country markets and another for a group of developing-country markets.

The impact of the Single Market in Europe was dramatic. Beginning in 1988, dozens of major advertisers from Japan, the United States, and Europe converted one or more of their products to pan-European campaigns and switched to a single agency for Europe.

Other Considerations

If market considerations permit similarity in international advertising, the marketer must then evaluate the other factors affecting its feasibility.

Economics. One of these factors is economics. Are there any gains in efficiency in taking an international approach to advertising? As long as agencies are paid on the commission basis, no savings would seem to result from a uniform international message because the payment would be the same whether an international agency or separate national agencies were used. Although this is true for commission payments, gains could still come in other areas. If the company uses a national approach to advertising, the creative work will probably vary greatly in quality from country to country. Small markets have small agencies and small budgets for doing creative work, not to mention a shortage of skilled personnel.

An international approach would permit more to be spent on developing a quality campaign with the best personnel. The best agencies in the larger markets could create the campaign and that expenditure could then be "amortized" over many countries. The better campaign should result in increased revenues. Grey Advertising produced an ad for 12 countries for a new Playtex bra. It cost $250,000 to develop. However, the average cost to develop a single U.S. ad was $100,000.

Agency Relations. A uniform approach is also facilitated by the use of the same agency in all or most of the company's markets. By using an international agency, the company gains efficiencies in communication and coordination. Additionally, the preparation of the international campaign, including inputs and testing in various markets, is much easier if the same agency is working in all the markets. The use of closed-circuit TV and the Web aid the preparation and coordination of international campaigns, eliminating time and travel costs involved in consultations among agencies in various nations. When Playtex wanted to create a global campaign for its previously mentioned new Wow bra, it switched from using 30 different agencies around the world to a single international agency—Grey Advertising.

Because Goodyear and Coca-Cola use McCann-Erickson as their major international agency, they can benefit from McCann's International Team, which has a staff of 25 "creatives" from Japan, Africa, Brazil, China, Britain, and the United States. It creates advertising for 43 clients in three or more countries.

Another factor affecting the feasibility of similar campaigns is the internal organization of the company. If the firm's international operations are very decentralized, international campaigns will be more difficult. Conversely, if the firm is centralized and has a marketing or advertising manager with global responsibility, international campaigns are easier.

Media Developments. The availability of media also affects the development of an international campaign. If the same media were available everywhere, international campaigns would benefit greatly. The fact that this situation does not exist hampers an internationally similar approach. The media do "massage the message" to some degree, and a campaign prepared for TV probably would not be identical to one prepared for radio or print media. This lack of media uniformity does not, in itself, prevent international campaigns, however, as is evidenced by domestic campaigns that use the same appeals in several different kinds of media simultaneously.

Similarity in international media conditions is increasing steadily. Commercial TV and radio are coming to more and more countries. Satellite TV is becoming a truly international medium, bringing to the whole world such events as the Olympic Games, the World Cup, or a space spectacular. Satellite TV in Europe will have a Europeanizing effect on campaigns there. Gillette, for example, signed with Sky Channel (now B Sky B) for advertising to 17 European countries. A study of European advertising and agency executives produced several predictions about the effects of satellite/cable TV in Europe:[3]

1. Brand awareness of non-European products will increase. It will be easier for non-European firms to break into Europe.

2. It will lead to the use of Europewide promotional campaigns and themes.

3.   Local ad agencies will lose out to those that operate across national boundaries.

Print media are going international also. *Reader's Digest* reaches 41 countries in their own languages, and other U.S. magazines and newspapers also have international coverage. European print media are going more Europewide and also beyond Europe. The internationalization of media ownership will reinforce this trend. Already, European groups are among the largest owners of U.S. magazines. Media internationalization will contribute to the internationalization of advertising messages.

Regional or Global Product Introductions.   Companies are going to more uniform campaigns as they develop products for a regional or global market, introducing them simultaneously (or sequentially) in the region or the world. An early example of this was the around-the-world send-off given the Instamatic camera by Kodak. Another one was by NCR in introducing its Century computer on all five continents, with simultaneous showings in 120 cities around the world. A more recent example is the global introduction by Microsoft of Windows 95. As product development becomes more international, and as firms Europeanize campaigns, there is more motivation to create advertising that is as international as the rest of the marketing program. Interestingly, however, regionally integrated advertising is coming only slowly to the Asian and Eastern European markets.

When Johnson & Johnson chose its Silhouettes sanitary napkin for its first Europewide product roll-out, it selected Saatchi & Saatchi to manage the campaign, in part because of that agency's good European coverage. When Philip Morris took Marlboro cigarettes into world markets, it successfully carried much of the "Marlboro Man" ad campaign along with it.

Even apart from global product introductions, global campaigns are increasing. Some examples of firms initiating their first global campaigns in the late 1990s are BMW, The Gap, Jaguar, Saab, Sony, Van Cleef and Arpels, and Volvo.

Government Regulations.   Government restrictions are a fact of life as countries regulate the content of advertisements. The Marlboro cowboy, for example, has been sidelined altogether by stiff regulations in Britain. The reasoning: Heroic figures in cigarette advertisements might have special appeal and encourage people to start smoking. The maze of government regulations makes it difficult to create a universal advertising campaign. One trend, however, has been to restrict advertisements for cigarettes, children's products, liquor, and pharmaceuticals.

In China, the explosion of advertising was accompanied by wild, extravagant ad claims made by many new agencies. China passed new regulations to control the problem and forced even the Western agencies in Beijing to redo hundreds of ads. For example, DDB Needham discovered that calling Budweiser the "King of Beers" was not acceptable.

◆   Kellogg found how European regulations would undermine a 30-second commercial produced for British TV. References to iron and vitamins would have to be deleted in the Netherlands; a child wearing a Kellogg T-shirt would be edited out in France, where children are forbidden from endorsing products on TV. And in Germany, the line "Kellogg makes their cornflakes the best they have ever been" would be dropped because of rules against making competitive claims. An executive of the Kellogg account at J. Walter Thompson discovered that after the required changes, the 30-second commercial would be about five seconds long.

◆   Benetton has been notorious for running ads that are controversial. They ran an ad in Europe showing a dying AIDS patient and another showing the blood-stained clothes of a dead soldier in Bosnia. The strong reactions included boycotts, lawsuits, and legal judgments. Ads were banned in Germany and Switzerland, and a French government minister urged people not to buy Benetton clothes.

Nationalistic policies also restrict advertisers' freedom. More countries now are requiring local production of at least a portion of TV commercials to build their film industries and create more jobs. When Playtex created the international ad for its new bra, it was filmed in Australia because Australian TV will run only those commercials produced there. The other markets for the bra did not have such a restriction.

Industrial Products. The industrial market is more homogeneous internationally than the consumer market. Therefore, industrial marketers are generally more able to implement international campaigns. For example, Siemens of Germany has been working on internationally coordinated advertising in 52 foreign markets ever since 1955. By contrast, IBM did not run a globally integrated campaign until 1995. This was for its AS/400 computer workstation.

Making a Choice

All the variables discussed above must be weighed in deciding what kinds of advertising appeals to use. Although agencies and subsidiaries in each country must help to determine the appeals for their market, it is unlikely that a purely national approach will be taken in many markets. Some internationalizing of the advertising will probably be done. For Europe, it has been suggested that a multinational campaign with a distinctive national touch in each country flatters national sensitivities.

The task is not to find global uniformity but to make the most effective advertising. Multimarket advertising on a regional basis may be desirable because of regional groupings, regional tourism, and media overlap. Or it may be possible to use common appeals in common-language areas. In any case, by seeking common denominators and by playing down national differences, a firm can probably be effective with similar appeals in many countries. We have mentioned a few firms that use basically the same appeals all over the world. Some others are Maidenform, Revlon, and Helena Rubenstein. Although the products associated with these names are of a personal nature, they succeed internationally with universal appeals.

Multinational Coordination in Practice: The Pattern, or Prototype, Approach

Because of client demands for more uniform international advertising, McCann-Erickson created a division called the International Team. Its membership with nationals from more than six countries was noted earlier. Since the "Coke Is It" ads of 1981, no Coca-Cola campaign has been created without using McCann's International Team. For each new campaign, variations on the standard theme are based on research on target markets. This allows much uniformity along with some localization.

Goodyear International provides a more detailed example. International advertising was guided from Akron, Ohio, using prototype campaigns based on common denominators drawn from consumer research in representative markets around the world. The finished ads were prepared nationally for a more effective result.

This prototype, "pattern standardization" approach was used in the firm's 11 major markets. Other developed markets, such as Brazil, Mexico, South Africa, and Japan, received copies of pattern campaigns and could adopt all or part of them. However, these markets had more discretion about adopting them. It should be recognized, however, that for less developed markets, the pattern itself became the best source of high-quality advertising material and strategy.

As Goodyear's international business grew, this pattern approach evolved with more input from the foreign markets. It also became a regional approach with emphasis on the three Strategic Business Units (SBUs) that replaced the former Goodyear International in the 1990s. The SBUs cover Europe, Asia, and Latin America. The goal continues to be the pattern approach, but now it's a regional pattern approach that recognizes the unique needs of each regional participant— a more democratic, participative kind of pattern standardization.

Union Carbide provides another example. Wanting to move its Prestone brand of car-care products into Europe, it called on its ad agency, Young & Rubicam, to survey dealers and consumers in 11 European countries. Research showed that the ideas and approaches that had been used in the United States would also be suitable for the European market. The basic U.S. advertising campaign was, therefore, used in Europe. It proved to be a successful illustration of the pattern approach.

Selecting the Media

A third decision in international advertising is the selection of media for each national market. The desirable media in every country are those that reach the target markets efficiently. The target markets—the purchase decision influencers—are not always the same individuals or groups as in the domestic market. The relative roles of different family members in consumer buying, or of the purchasing agent, engineer, or president in industrial procurement, vary from country to country.

Those most familiar with the local scene—the agency and the company representative within the country—do much of the local media selection. Studies have found the greatest role of subsidiaries in advertising is in media selection. To the extent that subsidiaries do the job, international managers need not get involved. However, international managers might wish to have some voice in local media selection. Through their experience in many countries, they may have insights to contribute.

Or managers may wish to use international media alongside of, or in place of, strictly national media. Because international media cover a number of markets, this combination would require some centralization. For example, Continental Bank, Deltona, and Monsanto handled their international media planning through Tatham-Laird & Kudner, a Chicago agency. Then, too, international managers may be able to contribute sophisticated techniques of media selection. Because more money is spent on advertising in the United States than elsewhere, the technology is generally more advanced here. International managers can ensure that these techniques are made available to company operations everywhere.

Media Diversity

International media selection is complicated by the international differences in media availability. One cannot take a successful media configuration from domestic operations and apply it abroad because the same facilities are often not available. We saw earlier how nations differ in their communications infrastructure, that is, the availability of TV, radio, and newspapers. In addition to that disparity, a great difference exists in how these media are used for advertising. The data in Table 12–4 illustrate these differences.

TV's share of the dollar ranges from 19 percent in Germany to 74 percent in Venezuela. Radio's share ranges from 2 percent in Sweden and Venezuela to 12 percent in Canada; the print media, from 16 percent in Mexico to 73 percent in Germany; and outdoor advertising from 2 percent in the United States and Venezuela to 21 percent in South Korea. Even within regions, media use differs greatly.

Diversity Means Adaptation. When media availability differs from market to market, international marketers have to decentralize media selection and adapt to local

TABLE 12-4	Media Advertising Expenditures for Selected Countries			
		Media		
Countries	TV	Radio	Print	Outdoor
United States	56	4	39	2
Canada	27	12	50	11
Asia				
India	21	3	67	9
Indonesia	43	10	41	5
Japan	47	5	40	8
South Korea	28	4	45	21
Thailand	51	11	34	4
Europe				
France	33	9	45	12
Germany	19	4	73	4
Italy	53	4	40	3
Sweden	24	2	69	5
United Kingdom	32	3	61	4
Latin America				
Argentina	60	7	21	11
Brazil	59	4	34	3
Mexico	68	11	16	4
Venezuela	74	2	23	2

Rounding may affect totals.
Source: International Marketing Data and Statistics 1998 (London: Euromonitor, 1998), 353.

possibilities. Because local managers cannot follow the media patterns used elsewhere, they must find the local media that reach their markets effectively.

In Peru, Orange Crush used a wide variety of media ranging from newspapers, TV and radio, to cinema and point-of-purchase materials. Outside the capital, Lima, the company used billboards more heavily because taxes on billboards were lower in the provinces. On the other hand, the use of cinema was reduced in the provinces because it was not found very effective.

Whom Does the Medium Massage?

Another factor hampering media decisions in many countries is the lack of reliable information on circulation and audience characteristics. Advertisers in the United States are accustomed to audited data on the size of audience reached by the various media. In addition, they often have a breakdown on audience characteristics, such as occupation, education, and income level. No other country has as much information, and the supply decreases rapidly with the level of economic development. In many countries, the only figures are those supplied by the media themselves. Such unaudited figures are suspect.

Another consideration complicating media evaluation is that whatever figures can be obtained for the circulation of a medium do not necessarily indicate its true coverage. In countries where data can be obtained as to the number of TV or radio sets, the true audience may be much larger than the figures suggest. For example, in countries with low literacy rates, the average number of viewers per TV set is apt to be at least twice as large as in the United States. This principle also applies to the number of radio listeners, especially in less developed countries where a few receivers may reach a whole village.

Even with print media, the average readership varies from country to country. In less developed countries, one literate villager will read a newspaper or magazine to illiterate neighbors. Even in developed countries, one issue may pass from the initial purchaser through several other readers. A French magazine with a circulation of 1.5 million estimated its total readership at 8.3 million.

This lack of accurate media information makes media selection difficult. The answer in the long run is to expand media auditing services. In the short run, advertisers must depend on their own ingenuity. As firms gain experience in a market, they learn about the relative effectiveness of different media there. Comparative analysis of similar markets can again be useful.

International or Local Media?

The manager sometimes has the alternative of using either national media or media that cover several markets; both print and broadcast media, for example, have multimarket coverage. The print media with international market coverage include such U.S. general-interest magazines as *Reader's Digest* and *Time,* which reach most of the world's major markets, and *Paris Match* or *Vision,* which reach several European and Latin American markets, respectively. *Elle,* the French women's magazine, has 28 editions worldwide. Numerous technical and trade publications (usually U.S.-based) in the engineering, chemistry, electronics, and automotive industry, and so on, also have an extensive and influential circulation around the world.

The scope of international media is rising steadily. Magazines, newspapers, and TV are all expanding in the Global Village, as we shall see. In each medium, the geographic coverage is expanding. For example, *Business Week, Forbes,* and *Fortune* all have European, Asian, and/or international editions.

Magazines, the First Internationalists. International magazines can offer advantages to the marketer where they correspond to target markets. Among these advantages are audited circulation and audience data, good-quality reproduction of advertisements, an influential audience, regional market coverage for marketing to specific areas, and the lending of the magazines' prestige to products advertised. An additional boon is that advertisements can be placed and paid for at one source.

The internationalization of magazines is increasing with the international consolidation of the industry. Through purchases of U.S. magazine publishers, Bertelsmann of Germany and Hachette of France have become the world's largest media companies after Capital Cities-ABC and Time-Warner. Hachette is now the publisher of *Woman's Day* and *Car and Driver,* for example.

Surveys of European executives continually show their cosmopolitan reading habits. Publications such as the *Financial Times* and *The Economist* (London), *Fortune* and *Business Week,* and leading European business publications are read in a number of countries besides their country of origin.

The drawbacks of international magazines are that they usually have only English, French, or Spanish editions (except for the *Reader's Digest*) and give only partial coverage of any national market. These advantages and limitations have to be evaluated in terms of the markets of the firm. International magazines are less likely to be used for mass-consumption items because of their limited coverage. However, for certain industrial goods, and for consumer goods and services that appeal to an affluent market, the international magazines may give just the right coverage.

Reader's Digest signed pioneering global advertising deals with Ford and General Motors and with several other international marketers, including Procter & Gamble, Warner-Lambert, and Bristol-Myers Squibb. The deals allow the firms to earn discounts and develop marketing programs involving any of *Reader's Digest*'s 41 editions worldwide.

The Internationalizing Newspapers. Whereas the *International Herald Tribune* was once the only international paper, it now has lots of company. The *Financial Times* covers Europe and the United States. *The Wall Street Journal* has European and Asian editions and also has special editions in 25 newspapers in 21 countries and 5 languages, including Turkish. Even the *China Daily*, the official English-language publication of China, is published simultaneously (by satellite) in China, the United States, and Europe. European integration is forcing major national papers to try to regionalize their coverage.

Radio. Although broadcast media traditionally have played a smaller international role than print media, their growing commercialization is increasing their importance. International commercial radio is most important in Western Europe, where at least four stations reach several nations. Because they have transmitting power up to 275,000 watts (the U.S. limit is 50,000 watts), these stations can cover most of Western Europe. The leading international and commercial station is Radio Luxembourg, which works three frequencies—long-wave, medium-, and short-wave—and broadcasts in five languages. It counts millions of listeners from the British Isles to southern France and eastward into Germany, Austria, and Switzerland. Many of the advertisers on this station are U.S. firms: Procter & Gamble, Colgate-Palmolive, Gillette, Nabisco, John Deere, 3M, and Coca-Cola. Radio Luxembourg's coverage corresponds to their markets.

If the national radio networks in the major European nations ever go commercial, it would threaten these "international" stations, all of which are located in tiny principalities. Until that time, however, they are the major commercial radio available in Europe; Latin America, by contrast, has many commercial radio stations. Clearly, commercial radio is especially useful for reaching nonliterate populations. As seen in Table 12–4, radio's share is limited in many countries.

A good example of radio as an international medium is the case of Saudi Arabia. Because of restrictions on broadcast advertising, the best buy for spot radio in Saudi Arabia is Radio Monte Carlo, one of the European international stations. It is a favorite of Saudis who have lived abroad.

Television. Commercial TV for international advertising is an area of great growth. Some such advertising occurs almost accidentally now as U.S. broadcasts reach into Canada (and vice versa) or German television commercials spill over into Austria and Switzerland. Today, however, there are more international commercial TV choices. CNN is the leader, reaching homes in over 100 countries, but there are many competitors. Europe has over 80 satellite TV channels now. Latin America has Univision plus Televisa and Globo, which joined with Murdoch's News Corp. to cover the continent. In Asia, Murdoch's Star TV covers 53 countries from Japan to the Middle East. The BBC has its World Service Channel, and MTV reaches almost 300 million in about 80 countries. See "Global Marketing," "The European Air Battle."

ABC, the U.S. company, pioneered a network of TV stations in Canada, Latin America, the Caribbean, Spain, Africa, the Middle East, the Far East, and Australia, an area of 25 nations. An advertiser can buy various packages of nations in this network for an international campaign. For example, Pan American Life Insurance sponsored the Academy Awards program, on a delayed basis, in 14 Latin American countries. Other firms that use parts of this international network include Ford, Sterling Drug, Nestlé, Goodyear, Kellogg, Quaker Oats, and PepsiCo.

Commercial television is expanding almost everywhere. The majority of nations have it, and the number increases each year. Also, a potentially large number of hours can be devoted to the same broadcasting material all over the world: for

GLOBAL MARKETING

The European Air Battle

CNN had built a strong European subscriber base following the Gulf War, but its success drew many competitors.

1. *European Business News.* A 24-hour business news channel; a joint venture of Dow Jones and Telecommunications, Inc.
2. *BBC World.* A 24-hour news and current events channel; a joint venture of the BBC, Pearson, and Cox Communications.
3. *Sky News.* B Sky B's news channel signed an agreement with Reuters to provide much of its international news coverage.
4. *CNBC Money Wheel.* A four-hour live news show put on by the *Financial Times* broadcast unit for NBC Super Channel.
5. Bloomberg has gone abroad with its financial information and business news.
6. Europe's public-sector broadcasters create "Euronews," which has now gone commercial.
7. In partial response to be competitive, CNN formed CNNFN for financial and business news.

example, programs on the Olympic Games, space shots, royal or presidential accessions (or funerals), and so forth. The international popularity of some U.S. television series is an indicator of the potential.

Other International Media. While magazines, radio, and TV are the major international media, other kinds exist as well. John Deere found no suitable medium in which to advertise to farmers, so it started a magazine called *Furrow* back in 1895. As Deere went international, so did the magazine, which now has 22 different editions in 10 languages and a circulation of about 2,500,000. It is easily the world's most widely read farm magazine and the most effective medium John Deere could use. An equivalent campaign in other farm periodicals would be at least twice as expensive. In a similar way, Abbott Labs reaches 300,000 doctors around the world with its quarterly magazine *Abottempo,* printed in nine languages.

Ronald McDonald, the clown, represents another kind of media. Used first in Washington, D.C., in 1963, he went national in 1967 and made his first international TV appearance in 1969. Today Ronald speaks a dozen languages, including Chinese, Dutch, French, German, Gaelic, Japanese, Papiemento, Portuguese, and Swedish. A clown seems to be popular everywhere, and Ronald may be the best-known character since Santa Claus. Ronald not only opens stores but also is a goodwill ambassador who visits hospitals and raises funds for children. (There are 90 Ronald McDonald Houses in countries abroad.)

Local Media. We have discussed international media at some length because they are an option peculiar to international marketing and because they will be more significant tomorrow. Nevertheless, the amount of advertising in national media is vastly greater than that done in international media. National media predominate, even for the international advertiser, because they offer certain advantages. They offer more possibilities, ranging from newspapers, magazines, direct mail, cinema, and billboards to the broadcast media. They use local languages and provide greater flexibility in market segmentation and test marketing. In general, local media do a better job of reaching and adapting to the local market, especially for consumer goods.

Disadvantages, however, occasionally arise in using local media. Although the industrialized countries frequently offer the same media quality as found in the United States, in many other countries print reproduction may be poor, rates may not be fixed, and audited circulation data may not be available. The need to place the advertising as well as pay for it locally can be a drawback if the firm has centralized control. Nevertheless, these disadvantages are not sufficient to seriously limit the use of local media.

Most companies do most of their advertising in the local media of the foreign market. Generally, the more decentralized the firm, the more it uses local campaigns, and the more it relies on local ad agencies, the more it will use local media.

◆ Colgate knows well how to use the local media in its foreign markets. It is credited with creating the Mexican soap opera and one of the more popular programs broadcast in Mexico. Thus, the company successfully carried to Mexico a form more commonly associated with its competitor, Procter & Gamble, in the United States.

Setting the International Advertising Budget

Among the controversial aspects of advertising is determining the proper method for setting the advertising budget. This is a problem domestically as it is internationally. Yet because the international advertiser must try to find an optimum outlay for a number of markets, the problem is more complex on the international level. In theory, it is not difficult to state the amount of money the firm should put into advertising abroad. In each of its markets, the firm should continue to put more money into advertising as long as an advertising dollar returns more than a dollar spent on anything else. In practice, this equimarginal principle is difficult to apply because of the impossibility of measuring accurately the returns, not only from advertising but also from other company outlays.

Because of the difficulty in determining the theoretically optimum advertising budget, companies have developed more practical guidelines. We will examine the relevance of these guidelines for the international advertiser. Although the equimarginal principle noted above is difficult to apply, it must nevertheless serve as an initial rough guide. In other words, the advertising budget is not set in a vacuum but is just one element of the overall marketing mix. Therefore, it is necessary to have some idea as to whether a sum of money should go into advertising or personal selling or price reductions or product or package improvements or something else.

Coca-Cola may be the world's most advertised product. The company yearly spends over $800 million, about half of it outside the United States. In addition, the bottlers approximately match the corporate outlay.

Percentage-of-Sales Approach

An easy method for setting the advertising appropriation in a country is based on *percentage of sales*. Besides its convenience, this method has the advantage of relating advertising to the volume of sales in a country and thus keeping advertising from "getting out of hand." This approach, perhaps the easiest to justify in the budget meeting, appeals to financially oriented managers who like to think in terms of ratios and costs per unit. And when the firm is selling in many markets, it has the further advantage of appearing to guarantee equality among them. Each market seems to get the advertising it deserves.

For the firm that centralizes control over international advertising, the percentage-of-sales approach is very attractive. A manager at headquarters would have difficulty using any other budgeting approach for 50 or 100 markets. Rabino studied 80 of the Fortune 1,000 companies and found this to be the most popular method.[4] The Europeans favor this approach as much as the Americans.

Despite its attractions, however, this approach has limitations. The purpose of advertising is to cause sales, but this method perversely makes the volume of sales determine the amount of advertising. When sales are declining, advertising declines, although long-range considerations might suggest that advertising should be stepped up. When a firm is entering a foreign market, it may need a disproportionate amount of advertising to break in. Limiting the advertising to the same percentage-of-sales figure used elsewhere would be undesirable during the firm's first years in the market.

The same is true in the introduction of new products into a market. As firms expand, they introduce more products into their markets. The advertising budget for these introductions should relate to the introductory needs rather than to some percentage of sales applied to existing products—or to the same products being sold in other countries. Significant advertising outlays are usually required of firms that want to expand their presence in world markets.

When Panasonic tried to launch its batteries into the U.S. market, it set an ad budget that was a small fraction of those of its competitors. Its success was limited. By contrast, when Nike and Reebok entered Europe, they each had a promotional budget approximately twice that of the well-entrenched Adidas. They succeeded in sharing 50 percent of the market in a few years.

The major weakness in applying a standard percentage-of-sales figure for advertising in foreign markets is that this method does not relate to the firm's situation in each market. The examples given—entering a market and introducing new products—are just two illustrations of the need for special treatment for special situations. In some countries, the firm may be well established with no strong competitors, whereas in others it may have difficulty getting a consumer franchise. Advertising needs are different in these two instances. For example, European firms increased their ad budgets for the Single Market.

Other factors differentiating the firm's situation from country to country are variations in media availability and the firm's level of involvement. Differences in media possibilities might mean that the firm will spend more on personal selling or other promotional tools and less on advertising. In countries where the firm has its own subsidiaries, the ad budget usually is determined differently from the way it is in countries where it has a licensee or distributor.

Until more sophisticated techniques are made operational, many companies will continue to use some percentage-of-sales method despite its limitations. This is not necessarily bad if the percentage is shown from company experience to be reasonably successful and if the method is somewhat flexible, allowing different percentages to be applied in different markets according to need.

Competitive-Parity Approach

Matching competitors' advertising outlays—the **competitive-parity approach**—is used by some companies. Although it may offer the firm a feeling that it is not losing ground to its competitors, the merit of this approach is dubious in domestic operations, and it is especially to be challenged in international marketing. As a practical matter, in most markets the firm is not able to determine advertising figures of competitors.

Another danger in following the practice of competitors is that they are not necessarily right. In fact, the international firm is almost always a heavier advertiser than national firms in the same industry. If anything, the international firm sets the standard for national competitors to follow rather than the reverse. This was evident in Procter & Gamble's entry into Europe, for example. The fact that different competitors may employ different promotional mixes also hampers the use of this approach. In the United States, for instance, Revlon is a heavy advertiser, whereas Avon relies more on personal selling. Who should follow whom?

A final limitation to the competitive-parity approach in foreign markets is the difference in the situation of the international firm. Since it is a foreigner in the market, its relationship with consumers may differ from that of national companies. This would be reflected in its promotion. Its product line and marketing program are also likely to differ from those of national competitors. For these reasons, it is improbable that matching competitors' outlays would prove to be a sound strategy in foreign markets.

Objective-and-Task Approach

The weaknesses of the above approaches have led some advertisers to the **objective-and-task method,** which begins by determining the advertising objectives, expressed in terms of sales, brand awareness, or something else, then ascertaining the tasks needed to attain these objectives, and finally estimating the costs of performing these tasks. If this approach includes a cost-benefit analysis, relating the objectives to the cost of reaching them, it is a desirable method.

The objective-and-task method is as relevant for markets abroad as it is at home. It logically seeks to relate the advertising budget in a country to the firm's situation and goals there. To use it satisfactorily, however, the firm must have good knowledge of the local market to set appropriate objectives. Unfortunately, except where it has local subsidiaries, the firm does not have intimate knowledge of the market, so setting specific objectives and defining the task of advertising may be difficult. In such cases, a percentage-of-sales method may be more feasible. It may be more important to be operational than to be "scientifically correct." Europeans and North Americans have equally low usage of the objective-and-task method.

Comparative-Analysis Approach

Between applying a uniform percentage to all markets and letting each market go its own way lies a middle ground: **comparative analysis,** in which markets are grouped into categories according to characteristics relevant to advertising. This method yields more flexibility than the uniform approach and more control than the laissez-faire approach. Categories might be based on size (markets with over $1 million sales and those with under $1 million), media situation, or other pertinent characteristics. Different budgeting methods or percentages could be tried for each group. One country could serve as a test market for its group. This technique can be useful for the advertiser who has a large number of markets.

Some Special Considerations

Several special factors affect the amount of advertising the firm will do in foreign markets.

Media Restrictions. In markets where certain media do not exist or cannot be used commercially, the firm's advertising budget is apt to be relatively low. For example, many firms that advertise heavily on TV in the United States have smaller relative outlays in markets where that medium is not available. Conversely, many firms greatly increase their budgets when commercial TV becomes available. When media regulations are very restrictive, the firm may place greater reliance on other promotional tools.

Low-Income Markets. Two-thirds of the world's countries are less developed. Generally, a limited amount of advertising is done in these economies, and consumers have limited discretionary income. Although these factors usually combine to cut the ad budget, exceptions do exist. Some firms selling low-priced consumer goods, such as Colgate-Palmolive and Unilever, have successfully used heavy advertising outlays in low-income countries.

Company Organization. The degree to which the firm is centralized will affect advertising budgeting. The more centralized, the more uniform the budget process is likely to be from country to country. The percentage-of-sales approach is probable in this case. If the firm has autonomous subsidiaries, however, each one is likely to determine its own advertising appropriation, resulting in greater variability.

Level of Involvement. A firm's involvement in foreign markets often ranges from a distributor in some markets to subsidiaries in others. As the firm's position and control vary greatly from one situation to another, so does its approach to budgeting advertising. Subsidiaries were discussed in the preceding paragraph. Advertising budgeting of joint ventures may be constrained by the other partner. Licensees may be entirely on their own, or the agreement may require them to do some advertising. Distributors also may be on their own or have a cooperative advertising program.

The Culligan Company provides a fairly typical example. Culligan adds 2 percent to the price paid by the distributor and matches this with an additional 2 percent from the corporation. This is a percentage-of-sales method of administering local advertising on a cooperative basis. In this case, 4 percent of sales is applied to local advertising.

Evaluating International Advertising Effectiveness

Testing advertising effectiveness is even more difficult in international markets than in the United States. One reason is that the markets are smaller and therefore budgets are smaller. A more important reason is that few markets have experience in this work. Consequently, in most markets marketers have to rely primarily on their own capabilities. Because they have less contact with foreign markets, their ability to investigate advertising effectiveness is limited. Thus, three factors restrict the measurement of advertising's effectiveness in world markets: (1) small size of the market, (2) lack of facilities, and (3) the distance and communications gap between the market and international marketers. As a result, many firms use sales results as the measure of advertising effectiveness.

In this area, international marketers must again exercise ingenuity. Some evidence of effectiveness is needed to develop sound advertising budgets. Once more, comparative analysis may be useful. If the firm's markets can be grouped according to similar characteristics, experiments with advertising programs can be conducted using one or two countries in a group as test markets. Variables to be tested might include the amount of advertising, the media mix, the appeals, the frequency of placement, and so on. Experience needs to be built up on a cross-sectional basis—that is, between countries—as well as on a historical basis. Such experience can help to overcome some of the handicaps in measuring advertising effectiveness in foreign markets. The continuing internationalization of marketing research and ad agencies will eventually help with this problem.

Organizing for International Advertising

The firm has basically three organizational alternatives: (1) It can centralize all decision making for international advertising at headquarters; (2) it can decentralize the decision making to foreign markets; or (3) it can use some blend of these two alternatives. Of course, the question of organizing for international advertising cannot be separated from the company's overall organization for international business. The firm is unlikely to be highly centralized for one function and decentralized for another. We discuss overall organization in Chapter 17. Here we consider the special factors affecting organization for international advertising.

Centralization

Complete centralization of international advertising implies that campaign preparation, media and agency selection, and budgeting are all done at headquarters. This might be necessary if the firm's international business is small or if it is confined to dealing with distributors or licensees. Complete centralization is less likely when the firm operates through foreign subsidiaries. In reality, control at headquarters of international advertising is seldom complete. We use the term *centralized* to refer to the situation where headquarters plays a major coordinating role, as in the Goodyear example cited earlier, or the ITT example below.

Centralized control of advertising is more feasible when the firm works with one international agency that has branches covering all of its markets, when the firm has standardized international advertising, and when market and media conditions are similar from market to market. As we saw, these conditions were met by American Express when it used Ogilvy & Mather to carry its message around the world.

On the personnel side, centralized control implies that staff at headquarters know foreign markets and media well enough to make appropriate decisions. Communications must be adequate for controlling the actual placement of the advertising in each market. It might be possible to rely on an international agency for help. Industrial marketers, such as Timken, Rockwell, and Du Pont rely on the U.S. office of their international agency. When subsidiaries are involved, there must be some authority over the subsidiary personnel, just as the agency works with its own people in the same market.

The centralized approach creates demands for advertising personnel at headquarters but minimal demands for them at the subsidiary level. Economies of scale in staffing and in administration are arguments for centralization. The potential dangers are rigidity, failure to adapt to local needs, and stifling of local initiative, which can lead to morale problems in the subsidiary.

◆ ITT provides an example of strong headquarters coordination of international advertising. ITT headquarters is in New York and so is its global advertising department. Under this office are advertising staff in the area organizations: Europe, Latin America, the Far East, and the Pacific. The department also monitors the efforts of the various advertising agencies for ITT worldwide. The global budget is over $400 million. The department's responsibilities include selection of ad agencies around the world and hiring and indoctrination of ad managers for ITT divisions.

Coordination starts with an annual subsidiary advertising plan, which is explained in its *Standard Planning Guide.* The guide also spells out standard practices. Another control device is the monthly progress report from each unit's ad manager. A final form of communication is the annual face-to-face group meeting. It is a two-day session where staff from New York meet with ad managers from the four regions.

The trend is increasing for centralizing international advertising as more companies push for regional or global marketing. The European Single Market has increased centralized control for European firms, as we have seen. Continuing integration of world markets is leading U.S. and Japanese multinationals in the same direction. For U.S. firms with well-established foreign subsidiaries, the main resistance comes from subsidiary managers who view global advertising as a threat to their autonomy.

Decentralization

With complete decentralization of international advertising, each market would make all its own advertising decisions. When this laissez-faire method is company policy, it may result from several considerations: (1) The volume of international business and advertising is too small to warrant attention at headquarters. (2) The communications problems between home and field render a centralized approach impossible. (3) The firm believes that local decision making gives a more national image. (4) The firm believes that nationals know the local scene best and will be more highly motivated if given this responsibility.

Decentralized control is likely to be associated with national rather than international advertising campaigns and with the employment of independent local agencies in each market. It requires more expertise and personnel at the subsidiary.

In markets where the firm does not have subsidiaries, performance depends on the advertising skills and interest of the firm's licensee or distributor. The advantages of decentralization are the motivation given to the national operation and the possibility of getting more effective tailor-made advertising programs. The dangers are duplication of effort and ineffective advertising, especially in smaller markets. Honeywell was a practitioner of the decentralized, or "hands off" approach, and when Microsoft entered Europe in the mid-1990s, its advertising was also prepared by national marketing teams.

A Compromise Approach

Between the extremes of complete centralization and complete decentralization are programs that use elements of both approaches. A compromise approach should entail finding the appropriate division of labor between headquarters and country operations, with each making its contribution according to its comparative advantage. One expert has called this *coordinated decentralization*. However, this same expert emphasizes the coordination more than decentralization. IBM, Matsushita, and Philips follow this approach, for example.

In a compromise approach, headquarters usually plays the more important role, being "more equal" than the national operations. The central advertising manager is responsible for international advertising policy and guidelines. The basic creative work and selection of overall themes and appeals are generally centralized. Headquarters also works with the coordinator from the international agency, if such an agency is used.

When the Kodak Instamatic was introduced around the world, the Kodak vice-president for marketing and the Instamatic account executive of J. Walter Thompson not only planned strategy together, but they also traveled around the world together, visiting local subsidiaries and agencies. Rank-Xerox had a similar collaboration with Young & Rubicam in Europe.

The advertising manager at headquarters establishes standard operating procedures and prepares a manual for subsidiary advertising management, including budget and reporting forms, as at ITT. Common formats make budgets comparable from country to country for better evaluation. The manager also acts as a clearinghouse, transferring relevant experiences between countries and from domestic operations, and organizing meetings of advertising personnel.

CPC International has held annual worldwide marketing conferences to help advertising coordination. These meetings sometimes took place in the United States, sometimes abroad. In addition, meetings were held on a regional basis where marketing personnel discussed advertising programs and agency operations. The company used more than one agency in many markets because of the number of different brands it sold. In Europe, the company's largest region, the firm had a consumer goods policy council, whose duties included selection of agencies and coordination of advertising programs.

In this compromise approach, the role of subsidiary personnel is strongest in media selection and in the adaptation of advertising appeals to local needs, while the role of headquarters is greatest in setting objectives and establishing the budget. Subsidiaries do not have major creative responsibilities, but they do have a voice in the decisions related to their own market. As compared with a decentralized approach, this compromise requires a smaller staff and less expertise within the subsidiary.

The U.S. auto companies practice central coordination, but in differing degrees and with different approaches. For example, General Motors markets in 176 countries and uses McCann-Erickson as the main agent of coordination. GM coordinates on a regional basis, that is, for Latin America, Europe, and Asia. McCann is GM's agency in 35 countries. Other agencies are used elsewhere, but they are in consultation with McCann and regional and corporate marketing staff in GM. Though control is regional, Detroit has final approval on campaign budgets. In

Europe, McCann's office in Zurich coordinates European advertising in conjunction with GM's European headquarters there.

Ford, on the other hand, markets in 185 countries and uses more agencies. Rather than using a single agency for coordination as GM does, Ford has its own international coordinating group in Detroit that coordinates, counsels, advises, and assists the other agencies. It does this through regular advertising exchange, including videos, advertising cost reviews, and annual agency reviews.

Chrysler was primarily only an export marketer and used a U.S. international agency. Their merger with Daimler-Benz changed that, of course.

Using Cooperative Advertising

A firm that sells through licensees or distributors can choose one of three ways to advertise in its foreign markets: (1) It can handle such advertising itself; (2) it can cooperate with the local distributor; or (3) it can try to encourage the distributor or licensee to do such advertising by itself. The last alternative is not really feasible, so the choice is primarily between going it alone or cooperating.

Advertising Made in the United States

When the firm chooses to handle its own advertising for distributor markets, it must arrange for the complete advertising program at home with few inputs from the markets concerned. Going it alone poses some difficulty because the firm is not very familiar with those markets where its only contact is a licensee or distributor. This problem is alleviated somewhat when the firm's agency has offices in those markets. However, the agency's network is unlikely to mesh very closely with the company's foreign markets. The agency tends to have offices in the larger markets, whereas many of the firm's distributors are likely to be in smaller markets. The company may have its own subsidiaries in the larger markets.

In spite of the problems in centralized management of advertising for distributor markets, some firms choose this approach, implementing it through an international agency. Their understanding is that even with its limitations, this way offers more control and greater effectiveness than the alternatives. Working on a centralized basis with its agency gives the firm a voice in the management of the advertising and general control over its quality and placement even in distant markets.

Cooperative Local Advertising

Many other firms choose the alternative of developing their foreign advertising programs in cooperation with their local distributors. They do so in an attempt to obtain the advantages claimed for coordinated decentralization—the appropriate division of labor and a contribution from each party according to its comparative advantage.

Several advantages are claimed for the cooperative approach. For one, the exporter hopes to get more advertising for the money, either through a greater amount of advertising or through the same amount done on a shared basis rather than solely by the exporter. Furthermore, the cooperative program itself may motivate the distributor to do more promotion. In markets where the distributor is well known, the exporter can trade on the distributor's reputation. The distributor, through knowledge of the local market and media, can help choose the advertising that best fits the local situation. The distributor may also get better media rates as a national.

One problem with cooperative advertising is that advertising quality is uneven from country to country. If the advertising is poor, it could be a waste. A related difficulty is that distributors sometimes emphasize their own business rather than the exporter's. Also, it is difficult to ascertain whether distributors actually spend their advertising allowance on advertising.

The problems of cooperative advertising need not prevent its being used. The manager can minimize the problems. Working with an agency with good foreign-market coverage can help to control distributor placement of ads. Development of prototype advertising helps standardize the quality. The exporter's partial payment of the cost provides for some control. Still another way to combat the problem of uncooperative distributors is to establish agreed-upon guidelines. If the firm can implement these steps, it has a good chance with a cooperative program.

- ◆ The Culligan Company prepared three different advertising approaches with its domestic agency. Then it met with its European licensees to review them. A majority vote by the licensees decided which approach should be used. The licensee's agency placed the ads.

- ◆ Another success story involved the MEM Company (maker of English Leather products), which distributed U.S. ad copy to licensees and allowed them discretion as to its use. Many did use these advertisements, finding them well done and convenient. If the licensee used its own ad material, it had to have it approved by MEM. Of course, to have this kind of control, the firm must pay for at least part of the local advertising. For example, both Culligan and MEM paid one-half of the expense.

SUMMARY

Several factors affect the job of the international advertiser. Languages vary by market, and the advertising must be in the local language. This requires local help, from the local ad agency or subsidiary of the firm. Media availability (TV, radio, newspaper) varies between countries, requiring adjustment by the advertiser. Governments restrict advertisers' freedom by limits on products advertised, appeals used, media use, and agency ownership. Competition in the local market influences the firm's advertising there. Agency availability differs between markets for political and economic reasons. This can hinder the firm's ability to find a good agency or get international coordination.

Major advertising decisions involve selecting the agency, the message, and the media; determining the budget; evaluating the effectiveness of the advertising; and determining the degree of centralization or decentralization appropriate.

Using its own international marketing criteria, the firm must choose an agency for each foreign market. The trend is to multicountry agencies that are gaining market share. However, some good local agencies will survive in most markets.

In choosing the message, the issue is whether the firm should use local or international campaigns. The use of internationalized campaigns is affected by language requirements, the existence of international market segments, the use of local versus international agencies, and the degree of decentralization in the firm. To maximize similarities, many firms use a pattern, or prototype, approach.

The firm's media configuration often varies from country to country because of government restrictions or media infrastructure in the country. Some firms are able to use international media for multicountry coverage, but local media predominate for most international marketers.

It is difficult to apply the various formulas for determining the ad budget in the firm's foreign markets. Because of this, the percentage-of-sales approach is the most common. The ad budget in a country is a function of its overall promotional mix there, local media availability, and the firm's own level of involvement in that country.

Evaluating advertising is more difficult in foreign markets than at home. For this reason, firms frequently use sales as the measure of effectiveness. The internationalization of research and advertising agencies is helping on this score.

A major question is, How centralized should the firm be for international advertising? Favoring centralization are potential economies, international coordination, and higher quality. Favoring decentralization are local adaptation and motivation of the local subsidiary. Most firms compromise between the two extremes, making coordination more common.

The firm must also decide how to advertise in markets where it is represented by independent licensees or distributors. Should it rely on them, go it alone, or co-operate? Cooperative programs with the local licensee or distributor appear to be the most common and effective approach.

QUESTIONS

12.1 Discuss government controls and agency and media availability as constraints on the international advertising manager.

12.2 Identify the seven advertising decisions facing the international marketer.

12.3 Home Care Products Co. just opened a marketing subsidiary in Spain. The company has been selling in 12 other European countries since 1950. The advertising manager at European headquarters must choose between the Madrid office of a large U.S. agency and a leading Spanish agency. What questions would you ask in advising her?

12.4 Why have the international agencies been growing so strong?

12.5 Why do local agencies survive in view of the internationals' growth?

12.6 What are the factors encouraging standardization of international advertising?

12.7 What are the factors encouraging localized advertising in a firm's foreign markets?

12.8 Explain "pattern" or "prototype" advertising.

12.9 Why is it difficult for the international advertising manager to use the same media configuration in all markets?

12.10 Discuss the growth of the international media.

12.11 Why do local media predominate, even for international marketers?

12.12 Evaluate the percentage-of-sales approach to setting advertising budgets in foreign markets.

12.13 What are the arguments for and against centralization of advertising decision making in the international firm?

12.14 Discuss the benefits and problems in a program of cooperative advertising with local distributors in export markets.

ENDNOTES

1 J. J. Boddewyn, "Barriers to Advertising," *International Advertiser,* May–June 1989, 21, 22.

2 Barry Rosen, J. J. Boddewyn, and Ernst Louis, "Participation by U.S. Agencies in International Brand Advertising," *Journal of Advertising* 17, no. 4 (1988): 14–22.

3 Donald G. Howard and John K. Ryans, Jr., "The Probable Effect of Satellite TV," *Journal of Advertising Research,* January 1989, 41–46.

4 Samuel Rabino, "Is Advertising Budgeting Changing?" *International Journal of Advertising* 3, no. 2 (1984).

FURTHER READINGS

Church, Nancy. "Advertising in the Eastern Bloc." *Journal of Global Marketing* 5, no. 3 (1992): 109–129.

Grein, Andreas, and Robert Ducoffe. "Responses to Market Globalisation among Ad Agencies." *International Journal of Advertising* 17 (Spring 1998): 301–319.

Ha, Louisa. "Limitations and Strengths of Pan-Asian Advertising Media." *International Journal of Advertising* 16 (1997): 148–163.

Harker, Debra. "Analysis of Advertising Regulation in Five Countries." *International Marketing Review* 15, no. 2 (1998): 101–118.

Hill, John S., and Alan T. Shao. "Agency Participants in Multicountry Advertising."

Journal of International Marketing 2 (1994): 29–48.

Quelch, John A., and Lisa R. Klein. "The Internet and International Marketing." *Sloan Management Review,* Spring 1996, 60–69.

Thomas, Amos Owen. "Advertising to the Masses without Mass Media." *Journal of Global Marketing* 9, no. 4 (1996): 75–88.

Whitelock, Jeryl, and Jean-Christophe Rey. "Cross Cultural Advertising in Europe." *International Marketing Review* 15, no. 4 (1998): 257–276.

Nestlé (A): The Case of the Dying Babies

In June 1976 Nestlé Alimentana S.A. (Nestlé) was told by a Swiss court to "carry out a fundamental reconsideration" of the methods it uses in Third World nations to sell milk powder for babies. The Nestlé managing director wondered what actions should be taken on the court judgment.

The Company

Based in Vevey, Switzerland, Nestlé is one of the world's largest food companies, with 110 years of history. In 1975 its group sales with 300 factories in 49 countries totaled 18.3 billion Swiss francs, and the number of employees reached more than 140,000, of which only some 7,000 actually worked in Switzerland. Nestlé's most important products are instant drinks and other beverages, which yield nearly one-third of sales, and dairy products, which account for one-fourth. Infant foods and dietetic products account for 7.5 percent of sales. Nestlé has many marketing and manufacturing facilities in the Third World, including 19 factories in 10 African countries.

Like other multinational giants, Nestlé is increasingly exposed to criticism from activists in the home country as well as nationalists in the foreign countries in which it operates. Nestlé has more reason for trepidation than most, however; only 3 percent of its business is in its home market.

The Libel Suit

In early 1974 the British aid-for-development organization War on Want published a report titled "The Baby Killer." As the picture on the first page showed, the killer was the baby's nursing bottle. The author, Mike Muller, stated that powdered formula manufacturers contributed to the death of Third World infants by hard-selling their products to people incapable of using them properly. Too often the powdered milk was mixed with impure water or excessively diluted in order to economize. In the 28-page pamphlet, he accused the industry of encouraging mothers to give up breast feeding but added the qualification that other factors, such as working at a job, also influence women to switch to bottle feeding.

In 1974 the World Health Organization had also called for a code of good practice in advertising of baby foods. In the same year, the Bern-based Third World Working Group (which lobbies in Switzerland for support of less developed countries) published the Muller pamphlet with a few changes. Muller had criticized the industry as a whole, but the Bern activists titled their pamphlet "Nestlé Kills Babies," making the killer the company rather than the bottle-feeding process. They also omitted some of Muller's qualifying remarks and included a preface that singled out Nestlé for an accusation of using dishonest sales techniques in the developing world. Nestlé sued for libel, and the trial took place in Bern.

One of the activists said that the powdered formulas should be provided in pharmacies or through doctors and that they should not be advertised on the radio in native languages such as Swahili, which are understood by illiterates. Nestlé's managing director countered, "No one has yet hit on the idea of demanding that wine be sold through doctors or pharmacies because hundreds of thousands of people get drunk on it and sometimes cause fatal accidents." Nestlé officials insisted that their advertising has always stressed, as one billboard in Nigeria put it, that "Breast Milk Is Best."

When the final hearing began, Nestlé withdrew three of the four libel charges it had made against the group. These charges had concerned the allegations that Nestlé dressed sales representatives as nurses to increase sales of its Lactogen milk powder and asserted in advertisements that Lactogen makes children healthier and more intelligent. The only charge retained by Nestlé involved the title on the pamphlet, "Nestlé Kills Babies."

In what *The Economist* (December 6, 1975, 92) called a "happy coincidence," a new ethical code drawn up by an international baby food makers' council appeared in November 1975. The code governs advertising and promotional materials for Third World consumers. It was adopted by nine infant food processors, including Nestlé. The code had been under discussion for five years.

The Decision

In June 1976 the court ruled that the pamphlet's title was indeed defamatory. In his decision, the judge stated that the cause behind the injuries and deaths was not Nestlé's products; rather it was the unhygienic way they were prepared by end users. However, the judge ordered the 13 members of the group found guilty to pay only token fines: $120 each plus an additional $160 toward Nestlé's legal expenses. Furthermore, the judgment then stated, "Nestlé has to carry out a fundamental reconsideration of its promotion methods if in the future it wants to avoid charges of immoral and unethical behavior."

The defendants indicated they would appeal the verdict.

Questions

1. What problem is Nestlé facing here?
2. In view of the judge's order to Nestlé, review its promotional program in detail (see the Appendix). Evaluate this promotional program and suggest potential changes in Nestlé's marketing program for the Third World.
3. What responsibilities do manufacturers have to ensure the safe usage of their products? Would your answer differ for developed and Third World markets? Why?

CASE 12.1 APPENDIX

Nestlé's Response

On November 28, 1975, Dr. Arthur Furer, Managing Director of Nestlé Alimentana S.A., held a press conference in Bern to defend the company against its attackers. Following are extracts from that press conference (from 1975 Annual Report supplement 1–4):

> We have been making and selling baby foods in the world for over 100 years. We have been doing the same in the developing countries for over 50 years. During this period, infant mortality has considerably declined in these countries. Our products have greatly contributed to this. So much so that the more zealous members blame us for the population explosion in the developing countries.
>
> In 1974, the British aid-for-development organization War on Want published a report titled "The Baby Killer." As the title on the first page shows, the target is the feeding bottle. The author, Mike Muller, refers in his report to mothers wrongly using baby milk in the developing countries; he blames the manufacturers who advertise these products.
>
> Professor Mauron and Dr. Muller have reminded you of the situation of babies in the developing countries. We have been concerned with this matter for several decades, not merely since the existence of "War on Want" and a group called, "Arbeitsgruppe Dritte Welt." The two speakers who have just addressed you have clearly explained that these countries need milk formula foods if many infants are to survive. The problem is not solved by ordering mothers to breast-feed their infants until they are four years old. Nor is the problem solved by having baby foods sold exclusively by doctors, pharmacies, and dispensaries. There are far too few of them. Nor would a ban on advertising help solve the problem, since there is an urgent need for these foods. Mothers must be made aware of these products and the manufacturer has the right to draw their attention to them. The governments of the countries concerned have always understood this.
>
> However, this right also creates obligations. The first obligation is self-evident. It is the obligation on the manufacturer's part to make good products.
>
> The manufacturer's second obligation relates to the advertising he does. In my opinion, it is obvious that the advertising must not contain

any false indications leading to possible error. In the developing countries there is the added fact that a fair percentage of mothers are illiterate, disregard the fundamental rules of hygiene and do not have the means to buy our products. To begin with—let's be quite open about it—we are not responsible for this state of affairs. We can help to keep children alive with our products, but we can't teach large sections of the population to read and write any more than we can radically change the living conditions of millions of people. The only thing the producer can do is to instruct and advise the mothers. We have been doing this for decades, and we shall improve our efforts in the light of experience as time goes on. The methods employed by our allied companies to sell milk foods for infants can be summarized as follows:

◆ Our subsidiaries take the greatest trouble to instruct expectant mothers by means of specialized brochures, tables, leaflets, and films on the care to be given to nursing infants. We have also consulted old brochures and found that for very many years we have drawn attention to the fact that breast feeding is best. We have always stressed the fact that infant milk formulas are primarily intended to supplement mother's milk which, if the mother is feeding the baby herself, is not always sufficient to meet the infant's growing needs.

◆ These brochures have been so clearly illustrated for many years that even the illiterate can understand them.

◆ The packages contain all the relevant instructions, set out in a simple manner, for preparing the food hygienically.

◆ Mothers and expectant mothers receive advice mainly through the clinics, doctors and consultations.

◆ To advise young mothers, we also engage the services of qualified midwives or nurses in various countries who work closely together with those responsible for consultation.

◆ Newspaper advertising seldom occurs.

◆ Slogans relating to our milk formula foods have been broadcast on the radio in various countries.

◆ The TV medium has been used only in a few countries.

In spite of everything, I am willing to admit that the War on Want report has made public opinion aware of a real problem. However, one fails to understand why the matter is blown up like this in a country such as ours where hygienic conditions are satisfactory.

There are plenty of other problems of hygiene and common sense that deserve attention in the developed countries.

But no one has yet hit on the idea of demanding that wine be sold through doctors and dispensing chemists because hundreds and thousands of people get drunk on it, cause fatal accidents, or take the risk of a cirrhosis, which may endanger their lives.

No one has called for a ban on automobile advertising, despite the fact that many drivers are really incapable of driving properly, with the result that hundreds of thousands of people are killed on the road every year.

No one has thought of banning television just because some program or other brings cruelty, violence, shooting, and murder to the remotest homes day after day. Such programs are jointly responsible for the increase in brutality and for corrupting the minds of viewers; thus the program sponsors bear their share of responsibility for the frequent crimes that are being committed in Switzerland.

These problems are serious—one man's meat is another man's poison—and no one can be prevented from drawing public attention to them.

But it is reasonable to expect that those who are criticized should deal with the matter and closely examine all possible ways and means of improving the situation.

This is what we ourselves did once again after the publication of the War on Want report, if only for the simple reason that even in a large organization there are matters that have not been given sufficient thought.

We are surprised at the extent to which some radio and television stations have been carried away by this flood of propaganda. It's no excuse to say that we were also invited to put forth our views. Firstly because this wasn't always the case, and secondly because when we were invited, the public could at least have been told of the reason for our absence, namely that we did not wish to make a public pronouncement before the initial hearings of the case.

The first act in the libel suit took place before the Court yesterday and the day before. At a public hearing the judge has listened to the plaintiff and the defendants. Thus, we now think it appropriate to take a public stand.

Finally, I should like to give those who claim they have interests of the Third World at heart, a little further food for thought:

The women of the Third World—they too have a right to avail themselves of modern feeding methods if they are unable to breast-feed their babies because of physical incapacity, because of the work they do, or for any other reason. Before insisting that they nurse their children for three or four years, one would do well to ask Swiss mothers what they think about it. White women are not the only ones entitled to some relief in feeding their babies or to keeping their figures attractive.

International Promotion

Other Factors

Advertising is a major but not the only form of promotion in world markets. In this chapter, we consider a number of other ingredients in the promotional mix: personal selling, sales promotion, marketing mix, and public relations.

The main goals of this chapter are to

1.   Explore the ways in which personal selling varies in world markets, requiring different methods of recruitment and management of the sales force.

2.   Describe how differing national cultures and requirements affect the possibilities for sales promotion in foreign markets.

3.   Explain how the firm can use the total marketing mix as a form of promotion in foreign markets.

4.   Detail special forms of promotion, such as government assistance, trade fairs, traveling exhibits, seminars, countertrade, and bribery.

5.   Answer the question of whether an effective public relations program in foreign markets can make the firm a better marketer there.

Although advertising is often the most prominent element in the promotional mix of the international marketer, for some firms, especially those in industrial marketing, it is a minor form of promotion. Certainly, in every case, a sound promotional program involves more than advertising. In this chapter, we will examine some of the other considerations, namely, (1) personal selling, (2) sales promotion, (3) the marketing mix as promotion, (4) special forms of promotion, and (5) public relations.

PERSONAL SELLING

After advertising, personal selling is the major promotional tool. Often it is more important in international marketing than in the domestic market. That is, it takes a greater percentage of the promotional budget, for two reasons: (1) Restrictions on advertising and media availability may limit the amount of advertising the firm can do, and (2) low wages in many countries allow the company to hire a larger sales force. This reason is especially applicable in less developed nations. Working in the opposite direction is the low status associated with sales work in most countries.

The experience of Philip Morris in Venezuela illustrates the role personal selling can have. Low wages permitted the sales department to employ 300 men. However, only one-third were salesmen. The rest were assistants who helped with deliveries, distribution of sales materials, and so on. The younger sales assistants were provided with bikes (a prized possession), which were cheaper than four-wheeled transportation. The missionary-selling activities of these younger sales assistants provided a very effective complement to the regular sales force.

Sunbeam also had success with its appliances in Peru with a heavy emphasis on personal selling. Sunbeam had a dual-brand policy. The distributor's sales force and the Sunbeam subsidiary's sales force overlapped in their market coverage—with the two different brands. This double coverage meant increased sales and increased market penetration.

National, Not International

The subject we are considering is essentially personal selling in the firm's foreign markets; it cannot really be called *international* personal selling. In discussing advertising, we could speak of international campaigns and international media, but personal selling involves personal contact and is more culture bound than impersonal advertising. As a result, even though international business has expanded tremendously in recent decades, personal selling activities are still conducted primarily on a national basis. In fact, many national markets are divided into sales territories served by salespeople recruited only from their respective territories. They do not even cover a national market.

A limited amount of personal selling does cross national boundaries, most commonly for industrial goods, and especially big-ticket items. However, as international as IBM is, it still uses national sales representatives in its markets. Although the growth of regionalism should encourage more international personal selling, economic integration is not the same as cultural integration. Experience in the EU shows that personal selling activities are very slow to cross cultural-political boundaries.

A study of international selling by the Fortune 100 made this observation:

"Foreign competition, expanding global markets, and the Single Market in Europe will cause U.S. firms to put significantly higher priority on sales force management in the 1990s."[1]

Observations about some other countries were as follows:

1. *Japan.* Individual recognition of sales reps is still at odds with the nation's team approach to business.

2. *Saudi Arabia.* Finding qualified sales reps is difficult because of a labor shortage and the low prestige of selling.

3. *India.* Sales force management is difficult in a market fragmented by language divisions and the caste system.

One task of the international marketer is to determine the role personal selling should play in each market. Once the role of personal selling has been decided, the administration of the sales force is similar to that in the home market. That is, the same functions must be performed: recruitment, selection, training, motivation, supervision, and compensation. We will touch on them here only as they take on special international dimensions.

Since the sales task varies by country and personal selling takes place on a national basis, sales management must be decentralized to the national market. International marketers do not have a sales force but generally serve as advisers to national operations. For example, Manufacturing Data Systems, Inc. (MDSI), a producer of computer software, found that a sale in the United States requires an average of two calls per firm. In Europe, there are frequent callbacks, each with a higher level of management. This means more time and higher cost. In Japan, MDSI's selling requires even more time than in Europe. In other Asian markets, Electrolux finds its direct sales force requires an average of only five demonstrations to make a sale in Malaysia but 20 demonstrations in the Philippines.

Recruiting and Selecting the Sales Force

Recruiting and selecting sales representatives are done in the local market by those who know the situation best. Two problems may arise in trying to find salespeople in certain markets: (1) Selling is a low-status occupation in many countries; the most attractive candidates seek other employment; and (2) finding people with the desired characteristics is often difficult. Shortcomings encountered in recruitment and selection have to be compensated for in training and managing the sales force.

NCR has been in Japan for over 75 years but only in the past 25 years has it been able to recruit college graduates for its sales force because selling was previously considered a low-prestige job. Recruitment is a major part of Electrolux's sales management task in Hong Kong, where it must interview 400 applicants to find 10 it accepts for sales training.

As an aid in recruitment and selection of salespeople, many companies develop job descriptions and specification lists. Both may vary internationally. In a foreign market, the sales job will be a function of the firm's product line, distribution channels, and marketing mix. Thus, the job will not be exactly the same in all markets. The greater the carryover from country to country, the more international direction is possible. The international marketer searches for similarities to aid supervision.

A question arises as to whether a universal "sales type" exists, even for one industry. As job descriptions and market situations vary from country to country, so do other cultural influences. In many markets, a variety of religious, educational, and racial or tribal characteristics must be considered. When markets are segmented in these dimensions, the sales force may have to be segmented also. Just as German sales representatives generally are not used in France, so salespeople from one tribal or religious group often cannot sell to another group in their own country. The world is full of examples of group conflicts that can be reflected in sales force requirements:

English versus Irish, French-speaking versus English-speaking Canadians, Hindu versus Muslim, Sinhalese versus Tamil, Croat versus Serb, and so on.

In some parts of the world, a particular group is the major source of businesspeople, as were the Jews throughout Europe prior to World War II. The Chinese are prominent merchants in many Asian nations. Within the nation itself, a particular group or tribe may play this role. For example, the Parsees are a chief supplier of business enterprise in India; in Nigeria, the Ibos occupied a majority of positions in government and business until the Biafran War. In many countries, the important commercial role played by a minority group, such as the Chinese, is resented by the majority. Laws may be passed forcing greater hiring of the major national group. In Malaysia the group favored by legislation is called "Bumiputra"—sons of the soil.

Although recruitment and selection are done in the host country, international marketers can make contributions. For example, they may introduce tests or techniques that have proved successful in domestic operations or in other subsidiaries. Each country is not completely different from all others, and some carryover of these techniques is possible. By analysis of company experience and by collaboration with subsidiary personnel, international marketers should optimize the use of these experiences in local operations.

When industrial marketers enter a foreign market, they often find their lack of a local sales force to be an important barrier. To accelerate and ease their entry, they may find it desirable to join with—or acquire—a local firm for its sales force capability. In Japan, where relationships are so important, personal selling is especially critical. When Merck wanted to expand in Japan, therefore, it acquired Banyu Pharmaceutical, which enabled it to field a sales force of more than 1,000.

IBM, long number one in Japan, dropped to number three, partly because it had only about 10,000 sales-engineer "hand holders," whereas Hitachi had 17,000 and Fujitsu, 23,000. Nomura Securities is famous for its 3,000-man sales force that meets demanding quotas. This is supplemented by a part-time force of 2,500 women who sell to the home. Toyota has over 100,000 door-to-door salespeople in Japan, and Amway has over one million.

Training the Sales Force

Training salespeople is done primarily in the national market. The nature of the training program is determined by the demands of the job and the previous preparation of the sales force. These vary from country to country. Nevertheless, the international marketer has a voice in local training. Because of the similarity in company products from market to market, national training programs have common denominators.

Drawing on the firm's multinational experience, the international marketer seeks to improve each training program. This can be accomplished in part by supplying training materials, program formats, and ideas to each country. International meetings of subsidiary personnel responsible for sales training can also promote the exchange of experiences.

Bristol-Myers Squibb gives special attention to sales training in developing countries. Training programs are developed by the corporate medical affairs division and product planning division. The company has medical directors in its Latin American, Pacific, Indian, and Middle East regions who help in subsidiary training programs. All national salespeople receive basic training in anatomy, pharmacology, and diseases, as well as in sales. Then they receive detailed information on drug products, including contraindications and possible complications in their use.

For some high-priced or high-technology products, sales training may be at the international or regional level. Because the industrial market has more similarities internationally and because selling is more complicated, centralizing training for

GLOBAL MARKETING

Personal Selling in India

New Delhi

India is one market where Coke trails Pepsi. As part of its catch-up strategy, Coke recruited paraplegics to sell Coke in New Delhi. They were encouraged in this by the New Delhi Handicapped Welfare Society. The Society supplies the hand-powered tricycles and Coke supplies the beverages and marketing aids. Coke expects public relations benefits as well as sales from these new vendors.

Rural India

Colgate is a strong leader in the toothpaste market in India, but most of its sales are in urban areas, which account for less than one-third of India's population.

To reach rural customers, Colgate began a program of traveling video-vans to the villages. The van arrives, playing music from a popular movie, and invites villagers to come. When the back door opens, there is a video screen and soon about 100 villagers gather. A 27-minute infomercial is shown. It is a romantic story about a wedding and wedding night where the message comes through that Colgate is good for your breath, your teeth, and your love life.

Free samples are given out after the video and there is a tooth brushing demonstration. A van will visit about three villages a day and returns to each village one month later. In one year, these vans reached over 16,000 villages and over 10 million people. Colgate attributes a doubling of rural toothpaste consumption to these efforts and expects over 50 percent of its sales from rural areas in the new millenium.

---

several countries is feasible. For example, a company's European or Latin American headquarters could conduct training. This would allow better facilities, highly skilled trainers, and economies of scale. IBM has a European training center with average attendance of 5,000 people a day. Bank of America managed its training from its Tokyo, Caracas, and London offices.

Another training technique is the traveling team of experts from regional or international headquarters. As the company finds new product applications, adds new products, or enters new market segments, the sales task might be changed. The new selling task usually requires additional training, which can be accomplished either at a regional center or by a traveling team of experts. As we have seen, Kodak and NCR used such extra training when they introduced new products into several countries simultaneously.

When the firm sells through independent distributors or licensees, it has little control over the sales force, except to some extent in the initial selection of the distributor. Nevertheless, it is not unusual for firms to give specialized training to the sales staff of their distributors or licensees. This is generally done at no charge and turns out to be a profitable expenditure because of its contribution to sales as well as to relations with the licensee or distributor.

A particular problem faces international companies in many markets. Because they are usually better marketers and have a better trained sales staff, they tend to be "raided" by national companies. This means that they must either train more salespeople than they need or find some way of keeping their sales force with them, usually with higher compensation.

Motivating and Compensating the Sales Force

Motivation and compensation of the sales force are closely related. Indeed, attractive compensation is often the chief motivator. Motivation can be more of a challenge abroad than at home, for two reasons: (1) the low esteem in which selling is held and (2) the cultural reluctance of prospective sales representatives to talk to strangers, especially to try to persuade them—two essential elements of selling.

Although compensation is a prime motivator, there are other ways to motivate. Since much depends on cultural factors, motivation must be designed to meet local needs. In countries where selling has especially low status, the firm must try to overcome this handicap. Training, titles, and perquisites are all helpful, as well as financial awards. In addition, special recognition can help the salesperson's self-image. For example, Philip Morris in Venezuela publicizes the achievements of its best salespeople and also gives them financial and other awards; periodically it gives a special party and banquet for the top four. Electrolux in Asia also finds such "hoopla" to be a major motivation for its sales force.

Foreign travel is another kind of reward employed by international companies. Few members of the sales force in foreign markets would be able to afford a trip to the United States or Europe. Their ability to earn such a trip through good performance is a strong incentive. In addition to providing access to tourist attractions, the company usually entertains the visitors at headquarters. International companies are able to do this, both because of their size and because their internal logistics facilitate such efforts. They also gain economies of scale by entertaining sales representatives from a number of countries at the same time. Electrolux rewards winning sales teams in Asia with international trips.

A British engineering firm was having trouble motivating its East European sales representatives. Direct cash bonuses were illegal, so it had to find something else. It came up with a program of periodic one-week training visits to the plant in England. Maximum benefit results when the company invites sales reps from Western countries at the same time. Much of the week is devoted to actual training on new products and applications, but ample time remains for shopping and tourism. The firm has found these visits an effective motivator.

Chesterton Packing & Seal Company, working through its Japanese distributor, Nitta, offered one-week vacation trips to those sales representatives who topped their quotas. The trips were to such Far East holiday spots as Hong Kong, Taiwan, and Manila. The first year of the program, sales of Chesterton products jumped 212 percent. The distributor, Nitta, was so impressed that it adopted an incentive program for its other products.

In motivating and compensating the sales force, one challenge is to find the mix of monetary and nonmonetary rewards appropriate for each market. Some nonmonetary factors are training, counseling, supervision, and the use of quotas and contests. In monetary compensation, the question usually arises as to whether payment should be a salary or a commission.

In many countries, salespeople are reluctant to accept an incentive form of payment such as a commission. They believe that this reinforces the cultural conflict and the negative image of personal selling. In such markets, the firm tends to rely on a salary payment rather than a commission. Some U.S. companies, however, have been able to introduce incentive elements into their sales representatives' remuneration even in these markets.

NCR, for example, pioneered the use of commission selling in Japan, a country where incentive payments were felt to be against the cultural pattern. However, a decade of experience in which NCR sales quadrupled and sales representatives were increasingly satisfied seemed to argue to the contrary. In fact, the evidence convinced others to follow. Not only foreign firms, such as IBM, but even a number of Japanese firms began to model commission systems on the NCR example.

Controlling the Sales Force

With a commission form of remuneration, close control over the sales staff is less necessary than with a straight salary. Regardless of the mode of payment, however, some control is necessary. Some control techniques are establishing sales territories, setting itineraries and call frequencies, using quotas, and reporting arrangements. Because these must reflect local conditions, they must be determined in part at the local level. For example, when some territories are less attractive than others, the firm may offer extra reward in those areas to ensure equal coverage. Philip Morris did this in Venezuela, offering higher commissions in rural provinces.

Even though this activity is decentralized, international managers should participate in establishing control techniques. They have contact with domestic operations, which are probably the most sophisticated in these techniques, and their experience can be a source of know-how for foreign markets. They can advise on establishing sales territories, norms for sales calls, reporting arrangements, and so on.

The local knowledge of national management is complemented by the international knowledge of the international marketer. A comparative analysis of similar markets provides a better idea of what range of performance is possible. Thus, international managers can aid local managers in setting appropriate norms. Especially when introducing a new product, local management can learn from experience in the firm's other markets. In the United States, firms make comparisons among sales territories. With appropriate modifications, the same kind of comparative analysis should be conducted for foreign markets. The comparisons should be among groups of similar countries. This is one way managers can realize the benefits of multinational experience in sales force management.

Evaluating Sales Force Performance

Although far removed from selling activities in foreign markets, international marketers have a twofold interest in evaluating them. First, the performance of the sales force helps determine the firm's success in a market. International marketers want to be sure that local management is getting good performance. To do this, they help locals to apply the best techniques of evaluation. They can assist with ideas, reporting forms, ratios, and other criteria used elsewhere in the company.

The second interest in evaluating performance is in making international comparisons. It is important to know not only how each country is performing in its local context, but also how it compares with other markets. Such comparisons identify the countries needing help. They can be used to motivate below-average markets to improve their performance. Some criteria for comparing countries can be personal selling cost as a percentage of sales, number of salespeople per $1 million sales (to eliminate differences in wage costs), or units sold per sales representative.

Obviously, many differences hinder such comparisons. In fact, the differences are so evident that some firms try to avoid comparing countries. We say "try to" because every international executive inevitably makes such comparisons subjectively. It is better that they be made explicitly, on the basis of criteria that take account of relevant differences. For example, the European division of Singer developed such a comparative framework for its 16 European subsidiaries, including such diverse countries as Sweden and Spain. This framework became operational in the sense that it was understood and accepted by management in the 16 subsidiaries.

Level of Involvement and Personal Selling

Our discussion until now has been concerned with markets where the firm has subsidiaries and, therefore, company sales forces. Where the firm sells through independent distributors or licensees, the international marketer has no line authority. Because of this, it is all the more important to exercise great care in the initial selection of a representative. One of the main things a distributor has to offer the international firm is a sales force, which makes quality of sales force a major criterion in choosing a distributor. The international firm usually can aid the licensee's or distributor's sales force by providing sales aids and even special training. This is useful but provides only a limited form of control.

The licensee's or distributor's sales force is important for another reason. When an international firm wishes to expand its involvement in a market, a common method is to take over the licensee or distributor. In such a case, the sales force becomes the company's own. Although it is theoretically possible to dismiss the acquired sales force, many political and marketing (and often legal) arguments militate against this.

In joint ventures, the international marketer may have a small or a large voice in selling, depending on the capabilities of both partners. The greater the control given to the international firm, the more the situation resembles that of a wholly owned subsidiary. The less the control, the more the situation resembles that in a licensing or distributor agreement.

SALES PROMOTION

Sales promotion is defined as those selling activities that do not fall directly into the advertising or personal selling category, such as the use of contests, coupons, sampling, premiums, cents-off deals, point-of-purchase materials, and so on. In the United States, sales promotion budgets have been larger than advertising budgets since 1980. The factors that created that situation are coming to other world markets too. For example, in Colombia, two-thirds of spending goes to sales promotions and only one-third to media.

The firm is interested in any approach that will persuade customers to buy. Firms that use sales promotion in the United States generally find it as effective in other markets, if not more effective. When incomes are lower, people are usually even more interested in "something for nothing," such as free samples, premiums, or contests.

Apart from economics, other constraints affect the international use of sales promotion, one of which is legal. Laws in foreign markets may restrict both the size and the nature of the sample, premium, or prize. The value of the item received free must often be limited to a percent (say, 5 percent, as in France) of the value of the product. In other cases, the item received free must be related to the nature of the product purchased, such as cups with coffee—but not steak knives with detergent. Such restrictions are limiting but not always crippling. For example, *Reader's Digest* successfully used contests in Italy even though they are taxed there, giving away such prizes as automobiles. Vicks was able to distribute over 30 million samples of Oil of Olay in many countries.

Another constraint is cultural. The premiums or other devices used must be attractive to the local consumer. For example, Procter & Gamble successfully used nativity scene characters in packages of detergent in the Spanish market for many years. Premiums may even require greater adaptation than products.

Another problem involves the capabilities of local retailers. Many sales promotion activities require some retail involvement, that is, processing coupons, handling odd-shaped combination or premium packages, posting display materials, and so on. Getting retailers to cooperate may be difficult where they lack appropriate facilities. Among the problems that arise with small retailers are that they are difficult to contact, they have limited space, and they often handle the materials in a way that the producer did not intend.

For a variety of legal and cultural reasons, sales promotions are primarily national rather than international. Even in Europe, for example, differences in advertising rules are not as great as differences in sales promotion rules. Thus, one sees much more pan-European advertising than pan-European sales promotions. Nevertheless, a number of organizations have been formed to facilitate multi-country sales promotions. KLP International of London brought together sales promotion groups from the United States and six European countries. The Point of Purchase Advertising Institute (POPAI) formed POPAI Europe with 200 point-of-purchase firms there.

GLOBAL MARKETING

Sales Promotion Goes International

Sales promotion has not only increased its share of the marketing budget, but sales promotions are increasingly crossing national borders.

141 Worldwide. This is a global sales promotion network created by the ad agency, Bates Worldwide. Bates claims this is the first worldwide sales promotion network. It is designed to help firms internationalize their promotions, instead of having to create unique ones for each market.

Hiram Walker. Kahlúa is a leading brand of coffee-flavored liquor but it was relatively unknown in Europe. Hiram Walker hired the KLP group (part of the Euro RSCG agency) to create a cross-border promotion aimed at 18–25 year olds. KLP designed a campaign with three elements: (1) a series of short programs on the MTV channel, (2) a sponsored music tour with popular music groups; and (3) a range of point-of-sale material.

Unilever. Clearblue One Step, Unilever's home pregnancy test kit, became Europe's market leader via cross-border sales promotion. The program was centrally designed but allowed for local adaptation because of regulatory difference still existing in the EU. It was aimed at pharmacies and pharmacist assistants. It included a magazine and a questionnaire and offered the chance to win a prize—even a car (a Renault Clio in France; a Fiat Uno in Italy).

IBM. Always considered a traditional marketer, IBM began to use sales promotions to sell its PCs, especially to the consumer market. Finding it difficult and inefficient to do these separately in each market, IBM consolidated all its international sales promotions with a single global agency, WPP Group.

The competitive situation in a market can also affect the firm's choice of sales promotions and the success they might have. General Electric provides an illustration: In Japan GE had noticeable success in breaking into the air conditioning market. Two factors behind the successful entry were offering (1) overseas trips as prizes to outstanding dealers and (2) a free color TV set to purchasers of high-priced models.

The result was that the trade association drew up rules banning overseas trips as prizes for sales of air conditioners and setting a limit on the size of premium that could be offered. These rules were approved by the Japanese Fair Trade Commission. Company complaints led to a modification of the rules—no overseas trips as prizes for *any* home electric appliance dealers.

The international firm should have some advantages over its national competitors in sales promotion. For example, economies of scale may exist in generating ideas and in buying materials. Ideas and materials may be suitable for several markets. One country can be used as a test market for others that are similar. Analysis of company experience in different markets helps in evaluating sales promotion and setting budgets. Though sales promotion has been discussed as a separate item, it obviously is part of overall promotion, as with Colgate in India, mentioned earlier.

MARKETING MIX AS PROMOTION

We have discussed the principal elements of promotion: advertising, personal selling, and sales promotion. The purpose of these activities is to induce purchase of the company's products. As marketers well know, however, other factors also help persuade customers to buy—or not to buy—the firm's products. All elements of the marketing mix influence the sale of goods and services. Because the elements of the mix have a different influence from country to country, the appropriate mix for a given market should have some degree of individuality.

The idea of the complementarity and substitutability of the various elements of the mix is familiar to students of marketing. What we note here are some of the international applications of the mix concept as related to promotion. Since we have already examined product policy and distribution, as well as the other elements of promotion, our treatment will be brief.

Product

Although the quality of the product is presumably the major reason a consumer buys it, consumer desires for a given product often differ from country to country. By modifying products for national markets, the firm can persuade more customers to buy. Affluent markets may demand more style and power, or larger size. Poorer markets may require smaller sizes, durability, and simplicity. Food products vary in the degree of sweetness or spiciness desired. Further differences are found in the form, color, and texture of products. In Britain, for example, Ocean Spray had to mix cranberry juice with black currant juice to gain acceptance.

Package

For many goods, the package is an important element of the product. Adapting packaging to the market may be effective promotion. In Latin America, Gillette sells Silkience shampoo in one-half-ounce plastic bubbles. In the Far East, Procter & Gamble sells most of its shampoo in single-use packets. In some markets, dual-use packages attract the consumer because they can be retained for some other use. Plastic containers are popular in some markets, whereas metal or glass are preferred elsewhere. Form and color are important, too. Ocean Spray, for example, had to change from bottles to juice boxes in Britain. The label on the package should also serve a promotional role in its design and color, in the language used, and in the text printed on it.

Brand

Brand policy can affect the attractiveness of the product. For some goods, an international brand name will be more prestigious and trusted than a national brand. On the other hand, for many products, such as food and household items, individualized national brands are favored by international companies. Johnson Wax and CPC International are examples of firms that pursue a national brand policy primarily.

Warranty and Service

Many companies use warranties defensively; that is, they meet competitors' warranties. Warranties, however, can also be used aggressively to promote sales. If the international company has stronger quality and a more reliable product than competitors, it may gain a promotional edge through a more liberal warranty. Many producers of electrical and mechanical products have used a strong warranty as part of their foreign-market entry strategy. When Chrysler re-entered Europe, it offered a generous three-year, 100,000-kilometer warranty.

Consumers everywhere are concerned about product service, which includes delivery, installation, repair and maintenance facilities, and spare parts inventories. International firms are handicapped in some markets because they are not represented well enough to offer service as good as that of national firms. A weakness in this area can offset strengths in other areas. By the same token, a strong service capability can be effective promotion. It has been a strength of Singer and IBM in many markets and of the German and Japanese auto producers in the U.S. market.

Distribution or Level of Involvement

Marketers are aware of the promotional implications of different distribution strategies. When convenience is important to the buyer, the firm must have widespread distribution. Where dealer "push" is important, more selective distribution is necessary. The same considerations apply in foreign markets. When the international firm sells through distributors, it usually gives them an exclusive franchise to encourage support. This exclusive franchise is almost always necessary to get cooperation.

When a firm goes from an indirect to a direct channel, the distribution system is bearing a greater part of the promotion. The more direct the channel, the greater push it gives the product. Going direct can have a special significance for the international firm in reference to its level of involvement in a market. An indirect channel means many intermediaries between producer and consumer. In international marketing, an indirect channel is exporting. Amway goes very direct. (See "Global Marketing," "Amway Goes Global.")

The way the firm can go more direct in export markets is to establish its own presence there with a marketing subsidiary. As with any more direct method, the firm's cost will increase. Many benefits are associated with such a move, however, one of which is a favorable promotional effect. One way of illustrating the benefits is to note the disadvantages of exporting, which are usually overcome by establishing a local subsidiary.

Studies have shown the following complaints expressed by foreign buyers in dealing with U.S. exporters.

1. U.S. exporters do not familiarize themselves with the market.

2. Management gives less attention to foreign business. Foreign inquiries are sometimes ignored.

3. There is a lack of reliability in delivery dates.

4. Price quotations are F.O.B.—U.S. plant.

5. Little or no local language material is available describing the firm's products.

6. Domestic customers get open account terms. Foreign buyers receive harsher terms, such as the requirement of a letter of credit.

The establishment of a foreign subsidiary is likely to eliminate these problems. It can be one of the most powerful promotional tools the firm can use.

Price and Terms

The idea behind the demand curve and the elasticity concept is that buyers are sensitive to price. By changing the price, the marketer affects the attractiveness of the product. In other words, pricing has promotional aspects. If consumers in different countries have differing degrees of price sensitivity, the marketer should try to adjust prices accordingly, if costs permit.

Price may be used promotionally in other ways. On products for which there is a price-quality association, the firm might wish to price above competitors to gain the quality image. Of course, this is most meaningful if the product in fact has a quality advantage. In countries where purchasing power is low, prices might be reduced by modifying the product, for example, giving it fewer features and greater simplicity, or using smaller sizes.

GLOBAL MARKETING

 Amway Goes Global

Amway began as a peculiarly American company, as its name indicates. The name may be less appropriate now because the firm is in over 50 countries and gets 70 percent of its sales abroad.

Japan. This is Amway's largest market, surpassing the United States. It is the second most profitable foreign company there. It has 1.2 million distributors there and sells over 160 Amway products. Two-thirds of the merchandise comes from the United States but there are also several uniquely Japanese products. Amway also piggybacks products from other firms. Amway benefits from Japan's inefficient retail structure. It also received a boost when it was a major sponsor of the 1998 Nagano Winter Olympics.

Malaysia. Amway was a surprising beneficiary of the Asian crisis. That made it much easier to get salespeople—distributors. The first year of the crisis, Amway's local currency sales were up 37 percent and it was one of the top 10 growth firms in 1998.

China. China is always considered as a land of great potential. That was proving true for Amway in its early years there. Its growth rate in China was faster than anywhere else. Suddenly, China outlawed its direct-selling approach, hurting Amway as well as Avon and Mary Kay. The future is uncertain now.

Philippines. Hundreds of Filipino distributors from the United States went back to the Philippines to recruit distributors for their homeland in 1997. With 70 million people and a love for things American, it was a natural target for Amway.

South Korea. This was Amway's third largest market so it had a great start here. Then groups of competitors, consumers, and environmental groups began attacking Amway on various grounds, including Amway's import drain on Korea's balance of payments. Amway said the attack was caused by its success in the market. In any case, the company had to try to regroup and maintain its place in this promising market.

As these examples show, Amway's products and methods have found success in a variety of cultures. In spite of occasional problems, the firm is continuing its foreign expansion, hoping for over 80 percent of sales abroad. Further expansion in Eastern Europe, India, and South Africa are current plans.

Export Pricing

Export prices and terms can be used to promotional advantage in several ways. One is in choosing the currency for the price quotation. Although exporters usually prefer to quote in their own currency, importers like price quotations in *their* currency because it protects them against variations in the exchange rate.

Another promotional aspect of export pricing is the specific quotation used. As noted in our chapter on pricing, F.O.B. plant prices are favored by exporters. However, there is a promotional advantage in using a C.I.F. quotation, which is preferred by importers.

A third promotional aspect of export pricing involves the terms extended to the buyer. Exporters often discriminate against foreign buyers. For example, domestic buyers may be given open account terms, whereas foreign importers have to pay by letter of credit. Foreign buyers would like the same terms as domestic buyers. Although this may not always be feasible, exporters who want to use pricing as a promotional tool will respond insofar as possible. They would move toward local currency price quotations, C.I.F. pricing, and more liberal payment terms.

Credit

A final promotional aspect of payment terms is the use of credit. The credit needs of buyers vary from country to country. Sellers of industrial equipment often find that the factor determining the choice of supplier is the credit terms. For some, it has meant greater working capital to cover more liberal credit. Cincinnati Milacron lost a contract to supply equipment for a factory in Georgia even though it had the low bid. The factory chose a Japanese supplier because it offered a complete credit package.

For consumer goods marketers, credit extension can be directed at both channel members and consumers. In many countries, wholesalers and retailers are financially weak. The seller has to cover their credit needs in what seems to be liberal fashion compared with domestic practices. Liberal credit may be needed to sell durable goods. For example, credit extension is one reason Singer has been able to maintain a market in sewing machines in spite of lower-priced competition.

Automobile dealers in Brazil found an ingenious way to sell cars in a money-tight economy without credit through a *consorcio,* or lottery. Each *consorcio* group member is guaranteed a new car within 60 months, and each group includes 120 people. The monthly payment is pegged to the price of the car divided by the number of members. At a monthly drawing two winners are selected. The members pay for the whole 60 months, of course. Members avoid Brazil's high interest charges and the large down payments normally required. They pay a 10 percent administrative fee, however. Ford's Brazilian subsidiary parlayed these clubs into a major marketing tool. Ford ran 2,300 such *consorcios* and sold one-fifth of its total Brazilian output this way.

The Total Mix at Work

We discussed the promotional aspects of the elements of the marketing mix taken in isolation. In reality, of course, these elements interact synergistically. Two examples illustrate the mix elements as part of an overall marketing strategy.

First, consider how Kodak adapted its marketing-mix elements to gain a stronger position in the Japanese film market.

1. *Product.* Conducted an early rollout of its new Ektar 25 film.

2. *Packaging.* Added Japanese-language labels to packaging. Only English was used before.

3. *Service.* Established a Kodak photofinishing operation to give one-day turnaround versus three days when competitor facilities were used.

4. *Level of involvement.* Greatly expanded commitment to the Japanese market: Work force was more than doubled, photofinishing operation was opened, and a $74 million R&D operation was established.

5. *Distribution.* Moved to direct distribution to retailers versus previous distributor. Marketed Kodak's increased commitment in Japan to encourage retailer support. Gave free trips to Olympics as dealer incentives for good performance.

6. *Promotion.* Expanded promotion generally: expanded advertising, used yellow Kodak blimp, set up Kodak neon signs on major streets, and offered free Kodak film with Kodak photofinishing.

Next consider how European Airbus Industries adapted its marketing strategy to sell beyond its European market. Airbus faced a challenge in non-European markets against mighty Boeing. Part of Airbus's product strategy was to design all planes using inches and feet instead of the metric system so that mechanics around the world accustomed to working with U.S. aircraft wouldn't have to deal with unfamiliar measurements and tools. It also aimed to have superior technology, which it achieved in certain areas.

As a completely European company, Airbus used local sourcing in foreign markets to please customers. To answer charges that Airbus was costing U.S. jobs, officials point out that 500 U.S. companies in 34 states produce components for Airbus. Local content varies from 20 to 40 percent on each plane.

To further entice foreign airlines, Airbus offered extremely attractive leasing deals, making it very easy for airlines to "buy" Airbus. In an extreme case, an upfront, low-cost $500 million loan was made to Northwest, which led to Northwest's purchase of an additional 75 A320 aircraft.

SPECIAL FORMS OF INTERNATIONAL PROMOTION

Certain forms of promotion have special international dimensions. Because they are not usually considered in the promotional mix, we discuss them separately here. They include the activities of governments, international trade fairs, and the Washington representative. Barter and bribery, along with other miscellaneous efforts, will also be discussed.

Government Assistance in Promotion

Many governments assist their industry in export marketing. This assistance usually takes three forms: information, financing, and promotion. Only the latter form will concern us here. The other forms of governmental assistance are discussed in Chapters 7 and 14. Since most readers of this book will be in the United States, we take that country as our example. Most developed and some developing nations have programs similar to those described here. In addition, the WTO-UNCTAD International Trade Centre in Geneva serves less developed countries for export promotion.

Federal-Level Assistance

In looking at the United States, it is necessary to distinguish between the federal and state governments. Promotional assistance for international selling is often available at each level. We will first look at the efforts of the federal government. The Commerce and State Departments are the major sources of help, but the Trade Promotion Committee also includes the Departments of Treasury, Defense, Interior, Agriculture, Labor, Transportation, and Energy.

Department of State
U.S. international trade promotion was affected by the presidential reorganization in 1980. Commercial activities previously administered by the Department of State in the leading 70 country markets were transferred to the Foreign Commercial Service under the Department of Commerce. The Department of State remains active in secondary markets and through projects administered by the Agency for International Development.

Although the U.S. program is large in absolute terms, it ranks near the bottom in relative terms. Many of America's trade competitors spend up to 10 times as much on a per capita basis.

Department of Commerce
The most active department in promoting the international business of U.S. firms is the Department of Commerce. We discussed in Chapter 7 how it supplies information on world markets. Equally active in promotion, it has several major promotional efforts:

GLOBAL MARKETING

Uncle Sam As International Marketer

Protection and promotion of a country's economic interests have long been a part of an ambassador's job but usually only a small part for U.S. ambassadors. After the collapse of Communism, economic matters have become a much more important part of a U.S. ambassador's job. This began in the Bush administration and continued under Clinton. Secretary of State Albright noted in her confirmation hearing that a major administration goal was to assure that "American economic interests can be pursued globally." Trade is now covered in the two-week seminar given new ambassadors before assignment. In recent years, embassies have helped U.S. firms win contracts in such diverse places as Belgium and Indonesia.

The Department of Commerce opened an Advocacy Center in 1994 as a new form of trade promotion. In its first year, it helped U.S. companies win 70 contracts with an export value of $20 billion.

Ron Brown, former Secretary of Commerce under Clinton, became an active "international marketer," flying to China and other countries with a planeload of CEOs to promote U.S. businesses abroad. Brown also helped get Ex-Im Bank support for some U.S. contracts abroad.

President Clinton himself became active in promoting U.S. businesses abroad. Some examples:

- Clinton called and wrote King Fahd of Saudi Arabia about a potential airplane contract. This was influential in Boeing and McDonnell-Douglas winning a $6 billion contract against Airbus.

- Clinton again intervened in a telecommunications contract in Saudi Arabia. AT&T won a $4 billion contract even though Ericsson and Northern Telecom claimed lower bids.

- In Brazil, Raytheon won a contract with Clinton's help.

- Chevron participated in a $20 billion oil deal in Kazakhstan aided by the president.

1. *Commercial News USA.* This monthly catalog/magazine contains hundreds of descriptions of U.S. products or services for export. It goes to foreign buyers, agents, and distributors who are prequalified by commercial specialists. It also has 2 million electronic subscribers. It generates export sales for about 1,500 U.S. firms annually.

2. *Foreign buyer program.* Exporters can meet qualified foreign purchasers for their product or service at trade shows in the United States. The department promotes the shows worldwide to attract foreign buyers, manages an international business center, counsels participating firms, and brings together buyer and seller.

3. *Overseas catalog and video-catalog shows.* Companies can gain market exposure for their product or service without the cost of traveling overseas by participating in a catalog or video-catalog show sponsored by the department. Provided with the firm's product literature or promotional video, the department sends an industry expert to display the material to select foreign audiences in several countries.

4. *Overseas trade missions.* Officials of U.S. firms can participate in a trade mission that gives them an opportunity to confer with foreign business and government representatives. Department staff will identify and arrange a full schedule of appointments in each country to be visited.

5. *Overseas trade fairs.* U.S. exporters can participate in overseas trade fairs to meet customers face-to-face and assess the competition. The department creates and promotes a U.S. pavilion at about 100 fairs annually. This aids U.S. firms in exhibiting and gaining international recognition. Cooperation with show organizers helps U.S. exhibitors to receive special services.

State-Level Assistance

States' Role in Promoting International Business

All 50 states have export development programs. Over half of the states operate a total of 108 offices in over 15 countries. Tokyo is the most popular location, with about 30 states represented. California is represented in Tokyo, London, and Mexico City; Michigan and Ohio each have offices in Tokyo, Brussels, and Lagos; Montana has an office in Taipei. Minnesota has eight offices abroad, four in Asia and four in Europe. The activities of state export agencies are expanding. Twenty-seven states have set up export financing programs, and several have set up export trading companies and/or shared foreign sales corporations (see Chapter 5). The range of their activities is shown in Table 13–1. As can be seen, state activities sometimes complement and sometimes overlap those of the federal government.

Relevance of Federal and State Programs for International Marketing

As a citizen and taxpayer, the firm is entitled to both federal and state assistance. Because both are subsidized efforts, the cost to the firm is usually low. Therefore, if there are benefits to be derived, the firm should make federal and state support a part of its own promotional mix.

International Trade Fairs

Several thousand international trade fairs occur annually in over 70 nations. Trade fairs are popular in the United States, too, but they often play an even greater role in other countries. In the United Kingdom, for example, manufacturing firms spend about one-fourth of their promotion budget on trade fairs, whereas American exhibitors spend 18 percent. In the United States, about half of the fairs are strictly business-to-business affairs with the rest designed with consumers also in mind. Abroad there is more of a business-to-business emphasis.

International trade fairs are either general, covering many product categories, or specialized, displaying the products of a single industry. The annual Hanover Fair in Germany is the largest of the general fairs, with over 5,000 exhibitors in 20 major categories, and 500,000 visitors. Because so many buyers and sellers from different nations gather at a big general fair, contacts can often be made that might take years otherwise. Said one marketer: "We had been trying to crack the European market for three years. After we came to the Hanover Fair last year, we soon had a complete network of European distributors lined up." Potential licensees or joint-venture partners might also be found at a fair.

Fair time can also be test-market time. A firm can test sales and potential distributor reactions in a market before committing itself there. If sales potential is proved, the firm can contact candidates for distributorships or licensing agreements. Potential distributors or licensees favor the fair for the same reasons. They can see the firm's products and observe the market reaction to them. The fair provides a test-market situation for both parties.

An additional value of trade fairs is the opportunity to do some research on the competition. Because of the strategic audience and the publicity given to the major fairs, firms use them to show their latest products and services. Therefore, a firm can note initial market reaction to competitive developments and get a comparative evaluation of its own offerings.

TABLE 13-1	State Foreign Trade Development Programs

Seminars/Conferences
One-on-One Counseling
Market Studies Prepared
Language Bank
Referrals to Local Export Services
Newsletters
How-to-Handbook
Sales Leads Disseminated
Trade Shows
Trade Missions
Foreign Offices Representation
Operational Financing Program

Source: National Association of State Development Agencies.

The specialized, or vertical, fair fulfills basically the same role but for a single product category. Two of the more famous specialized fairs are the Paris Air Show and the *Fotokina*, or photo products fair, in Cologne. The *Fotokina* is the major international showplace and battleground of German, Japanese, U.S., and other producers of photo products.

The Paris Air Show is a giant biennial event running more than a week. About 150 U.S. firms are represented in the USA National Pavilion. This includes small firms as well as the aerospace giants. Thousands of visitors from around the world produce thousands of sales leads as well as off-the-floor sales. As Rosson and Seringhaus have noted, most of the sales do not take place at the fair but in the following 12 months.[2]

East European Fairs. With the collapse of Communism in Eastern Europe, governments there have dismantled some of their centralized control over the economy and trade. They want to trade more with the outside world than ever, so they are continuing their own trade fairs to sell their products and to entice Western firms to their markets. Several hundred trade fairs are held in Eastern Europe annually. Western firms attending these fairs find them more important for making contacts than for making direct sales.

The Use of Trade Fairs. International trade fairs can offer many advantages, and international marketers must consider them when planning promotional programs. If the decision is made to use fairs, the first step is to identify those relevant to their products and markets. The publication of the Department of Commerce, *Business America,* has a periodic listing of international trade fairs. Then the firm's participation in the selected fairs must be incorporated into the planning of the annual promotional mix.

The firm should include its subsidiaries, distributors, and licensees so that maximum value can be obtained by all of the firm's operations. An annual review of international fairs will indicate some that might be added and others that might be dropped.

The Washington Representative

More than 700 U.S. firms maintain Washington offices, and more than 15,000 lobbyists work the halls of Congress and the regulatory agencies. More than 100

Japanese firms also have representatives in Washington. When the office has several people, one is usually responsible for the firm's international interests. Washington, D.C., is one of the largest markets in the world. The international side includes the foreign embassies, the World Bank, the Inter-American Development Bank, and the continuing flow of high-level visitors. Together, these banks (with the Export-Import Bank) add up to billions of dollars in sales opportunities. The Washington rep is a high-level salesperson in a very strategic market.

The task involves marketing to purchase influencers. This is the international part of the job: to cultivate the market among international agencies, embassies, and important foreign visitors. After a sale, the representative may even help customers arrange financing with the Export-Import Bank. Some of the work is long-range market development and may not result in immediate sales. The goal is the same, however: to increase the company's international business.

Miscellaneous Efforts

Because each market is to some degree unique, the varieties of promotional efforts possible are limited only by the ingenuity of the marketer. Special programs can be designed to meet particular situations. The international marketer is interested in these promotions not only for their success in one country but also in terms of their potential application in other markets. One country or region may serve as a test market for such promotions. Here we note briefly a few of the diverse efforts.

The Traveling Exhibit

Some firms and industries have organized a traveling exhibit that can be a one-company or industry trade fair covering countries or products not normally covered by trade fairs. This can best be illustrated by examples.

- Automatic Radio International (ARI) organized a 10-week flying-showcase promotion for 22 Western Hemisphere nations from Canada through Latin America. The 37,000-mile promotion to 27 cities attracted more than 6,000 visitors, including presidents and prime ministers as well as business prospects. All of these visitors saw and heard demonstrations of ARI's full line of radio, stereo, air conditioning, and refrigeration equipment.

    The results met ARI's goals. Eleven new distributors and licensees were acquired, dealers were added in existing markets, and several agreements were expanded. The firm considered the publicity received a valuable extra benefit for its continuing operations.

- Westinghouse chartered a cargo jet and sent 25 tons of equipment to stage what it called the largest private exhibit ever presented in Saudi Arabia. Displays featured virtually all of the company's products and services applicable to current or anticipated projects in the development of Saudi Arabia's infrastructure. Many Westinghouse divisions had products in the exhibit.

- Rank-Xerox used an exhibition train to promote products in countries of Eastern Europe. This was rather expensive, so it later replaced the train with mobile display vans that ran twice a year.

Traveling exhibits share features of international trade fairs. For a single company, they are more costly than participation in trade fairs. However, they can cover market opportunities not available otherwise and give one company a monopoly of the exhibit.

International 800

Telemarketing is now international. AT&T International Service 800 S.A. offers toll-free dialing in more than 50 countries on five continents, much as firms use

800 numbers in the United States. The service is available in over 110 cities around the world. Financial services account for 40 percent of clients; many others are in the travel industry. However, firms such as Du Pont, Digital Equipment, and Lee Jeans are among the U.S. clients. Many firms use this service as an intermediate step before establishing a sales office in a country. If the volume of business reaches a certain level in one location, a sales office can be justified there. Harrod's of London has an 800 number for customers in America.

While language barriers can pose a problem for international 800 numbers, firms such as AT&T, American Express, and R.R. Donnelly already have translators to handle telemarketing inquiries in as many as 100 languages. AT&T Language Line Service provides for on-phone translation in more than 140 languages. The service is available 24 hours a day, seven days a week.

The Internet

One of the fastest-growing areas is the Internet, and as the initials WWW indicate, it is worldwide. It offers intriguing opportunities—and challenges. For a fuller discussion of this revolutionary tool, see Chapter 18.

Videodisk Marketing

Another marketing device is the videodisk. IBM Europe is using videodisks linked to touch-screen TV to market its personal computers. The sales/training message is interactive, allowing the viewer to call up various programs. This means that the PC can be demonstrated at a uniformly high level in all European countries. IBM has supplied videodisks in Danish, Dutch, English, French, German, Italian, and Spanish.

Reducing Level of Involvement or Sharing Production

A firm's level of involvement in foreign markets is a critical determinant of its marketing program there. Here we consider its use as a form of promotion. We've noted how an exporting firm can increase its credibility in a country by establishing a subsidiary there. Interestingly, a firm can also promote its business by reducing its level of involvement in a market.

Many countries want to reduce the power of multinational firms in their countries. Foreign firms with wholly owned operations in such countries may find that their business opportunities increase as their equity percentage decreases. This can be true for diverse markets including Canada, Europe, India, and Latin America.

- ♦ Hindustan Ciba-Geigy reduced its equity from 65 percent to 40 percent. This allowed it to be classified as an Indian company. Effectively, its equity dilution strategy allowed Ciba-Geigy to double its pharmaceutical sales.

- ♦ ITT was induced by the French government to sell to a French firm one of its two French subsidiaries. One return to ITT was $160 million for its interest in the subsidiary. The primary gain by ITT, however, was the right of its other subsidiary to share in $10 billion of telecommunications business budgeted by the government.

The aerospace industry illustrates another kind of "sharing as promotion." Such firms as Boeing, General Electric, and McDonnell-Douglas have formed joint ventures in Europe, China, and Japan to land business there. By guaranteeing employment, research, and value added in the host country, the firms can be assured of continuing business in these markets. In getting this business, the major promotional tool is the agreement to joint-venture and subcontract rather than exporting finished products from the United States. To sell in the United States, Airbus stresses the large number of American suppliers it employs and the local value added.

McDonnell-Douglas won a $1 billion military airplane contract in Britain over a British competitor. Critical to the success of its bid was its promise to build the 60 planes in the United Kingdom and to use Rolls Royce engines in planes sold to the

GLOBAL MARKETING

Carpeting the World, Electronically

Domotex is the world's largest trade fair for the rug, carpet, and flooring industries. Held annually in Hanover, Germany, it gathers more then 1,000 exhibitors from over 50 countries. In 1998, for the first time, buyers and sellers from several continents were brought face-to-face electronically through videoconferencing.

RECoN, the Regional Export Conferencing Network, was developed by the Georgia Department of Industry. It is a videoconferencing and data transmission network designed to enhance federal, state, and private-sector teamwork in in-ternational trade. It received a grant from the U.S. Department of Commerce.

At Domotex, RECoN enabled buyers from four continents to engage in meetings and negotiations with 19 American carpet manufacturers and distributors from Dalton, Georgia—center of the U.S. carpet industry. Sellers also received instant status reports from their representatives at Domotex, and these reps could receive immediate answers to questions about pricing, production schedules, delivery terms, and financing.

Many of the American firms made export deals at Domotex. Following its initial success at Domotex, RECoN was used at a Mercosur Conference and trade fairs in the Netherlands, Poland, and Hong Kong.

Source: *Business America,* July 1998, 13, 14.

U.S. Marine Corps. As another example, to clinch an AWACS sale to Britain and France, Boeing agreed to local offsets of $1.85 billion on a contract valued at $1.5 billion.

Seminars

Industrial marketers find that company-sponsored seminars can be effective marketing tools internationally. A company seminar usually includes lectures as well as demonstrations and/or films of new products, applications, or developments in the industry. The firm invites customers and potential customers, and perhaps purchase influencers. At one seminar, for example, Caterpillar had 425 users in attendance, plus 59 bankers. Also included are the company's own distributors and personnel, both for updating and for marketing contact at the seminars.

Seminars may cover just one country or a whole region. Alcan found its seminar in Indonesia to be the most important factor in its sales one year and has them there every couple of years. 3M uses them in Hong Kong but includes participants from China. Caterpillar has had seminars in Singapore for all 10 Asian countries in its Far East division.

Bribery?

Without question, bribery has been an effective and extensive form of promotion in international marketing. The SEC estimated that U.S. corporations alone made over $400 million in questionable payments in the years 1970 to 1976. The questions concerning bribery are not about its effectiveness but about its legality and morality. For U.S. firms, bribery of foreign government officials or political parties has been illegal since the passage of the 1977 Foreign Corrupt Practices Act (FCPA). The law makes it a crime to make payments to anyone if the firm has reason to believe that some of the money will go to a government official. Excluded from the act are payments made to lower-level government officials for the purpose of obtaining permits or expediting goods through customs, so-called "grease" payments.

The fact that bribery is illegal for U.S. firms should simplify decision making. Do not act illegally. One problem for U.S. firms, however, was that their competitors from other countries were not forbidden to bribe in their foreign business. Italy passed a law in 1980 saying that payoffs were a legal way of doing business abroad. A German government memo suggested firms be prepared to pay up to 20 percent of the contract price. It is not surprising, then, that American firms lost business to their competitors—$15 billion in 1997 alone.[3] Airbus increased its global market share against Boeing in part because it could offer "financial incentives" that Boeing could not. The director of the IMF estimated money-laundering transactions at 2 to 5 percent of global GDP in 1998.

The situation took a potentially big change for the better in December 1997 when the 29 members of the OECD passed "The Convention on Combating Bribery of Foreign Public Officials in International Business Transactions." It calls on all member countries to enact legislation in 1998 to criminalize foreign bribery. As of February 1999, only 12 of the member countries had ratified the Convention. If all of them ratify it, there remains the question of how well it is monitored and enforced.

There are some reasons for optimism. The fact of bribery and its costs to society have gained public attention and caused discontent, not only in countries like Congo, Indonesia, and Nigeria, but also in European countries like Germany and Italy. Note also the Salt Lake City Olympics scandal. Furthermore, the World Bank, the IMF, and the WTO now all have policies to combat bribery. The International Chamber of Commerce has also recently adopted new antibribery standards.

U.S. firms were learning to live with the U.S. law and are happy to see the OECD Convention. Many major firms wrote company codes of conduct. Some enforce them severely. Rand Araskog at ITT did not hesitate to fire high-level executives who did not comply with company policy. Boeing has 50 Ethics Coordinators to monitor compliance with its code. In closing our discussion, we quote from Eaton Corp's code, which had to be signed by managers.

> Bribes and illegal payments subvert the very essence of competition and erode the moral fiber of those involved. Such activities are not condoned and will not be tolerated.

Barter and Countertrade

One of the biggest markets in the world is the nonmonetary world of barter and countertrade. Modern countertrade is much more complex than the barter trade of ancient times. It includes barter, compensation deals, counterpurchase, and product buy-back. Whatever form it takes, the basic principle is the same—the exporter agrees to take products from the importer in full or partial payment for its exports. Instead of the convenience of money, the exporter accepts, at least partially, the awkward form of payment in goods.

Countertrade is truly a giant market. Estimates of its size range up to 10 percent of world trade. More than 100 countries practice countertrade, and over 90 have government-mandated countertrade. There are many participants on the export side also. In the United States, about one-half of the Fortune 500 companies are involved in countertrade. Of GE's exports one year, over 40 percent depended on countertrade. Not only large firms are involved, however. Bates found that half of the countertrading firms in Florida had fewer than 100 employees.[4]

Why is such an awkward form of commerce a major market in world trade? A primary reason is that many would-be importing countries lack the international money (foreign exchange) to buy the foreign goods they want. Therefore, they seek to use their goods as a means of payment. Countertrade is most prominent in Eastern Europe and the developing countries because they have chronic balance-of-payments deficits and consequent shortage of foreign exchange. It is not limited to these countries, however. Even Switzerland used countertrade when it bought Northrop fighter planes with GE engines. It required the two firms to find markets

GLOBAL MARKETING

The Olympics—International Marketing Tool

The Olympics are easily the world's premier sporting event. It is not surprising that firms try to benefit from association with such a globally popular phenomenon. In 1984 the Los Angeles Olympic Organizing Committee raised an unprecedented $127 million from corporate sponsors. Given that example, the International Olympic Committee (IOC) decided it was time for all countries to get a share of the corporate bounty.

After the 1984 Olympics, the IOC hired ISL Marketing, a sports marketing firm based in Lucerne, Switzerland, to set up and sell an international Olympic sponsorship program. This marketing arrangement has proved successful for IOC, ISL, and presumably, the corporate sponsors, although success in sponsorship terms is not easy to measure.

More than 300 sponsorships were sold for the 1980 Olympics. Little money was raised, and the large number of sponsors meant too much clutter for any meaningful return for the sponsors. Under ISL's management a severely restricted number of global corporate sponsorships were sold for succeeding Olympics. For its 1996 comprehensive global package the firms paid up to $40 million each. Sponsors received a global monopoly for Olympic advertising in certain product or service categories.

Global marketers such as Coca-Cola, Kodak, Visa, and Xerox are among the repeat sponsors for the Olympics. IOC raised $500 million for the 1992 Olympics through this program and $650 million for 1996. Companies develop related programs to help them make business deals, launch new products, motivate employees, and wrap their advertising in the glory of the gold. NBC, for example, had record ad sales for the 1996 Olympics.

Xerox, the "official document processing company" of the Summer Olympics, began its commercial broadcasting in June, before the games began. Young & Rubicam, its agency, prepared the campaign, which ran in European media and CNN International as well as in the United States.

Visa, which claimed that its 1988 Olympic sponsorship increased sales by 16 percent, was an enthusiastic repeater. For the 1996 Games in Atlanta, Coca-Cola spent over $200 million in related promotions, in addition to its $40 million fee.

Sponsors gained more bargaining power with IOC after the Salt Lake City scandal. Only time will tell how this will affect sponsor participation.

---

for Swiss products equal to 50 percent of the value of the planes. They had to be products the Swiss could not sell themselves.

Why are firms willing to supply their goods for such an inconvenient form of payment? The major reason is that they would miss out on many sales and many markets if they insisted on monetary payments. Obviously, any firm that can make all the sales it wants for hard cash should do so. In today's competitive world, with a majority of countries short of foreign exchange, few firms are in that ideal situation. The alternative then is some form of countertrade or nothing.

For the exporting firm, the use of countertrade becomes a major form of promotion. In countries with chronic foreign-exchange shortages, the most persuasive argument to choose the firm's products will be acceptance of a nonmonetary form of payment. A country faced with two suppliers offering equivalent goods and prices will invariably choose the supplier who will countertrade over the one demanding money payment. In other words, a firm's willingness to countertrade is often its major form of persuasion and may even offset competitive handicaps in price and quality.

Because of the great variety and complexity of countertrade transactions, we have gathered a series of examples to convey some of the flavor of this important kind of international marketing. See also Chapter 15.

- ◆ NEC, which assembles TVs in Egypt, has half the market there. To keep the business, NEC agreed to transport Japanese tourists to Egypt on Egypt Air

(3,000 yearly). Half of the airfare and all local spending by the tourists is used to buy parts from NEC.

◆ Coca-Cola operated a tomato paste factory in Turkey, sold Polish beer in the United States, and marketed Yugoslavian wine in Japan—all to sell Coke in Eastern and Southern Europe.

◆ Singer supplied its name and technical expertise for a sewing machine plant in Poland. As payment for its name and services, Singer receives part of the plant's output for sale in Singer's other markets.

◆ Gillette's British subsidiary was selling 20 percent of its exports to Eastern Europe. Barter deals were an important factor in its success there. The company has taken anything from rabbit skins to butter, from carpets to pajamas in exchange for razor blades. However, it relied on a specialized London barter house to handle the mechanics of the trade.

PUBLIC RELATIONS—CORPORATE COMMUNICATIONS

Public relations is concerned with images. The firm is trying to present itself in a favorable light with one or more of its constituencies. Too often it has meant telling the world how good the company is or explaining away the company's mistakes. In an ideal sense, good public relations is corporate diplomacy—the firm seeking to relate constructively to its various stakeholders to the benefit of both parties. Thus, it involves more than corporate communications—it requires appropriate corporate behavior. Public relations is often more important in a foreign market than it is domestically. A Conference Board survey that identified the problems facing international executives found that number one was relations with governments and number two was marketing. The two are often related.

Public relations is not marketing, but good relations with the public are essential to marketing success. A firm that is seen as a bad citizen may find itself *persona non grata* in the marketplace; one reaction could be a boycott of its products. In another sense, public relations can be considered as the marketing of a product, the product being the firm itself. The firm's products can enjoy continued success only because of their performance. The image of the product cannot be maintained if product performance is not consistent with it. The same reasoning applies to the image and behavior of the firm. Public relations cannot be more effective than the corporate behavior behind it.

The firm must obviously behave in a legal manner in all of its markets. It also must be perceived as behaving in an ethically correct and environmentally friendly way. A problem can arise here because what is "ethically correct" and "environmentally friendly" may be defined somewhat differently by different observers. These observers include the firm's various publics. The Shell and Marketing Ethics cases at the end of this chapter probe these issues.

The publics of the firm are broader than its market. They include all those who are affected by the firm's operations—and all those who can have an effect on the firm's success. These publics, stakeholders, or constituencies include the following:

1. Customers
2. General public
3. Stockholders
4. Government
5. Media

6. Suppliers
7. Employees
8. Activist groups
9. Financial community
10. Distributors

The importance of any particular group varies from country to country. The firm's level of involvement in a market also affects the publics with which it must deal.

The Public Relations Task Today

Research

Just as the first job in marketing is to become familiar with the market, so the first task of international public relations is to become familiar with the various publics of the firm in each of its markets. This involves two processes: (1) seeing others as they see themselves, rather than using a foreign viewpoint or stereotype and (2) seeing the company as others see it. Thus public relations should begin with market intelligence. By being informed, the firm can practice preventive medicine rather than finding itself forced into drastic surgery after serious trouble has developed. Too often, public relations is used to fight fires rather than to prevent them. Inadequate intelligence can lead to many problems.

Response to the Public

The purpose of intelligence gathering is to serve as a basis for action. The appropriate action depends on the nature of the intelligence. Occasionally, the appropriate action involves a statement or press release by the firm as, for instance, when false statements are circulating. In other instances, it may be a change in the behavior of the firm. When change is inevitable, it is preferable to initiate the change voluntarily rather than to be forced into it. For example, Nestlé was reluctant to change its baby-food marketing in developing countries. This led to a boycott of its products. On the other hand, Procter & Gamble immediately withdrew its Rely tampons from the market when unwanted side effects were discovered. This quick action minimized the problem and maintained customer goodwill. (See "Global Marketing," "McDonald's in Thailand.")

Avon Products took a proactive response to the rise of consumerism: (1) It created Avon Cares Network to respond to inquiries and complaints, (2) it published consumer information pamphlets, (3) it sought out consumer leaders and groups, (4) it held conferences on consumer issues, (5) it invited consumer leaders to meet Avon managers, and (6) it sought guidance from experts.

Noting host-country complaints about the "foreign" company is a helpful way to see problems the firm must deal with. In addition to problems peculiar to individual countries, certain complaints tend to appear in most foreign markets. They arise primarily because the international firm is a foreigner in the market, and the common thread among them is that the foreign firm takes unfair advantage of the host country and otherwise abuses its position as a guest. These complaints are often expressed in emotional language, such as "imperialistic exploitation." A reasonable statement of the kinds of things a host country wants from a foreign firm is given in Table 13–2. It is based on an advisory of the Canadian government.

The best defense probably is a good offense. An imaginative public relations program is the best way to reduce the probability of reaction against the company. Many companies have won praise and awards from host governments for their behavior. Thomas Watson, former chairman of IBM, was decorated by no fewer than nine governments. Esso has a better image in Colombia because it organized a collection of Colombian art and sponsored its tour in the United States. The acclaim this exhibit received led to the Colombian government's highest decoration for Esso. Obviously, the marketing task is easier for a company that enjoys an attractive image.

Organizational Aspects

Because of its need to be sensitive to local publics, the firm must rely heavily on local staff. BASF and ITT are firms with centralized control of public relations, while Citibank and John Deere exemplify the decentralized approach. The firm

GLOBAL MARKETING

McDonald's in Thailand

After the Asian crisis began in 1997, the Thai baht dropped dramatically in value. A government campaign was launched urging consumers to "buy Thai, eat Thai." Even the revered Thai king urged his subjects to "buy Thai." Research by Damask/BBDO Thailand showed that 98 percent of the respondents believed that buying "foreign" products hurts Thailand. Thai TV news broadcasts on this issue frequently used McDonald's "golden arches" as a backdrop.

Instead of fighting the campaign in a direct way, McDonald's began to promote the idea that it contributes to Thailand's foreign exchange reserves rather than draining them. Dej Belsuk, CEO of McThai, the joint venture with 51 percent Thai ownership, noted that for every dollar of imports, McDonald's exports seven dollars worth of goods. They export everything from chicken nuggets to apple pies to Ronald McDonald statues to McDonald's in other Asian countries. Their shrimp nuggets sell as far away as Germany.

Customers didn't know that up to 90 percent of a typical meal is locally grown products. French fries are the only main item imported. McDonald's used tray mats to convey such information and also used TV and the press. After Dej Belsuk was interviewed on TV, there was a noticeable recovery in sales. The company also launched a "Thai-style" hot-basil pork burger. The supporting advertising campaign is built around traditional Thai images.

Source: Extracted from *Business Asia*, June 29, 1998, 3.

can centralize policymaking, but day-to-day operations are left to people in the market. The firm has nationals on its staff and may use a local public relations agency. The international corporate communications manager ensures consistency from country to country and also acts as a clearinghouse of ideas and experience. Aiding in this task is the increasing availability of international public relations firms, even in China and Russia. Such groups can aid coordination much as the multinational agency does in advertising.

A promising development for external affairs is the European Advisory Committee. Many large firms, such as Exxon, General Motors, IBM, ITT, and Thyssen, have formed such committees. The groups are composed of prominent European leaders from various countries. They meet regularly and advise the company on economic, social, and political trends. The group also acts as a sounding board, interprets events, and contributes to strategies. A major value of such committees is the members' independence from company management. They do not "rubber stamp" but give the outsider's objective view.

Public relations is important to effective marketing, but the two functions should be organizationally separate. Although public relations is a profitable activity, its purpose is not immediate sales. By lumping the public relations and marketing functions together, the firm runs the risk that public relations might take a short-run view, focusing on the annual profit-and-loss statement. Public relations should be sufficiently independent to be able to consider the interest of the public as well as the long-run interest of the firm.

Megamarketing

Public relations (external relations or corporate communications) has evolved into a new kind of role called **megamarketing,** or the "fifth P" of marketing. The idea is that marketing today must do more than manage the four Ps of marketing; it must also try to manage the environment—political power and public opinion—a much broader role than traditional public relations. In megamarketing, in other words, the firm attempts to make changes in the external environment so that the market

TABLE 13–2	**Ten Commandments for the Foreign Firm**

1. Maintain a high degree of local autonomy in decision making.
2. Retain some earnings within the country.
3. Allow and encourage exports.
4. Process locally the natural resources of the country.
5. Conduct local R&D.
6. Search out and develop local sources of supply (local content).
7. Offer equity to national investors.
8. Provide employment and career opportunities at all levels.
9. Maintain fair prices locally and in transfer pricing.
10. Provide information and maintain transparency in company operations.

will be more receptive to the firm, its products, and marketing program. This new function is implemented in a variety of ways:

1. *Developing a statement of company philosophy and strategy.* See Table 13–3 for an example.

2. *Making the chairman or chief executive officer the principal communicator for the company.*

3. *Investing in corporate advertising.* Some U.S. and Japanese firms are advertising in China even though their products are not available there. They are trying to create familiarity and an image that will facilitate their eventual entry into that market. Hitachi took out full-page ads in major U.S. papers. They showed a picture of Tsuneo Tanaka, president of Hitachi America. The heading read, "Toward a Truly American Corporation," and Tanaka discussed Hitachi's "commitment to becoming an active member of America's corporate community."

4. *Using the home government to support the firm's sales abroad.* AT&T entered the Italian market with President Reagan's support, and the Saudi Arabian market with President Clinton's support. England's Queen Elizabeth entertained Saudi Arabia's Prince Abdullah in her box at the Ascot races; this fraternization led to the Saudis' agreement to purchase $25 billion in English weapons over a 10-year period.

5. *Developing government negotiation and lobbying skills.* In Japan, Motorola retained as advisers former officials of MITI and the Ministry of Post and Telecommunications. In Korea, Goodyear received permission for a wholly owned plant rather than the suggested joint venture because of extensive negotiation with different parts of the Korean government.

In recent years, Japanese firms have learned that efficient production is not sufficient for success. The public/political environment must also be managed. As a result, the Japanese have become adept at public relations (including corporate philanthropy) and lobbying.

Japanese philanthropic giving in the United States averages over $500 million annually since Keidanren (Japan Federation of Economic Organizations) declared 1990 as the inaugural year for Japanese corporate philanthropy. The Japanese gov-

TABLE 13-3	**Procter & Gamble's Ethical Philosophy**

Constituent Groups	*Company Responsibilities to Each Group*
Customers	◆ To provide products with superior benefits
	◆ To listen and respond to customer opinions
	◆ To ensure products are safe for intended use and anticipate accidental misuse
Suppliers *and*	◆ To strive for fair and open business relationships
Channel Members	◆ To help business partners improve performance
	◆ To reject illegal or deceptive activities anywhere in the world
Employees	◆ To provide a safe workplace
	◆ To show concern for the well-being of all employees
	◆ To create opportunities for individual achievement, creativity, and personal reward
Shareholders	◆ To provide a fair annual return to the owners
	◆ To build for the future to maintain growth
	◆ To safeguard the environment
Society	◆ To encourage employees to participate in community activities
	◆ To be a good neighbor in communities in which business is done

ernment also began especially favorable tax treatment for foreign charitable contributions. The order of priority for Japanese philanthropy in the United States is (1) higher education, (2) arts and culture, (3) local communities, (4) schools and social programs, and (5) international exchange programs.

Japan also spends an estimated $400 million in the United States for lobbying activities, more than the combined total of the U.S. Chamber of Commerce, National Association of Manufacturers, the Business Roundtable, Committee for Economic Development, and the American Business Conference—the top U.S. business organizations. The U.S. business community is becoming more active in Japan, but nothing like the Japanese activity in the United States. The EU headquarters in Brussels is perhaps the most active business lobby target (after Washington, D.C.) with 400 trade associations, 300 companies active there, and 13,000 lobbyists.

SUMMARY

Personal selling is often more important in the promotional mix abroad than in the domestic market. Although it is done almost entirely on a national basis, headquarters management can contribute something to almost all the tasks of sales force management in the firm's foreign markets: recruitment and selection, training, motivation, compensation, control, and evaluation. Successful techniques can be transferred from the home market to similar foreign markets. Economies of scale can be realized for some tasks. The firm will also frequently train or assist distributors' or licensees' sales forces. And international comparisons help in evaluating and thus improving international performance.

Sales promotion is usually effective in most foreign markets in spite of national restrictions. It must be adapted to meet local legal and cultural differences, but it plays the same role in the marketing mix abroad as at home.

Each of the four Ps of the marketing mix can attract the customer and therefore serve as promotion. Product modifications abroad (including package, brand, warranty, and service) can persuade customers to buy the firm's products. By going to more direct distribution abroad, the firm can usually increase sales and respond better to the local market. Various pricing and credit terms can make the firm's marketing more productive, such as C.I.F. quotes and open account terms.

Government assistance is a special form of promotion in international marketing. Many governments support the export sales of their companies. In the United States, the Department of Commerce is the main supporter and has several programs—publications, shows, and missions. All 50 state governments also have support programs, sometimes overlapping and sometimes complementing those of the federal government.

International trade fairs are valuable marketing tools, not only for market entry but for keeping up in markets abroad. They can also be used in Eastern Europe and China.

The Washington representative can market to a critical clientele in Washington, D.C.

Other special forms of promotion include (1) traveling exhibits that involve extra costs but special advantages; (2) international 800 numbers for distributors or customers (these should become more popular); (3) reducing the level of involvement in a market to give a firm a bigger market share because of favorable government treatment; (4) seminars and symposia offering a special entry to some countries and some industry sectors; (5) bribery, which, though illegal for U.S. firms, is used by competitors; and (6) barter and countertrade, which are enormous markets today. The firm will often find its willingness to countertrade is its most persuasive marketing tool.

Public relations is a very important and sensitive task for international marketing. The first step in successful public relations is research to familiarize the firm with all the constituencies that can affect its success in the market. The second is designing a company program and behavior appropriate to the market. The new megamarketing concept suggests that firms should not only respond to the environment but should try to manage it, thus achieving more favorable outcomes in the marketplace through political power and public opinion—the "fifth P" of marketing.

QUESTIONS

13.1   Why does personal selling often play a proportionately larger promotional role in foreign markets than in the domestic market?

13.2   Why is personal selling done largely within national boundaries rather than internationally?

13.3   Since most of the task of sales force management must be done within the national market, what contributions can the international marketing manager make?

13.4   How can comparative analysis of the firm's foreign markets help the international marketer with local sales force management?

13.5   Explain how the multinational firm may have an advantage over local firms in training the sales force and evaluating its performance.

13.6   Discuss the influence of the firm's level of involvement on the personal-selling function in foreign markets.

13.7   Discuss the potential competitive advantages of the multinational firm in sales promotion activities in foreign markets.

13.8   How does the establishment of local operations aid the firm's promotion in foreign markets?

13.9   Review the promotional services of the U.S. Department of Commerce. Who might use them, and how?

13.10   How might the firm take advantage of international trade fairs?

13.11   Discuss the role of the Washington representative in international marketing.

13.12   Identify the various publics of the firm in foreign markets.

13.13   What are the elements of a sound public relations program?

13.14   What is the relationship of public relations to marketing?

13.15   What constitutes megamarketing for the international marketer?

ENDNOTES

1 *Marketing News,* May 8, 1989, 7.

2 Philip J. Rosson and Rolf Seringhaus, "International Trade Fair Performance," *Dimensions of International Business* (Ottawa, Canada: 1989), 13–25.

3 Department of Commerce, 1998.

4 Constance Bates, "A Study of Countertrading Firms in Florida," Paper presented at the Academy of International Business, New York, October 1985.

FURTHER READINGS

Amine, Lyn S. "The Need for Moral Champions in Global Marketing." *European Journal of Marketing* 30, no. 5 (1996): 81–94.

Asugman, Gulden, Jean Johnson, and James McCullough. "The Role of After-Sales Service in International Marketing." *Journal of International Marketing* 5, no. 4 (1997): 11–28.

Dubinsky, Alan, J., and Abdalla Hanafg. "The Super Sales Force—Politicians in the World Market." *Journal of International Marketing* 4, no. 3 (1996): 73–87.

Erffmeyer, Robert C., Jamal Al-Khatib, Mohammed Al-Habib, and Joseph Hair, Jr. "Sales Training Practices: A Cross-National Comparison." *International Marketing Review* 10, no. 1 (1993): 45–57.

Hahn, Minhi, Dae Ryun Chang, Ik-Tae Kim, and Yup Kim. "Consumer Response to Coupon Advertising." *Journal of International Advertising* 14 (1995): 41–53.

Paun, Dorothy A. and Aviv Shohan. "Marketing Motives in International Countertrade." *Journal of International Marketing* 4, no. 3 (1996): 29–47.

Serringhaus, Rolf, and Philip J. Rosson. "Management and Performance of International Trade Fair Exhibitors." *International Marketing Review* 15, no. 5 (1998): 398–412.

Zalka, Lori, Meredith Downes, and Karen Paul. "Measuring Consumer Sensitivity to Corporate Social Performance across Cultures." *Journal of Global Marketing* 11, no. 1 (1997): 29–42.

Nestlé (B): More Trouble in the Baby Market

On October 12, 1988, the International Organization of Consumers Unions (IOCU) called for a renewal of the boycott against Nestlé. Because of the deaths of babies in developing countries that were alleged to be related to the use of infant formula (see Case 12.1), IOCU encouraged an international boycott of Nestlé products from 1977 to 1984. During that time, Nestlé responded by changing its marketing practices for infant formula, working with the industry and the World Health Organization (WHO) on a code for marketing infant formula and forming a prestigious committee (headed by Senator Muskie) to investigate the claims and advise Nestlé. By 1984 the company was perceived as a leading firm in support of the WHO code, and the boycott was dropped.

Calls for a renewed boycott arose because some observers claimed that Nestlé and some other firms were breaking the spirit of the code by supplying large amounts of free formula to hospitals in developing countries with the result that too many mothers became dependent on formula and lost the ability to nurse their babies. Nestlé's response was that the WHO code allows the free distribution of supplies to hospitals that request it and that the amounts supplied were not excessive.

Nestlé in the U.S. Baby Market

The U.S. market for infant formula amounts to over $1.6 billion, and until 1988 none of it belonged to Nestlé. (Abbott and Bristol-Myers had 90 percent of the market between them.) In June 1988 Nestlé introduced Good Start H.A., which it said was able to prevent or reduce fussiness, sleeplessness, colic, rash, and other worrisome ailments because it is hypoallergenic—which the labels indicated in bold type. Carnation, Nestlé's U.S. subsidiary, introduced the product and called it "a medical breakthrough."

The market-entry strategy for Good Start H.A. included the product-differentiation feature of being hypoallergenic while having a taste similar to other infant formula products. By contrast, Nutramigen, another hypoallergenic product, had a distinctive, less pleasant taste. Good Start H.A. was priced competitively with the leading infant formula brands, although Bristol-Myers' hypoallergenic Nutramigen, a niche product, cost twice as much as Good Start H.A. To further speed market entry, Carnation broke with industry practice and publicized the hypoallergenic feature directly to parents without waiting for pediatricians to recommend it.

About three months after the introduction of Good Start H.A., there were scattered reports of severe reactions. Some mothers of severely milk-allergic babies tried the formula and reported that their babies vomited violently and went limp. Nestlé's competitors helped to publicize these incidents. Some leading pediatricians criticized Nestlé's marketing as misleading, and the American Academy of Pediatrics strongly protested against advertising directly to mothers and bypassing the physician. James Strain, director of the academy, said, "These ailments (fussiness, colic, etc.) happen to 90 percent of all babies and aren't really symptoms of anything. The advertising just raises the level of anxiety in mothers about something being wrong with their babies."

One mother, Mrs. Elizabeth Strickler, was interviewed by *The Wall Street Journal.*[1] Her son, Zachary, hadn't tolerated other formulas well, so she was eager to try Good Start H.A. After two weeks of use, Zachary had severe vomiting. She discontinued usage, but for two months she had to feed him Maalox to soothe his gastrointestinal tract, "If you call something hypoallergenic, that means a lot to me," she said. "I thought it was the best thing and that's why I bought it."

William Spivak, pediatrician and Mrs. Strickler's doctor, said, "My concern is that long after physicians realize that this formula isn't as hypoallergenic as claimed, parents with milk-allergic babies will be grabbing it off the shelf because of its attractive hypoallergenic labeling, and thereby exposing their babies to a potentially dangerous formula without physician supervision." Other pediatricians pointed out that while Good Start is easier to digest than ordinary milk-based formulas, it isn't mild enough for the approximately 2 percent of babies who, like Zachary, are severely allergic to cows' milk. The mothers of these babies were most likely to be attracted by the hypoallergenic claim.

Good Start had received preliminary approval of the Food and Drug Administration (FDA) before introductory marketing, but the FDA had asked for more data backing up the formula's extra claims that it could reduce allergies. After the severe reactions were reported, the FDA began a new investigation of the company's claims as well as of the six reports of severe reaction.

Following the widespread publicity given to the cases of severe reaction to the Good Start formula, several state attorneys general also began an investigation of Nestlé's Good Start marketing. The company had to submit copies of Good Start's print, radio, and TV advertising that had appeared in California, New York, and Texas. It also had to provide scientific studies supporting the formula's health and nutrition claims as well as studies showing consumer perception of the term "hypoallergenic."

Robert Roth, an assistant attorney general in New York, said, "This case is a little unusual in that it involves the health of infants. We are pursuing it more urgently than we would a matter which is purely economic."[2]

In responding to the publicity and the criticisms, Nestlé and Carnation pointed out that all formulas have isolated cases of bad reactions. They argued that the severe reactions to Good Start resulted from its misuse with highly milk-allergic babies. Pierre Guesry, a Nestlé vice-president in Switzerland, said, "I don't understand why our product should work in 100 percent of cases. If we wanted to say it was foolproof, we would have called it allergy-free. We call it hypo- or less-allergenic."

A Product from Europe

Nestlé, which has the largest share of the infant formula market outside the United States, had introduced Beba H.A., a version of Good Start H.A., in Germany two years before bringing it into the U.S. market. While mothers are in the hospital after giving birth, Nestlé supplies them information about hypoallergenic formulas and infant allergies. It doesn't name the company or the product, but Beba H.A. is the only major hypoallergenic brand available. Other formula makers also distribute information to mothers, but some critics say Nestlé goes too far. Judith Phillipoa of the Geneva Infant Feeding Association, an anti-Nestlé activist group, said, "In Europe, Nestlé is blowing up the allergy problem as a way of creating demand for their product. Now they're exporting this system to the United States."

Pierre Guesry said that Good Start was introduced in the United States because "we felt American babies should have the same rights to a good formula as German, Belgian, or French babies." He pointed out that no problems were reported in Europe as have occurred in the United States and that most of the 40,000 U.S. babies who had tried Good Start had no problems with it.

Nestlé Responds

Nestlé's first response to the publicity and criticism was to remove the term "hypoallergenic" from the front of the can where it had been displayed in large type. Some critics were not satisfied, because H.A. was still in the product name—Good Start H.A.—and "hypoallergenic" was in the fine print on the back of the can. Also, Good Start was still advertised in medical journals as a "breakthrough hypoallergenic infant formula."[3]

In July 1989 Nestlé reached a settlement with nine states attorneys general about its Good Start marketing. The agreement specified (1) Carnation could not use the word *hypoal-*lergenic in advertising Good Start; (2) it could not use expert endorsers that had been paid by the company; and (3) it could not make claims that were not scientifically supported. Carnation also agreed to pay $90,000 to cover the costs of the investigation.[4]

Nestlé also hired Ogilvy & Mather's public relations unit to help its relations with the FDA and the other publics involved. Among Ogilvy's proposals were these:

1. Get people into the groups organizing and supporting the boycott. This was meant to be an early warning system for Nestlé.
2. Create a Nestlé positive image campaign—a daily 12-minute news program to reach 8,000 high schools. This was not to advertise but to buy public service time such as a "Nestlé News Network."
3. Create a Carnation image campaign to inoculate the Nestlé subsidiary from any negative effects of the boycott.

The game plan included a Carnation National Homework Help Line and a foster care fund for children with AIDS.

Questions

1. Identify in some detail and evaluate Nestlé's marketing strategy (the four Ps) for entering the U.S. infant formula market.
2. Suggest a program for Nestlé to deal with its public relations problems, for example, the renewed boycott and the negative publicity about Good Start. Would you use the Ogilvy & Mather recommendations?

Endnotes

1. *The Wall Street Journal*, February 16, 1989, A1.
2. Ibid., February 24, 1989, B6.
3. Ibid., March 13, 1989, B6.
4. Ibid., July 7, 1989, B4.

Eberhard Faber's Special Forms of Promotion

The board of directors of Eberhard Faber, Inc., was discussing the matter of establishing a joint venture in a Third World country. The joint venture was to supply the know-how to enable a local pencil company there to expand and improve its operations and to use Eberhard Faber's name. In return, Eberhard Faber would receive 35 percent equity of the local company, which could be expected to provide dividend income in the years ahead. However, no cash was required of Eberhard Faber for the equity position. The deal also envisaged that Eberhard Faber would supply equipment for the expected venture over a five-year period at a pretty good profit. After two years' effort, the deal was consummated in principle. Only the approval of the board was lacking.

The Company

Eberhard Faber, Inc., was founded in 1849 by the original Eberhard Faber. It is known for high-quality pencils and other stationery supplies including the well-known brands Mongol and Colorbrite pencils, Dart pens, Pink Pearl erasers, and Star rubber bands. It is owned by the Faber family, and the present chairman is the fourth Eberhard Faber. It has no immediate plans to go public.

Although sales were only $30 million, the company did business in many countries. In addition to the U.S. operation based in Wilkes-Barre, Pennsylvania, it had wholly owned subsidiaries in Canada and Germany and joint ventures in Venezuela and Colombia. There were also licensees using its name and know-how in Argentina, Brazil, Central America, Peru, Syria, and the Philippines. Eberhard Faber's board of directors has been on record for several years in favor of further expansion into foreign markets.

Following the board's policy of international growth, a substantial contract that included know-how for a factory to make Eberhard Faber products was signed with the Syrian government. Soon after, there was an expansion of the licensing agreement in Brazil. The proposed joint venture was the next step in this program of international development.

The company had a good reputation, both for product quality and business dealings. Recently, for example, it refused to ship large quantities of its newest Dart pen because the quality didn't meet its standards—even though the company knew that its customers would accept the merchandise. The board of directors was always very concerned for the company's reputation.

The Board Meeting

After discussing the other major agenda items, Eberhard Faber, chairman and chief executive officer, introduced the proposal for the joint venture with a 10-minute summary of the conditions of the deal. He explained that it would increase this year's budgeted profit by more than one-quarter. In addition, he mentioned that the local pencil company under consideration was paying off the government of its country in order to do business. Although the laws of the country prohibited bribery, it was a common and accepted practice there. Eberhard Faber, Inc., however, would be a minority shareholder in the venture, so there seemed to be no legal exposure. (Later it was confirmed by legal counsel that there was no legal exposure, and the company had informal advice from the IRS that its concern was primarily with U.S.–controlled companies that made illegal payoffs and deductions.)

A number of board members insisted that the problem was not the legal exposure but the ethics of taking an equity position in a company that was paying off its country's government. Faber argued, however, that aside from the rights and wrongs of payoffs in a country where they were common practice, the board's own company would be doing no paying off. Furthermore, it could not hope to change the practices of another company in which it held only a minority stock interest. He also said, "Don't you realize that if we adopt this type of policy, we'll be shut out of half the world? Don't you realize that our competition in Europe, if not the United States, won't have any such ethical qualms and will take over this opportunity in a flash, shutting us out of this market permanently? Whatever happened to our policy of international expansion?"

Questions

1. If you were a board member, what would be your decision? Why?
2. What guidelines for international business expansion would you suggest for Eberhard Faber, Inc.?

Source: *Fortune,* November 1982.

disposal plan for the Brent Spar, they studied it and argued that Brent Spar's use as an oil-holding pen made it too contaminated to sink into the ocean. While the structure was technically empty, it still contained an estimated 100 tons of oil-related sludge. Most of that was simply sand, but about 10 percent was made up of toxic heavy metals. Shell had concluded a plume of pollution would result, but that it would be so deep that it wouldn't affect much marine life.

On April 30, 1995, as Shell was towing the Brent Spar in the North Atlantic, Greenpeace landed two activists, by helicopter, on the rig who were eventually joined by 14 activists and nine journalists. They stayed for three weeks. There was also a Greenpeace boat nearby taking videos and sending satellite reports back to the news media on the Continent. The event was a public relations coup for Greenpeace. Across environmentally conscious northern European countries, the media coverage aroused a tremendous public reaction. Greenpeace was portrayed as being in a David-versus-Goliath situation. They conveyed the simple message "a poison bomb in the ocean, and a precedent for 400 other platforms." They also pointed out that Shell had chosen the least costly solution, suggesting that the company's decision was based more on economics than science.

Shell disagreed with the Greenpeace complaints and activities and continued towing the Brent Spar. The company tried to prevent the activists from landing or staying on the rig by using high-powered water cannons. All of this was captured on film and beamed around the world, reinforcing the David-versus-Goliath analogy. The growing publicity in Europe stimulated a variety of reactions from many different groups, almost all against Shell's decision to sink the Brent Spar at sea.

The most violent reactions against Shell occurred in Germany, where some Shell stations were firebombed and others were shot at. A more moderate reaction was the boycott of Deutsche Shell that was called for by German environmentalists and politicians. For example, the mayor of Leipzig banned all city vehicles from using Shell stations, and Chancellor Kohl complained to Prime Minister Major about Shell's plans having been approved by Britain. (The Green Party is especially strong in Germany.) Shell sales in Germany plummeted more than 20 percent after the boycott got underway.

Other peaceful protesters in Germany included talk-show hosts, industrialists, and even Protestant churches. Perhaps most embarrassing for Shell was the reaction of some Shell managers and other employees in Germany. In Koblenz, five Shell stations closed for 24 hours to protest the company's plan. The worker representatives on Shell's supervisory board in Germany sent a letter to Greenpeace expressing "concern and outrage" at Shell's plans to "turn the sea into a trash pit." The head of Shell-Austria described the plan to sink the Brent Spar as intolerable.

The reaction in other northern European countries was less strong and pervasive than in Germany, but was important—and negative—nonetheless. The boycott spread to Denmark and the Netherlands. In Denmark, the environment minister urged a boycott of Shell stations. In Britain, demonstrators showed up at a number of Shell stations.

Shell was very surprised at the extent and pervasiveness of the public reaction. This had become more than a Shell-Greenpeace battle. Initially, Shell planned a high profile campaign in its own defense. Shell had placed some newspaper ads and distributed leaflets to customers at its stations. It planned to lobby politicians, also. The intensity of the public furor, however, shocked the company into a rather abrupt withdrawal. On June 20, Shell announced that they would seek a license from the British government to dismantle the rig on shore. It said strong objections to its original plans from some governments had placed Shell's European subsidiaries in an untenable position.

Questions

1. How did Shell get into this public relations disaster?
2. How can Shell now argue for land disposal after their previous position?
3. How can Shell repair its battered image?
4. How can Shell avoid similar problems in the future?

Sources: *The Wall Street Journal,* June 19, 1995, A6, B7; June 21, 1995, A10; July 7, 1995, A1; *Financial Times,* June 20, 1995, 10; June 21, 1995, 1, 11.

Marketers Can't Ignore New Ethics Issue

A new dimension of ethics and corporate social responsibility has surfaced in the world of marketing.

According to this emerging doctrine the products that we sell must be made under appropriate and acceptable working conditions, whether they are made in our own factories or those of our suppliers and contractors.

Levi Strauss, which takes pride in its reputation for being on the cutting edge of business ethics issues, insists that its contractors, whether in Latin America or Southeast Asia, follow strict contractual terms that go well beyond the number of stitches to the inch in a garment. The contractors must also meet standards regarding the minimum age of employees, overtime pay, plant safety, and healthful working conditions.

This is not strictly an international issue. A few years ago it was discovered that the immigrant laborers who pick strawberries in the fields near Watsonville, Calif., were actually living on the periphery of those fields in shacks made of cardboard cartons, sometimes in bare caves dug into the ground, with absolutely no sanitation facilities.

The growers were owners of relatively small businesses and did not have the capital to provide decent housing. The large corporations that bought the strawberries, processors such as Smuckers and retailers such as Safeway, accepted no responsibility because the laborers were not their employees.

It is difficult enough for marketers and managers to reach consensus regarding the extent of their responsibility to their own employees. Beyond legal requirements, what must employers offer in the way of employee benefits to satisfy their social obligations? Just how comfortable or how safe must working conditions be?

The idea that they must accept responsibility for their suppliers' and contractors' employment conditions is a new dimension of responsibility.

If we make sure that our own employees are paid a decent wage and work under safe conditions, is that not enough? Hanging in the air is the Old Testament query, "Am I my brother's keeper?"

This idea of extended responsibility is not entirely new. For the better part of two decades marketers have wrestled with the problem of whether to sell goods manufactured in South Africa under the laws of apartheid. But this question, now moot since the democratic transfer of power to black South Africans, was of a different sort because it involved a heinous governmental and legal system.

The new dimension of ethics under review here focuses on the working conditions allowed by individual employers. There is little question that this new dimension of ethical concern will grow.

International trade is sure to accelerate as the European Union expands beyond its original 12 members, as NAFTA encourages trade among the North American countries and, perhaps in time, with other Latin American nations, and as a new GATT agreement lowers trade barriers around the world still further.

Nevertheless, this new dimension of ethics and responsibility, a concern for the benefits and working conditions of ones' suppliers and contractors, is fraught with unanswered questions that fall into four categories.

1. What constitutes unacceptable employment practices and working conditions? In recent months, considerable attention has focused on "slave labor" and "prison labor" conditions in China. Few people disagree that these are abhorrent practices and that we should not trade in merchandise made under such conditions, although the political problems of dealing with such matters have proved to be rather sticky.

    Agreement on other standards would be more difficult to achieve. There might well be a general condemnation of the use of child labor, although agreement on some of the specifics—minimum age, physical demands of the job, education alternatives—might be difficult to reach. More difficult yet would be to achieve consensus on such matters as appropriate wage rates (just what does exploitation mean?), necessary benefits, and rights to organize.

2. When does a product become tainted or unacceptable? For example, if a dress has been cut and sewn by 12- and 13-year-old girls in Honduras, we might agree that accepted ethical standards prohibit us from participating in the marketing of the dress. But what if the body of the dress is produced in our own factory in the U.S. under appropriate working conditions, and what if just the shoulder pads or the belt or the buttons are imported from a manufacturer where the working conditions are not acceptable? What then are our ethical obligations?

3. Just how far back along the supply chain do our responsibilities extend? To our suppliers or contractors? To the suppliers of our suppliers?

4. What is our responsibility for conditions in the factories of our suppliers? Levi's regional supervisors have as an integral part of their job responsibilities the monitoring of contractors, plant safety, and working conditions as well as quality control of the actual garments. To what extent are we obligated to police the facilities of our trading partners?

    These are troubling questions; acceptable answers or a degree of consensus will not come easily. But the warning flags have been raised. Wal-Mart already has been embarrassed by selling merchandise allegedly manufactured by young children earning 5¢ an hour in Bangladesh, where there are no child labor laws.

Levi Strauss, Gillette, Nordstrom, and others have taken the lead in developing policies for managing this issue, although their policies will not be appropriate for every company. Nevertheless, all manufacturers and retailers involved in international purchasing are now confronted with this new ethical dimension.

They must not ignore it; it will not go away.

Question

1. Address the four questions raised by the author. Suggest appropriate policies and practices.

Source: D. Kirk Davidson, *Marketing News,* February 27, 1995, 48. Used by permission.

Pricing in International Marketing

I

We now examine price-setting in international markets. International pricing is complex, influenced by differences in consumer behavior across markets, competitive response, the firm's own cost structure and profit objectives, and government regulation. Exchange-rate fluctuations add spice to this mixture.

The main goals of this chapter are to

1. Establish a framework covering the broad principles governing international pricing.

2. Compare export prices to domestic prices.

3. Explain why and how prices escalate in export selling.

4. Discuss how exchange-rate fluctuations challenge the export marketer.

5. Explain how export price quotations are used in export marketing.

6. Discuss the importance of export credit and financing for successful export marketing.

7. Explore the special roles and problems of transfer pricing in international marketing

Pricing is part of the marketing mix. Pricing decisions must therefore be integrated with other aspects of the marketing mix. And since price is just one attribute of a product, along with others such as quality, reliability, service, and user satisfaction, trade-offs are necessary. A lower-priced product may be offered with lower quality or a less comprehensive warranty policy, for example.

The most useful way to deal with the complexities of pricing internationally is to consider the kinds of pricing situations and decisions the firm faces in international marketing. We will consider the following international pricing problems: (1) export pricing and terms, (2) transfer pricing in international marketing, (3) foreign-market pricing, and (4) coordination of prices in world markets. But first, we develop a conceptual framework for analyzing international pricing.

FACTORS IN INTERNATIONAL PRICING

Several factors are important in international pricing:

1. Setting pricing and strategic objectives.

2. Monitoring price-setting behavior by competitors and assessing their strategic objectives.

3. Evaluating consumers' ability to buy in the various country markets.

4. Relating price to a firm's costs and profit goals.

5. Understanding the product-specific factors, including product life cycle stage, that affect pricing. Generally, prices are reduced on mature products as they become more commoditylike and face increased competition.

6. Recognizing differences in the country environment governing prices in each national market—differences in the legal and regulatory environment, the volatility of foreign-exchange rates, market structure (especially distribution channels), and competitive environment.

Each of these differences influences the firm's price-setting behavior in each market.[1] Figure 14–1 sets out the framework.

Price, Competition, and Strategic Objectives

Pricing affects realized demand and hence is an influential tool in gaining market share. Or, thinking in reverse, competitive objectives toward gaining market share determine pricing. Therefore, as market share and competitive positions differ from country to country, so do prices.

Note that competitive objectives do not always demand a lowered price. In an oligopolistic environment with few competitors, for example, a company may attempt to head off ruinous price-cutting by signaling its intent to keep prices steady or even raise them. A case in point is an airline that might file a fare increase in a computer reservation system for the following week to see if its competitors raise prices, too. Such signaling is part of the role played by prices in affecting competitive position.

The strength of competition and the firm's objectives interact in determining how a firm sets its international prices. We can distinguish among several types of pricing strategies:

- ◆ *Setting low prices that result in low margins.* The firm expects that elasticity of demand will result in increased volume so that overall contribution from

FIGURE 14–1   Framework for International Pricing Strategy

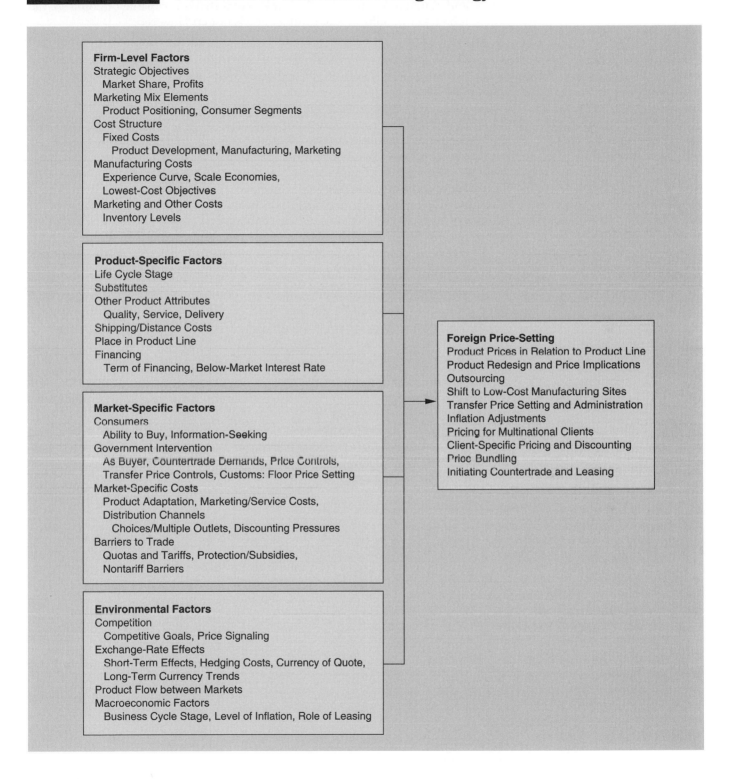

the product (volume in units times margin per unit) is sufficient to meet profit and contribution targets for that product or product line. If the firm already has a large installed base and enjoys scale economies, such a strategy hinders the competition from becoming strong.

♦ *The firm as price taker.* Stronger competitors set prices and the firm follows and matches the price leader to the extent that it is capable of doing so. Its long-term viability in that product line is not endangered.

♦ *Pricing at a premium to the market.* The firm avoids the commodity end of the market and caters to niche segments where the higher price is acceptable in return for features and product characteristics needed and desired by customers.

♦ *Pricing on a cost-plus basis.* Overall costs and a desired profit margin determine the level of prices. In the long run, prices should cover costs to yield a reasonable return on investment. Hence, in making a long-term decision such as whether to go ahead with a new-product proposal, such a cost-plus pricing approach may play a role; that is, it may determine at what level prices *should be set* in order to earn a given rate of return (often the hurdle rate). In practice, such an approach is only possible in industries with limited competition, such as regulated utilities. International long-distance rates come to mind, with the total market split between a few providers. Even here, however, international call-back systems undercut the "cartel" price and force prices to respond to competition.

In summary, the intensity of competition determines prices, and differentiating a product to command a higher price is more of a strategic positioning approach to reduce competition in order to gain greater leeway in setting prices.

Consumer's Ability to Buy

Incomes, cultural habits, and consumer preferences differ from country to country. Thus, for the same price in two different country markets, different amounts of products may be demanded.

Furthermore, extending pricing strategies from more information-saturated markets to markets where a consumerist movement is just starting might not be appropriate. Shoppers in country markets that lack cut-priced distribution channels, for example, may not have formed the habit of waiting for sales when making large purchases. Consumers may not have developed the habit of obtaining information about competing brands.

Target Pricing and Product Development

One way to be responsive to consumers' ability to buy is to use a target price approach, like the one implemented by Canon in developing a personal copier for under $1,000. This decision guided the entire product-development process. (See Chapter 9.) Such target pricing is necessarily a long-term pricing strategy because it envisions modulating the entire design, procurement, and manufacturing process in order to meet the target price. Implicit in the idea of a target price is the notion that the target price is for a product for a certain market segment and that the product can achieve long-term profitability at the target price.

Another example of using target pricing comes from Japan's Olympus Optical Co., which makes high-quality, single-lens reflex cameras (SLRs). The market for SLRs began to erode as compact cameras with auto-focus, built-in flash, and zoom lenses began to be sold at attractive prices. Olympus realized that the new generation of compact cameras was determining what price consumers were willing to pay for cameras, and that Olympus had to offer its SLRs at such a target price if it wanted to remain competitive and obtain market share. Working backward from the target price, Olympus developed (1) a set of features prioritized from must-have to nice-to-have, (2) the components and subassemblies needed to build such a camera, and, eventually, (3) the target costs that had to be attained to sell the camera at the target price, allow dealer and distributor margins, and still have a satisfactory margin left over for Olympus. Such an approach is iterative and products cannot always be designed to meet both the target price and the desired functionality at an acceptable cost. Olympus's efforts, however, demonstrate an approach to integrating product development, pricing, and targeted market share when product cycles are fairly short—about three years for a camera model.[2]

Figure 14–2 illustrates how a target-pricing approach interacts with product design and manufacturing to iteratively set product functionality and features so that target prices may be met. If careful study shows that target prices may have to be adjusted upward, the firm can then rethink whether satisfactory markets exist at the new target price. If not, it may consider cancellation of that particular product development effort.

Price in Relation to a Firm's Costs and Profit Goals

In the long term, prices must be set to cover full costs. In the short term, however, prices may be set below that level in order to gain market share and to accommodate economic recessionary cycles in particular markets. Also, the company may decide to accept losses from low prices in certain markets because these losses can be offset with profits from other markets.

In a similar vein, a company may deliberately price below costs in anticipation of reducing costs through increases in manufacturing volume. It thus gambles on gaining learning- and experience-curve efficiencies[3] to produce long-run profits. The Japanese have used this method to penetrate a number of industries, such as motorcycles.[4]

Shipping and transportation are further elements of costs specific to international pricing. Such additional "distance" costs are a deterrent to gaining market share in overseas markets and a difficult problem to overcome.

In thinking about the relation between prices and a firm's costs, it is important to focus on costs that are *relevant* to a firm's international marketing effort. Relevant costs, that is, costs specific to marketing a product in a specific international market, should be used in examining the price-cost relationship. Distributors in export markets may often ask for additional discounts because of the incremental costs of developing a new market, and a full-cost–based analysis may indicate that such a discount results in losses, suggesting that the distributor's request for an additional discount be denied. If the discount were granted, however, for specific market development and seeding activities, exports may still generate a positive contribution to fixed costs. As volume builds up, the additional discounts can be phased out. Such an approach builds long-term market share but recognizes that the relevant costs in the early stages of international marketing are higher for the distributor and require some concessions from the exporting firm.[5]

Price and the Product Line

Products within a product line with less competition may be priced higher to subsidize other parts of the product line. Similarly, some items in the product line may be priced very low to serve as loss leaders and induce customers to try the product, particularly if the company and its products are recent entrants into that country market. Another variant of such strategies is **price-bundling**—that is, a certain price is set for customers who simultaneously buy several items within the product line (i.e., a season ticket price or a personal computer package with software and printer). In all such cases, a key consideration is how desirous consumers in diverse country markets are to save money, to spend time searching for the "best buy," and so forth.

Price-Bundling in the Software Industry

Examples of price-bundling come from the software industry, which has experimented with several innovative approaches to pricing:

FIGURE 14–2   **Target Pricing and Product Development**

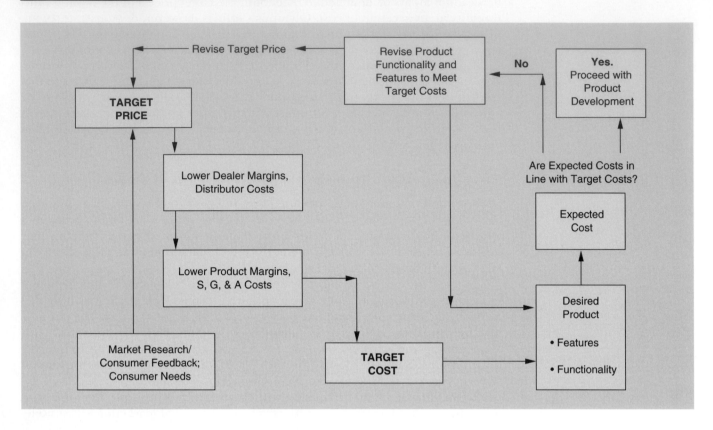

◆ *Basing prices on the power of the processor utilizing the software.* Thus, a software package used on a mainframe or workstation would command higher prices than one used on a personal computer.

◆ *A metering approach,* whereby a separate computer program keeps track of the number of users accessing a particular software package as well as how long they are using the package, resulting in a variable price that generally increases with greater usage.

◆ *A site license,* whereby individual corporate users negotiate a fixed, lump-sum price, perhaps payable once a year, based on the organization's size, number of computers, and relative demand for computer utilization.

◆ *Sale of "suites,"* such as Microsoft's Office suite, whereby users get significant price concessions for buying a related set of different software packages from one vendor. In this case, the Microsoft Office suite contains word processing, spreadsheet, database, and other utility packages.

Price and Flexible Service Offerings

All of these approaches develop prices based on an assessment of the value derived by the consumer from using the company's products or services. A corollary of thinking in terms of value to the customer is to break out the total product offering into tiers of value, and to charge price increments for delivering additional value beyond a base package provided to all customers. This approach, termed the flexible service offering model, allows users to pick the precise configuration of values they seek and pay accordingly.[6] This approach allows a company to offer a bare-bones model at a lower price, attracting new customers, who might then trade up and pay more for additional features that they deem particularly desirable. The sticking point here is how the bare-bones model is arrived at. If it is designed so that very few customers will settle for a bare-bones model but must add options to obtain an acceptable product, then the pricing model might breed resentment and be seen as a transparent attempt to gouge the customer. If a company moves to the flexible service offering model, therefore, it must guard against offering a base-line model for which there are no buyers.

EXPORT PRICING AND TERMS

In this discussion, we assume that the firm is committing itself to exporting on a continuing basis and thus is aiming for long-term profits and market position. The firm must answer a number of questions specific to international marketing that concerns the relationship between export prices and domestic prices, tariffs, transport costs, export packaging, insurance, and foreign taxes.

Export Prices in Relation to Domestic Prices

Should export prices be higher than, equal to, or less than domestic prices? If costs associated with export sales are greater than those associated with domestic sales, perhaps prices should be raised by these incremental costs. For example, exports may require special packaging and handling. Extra costs may arise in translating and processing export orders, and credit and collection costs may be higher. If the company has an export department, its operating costs may be higher as a percentage of sales.

Careful cost analysis is needed, however, before concluding that costs are higher for exports. Some costs allocated to domestic sales, such as domestic promotion or marketing research, do not apply to export sales. For example, foreign distributors may buy in larger quantities, assume warranty responsibility, and provide their own advertising and trade-show support. Exports should bear only those costs for which they are directly responsible plus, perhaps, a share of general overhead.

Even if export sales have higher costs, it does not follow necessarily that the export price should be higher than the domestic price. The best export price is the one that maximizes long-term profits. If foreign markets have lower income levels or more elastic demand curves, the most profitable export price may be lower than the domestic price. The firm may even find it necessary to modify the package or simplify the product to get the lower price needed for foreign markets.

Export Price Less Than Domestic

Setting the free on board (FOB) plant price lower on exports than on domestic products favors export sales. Some good reasons exist for such an approach:

1. The lower income levels in some foreign markets may require the firm to set a lower price to achieve sales.

2. Foreign competition may dictate a lower price.

3. The firm realizes that even with a lower FOB plant price, the product still can be more expensive in the foreign market because of the transport and tariff costs and other add-ons. All these add-ons could price the product out of the market if the FOB plant price were high.

4. The firm may consider that costs of export are actually less because research and development, overhead, and some other costs are already covered by domestic sales.

The firm that sells abroad at less than domestic prices may be accused of **dumping,** selling goods in foreign markets at prices lower than those in the producer's home market. Recipient nations may complain because national producers claim that such low-price competition is unfair to them. To avoid this type of producer resentment, countries tend to penalize imports sold at dumping prices.

Marginal cost pricing for exports may be appropriate when there is excess capacity; if new investment is needed, however, company profit goals will dictate full cost pricing for exports. The excess capacity justification for lower export prices will no longer be reliable.

Another problem with export prices that are lower than domestic prices is that the producing division has less interest in export sales. Only when no domestic alternative presents itself do export sales become interesting.

One of the largest U.S. electrical equipment manufacturers, for example, noted that its producing divisions used incremental pricing (marginal cost pricing) when domestic demand was lower. The export department thus found itself in a stronger market position when domestic sales were weak. Unfortunately, its position would reverse itself when domestic sales were strong. Because this pricing practice was based on domestic supply and demand conditions, it is not surprising that the firm was having trouble maintaining a consistent position in foreign markets.

Market-Oriented Export Pricing

A good starting point for export price analysis is the determination of conditions in foreign markets: What are the demand and competitive situations in the target markets? Within what price range could the firm's product sell? By determining the demand situation in foreign markets, the export manager can get a base price for evaluating export opportunities. Having figured out what the market will pay, the firm must see if it can sell at that price, a determination it makes by working back from the market price (base price) to the cost structure of the firm. The various intermediary margins, taxes, duties, and transport and handling costs must be subtracted from the consumer price. The resulting figure will help determine the firm's FOB plant price for exports.

Price Escalation in Exporting

Because of the additional costs and steps involved in exporting, the final price to a consumer in the importing country often increases significantly. There are incremental transportation and insurance costs, and more intermediaries such as freight forwarders involved in the channels of distribution. There are charges for export documentation, specialized packaging, and import duties. Table 14–1 illustrates this phenomenon.

The implication from Table 14–1 is that an exported product typically is sold for a higher price than the same product sold domestically. The higher price in turn raises two questions: (1) Can foreign consumers afford to buy the product at the higher price? Will demand be lowered because of it? (2) Will the higher price make imports less competitive against domestically produced products? The incremental distance costs associated with exporting allow domestic producer costs to be higher but to remain competitive.

In reality, shipping costs and tariffs totaling $2.04 in the table represent the true higher cost of the imported product. A manufacturer in the importing country can have higher production costs of up to $2.04 and still match the import price.

If, in fact, the manufacturer's costs in the importing country are only $1 higher, then it can offer a price cut of about $2.20.[7] In that case, the exporter must consider several alternatives:

1. It can discard exporting as an option, which may be a wise decision if it has plentiful opportunity for profitable growth in the domestic market.

TABLE 14–1	Export Price Escalation			
		Export Price		*Domestic Price*
Manufacturer's FOB price		$ 9.60		$ 9.60
Ocean freight and insurance		1.08		—
Landed or CIF value		10.68		—
Tariff: 9% on CIF value		.96		—
CIF value plus tariff		11.64		—
12% value-added tax (VAT)		1.40		—
Distributor cost		13.04		9.60
Distributor markup @ 15%		1.96		1.44
Retailer cost		15.00		11.04
40% retail margin		10.00		7.36
Consumer price		25.00		18.40

2. It can consider marginal cost pricing for exports if it has excess capacity that is expected to continue. This would allow exports to increase profits as long as more attractive domestic opportunities do not arise.

3. It can try to shorten the distribution channel, for example, by selling direct to wholesalers or large retailers. Each step in the channel costs the firm something extra. Whether elimination of certain steps lowers costs for the exporting firm depends on how well it can perform the functions eliminated.

4. It can modify the product to make it cheaper. A stripped-down model and smaller sizes or packaging are ways to achieve this. The company may also try to change the product for a lower duty classification.

5. It can consider foreign manufacturing, assembly, or licensing as ways to tap foreign markets, avoiding many of the steps that inflate export prices. Although foreign manufacturing involves greater commitment, it could be the most profitable method if markets are large enough.

Impact of Exchange-Rate Fluctuations

Currency instability presents one of the central challenges to a firm in its price-setting efforts in international markets. Table 14–2 shows how major currencies changed value against each other over the period of February 1998 to February 1999. The U.S. dollar lost value against every currency in the table except the British pound, while the Japanese yen gained in value against every currency in the table, appreciating as much as 11 percent against the British pound. The British pound was notably weak, perhaps because it had opted to stay out of the Euro zone. The Euro is the common currency being adopted by most of the European Union members, which explains the relative stability of the mark, the lira, and the franc against each other as these countries align their economic policies more closely to support a common currency.

As can be seen in Table 14–2, U.S. exporters, while maintaining their U.S. dollar prices constant, have seen their products available for 4 to 11 percent against their major international trade partners. Normal price elasticities should cause

TABLE 14–2	Potential Effects of Currency Movements on Sales Prices Percentage Changes in Exchange Rates, February 1998 to February 1999

	France	*Germany*	*Italy*	*Japan*	*Switzerland*	*U.K.*	*United States*
France	—						
Germany	+0.4	—					
Italy	–0.1	–0.5	—				
Japan	+5.6	+5.2	+5.7	—			
Switzerland	–1.2	–1.6	–1.1	–6.5	—		
U.K.	–6.1	–6.5	–6.0	–11.1	–4.9	—	
United States	–4.8	–5.2	–4.7	–10.7	–3.5	+1.6	—

Source: Derived from exchange rates published in *The Economist*, February 6, 1999, 109.
Table is read as follows: Germany's currency gained 0.4 percent against the French currency; thus, the French franc lost 0.4 percent against the deutsche mark. Similarly, the U.S. dollar lost 4.8 percent against the French franc, and the French franc gained 4.8 percent against the U.S. dollar.

demand for their products to rise. By the same token, Japanese, French, German, Italian, and Swiss exporters face loss of market share for products exported to the United States as the exchange-related price rise will reduce demand for their products. Within the European Union, Italy and the United Kingdom saw their currencies depreciate against the stronger deutsche mark (DM) and French franc (FF). Given the European Single Market, this meant that British and Italian producers could grab market share in competition against German and French suppliers, without barriers such as customs duties and border controls. The British pound was the weakest currency during the period, falling in value against every other currency in the table, including the weak U.S. dollar. Table 14–2 clearly demonstrates that a world of volatile and fluctuating exchange rates results in unexpected price rises and declines, even though exporters may not have changed list prices in their domestic currencies.

The data from Table 14–2 present an interesting decision for exporters. The average Japanese exporter faces an 11 percent price rise for its goods when sold to the United States. It may lose some sales because of this price increase, and it might want to consider lowering its yen price so that the price increase in U.S. dollars is less than the total 11 percent appreciation of the yen against the dollar. Conversely, the U.S. exporter to Japan has the option of passing on the full 11 percent decline in the value of the dollar in the form of a price cut in yen, or allow the U.S. dollar price to rise somewhat, retaining some of the windfall gains from the appreciation of the yen. The U.S. exporter has to decide whether to gain market share or to increase its profit, while the Japanese exporter's problem is to choose between losing U.S. market share or sacrificing some profit to retain U.S. customers.

In their global marketing efforts to hedge against exchange-rate fluctuations, multinationals have developed some practical solutions (see "Global Marketing," "Using European Currency Units to Reduce Foreign-Exchange Risk."):[8]

◆ Reduce the time lag between order fulfillment and payment receipt to reduce exposure of accounts receivables; similarly, reduce payables exposure with timely payment.

◆ Since hedging is costly, consider balancing receipts in one currency with equal amounts of payables in that currency; that is, balance sales in a country with equal amounts of supplier sourcing in that country.

GLOBAL MARKETING

Using European Currency Units to Reduce Foreign-Exchange Risk

Mattel is a vertically integrated toy company that manufactures about 70 percent of its needs in Asia, with the remaining 30 percent coming from Mexico for the U.S. market and from Italy for the European market. The manufacturing units bill in dollars, and the marketing units must then decide how to hedge their dollar payables against receipts in their local currencies. In Europe, however, Mattel allows the Italian manufacturing subsidiary to bill in European currency units (ECUs), while also allowing it to borrow in ECUs for its working capital needs. The European marketing units thus owe ECU payables, but European currencies fluctuate against each other within a narrow band; hence, their exchange-rate volatility is reduced because their domestic European currencies will fluctuate only slightly against the ECU.

A similar ECU orientation is used by Eurocontrol, the European intergovernmental agency that is in charge of European airspace. It bills for use and then distributes the revenues to the member states whose airspace has been used. The revenues are also used to pay for air traffic control systems. Users are billed based on how many airspace service units they used on each flight, with a per unit charge established each year in

dollars. As the dollar started fluctuating against European currencies, however, Eurocontrol moved to adjust the unit rate each month, which led to wildly varying unit rates: from $37.47 per unit in 1984 to a peak of $49.08 in 1987, then gradually declining. Hence, Eurocontrol decided that as of July 1989, the ECU would be used as the basis for pricing service units and as the currency of billing and payment.

Of course, using ECUs reduces volatility as long as the European currencies fluctuate against each other in a narrow band. In 1992, the European monetary system collapsed, with several currencies including the pound sterling and the lira having to be devalued significantly against the strong D-mark. As the European economies settle into a trading range, however, ECU-based pricing may seem to be the right choice.

A recent development is the move to a single European currency as part of the European Monetary Union. When the EMU comes to pass, it will simplify operations within the EU as foreign-exchange fluctuations within it will disappear. However, while there is considerable enthusiasm for the EMU in Brussels, national politicians are loath to give up control of their monetary and fiscal policy to the bureaucrats in Brussels. Moreover, for a country to enter the EMU, it needs to put its fiscal and monetary house in order, covering inflation rates, budget deficits, and total public debt to GDP. Very few of the EU member nations qualify to become part of the EMU under these conditions.

Sources: "Mattel: Wedding FX Management with Global Intercompany Pricing," *Business International Money Report*, March 25, 1991; and "Eurocontrol: A Model for Using the ECU in International Transactions," *Business International Money Report*, September 3, 1990.

Commodity hedges—owning commodities whose world price in local currency will go up following a devaluation—can be a hedge against local currency financial asset exposure. Similarly, real asset investments, such as in land or plant, can be a hedge in an inflation/devaluation scenario.

♦ Hedge longer-term exposure, although the cost of hedging goes up with the period of coverage desired.

♦ Reassess sourcing decisions to switch to suppliers in weaker currencies, when appropriate. This includes the possibility of switching internal sourcing to plants located in weaker currency countries.

♦ Increase marketing in countries with strong currencies.

♦ Assess how exchange-rate volatility affects competition. Which competitors are in a stronger or weaker market position, and how might they take advantage of this? Will they seek market share or higher profits?

Export Price Quotations

The base foreign-market price described in the previous section was a consumer price. Here we consider the price and terms to the importer-buyer, who is usually the final buyer insofar as the exporter is concerned.

Currency of Quotation

A first question concerns the currency used for the price quotation. The U.S. firm quotes in U.S. dollars domestically and would like to do the same on exports. Quoting dollar prices is less risky for the exporter and easier. Two other aspects have more influence on the choice of currency for quotation. First, importers prefer all quotations in their own currency for easier comparison of the offers of various foreign and national suppliers. Second, both exporters and importers worry about the foreign exchange risk. If the importers' currency is susceptible to devaluation or depreciation, they would prefer the price quote in their own currency so that on the due date of their invoice, they will not have to pay a larger number of francs or lira for a given dollar amount. Similar reasoning lies behind U.S. exporters' preference for a dollar quote: Exporters do not want to receive fewer dollars when payment is finally made.

Assume, for example, that a U.S. exporter has a shipment for France worth $10,000, or 70,000 French francs, with payment due in 90 days in francs. If the French franc depreciates by 15 percent during that period, the importer will still pay 70,000 francs, but this now translates into only $8,500. In this case, the exporter has a big loss. Conversely, if the quote had been in dollars, the importer would still pay only $10,000, but this would now cost him 80,500 francs instead of 70,000. The importer would be the loser. Although each party could hedge its position in the forward exchange market, hedging has a cost.

How is the conflict resolved? The choice of currency for the price quotation depends partly on trade practice in the country and industry in question, but also partly on the bargaining position of the parties. In a buyer's market, the exporter will be anxious for sales and will tend to yield to the importer's desires. In a seller's market, the situation will be reversed.

Since 1973, most major currencies have been floating, so exchange-rate changes are a daily occurrence. Export pricing has consequently received much more management attention. Companies have adapted in several ways to pricing with floating exchange rates:

1. Decision making becomes more centralized; headquarters exercises more control.

2. Sources of supply and prices to customers are more tightly controlled.

3. Credit terms are cut back.

4. There is more hedging, and there are more renegotiation clauses in long-term contracts.

5. Price lists are reviewed more frequently.

6. More sales are on a "spot price" basis—the firm uses the exchange rate on the day of order.

The advent of the Euro, a single European currency, means that exchange risks in intra-European transactions disappear, while possibly reducing the volatility of the Euro against the dollar, making international trade less subject to exchange rate fluctuations. A recent study considered differences in currency choice across countries. Factors affecting currency choice include avoidance of exchange rate exposure, relative bargaining power, predicted currency strength or weakness, market conditons, industry practices and competition. After considering these factors, Samiee and Anckar divided the relevant factors into firm-level and market-based factors:

Variables Affecting Currency Choice in Export Transactions

Firm-Level Factors	*Market-based Factors*
Customer Orientation	Competition
Bargaining Power	Relative Importance of Product to Customer
Product Differentiation	Product Characteristics—Commoditization, Customization
Relative Price Control	
Relative Importance of Customer	
Firm and Transaction Characteristics	
Long-term Nature of Relationship	

Source: Derived from S. Samiee and P. Anckar, "Currency Choice in Industrial Pricing: A Cross-National Evaluation," *Journal of Marketing* 62 (July 1998): 112–127.

Export Price Quotations Defined

Export price quotations are more complex than those used in domestic selling. It is important for exporters to ensure agreement on the exact meaning of the terms being used so that they and their importers both know their respective duties and liabilities. See Table 14–3 for a listing of terms.

Price quotations are important because they spell out the legal responsibilities of each party. Sellers favor a quote that gives them the least liability and responsibility, such as free on board (FOB) their plant. In this case, both the exporters' responsibility and liability end when the goods are put on a carrier at their plant. Importer-buyers, on the other hand, favor a cost, insurance, and freight to port of discharge (CIF) price, which means that their responsibilities begin only when the goods are in their own country. Importers favor CIF pricing also because it facilitates price comparisons of different exporting nations and of national suppliers.

Generally, a market orientation indicates CIF (port of importation) pricing by the exporter. Note that the price quotation does not affect the total amount paid or received but merely indicates the division of labor in providing for various transportation, handling, and insurance arrangements. It may be that the total burden of these arrangements is lessened when exporters and importers do what they are most qualified to do. Exporters deal with their fellow nationals in arranging transportation to the port, insurance, and overseas shipping, whereas importers would deal with their compatriots in the unloading and transportation in their country. Occasionally, the importer is a large international organization—one of the Japanese trading companies, for example—that is better qualified to handle insurance and transportation than the exporter. That importer can gain economies of scale by taking these tasks out of the exporters' hands.

Raising Prices Because of Exchange-Rate Changes

Figure 14–3 illustrates how nations have dealt in the past with appreciation of their currencies. The graph in the top portion of the figure shows the extent to which price increases were less than or greater than exchange-rate appreciation. Although countries such as the United Kingdom, France, and Canada had increased their prices by more than the rate of exchange-rate appreciation, Japan had passed on only about half of the appreciation of the yen in the form of a price rise. Japanese exporters were willing to retain market share by absorbing some of the impact of yen appreciation.

The bottom graph in the figure relates price increases to increases in a country's unit labor cost, which is an important element of total costs. On this basis, too,

TABLE 14–3	Export Price Quotations

I.   Ex (point of origin)
        Ex factory, ex mine, ex warehouse, and so on
II.   FOB(free on board)
        1. FOB (named inland carrier)
        2. FOB freight allowed to (named point of exportation)
        3. FOB vessel (named port of shipment)
        4. FOB (named inland point in country of importation)
III.   FAS (free alongside)
        1. FAS vessel (named port of shipment)
IV.   C &F (cost and freight)
        1. C & F (named point of destination)
V.   C.I.F. (cost, insurance, freight)
        1. C.I.F. (named point of destination)

Japan did not raise its export prices by the full amount of cost increases, but only by about 60 percent, absorbing about 40 percent. If in fact prices of imports are being raised because of exchange-rate appreciation, this presents a golden opportunity for companies from countries with weak exchange rates to grab or regain market share by keeping their prices constant and thus gaining a price advantage.

Figure 14–4 shows how U.S. car prices evolved in relation to prices of their foreign competitors over the 1980–87 period, a time when the Japanese yen, after years of weakness was steadily gaining strength. The prices of imported autos went up over the 1980–1985 period even though the dollar was gaining strength. The voluntary quotas on Japanese autos led Japanese car manufacturers to ship more expensive models, creating the price rise. In response, U.S. auto manufacturers had two choices: Keep prices steady and attempt to win back market share, or raise prices in lockstep with the Japanese. As Figure 14–4 shows, U.S. auto price increases kept step with import prices through 1985, when the dollar reached its peak. After that, import prices rose faster than domestic car prices, as the foreign currencies appreciated against the dollar, giving U.S. cars a relative price advantage.

Combining the insights from Figures 14–3 and 14–4 we can surmise that Japanese price strategy was to match domestic price trends when the dollar was strengthening but to absorb some of yen price appreciation when the dollar began weakening. In sum, the Japanese prefer to hold onto market share rather than try to recover the full impact of any exchange-rate appreciation from their foreign customers. This strategy is relevant to firms from almost every advanced industrial nation, as in each of these countries, there are periods when their currency strengthens, followed by later periods of currency depreciation. Firms therefore constantly face the temptation to reap windfall profits when their currency weakens and the prices of their goods in the strong foreign currency is unchanged; the opposite is true when they are faced with a strong domestic currency and their choice is between raising foreign currency prices or keeping them steady and incurring losses.

Strategies for Coping with Foreign-Exchange Risk

Subaru of America (the U.S. distributor of Subaru cars) is an example of a company that was seriously affected by exchange-rate changes. It was one of the most profitable companies in the United States for over a decade. Then the yen ap-

FIGURE 14–3   **Price Increases in Relation to Rising Exchange Rate and Unit Labor Costs**

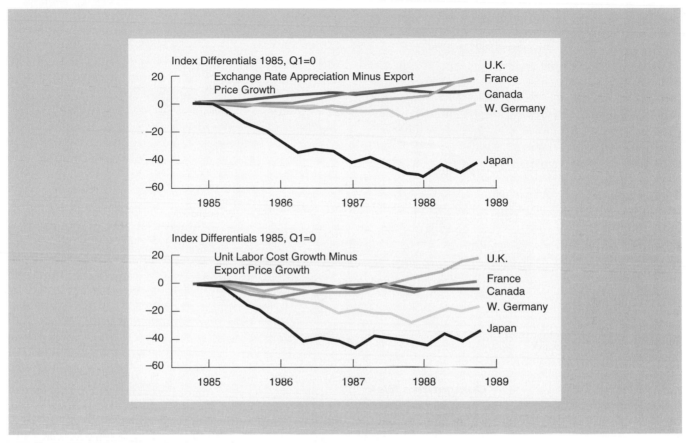

Source: Steven Strongin and Jack L. Hervey, "The Dollar Can Only Do So Much." *Chicago Fed. Letter,* October 1989.

preciated almost 50 percent against the dollar from the end of 1985 through 1987, and the dollar price of Subaru cars had to go up because of yen appreciation. Suddenly, Subaru sales dropped by over 20 percent, and it began registering large losses.

As the Subaru example shows, even highly profitable companies can be devastated by exchange-rate changes. Three areas of risk are involved: transaction risk, competitive risk, and market-portfolio risk.[9]

Transaction Risk

When a firm makes a transaction denominated in a foreign currency, it exposes itself to **transaction risk,** meaning that changes in the value of the foreign currency may diminish the financial results of the firm. For example, if a firm purchases supplies from Germany totaling 100,000 DMs, and the exchange rate is 2 DMs = \$1, the dollar value of the purchase is \$50,000. Further, if the period of credit granted is 90 days, and the DM appreciates so that the rate at the end of 90 days is 1.80 DM = \$1, the debt is now equal to \$55,556. The importer is thus required to pay more dollars, raising its costs and reducing profits. The exporter has gained by holding an asset denominated in DMs at a time when it has been appreciating against the dollar. Such transaction risk can be guarded against by hedging, through the use of forward markets, and the purchase of futures and options contracts.

FIGURE 14-4   **Auto Prices for United States and Foreign Competitors, 1980–1987**

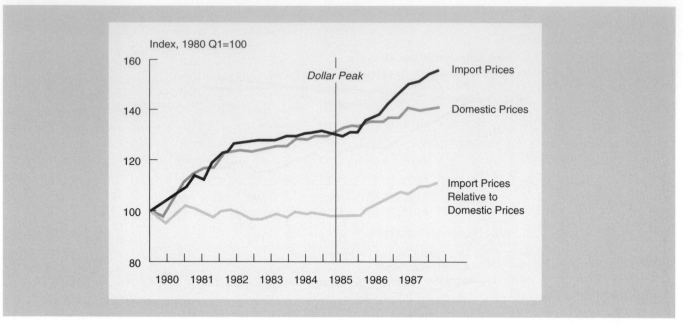

Source: Jack L. Hervey, "Dollar Drop Helps Those Who Help Themselves," *Chicago Fed. Letter,* March 1988.

Competitive Risk

The geographic pattern of a company's manufacturing and sales configuration, when compared to that of its key competitors, can cause **competitive risk** to arise. Thus, if Firm A manufactures in a country with depreciating exchange rates and sells to a country with appreciating exchange rates, it stands to gain considerable market share without raising prices. Now suppose Firm B does exactly the opposite, manufacturing in a country with appreciating exchange rates and selling to a country whose exchange rate is depreciating. In this situation, Firm A could gain market share at the expense of Firm B without having to change its prices in its own domestic currency.

Subaru's problem in 1987 stemmed from the fact that it sourced its cars from Japan and sold into the United States at a time when the dollar was weakening significantly against the yen. Thus, Subaru was influenced by the performance of two currencies, the yen and the dollar. All Japanese manufacturers importing cars from Japan for the United States had a greater competitive risk than the European car makers such as Volvo of Sweden (the kroner did not appreciate as much as the yen against the dollar).

Market-Portfolio Risk

The third kind of risk, **market-portfolio risk,** arises from a firm's export markets as compared to the country-market portfolio of its global competitors. A more diversified company, one that sold to several country markets, would not be as influenced by changes in the yen/dollar rate. Subaru of America manufactured in Japan and sold 75 percent of its cars in the United States, with the remainder going to Canada and Europe. In contrast, BMW manufactured in Germany and derived only 36 percent of its sales from the United States. Since BMW manufactured in Germany, whereas Subaru manufactured in Japan, to the extent that the mark appreciated less than the yen, BMW would be less affected by the devaluation of the dollar. This is the difference in the two companies' competitive risk.

In addition, Subaru concentrated most of its export output on the U.S. market. By putting all its eggs in one basket, therefore, it was more vulnerable to changes in the value of the yen versus the dollar. In contrast, BMW exported its output to other countries in addition to the United States, including Japan. Thus, its market-portfolio risk was different from Subaru's since its foreign revenues were not affected only by the dollar's performance. BMW has a more diversified portfolio of markets and hence faces less risk. One solution for Subaru would be to similarly diversify markets, either by selling to many more countries and/or by manufacturing in major markets. Subaru's decision to produce its new Legacy model in a U.S. plant is an example of such a solution.

Subaru, however, would not be likely to lose market share if all other car manufacturers were similarly affected. Subaru's problem was that it competed against U.S.–made subcompacts manufactured by U.S. car companies and by Japanese firms such as Mazda. In addition, imports of subcompact cars were also increasing from countries such as Brazil, Mexico, and South Korea. These countries did not have the exchange-rate disadvantage of Japanese manufacturing. In response, all of the major Japanese car companies began manufacturing cars in the United States. This changes both their competitive and their market-portfolio risk, with all of the manufacturers seeing a reduction in their exposure to yen appreciation; this decision also changed their competitive risk compared to their European competitors that did not have such U.S. manufacturing facilities.

Companywide Models for Revenue Hedging

An innovative corporatewide approach to managing the impact of volatile exchange rates is Merck's revenue hedging model, set out in Figure 14–5.

Merck's model attempts to gauge the impact of foreign-exchange volatility on Merck's long-term capital and research and development (R&D) expenditure programs. To do this, the model accepts as input the planned capital and R&D outlays and the forecasts of anticipated cash flows in multiple local currencies; it also adds forecasts of exchange rates for all the relevant currencies over a five-year planning horizon and equations that link foreign-exchange changes with forecasted earnings and cash flows. Stage 2 then simulates the impact of different hedging strategies, through the input of purchases and sales of foreign-exchange forward contracts, as well as the use of theoretical option pricing models to calculate the value of the hedges purchased. Stage 3 is the actual simulation, whereby for each iteration of estimated cash flows and forecasted foreign-exchange rates, U.S. dollar cash flows are calculated and compared to programmed expenditures. Furthermore, the statistical distribution of earnings, both hedged and unhedged, are compared under different hedging and foreign-exchange scenarios, possibly resulting in revised hedging strategies. The simulation model ends with a set of suggested hedging policies.[10]

Merck's model to cope with exchange-rate volatility has many outstanding features, including a long-term simulation approach to measuring the impact of exchange-rate volatility, the use of option pricing models to value hedged positions, and a recommended set of hedging policies as output. Last, the model is not deterministic, but instead provides executive users with a range of outcomes and a statistical probability distribution of the expected cash flows and earnings from following the recommended hedging strategies. The model is also heuristic in that it suggests new hedging strategies until a combination of strategies is found that matches simulated hedged cash flows with the amount of funds needed based on capital spending and R&D programs already committed to.

While the Merck revenue hedging model is a headquarters model intended to approach the optimum for the company as a whole, Merck is also committed to using regional and national strategies to reduce the impacts of foreign-exchange volatility. For example, during the 70s, Merck had a range of controlled assembly

FIGURE 14–5   Merck's Revenue Hedging Model

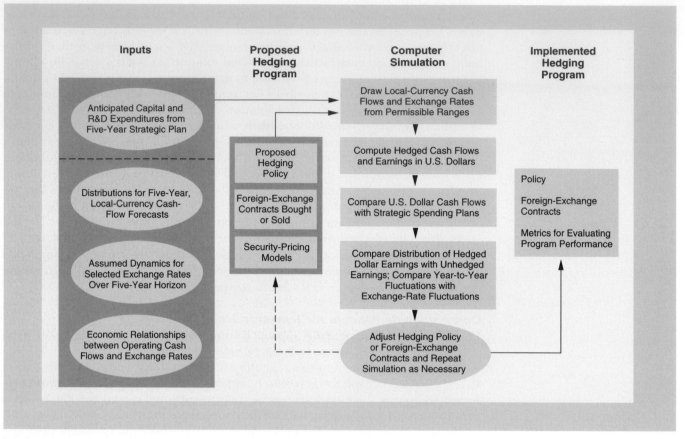

Source: Nancy A. Nichols, "Scientific Management at Merck: An Interview with CFO Judy Lewent," *Harvard Business Review* (January–February 1994), 96.

operations across Latin America that imported active chemical ingredients from Merck facilities in the United States and elsewhere and locally assembled the raw materials into tablets, capsules, and injections for local sale. During the 80s, the Latin American economic climate deteriorated, and Merck decided to pull out of manufacturing operations in Latin America. It preferred to license independent local companies who purchased the same raw materials but now assembled them into pharmaceutical tablets and capsules and then sold them in Latin American markets. Once Latin economies moved to privatization—a reining in of inflation and government deficits and a greater reliance on the private sector—Merck once again changed course, buying back the rights to the various Latin markets from its licensees and beginning to manufacture once again for its own account. Merck's example suggests that foreign-exchange rates have a deep strategic effect on long-term multinational operations.[11]

Options for Realizing Foreign-Exchange Receivables[12]

Firms with export or foreign sales often face the problem of realizing their foreign client receivables. Normal commercial credit terms when combined with additional delays in the international receivables collection process can strain a company's working capital availability. Hence, many firms, especially smaller ones, seek to accelerate foreign receivables realization. Short-term receivables may be factored; that is, factors will exchange a receivable for cash at about 85 to 90 percent of the value, particularly if the transaction has been insured by an agency such as the Eximbank (Export-Import Bank of the United States). Upon collection, the company receives the balance less the factor's commission, which may be between 1 and 3 percent.

Forfaiting is more common with longer-term receivables, such as those associated with capital goods projects. Specialized forfait companies such as London Forfaiting work with receivables guaranteed by foreign banks and governments, again charging a commission that may be around 3 percent of the transaction value. Forfaiters often work with the exporter to decide the terms of the sale so that the forfaiter's interests are covered, making the forfait agreement more likely. The exporter can then try to negotiate an export price that covers the forfaiter's commission. Forfaiters place the guarantee received from the foreign bank or government agency (known as avalizers) as an endorsement on the bill of exchange or other document evidencing the debt. This allows resale of the document on financial markets and enhances liquidity. A number of forfaited loans may be bundled together and sold on the secondary market to portfolio investors. This increases the total capacity of the world market for forfaits and reduces forfaiting commissions, making forfaiting more attractive to smaller firms. Forfaiting commission is also influenced by risk factors such as the debt rating for the debtor and its country, foreign-exchange volatility, and overall debt-service ratios. Forfaiting instruments are medium- to long-term instruments, with repayment in installments stretching over several years. The upfront fixed costs of setting up the forfait instrument and perhaps repackaging it for sale to secondary investors also sets a floor for transaction size, making forfaiting transactions economical only for large amounts over $1 million.

Export Credit and Terms

Export credit and terms constitute another complex area in pricing for the international market. The task is to choose payment terms that satisfy importers yet safeguard the interests of the exporter. On purely financial considerations, the exporter would favor very hard terms, that is, cash in advance of shipment—or even in advance of production for custom items. Because importers dislike bearing the financial burden implied in cash-in-advance terms, the exporter normally can demand prepayment only when producing merchandise to an importer's specifications.

In lieu of cash in advance, the export marketer can consider a range of terms that generally add to the convenience of the buyer while increasing the risks and financial burdens of the exporter. In order of increasing attractiveness to the *importer* are several common payment methods:

1. Cash in advance

2. Letters of credit

3. Time or sight drafts (bills of exchange)

4. Open account

5. Consignment

Letters of Credit and Drafts

Letters of credit and drafts are the most common forms of export financing. A **draft** is drawn by the exporter on the importer, who makes it into a trade acceptance by writing on it the word "accepted" and signing it. The signature makes payment a legal obligation. The **letter of credit** is similar, except that it is drawn on a bank and becomes a bank acceptance rather than a trade acceptance. The bank's entrance into the payment process means greater assurance of payment for the exporter.

The terms of both are relatively strict and favor the exporter in that they spell out specific responsibilities and payment times for the importer, although they do not preclude credit extension. For example, time drafts are customarily drawn for periods ranging from 30 to 180 days after sight or after date. The exporter usually feels more secure with a letter of credit than with a draft. It is safer for the exporter, but it is more costly for the importer to get a letter of credit.

Open Account

In **open account** sales, terms are agreed to between buyer and seller but without documents specifying clearly the importer's payment obligations. Open account terms involve less paperwork and give more flexibility to both parties. However, the legal recourse of the exporter in case of default is less satisfactory than under the methods discussed above. Open account sales are more attractive to the importer, but because of the risks to the exporter, they tend to be limited to foreign subsidiaries, joint ventures or licensees, or foreign customers with whom the exporter has had a long and favorable experience.

As a further precaution in open account sales, the exporter must consider the availability of foreign exchange in the importing country. In countries with tight foreign-exchange positions, imports covered by documentary drafts generally receive priority in foreign-exchange allocation over imports on open account.

Consignment

Since the exporter retains title until the importer sells the goods, **consignment** sales are not really sales. Because exporters own the goods longer in this method than in any other, their financial burdens and risk are greatest. In addition, legal recourse in case of misbehavior by importers and foreign-exchange allocations are more difficult to obtain. Because of these problems, exporters tend to limit consignment arrangements to their subsidiaries abroad.

When exporters want to introduce goods to a new market, a consignment arrangement might be necessary to encourage importers to handle the new merchandise. Furthermore, if exporters wish to retain some control over the foreign market price, this is most feasible under a consignment contract. They can set the price when they own the goods, as they do under a consignment contract.

FINANCING INTERNATIONAL SALES: A COMPONENT OF INTERNATIONAL PRICING

The terms of financing determine the final effective price paid by a buyer. If the cost of capital is 12 percent per year, and a buyer is allowed to pay its bill in 90 days, this 90 days' free credit amounts to a 3 percent discount on the purchase price. When products from international competitors are perceived as being reasonably similar, the purchaser may choose the supplier that provides the best financing terms resulting in the greatest effective discount. Thus, when Embraer, a Brazilian manufacturer of small aircraft, wanted to introduce its 19-seat commuter plane to the United States, it offered long-term (six years or more) financing at around 8 percent. Because it was a state-owned enterprise, it could guarantee the availability of such credit. Fairchild Aircraft, a U.S. competitor, filed an "unfair trade practices" complaint with the U.S. International Trade Commission because of this low-interest-rate financing, offered at a time when U.S. interest rates were around 12 percent.[13]

Without government help, U.S. firms might find it impossible to offer the necessary financing. Ellicott Machine Corporation of Baltimore could not have sold its dredges to the former Yugoslavia without such help. It had bid on a project to supply a dredge to mine coal near the Danube River, but the customer needed financing. Ellicott was able to get a State of Maryland guarantee from the Maryland Industrial Development Financing Authority and was thus able to offer 100 percent financing. Further, with the help of the Maryland Office of International Trade, it was able to get a Maryland State grant to offer training to customer personnel. This led to scholarships at the University of Maryland to train Yugoslav engineers in disciplines relevant to the project. Such government help led to an initial contract of $25 million awarded to Ellicott, with add-ons possible that could total nearly $100 million.[14]

To successfully use financing as a competitive weapon in international marketing, two conditions are typically necessary. The firm must have the ability to fund the long-term receivables at below-market interest rates; this condition usually favors state-owned enterprises and larger multinationals, which can borrow at lower rates and in countries where borrowing costs are low. Second, official government backing to subsidize the lower interest rates offered, as well as guarantee the loans, is necessary to match the best offers made by international competitors. Without government guarantees, private (U.S.) banks will not make the loan, and without a government subsidy, below-market rates cannot be offered. Several nations have an established policy of offering such favorable financing as part of packages designed to promote exports from their countries.

A related problem for U.S. firms is the relative lack of interest on the part of commercial banks in trade finance. Banks can make as much money on residential mortgages as they can on government-guaranteed export loans. Making export loans is also a labor-intensive business, requiring manager expertise. As a result, several large money-center banks have deliberately reduced their trade finance activities. Firms must therefore turn to the branches of foreign banks that may be interested primarily in financing exports to countries near their home base or certain geographic areas deemed to be in their strategic interest.[15] A stunted U.S. institutional structure for trade finance is an obstacle that U.S. firms face in the global competition for markets. And subsidized financing from other nations rubs salt in the wound.

Twenty-two industrialized countries met in the early 1980s to limit such credit subsidies, and the result was an agreement that specified minimum interest rates and maximum repayment periods for most categories of exports sold on credit terms of over two years.[16] However, a loophole is the use of **tied aid,** in which foreign aid is granted with the condition that a portion of the aid be used to buy goods from the aid-granting country. Thus, an exporter seeking a sale of $1 million might be able to allow the importer to use $100,000 of aid granted by the exporter's government to pay for part of the sale. This way, the exporter is offering a price cut of $100,000, or 10 percent, which is equivalent in effect to a direct interest rate or price subsidy. A 1989 Eximbank study estimated that $400 million to $800 million in potential U.S. exports were being lost because of tied aid in industries such as telecommunications, electric power systems, computers, and heavy earth-moving vehicles. Countries such as Canada, France, Germany, Italy, Britain, and Japan account for about 75 percent of all such credits.

While decrying such practices, the United States has, in self-defense, begun providing some tied aid on a limited scale. Yet the United States accounted for only about 2 percent of the world volume of tied aid. Eximbank is the main U.S. financing agency for international trade.

Other forms of government-supported trade development can help a firm make international sales. The U.S. Trade Development Agency offers funding to carry out market feasibility studies when matched with private funds. Thus, ABB Lummus of New Jersey obtained $300,000 in funds to study the feasibility of modernizing the Lukoil oil refinery in Russia; with the study complete, Lukoil signed contracts for over $21 million for U.S. technology licenses and engineering services.

As suggested above, governments routinely offer "tied aid" as a means of export promotion. A Government Accounting Office study noted that OECD nations typically tied over half of their capital project aid to purchases from the donor countries' firms. Compared to tied-aid percentages as high as 91 percent for Germany, 76 percent for Japan, and 73 percent for France, U.S. tied aid represented only 17 percent of capital project commitments over the 1988 to 1991 period.[17] In response, the U.S. Eximbank set up a war chest to counter other nations' tied-aid subsidies and was funded with $200 million in 1993, with Eximbank disbursing war chest funds equal to about 30 percent of export value over the 1987 to 1993 period.

Transfer Pricing in International Marketing

Transfer pricing (intracorporate pricing) is an area that has special implications for international marketing. It refers to prices on goods sold within the corporate family, that is, from division to division or to a foreign subsidiary. (See "Global Marketing," "Transfer Pricing at Hewlett-Packard.")

Product Division to International Division

The transfer price paid by the international group to the producing division should have certain characteristics if it is to optimize corporate, rather than divisional, profit. For the producing division, the price should be high enough to encourage a flow of products for export. The transfer price does this if sales to the international division are as attractive as sales to other parties. The price to the international division may be even lower than to other parties if the services the international division renders (market research, promotion, and so on) warrant this.

For the international division, the transfer price should be low enough to enable it to be both competitive and profitable in the foreign market. Obviously, there is room for conflict here. The producing division wants a high price, and the international division wants a low price. The transfer pricing mechanism must be such that the overall corporate interest is not ignored in the divisional conflict. Quite possibly a profit margin that is unattractive to one or the other division, or to both, might be worthwhile from the overall corporate viewpoint.

Assume that the producing division makes a product at a full cost of $50. It sells this to outside buyers for $60, but the transfer price to the international division is $58. The producing division may be unhappy because the markup is 20 percent lower to the international division ($8 versus $10). The international division adds its various export marketing expenses of $10 for an export cost of $68. For competitive reasons, the international division cannot sell the product for more than $72, or a $4 return. Since this is less than 6 percent of sales, the international division is also unhappy. However, the return to the corporation is $12 on $72, or almost 17 percent ($8 from the producing division plus $4 from the international division). The corporation may find this attractive, even though both divisions are unhappy with it.

Different approaches can be taken to solve this problem. One solution is to eliminate one division or the other as a profit center. The producing division can be judged on the basis of costs and other performance criteria instead of profit. Then it can sell to the international division at a price enabling the latter to be competitive in foreign markets. Market pricing will not be handicapped by their internal markups of the transfer pricing process, and the total corporate profit will be given greater attention.

On the other hand, the international division can operate as a service center rather than as a profit center, thus eliminating one source of conflict. A question arises, however, about whether a selling organization can be as efficient and as motivated when it is not operating under a profit constraint. A related possibility is to have the international division act as a commission agent for the producing divi-

GLOBAL MARKETING

Transfer Pricing at Hewlett-Packard

Transfer pricing plays a key role in coordinating numerous and distant profit centers at Hewlett-Packard (IIP), a multinational firm that gets over half of its sales from outside the United States. HP's transfer pricing objectives include (1) motivating local managers who wish to show large profits, (2) minimizing the chances of a tax audit, and (3) moving profits to low-tax jurisdictions while satisfying tax authorities of the business reasons for such moves. HP's accounting and finance manual describes the basis for transfer pricing, using either a list price minus a discount or a cost-plus method. HP typically uses cost plus 10 percent as the desired company rate of return. The U.S. Internal Revenue Service (IRS) generally advises corporations to base transfer pricing markups on a return on assets method.

HP believes, however, that such a return on assets method is more appropriate to capital-intensive and machinery-based industries; HP and other high-tech companies spend an enormous amount on R&D, which is often expensed. Thus, capital assets may be understated. Hence, HP argues that using a cost-plus method allows adequate return to R&D. HP's tax department breaks down the profit from each product line and shows how it is allocated among R&D, manufacturing, and sales.

To avoid ongoing conflicts with the IRS over transfer pricing, however, HP has considered whether to adhere to the new IRS approach to transfer pricing, called advanced determination rulings (ADR). The ADR method suggests that companies submit proposed transfer pricing plans to it to determine whether they comply with IRS regulations rather than wait for an audit to rule on the acceptability of a formula already in use. However, HP believes that the ADR approach needs to be modified to make it more attractive. Several areas of concern exist:

1. The amount of detailed information and economic analysis required by the IRS; HP found this burden to be as great as the requirements of a tax audit.
2. The financial information disclosed might become available to competitors.
3. The information submitted would later be used by other parts of the IRS in a tax audit. HP wanted the department carrying out the ADR to be in a different jurisdiction from the one doing previous years' tax audits. Similarly, HP wanted IRS agents involved in the ADR to agree not to disclose information gained from the ADR to agents conducting an audit.

Given the importance of transfer pricing, ADRs look promising, especially because other countries such as Japan and Germany use them, and bilateral agreements are being developed. Under bilateral agreements between two countries, the results of one country's ADR investigations would be accepted in the other country.

Sources: "Hewlett-Packard: Making Transfer Pricing Work," *Business International,* November 12, 1990; and "Hewlett-Packard: Jousting with the IRS over Transfer Prices," *Business International Money Report,* June 11, 1990.

---

sions. When the international division is not a profit center, its expenses can be allocated back to the product divisions.

Transfer pricing can be established in three ways: at manufacturing cost, at arm's length, and at cost-plus.

Transfer at Manufacturing Cost

When profit centers are maintained, several alternatives are possible. At one extreme, and favoring the international division, is the transfer at direct manufacturing cost. This would be the lowest cost, probably well under what the producing division could obtain from other customers. The producing division dislikes selling at manufacturing cost because it believes it is subsidizing the international division and thereby taking a loss when compared with other profit centers. The firm may offset this by an accounting or memorandum profit to the producing division on its sales for export. Such memorandum profits, unfortunately, are never as satisfactory as the real thing. When the product division is unhappy, the international division may get sluggish service because the product division is servicing more attractive domestic opportunities first.

GLOBAL MARKETING

Tuna Prices in Japan: Price and Value

As connoisseurs of fish, the Japanese are finicky about the quality of the raw fish used to make *sashimi*, a national favorite. Tuna is one of the major fish varieties commonly used in *sashimi*, and both yellowfin and bigeye tuna are found in quantity off the coast of Australia in the Coral Sea. The Australians have been encouraged to export chilled fresh tuna to Japan for consumption raw as *sashimi*. Chilled tuna must be exported by air, but auction prices in Japan are attractive: about A$80 (Australian dollar) per kilogram (in 1987) in Japan, versus A$1 per kilogram in Australia. The economic incentive is clearly high. Australian exports of such tuna have been low, however, even while Japanese fishing boats have been active in these waters.

It seems that the Australian fishing industry was discouraged by the high variation in prices received at the Tokyo fish auctions, and this led them to believe that Japanese auction buyers colluded to keep Australian imported fish out of the market and hence favor the Japanese fishing fleet in the Coral Sea. Australian researchers, therefore, meticulously studied auction prices for 27 days in October 1985, attempting to relate prices (in yen per kilogram) to factors such as fish meat color, freshness, condition (degree of carcass dam-

age, bruises, etc.), weight of the whole fish, and origin (whether the tuna was caught in the waters off Japan, the Philippines, Taiwan, or Australia). Since *sashimi* is eaten raw, consumers are willing to pay more for "good" meat color, such as the absence of a concentration of red meat pigments in the flesh of the tuna. They also want the freshest fish possible. (The degree of freshness can be measured by the presence of breakdown products, such as adenosine triphosphate, which increase with length of time.)

Aside from the importance of freshness and color, the study found that auction prices were lower for bigeye tuna caught in non-Japanese waters. However, research could not determine the reason. Bigeye tuna have high fat content, and one possibility was that the food organisms found in the particular feeding grounds off the waters of Taiwan or the Philippines may be absorbed into the fat, yielding flavors that are less acceptable to the discerning Japanese palate. The main conclusion of the study, however, was that Japanese consumers choose raw fish for their *sashimi* on the basis of its appearance. Hence, buyers at auctions are willing to pay more for tuna that has good color. The implication, then, is that the Australians must select tuna of the requisite freshness and meat color for export to the chilled tuna auction in Tokyo if they want to get high prices.

The researchers also found that although the Tokyo market accounted for nearly 60 percent of all chilled bigeye tuna sold in Japan, two other markets, Nagoya and Osaka,

Transfer at Arm's Length

The other extreme in transfer pricing is to charge the international division the same price any buyer outside the firm pays. This price favors the producing division because it does as well on internal as on external sales, or even better. The services rendered by the international division and the elimination of the credit problem can make export sales especially profitable.

If the product has no external buyers, however, a problem occurs in trying to determine an arm's-length price. An artificial price must be constructed. Further difficulties arise because such a price fails to take into account the services performed by the international division and because the international division may be noncompetitive with such a price. Finally, there is no real reason that the price to foreign buyers should be determined by the domestic market.

Transfer at Cost-Plus

Between the transfer pricing extremes just discussed is a range of prices that involves a profit split between the producing and international divisions. Starting from the cost floor, cost-plus pricing attempts to add on some amount or percentage that will make the resulting price acceptable to both divisions. The "plus" may

accounted for about 40 percent of all chilled yellowfin tuna, as compared to the Tokyo market's 16 percent. Thus, the Australians were erroneously concentrating on the Tokyo market alone because of lack of information.

The market for tuna in Japan may be of little interest to most people. The principle that emerges from the study, however, is important: The price that people are willing to pay for a product depends on the value perceived. Careful market research can uncover what consumers in different countries look for in a product. The price set for a particular country market must be appropriate to the value delivered in that market if the company wishes to avoid over- or underpricing the product.

Another Australian study focused on prices paid in Japan for wild shrimp exported from Australia to Japan. Wild shrimp are harvested at sea and used to be sold primarily to high-priced Japanese restaurants. Then, Taiwanese research led to the cultivation of pond-reared, high-yield shrimp similar in taste to the Japanese *kuruma ebi,* which is a favorite among Japanese consumers, with about 25 to 30 shrimp per pound. The lower shrimp prices resulting from pond culture and higher yields increased Japanese demand considerably, with Japanese homemakers now buying shrimp for home cooking and consumption. In 1990, Japan imported 287,000 tons of shrimp valued at $3.6 billion.

A direct consequence was that new producers, such as shrimp farmers from Vietnam, entered the market, and wild shrimp prices began dropping. Australian wild-shrimp fishing costs increased, while prices for their catch dropped 25 percent in Tokyo. Even so, wild shrimp prices were double farmed shrimp prices. While connoisseurs could distinguish between wild and farm shrimp, few consumers could, especially since shrimp is often cooked in spicy sauces, further masking the taste.

Australian shrimp producers began considering an advertising campaign to build up a brand image for Australian shrimp, stressing that it was wild shrimp, harvested at sea in clean, cold, unpolluted waters, and that it had a distinctive and superior taste. The question was whether the expense of an advertising campaign could lead to a differentiated image for Australian shrimp and convince Japanese consumers that Australian-origin shrimp justified a higher price. The Australian producers also considered other alternatives, including switching their export focus to less competitive markets in the United States and Europe; this would further reduce Australian market share in Japan, because Japanese shrimp dealers would not look kindly on suppliers who walked away from long-standing business arrangements. Another alternative was to form a Japanese distribution joint venture and sell directly to higher-priced Japanese restaurants whose chefs might be willing to pay higher prices for larger and more distinctive-tasting shrimp.

Sources: Stephen C. Williams and John W. Longworth, "Factors Influencing Tuna Prices in Japan and Implications for the Development of the Coral Sea Tuna Fishery," *European Journal of Marketing* 23, no. 3 (1989); and Steve C. Williams, "Prospects for Promotion of 'Wild' Shrimp in Japan: Implications for Australian Exporters," *European Journal of Marketing* 26, no. 10 (1992).

be a percentage negotiated between the divisions, a percentage of product division overhead, or a percentage return on product division investment. Further variation can be caused by using different definitions of cost. In any case, the pricing formula is less important than the results obtained. A good transfer pricing formula should consider total corporate profit and encourage divisional cooperation. It should also minimize executive time spent on transfer price disagreements and keep the accounting burden to a minimum.

Other factors affecting the transfer price charged include the existence of restrictions on capital outflows from a market, the level of customs tariffs in each market, and whether the two transacting parties are both wholly owned by the firm, or whether one of the two entities is a licensee, a joint-venture, or a minority-owned partner.

The Tax Authority's Interest

When countries have different levels of taxation on corporate profits, firms may wish to accumulate profits in countries with low taxes. They would like to use a low transfer price to subsidiaries in low-tax countries and a high transfer price to subsidiaries in high-tax countries. U.S. companies, for example, are tempted to sell at low transfer prices to countries that have lower corporate tax rates than the United States. The IRS, however, is on guard against this because it does not want to lose taxable income to other countries. Therefore, it carefully scrutinizes the transfer prices of international companies to ensure that they are not too low. One specific demand of the IRS is that export prices bear a share of domestic R&D expenses. The IRS wants to be sure that an equitable portion of the income remains under U.S. tax jurisdiction. Transfer pricing cases can drag on for years and hence corporations and the IRS have begun establishing procedures whereby the firm sets out the transfer pricing scheme it wishes to pursue and tries to get the IRS to agree that such a scheme results in a fair price. At the same time, the firms are anxious to prevent too much sensitive financial information from being handed over to the IRS. Similar problems confront firms using transfer pricing in other tax jurisdictions, especially when the tax authorities of various countries begin to share transfer pricing data and attempt joint regulation of transfer pricing.

SUMMARY

Pricing in international markets is affected by the firm's strategic objectives, competitive behavior, consumers' ability to buy, the product life-cycle stage, and market-specific environmental considerations such as government regulation.

Export prices should be set so that export sales are at least as rewarding as other sales outlets. Export sales prices may be less than domestic prices because of the additional costs involved and the need to keep the final consumer price affordable. Export prices in the short run can be set at just above marginal cost, though this could invite government accusations of dumping. Shipping and insurance costs, tariffs, market-specific taxes such as VAT, and distributor markups all add to the cost of exported products.

Exchange-rate fluctuations can affect consumer prices, too. Offsetting such fluctuations may entail the sacrifice of profit margins to maintain market share. Quoting prices in a firm's domestic currency may seem to avoid exchange-rate–related problems. Whether buyers will accept such quotes, however, depends on the relative strength of demand and supply, as well as competitive behavior. Export price quotations specify which services, such as shipping, insurance, and documentation, are included in the quoted price.

When currencies appreciate, firms often raise prices by less than the amount of appreciation. Japanese firms are prone to such pricing behavior. Exchange-rate risk can be classified into transaction risk, competitive risk, and market-portfolio risk; each of these risks suggests different strategic actions.

How sales are financed is crucial to winning export orders. Hence, financing terms and conditions form an integral part of international pricing policies. Government help to exporters often comes in the form of subsidies that allow the firm to offer below-market rates of interest on customer receivables, thus offering a hidden price discount.

Transfer pricing becomes relevant when a product division in one country supplies another division located in a foreign market. Transfer prices must be set so that they yield a satisfactory profit but are not high enough to discourage sales.

Common transfer pricing formulas are based on arm's-length market prices, cost-plus pricing, negotiated prices, and transfers at cost with shared profits. In all cases, motivation is as important as the profit accruing to each division.

Governments often intervene in international transfer pricing to ensure that prices are not set so low as to avoid taxes. Customs authorities may set a floor on the transfer price to prevent tariff avoidance.

QUESTIONS

14.1 What are some of the major factors affecting international pricing? In particular, how are prices influenced by the firm's strategy, its competition, consumers' ability to buy, the firm's cost and market structure, and the complete product line?

14.2 What should be the relationship between export and domestic prices?

14.3 What are the consequences of charging an export price below the domestic market price?

14.4 Are there reasons why export prices should be higher than domestic prices? What are the marketing implications of export price escalation?

14.5 How do exchange rates affect international pricing? Why might a firm with an appreciating currency not raise its export prices?

14.6 Is quoting export prices only in the firm's domestic currency a viable strategy to avoid the impact of exchange rates?

14.7 What are the different ways in which export prices can be quoted?

14.8 What are the different risks that a firm marketing its products internationally faces because of exchange-rate fluctuations? How might it cope with these categories of risk?

14.9 How and why are export credit financing terms and conditions relevant to international pricing?

14.10 How can governments help in financing international sales?

14.11 What is transfer pricing? Why is it taken into consideration in international pricing?

14.12 What are some useful formulas in setting transfer prices?

14.13 Why do the tax authorities of both the parent country and the host country concern themselves with transfer prices? How might such intervention affect the multinational corporation?

14.14 What are the factors affecting prices received for export of tuna from Australia to Japan? What generalizations concerning pricing in foreign markets may be drawn from this illustration?

ENDNOTES

[1] For reviews of pricing in the marketing mix, see Vithala R. Rao, "Pricing Research in Marketing: The State of the Art," *Journal of Business* 57 (1984); and Gerard J. Tellis, "Beyond the Many Faces of Price: An Integration of Pricing Strategies," *Journal of Marketing* 50 (October 1986).

[2] Robin Cooper and W. Bruce Chew, "Control Tomorrow's Costs through Today's Designs," *Harvard Business Review,* January–February 1996, 88–97.

[3] Boston Consulting Group, *Perspectives on Experience* (Boston: BCG, 1972); and Robert Dolan and Abel Jeuland, "Experience Curves and Dynamic Demand Models: Implications for Optimal Pricing Strategies," *Journal of Marketing,* Winter 1981.

[4] See "Note on the Motorcycle Industry," Harvard Business School Case Services, No. 578–210.

[5] John A. Boyd, "How One Company Solved Its Export Pricing Problems," *Small Business Forum,* Fall 1995, 28–38.

[6] James C. Anderson and James A. Narus, "Capturing the Value of Supplementary Services," *Harvard Business Review,* January–February 1995, 75–83.

[7] That is, $10.60 local manufacturer's price plus 12 percent VAT equals $11.87; plus 15 percent distributor markup equals $13.65; plus 40 percent retail margin on price equals $22.80. Since the import price is $25, the domestic manufacturer can undercut the import price by up to $2.20, that is, $25 minus $22.80, or $2.20.

[8] "Coping with Currency Turmoil," *Business Europe,* September 25, 1995.

[9] Staffan Hertzell and Christian Caspar, "Coping with Unpredictable Currencies," *The McKinsey Quarterly,* Summer 1988.

[10] Nancy A. Nichols, "Scientific Management at Merck: An Interview with CFO Judy Lewent," *Harvard Business Review,* January–February 1994, 89–99.

[11] "Merck Renews Its Vows," *Business Latin America,* February 6, 1995.

[12] "Congratulations, Exporter! Now about Getting Paid . . ." *Business Week,* January 17, 1994; and "Forfait," *Finance & Treasury,* July 17, 1995.

[13] Ravi Sarathy, "High-Technology Exports from Newly Industrializing Countries: The Brazilian Commuter Aircraft Industry," *California Management Review* 27, no. 2 (Winter 1985): 60–84.

[14] Peter Bowe, president, Dredge Division, Ellicott Machine Corporation, as reported in *Maryland Trader,* 1987.

[15] "Financing for Exports Grows Harder to Find," *The Wall Street Journal,* May 14, 1987.

[16] See *Trade Finance: Current Issues and Developments,* International Trade Administration (Washington, DC: U.S. Department of Commerce, November 1988), 34–43.

[17] *International Trade: Competitors' Tied Aid Practices Affect U.S. Exports* (Washington, DC: U.S. General Accounting Office, May 1994) GAO/GGD-94-81; and *Combating U.S. Competitors' Tied-Aid Practices* (May 1994), GAO/T-GGD-94-156.

FURTHER READINGS

Anderson, James C., and James A. Narus. "Capturing the Value of Supplementary Services." *Harvard Business Review,* January–February 1995, 75–83.

Arpan, Jeffrey. "International Intracorporate Pricing." *Journal of International Business Studies,* Spring 1972.

Cooper, Robin, and W. Bruce Chew. "Control Tomorrow's Costs through Today's Designs." *Harvard Business Review,* January–February 1996, 88–97.

Dolan, Robert, and Abel Jeuland. "Experience Curves and Dynamic Demand Models: Implications for Optimal Pricing Strategies." *Journal of Marketing,* Winter 1981.

Hertzell, Staffan, and Christian Caspar. "Coping with Unpredictable Currencies." *The McKinsey Quarterly,* Summer 1988.

International Trade Administration. "*Trade Finance: Current Issues and Developments.*

Washington, DC: U.S. Department of Commerce, November 1988.

Nichols, Nancy A., "Scientific Management at Merck: An Interview with CFO Judy Lewent." *Harvard Business Review,* January–February 1994, 89–99.

Rao, Vithala R. "Pricing Research in Marketing: The State of the Art." *Journal of Business* 57 (1984).

Sarathy, Ravi. "High Technology Exports from Newly Industrializing Countries: The Brazilian Commuter Aircraft Industry." *California Management Review* 27, no. 2 (Winter 1985): 60–84.

Tellis, Gerard J. "Beyond the Many Faces of Price: An Integration of Pricing Strategies." *Journal of Marketing* 50 (October 1986).

Walters, Peter G. P. "A Framework for Export Pricing Decisions." *Journal of Global Marketing* 2, no. 3 (1989).

CASE 14.1

Subaru of America*

Subaru of America (SA) distributes cars manufactured in Japan by Fuji Heavy Industries, which is itself one of Japan's smallest car manufacturers. Fuji has majority control of SA. SA had been one of the most profitable companies in the United States, as the first two tables show.

Subaru was popular for its subcompact four-wheel-drive cars that were built well and priced low. It was the first auto firm to make four-wheel drive available on a low-priced compact car. The United States was an important and profitable market for the parent Fuji company in Japan, accounting for between 32 and 35 percent of total Fuji shipments.

Subaru's U.S. sales peaked at 183,242 units in 1986. Since then, sales fell to only about 150,000 units in 1989.

Several problems contributed to the declining performance at Subaru, primarily the declining dollar. Between the latter part of 1984 and the end of 1988, the dollar declined from a peak of about 250 yen to the dollar to as low as 120 yen to the dollar in 1989 (see Table 1). Thus, dollar prices effectively doubled for a Japanese product priced in yen unless the Japanese manufacturer chose to absorb some of the effects of a rising yen.

Fuji, which controlled SA, wanted Subaru to be seen as a U.S. company with U.S. management. Its agreement was that Fuji and SA would negotiate transfer prices for each model on an annual basis. However, Fuji could renegotiate the prices based on its cost structure.

Within Japan, Fuji is one of the smaller automakers, with a limited number of models in the subcompact segment of the market. When overcapacity in Japan led to price-cutting, thus putting pressure on profits, Fuji was trapped by a series of developments:

Year (Ended October)	Net Income (Millions of Dollars)	Return on Equity
1978	$ 7.2	70%
1979	10.4	62
1980	17.7	68
1981	26.3	62
1982	39.4	59
1983	49.5	48
1984	60.0	41
1985	77.1	39
1986	94.0	35
1987	−30.0	−9
1988	−57.9	−22

Source: Subaru of America, Inc., 1988 Annual Report.

Fuji Heavy Industries Auto Exports					
	1984	1985	1986	1987	1988
Exports as percent of total sales	54.5	46.8	49.1	50.6	49.0
Exports to U.S. as percent of total sales	Not available	Not available	35.2	34.5	32.3

1. Overcapacity in Japan and slowing growth in demand for cars in Japan.
2. A swiftly appreciating yen.
3. Price cutting in Japan.
4. Increasing wage costs in Japan, as the older work force received raises based on seniority.
5. Fear of losing quotas to the United States, putting pressure on Subaru to accept cars in excess of normally sustainable demand.

Under these circumstances, Fuji chose to pass on some of the price increases forced by yen appreciation. In effect, Fuji and Subaru agreed to share the pain of a stronger yen, with each side absorbing half the price rise implied. Thus, if the yen rose by 20 percent, Fuji would raise transfer prices by 10 percent, and in turn, Subaru would not pass on the full increase in transfer prices in the form of increased U.S. car sticker prices.

Table 1 summarizes the cost of goods sold, gross margin percent, unit revenue, and total sales at Subaru, as well as the number of units sold and the changing value of the dollar against the yen. In 1986 alone, adjusting inventory values to reflect the changing value of the yen would have meant increasing the value of inventory by 97.5 percent (see Table 2).

Thus, if the FIFO (first-in first-out) method of inventory had been used, inventory values in 1986 would have been shown at $155.24 million, a 97.5 percent increase (meaning that because of yen appreciation, delivered cost in dollars had risen by that percent).

The quota system also affected Subaru's inventories. The Japanese voluntary export restraints on cars sold into the United States had limited each individual Japanese firm's unit exports to the United States; hence, most of them moved upscale, selling higher value-added and more profitable models, at higher prices. Fuji's U.S. quota had been steadily increasing: It went up from 148,000 cars in 1981 to 199,000 in 1985. If Fuji did not ship the total number of cars allowed to it under the voluntary quotas assigned to Japanese car companies by the Ministry for International Trade and Industry (MITI), it would face cuts in the quota for the ensuing year. To avoid this, Fuji shipped cars in excess of demand, with Subaru of America having to stockpile these cars in its inventory and with its dealers. By April 1988, dealer inventory had risen to 110 days, from a level of just 53 days in October 1987.

| **TABLE 1** | **Subaru of America, Inc.: Years Ended October 31, Millions of Dollars** |

	1988	*1987*	*1986*	*1985*	*1984*	*1983*	*1982*	*1981*	*1980*
Total sales	$1,673.2	$1,785.0	$1,939.3	$1,502.3	$1,174.9	$1,057.5	$977.6	$916.1	$744.2
Cost of goods sold	1,584.8	1,688.8	1,680.1	1,286.5	996.8	908.4	848.5	823.4	671.6
Gross margin	88.4	96.2	259.2	215.8	178.1	149.1	129.1	92.7	72.6
Gross margin (%)	5.28	5.39	13.37	14.36	15.16	14.10	13.21	10.12	9.76
Selling & general expenses	203.9	170.2	116.1	98.5	81.3	67.1	59.9	43.6	38.7
Net income	-57.9	-30	94	77.1	60	49.5	39.5	26.3	17.7
Cars sold (thousands)	156	177.1	183.2	178.2	157.4	156.8	150.3	152.1	143
Revenue per car	$10,726	$10,079	$10,586	$8,430	$7,464	$6,744	$6,504	$6,023	$5,204
Exchange rate: yen/ dollar	125.16	135.54	160.38	207.03	237.31	237.37	248.24	220.11	225.68

TABLE 2	Impact of Yen Appreciation on Inventory Values: Subaru of America		
	1988	*1987*	*1986*
Inventory values (LIFO, millions of dollars)	210	133.4	78.6
Percent increase in value to reflect yen appreciation (FIFO value increase)	40	57.2	97.5

The U.S. car industry was also on the brink of a recession. Over the period 1983 to 1987, more than 70 million cars and trucks had been sold in the United States, the most in any five-year period, but it was time for a pause. The 20 percent reduction in sales (from peak-year sales) that Subaru experienced may have been partly due to this weakening of demand; in comparison, Porsche sales declined over 50 percent, Jaguar's sales by 20 percent, and Mercedes-Benz by about 10 percent. Overall, auto imports were affected by the weak dollar.

Subaru's problems were compounded by a product line reaching maturity: Its models were nearly five years old, and it had to introduce newer models. In addition, it began facing competition from models such as the Jeep Cherokee and the Ford Bronco II, both U.S.-made, competitively priced, and also offering four-wheel drive. Further, its models were predominantly lower-priced subcompact cars. Subaru had been advertised as "inexpensive and built to stay that way." Therefore, SA experienced much consumer resistance to price rises and the adding on of extra (and profitable) options.

Another problem was rising labor costs in Japan, while countries such as South Korea were challenging Subaru with their own subcompacts manufactured with lower-priced labor. The Hyundai Excel was introduced to the United States in early 1986, and sales had reached 250,000 units by 1987. In response, the other Japanese car companies had moved upscale, selling compact sedans averaging $15,000 in price. Subaru as a sales subsidiary, however, was limited by its parent company Fuji's focus on producing subcompact cars.

As did most car companies, Subaru was forced to use incentives to sell cars. It began offering rebates to buyers of its cars, averaging about $500 per car sold. Such incentives temporarily increased sales. In August 1987, the first month that incentives were in effect and heavily advertised, 17,745 cars were sold, as compared to 14,436 the previous month. These incentives also decreased gross margins, however, and reduced profits. Subaru also had to advertise heavily to move inventory and maintain market share. The total scale of additional selling effort can be seen in the trend for selling expenses in Table 1.

Fuji initially responded by supplying Subaru in 1988 with four-wheel-drive Justy models (its most popular compact car) from Fuji's Taiwan factory. Lower Taiwanese wages meant lower prices, and cars imported from Taiwan also fell outside the Japanese quota granted Fuji. In theory, Fuji could continue to ship its full quota from Japan in addition to the Taiwanese shipments. The goal was to bring in 30,000 to 40,000 cars a year from Taiwan. However, the dollar had been depreciating significantly against the Taiwanese currency, which tended to undercut the benefits of importing from it.

Fuji also initiated a joint venture with Isuzu Motors to open a car factory in the United States—Subaru/Isuzu Automotive, Inc. (SIA)—to produce 120,000 cars annually, including 60,000 new Subaru Legacy model cars. Plant construction was begun in May 1987, with production scheduled to begin in October 1989. A total of $550 million was invested, employing 1,700 workers. Fuji provided the investment funds and hence bore all of the risk. Thus, Subaru could get U.S. made cars and overcome the yen disadvantage, with its parent company bearing the financial risk.

The Legacy model was part of Subaru's response: a new entry in the compact sedan and station wagon segment to compete against cars such as the Honda Accord, the Toyota Camry, and the Mazda 626. This allowed Subaru to move into the higher-priced and less price-sensitive market segment. The Legacy was to feature antilock brake systems, a 2.2 liter 130 HP engine, European styling, and four-wheel drive. It would be priced between $11,000 and $19,000. Coming from a factory incorporating the latest technology provided by the Fuji factories in Japan, it would carry a "Made in America" label. Harvey Lamm, SA CEO, contended, "We have a car in technology that the Germans can't match at twice the price."[1]

SA saw several benefits coming from starting U.S. production: shelter from the ravages of a strong yen, freedom to operate without the constraints set by the voluntary export quotas agreed to by the Japanese car manufacturers, lower costs and more efficient distribution from the central U.S. factory location, larger gross margins, quicker reactions to changing market conditions, and the ability to add the "Made in America" label to the new Legacy product.

However, the U.S. car industry was on the verge of a recession in 1989. Sales were declining even as an additional capacity to manufacture 2 million cars was promised for 1990 by new factories owned by the Japanese. It was an open question when Subaru might achieve a turnaround in sales and profits, even if the yen weakened. Yet, at the end of 1989, Fuji decided to convert Subaru of America into a wholly owned subsidiary. It offered to buy up all the shares held by the public, thus making the U.S. sales operation an integrated part of Fuji's operations.

Questions

1. Explain how the yen appreciation hurt Subaru.
2. How did Fuji's transfer pricing policies affect Subaru's U.S. prices?

3. What other factors may have contributed to Subaru's declining sales in the United States?
4. How did Subaru respond to the problems created by the yen price rise? And how did the Fuji parent company respond?
5. Were Fuji's other Japanese auto-industry competitors similarly affected by the yen appreciation? And how might the dollar devaluation have affected other auto importers from areas such as Mexico, Brazil, South Korea, and Europe?
6. What is your assessment of Subaru's future? How might the future outlook have affected Fuji's decision to convert Subaru into a wholly owned subsidiary?

Endnote

[1]"Counterattack," *Forbes*, November 13, 1989.

*Case prepared by Ravi Sarathy for use in classroom discussion. All rights reserved.
Sources: "Counterattack," *Forbes*, November 13, 1989; Fuji Heavy Industries, Annual Reports; and Subaru of America, Inc., 1988 and 1989 Annual Reports.

CASE 14.2

Federal Cash Registers: Price Competition Overseas*

Supermercados Mundiales, S.A.
1, Avenida Bolivar
Caracas, Venezuela
May 17

Señor Donald Fraser
Presidente
Federal Cash Registers de Venezuela, S.A.
247, Calle Libertad,
Caracas, Venezuela

Dear Donald:

It is with great regret that I have to inform you of our decision to equip our new supermarket with cash registers from the Japanese firm Nippon Business Machines. As I told you

over the telephone yesterday, I cannot wait until you make another trip to Chicago to see if your head office will give a lower price; I have given my word to the Nippon sales manager, and there is no likelihood, if you will forgive my saying so, that you could ever come close enough to their prices to secure our business in future stores. At least not as matters now stand.

I am, however, concerned about your inability to compete, for, as you know, I have friendly feelings toward Federal, and personally I and my brothers have benefited greatly from our attendance at your seminars in Chicago. We have also found the training you offer here to our checkers to be most useful, and I think you will admit that in our earlier stores we showed our gratitude tangibly by installing your machines. However, that was before Nippon began to market here and during a time when you had things pretty much your own way.

But not only am I disturbed about your apparent inability to compete but also about the way in which other American firms are being underpriced. We here have good feelings toward the United States, except for some foolish ones, and we know that you buy most of our oil, so we should buy from you in return. But, leaving apart any difficulties over oil quotas and restrictions, how can we buy from you when other countries, with whom we are also friendly, can outsell you and, I conclude, still make profits? I have certainly not rushed into this purchase of Nippon registers, as you must admit, for I have waited a long time for your counteroffers. It is only now that your offers are still above Nippon's by a substantial margin that I have decided I must act.

Let me review the history of the situation with you, and perhaps you can draw from it some help for the future. I assure you that we will always give you the chance to offer for the business, and I hope you will be able to persuade Chicago to support you.

As you know, when I called for the bid on the registers, your original price was well above the other price, by an outlandish figure. You took it up with Chicago and succeeded in getting the difference reduced, but not sufficiently to be interesting. You went back again for help, and this time the suggestion was that you send in Italian registers from your factory there (which I must say I found a curious thing). But even then, though the difference was reduced from $30,000 for the American machines to $19,000 for the Italian ones, you were still way over the other price.

You asked me yesterday what the competitor's edge was. I can tell you now that his price is better than yours by $9,000, and I think you must agree that that amount is too much to be sacrificed to sentiment. How he does it, I don't know, nor do I much care. So we have gone ahead and placed the order.

You brought up the question of parts and service, particularly in wartime. To the first, I must in all logic point out that the kind of war that seems likely will make the problem of parts an academic one, but in any event, the chances of our getting parts from Japan are as good as they are of getting them from a U.S. firm, which is sure to be at war.

As to service, I have this to say. We keep open on Saturdays and Sundays in many departments, as you know. We have had occasion, in other stores, to call your company on Friday afternoons for service and to be told that you don't work the "American weekend" and nobody will be available until Monday. You explain this as being because of labor restrictions and the like. About this I don't care. I do care that Nippon, called on Friday, or any time, will come on Saturday, Sunday, or in the middle of the night. The general sales manager himself will come and work on the register, and it is this that we want, not excuses about "American weekends." If you want our business, you must be prepared to work for it.

So this is the story. If you want to discuss it with me further, I shall be happy at any time to see you. I hope we can remain friends, but I am not sure that we can remain in the position of doing business with each other.

My warm regards to your esteemed señora.

With great cordiality,

Jaime Aragon
Presidente

Questions

1. What action should Donald Fraser take with regard to this letter: (a) Should he take the matter up with Jaime Aragon again? (b) Should he send the letter on to his Chicago headquarters?
2. What bases for action with regard to new business are suggested by the letter?
3. What is the significance of this letter in terms of U.S. business operating abroad?

---

*Source: This case was prepared by John S. Ewing, Department of Marketing, California Polytechnic State University, Chico, California. Used by permission.

Chapter

15

Pricing in International Marketing

II

Going beyond export pricing and transfer pricing, this chapter considers other aspects of pricing in international marketing.

The main goals of this chapter are to

1.   Determine the influence on pricing of foreign-market variables such as government, inflation, local demand, and costs.

2.   Discuss how a firm deals with international competition—the pressure to cut costs and prices—and how manufacturing decisions and product design meet low-cost competition.

3.   Define gray markets and explain how to deal with them.

4.   Explore the dimensions and implications of countertrade, a sizable segment of world trade.

5.   Discuss the role of leasing in international marketing.

6.   Explain when and why coordinating prices is necessary in international marketing, and describe how it is done.

FOREIGN-MARKET PRICING

Management concern in both export pricing and international transfer pricing is with getting goods into foreign markets at a competitive price. In both cases, the problem is one of international pricing. Foreign-market pricing is concerned with pricing within foreign markets; as such, it is a matter of domestic pricing. However, it is a concern of the international marketer for two reasons: (1) The firm's prices in any market are usually related to supply and demand factors beyond that market and (2) an important part of international marketing is the coordination of domestic marketing in each of the firm's markets, which includes pricing policy.

Because foreign-market pricing is pricing for a national market, relevant pricing considerations include pricing over the product life cycle, product-line pricing, first-time purchasers versus replacement sales, pricing to intermediaries, and skimming versus penetration strategies. The determinants of a firm's prices in a market are indicated in Table 15–1.

Foreign-Market Variables

Company Goals

A firm's objectives generally vary from country to country. In growth markets, the firm probably stresses market share and may have a penetration pricing strategy. In mature slow-growth markets, the firm may try a holding pattern with pricing strategy appropriate to that goal. A joint venture puts a special constraint on pricing because the firm must consider the desires of its national partner as well as its own.

When a firm first enters foreign markets, it sets goals appropriate for the then-prevailing economic situation. As the environments in these markets evolve (e.g., political changes such as in Lebanon, South Africa, or the Philippines, or economic development such as in China or South Korea), the firm's goals for these markets will also change. This leads to modifications in pricing strategy over time.

Costs

The costs relevant to foreign-market pricing include all costs necessary to get the product to the ultimate buyer. When a firm operates in just one market, the relevant costs are easy to determine. In the international firm, it is not easy to determine the relevant costs for a particular market. A subsidiary in one country is usually part of an international network on both the supply and the demand sides. Allocating indirect costs among countries is similar to the problem of allocating them among different product lines. In addition, the international firm has a different cost structure in each of its markets.

Manufacturing Costs. When the products sold in a market are produced there, determination of manufacturing costs is no problem. Questions arise, however, when a market is served by other production sources: If a firm has several plants, which plant's costs should be used? Should variable or full cost be used? What does "full cost" mean for a product coming from a plant in another country; that is, what portion of that country's costs should be allocated? Obviously, some costs, such as local advertising or marketing research, do not apply to products sold in another country.

Marketing Costs. Distribution and marketing costs also must be covered in the foreign-market price. Because tariffs can be an important part of delivered cost, the subsidiary tends to prefer a source from a country having favorable tariff relations with its own. Thus, a subsidiary in the European Union (EU) usually chooses another EU subsidiary because no tariff barriers exist.

Marketing costs in the foreign-market price are primarily those generated within that market by the national subsidiary. Occasionally, however, the firm incurs costs for marketing research or other services rendered by a regional division (or international division) for the subsidiary. Local marketing costs vary from one

TABLE 15-1	Determinants of Foreign-Market Pricing
Company goals	Market share; profits; discounting for specific customers; competitive response; response to gray markets
Costs	
Manufacturing	Scale economies; lower factor costs; productivity
Transportation	Long-term shipping contracts; alternative modes of transport; scale economies
Marketing	Direct vs. indirect distribution; start-up marketing costs in new country markets; short-term promotions
Demand	Elasticity; cyclicality; product cycle stage
Competition	Their goals: seeking market share; cross-subsidization of markets; segment strategy
Government	Government as buyer; price controls; attitude to profits (deemed excessive?); demands for reinvestment
Taxes and tariffs	Duty-free imports; reclassifying goods to lower duties; taking advantage of regional integration, offset, and countertrade possibilities; incentives for re-export
Inflation	Inflation rate; level and trends; possible impacts; use of barter; pricing in hard currencies; unbundling
Product line	Extent of product line; bundled pricing; volume discounts across product line
Distribution channels	Differential pricing by channel based on value-added services specific to the channel; volume discounts
Marketing mix	Additional costs of local advertising and promotions, service, training; local cooperative advertising; commission structure and local cost levels

country to another. This variation derives in part from differing product lines and company goals in each market.

Inflation. Almost all countries face some gradual increase in prices over time. However, continuing strong inflation characterizes a limited number of countries. In those markets where price levels rise by 20 percent or more every year, pricing is a different problem. Selling in an inflationary market might well appear to be a marketer's dream. People are anxious to exchange their money for real assets that do not depreciate quickly. Indeed, it would be a good situation for sellers if it were not for other factors that usually accompany high rates of inflation. First, costs may go up faster than prices. Second, countries with high rates of inflation are usually those with strong price controls. Third, countries with rampant inflation usually have strict controls over foreign exchange. Profits earned in those countries may not be remittable, at least not until they have been eroded by the devaluations that usually accompany inflation.

Pricing for inflationary markets requires accounting for changing values over time. Material and other costs of a product must be recovered (plus a margin for profit) at the time of sale—or at the time of payment, if credit is extended. If prices are stable, pricing can be a simple process of addition. If prices are rising rapidly, addition of the various cost elements at the time they were incurred will not ensure that the *current* value of these costs is recovered.

The following examples illustrate these contrasting situations.

Stable Currency Situation

Raw materials	250 pesos
Overhead	100
Labor	100
Packaging	50
Total costs	500 pesos
Gross profit (20%)	100
Selling price (cash sale)	600 pesos

Inflation Rate of 84 Percent per Year

Assume that raw materials were purchased four months before being used in the product, labor costs were incurred one month before product sale, overhead was charged for a one-month period, and packaging materials were purchased three months before sale.

Raw materials	250 + 70 (28% inflation—4 months)	320 pesos
Labor	100 + 7 (7% inflation—1 month)	107
Overhead	100 + 7 (7% inflation—1 month)	107
Packaging	50 + 10.5 (21% inflation—3 months)	61
Total costs		595
Gross profit (20%)		119
Selling price (cash sale)		714 pesos

As shown in the preceding tables, selling price must be increased by 19 percent to reflect current cost levels.

In reality, many more cost elements go into a product than the four general headings given here; for example, marketing costs are not mentioned. In addition, each of the cost elements has a rate of inflation different from the average (here 84 percent a year increase in the *general* price level). Finally, time may elapse between production and sale—as well as between sale and payment. This additional time is a further inflation cost to be considered in the price.

Another problem arises if government price controls prevent raising the price. When the firm does have freedom to raise prices, it often fares better by making frequent small price increases than occasional large increases that jolt the consumer. Such was the experience of companies in Brazil. During one period, for example, companies raised their prices 7 percent on the first of every month. At one time, General Foods' Brazilian subsidiary, Kibon, had to raise prices on popsicles from 10 cruzeiros to 60 cruzeiros in just two years. The buyers were mainly children whose income had not risen anywhere near six times the product's original cost. Kibon tried to raise prices by small steps and undertook special promotions each time to minimize the shock. In one such promotional program, those who got a marked popsicle stick won a free bike.

Pricing in inflation will never be easy, especially if there are price controls. However, certain guidelines can help:

1. Good cost accounting is critical, especially in forecasting of costs for pricing.

2. It may be possible to source materials or components from lower-cost suppliers in other countries.

3. Long-term contracts may need escalator or reopener clauses.

4. Credit terms can perhaps be shortened.

5. Product ingredients and/or the product line can perhaps be changed to items less subject either to inflation or government price control.

Demand

The international firm faces a different demand curve in each of its markets. Demand for the firm's products is a function of the number of consumers, their ability to pay, their tastes, habits, and attitudes relating to the product, and the existence of competing products. It is improbable that these are identical in any two markets. U.S. firms find that another variable affecting demand is the attitude toward the United States and products made there.

One implication of differing demand is that the firm must charge different prices in each market. Patterns of demand can also change in reaction to cyclical economic conditions within a country. Consider the evolution of U.S. goods and pricing in Japan. Imported U.S. goods such as brand-name sweaters and cosmetics and software have all been priced significantly above U.S. prices. Part of the reason for higher Japanese prices has been the higher local costs of rent, sales force, advertising, and multiple-layered distribution margins. However, when Japan underwent a deep recession, depressed incomes led Japanese buyers to seek bargains. Discounting and value pricing strategies took hold. Gray-market pressures and increased public consciousness of high Japanese prices also led to lowered prices, with U.S. companies following the general trend.[1]

Competition

In a purely competitive market, all producers would sell at identical prices. In the imperfectly competitive real world, the firm must take note of competitors' prices. However, it has some freedom to sell above or below these prices. Firms marketing internationally may prefer to compete on a nonprice basis. A study by Lecraw found that U.S. firms tended to set their prices in relation to an industry leader in the foreign market.[2]

The nature of competition is another variable. The number of competitors and the way they compete differ between Belgium and Brazil, or between Italy and India. A state-owned enterprise, for instance, may prefer to set prices low to maximize sales and employment, even though this reduces profits and may even result in losses. The U.S. firm often finds that its chief competitors in a market are multinationals from Europe or Japan, which exhibit differing competitive behavior. Lecraw found, for example, that Japanese multinationals "tended to set prices to achieve market penetration," that is, set low prices.[3]

Government

Governments also influence the firm's pricing in a variety of ways. Some influence is exerted via tariffs, taxes, and competition policy. Some governments have specific legislation, such as those governing resale price maintenance or restraint of trade. Most commonly, however, governments have the power to control prices directly if they so choose, and they use their power in varying degrees. In the United States, public utility pricing has been regulated, and price freezes have been occasionally employed. Other governments also regulate specific prices, or occasionally all prices, in their country.

The purpose of price controls is generally to limit price increases. In such an environment, the manufacturer generally must apply for a price increase with data to support the request (increased costs of energy or materials, higher wages, etc.); then there will be a waiting period before the price can be raised, if the request is approved. There is also usually a limit to how frequently the firm can apply for a price increase.

Government controls obviously limit the firm's freedom in setting prices. They raise the cost of price administration by requiring more record keeping and management time. They also probably result in lower prices and less frequent price increases. The government limit to approved price increases may, in fact, be quite arbitrary. The greatest challenge to the firm, however, arises when its request for a price increase is denied. Inability to raise prices in an inflationary environment threatens the very survival of the firm.

Government price controls are often limited to selected product groups. Some products are perceived as being more strategic or sensitive and are more susceptible to government regulation. Pharmaceuticals have the unenviable position of being the most frequently subject to price controls. Even countries that don't control other prices usually control pharmaceutical prices. It is interesting to note, however, that drug firms manage to show consistently good profits.

The reactions by firms to such government-imposed price controls vary. Companies may question a government-mandated policy of unit price disclosure, because they may claim that this draws consumers' attention to price alone and does not make any allowance for quality or brand name–based strategies. Companies would prefer to let retailers decide whether they wish to compete on price, letting price-conscious consumers patronize shops where such information is disclosed.[4]

Because price controls usually apply to the basic product, firms can charge an additional sum for services such as delivery, warranty, on-site service, and installation. A similar approach is **unbundling,** in which the product is broken down into separate components and a separate price charged for each component such as add-on tools and peripherals. Another technique is the **matched-sales technique,** in which sales of the price-controlled product are coupled with purchases of another, perhaps complementary, product not subject to price controls.

Firms may also deliberately change their product line to move away from items that are price controlled and then continue featuring "phantom" products on which price controls are exercised. Another technique is defining orders as "special orders" by adding product features and customization. Prices can generally be negotiated free of price controls on such custom products. Finally, companies can try to increase transfer prices on imported products to raise the base price because price controls generally allow increases in product costs to be passed along to the consumer.[5]

Distribution Channels

A final determinant of the firm's price to consumers in a foreign market is its distribution channels in those markets. The costs and margins of a given channel are not the same from country to country. This suggests that a channel decision may also be a pricing decision. The firm may be forced to choose a particular channel in a market to get the consumer price it needs. Table 15–2 illustrates the intercountry variability of channel costs.

Distribution channels may also differ across countries in their relative demand for discounts. Customary business practices and longstanding relationships in a country may mean a series of additional discounts that reduce the ultimate price realized by the firm, the amount that Marn and Rosiello term the *pocket price.*[6] Firms grant a variety of discounts for a number of reasons:

Order size	Co-op advertising
Response to competitive price cuts	Shipping charges
Early payment	Special customer relationships
Cumulative volume	Product-line promotions

Such discounts need not be offered to all customers in all markets. It is useful, however, to monitor what the various discounts offered in each market are and to establish norms under which such discounts are granted. Otherwise, it is the knowledgeable customer who is able to negotiate additional discounts because of knowing when and whom to call asking for discounts. A firm that develops information on its price waterfall—the sequence of discounts leading to the pocket price—is more able to decide which customers are to be rewarded and which distribution channels should get the most discounts. Marn and Rosiello suggest that careful analysis can result in an overall reduction in discounting and significant gains in the pocket price achieved by the firm. Its sales margins will, therefore, be enhanced.

| TABLE 15-2 | Cost Variability of the Same Channel in Different Countries: Medicines (U.S. Dollars) | | | | |

Country	Manufacturer's Price	Wholesaler's Markup	Retailer's Markup	VAT	Total
Germany	$100	$25	$92	$24	$241
Switzerland	100	21	99	none	220
France	100	12	56	34	202
United Kingdom	100	18	59	14	191
Italy	100	10	38	9	157

Currency Inconvertibility

Most free-market economies follow a regime of freely floating exchange rates with complete convertibility of the currency. However, many countries, including key emerging markets such as China, still have restrictions on the convertibility of their currencies, allowing the governments to maintain artificial exchange rates that may diverge significantly from a freely floating or black-market exchange rate. Such currency inconvertibility also poses problems for multinationals seeking to integrate myriad multinational operations and transfer payments for goods and equipment supplied, as well as payment of dividends and capital repatriation.

Figure 15–1 provides an example of different approaches used by Pepsi in China. Shown are some of the stresses and creativity that currency inconvertibility fosters.

China's exchange controls are due to its desire to conserve scarce foreign exchange and use it for approved purposes such as imports of capital equipment and essential raw materials. The Chinese government prefers that multinationals become self-sufficient in foreign exchange by exporting sufficient amounts to generate the foreign exchange needed to pay for their imports and foreign-exchange outflows. Figure 15–1 shows some alternatives developed by Pepsi to handle exchange controls.[7]

Model A of Figure 15–1 shows how Pepsi can use surplus cash generated in one Pepsi subsidiary to fund the capital needs of another Pepsi subsidiary, thus obviating the need to send into China additional foreign-exchange capital contributions. However, this runs up against the desire of Chinese states to conserve capital for use within the state. Thus, a state could prevent Pepsi from transferring capital out. More generally, such a solution only works as long as a multinational can use local funds to continue expanding within the country. Imports of machinery and components would still have to be paid for with additional foreign exchange. In Pepsi's case, it needs to expand across China because soft drink consumption is still at low levels, and there is considerable room for growth. Other companies, however, may not find enough attractive investment opportunities.

Model B shows how Pepsi can tap additional local currency (LC) sources to meet its capital needs without having to bring in foreign exchange. In this instance, Pepsi relies on its connections with foreign banks to borrow hard currency (HC), which is then used as collateral to borrow LC from a Chinese bank. As Pepsi's units generate funds from operations, the LC loans can be paid off, releasing the HC collateral, which, in turn, can then be repaid to the foreign bank. The cost is higher because Pepsi has to pay interest on two loans, both the HC and the LC loans. This method, however, allows Pepsi not to have to make additional HC contributions to its Chinese operations.

Model C is an illustration of how Pepsi might use surplus LC funds to source goods in China that can be used by Pepsi subsidiaries overseas. For example, Pepsi

FIGURE 15-1   **Pepsi in China: Dealing with Currency Volatility and Inconvertibility**

The problem: Inconvertibility of the Chinese currency (Renminbi) makes it difficult to remit dividends, repatriate capital, and import needed materials, parts, and capital goods.
The Chinese government solution: Earn export revenues sufficient to pay for imports and foreign currency outflows (dividends, imports, and capital repatriation).

A.

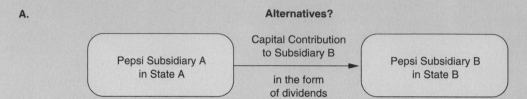

Alternatives?

States Reluctant to Allow Interstate Transfers of Capital

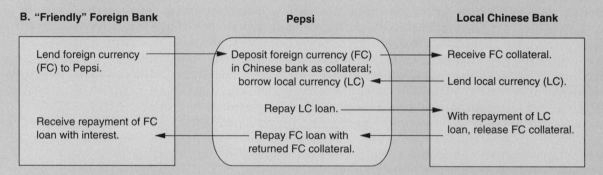

B. "Friendly" Foreign Bank   **Pepsi**   **Local Chinese Bank**

Net Cost to Company: Interest on FC and LC Borrowing, Less Interest Received on FC Collateral

C.

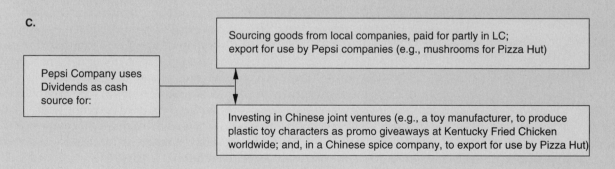

Source: Derived from "Learn from Russia," *Business China*, September 5, 1994, 1–3.

might use surplus LC to buy ingredients such as mushrooms for its international chain of Pizza Hut shops. Alternatively, Pepsi can use its surplus LC funds to invest in joint ventures with Chinese partners to start up new ventures that can supply goods to Pepsi's overseas subsidiaries or for general export purposes. China prefers this third alternative because it deepens China's business base and capabilities.

As the three models in Figure 15–1 show, getting paid becomes at least as important as the basic pricing decision in major emerging markets. Pricing executives need to carefully think through how the foreign-exchange situation can affect their pricing flexibility.

PRESSURES FOR UNIFORM PRICING IN INTERNATIONAL MARKETS

Customers of the multinationals who pay different prices in different countries for essentially the same product or service can be expected to press for a uniform global price. Better information systems and sharing of data across national subsidiaries allow multinationals to see when differential pricing exists and allow them to pool their purchasing to command a single price and even volume discounts. In response, suppliers have begun a move to uniform pricing. For example, Fujitsu sells its computers across Europe at a price fixed in dollars, with a goal of keeping price variations across countries within a 3 percent band. This policy also prevents gray marketing such as when U.S. distributors ship products to Europe to take advantage of price differentials between the United States and Europe.

Similarly, Novell charges a standard worldwide price set in dollars. This places the onus on the distributor to decide how to adjust LC prices in response to exchange-rate changes. Novell moved to its global uniform price because users could easily buy software in lower-priced markets. Once customers use Novell networking software, switching costs ensure that Novell retains a significant portion of its clients, resulting in a recurring income stream. Novell's competitor 3Com has a similar dollar-based pricing policy, with all customers being charged U.S. dollar prices. The impetus was complaints from European customers who were sometimes being charged 50 percent more than comparable U.S. prices for 3Com routers and hubs.[8]

The threat from multinational customers needs to be taken seriously. British Polyethene (BPI), one of Europe's leading consumers of polyethene (PE), publicly told its European suppliers that it had moved some production to China because Asian PE prices were 10 percent lower, thereby allowing BPI to be competitive in a global commodity business. PE prices rose in Europe because tariff preferences on PE imports from countries such as Russia, South Korea, and Mexico had lapsed and the resulting higher tariff walls created a protectionist barrier for European producers.[9]

The methanol industry faces similar global uniform pricing pressures. The U.S. industry sets methanol prices monthly, while quarterly prices are normal in Europe. Spot business is more common in Asia. Since Asia is a net importer of methanol, the different pricing schemes lead to market instability and price fluctuations. An industrywide global agreement on a common approach to pricing is one solution.[10]

Multinational clients can also force a company to share in exchange-rate risk. That is, a large customer can insist that any windfall gains from exchange-rate changes be partially passed back to the customer. For example, one U.S. drug manufacturer manufactured drugs in Ireland for a Japanese customer and invoiced in yen when the yen was 125 to the dollar. When the rate dropped to below 90 yen, the Japanese customer asked that yen prices be dropped. The same problem arises in transfer pricing with a volatile currency changing the relative allocation of profit between the subsidiary and the parent company. In such cases tax authorities in the jurisdiction where profits have dropped are likely to want prices to be adjusted so that profits and the tax payments remain constant.

Japanese semiconductor companies have developed an interesting response to the problem of price changes caused by exchange-rate shifts. Their client contracts include cost-sharing agreements. The Japanese companies know from internal profitability assessments that they can earn a reasonable rate of return on dollar-based contracts as long as the yen sells above 75 to the dollar. Hence, they negotiate contracts that guarantee a price as long as the yen remains between 75 and 95 yen. If the yen falls below 75 yen, however, the dollar price goes up. Similarly, if the yen rises above 95 to the dollar, the dollar price to the customer is cut. This flexibility is fair to both buyer and seller and enhances long-term relationships between supplier and client.[11] Of course, price changes also signal information about product characteristics to the customer. For example, do price reductions increase sales of high-quality brands more than lower-quality products? Under certain circumstances, price changes can affect consumer choices of the kind of product to consume and the specific brand chosen.[12]

The Influence of Competition on Pricing

As competition in the luxury segment of the automobile market intensifies, Jaguar's U.S. sales have dropped by nearly two-thirds since 1986, its peak year. A poor-quality image coupled with new cars and aggressive pricing from Japanese companies are partly responsible for Jaguar's decline. Jaguar last offered a new car to the U.S. market in 1987.

In response, Jaguar cut the price of its 1993 XS coupe to $49,750 from $60,500 the previous year. To sustain such a cut, Jaguar offered a smaller engine: a 4 liter, 219 HP, 6-cylinder engine rather than the 5.3 liter, V-12, 260 HP engine formerly available. But Jaguar did not rely on price alone to win back market share. It simultaneously launched a new advertising campaign underlining Jaguar's long history of making luxury cars while reducing defects by 80 percent under a new quality control program, and adding standard equipment such as a driver's-side airbag and CFC-free air conditioners. Price is being used as part of a marketing mix in developing competitive marketing responses.

General Motors also used pricing as part of its marketing strategy in competing with Japanese companies. The strong yen had forced Japanese automakers to raise their U.S. dollar prices. GM saw this as an opportunity to raise prices on its better-selling models by 2 to 6 percent, less than the price rise

Exchange-rate volatility can also force firms to consider hedging strategies as part of overall pricing strategy. During 1995, for example, the yen appreciated from 100 yen to the dollar to nearly 80 yen to the dollar by mid-1995. Then the yen began depreciating, rising to above 100 yen to the dollar by year-end. Since Japanese corporations are major exporters, firms such as Nissan process $8 billion in foreign receivables. Such large foreign balances led many Japanese firms to hedge their foreign short-term assets (and liabilities). During 1995, however, a hedging strategy meant that Japanese firms may have locked in rates that prevented them from exploiting the dollar appreciation. For example, a hedge on dollar receivables at 90 yen to the dollar meant that the firm lost out on dollar appreciation to 107 yen to the dollar in January 1996. Because the Japanese fiscal year begins in April, treasurers all across Japan had to consider whether the steady weakening of the yen from mid-1995 was a secular trend reversing a decade-long strengthening of the yen or a short-term fluctuation.

Some firms such as Hitachi follow a simple decision rule: Always hedge half of all outstanding FC receivables.[13] Smaller firms may find even this degree of risk hard to accept, and prefer a 100 percent hedging strategy. After all, hedging is about passing on FC risk to a third party, and it is disingenuous to hope to pass on the downside risk but retain upside risk for the firm through simple hedges such as forward contracts. Hedging strategies such as selling FC puts do exist and incur costly premiums, but can be used by a firm that desires to take on some degree of FC exposure.

Uniform pricing also allows a firm to set pricing policy centrally and decide the role that price should play in the overall marketing mix. Headquarters may then decide that the company will not indiscriminately cut prices to win market share and prevent inconsistencies cropping up under which one subsidiary might cut prices excessively whereas another might prefer to cater to fewer clients at a higher margin.[14]

Hermann Simon suggests that pricing in a global setting consists of resolving the tension between the desire to charge different prices and the pressure to

for Japanese cars, while keeping prices constant or even cutting them on older and less successful models. The following table shows how GM's 1993 prices compare with its major competitors.

Automobile Prices for 1993 Models

Midsize Sedans	Price	Minivans	Price
Chevrolet Lumina	$13,400	Plymouth Voyager	$14,076
Honda Accord	13,500[a]	Ford Aerostar	14,416
Pontiac Grand Prix	14,890	Chevrolet Lumina APV	14,695
Toyota Camry	15,598[a]	Mazda MPV	16,555
Ford Taurus	15,623	Toyota Previa	17,518[a]
Dodge Intrepid	15,930	Oldsmobile Silhouette	19,499

[a]1992 prices.

Sources: "GM's Price Strategy for 1993 Reflects Detroit Bid to Squeeze Japanese Rivals," *The Wall Street Journal*, August 14, 1992; and "Jaguar Pulls in Its Car-pricing Claws," *The Wall Street Journal*, October 14, 1992.

charge one price in all markets.[15] Multinational clients who want to buy all their product needs at the lowest price prevalent within a group of countries and gray marketers indulging in price arbitrage are the two forces leading to a uniform price. Consumers in different markets may have different elasticities of demand, however, and some groups may be willing to pay higher prices.

As important, consumers may differ in the value they perceive in a product and its features. Conjoint measurement allows the firm to see the differences in perceived value. Coupling this information with differing elasticities can justify higher prices in certain markets. The solution, according to Simon, is to set up an "international price corridor" within which band prices can vary across countries. The width of the band would be set centrally at headquarters. If some low level of gray marketing ensues, the firm can tolerate it. Simon emphasizes that "a global product and local price are incompatible," and if low income and positioning strategies suggest that different prices need to be charged, then a multiple brand policy can prevent the low price from diluting the brand equity of the higher-priced brand.

INTERNATIONAL COMPETITION AND PRICE-CUTTING PRESSURES

Comparative-advantage concepts indicate that developing nations with their lower labor costs are likely to have an advantage in world competition in labor-intensive products. Such advantages also arise when foreign companies gain a technological advantage or obtain higher productivity. The resultant lower prices allowed can give the foreign firm a toehold in the market. For example, a Russian-made Belarus 85-horsepower tractor sold for about $15,000, compared to about $30,000 for a comparable John Deere machine. Raw-material costs were subsidized in the Russian factory, and labor cost about $2.25 an hour. The machines were simple, of older design. The Deere tractor was "quiet, smooth-shifting, with a short turning radius, a steering wheel that responds to one finger and pushbutton four-wheel drive"; the Belarus was "loud, smoky, and cantankerous." The tractors were shipped from Russia, unloaded, inspected, and repainted orange, with English-language instruction decals. The marketing was price based, with ads in local farm papers such as *Focus on Farming* and *Country Folks*. The ads said: "Get a new $30,000 to $40,000 tractor and pay only $13,900 for it."[16]

Regardless of the source of comparative advantage, the end result is that foreign firms may have lower prices. The dilemma then facing the domestic (U.S.) firm is whether it should respond by also cutting prices. Suppose that a U.S. manufacturer of machine tools bids on an order. The salesperson calls the purchasing agent to check on the status of the bid and is told that a Japanese company has submitted a lower bid and that the U.S. firm must cut its prices by a certain amount to get the order. The salesperson's boss, however, is adamant that company policy is not to compete on prices and that the salesperson must convey other advantages of the U.S. firm, such as its position as long-term supplier to the client, its greater experience, its location closer to the client, its reputation for better service, and so forth.[17]

The problem here is in judging how the role of price as an attribute of the product has changed. That is, as the technology inherent in a product is diffused, there are fewer differences in the product itself than between the U.S. firm and its foreign competitors. As the product becomes less differentiated, price-cutting is more likely. Then, if the foreign firms can also match the U.S. firm on other attributes of the product such as service, quality, and delivery terms, price becomes more influential in the decision to buy.

To generalize, U.S. firms must constantly monitor the prices charged by their foreign competitors and understand the reasons why foreign firm prices are lower. Are the price cuts of a temporary nature, designed to aid in initial market penetration? Or do they represent the net cost advantage enjoyed by the foreign competitors? In other words, price-cutting is the symptom. The correct response to such price cuts requires understanding the cause.

PRICE PRESSURE AND THE NEED TO CUT COSTS

If the U.S. firm must lower its prices, it will be able to do so only after cutting its costs—either by redesigning the product to cut component and direct labor costs or by moving manufacturing overseas to a location with lower labor costs. However, this last, and seemingly obvious, choice can backfire on the company. Quality may be lower and delivery may be delayed. The cost savings on the labor side may be eaten up by the need to maintain larger U.S. inventories; otherwise, the company may lose sales because its inventory is inadequate to meet orders on a timely basis. Manufacturing in a distant overseas location also makes it harder to respond to changing customer needs.

Consider the garment industry, in which low labor costs have led many U.S. firms to manufacture clothes in plants in the Far East. However, designs must be sent to these Far East plants in the spring for clothes meant to be sold in the fall in the United States. Then, in September, when the company finds out that certain designs are selling well, it is too late to attempt to increase production, and potential sales are lost. Similarly, if some items are poor sellers, the company is stuck with excess inventory that must be sold off through sales at price discounts; the reduced profits caused by such discounting offset the gains from manufacturing overseas with lower labor costs.

A compromise between using overseas manufacturing and staying at home is the development of **maquiladora plants,** which are set up along the Mexican border by U.S. firms using Mexican labor that averages approximately $2 an hour. These workers perform assembly operations on parts and components imported from the United States; tariffs are paid when the completed product is brought back into the United States, but only on the value added by Mexican labor in Mexico. Such factories allow U.S. firms to become more competitive with imports from low-wage countries in the Far East.

The idea that prices must be set in relation to foreign competition applies to all products, whether they are consumer goods or industrial products such as machine tools. How Jaguar prices its cars is an illustration of this concept. Traditionally, Jaguar has always priced its cars in relation to Cadillac prices. As Mike Dale, senior vice-president of marketing, explains it, "Cadillac has always been Jaguar's major source of growth." The goal is to let the Cadillac owner take a two-year-old car and $23,000 and step into a Jaguar. Thus, in 1986, the Jaguar was priced at $12,610 over a Cadillac. But as the dollar weakened in subsequent years, the price differential increased to almost $20,000. Jaguar had to cut prices to bring the price differential back to about $12,000. It achieved this by introducing a modified 1990 model version of the Jaguar XJ6 priced at $37,900, as compared to a 1989 model price of $44,000. To get such a price reduction, it had to redesign the car. Price had become even more important after the introduction of two new Japanese luxury cars, the Nissan Infiniti and the Toyota Lexus, both priced between $35,000 and $40,000.[18]

High domestic prices relative to world market prices invite foreign competition. An interesting example of this issue is Japan. At a 100-yen exchange rate to the dollar, nearly all goods and services are more expensive in Japan than in the United States: housing, office space, cab fares, cars, VCRs, food and beverages, shoes, and so on. A survey by Japan's Economic Planning Agency for a broad sample of 306 goods and services showed Tokyo prices to be between 26 and 48 percent higher than in New York.[19] This price disparity may be due to the Japanese deliberately charging higher prices at home, and it may also be partly due to the less-efficient Japanese distribution system. Japanese consumers, however, seem less sensitive to price, showing loyalty to high-quality products, especially if they are of Japanese origin.[20]

Despite this, Japanese consumers are beginning to pay attention to the lure of lower prices. This is particularly true of low-priced electronic product imports from South Korea, Taiwan, and Hong Kong. Such imported products are simpler, with fewer features, and are attractively priced. One of the hardest-hit industries was the electric fan industry, with 2 million imported units out of a total market of 3.8 million units. Imported fans were selling at 7,000 to 8,000 yen, compared to prices on Japanese fans of around 20,000 yen. The major conclusion to draw is that the Japanese market presents an opportunity due to its domestic high prices.[21] Such opportunities increased with continued Japanese economic stagnation, with Japanese consumers facing years of flat earnings seeking lower prices as a way of improving their consumption capabilities.

PRICING IMPLICATIONS OF INTERNATIONAL MANUFACTURING DECISIONS

Switching manufacturing locations to take advantage of lower labor costs or other factor costs is a long-run solution. It is costly and irreversible, but it is becoming increasingly common. Bosch GmbH is the world leader in automotive electronics, with over 50 percent world market share in fuel injectors and antiskid brakes. But two-thirds of its output was manufactured in Germany, where wages were high and unions strong. Hence, Bosch selected Wales as the site for a major new 320-million-mark factory. Car manufacturing capacity will exceed demand worldwide in the 1990s, which means that price competition will be strong, and cost efficiency will be rewarded.[22]

As noted earlier, price-setting is partly determined by the company's cost structure. In competing in global markets, the firm must contend with the cost structure of its international competitors. Factor endowments and factor prices affect the cost structure of all companies, so an international competitor with lower-cost labor or capital can have a comparative advantage because its overall total costs are lowered to whatever extent its labor and capital costs affect its total cost of production.

However, while low-cost labor is an important factor affecting total costs, so are technology, the experience curve, and the capital intensity of manufacturing. As technology and capital equipment substitute for lower-cost direct labor, therefore, the paradoxical situation emerges that the country with the lowest-cost labor does not necessarily have the lowest total costs of production. A case in point is the example of the iron.[23] Table 15–3 gives the statistics, which show how innovative manufacturing can overcome higher labor costs.

Product Redesign and Pricing Implications

Table 15–3 compares the cost structure for irons manufactured by different companies in various locations. The irons are (1) Sunbeam's traditional product, the old iron; (2) a redesigned iron; (3) the Black & Decker iron, designed to be manufactured in Singapore; and (4) Sunbeam's latest product, the "global" iron, designed to be manufactured at low cost and sold around the world.

Sunbeam's old iron had an enormous cost disadvantage based on both the design (using more materials) as well as the higher labor costs and manufacturing overhead. Black & Decker's approach was to manufacture an iron in Singapore using almost the same design (the high number of parts needed and assembly operations indicated by the number of screws needed), but with lower-cost materials, overhead savings, and lower-cost labor. The unit cost advantage seems insurmountable. Sunbeam was able to respond to the competitive challenge, however, with a multipart strategy:

- ◆ Redesign of the product to reduce the number of parts and assembly operations needed, thus reducing the use of direct labor.

- ◆ Reduction in the cost of materials.

- ◆ Reduction in the cost of direct labor, although overhead is higher than in the case of Black & Decker in Singapore, reflecting the more capital-intensive nature of the manufacturing process used.

Overall, the data in the table underline the importance of cost structure in competing in product areas that are mature and subject to global competition where low-cost labor is significant. In such circumstances, pricing strategy becomes relevant only after the cost disadvantage can be overcome, which means paying attention to reducing labor cost, manufacturing overhead, materials cost, and redesigning the product so that it can be manufactured at a lower cost. Pricing strategy thus becomes closely linked to the firm's overall manufacturing strategy.

Changing manufacturing locations is, therefore, not the only way to cut costs. Product redesign and more capital-intensive manufacturing are also options. Baldor Electric, a manufacturer of industrial electric motors, faced severe competition from Taiwan, South Korea, and Japan but was unwilling to move to an overseas low-wage location. It feared that quality of its product would go down and that a weakening dollar would diminish the gains from manufacturing overseas. Hence, Baldor tripled its rate of capital investment, using an adaptation of just-in-time manufacturing. Each worker assembles a complete motor from the full set of parts on a tray, with a computer printout giving him or her information on the motor and how to assemble and test it. Four of five workers attended in-house quality control seminars. The capital spending, new manufacturing methods, and focus on quality all helped Baldor innovate and stay in business while continuing to manufacture in the United States.[24]

Remember, *pricing problems are symptoms*. In the short term, price-cutting and adjustment might be the answer to them, but over the longer term, solutions lie in analyzing their causes. As shown, exchange rates may be the initial cause of pricing

TABLE 15-3	Cost Structure of Irons Manufactured at Various Locations					
	Unit Cost	Materials	Labor	Manufacturing Overhead	Number of Parts	Number of Screws Needed
Sunbeam (old model)	9.50	4.32	1.06	4.12	73	13
Sunbeam (redesigned model)	6.66	4.10	.48	2.08	68	13
Black & Decker (Singapore)	5.98[a]	3.40	.53	1.25	74	19
Sunbeam (global model)	5.33	3.40	.35	1.58	52	3

[a]Includes .80/unit of transportation costs.
Source: M. Therese Flaherty, "Emerging Global Business Environment and Managerial Reaction to It," Paper COF-8, presented at the Ministry of International Trade and Industry Conference, Tokyo, 1988.

problems, but a fundamental solution to these problems requires comparing the firm's cost structure with that of the competition and then taking actions to reduce or nullify the effects of a cost disadvantage.

Gray Markets

An additional pricing problem in international marketing is the incentive that the consumer price differential between countries creates to shop for a given product in a country with lower prices. For example, it was common for planeloads of Japanese tourists (in times of economic prosperity in Japan) to take weekend shopping trips to Taiwan and Hong Kong to buy goods such as consumer electronics, perfumes, and clothes to take advantage of price differentials.

In international marketing, when a product may be manufactured in more than one location, currency fluctuations can make gray marketing profitable. **Gray marketing** is the unauthorized import and sale of products intended for one market in another, higher-priced market. When the dollar was appreciating in the early 1980s, it was profitable for dealers to bring in unauthorized imports of Caterpillar tractors from Europe because of the weak European currency. In such cases, even after shipping and tariffs, the landed cost in the United States of such imported Caterpillar tractors was less than the price charged for U.S.–made Caterpillar tractors.[25]

The major problem with gray marketing is that established distributors lose motivation to sell the product because they see their margins eroded by low-overhead gray marketers. (Consider, for example, the mail-order PC resellers, whose main expense is telemarketing.) Meanwhile, the gray marketer is primarily interested in quick sales and short-term profits. Over time, the manufacturer could lose markets because the gray marketer competes only on price and drives away customers who seek after-sales service and other forms of support. This issue is particularly serious for industrial products. On the other hand, gray markets provide an outlet for excess production and, indeed, allow a firm to gain economies of scale by deliberately increasing production, some of which will go into the gray market. And when product life cycles are short, gray markets allow a firm to gain market share and not be stuck with obsolete inventories.

Ultimately, gray marketing arises because of unsustainable price differences between two markets. When a perfume manufacturer charges U.S. wholesale prices that are 25 percent higher than similar prices in Europe, it is not surprising that some of the product sold to European wholesalers leaks into the United States, and such importing is legal under U.S. law. Companies must carefully examine their pricing policies in different markets and their attempts to maintain a price differential. Otherwise, gray marketing is merely an efficient market response to ill-thought-out attempts to charge higher prices in certain markets.

Strategies for Foreign-Market Pricing

We will review pricing strategies that follow from the preceding discussion. First, in dealing with costs in a foreign market, international marketers have options not available to national firms. They may control costs through a choice of supply sources with differing production costs, tariffs, and transportation charges. They may further affect costs by changing the firm's level of involvement in a market. Changing from exports to some form of local production changes not only tariff and transportation charges but production costs as well.

In dealing with inflation, a replacement cost formula was suggested along with careful cost accounting, escalator clauses in contracts, and a shortening of credit terms. Changing the input mix should also be considered because not all the firm's inputs have the same rate of inflation. If the firm can use inputs with lower-than-average inflation rates, it will have an advantage in its pricing. Changing the product mix is another possible approach because not all of the firm's products are equally buffeted by inflation or price controls. In India, for example, multinational drug companies expanded into areas of the pharmaceutical business, where price controls were less stringent. In Mexico, under price controls, appliance manufacturers were offered very attractive prices if they would concentrate production on a limited number of basic models of eight kinds of appliances.

In facing demand in a market, the firm has less flexibility than in facing costs. The marketer must adapt the price to the local demand. Of course, demand occasionally can be influenced through promotional activities, or there may be a price-quality association concerning the firm's product, enabling it to sell above competitors' prices.

In regard to competition, the marketing firm must determine the appropriate relation between its own and competitors' prices. It may have some flexibility in meeting national competitors' pricing through the logistics arrangements possible in the international company. There should be economies of scale through multinational production sources and markets. Using nonprice competition may offer further pricing flexibility.

Government is a powerful constraint on pricing, but the firm does have some freedom. It can, of course, avoid those markets where government price controls are too rigid. If it is already in such markets, the extreme alternative is to withdraw. A more common and generally more desirable alternative is to cooperate with the government, presenting the company's arguments and working toward a compromise. Drug companies in Brazil provide an example. They finally gained some relief from stringent price controls by acting through their professional association, Abrifarma. The government was suspicious of drug company pricing and profits and was refusing requests for price increases. Abrifarma hired an independent firm (Price Waterhouse) to audit the pricing of 33 major drug firms. When this analysis was presented to government price controllers, they approved some drug price increases larger than the amount of inflation for the first time in four years.

COUNTERTRADE

As discussed previously, countertrade is a form of financing international trade wherein price-setting and financing are tied together in one transaction. It is essentially barter, the exchange of goods for goods, but with some flexibility. In barter, the exact item to be exchanged is specified, such as oil for machinery. In countertrade, a range of goods is specified that can be taken in exchange for exports from a Western supplier. For example, Catalyst Research of Maryland had begun selling specialized batteries for pacemakers to Tesla, the Czech electronics collective. In 1986 Tesla bought the rights to manufacture the pacemaker battery, with Catalyst selling the equipment, supplies, and raw materials needed. As part of the agreement, Catalyst Research started buying product inventions from the Czech Academy of Sciences to fulfill its countertrade obligations.

A typical transaction might be as follows: A Polish apple juice factory may need new equipment but be unable to buy from a U.S. supplier because no U.S. bank will lend it money. However, an Austrian bank is willing to guarantee its debt; hence, the order goes to an Austrian manufacturer. The Austrian bank undertakes to buy a large portion of the apple juice produced for resale on Western markets. It is able to do this because most Austrian banks have their own in-house trading companies (Austria's proximity to the Eastern European countries has led to a concentration of countertrade expertise in Vienna). Through this convoluted chain, the Polish factory gets the equipment, the Austrian manufacturer an order, and the bank makes fees from the loan guarantee and commissions on sale of the apple juice.[26]

A U.S. International Trade Commission study showed that $7.1 billion of U.S. trade in 1984 was through countertrade, although 80 percent of such countertrade was for defense goods and armaments.[27] The role of countertrade in world trade is increasing, accounting for about 15 percent of all world trade in 1996. Much of the growth in countertrade has occurred because of the domination of the former Communist bloc economies by state trading. Such government monopolies use countertrade to make up for economic inefficiencies, while using their ability to control access to their domestic markets as a way to convince Western suppliers to agree to countertrade. These trends have been exacerbated by uneven economic growth and shortages of foreign currency caused by a lack of creditworthiness and past over-borrowing.

There are several forms of countertrade:

1. *Barter,* the simplest, is the direct exchange of goods for goods. It is cumbersome, since each party must have goods that the other party wants, in the exact quantities. It is the least attractive form of countertrade.

2. *Counterpurchase* is reciprocal buying to be fulfilled over some time period in the future, with flexibility as to the actual goods to be purchased. In such transactions, a majority of the purchase price is paid in cash. An example of this is the way in which Lurgi, a European construction and engineering firm, built a methanol plant for East Germany. In return for the 400 million deutsche mark contract to build the plant, Lurgi took back 408,000 tons a year of methanol, out of its total capacity of 800,000 tons. At the time the contract was signed, there was excess supply, which eased only gradually as older, environmentally unacceptable plants were closed in Western Europe. Heinz Schimmelbusch, chairman of Metallgesellschaft A.G., however, sees such deals as the major growth path for his Lurgi subsidiary because Eastern Europe is more willing to accept polluting plants if Western companies can solve their foreign-exchange shortages.[28]

3. *Offset* is similar to counterpurchase and is more likely at the government level. In dealing with government buyers, the other party has a generalized commitment to buy a certain percentage of the initial export transaction from the country. Thus, when Boeing sold AWACs to the British defense department, it agreed to buy 130 percent of the value of the transaction in British goods.

4. *Buyback* occurs when capital equipment sales are sold with a counterpurchase clause that can be fulfilled by buying some of the output of the plant that is set up with the imported capital equipment.

5.   *Switch trading* involves a third party, usually a specialized trading house with expertise in certain industrial sectors and with certain countries, usually centrally planned economies. Austria and Switzerland are two sources of expertise, with several such switch trading firms located in these two countries.[29]

Countertrade involves forced sourcing, often from centrally planned economies and newly industrializing nations. Such sources of product may not have advanced technology and high-quality products. By default, then, countertrade forces the exporter to develop a strategic purchasing policy for countertrade opportunities.

Before deciding to enter into countertrade, the exporter should scout firms in the targeted country to decide whether reliable suppliers (of raw materials or components) can be developed. It also should be willing to help upgrade the manufacturing capability of potential suppliers so that the countertrade opportunity results in obtaining useful raw materials and components at reasonable prices; otherwise, the firm is likely to be stuck with poor-quality goods that are difficult to trade.

Countertrade, then, should be viewed as the initiation of a long-term relationship with a country and its firms. This is turn will satisfy the needs of the countries that resort to countertrade. Typically, such developing nations use countertrade for several reasons:

1.   They lack foreign exchange.

2.   Just as important, they want as partners multinationals that will help sell their goods overseas.

3.   They hope that successful technology transfer will take place as multinationals work with domestic firms to transform them into reliable suppliers of high-quality raw materials and components.

4.   All of this, they hope, will increase domestic employment and incomes and lead to economic development.

Creativity in Countertrade

As countertrade evolves, Western firms often have to develop new forms of the countertrade model to adapt to changing circumstances in the foreign currency–constrained buying nations. Several new forms of countertrade have been developed: the advance purchase model, the letter-of-credit model, the blocked evidence account, and the export prefinancing method.[30]

A new form of countertrade is the advance purchase model. The Western firm first buys locally manufactured goods from a company in a countertrade country, such as an East European economy. This Western purchase provides hard currency. However, the hard currency is put into an escrow account with a Western bank. The local firm then buys goods from the Western firm, which is paid for out of the escrow account. The local government may not be totally accepting of this advance purchase-escrow account model because it involves opening a foreign account in the name of a local citizen or entity. This can raise fears that such a foreign currency account can become a conduit for illegal payments and unauthorized retention of foreign currency earnings. Governments may also be able to exercise sovereign authority and request sequestration of such accounts, blocking access to the account by both the local company and the Western firm.

A second approach to countertrade is the issuance of back-to-back letters of credit, under which the Western firm opens a local currency (LC) account in the name of the local firm but stipulates that funds may not be released until the local firm fulfills its side of the bargain, namely, exporting the local goods under contract terms and furnishing its own LC for purchase of the Western company's goods.

A third approach is the blocked evidence account, which allows a Western firm to transact multiple countertrade deals without having to balance each deal separately. The deposit by the Western company is "blocked," and the local company cannot get access to the funds until certain terms are met. A sequence of steps must occur:

1. The Western firm exports goods to the local firm.

2. The local firm receives goods from the Western firm and pays in LC into a blocked account with a local bank.

3. An independent trading company (acting as intermediary for the Western firm) buys goods from the local firm and pays for it with the LC in the account.

4. The trading company then pays for the goods in hard currency into the blocked account (possibly following successful export of the goods to a hard currency market).

5. The hard currency is received by the Western firm.

With such a complex chain of transactions, the main risk to the Western firm is that the local firm will not deliver goods as contracted for to the trading company. If this happens, the LC deposit in Step 2 can be used by the Western firm to purchase different goods for possible export.

A fourth method is the export-prefinancing method, shown in Figure 15–2. This method is appropriate when a local firm has a Western buyer for its goods but needs help in setting up its manufacturing facility to produce the goods. The Western firm that can supply machinery and components to fulfill the order sells them in return for having the sales contract for final goods transferred to a Western bank. When the local firm produces and exports the final goods, the Western buyer then pays hard currency to the Western bank holding the sales contract. The bank, in turn, remits hard currency to the Western supplier of equipment and components. While it is apparent that all of these methods are "second-best," tortuous, and cumbersome, they are creative responses to develop customers who have hard currency resource restraints.

In addition to being creative, success in countertrade requires a company to develop a strategic plan. Figure 15–3 outlines the major steps in implementing countertrade:

1. Ensure that the benefits outweigh the costs of carrying out countertrade.

2. Develop a countertrade strategy, including the development of foreign countertrade suppliers.

3. Get top management support by explaining to them the task involved and why countertrade will benefit the company.

4. Develop an organization structure for countertrade; this will include deciding whether to rely on outside help or to keep the entire effort in-house. Outside help is particularly useful when goods obtained in countertrade are not needed by the exporting firm.

FIGURE 15-2   The Export-Prefinancing Method of Countertrade

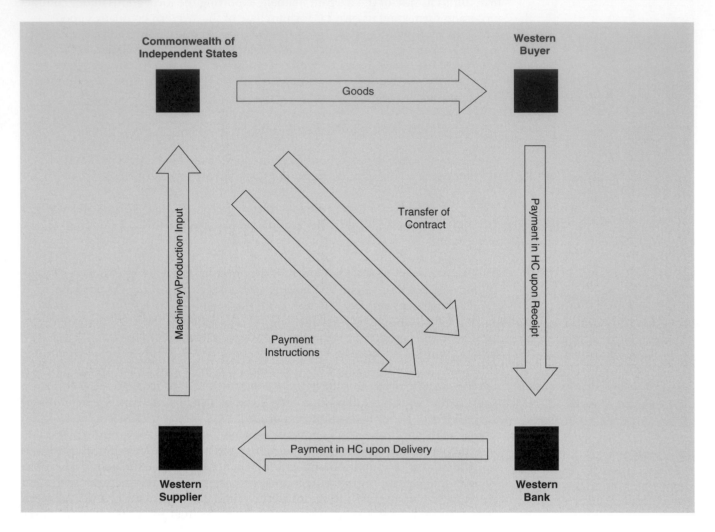

Source: "Countertrade," *Business Eastern Europe,* January 17, 1994.

Separate contracts for the sale of goods and for the receipt of goods in countertrade can also help make the operation successful. The contract should specify the
quality and the nature of goods to be received in countertrade; and it should clarify any restrictions that might be sought on the resale of Western goods and into
what territories such goods may be resold. Penalty clauses and bank guarantees
may be necessary to protect against noncompliance.[31]

It is difficult to ascertain the ultimate profit from a countertrade transaction.
Several relevant payment streams must be examined:

1. Net profit from the export of goods.

2. Plus/minus the profit or loss on disposition of goods received in
   countertrade (in the case of commodities such as oil, prices can fall rapidly,
   reducing the sales proceeds of the goods received in countertrade).

FIGURE 15-3   **Countertrade Implementation**

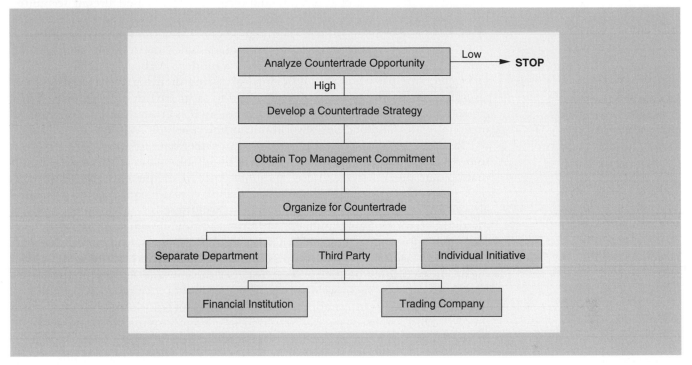

3. Less the imputed interest on the capital tied up in inventory of goods received in countertrade until disposed of.

4. Less the commissions paid to third parties, such as trading companies to help in disposing of goods received in countertrade. A World Bank study on countertrade deals in Indonesia found that about 85 percent of the total commissions went to brokers and intermediaries who arranged the various steps in the countertrade transaction.[32]

5. Less the incremental marketing expenses associated with countertrade.

These factors help determine the short-term profit associated with a countertrade transaction. Generally, the profit will be lower than a straightforward market-based transaction, reflecting the second-best and inefficient nature of the countertrade approach. However, countertrade does have a strategic aspect—as a long-term source of materials and components and as a way of breaking into new markets. Hence, the opportunity costs of a countertrade transaction can be viewed as a strategic investment in gaining long-term market position. Countertrade as an isolated transaction makes little business sense.

Leasing in International Markets

Leasing—an alternative to outright purchase—is an important pricing-financing-marketing device for expensive equipment. Offering competitive leasing terms can be crucial to winning orders in international markets.

For example, GPA Group Ltd., an aircraft leasing firm, placed a $16.8 billion order in 1989 for over 300 jet aircraft, one of the largest orders ever. Its order accounted for 10 percent of all aircraft built through 1995. Leased aircraft accounted for about 14 percent of all aircraft worldwide in 1989, compared to 6 percent in 1985. Leased aircraft accounted for about 20 percent of the world aircraft fleet in 1991.[33] In 1988, 24 percent of McDonnell-Douglas sales was to leasing firms. Jet aircraft are expensive, at about $35 million for a modern Airbus A320, and climbing to $145 million for a long-range Boeing 747. Given their high capital cost, leased aircraft appeal to small start-up airlines and to large carriers. In both cases, precious capital can be conserved for other areas, such as ground support, acquisition of aircraft gates, and building a worldwide airline reservation system.

In effect, airlines are deciding that it is not necessary to own aircraft in order to provide airline service. The separation of ownership of aircraft from the airlines that operate them, however, raises questions. Will an adequate inventory of spares be kept? Will the lessee provide the same quality of maintenance services to leased aircraft? If leased planes are quickly available, will there be enough time for training flight crew? Aircraft manufacturers have traditionally relied on the airlines to give them information about their needs and market trends, which are used in designing new aircraft. If manufacturers cannot get direct market information from the airlines, deciding on the correct passenger capacity and flying range for a new model aircraft may be more difficult. Also, the emergence of a few large buyers such as GPA, ILFC (International Lease Finance Corporation), and Ansett, who then lease the purchased aircraft, results in an oligopoly on the buy side. Such clout can help drive down prices and reduce margins for aircraft manufacturers.

As in the aircraft example, leasing is most likely with expensive capital equipment and undercapitalized purchasers in an environment in which credit is tight. Leasing can be seen as an opportunity; it is less risky to the purchaser, and firms can use this lessened risk to convince would-be buyers to try new equipment. In new markets, leasing can be the avenue to obtaining the first few sales, thus providing an installed base. Then subsequent sales prospects can be referred to these initial lease sales to get data on machine performance. In industrial selling, demonstrations of equipment in a practical real-life environment can be a powerful motivator to closing a sale.

Leasing can also help cope with downturns in an economy because corporations might find it easier to take on moderate-sized lease payments if obtaining approval of large capital investments might not be possible. A number of such leases can also lead to a predictable and recurring revenue stream in the form of lease payments. Another advantage to the lessee is the better maintenance available under the lease contract. In countries with shortages of trained service personnel, service facilities, and spare parts, such maintenance service can be important. Finally, when product life cycles are short, customers may be unwilling to purchase high-priced equipment that might become obsolete. Leasing allows the sale to be made, with the manufacturer sharing a portion of the risk from obsolescence.

A complicating factor in international leases is the currency in which the lease is denominated. If local currency leases are allowed, issues such as the expected pace of local inflation and expected future devaluations are relevant. Clauses allowing for adjustment to such anticipated or expected inflation and devaluation are a must. Also the company must obtain the necessary permissions to ensure conversion into a foreign (hard) currency and repatriation of the lease payments to the parent company headquarters, if desired. Again, competitive behavior should be a reference point. If competition does not press the local government to allow repatriation, but instead permits lease payments in local currency to be accumulated in the economy for later local investment, then the company may have no choice but to do the same thing. Then long-run strategic intent becomes important: Why are we in this particular country market? Why are we permitting leasing in this market? And what are our long-range strategic market-share goals for this market? Needless to say, short-term leasing objectives should fit into the overall long-term market strategy.

Pricing Coordination in International Marketing

The final pricing question is the degree to which the international marketer must coordinate prices in different markets. For most marketing functions, the firm faces the issue of international standardization versus local adaptation. The same issue arises in pricing.

Final Consumer Prices

We noted that the international firm faces a different supply and demand situation in each market. This indicates different optimum prices for each country. If the firm has national subsidiaries operating as profit centers, this also suggests the use of national rather than international prices. Profit center operation would lead to different subsidiaries having different prices.

In addition to the situation of the individual firm, external factors cause price variations between markets. For example, although the EU is an economic union, studies have shown repeatedly that no economic union exists in pricing. Even with tariffs eliminated and value-added taxes subtracted, there remain great disparities in the prices of widely traded goods. These disparities result from variations in competition, distribution efficiency, and national tastes, as well as manufacturers' pricing policies. To be sure, as economic union proceeds, with the advent of the Euro, such discrepancies in pricing will become more obvious, and prices will tend to equalize over time.

When consumer prices on a product vary significantly, consumers may undertake some price arbitrage on their own by resorting to the gray market. When the markets can be kept separate, differential pricing is usually successful. When the markets cannot be kept separate, it may not be successful. It is frequently employed in Western European countries but is often unsuccessful there because of the growing integration of these markets in the European Union. An example of how firms can run into trouble trying to have different prices in differing EU countries is provided by Kawasaki. Prices on its motorbikes varied from $500 to $1,300 in different EU markets, with the United Kingdom market being the cheapest. Kawasaki enforced these differences by a contract with its dealers prohibiting them from exporting. When a Belgian consumer tried to buy a bike in Britain to take back to Belgium, the dealer refused to sell. The consumer complained to the European Union, which found this practice illegal and fined Kawasaki $130,000.

The difficulty of maintaining uniform consumer prices in different markets does not mean that pricing strategies cannot be consistent. A company can maintain a uniform policy of pricing at the market level, above it, or below it. Even though final consumer prices differ, the firm can be consistent in being at the same particular part of the price spectrum in each country.

Control Techniques

Apart from external pressures toward or away from uniform international prices, the firm itself must play a conscious role. To obtain optimum performance, some central coordination is necessary. Various methods are available to control pricing in international operations. Consumer prices are least susceptible to control, except where the firm has direct distribution to consumers. Singer, Avon, and Tupperware are examples in this category, as well as many firms selling to the industrial market. Similarly, the firm has greater control over pricing when it has its own sales subsidiary than when it sells through distributors.

Drug Pricing and Social Pressures

Health care accounts for about 15 percent of U.S. government spending, and health care costs have risen at twice the rate of U.S. inflation. Controlling U.S. health care costs, therefore, is a major national priority. Aside from economics, there is considerable social pressure against drug price increases, particularly when expensive life-saving drugs become out of reach of lower-income patients. Wellcome PLC's experience with AZT, an AIDS drug, is instructive.

Wellcome has been tagged as a corporate extortionist and AIDS profiteer by AIDS activists. Ironically, Wellcome is owned by the Wellcome Trust, a charitable organization. Initially, AZT was priced so a year's treatment cost about $8,000. As FDA tests verified the drug's efficacy and as production costs were lowered due to experience curve and economies of scale, Wellcome began lowering the price to about $6,400 per patient per year by the end of 1989. The original research that developed AZT was done in the United States under U.S.

government sponsorship, and the U.S. government will be one of the biggest purchasers of the drug through its Medicaid program.

Although activists want the drug price lowered and Congress held hearings, experts from the National Cancer Institute suggested that price control could be best achieved through competition. As competitors developed alternatives to AZT, market pressures could bring lower prices.

Sandoz, the Swiss drug firm, faced similar price control pressures over its schizophrenia treatment drug, Clorazil. Sandoz decided to market the drug only when tied to mandatory weekly blood tests performed by a company named Caremark under contract with Sandoz. Annual patient costs approached nearly $9,000. As a result of the high cost, states have limited the availability of the drug under Medicaid, with only about 7,000 patients using it in 1990 against an estimated market of over 100,000 candidates for the drug. Sandoz instituted the weekly blood monitoring because of concern over potentially harmful side effects. Critics suggest that by limiting the blood monitoring to one company working for Sandoz, the total cost of using Clorazil is unduly high. As a result, 22 U.S. states filed suit against Sandoz, charging it with violating antitrust laws.

Sources: "Burroughs Wellcome Reaps Profits, Outrage from Its AIDS Drug," *The Wall Street Journal,* September 15, 1989; "Burroughs Wellcome Cuts Price of AZT under Pressure from AIDS Activists," *The Wall Street Journal,* September 19, 1989; and "Sandoz Unit Faces States' Antitrust Suit over Marketing of Schizophrenia Drug," *The Wall Street Journal,* December 19, 1990.

Few countries allow resale price maintenance as a form of control. With resale price maintenance, the manufacturer sets prices below which the product cannot be retailed. When this is not available, the firm is concerned both about distributors that price too high—and limit the market—and those that price too low—and cause an erosion of prices and margins. Use of recommended, listed, or advertised prices may help to restrain distributors' pricing independence. Use of consignment selling is also an effective, though costly, way to control prices. Extension of credit to the buyer may be another way of maintaining greater control over prices. In general, anything that ties the seller to the producer gives the producer some control.

Subsidiary Pricing of Exports

When subsidiaries are profit centers, they need reasonable pricing freedom on sales within their own market. In this case, the annual budget and product margin agreed upon by parent and subsidiary may provide sufficient control. When several subsidiaries export the same product, central control over export prices is needed to avoid suboptimization. If each subsidiary tries to maximize its own sales and profits, the total company may suffer as the subsidiaries compete against each other.

When the firm has different production sources for a product, coordination of export prices is essential. In the absence of coordination, each subsidiary producing the good sets its own price, and buyers choose the plant offering the lowest delivered cost. The result is that buyers determine the logistics of the producing company, that is, which plant is the supplier. This may result in suboptimization. To avoid this, firms sometimes set uniform FOB plant prices on exports for each producing subsidiary. The customer still chooses the source offering the lowest delivered cost, but the parent firm has greater control. The subsidiary also has an incentive to reduce costs because with a fixed export price, any cost reduction is added to its profits.

Another way of controlling export prices is to require all exports to be handled through one export organization, regardless of source or destination. This is occasionally applied to licensee and joint-venture exports, as well as to wholly owned operations. Such an organization may be located in Switzerland or Panama, New York City or Midland, Michigan (as with Dow Chemical Company). The centralized export operation can set prices and determine logistics to get the most efficient source, lowest landed cost, and greatest total company profit. Such a centralized operation can offer both economies of scale in logistics administration and optimization of global supply and demand.

SUMMARY

Foreign-market pricing is affected by many variables. Rapid inflation, coupled with government controls on price increases, erodes profits and is a major problem.

International competition also creates worldwide pressure to cut prices. Firms must rethink the role of price as a product attribute. Alternatives to matching price cuts are competing with differentiated products and relying on a technological or marketing edge.

If competitive price cuts must be matched, firms need to cut their costs of production. A common solution is to shift production to low-cost overseas locations. Such cost reductions may be achieved, however, at the expense of new problems with quality and timely delivery.

Currency inconvertibility can affect the profitability of international operations and require creative solutions, as did Pepsi in China.

Better informed multinational consumers prevent firms from charging different prices for the same good in different markets, instead moving to uniform pricing.

Price differentials between country markets lead to arbitrage attempts. Gray marketing, the unauthorized import of cheaper goods from other foreign markets, can create problems with distributor channels and affect product image.

Product redesign is another avenue to providing customer value and cutting costs without necessarily competing with cheap-labor manufacturing solutions.

Countertrade is a form of pricing because the sale is tied to accepting other goods in exchange. Creativity and a strategic plan for implementation are necessary for success. Countertrade is rapidly growing in importance and should be viewed as an opportunity to nurture a long-term source of quality raw materials and components.

International leasing is an alternative to outright sale and is important in the international capital goods market. Firms must be able to offer leasing alternatives as part of their international pricing policies to compete effectively in such cases.

Finally, to respond to competition, careful coordination is necessary to manage the conflicting demands of export pricing, foreign-market pricing, and global pricing policies.

QUESTIONS

15.1 How can the level of inflation affect the setting of prices in different country markets?

15.2 How should a firm cope with government price controls in foreign markets?

15.3 Why might international competition force a firm to consider price cuts? What are other alternatives open to a firm facing such price pressures in international markets?

15.4 What are the advantages and disadvantages of moving production off-shore to a low-cost production site?

15.5   What is gray marketing? How does it affect international marketing and price setting?

15.6   How is product redesign relevant to international pricing?

15.7   What is countertrade? Why should firms be willing to consider countertrade arrangements in their international marketing efforts?

15.8   Why do countries seek countertrade? How can the firm assess the profitability of a proposed countertrade transaction?

15.9   How should a firm organize itself to deal in countertrade?

15.10   What are some creative ways to approach currency inconvertibility and countertrade?

15.11   How does international leasing form part of the global pricing decision?

15.12   What are some organizational issues relevant to international pricing?

ENDNOTES

1   "Luxury Prices for U.S. Goods No Longer Pass Muster in Japan," *The Wall Street Journal,* February 8, 1996.

2   Donald J. Lecraw, "Pricing Strategies of Transnational Corporations," *Asia Pacific Journal of Management,* January 1984, 112–119.

3   Ibid., 117.

4   "Knowing the Price," *Business Europe,* July 24, 1995, 3.

5   "Price Control Strategies," *Business Latin America,* September 12, 1988.

6   Michael Marn and R. L. Rosiello, "Managing Price, Gaining Profit," *The McKinsey Quarterly* (no. 4), 1992.

7   "Learn from Russia," *Business China,* September 5, 1994, 1–3.

8   "Global Networks, Global Prices," *Data Communications,* July 1993, 18.

9   *European Chemical News,* 64 (no. 1686).

10   "Pacific-Asia Revamp for Methanol," *Asian Chemical News* 1, no. 22.

11   N. Ostro-Landau, "Currencies, Prices, and Profits," *International Business* 83, no. 8 (July 1995): 16–19.

12   K. Sivakumar and S. P. Raj, "Quality Tier Competition: How Price Change Influences Brand Choice and Category Choice," *Journal of Marketing* 61 (July 1997): 71–84.

13   "As Yen Oscillates, Japanese Firms Mull Risks of Hedging Bets against Dollar," *The Wall Street Journal,* February 8, 1996.

14   "Is the Price Right?" *Business Europe,* February 6–12, 1995, 6–7.

15   Hermann Simon, "Pricing Problems in a Global Setting," *Marketing News,* October 9, 1995.

16   "It Was a Matter of Economics," *Forbes,* February 22, 1988.

17   Mary Karr, "The Case of the Pricing Predicament," *Harvard Business Review,* March–April 1988.

18   See "Jaguar Is Taking the Aggressive Tack to Claw Its Way Out of Sales Sag," *The Wall Street Journal,* September 12, 1989; and "Jaguar Has a New Pride of Cats on the Prowl for Cadillac, Lexus," *The Boston Globe,* September 17, 1989.

19   Charles Wolf, "The Weaknesses Amid Japan's Economic Strengths," *The Wall Street Journal,* May 19, 1989.

20   Robert Weigand, "So You Think Our Retailing Laws Are Tough," *The Wall Street Journal,* September 13, 1989.

21   Takahiro Takesue, "Cheap Imports That Signal a Quiet Revolution," *Journal of Japanese Trade and Industry,* July–August 1988.

22   "A Booming Bosch Frets about the Future," *The Wall Street Journal,* April 19, 1989.

23   M. Therese Flaherty, "Emerging Global Business Environment and Managerial Reaction to It," Paper COF-8, presented at the Ministry of International Trade and Industry Conference, Tokyo, 1988.

24   "Baldor's Success: Made in the U.S.A.," *Fortune,* July 17, 1989.

25   F. V. Cespedes, E. Raymond Corey, and V. Kasturi Rangan, "Gray Markets: Causes and Cures," *Harvard Business Review,* July–August 1988.

26   Stephen S. Cohen with John Zysman, "Countertrade, Offsets, Barter, and Buybacks," *California Management Review* 28, no. 2 (Winter 1986): 43.

27   Joseph R. Carter and James Gagne, "The Do's and Don'ts of International Countertrade," *Sloan Management Review,* Spring 1988.

28   George Melloan, "Countertrade Suits Metallgesellschaft Fine," *The Wall Street Journal,* August 2, 1988.

29   Countertrade has become sufficiently important that DeBard, a Swiss company operating in Britain, has published *The Oxford International Countertrade Directory,* listing participants in the business worldwide.

30   "Reinventing Countertrade," *Business Eastern Europe,* January 17, 1994.

31   Sarkis Khoury, "Countertrade: Forms, Motives, Pitfalls, and Negotiation

Requisites," *Journal of Business Research* 12 (1984).

[32] "Too Much Barter Is Bad for You," *The Economist*, May 9, 1987.

[33] "GPA Group Becomes Leader in Plane Leasing," *The Wall Street Journal,* May 1, 1989.

FURTHER READINGS

Carter, Joseph R., and James Gagne. "The Do's and Don'ts of International Countertrade." *Sloan Management Review,* Spring 1988.

Cespedes, F. V., E. Raymond Corey, and V. Kasturi Rangan. "Gray Markets: Causes and Cures." *Harvard Business Review,* July–August 1988.

Cohen, Stephen S., with John Zysman. "Countertrade, Offsets, Barter, and Buybacks." *California Management Review* 28, no. 2 (Winter 1986): 43.

Khoury, Sarkis. "Countertrade: Forms, Motives, Pitfalls, and Negotiation Requisites." *Journal of Business Research* 12 (1984).

Marn, Michael, and R. L. Rosiello. "Managing Price, Gaining Profit." *The McKinsey Quarterly,* no. 4, (1992).

Rabino, Samuel, and Kirit Shah. "Countertrade and Penetration of LDC's Markets." *Columbia Journal of World Business,* Winter 1987.

C A S E   1 5 . 1

Alimentaires de Barria S.A.: Operating in an Inflationary Economy

Alimentaires de Barria is a leading food processor in the Barrian market. Its primary products are canned fruits and juices, vegetables, and meats. Through an acquisition a few years ago, it is now also a factor in processed dairy foods. Mr. Piperno has been considering diversifying into frozen foods as well, because the nature of the raw materials would be much the same as the present product line. Most of the food products canned come from Barrian sources. Some things are imported, however: sugar for the syrups, tin plate for the cans, and some subtropical vegetables and fruits, such as papaya and pineapple. Furthermore, most of the specialized production equipment was imported from Europe or the United States.

Although it was a subsidiary of a Europe-based multinational firm, Alimentaires de Barria was largely autonomous and responsible for its own operations. Normally, Mr. Piperno enjoyed this independence, but occasionally he felt they could use some help. The spring of 1996 was one of those times. Mr. Piperno had been in Barria for eight years and had faced many problems with reasonable success. In addition to the "usual" problems, he had to deal with the chronic inflation that characterized so many Latin American countries, including Barria (see Table 1). Compounding the problem of inflation was the government policy of imposing price controls on some of the company's products. Inflation was driving up costs, while the government was putting price controls on most of the company's products.

Alimentaires de Barria is the Barrian subsidiary of a large European multinational food processor, Produits Alimentaires. Barria is a Latin American nation of 19 million people. The Produits Alimentaires subsidiary has been in Barria for over 35 years, but Mr. Bruno Piperno, the manager of Alimentaires de Barria, was concerned about the future prosperity and survival of the subsidiary because of the great increase in inflationary pressures in the mid-1990s. He was wondering what pricing and other operating policies he should follow to ensure the continued success of his company.

Inflation had a mixed impact on the firm's operations. On the one hand, it raised costs, and, on the other hand, it raised company sales. On the cost side, the impact of inflation fell differently on different ingredients. This was partly because these ingredients had differing rates of inflation and

partly because some ingredients had their price controlled at times by the government (see Table 2).

As Mr. Piperno considered the inflationary cost picture, he knew he faced a complex problem because each ingredient had different determinants and constraints. In the case of wages, for example, a strong government had kept wage increases below the inflation rate in his early years in Barria. In recent years, however, wage increases surpassed the rate of inflation as the new government felt less secure in office. As an important dietary item, sugar was price controlled, so its cost lagged behind other items in the general cost of living. The price of tin depended on (1) its price on the world market and (2) the Barrian exchange rate, since all tin was imported. Both of these factors were subject to abrupt fluctuations.

The price indexes for vegetables, fruits, and meats were averages because many different kinds of vegetables and fruits as well as three different kinds of meats were canned by Alimentaires. The inflation rate between different vegetable products did not vary as much as that for fruits and meats. Some of the fruits were imported, and their prices varied according to both the Barrian exchange rate and regular supply conditions. The various meat products had a more irregular supply. Suppliers would produce large quantities when the prices were high. This would tend create for an excess supply and a decline in prices. This action led in turn to a decline in supply in a later year.

The bright side of Mr. Piperno's experience in Barria was that he had expanded the sales and market share of Alimentaires' products. Unit sales of all three of the firm's product categories had more than kept up with the growth in population and real income in Barria. Even in competition with other food processors, local and foreign, Alimentaires' market share had gradually increased over the years. This was a source of satisfaction to Mr. Piperno, and it was appropriately noted back at corporate headquarters.

While Mr. Piperno felt he had done a good job in Barria with those things he could control, he was disturbed by the many things beyond his control. One of these "uncontrollables" was the availability of foreign exchange. Certain fruits and tin had to be imported. Also, any new equipment had to come from abroad. Because of its international debts, Barria had tight exchange controls. Every year Mr. Piperno had to battle with the Central Bank to get the foreign exchange he needed. Companies that exported received better treatment in getting foreign exchange, but Alimentaires had no exports.

Another "uncontrollable" that bothered Mr. Piperno even more than the foreign-exchange problem was the exis-

TABLE 1   Cost-of-Living Index in Barria

Year	Index
1986	100
1987	123
1988	148
1989	179
1990	211
1991	255
1992	312
1993	398
1994	675
1995	1,220

tence of government price controls on most of Alimentaires' products. Not all products in Barria were price controlled, but a great many were, especially so-called necessities, the items that entered into the cost-of-living calculation by the Central Bank. Since Alimentaires' products were food items, they were subject to price controls of varying rigidity. Some items, such as pineapple slices and the fancier meat products, were considered more like luxuries and therefore less tightly price controlled than the more prosaic products of everyday consumption. Also, the older the product, the tighter the price controls generally were. For Alimentaires this meant that its original canned vegetable line had generally more rigid price controls than its fruit products, which were a more recent part of the product line, especially certain new varieties and the juices that had been added only in 1990.

Mr. Piperno had been intrigued by the patterns of government price control and had ordered an internal study of its effects on Alimentaires. He found strong correlation between the degree of price control and unit sales growth of a product—the products most tightly controlled in price experienced the fastest unit sales growth. He wondered if this sales pattern meant that Alimentaires was subsidizing the consumption by Barrian consumers of these products.

Inventories were another aspect of operations only partly subject to management's control. A seasonal aspect characterized the supplies of some of the vegetables, fruits, and meats processed by Alimentaires. The people would tend to buy fresh products when they came on the market

TABLE 2   Price Indexes of Various Cost Factors

Year	Wages	Sugar	Tin	Vegetables	Fruits	Meats
1986	100	100	100	100	100	100
1987	110	100	114	109	134	140
1988	130	128	122	120	158	176
1989	155	128	141	135	187	168
1990	210	128	241	182	216	251
1991	243	190	313	212	269	245
1992	328	227	462	351	327	349
1993	435	285	614	377	409	418
1994	750	401	889	474	695	462
1995	1,318	752	1.602	768	1,229	891

and buy canned products during the other seasons. Alimentaires had to schedule its procurement and production according to these patterns of supply and demand. Another inventory problem arose because of the uncertainty of foreign-exchange allocations. Imported items had to be purchased when foreign exchange was available even if they were not needed at that time.

The net effect of all these conflicting forces was not positive for Alimentaires or Mr. Piperno. Even though unit sales had grown steadily and market share had increased, Alimentaires' total sales had not kept pace with the rate of inflation. In other words, government price controls had kept Alimentaires' selling-price increases below the increases in its costs. This meant a steady erosion of profit margins that had become especially worrisome in the past few years of more rapid inflation.

Mr. Piperno was very aware that a U.S. producer of baby food had left the Barrian market in 1995 after 10 years of struggling with these problems. The U.S. firm faced particularly tough price controls because of the sensitivity of its product line. Mr. Piperno didn't feel that Alimentaires was in the same situation as the U.S. firm, but he felt that it might be if inflation continued at its present frantic pace. Therefore, he was trying to think of possible adjustments he could make in Alimentaires' operations to meet these challenges.

Questions

1. What problem does Mr. Piperno face?
2. Identify and evaluate various courses of action Mr. Piperno might consider in attacking his problem.
3. What generalizations can you make about operating in an inflationary economy such as Barria?

International Marketing of Services

Learning Objectives

Trade in services is growing faster than the international trade in goods. Services have special characteristics that pose special problems in international marketing.

The main goals of this chapter are to

1. Identify the characteristics that distinguish services from goods and that influence the way they are marketed internationally.

2. Determine the basis of comparative advantage in service industries.

3. Define the roles played by governments and WTO in the service trade.

4. Discuss the following industry examples:

   ◆ Media and entertainment
   ◆ Airlines
   ◆ Professional services
   ◆ Retailing
   ◆ Hotel industry
   ◆ Financial services

What are services? Industries such as wholesaling and retailing, communications, transportation, utilities, banking and insurance, tourism, and business and personal services are all service industries. Services account for the largest portion of output and employment in the advanced industrialized countries. In 1994, services as a percent of gross domestic product (GDP) were 62 percent in Germany, 69 percent in France, 75 percent in Canada and the United States, 66 percent in Japan, 69 percent in Italy, and 77 percent in the United Kingdom. Services typically become more important as an economy becomes more developed. Thus, U.S. employment in service industries was 24 percent of total employment in 1870, 31 percent in 1900, 55 percent in 1950, and 72 percent in 1985, stabilizing around 75 percent in the mid-90s.[1] Similar increases were recorded in Japan, Germany, France, and Britain. The service industry as a whole has been increasing in importance for almost a century in the advanced industrialized nations.

Given the importance of services in the national economies, it is not surprising that they are becoming increasingly important in world trade. Trade in services accounts for between 20 and 25 percent of all world trade, having grown at about 16 percent a year for the past decade compared to a 7 percent growth rate for merchandise trade.

Table 16–1 shows that the United States has a trade surplus in services, unlike its overall balance-of-trade deficit. This reflects the greater competitiveness of U.S. services providers such as U.S. airlines, insurance companies, and banks. Equally interesting, however, is the relationship between services exports and foreign services sales. In 1993, subsidiaries of U.S. companies overseas generated $143.1 billion in services sales, about 80 percent of services exports. On the import side, U.S. subsidiaries of foreign companies sold $140.5 billion of services, exceeding the services imports for 1993 of $115.4 billion. This suggests that international marketing of services is done as much through foreign direct investment, franchising, and joint ventures as through exporting. Hence, the $750 billion estimate for services exports worldwide underestimates the total size of the international market for services.[2] U.S. services that have been exported include the following:

- Construction, design, and engineering services
- Banking and financial services
- Insurance services
- Legal and accounting services
- Computer software and data services
- Training and education
- Entertainment, music, film, and sports
- Management consulting
- Franchising
- Hotel and lodging services
- Transportation services, including airline and maritime services, and both passenger and cargo service

As this list indicates, the United States exports a wide variety of services. It is interesting to note, however, that some major service sectors within the United States are not represented in the list. For example, the utility sector, auto repair services, and personal services (laundry, barber shops, home-cleaning services) are not well represented in U.S. service exports. In the next section, we review some service industry characteristics that make international trade difficult.

SERVICES: HOW ARE THEY DIFFERENT FROM PRODUCTS?

Services have been defined as "those fruits of economic activity that you cannot drop on your toe: banking to butchery, acting to accountancy."[3] Indeed, services

| TABLE 16-1 | U.S. Imports and Exports of Services ($ Billions) |

	Exports		Imports	
	1993	1994	1993	1994
Total Private Exports and Imports	$174.2	$185.4	$115.4	$125.9
Travel	57.9	60.4	40.7	43.6
Passenger fares	16.6	17.5	11.3	12.7
Other transportation	23.9	26.1	26.6	28.4
Royalties	20.6	22.4	4.9	5.7
Other services	55.1	59.0	32.0	35.6
Foreign Services Sales[a]	143.1	NA	140.5	NA

[a]Represents foreign services sales by foreign affiliates of U.S. companies (equivalent to exports), and U.S. services sales by U.S. affiliates of foreign companies (equivalent to imports).
Source: Michael Mann and Sylvia E. Bargas, "U.S. International Sales and Purchases of Private Services," *Survey of Current Business,* September 1995.

are mostly intangible. The distinguishing characteristics of services include intangibility, heterogeneity, perishability, and, often, simultaneous production and consumption.[4] These characteristics are outlined in Table 16–2 and discussed further below. Because of these characteristics, services are more difficult to price and measure than products.

Intangibility

Services are often performances, such as performing an audit, designing a building, fixing a car. In this sense, they are intangible. Questions pertinent to the international marketing of services would include (1) whether actions are being performed on people (e.g., education) or things (e.g., air freight),[5] (2) whether the customer needed to be physically present during the service or only at initiation and termination of the service, and (3) whether it is enough that the customer be mentally present—that is, can the service be performed at a distance?

Heterogeneity

Different customers going to the same service company may not receive exactly the same service. This quality of heterogeneity occurs because different people perform the service. It is therefore impossible to make sure that the service is performed in exactly the same way each time. One sales clerk may be less polite or amiable than another, resulting in consumer dissatisfaction. The implication of heterogeneity is that quality is difficult to control.

A logical response is to attempt to standardize the service. One way is to develop a detailed blueprint of the steps in providing the service and then analyze results as these steps are taken to ensure that quality standards are maintained. This may mean changing the way the service is performed to reduce complexity and the possibilities for divergence among different service providers.[6] But it is exceedingly difficult to standardize services when the personnel providing them must exercise a high degree of judgment. When a firm's advantage is based on customizing the service, any attempt at standardization means that the fundamental strategy of the business is being changed.

When extending the service to international markets, there is also the question whether the service standardized for one national market will satisfy customers in other markets. For example, one way to standardize a service is to personalize the interaction between customer and service provider by training retail salespersons to

TABLE 16-2	Services Characteristics and Their Implications for Globalization

Service Characteristics	*Implications for Globalization*
Intangibility	How to differentiate the service? Advertising mainly through word of mouth: Who are the influential opinion makers in each market? Validity of a *follow-the-client* strategy in entering international markets? Manage corporate image in multiple markets.
Heterogeneity	How to reduce across-country variations in service quality influenced by variations among service providers? Can all service personnel in several countries be trained to the same level and quality of performance? Impact of cultural differences affecting extent and kind of training in each market. *Develop ownership and control stake sufficient to influence recruitment and training.*
Perishability	Can excess capacity in one market be used to satisfy demand in another? How to forecast service demand patterns in different markets? Are there similarities in the model for service demand across countries? Can standardized incentives be used to manage demand across countries? *Create cross-country databases, raise switching costs, ownership, and franchise strategies.*
Inseparability: The simultaneity of production and consumption	Can service be provided at a distance internationally? *Enhancing role of technology, electronic delivery* (e.g., ATMs—automatic teller machines). How much of service production can be placed in the "back office"? *Sharing of back office functions across markets.* The need to find service providers places a constraint on the pace of international expansion. If technology cannot facilitate service exporting, then *franchising, licensing, joint venture, and foreign direct investment are better avenues.*
Service quality and consumer participation in service creation/delivery	How do consumers determine service quality? A matter of consumer perceptions. Moreover, are customers in all markets equally willing to participate in the service creation process? What turns off the customer (variations in customer defection rates across markets)? How to ensure customer loyalty and repeat business? Developing market-specific plans to maintain customer loyalty. Customer perceptions of service quality may be affected by culture.
Implications of fixed-cost structure for pricing	Can scale economies lower costs of international entry? Will price-bundling strategies work in all markets? Can price discrimination be practiced across markets? Prioritizing markets by volume necessary to reach break-even. *Scale necessitates internationalization, and hence foreign direct investment, joint ventures.*
Service as a process	Is the service concept culture-bound? Adaptation versus standardization of the service concept for overseas markets. Can standardized "scripts" for the service encounter be used across countries? *Franchising and licensing more appealing as greater adaptation needed.*

Source: Adapted from R. Sarathy, "Global Strategy in Service Industries," *Long Range Planning* 27, No. 6 (1994).

greet customers by name and use certain standard conversational gambits. When such "scripts" are to be followed,[7] though, cultural factors probably demand a somewhat different "script" for each country market.

Also, it is reasonable that the training of customer-contact personnel should be conducted differently in different cultures. For example, the two-week training given to Kentucky Fried Chicken workers in Japan would be uneconomical in the context of high labor turnover in the United States; but it is appropriate for Japan, given the greater job loyalty among workers and, more important, Japanese customers' expectations of high levels of politeness and courtesy from Japanese service workers.

Perishability

Services are perishable in that they cannot be inventoried, saved, or stored; thus a plane seat that is not sold when the flight takes off is lost forever. This makes it harder to adjust the supply of a service to fluctuating demand, especially at times of peak demand. Service companies therefore seek innovations that allow the service to be "inventoried" in some fashion, or that allow demand to be managed so that the supply of services is adequate and can be economically provided. An example would be providing a restricted number of reduced-fare, advance-purchase seats on flights, with the number of such seats being increased if seats on the flight do not appear to be selling as forecast.

Marketing services internationally makes the task of forecasting demand for services more complex because the vagaries of individual national markets affect demand in unique ways. Further, service must match demand in many different markets. It is likely that idle capacity exists in some markets while excess demand is encountered in other markets.

Simultaneous Production and Consumption

Production and consumption of the service often take place at the same time; that is, the producer and the seller of the service are often the same person. Moreover, the customer must often be present for the service to take place. Unlike products, services usually cannot be exported, so international marketing means that the service must be performed by the firm itself in the country market, whether through franchising, licensing, a direct investment, or an acquisition. The fundamental question is, Can the service be performed at a distance? And if not, how should the firm position itself in a distant market in order to offer the service? An example would be the use of ATMs (automated teller machines), which allow customers to conduct certain banking transactions without a teller being present.

Pricing Services

Services are difficult to price because calculating the cost of producing them is difficult.[8] Price can be set in relation to full costs, based on what the competition charges, or simply set at whatever the customer is willing to pay. Service businesses have a high fixed-cost ratio. Hence, if the service can be offered without much modification in many national markets, prices can be lower because the fixed costs have presumably been recovered in the home market. Some advantages of scale therefore accrue to the company that is first to market with a new service. For example, in the case of a banking innovation such as a credit card, U.S. firms have already recovered much of their fixed costs of developing the credit-card concept through sales in the U.S. market. Hence, their foreign credit-card service prices can be lower because they do not have to incur the fixed costs of product development a second time.

Measuring Service Quality

Service quality is difficult to measure because it is often unclear what the consumer expects, yet quality is a matter of meeting customer expectations. In other words, it depends on consumer perception, which in turn is determined by the following:[9]

1. The person doing the service

2. The technical outcome of the service

3. The overall image of the company whose employee is carrying out the service

Technical quality may be amenable to traditional quality-control approaches borrowed from a manufacturing setting, but only if the service process is standardized. If corporate image affects the perception of quality, the firm must decide whether the same corporate image is needed in all countries. Should all employees wear the same uniforms? Should the physical facilities look the same in all national markets?

Consumer dissatisfaction may result from unrealistic expectations. Other reasons for the gap between desired quality and perceived quality include not understanding what consumers expect from a service, inability, or unwillingness to meet customer expectations; problems with service delivery; and communications gaps

GLOBAL MARKETING

McDonald's in Hungary and Russia

McDonald's began operations in Budapest, Hungary, on April 30, 1988. On its first day of operation, it broke a McDonald's record for the most transactions. Today it is one of the busiest McDonald's in the world, with 9,000 transactions daily.

Plans to establish a McDonald's in Hungary began with a joint-venture agreement in November 1986, although negotiations began back in 1985. McDonald's is a 50 percent owner, its partner being Hungary's Babolna Agricultural Cooperative.

McDonald's supplied all of the restaurant equipment, including equipment to established sources of supply such as a bakery to make hamburger buns. McDonald's also contributed something intangible: a standard of quality for the fast-food industry. It had to develop a supplier infrastructure by introducing new food-processing techniques and forcing development of new products in Hungary, as well as insisting on the improvement of existing products to meet world standards of quality. Products such as hamburger buns, the kind of cheese used in its cheeseburgers, and orange juice concentrate were unavailable in Hungary. Ketchup was available, but it did not meet McDonald's quality standards. It took over a year to develop supply sources. McDonald's experts in purchasing and quality control then worked with suppliers on a monthly basis to get the desired product and quality.

Locally produced food products are used, except for Mc-Cormick spices, which are used exclusively by McDonald's around the world, and sesame seeds, which cannot be grown in Hungary. Paper products such as paper cups are imported.

McDonald's opened with seven partially trained managers and with another 20 employees loaned from stores in other countries. Most of the loaned employees returned home after a month, with the exception of a U.S. manager who stayed on as an adviser and trainer. New employees had training, but little experience, and had to learn on the job in the middle of huge crowds. During the first few days, a line was always outside the store. Some of the training focused on incul-

when the firm fails to communicate realistic expectations about what service quality will be offered.[10]

Importance of Customer Loyalty to Services

Because services cannot be stored, a basic marketing strategy is to ensure repeat business by generating loyalty in existing customers. Devices such as frequent-flyer plans may be used to reward customer loyalty. But given that consumers have different characteristics in different countries, are such plans necessary for all national markets, or should they be shaped mainly by competitive variations in each market? Loyalty can also be maintained and rewarded through pricing, and the question for each national market is whether volume discounts and membership strategies work equally well in all markets.

ADDITIONAL DECISION AREAS

Advertising

How are services best advertised? By word of mouth, direct mail, satisfied customer referrals, or ads in newspapers and on television? Are there national differences in the relative appeal of these different forms of advertising of services? What should the focus of advertising be? Which is more important, the image and name of the company providing the service, or facets of the service being sold? These questions will have to be answered for each country market.

cating attitudes of customer service. In a country of shortages where people are accustomed to waiting, customer service was to some degree an unfamiliar concept. McDonald's found it impossible to get part-time help, which it relies on in most countries. However, with a successful opening behind it, McDonald's plans to open another five outlets in the next five years in Budapest. Real estate is difficult to buy at any price, so the company must build its restaurants in existing buildings. As yet, McDonald's has not chosen franchisees but plans to do so for perhaps three of the proposed five restaurants.

After its Hungarian experience, McDonald's natural response was to turn to Russia. McDonald's Russian entry was shepherded by its head of Canadian operations, Mr. George Cohon, who had made initial contact with some Russian delegation members during the Montreal Olympics in 1976! But the joint-venture agreement was not signed until April 1988 because of intervening events such as the U.S. Olympic boycott. McDonald's Russian venture had some unusual features. Its joint-venture partner with a 51 percent ownership was the food service department of the Moscow City Council. Normally, Mc-

Donald's worked with entrepreneurs, but in Russia in the late 1980s they had no choice but to work with a leading entity within the Communist party. The joint venture was also a "rubles-only" joint venture at a time when the ruble was inconvertible. This meant that McDonald's would sell its hamburgers to Russians for rubles and would buy mostly local supplies paid for in rubles. As in Hungary, the company had difficulty maintaining its reputation because of poor-quality local suppliers.

Ultimately, McDonald's had to invest over $40 million in setting up a raw-material processing plant to supply it with the requisite buns, french fries, hamburger patties, and so forth. Amortizing this large injection of foreign capital at a time when the ruble was rapidly devaluing meant that McDonald's was making no money in the short run. It might well have been selling Ray Kroc's original dream of 15 cent hamburgers. But overall, McDonald's is hugely profitable and was planning to open over 2,000 restaurants outside the United States in 1995 alone. If one has faith in the long-term promise of Russia, losing money for a few years might seem a reasonable investment to ensure front-row seats for the Russian renaissance.

Sources: "Joint Ventures in Hungary," *CW Informatika Ltd.* (Budapest) 2, no. 1 (1989): 9–10; Peter Foster, "McDonald's Excellent Soviet Venture," *Canadian Business,* May 1991; and "McDonald's Accelerates Store Openings in U.S. and Abroad, Pressuring Rivals," *The Wall Street Journal,* January 18, 1996.

Organization

A decentralized organization seems more apt for service industries, given the inherent heterogeneity of the product and the customer base. But if a firm moves to standardize the service performance, can it do so without considerable centralization? This is a key decision for the firm that chooses to market its services internationally.

Cultural Variables

Because services generally involve close interaction between the service provider and the customer, cultural variables affect user satisfaction; they also affect service design and the nature of interaction with the customer. An interesting illustration involves the signing of a book contract in Russia.

Little, Brown, a U.S. publishing house, wanted to obtain the rights to Anatoli Ryabakov's *Children of the Arbat,* a novel about life in Stalinist Russia. As is the norm in Russia, Little, Brown had to negotiate with the state-owned copyright agency, VAAP, represented by a team of eight officials, two translators, and the author. Settling on the amount of advance was easy, but royalties created some difficulties. U.S. royalties are tied to the mode of selling; thus, they may be lower on discounted sales to book clubs, direct-mail sales, and to large wholesalers. But VAAP would accept a reduction only for paperback and book club sales. It also wanted to have the right of approval over the translation, book jacket, flap copy, and promotional material.

VAAP also wanted to insert into the contract a clause that the publisher would do no harm to "VAAP, the author, or the book." When Roger Donald of Little,

Brown responded to this demand by discussing the acceptable amount of monetary damages, VAAP countered that this was not the meaning of injury to reputation. When Donald asked how the clause was enforceable without a monetary provision, he was told that this would be based on honorable behavior. The difficulty was solved by inserting a clause vowing never to inflict "intentional harm." When, at the end of successful negotiations, Donald invited the VAAP team to a fancy dinner, he found that all members spoke English.[11]

COMPARATIVE ADVANTAGE AND THE SERVICE INDUSTRIES

Why do the advanced industrialized nations dominate services exports? What factors lead a nation and its firms to have a comparative advantage in services? Clearly, each service industry is distinct, with a different production function; that is, each service industry uses technology, labor, capital, and management in different proportions to deliver the service. Still, we can examine the role that factors of production play in service industries.

Labor

Service industries are generally labor intensive, with both highly skilled and unskilled labor being used. In services such as retailing, barber shops, and florists, labor may not need much training and is likely to be low paid. In such cases, countries with low labor costs would have an advantage. At the other extreme are legal and accounting services that require highly educated and highly paid personnel such as lawyers and accountants. It is likely that advanced countries would have an advantage in such services. However, such high-level skills may be country-specific and not easily transferable to other countries. Expertise in U.S. tax law may not be meaningful to tax practice in Europe; however, the *methodologies* used by U.S. law firms to research and argue tax issues may indeed be pertinent to tax law practice in advanced nations.

Capital

Traditionally, services have low capital-to-labor ratios. Lower amounts of capital are used per worker than in manufacturing industries. Service productivity has been lower than in manufacturing, and the future growth of service industries will require larger amounts of capital per worker to raise productivity and quality. In banking, for example, increased use of computers results in more productive workers, faster transactions, and more satisfied customers. If this trend continues, countries and firms with lower costs of capital will gain an advantage in international markets.

Technology

Services vary in their use of technology (although it is an increasingly pervasive influence in all industries). Services such as airlines and shipping, custom computer software, and banking can be termed high-technology services compared to, say, interior decorating, which uses less sophisticated technology.

A case in point is the use of Integrated Services Digital Network (ISDN) networks by a French maintenance company to provide maintenance services at a distance. ISDN networks integrate voice, data, and graphic images in communication networks, allowing pictures to be sent with text and numbers. Service S.A. has developed its Service Expert System to provide technical assistance to dealers for the maintenance of compact disk (CD) players sold to customers throughout France under terms of a customer warranty.[12]

Service staff affiliated with dealers needed help in repairing the CD players, and a previously established interactive computer network handled only data. A videotape had to be shipped to handle visual images. But with the new Service Expert System, pictures are stored with reference numbers as part of the maintenance manual. Then, as the mechanics need help, they can call up both the relevant portions of the manual and the pictures from the central database maintained by Service S.A. This allows Service S.A. to update both the manual and the pictures at will.

The major saving is the reduction in the direct labor cost of the repair because diagnostic time is cut in half. Not only is the latest information sent quickly to dealers but also statistical information on product defects and repairs is fed back to quality control at the factory. This immediate feedback of problems and repairs enhances the manufacturer's ability to redesign the product.

Clearly, the capital investment in research and development (R&D) that allowed the creation of this technology application led to a comparative advantage for the company—and for the country because it can use the technology to enter the global maintenance industry in a new fashion, bypassing former barriers.

Transfer of Information, Technology, Capital, and People

Very important in the export of services is a global communications network. In essence, such transborder data flows have created a whole new category of industries, enabling previously nontradable goods to enter international trade. The provision of custom software programming services by teleports is an example of this phenomenon. Companies such as Hewlett-Packard and Texas Instruments have set up software development labs in India using Indian programmers, who maintain and upgrade mainframe software for the parent company and other clients in the United States by means of remote terminals and computers and telecommunications links.

Of course, services need not be provided solely through information transfer. Foreign direct investment involves the transfer of capital and ideas, often technology through which the service is provided. The Service Expert System described earlier is one example of the role of technology in deriving competitive advantage in services. Another is the use of laser scanners and bar codes, with which checkout at grocery stores and other retail outlets is speeded up. Going a step further, companies such as Information Resources have developed proprietary databases of the information gleaned from laser scanning the entire sales volume of a store. These data are analyzed and sold to companies seeking more information about their consumers. As these companies begin selling such services outside the United States, they must first ensure that the technology of bar codes and laser scanning is available in that country, as well as the computer software used to analyze the raw data to prepare reports.

Thus, for services to be provided in foreign countries, there must also be a transfer of information (or other intangible assets), technology, capital, and people—the service providers who interact with customers.[13] However, barriers to labor mobility across countries exist; hence, services will export capital, technology, and information to be combined with local labor.

Other Bases for Comparative Advantage

Other bases for comparative advantage include (1) management skills specific to service industries, (2) size, (3) experience in a particular service sector, and (4) the firm's global reputation. Thus, U.S. firms have been able to dominate the world software industry because of their long experience and skilled management developed through years of being in business. Specific skills that U.S. firms have developed include transforming custom software into packages that have the widest customer-base appeal, supervising the development of complicated software within large teams of programmers, and marketing software to an end-user base that is technologically unsophisticated through indirect channels of distribution such as computer industry retailers and department stores.[14]

In short, services can be more or less capital intensive and technology intensive, along with greater or lesser reliance on skilled labor. Advanced nations such as the United States and France are likely to have a comparative advantage in the more capital-intensive, skilled labor-intensive, and technology-intensive service industry sectors.

Sustainable Competitive Advantage in Services

Beyond country-specific advantages, service companies seek to build a sustainable competitive advantage in order to enhance long-term performance. Bharadwaj and others[15] have developed a conceptual framework that links the resources and capabilities of a service firm together with the nature of the service offered and certain firm characteristics, resulting in a competitive positioning advantage. Whether this advantage can be sustained depends on whether barriers exist to the diffusion and imitation of firm-specific capabilities and resources. This model is set out in Figure 16–1.

GOVERNMENT INTERVENTION IN THE TRADE IN SERVICES

As is true for goods, international trade in services is also subject to government interference and protection. U.S. manufacturers in a survey noted several government barriers:[16]

- Rights of establishment (meaning the right to establish a branch or subsidiary in a foreign country; for example, many nations ban ownership of television stations by foreigners).
- Trade barriers, including limitations on the proportion of a market that can be served by a foreign company, and discriminatory taxation of services provided by a foreign company.
- Foreign exchange controls; limits on remitting profits from service businesses.
- Government procurement barriers because government buys services only from "national" companies.
- Technical issues that may serve to keep out foreign firms, such as through the use of standards and certification conditions.
- Government subsidies, countervailing duties, and high customs valuation of foreign services, leading to higher total tariffs.
- Licensing regulations that impose unreasonable terms of entry or insist on licensing as the only mode of entry.
- Restrictions on professional qualifications, including ban on entry of qualified service company personnel.
- Tolerance of commercial counterfeiting.

Further, U.S. managers of service industries indicated that although the key reasons for the success of other countries' service firms in world markets were factors such as experience, technology expertise, and superior quality, some of their success was also attributable to lower price, government support, preferential financing, political or regional bias, and U.S. government restrictions (particularly in reference to selling to formerly Communist countries).

Telecommunications is an industry in which government intervention is particularly important. U.S. deregulation and the breakup of the AT&T Bell system have created many opportunities for foreign firms to participate in the U.S. market for telecommunications services. A major growth segment is value-added networks (VANs), for which private firms provide services and information over public

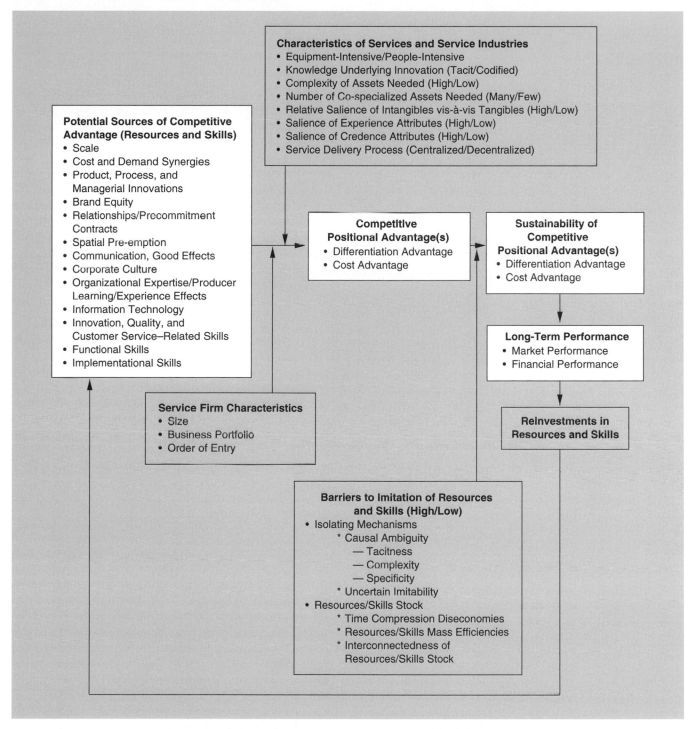

FIGURE 18-1 A Contingency Model of Sustainable Competitive Advantage in Service Industries

Characteristics of Services and Service Industries
- Equipment-Intensive/People-Intensive
- Knowledge Underlying Innovation (Tacit/Codified)
- Complexity of Assets Needed (High/Low)
- Number of Co-specialized Assets Needed (Many/Few)
- Relative Salience of Intangibles vis-à-vis Tangibles (High/Low)
- Salience of Experience Attributes (High/Low)
- Salience of Credence Attributes (High/Low)
- Service Delivery Process (Centralized/Decentralized)

Potential Sources of Competitive Advantage (Resources and Skills)
- Scale
- Cost and Demand Synergies
- Product, Process, and Managerial Innovations
- Brand Equity
- Relationships/Precommitment Contracts
- Spatial Pre-emption
- Communication, Good Effects
- Corporate Culture
- Organizational Expertise/Producer Learning/Experience Effects
- Information Technology
- Innovation, Quality, and Customer Service–Related Skills
- Functional Skills
- Implementational Skills

Competitive Positional Advantage(s)
- Differentiation Advantage
- Cost Advantage

Sustainability of Competitive Positional Advantage(s)
- Differentiation Advantage
- Cost Advantage

Long-Term Performance
- Market Performance
- Financial Performance

Reinvestments in Resources and Skills

Service Firm Characteristics
- Size
- Business Portfolio
- Order of Entry

Barriers to Imitation of Resources and Skills (High/Low)
- Isolating Mechanisms
    * Causal Ambiguity
        — Tacitness
        — Complexity
        — Specificity
    * Uncertain Imitability
- Resources/Skills Stock
    * Time Compression Diseconomies
    * Resources/Skills Mass Efficiencies
    * Interconnectedness of Resources/Skills Stock

Source: From S. G. Bharadwaj, P. R. Varadarajan, and J. Fahy, "Sustainable Competitive Advantage in Service Industries: A Conceptual Model and Research Propositions," *Journal of Marketing,* October 1993, 85.

telecommunication networks. An example is an on-line credit-reporting and credit-verification service for credit-card customers. The problem here is that European and Japanese markets have been slower to deregulate, creating inequality of opportunity for U.S. firms.[17]

GLOBAL MARKETING

Selling Telecommunications in China

China has a fast-growing economy, with average growth rates exceeding 8 percent a year since 1980. Its income has tripled and it is modernizing rapidly. As part of its modernization, it needs telephones. There are approximately two telephone lines per 100 people in China, compared to about 51 lines per 100 people in the United States. A modern telephone system is essential for the smooth functioning of a country's economy, particularly its foreign trade and foreign investment activities. China hopes to achieve between five to eight lines per 100 people by the year 2000. This implies installing approximately 100 million telephone lines and would represent between 20 and 30 percent of the world's demand for telecommunications equipment, representing the world's largest market for telecommunications equipment over the next decade.

All of the world's major telecommunications multinationals, including Ericsson, Siemens, NEC, and Alcatel, a French company, are competing for this inviting market. When Alcatel purchased ITT's telecommunications business in 1987, it obtained a minority interest in Shanghai Bell, with China's telecommunications ministry owning 60 percent. Its new factory in Shanghai's industrial zone has a capacity of 4 million telephone lines annually.

China's shortage of foreign exchange leads it to favor local manufacturing over imports. At the same time, it wants technology transfer, even though it results in higher domestic prices. In response, Alcatel is manufacturing semiconductors for telecommunications use in another joint venture, Shanghai Belling Microelectronics. Alcatel expects that its local manufacturing and its continued presence in China through the Tiananmen Square incident will allow it to win a considerable portion of Chinese government contracts for telecommunications equipment. Selling to any government is not easy: In the Chinese case, Alcatel must deal with several deci-

Fair Trade in Services: The Uruguay Round

As services grow in importance in world trade, nations have begun seeking a consensus on fair trade practices with regard to services. The last round of GATT (now the WTO) talks, the "Uruguay Round," gave special attention to protecting intellectual property rights, referring to the ideas that form the basis for many high-technology services, such as custom software. These provisions address the issues of barriers to trade in services, national treatment of foreign firms, allowance of FDI in services without undue restrictions, temporary admission of foreign-service workers, international agreement on the extent of regulation of international data flows and ownership rights in international databases, and the importation of materials and equipment necessary for provision of services. Other thorny issues included establishing a framework to control restrictive licensing practices and the right of "nonestablishment," which is growing increasingly important as service firms deliver their services electronically or through the mail without being physically present in a country. This governs the conditions under which a foreign firm can be said to have established a presence in a foreign market, which may determine whether the foreign firm qualifies for treatment as a domestic firm; similarly, establishing a domestic presence is often necessary to qualify for protection under the laws of intellectual property rights in that country.[18]

The U.S. government offers some specialized help to service industries. Within the Department of Commerce, the Office of Service Industries has divisions covering specific industry sectors such as the information industries, transportation and tourism, and finance and management.

In the remainder of this chapter, we examine the global marketing of a variety of service industry sectors.

sion makers, including the central government, telecommunications ministry, other ministries, the Cabinet of Ministers, and provincial governments that control finances, as well as state-owned banks.

Political issues also affect Alcatel's chances of winning telecommunication contracts. France sold Mirage jet fighters to Taiwan, whereupon China closed France's consulate in Guangzhou. GEC-Alsthom, half owned by Alcatel, had hoped to bid on a new $1 billion underground railroad in Guangzhou, but the fighter sale jeopardized bidding on and winning this contract.

While China is attractive to Western companies because of its growth potential, from a low base of less than two phones per 100 people, the Chinese government has been adept at obtaining Western technology and capital without giving up control of its telecom sector. China does not allow foreign ownership of its telephone networks. However, economic growth in China, exceeding 10 percent a year for several years, has strained its telephone capacity, and the need to offer better and more phone service may be the reason why this ban may be relaxed. Given that it costs $10 billion a year to add the 10 to 15 million new lines that China needs every year, it might be necessary to offer private Western capitalists more incentives to invest in China. One approach that reduces risk is the "build-lease-service" approach, whereby Western capital builds and leases the network, receiving a rental income for use of the network while also getting paid to maintain it so that the network works as planned.

Motorola, which is a major supplier of cellular phone systems to China, faces similar pressures to transfer technology. It has invested $720 million in a semiconductor factory, together with 2,200 apartments, schools, and a management training program. Over time, such a show of commitment, coupled with an early presence, could pay off as China modernizes and relaxes state control over key sectors such as telecommunications.

Sources: "Alcatel in China: The Biggest Prize," *The Economist*, January 16, 1993; "China's Telecom Industry: Hung Up," *The Economist*, July 22, 1995; and "Tough at the Top," *The Economist*, January 6, 1996.

GLOBAL MEDIA AND THE ENTERTAINMENT INDUSTRY

In the United States, entertainment has always been one of the largest exports. In 1988 the United States earned $5.5 billion in entertainment industry exports, second only to its aerospace industry.[19] By 1994, U.S. entertainment exports were up to $9 billion. The private-enterprise system governing U.S. television and the burgeoning of alternative channels, first on pay-TV, then on cable television, and now on satellite television, has led to fierce competition. Each station seeks larger audiences to sell more commercials and charge higher prices for commercial time: this means showing the programs that attract the largest audiences. Over time, U.S. firms have become very adept in producing such mass audience–pleasing programs. This is their competitive advantage in world markets.

Deregulation of U.S. television, the large U.S. population, the large number of available programming hours, and the multiplicity of TV channels and theaters all combine to make it worthwhile for U.S. companies to invest additional resources in TV and film production since the potential audience for any hit program is enormous. These investments also become a comparative advantage because the U.S. industry enjoys economies of scale arising from a multiplicity of "customers," both in the number of TV channels and movie theaters and in the large English-speaking audience.

European Media Environment

In sharp contrast to the United States, European television was at one time largely government controlled. Basically, government ownership of stations meant noncommercial television except for rare and restricted instances. In West Germany, for example, television advertising was restricted to 40 minutes a day; in Switzerland, 20 minutes a day.

Deregulation of European television has changed the competitive environment. The use of new technologies (satellite broadcasting, cable, and pay-TV) has increased the number of channels. For example, in Japan, since 1990, 24-hour satellite TV broadcasting has increased the number of channels available from 7 to 12 or 13.

Now that there are more TV stations in Europe and Japan and more air time to fill, there will be a greater demand for TV programming. Also, deregulated TV stations and channels will show more commercials, so advertising by firms seeking a European market will increase. This, in turn, means more business for advertising agencies and their suppliers. The market for exports from U.S. producers of films and TV shows will grow, and, in response, government attempts at protection are likely to stop the onslaught of U.S. companies and allow the emergence of a "European" TV industry.

Such changes broaden the scope of the media industry, which now encompasses broadcasting and production of TV and motion picture films, and also includes books and newspapers, printing services, and alternative modes of information delivery such as the creation and sale of proprietary databases. Information and entertainment can be delivered in so many ways: by record and cassette, by television and movie theater, in book form, and as data that can be downloaded from on-line databases.

An example of the response to the growing appetite for program content in Europe is the rise of Endemol, a Dutch independent television production company. Endemol focuses on producing pan-European programs with tight budgetary control so that the excesses of Hollywood are avoided. Like its larger U.S. brethren, Endemol has begun integrating content with access to channels, forming a consortium with Dutch publisher VNU and local media interests to manage a group of three Dutch TV stations that reach 41 percent of the European population. Content will be principally supplied by Endemol.[20]

Satellite TV and a Pan-European Audience

Technology has played a key role in changing the nature of the industry. The Europeans are creating new TV channels by using high-power direct-broadcast satellite (DBS) systems that can beam programs from satellites directly into the home via a small receiver. Satellite TV promises the possibility of creating a pan-European, cross-cultural audience. In response, companies such as BBC and BskyB have merged to obtain scale economies and better market to the growing European audience.[21]

Pay-TV in Europe

Unlike the United States, where cable TV has over 60 percent penetration of households and routinely offers 50 or more channels, European households will move from a situation in which they had access to only a few over-air or cable channels to a pay-TV–channel world with hundreds of digital TV channels via satellite, offering superior picture and sound quality. To attract viewers, companies offer video on demand, whereby viewers can watch relatively new films on a flexible schedule, with the film broadcast at staggered starting times. Initially, the competition to show new films means that the bulk of the profits accrue to the film's owners, primarily Hollywood studios. Over time, the presence of a large European market can stimulate the emergence of focused European companies providing home-grown programs and entertainment.[22]

What decisions are involved in reaching a pan-European audience? First, the firm must try to predict which programs are likely to appeal to viewers from different European countries. Second, it must determine the appropriate forms of advertising for those viewers Companies must also develop one brand name to push in their pan-European commercials. Thus, Unilever cannot easily advertise its cleaning fluid branded as Vif in Switzerland, Viss in Germany, Jif in the United

Kingdom and Greece, and Cif in France. And nationalistic country managers must be persuaded to use standardized brand names and advertising channels.

Before the advent of television deregulation in Europe, European companies spent about $5 billion a year on advertising, compared to the U.S. level of nearly $20 billion with a quarter less population.[23] The proliferation of media can only motivate European firms to significantly raise their media spending plans.

Cable TV is not as widespread in Europe as in the United States and may never become as strong because of competition from direct-broadcast satellite television. One of the more successful cable TV stations in Europe is MTV Europe, itself a joint venture of U.S. and European partners. Understanding why MTV has been successful is the key to understanding the potentials and pitfalls of a pan-European television network. So let's examine its history.

MTV President Tom Freston has said, "Music crosses borders very easily, and the lingua franca of rock 'n roll is English. Rock is an Anglo-American form; German rock bands sing in English; Swedish rock bands sing in English." Not surprisingly, MTV is now available all across Europe. It is particularly interested in Europe because of the proliferation of TV channels there. MTV's mission? "We want to be the global rock n' roll village where we can talk to youth worldwide."

The key to cross-national TV networks is language. People seeking entertainment are not likely to choose a foreign-language show. In contrast to MTV's success, SuperChannel, an English-based satellite and cable station, lost nearly $100 million in two years for this reason. It then changed ownership and format, emphasizing sporting events, where language is less important. As *The Economist* puts it, entertainment in a foreign language is seldom "light." The Germans were glad to watch Sky and SuperChannel for a while until the two German satellite stations RTL Plus and SAT1 were available. Rock-music videos on MTV succeed mainly because language is irrelevant. But even here, cultural preferences are important: Teenagers in different countries may prefer different kinds of rock music.[24] To overcome the language problem, cross-national TV channels must focus on special-interest programs, such as sports, business news, and first-run movies.

Satellite TV and Cable TV in Asia

Over a dozen satellites are available to beam TV programs into Asia. The signals then have to be received in the home, either through small antennas, "dishes," affixed outside the home or apartment, or redistributed by cable TV operators, particularly likely in large apartment buildings common in Singapore, Hong Kong, and Taiwan. TV companies seeking to offer their programs, therefore, may have to make alliances with local cable TV operators. Furthermore, as more moderate-income households become satellite and cable TV customers, they seek out native-language entertainment. As a result, Star TV has divided its programming into two segments, one aimed at India, and the other at China and surrounding countries. In addition to MTV, a new offering, called Channel V, provides music in Chinese, Hindi, and other Asian languages.[25] Advertisers prefer local programming because it is more likely to attract large audiences. Of course, no "right" formula exists. A mix of Western hits, sports with wide appeal such as soccer or basketball, coupled with judicious local programming, may be the recipe to attract and maintain the large audiences that in turn bring in the advertising dollars.

ENTERTAINMENT INDUSTRY ECONOMICS

The media industry has some significant cost-structure characteristics that interact with the environmental changes discussed thus far to create the need for new global strategies.[26]

First, this is an industry with a *high fixed-cost structure.* Most costs are incurred in the production of programs and in the establishment of the distribution system, that is, the TV network, be it via satellite, on-air, cable, or pay channels. These high fixed costs place a premium on obtaining a large subscriber base and create high leverage with handsome profits occurring once break-even levels are reached.

The media industry is also *cyclical,* at least in the United States, with sudden jumps in revenue being derived from *hit* films, TV programs, books, and records. Thus, the industry has a high level of *risk* and requires *abundant capital* to survive long periods of negative cash flow. In turn, this creates a bias within the industry to *control distribution channels,* that is, media outlets, be they book publishers, TV channels, or record clubs.

The maturation of the U.S. market has brought lower growth rates and an abundant supply of TV channels as compared to markets in Europe or Japan and the Far East, where fewer channels are available and growth rates are higher because market saturation is low. This situation, together with the cyclical nature of the industry and its high fixed costs, results in a bias toward *larger companies* and produces a strategic advantage for those able to control distribution channels as well as produce programs for them. That is, companies that own both TV stations and TV film production companies tend to enjoy higher profits, less risk, and faster rates of growth.

Global Mergers in the Media Industry

A conjunction of environmental change and industry characteristics has led to the globalization of the media industry, with a concentration of acquisitions by foreign companies of major U.S. media companies. Table 16–3 summarizes some of the major acquisitions that have taken place since 1988 in the media industry.

As the table shows, the bulk of activity has been concentrated in the United States. Several reasons exist for this U.S. focus:

1. The United States has had long experience in developing films and TV programs, and Hollywood and U.S. productions have enjoyed worldwide success. Owning these facilities would deliver a stream of films and TV programs, books, records, and magazines then to be marketed around the world.

2. The U.S. market is huge, offering high potential profits. It is also a lead market, so programs successful here can easily be sold in Europe.

3. U.S. film and TV production technology is to be desired, as well as the talent and experience of U.S.–based film and TV production crews. Rather than try to transport talent to European markets, companies may prefer to obtain it by acquiring a U.S. company.

The best example of this globalization phenomenon is News Corp., controlled by Australian entrepreneur Rupert Murdoch. He first expanded from Australia to the United Kingdom, primarily in TV and newspapers. He built Sky Channel as a pan-European service using both cable and satellite delivery; next, he developed a U.S. base, buying several independent TV stations and 20th Century Fox film production company, along with its library of films, as the nucleus for creating a fourth U.S.–wide, on-air TV network. The Fox network would distribute (i.e., show) films produced by 20th Century Fox, and the same material could appear in England and Europe on Sky Channel. Then he acquired *TV Guide* and created *Premiere* magazine, both vehicles to appeal to the U.S. national TV audience and further publicize his network. Murdoch's News Corp. is an example of the implementation of a globalization strategy in a global services in-

| TABLE 16-3 | Global Media Empire Building: Major Acquisitions Since 1988 |

Acquirer	Acquisition
Sony Corp.	CBS Records, Columbia Pictures, Gubers-Peters Productions. Disappointing results at Sony Pictures led to a $3.2 billion loss in 1994.
Seagram	Acquired 80 percent of MCA for $5.7 billion, from Matsushita, which had earlier acquired MCA in response to Sony acquiring its media interests. Matsushita is reputed to have lost $3–4 billion on purchase & sale of MCA.
Time-Warner	Merger combining books and magazines, pay and cable TV, film production, records, and movies. U.S. West invested $2.5 billion for 25 percent of Time-Warner entertainment unit. In 1995, acquired Turner Broadcasting for its cable operations, film library, and CNN.
Bertelsmann	RCA Records, Bantam Books, and Doubleday Books. $360 million joint venture with Canal+ to develop digital pay-TV in Europe; similar accord with British Sky Broadcasting; merger with Luxembourg-based CLT to gain presence in European over-the-air "free" TV.
News Corp.	20th Century Fox films, several TV stations: The Fox network, British Sky Broadcasting in Europe, *TV Guide* (Triangle Publications) and *Premiere* magazine. 1993, acquired control of Star TV, Asia's satellite TV channel. Joint venture with MCI to launch global multimedia network, and with Televisa and Globo to launch a satellite direct-to-home TV service for Latin America.
Hachette	Diamandis (magazines), Grolier (encyclopedias).
Maxwell	Macmillan Publishing, *Official Airline Guide* (subsequently divested with the collapse of the Maxwell companies).
Disney/Cap Cities	Acquired Cap Cities and ABC Television for $19 billion, controlling both channels and content, with synergies in international markets, and between cable and over-the-air TV networks in the United States; main properties include ESPN, UK cable properties, and joint venture with Luxembourg-based CLT.
U.S. West	A joint-venture cable TV franchise for all of Hong Kong (1.5 million homes) and cable TV properties in the United Kingdom and France. Similar moves by NYNEX and Bell Canada.
Fujisankei	Virgin Records, David Puttnam's Enigma Productions.
Viacom	Paramount Pictures acquisition, resulting in ownership of MTV Networks, Paramount Pictures, and Blockbuster Video stores. Viacom plans to sell cable systems to Telecommunications Inc. for $2 billion, diversify into music; MTV partnership with Polygram to launch two music channels in Asia. NYNEX invested $1.2 billion in Viacom.
GM-Hughes DirecTV	Partnership with Cisneros (Venezuela), Abril (Brazil), and MVS Multivision (Mexico) to launch "Galaxy" Latin American satellite TV service.
Television South Plc.	MTM (Mary Tyler Moore) Productions.

dustry. The principal points of his strategy include a physical presence in two major markets, Europe and the United States, and combining distribution channels, TV stations, and channels themselves, with production facilities and "software" (the actual programs) in the form of a list of films and TV programs to be continually resold.

Subsequently, News Corp. purchased 63.6 percent of Star TV (from Hutchison Whampoa of Hong Kong) for $525 million, plus another $40 million for a similar stake in its programming affiliate, Media Assets Ltd. Star TV represents the missing piece in creating a global network. Star reaches an audience ranging from the Middle East to New Zealand, which potentially includes two-thirds of the world's population and complements Fox Broadcasting in the United States and British Sky Broadcasting in Europe. The latest moves include attempts to merge with major European competitors such as Canal Plus.

Just as important as creating a global network is control of Star's programming assets: Star had signed up five Hollywood studios and three international news programmers to supply content for a series of pay channels it controls. Star also had a contract with Taiwan-based Golden Harvest group, which would supply Chinese-language films, TV shows, and other programming. A library of Chinese movies and programs will help News Corp. immeasurably in gaining audience share in mainland China and in the Chinese-speaking portions of Southeast Asia.[27]

Cable TV

Cable TV is another area in which major U.S. companies are looking for growth overseas as cable penetration rates in the United States exceed 70 percent and the market is near saturation. Foreign government regulations limit its profitability, however. In many countries, cable TV is viewed as a public utility and controlled by a utility company. In others, cable fees are set by the government. Still, the U.S. cable companies' extensive experience gives them an edge in countries where regulation has not reduced cable's attractiveness. The real issue is competition in the form of satellite DBS systems that can be picked up with satellite dishes.

Cable TV in the United Kingdom

An interesting case is the United Kingdom, where NYNEX, and U.S. West, both major U.S. telephone companies, have invested to build two of the largest cable systems. Until 1995, "Baby Bells" were not allowed to enter the U.S. cable TV market. Hence, they have resorted to the U.K. market, where they offered a combined telephone and cable TV service. That is, telephone calls as well as cable TV programs could be carried over the same wires. Thus, NYNEX and U.S. West hoped to learn how to develop two income streams from the same basic capital investments and use such expertise in the United States when the telecommunications markets became deregulated, as they were in 1995. In the United Kingdom itself, while sales have been growing—up nearly tenfold between 1991 and 1995—companies such as Telewest have only shown losses as capital expenditures have exceeded sales in every year since inception. In response, the major U.S. cable firms in the U.K. decided to merge, to reduce losses, obtain significant market clout and position themselves better to compete with dominant phone companies.

Sports

Sports is an area of the entertainment industry that is rapidly becoming globalized, principally because of the media industry itself. ESPN, for example, took a 40 percent share in Japan Sports Channel in a joint venture with C. Itoh Corporation, the Japanese trading company. It plans to derive additional revenues overseas by broadcasting U.S. sports for which it has already obtained rights, such as National Football League games. At the same time, it hopes to get rights to foreign sporting events and show them to both U.S. and worldwide viewers.

It is interesting to consider how the U.S. sports industry itself has been changed by the globalization of the media industry. A sporting event would generally be considered a nontradable good, perishable and evanescent, yet TV media have made it commonplace for sporting events to be seen around the world, so now the sports industry has begun to ask, Why not move players and the games to foreign locations?

While both American football and basketball are being marketed aggressively around the world, with basketball being Italy's number two spectator sport after soccer, equally significant is the rise of sports that have generally greater appeal in Asia. Cricket, for example, is only played in the former Commonwealth countries, and one would be hard pressed even to find test match scores reported in United States newspapers or on ESPN. But cricket has huge appeal across India and with the advent of satellite TV and access to the middle class on the Indian subcontinent, ESPN has formed a joint venture to broadcast cricket games in both Hindi and English. It is Cleveland-based International Management Group that produces the cricket programs and sells them to stations in Australia, Europe, and to ESPN. IMG has similarly started popularizing the World Cup Badminton series across Southeast Asia through Star TV's Prime Sports channel. IMG has also established a Chinese pro soccer league and an Asian soccer tournament, all designed to feed the increasing number of TV channels across Asia.[28]

Music

The music industry is also rapidly becoming global; the worldwide popularity of rock 'n roll owes much to MTV. Bertelsmann, a German company and music conglomerate, acquired RCA Records to sell pop music around the world because it saw the U.S. music industry as the primary source of innovation in the international music business. Upon acquiring RCA, Bertelsmann moved its music division headquarters to New York. Michael Dornemann, its CEO, follows a policy of "breaking" an artist into a country's market by launching the act on TV and on stage and through publicity in newspapers and magazines. Only then will he begin to bring in records and tapes. In effect, he designs a separate marketing program for each artist for each country.[29]

At the same time, as in the growing popularity of Asian sports, there is rising demand for local-language musical acts. Again, two big markets in Asia stand out: Mandarin Chinese–based music programs beamed from Hong Kong and Taiwan and now mainland China to attract the vast numbers of Chinese speakers; and Hindi language musical acts aimed principally at the Indian subcontinent. Even Western channels such as MTV have become localized, with local hosts presenting several hours of shows featuring local acts singing in local languages. As explained earlier, entertainment is most appreciated in one's native language. Initially, when TV channels were received primarily by upper-income segments, imported Western programs worked well, because much of the audience had some understanding of English. But with TV spreading rapidly and mass markets emerging, local interests and local languages are becoming the key to gaining audience share.

European Trade Barriers in Entertainment

However, although foreign companies buy U.S. companies and get market share as well as production capabilities, there is alarm in Europe about the domination of TV channels and air waves by U.S. products and, by extension, U.S. culture. As European governments respond to the opportunity they have created for new television programming, they have begun to favor home-grown shows. Smaller countries fear that their culture will be overrun by programs from countries with large internal markets such as the United States. The French fear that English will become even more accepted as a world language. In May 1989 the European Community adopted a directive requiring that a majority of the shows on European television be European "where practicable." The French consider television to be Europe's cultural cement and see the issue as one of cultural imperialism.[30] But the effect of quotas and subsidies for production in Europe is that U.S. production companies, such as MTV Europe, which produces a non–MTV series youth program in London called "Buzz," set up shop in Europe.[31]

European media companies are not necessarily welcoming of EU restrictions on the use of imported programs. From the perspective of major European media firms such as Havas, Bertelsmann, or BSkyB, such restrictions make it harder for them to put on attractive programs that will attract viewers, increase their advertising and subscriber revenues, and, ultimately, enhance their returns to investment. While program producers such as Endemol benefit from the quotas on imports and the captive market that they can sell to, the Association of Commercial Television in Europe has said, "The culture committee's amendments signal a death sentence for the European audio-visual sector."[32]

Future Outlook for Globalization of Media and the Entertainment Industry

In sum, the globalization of the media industry, together with the proliferation of TV channels and other media overseas, presents enormous and growing markets for U.S.–made entertainment, sports, and news programming. The opportunities are there for U.S. firms to reap profits from their comparative advantage in this industry. So far, foreign companies have been aggressive in obtaining ownership in U.S. media properties.

INTERNATIONAL AIRLINE INDUSTRY

International marketing in the airline business mainly consists of offering air transportation services on foreign routes. However, foreign governments have traditionally regulated access to domestic routes by foreign competitors. They have also regulated the right of foreign airlines to offer service to their international passengers. Such traffic rights have generally been subject to bilateral negotiation between governments.

Governments have also regulated the fares charged, the routes airlines may fly, and which airlines will be allowed to compete in the market. Many countries have one or two dominant airlines, either owned by the government or having quasi-public status; such "flagship" carriers are given preference in allocation of new routes, finances, and fare increases. Examples of such flagships are Lufthansa, Air France, Japan Air Lines, Royal Jordanian, and Air India. Thus, if a U.S. airline wishes to compete for foreign passenger traffic, it has to wait for the U.S. government to negotiate a bilateral agreement.

Deregulation of the U.S. airline industry facilitated entry by foreign airlines and led many to seek a portion of U.S. air traffic, such as KLM acquiring a stake in Northwest Airlines, and a joint-marketing agreement between British Airways and American Airlines. In the latter agreement, each airline agreed to use the other airline for ongoing service on complementary routes and to list each other's flights in the computer reservation system, which is the heart of competitive advantage in the industry (airlines that own such systems can more easily fill seats on a flight).

The major industry trend is faster growth outside the United States. In such a regulated industry, the dilemma for U.S. airlines is how to obtain and increase market share in these fast-growing overseas markets when host governments seek to favor their domestic flagship carriers.

Table 16–4 summarizes global airline traffic growth trends. Note that although the North American market is growing, it will register the lowest estimated rates of growth, while the Asia/Pacific region will have some of the highest growth rates. Hence, airlines around the world will be seeking route authority to permit them to fly passengers on Pacific routes. Of course, factors such as airspace congestion and airport capacity limitations also hinder efforts at route expansion by airlines.[33] Yet government regulation will not disappear overnight. U.S. and other airlines must therefore seek alliances with carriers from the Far East while requesting U.S. government help in obtaining fairer access to these burgeoning markets.

Air transportation also includes cargo traffic. The international express-delivery market was estimated at about $6.5 billion in 1988, with growth at 20 percent per year through the 1990s. And the top 15 companies together accounted for only about 50 percent of the total international market. An example of global thinking in this industry is Federal Express's acquisition of the Flying Tiger line in order to gain access to its worldwide delivery route system built over 40 years. Tiger was the world's biggest heavy-cargo airline, flying from the West Coast of the United States to all of the Far East and Australia, and from the East Coast to Brazil and Argentina, Europe, and the Persian Gulf. It planned to use the acquired routes to offer global delivery of small packages, its major strength.[34]

In response to competition from Federal Express, Japan Air Lines began negotiating with Lufthansa and Air France to establish an international airfreight company, integrating their ground cargo and aircargo systems. This combination would result in a company that carried 1.8 million tons of freight in 1988, as compared to

TABLE 16–4	Past Growth and Forecasted Growth Rates of Airline Passenger Traffic by Region (Percentages)					
	North America	East Asia/ Pacific	Europe	Latin America	Middle East	Africa
1976–1986	7.3%	9.5%	6.5%	8.1%	11.5%	8.0%
1986–1996	5.1	6.8	5.8	6.4	5.0	5.5
1996–2006	4.6	6.5	5.5	6.3	5.4	5.5

the Federal Express/Tiger combination's volume of 2.6 million tons in 1988.[35] Further, the combined company would have global reach and be able to deliver a package anywhere in the world.

Not all mergers and alliances result in a stronger international position, however. A cautionary tale is British Airways' acquisition of a 22 percent ownership interest in USAir in order to be able to offer through service to many U.S. destinations. However, British Airways was forced to write off over $200 million due to recurring losses at USAir. USAir is among the highest cost carriers in the United States, and while BA may have received marketing benefits, it came at a high cost. Iberia, a loss-plagued Spanish government-owned airline, similarly had to dispose of its 85 percent ownership in Aerolineas Argentinas because of 1994 losses of 41.5 billion pesetas. It needed a subsidy of nearly $700 million from the Spanish government, and a condition for receiving the subsidy was that it dispose of some of its international assets and focus on restoring its core operations to profitability.[36]

INTERNATIONAL PROFESSIONAL SERVICES

Professional services such as accounting and management consulting, legal counsel, advertising, and public relations are driven by growth among their business clients. Their international expansion is therefore driven by the overseas growth of their clients. As their clients open offices and factories and set up joint ventures abroad, they will demand help in the law, advertising, accounting, and so forth. At the same time, as the foreign economies grow and begin adopting professional management habits, they, too, will seek professional services with global networks. Again, the market growth will be higher and more attractive outside the United States. The question is, How can a firm market overseas?

As an example, how does one export legal services? Jones, Day, Reavis, and Pogue provide a model. Initially a regional law firm, it began by acquiring a New York law firm with a primarily international practice. Since then, it has opened offices in Geneva, Hong Kong, London, Paris, and Riyadh, with new offices opening in Tokyo and Brussels. The firm's "product" strategy is interesting: "We are an American firm using American methodology for solving legal problems." Foreign offices are staffed with U.S. citizens and foreign nationals with U.S. education and extensive experience. For example, the company does not attempt to practice Japanese law for Japanese clients because local firms could do this more effectively. Instead, its goal is to provide a world view, helping Japanese clients in Europe and U.S. and European clients in Japan. A key aid is an in-house computerized communication system to allow the lawyers in the firm almost instantaneous contact with one another around the world.

Globalizing Services: Federal Express

Federal Express is the U.S. market leader, holding nearly half of the market for overnight package delivery. While it seemed logical to offer that service concept to foreign markets, Federal Express has found it difficult to duplicate its U.S. success, for several reasons:

Its late start. By the time Federal Express made its move overseas, competitors such as DHL and TNT were already providing such service.

Difficulties in duplicating the U.S. approach to overnight service. In the United States, Federal Express used its own fleet of planes and trucks, preferring to control its shipping rather than contract with others; this was a high-cost solution that necessitated high-capacity utilization for profitability; competition and the late start-up meant lower traffic volumes for Federal Express.

Difficulties in using hub-and-spoke operations overseas. Federal Express shipped all its packages to Memphis, where packages were sorted, regrouped, and rerouted; this permitted standardized sorting and tracking of packages. Overseas regulators were in no hurry to let Federal Express develop an efficient international hub-and-spoke system, often preferring to nurture their own companies.

Protectionism. Just three days before scheduled start of operations, Japan prevented Federal Express from shipping packages over 70 pounds through Tokyo,

INTERNATIONAL RETAILING

Retailing, one of the major sectors of any economy, typically requires contact between retailer and seller. It is generally a labor-intensive and geographically diffused activity, with considerable national and regional variation in business practices. It is also an industry subject to considerable government regulation. Finally, it is a major generator of jobs and requires considerable management time and attention. Now let us consider how internationalization of retailing services can proceed.

Two major avenues can be pursued. One is to obtain control of retailing channels through direct investment, with joint ventures and franchising being modified approaches to the overseas retailing industry. The key objective is to have a degree of control over the retailing channel and also receive as much market information as possible from retailers about the ultimate consumer. Such control is often linked to a vertical-integration strategy. Retailing offers attractive returns in its own right, however, as a means of participating in the growth of an economy. From this angle, the foreign retailer hopes to bring a competitive edge to the domestic industry in the form of more efficient management, greater worldwide purchasing clout, and superior retailing technology and information systems.

The second avenue for internationalization of retailing services lies in using technology to diminish the need for direct contact between retailer and customer and thus allow for long-distance retailing. Computerized electronic shopping and direct mail are two instances of such an approach. Foreign retailers can service domestic customers in another country market this way without physically entering the domestic retail industry.

The Changing Face of Retailing

In 1987, 3 percent of Taiwan's population shopped in modern supermarkets and grocery stores.[37] Today, over half of all shopping is done in modern department

and three years elapsed before Federal Express received permission to fly four times a week from Memphis to Tokyo.

Hence, Federal Express has begun to adapt to overseas environments. For example, in the United States, it stops picking up packages after 5 P.M., but it had to modify this overseas, where later business hours are the norm, as in Spain where business is conducted as late as 8 P.M. In Japan, Federal Express began offering an express freighter service to appeal to computer manufacturers who wanted to ship heavy cargo to the United States faster. Federal Express also decided to use alliances, such as teaming up with Qantas in Australia, and considered using local companies to handle the local transportation end of the overall business. Federal Express also began acquiring overseas companies, including Tiger International, which it bought for $880 million. Ultimately, Federal Express hopes for a profitable worldwide operation rivaling the U.S. operations. But being number one at home is no guarantee that foreign success is ensured.

An additional complication for Federal Express is the threat that it poses to Japanese cargo operators. This led Japanese air traffic rights negotiators to threaten to take away the rights of Federal Express (and other U.S. operators) to pick up cargo and passengers in Japan during stopovers, and transport them onwards to other points in Asia. Such threats are often bargaining ploys to extract greater concessions for that country's companies but highlight the uncertainty and dependence on government support that Federal Express faces in order to fully implement its global strategies.

Sources: "Innocents Abroad: Federal Express Finds Its Pioneering Formula Falls Flat Overseas," *The Wall Street Journal,* March 15, 1991; and "U.S.–Japanese Air-Cargo Accord Gains as Tokyo Drops Threat Against FedEx," *The Wall Street Journal,* March 4, 1996.

stores and supermarkets. All across Asia and Latin America, as incomes rise and more two-income families emerge, time has become scarcer. Shopping at modern stores with large assortments of goods, fairly priced and fresh, with amenities such as debit-card shopping and home delivery, has caused a major shift in shopping habits and preferences. As shopping volumes increase, prices can be lowered as fixed costs of warehouses and computerization can be spread over a larger sales base; the net result is a virtuous cycle wherein low prices, convenience, larger choice, and high quality combine to continually attract more customers, allowing owners to continually upgrade the shopping parameters that initially attracted shoppers. Western-style enclosed shopping malls, with their temperature-controlled, safe, well-lit ambience, offer variety and entertainment and increasingly attract the patrons of small street-side shops.

China, for example, has seen the opening of stores by the Japanese chains Isetan and Yaohan, as well as by Hong Kong–based A. S. Watson. Local chains have also been developing, such as Giordano; these chains are adapting to local cultural realities, such as the traditional Chinese preference for "wet" markets, where shoppers can inspect live fish, chicken, and other food. Taiwan's local chain, Dairy Farm International, has seen competition from the European retailers Makro and Carrefour. The latter two stress the hypermarket model, offering a huge assortment and accepting very low margins. Makro, for example, sells groceries in bulk, office supplies, and computers, selling both to individuals as well as local wholesalers and small retailers.

Regional integration has seen similar cross-border forays: Promodes from France has opened up stores across Spain, and Wal-Mart, partnering with Cifra, is populating the Mexican countryside. Blockbuster Video's expansion across Europe is another case in point. It has 4,000 stores across Europe in 16 countries, but has concentrated both on developing a strong U.K. base and building the Blockbuster retail brand image. It had acquired the Ritz chain a few years earlier, and its focus on branding led it to unify all the stores and develop two formats, the Blockbuster

Superstore with a very large assortment, and the Blockbuster Express, smaller stores at convenient locations with an assortment of titles in greatest demand. Its European strategy focuses on training retail salespeople to keep the customer in mind and offer superior service, such as allowing store-level decisions to waive late-return fees or order special titles. Blockbuster is flexible in growing through company-owned stores, franchises, and joint ventures. It has grown slowly outside the United Kingdom, and part of the reason is its desire to fully understand the best markets for expansion. Much of Europe prefers to buy videos rather than rent them, and Blockbuster makes more profit through rentals. Blockbuster, therefore, launched ad campaigns to change customer preferences toward rentals, stressing the rapid availability of new releases, the convenience, and the low prices. It also created business managers responsible for groups of six stores, charged with maintaining customer databases and encouraging infrequent customers to shop more often at Blockbuster, as well as rent more titles at a time. Blockbuster clearly understands the need to have a unified brand and retail strategy, which is then adjusted for local market differences by empowering and relying on local retail managers.[38]

One consequence of the proliferation of large chains is a gradual seeping of power from manufacturers to retailers. This is exemplified in the rising sales of private, or store-brand, items, with the foremost exponents of private brands being the U.K. chains Tesco and Sainsbury. (See the discussions in Chapters 8 and 9 on private label versus branded goods and the implications for brand equity.)

Entering the Japanese Retail Industry

We have discussed the rapid growth of Japanese incomes and the willingness of Japanese consumers to step up consumption. This may be the reason that Aeon Corp., a Japanese retail conglomerate, decided to buy the U.S.–based Talbots chain consisting of about 150 clothing stores in the United States. Talbots has a specific image—preppy clothes, the classic New England look. The Talbots stores in Japan were to feature the same clothing, trademark red storefront, and maplewood floors as in the United States, in an attempt to appeal to working women and housewives. (Aeon has had much success with Laura Ashley boutiques in the best Japanese department stores, and Talbots is positioned as more middle market than Laura Ashley.) As Michael Golding of Access Japan, Inc., notes, however, Japanese women in their late 20s who are not married and still live at home have the most money to spend, and this group, with perhaps $25,000 in the bank, is more sophisticated in its tastes than U.S. women. Furthermore, Japanese women are reputed to be label conscious and willing to pay premium prices for quality and snob appeal.

Bearing this in mind, Japanese managers select garments from the Talbots line that they thought would sell in Japan. They established the Talbots brand name in Japan by sponsoring a classical music radio show in Tokyo in much the same way that Talbots sponsors the morning classical music show on WGBH in Boston. They also borrowed direct-marketing techniques from Talbots USA in selling from catalogs. Rosy Clarke of ASI Market Research (Japan) noted that catalogs have become a hip way to shop in Japan. Stores close by 7:00 P.M., and catalogs might appeal to working married women who have less time to shop.[39]

Another approach is the joint venture between Toys 'R Us and McDonald's Co. of Japan. This joint venture would allow McDonald's to operate restaurants at toy stores. Toy 'R Us plans to rely on McDonald's expertise in picking Japanese retailing sites. (McDonald's had 675 stores in Japan by 1989, and this is Toys 'R Us's first move into Japan.) Although Japanese stores were forecast to do twice as much business as the average U.S. store, margins were expected to be lower because of high real estate costs. Toys 'R Us was basing its Japanese expansion on the long-term potential of the Japanese market, banking on a competitive edge derived from offering low prices and a large selection of toys.[40]

Although Japan is a large and growing market, the United States is always an attractive retail environment for foreign companies. Thorne EMI, a British electronics and entertainment company, has rented TV sets and VCRs for a long time in the United Kingdom. It wanted to enter the similar "rent-to-own" retailing segment in the United States. About a third of U.S. households cannot obtain credit and hence have little alternative to renting if they want to purchase a TV or other appliance. The business may sound pedestrian, but it has strong cash flow. The stream of weekly rental payments added up to 2 to 3.5 times the retail price. Given the fragmented nature of the industry, Thorne decided to enter the U.S. market by buying out Rent-a-Center, Inc., of the United States, a company that rented video equipment, appliances, and furniture to middle- and lower-income households. Speed of entry and an established market share were the motivations behind Thorne's acquisition mode of entry into the rental retailing environment in the United States.[41]

The rapid expansion of retailing chains internationally raises this question: What are the critical steps in developing an internationalization strategy? Several variables must be kept in mind:[42]

1. An understanding of the market, either by careful observation over an extended period or through pilot expansion.

2. A measured pace of expansion, within constraints of capital and management.

3. A clearly defined role for local partners, after careful consideration of whether they are needed.

4. The importance of planning the assortment of goods to be carried, which should vary with the preferences of each local market. Stores such as Marks & Spencer carry a core of best-selling products across borders, supplemented by products adapted to local preferences.

5. The extent to which goods are sourced locally, affected by local quality and availability considerations, as well as exchange-rate volatility. Cost reduction pressures move a company such as Benetton toward centralization, with customization for individual markets happening at the last minute, when up-to-date point-of-sale information is used to dye clothes in the colors that sell the best in each individual market. Of course, this can work only if the basic product concept, namely, the style and design, have strong multicultural acceptability.

6. Scale economies, as evidenced by the merger of Kingfisher, a U.K. consumer electronics retailer, and Darty, a leading French retailer of consumer electronics and appliances (white goods) through warehouse-style stores, with 12 percent market share at the time of the merger.

7. The development of local management for both day-to-day supervision as well as strategic expansion.

Direct Mail Selling to Japan

Japan's labyrinthine retailing system has always posed distribution barriers to U.S. and other foreign retailers seeking to enter Japanese markets.[43] Japan's direct-marketing sector is undeveloped, about one-twentieth the size of the US. direct-marketing industry. U.S. direct marketers have an edge in that their prices are generally lower than Japanese retail prices. Companies that have been successful in direct marketing in Japan have undertaken several steps:

Japanese-language catalogs and inserts and forms to cover sizes, shipping, customs, and tariffs.

24-hour, toll-free ordering and hot lines, phone, and fax, to enable Japanese customers to conveniently reach sales representatives, particularly important given the 12-hour time-zone differences from the United States to Japan. Japanese-speaking phone agents are, of course, a plus.

A local Japanese office to handle customer complaints and returns; developing and maintaining mailing lists because few Japanese mailing lists are available for purchase.

INTERNATIONAL HOTEL INDUSTRY

The hotel industry is another sector whose growth is fueled by the growth of international business. As more businesspeople travel internationally, they demand lodging on a scale comparable to that experienced at home. Similarly, increasing international tourism leads to greater demands for hotel beds, again with amenities comparable to home. In addition, a need exists for more hotels in the towns of fast-growing countries in the Third World, in Eastern Europe, and in the smaller cities of Europe and Southeast Asia. Here the demand is domestic, which can be satisfied by international hotel chains. Thus, business and leisure travel represent two major segments, as do foreign and domestic guests.

Hotels have a tangible side: their construction and ownership. The intangible side is their management, including marketing hotel rooms worldwide and providing the hotel service itself, as well as offering related services such as ongoing maintenance. The internationalization of the hotel industry means a separation of these two aspects, with domestic investors often building and owning the hotel, while foreign hotel conglomerates provide hotel management services on a commission fee and profit-sharing basis.

As in the case of airlines, a key element in marketing hotel services worldwide is the use of computerized reservation services. This is a way to capitalize on brand image. With such systems, a businessperson can book rooms in any city in the world where the hotel chain has a presence with one local phone call. This ease of use leads travelers to favor such hotel chains as the Hyatt or Westin, giving them a competitive edge over more isolated hotels.

The other major variable is service. Top-notch service is labor-intensive and requires considerable training. Thus, Tokyo's Hotel Okura has 1,600 workers for 880 rooms, compared to about 1,000 workers for 1,008 rooms at the Helmsley Palace in Manhattan, both among the world's most prestigious hotels. Around-the-clock room service and a business center for sending international messages and translating documents are examples of the expected levels of service, even though these operations lose money themselves.[44]

INTERNATIONAL FINANCIAL SERVICES

International financial services are also growing rapidly. In this segment, availability of low-cost capital is a critical advantage. Following clients as they enter foreign markets becomes a major influence on international expansion. Two other critical variables are innovation—coming up with ideas for new financial services—and technology—being able to deliver innovative new services at arm's length, at low cost, and with high quality.[45] Twenty-four-hour trading, international bank lending, global foreign exchange trading, and hedging products to manage interest and currency exposure are services demanded by multinationals as they spread around the world. Japan, the United States, and the United Kingdom account for over 50 percent of all international bank lending and are the major financial centers of the world. Any company wanting to operate in the international financial services market needs to have a presence in each of these markets.

Table 16–5 lists the world's largest global banks, and the omission of Japanese banks from this list is notable. The list includes banks based on the percentage of overseas sales, income, and staff to totals. The U.K.– based Standard Chartered tops the list because it has over 70 percent of its assets "overseas," that is, outside the United Kingdom in its case. For banks from countries with small internal markets, one might expect such a distribution of assets. Yet, several U.S. banks figure on the list even though their home country represents one of the world's largest financial markets.

The battle for market share in key overseas markets is seen in the duel between Citicorp and HBSC.[46] While HBSC branched out from its original Hong Kong base to acquire U.K. and U.S. banks, Citicorp was deepening its market share in Asia. As more people enter the middle class and become the newly rich, both Citicorp and HBSC try to increase their business with this segment, selling credit cards, mutual funds, and "smart cards." Both offer a form of specialized private banking type services for the more affluent client, with amenities such as a personal banker and free advice. A particularly important segment is the entrepreneur who needs both business and personal banking.

Another aspect of banking is private banking, in which banks tailor their banking services for very rich individuals. For banks looking for rich people, there are few places like Japan. Foreign banks such as Citicorp are in the forefront of competing for rich Japanese clients. Again, this is a labor-intensive business, with highly qualified and specialized staff needed who can develop customized financial packages for each client. U.S. banks are aggressively pursuing this opportunity in Japan, using their global networks to win clients by offering opportunities for global investment and tax minimization. Of course, the Japanese banks have extensive branch networks in Japan and a reputation for service. Therefore, they will make every effort to provide similar quality banking services, and the competition will be keen, both in Japan and in other countries.[47]

The International Credit-Card Market

U.S. banks are similarly targeting the Japanese credit-card market. Penetration of that market in Japan has been only one-third of U.S. levels, even though the two countries are comparable in terms of per capita incomes and purchasing power. Segments are important, with American Express and Diners Club dominating the upscale market. Because credit-card companies get their income from the commission received on purchases with credit cards, companies such as Diners benefit from the fact that their cardholders spend about three times as much as holders of the average bank card.

In the lower-spending segments, the issue is market penetration. About one-third of all individual savings in Japan is held by the post office savings system. When Visa wanted to increase its penetration of the Japanese market, it struck an agreement allowing it to market Visa cards to the 70 million savings account holders. Since Japanese banks compete with the post office system, this made them less willing to offer Visa cards through their branch networks. In contrast, Mastercard uses an indirect entry method, with Japanese banks acting as franchisees, issuing bank cards under their own names, as part of the international Mastercard network.

All of the international entrants must compete with Japan Credit Bank (JCB), which is Japan's top-selling card and chief domestic competitor. JCB is planning to expand into international markets, with the idea of protecting and even increasing

TABLE 16–5	World's Major Global Banks, 1997–98			
	Total Assets ($ Billions)	*Percentage Overseas Assets*	*Percentage Overseas Income*	*Percentage Staff Overseas*
Standard Chartered, U.K.	$ 78	74%	84%	89%
Crédit Suisse Holdings, Switzerland	438	73	45	54
Hong Kong Shanghai Bank Corp.-HBSC, U.K.	438	65	52	65
Union Bank of Switzerland	397	68	40	30
ABN-AMRO Bank, Netherlands	415	57	60	57
Bank of China	306	24	61	NA
Credit Lyonnais, France	250	54	42	32
Société Générale, France	441	41	1	20
J.P. Morgan Co., U.S.	262	53	50	47
Bankers Trust, U.S.	140	52	36	27
Paribas, France	245	55	39	40
National Westminster, U.K.	307	48	32	NA
Swiss Bank Corp.	302	67	39	37
Citicorp, U.S.	311	63	70	58

Source: "Global Banking," *The Banker,* February 1999, pp. 40–41.

market share when its JCB cardholders begin to travel and spend money overseas. Another source of competition is retailers who issue their own store cards. An anomaly in Japan is that holders of store credit cards can pay off their outstanding balances in installments, but owners of bank credit cards must pay their balances in full.

International Investment Banking

Investment banking and brokerage services are another attractive international services industry. It is generally accepted that investment portfolios must be diversified internationally for superior performance, which means that there is a need for information about, and access to, investing in foreign stock markets around the world. The question for U.S. brokerage houses is how they might go about selling brokerage services in Japan in the face of intense competition from giant Japanese brokerage houses with extensive retail networks. It is expensive to do business in Japan: Salaries, rents, and overhead costs are all high, and large volumes of business are needed to break even and make profits.

Foreign firms can either concentrate on a specialty or, if they are large, offer the breadth of global investment opportunities. Accordingly, some large firms offer Japanese institutional clients the options of investing in U.S. Treasury securities, trading in futures and options, hedging currencies, and investing in the major stock markets of the world. Smaller companies usually specialize. Because Japanese companies routinely issue warrants with their bonds, some foreign companies have decided to become expert in this narrow niche in the market.

Over the past several years, Japanese financial markets have performed poorly, leading Japanese investors to question the advice and returns turned in by their own predominantly Japanese brokers and mutual funds. That is, Japanese protectionism had kept out the technologically advanced and aggressive U.S. pension fund managers such as Fidelity. As Japanese investors began to seek better returns, their pressure as well as that from the U.S. government opened up Japanese fund-management markets slightly, allowing U.S. funds to begin to offer their greater experience in global investing, their use of quantitative investing, and their skills in analyzing companies. Such liberalization points to another critical aspect of trade in services: Open markets are not always adhered to, and deregulating financial services can result in enhanced global market share.

Aside from the product, however, patience and cultural sensitivity are crucial to success because personal relations with individual clients determine the volume of business. Salomon Brothers in Tokyo has been successful because of its autonomy and Japanese orientation. It is run largely by Japanese managers, including three of Japan's top securities experts from major Japanese firms. Salomon benefits from the personal contacts built by these employees through the years in the profession and through college ties. Their colleagues manage the portfolios at Japan's life insurance and trust companies and thus determine the amount of institutional funds invested through Salomon. Also, Japanese managers make Salomon more Japanese and therefore more successful in recruiting qualified young Japanese analysts and managers.[48]

International Insurance Markets

Insurance, another segment of the financial services industry, is growing much faster in international markets than in the U.S. market. The United States accounted for about 40 percent of premiums collected worldwide, but it is a saturated market, especially in life insurance. The potential for future growth lies primarily overseas, in markets where incomes are rising and individuals and heads of families are beginning to purchase insurance products. U.S. insurance companies have little foreign penetration, however. Only about 2 percent of sales come from foreign markets and consist mainly of business from U.S. clients who have multinational operations.

The integration of Europe presents an opportunity for U.S. companies to offer lower prices and to take advantage of inefficient local competition; for example, insurance products in Italy were priced between 77 percent and 245 percent higher than the average of the four European countries with lowest prices in areas such as life, home, automobile, commercial fire and theft, and public liability insurance.[49]

Competition from European companies will be strong, however, and greater opportunities might be found in the Far East. Aetna, for example, has had success selling U.S. dollar–denominated insurance to Hong Kong natives worried about the Chinese takeover, and Japan is even more attractive due to its high rate of savings. Insurance is generally sold in Japan by women; however, one U.S. company, Equitable, plans to approach the Japanese market by selling investment-based insurance products such as annuities to wealthy Japanese using a sales force that is 85 percent male and trained in financial planning. Although U.S. insurance companies may face a fight for market share in advanced economies that have their own entrenched domestic insurance firms, this might be the opportune time to position themselves in the newly industrializing countries.

AIG in China

The market for life insurance in China is large and mostly untapped. The market is dominated by the state-owned People's Insurance Co. of China (PICC), which has about 75 percent of the market. Founded in Shanghai in 1919, AIG operated in China until it was forced out in 1950. To win permission to re-enter, it lavished attention on China, winning goodwill by setting up a $1 billion infrastructure fund, and buying and restoring to China ancient pagoda windows from Beijing's Summer Palace. It finally received permission to sell life insurance in China in 1992. While its current premium revenues are small—under $100 million—the market is expected to grow to $75 billion by 2005. To prepare for such high potential, AIG carefully screens and hires salespeople and trains them in great detail. This allows its 5,000 plus sales force to sell 55,000 new policies a month.[50] Until AIG came along, such door-to-door selling, with a commission on the first year's premium income, was not common. AIG's success motivated rivals such as PICC to use a field sales force, offer them training to call on potential customers in their homes or offices, and reward them with commission-based incentives.

Other Opportunities in International Services

Many more opportunities than those discussed thus far are available in international services. Century 21, the U.S. real estate franchise chain, has been growing steadily in France. The chain found the U.S. real estate market saturated and therefore began looking overseas, first selling a master Japanese franchise to C. Itoh, the trading company. Cultural differences made it difficult to sell real estate the Century 21 way, however. M. Evans, senior vice-president of foreign operations for Century 21, noted that selling property is sometimes considered a disgrace among Japanese families and so must be done secretly and with confidentiality. Century 21's banners, open houses, and lawn signs are embarrassing in this Japanese context.

The company next expanded to England and France. The French market was fragmented, with many small "mom-and-pop" shops surviving on low volume. The U.S. parent believed that conditions were right to introduce modern real estate selling techniques, such as blanket mailing to all the homeowners in a neighborhood and notices of recent house sales and the price at which the sale took place, both techniques geared to "farming" an area to drum up new business. The goal is to generate larger volumes per broker and thus raise profits from economies of scale.

A joint venture formed the basis for bringing circus artists from the former Soviet Union to the United States. Steven Leber had gained experience with U.S. tours of rock 'n roll groups and with marketing musicals such as *Jesus Christ Superstar* and *Beatlemania*. He visited Russia to consider importing Russian rock groups but ended up being impressed with the huge Russian circus industry. He negotiated with Soyuzgoscirk, the national circus authority, to obtain the rights to promote the Moscow Circus in the United States. Then he obtained corporate sponsorship, initially from Unilever and American Express. The result has been a growing U.S. interest in Russian circuses. Putting the package together, however, required considerable flexibility and sensitivity to Russian ways of doing business.[51]

Death and taxes are universal, and in affluent countries survivors rarely wish to skimp on funerals. This reasoning led Service Corp. International, the leading U.S. funeral home operator, to aggressively expand overseas. "People aren't going to quit dying," says CEO Robert Waltrip. With 10 percent of the U.S. market and a steady cash flow, Service Corp. has the cash to move into overseas markets. In 1993, it acquired Australia's largest funeral home and crematorium operator. It transplanted U.S. methods, such as sharing hearses, personnel, accounting staff, and embalming facilities across funeral homes within a city, thus reducing costs and raising profits without touching prices. This allowed it to increase Australian profits by 40 percent, which were used to acquire a second company in Australia, giving it a total 20 percent market share. It then turned to the United Kingdom, buying the second and third largest operators of funeral homes for over $500 million, to give it a 15 percent U.K. market share. Next was France, where it bought out two of France's largest funeral home chains from the French utility Lyonnais des Eaux for a net price of over $400 million, giving it a 30 percent share. Service Corp. is bringing its American approach of focusing on scale and efficiency to dominate a fragmented industry of traditionally family-owned, small businesses around the world.[52]

Finally, one of the more arcane examples of international services is the Swiss company, Société Générale de Surveillance (SGS), which inspects goods shipped between countries. It checks measures, quality, invoices, and prices of imported and exported goods, typically on behalf of governments. Such inspection is necessary to allow proper application of tariffs because tariff rates often vary with the exact category into which the traded goods fall. The most important reason for inspection, however, is to prevent underinvoicing, by which the price is set below what the exported goods are worth, with the difference being credited to the exporter's overseas bank accounts. Underinvoicing thus becomes a means to smuggle capital out of a country, and SGS has contracts with governments to prevent such practices. Inspection also helps governments prevent transfer pricing from being used to avoid or reduce duties and taxes on profits.[53]

MARKETING SERVICES OVERSEAS: WHAT HAVE WE LEARNED?

Experience has taught that because services are intangible, exporting them is often unfeasible without also exporting the personnel to provide them. Hence, foreign direct investment, licensing and franchising, and joint ventures are common vehicles for providing services in international markets.

Intangibility makes selling services overseas more difficult because the buyer must take the quality of service on faith. Corporate brand name and reputation sometimes help.

Financing the overseas expansion of services can be difficult, with the cost structure leaning toward fixed costs. Although heavy capital investments may not be necessary, working capital needs may be high initially, especially in regard to the personnel required to provide the service. This is another reason that joint ventures and strategic alliances are common when a firm seeks to sell services overseas.

Clearly, because direct interaction between buyer and service provider is essential to marketing services, cultural differences must be accounted for in seeking buyer satisfaction. Establishing a local presence and using local personnel are usually recommended for this reason. And if the service must be adapted to the foreign market, the interaction between buyer and foreign provider takes on additional importance because direct contact can facilitate cooperation and result in more appropriate adaptation.

Service markets are largest in the advanced industrial countries. The U.S. market is generally saturated for a variety of services, making foreign expansion attractive. Even with stiff competition in the advanced industrial nations, service markets as a whole offer greater unrealized potential than goods markets, especially for U.S. firms with their accumulated experience in service industry sectors.

However, service exports or foreign sales do not take place in a vacuum. They often accompany sales of goods. Thus, if exports of goods are faltering, service sales will be affected. For example, the billings of U.S.–based advertising agencies overseas depend somewhat on the success of their U.S. clients overseas. To the extent that a client such as IBM or Coca-Cola generates overseas sales growth, U.S. advertising agencies are more likely to have opportunities to increase their overseas billings.

This last point also suggests a path of least resistance for overseas growth: Follow the client! Such a strategy has been successful for Japanese auto parts companies in the United States and for Japanese banks providing Japanese-language, yen-based financial software and services to their Japanese clients.

Concepts from the international marketing of goods can be carried over to services. For example, gap analysis (see Chapter 7) can be used to determine whether the actual market for a particular service (say, the use of overnight parcel and small package delivery) is below the forecast potential. Similarly, the international product life cycle model can be used to predict, for example, when a developing nation will begin accelerating its consumption of long-distance phone and facsimile services based on the experiences of the more developed nations.

GLOBAL MARKETING

Designing Golf Courses for Southeast Asia

As Southeast Asia modernizes, incomes are rising over the longer term, with per capita income reaching approximately $10,000 in countries such as South Korea, Taiwan, Singapore, and Hong Kong. Japan is the most prosperous country, of course, with per capita income over $20,000. With the rise in disposable income, the Japanese have more interest in leisure products and services. Golf falls within this consumption pattern, and designing new golf courses is a major growth business for U.S. golf course architects.

Japan is primarily a mountainous country; all flat land is earmarked for agriculture. Golf courses were thus built into hillsides, taking the terrain as is. This led to courses with steep holes; in one instance, golfers had to hold on to ropes to reach some holes. The Japanese first built golf courses as if they were highways, bulldozing away the earth and any obstacles. But once the Japanese began traveling and played the world's famous courses at St. Andrew's, Pebble Beach, and Augusta, they raised their sights considerably. Hence, Japanese project developers began approaching U.S. architects, with their long experience in building championship golf courses in the United States, to develop top-notch golf courses in Japan. Japanese developers vied for their services, which are noted for excellence in design.

J. Michael Poellot is one such architect. He has been involved in golf course projects that together totaled $1 billion in construction costs. He has built golf courses in swamps, in rice paddies, and near the Great Wall of China.

In conclusion, the ways in which the international marketing of services differs from that of goods create closer links to an overall strategy, with issues such as acquisitions and joint ventures being as important as pure marketing issues.[54]

SUMMARY

Services are offered by a number of industries, including wholesaling and retailing, communications, transportation, utilities, banking and insurance, tourism, and business and personal services. Services account for an increasing portion of output and employment in all of the industrialized nations and, consequently, are becoming increasingly important in international trade.

In the United States, nearly three of four jobs outside agriculture come from the service industries. The most important service sectors in the United States (other than government) are the retail and wholesale trade, finance and insurance, health care, and business services.

All of the major service exporters are developed, industrialized nations. Service exports do not tell the whole story, however, because many services can be provided only from within a foreign market.

Services are difficult to market because of their special characteristics: intangibility, heterogeneity, variability in service quality, perishability, simultaneity of production and consumption, and the predominance of fixed costs.

Challenges in international services marketing include how to standardize services and how to manage demand to match supply and generate repeat business. Cultural variables are an important factor in user satisfaction.

Comparative advantage in services marketing can arise from labor, capital, technology, or management skills. Technology, in the form of computer hardware and software, and communication networks are useful in providing services at a distance. Services are information-intensive.

Government intervention in trade serves to keep out foreign competition from domestic markets. Restrictions are placed on the right of foreign firms to do busi-

He has had to move mountains, drain seas, and re-create the landscape to build world-class golf courses. This raises costs; an average golf course in Japan may cost $30 million to build versus about $5 million for U.S. courses. Poellot notes that Japanese golf courses are meant for golfers with high handicaps because Japanese golfers take up the game late and have little time to practice. Because most Japanese live in cramped quarters, they want opulence during their leisure time. Clubhouses must be huge. Their cramped living spaces may also explain why the wide-open spaces of golf have such appeal for Japanese men. Another unusual feature is that golf courses must have large reservoirs to hold water in case of torrential rainfall and typhoons, which are common in Japan.

Poellot got his start when serving in the military, and his offer to review golf course plans for a Bangkok developer led to a meeting with Robert Trent Jones, one of America's foremost golf course designers. He began working for Jones and became responsible for Asia/Pacific work. Japanese businessmen who played at the Gainey Ranch golf course, designed by Poellot, were sufficiently impressed to seek out the architect and offer a contract to design six golf courses. Poellot was on his way. Among his recent triumphs is a golf course for the Beijing Golf Club, which was voted the best new golf course in Asia for that year. Poellot attributes some of his success to his love of nature and landscape, a feeling that reflects Japan's age-old traditions of formal gardens renowned for their meditative beauty.

As Japan begins importing rice, agricultural land will be freed to build even more golf courses, a prospect that brings delight to Poellot's eye.

Source: Walter Roessing, "Master Planner," *Northwest Airlines Inflight Magazine.*

ness, sell to the government, repatriate profits, and transfer personnel. Trade barriers, licensing regulations, and divergent technical standards are also used to limit competition from foreign firms.

The Uruguay round of talks on trade focused on removing barriers to trade in services, with emphasis on protecting intellectual property rights and on setting parameters for government intervention in trade in services.

Entertainment is one of the largest U.S. exports. Deregulation of TV in Europe is increasing the demand for U.S. programs. However, European "local content" laws applied to TV programs may diminish the market opportunities.

The emergence of a global entertainment industry has also led to mergers, with multinationals jockeying to obtain global competitive advantage and representation in the key triad markets. All of the major firms seek to control both production and distribution of entertainment programs, whether it be films, TV programs, sports events, or news and variety shows.

Foreign airline markets are growing faster than the U.S. market, with highest growth occurring in the Pacific Rim area because of economic growth in Japan and in its neighboring countries. Joint marketing and strategic alliances are being used to obtain market share.

Professional services are a growth market overseas, particularly as multinationals expand operations around the world, placing domestic professional service providers in various foreign markets. Retailing offers considerable growth opportunities overseas as incomes rise around the world. Technological innovations allow retailers to offer their services at a distance. Acquisitions are the major mode of participating in retailing in foreign markets.

The international hotel industry is expanding because of growth in business and tourist travel internationally. Management skills and computerized global reservation systems provide U.S. hotel chains with a competitive edge.

The globalization of industry leads to growing demand for international banking services, such as global foreign exchange trading and international lending and hedging services to manage interest rate and currency exposure. Innovative new services and possession of a low-cost source of funds are both critical to competitive advantage in overseas markets.

Firms can profit from targeting niches within financial services, such as private banking, credit cards, investment banking and brokerage services, and insurance. Because client contacts are important in finance, cultural sensitivity is as important as financial know-how.

Considerable untapped market potential exists for insurance products in the newly industrializing countries of Asia, in the Single Europe, and in Japan. These foreign markets are characterized by high prices and have fewer innovative products available. Experienced U.S. insurance companies may have a competitive edge, although they have not been active in seeking foreign markets.

A few generalizations can be made about the service sector: (1) Foreign markets offer attractive growth prospects; (2) following domestic clients overseas is one avenue to gain foreign sales; and (3) some form of direct involvement in the foreign market is necessary to gain significant market share.

QUESTIONS

16.1 What are services? Why are they important in industrialized nations?

16.2 Which service industry sectors are important in the U.S. economy? Can these sectors easily enter into foreign trade?

16.3 What are the major service-exporting nations? What might explain the number of advanced industrialized nations that appear on this list?

16.4 Explain the steps by which McDonald's was able to initiate operations in Hungary. What difficulties did it face, and how did it solve them? What generalizations can you make from the McDonald's example?

16.5 What are some distinguishing characteristics of services? Explain why these characteristics make it difficult to sell services in foreign markets.

16.6 Discuss how culture can affect the sale of services overseas. Use the Little, Brown–Russian negotiation as an illustration.

16.7 What are the bases of comparative advantage in services? Explain how capital and technology have transformed global competition in services.

16.8 Why and how do governments intervene in services? How is GATT (now the WTO) attempting to create freer trade in services?

16.9 What is intellectual property? Why is it the focus of GATT-WTO negotiations in the services area?

16.10 Why are U.S. firms dominant in the world entertainment industry?

16.11 How is environmental change in the television industry in Europe creating opportunities for U.S. firms?

16.12 How does the spread of satellite TV and cable TV affect pan-European advertising by multinational firms?

16.13 Why has MTV been successful in Europe?

16.14 Explain the reasons behind the rise in global mergers in the media industry. How do such mergers help the firms sell more entertainment services around the world?

16.15 Where is airline traffic growing the fastest? How should U.S. airlines respond in order to obtain a share of passenger traffic growth overseas?

16.16 What are the problems of expanding professional service operations overseas? Illustrate your answer using Manpower's experience in Japan.

16.17 How can retailing services be expanded overseas? Why is acquisition a popular approach?

16.18 What are the forces creating greater demand for hotel services in foreign markets? How can multinational hotel chains profit from such growth?

16.19 How is banking becoming a global business?

16.20 Analyze multinational competition within the credit-card industry in Japan. What are the respective competitive advantages of foreign and Japanese banks? How do these advantages affect the marketing of credit-card services?

16.21   Comment on how foreign brokerage and investment banking firms have marketed in Japan. Why is culture important in selling financial services?

16.22   What are the prospects for the international marketing of insurance products and services?

16.23   Can any generalizations be made about the international marketing of services?

ENDNOTES

1   Mack Ott, "The Growing Share of Services in the U.S. Economy— Degeneration or Evolution?" *Federal Reserve Bank of St. Louis Review,* June–July 1987.

2   Irving Kravis and Robert Lipsey, *Production and Trade in Services by U.S. Multinational Firms,* National Bureau of Economic Research Working Paper No. 2615.

3   "Service Area in a Fog," *The Economist,* May 23, 1987.

4   V. Zeithaml, A. Parasuraman, and Leonard L. Berry, "Problems and Strategies in Services Marketing," *Journal of Marketing* 49 (Spring 1985).

5   Christopher Lovelock, "Classifying Services to Gain Strategic Marketing Insights," *Journal of Marketing* 47 (Summer 1983).

6   G. Lyn Shostack, "Service Positioning through Structural Change," *Journal of Marketing* 51 (January 1987).

7   Carol F. Suprenant and Michael R. Solomon, "Predictability and Personalization in the Service Encounter," *Journal of Marketing* 51 (April 1987).

8   Joseph P. Guiltinan, "The Price Bundling of Services: A Normative Framework," *Journal of Marketing* 51 (April 1987).

9   See C. Groonroos, "A Service Quality Model and Its Marketing Implications," *European Journal of Marketing* 18, no. 4 (1984).

10   A. Parasuraman, V. Zeithaml, and Leonard L. Berry, "A Conceptual Model of Service Quality and Its Implications for Future Research," *Journal of Marketing* 49 (Fall 1985).

11   Helen Dudar, "Moscow Rights: Doing a Book Deal with the Soviets," *The Wall Street Journal,* February 23, 1988.

12   "ISDN Executive Report: Snapshot of the French Scene," *Computerworld,* December 12, 1988, 80.

13   Geza Feketekuty, *International Trade in Services: An Overview and Blueprint for Negotiation* (Cambridge, MA: Ballinger, 1988).

14   Ravi Sarathy, "The Export Expansion Process in the Computer Software Industry," in *Managing Export Entry and Expansion,* ed. Philip Rosson and Stan Reid (New York: Praeger, 1987).

15   S. G. Bharadwaj, P. R. Varadarajan, and J. Fahy, "Sustainable Competitive Advantage in Service Industries: A Conceptual Model and Research Propositions," *Journal of Marketing,* October 1993, 83–99.

16   U.S. International Trade Commission, *The Relationship of Exports in Selected Service Industries to U.S. Merchandise Exports,* USITC Publication No. 1290, Washington, D.C., September 1982.

17   J. Aronson and P. Cowhey, *When Countries Talk: International Trade in Telecommunications Services* (Cambridge, MA: Ballinger, 1988).

18   Geza Feketekuty, *International Trade in Services: An Overview and Blueprint for Negotiation* (Cambridge, MA: Ballinger, 1988).

19   "Fancy Free: A Survey of the Entertainment Industry," *The Economist,* December 23, 1989.

20   "Endemol Feeds Growing TV Appetite across Europe amid Media Revolution," *The Wall Street Journal,* September 11, 1995.

21   "Murdoch's Empire: The Gambler's Last Throw," *The Economist,* March 9, 1996.

22   "Let a Hundred Channels Bloom, But Mind the Thorns," *The Economist,* November 25, 1995.

23   "Cable and Satellites Are Opening Europe to TV Commercials," *The Wall Street Journal,* December 22, 1987.

24   "Beaming Soap to Babel," *The Economist,* October 22, 1988.

25   "Satellite Television in Asia: A Little Local Interference," *The Economist,* February 3, 1996.

26   "Meet the New Media Monsters," *The Economist,* March 11, 1989.

[27] "News Corp. Buys 63.6 percent of Star TV for $525 million," *The Wall Street Journal,* July 27, 1993.

[28] "Sticky Wickets, but What a Future," *Business Week,* August 7, 1995.

[29] "Going Global with Rock and Roll," *The Wall Street Journal,* December 20, 1988.

[30] "The Battle for Europe's TV Future," *The Wall Street Journal,* October 6, 1989.

[31] "Empty Threat," *Forbes,* November 13, 1989.

[32] "European Companies Lobby to Defeat Proposed Controls on Media Industry," *The Wall Street Journal,* February 12, 1996.

[33] See Daniel Kasper, *Deregulation and Globalization: Liberalizing International Trade in Air Services* (Cambridge, MA: Ballinger, 1988).

[34] "Mr. Smith Goes Global," *Business Week,* February 13, 1989; "Federal Express Corp. Agrees to Acquire Tiger International in $800 Million Deal," *The Wall Street Journal,* December 19, 1988; and "Battle Heats Up over Global Air Delivery," *The Wall Street Journal,* December 19, 1988.

[35] "JAL, Lufthansa and Air France Discuss Venture," *The Wall Street Journal,* October 19, 1989.

[36] "Iberia Airlines to Sell Argentine Unit," *The Wall Street Journal,* February 5, 1996.

[37] "A Survey of Retailing: Change at the Checkout," *The Economist,* March 4, 1995.

[38] "Expanding across the EU," *Business Europe,* July 10, 1995.

[39] "Dressed for Success in Japan," *Boston Globe,* November 3, 1989.

[40] "Toys 'R Us Sets Venture in Japan with Food Chain," *The Wall Street Journal,* September 27, 1989.

[41] "Thorne Purchase Would Mark End of Retreat," *The Wall Street Journal,* July 30, 1987.

[42] "Lessons for Us All," *Business Europe,* March 6–12, 1995.

[43] "Japan Is Dialing 1 800 Buyamerica," *Business Week,* June 12, 1996.

[44] "How Hotels in Japan and the U.S. Compare in the Services Game," *The Wall Street Journal,* September 21, 1988.

[45] See Olivier Bertrand and T. Noyelle, *Human Resources and Corporate Strategy: Technological Change in Banks and Insurance Companies.* (Paris: Organization for Economic Cooperation and Development, 1988).

[46] "Hong Kong & Shanghai vs. the World," *Business Week,* August 7, 1995.

[47] "In Japan, Banks Get Personal to Get Rich," *Business Week,* November 28, 1988; and "U.S. Banks Are Losing Business to Japanese at Home and Abroad," *The Wall Street Journal,* October 12, 1989.

[48] "Trading in Tokyo: U.S. Brokerage Firms Operating in Japan Have Mixed Results," *The Wall Street Journal,* August 16, 1989.

[49] P. Cecchini, *The European Challenge: 1992, The Benefits of a Single Market* (Brookfield, VT: Gower Publishing, 1989), table 6.1.

[50] "How Beijing Is Boosting AIG," *Business Week,* November 13, 1995; and "AIG Reshapes China's Insurance Industry," *The Wall Street Journal,* February 9, 1996.

[51] "Entrepreneur Is Ringmaster of U.S.–Soviet Promotions," *The Wall Street Journal,* October 4, 1989.

[52] "The Loved Ones," *Financial World,* September 12, 1995.

[53] "SGS: Inspectors General," *The Economist,* May 16, 1987.

[54] For more on the subject, see Office of Technology Assessment, *International Competition in Services* (Washington, DC: Government Printing Office, 1987).

FURTHER READINGS

Bertrand, Olivier, and T. Noyelle. *Human Resources and Corporate Strategy: Technological Change in Banks and Insurance Companies.* Paris: Organization for Economic Cooperation and Development, 1988.

Bharadwaj, S. G., P. R. Varadarajan, and J. Fahy. "Sustainable Competitive Advantage in Service Industries: A Conceptual Model and Research Propositions." *Journal of Marketing,* October 1993, 83–99.

"Fancy Free: A Survey of the Entertainment Industry." *The Economist,* December 23, 1989.

Feketekuty, Geza. *International Trade in Services: An Overview and Blueprint for Negotiation.* Cambridge, MA: Ballinger, 1988.

Foster, Peter. "McDonald's Excellent Soviet Venture." *Canadian Business,* May 1991.

Groonroos, C. "A Service Quality Model and Its Marketing Implications." *European Journal of Marketing* 18, no. 4 (1984).

Lovelock, Christopher. "Classifying Services to Gain Strategic Marketing Insights." *Journal of Marketing* 47 (Summer 1983).

Mann, Michael, and Sylvia E. Bargas. "U.S. International Sales and Purchases of Private Services." *Survey of Current Business,* September 1995.

Office of Technology Assessment. *International Competition in Services.* Washington, D.C.: Government Printing Office, 1987.

Parasuraman, A., V. Zeithaml, and Leonard L. Berry. "A Conceptual Model of Service Quality and Its Implications for Future Research." *Journal of Marketing* 49 (Fall 1985).

Sarathy, Ravi. "The Export Expansion Process in the Computer Software Industry." In *Managing Export Entry and Expansion,* ed. Philip Rosson and Stan Reid. New York: Praeger, 1987.

Sarathy, Ravi. "Global Strategy in Service Industries." *Long Range Planning* 27, no. 6 (1994).

Shelp, R. *Service Industries and Economic Development.* New York: Praeger, 1984.

Shostack, G. Lyn. "Service Positioning through Structural Change." *Journal of Marketing* 51 (January 1987).

"A Survey of Retailing: Change at the Checkout." *The Economist,* March 4, 1995.

Zeithaml, V., A. Parasuraman, and Leonard L. Berry. "Problems and Strategies in Services Marketing." *Journal of Marketing* 49 (Spring 1985).

CASE 16.1

Baseball: The Japanese Game

Babe Ruth toured Japan with an All-Star team in 1931. Pro baseball resumed in Japan after the war in 1950. Japanese teams play each other all the time. There are 12 professional teams, divided into two leagues, the Pacific and the Central. The champion from each league plays in an end-of-season playoff, a Japanese "World" series. The teams are:

Central League	Pacific League
Yomiuri Giants	Nippon Ham Fighters
Yakult Swallows	Lotte Orions
Taiyo Whales	Seibu Lions
Chunichi Dragons	Nankai Hawks
Hanshin Tigers	Kintetsu Buffaloes
Hiroshima Carp	Hankyu Braves

Four of these teams are located in Tokyo and four in Osaka; all teams are owned by corporations. The Yomiuri Giants are owned and run by Japan's leading newspaper chain, the Yomiuri. The Chunichi Dragons are owned by another newspaper chain. Five teams are owned by railroads: Seibu, Hankyu, Kintetsu, and Nankai, all in the Pacific League, and the Hanshin Tigers in the Central. Other team owners include Taiyo, a fish producer; Nippon Ham, a meat producer; Lotte, a chewing gum manufacturer; Yakult, a soft-drink company; and Mazda, which owns the Hiroshima Carp. The Central League is stronger, with an attendance of 12 million compared with 7 million for the Pacific League in 1987. The Yomiuri Giants alone are on TV five or six nights a week, and all 65 of their home games and most of their away games are covered. Similarly, Taiyo and Yakult both have separate TV contracts and hence strong fan loyalty, and home attendance is high.

The Japanese players are smaller in size. They come up the traditional way: through high school baseball and then into Japan's only minor league or through four years of college. Once in college, they cannot be drafted for four years. Japanese players know that the Americans are better paid and accept that the current generation of U.S. players is bigger, stronger, and faster and hits with more power than most Japanese players. Mike Lum, a hitting coach with Kansas City who played in Japan, noted, however, that Japanese pitching is good. It helps that the Japanese strike zone is wider and deeper, from below the belt to the armpits.

As in the United States, TV is a strong influence on baseball. The Yomiuri Giants have a national following because of

TV and with Sadaharu Oh (who has 868 home runs to his name) they won nine straight national championships between 1965 and 1973. They play in the new Tokyo Dome, modeled after the Metrodome in Minnesota, which they share with the Nippon Ham Fighters.

Built by the Korokuen Corp. for about $280 million, the new Tokyo Dome produced first-year revenues of over $325 million. It can draw on a population of nearly 30 million in a 100-square-mile radius (due to Japan's excellent and fast public transportation system). The 56,000-seat arena also hosts track meets, bicycle races (on which big bets are placed in Japan), rugby matches, and events that have been as diverse as Michael Jackson concerts and Mike Tyson boxing matches.

To combat the greater financial strength of the Central League, the Pacific League began importing U.S. players. The practice is now standard in both leagues. Each team can have two active foreign players, with an additional "imported" player in the minor leagues who can be called up in case of injury. Japanese baseball now offers an opportunity for the young U.S. ballplayer who *almost* makes the U.S. major league teams. An example is Jim Paciorek, who played in the Milwaukee Brewer farm club organization for five years. Unable to make the Brewer team, he moved to Japan to play for the Taiyo Whales in Yokohama.

The foreign players, *gaijin senshu,* are well paid, with the appreciating yen making Japanese salaries look even better. For example, Mike Easler signed with the Nippon Ham Fighters in May 1988 for $975,000 for one year. He had been cut by the Yankees and, at age 37, saw Japan as his only chance to continue playing in the majors. Others signing the same year were Doug DeCinces, Bill Madlock, and Bill Gullickson. The transition was made easier by playing in the Tokyo Dome, the only real major-league facility in Japan. It may have helped that Easler had played 10 seasons of winter ball in Mexico and Venezuela, thus becoming more comfortable with foreign cultures. Salaries for U.S. baseball players are high when compared with the following average 1988 salaries for Japanese players: $93,680 for pitchers, $76,160 for catchers, and between $112,000 and $113,000 for infielders and outfielders in the Central League.

But for the Japanese player, the pay difference is not a major bone of contention: The player is ultimately a company employee who knows that the company that owns his team will absorb him into the company culture and find him a position if he quits baseball.

The pay is good, but life is not easy for the U.S. ballplayer in Japan. For one thing, the entire team relies heavily on him. For another, although teams hire interpreters who work with the player nonstop, he and his family must adjust to the culture, the scarce housing, and the expensive way of life. Then there are the playing fields themselves. The Tokyo Dome is fine, as are three other stadiums that have artificial turf. But the remaining clubs have all-dirt infields and grass outfields, or even all-dirt fields. When it rains, the field can be a swamp, and playing during the hot season has been compared to playing on a basketball court. The work ethic, quintessentially Japanese, often is the undoing of the aging U.S. baseball player who comes to Japan expecting some easy money. It is not surprising that, faced with the demand to believe that the company or team is what matters and that the manager must be listened to, many U.S. players quit after a year.

Randy Bass's story is an example of the culture gap. He became Japan's leading slugger, winning the Triple Crown in both 1985 and 1986. He became the highest-paid player in Japan, but he left the Hanshin Tigers for San Francisco in May 1988 when his son was hospitalized. He was contravening the Japanese cultural code that puts loyalty to the company above personal considerations. When he did not return by June 17, as he had agreed, he was released.

Unlike U.S. baseball, Japanese teams play each other frequently because there are only six teams in each league. Pitchers watch and learn about batters. The pitcher's chief weapons are the curve, the slider, and the forkball—in other words, control. After facing a hitter so many times during the Japanese season (and studying him like a hawk), the better pitcher has a distinct advantage. As Easler puts it, "They know everything about you—what you can hit, what you can't; before the game, you have a video of each team that you play. We go over everything in great detail. The practice habits and work habits here are just exceptional. . . . It's like spring training every day."[1] One other difference is the stress on pitching complete games. Easler thinks that this builds confidence because the pitcher learns to bail himself out. "Patience is the key to hitting in Japan. You are definitely going to have to hit the ball the other way. If you don't, you'll die here." Easler, who used to be a dead pull hitter, has returned to the spray hitting style that he learned under Walter Hriniak with the Boston Red Sox. As a result, he was hitting .312 after 39 games by mid-July 1988.

Will There Be a True World Series Some Day?

What of the future? Because of the strong yen, Japanese clubs can bid more dollars for better U.S. players if they so choose. The concentration of teams in Tokyo and Osaka may hinder attempts to expand baseball in Japan by adding new teams in other cities. On the other hand, the success of the Tokyo Dome points to the possibility of moving franchises and creating expansion teams linked to new major league–quality stadiums. And now that baseball is an Olympic sport, on the horizon is the possibility of a Japanese–U.S. world series, with the Japanese champions challenging the U.S. World Series winners. This means raising the quality of Japanese baseball, increasing the size of the roster from the present 25 men, and perhaps raising the current three-man ceiling for foreign players.

Baseball Trade Opportunities

Selling U.S. baseball to Japan is an "export" possibility. Growing TV revenues in the United States may indicate that a similar high-paying market might exist in Japan. TV rights for baseball games to be shown on Japanese TV might bring yen-based revenues for U.S. entrepreneurs. Promotional opportunities for ballplayers in Japan are underexploited, being currently under control of the company owning the team. There are no Japanese baseball cards. And if baseball can be exported, can ownership rights be far behind? Would Sony buy up a U.S. baseball team? After all, the owner of Nintendo was given permission by U.S. baseball team owners to purchase the Seattle Mariners when the team was for sale. If the two richest markets in the world are baseball crazy, there are surely opportunities for further trade in baseball between these nations.

Questions

1. How is Japanese baseball marketed? In what ways does it differ from the selling of U.S. baseball?

2. How would an aging U.S. baseball player market himself to a Japanese team?

3. How is the growing popularity of baseball in Japan likely to affect U.S. baseball?

4. Does U.S.-Japanese collaboration change the market for U.S. baseball players? How should the Major League Players Association (the union) react to protect its member interests?

5. Why would U.S. entrepreneurs and agents be interested in Japanese baseball players?

6. Why would someone in Japan want to buy a U.S. baseball team? What are the implications of an internationalization of the baseball scene?

7. How can trade in baseball be seen as an example of trade in services?

Endnote

[1] Larry Whiteside, "He's Still a Big Hit," Boston Globe, July 18, 1988, 45.

Sony Corp

Sony has long been known for its innovative consumer electronics products, such as the pioneering Walkman. It is an international corporation, with 70 percent of its sales coming from outside Japan, and non-Japanese owners owning 23 percent of its stock. Sony manufactures about 20 percent of its output outside Japan. As of 1986 its sales mix was video equipment (VCRs) 33 percent, audio equipment (compact disk players) 22 percent, TVs (the Trinitron) 22 percent, and other products (records, floppy disk drives, and semiconductors) 17 percent. Sony has always emphasized R&D, spending about 9 percent of sales on it.

The Betamax Experience

Sony has been facing increasing competition from other Japanese companies and from countries with lower labor costs, such as Taiwan and South Korea. Its strategy of inventing new, advanced-technology products and then waiting for the market to buy seemed to be faltering. Sony's biggest failure was the Betamax, however. Having invented the Betamax format for VCRs, it refused to license the technology to other manufacturers. Betamax was higher priced, and recording times were somewhat shorter than those of the competing VHS format, although quality of the images was better.

Sony's competitors, such as Matsushita (Panasonic), Hitachi, and Toshiba, all banded together around the VHS format. They licensed the format to any manufacturer who wanted it. Consequently, the total number of VHS sets produced and sold was far higher than the Betamax-format VCRs, which meant lower retail prices because of accumulated volume and resulting economies of scale. Also, far more "software" was available for the VHS format; that is, movie producers were more likely to make home video copies of their films available for purchase and rental on VHS tapes. This further increased demand for VHS-format VCRs. The net result was that Betamax gradually faded, and Sony stopped its production in 1988.

Rethinking Basic Strategy

The difficulty of selling advanced technology coupled with the speed of imitation and the impact of low-wage country competitors led Sony to change its basic corporate strategy. The CBS/Sony Group, Inc., a 50-50 joint venture between Sony and CBS, Inc., has grown dramatically over a 20-year period to become an industry leader in the multibillion yen Japanese music industry. It releases recordings in Japan, Hong Kong, and Macau, on compact disk and other formats, by popular Japanese artists such as Seiko Matsuda and Rebecca, as well as foreign artists.

Sony's Diversification into the Entertainment Industry

Sony's diversification into the global music industry is, therefore, not unexpected. In January 1988 it agreed to buy CBS Records worldwide for $2 billion. But subsequent moves have dramatically transformed Sony as it moves to become more a service company. Table 1 summarizes the major entertainment industry acquisitions made by Sony since 1988.

TABLE 1		

From Electronics to Entertainment: Sony's Acquisitions since 1988

Date	Company Acquired	Price
October 1989	Guber-Peters Productions	$200 million
September 1989	Columbia Pictures	$3.4 billion
January 1989	Tree International country music publishers	$30 million
January 1988	CBS Records	$2 billion

The acquisitions themselves are large, totaling over $5 billion, or about half of Sony's total assets. More interesting is the reasoning behind Sony's decision to acquire a slew of entertainment companies. A summary of the acquisitions follows:

CBS Records For $2 billion, Sony was able to acquire control of the world's largest record company, CBS Records. CBS Records, Inc., consists of CBS Records (Domestic), CBS Masterworks, CBS Records International, CBS/Sony, Columbia House, and CBS Musicvideo. The acquisition gave Sony an immediate international presence in the music industry. Traditionally selling music hardware, Sony was one of the world's largest producers of compact disk players (CDs), tape recorders (including the phenomenally successful Walkman), and stereo television. But all of these products were subject to competition because innovative ideas could be imitated and prices cut. Sony realized that being in the music business allowed it to take advantage of the entire installed base of compact disk players around the world, not just those it alone manufactured. Imitation was impossible because each musical performance was unique; however, managing such a creative business required great cultural sensitivity and the use of local managers rather than predominantly Japanese management.

The music industry is a fast-growing business. In 1988 over 150 million CDs were sold in the United States alone, and there were over 11 million CD players in households.

Columbia Pictures The major attraction of Columbia Pictures was its large library of movies that continue to earn revenues every time they are shown at cinemas and on video around the world. Columbia also had a profitable TV production and syndication business. Thus, the acquisition gave Sony products to sell to owners of TV sets and VCRs in a manner analogous to providing music on record and tape for owners of CD players and tape recorders.

There are two other reasons that Sony might have found Columbia Pictures attractive. First, TV in Japan is being liberalized, with a doubling in the number of TV stations and on-air time because of the launch of satellite television. There will be a sudden increase in demand for product, such as films and TV shows, to fill air time on Japan's satellite stations. Sony will be in a position to supply such product for premium prices in yen at a time when demand will be increasing.

The other reason is hardware related. Sony has been trying to establish its 8 mm camcorder format, again in competition with a VHS-C–based format from competing Japanese producers. This standards battle is reminiscent of Sony's experience with Betamax. This time, however, Sony realizes the need to build the installed base. Hence, it has licensed the 8 mm technology to other producers and is willing to manufacture the camcorders for sale by others under their brand names. Sony is thus making sure that volume sales of the 8 mm camcorder will be achieved, resulting in economies of scale and lower prices. The next step is to stimulate demand by making available a variety of movies in this format. Sony can do this by putting the entire Columbia Pictures catalog on 8 mm video, thus giving consumers a reason to buy the camcorder, which can also be used as a video player. This availability will be crucial to the success of Sony's newly introduced 8 mm video Walkman, a pocket-sized portable color TV set that will appeal to the extent that videos are available for use with the video Walkman.

Thus, with the CBS Records and Columbia Pictures acquisition, Sony becomes one of the world's major producers of entertainment hardware and software: record producer and CD player producer; a leading manufacturer of TV sets and an owner of a library of classic films.

Guber-Peters Productions When Sony purchased Columbia Pictures, it obtained a film library as well as a studio for film production. Columbia had gone through four producers in five years, however, and needed more capable film production management. The logical step was to take over one of Hollywood's most successful film production companies, Guber-Peters (G-P) (formerly Barris Productions), which had been responsible for Batman, one of Warner Communications' all-time best selling films. In fact, G-P had signed a five-year exclusive agreement with Warner to produce movies on its behalf. G-P's expertise lay in spotting hot properties, signing them, and then convincing major studios to bankroll the films and distribute them. G-P had a unique culture-specific talent for working in and with Hollywood, producing successful films for the huge U.S. TV and film audience. Sony acquired G-P for over $200 million, or about five times G-P's latest-year revenues. The two key producers, Peter Guber and Jon Peters, received about $50 million for their stock in G-P, a 10 percent stake in future profits at Columbia Pictures, 8 percent of the future appreciation of Columbia Pictures' market value, and about $50 million in total deferred compensation.

Warner immediately sued Sony for acquiring G-P. Warner refused to release Peter Guber from a long-term contract. Of course, Sony and Warner ultimately settled out of court, exchanging valuable assets such as a share of the movie studio, video rights, and so on. Clearly, Sony wanted the management talent, Americans who knew Hollywood and could hire the right people, had the appropriate financial and creative contacts, and, most important, knew how to make hit films.

Tree International Sony also acquired, through CBS Records, the ownership of Tree, the premier country music publishing company. The ownership of rights to several generations of hit country songs guarantees a steady stream of revenue, especially as the catalog becomes popular around the world and in Japan through Sony's music and video production divisions. This is a minor acquisition, but it may point to a trend toward acquiring other music publishing companies as a means to further control the software end of the entertainment business.

Sony's Future

Looking to the future, Sony's heavy involvement in new hardware technologies such as advanced high-definition TV, computer workstations, and compact disk interactive technology will require further research and development; but their acceptance by consumers will depend equally on the availability of software products that showcase the new hardware products. Sony's long-term plans focus more on services and entertainment; paradoxically, this will help it to become a stronger hardware company and to reduce risk by smoothing revenue fluctuations and providing the stability of recurring earnings from sales of music, film, and videotapes.

Questions

1. What were the threats facing Sony?
2. Trace the various entertainment industry acquisitions made by Sony. Why did Sony make these acquisitions? Have they helped the company compete more effectively in international markets?
3. What are the risks of Sony's strategy of buying U.S. entertainment companies?
4. What would you recommend that Sony do next? And how do you think Sony's Japanese competitors might respond to its action?
5. Is Sony becoming a global company, or is it becoming a company with products adapted for each specific country market?
6. What generalizations can you make about the global service industry from Sony's experience?

Case prepared by Ravi Sarathy for use in classroom discussion. All rights reserved.
Sources: "Sony Sees More Than Michael Jackson in CBS," *The Economist*, November 28, 1987; "A Changing Sony Aims to Own the Software That Its Products Need," *The Wall Street Journal*, December 30, 1988; "Sony Sets Pact with Coca-Cola for Columbia," *The Wall Street Journal*, September 28, 1989; and "Dynamic Duo: Producers of 'Batman' Stir Whammo Battle over Future Services," *The Wall Street Journal*, October 20, 1989.

CASE 16.3

Sony in 1996

In December 1994, Sony announced that it was taking a $2.7 billion write-off in connection with its 1989 acquisition of Columbia Pictures. Furthermore, Sony Pictures reported a loss of $500 million for the year; the combined losses of $3.2 billion were some of the largest losses incurred in Hollywood. Shortly thereafter, Matsushita, which had copied Sony by buying MCA, announced that it was selling MCA to Seagram, incurring a large loss in the process. MCA's top management had threatened to leave MCA because Matsushita did not wish to invest additional funds into MCA. MCA's main film-producing partner, Steven Spielberg, would have accompanied MCA's management and stopped distributing his films through MCA.

Back in Japan, meanwhile, an appreciating yen made Sony's consumer electronics products more expensive in its export markets. It was facing competition from producers in South Korea and Taiwan that could offer a basic VCR in U.S. stores such as Circuit City for $99, a price at which Sony could not compete.

Changes at the Top

Major changes occurred within top management ranks at Sony. Mr. Morita, Sony's founder, had suffered a stroke and

withdrawn from management involvement. Mr. Ohga, the CEO, who had himself undergone a bypass operation, missed being able to chat with his mentor, and the gradual decline in Sony's fortunes led him to think carefully about what sort of person should lead Sony into the 21st century. Both Morita and Ohga had agreed years earlier that they would step down as President of Sony at age 65. It had been widely assumed that an engineer, Mr. Minoru Morio, the president of Sony's audio-visual products and head of Sony's Digital Video Disc (DVD) efforts, would step in. Ohga, however, turned to a marketer, Mr. Nobuyuki Idei, as Sony's next president. Mr. Idei had worked for Sony in overseas locations and been in charge of marketing Sony's audio-visual products. In 1990, he had become head of Sony's Design Center, responsible for Sony's merchandising and product promotions and corporate communications. As such, he represented Sony across the world at major trade shows and industry gatherings. His appointment signaled a major change in Sony's strategic direction and vision of itself. Mr. Idei was an enthusiastic proponent of digital video, and saw opportunities for Sony in the convergence of entertainment, consumer electronics products, and PCs.

The Digital Video Era

Digital video could be to VCRs and films on videotape what CDs were to the older analog LPs (long-playing records). Digital video allows entire films to be stored on CD-ROM–sized disks and accessed at any point, manipulated and reused.

Sony had been working with the Dutch company Philips in developing a DVD standard that would be used in digital video devices. Sony's standard called for a single-sided disk containing about 3.7 gigabytes of information, equal to about 135 minutes of video.

Establishing an industry standard can be enormously profitable, as can be seen in the examples of Intel and Microsoft—Sony (and Philips) earned a nickel in royalties for each CD sold. But in 1993 Sony found out that Toshiba and Time Warner were working on a DVD standard of their own. Their Super-Density, or SD, format would use both sides of the disk and store five gigabytes on each side; Time Warner also found it easier to get the attention of movie studios in Hollywood and get them to clarify what performance criteria they expected from DVD. (Mr. Morio, who headed Sony's DVD effort, in contrast, spoke little English and came from an engineering, not marketing, background.) With mounting competition from Toshiba and Time Warner, Mr. Idei was asked to formulate a new DVD strategy, which he crafted by stressing the role of DVD as a format for multimedia PCs. By January 1995, Matsushita had joined Hitachi, Pioneer, JVC, Thomson, and Mitsubishi in supporting the Toshiba SD standard. With the Betamax fiasco possibly in mind, Sony ultimately compromised and agreed to work out a unified DVD standard.

New Business Directions

One of Sony's successes has been the Sony Playstation, which competed against the Nintendo and Sega 16-bit game machines, but offered superior video and sound and faster speed through 32-bit processors. Planning for the Playstation began in 1988 when Ken Kutaragi, who was designing Sony workstations using advanced chips, realized that the prices of these chips would fall to the point that it made sense to build a game machine around these 32-bit semiconductors, with added features such as a CD-ROM input device and superior graphics screen. However, game machines sell because their customers want the hit games that are exclusive to that platform. Hence, an executive from Sony Music, which was a distributor of Nintendo machines, suggested that Mr. Kutaragi think about building reusable modules that programmers could use to quickly create entertaining and impressive new games. Based on this, Mr. Kutaragi built a dictionary of images that could be combined on the fly to build game characters who could exhibit subtle and lifelike movements, while cutting game development time by half. Sony also created a joint venture within the company with Sony Music to focus on selling both hardware (the Playstation) and software (that is, newly developed games). This allowed the Playstation to be priced at $299 in the United States, a full $100 below the competing Sega Saturn (with the expectation that a growing installed base offered a fertile and captive market for the sale of high-margin hit games; the typical Nintendo owner purchased 6 to 12 games for a machine). Sony's Playstation became the best-selling 32-bit game machine in Japan and the United States in 1995. About a year later, Nintendo introduced its N64 machine and both companies reduced their game machine prices to under $150. Loyal Nintendo fans bought its new machine in large numbers, but Sony's lead and larger number of games available ensured that it continued to hold a larger market share over Nintendo in the new generation video game segment of the market.

Under Mr. Idei's leadership, Sony entered into an alliance with Intel to make multimedia PCs, what he termed "Intelligent TV." He visualized "the intelligence of computers, the access power of on-line communications, and the visual power of full-motion video integrated into a new form of viewing experience." Other new products that Sony targeted for the age of digital TV included wide-screen living room televisions that could access the Internet using Web browsers, eyeglasses onto which TV and E-mail could be projected using wireless technology, as well as low-cost computers acting as Web browsers. The new Sony PCs could include Sony Playstation game-playing abilities as well as the ability to access digital TV programs, and use screensavers featuring images and sound from Sony films and Sony music acts. Moreover, Sony's library of 3,000 films and over 35,000 hours of TV programs would be a valuable resource for an age of digital TV.

Outside the United States, Sony saw strong growth possibilities in satellite TV. It formed a joint venture with Singapore-based Argos Communications to launch a Hindi-language satellite TV channel beamed to India. The channel would feature locally produced Indian shows and movies, as well as films and programs from Sony's library. Initially, the channel would be offered free to cable TV operators who would redistribute it; Sony expected to generate revenues from sale of advertising time. Sony also became a partner in HBO OIC, a Spanish-language service aimed at Latin America.

Management Shake-up in the United States

Mr. Schulhof, a physicist and jet pilot (like Mr. Ohga), was the head of U.S. operations and a close ally of Morita and Ohga. He had authorized the payment of $200 million to buy Guber-Peters Entertainment and to buy out their contract with Warner Brothers. He allowed Guber and Peters to choose their managers, sometimes resulting in the appointment of friends and associates (Guber named his lawyer as the number two executive). This may have resulted in an atmosphere where politics and whom one knew became important.

Guber and Peters had little management experience in running a studio, but spent lavishly, updating the Culver City studios at a cost of $200 million. There were no cost controls, and several new films released were expensive failures such as the *Last Action Hero, Hudson Hawk, Geronimo,* and *Frankenstein.* Mr. Schulhof also backed Sony's entry into programs for radio syndication and into theme parks featuring Sony characters and goods. He did not agree with the move into PCs, which he characterized as a low-margin business with very rapid change and short product cycles—an environment with which Sony had no experience. By the end of 1995 he had resigned from Sony, as Mr. Idei moved to re-establish Japanese headquarters control over Sony Pictures and U.S. operations.

Sony Finances

Table 1 summarizes Sony's financial performance between 1986 and 1995. Sales grew dramatically, from $7.7 billion to over $46 billion in the decade. 1995 sales were nearly evenly distributed across Japan, the United States, and Europe, with sales of $12.3, $13.9, and $10.2 billion respectively. However, net income was at half the profitability levels of 1986, and long-term debt grew tenfold. Sony had to choose in allocating its cash flow between the entertainment division and the support of R&D in the hardware divisions. In 1995, sales of TV, audio, and video equipment were about 58 percent of total sales, compared to about 20 percent from music and films. In 1995, U.S. consumer electronics revenues actually exceeded U.S. music and film revenues.

Alternatives for Sony's U.S. Entertainment Operations

Matsushita's sale of MCA immediately raised questions as to whether Sony should do the same. Mr. Idei remarked that

Matsushita was shortsighted in selling its film division. In a digital age, content and copyrights can be distributed in myriad formats, and the large film library that came with the Columbia Pictures acquisition was a valuable and scarce asset. There are few Hollywood film studios left to buy for any media company eager to enter into the software or content-generation side of the business. When Mr. Idei took over as president of Sony, he indicated that he wanted to hold on to his entertainment division in the United States. His priority, however, was restoring profitability at Sony Pictures. He wanted to see more pictures made with lower budgets, stressing cost controls. When Mr. Schulhof, head of Sony U.S. operations, mentioned that Sony's market share was rising, Mr. Idei remarked that he was more interested in profits.

If Sony were to sell, several choices existed: Should it sell all of the entertainment business? If so, who should it sell to, mindful that it did not want to create a strong competitor down the road. Interested parties included GE, which owns NBC-TV, News Corp., which already has the Fox studios, and overseas buyers such as Polygram and Bertelsmann, neither of which had a major Hollywood studio. Another alternative was to sell only part of the U.S. entertainment business, perhaps selling a portion in a U.S. public stock offering, or, selling a stake in the company to a strategic partner.

Mr. Idei had specific ideas on how Sony should be run. He expressed little interest in buying media channels as Disney did with ABC—"Buying a network in a digital age with so many channels won't bring any benefits to us." He disliked the idea of selling the U.S. music and film business and the taking on of a partner for fear of losing control and having to put up with interference from U.S. owners with different perspectives. "I also want to set a new future direction for our R&D, so that it is not merely trying to extend our current business, but attempting to identify new opportunities for the

| TABLE 1 | Sony Corporation: 1986–1995 Financial Statements ($ Billions) |

	1986	1987	1988	1989	1990	1991	1992	1993	1994	1995
Sales	7.700	10.700	17.100	20.500	26.100	29.600	32.200	34.800	40.40	46.200
Operating income	0.200	0.400	1.200	2.100	2.100	1.400	1.00	0.900	−1.70	2.300
Net income	0.245	0.269	0.562	0.717	0.827	0.904	0.292	0.143	−2.97	0.683
Long-term debt	0.880	1.580	1.670	4.100	4.910	6.650	7.650	9.360	10.49	8.470
Net worth	3.700	5.200	6.900	9.100	10.400	11.600	12.400	12.600	11.70	10.700

21st century. And of course DVD is a very high priority because setting a format standard energizes the company."[1]

Questions

1. Evaluate the performance of Sony's U.S. entertainment division. Why did they do poorly?

2. What are the challenges facing Sony in 1996? Assess its strategy for coping with these challenges.

3. Looking back, would Sony have been better off not buying into the U.S. film and music businesses?

4. What do you think of Mr. Idei's approach to running Sony?

Endnote

[1] Brent Schlender, "Sony on the Brink," *Fortune,* June 12, 1995, 78.

Case prepared by Ravi Sarathy for use in classroom discussion, 1996. All rights reserved.
Sources: *The Wall Street Journal:* "Ouster of Schulhof Leaves Focus Fuzzy at Sony Entertainment," December 6, 1995; "Sony Heads Down Information Highway and Decides Not to Go It Alone," April 14, 1995; "Sony President Rules out Buying American Network," November 21, 1995; "Sony May Sell Stake in U.S. Operations," October 30, 1995; "Sony Resignation Brings Speculation about Possible Suitors for Movie Unit," December 7, 1995; "Sony Unit Plans Venture to Launch Hindi-Language TV Channel in India," August 14, 1995; "Sony President Seeks to Quash Rumors about Sale of U.S. Entertainment Unit," January 15, 1996. *Business Week:* "Sony's Headaches in Hollywood," December 5, 1994; "It's Nobuyuki Idei's Sony Now," December 18, 1995; *Fortune:* Brent Schlender, "Sony on the Brink," June 12, 1995; *Financial World:* "Lonesome Samurai," May 23, 1995; and "Sony Outside, Intel Inside," January 2, 1996.

CASE 16.4

Enron: Supplying Electric Power in India

Rapid economic growth in emerging nations, principally in Southeast Asia, has taxed their existing infrastructure. Their future growth is dependent on resolving bottlenecks in critical infrastructure industries such as electricity generation and transmission, roads, telecommunications, port facilities, railroads, and airline service. A particularly pressing need is to increase electricity power generation and availability. Table 1 sets out the relationship between GDP per capita and energy production as well as energy consumption. Both energy production and consumption rise with growing incomes, and the current levels of energy consumption in countries such as India and China are far below levels in countries such as the United States. China's consumption (below 600 kwh per capita) is at about one-quarter of the world average, while India's (below 300 kwh per capita) is at about one-eighth of the world average.

There is no question that energy consumption and production must rise if these emerging nations are to continue their rapid growth. If not, energy shortages will pose bottlenecks, impeding and arresting growth and putting a damper on the rising prosperity of people all across Asia. The World

Bank estimates that Asia will need 290,000 megawatts (mw) of new generating capacity until 2004, which works out to new capacity coming on line at the rate of 2,000 to 2,400 mw a month! Such a pace of new capacity build-up will require investments of $35 billion a year;[1] emerging nations cannot finance the level of investment needed by themselves.[2] A typical 300 mw plant could cost $500 million, and China alone might require around 300 plants over the next decade, implying $150 billion for investment in electricity generation in China alone!

Therein lies the promise and the risk of international energy investments for private-sector, independent power producers (IPPs) and energy multinationals. The high-growth potential markets of Asia offer electric utilities (and other firms) the opportunity to significantly increase sales and profits.

Enron's Dabhol Power Project in India

Enron, a Texas-based utility, launched a separate subsidiary to begin to sell its power-generating expertise in international markets. One of its first major projects was in India. India has a great need for power, with per capita consumption of only 270 kwh per capita, capacity shortages of 23 percent at peak utilization, and transmission and distribution losses of 22 and 24 percent. While installed capacity in India was at 80,000 mw in 1994 (a doubling of capacity since 1985), an additional 142,000 mw is forecast to be needed by 2005 to keep pace with

TABLE 1	Electricity Consumption, Production, and GDP per Capita		
Country	**GDP per Capita (US$, 1991)**	**Electricity Production (Billions KWH, 1991)**	**Energy Consumption (Kg. Oil Equivalent per Capita, 1990)**
United States	22,449	3,079.0	6,971
Japan	27,005	857.0	2,904
India	350	286.0	217
China	600	671.0	569
Indonesia	620	44.0	211
South Korea	6,540	119.0	1,731
Philippines	720	22.5	210
Thailand	1,623	50.1	516
Hong Kong	14,500	28.4	1,240

demand growing at 8 to 10 percent a year; this implies investments of around $165 billion, of which over half has to come from outside India.

The Indian government announced policies that would allow IPPs to receive prices for electricity such that full costs would be recovered with a 16 percent rate of return at a 68.5 percent load factor.[3] Foreign participation has been welcomed, and India's central government has offered counter-guarantees concerning power purchase agreements by local State Electricity Boards (SEBs) to eight "fast-track" sole-source projects, Enron being one. Enron chose to receive an Indian government guarantee covering the price it would be paid for fuel during the first 12 years, hoping to earn returns in excess of 16 percent on capital by operating above 90 percent of capacity and achieving higher thermal efficiency.

Enron announced a $2.8 billion, 2,015-megawatt (mw) gas-fired plant to be built in Dabhol in Maharashtra State on the west coast of India. The build–operate–transfer (BOT) plant was to be operated by Enron for 20 years, with power sold at a fixed rate of 7.47 US$ cents per kw hour. Enron holds 80 percent of the equity, with 10 percent each held by GE and Bechtel. The project was to be implemented in two stages, based on fuel availability and growth in demand for energy, with the plant switching to imported liquified natural gas (LNG) in the second stage. Enron hoped to supply the LNG from its fields in Qatar in the Persian Gulf. Debt is 70 percent of the project, to be supplied by the U.S. Eximbank, IFC, and others, including Indian financial institutions.

The project attracted opposition from the start, including a negative report by the World Bank, which refused to par-ticipate in financing the project. More important, the opposition party began campaigning against the Enron project during the run-up to state government elections in 1994–1995. They alleged that Enron had indulged in bribery to win the contract and that the project was costly and not in the best interests of the state of Maharashtra. Several major criticisms of the Enron project (see Table 2) existed:

1. *High capital cost of the project.* Enron justified the cost by citing the need to create special additional infrastructure, for example, new port facilities to handle imports of LNG (needed in the second stage). Enron's cost to produce energy has been judged to be high. It is estimated, for example, that Dabhol's power will cost around $1,300 per kw, while a new-technology, combined-cycle gas-fired plant should cost between $700 and $800 per kw.[4]

2. *High price of energy.* To be sold at 7.47 cents per kw hour, the price of energy was also criticized as high, being above the existing electricity prices charged by the MSEB (Maharashtra State Electricity Board). Further, since the capital recovery charge was backloaded, rates would increase as the capital charge was added to the electricity tariff down the road. Market pricing of energy may have salutary effects on the efficient use of energy (the OECD average is about 8 cents per kw hour). However, market-driven price increases in the price of a basic input such as electricity may be politically

TABLE 2	Enron's Dabhol Power Project in India

Perceived Negatives	Enron's Rebuttal
High capital cost, averaging about $1.4 million per mw.	Due to additional infrastructure, including a port facility to handle LNG, new roads, schools, hospital, water supply, and housing.
High cost of power to MSEB, fixed in US$ at 7.47 cents, forcing MSEB to reduce power intake from older cheaper plants	Inflation will bring up power costs from older plants to the 7.47 cent level; also relevant are the greater inefficiency and environmental cost of the old plants.
Produce power in excess of MSEB base-load requirements.	Maharashtra is expected to receive about 1/3 of all FDI in India; hence its power needs will grow sufficiently over time to use up plant capacity.
Plant's inflexible design, leading to uneconomical load dispatch, financial burden on MSEB.	Older obsolete plants are wasteful and would have to be upgraded at some point.
Technology: Why not use coal, even imported coal, rather than oil and imported LNG?	Cost of a coal-fired plant with scrubbers would be higher; if such pollution control were to be ignored, there could be negative environmental impact on an agricultural region.
Favoritism and corruption in granting the project to Enron without competitive bidding; opposition politicians suggested the collusion of the Maharashtra State government, controlled by the Congress Party then in power.	Exhaustive investigation conducted by the U.S. government prior to granting Eximbank financing, to ensure that the U.S. Foreign Corrupt Practices Act has been scrupulously adhered to.

unpalatable. The problem is political readiness of the market to accept higher market prices for a good that has long been subsidized. The Indian government has been subsidizing energy for farmers for 40 years, and a sudden withdrawal is not in the cards. Indian electricity tariffs are among the lowest in the world, presenting a problem for private power production.[5] In 1994–1995, electricity rates were about Indian rupees (Rs.) 1.74 per kw hour against the Rs. 2.40 that MSEB would have to charge in 1997. It is conceivable that Indian inflation, however, could raise current rates to the Rs. 2.40 level anyway.

3. *A poor bargain for the MSEB.* The MSEB is committed to buying electricity up to a plant load factor (PLF) of 90 percent, and it has been suggested that such a volume is greater than that required by consumers;[6] as a result, MSEB would have to cut back purchases of energy from older plants with cheaper electricity. Moreover, LNG-based plants—which is what Dabhol is—are more suited to be run as peak-load plants, adding energy to the grid during periods of high demand (that is, in peak hours); however, the 90 percent PLF means that Dabhol will be operated continuously as a base-load–supplying plant, and other older plants would have to be turned on and shut down to accommodate peak demands, with

deleterious consequences on their efficiency and economic life.

4. *MSEB bears the foreign exchange risk.* Guaranteeing the price of electricity in foreign currency has insulated Enron from the problem of local currency electricity tariffs not keeping pace with local inflation. MSEB would be paying Enron for its electricity at a rate guaranteed in U.S. dollars, but might not be able to pass on foreign exchange rate increases through higher tariffs, thus facing the prospect of absorbing exchange rate rises and increasing its losses.

In March 1995 the opposition party won the election, somewhat unexpectedly. One of their first acts was to repudiate the contract with Enron. Enron had spent about $300 million and almost a year working on the project. Enron proceeded to place the case before arbitrators in London while continuing to negotiate with the newly elected government. The cultural background to this opposition was the adherence by many political parties and intellectuals to the Gandhian ideals of "swadeshi"—self-reliance—who are loth to depend on and allow entry of multinationals into spheres such as electricity. Local business interests can also hide behind such populist appeals as a way of avoiding strong foreign competition.

Given that construction had begun and that contracts had been signed, a cancelation of the Dabhol project would have had serious impact on the willingness of other foreign IPPs to enter the Indian energy market.[7] A walkout by Enron would also have kept it from participating in future development of the Indian energy sector. Hence, Enron announced a willingness to renegotiate some of the terms of the Dabhol project, while preserving its rights to seek mediation in London as agreed upon at the time of project negotiations.[8]

In January 1996, Enron and the local state government settled their differences, allowing the project to restart. Enron made concessions by lowering the selling price of energy to 5.2 cents (a 22.5 percent reduction), increasing the size of the project to 2,450 mw, and lowering the capital cost by $300 million. Enron also reduced its equity stake to 50 percent, selling 30 percent ownership of the project to the state-owned MSEB.[9] The renegotiated terms, which probably lower Enron's return from the project, also demonstrate the increased willingness of nation-states to drive hard bargains as more Western suppliers seek to participate in the high-potential Asian energy markets.

Questions

1. What are the opportunities for electricity generation in emerging markets such as Asia?
2. Discuss the terms Enron agreed to initially in starting its Dabhol project in India. Were these terms fair to India? To Enron?
3. Are the criticisms of the Enron Dabhol project in India valid?
4. Do you agree with Enron's decision to renegotiate with the state government? What is your assessment of the renegotiated deal?
5. What lessons can be learned from Enron's experience in India about the advisability of participating in the markets for electricity generation in Asia and elsewhere?

Endnotes

1. Michael T. Burr, "Asia: Institutional Restructuring," *Independent Energy,* July/August 1995.
2. "A Survey of Energy," *The Economist,* June 18, 1994, 7.
3. Donald Marier, "India: Policy Evolution," *Independent Energy,* July/August 1995.
4. See A. K. N. Reddy and A. D'Sa, "Enron and Other Similar Deals vs. the New Energy Paradigm," cited in C. R. Reddy, "Power at What Cost?" *The Hindu (Madras),* July 2, 1995, 12.
5. D. Marier, 34.
6. Maharashtra State's shortfall of electricity supply in relation to peak demand of about 8 percent in April 1995 was the lowest among all of India's industrialized areas; see "Dabhol Debacle Undermines Reform Programme," *Petroleum Economist,* July 1995, 30.
7. "Enron in India: Pioneer Takes the Flak," *Business Asia,* April 11, 1994; and "Clash over Power Plant Reflects Fight in India for Its Economic Soul," *The Wall Street Journal,* April 27, 1995.
8. "Enron Pursues Arbitration in Dispute over Project Canceled by Indian State," *The Wall Street Journal,* August 7, 1995; "Enron Sees Compromise on India Plant," *The Wall Street Journal,* August 23, 1995; and "Enron: Maybe Megadeals Mean Megarisk," *Business Week,* September 4, 1995.
9. "Enron of U.S. Settles India Power Dispute," *The Wall Street Journal,* January 9, 1996; and "More Power to India," *Business Week,* January 22, 1996.

Case prepared by Ravi Sarathy for use in classroom discussion, 1996. All rights reserved.

PART THREE

COORDINATING INTERNATIONAL MARKETING

I n Part 1 we looked at the world environment that shapes international marketing. In Part 2 we looked at how managers perform the functional tasks that constitute international marketing —that is, marketing intelligence, pricing, and so forth. In Part 3 we are concerned with how the separate functional tasks of organization, planning, and control are blended together into an effective international marketing mix. Part 3 also includes a chapter on the future of international marketing.

◆   ◆   ◆

Planning, Organization, and Control of International Marketing

Learning Objectives

In previous chapters, we discussed global strategy and its marketing implications. We dwelt at length on specifics of marketing internationally. However, the proof of the pudding is in the eating; a recipe alone does not yield a feast. The implementation of plans and strategies determines how well the firm functions in the global marketplace. Therefore, this chapter is concerned with implementation, which entails planning, organization, and control.

The main goals of this chapter are to

1. Identify the elements of the planning process.

2. Describe how firms develop and coordinate plans for national markets.

3. Describe the nature and role of long-range planning.

4. Identify the variables that affect organization design.

5. Describe the alternative designs available for international organization.

6. Examine how companies really organize internationally and what roles headquarters can play.

7. Discuss how companies control international marketing.

8. Explain the role of the information system in international control.

PLANNING FOR GLOBAL MARKETING

Planning consists of identifying systematic steps that will help the company formulate detailed actions to implement broad strategies. Thus, the stages of planning should mirror the steps used in formulating strategy as set out in Figure 6–1 in Chapter 6. Planning can be for the short or long term. Typically, firms plan for three to five years, with the long-term plan being revised annually. Then the year immediately ahead becomes the short-term plan, with more detailed strategies.

There is an advantage in having the annual plan be part of a longer planning horizon. It keeps planners from being shortsighted by forcing them to consider the future impact of each year's operating plan. The short-range plan for international marketing can be composed of several elements, including, for example, a marketing plan for each foreign market, plans for individual product lines, and a plan for international product development.

There are several elements of the marketing plan:

1. *Situation analysis: Where are we now?* The company must analyze its current environment in each of its markets: What are the important characteristics of demand, competition, distribution, law, and government? What problems and opportunities are evident in the current situation?

2. *Objectives: Where do we want to be?* Given an understanding of the firm's current situation in markets around the world, management can propose objectives that are appropriate for each country market and region. While these objectives should be challenging, they should also be reachable. And they must be specific if they are to be operational.

3. *Strategy and tactics: How can we best reach our goals?* Once the firm has identified concrete objectives for foreign markets, it must prepare a plan of action to meet them. The approach includes assigning specific responsibilities to marketing personnel and to the marketing functions.

These three basic elements—situation analysis, objectives, and strategy and tactics—provide an adequate framework for discussing the planning problems of the international marketing manager. The short-range planning task of the international marketer has two basic parts: (1) developing the plan for each foreign market and (2) integrating the national plans into a coherent international plan, both regional and global.

Developing Plans for Individual Markets

The mode of entry affects the extent to which the firm takes responsibility for and control of planning. Exporting may rely more heavily on export intermediaries for planning; similarly, licensing cedes principal control and responsibility to the licensee. In a joint venture, the partner may share or take a controlling role in planning, depending on how the joint venture has been structured. It is in wholly owned subsidiaries that the firm's planning role is realized.

Setting Objectives for a Subsidiary

As outlined in Chapter 6, the firm must first evaluate the environment and industry context, which can be unique for each subsidiary. It must also clarify the governmental actions and role that may affect the subsidiary, and what competitors are up to, their strengths and weaknesses, the threats they pose, their strategic actions and tactics. The firm can then set detailed subsidiary objectives, including:

- ◆ Target sales, in units, in local currency and in the parent company's home currency, possibly at a predetermined exchange rate

- Target market share by product and line of business
- Goals for distribution channel penetration, coverage, extension to new distributors and channels
- Goals for brand image creation and awareness
- New-product introduction plans, as appropriate, with detailed marketing plans for launch, covering issues such as pricing, positioning, channels, media plans and spending, target sales, logistics, and marketing service and support
- Export and international marketing plans, including countries and regions to be addressed
- Marketing research goals and specific programs
- Marketing personnel training, hiring, and motivation, including salesforce plans

From Strategy to Tactics and Budgets

Each of the above planning goals can be broken down into more detailed targets, with operational plans spelling out details of implementation, budgets, and managerial responsibilities. At this stage, individuals within the marketing department can receive specific assignments with details worked out for working with third parties such as advertising agencies, market research firms, value-added distributors, product servicing companies, and so forth.

Stages in the Planning Calendar

Thus, a series of typical planning steps can be constructed:

1. *Communication of companywide goals,* subsequently broken down into global, regional, and country-specific goals, and goals for product lines

2. *Detailed country and product-manager plans* showing how goals such as market share, competition containment, and return on investment will be achieved

3. *Aggregation of detailed country and product-line plans* to determine whether the overall result is compatible with corporate headquarters' goals

4. *Translation of plans into budgets,* setting out quantitative and qualitative targets in terms of market share, unit volume growth, prices, target-market segments, distribution channels, advertising budgets, new-product introductions, and personnel and training needs

5. *Actions by product-line and country managers* based on plans and budgets, which also form the criteria used to judge performance

Adapting Plans to Individual Countries

A centralized coordination of programs is necessary so that, for example, global products can be introduced into different markets on a staggered basis. The experience of lead markets may be used to tailor product-introduction programs for other markets. In addition to country and product-manager initiatives, some programs may be initiated at headquarters and communicated to subsidiaries.

Consider the example of Avon's planning process for Latin America.[1] Local executives gather information and develop preliminary country business strategies. Scrutiny of the operating environment is given precedence, focusing on the political, economic, and regulatory environment in each market, as well as making forecasts for the next five years. Next, competitors are identified, their products, market share, strengths, and weaknesses assessed. Avon seeks to learn the sources of its competitors' competitive advantages and compare them with Avon's own competitive advantages. Out of such analysis emerges a plan designed to capitalize on opportunities and competitive weaknesses. Contingency planning is emphasized, the question being, what actions are necessary to achieve planned results in the face of unforeseen events.

The Avon planning process is initiated by its top management, which visits each of the firm's key country subsidiaries over a period of two months. While each country subsidiary's general manager prepares the plan, headquarters planning staff, including the planning director, help key markets with their plans. Once all the plans are completed, they are forwarded to headquarters for review and integration. Country proposals are reviewed and prioritized, and through comparison, headquarters can detect unexploited opportunities and suggest imitation or adaptation of plans currently scheduled for implementation in one country.

Division of Labor in International Planning

Avon's approach highlights the importance of organizational arrangements in international marketing planning. How the company is organized will affect the quality of the plan and whether it can be implemented. *Who* contributes *what* to national operating plans? What are the respective roles of corporate headquarters and the national subsidiaries? Usually corporate headquarters can contribute planning know-how based on its domestic and international experience. This would include planning guidelines, a planning schedule, and training of subsidiary personnel.

The national subsidiary should do most of the actual planning. Whereas the international parent has planning expertise, only the subsidiary has the intimate local knowledge needed. Most of the data for the plan, therefore, must be supplied locally. The resulting plan is more effective because of the complementary contributions of the two parties.

Nestlé provides an example of interactive planning, but with a bias toward decentralization. Some guidance comes from headquarters, but each national company essentially prepares the annual marketing plan and budget. Once a year each affiliate comes to Vevey, Switzerland, to review the plan with headquarters specialists. Compromises and adjustments are made at that time.

International Coordination of National Plans

The final role of the international planner is to coordinate the national plans into an international plan. This coordination is not done after the national plans have been completed; rather, it must start at the beginning of the planning process. Otherwise, national plans will make conflicting claims on company resources and require time-consuming revision. Therefore, coordination begins with guidelines sent to each national operation at the beginning of the planning period. National plans may be modified during the planning process, but good communications will ensure that these changes can be coordinated within the overall international plan.

For example, a company could begin its planning cycle in August. Each country prepares its plan, which would go to its regional headquarters and then to international headquarters in the United States. Between September and November, continuing exchange of information might occur among these three levels. The final coordination would take place at areawide meetings in December, where country managers, regional managers, and headquarters staff would meet for one or two weeks. These meetings could be held in the area—Europe, Latin America, and so forth—and sometimes in the United States.

TABLE 17–1	AM International's Global Markets Analysis			
Market Segment	Market Growth Rate (%)	AM Growth Rate (%)	International Division Presence	
Traditional				
Offset Printing	5%	4%	X	
Engineering/Graphics	0	0	X	
Growth				
Bindery	9	13	X	
Imagesetting	7	13	X	
Forms Press	6	3	X	
Newspaper Inserts	14	19	X	
Computer Graphics	9	18		
Copiers	9	None	X	

Source: AM International Stockholders Meeting Presentation, December 1, 1988.

Comparative Analysis for International Planning

As firms increase their multinational presence and the number of subsidiaries increases, regional and headquarters managers will begin comparing subsidiaries against one another, by region, by product line, and by stage of evolution of their respective markets. Such comparisons can help decide if targets set for individual subsidiaries represent challenging but achievable goals. Comparisons can be helpful if the subsidiaries being compared are similar in their markets and competitive environments and face roughly the same degree of governmental controls. Thus, it may make sense to compare marketing plans for marketing blades in Brazil, Argentina, and Mexico, and perhaps extend this to Turkey and the Philippines. Nevertheless, including significantly poorer countries such as China and India, with their larger populations and lesser degree of infrastructure development, may blur the comparisons. Hence, care is necessary in choosing subsidiaries to be compared.

AM International provides an example of an analytical approach to international markets planning. It is a leader in the world graphics industry, with divisions including offset presses and printing equipment, engineering and architectural market graphics equipment, and duplicating equipment. International sales are about 40 percent of total sales, and AM's strength is its worldwide sales and service infrastructure, with sales branches in countries on six continents, and a worldwide base of installed equipment that is a continuing market for supplies and service. To manage this global business, it operates warehouses, has a worldwide logistics system, and offers worldwide service capabilities, including training. A large portion of the costs of this infrastructure is fixed, and hence its primary goal is to maximize sales from the worldwide infrastructure already in place. In practical terms, this means selling more products through the sales and service organization. To accomplish this, AM analyzes the outlook for international markets for each of its market segments as shown in Table 17–1.

As can be seen in the table, AM has developed a new international presence in copiers, an area in which it had not been active previously. The AM International division agreed to market the entire line of Konica copiers in Europe under the AM label. This was part of the plan to leverage the existing distribution channel by taking on worldwide distribution rights to market "contiguous" products under the AM brand name. Copiers are considered contiguous to duplicators, and AM expected considerable overlap with its current customer base.

Long-Range Scenario Building at Shell and at the Salim Group

Shell Oil has long been renowned for its use of scenarios in its long-range planning. The oil industry requires long-term forecasts when examining investment decisions in new energy and exploration projects. An oil field can yield output for 20 years or more, and long-range scenarios covering that time period are common at Shell. The Middle East is critical to oil; hence, scenarios envisioned by Shell often study the consequences for the oil industry of volatility in the Middle East. When the Gulf War broke out, for example, even though Shell scenarios did not specifically address such a war, they did have unknown events leading to volatility in oil prices and supply uncertainty. As a result, Shell was able to implement contingency plans immediately when war did occur.

Shell typically develops global scenarios every two years, with more detailed regional scenarios developed as needed. The scenarios address issues important to Shell senior management. World experts work with in-house staff to develop "branching points," from which the business environment might be changed significantly. Plans are then developed to cope with such shifts in the environment. The hope is that if the business can be prepared to accept and live with major paradigmatic change, it can more easily accommodate lesser degrees of change. For example, recent scenarios addressed the growth of the environmental movement and the increase in mercantilism and protectionism by the world's leading economies. Other interesting scenarios might be a shift in the center of economic power to the Pacific Rim countries, the emergence of China as the world's largest economy, and another world war brought on by religious intolerance and conflict between the West and Moslem countries.

AM further analyzed markets by geographic area, with a recognition that growth rates of over 30 percent per year registered in the Asia/Pacific region would continue and should be exploited aggressively. At the same time, the above analysis, extended to include current market share and future potential, disclosed areas for further attention. Such comparative information gathering is the cornerstone of successful planning for international markets.

Long-Range Planning

Long-range planning deals with the future of the company over a period of 5 to 10 years. Uncertainty is high, and the level of detail that can be forecast is low. The major concern is with determining the shape of future markets and competition. How will the environment change, how will competition change, how will our customer base change, and what will their needs be in the future? The firm seeks to learn enough about the future to prevent unpleasant surprises that can cut the firm's competitive advantage.

The flavor of long-range planning can be seen in TRW's approach, which extends its planning beyond the year 2000. It addresses questions such as the following: What markets should we be in at that time? What products should we be making then? What business and operations methods will be valid then?

In TRW's Automotive Worldwide Group, the plan is prepared at group headquarters in Cleveland by the Planning and Development Department. It draws on data assembled by the group's product divisions and foreign subsidiaries. The plan covers several variables:

1. Historical trends in the automotive industry

2. Forecasts of demand for cars, trucks, and off-road vehicles

Within scenarios, econometrics and system dynamics models are used to study economic and energy situations in different countries. Users comment on the scenarios as they are developed so that the scenario itself undergoes several iterations. The final result is a 100-page book for top management that summarizes the key scenarios, statistical data, and strategic implications for Shell's lines of businesses.

A different tack to long-range planning is illustrated by Indonesia's Salim Group, which relies on Indonesian government goals and national plans. Once the world's largest rice importer, Indonesia then became self-sufficient in rice before beginning to import again, an amount equal to 8 percent of its needs in 1995. It would like to regain self-sufficiency, but a growing population has led to the loss of arable rice-growing land to urban development, even as rice consumption increases. Indonesia's national plans call for rice to be grown on less suitable swampy land in Borneo, asking Indonesia's conglomerates to help. The Salim Group responded by announcing plans to invest over $500 million in cultivating rice on about 300,000 hectares of land. This decision is of interest because Salim has palm-oil and sugar plantations but no experience with rice.

Salim also plans to diversify into supplying clean water to half of Jakarta. As part of a privatization move, the Salim Group was awarded a water utility franchise in a joint venture with the French water company Lyonnaise des Eaux, and will invest $500 million to supply the western half of the capital city. The Salim Group is a family-controlled company and Mr. Anthony Salim, the founder's eldest son, indicates that he is personally keen on these two projects not because they were particularly profitable but because they tackled essential needs of the country.

Sources: "Shell Pioneers Use of Scenarios to Enhance Its Long-Range Planning," *Business International,* November 12, 1990; and "Indonesia's Salim Group Plans to Invest in Rice, Join Others on Water Project," *The Wall Street Journal,* March 1, 1996.

3. Forecasts of the economics of the countries where the group has operations

4. The competitive situation in those countries

5. Possible future modes of transportation

6. Possible future energy problems

Both short-range and long-range plans reflect the automotive supplier's dependence on the plans of the major auto companies. The planners rely heavily on contacts within these companies for inputs to the plan.

Responding to Competition: Strategic Alliances

A central aspect of planning is responding to competition. In a global context, this may involve actions in more than one market, making integration of activities across markets essential. Response may be defensive or aggressive and may involve waiting for a competitor to act, or it may be preemptive, seeking to ward off or warn competitors against certain actions such as price cuts, competitive product introductions, and expansion of dealer networks.

Being ready to respond to competition is partly a matter of contingency planning. Although a firm does not know what a competitor will do, it can make reasonable guesses as to that competitor's options over the planning horizon. Planning should therefore include appropriate responses to those options. Models such as DEFENDER[2] allow the firm to play out these scenarios.

Strategic response may sometimes entail cooperating with the competition—termed **strategic alliance.** This action is becoming increasingly popular as companies realize the importance of having a global strategy. The problem for many companies is that their global ambitions exceed their resources, and if they move too slowly in developing global markets, they may be swallowed up by stronger and already established global competition. Strategic alliances sometimes solve this problem. We will review a variety of strategic alliances, with examples from the pharmaceutical and tire industries.

Competitive Response in the Pharmaceutical Industry

The pharmaceutical industry presents an interesting arena for competitive response. It is stable, with an aging population in the rich countries, boding well for growing demand. Major markets include the triad economies of Japan, Europe, and the United States. However, developing a new drug is costly, exceeding $350 million, and taking 10 years. Drug companies must be able to sell the drug quickly in all three triad economies and therefore may need partners to help them market a drug or defray the cost of developing a new one. And they may want partners who have something of their own to offer: ideally, a new drug of their own, marketing rights for which can be swapped for the firm's own new drugs.

Pressure also exists on drug companies to reduce costs because governments pay for many health care costs and want to keep drug prices low. Hence, drug companies have to increase sales volume to make up for lower margins. Price pressures are also a threat from generic drug companies, which make drugs no longer protected by patents. Because these generic drug companies do not have to invest in R&D, they can charge lower prices.

The merger of SmithKline Beckman with Beecham PLC of the United Kingdom is an example of partnership cost reduction.[3] The combination created the world's then second largest drug company with sales of $6.7 billion, 6,000 salespeople in the United States, Japan, and Europe, and an R&D budget of over $500 million per year.

Sales of SmithKline's major drug, Tagamet, an antiulcer drug, were falling, and no new drug was ready for introduction; worse, patents on Tagamet were to expire in 1994. Beecham had some promising new drugs, including Eminase, for treating heart attack victims, and Reliflex, an antiarthritis medicine. It needed more marketing power, which SmithKline could provide. Also, Beecham is strong in the over-the-counter drug market (Sucrets and Geritol, for instance), especially in Europe (and its Tums antacid had 27 percent of the U.S. market). It could help sell an over-the-counter version of Tagamet that SmithKline was developing. Thus, each party had something to offer.

Of course, mergers are not necessary to form strategic alliances. Glaxo, another British drug firm, contracted with Hoffman-La Roche, a Swiss pharmaceutical company, to sell Zantac, an antiulcer drug and a competitor for Tagamet, in the United States. Glaxo used La Roche's 800 U.S. salespeople to augment its own salesforce of 400, and within three years it had captured the lead from Tagamet.[4] Glaxo has done much the same in Japan, using a partner to sell in Japan (Glaxo would otherwise need its own sales force of over 1,000 to reach the Japanese medical establishment) while focusing its scarce resources on European marketing. Similarly, DuPont has been the leader in developing new drugs to combat high blood pressure and heart disease. DuPont will use Merck, the world's largest prescription drug company, to market these new drugs; it expected that the alliance would save it about two years in bringing the drugs to market.[5]

The global pharmaceutical industry has seen a changing environment in which customers are gaining power, forcing down prices and profit margins. The growth of large buyers such as health maintenance organizations (HMOs) has increased their power vis-à-vis the pharmaceutical suppliers. Patents on many major drugs are expiring in the industry and the industry is fragmented with the largest company, Novartis, controlling about 6 percent of the global market. The drug companies need to become larger in order to reap scale economies and possibly diversify so that they are not dependent solely on research success within pharmaceuticals.

Glaxo itself became the industry's largest company by acquiring the British competitor Wellcome in a hostile takeover valued at nearly $15 billion. Other pharmaceutical companies have followed similar strategies of acquisition, as shown in Table 17–2.

TABLE 17-2	Pharmaceutical Company Acquisitions

Company	Percent Market Share	Strategic Moves
Glaxo Wellcome	5.8	Acquired Wellcome for $15 billion.
Merck	5.5	Acquired Medco Containment Systems in the United States to control marketing of drugs there and to build a database of drugs prescribed.
Sandoz-Ciba-Geigy	5.5	Merger between Sandoz and Ciba-Geigy, both Swiss firms, with sales totaling $30 billion, of which one-third comes from drugs. Sandoz had earlier acquired Gerber Products, the U.S. baby-food company.
Hoechst	4.7	Became a major drug company with acquisition of U.S.–based Marion Merrell Dow.
Roche Holding	3.9	Acquired U.S.–based Syntex for $5.3 billion.
Bristol-Myers Squibb	3.9	Formed by merger between Bristol-Myers and Squibb.
SmithKline Beecham	3.3	Merger between the United States' SmithKline and U.K.'s Beecham.
Pharmacia & Upjohn	3.1	Merger between Swedish and U.S. firms to gain size and ward off hostile takeovers.
American Home Products	3.1	Acquired American Cyanamid, including its Lederle drug division.

The 1996 merger between Ciba-Geigy and Sandoz illustrates why mergers have become the central strategic response to pharmaceutical industry change and globalization. It is instructive to consider the strengths and motivations that each company brings to the merger. Both companies faced threats from generic drugs to their own lines whose patents were expiring. They did not have blockbuster drugs in their research pipeline, and Ciba had experienced negative clinical results in two major research efforts on acute heart disease and therapies to limit damage from head injuries and strokes. A merger would allow for elimination of redundancies and lead to cost reduction. Moreover, neither company would have to take on debt or spend large sums of money, as the merger was a friendly one.

Ciba-Geigy	Sandoz
Two strong divisions: over-the-counter medication and eye care	Strong gene therapy research
	80% global market share in drugs to prevent rejection in organ transplants
49% ownership of U.S. biotech leader, Chiron	$1 billion research on animal organ transplants in humans
Respected worldwide marketing capability	Owns Gerber Products (acquired in 1994 for $3.7 billion); strength in nutrition products for babies and aging population

Corporate culture clashes, while inevitable, might be reduced because of a shared Swiss culture, with companies headquartered in Basel, Switzerland. The merged company would be diversified with 40 percent of total revenues coming from agricultural chemicals and human nutrition. Lastly, power would be shared, with each company contributing eight members to a joint executive board. Aside from these merger synergies, each company had certain strengths:

The Sandoz-Ciba-Geigy merger illustrates one effect of globalization on strategy: Fragmented industries begin to consolidate in order to approach the requisite size and to obtain scale economies necessary to be competitive in the global arena.[6]

Why Form Strategic Alliances?

In a strategic alliance, firms join together in some area of their business to reduce risk, obtain economies of scale, and obtain complementary assets, often intangible ones such as market access, brand names, and access to government procurement. The allure of acquiring technology and the pressures of government are also reasons for such alliances. They are typically formed in one of three broad areas: technology, manufacturing, and marketing.

Another reason for alliances is that consumers are becoming alike in the developed nations. They tend to receive the same information, and their discretionary incomes are roughly equal. As a result, tastes are becoming homogenized. As Kenichi Ohmae puts it, "Everyone in a sense wants to live and shop in California."[7] But no one company can expect to dominate all technologies and create entire product lines for the developing global market. A likely solution, therefore, is to swap products.

Another factor concerning alliances is that fixed costs account for a larger proportion of total costs. Global sales help recover these higher fixed costs even when lower prices are charged. (Volume compensates for a smaller contribution per unit.) The reason to lower prices and sell globally is that product life cycles are becoming short, and fixed costs are more likely to be covered by resorting to global markets. It is difficult to exploit worldwide markets without global alliances, however. Short product life cycles mean that firms must move quickly to exploit their technological lead, which is actually a disappearing asset, diminishing in value with the passage of time. Strategic alliances allow a firm to simultaneously penetrate several key markets. Table 17–3 summarizes these motivations.

Alliances, however, require that each party has something to swap. In the tire industry, General Tire supplies Japanese auto companies in the United States on behalf of Japanese companies, which in turn supply companies in Japan on behalf of General Tire and Continental. Several alliances can be formed within the same country. IBM, for example, works in Japan with Ricoh to distribute its low-end copiers, with Nippon Steel to sell systems integration services, with Fuji Bank to sell financial systems, with OMRON to penetrate the computer-integrated manufacturing market, and with NTT (Nippon Telephone) to sell value-added networks.

Technology sharing, joint marketing, and supply arrangements are the main foci of such alliances. What is interesting is that such alliances often occur between companies that also compete with each other in other markets. In choosing such partners, several criteria are useful:[8]

- The competitor should have a competitive advantage—economies of scale, technology, or market access—and these areas should be critical in the value-added chain.

- The contributions of each partner should be complementary or balanced.

- The two partners should agree on the global strategy to be followed.

- The risk that the partner will become a future competitor should be low.

- There should be a pre-emptive value in having the firm as a partner rather than as a rival.

- There should be compatibility of organizations, as well as of top management of the two firms.

ORGANIZING FOR GLOBAL MARKETING

All the planning in the world will be in vain unless the company is organized to implement these plans. Organization structure determines who does what, including which employees exercise gatekeeping power in supporting or undermining

TABLE 17-3	Motivations to Form Joint Ventures and Strategic Alliances

Motivations	*Results*
Complement weaknesses in the value chain	Obtain complementary competences in R&D (basic research and/or applications development) and manufacturing (scale/scope economies, new processes, cost reduction).
Take defensive position to protect market	See examples from the pharmaceutical industry, such as the Sandoz-Ciba-Geigy merger.
Be proactive by developing new businesses	Keep pace with new technologies and new customer segments.
Take a product line or geographic focus	Enhance market access to specific countries, brands, distribution channels, service capabilities. Enhance product line with partners possessing complementary products and services.
Think strategically of core and peripheral operations	Decision will have implications for growing dependency on alliance partner and possible hollowing out of the corporation.
React to government-imposed regulations	Offer legally necessary ownership stakes in return for political ties and local influence, as in several Asian private energy infrastructure projects.
Reduce/share risk	Reduce ownership with attendant reduction in share of profits and losses.
Overcome resource scarcity with partner contributions	Obtain resources (materials, components, capital, management, and information technology, such as Computer Reservation Systems in airline and hotel businesses).
Learn from partner	Seek partners from related or unrelated industries, from supplier and customer segments, or possible multiple partners and coalitions (e.g., telecommunications firms bidding for licenses in the nascent U.S. wireless industry).
Obtain fit with global strategy alternatives through licensing, foreign direct investment, and acquisitions	Act cautiously, for alliances are not the universal panacea (over half of all joint ventures and alliances are dissolved within a few years).

decisions made by others. Organization structure also sets up the rewards that motivate performance and determines the degree to which activities can be integrated, which is particularly important in global strategy, since implementation must be carried out by subsidiaries in different countries, without many opportunities for face-to-face communication. Indeed, some of the worst problems facing international marketers result from the friction between headquarters and foreign subsidiaries.

The basic issue for all organization structure in global corporations revolves around centralization versus decentralization. Global corporations need strong coordination at headquarters to provide and supervise implementation of global strategy. Local subsidiary managers may have different opinions, however, and pull away from that strategy. Or, local government pressures may require greater local responsiveness, even if it means diverging from global strategy. Thus, the major task for organization structure is to mediate between the opposing needs for centralization and local responsiveness.[9]

Research has suggested that in some industries where consumers around the world buy essentially the same product, as in consumer electronics, centralization and large-scale manufacturing are the key to success. In industries in which national consumers have distinct product preferences and much product adaptation is necessary, as in branded packaged goods such as detergents, a large degree of national subsidiary autonomy is needed. Then there are industries in which scale economies demand centralized large-scale manufacturing, yet monopolistic consumers have distinct product preferences, as in the telecommunications industry. Here, both centralization and local responsiveness are needed.[10]

GLOBAL MARKETING

Internationalizing the Company: Staffing Issues

Organizing the international marketing function is partly a matter of hierarchies and power and control. But it is also about finding and putting the best people in key positions. Staffing international positions raises tricky issues not found in the domestic arena. Foremost is the danger that the executive assigned overseas will get "lost," forgotten by colleagues and bosses. In turn, this makes re-entry into domestic operations difficult. Very often, the returning expatriate may find no job available that makes use of the incremental international business skills gained during the overseas as-signment. Overseas executives also supervise large staffs, enjoy high pay and fringe benefits, and have considerable autonomy; returning to headquarters may mean lower pay and less prestige. Unless they have a mentor or champion at home who smooths re-entry and finds them a position commensurate with their new skills, returning managers often believe that their careers are at a dead end and that the firm does not appreciate them, or want them. They often resign, which is a waste because the international skills are hard earned and necessary to the corporation competing in the global arena. Hence, firms need to set up programs that consciously choose the best younger managers for overseas assignments and establish a clear career path including identifying jobs that will be open and available for the re-turning managers.

Approaches to Organizing International Operations

A company can organize its international operations as a separate international division, with further subunits within the international division consisting of re-gional and subunits. Alternatively, it may prefer to create organizational units structured along products and lines of business. A third approach is to create functional units, with distinct *global* responsibilities for research, marketing, manufacturing, logistics, and other functions. Finally, a company may decide that proper planning and execution of tasks require cooperation between man-agers and foster such cooperation by resorting to a matrix organization, where responsibilities for achieving goals is jointly allocated to managers with country, functional, and product-line responsibilities.

The International Division

Creating a separate organizational unit to focus on international business and op-erations allows international expertise, personnel, and vision to be concentrated in one part of the company. It creates a unit with a sole focus on international busi-ness, one that would stand up for international operations and seek human and capital resources for this activity. Such an approach is more likely in companies with relatively limited international operations, where domestic concerns predomi-nate, and where product-line complexity is limited. Figure 17–1 illustrates the in-ternational division structure.

However, a separate international division faces several problems: It may receive a lesser share of resources than its markets warrant, may be perceived as a backwater that is less relevant to the future of the company, and may have less political clout in the fight for top management attention and budget allocations. Resolving interna-tional business issues without regard to their integration into the overall company's strategy may result in suboptimization.

As the global economy continues to become more important, one condition to attain top management positions at large U.S. multinationals is substantial international experience. For example, all eight members of Tupperware's executive committee speak two to four languages and have worked overseas. Samir Gibara, CEO of Goodyear Tire, spent 27 years in management positions outside the United States. The COO at Gillette, and the CEOs at Outboard Marine, Case Corporation, and Mobil have all spent over half their management careers outside the United States. Twenty-eight percent of all senior management searches now require international experience. Companies seem to be looking for substantial international experience in which the executives have spent several years overseas immersing themselves in the culture while running operations. U.S. companies seem to particularly value experience in emerging markets such as China, India, and Brazil. The difficulty, of course, is how does an executive who spends all his time overseas become visible to the top management at headquarters in the United States. The answer, presumably, is to also spend some time at home in a job with significant managerial responsibilities.

Sources: "Grappling with the Expatriate Issue: Little Benefit to Careers Seen in Foreign Stints," *The Wall Street Journal,* December 11, 1989; and "An Overseas Stint Can Be a Ticket to the Top," *The Wall Street Journal,* January 29, 1996.

Structuring by Area

Rather than have a separate international division, a company may develop an organizational structure with distinct responsibilites for each major geographical area. What is international is not relegated to second division status, and instead, world markets are broken up into a series of geographical divisions, one of which happens to include the company's home or domestic market.

When the company is structured by area, the primary basis for organization is by divisions for major regions of the world. For example, when CPC International reorganized from an international division to a world company approach, it set up five operating companies—one for Europe, one for Latin America, one for the Far East, and two for North America (consumer products and industrial products). Although this is primarily a regional form of organization, the North American area is divided on the basis of product. The regional organization form is used primarily by companies that are highly oriented to marketing with relatively stable technology, such as those in consumer nondurables, pharmaceuticals, and automotive and farm equipment.

Several factors favor a regional approach to organization. The growth of regional groupings is one. As nations within a region integrate economically, it makes more sense to treat them as a unit. The proximity of countries provides one logical basis for organization. Certain kinds of expertise can be grouped within the region for the benefit of individual country operations. Communications are easy, and there can be coordination of product and functional know-how in the region. A narrow product line and similarity in technology and methods of operation also favor regional organization. The greater the international similarity of the firm's products, the greater the importance of area knowledge.

In spite of its popularity, the regional organization has drawbacks. It ensures the best use of the firm's regional expertise, but it means less than optimal allocation of product and functional expertise. If each region needs its own staff of product and functional specialists, duplication—and also inefficiency—may result if less than the best staff is available for each region. This inefficiency is most likely if the

FIGURE 17–1   **International Division Approach**

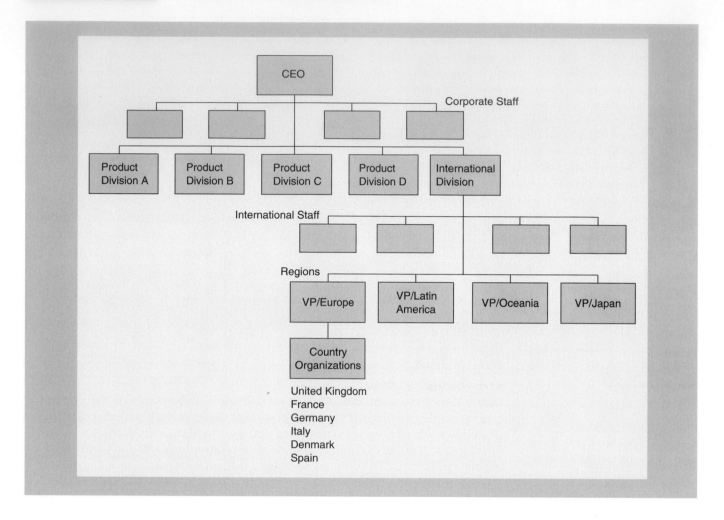

regional management is located away from corporate headquarters. If regional management is at corporate headquarters, centralized staff can serve all regional units, providing some economies of scale. A regional organization may optimize performance within the region, but there is danger of global suboptimization if there is no coordination among the regions. Each region must blend into a global operation. Figure 17–2 illustrates a regional organization structure.

Structuring by Product

Organizing by product line means that product groups have global responsibilities for marketing; thus, it is a global company approach by product division. An international division can be organized along product lines too, but by its very nature it also includes area expertise. Structuring by product line is most common for companies with several unrelated product lines because their marketing task varies more by product line than by region. As Figure 17–3 shows, the global product structure gives each product group what amounts to its own international division.

Structuring an organization along product lines has the merit of flexibility, in that the firm can add a new product division if it enters another business unrelated to its current lines. However, the product division approach has several potential limitations. When the domestic market is more important to a product division, international opportunities are likely to be missed. Shortage of area knowledge is a

FIGURE 17-2 **Worldwide Regional Organization Structure**

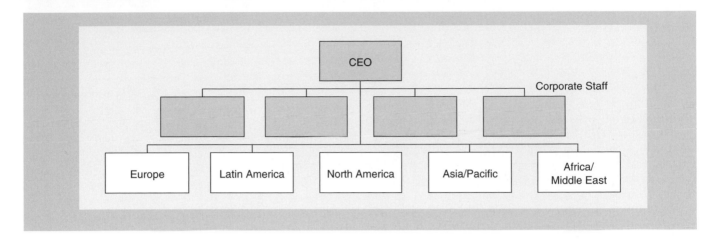

common weakness of product-structured organizations. Each product division cannot afford to maintain its own complete international staff.

Another problem in a product-structured approach is the difficulty of achieving companywide coordination in international markets. If each product division goes its own way, the firm's international development will encounter conflicts and inefficiencies. The organization must provide for global coordination to offset the sometimes contradictory international plans of individual product divisions. For example, it is probably unnecessary for each producing division to have its own advertising agency, service organization, and government relations staff in every market. When foreign plants manufacture products of different divisions, coordination among these divisions also is usually a problem for a product organization.

Eaton provides an illustration of how companies with global product organization try to overcome some of its weaknesses: It is highly diversified in the capital goods and automotive industries. It has five worldwide product groups and each has a managing director for European operations. To get a better overall corporate understanding and response to European problems in such areas as legislation, labor, and taxes, Eaton formed a European Coordinating Committee (ECC), composed of the five product division managing directors, several European staff, and one executive from world headquarters.

The chair responsibilities of the ECC rotate among the managing directors, and meetings are at different European facilities. Eaton was satisfied enough with this arrangement to set up Country Coordinating Committees to coordinate the product groups within each European country. It also formed a Latin American Coordinating Committee to achieve the same integration in Latin America.

Structuring by Function

A functional structure, whereby top executives in marketing, finance, production, and so on, all have global responsibilities, is most suitable for firms with narrow, homogeneous product lines, when product expertise is not a variable. It is also helpful if regional variations in operations are not great, thus lessening the need for regional expertise. Because these conditions are not usually met, the functional form of organization for international operations is not common among U.S. firms except in extractive industries. It is more common for European companies. Although functional executives in U.S. firms do have international responsibilities, these are usually in conjunction with a product or regional form of organization.

FIGURE 17-3   **Worldwide Product Organization Structure**

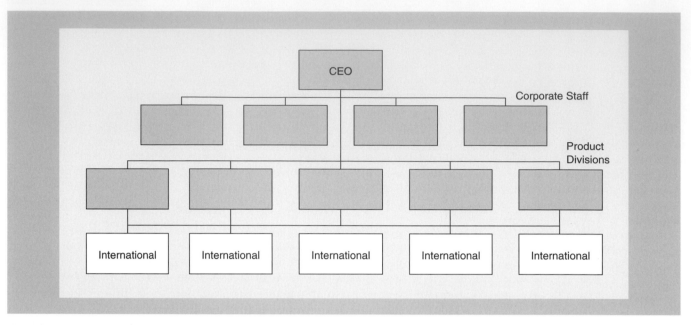

Note: Each product division will have similar parallel international divisions.

The Matrix Organization

One of the more interesting organizational developments in recent decades is the **matrix** form of organization. Companies became frustrated with the shortcomings of unidimensional organizational structures (product, area, function) that we noted above. They, therefore, moved to a more complex organizational form that allowed two dimensions to have more or less equal weight in their organizational structure and decision making. A matrix organization has a dual rather than a single chain of command. That means that many managers have two bosses. Matrix also involves lateral (dual) decision making and a chain of command that fosters conflict management and a balance of power. Product and market (geography) are the two dimensions receiving equal emphasis in matrix organizations in international business.

Matrix can help answer some problems of the simple product or area structure, but matrix organizations had many problems of their own arising from inherent conflicts and complexity. One study of 93 multinationals found that unitary reporting structures still prevailed because dual reporting was perceived as too problematic. Also, unitary structures could be altered to obtain the benefits espoused for matrix organizations.[11]

Evolving to a Transnational Organization

To summarize, multinationals evolve from a structure consisting mainly of domestic operations with some overseas business, to the multinational stage in which international business becomes more important. This typically results in independent, locally responsive subsidiaries, which display greater sensitivity to local customers, governments, and culture, and which are headed by local country managers with an entrepreneurial bent. At some point, competitive forces and environmental pressures from globalization of the industry lead headquarters to desire greater global integration of relatively autonomous local subsidiaries. One solution is to implement a matrix approach. The problem, however, is that a global matrix organization is both complex and bureaucratic, with its two-boss structure. The possible consequence is conflict and confusion, with overlapping responsibilities. Negotiation is necessary, and the organization may become bogged down in information, while multiple time zones and distances render face-to-face conflict resolution difficult. Hence, top management attempts to rein in national subsidiaries and begins to eliminate redundancies that may have developed in products, manufacturing sites, and staff functions. Greater centralization focuses on developing global products and rationalized global manufacturing. Such steps require more central coordination and control. At this point, local managers begin to chafe against central headquarters dictates, and market forces lead top management to realize that some local responsiveness and autonomy are necessary. *This is the emergence of the transnational form of organization,* with the goal of mediating between the conflicting drives of global integration and local responsiveness.

Why become transnational? The multinational can achieve scale and scope economies, and obtain lower factor costs for factors such as raw materials, labor, and capital. At the same time, growing convergence of tastes allows the multinational to concentrate on developing global products and standards, with some local variation. The multinational is better able to confront global competitors with cross-subsidization of weaker or embattled subsidiaries with cash flow from stronger subsidiaries in healthy markets. Such a structure also allows the multinational to respond to environmental volatility, including local government discriminatory industrial policies, currency volatility, short product life cycles, economic cyclicality, and cultural differences. The challenge facing the transnational organization is to continue to stimulate worldwide innovation and organizational learning, while maintaining organizational flexibility, because the environment is constantly changing.[12]

Transnational corporations are the conceptual translation of the rule to think local, act global. Transnationals often have products that require adaptation to the needs of local markets. At the same time, their size leads to benefits from the centralization or regionalization of certain functions such as finance or product development. And, as ideas can develop anywhere in the world in a large, far-flung corporation, the transnational form of organization creates communication links that encourage the sharing of information and ideas across entities, whether demarcated by function or geography or product line. Transnational organization is an evolution of the matrix form of organization with responsibility and authority clarified.

Examples of Global Organization

It is difficult to appreciate arguments about organization structure in the abstract. The subtleties of structure are more easily grasped in the context of a product and a market. Hence, in this section, we discuss specific examples of organization structure evolution to show how market realities are incorporated in the process of organizational change.

Reynolds: European Regional Autonomy
The Single Market in Europe has led many global corporations to re-examine how they structure their European operations. Reynolds Metals used to have 25 European subsidiaries report to the International Division located at headquarters in Richmond, Virginia. This meant that each European country manager dealt directly with the United States and rarely attempted to coordinate operations with the other European countries. Thus, salespeople from different national units would compete against one another for the same multinational client. There was duplication of manufacturing operations and differences in cost and quality. The pending changes in Europe meant that Reynolds had to integrate European operations because it would be facing intense competition from pan-European companies such as Pechiney and Alusuisse.

Consequently, Reynolds created a European headquarters in Lausanne, Switzerland, to oversee all European operations, so that they would have a "single voice."[13] Lausanne was headed by a top management team consisting of a president, a chief financial officer, an executive vice-president in charge of manufacturing, and several vice-presidents with responsibilities in areas such as marketing. Lausanne was chosen as a neutral site, unlikely to create regional tensions that a country with a strong national unit, such as France or Germany, might. Reynolds (Europe) Ltd. had direct responsibility for manufacturing facilities.

Reynolds plans to focus on downstream, household-oriented products, as well as the aluminum can market: Europe consumes only 6 billion cans, compared to about 74 billion sold in the United States. Reynolds expects several benefits to flow from the organization change:

◆ Rationalized manufacturing, lowering costs

◆ Faster decision making

◆ A pan-European thrust in production, marketing, and advertising

◆ Greater influence in Brussels, which is fast becoming the seat of European government

Unilever: Transnational Organization

In Unilever's transnational organization, product groups are responsible for profits in Europe and North America while geographically based regional organizations have profit responsibility elsewhere in the world. Unilever's transnational organization is the result of a long evolution lasting several decades. Initially, Unilever was organized as a series of relatively independent country subsidiaries with strong local management. Later, product groups took over worldwide profit responsibility, divided into three major groups: edible fats, frozen food and ice cream, and food and drinks, such as tea and soup. Raw materials and distribution systems determined the makeup of these three groups. This change took many years of "patience, persuasion and even some early retirements."[14]

As markets changed, consumer-driven products such as low-calorie, health, and convenience foods, and the use of natural ingredients became important. Unilever's response was to form an executive triad of three board directors responsible for all of Unilever's food businesses. Each director received profit responsibility for a group of countries in a region. Five strategic groups centered around edible fats, ice cream, beverages, meals, and professional markets. These groups advise the "Food Executive," providing product expertise, but without having profit-center responsibilities. Unilever's newest transnational organization structure seeks to preserve unity within diversity. It well understands that major, current, food market trends such as global fast food, national foods that cross country boundaries (such as Chinese or Mexican food), and purely national foods might require continued organizational evolution, which, in turn, means maintaining a work force that can be flexible.

Such flexibility is achieved by careful recruitment and training of managers. Unilever managers constantly watch for bright young local university graduates and scientists. Recruits go through in-house training programs on a continuing basis, maintaining contact with their peer cohorts across countries. Job rotation across product groups and countries, and use of third-country nationals in high-level executive positions in country subsidiaries, further cement informal transnational network ties across various country units. Unilever also uses international working groups to work on specific tasks and issues, and international conferences that bring together managers from all over the world on a twice yearly basis to listen to top management plans and to meet and renew old friendships.

General Motors: Reducing U.S. Control

General Motors is another company that for the first time in its history is decentralizing authority from Detroit. It is setting up European headquarters in Zurich (to

Bringing Global Vision into the Company

Global companies face a problem in that their top management is predominantly a national one; that is, most top managers at U.S. companies are Americans; in Japanese companies, they are predominantly Japanese. How can such companies not allow a purely nationalistic perspective to bias their attempts to develop a global vision in their planning? The answer may lie partly in adding nondomestic members to the firm's board of directors. In 1989, only one-sixth of about 600 firms surveyed had one or more non–U.S. citizen directors. Because they have operated in international markets a longer time, European companies have a larger proportion of foreign directors. The difficulty lies in getting the closed-club world of top executives in one country to accept outsiders from another country. Then there is the matter of finding the appropriate people who are willing to serve. Firms need to establish criteria that are especially relevant for choosing a foreign director, such as close ties to local government, considerable experience in economic planning, or years of top management experience running a global company in a related industry. U.S. directors' liability laws can lead non–U.S. citizens to be reluctant to serve. Scheduling meetings is another difficulty: A foreign director must fly to the United States for one- or two-day meetings several times a year.

Just as U.S. companies need Europeans and Asians to bring in a fresh perspective, Asian family-owned firms similarly need Western multinationals and their managers to bring in professional management techniques, and a taste for open communication and meritocracy. Of course, as Asian firms begin to launch factories and sales offices across Europe and the Americas, such Western contacts help them find their way. Cultural clashes abound, however, particularly in the contrast between the stress on personal relationships in Asian family businesses and the Western preference for legal contracts and agreements.

Sources: "Globalizing the Company with Foreign Board Members," *Business International*, March 4, 1991; and "Asia's Family Empires Change Their Tactics for a Shrinking World," *The Wall Street Journal*, April 19, 1995.

---

be known as GM European Passenger Cars: GMEPC).[15] The head of GMEPC is from Opel (West Germany), GM's largest subsidiary, with other top management coming from Vauxhall (the British sub), GM-Canada, and the Saginaw, Michigan, plant. GMEPC will coordinate European planning and operations, with a strict division between national and European HQ tasks. Thus, Zurich will focus on Europewide planning and strategy, environmental matters, personnel, and relations with the EEC in Brussels and other European capitals.

Shell: Relying on Matrix Organization

The Royal Dutch/Shell Group of companies has also adopted a matrix structure, with the additional innovation that the matrix involves three dimensions:[16] regions, industry sectors, and functions. Shell's several hundred operating companies, which are autonomous, can then draw on global resources of the "service" companies, including regional, sectoral, and functional management.

Shell has nine service companies providing specialized advice and services and consisting of executives that have considerable operating experience in the field. Thus, an operating company could call on experts in petroleum-exploration techniques, in financial management, or in managing a chemical plant. The service companies include trading companies dealing in oil, chemicals, and coal.

The three dimensions of the service companies include five regional coordinators who monitor the profits of the operating companies and approve investments, and six business sectors, consisting of upstream oil and gas and downstream oil, including marketing, natural gas, chemicals, coal, and metals. Sectoral panels supervise strategy for national, regional, and worldwide lines of business. Further, nine specialized functional departments exist: finance, legal affairs, materials, planning, public affairs, research, safety and environment, information systems, and human resources and organization. The CEO of each operating company must draw up

Reorganization at Square D Company and Ciba-Geigy

Square D Company is another example of the role of organization structure in mediating headquarters and regional interests. Square D manufactures electrical products in over 100 factories, including 31 outside the United States. Until recently, international responsibility had been based at U.S. headquarters. The work was divided between vice-presidents for international marketing and international manufacturing. U.S. products were sold overseas, foreign subsidiaries had little authority, and communication with the United States was infrequent.

To implement a global strategy, the electrical group was divided into three business units: distribution equipment, power equipment, and controls. At the same time, five regional divisions were created: U.S., Asia/Pacific, Canada, Europe, and Latin America. The result was a product/region matrix with the following structure:

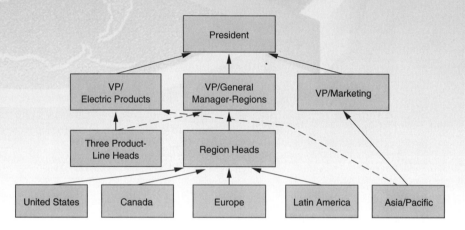

the annual plan, however, calling on any of the service companies for assistance if desired. The quality and experience of the service companies are what make the system work; a drawback, however, is the vast quantity of information that flows to headquarters. All in all, Shell believes that the gains from giving autonomy to operating companies provide a compensatory quick-response capability.

Philips: Global Product Divisions

Philips, the Dutch electronics multinational, also stresses quick local responses and a marketing orientation as it reorganizes for global operations.[17] Philips has been reducing local subsidiary autonomy to focus on three core global-product divisions: consumer electronics, electronic components, and information technology/communications. National subsidiary autonomy was reduced to allow a global manufacturing and marketing strategy to be formulated for each product division. The importance of the product line is stressed by bringing product division directors on board. At the same time, central control allows for rationalized manufacturing on a global scale for each product line to gain economies of scale.

How can such a system not stifle local subsidiaries? Philips wants to be creative in creating new products and wants input from key markets for this decision. At the same time, central control is needed to prevent inventing different national products for each market. Philips has located "competence centers" in crucial markets—car electronics in Germany and domestic appliances in Italy, for example. Also, it

The matrix consists of product-line heads and regional managers, except for Asia/Pacific, which reports directly to a vice-president of marketing because Square D's manufacturing presence in Asia is limited. Quarterly meetings are held in the United States with the product-line and regional heads as well as domestic marketing managers. Communications are emphasized through a quarterly videotape and an in-house magazine distributed worldwide.

The benefits from this reorganization include

- Greater regional autonomy with profit and loss responsibility

- Timely relay of market information about electrical standards, priorities for each market, and feedback on demand trends and competition, to benefit manufacturing worldwide

- Ability to design a global product effectively and at low cost; the smooth flow of information from around the world helps determine global product requirements and allows pooling of manufacturing and engineering capabilities

- An emphasis on cooperation and global line responsibilities, fostering a global corporate culture

Ciba-Geigy (C-G) presents an alternative approach to using regional managers. C-G is divided into 14 major worldwide product lines and 34 profit centers. If a country has only one product subsidiary, that division reports directly to the worldwide product division manager, who in turn reports to an executive committee member responsible for that product line. When countries have multiple product divisions, however, they are supervised by a regional manager who in turn reports to an executive committee member who has responsibility for a geographical area. C-G has three broad geographic areas: Europe, the Americas, and Asia/Australia. Thus, executive committee members have both product and geographic responsibilities. C-G's regional managers are responsible for local management of areas such as legal, personnel, quality and security, management development, and performance measurement. They also represent C-G in interaction with local governments, unions, and the media. Both the regional manager and the local product division manager are *jointly responsible* for profits. Bonuses for regional managers are based on a combination of local country profits and worldwide profits, and also division profits (in cases where the regional manager has local product division responsibility).

Sources: "Square D Unites Managers to Compete Globally," *Business International*, September 21, 1987; and "The Role of the Country Manager," *Business Europe*, March 27, 1995.

uses multidisciplinary teams with expertise in development, design, manufacturing, and marketing, thus keeping in mind technical and manufacturing as well as marketing considerations. As Dr. van Hamersveld, marketing manager at Philips, puts it, "The international product axis underlies corporate policy, but the contribution of national organizations is vital for local marketing and distribution and in dealing with national regulations and handling relationships with governments."

Philips takes care to balance the opposing demands of centralization and local responsiveness over the stages of the product life cycle. In the early stage, product launch is centrally coordinated in Europe, the United States, and Japan, while centralized manufacturing and standardization reduce costs. In the maturity phase, local subs play a larger role, tailoring local marketing, possibly including some product modifications. In the decline phase, emphasis shifts to centralized manufacturing and cost saving. Local subsidiaries make the greatest contribution and have the greatest autonomy in choosing distribution channels, which Philips believes must be adapted most to local conditions. The powerful distribution and dealer networks built up by local subs become a key competitive advantage in Philips' global strategy.

An important element in developing new products is the R&D lab. As firms try to decide whether to customize products for individual products, they also must decide how to organize the R&D function. If it is centralized, there needs to be organizational procedures to allow product customization requests to come in from the various subsidiaries and a way to prioritize such requests and respond in a timely manner. One approach is to appoint a marketing executive to serve as liaison between marketing subsidiaries and the central R&D lab, channeling and prioritizing customization requests. Then, the actual development can be carried out at the central lab or at regional sites, serving specific clusters of markets. Such ventures also require the fomation of virtual teams, established on a project basis, using communication networks, E-mail, and videoconferencing to allow exchange of information and debate on major issues.[18]

Organizational flexibility will be the necessary ingredient as organizations change to meet the challenges of a global economy and new forms of competition from knowledge-rich and Internet-based companies. Organizing to harness knowledge from around the challenge is the critical dimension; building and using knowledge bases, motivating people to contribute to and use shared knowledge, and fostering interaction among virtual organizational units and teams that dominate specific forms of knowledge such as customer knowledge, business processes, and product-based knowledge are all part of these new organization structures.[19]

Organizational Responses to Asian and Latin American Markets

GE has 12 major lines of business in Asia, but unlike many Asian conglomerates that cross-subsidize their disparate lines of business, GE insists that each line of business be independent. In practice, this means that GE has a country manager for each country, who can give a common face to all of GE's businesses in that country. However, the country manager at GE works in a matrix context, with each line of business evaluated on how it contributes to global profits of that line of business and to the country unit's profits. Another critical element of GE's Asian focus is the rotation of managers across GE's various Asian country units, because human resources is a scarce and limiting factor and the executives bring varied experience but a common GE perspective to each business they are assigned to.[20]

Sometimes a company's situation and strategic need may dictate that it stop the process of using mostly local managers and bring in more expatriates. For example, as China began to move to GSM-based cellular phones, Motorola saw its phone division sales drop precipitously, because it did not have a GSM switch to sell with its phones, thus losing out to competitors who could offer a complete turnkey system. To turn around its business, it brought back senior-level expatriates, replacing some high-level local managers, as well as selling older models at steep discounts so that they were able to compete with traditional land-line phones, increase market share, and hold off competitors while Motorola brought in newer technologies. This involved licensing a local Chinese company, Da Tang, to produce CDMA switches, a new U.S. technology intended to replace the GSM standard that was becoming widespread in China.[21]

A similar matrix structure is used by DuPont in South America. Responding to the formation of Mercosur, DuPont integrated its South American operations, with headquarters outside of Sao Paulo, where all product-line managers are typically based, each also having responsibility for a country in Mercosur and in the smaller markets of Venezuela, Colombia. Such regional integration allows products to be specialized by plants located in different countries with between plant transfers of goods to meet various market needs. An interesting issue in organizations where matrix structures exist and where country managers work closely with several product-line managers is how to measure performance. Budgets can be set and performance against budget used to evaluate performance. Beyond financial targets, country managers are responsible for soft variables such as government relations and maintaining corporate culture, nurturing managers, and so forth, in such areas; each region and country may have to develop specific measures adapted to that country's needs and to that country's cultures.[22]

What Role Should Headquarters Play?

A constant theme running through the various attempts at creating an organizational structure appropriate for global strategy and marketing is the role that the parent company headquarters should take. Corporate headquarters can play three roles in its dealings with subsidiaries around the world: controller, coach, or orchestrator.[23]

A **controller** gives considerable autonomy to subsidiaries and uses measurements such as profits by a small business unit to determine when to intervene. This is classic management by exception.

The **coach** also decentralizes authority to subsidiaries but is available to provide support and advice, somewhat along the lines of the Shell example described above. This means that the coach will intervene when it appears necessary, attempting to strike the right balance between decentralization and central control.

The **orchestrator** is an interventionist with central control and responsibility for activities such as manufacturing, R&D, and finance. Subsidiary managers, therefore, have less autonomy. Such a style may be appropriate for industries for which global integration is important and investment needs are large, as in oil, steel, mining, and financial services.

In addition, headquarters can play two other temporary roles: surgeon and architect. When major upheavals threaten the firm and its industry, the company may have to be restructured with many units divested, product lines dropped, and workers laid off. Responses to corporate raiders at companies such as Gillette are typical of such a stance. The other extreme is restructuring through acquisitions, as in the case of Sony, which reacted to the failure of the Betamax video format by deciding to emphasize "software," that is, music and film production. This has led it to acquire United States record companies and film studios. This phase also requires strong central direction from the **architect,** who reshapes the company according to a global vision before returning to the mode of coach or orchestrator.

Company roles should be consistent with the nature of businesses within the global firm. The degree of synergy between the various lines of business in a firm, the level of risk facing it, and the intensity of competition determine which headquarters style is appropriate for a specific firm (see Table 17–4).

If a company's lines of business are such that both high and low risk are present, headquarters' task becomes blurred for the high-risk business because it may have to play the role of orchestrator, while for a low-risk business, a controller role is more appropriate. Unless the company then restructures so that only one kind of business-line profile prevails across the firm, it must live with multiple roles. This implies that no one organization structure is appropriate for a global firm with many lines of business. This is the reason that large global firms seem to be constantly changing their organization structure. As the profiles of the various lines of business change, new organization structures are necessary.

The Country Manager

A key element in the growing multinational company is the Country Manager (CM).[24] What does the CM do? The CM will often be given local profit center responsibility, be responsible for multiple functional areas, and be the liaison with regional and HQ management. Expected to be as much an entrepreneur as a manager, the CM seeks to increase local autonomy.

Factors changing the role of a CM include demands for greater global integration, for example, of R&D and manufacturing; the subordination of national interests; the rise of product-based global organizations and global customers; and regional integration policies such as the European Union and NAFTA. How do these forces impact on the CM? They tend to reduce the CM's local authority to implement global and regional policies in the national sphere. The CM's main focus becomes local sales

TABLE 17–4	Headquarters' Roles and Line-of-Business Characteristics		
	Controller	*Coach*	*Orchestrator*
Synergy	Little/None	Medium	High
Risk	Low	Medium	High
Competition	Stable	Open	Intense

Source: M. Goold and A. Campbell, *Strategies and Styles* (United Kingdom: Ashridge Management Centre, 1989).

and distribution, along with local planning, forecasting and budgeting, financial management and control, personnel and labor relations (including training local managers), and government relations. Public relations is another area of activity, particularly representing the parent company in meetings with local trade and industry officials, and in community relations. The CM may have more autonomy, however, if the local subsidiary is more important, typically determined by the subsidiary's size, age and experience, its total sales revenues and market position, overall performance, and the ability and effectiveness of local management. The cultural distance of the local subsidiary from its parent is also relevant.

As outlined below, the CM's responsibilities and roles change as the firm's international business position changes:

Stage of the Firm's Internationalization	*CM's Role*
International	*"Trader"*: Sales and distribution of products principally exported from HQ
Multinational	*"Potentate"*: A local czar, with local products, manufacturing, profit and loss responsibility, particularly in countries with barriers to free trade
Transnational	*"Cabinet Member"*: A team player, subordinating local subsidiary to the needs of global integration; reduced authority in some areas (e.g., R&D, manufacturing); greater role for regional manager
Global	*"Ambassador"*: The CM works with product and line-of-business global managers, focusing principally on local government and trade issues; often a local national

CMs can draw on local roots to build businesses. For example, Richardson Hindustan's CMs were able to highlight the role of natural herbs used to formulate Vicks Vaporub cold medicine, which appealed to Indian consumers because they could see connections to the age-old Indian Ayurvedic traditional system of medicine that also draws on native herbs and plants. At the same time, the parent company's transnational approach allows learning from local solutions and applying them in other national markets; for example, the success to be had from year-round advertising or from using traditional distribution systems in emerging markets.[25]

As we have suggested above, multinationals constantly change their organizational structure as environmental change and daily operations disclose weaknesses in the way the firm is organized. Organizational fashions can exist, such as the trend to develop worldwide product-line operations and subordinate country managers to the product-line leaders. McKinsey[26] studied 43 U.S. consumer companies to see if organizational changes could be linked to international success. The study found that superior international growth in sales and profits seemed to be linked to several traits:

- Centralized international decision making except in new-product development
- Requirement that top management have international experience
- Use of videoconferencing and E-mail to link international managers
- Successful integration of international acquisitions
- Reporting by multiple product managers in a country to a country manager, as shown in the Ciba-Geigy example earlier.

Regardless of which organization structure is chosen, the central problem is that organization structure is static, while the environment is dynamic. How is the multinational to preserve strategic and organizational flexibility? *The answer is to go beyond the formal organization.* Beyond organization structure, the firm must focus on communication channels, interpersonal relationships, and changing individual perceptions. The goal should be to let the informal organization bloom. Overall, an environment of intense competition, overcapacity, and technological change means that companies that succeed will do so because of clarity of corporate *purpose,* effective management *processes,* and ability to develop *people*—employee capabilities and perspectives. Instead of sweeping strategic visions, employees who believe in what the company is trying to achieve are more likely to move the company to success.[27] An example is The Body Shop, whose employees share Body Shop founder Anita Roddick's interest in selling natural products, helping the environment, and backing causes such as Third-World development and shelters for battered women. Such shared values make Body Shop employees loyal and committed to making The Body Shop a success.

Forming Industrywide "Webs": Going beyond a Company's Organizational Boundaries

A further facet of organization structure is how a company is organized to deal with outsiders. As companies begin to work more closely with entities such as suppliers and competitors, a network approach is becoming more common. Such network linkages go beyond purely commercial links, and encompass a larger relationship wherein the two partners attempt to share resources and harmonize competitive strategies for competitive advantage. Such networks can include key suppliers and customers, competitors, and entities such as governments, unions, universities, research institutes, and trade associations.[28]

Such networks are particularly interesting in technology-based industries where companies form a "web" linked together without any formal agreement, but built around a common technological standard. An example would be the number of companies developing software built around the Windows-Intel standard or, more recently, around the Netscape Internet browser. Coalescing around a technological standard reduces risk because greater assurance exists of larger market size, while the web of informal linkages allows individual firms to focus their strategy and concentrate on relatively narrow segments of the value chain. Because the technological standard reduces risk, the web shapers, who set the standard, have the option of keeping the standard to themselves (that is, creating a proprietary standard as Apple attempted to do with the Macintosh). The trade-off here is between increasing the size of the web by freely giving away the standard versus attempting to capture profits while reducing the size of the web. It is estimated that Microsoft captured only 4 percent of the total revenues created by the Wintel standard, but it is debatable whether the Wintel standard could have generated total web revenues of over $120 billion without facilitating creation of the web of Wintel companies. Webs are a further extension of the business networks idea, with the added complication that association is primarily voluntary, with companies joining the web because of the profit potential that they see in adhering to such voluntary webs.[29]

Implementation and Organization

A global strategy makes it inevitable that some headquarters intervention will be necessary, ranging from informing, to persuading, then coordinating, to approving, and culminating in directing.[30] As headquarters moves from informing to directing, it is taking greater control and lessening autonomy at the subsidiary.

Headquarters involvement may vary from country to country, with greater intervention occurring in regions experiencing troubles. However, greater autonomy may be given to some subsidiaries for certain elements of the marketing mix. Table 17–5 sets out a hypothetical example of how a company might arrange headquarters' role in implementing strategy.

Five modes of involvement exist:

1. *Informing.* Headquarters management informs subsidiaries of news, statistics, market research findings, corporate goals and objectives, and competitive developments. Successful experiences in a country or product line are disseminated throughout the organization, with top management relying on the business judgment of subsidiary managers to pick up relevant ideas for adaptation into their own lines of business. An example would be the use of a quarterly videotape by Square D to communicate developments in the electrical products group worldwide.

2. *Persuading.* The three-dimensional service groups used at Shell provide an example of this approach, with autonomy still resting at the subsidiary level. Much of matrix management involves persuasion and can be a slow process, although long-term results are more likely because the subsidiary managers will have been convinced of the merit of the actions taken.

3. *Coordinating.* This is the approach used by Avon in which subsidiary managers in Latin America develop their own plans, but headquarters coordinates the various country plans. Notably, Avon uses a bottom-up approach, preferring that plans originate with the national managers; this allows good managers to develop at subsidiaries and heightens the chances of their retention.

4. *Approving.* Headquarters must approve plans drawn up by subsidiaries. This allows for global strategy, influenced by competitor response, to take precedence over plans tailored to the needs of a specific subsidiary.

5. *Directing.* Subsidiary managers do as they are told by headquarters. This approach may be necessitated by a critical situation, because of a lack of seasoned managers, or because the issue must be standardized on a global basis. The effect on manager motivation can be damaging. Those who are competent may chafe at the restraint and move on to other companies. It is also unlikely that top management's decisions will always be right. What is lost in this approach is the sensitivity of local managers to the adaptation needs of the local market.

A global company needs strong local managers, but managers need experience to become strong. As Table 17–5 makes clear, some products, functions, and marketing activities can safely be left to subsidiary managers. Indeed, companies should seek to create some areas where such autonomy is fostered.

| TABLE 17–5 | Global Marketing Strategy Implementation: Headquarters' Role |

	Informing	Persuading	Coordinating	Approving	Directing
New-Product Development					X
Product Line					
Marketing Mix					X
Product Characteristics			X		
Product Segmentation			X		
Brand Policy			X		
Packaging				X	
Advertising			X		
Promotion		X			
Distribution Channels		X			
Pricing				X	
Customer Service			X		
Country Markets					
Market 1		X			
Market 2			X		
•					
•					
•					
Market *n*					X

Source: Adapted from John Quelch and E. Hoff, "Customizing Global Marketing," *Harvard Business Review,* May–June 1986.

Regional Headquarters: A Halfway House

We have considered decentralization in terms of the division of labor between corporate headquarters and the units in foreign markets. Frequently, however, as the firm's business in a region such as Europe or Latin America grows larger, it becomes important enough to warrant separate attention. This could lead to the establishment of a new level in the organization between corporate headquarters and the foreign markets, that is, a regional headquarters. A **regional headquarters** is not necessarily located within the region, although usually it is for the larger regions, such as Europe. Many U.S. companies, for example, have their Latin American headquarters in Coral Gables, Florida, truly a halfway location between corporate headquarters and country operations. Regardless of location, however, regional headquarters gives undivided attention to the affairs of the region.

Almost all the world's major computer companies find it necessary to have a regional headquarters *within* Asia for the important Asia/Pacific market. Based in Hong Kong are such firms as Apple, Unisys, DEC, Hewlett-Packard, and Wang. AT&T is in Singapore, IBM is in Tokyo, and ICL is in Australia.

Conclusions on Organizational Structure

From the preceding discussion, three generalizations can be made about organizational structure. One is that structure must be tailored to the situation and needs of the individual firm. No standard model exists. Second, changing conditions require adaptation by the firm, so organization structures are in almost continual evolution. Perhaps the most important conclusion, though, is that firms are now recognizing that organizational structure can never be a complete and satisfactory means of coordinating their international operations. Accordingly, they are now trying to incorporate the product, geographic, and functional dimensions into their decision making *without changing their organizational structure.* In other words, other things besides organization structure can be used to coordinate international business.

Stopford and Wells studied structural changes but noted that "management skills" were more important than the formal organization structure.[31] In a later study, Bartlett found that many successful firms did not worry about structural change but focused attention on the individual tasks facing their companies. "Instead of joining the quest for the ideal structure, they looked at the connection between environment, strategy, and the 'way of managing.'"[32] Hedlund found the same story for Swedish multinationals. Instead of introducing matrix structures, they complemented their simple organization forms by changes in information systems, budgeting, rotation of personnel, and so forth.[33] These changes and what Bartlett calls the "way of managing" include a variety of things that can best be considered as control devices, a topic to which we now turn.

CONTROLLING INTERNATIONAL MARKETING

Companies market internationally to attain certain corporate goals. The purpose of control is to direct operations to achieve the desired objectives. Considered in this way, control is the essence of management. According to Koontz and O'Donnell, the basic control process involves three steps:[34]

1. Establishing standards

2. Measuring performance against the standards

3. Correcting deviations from standards and plans

Control is inextricably related to the previous topics, planning and organization. Indeed, Koontz and O'Donnell call planning and organization prerequisites of control systems. Planning involves setting standards and goals, the first step in the control process. The organization of the firm establishes the hierarchy, division of labor, and the communications channels for management control. Furthermore, the degree of decentralization affects the control task. General control principles are as valid internationally as domestically. The special problems arise from the different environments in which these operations occur. The communication gaps—the distance between the firm's different markets and the differences in language, nationality, and culture—are the major causes of difficulty. Problems also arise from differences in financial and monetary environments. For example, government supervision, exchange controls, and differing rates of inflation limit the firm's ability to control transfer prices, remittances, and logistics, that is, limit where it will buy and sell internationally.

The following discussion is organized around the three steps of the control process: (1) establishing standards, (2) measuring performance against the standards, and (3) correcting deviations from standards and plans.

What we refer to here as the *control process* has been referred to by others as *coordination,* or *integration,* of international marketing. A *Business International* study mentions a number of methods for "integrating" international marketing:[35]

1. Standard planning systems

2. International product management

3. Marketing committees

4. International marketing meetings

5. Task forces

6. Marketing support services

7. Internal marketing publications

8. Rotation of marketing personnel

Special Measurement Techniques

In addition to regular reporting, specialized techniques exist for evaluating marketing performance. Two of the most noteworthy are distribution cost analysis and the marketing audit.

Distribution cost analysis is a technique for analyzing the profitability of different parts of the marketing program. It can be used to study product lines, distribution channels, customers, or territories. Through comparative distribution cost studies of markets, international marketers can recognize weaknesses in marketing programs and find solutions to recommend for markets having problems.

The **marketing audit** is a methodical examination of the total marketing effort, often by some outside expert.[36] Such an audit perhaps could be done by international marketing managers for each market every few years. Certainly the audit would add to management's understanding of the firm's foreign marketing and aid in improving it.

A marketing audit would be especially useful when the firm is changing its involvement in a country. At a higher level, an audit could be made of the total international marketing of the firm.

Organization

The purpose of organization is to facilitate management control. The organization structure shows the lines of authority, the hierarchy of control. Going beyond organization structure, a study by Doz and Prahalad emphasizes *organizational context* as a means of maintaining strategic control.[37] By organizational context they mean that administrative mechanisms exist (apart from changing the organization structure) that allow headquarters to maintain control in changing environments and circumstances. Table 17–6 gives an overview of these administrative mechanisms. Their argument is that headquarters must maintain strategic control if international operations are to be optimized; to achieve this, organizational context (these administrative mechanisms) is more effective than structural change. Dow, for example, refuses to create a written organization chart because this would de-emphasize the nonstructural methods it uses to deal with competing strategic imperatives.

For example, in executive placement, it may be necessary to consider the propensity of individual managers to take a headquarters/business perspective versus a subsidiary/market perspective. Reporting relationships may be made to encourage greater or lesser local autonomy. Management accounting and reward systems may be used to enforce a strong national profit center mentality or to create an international perspective. Membership in critical committees may be adjusted to recognize either global or foreign national concerns. Critical functional staff groups may be centralized at headquarters or attached to local operating units.[38] Table 17–7 provides additional positive and negative control mechanisms.

Budget

The budget is the basic control technique used by most multinationals. The control offered by the budget is essentially negative; it may prevent excessive expenditure,

TABLE 17-6	Administrative Mechanisms for Strategic Control	
Data Management Mechanisms	*Managers' Management Mechanisms*	*Conflict Resolution Mechanisms*
1. Information systems	1. Choice of key managers	1. Decision responsibility assignments
2. Measurement systems	2. Career paths	2. Integrators
3. Resource allocation	3. Reward and punishment systems	3. Business teams
4. Strategic planning	4. Management development	4. Coordination committees
5. Budgeting process	5. Patterns of socialization	5. Task forces
		6. Issue resolution process

Source: Yves L. Doz and C. K. Prahalad, "Headquarter's Influence and Strategic Control in MNCs," *Sloan Management Review,* Fall 1981, 16. Copyright 1981 by the Sloan Management Review Association. All rights reserved.

but it does not ensure that goals will be reached. Furthermore, if the foreign subsidiary is substantially independent financially, control from headquarters can be difficult. In this case, the administrative mechanisms mentioned by Doz and Prahalad become especially important.

Subsidiaries as Profit Centers

One way to minimize the control burden on corporate headquarters is to have each subsidiary operate as a profit center. Profit centers can take on varying degrees of responsibility. With a high degree of delegation, the subsidiary handles most control problems. Headquarters may enter the scene only if profits are unsatisfactory. Most U.S. companies operate their foreign subsidiaries as profit centers but with differing degrees of decentralization.

The profit center approach to controlling subsidiaries has several advantages. It maximizes the use of local knowledge and on-the-spot decision making and minimizes the frictions of absentee management. It is good for subsidiary morale because local management likes to "run its own shop."

On the negative side, local management, evaluated on short-term profitability, may act in ways that endanger long-term profits. Very autonomous subsidiaries are difficult to integrate into a coherent international operation. Therefore, a high degree of decentralization is most feasible when the subsidiaries are most self-contained in buying and selling and have minimal reliance on the corporation for other inputs.

Information Systems for Control

Information is needed to plan, to assess performance against plans, and to monitor changes in the competitive and client environment. The company's planning and organization structure determine what information is gathered and how it will be channeled through the organization. The amount of information collected can be enormous. Table 17–8 outlines some categories of useful information.

Without information, global corporations cannot be integrated efficiently. Mattel, a U.S. toy company, is a good example of this. Toy sales are concentrated around the Christmas season, with 60 percent of sales between late September and mid-December. Toy makers must be able to stock sufficient quantities of the best-selling toys in order to do well. Mattel produces most of its toys in plants in the Far East and needs to be able to change production plans to take advantage of new sales forecasts, which in turn are based on sales figures. That is, if a certain toy is sold out by early November, Mattel needs this information and must be able to change production in Hong Kong to produce more of the best-selling toy and then ship it where demand is greatest. Dakin, another toy company and maker of stuffed

TABLE 17-7	Control Mechanisms in Joint Ventures

Positive	*Negative*
Ability to make specific decisions	Board
Ability to design:	Executive committee
Planning process	Approval required for:
Appropriation requests	Specific decisions
Policies and procedures	Plans, budgets
Ability to set objectives for joint-venture general manager (JVGM)	Appropriation requests
	Nomination of JVGM
Bonus of JVGM tied to parent results	Screening/No objection of parent before ideas or projects are discussed with other parent
Ability to decide on future promotion of JVGM (and other JV managers)	
JVGM participation in parent's worldwide meetings	
Relations with JVGM; phone calls, meetings, visits	
Contracts:	
Management	
Technology transfer	
Marketing	
Supplier	
Participation in planning or budgeting process	
Parent organization structure	
Reporting structure	
Staffing	
Training programs	
Staff services	
Feedback; strategy/plan budgets, appropriation requests	
Staffing parent with someone with experience with JV	
MNC level in Mexico	
Informal meetings with other parent	

Source: J. L. Schaan, "Parent Control and Joint Venture Success: The Case of Mexico," cited in J. M. Geringer and L. Hebert, "Control and Performance of International Joint Ventures," *Journal of International Business Studies,* Summer 1989.

animals, faced such a situation when it introduced its Garfield "Stuck on You," a stuffed animal with suction cups on the paws. Dakin had an initial inventory of about 12,000 units, but initial orders exceeded 40,000.

Equally important, if a toy is not selling well, the company needs to know so that production can be stopped. Mattel had increased production of its Masters of the Universe toy line because of excellent 1983 sales. Then 1984 sales dropped to $40 million, from $300 million in 1983; as a result, Mattel had to write off inventory.

Mattel also needs updated figures on toy inventory at its warehouses around the world so that it can shift excess inventory from slow-selling areas to markets where demand is high. All this requires a global computer and communication system that can track production of several thousand individual toy items and inventories at warehouses in various countries, plus retail stocks, again, for each of several thousand individual toys. Hence, Mattel built a global information system linking headquarters with distribution centers and the Far East plants. Now the company knows what finished goods are due from which plant on a daily basis, and where inventory is located.[39] This allows for "better alignment of the production schedule, market forecast, and real orders." Another benefit is that engineers can quickly exchange product specifications with plants, reducing the time it takes for a toy idea to become a product.

TABLE 17-8	**Categories for a Global Marketing Information System**
Market Information	Market potential, consumer behavior and attitudes, channels of distribution, communications media, market information sources, and new products launched
Competitive Information	Competitors' objectives; goals and strategies in the areas of technology, manufacturing, and marketing; and details of competitor operations (logistics, human resources, etc.)
Environmental Information	Foreign exchange perspectives, foreign government regulation, taxes and attitudes to foreign firms, U.S. government regulations
The Firm's Resources	Available human and financial resources, technology, raw materials, strategic partners
General Information	Macroeconomic trends, social structure, political climate and risk, technological advances, management trends

Source: Adapted from Warren J. Keegan, *Multinational Marketing Management* (Englewood Cliffs, NJ: Prentice-Hall, 1984).

The global information system allows Mattel to update inventory, production schedules, and engineering specifications on a one-day turnaround basis, as opposed to between 7 and 30 days formerly. In addition, the system allows Mattel to reduce inventories significantly. Without such systems, global strategy and its implementation would remain a dream.

Once such networks are in place, they can be used for other purposes. Conversational interaction through electronic mail facilities allows for closer coordination of international marketing, making local autonomy and centralized coordination simultaneously achievable. Such systems also allow for close monitoring and exchange of information about competition from around the world, which can be invaluable in determining competitive response.

SUMMARY

Planning for international marketing follows the steps by which strategy is formulated as outlined in Figure 6–1 in Chapter 6. The basic elements of the marketing plan include the environment and the company situation in each market, the firm's objectives, and the strategy and tactics that will help it achieve its objectives.

Plans have a short-range and a long-range component. They should be developed for each foreign market and within the context of a global plan integrating country markets and other areas of activity, such as manufacturing, technology planning, and R&D.

A comprehensive operating plan is necessary to help achieve the firm's objectives in the short term. It should include elements such as detailed sales and market-share targets, planned new distribution outlets, brand awareness goals, new-product introduction plans, test-marketing plans, and other market research activities.

A planning calendar typically requires reconciliation of national plans with headquarters' goals. Once headquarters accepts the plan, budgetary targets are derived and become the basis for managerial action and evaluation.

Broad companywide plans must be adapted to individual markets. Local participation is necessary, and additional information gathering and analysis will ensure a plan better adapted to individual market realities.

Long-range planning deals with uncertainty. The focus is on developing scenarios in basic areas such as technology, market growth, competitive change, and the firm's resources. The goal is to be prepared for contingencies and be alert to major opportunities.

Responding to competitive moves is another essential aspect of planning. This is in the nature of contingency planning, with the firm deciding how it will react if competition cuts prices, launches a new product, or strikes up a strategic alliance.

Paradoxically, the best way to counter competition might be through a strategic alliance with other competitors. Such alliances reduce risk, save time, provide access to technology and markets, and even secure sources of supply. The main question is whether it is better to have a competitor as a partner. Generally, the competitor must possess a complementary asset for a strategic alliance to work well.

Planning cannot work without a well-designed organization structure to implement plans. The basic choice is between centralization and decentralization; in some cases, manufacturing may be centralized, with technology development, product adaptation, and marketing decentralized.

Multinational organizations can be structured along geographic, product, or functional lines. The chosen structure may then evolve to a matrix organization. As the environment changes, organization structure will also have to change.

Examples of companies such as Reynolds Metals, Unilever, General Motors, Square D Co., Royal Dutch/Shell, the Salim Group, and Philips show that there is no one way to structure an international organization. The examples also show that firms do change their structure over time.

A central issue is the role that headquarters should play. One approach is to view headquarters' roles as controller, coach, or orchestrator. In addition, when major changes are occurring in the environment, headquarters may play the role of surgeon or architect.

Further, headquarters' styles must be consistent with the nature of the firm. Firms may be grouped according to three criteria: synergy between lines of business, level of risk, and intensity of competition facing the firm.

Headquarters can affect the quality of implementation, taking a stance ranging from informing, to persuading, coordinating, approving, and directing subsidiary actions. It must decide how much autonomy to grant subsidiaries. In some cases, it may want to direct new-product development while using persuasion in the area of pricing.

Control is necessary to monitor progress against plans and budgets. The chief control tasks are establishing performance standards, measuring performance against standards, and taking corrective action in the case of deviations. Marketing audits are useful in looking at foreign-market performance.

Global information systems are a necessary component of international planning. A wide variety of information can be gathered, and, if usefully organized, can help increase sales, manage global factories and inventories, and ultimately give the firm a competitive edge.

QUESTIONS

17.1 What basic elements should be included in a company's international marketing planning?

17.2 What distinguishes a short-range plan from a long-range plan? What sort of activities are appropriate for inclusion in a short-range plan?

17.3 How should the marketing plan be integrated with other aspects of the firm such as technology and manufacturing?

17.4 What elements would you include in a firm's operating plans for international markets?

17.5 What is the appropriate relationship between a national subsidiary's marketing plans and headquarters' broad goals?

17.6 Why should headquarters' broad plans uniquely be adapted to individual country markets?

17.7 Why should future scenarios be incorporated in a firm's long-range marketing plan?

17.8 How does competition affect international marketing planning?

17.9 Why would a firm consider forming partnerships with competitors?

17.10 Analyze the tire and pharmaceutical industries as examples of strategic alliance formation. What general principles emerge from your analysis?

17.11 How is a firm's organization structure relevant to its international market planning?

17.12 "Organization structure is essentially a choice between headquarters centralization and local autonomy." Discuss.

17.13 What are the merits of choosing functions, products, and geographic areas as the basis for organizational structure?

17.14 Compare the organization structures chosen by Reynolds Metals, Unilever, General Motors, Square D Co., Royal Dutch/Shell, the Salim Group, and Philips. Explain why each organization has chosen a different path for its organization structure. Is there an ideal structure?

17.15 How can headquarters influence the implementation of plans? Under what conditions will it be more or less directive?

17.16 What is control? How is control related to multinational planning?

17.17 What are some measurements that could be useful in controlling a multinational marketing subsidiary?

17.18 What is a marketing audit? How might such an audit be useful in international markets?

17.19 What are the components of a global information system? How do such systems fit in with international market planning?

17.20 Explain how Mattel's global information system gives it a competitive edge in the global toy industry.

ENDNOTES

1 "How Avon Tackles Strategic Planning for Latin America," *Business International,* December 5, 1988.

2 J. P. Hauser and S. M. Shugan, "Defensive Marketing Strategies," *Marketing Science,* Fall 1983.

3 "Global Drug Industry Appears to Be Headed for Big Consolidation," *The Wall Street Journal,* April 13, 1989.

4 "Never Mind the Analysts," *Forbes,* June 13, 1988; and "SmithKline's Case of Ulcers," *Business Week,* October 10, 1988.

5 "Du Pont Signs Agreement with Merck in Effort to Speed Up Drug Marketing," *The Wall Street Journal,* September 2, 1989.

6 "In Huge Drug Merger, Sandoz and Ciba-Geigy Plan to Join Forces," *The Wall Street Journal,* March 7, 1996; and "Multibillion-Dollar Creation of a Drug Colossus," *The Wall Street Journal,* March 8, 1996.

7 Kenichi Ohmae, "The Global Logic of Strategic Alliances," *Harvard Business Review,* March–April 1989.

8 M. E. Porter and Mark Fuller, "Coalitions and Global Strategy" in *Competition in Global Industries,* ed. M. Porter (Boston: Harvard Business School Press, 1986).

9 See C. K. Prahalad and Yves Doz, *The Multinational Mission* (New York: The Free Press, 1988).

10 Chris Bartlett and Sumantra Ghoshal, "Managing across Borders: New Strategic Requirements," *Sloan Management Review,* Summer 1987.

11 R. A. Pitts and John D. Daniels, "Aftermath of the Matrix Mania," *Columbia Journal of World Business,* Summer 1984, 48–54.

12 C. Bartlett and S. Ghoshal, "Organizing for Worldwide Effectiveness: The Transnational Solution," *California Management Review,* 1988.

13 "Reynolds Metals Selects Lausanne As Nerve Center for Its European Operations," *Business International,* March 20, 1989; "Reynolds Metals Plans Unit to Better Tap Hard-to-Reach Can Market in Europe," *The Wall Street Journal,* January 27, 1988.

14 Floris A. Maljiers, "Inside Unilever: The Evolving Transnational Company," *Harvard Business Review,* September–October 1992.

15 "General Motors Sets Up First European Regional HQ," *Business International,* October 20, 1986.

16 "Shell: A Global Management Model," *Management Europe,* March 13, 1989.

17 "Philips: Thinking Global, Acting Local," *Management Europe,* April 10, 1989.

18 "Issues for the European CEO (4): New Products," *Business Europe,* February 12, 1997.

19 "Building Tomorrow's Global Company," *Crossboarder Monitor,* October 15, 1997.

20 "GE's Asian Units: Rugged Individuals," *Crossboarder Monitor,* November 5, 1997.

21 "Comeback Kid in China," *Business China,* May 25, 1998.

22 "Mercosur: The Right Fit," *Business Latin America,* September 7, 1998.

23 M. Goold and A. Campbell, *Strategies and Styles* (United Kingdom: Ashridge Management Centre, 1989).

24 John A. Quelch, "The New Country Managers," *McKinsey Quarterly,* 1992.

[25] Gurcharan Das, "Local Memoirs of a Global Manager," *Harvard Business Review,* March–April, 1993.

[26] "Study Sees U.S. Businesses Stumbling on the Road toward Globalization," *The Wall Street Journal,* March 22, 1993.

[27] Chris Bartlett and Sumantra Ghoshal, "Beyond Strategy to Purpose," *Harvard Business Review,* November–December 1994.

[28] Joseph D'Cruz and Alan Rugman, "Business Networks for International Competitiveness," *Business Quarterly,* Spring 1992, 101–107.

[29] John Hagel III, "A Web that Supports Rather than Traps," *The Wall Street Journal,* March 11, 1996.

[30] John Quelch and Edward Hoff, "Customizing Global Marketing," *Harvard Business Review,* May–June 1986.

[31] John Stopford and Louis T. Wells, Jr., *Managing the Multinational Enterprise* (New York: Basic Books, 1972).

[32] Christopher A. Bartlett, "Multinational Organization: Where to after the Structural Stages?" (Cambridge, MA: Harvard Business School, 1981).

[33] Gunnar Hedlund, "The Evolution of the Mother-Daughter Structure in Swedish Multinationals," *Journal of International Business Studies,* Fall 1984, 109–123.

[34] Harold Koontz and Cyril O'Donnell, *Management,* 6th ed. (New York: McGraw-Hill, 1976), 640–642.

[35] Business International, *Managing Global Marketing* (New York, 1976), 103.

[36] Philip Kotler, W. T. Gregor, and W. H. Rodgers III, "The Marketing Audit Comes of Age," *Sloan Management Review,* Winter 1989.

[37] Yves L. Doz and C. K. Prahalad, "Headquarters' Influence and Strategic Control in MNCs," *Sloan Management Review,* Fall 1981, 15–29.

[38] Gary Hamel and C. K. Prahalad, "Managing Strategic Responsibility in the MNC," *Sloan Management Journal* 4 (1983): 348.

[39] See "Mattel Net Chases Xmas Blues," and "The New On-Line World of Santa's Helpers," *Computerworld,* December 19, 1988.

FURTHER READINGS

Bartlett, Chris, and Sumantra Ghoshal. "Managing across Borders: New Strategic Requirements." *Sloan Management Review,* Summer 1987.

Bartlett, Chris, and Sumantra Ghoshal. "Organizing for Worldwide Effectiveness: The Transnational Solution." *California Management Review,* 1988.

Bartlett, Chris, and Sumantra Ghoshal. "Beyond Strategy to Purpose." *Harvard Business Review,* November–December 1994.

Calantone, Roger, and C. A. di Benedetto. "Defensive Marketing in Globally Competitive Industrial Markets." *Columbia Journal of World Business,* Fall 1988.

Daniels, John D. "Bridging National and Global Marketing Strategies through Regional Operations." *International Marketing Review,* Autumn 1987.

Das, Gurcharan. "Local Memoirs of a Global Manager." *Harvard Business Review,* March–April 1993.

Diamantopoulos, A., and B. Schlegelmilch. "Comparing Marketing Operations of Autonomous Subsidiaries." *International Marketing Review,* Winter 1987.

Goold, M., and A. Campbell. *Strategies and Styles.* United Kingdom: Ashridge Management Centre, 1989.

Hulbert, James M., William K. Brandt, and Raimar Richers. "Marketing Planning in the Multinational Subsidiary." *Journal of Marketing,* Summer 1980.

Kotler, Philip, W. T. Gregor, and W. H. Rodgers III. "The Marketing Audit Comes of Age." *Sloan Management Review,* Winter 1989.

Maljiers, Floris A. "Inside Unilever: The Evolving Transnational Company." *Harvard Business Review,* September–October 1992.

Ohmae, Kenichi. "The Global Logic of Strategic Alliances." *Harvard Business Review,* March–April 1989.

Porter, M. E., and Mark Fuller. "Coalitions and Global Strategy." In *Competition in Global Industries,* ed. M. Porter. Boston: Harvard Business School Press, 1986.

Prahalad, C. K., and Yves Doz. *The Multinational Mission.* New York: The Free Press, 1988.

Quelch, John. "The New Country Managers." *McKinsey Quarterly,* 1992.

Quelch, John, and Edward Hoff. "Customizing Global Marketing." *Harvard Business Review,* May–June 1986.

Verhage, Bronislaw, and Eric Waarts. "Marketing Planning for Improved Performance." *International Marketing Review,* Spring 1988.

Pall Corporation

Pall Corporation makes filters to purify liquids and gases. Its customers are global and come from a variety of industries. Pall's foreign sales were 40, 45, and 51 percent of total sales of $332 million, $385 million, and $429 million for the years 1986, 1987, and 1988. Foreign sales nearly doubled, from $131.8 million to $220.2 million, from 1986 to 1988. In 1988 three-quarters of its overseas sales came from Europe and the rest from its Asia/Pacific region.

Filters for All Occasions

Pall's products have numerous applications. The company sells filters to remove contaminants from hydraulic fluid used in aircraft engines. (The hydraulic fluid allows the pilot to control the plane.) Its filters are also sold to the wine and beer industries to remove bacteria, yeast, and contaminants, often replacing cumbersome older-generation, low-technology, sheet filters. Makers of Blue Nun wine at Sichel Winery prefilter and cold-sterilize wine with Pall filter systems. Coty, a perfume maker, uses Pall filters to clarify perfumes at its Montreal operations before bottling. SmithKline Beecham pharmaceuticals uses Pall filters in producing penicillin.

Hospitals and blood banks use its filters to remove leukocytes (white blood corpuscles) to prevent rejection during blood transfusions. Its filters are used to prevent bubbles in blood from reaching the brain during open heart surgery. Auto and truck manufacturers such as Volvo in Sweden and Honda in Suzuka, Japan, use Pall filters to remove contaminants and provide a better paint job and clear coat finishes on auto and truck bodies. Manufacturers of photographic film, floppy and hard disks, compact disks and videotapes, pharmaceuticals, even household water purifiers, all use Pall filters. Industrial uses include paint and chemical processing, nuclear power plants, and natural gas and oil well operations.

Finding and Keeping Customers

Pall's customers are global, and the company develops new filters based on information gained by close interaction with leading-edge customers around the world, be it IBM, Siemens, or Hitachi. Much of the electronic industry is concentrated in countries such as Japan, South Korea, and Taiwan, and Pall has set out to provide enhanced distribution and service, as well as product breadth in this region. It has a Japanese subsidiary, Nihon Pall, to supply the Japanese market. Its products are used by Japanese breweries, including

Asahi's dry beer manufacturing plant. Other clients include Japanese photographic film, lithographic plate, and automotive companies, which use Pall products in Japan. As Japanese auto companies have begun manufacturing automobiles in the United States, they have continued to specify Pall equipment for their new factories.

Drawing on such experiences, Pall plans to increase original equipment manufacturer (OEM) sales by convincing industrial equipment firms in Japan and elsewhere to incorporate Pall filters into their products. By thus making indirect sales, Pall can grow even when more of the market share for industrial equipment sold worldwide goes to foreign equipment manufacturers.

Government clients include hydraulic fluid filter sales to Taiwan for its defense aircraft fighter program, to Argentina for its jet trainer IA63, and to the Brazilian aircraft company, Embraer, for its 19-seat turboprop CBA123. Pall supplies filters for all of Aerospatiale's Airbus planes, which are gaining market share worldwide against Boeing.

Global Vision

Pall Corp.'s 1988 annual report is titled "Focusing on Global Opportunities." When Pall was formed in 1961, its point of view was that (1) it was a technology company, (2) technology is used worldwide, and (3) the world outside the United States is larger than the United States. Hence, right from the beginning, Pall has been aware of the importance of international markets and has focused on global opportunities. Pall forecasts high growth likely in Asia and Eastern Europe now that countries such as China, India, and Russia have each announced a move to "quasi-democratic, semi-capitalistic" systems.

Pall's competitors are global, including firms such as Sartorius, Hydac, and Mann & Hummel in Germany; Koito, Taisei, Shoketsu, and Teijin in Japan; SoFrance in France; and Fairey-Vokes, Fairey-Arlon, and Normalair-Garrett in the United Kingdom. Pall's goal is to meet the competition on their turf, investing heavily to build manufacturing, marketing, sales, and scientific capability in key markets. It plans to establish a physical presence wherever there are budding competitors.

The Challenges of a Global Market

However, being a global company means changing its ways of doing business to accommodate foreign governments. Pall gets nearly 40 percent of its sales from Europe and sees the integration of the European countries in 1992 as being achieved at the expense of outside interests. With Europe growing more protectionist, it plans to adapt by increasing its manufacturing within Europe so that nearly all products sold there are also manufactured there.

At present, Pall divides its manufacturing equally between Europe and the United States and ships components from the United States to Britain, producing in Britain for the European market. Its goal is to be equally represented in the United States and in Europe, being capable of making everything it sells in each market separately. This course of action may be less efficient than others, in that capacity is duplicated and smaller-scale multiple plants have to be built, reducing gross profit and leading to unnecessary capacity because politics rather than immediate demand dictates the plant-expansion decision.

Pall's future growth and new-product development depend highly on customer relations. It has put in place a scientific and laboratory services unit (SLS) that calls on customers only to solve technical problems, never to make a sale. Pall uses these globetrotters solely to gather information from customers and feed it back to research and production personnel. There are about 300 scientists helping connect clients to Pall's leading-edge R&D. The company believes it is important to work with its leading-edge customers all over the world including IBM, Hitachi, and Siemens, for example.

Selling to Japan and Europe   Pall is a leading supplier in Japan to the biotechnology industry. It sells to multinational biotechnology firms such as Sumitomo, Takeda, Hoechst, and Wellcome. Selling the Japanese market is a challenge. A. Krasnoff, Pall's CEO, resignedly jokes about delays in certification in Japan that typically add six months to a year before market entry into Japan is possible.

Government procedures and regulations for receiving certification in health-related products differ from country to country, and Pall must be patient in winning government approval to sell its filters for the pharmaceutical and health-care markets. In Europe, Pall has allied itself with major vendors of intravenous sets and solution suppliers to speed up the certification process. The alliance also helps to obtain greater sales of its intravenous (IV) filters that remove pyrogens (fever causers) for up to 96 hours before they have to be changed. IV filter use is not as widespread in Europe, and Pall hopes that such an alliance will increase market penetration.

Exchange-rate fluctuations also affect profitability at Pall because over half of its sales are realized overseas; thus, changes in the dollar versus other foreign currencies affect the translated dollar value of total sales, with a dollar that is getting weaker magnifying the sales and profit impact of foreign sales. Given the importance of its manufacturing facilities in Britain and its function as a source of products for the European market, Pall also benefits from a lower sterling against continental currencies.

Organizing for Global Markets

Going global involves considerable coordination. Pall must meet the needs of diverse customer segments in different industries in each country; for example, it has developed transmission fluid filters for use with General Motors Detroit Diesel Allison engines used in large off-highway vehicles. To capitalize on this opportunity, Pall must put in place a worldwide distribution network, distinct from that used to market, say, its cabin air-purification filters used on commercial aircraft or its blood and IV filters. In many cases, this will mean forming parallel organizations in the same country pushing distinct product lines from different divisions within Pall.

Thus, within the market region denoted "the Americas and Pacific Basin," Pall has group vice-presidents in charge of aerospace, industrial, and biomedical segments; subordinate to them are senior vice-presidents for marketing and for Pacific Basin operations; at the next level are vice-presidents in charge of fluid process manufacturing, fluid power manufacturing, biomedical, and scientific and engineering services. Nine senior executives have responsibility for the Americas and Pacific Basin region. Coordination and communication of information can be difficult, especially when a client company buys filters from more than one division of Pall.

Pall has launched a worldwide information system to link itself to customers (to permit payment of invoices, place orders, and access inventory and engineering data). The same system will link Pall to suppliers and distributors, as well as provide an internal network for exchange of management and scientific information.

Questions

1. How should Pall be organized in light of its international goals?

2. For the organization structure that you recommend, note the impact on new-product development, client relations, government relations, regional emphasis on Europe and Asia/Pacific regions, and countering competition.

3. Several aspects are critical to Pall's functioning, such as catering to different end-user industrial markets, managing an international manufacturing network, and monitoring international financial flows. How would your proposed organization structure affect these areas?

4. What are the broad information needs of Pall's senior management?

5. Are Pall's organizational structure needs typical of a medium-sized technology corporation? What generalizations can you draw from the Pall experience about organization structure issues over the next decade?

Case prepared by Ravi Sarathy for use in classroom discussion. All rights reserved.
Source: Pall Corporation Annual Report 1987, 1988, and 1989; presentation to the New York Society of Security Analysts, January 5, 1989; and First Quarter Report to Shareholders, October 28, 1989.

Catalina Lighting: "Quality Lighting at *Very* Affordable Prices"

Catalina Lighting began importing and distributing lighting fixtures into the United States in 1985 and has grown rapidly, from $3 million in sales in 1985 to $27 million in sales in fiscal 1988. It has concentrated on carving out a niche as an intermediary, handling design and distribution, while leaving manufacturing to subcontracting factories in the Far East.

The overall U.S. market for lighting fixtures in 1987 totaled $7.3 billion, of which residential lighting accounted for the largest portion at $2.7 billion. There are over 150 domestic manufacturers and about 200 importers, making for a competitive market. New entry is easy because capital requirements are not high and technology is not a barrier. Design is all-important, with new styles sweeping the market, particularly in the United States; but individual product life cycles are short because designs are fairly easily copied and retailers and customers continually move on to new ideas. Delivery times become crucial when new models have short lives; the first manufacturers to ship new models to retail stores can garner larger market shares. Innovative new designs tend to achieve the greatest portion of total sales during the first year that they are on the market.

Manufacture of lights is labor intensive, and imports have been taking an increasing share of the U.S. market, to the point that 10 percent of lighting fixtures sold in the United States in 1987 were imported. Most imports come from Asia, about half from Taiwan. There are about 350 registered lighting manufacturers and at least as many unregistered ones. When a new design appears to be successful, it is quickly copied, with the result that Taiwanese firms cut prices to gain sales of essentially similar products: The cost of producing a Taiwanese lamp is estimated to be one-third of that of a similar U.S. product. Further, most of the Taiwanese industry's output (about 75 percent) is sold to trading companies.

Annual wages in Taiwan and South Korea were about $3,800 and $2,600, respectively, in 1985, and the lack of regulation of the labor market means that overall wage costs are not increased by the costs of compliance with government standards on matters such as fringe benefits, job safety, and EPA regulations. Europe is another major source of imports, accounting for 24 percent of total U.S. imports, principally from Italy (10 percent) and Spain (7 percent).

Having rapidly grown as a purveyor of fashionable lighting at low prices, Catalina's ways of doing business are worth examining.

Design/New-Product Ideas

David Moss, chairman of Catalina, has said, "A pioneer is a guy who walks around with arrows in his back. I might try to make it better, but I only offer to the mass market what I know will sell." Catalina's designers visit lighting trade shows in the United States and Europe to identify new styles most likely to appeal to fashion-conscious consumers. Catalina then designs similar fixtures based on ideas derived from the shows. It provides these designs, shipping drawings and pictures taken from catalogs, to factories in the Far East. Catalina does not pretend to be original, seeing its ability to market proven designs that sell well as a reason for its success. Thus, a European chandelier that retails for $350 in a traditional lighting store can be found in a Catalina clone version for about $125 retail.

Catalina devotes development efforts to ensure a constant stream of new products. Over 100 new products are introduced annually, with current emphasis on outdoor lighting products, such as a motion-sensing infrared model, as well as solar-powered lighting products. It has over 850 different models in its current product line, including chandeliers, recessed lighting, track lighting, security lighting, and table and floor lamps, pole lamps, and torchieres ranging in price from $1.50 to $400.

Catalina Product Categories, June 1987 to June 1988

Outdoor lighting	40
Ceiling fans	20
Bathroom fixtures	15
Table lamps	10
Others	15

However, sales within product categories can change considerably from year to year. For example, as homeowners spend more on remodeling bathrooms, Catalina has added new bathroom fixture products to expand sales and take advantage of this fad.

In the outdoor lighting area, both lighting and security are being sold. Catalina introduced a product retailing for under $30 in which passive infrared motion-sensor switches go on when there is motion within range of an infrared sensing field. Such products had been selling for over $100 a unit, and Catalina's launch of a fashionable product at low prices was an immediate success, garnering sales of over $2 million.

A similar strategy of introducing a lower-priced version of a successful new idea can be seen in Catalina's solar-powered outdoor light, which uses photoelectric cells, turning on automatically at dusk and off at dawn.

Safety/UL Seal of Approval

Catalina has worked with Underwriters Laboratories (UL) to make sure that its products get speedy UL approval (within two to three months), which is important in marketing electrical products. Catalina assigns engineers solely to this responsibility. Two of Catalina's employees worked previously at UL.

Manufacturing: Subcontracting in the Far East

Catalina does not manufacture anything that it sells. After lamps are designed in Miami, the design is submitted for UL testing, while, concurrently, manufacturing planning begins with manufacturers in the Far East, overlapping with the UL process and thus reducing manufacturing lead time to about one to two months. Catalina can get a new product from initial design to display at retailers in three to six months. As noted earlier, being first to market can generate additional sales. Quotations from the manufacturers are priced in dollars, as are customers' orders, to avoid exposure to exchange-rate fluctuations.

Manufacturing Control/Independent Agents

Fourteen independent agents based in Taiwan and Hong Kong work with Catalina to supervise manufacturing; they frequently visit plants to ensure that they meet the company's and UL specifications and expedite orders so that delivery times can be met. Most important, they inspect the finished product before shipping. When UL certification is obtained, UL issues a listing report that provides a technical description of the fixture. It provides manufacturers selected by the company with procedures to follow in producing the products and periodically requires inspections of products at such manufacturers. Catalina uses over 70 independent plants in Taiwan, South Korea, Hong Kong, and the People's Republic of China. To lower risk, Catalina always uses at least two factories in different countries to manufacture fixtures under contract. However, its upper management is directly involved in major buying decisions (signing subcontracting manufacturing contracts), and buying decisions can be made quickly to take advantage of opportunities.

Direct Sales to Large Clients (Home-Improvement Stores)

Catalina uses a direct sales method whereby large clients buy container lots, shipped directly from the Far East manufacturers to the clients. The goods become the responsibility of the retailer once they leave the foreign port, with the retailer responsible for all freight costs, insurance, customs clearance, and payment of customs duties.

Catalina pays manufacturers after receiving payment itself. That is, upon receipt of a customer's letter of credit, Catalina establishes a separate letter of credit payable to the manufacturer. But a key proviso is that draws may not be made by the manufacturer until Catalina is entitled to be paid under the terms of the customer's letter of credit. Catalina draws on its customers' letter of credit once the goods have been inspected by its agents and accepted, delivered to the overseas ports, and the appropriate documentation (title to goods) presented to the bank that issued the letter of credit within the established time period.

This system developed because Catalina at start-up had little working capital. It therefore attempted to work with clients who were willing to finance the entire shipment. These large clients are home-improvement stores catering to the do-it-yourself (DIY) market; Catalina's first such customer was Pay'n Pak, a chain store based in Seattle. Such clients accounted for 65 percent of revenues in the year ending September 30, 1988.

Innovation in Distribution Channels and Packaging

Selling through home-improvement chains is itself an innovation. Light fixtures were traditionally sold through lighting showrooms, which provided advice and information about the product, delivery, and installation service. Catalina pioneered in selling lighting fixtures through home-improvement stores. Its largest clients are Payless Cashways, Lowe's, Wickes, Home Depot, Grossman's, Hechinger, Channel Home Center, Builder's Square, Rickel, and Home Club. DIY chains have themselves been growing as more homeowners have taken up remodeling. Products sold through such stores must then be designed for easy assembly.

When sold through lighting showrooms, the fixtures were packaged in plain cardboard boxes, with salespeople describing product features and charging for installation. With the move to home-improvement stores, clerks had to educate customers about the product as well as provide instructions on installation. This proved burdensome, and the stores needed a way to stress self-service and convenience. This change in the channels of distribution for lighting fixtures led Catalina to repackage the goods in full-color litho boxes, enabling retailers to develop self-service lighting departments for their stores. Assembly instructions were printed directly on the colorful and attractive boxes designed to stand out on crowded shelves.

Catalina has achieved considerable penetration in the large home-improvement segment, selling to 16 of the 20 largest chains, but only having 14 of the next 80 retailers as clients. Future growth could thus come from greater penetration of the small retailer segment. Catalina has begun targeting mass merchandisers and department stores as outlets for its products.

Warehouse Sales to Smaller Clients

Catalina also sells from warehouses in California, Florida, New Jersey, and Dallas, to smaller companies that cannot afford to buy in container lots and do not want to provide letters of credit. They are willing to pay a higher price for the privilege of not having to place orders many months in advance and being able to buy a larger assortment but in smaller quantities. In this case, Catalina is responsible for all shipping and customs costs, and risk is higher because Catalina carries the full inventory necessary to speedily ship orders from stock. Catalina must also issue letters of credit and banker's acceptances to get inventory for its warehouses because it is now buying for its own account. It went public in May 1988, selling 920,000 shares for $2.6 million net, and it used $2 million of the proceeds to buy inventory in order to expand its warehouse operations.

Such warehouses also allow Catalina to provide emergency shipments of items in demand that retailers have run out of. In return, it gets a higher margin on such sales. It has been trying to increase the portion of its total sales made to smaller clients from its warehouses as a way of increasing profit margins. In the year ending September 1988, warehouse sales were over $9 million, 136 percent higher than in 1987.

These sales to smaller clients are handled through 15 manufacturer's representatives, who are nonexclusive and sell from the company's catalog, being compensated on a commission basis. Catalina also carries out some private-brand sales.

Low Prices: Economies of Scale in Outsourcing

Initially, Catalina bought from a few factories in Taiwan. Over time, it became the largest buyer of lighting fixtures in Taiwan, and it currently subcontracts manufacturing with over 70 factories in four countries. As the largest buyer, it has gained considerable negotiating clout, and negotiating low prices from the manufacturers translates into lower purchasing costs. Thus, a fixture that might sell for $200 in a lighting showroom would retail for around $79.95 at Home Depot, courtesy of Catalina's economy-minded approach to design and manufacture.

However, as Mike Gaines, a merchandising manager for Grossman's, points out: "We use Catalina because it offers a quality product at an excellent price." And Mr. Kirchner, merchandising manager with the midwest Handy Andy chain, notes, "There are plenty of low-cost importers who offer lighting out of the Orient. But none except Catalina offers a complete program, and if we run out of a product, they can deliver extra product in a hurry" (from its large and complete line of inventory maintained in warehouses).

A characteristic of its outsourcing is a no-return policy on direct sales once the manufacturing agent has inspected and approved a shipment. Under the retailer agreement, a "defective" allowance is netted from the invoice for any unsalable product. Retailers cannot return a product once it is delivered unless they can prove that the lot had an unusually large number of unacceptable products. It is notable that Catalina manufacturing agents reject nearly one-third of all products inspected prior to shipment.

Cooperative Marketing with Windmere

As Catalina relies heavily on low-cost imports to compete in U.S. markets, efficient outsourcing becomes critical. Windmere, with its long experience in the People's Republic of China, where it employs 10,000 people in its factory in southern China, has agreed to produce quality products for Catalina in its mainland China factories. Because wages there are even lower than in South Korea and Taiwan, this could help Catalina cut labor costs by about a third over that of Taiwan, which will be important as competition increases. Windmere has also provided advice in establishing a subsidiary in Hong Kong to cut taxes paid by 20 to 30 percent.

Catalina recently arranged to let Windmere buy a 19 percent ownership share and has signed a cross-selling agreement. Windmere, which sells low-price hair-care appliances, will introduce Catalina products into its channels of distribution, mainly drugstores and catalog showrooms; it will also help market Catalina products in Canada, while Catalina will attempt to persuade its clients, the home-improvement chains, to carry Windmere hair dryers, fans, and air cleaners. This agreement has led to the sale of Catalina products through the catalog retailers that currently handle Windmere products.

Customer Service

Manufacturer's representatives service about 150 accounts. David Moss, CEO, and Robert Hersh, executive vice-president, personally service the top 25 accounts. Customers are naturally concerned about importing large quantities of product manufactured in distant Asia. Hence, Catalina schedules customer trips to Asia to permit first-hand observation of manufacturing facilities and products prior to shipping.

Distribution Channels for Lighting Products (Based on Units)

Distribution Channel	1970	1987
Lighting Showrooms	61%	28%
Home-Improvement Stores	10	35
General Merchandise	12	17
Other	17	20

Source: Quoted in Ed Cabrera, "Catalina Lighting: Detailed Study," *Home Lighting & Accessories*, Raymond James & Associates, St. Petersburg, FL, December 16, 1988.

Geographic Expansion by Acquisition

With a supply pipeline in place, Catalina began focusing on expanding its distribution. In this effort, it purchased Unitex sales, a Dallas-based firm that sells light fixtures and ceiling fans under the Christina brand name. The acquisition would add about $18 million to sales in fiscal 1989, with some seasonal diversification in that ceiling fans are mostly sold in the April-to-June period. Further, Christina products were sold in some home-improvement chains not yet penetrated by Catalina; thus, Christina was strong in sales to Payless Cashways, Lowe's Co., Channel Home Center, Builder's Square, and Rickel.

Much of Catalina's success is due to its chairman and president, David Moss, who is the largest shareholder in the firm, with about a one-third ownership. Moss worked as senior vice-president at Keller Industries, an aluminum processor, where he managed sales growth from $85 to $130 million in three years. He then went on his own, importing wooden doors, lock sets, and electric heaters. Moss Manufacturing was established in 1980, doing $70 million in sales of ceiling fans within three years. Moss then turned to light fixtures, in part because he would be selling to the same buyers he had dealt with when selling ceiling fans. Moss humorously observes that when he was in the ceiling fan business, he was always praying for hot weather. And when he used to sell heaters, he wanted cold weather. But in the lighting business, he does not have to worry because it always gets dark.

Margins were high in the lighting industry, and Moss believed that he could break into the industry by shaving margins, grabbing chain-store buyers' attention (and getting initial orders) with prices half that of competition. Low prices and a high-quality product, bright and colorful packaging, understandable assembly instructions, and a large variety of products (over 500 styles of lighting accessories) all helped Catalina obtain shelf space.

Catalina's planning of sourcing and marketing have enabled it to capture about 2 percent of the U.S. market. Tables 1 and 2 provide income statements and balance sheets for Catalina showing that it doubled its profit from 1987 to 1988, with return on equity of 27 percent in fiscal 1988.

Looking to the future, Catalina plans to expand into Canada with Windmere's help. Windmere already has experience and a distribution system in place in Canada. Catalina has also begun exporting to the European market, with orders for $2 million from British and Belgian customers. This includes orders from G.B. Inno, Belgium's largest retailer and owner of major interests in Scotty's and Handy Andy, themselves among the major home-improvement chains in the United States, and established Catalina customers. In Britain, direct sales are made to an independent distributor. The Catalina trademark is registered in the United States, Germany, France, and the Benelux countries, with trademark applications pending in other countries in Europe and the Far East. Catalina has established European offices in Germany and Belgium. Beyond that, warehouses are planned for Perth, Scotland; Sydney, Australia; and Tokyo to aid in developing sales in these market regions. It has also begun factoring receivables to reduce risks of exposure to a few large clients (the major home-improvement chains) while also conserving working capital.

Questions

1. Discuss the comparative advantage and the competitive advantage possible in the lighting fixture industry.
2. How has Catalina Lighting taken advantage of the comparative and competitive advantage features noted in your answer to Question 1 to configure and coordinate its value-added chain?
3. What are some of the major strategic choices at Catalina that help make a success of its basic philosophy of sourcing overseas?
4. What are some of the weaknesses of Catalina Lighting?
5. What are the sources of potential competition for Catalina?

TABLE 1	**Catalina Lighting, Inc. Income Statement: Year Ended September 30, 1986, 1987, 1988, and First Half of 1989 (Millions of Dollars)**			
	1989 (Six Months)	*1988*	*1987*	*1986*
Net sales	$22.1	$26.9	$19.8	$11.8
Cost of sales	18.3	22.3	16.9	10.2
Gross profit	3.8	4.6	2.8	1.6
SGA expense	1.9	2.9	2.0	1.3
Operating income	1.9	1.7	0.8	0.3
Other expenses	0.3	0.1	0.1	0.1
Profit before tax	1.6	1.6	0.7	0.2
Net income	1.1	1.0	0.4	0.2

6. Could Catalina's customers bypass Catalina and buy direct from Taiwan, South Korea, and other countries?

7. What do you see as problems facing Catalina? How should Catalina plan to change in the future?

8. Are you optimistic about Catalina's prospects for the future? What would you recommend?

TABLE 2	**Catalina Lighting, Inc. Balance Sheet: Year Ended September 30, 1986, 1987, 1988, and First Half of 1989 (Millions of Dollars)**			
	1989 (Six Months)	*1988*	*1987*	*1986*
Current assets:				
Cash	$ 1.2	$ 0.2	$ 0.7	—
Accounts receivable	7.0	3.7	1.4	$1.8
Inventory	12.3	6.7	1.2	0.4
Other	0.4	0.2	—	—
Total current assets	20.9	10.8	3.3	2.5
Plant and equipment	0.7	0.3	0.2	0.1
Other	0.6	0.5	0.1	—
TOTAL ASSETS	22.2	11.6	3.6	2.6
Current liabilities:				
Notes payable	11.3	4.2	1.0	—
Accounts payable	2.2	2.0	1.2	—
Other	0.2	0.5	0.4	—
Total current liabilities	13.7	6.7	2.6	2.0
Long-term debt	0.1	—	—	0.2
Convertible debentures		—	0.1	0.2
Stockholders equity	8.4	4.8	0.8	0.4
TOTAL LIABILITIES	22.2	11.6	3.6	2.6

Case prepared by Ravi Sarathy for use in classroom discussion. All rights reserved.
Sources: Ed Cabrera, "Catalina Lighting: Detailed Study," Raymond James & Associates, St. Petersburg, FL, December 16, 1988; R. Jerry Falkner, "Catalina Lighting, Investment Opinion," Gulfstream Financial Associates, Boca Raton, FL, January 17, 1989; *Catalina Lighting Prospectus,* May 9, 1989; *Catalina Lighting Annual and 10-K Report,* year ended September 30, 1988; Larry Birger, "Catalina Lighting on Orient Express," *Miami Herald,* February 13, 1989.

Information Technology:

The Internet and International Marketing

Learning Objectives

Information technology has changed the way marketing is conducted, and information has become a strategic weapon.

The main goals of this chapter are to

1. Describe recent major information technology innovations, divided into global linkages with customers and with suppliers.

2. Develop information about customers around the world using Internet-based interaction and point-of-sale information-gathering techniques.

3. Involve customers in new-product design and interact with them after the sale, enhance customer loyalty, and stimulate repeat business.

4. Use information technology to develop new international market research techniques based on developing virtual shopping environments and tracking customer behavior on the Internet.

5. Use the Internet as a new marketing paradigm to communicate with and sell to customers around the world.

6. Use the Internet and electronic data interchange (EDI) to communicate with and conduct business transactions with global suppliers, while also enhancing their efficiency.

GLOBAL LINKAGES

Information technology has changed the way in which companies conduct their international marketing. These linkages can be considered to be a form of virtual international marketing.[1] Significant linkages include: (see Figure 18–1)

1. The company can **monitor the point of sale (POS)** to obtain detailed information on consumer purchase behavior; POS information systems, including data on sales desegregated by brands, quantities, prices, package size, time of day and day of week, month, and so forth, whether coupons were used and other competing products purchased in the category, provide instantaneous feedback about customer decisions, letting the firm know exactly what was sold, at what prices, in what quantities, and at which location. Such information can be used to update inventory records, make decisions about additional production runs, adjust prices and launch sales, and it can be used in designing new products.

    Information thus collected feeds into **database marketing,** where vast stores of knowledge built up about customers and potential customers are analyzed and utilized to develop products and marketing strategies. Such information, aggregated by individual store, and then by other groupings such as by city, region, sales territory, and so on, allows marketing managers to relate actual sales to historical data, competitive market share, advertising, promotion and pricing actions, and so forth, all resulting in better information on the links between marketing mix strategy and effectiveness.

2. The company can **interact with the customer on both the pre-sale and post-sale end:** pre-sale, allowing customers to communicate desires and wants and to be involved in designing and testing the product, and post-sale, providing information on satisfaction with purchase, post-sale use experience, events and problems surrounding post-sale service, and training; the goal is to enhance customer loyalty and encourage repeat purchase behavior.

3. The company can use information technology to develop **new international market research techniques** based on developing simulated, or **virtual shopping environments;** consumer behavior in the virtual shop can be monitored using design of experiment techniques such as fractional factorial design to trace the direct and interaction effects of marketing variables such as price, packaging, promotions in a simulation environment.

4. The company can **use information networks, principally the Internet, to sell and develop a new direct channel of distribution to the customer,** allowing customized shopping at the convenience of the customer; the Internet allows even small firms to directly interact with customers around the world as long as they have access to the Internet, which of course is not always the case.

5. The company can use **the Internet and EDI (electronic data interchange) to deal directly with business partners, both large customers and suppliers.** The Internet is the central medium for this purpose—ubiquitous, cheap, and available nearly all over the world, and to small as well as large companies. Combining the Internet with the Intranet (Internet-based internal corporate networks protected by "firewalls" against intrusion by outsiders) allows a company to develop networks to communicate both

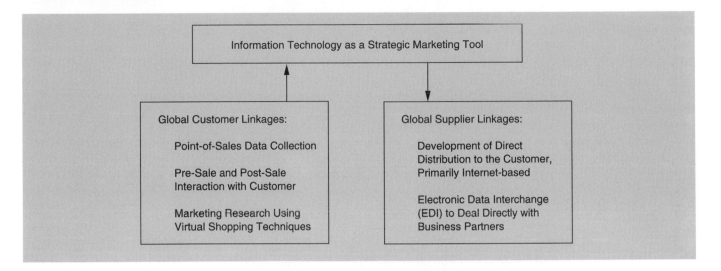

FIGURE 18-1   **Information Technology and International Marketing**

internally and externally. Such networks can be used to send out orders, negotiate prices, set up auctions at which prequalified suppliers bid, exchange product specs, track production status, keep track of shipment status and arrivals, and carry out billing and payments. Advanced use would include interaction at the product design phase ("design for manufacturability") whereby suppliers and customers interact with the firm in developing new products, with a view to reducing time to market, and reducing cost to manufacture. **EDI is the principal technical communication vehicle for such information exchange between a company and its business partners.** Corporate data networks and EDI facilitate accurate interaction, making easier the use of techniques such as quick response production planning based on up to date sales figures; and just-in-time supply chains, with EDI allowing communication of quick response production schedules and required delivery quantities.

Glazer has noted that changes in the information environment can have dramatic implications for marketing strategy, in that information intensity affects a firm's evaluation of both market attractiveness and competitive position.[2] Information systems development also influences the firm's marketing organization structure, dissolving to some extent the boundary between the firm and its environment, its suppliers, competitors and customers, and also within the firm, in reducing the importance of organizational demarcation between, say, marketing and manufacturing. Information content also becomes a feature of the product, a product in its own right and can affect the performance and delivery of elements of the marketing mix, such as service, distribution, marketing communication and promotion, and marketing research. Moriarty and Swartz[3] stress how marketing and sales productivity systems can upgrade the efficiency of sales and marketing staff and also improve the timeliness and quality of marketing and sales executives' decision making.

Figure 18-2 is an example of the global networks being discussed in this paper, describing global linkages at Mattel. As shown in the case of Mattel Corp., its U.S.–based toy designers depend on customer feedback from customers around the world in coming up with new-product ideas. U.S. headquarters management uses these new toy ideas and selects independent Far East–based manufacturing

FIGURE 18–2   **Global Linkages at Mattel**

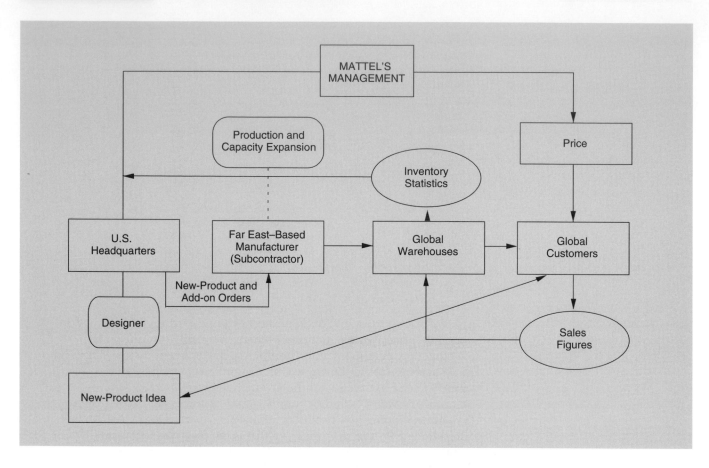

subcontractors, who are given new-product as well as follow-on orders for existing toy products. Inventory statistics from a network of global warehouses are analyzed at U.S. headquarters in arriving at follow-on orders given to their manufacturing subcontractors. Shipments of finished products go directly from the Far East subcontractors to the various global warehouses, with allocations based on sales figures from global customers, which are also analyzed at headquarters and at regional offices. Sales figures and inventory levels are also relayed to and analyzed by management in monitoring and changing prices in order to achieve increased sales in an industry where the bulk of demand is concentrated in a short selling season; in such an environment, management's twin imperatives are (1) to ensure that popular toys are available in sufficient quantities around the world to satisfy demand (hence, the need to transmit rush follow-on orders to distant manufacturing subcontractors) and (2) that pricing policies are used to clear inventory of toys to prevent losses from obsolescence of outdated toy inventories. Without the global marketing information network in use at Mattel, such market responsiveness would be difficult.

Developing such global networks is complicated by the very nature of the international environment. Difficulties arise from:

- Differences in the level of infrastructure across countries, including the depth and sophistication of computer networks; availability, reliability, and cost of local phone systems; and the penetration of computer hardware and software usage across companies. Arguably, these three areas are fundamental to the development of information technology–based marketing.

- Traditional barriers, such as tariffs, quotas, and non-tariff barriers such as customs formalities and local-content laws.

- Cultural differences such as those created by language and different business practices.

- Legal differences that complicate establishing commercial relationships with overseas partners and require close attention to questions of data security and network access.

- Geographical distance and differing time zones, which make communication difficult.

- Barriers created by government regulation, such as limits on transborder data flows (TDFs) and on using value-added networks (VANs).

- Differences in the level of technological sophistication of overseas partners, such as in the use of information systems, computer hardware and software, incompatible standards, and differences in managerial expertise brought to bear on subjects such as quality control, inventory management, customer service and support, and market research; these differences complicate efforts to tie in partners into the global network.

GLOBAL NETWORKS: A CONCEPTUAL FRAMEWORK

Figure 18–3 outlines a conceptual framework for global marketing networks that would include the following major elements:

1. A core subsystem, linking the firm with global customers and suppliers.

2. A subsystem establishing linkages with marketing support, particularly, multinational salesforce teams, overseas distributor organizations, integrated marketing communications (principally advertising and promotion) aimed at global markets, and global service needs.

3. A set of major environmental linkages with outsiders, including host governments, multinational competitors, and the global logistics infrastructure, both with in-house entities and with independent third parties.

4. Linkages to the implementation aspects of such global marketing networks, comprised principally of marketing control, organizational structure, and personnel. Equally important are technical issues crucial to the smooth functioning of such global networks.

In the remainder of this chapter, we examine the various elements of such a global marketing network in greater detail. Table 18–1 sets out the typical information needs of the various strategic areas within a global marketing network.

LINKAGES WITH CUSTOMERS

As information technology becomes more closely intertwined with the very fabric of doing business, information becomes both a critical resource enabling a company to compete in the marketplace and a service in its own right that the company can offer and sell to its customers. Rayport and Sviokla[4] assert that a company competes in two worlds: a world of physical resources, the *marketplace,* and, a virtual

FIGURE 18-3   **A Conceptual Framework for Global Marketing Networks**

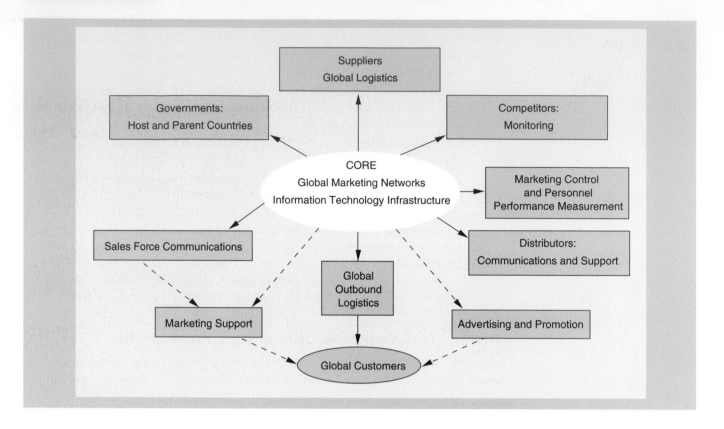

world of information, the *marketspace*. Information changes the way a company creates value and competes within the virtual value chain. A well-known example is Federal Express's system, which allows its customers to dial into the FedEx database and verify where a letter or parcel is in the system: whether it is en route, whether it has been delivered, who received it, when it was delivered. Providing such information allows FedEx to provide an additional service of value to the customer, differentiating itself from competition and building customer loyalty and increasing repeat business. Value chain activities in the virtual world include *gathering, organizing, selecting, synthesizing, and distributing information.* Often, these steps result in a company entering a new business. Rayport and Sviokla cite the opportunities offered by developing a central database of digital music:

1. Customers can download and listen to samples of new music before deciding whether to buy it.

2. Based on a customer's choices of music samples to download, the company can construct listener profiles and offer additional music samples that are likely to appeal to the customer; as important, customers can choose which tracks, which musical selection they wish to include on the CD they purchase. Thus, they can customize CDs with music they like, drawn from different artists and perhaps different producing companies.

3. The company can audition and sign up new music groups by receiving digital "demo tapes."

| TABLE 18-1 | Global Marketing Networks and Information Needs |

Strategy Area	Information Needs
Global Sourcing	Manufacturing lot sizes of parts and subassemblies, by location; monitoring of inventory, costs, and quality; allocation of production, exchanging design information, and product specification changes.
Global Logistics	Servicing overseas subsidiaries: up-to-date information on inventory, manufacturing output, demand in various markets, shipping details, delivery dates, all categorized by finished goods and parts numbers.
Global Servicing	Service quality levels achieved, warranty/service offered, worldwide personnel and parts availability, training and documentation, including service updates.
Global Competitors	Monitor competitive new product offerings, analyze competitor market share, cash flow, and profits.
Strategic Partners	Exchanging R&D results, communicating strategic goals and tactics, coordinating transfer of technology, manufacturing, and marketing.
National Governments	Local output and value-added statistics, company-specific export and import flows, local pricing, promotion, and service; compliance with national interest.
Global Customers	Coordinating multinational marketing: product adaptations, discounts, coordinating pricing and credit, allocating product to markets; developing and maintaining customer and sales leads databases. Global salesforce and distributor management.

4. The company can store all of its recorded music in digital archives and offer a complete catalog of new as well as old music, reducing risks of stockouts and avoiding the discontinuance of music that does not sell well.

5. With direct links between store and customer, intermediaries such as record chains become less important; as distribution costs are reduced, music prices can be lowered; and detailed customer databases can be built up containing information on their music preferences and purchasing behavior. Customers can contribute reviews that can help sell the music to other customers with similar tastes.

6. Additional value-added services can be offered, such as allowing listeners to sit in on recording sessions, eliciting their feedback on different studio takes of the same song, facilitating their interaction with their favorite artists, and allowing them to offer suggestions for new music and acts to be signed.

The virtual marketspace opportunities described above are available to consumers anywhere in the world who have access to the Internet and can access the company's databases and home page. Suddenly, the company can be close to customers in distant lands, to teenagers in Tokyo as well as in Tucson. Imagination and creativity are the only limits on the ability of firms to use the virtual marketspace in attracting and serving international customers. As the previous example shows, companies can:

1. Develop new products and services tailored to the needs of small customer segments and even individual customers.

2. Interact directly with customers to capture and store information about them and use such information to better serve them; a major gain is that such information allows the firm to more precisely forecast demand and shifts in preferences, avoiding both stockouts and excess inventory that could become obsolete and perhaps would have to be discounted.

3. Move a product's utility from the physical to the virtual world, affecting scale and scope economies; in general, such a move makes it easier for small companies to sell in world markets; information-based products and services have low to zero variable costs of production while the fixed costs of production are high; such products are often patentable, and the patent can serve as a barrier to entry.

Virtual Shopping Environments and Experiments

Information technology advances allow companies to simulate marketing environments and learn from watching customers interact with such simulated or "virtual shopping" experiments.[5] Traditional field marketing research uses techniques such as local and regional marketing tests, controlled field experiments, and focus groups. Such approaches are costly, and results from such tests can be contaminated by "noise," that is, by uncontrollable background influences and may be deliberately disrupted by competitors. Such tests take time to implement, are difficult to modify, and may not truly represent consumer behavior under actual product launch conditions. Virtual shopping is a promising alternative.

In a virtual shopping environment, the customer interacts with a grocery store or other retail outlet as simulated on a computer. The customer can survey the layout of the store, pick directions to walk in, stroll down an aisle, and watch the display of goods on shelves unfold. The customer can stop and examine a product on a shelf more closely, read the label, and perhaps peruse product literature. The customer can find out the price, do comparison shopping, look for promotions, and perhaps buy the product. The computer can record customer behavior, including the decision to purchase, quantity and price, alternatives compared, the time spent shopping, the order in which products and categories were examined, and so on.

The simulation can be quite realistic, offering 3-D representations of the product. Such tests may be costly to set up initially, but once the store layout and product assortment has been digitized and stored in the simulation database, experiments can be conducted that monitor customer response to variables such as changes in price, packaging, promotions, new display techniques, and response to displaying new products. Companies and researchers can explore questions such as the drawing power of a brand under different competitive conditions such as price cuts and expanded offerings; study whether the firm's product line meets customer needs; and understand which display mode (arraying a firm's products all together, or next to competition, or by size of package, etc.) most elicits desired customer purchase behavior.

Virtual shopping experiments have many advantages: they are easy to set up, can be modified easily, can be kept secret from competition, and experimental design methodology can be used to study both the main and interaction effects of key variables such as price cuts or package size. Such experiments can also help understand the shopping process—that is, how customers buy products. Virtual shopping makes international marketing relatively easy, because the virtual shop can be presented to customers in different countries through a computer network, and the shop can be modified to offer local products priced in local currencies and in the local language. This approach makes it easier to test standardization versus adaptation questions. Of course, not all products can be tested or sold in virtual shopping environments. Products that customers want to touch or smell or taste would be harder to simulate; the computer-based shopping experience is most useful in providing visual cues and furnishing large quantities of information relevant to the purchase decision. A strong consumer rights movement is also necessary. If consumers cannot seek redress when a product or service is unsatisfactory, they are unlikely to embrace on-line shopping where they have to buy on faith and trust the long-distance unfamiliar supplier. Nevertheless, virtual shopping illustrates the gains to be had from using information technology in conducting international marketing research.

On-line and Internet-Based Shopping

With the creation of virtual shops, it is a short step to actually allowing customers to do their shopping in such on-line shops. The difference is that in virtual shops customer shopping is simulated, while in on-line shopping actual transactions take place with money being exchanged for goods and services. On-line shopping is becoming increasingly important. As issues such as preserving confidentiality and security of payment are addressed to the customers' satisfaction, more companies and customers will begin offering on-line shopping possibilities. On-line shopping is an evolutionary response to a number of market trends:[6]

- Large retailers have become more influential in determining which products are made available to consumers, and they can squeeze suppliers to get better margins for themselves. On-line shopping allows suppliers to bypass the retailer and go directly to the customer.

- Consumers are getting older and revising their budgets to allocate more toward areas such as education, health care, and savings for retirement. Hence, they are becoming smarter shoppers, while simultaneously having less time to shop. On-line shopping offers convenience and value, because part of the savings from not incurring retailer's margins can be passed on to on-line shoppers. On-line shopping also allows more customization to customer needs, in product areas as diverse as computer systems, clothing, and home furnishings. However, on-line shopping must be user friendly and relatively quick and easy to use. Customers face a problem of information overload, and if it takes too long to locate the precise product category and configuration required on an on-line shopping site, customers may never come back.

The Internet's Impact on Marketing[7]

As customers gain increased access to the Internet, it becomes a more viable approach to interacting with customers and their households. Through the Internet, a company can: (See Figure 18–3b)

1. Develop a presence on the Internet, enhancing its image and using the Internet as a vehicle for advertising, both broad corporate image advertising as well as product and service specific advertising. When all is said and done, a company's image is a precious asset, difficult to replicate but easy to lose.[8] However, customers on the Internet typically approach sites because they are looking for information, interaction and communication, entertainment, or to close a transaction. Advertising is likely to be bypassed with a mouse click unless the message is informative and helps the customer in his or her decision process. A danger is that advertising may be difficult to separate from provision of more objective content, leading consumers to question the validity of information provided at that company's site.[9]

2. Provide information about its products and services, its prices, product availability, order status, access to its databases, and links to other useful sites on the Web. The more useful such information is to customers, the more customers will visit the site and the longer they will stay at the site, making the site "sticky" and allowing the company more time to capture that customer's business.

FIGURE 18–3b   **A Strategy for Web-Based International Marketing**

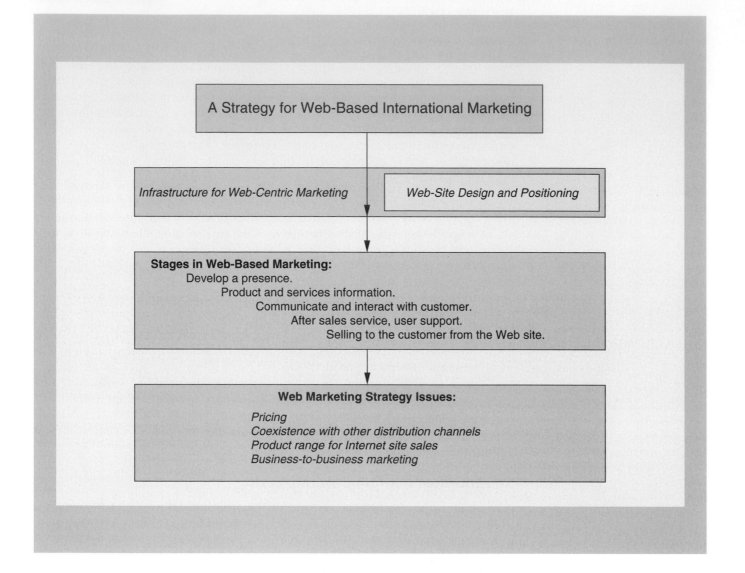

A Strategy for Web-Based International Marketing

Infrastructure for Web-Centric Marketing

Web-Site Design and Positioning

Stages in Web-Based Marketing:
Develop a presence.
Product and services information.
Communicate and interact with customer.
After sales service, user support.
Selling to the customer from the Web site.

Web Marketing Strategy Issues:

Pricing
Coexistence with other distribution channels
Product range for Internet site sales
Business-to-business marketing

3. Communicate and interact with the customer, receiving queries from the customer, handling complaints and feedback on product use, and conducting market research by persuading the customer to respond to queries and forms on the Web, giving the firm the ability to conduct market research in real time and continuously update its market information.

4. Provide after-sales service to the customer, providing product bug fixes, giving the customer access to its experts and facilitating the formation of user groups. Providing a chat environment in which users can talk to one another about product use, new features desired, and can air complaints and ask questions is a value-added service that enhances customer loyalty and encourages repeat business even as it builds confidence in the company. Adding free E-mail services is an example of providing clients with reasons to keep coming back to a company's Web site.

5. Sell to the customer. The most enticing aspect of the Internet is its ability to close commercial transactions with clients, making a sale and obtaining payment. Having said this, few Internet sites have reached the point where the volume is sufficient to make a profit. Even as companies commit large sums of capital to building their Web presence, they continue to rack up losses as the fixed costs and investments needed to become Web-centric far outpace the current revenue streams. The hope, of course, is that once the investments have been made, low operating and variable costs coupled with larger volume and repeat sales will yield a profit.

Pricing on the Internet

The Internet allows customers to be fully informed. They can use agents to learn about competing products' features, develop a best buy, and then conduct comparison shopping on the Web to determine the best price. This means that companies will find themselves competing on price and customers, often gravitating to the lowest price—from sites such as *Buy.com*. How does this help a firm selling a product differentiated by superior quality and service?[10] Firms need to communicate and educate customers about why the lowest price may not provide the desired bundle of attributes, but companies must also realize that price competition is here to stay. This means developing business models that allow profitable operations at lower prices, through cost economies realized from lower distribution costs, savings from bypassing channel intermediaries, and savings from lower inventories and from reducing losses caused by obsolete inventories, as the closer interaction allows companies to practice just-in-time manufacturing and customization of product to customer specifications. Innovative responses such as Barnes & Noble's buying a major channel intermediary, Ingram Books, are influenced in part by the need to cut costs as lower prices become the norm. A related question is the ability to use electronic cash to make payments for small purchases on the Internet—that is, when a customer wishes to read a single news item for which the charge might be five U.S. cents. As E-cash becomes established, new approaches to pricing will also be desirable.[11]

Can the Internet Coexist with Other Channels?

Many large firms that dominate their industries have assiduously developed close channel relationships with distributors, wholesalers, and retailers. The major U.S. car companies are an example, relying on a nationwide network of car dealers who sell in a time-honored ritual of haggling over the car price, options package, and financing. Such firms are loth to destroy decades of effort and are fearful of the impact of demotivated channel intermediaries on their competitive position. Their dilemma is that, as they develop Internet-based marketing to their consumers, they may cannibalize sales from their existing channels, upsetting dealers and salespeople. The new Internet channel can also upset corporate culture built up over a long period. Firms unfortunately do not have an alternative. Indecision caused by current channel relationships simply allows unencumbered newcomers to obtain first mover advantages with the new Internet channel, such as in the competition between Amazon and Barnes & Noble in selling books. The Internet will become a dominant new channel and firms must establish their positions, while working with their existing channels, perhaps by giving them a portion of sales commissions during a transition period. Otherwise, the firm is likely to disappear and their existing channels will have nothing to sell.

Can Everything Be Sold on the Internet?

Products such as books, airline tickets, hotel rooms and vacations, and stocks and bonds are some of the products that first made a splash using the Internet as a channel of distribution. As customers have become more comfortable with shopping on the Internet, new products have begun using this channel: flowers, mortgages, insurance, and office products. It may be that products whose features can be assessed on-line, products in which competing offerings can be ranked, products that are non-perishable, light in weight, and thus easy to ship, can be shipped off the shelf, and are familiar to the customer lend themselves more easily to Internet shopping. Consumers must also be willing to postpone consumption gratification till the product arrives; thus, buying a bottle of wine to take to a dinner that evening would still be purchased at the corner store. But the expanding range of products sold on the Web suggests that merchants are using their ingenuity to adapt their products for sale on the Web: even products such as pharmaceutical drugs, expensive houses, furniture, and designer dresses.

Business-to-Business Marketing on the Web

Even while firms grapple with consumer marketing on the Web, over half of all Internet transactions are between businesses. Businesses find that procurement of product inputs, supplies, and components can be more easily done on the Web. Specs can be clearly laid out, suppliers can be prequalified, and bids can be taken, with due dates for a tender or by auction. Such procurement saves immensely on product purchasing costs, can be speedy; and EDI allows for rapid interchange of information and payment.[12]

Infrastructure for Web-Centric Marketing

Secure networks are a must to preserve company confidentiality and to provide peace of mind to customers as they arrange to pay for their purchases. Speed of Web response is also important, because customers are likely to get impatient and move on if secure transactions processing networks are slow. Consumers also worry about the integrity of the companies they buy from; arrangements that guarantee customer rights, the ability to effect product returns and exchanges, and settle disputes will help alleviate such worries and win the customer's trust. Also essential are measurement tools to gather data on visitor traffic and interest, using services such as Media Metrix and feedback on customer satisfaction with the Web site and with the on-line shopping experience, often using unobtrusive measures such as "cookies."

Web Site Design and Positioning

Attractive, well-designed Web sites are a must in holding the customers' attention and getting them to browse the company's offerings, perhaps making a purchase. Sites that load quickly are a must, as are sites that are well arranged so that clients can quickly find the information they are seeking. The site is an ad as much as it is a source of information about the company and its products, and the same level of attention and graphic design expertise devoted to print and other media ads should also be given to Web site design.[13] Major firms attempt to make their sites comprehensive so that visitors stay as long as possible; for example, Microsoft provides one-stop access from its *msn.com* site to E-mail, chat facilities, travel, brokerage, news, and entertainment links, all under its aegis. Smaller companies have formed consortia linking each other's sites, such as those between purveyors of books and CDs, software, movies, travel services, toys, and brokerage services. The other extreme is firms such as Amazon, which tries to be a one-stop shop on the Internet, expanding from books into movies, music, and related products. The chief competitive advantage in this situation is not so much the range of product offerings as it is a base of shoppers who like on-line shopping, are early adopters of this technology, and are repeat buyers, likely to exhibit loyalty as long as their shopping experience is satisfying. Schwab, the American brokerage house, similarly added services such as retirement products, tax advice, personal finance modules, and mortgage and insurance products to its base of investment products and databases.[14]

Customization

One of the most exciting and promising aspects of using information technology in marketing is the ability to find out exactly what customers want, and then customize to meet each individual customer's needs. What can be digitized can be customized! Pine and his coauthors[15] describe this as becoming a *mass customizer and a one-to-one marketer.* Such an approach allows for continuous learning on both sides, by both the company and its customers. Furthermore, customers who are listened to are more likely to be loyal and buy repeatedly from the company. Of course, this built-in loyalty advantage must be supplemented with competitive quality products at matching prices, and products must evolve to accompany technology generations.

An example of such customization is *Peapod,* a company which allows customers to buy groceries on-line. Peapod works with grocery chains to present the available assortment of goods and services on-line. The products are displayed in whichever format the customer requests: displayed by produce category, by items on sale at that point in time, by brand name, package size, and so forth. Then, the customer indicates which items he or she wants to buy. Peapod's buyers purchase and deliver the groceries for an additional charge, and despite the higher price, customers find that the service saves time and money, by taking advantage of sales, doing comparison shopping, and avoiding impulse purchases. Peapod has a high rate of repeat business and, by constantly asking its customers to rate their shopping experience, it learns from its customers. This allows it to modify and improve its service, particularly in critical areas such as the handling of customer complaints and correcting erroneously filled orders.

An important issue is who controls and learns from the interaction with customers: the retailer or the manufacturer? Whichever party controls the information gains power. One solution is an alliance, as in the auto industry, where car manufacturers work with dealers to deliver mass customization. In such instances, dealers have to receive special training to understand the implications of customers armed with information about buying cars gleaned from the Internet and the need to respond quickly to customer on-line and E-mailed queries.

What Are Some Key Steps in Developing an Information-Based Mass Customization Approach?

1. The company must gather information to learn about the customer; however, not all customers are equally important; initially, companies need to concentrate on large-volume customers and customers who are at the user frontier, enabling the company to learn from them (i.e., beta site software customers). The company can benefit from collaborating with such customers in jointly creating new products. "Technology-facilitated conversation . . . (can) establish binding relationships with customers."[16] Involving customers in the design process can result in better product and win their loyalty and their willingness to buy the new product, reducing *time to acceptance.* Beyond individual product design, the company can maintain a continuous dialog. This implies accepting and encouraging interaction instead of one way broadcast.

    It is therefore important to train front-line salesforce and others who interact with the customer to gather and transmit information. Unsurprisingly, customers are resistant to giving out such information because of all too realistic fears of being deluged with junk mail. Micromarketing can lose effectiveness if every company, armed with the same databases, bombards the customer with multiple direct mail pieces, causing fatigue and anger. Companies need to make special efforts to respect customers' privacy if they are to gain the customer as an ally. The information gathering needs to focus on two separate areas: How hard

is it for the customer to do business with me? (customer sacrifice);
and how much of the customer's total business does my company get?
(customer share)

2. Information technology can be used to facilitate the purchase and delivery
    of goods and services. This suggests that there are two distinct sets of skills
    that are relevant to satisfying customers. Pine and his coauthors suggest
    that two categories of managers are equally important, *customer* managers
    and *capabilities* managers. Customer managers determine what new
    products and services should be offered and customized, while the
    capabilities managers have to discover how to deliver the goods, whether it
    is possible, and whether the new customized offerings should be produced
    in-house or subcontracted.

3. The company can offer information technology–based follow-up services,
    including complaints handling and customer retention campaigns. British
    Airways has a department whose sole responsibility is to follow up on
    customer complaints, trace the internal cause of the problem so that it can
    be corrected, and then provide feedback to the customer about how the
    problem was handled.[17] Customer problems can form the basis of new-
    product modifications and better customer service. But increased
    customer access raises their expectations and customers will get frustrated
    if there is no immediate response.

4. The company can organize and store information for ease of retrieval, for
    use in distinct phases of the marketing process such as new-product
    development, information gathering prior to purchase decision making,
    current product purchases, and post-purchase follow-up, broken into after-
    sales training and service, and generating repeat business and enhancing
    retention. Successful database marketing requires that a database design
    be linked to marketing decisions that use such information. The best
    known example of this approach might be FedEx, which offers Internet-
    based tracking of packages sent through it so that customers and suppliers
    know exactly where a critical shipment is in transit and when it might
    arrive at the customer site.

The studies and concepts reviewed above suggest that we can divide customer
linkages into two broad categories: *customer interaction variables* and *customer information variables*. Customer interaction variables affect the nature of the relationship
established with the customer and shape the parameters of the network to be developed. Customer information variables concern the information content of the
network: that is, what kinds of information will flow from the firm to the customer
and vice-versa. The information content aspect is mainly concerned with understanding the buyer and what role the firm's product plays in helping the buyer improve his business performance. Table 18–2 summarizes how these two categories
of variables shape global linkages with customers.

EXAMPLES OF GLOBAL CUSTOMER LINKAGES

Liz Claiborne has been developing links with retailers that allow the retail store
buyer to view new fashion lines and specific styles on a high-resolution graphics
computer. Here, the high-definition image is digitized and transmitted to the retailer, saving time and allowing for feedback as the design process is occurring.
The idea here is that the retailer does not have to wait for occasional visits from a
factory representative but can view the line as often as desired. Such a system

TABLE 18-2   Variables Affecting Global Linkages with Customers

Customer Interaction	Customer Information
Relationship: one-time, ongoing.	Customer database and buying history; market demographics.
Product complexity: straight sales vs. requiring after-sales support and complex service.	Customer segment positioning, vertical industry segments.
Length of selling cycle: Is repeated interaction necessary to close the sale? Team selling effort?	Key decision makers; team buying?
Intensity of competition for order; first-time or repeat sale?	Client importance: size and frequency of order, lead user.
	Competitive presence among: ◆ Existing customers ◆ New prospects/sales leads
Price: fixed or negotiated, volume and use-based pricing.	Differences across country markets.
Upstream involvement: customer participation in product design, modification, and customization.	Customer input and feedback during product design, role in prototype (beta site) testing, feedback on product performance.
Distribution channel in reaching customer: independent distributors, personal selling, direct mail, telemarketing, or in an OEM arrangement?	Channels used to reach customer: alternative distribution approaches, volume and efficiency.
Downstream involvement: customer participation in joint selling, promotion.	Customer capabilities, convergence of interests, perceived strategy development.
Service relationship: extent of service interaction, quality of service, parts shortages; debriefing service personnel.	Customer service: monitoring service quality.
Other: exchange rate risk and risk-sharing.	Monitoring exchange rate changes and effects on customers; developing risk-sharing formulas based on exchange rate bands.

would also allow the retailer to zoom in on details of a product, such as detailing over pockets or the weave of the fabric, and then transmit an order if they so desire. Similar CAD/CAM-based linkages allow such design information to be transmitted to Liz Claiborne's overseas suppliers; this allows interaction between retail buyers, Liz Claiborne executives, and representatives of its manufacturing subcontractors in shaping the final product. Figure 18–4 graphically displays Liz Claiborne's global network.

K-Line: Shipping Freight for Customers

Customers of freight shipping firms want constantly updated information on the status of their shipments. In response, K-Line, a Japanese shipping firm, developed a global network integrating voice, data, telex and fax traffic. The network connects North America on to Tokyo via trans-Pacific fiber cable, and then on to Hong Kong, Taiwan, Singapore, Korea, and Thailand. The network will soon expand to Europe, and users can query the system for updated shipping information,[18] with user-friendly features such as color graphic maps facilitating communication. Figure 18–5 indicates the workings of this system.

A central problem in such a system is identifying the exact location of a container, one out of hundreds of same-sized red or yellow or green rectangles. The

FIGURE 18-4 **Linkages with Retailers and Suppliers: Liz Claiborne**

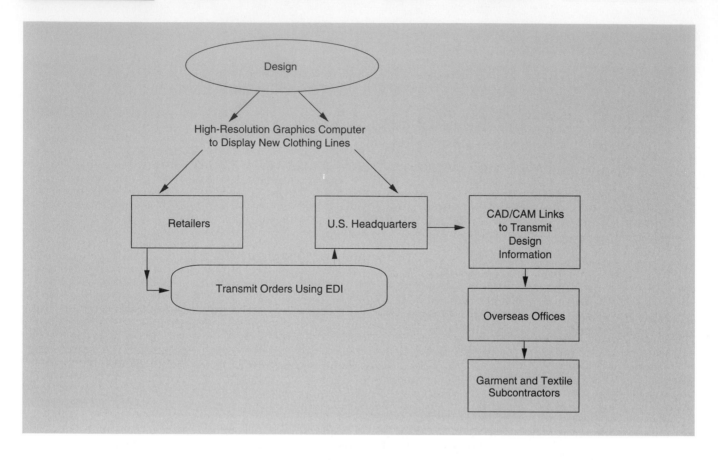

solution is to use remote radio tagging, similar to the technique used to track animal movements in the wild. Electronic tags are attached to each container containing specific information on that container. A receiver at the shipyard or on board can read the tags and feed the information to a computer at the terminal and, from there, to a central computer that updates container information and location throughout the company. The information is collected almost instantaneously and continuously updated. Such a system is in use at American President Companies in their Seattle shipyard.[19]

Gould Pumps manufactures many varieties of industrial pumps, and because pumps wear out, replacement demand is a major component of sales. Gould had five geographically separated product divisions, which meant that salespeople might have to place five separate orders (with each manufacturing division) for one customer order. Dispersed sales offices, 34 in all, including seven international offices further delayed order processing and sometimes resulted in nonstandardized price quotes. Gould wanted to create a system to retain customers, increase sales, and speed up shipping and delivery. It wanted to provide customers immediate information on pricing, order status, inventory availability, and shipping schedules and allow customers to dial into Gould's computers and look up the information themselves. The goal was a centralized system that would bypass and reduce the load on local sales offices, agents, and distributors.

Further, Gould wanted an international order-entry system that would eventually be integrated with inventory, plant scheduling, and shipping systems. The global network will link markets in the United States, Canada, Italy, West Germany, and Hong Kong. A planned next stage will link the customer order to bill of mate-

| FIGURE 18-5 | K-Line's Shipment Locator/Status Information System: A Global Network Integrating Voice, Data, Telex, and Fax Traffic |

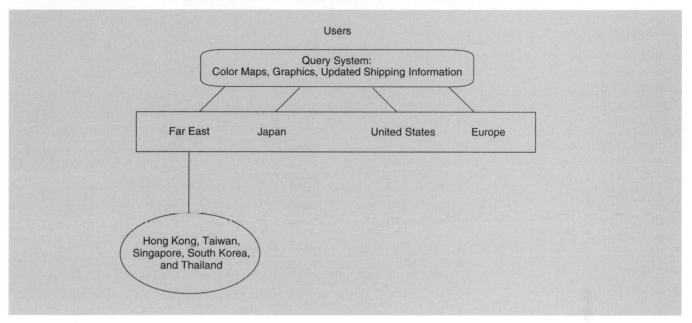

rials for the factories producing the pumps, especially as a pump's features and options vary, thus automating purchasing and providing links with preferred suppliers for components and subassemblies. In turn, this could lead to integrating all the manufacturing plants to provide just-in-time deliveries to customers. In short, an attempt to provide better customer service could lead to integration of several parts of the company, including purchasing, material requirements planning, outside sourcing, production control, and costing.

In summary, combining an understanding of the buyer together with interaction variables (described previously) helps shape a global network that can aid a firm in improving the quality of its relationship marketing to industrial customers worldwide. A supplementary benefit is that aggregating information gathered from customers scattered around the world will result in developing data about individual country markets, as well as about individual products in a product line.

LINKAGES WITH SUPPLIERS

The second major focus of global networks is linkages with suppliers. Several factors mediate this relationship. Foremost is the intent behind the business purchase transaction. Is the relationship intended to be a long-term one, a strategic partnership? Why does the client firm seek a supplier? A strategic orientation arises out of a clear client firm mandate to reduce fixed costs and investments while seeking quality and lowered outsourcing costs; in turn, this may often lead to favoring one or a few suppliers in an effort to gain improved quality and closer coordination in design and manufacturing, as well as the traditional economies of scale. Table 18–3 outlines the variables affecting global linkages with suppliers.

Arising out of such a strategic orientation in seeking suppliers, the next question is, When does the supplier become involved? A critical concern is whether the supplier becomes involved at the design stage of a product's development, thereby affecting its integration into the buyer's final product, its manufacturing cost, manufacturable quality, ease of service, and so forth. Other kinds of involvement could

TABLE 18-3	Variables Affecting Global Linkages with Suppliers

Strategic Orientation	*Subcontractor or Partner?*
Stage of Involvement	At Design? (design for manufacturability)
Pricing Relationships	Sharing in cost reduction achieved by supplier, purchase volume-based price discounts
Delivery Terms	Just-in-time
Quality Standards	Contracted for targeted improvement
Compatibility of Capital Equipment and Communications Networks	CAD/CAM standards, EDI, transparent document interchange
Service Responsibilities	Subassemblies replaced by suppliers, joint service teams, spare parts provision, service data interchange and sharing with manufacturing
Technology Transfer	Safeguarding technology, technical assistance in implementing technology, second-sourcing

include supplying a long-term open order, guaranteeing incremental product performance improvements over the life of the order, providing customer support and warranty services and engaging in joint promotion.

Blenkhorn and Noori[20] break out the stages of involvement by Japanese suppliers with their OEM clients as follows:

- Market needs assessment
- R&D
- Design
- Test
- Product specification
- Make-or-buy decision
- Final assembly and shipment

They found that Japanese OEMs typically concentrate on market needs assessment and final assembly and shipment, leaving all other stages to the supplier, with the make-or-buy decision going in favor of outsourcing. They contrast this with a typical North American pattern, where suppliers mainly perform as subcontracting manufacturers, with all product design and test phases carried out by the client (OEM) firm itself. While this dichotomy represents two extremes, the point is that outsourcing as a strategic decision requires greater supplier involvement and is the first and key question to be asked. Several other consequences follow from this first strategic decision.

EXAMPLES OF GLOBAL SUPPLIER LINKAGES

We now briefly review case studies of recent corporate attempts to develop global networks with overseas suppliers.

Mast Industries

Mast is the manufacturing and sourcing arm of The Limited, responsible for supplying Limited subsidiaries such as Limited, Lerner, Abercrombie & Fitch, Victoria's Secret, and various catalog businesses. Mast does not generate clothing ideas itself. Instead, buyers for the various Limited retail subsidiaries come to Mast with garment ideas for their stores. Mast's job is to get the clothing produced and make it available on time for the various Limited subsidiaries. Mast works with independent factories in Hong Kong, Taiwan, Singapore, Korea, and in Europe. One of its objectives is to reduce the turnaround time it takes to get the items into the stores (i.e., reduce the off-shore production and sourcing time). Mast has gradually evolved a system that allows requests to be filled within 30 to 60 days compared to 3 to 10 months taken by competing specialty and department stores.[21] This allows buying decisions to be delayed until consumer needs can be more clearly assessed. The short production time also means that smaller repeat orders can be placed, instead of one large order early in the buying season. In turn, this reduces the risk of having excess unsold inventory at the retail stores, which consequently obviates the need for end-of-season sales at discount prices. Thus, initial prices need not be as high, as they would not have to be to absorb the losses on unsold end-of-season merchandise. These lower initial prices can translate into increased market share. Figure 18–6 details the workings of Mast's global supply network.

Mast's system uses videoconferencing and high-definition TV (HDTV) to facilitate global discussion on fabric colors and textures. The 35 mm photograph quality of HDTV allows fabric comparisons between the Far East and the United States, allowing buyers and suppliers to zoom in on a complex print with enough detail to count the stitches in the cloth. This cuts down on travel time and, more importantly, allows for quick decisions: Instead of five days, the fabric decision can be made in a few hours, through such global teleconferencing. Similar results come from an electronic mail system linking Mast to its suppliers; it can request a quote from its overseas production network and receive a cost sheet overnight through the E-mail system, which increases the overall system responsiveness while also dealing with the major time difference between Mast's East Coast U.S. offices and the Far East suppliers.

Developing such global networks means overcoming several problems such as building or leasing high-speed communication facilities, which are not universally available worldwide. There are also regulatory problems, ranging from government controls over the kind and type of equipment to be used on a network to controls over the transmission of data across borders (transborder data flows). Customs clearances can hold up shipments, in response to which Mast has developed artificial intelligence systems to automatically determine the tariff classification of a garment and its duty rate, in order to expedite import and export of garments between Hong Kong and the United States (since quotas and tariffs are important in garment exports to the United States and Europe).

Texas Instruments

Texas Instruments has one of the most developed global networks, connecting 20 centers around the world with customers and suppliers. The system has been under development and evolution for over 20 years. The main goals are to maximize cost savings from manufacturing in the Asia/Pacific region and to create a design, manufacturing, and marketing presence close to customers throughout the world. Each business group, such as the semiconductor group, carries out marketing, production scheduling, and control on a worldwide basis. Orders from all over the world are aggregated each night, and then assembled materials, packing lists, and shipping orders are sent to the appropriate factory or warehouse. A product designer in Tokyo could transmit his specs to a fabrication facility in Texas, from which slices of silicon can be shipped to Malaysia for assembly and testing and then shipped directly to customers. Future goals include creating a single European customer database instead of separate ones for each business group; this would eventually become a global database.[22]

Benetton

One of the more advanced systems linking a firm with suppliers and customers is at Benetton, which is set out in Figure 18–7. Benetton's network is interesting because

FIGURE 18-6   **Mast Industries' Global Supply Network**

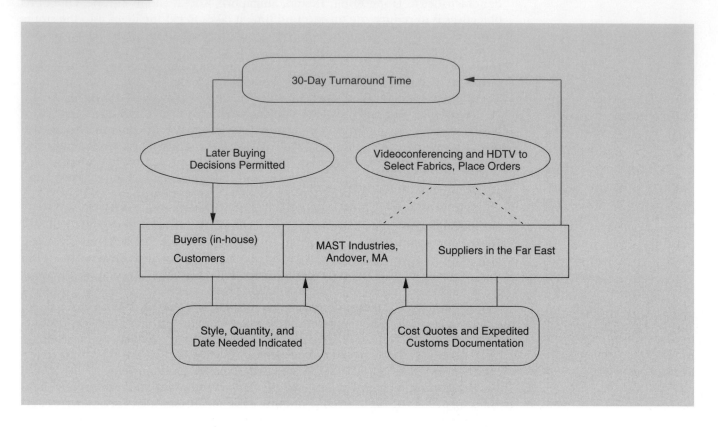

it has both company-owned retail outlets and franchisees and uses both in-house and subcontract manufacturing. As shown in Figure 18–7, Benetton analyzes sales from its owned outlets to forecast sales by product lines; this information is relayed to independent agents who use such information to increase orders from franchisees. Such orders are grouped and transmitted to Benetton factories and to subcontractors; up-to-date information allows for orders to be closed closer to the selling season, cutting down on unsold goods, and the speed of the system allows smaller orders to be placed later in the season. Close ties to manufacturing allows headquarters to respond to order status inquiries, and a subsystem allows Benetton to automate preparation of shipping and customs documents for a large number of countries, each with its own import, tariff, and shipping rules.

Information Technology and the Obsolete Inventory Problem

Information technology can help alleviate a serious problem that consumer goods marketers face: goods with short product life cycles that become obsolete, resulting in large losses to the firm because they have to write off excess inventories that cannot be sold through regular channels at normal retail prices. Firms have typically responded to this problem by trying to reduce production quantities, in which case they run the risk of lost sales on popular products whose demand exceeds the supply produced. Fisher et al.[23] have developed an interesting quick response production planning technique in which early market sales figures are used to adjust subsequent production schedules. Their approach was used to reduce losses from obsolescence for a company selling fashionable adult and children's ski-wear whose manufacturing was primarily subcontracted in Asia; a lengthy supply chain, the need to obtain raw materials such as fabric, zippers, and insulating materials from

FIGURE 18-7   **Supplier–Customer Linkages at Benetton**

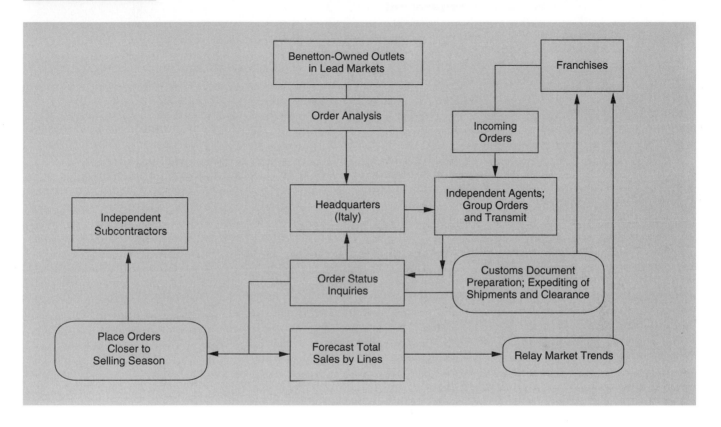

multiple geographically scattered sources, and the need to begin production eight months to a year ahead of the actual selling season all contributed to the complexity of the problem. The authors' solution, which is graphically displayed in Figure 18–8, encompasses the following steps:

1. Divide the product line into two categories, with one category containing items with more predictable demand, while the other includes products with more volatile demand.

2. Develop a team of seasoned marketing professionals who are asked to individually develop a sales forecast for the more volatile products, with specific forecasts for each product subdivided by color and style.

3. Statistically analyze the forecasts to develop a group mean or average forecast, as well as a measure of the dispersion or variance of individual forecasts about the mean. A larger variance indicates a product with highly volatile demand.

4. Use these initial forecasts to develop production schedules; the firm then contracts to buy a certain total amount of production capacity to be used over a period of months; some of this reserved production capacity is used during the initial months to produce products with less volatile demand as well as a portion of the total forecasted demand for the more fashionable items; that is, not all of the forecasted demand is scheduled for production.

FIGURE 18-8   **Reducing Risk of Obsolete Inventory through Multi-Stage Production Sequencing**

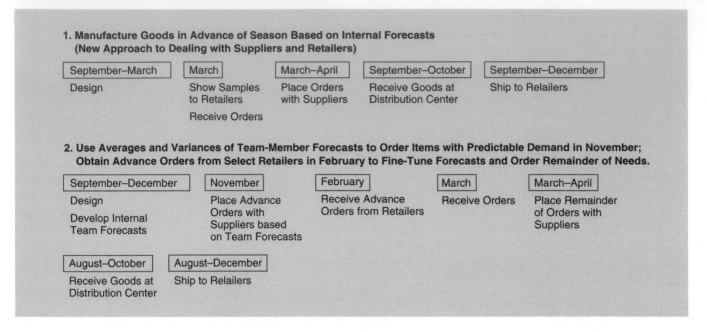

1. **Manufacture Goods in Advance of Season Based on Internal Forecasts (New Approach to Dealing with Suppliers and Retailers)**

September–March	March	March–April	September–October	September–December
Design	Show Samples to Retailers	Place Orders with Suppliers	Receive Goods at Distribution Center	Ship to Relailers
	Receive Orders			

2. **Use Averages and Variances of Team-Member Forecasts to Order Items with Predictable Demand in November; Obtain Advance Orders from Select Retailers in February to Fine-Tune Forecasts and Order Remainder of Needs.**

September–December	November	February	March	March–April
Design	Place Advance Orders with Suppliers based on Team Forecasts	Receive Advance Orders from Retailers	Receive Orders	Place Remainder of Orders with Suppliers
Develop Internal Team Forecasts				

August–October	August–December
Receive Goods at Distribution Center	Ship to Relailers

5. Obtain advance orders from a select group of influential retailers who together account for a significant portion of annual sales. Use these early orders as additional information to help team members develop revised forecasts. Based on these revised demand forecasts, the remaining production capacity is allocated among the various fashion products in accordance with the revised demand figures.

The net result of the above system, described by the authors as "risk-based multi-stage production sequencing," is fewer losses due to write-off of obsolete goods in inventory. At the same time, POS information and order-taking systems allow the firm to keep track of stockouts so that the forecasting system can be continually revised to ensure that foregone profits because of stockouts are balanced against losses caused by excess inventory. The heart of the system is the development of timely information and letting production schedules react to such timely market information.

In sum, industrial buyers throughout the world are seeking to reduce the number of suppliers they buy from, while negotiating longer-term agreements. They seek to link manufacturing with product design, inventory and shipping, and customer information. Designers seek closer links to suppliers to reduce excess inventory that could become obsolete. Not only does the firm have to communicate with outsiders, but it must also break down functional barriers within the organization. At a minimum, marketing and manufacturing will have to work together to design products that can be manufactured at low cost (the design for manufacturability environment) and together choose and coordinate working relationships with outside suppliers. Such networks are complex and costly, but seem quite necessary to doing business as a multinational.

SUBSIDIARY LINKAGES: SALES FORCE, DISTRIBUTION, SERVICE

While buyers and suppliers represent two principal nodes of the global network, there are other interests that must also be integrated. These include sales force interests, distribution and other aspects of the marketing system (promotion, for example), and service.

Sales force interests tend to concentrate on generating sales leads, obtaining up-to-date customer profiles and sales histories, a sales call scheduling and monitoring system, inventory availability and shipping dates, prices and discounts or deals allowable, and competitive pressures pertinent to each sales lead. In global industrial markets, a special issue is the use of multinational and multifunctional leads, with a drawn-out selling cycle. A progress reporting subsystem to monitor and summarize progress made at each visit with a sales lead, as well as communication capabilities between members of the sales team are necessary elements of the network.

Service tends to be a major element of successful industrial selling. Hence, global networks must include service subsystems. Pertinent issues include maintaining failure and service records, forecasting future failures from the service history of a product or parts family, keeping track of the cost of service, facilitating feedback to product design in order to facilitate incremental product improvements, and similar feedback to parts and subsystem suppliers for similar corrective action. Also important is record keeping on the cost of providing service, customer satisfaction with service, field parts inventory adequacy for service calls, and comparative competitor performance in the service area, including comparative warranty information and comparative mean-time between failure statistics. Providing service in the international arena is complicated by distance, the number of locations from which service is provided, location and availability of warehouses and parts, training and dispatch of technical personnel, and providing technical information in enhancing the quality of service performed. Basically, there are two central service issues: providing field service to enhance customer satisfaction at reasonable cost and using service feedback to enhance product design and quality of next-generation products, particularly through incremental improvements. Rather than providing some absolute level of service, the cost of downtime to the customer can be used to tailor the quality and intensity of service provided.[24]

GLOBAL NETWORKS AND MANAGEMENT CONTROL ISSUES

The shape of global networks is also affected by organization structure and management control needs.[25] These management control and organizational issues surrounding the implementation of global marketing systems are summarized in Table 18–4.

Critical points outlined in Table 18-4 include:

- ◆ Enhancing management efficiency through applications in areas such as order entry, sales calls, and expense reporting, product profitability analysis by region and customer, databases of technical product specifications, and so forth.

- ◆ Managing the selling process, through information that permits client and product profitability analysis, comparing actual sales with targets or quotas, and sales trend forecasting.

- ◆ Managing the manufacturing subcontracting process, with data on costs, quality, and delivery performance; spending on joint design and research, and comparative information on product and process improvement.

- ◆ Managing the customer relationship, through databases of customer purchases, customer complaints, and other feedback; and direct links with customers using approaches such as EDI (covered in detail in a subsequent section).

- ◆ Facilitating management control, with immediately accessible up-to-date information allowing managers to perform the computer equivalent of management by walking around; strolling through successive levels and

TABLE 18–4	**Implementing Global Marketing Systems**
Managerial Issues	Managing customers, suppliers Marketing efficiency: sales force control; forecasting, analysis, and planning; statistical capabilities; competitive assessment Environmental monitoring: governments, consumers, competition, technology, and legal aspects Database commonality
Organizational Issues	Opening up the firm: ◆ Externally, with customers/suppliers ◆ Internally, with manufacturing and others Sharing data: value of information; availability of information, access levels, frequency of access
Technological Issues	Use of EDI, data transfer problems, transmission protocols Data networks: use of third party VANs, VSAT private data (satellite-based) networks Data security, controlling access—hackers and viruses Government regulation on transborder data flows; data privacy issues Compatibility of equipment: computers, data transmission Legal responsibilities in using computer linkages with suppliers and customers

finer decompositions of a customer database can help trace causes of sales declines; for example, a shortfall in a regional quota can be traced to a particular customer, and to a division at a customer, where a change in the manufacturing process has led to a switch in the raw material specifications, resulting in a competitor's product being preferred. While the salesman might know this information, having such information reside in a central database might permit faster reaction and more appropriate response at a higher level of the organization.

◆ Environmental monitoring, particularly important with diverse country markets and national differences in regulations and standards.

◆ Statistical analysis capabilities, in areas such as market share shifts, the isolation of market segments across countries, and customer reaction to management actions such as promotions, new product improvements, changes in service levels, enhanced delivery and the like. For example, Frito-Lay, the snack foods company, used such capabilities to trace reduced market share in a region to the introduction of a generic store brand; having such data allowed a quick counter-response and elimination of the problem.

It should be apparent that management control draws on a set of databases and statistics that is also relevant to linkages with customers and with suppliers. The difference is in the level of aggregation and analysis to which such data are subject; timeliness and speed of response are what interests management. Hence, from the management control perspective, greater emphasis will be placed on the communication network itself and on cost/benefit trade-offs in articulating the database and communications network configuration. Implementation is always a management preoccupation, and it is clear that a full-blown global network is a major corporate undertaking, requiring considerable analysis and commitments of time and money. Hence, management is more likely to opt for a phased implementation approach, in the sense of building a full-scale global network for one product line, then, using the learning from this effort to extend the concept to other product lines at the firm. Such an approach will more clearly identify the difficulties involved in extending global networks to various countries, and also the coordination required to tie suppliers and customers into such a network.

An important question is the value of information, and firms must decide how much information to make available to outside partners such as customers or suppliers. Often, a hierarchical system of differential levels of access is set up, with a larger quantity and more sensitive information being provided to partners and clients where the strategic relationship is stronger and of greater duration. The firm must also be concerned about the cost and time required to implement such networks, including finding or designing appropriate software and getting partner collaboration in implementing such efforts; the technologies and management styles inherent in using a global network are being adopted at different rates in various overseas markets. As a consequence, overseas suppliers may be unable to successfully implement their end of a network. Their relative ignorance may also lead them to oppose such networking attempts. Such reluctance slows down the pace of implementing a global network, and the firm must then be willing to spend time and effort on training its partners to make full and effective use of global networks. One such example is Pier 1's approach to supply and distribution networks, which is set out in Figure 18–9.

Technological Issues in Developing Global Networks

Developing global networks is partly an exercise in developing a global information and communications network. Several computer-related technical issues affect such network development. Foremost is the growing global use of electronic data interchange (EDI), and of third-party value-added networks (VANs). Figure 18–10 summarizes the basic characteristics of using EDI. "Seventy percent of one business computer's input is actually the output of another business computer" (Jerry Hershney, systems analyst at Sears Chicago). If the data could be directly transferred, time, errors, and expense are all saved. EDI has grown from this premise.

EDI can be described as computers doing business with one another, or more accurately, the transfer of business transactions directly between computers. EDI is a process used to automate standardized data exchange between business partners. Thus, a buyer could set up EDI with his vendors to buy on a just-in-time basis, with all orders being electronically transmitted directly to the vendor's computer systems; in turn, he could directly query the vendors' manufacturing database to ascertain the status of his order, how far along it is, and when delivery is likely to be scheduled. Then, upon shipment, the buyer uses EDI to instruct his bank to electronically transfer funds in payment.

The potential advantages from EDI are immense,[26] because it can save on duplication of data entry, decrease errors, and raise productivity. EDI can reduce pipeline inventory and the time goods wait at loading docks and in warehouses. The problem in implementing EDI globally is that foreign suppliers, who may be small in relation to the client firm, do not have EDI capability and have to make an effort to learn how to do business using EDI. EDI, of course, cannot happen without a telecommunications network that can hook up users on disparate computer systems. Such networks have developed to a far greater extent in the United States than in Japan or Europe, with the smaller emerging markets lagging. Access to a network through which to send and receive data, compatibility with the existing order entry and inventory systems, data security (outsider access to a host computer via a network), and the cost of computing equipment and associated software are all factors impeding use of EDI by users around the world. Table 18–5 outlines some of the managerial and technical network issues relevant to EDI implementation. But the biggest factor hindering widespread adoption is a lack of confidence in a system that does away with paper forms in triplicate and with tried

FIGURE 18-9   **Pier 1's Supply and Distribution Network**

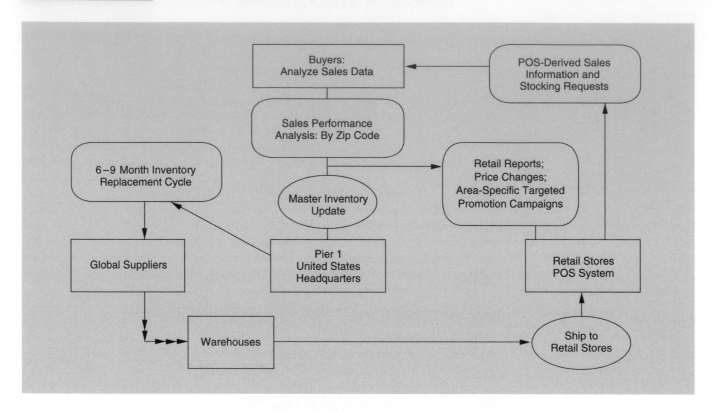

and trusted accounting systems. In conducting such data interchanges, a common data format is essential. When Greenwood Mills, a fabric producer, used EDI to link up with customers, an impediment was fabric bolt sizes. Greenwood used standard measurements such as 36" and 48" fabric sizes, these being minimum measurements. But customers who used numerical control machines needed to communicate exact sizes to their fabric-cutting machines, whether the bolt was actually 37 or 37.5 inches wide. Hence, they had to remeasure the shipments. Fabric color needed similar standardization as Greenwood used names for different colors, while customers measured fabric color by its variance from a standard color such as red. In order to use EDI with customers, Greenwood had to reconfigure the product database for exact bolt sizes and color variances. A Textile Apparel Linkage Council (TALC) has been formed to standardize terminology among the various companies, suppliers and customers in the U.S. textile industry. Similar vertical industry groups have formed across industries both in the United States and in Europe and the Far East, and a major implementation problem is reconciling incompatible standards within industries and across industries.

SUMMARY   Multinational corporations face an increasingly complex task of communicating and coordinating with their global customers and suppliers. The main components of such a network include linkages with customers, with suppliers, with the sales force and other elements of the marketing system, including distribution, promotion, and after-sales service. Factors such as customer profiles, the complexity of the product and the selling cycle, the strategic nature of the partnership, and the level of interdependence all influence the design and detail built into the network. Another set of influences on the network are managerial issues such as efficiency, mar-

FIGURE 18-10   **A Basic Approach to EDI**

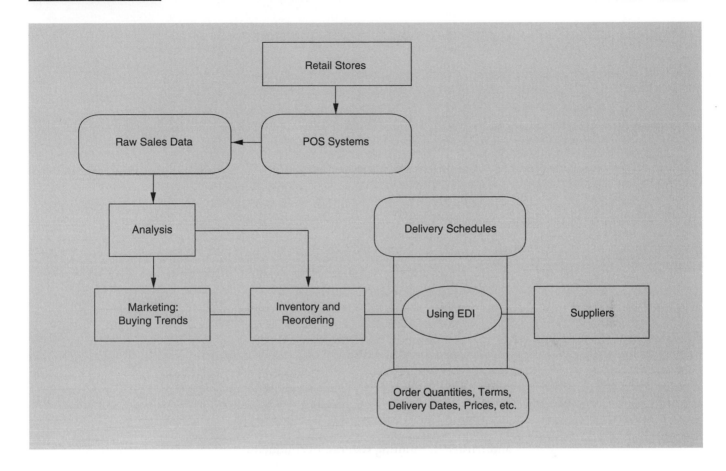

ket research needs, forecasting and analysis and planning, environmental monitoring and competitive assessment, and sales force and marketing control. Just as important are organizational issues, since creating such a network forces greater openness with customers and with other functional areas within the corporation. Technical issues such as the value of information made available to outsiders, the use of technologies such as electronic data interchange (EDI), third-party value-added networks (VANs), data security problems and controlled access, and government regulations limiting freedom of transborder data flows are also pertinent.

QUESTIONS

18.1   How can information technology (IT) change the practice of international marketing?

18.2   How did IT help Mattel become a more efficient global marketer?

18.3   What are some principal features of a global marketing network? What obstacles make it difficult to create such a network?

18.4   What are the different kinds of information needed by global marketing networks?

18.5   How can a company be said to compete in both the marketplace and the marketspace?

18.6   What is a virtual shopping environment? How can it be used by international marketing managers?

18.7   How does IT help implement the concept of mass customization? Discuss Peapod's approach to mass customization.

TABLE 18–5	EDI: A Checklist

Managerial Issues	Technical Network Issues
◆ Get orders right: timely receipt of and acknowledgement of orders. ◆ Accurate remittance notices, advising that a payment has been made. ◆ Payments made with EDI to suppliers must be 100 percent accurate. The correct amount must be credited to the correct account on time. ◆ Separation of payment details from remittance data (information on what is being paid for, which account should be credited, etc.). Separation creates a reconciliation problem: payments to client accounts. ◆ Ample time for implementation, permitting a careful evaluation before move from pilot use to full-scale volume and time for installation, training. ◆ Expandability, to be able to add new trading partners. Low cost of adding partners is a must, facilitated by VAN support programs to educate new trading partners and get them up and running. ◆ Confidentiality and data ownership issues. Sensitive firm and client data are being sent on the network, and confidentiality must be preserved. ◆ Security, preventing unauthorized access, error correction, and providing audit trails. ◆ Legal responsibility: When errors are made, who is responsible for consequences? The firm, the client, the provider of the physical VAN? ◆ Government regulations governing access to and the cost of using data networks and satellite communications; also, national data privacy laws affecting the database design of such networks. ◆ Build your own, or use a third party network (VAN)? As the volume of EDI transactions increases, larger EDI users will find it more economical to develop their own EDI transmission networks, though this means investing in special fault tolerant hardware and software combinations.	◆ Volume of data transmitted: network must be able to handle peak data traffic. ◆ 24-hour access to the network, 24-hour uptime (i.e., using alternate routes to avoid parts of the network that are defective, guarding against disasters such as power outages, electrical storms, hurricanes, etc.). ◆ Store and forward capability so that users can access data and documents at their convenience. This means building fast search and query capabilities when dealing with diverse databases and database software. ◆ Ability to handle different physical data characteristics, such as SNA, asynchronous, and so forth. ◆ Ability to handle different rates of data transmission speeds. ◆ Data standards and security of payment: There are competing and sometimes incompatible standards between the United States and Europe. ◆ Cost: generally, a fixed fee plus charges based on volume of data traffic, plus software to handle EDI, covering the technical issues outlined above. ◆ EDI software supporting multiple software platforms such as workstations, mainframes, Windows, and Unix; and integration with in-house financial software so that one company's purchase order system can communicate with another company's order recipt and processing system. ◆ Inter-networking capability (when a trading partner works through a different third-party EDI network). This is crucial for global EDI, since local VANs will often provide EDI services in their countries and may have incompatible equipment and standards.

Source: Developed from various sources including: "Product Spotlight: Electronic Data Interchange," *Computerworld*, March 26, 1990, October 5, 1992; and, Electronic Data Interchange Association documents.

18.8   Distinguish between customer information and customer interaction variables.

18.9   Discuss how companies such as Liz Claiborne, K-Line, and Gould Pumps have used global customer linkages to enhance their international marketing efforts.

18.10   What variables should a company keep in mind in designing global supplier linkages?

18.11   Discuss the examples of Texas Instruments, Benetton, and Mast Industries as models for developing global supplier linkages.

18.12   How can IT help firms reduce losses from obsolete goods?

18.13   What are some management control and organizational issues underlying the implementation of global marketing networks?

18.14   What is electronic data interchange (EDI)? How can it help a firm's international marketing efforts?

18.15   How do technical and managerial issues affect the creation and implementation of EDI networks?

ENDNOTES

[1] Cheri Speier, Michael G. Harvey, and Jonathan Palmer, "Virtual Management of Global Marketing Relationships," *Journal of World Business* 33 no. 3 (September 22, 1998): 263.

[2] Rashi Glazer, "Marketing in an Information-Intensive Environment: Strategic Implications of Knowledge as an Asset," 55, no. 5, (October 1991): 1–19.

[3] Rowland T. Moriarty, and Gordon Swartz, "Automation to Boost Sales and Marketing," *Harvard Business Review,* January–February 1989, 100–108.

[4] Jeffrey Rayport and John J. Sviokla, "Exploiting the Virtual Chain," *Harvard Business Review,* November–December 1995, 75–85.

[5] Raymond R. Burke, "Virtual Shopping: Breakthrough in Marketing Research," *Harvard Business Review,* March–April 1996.

[6] "A Survey of Retailing: Change at the Checkout," *The Economist,* March 4, 1995.

[7] "The Internet: Selling Points," *The Wall Street Journal,* Special Report, December 7, 1998; and Gary Hamel and Jeff Sampler, "The E-Corporation," *Fortune,* December 7, 1988.

[8] Bernice Kanner, "The Bad Man Cometh: Interview with Saatchi and Saatchi Worldwide CEO Kevin Roberts," *Chief Executive,* December 1998.

[9] Michelle Wirth Fellman, "Globalization: Worldwide Economic Woes Force Global Marketers to Seek New Opportunities— or Ways to Ride Out the Storm," *Marketing News,* December 7, 1998.

[10] "Amazon Denies Euro Debut Will Spark Price War," *Marketing,* May 7, 1998.

[11] "Smart Cards: Who Needs Them?" *LatinFinance,* September 1, 1998.

[12] Gwendolyn Smith, "Mastering the Art of Global Marketplace Exposure," *Marketing,* July 20, 1998.

[13] Warren R. Ross, "Networks Can Beat the Conflict Taboo; Interview with Torre Lazur Healthcare Group CHMN and CEO Joe Torre," *Medical Marketing & Media,* December 1998.

[14] See also R. Benjamin, and R. Wigand. "Electronic Markets and Virtual Value Chains on the Information Superhighway," *Sloan Management Review,* Winter 1995, 62–72.

[15] B. Joseph Pine II, D. Peppers, and Martha Rogers, "Do You Want to Keep Your Customers Forever," *Harvard Business Review,* March April 1995.

[16] Regis McKenna, "Real-Time Marketing," *Harvard Business Review,* July–August 1995.

[17] Steven E. Prokesch, "Competing on Customer Service: An Interview with British Airways' Sir Colin Marshall," *Harvard Business Review,* November–December 1995.

[18] "Tracking Freight Ship-to-Shore," *Computerworld,* June 11, 1990.

[19] "Freighter Plays Electronic Tag," *Computerworld,* May 7, 1990.

[20] David L. Blenkhorn and A. Hamid Noori, "What It Takes to Supply Japanese OEMs," *Industrial Marketing Management,* 19, no. 1, (1990): 21–30.

[21] "A Classic IS Approach to Fashion," *Computerworld,* April 2, 1990, 50.

[22] A. Pantages, "TI's Global Window," *Datamation,* September 1, 1989.

[23] Marshall L. Fisher, J. Hammond, W. Obermeyer, and A Raman, "Making Supply Meet Demand in an Uncertain World," *Harvard Business Review,* May–June 1994, 83–93.

[24] M. Cohen and Hau Lee, "Out of Touch with Customer Needs? Spare Parts and After-sales Service," *Sloan Management Review,* Winter 1990, 55–66.

[25] Don E. Schultz, "Structural Straitjackets Stifle Integrated Success," *Marketing News,* March 1, 1999.

[26] Robert Benjamin, David W. de Long, and M. S. Scott Morton, "Electronic Data Interchange: How Much Competitive Advantage?" *Long-Range Planning* 23, no. 1 (February 1990): 29–40.

FURTHER READINGS

Benjamin, R., and Wigand, R. "Electronic Markets and Virtual Value Chains on the Information Superhighway." *Sloan Management Review,* Winter 1995: 62–72.

Bishop, Bill *Global Marketing for the Digital Age: Globalize Your Business with Digital and Online Technology.* Canada: Harper Collins, 1998.

Bishop. Bill and W. Bishop. *Strategic Marketing for the Digital Age.* NTC Business Books, 1998

Bishop, Mark. *How to Build a Successful International Web Site.* The Coriolis Group, Bk&CD-Rom edition, February 1998.

Burke, Raymond R. "Virtual Shopping: Breakthrough in Marketing Research." *Harvard Business Review,* March–April 1996.

Cronin, Mary. ed. *Banking and Finance on the Internet.* John Wiley & Sons, 1997.

Cronin, Mary. *Global Advantage on the Internet: From Corporate Connectivity to International Connectiveness.* John Wiley & Sons, 1995.

Cronin, Mary. *The Internet Strategy Handbook: Lessons from the New Frontier of Business.* Harvard Business School Press, 1996.

Fisher, Marshall L., J. Hammond, W. Obermeyer, and A. Raman. "Making Supply Meet Demand in an Uncertain World." *Harvard Business Review,* May–June 1994, 83–93.

Glazer, Rashi. "Marketing in an Information-Intensive Environment: Strategic Implications of Knowledge as an Asset." 55, no. 5 (October 1991) 1–19.

Kosiur, D. *Understanding Electronic Commerce. Strategic Technology Series.* Microsoft Press, 1997.

McKenna, Regis. "Real-Time Marketing." *Harvard Business Review,* July–August 1995.

Mougayar, W. *Opening Digital Markets : Battle Plans and Business Strategies for Internet Commerce.* 2nd ed. McGraw-Hill, 1997.

Nemzow, M. *Building Cyberstores: Installation, Transaction Processing, and Management.* Bk&CD-Rom ed. Computing McGraw-Hill, 1997.

O'Mahoney, Donald et al. *Electronic Payment Systems.* Artech House, 1997.

Pine II, B. Joseph, D. Peppers, and Martha Rogers. "Do You Want to Keep Your Customers Forever?" *Harvard Business Review,* March–April 1995.

Silversteain, Barry. *Business-to-Business Internet Marketing: Five Proven Strategies for Increasing Profits through Internet Direct Marketing.* Maximum Press, 1998.

Rayport, Jeffrey and John J. Sviokla. "Exploiting the Virtual Chain." *Harvard Business Review,* November–December 1995, 75–85.

Rockwell, Browning. *Using the Web to Compete in a Global Marketplace.* John Wiley & Sons, 1998.

Szuprowicz, Bohdan. *Extranets and Intranets: E-Commerce Business Strategies for the Future.* Computer Technology Research Corporation, 1998.

Tapscott, Doan, A. Lowry, and D. Ticoll. eds. *Blueprint to the Digital Economy: Wealth Creation in the Era of E-Business.* McGraw-Hill, 1998.

Thomas, Jerry W. "Brave New World: Strategic Impact of the Internet." *Communication World,* no. 4 (March, 1998), 15, 38.

Vartanian, Thomas P., R. H. Ledig, and L. Bruneau. *21st Century Money, Banking and Commerce.* Fried, Frank, Harris, Shriver & Jacobson, May 1998.

Whinston, Andrew, D. O. Stahl, and S-Y Choi. *The Economics of Electronic Commerce.* Macmillan Technical Publishing, 1997.

Romm, Celia and Sudweeks, Fay. eds. *Doing Business Electronically: A Global Perspective of Electronic Commerce.* Springer Verlag, 1998.

The Future of International Marketing

International marketing is about identifying the needs of customers around the world and then satisfying these needs better than one's competitors. Consequently, the future of international marketing will be shaped by how global customer needs are changing and how global competition is evolving to satisfy those needs.

The main goals of this chapter are to

1. Describe what is happening in global markets and how global customers are changing.

2. Describe how the global competitive system is evolving.

3. Discuss the ways in which a firm can respond in order to gain a competitive edge in global markets.

GLOBAL CUSTOMERS AND GLOBAL MARKETS

The term **global markets** points to a major evolution of the global economy. The world is truly composed of many markets. It used to be that firms could prosper by selling mainly to the U.S. market. The triad economy is now a fact of life, however. Japan and its neighboring countries constitute a bloc of fast-growing economies with considerable discretionary incomes. A second major bloc is Europe, poised for further growth and prosperity with the formation of the European Union and the adoption of the Euro. The third bloc is NAFTA—United States, Canada, and Mexico—also a pool of wealth and purchasing power. Table 19–1 summarizes the size and wealth of the three major developed economies.

The Japanese Opportunity

Japan offers one of the most attractive and difficult markets of the world. It ostensibly has one of the highest per capita incomes in the world, but standards of living are not as commensurately high. A study by the Union Bank of Switzerland (UBS) found that net domestic purchasing power in 1987 was twice as high in the United States as in Japan,[1] even though the yen had been appreciating against the dollar for the previous two years. By adjusting for what the Japanese could buy with their yen, UBS found that high prices in Japan canceled out the effect of high incomes.

Japan's attraction lies partly in its steady long-term growth. Between 1967 and 1993, Japan's GDP grew over 6 percent a year, the highest among the advanced industrial nations. Adjusting for purchasing power parity, Japan's GDP per capita was 87 percent of U.S. levels by 1992 and has stayed at approximately these levels for the past few years because of economic recession in Japan. High Japanese prices represent a major opportunity for foreign companies. Japanese savings rates are still high, but domestic consumption and spending have been growing rapidly. The Japanese have begun to spend heavily on housing, consumer durables, and luxury goods, though recent economic stagnation has caused them to become cautious and seek value, becoming more price conscious. If foreign companies can penetrate the Japanese market and can match Japanese products in quality, high domestic prices will provide a wedge with which to gain market share from Japanese firms.

Domestic prices are high in Japan because of its internal distribution system, with far too many small retailers tied to specific suppliers and granted liberal credit and offered liberal sales-return policies. The system is inefficient, and only now has slowing GDP growth created pressure to discount prices.[2] Thus, if foreign companies can penetrate the Japanese market and if they can cut prices while matching quality, they stand to gain significant market share. This is the Japanese challenge and opportunity.

Japan's Neighbors

While Japan is important in itself as one of the wealthy nations of the world, its neighboring countries are growing even more rapidly. South Korea, Taiwan, Hong Kong, Singapore, Malaysia, and Thailand are among the fastest-growing countries of the world, with Taiwan's per capita income exceeding $10,000. Taiwan is now becoming actively involved in providing foreign aid to developing countries. Then there is China, where incomes have tripled since 1979, with southern China's Pearl River delta being the fastest-growing region in the world—12 percent annually! Even India, after nearly 50 years of socialism, seems to be waking up to the positive benefits of opening up its economy and letting multinationals in to compete with formerly protected domestic firms.

Simply put, the growth in discretionary incomes in these areas makes them attractive to companies whether they be from the United States or elsewhere. The Asian crisis beginning in 1997, while serious, should not call into question the true

TABLE 19-1	The Triad Economy, 1994	
	GDP (Trillions of Dollars)	*Population (Millions)*
United States	$6.6	265
European Union	7.0	368
Japan	4.3	125

long-term growth potential of these economies. The net result of economic growth around the world is that in nearly every industry sector over half the potential world demand is outside the United States; this is why global markets and global marketing are important.

The Opportunities of European Union

Europe has always been an important market for U.S. companies because of geographic and cultural proximity. The passage of the Single Europe Act and the creation of European Union have raised worldwide interest in European markets. Many barriers that are physical, technical, and fiscal in nature are gradually disappearing:

♦ Border controls

♦ Divergent product standards

♦ Different technical regulations

♦ Conflicting business laws

♦ Protected public procurement

♦ Differences in taxation (value-added taxes, or VAT, and excise taxes)

The real gains of European Union may lie in the removal of these barriers, which together have served to stop entrepreneurs in one European country from entering the same business in other European countries. The removal of barriers can also benefit non-European companies, however, provided they receive the same treatment as European firms. From a marketing perspective, the gains are great from not having to adapt a product to the divergent standards of 12 different countries. Similarly, companies will benefit from being able to compete for government orders with a superior product; this was a market segment formerly closed to all but national companies.

The reasoning behind creating European union is that the enlarged single market will lead to more competition; at the same time, the larger market created through merging the various national markets will allow larger-volume production, leading to economies of scale and thus bringing down costs. Enhanced competition, economies of scale, and the drive to greater efficiency should all lead to lower consumer prices, more jobs, higher profits, and ultimately, a more prosperous Europe.[3] Not surprisingly, companies from the United States and Japan, as well as from other countries, have been busy establishing themselves in Europe as its Single Market is established. The concern here is that they be treated as insiders and not discriminated against in case a fortress-Europe mentality sets in.

Liberalization in Eastern Europe

Another interesting market trend is the liberalization movement in Eastern Europe and in Russia itself. After decades of stagnation and dead-end economic philosophies, these nations have suddenly decided on a free-market orientation. The Eastern European nations are relatively small in size and population, but they all possess a relatively well-educated work force. In addition, Russia has the attraction of a large domestic population, the world's largest reserves of unexploited natural resources, and significant technological capabilities in some areas. Participating in their economic growth will mean getting direct access to a market with increasing purchasing power and long-repressed consumption desires.

Although these internal markets may be slow to develop, they represent an intriguing challenge. The Eastern European countries and their firms are not accustomed to working with Western-style, profit-oriented enterprises, and this could be an obstacle to growth initially. Helping these economies to develop through participating in their export-oriented industries, however, and supplying them much-needed hard currency will prove to be an advantage at a later stage when their domestic market begins to grow. Russia's severe economic difficulties have raised questions about the permanency of its transition to capitalist modes of operation. Political risk is high and it may take some years before Russia regains an even economic keel. But many of its Eastern European neighbors are progressing more smoothly and the opportunities are undeniable. Table 19–2 summarizes the promise of Eastern European markets.

Incidentally, developing countries present much the same opportunity profiles as Eastern European countries. They are also similarly beset with the need to grow and raise domestic standards of living while suffering from shortages of capital, outmoded ideologies, and wasteful antibusiness bureaucracies. As they strive for economic growth, less developed countries also offer immense market potential, particularly for basic products and consumer durables.

GLOBAL TRENDS

Global Markets, but Distinct Markets

Significant differences exist among the growing markets in Europe and the Far East. Even within the United States, a large and growing Hispanic market is attracting distinct marketing and advertising themes. Hence, a continuing basic issue for companies will be that of standardization versus differentiation. Homogenization of tastes and moves such as the creation of a Single Europe encourage product standardization, but cultural and historical differences are sufficiently strong that some adaptation will be beneficial to increasing market share. The marketing challenge lies in knowing how much standardization is appropriate and in deciding which elements of the product mix should be adapted to individual country and regional markets.

More Customers for New Products

The rise of global markets means that the total market size for new products is expanding. In looking over new-product introductions of the past decade, we find several new products that have been successful in all of the triad economies, including the following:

♦ The personal stereo popularly known as the Walkman
♦ The fax machine
♦ Express mail and overnight small-package delivery services
♦ The entire packaged software industry (as opposed to developing custom software for individual clients)
♦ Compact disk players and compact disk recordings
♦ Mountain bikes

TABLE 19-2	Marketing Implications of Change in Eastern Europe

1. Eastern Europe is backward and wants to develop. It will be a market for capital goods and technology.

2. The private sector is just beginning to emerge. A market for consumer goods may be slow to develop, though there is much repressed demand.

3. Wages are low; hence, they can be a source of low-cost production. GM produces autos in Hungary for this reason.

4. Health care and food products are likely to be growth markets.

5. The main mode of entry is likely to be joint ventures and countertrade. Eastern Europe lacks capital with which to buy foreign goods: hence, the importance of countertrade. Export-oriented ventures will receive high priority.

The list includes consumer products, business products, and services. Clearly, a market will always exist for well-thought-out new products. The difference is that these new products can now be sold in several middle- and upper-income countries in the Far East, Europe, and North America. A successful product can yield even higher profits, and the larger total market justifies taking more risk and spending larger amounts on R&D.

The Newly Rich: A Growing Global Market Segment

A striking aspect of new products is the entire category of "luxury goods."[4] By this we mean products such as Chanel perfumes and scarves, Gucci shoes and handbags, Lalique crystal, Vuitton luggage, haute couture in Paris, and Patek Phillipe watches. Common to these products is the idea that price is irrelevant. These products are as likely to be purchased in Japan, Taiwan, and Hong Kong as in Europe or the United States. Their market has expanded enormously. We can talk of a homogenization of taste for luxury products. More to the point, however, is the spread of a profitable consumer market segment across countries, a spread from the Old World to the New, and then to the newly rich Orient. The rise of global markets is also resulting in new and larger market segments across countries, which may have been ignored previously as too narrow to be profitable. Firms need to be attentive to these emergent phenomena of the global marketplace.

Services

As noted in Chapter 16, services are becoming increasingly important in world trade. As in the goods sector, foreign multinationals are beginning to challenge U.S. dominance in services. In some sectors, such as banking, European and Japanese banks have already caught up with U.S. firms. In others, such as international airlines, foreign airlines are moving fast to establish international networks as they seek market share in the growing Pacific Rim markets. Marketing services internationally is a major growth and profit opportunity and a sector that will become more intensely competitive.

The Infrastructure Projects Market

Development is impossible without adequate infrastructure, and emerging nations in Asia and South America are racing to build infrastructure such as electricity plants, telecommunications networks, airports and roads, and water-supply facilities. The capital needed to build such large projects is far beyond the available financial resources in these countries. As a result, many of these countries, such as

China, India, Mexico, and Indonesia, have turned to foreign capital. They have encouraged the participation of Western enterprises in building their infrastructure, often inviting them as partners in joint ventures with local companies.

A parallel endeavor that also attracts Western capital is privatization wherein state-owned companies and facilities are sold to private capital. The general presumption is that profit-oriented owners are likely to be more efficient as well as responsive to customers. The twin lures of privatization and the profit potential of emerging market infrastructure have lured many Western companies into countries such as India and China; an example is Enron's $2.8 billion Dabhol electricity project, which nearly ended in failure because of political opposition to profit-seeking Western corporations in the visible electricity-generation sector of India's economy.[5] As Wells and Gleason point out, Western infrastructure investment has all the characteristics of an **"obsolescing bargain,"** and Western firms have the greatest leverage when they are negotiating to bring in capital and technology to help build a nation's infrastructure. Once the plant has been built and is operational, the Western firm is on less solid ground, as its continued ownership is not as necessary to the continued functioning of the project.[6] Hence, new modes of operation have developed, such as the *build-operate-transfer (BOT)* mode, in which the Western partners build and operate the utility or infrastructure project for a determined period and then sell the plant to local authorities or companies for a fee often agreed upon in advance.

A second aspect of such projects is reliance on **project financing,** whereby a considerable proportion, perhaps 80 percent, of the cost of the project is financed by loans often backed by government guarantees. Furthermore, loans may be provided by government export-import banks and by multilateral agencies such as the International Finance Corporation. Such projects are often bid on by consortia, such as in Indonesia's Paiton project, in which equity owners included Mission Energy from the United States and Mitsui Co. from Japan, with debt funding from the Exim banks of both the United States and Japan.[7] Such infrastructures represent attractive opportunities but also political risk. Western companies seeking to enter this market must ensure that national interests are addressed and given equal weight with their own profit-seeking motives. This is more likely to ensure a long-term, profitable relationship.

How Is Global Competition Evolving?

What makes a firm competitive in world markets? Table 19–3 summarizes the key factors. Global competition is intense and likely to become more so. As firms become larger in size, they seek to sell to all major markets in order to spread their growing fixed costs over a larger sales volume.

Global competition is not limited to competing for sales and market share, however. It also involves competing for knowledge and scarce resources. In any industry, multinationals avidly seek to nullify their competitors' technological edge.

Technology in the Global Marketplace

The search for information by multinationals leads to rapid spread of scientific knowledge and reduces the long-term competitive edge of having proprietary knowledge.[8] This fact of life in the global arena has two implications: One, a firm with proprietary knowledge had better constantly innovate and produce new technology, and two, if a technology advantage will be short-lived, the firm should earn rents from it by rapidly marketing it in the global marketplace. This can be accomplished by manufacture and worldwide sale of products embodying the technology, perhaps with joint-venture partners or by licensing it. What matters is that the technology be marketed in a timely enough manner to reap its benefits.

TABLE 19-3　　**Factors Affecting Competitiveness**

1. *Wage rates.* If a product is labor intensive, a low-wage country has an advantage.

2. *Productivity.* If workers work harder, produce better-quality products, using more up-to-date machines, the company/country is more efficient.

3. *Cost of capital.* If it costs less to borrow money or raise equity capital, a company can invest more and accept lower returns.

4. *Technology.* A country or company that is the first with an advanced-technology product, which can be protected by patents, has an advantage.

5. *Management.* This covers a variety of skills, including manufacturing and marketing skills, as well as ability to organize for worldwide operations. This is primarily a firm-specific issue, arising out of the quality and experience of its human resources.

6. *Government.* Domestic companies can be helped by their government's industrial policy providing subsidized funds for new-product research, development, and marketing. Government can also be a negative factor by imposing overregulation, high taxes, and controls on industry. In particular, the U.S. government, by running a budget deficit, drives up interest rates and hence the cost of capital.

7. *Exchange rates.* Prices charged in world markets are affected by exchange rates. As a currency gets stronger, it is harder to sell overseas; at the same time, the strong currency makes imports cheaper, driving up demand for imports.

8. *Country-specific factors.* A better-educated population, with a culture that stresses hard work, savings, and a concern for society at large is more likely to be competitive in world markets.

Environmental Factors Affecting Global Competition

Several environmental forces affect the firm's success in global markets:

- Government intervention, protection, and subsidies
- Fluctuating exchange rates
- High uncertainty caused by rapid, unforeseeable change

These environmental forces will either undercut or enhance the firm's marketing and managerial efforts in the same way that a headwind or a tailwind can slow down or speed up an aircraft. Their impact will be even greater in the future so marketing managers must be ever more alert to incorporating environmental effects in formulating their marketing plans and tactics.

For example, government intervention may result in more managed trade. In such cases, the firm's own government must be enlisted as a player to obtain support and win market share overseas. Government intervention may also be defensive, providing subsidies to enable the firm to recover from overwhelming foreign competition. If a system of tailored trade gains dominance, firms might be best off deciding to locate manufacturing and marketing facilities in each of the three triad economy blocs—Japan, the United States, and Europe. This may be suboptimal yet pragmatic.

Firms also need a long-range strategy to cope with exchange-rate fluctuations, paying heed to short-term transaction effects and also to longer-term competitive and market portfolio exposure. An environment with increased uncertainty places a premium on cautious management, one that avoids leverage, shares risk, and aims for steady long-term results rather than attempting to buy short-term market share and manage short-term earnings.

HOW CAN THE FIRM GAIN AN EDGE IN GLOBAL MARKETS?

A firm's competitive advantage derives from four sources:

- Labor productivity and labor costs.
- The cost of capital.

- ◆ Technology, both product and process, including information technology.
- ◆ Management and marketing skills, including speed of response, process manufacturing skills, and design skills, and managerial experience; the entrepreneurial spirit also falls into this category.

We have just seen that the technology is not long lasting and by itself is a precarious basis for long-term competitive advantage. Both cost of capital and labor cost are comparative advantages accruing to an entire economy rather than to one particular firm in a specific country. This leaves labor productivity and management skills, including marketing, as the central source of firm-specific and firm-controllable competitive advantage. *In other words, the company that markets the best will win out.*

The Strategic Challenge of European Union

One of the notable examples of government intervention affecting corporate strategy is the creation of a single European market. Table 19–4 summarizes some of the strategic implications of this event for U.S. corporations. As it indicates, a unified European market requires responses in all areas, not just marketing. Firms can best exploit the market potential of a single Europe by being aware of all strategic ramifications. The strategic issues outlined here have relevance beyond the European Union, however. Multinationals face similar issues stemming from new regional integration attempts such as NAFTA (North American Free Trade Association); Mercosur (the alliance among Latin American countries around the southern cone—Chile, Argentina, and Brazil); and APEC (Asia-Pacific Economic Cooperation, a loose grouping of 18 nations around the Pacific Rim, including the United States, Canada, Japan, and China).

Future Strategic Areas of Prime Importance

Looking to the future, global marketing strategy will be affected by certain strategy areas:

- ◆ Technology, radical innovation, and the related areas of incremental innovation and time-based competition
- ◆ Marketing itself, principally the question of global brands and their relation to other product attributes; also, customer orientation and the building of long-lasting relationships with customers, with benefits flowing from customer loyalty
- ◆ Organization structure and adaptation to strategic alliances, as well as the role of personal contacts in international markets
- ◆ Control issues, including the role of global information systems

Technology

We begin with technology because it is a fundamental source of new products. The pressing need is for applied technology that can be used to develop consumer and industrial products, rather than one-of-a-kind custom military products. Ideally, technology should be produced to serve customer needs rather than technological advances determining what products are developed. Furthermore, with consumer products, it is incremental innovation that matters rather than being the first to market with a new product. Companies must monitor new-product introductions by competition and then not only match them but improve on them.

If a new product is protected by patents,[9] competitors might try engineering around the innovation or perhaps mount a challenge to the patent—a viable strategy only for large companies competing against minnows. The real solution is to buy the needed technology, deliberately developing a strategy of cross-licensing. We earlier made reference to the quick spread of knowledge. One result is that no

TABLE 19-4 **The Single European Market: Strategic Issues for U.S. Corporations**

Competition
Stronger European companies.
Less allowance for inefficiency.
Europewide, not national, competition.

Entry Strategies
Expansion and acquisition.
Foreign direct investment.
Joint ventures and alliances.
Shakeouts and restructuring.

Government Relations
Government and industry associations to counter protectionism.
Lobbying in Brussels.

Manufacturing
Rationalization; larger, flexible plants.
Plant location; "greenfield" (starting from scratch) versus acquisition.
Logistics and JIT (just-in-time) implications.

Marketing
Sheer size: Europe will be as large as the U.S. market.
Aim at European rather than discrete national markets.
Europewide coordination and planning, restructuring of existing organization.
Europewide brands, distribution, pricing, and servicing.
National cultures will not disappear.

R&D
The effects of European government programs and subsidies.
"Local content" applied to R&D activities.
Cross-licensing.
The standards issue: global versus European versus U.S. standards.

one company can expect to dominate all technologies. Even IBM has begun forging strategic alliances to obtain crucial technologies not available in-house. Developing new semiconductor chips is becoming so risky that IBM teamed up with Siemens to develop 64 megabit DRAMS for sale in the mid-1990s.[10] Thus, cross-licensing and strategic alliances, together with incremental innovation, will become the backbone of new-product development efforts in the future.[11] Strategic alliances are particularly important to small firms, where resource scarcity and a lack of capital may hinder attempts to penetrate overseas markets. Such alliances also allow the smaller firm to share the risk of global market entry and allow it to enter several country markets in a timely, nearly simultaneous manner.

Incremental innovation is about making things better than the competition: better quality, more features, at lower cost, providing better service, and for longer periods. Manufacturing is involved here. Engineers working with salespeople and product designers increase the probability of creating new products that appeal to customers yet can be produced at high quality and reasonable cost. As suggested earlier in this text, marketing has linkages with other areas of the enterprise, notably technology and manufacturing.

Another emerging basis for competition is **time.** Being able to respond quickly to the marketplace and to competitive moves gives a firm a competitive edge. Such a quick-response capability depends heavily on design engineers and process technology. For example, new developments in flexible manufacturing allow companies to manufacture small batches of products quickly and economically. This reduces the importance of economies of scale and gives an advantage to the firm that can satisfy customers with a large variety of products.

Marketing

What about marketing itself? Are there crucial aspects of international marketing strategy that can help firms in the global marketplace? Global brand development is certainly one such concept.[12] There are few truly global brands, perhaps only one—Coca-Cola. A Landor Associates study showed Coke to have the number one brand awareness and esteem position in the United States, number two in Japan, and number six in Europe. No other brand comes even close to being in the top 10 in all three market areas. The only other global "brands" are media stars, such as Mick Jagger. Why is it so desirable to have a global brand?

A brand name allows a firm to charge more. Brands also ensure a certain degree of repeat purchases from loyal customers. Thus, a global brand could yield handsome returns on the investment necessary—through advertising and establishing a reputation for quality—to create it. Having a global brand means additional volume sales overseas, which in turn justifies additional expenditures to create new global brands and defend the established one.

There are many aspects to pursuing a global brand policy. Acquiring brands is one way to establish market position quickly. Creating new brands is another, as Toyota seems to be doing with Lexus in the United States, and as Honda has accomplished with immense success with the Acura car line. (These brands seem to be approaching global status.) Once created, brands must be defended; they can wither away unless continually tended to. Brand families are important, as shown by U.S. cereal companies that have been creating new cereals in response to such fads as the oat bran obsession. And global brands can be applied to services as well as products; Singapore Airlines is an example of an attempt to create a global service brand.

Aside from branding, global marketing must pay attention to all of a product's attributes. Global firms are increasingly competing on the basis of quality, design, and service, more than on the basis of low prices. These attributes are what a brand often stands for: dependability, reliability, and safety, with an implied warranty as to performance. It is not surprising that global firms seek to make explicit their product's merits in these areas.

The other critical aspect of marketing is *rapid product development*. Products that get to the market on time, even if they exceed development costs by 50 percent, eventually earn only 4 percent less than those that are on time and within budget. In contrast, product-development projects that are six months late to market, even if within budget, earn a third less than those that are on time. The clear lesson is that in rapidly changing market environments—that is, the high-technology product field—it is more important to be on time. Firms around the world have been focusing attention on rapid product-development efforts, on rapid prototyping.[13] Using sequential methods such as making models and mock-ups, stereolithography, subsystems prototypes, and finally full production prototypes allow for faster product development while also integrating the new product with other interrelated aspects such as equipment acquisitions and supplier development.[14]

Overall, global marketing may be becoming more centralized, particularly in functions such as product selection and positioning in key country markets, standardized packaging, and uniform pricing. We should recognize, however, that the swing from decentralization to greater central control is cyclical, a reaction to the opportunities posed by regional integration and emerging markets. It is just as likely that in a few years decentralization will become all the rage.[15]

Organization

Global marketing requires people to implement plans, and coordinating their activities is of paramount concern. Companies have to balance the desire to centralize activities at headquarters and at regional centers against the demand for local autonomy and the desire of governments that the company be responsive to local concerns. Companies therefore have to determine which activities need centralized direction and which would benefit from scale economies. Sensitivity to local concerns will shape the extent of decentralization.

An organization that can respond quickly must necessarily have few layers of management and be less hierarchical. The use of teams, greater autonomy for lower levels of the organization, and widespread dissemination of information and in-house expertise throughout the organization can speed up the response capability of the global organization.

Companies also need an organization conducive to managing strategic alliances, where the interests of two or more separate companies must be meshed and reconciled. When two major multinationals such as Siemens and IBM become partners in a major venture to produce 64-megabit DRAMS, both parties will want control. In practice, control will be shared. How should such shared-control structures be designed, however? What does centralization mean in such a context? Trust, shared goals, and informal communications are at least as important in such instances as the formal organization that is imposed.

Similarly, as the organization becomes global, a global network of personal contacts becomes important. An illustration of this fact comes from Chrysler's reentry into Europe. Chrysler had to leave Europe in the mid-1970s because of financial problems. In 1986, when it decided to sell in Europe again, it first called on an ex-Chrysler employee who was heading up Ford's operations in Europe. Next, it contacted all the auto distributors that had been selling Chrysler products in the 1970s. Through this network, it was able to find qualified people and in some cases, finance their entry into business as Chrysler distributors in Europe. Personal contacts allowed Chrysler to put in place a distributor organization spanning Germany, France, Switzerland, Holland, and Belgium within a short period of time, ready for the launch of the Plymouth Voyager wagon and the Jeep Cherokee.[16]

Control

Going global requires greater attention to performance evaluation in order not to fritter away scarce resources in unpromising markets and on failing products. The major issue here is to allow for long-term thinking rather than be swayed by short-term results and setbacks. U.S. publicly held firms have the unfortunate problem of being in the grip of pension fund managers' obsession with quarterly earnings progression. Yet they cannot compete against long-term–oriented German and Japanese companies unless budgets and reward systems focus on long-term results. One proposal, put forth by Peter Drucker, is the use of a **futures budget,** amounting to about 10 percent of total expenses, that seeks to build and preserve a company's long-term competitiveness. Such a futures budget would neither be cut in bad times nor raised because results are good.[17] The concept is one that exemplifies the innovation in control systems that will be required to ensure that global marketing plans are not crippled by unrealistic budget expectations.

Innovation is also needed in the area of marketing measurements, such as in the development of product profitability analysis. Here the goal is to derive a product's contribution after adjusting for factors such as margins, amount of time product is in inventory, the shelf space that it takes up, its share of direct advertising costs, direct service and warranty costs, and so forth. Modeling in domestic marketing is fairly advanced, and similar efforts will be of great help in the global arena.

Global Information Systems

Without constantly updated information from global markets, the company is driving in the dark without lights. The technological advances in point-of-sale systems, the use of scanners, and the availability of global computer networks that link factories, warehouses, salespeople, and retail establishments all allow a firm to get timely information on the evolution of demand and customer tastes. Such systems allow responsive pricing, facilitate just-in-time purchasing systems with suppliers, and guide the product-development process. The use of EDI (electronic data interchange) with suppliers dispenses with paperwork and speeds up order transmission direct from the factory floor as production progresses. Such EDI systems are beginning to be used at ports and by customs authorities in countries such as Singapore to speed up product flow into and out of the country and to reduce bureaucracy. These systems also allow error-free application of tariffs and checks for compliance with documentation requirements.

When tied to the service network, an analysis of recurring product problems allows for better design and manufacturing. Such systems are needed to allow a firm to customize its production for individual customers and to compete on the basis of variety rather than mass production. Information systems can build up customer histories, and these databases can be accessed to develop relationship marketing, with directed marketing appeals to narrow segments of customers. Without detailed customer histories, such advances are not possible. Information is a strategic weapon, and in global marketing, it can give a firm the competitive edge.

In sum, companies must compete globally. They must strive to be different from their competitors, and a focus on marketing and its linkages to the rest of the firm is essential to global marketing success.

The "Green" Consumer

Green consumers, earth-conscious consumers, save-the-dolphins consumers, recycling-preaching children, the Rio summit on the environment—all are signs pointing to a major revolution in consumer consciousness, particularly in developed country markets. How does this green movement affect marketing? Some examples follow:

- *White paper products have become unpopular.* Because the manufacture of white paper uses chlorine bleaches, "natural" is in; Melitta's natural brown coffee filter is a best seller.

- *Negative connotations of excess packaging.* Refill packages offered by The Body Shop, and superconcentrated laundry detergents are examples of products that assure consumers that solid waste disposal is being controlled.

- *Acceptance, even approval, of recycled goods.* Burger King advertises that its paper carryout bags are being made from recycled paper, enhancing their appeal to consumers.

- *A preference for durable rather than disposable goods.* To reduce garbage, consumers are willing to trade some convenience for durable goods.

The green movement means that marketers have to re-examine materials, packaging, pricing, product formulations, advertising appeals, and even use of profits to appeal to the green consumer.[18] Walley and Whitehead[19] sound a cautionary note, however, as they point out that easy fixes to make a company green may have all been attended to, but that future choices may involve being more environmentally conscious at the expense of value destruction. That is, meeting environmental regulations may render certain activities uneconomic to the point that they are no longer carried out, with the loss of both jobs and profits. The principal reason why this might happen is increasingly onerous regulations—U.S. environmental costs are expected to be about 2.5 percent of GDP by the year 2000, as compared to 0.9 percent in 1972. There are 40 U.S. environmental laws in force as compared to five in 1972. To avoid value destruction, the authors suggest breaking down environmental issues into three categories: strategic, operational, and technical.

Strategic decisions are those that fundamentally affect the ability of the company to be competitive and continue as a going concern. In such matters, firms can consciously choose to shape events, such as influencing the nature of regulations enacted, as well as to develop an optimal response to such laws by reallocating resources and redesigning production processes. Operational issues are those in which management has little discretion in responding to the laws, and the goal is to minimize expenditures to maximize environmental impact. Technical decisions are those in which managerial discretion varies, and the financial consequences are not large, although the cumulative impact of the decisions in total could be considerable. Here the managerial job is to develop detailed information, a sort of environmental cost accounting so that compliance can be ensured in an economically efficient manner.

Such an integrated approach to environmental matters is illustrated by the example of Daimler-Benz.[20] The starting point is its environmental code, consisting of several tenets:

1. "Preserve the natural foundations of life."

2. Minimize environmental strain by fostering environmentally compatible products and processes.

3. "Inform candidly" by providing pertinent comprehensive information on the environmental impact of its plants, processes, and products.

4. "Involve every employee" through continual training and consultation.

5. Appoint chief environmental officers who are independent of operating management and report directly to the chairman of the board or to the president of each of the four corporate units' boards of management.

To fulfill these principles, Daimler-Benz has developed an environmental information system to gather data on energy, hazardous materials, emissions, effluents, and wastes at the plant level and at the corporate unit level. Results of its environmentally sensitive product development efforts include:

- Research on zero emission fuel-cell technology as a source of electric power. The goal is to develop small cells that can combine hydrogen and oxygen into electricity to power an automobile. Daimler-Benz expects that it will be 20 years before an economic and viable fuel cell will be available.

- The use of biofilters to reduce odor in metal foundry exhausts. Three vat-shaped biofilters contain moist wood chips inoculated with microbes that absorb the exhaust and convert it into heat, carbon dioxide, water, and cellulose, thereby deodorizing air by up to 75 percent, and scrubbing 240,000 cubic meters of it per hour.

- The replacement of high-performance plastics in parts such as vehicle moldings with natural fibers such as flax. Sisal, flax, and coconut fiber are used in Mercedes-Benz cars in interior door panels, head rests, rear shelves, and insulating mats.

- A "green design" approach to the product life cycle. This methodology takes environmental considerations into account in all stages of a product's life, as set out in Table 19–5.

TABLE 19-5	Green Design at Daimler-Benz

Stage of Product Cycle	Green Design Considerations
Development	Design to use fewer materials, less energy, natural components
Manufacture	Focus on raw materials, components, energy use; control of wastes and emissions
Use	Operating materials, energy use, spare parts, emissions, disposal of faulty and worn parts, packaging
Recycling, disposal	Collection, recovery of materials, recycling, waste

As can be seen from Daimler-Benz's example, an integrated approach that stretches across the company is necessary if a firm desires an economically viable green policy. In other words, green marketing cannot be separated from other aspects such as manufacturing, use by the customer, and eventual disposal.

The Aging Consumer

The developed world market is getting older. In the 1990s, more than 20 percent of the population will be 60 years or older in the European Community, Japan, and Austria. Over the period 1990 to 2000, the age group 70 to 74 years old will increase by 41 percent in the EU. These are consumers with considerable disposable incomes. Industries that will benefit include health care, convenience items, premium-priced quality products, and financial services.

At the opposite end of the spectrum in developing countries are an increasing working-age population and rising levels of personal consumption expenditure. The highest rate of consumption expenditure growth over 1987 to 1991 occurred in Taiwan (56.5 percent), South Korea (47 percent), and Malaysia (47 percent). Thus, as marketers target the world market, opportunities in the developed country markets will be significantly different from those in newly industrializing countries.[21]

Women in International Marketing

As more females enter the business world, they face the problem that the business environment is a male world outside the United States, and that appropriate roles for females vary according to culture. Moslem countries such as Saudi Arabia represent one extreme in which religious law forbids females from associating with unrelated males. This can result in a situation such as U.S. businesswomen being asked to leave officially sponsored trade shows, being denied visas, and being prevented from traveling alone in those countries.

At the other extreme, foreign males in business may be unwilling to treat females as their peers and refuse to accept their status in business. This may lead to lost orders because females are not being taken seriously. Jan Eddy, founder of a software company, had to have male executives offer discounts to an Australian distributor, although she—not the males—had the responsibility for approving the discount request. Foreign countries are changing and as more females in their environments enter business, men are likely to be more tolerant of the businesswomen from overseas. Such change is slow in coming, however, and small consolation to the hard-driving female executive.[22]

As Table 19–6 indicates, because of cultural and country-specific differences, women participate in the work force in varying degrees and at varying levels around the world. In Japan, for example, women are not expected to work after

	Japan	United States	Sweden	Mexico
TABLE 19–6 Working Women around the World				
Percent of work force that is female	41	46	50	37
Percent of all women aged 20–64 in work force	64	65	85	40
Percent of managerial jobs held by women	9.4	43[a]	17	NA
Women's wage as percent of men's	62	76	77	68
Female-headed businesses, including self-employed	30	30	NA	16
Working mothers with children under age 7	10	42	22	NA

[a]Includes executive, administrative, and managerial jobs.
Source: "Women in Business: A Global Report Card," *The Wall Street Journal,* July 26, 1995.

about age 30 and are likely to be laid off or put on part-time status if their employer runs into trouble.

A perennial issue is the availability of child care. Sweden has some of the most liberal child care in the Western world, with parents eligible for a year-long paid parental leave, as well as a government-guaranteed right to work part-time for up to 12 years after the child's birth. In consequence, women are more likely to take time off to be with their children, interrupting their careers and falling behind their male counterparts. Managers express the concern that as women spend more time at home with their families, they may become less ambitious about work, balancing it more easily with the satisfactions of a family and home.[23] It is an interesting and open question whether executive women, in the United States or elsewhere, put careers in a position of primary importance.

Ethical Considerations in International Marketing

Under-the-table discounts, shoddy merchandise, false advertising claims, and a lack of respect for overseas consumer rights are examples of unethical international marketing. Cultural differences about what is acceptable behavior, the attitude that lower standards are acceptable in foreign markets, and lack of immediate supervision can lead to ethical problems.

Ethical dilemmas in international marketing are exemplified by the unfair trade complaint filed by the U.S. Cigarette Export Association. Thailand has a state-run tobacco monopoly, which bans imported cigarettes. The U.S. association claims that such a ban deprives U.S. companies of a fair share of the Thai market, with an estimated size of $750 million. However, some U.S. representatives and antismoking lobbyists do not believe that Thailand should be punished for resisting U.S. cigarettes. The logical result of this view would be that U.S. antismoking laws help preserve the Thai monopoly, channeling revenue from smoking principally to Thai suppliers, rather than attempting to prevent people from smoking and ruining their health.

Salespeople will be quick to point out that bribes are necessary to win orders in some cultures, where it is customary to grant gifts to speed up approvals, and that U.S. standards of ethical behavior cannot and should not be applied in other cultures, especially in developing nations. Yet this is a slippery road to travel, and corporations are best off sticking to a uniform code of ethics worldwide. For example, because smoking is increasingly being regarded with disfavor in the United States, it would be unethical to encourage cigarette export to other countries.[24]

Given that the United States was the birthplace of scientific management, it is not surprising that it has also given rise to an ethics audit, designed to create "the moral organization." KPMG Peat Marwick wants to sample, test, and measure ethics process management, concentrating on the risks that a corporation's lawyers are most afraid of: sexual harassment, environmental contamination, antitrust infractions, corrupt foreign payments (bribery), fraudulent financial reporting, and racial discrimination problems.[25] These problems can arise as much in the global marketing function as in other parts of the organization. A more interesting question is whether these ethical "problems" are likely to be seen as such elsewhere in the world. Or is ethics simply a matter of the legal situational context varying across countries, depending on what is defined as illegal and likely to attract legal sanctions?

A different sort of ethical dilemma is the condemnation heaped on Royal Dutch Shell for not using its influential position in Nigeria to save human-rights activist Ken Saro-Wiwa from being hanged. (Shell pumps about half of Nigeria's oil and earns about $300 million a year in profits from its Nigerian activities.) Mr. Saro-Wiwa, a member of the Ogoni tribe, a small minority of 500,000 people in a country of 100 million, had tried to improve the lot of his ethnic group by getting access to some of the oil revenues from oil extracted from Ogoni lands in the Nigerian delta. A militant accused of murdering his political opponents, he was hastily tried and executed. Shell defended its position in full-page ads throughout Europe indicating that it would not pull out of a $4 billion LNG project with the Nigerian government because such a move would hurt Nigerians working on the project and withhold benefits from the local economy. Shell may have little to do with the facts of the case, but the incident highlights the delicate role that major foreign multinationals must play when they invest in emerging nations.[26]

As we enter the new millenium, we should remember that consumers will continue to exercise their prerogatives and whims. They will be more aware consumers, more knowledgeable and wealthier. Marketing to the world will continue to be of importance, but require greater diligence, tact, and knowledge.

> They denied that the Moon was Stilton;
> they denied that she was even Dutch.
> They denied that Wishes were Horses;
> they denied that a Pig had Wings.
> So we worshipped the Gods of the Market
> Who promised these beautiful things.
>
> *Rudyard Kipling*
> *The Gods of the Copybook Headings*

ENDNOTES

1   "Pity Those Poor Japanese," *The Economist,* December 24, 1988.

2   "Japan's Consumer Boom: The Pricey Society," *The Economist,* September 9, 1989.

3   P. Cecchini, *The European Challenge: 1992, the Benefits of a Single Market* (Brookfield, VT: Gower Publishing, 1989).

4   See, for example, "Lace at $300 a Yard," *Forbes,* October 23, 1989; and "French Luxury Firms Are Merging, Turning into Big Multinationals," *The Wall Street Journal,* December 28, 1987.

5   "Enron in India: Pioneer Takes the Flak," *Business Asia,* April 11, 1994; and "Enron of U.S. Settles India Power Dispute," *The Wall Street Journal,* January 9, 1996.

6   Louis T. Wells and Eric Gleason, "Is Foreign Infrastructure Investment Still Risky?" *Harvard Business Review,* September–October 1995, 44–55.

7   M. T. Burr, "The Two Paitons," *Independent Energy,* July–August 1995.

8   Kim B. Clark, "What Strategy Can Do for Technology," *Harvard Business Review* November–December 1989.

9   The fact that technology cannot be the basis of long-term competitive advantage does not mean that patent protection is not a strategic weapon. See Robert J. Thomas, "Patent Infringement of Innovations by Foreign Competitors," *Journal of Marketing,* October 1989.

10 "IBM Joins with Siemens AG to Develop Advanced Chips, Hoping to Share Risk," *The Wall Street Journal,* January 25, 1990.

11 Ralph E. Gomory, "From the 'Ladder of Science' to the Product Development Cycle," *Harvard Business Review,* November–December 1989.

12 "The Year of the Brand," *The Economist,* December 24, 1988.

13 H. Kent Bowen, K. Clark, C. Holloway, and S. Wheelwright, *The Perpetual Enterprise Machine: Seven Keys to Corporate Renewal through Successful Product and Process Development,* The Vision Group, 1994.

14 Tom Peters, "Do It Now, Stupid!" *Forbes ASAP,* August 28, 1995.

15 *The Changing Global Role of the Marketing Function* (New York: The Conference Board, 1995).

16 Michael Hammes, "Chrysler Kommt! Re-establishing a Brand in Europe," *The Journal of European Business,* January–February 1990.

17 Peter Drucker, "The Futures That Have Already Happened," *The Economist,* October 21, 1989.

18 Jacquelyn Ottman, "Consumer Attitude Shifts Provide Grist for New Products," *Marketing News,* January 4, 1993.

19 Noah Walley and B. Whitehead, "It's Not Easy Being Green," *Harvard Business Review,* May–June 1994, 46–52.

20 Daimler-Benz, *Environmental Report, 1995,* Stuttgart, Germany, 1995.

21 "Consumers in the 1990s: Older, Richer, and More Numerous," *Business International,* April 1, 1991.

22 Barbara Marsh, "Gender Gap," *The Wall Street Journal,* October 16, 1992.

23 "Sweden: Laws Help Mom, but They Hurt Her Career," *The Wall Street Journal,* July 26, 1995.

24 "Thais Gain Help of U.S. Smoking Foes in Fight to Keep Out Foreign Cigarettes," *The Wall Street Journal,* September 19, 1989.

25 "This Auditing Team Wants You to Create a Moral Organization," *The Wall Street Journal,* January 19, 1996.

26 See "After the Hangings," 41–42, and "Nigeria Foaming," 15–16, *The Economist,* November 18, 1995. Also, "Shell Boldly Defends Its Role in Nigeria," *The Wall Street Journal,* November 27, 1995.

FURTHER READINGS

"Oriental Renaissance: A Survey of Japan." *The Economist,* July 9, 1994.

Bowen, H. Kent, K. Clark, C. Holloway, and S. Wheelwright. *The Perpetual Enterprise Machine: Seven Keys to Corporate Renewal Through Successful Product and Process Development.* The Vision Group, 1994.

The Changing Global Role of the Marketing Function. New York: The Conference Board, 1995.

"Women in Business: A Global Report Card." *The Wall Street Journal,* July 26, 1995.

Daimler-Benz. *Environmental Report, 1995.* Stuttgart, Germany: 1995.

Gucci

Gucci in 1996

Since Gucci's acquisition by the investment bank Investcorp in 1993, sales have doubled. Gucci, embroiled for years in family feuding, seems to have improved its management and created a new sense of styling, backed up by innovative advertising and promotion.

Gucci's overhaul took place in the context of rapid growth in luxury goods sales during the 1993–1995 period. This growth may have been fueled by the rise in international demand, and may also reflect baby boomers' renewed desire to stuff their closets with easily recognizable status symbols.[1] According to Gucci CEO William Franz, "The luxury of quality is modern. And we're seeing a real resurgence in the luxury goods business now because I think people are responding to quality more than ever before. People really want to put quality and beauty back into their lives."[2]

The Company

Gucci is one of the world's leading designers, producers, and distributors of high-quality personal luxury accessories and apparel. It is one of the best recognized and most prestigious luxury brands in the world. Gucci's products include handbags, small leather goods, luggage, shoes, ties, scarves, ready-to-wear, eyewear, and perfume. Gucci manufactures a small portion of its leather goods, with the majority manufactured by third parties. The company directly operates 63 stores in major markets throughout the world. Products are also sold through 75 franchise stores, 74 duty-free boutiques, and 60 leading department and specialty stores.

Gucci has experienced growth in net revenues across all the company's product categories, distribution channels, and geographic markets. Net revenues grew 87.1 percent in the first half of fiscal 1995 to $206.2 million, as compared with $110.2 million for the first half of fiscal 1994. Annual net revenues grew 30 percent in fiscal 1994 to $263.6 million as compared with $202.9 million for fiscal 1993.[3] (See Tables 1–4.)

Company Background/History

Gucci was founded in 1923 as a sole proprietorship by Guccio Gucci. The company designed, produced, and sold exclusive

leather products. As its reputation in the Italian marketplace grew in the 1930s and 1940s, flagship stores were opened in major Italian cities, including Rome and Milan.

In 1953, following Guccio's death, ownership of the family business passed to his three sons. Under their management, the company began to expand internationally into the United States, France, England, and Hong Kong. As a result of this expansion, Gucci became known as one of the first truly global luxury brands.

By the late 1970s, ownership and management of Gucci broadened to the third generation of the Gucci family. During these years, despite the business's success, a series of shareholder conflicts arose among family members. By the mid-1980s, these conflicts erupted into a broadly publicized series of lawsuits that adversely affected the company.

In 1987, Bahrain-based Investcorp International, the secretive investment group bankrolled by Gulf Arabs, was enlisted by Maurizio Gucci, 50 percent owner of the company, to acquire the remaining 50 percent ownership interest. Investcorp, Maurizio hoped, was going to help end the shareholder conflicts among family members and restore the company to its former prominence among the world's elite retailers.

But as 1993 dawned, serious conflicts became apparent between Maurizio and Investcorp regarding Maurizio's role in the management and implementation of the company's strategy. Investcorp claimed that Gucci had wasted money with his lavish management style, breached contracts, and failed to return the company to profitability. For his part Gucci claimed that "Investcorp is a collection of ruthless financiers who want short-term gains but do not care about long-term strategy."[4] This conflict disrupted management continuity. By September 1993, Investcorp acquired Maurizio's 50 percent interest in Gucci, and Maurizio resigned as the chief executive officer and chairman of the company.

Gucci's Product Lines

The company's mission is "the continuing development of a profitable, growing luxury business worldwide through the continuing restoration and enhancement of the Gucci brand."[5] To accomplish this mission, the company seeks to have a diverse and popular product line.

Design   The heart of Gucci is design and style. Tom Ford, the creative director of Gucci, studied at the Parsons School of Design in New York City and went to work for Perry Ellis

TABLE 1	Combined Statement of Income Data

	Fiscal				First Half Fiscal	
	1991	1992	1993	1994	1994	1995
	(in Millions, Except per Share Data, Ratios, and Other Data)					
Amounts in accordance with IAS						
Net revenues	$208.0	$198.6	$202.9	$263.6	$110.2	$206.2
of which royalties	25.1	24.6	25.1	25.5	10.0	12.4
Cost of goods sold	99.1	84.3	82.8	95.5	43.2	70.2
Gross profit	108.9	114.3	120.1	168.1	66.9	136.0
Selling, general, and administrative expenses	150.6	143.9	115.9	136.6	60.6	93.9
Operating profit (loss)	(41.7)	(29.6)	4.3	31.5	6.4	42.1
Income (loss) before income taxes	(49.0)	(31.7)	(21.2)	19.0	5.2	33.1
Net income (loss)	(46.4)	(32.3)	(22.8)	17.3	4.7	24.8
Net income (loss) per share	$ (1.03)	$ (0.72)	$ (0.51)	$ 0.38	$ 0.10	$ 0.55

Source: Gucci Prospectus, 1995, 12.

TABLE 2	Combined Balance Sheet Data

	Fiscal				July 31, 1995	
	1991	1992	1993	1994	Actual	As Adjusted
	(in Millions, Except per Share Data, Ratios, and Other Data)					
Amounts in accordance with IAS						
Cash and cash equivalents	$ 9.8	$ 12.8	$ 22.6	$ 38.5	$ 51.0	$ 69.3
Working capital	42.8	38.8	4.4	4.8	(1.0)	25.9
Total assets	258.1	213.2	180.2	197.5	251.6	265.9
Debt						
Third parties	73.3	93.2	85.8	26.3	9.7	9.7
Related parties	2.0	1.6	1.3	228.5	251.4	0.0
Accumulated deficit	(32.9)	(65.3)	(88.1)	(202.0)	(177.2)	(177.2)
Shareholder's equity (deficit)	$ 90.4	$ 48.5	$ 15.0	$(142.5)	$(126.8)	$142.9

Source: Gucci Prospectus, 1995, 12.

TABLE 3	Ratios and Other Data					
			Fiscal		*First Half Fiscal*	
	1991	*1992*	*1993*	*1994*	*1994*	*1995*
	(in Millions, Except per Share Data, Ratios, and Other Data)					
Gross margin	52.4%	57.6%	59.2%	63.8%	60.8%	66.0%
Operating margin	(20.0)%	(14.9)%	2.1%	11.9%	5.8%	20.4%
Capital expenditures	$9.8	$6.5	$3.8	$4.5	$1.8	$3.1
Directly operated stores at period end	82	71	66	62	65	63

Source: Gucci Prospectus, 1995, 12.

TABLE 4	Net Revenue by Product Category (In Millions)				
		Fiscal		*First Half Fiscal*	*First Half Fiscal*
	1992	*1993*	*1994*	*1994*	*1995*
Leather goods	$80.8	$81.3	$110.6	$44.3	$103.4
Shoes	21.9	24.4	38.8	15.7	36.9
Ties and scarves	19.7	20.7	22.7	10.7	15.1
Ready-to-wear	31.6	33.5	44.4	19.1	25.7
Watches	11.8	9.9	11.3	4.9	6.2
Other	8.2	8.0	10.3	5.5	6.5
Royalties	24.6	25.1	25.5	10.0	12.4
Net revenues	$198.6	$202.9	$263.6	$110.2	$206.2

Source: Gucci Prospectus, 1995, 24.

America. When Dawn Mello came to work for Gucci in 1989, one of her first acts was to hire Tom Ford. Mello and Ford carefully studied the archive of Gucci designs before deciding to revive its classic Gucci loafer. That choice marked the beginning of the restoration of Gucci's lost lustre. Today, five primary designers work under Ford's direction. Together, they are responsible for the design of the company's core product categories as well as Gucci ready-to-wear. For each new collection, the team's goal is to develop a well-defined concept that establishes the feel, direction, and image for the collection. Ford created a sensation with his Fall 1995 and Spring 1996 collections, resulting in explosive sales growth.

He was honored in 1995 by the Council of Fashion Designers of America and VH1 Television for his innovative work.[6]

Ford and his team utilize Gucci's extensive archives as valuable inspiration for new or redesigned products, such as the revamped classic Gucci loafer and the bamboo handle bag. (See Exhibits 1 and 2.) Core products are the heart of Gucci and always will be; restyling keeps the products interesting and maintains the Gucci image. About his current designs, Ford states, "As a culture we are rapidly running through the second half of the 20th century. And for some reason we have to go back and relive it. But when we do, it's different. There's an underlying cynicism, a kitsch quality, an

EXHIBIT 1   Gucci Loafer

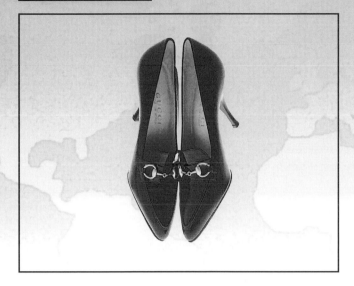

Source: Gucci Prospectus, 1995.

EXHIBIT 2   Gucci Bamboo Handle Bag

Source: Gucci Prospectus, 1995.

edge, a certain sinister feeling, because our society has become somewhat sinister. That's why when, for instance, you take a shoe from 1973 and pants from 1968 and combine them with hair from 1995, it is all put together in a slightly harder way."[7]

In addition to working directly with the design team and the product managers, Ford ensures quality and consistency through redesigning stores and supervising the 11 collections that appear in the stores. As for merchandise, every sample—women's and men's clothing, neckties, shoes, bags, belts, gloves, scarves, luggage, housewares, even candles and key rings—eventually comes across his desk. In addition, Ford controls advertising and public relations. (See Table 5.)

Manufacturing Gucci's manufacturing process is similar to that of other luxury goods manufacturers. Most of Gucci's leather goods suppliers are located in the Tuscany region of Italy and many work exclusively for Gucci. Gucci purchases the leather required for the production of leather goods, cuts it, and provides it to suppliers, who manufacture the products and return them to the company for distribution. Certain elements of the process, such as bending of bamboo and hand stitching, are labor intensive and require skilled craftsmanship. Gucci employs approximately 2,000 workers and intends to increase that number and work with them to increase productivity.

Gucci uses 18 shoe manufacturers who produced over 30,000 units each in 1995 versus 14 manufacturers who produced 11,000 units each in 1993. Gucci maintains a close relationship with its shoe suppliers, all of whom are located in Italy. Gucci also has eight suppliers of ready-to-wear, and five suppliers of ties and scarves. In addition, the company has 30 suppliers of gifts and jewelry.

Handbags Gucci's original business was the design, manufacture, and distribution of fine handbags. Today, they remain one of the most highly recognized luxury handbags in the world and one of the company's key products. Gucci presents approximately 80 classic styles and 60 new fashion-oriented styles per collection. Some of the more popular classic handbags include A-frame and bamboo handle bags, as well as knapsacks and bamboo, hobo, and dome handbags. The fashion handbag collection includes the Avant Garde, Bridal, Cosmopolitan, and Vernice lines. Prices range from $255 to $10,800.

Small Leather Goods and Luggage Small leather goods consist of ladies' and men's wallets, card cases, belts, and cosmetic cases, and utilize many of the same colors, materials, and motifs used in the handbag collection. This collection has over 250 styles, with 140 introduced since 1994. Prices range from $65 to $1,990. Luggage is another popular Gucci item, with prices ranging from $150 to $4,695.

TABLE 5	Division of Functions between Gucci and Its Business Partners				

Functions	*Leather Goods*	*Shoes*	*Ties/Scarves*	*Ready-to-Wear*	*Watches*
Collection Concept	Gucci	Gucci	Gucci	Gucci	Licensee/Gucci
Product Design	Gucci	Gucci	Gucci	Gucci	Licensee/Gucci
Product and Prototype Development	Gucci	Supplier/Gucci	Supplier/Gucci	Licensee	Licensee
Technical Advice	Gucci	Gucci	Gucci	Licensee	Licensee
Vendor Selection	Gucci	Gucci	Gucci	Gucci	Licensee
Production	Gucci/Supplier	Supplier	Supplier	Licensee	Licensee
Quality Control	Gucci	Gucci	Gucci	Licensee/Gucci	Licensee

Source: Gucci Prospectus, 1995, 40.

Shoes Gucci's shoe collection is probably best known for the horse bit loafer, although the collection offers 150 styles each year. Because the horse bit loafer represents 40 percent of shoe sales, emphasis has been placed on extending the line to include a silver and half horse bit. Overall, Gucci loafers have always been known for their quality, comfort, elegant styling, and, in the ladies' collection, an array of colors. Prices range from $160 to $1,050.

Ties and Scarves As with all Gucci products, ties and scarves are known for meticulous quality. The ties are hand folded and finished, and are distinctive for their attention to detail and use of color. Ties and scarves are design and color coordinated with Gucci's ready-to-wear, handbags, and shoes. Prices range from $95 to $395.

Ready-to-Wear Every year Gucci offers two major ladies' and men's ready-to-wear collections, as well as a cruise collection. These collections feature 60–80 new styles based on high-quality materials, such as silks, leather, cashmere, and knits. Prices range from $600 to $2,000.

Watches The Gucci watch line was one of the first luxury brand watches introduced into the international market and enjoys a leading position in that market. Severin Montres has been the Gucci watch licensee for the past 20 years. The Gucci watch line offers over 30 styles with prices ranging from $195 to $8,650.

Other Gucci sells a variety of personal items, including key chains, money clips, cuff links, and silver pens, as well as a wide variety of tableware and giftware. Prices range from $25

to $495. Gucci eyewear was introduced in 1987 and currently has 70 styles. Prices range from $95 to $250. The Gucci perfume line consists of "Eau de Gucci," "Gucci No. 3," "Accenti," and "Nobile." Retail prices range up to $228 per ounce.

Distribution Channels

Gucci distributes its products through directly operated stores, franchise stores, duty-free boutiques, and department and specialty stores. The core distribution channel for Gucci is its directly operated stores, which accounted for 70 percent of net revenues in fiscal 1994 (see Table 6).

Directly Operated Stores Gucci's stores include flagship stores located in premier retail sites throughout the world, as well as shop-in-shops located in prestigious locations, such as Harrod's in London and Isetan in Tokyo. In addition, all of Gucci's directly operated stores in Japan are located in premier department stores as is customary in the Japanese market.

Gucci has been attempting to offer a wider product assortment, better merchandising, enhanced customer service, and improved delivery and order times. Plans are in place to refurbish flagship stores in New York, Paris, and Rome, as well as 10 other directly operated stores, and to open 16 new stores during the next three years, including seven new stores located in major department stores in Japan.

Franchise Stores Currently, 75 Gucci stores are being operated by 37 franchises in smaller markets or in markets where Gucci believes it does not have sufficient local expertise or where, for governmental reasons, it would be impractical to

TABLE 6	Net Revenue by Distribution Channel (Millions of Dollars)				
		Fiscal		*First Half Fiscal*	*First Half Fiscal*
	1992	*1993*	*1994*	*1994*	*1995*
Directly Operated Stores	$134.9	$137.7	$183.7	$73.4	$153.3
Franchise Stores	24.4	17.5	20.4	10.7	16.6
Duty-Free Boutiques	6.9	7.1	11.2	5.5	10.1
Department and Specialty Stores	0.0	0.0	2.1	0.3	6.1
Other	7.8	15.5	20.7	10.3	7.7
Royalties	24.6	25.1	25.5	10.0	12.4
Net Revenues	$198.6	$202.9	$263.6	$110.2	$206.2

Source: Gucci Prospectus, 1995, 24.

establish directly operated stores. For example, in the Far East the Company has franchise stores in Guam, Indonesia, Malaysia, the Philippines, Singapore, South Korea, Taiwan, and Thailand. Merchandise assortments, store image, window display, and service standards are constantly monitored.

In general, Gucci's franchise agreements provide for the right to operate a specified number of Cucci stores or bou tiques in specified locations, and require the franchisee to sell Gucci products exclusively, purchased from Gucci, and licensed products purchased from Gucci's licensees. The Company's franchise agreements have a limited duration, with an initial term generally not in excess of five years, and stipulate the conditions of operation and merchandise assortments.

Duty-Free Boutiques A limited range of Gucci products are distributed through 74 duty-free boutiques operated worldwide by 28 companies. These boutiques provide Gucci with a strong sales channel for certain of its core products (handbags, small leather goods, ties, and scarves).

Department and Specialty Stores Between 1991 and 1994, Gucci stopped selling through department and specialty stores. Beginning in 1994, Gucci began selectively reentering those stores that offered image and merchandising expertise that Gucci required for the presentation of its products.

Geographic Areas

Luxury Goods Consumers As shown in Table 7, the main markets for luxury goods are North America, Japan, the Far East, and Europe.

The Asian Luxury Goods Market The current demand for luxury goods in Asia is very high, with many brands, including Gucci and Chanel, achieving a cult-like status among teenagers. According to Yukio Yanbe, chief economist at DKB Research Institute, "Increases in bonus money and overtime pay have been having a positive effect on consumption."[8] The Japanese economy has finally entered a recovery period and people are buying luxury goods again. The most impressive indications are in apparel sales. For many years, Japanese consumers dropped Gucci and Versace for discount labels. Now, however, many consumers seem to be moving back to high-priced brands. In 1995, sales increased 20 percent over 1994 in the Chanel, Louis Vuitton, and Hermes clothing lines in Japan.[9] Due to the importance of the Japanese market, Gucci added seven new stores to be located in major department stores in Japan.

The popularity of these luxury brands among teenagers, while significantly increasing sales, has also caused a rise in counterfeit products. Many teenagers cannot afford the real thing and are turning to cheaper fakes. For example, some 80 percent of Chanel tote bags bought by Japanese consumers are counterfeits.[10]

Luxury Goods Marketing

To promote a highly focused and consistent image throughout its international markets, Gucci has centralized control. To ensure consistency of image, Gucci produces all the creative materials for its campaigns. All worldwide marketing activities, including advertising, public relations, special events, and window display, are managed from Gucci's offices in

TABLE 7	**Net Revenue by Geographic Markets (Millions of Dollars)**				
	Fiscal			*First Half Fiscal*	*First Half Fiscal*
	1992	*1993*	*1994*	*1994*	*1995*
United States	$69.6	$66.8	$87.4	$34.8	$70.9
Italy	21.1	20.0	27.6	11.6	23.4
Europe (excluding Italy)	19.6	20.6	25.4	10.9	17.3
Japan	31.6	34.9	49.2	21.0	48.0
Far East (excluding Japan)	20.9	21.4	30.8	12.2	25.9
Rest of the World	11.2	14.1	17.7	9.7	8.3
Royalties	24.6	25.1	25.5	10.0	12.4
Net Revenues	$198.6	$202.9	$263.6	$110.2	$206.2

Source: Gucci Prospectus, 1995, 24.

Florence. The company's marketing strategy is designed to maintain a high profile and consistent visibility on international, national, and local levels, thus enabling Gucci to strengthen its position as a leading, worldwide, luxury goods brand. In addition, advertising and communication programs aim to reaffirm Gucci's leadership in leather goods, increase awareness of its merchandise range, and establish its authority as a leading luxury goods and fashion brand. Gucci has increased its total advertising and communications expenditures from $5.9 million in fiscal 1993 to $11.7 million in fiscal 1994, and expects to spend $26 million in fiscal 1995. The Company plans to continue increasing its spending on advertising and communications.[11]

Advertising The timing of media placements is carefully coordinated with product deliveries, international fashion calendars, and buying seasons in an effort to ensure that placement maintains the Gucci image and reaches potential customers at the most appropriate time. Advertising is placed mainly in national and international fashion, lifestyle, and business magazines, with newspapers used for store openings and other short-term marketing objectives. (See Exhibit 3.)

Catalogs The recent surge in catalog use comes mainly from direct marketing to existing and prospective customers. The company believes that increasing the utilization rate of its catalogs is an effective way to increase sales of Gucci products, enhance the Gucci image, and promote customer loyalty.

Public Relations A team of public relations professionals based in London, Milan, New York, Paris, and Tokyo is supplemented with select outside professionals. Efforts target the fashion press, such as national fashion magazines and trade publications. In addition, the company stages four ready-to-wear shows annually in Milan. These shows present a unique opportunity for Gucci to assert its style and quality leadership and to obtain coverage and endorsements from the fashion press.

Organizational Structure

In 1994, the company reorganized its management structure and appointed managers responsible for each of its product categories worldwide. (See Table 8.) As part of that change, Domenico De Sole was named as the company's president and CEO in July 1995. Prior to this appointment, De Sole was president and CEO of Gucci America, Inc., from 1984 to1994; from October 1994 until his appointment in 1995, he was COO of Gucci.

Robert Singer joined Gucci as the CFO in September 1995. Prior to this appointment, Singer served for over eight years as an audit partner and, since 1994, a member of the managing committee of Coopers and Lybrand, Italy. As the audit partner he was responsible for the Gucci account from October 1993 until he was appointed CFO.

Brian Blake was named president and CEO of Gucci America, Inc., in November 1994. Blake has been with Gucci

EXHIBIT 3   Full Page Gucci Ad, 1996

TABLE 8	**Executive Officers of Gucci, 1996**	

Name	*Position*	*Age*
Domenico De Sole	President and Chief Executive Officer	51
Robert Singer	Chief Financial Officer	43
Brian Blake	President and Chief Executive Officer, Gucci America, Inc.	39
Claudio Degl'Innocenti	Director of Integrated Logistics	41
Tom Ford	Creative Director	33
Marco Franchini	General Manager of European Retail	39
Jean Klee	Director of Pacific Region	49
Arthur Leshin	Group Controller	48
Patricia Malone	Director of Merchandising and Sales	41
Mario Massetti	Director of Legal Affairs and Administration	43
Renato Ricci	Director of Human Resources	50
Richard Swanson	Director of Strategic Planning	38
Enrico Ziliani	General Manager of Franchise, Duty Free, and Distribution	43

Source: Gucci Prospectus, 1995, 52.

America since 1987, serving in a number of positions, including general manager of the New York store, vice-president of wholesale operations, and senior vice-president of retail operations. Prior to joining Gucci, he was with Lord & Taylor from 1977 to 1987 as a merchandise buyer and later as the managing director of two of its stores.

Tom Ford was appointed creative director of Gucci in April 1994 and is responsible for product design, image, advertising, and visual display. Ford began his career with Gucci in 1990 as the company's chief ladies' ready-to-wear designer and later was appointed design director. Prior to joining Gucci, Ford was the design director of Perry Ellis Women's America Division from 1988 to 1990 and senior designer of Cathy Hardwick from 1986 to 1988.[12]

Competition in the Luxury Goods Market

Gucci faces substantial competition in all product categories and markets. The company competes with such well-known, high-quality, international luxury goods companies as Chanel, Ferragamo, Hermes, Louis Vuitton, and Yves Saint Laurent. Gucci believes it competes primarily on the basis of brand image, product design, reputation for quality, and product assortment. Some of Gucci's most intense competition comes from the following luxury goods companies:

Louis Vuitton This corporation has essentially two products—champagne and leather goods; the latter is in direct competition with Gucci. LVMH has the advantage of being able to leverage its strong champagne market even at times when Louis Vuitton may suffer setbacks. It competes mainly with Gucci in luggage and handbags.

Chanel Chanel competes with Gucci in ready-to-wear, leather goods, and other fashion items. It carries product lines very similar to those of Gucci. Its marketing challenge is to rethink marketing strategy in response to changing industry trends without tampering with the legend that Chanel has built over 100 years. In addition, Chanel is realizing that using the same name, packaging, and advertising globally does not always work. The company has experienced this firsthand in Asia.

Ferragamo Ferragamo manufactures elegant men's and ladies' shoes, ready-to-wear, silk scarves, leather bags, luggage, robes, and ties. The company competes with Gucci on most product lines.

YSL In January 1993, Elf Sanofi, a pharmaceutical company, acquired YSL (formerly Yves St. Laurent). In general, the couture houses in Paris that experienced a designer licensing boom beginning in the 1970s have now lost their leadership position. Although France remains the capital for servicing fashion, it now must compete with designers from Germany, Italy, the United Kingdom, the United States, and Japan.

Hermes Hermes, a luxury goods company with more than 50 stores worldwide, competes with Gucci in several product lines, including silk scarves and ties.

Counterfeiting of Luxury Goods and Trademark Infringement

Sales of counterfeit luxury merchandise have been on the rise over the past several years. Gucci and its competitors all experience trademark infringement and have attempted to control counterfeiting. Fake Louis Vuitton luggage and Chanel handbags are among the most popular items. In addition, fashion knockoffs tend to hit stores before the originals do, thanks to spies, FedEx, and fax machines. These look-alike, cheaper fashions are not usually in danger because U.S. trademark law protects only distinctive styles. It is difficult to prevent knockoffs, which do not masquerade as the real thing. Many retailers sell designer fakes to an unknowing public. Consumers who purchase what they believe to be the real thing in a department store do not get what they pay for. As a result of the flourishing counterfeit trade, the luxury goods manufacturers are suffering a loss in brand image.

The courts and the companies are attempting to deal with this situation. For example, in June 1994, a federal judge held that landlords can be held liable for trademark infringement carried out by their tenants if they had reason to know about it.[13] In addition, Chanel strives to protect products from being duplicated outside the country by limiting purchases of handbags to no more than three per foreign visitor.[14] Due to the importance of trademarks to the business, Gucci prosecutes trademark infringement vigorously. The company employs investigators in many parts of the world to report cases of infringement. Licensees, local distributors, and franchisees also report any infringement that they might identify. Gucci believes that these actions have been successful, although it is impossible to estimate the extent of counterfeiting, the amount of lost revenue, or the extent of any other damages suffered by Gucci as a result of counterfeiting.[15]

The Future of Gucci

What does the future hold for Gucci, the company that has become the talk of the luxury goods industry? It is difficult to speculate, but there appear to be several challenges that the company will have to consider if it desires to maintain its success into the next century: (1) how to maintain quality and prices while limiting volume; (2) how to plan for Asian and Latin American markets; (3) whether to extend product lines and licensing directions; and (4) how to monitor new competition from Asia, specifically Hong Kong, Taiwan, and Japan. If Gucci is able to keep abreast of these challenges and is able to retain Tom Ford's creative genius, the company should be able to continue surprising the luxury goods industry with its creativity.

Questions

1. What is Gucci's formula for marketing luxury goods?
2. Where are the growth markets for luxury goods likely to be in the future? How should Gucci plan for such market trends?
3. Can luxury goods marketing be standardized? What would you recommend to Gucci regarding the product-line assortment, promotions, and advertising in its major markets in Asia, Latin America, North America, and Europe?
4. Are there any generalizations that can be drawn from the luxury goods industry for global marketing of consumer products?

Endnotes

1. Linda Bird, "Retailing: Tired of T-shirts and No-name Watches, Shoppers Return to Tiffany and Chanel," *The Wall Street Journal,* September 6, 1995, B1, 3.
2. Sara Gay Fordon, "Keeping the Gucci in Gucci," *Daily News Record,* January 2, 1995, 20.
3. Gucci Prospectus, October 23, 1995, 34.
4. Peter Truell, "Legal Battle Wears on Gucci's Image—and Operations," *The Wall Street Journal,* August 6, 1995, B4.
5. Gucci Prospectus, October 23, 1995, 35.
6. Brooke Hayward, *Elle,* March 1996, 262.
7. Ibid., 263–264.
8. Akira Ikeya, "Spending Gives Momentum to Recovery," *The Nikkei Weekly,* February 5, 1996, 1.
9. "Trendy Clothing Purchases Lead Pickup in Retail Sector," *The Nikkei Weekly,* October 9, 1995, 3.
10. Emiko Terazono, "Craze for Chanel Causes Concern," *The Financial Times Limited,* November 4, 1995, 20.
11. Gucci Prospectus, October 23, 1995, 45.
12. Gucci Prospectus, 1995, 52–53.
13. Andrea Gerlin, "Legal Beat: Trademark Infringement," *The Wall Street Journal,* June 23, 1994, B9.
14. Warren-Walsh Brown, "The Bag Limit Is Three," *Washington Post,* August 13, 1990, 3.
15. Gucci Prospectus, October 23, 1995, 46.

Case prepared by Professor Ravi Sarathy, with the research assistance of Heather Sopczynski, for use in class discussion. 1996, all rights reserved.

Credits

Figure 1.1: Excerpted from "Annual Attendance for Amusement Parks in Western Europe," *The New York Times*, August 23, 1995, C-19. Reprinted with permission. **Table 1.5:** "Foreign Sales of U. S. Multinational Corporations, 1997," *Forbes,* July 27, 1998. Reprinted by permission of Forbes Magazine © Forbes, Inc., 1997. **Table 2.4:** "Central Europe and the Newly Independent States of the USSR," from *1998 World Bank Atlas*, 24, 25. (Washington, DC: World Bank, 1998). **Table 3.1:** "The World's Most Populous Nations," from *1998 World Bank Atlas*, 24, 25. (Washington, DC: World Bank, 1998). **Table 3.3:** "Per Capita Income," from *1998 World Bank Atlas*, 38. (Washington, DC: World Bank, 1998). **Table 3.4:** "Per Capita Income Measured Two Ways," *1998 World Bank Atlas*, 42, 43. (Washington, DC: World Bank, 1998). **Table 3.5:** "Countries with Gross National Product over $100 Billion," *1998 World Bank Atlas*, 42, 43. (Washington, DC: World Bank, 1998). **Table 3.6:** "Share of Agriculture in Gross Domestic Product, 1998," from *World Development Indicators 1998* (Washington, DC: World Bank, 1998), 12–14, 180–182. **Table 3.7:** "Energy Consumption Per Capita," *World Development Report 1998/99* (Washington, DC: World Bank, 1998), 224, 225. **Table 3.10:** "U.S. Firms Operating in Selected Foreign Countries, 1975 and 1996," from *Directory of American Firms Operating in Foreign Countries*, 8th & 13th eds. (New York: UniWorld Business Publications, 1975, 1994). **P. 134:** "Disney as Cop," from *Business Asia*, September 23, 1991, 329. Reprinted with permission of Business International Asia/Pacific, Ltd., Hong Kong. **Figure 6.3:** Susan P. Douglas and C. Samuel Craig, "Evolution of Global Marketing Strategy," *Columbia Journal of World Business,* vol. 24, no. 3 (Fall 1989). Copyright © 1989. Reprinted with permission. **Figure 6.4:** Szymanski et al., "Standardization versus Adoption of International Marketing Strategy," *Journal of Marketing*, vol. 57 (October 1993), 4. Reprinted with permission of the American Marketing Association. **Table 6.3:** "Global Marketing Strategy Choices" adapted from John Quelch and E. Hoff, "Customizing Global Marketing," *Harvard Business Review* (May–June 1986). Copyright © 1986 Harvard Business School Press. All Rights Reserved. **Figure 7.2:** Excerpted from "Investing in Neglected Stocks," *The Wall Street Transcript*, July 31, 1995, 119, 364. Reprinted with permission. **Figure 7.4:** "A Conceptual Framework for Assessing the Country-of-Origin Influence" from Saeed Samiee, "Customer Evaluation of Products in a Global Market," *Journal of International Business,* 25, no. 3 (1994), 587. Copyright © 1994 Association for Education in International Business. **P. 234:** Melissa Malhame, "The National Trade Data Bank: A Valuable Resource for Exporters," from *Business America*, April 1991. U. S. Department of Commerce. **Figure 8.1:** "A Testable Framework of Product and Promotion Adaptation" from S. T. Cavusgil, Shaoming Zou, and G. M. Naidu, "Product and Promotion Adaptation in Export Ventures: An Empirical Investigation," *Journal of International Business,* 24, no. 3 (1993), 485. Copyright © 1993 Association for Education in International Business. **Figure 8.2:** "An Eclectic Framework of the Entry Mode Choice" from W. Chan Kim and Peter Hwang, "Global Strategy and Multinationals' Entry Mode Choice," *Journal of International Business,* 23, no. 1 (1992), 33. Copyright © 1992 Association for Education in International Business. **Table 8.2:** "A Perspective on Branding" from Sak Onkvisit and John J. Shaw, "The International Dimension of Branding," *International Marketing Review* 6, no. 3 (1989), Table 1.24. Copyright © 1989 Association for Education in International Business. **Table 8.4:** H. Takeuchi and M. Porter, "Three Roles of International Marketing in Global Strategy," in *Competition in Global Industries*, M. Porter, ed. (Cambridge, MA: Harvard Business School Press, 1985), 140. Reprinted with permission. **Table 9.1:** "Market Characteristics and Product-Line Strategies," from Warren J. Keegan, "Multinational Product Planning: Strategic Alternatives," *Journal of Marketing* (January 1969). Reprinted with permission of the American Marketing Association. **Figure 9.4:** Raymond Vernon and Louis T. Wells, Jr., *Manager in the International Economy*, 5th ed. (Upper Saddle River, NJ: Prentice-Hall, 1986), 83. Reprinted by permission of Prentice-Hall, Inc. **Figure 9.5:** "Example of the Product Life Cycle: U.S. Music Sales (Millions of Units)," from *The Economist*, December 23, 1995, 78. Reprinted with permission. **Table 9.7:** "Consumer Product Export Opportunities to Liberalizing LDCs: A Life-Cycle Approach" from Kate Gillespie and D. Alden, "Consumer Product Export Opportunities to Liberalizing LDCs," *Journal of International Business Studies* (Spring 1989). Copyright © 1989 Association for Education in International Business. **Figure 9.7:** "Merck's R&D Planning Model" from Nancy Nichols, "Scientific Management at Merck," *Harvard Business Review* (January–February 1994), 95. Copyright © 1994 Harvard Business School Press. All Rights Reserved. **Case 13.2:** "Eberhard Faber's Special Forms of Promotion," from *Fortune*, November 1982. Reprinted by permission of Fortune Magazine © 1982 Time Inc. All rights reserved. **Figure 14.5:** "Merck's Revenue Hedging Model" from Nancy Nichols, "Scientific Management at Merck: An Interview with CFO Judy Lewent," *Harvard Business Review* (January–February 1994), 96. Copyright © 1994 Harvard Business School Press. All Rights Reserved. **Figure 15.2:** "The Export–Prefinancing Method of Countertrade," from "Countertrade," *Business Eastern Europe*, January 17, 1994. Reprinted with permission of Business International S.A., Geneva. **Figure 15.3:** Reprinted from "The Dos and Don'ts of International Countertrade" by Joseph R. Carter and James Gagne. *Sloan Management Review*, (Spring 1988), by permission of the publisher. Copyright © 1988 by Sloan Management Review Association. All rights reserved. **Figure 16.1:** "A Contingency Model of Sustainable Competitive Advantage in Service Industries," from Bharadwaj et al, "Sustainable Competitive Advantage in Service Industries: A Conceptual Model and Research Propositions," *Journal of Marketing* (October 1993), 85. Reprinted with permission of the American Marketing Association. **Table 17.5:** "Global Marketing Strategy Implementation: Headquarters' Role" adapted from John Quelch and E. Hoff, "Customizing Global Marketing," *Harvard Business Review* (May–June 1986). Copyright © 1986 Harvard Business School Press. All Rights Reserved. **Table 17.6:** Reprinted from "Headquarter's Influence and Strategic Control in MNCs" by Yves L. Doz and C. K. Prahalad. *Sloan Management Review*, (Fall 1981), by permission of the publisher. Copyright © 1981 by Sloan Management Review Association. All rights reserved.

Subject Index

Caste system
  elements of, 111
  Hinduism and, 103, 108
Catholics, 105
Central American Common Market, 52, 136
CETSCALE, 221
Change, attitudes toward, 109–110
China
  advertising regulations in, 140, 463
  arbitration in, 143
  dolls for children in, 14–15
  economic growth in, 708
  entry strategies for, 376
  exchange controls in, 561, 562
  insurance market in, 613–614
  language use in, 96
  marketing strategy and, 156–158
  multinational companies in, 66
  piracy in, 135
  population growth in, 65
  price controls in, 139
  product liability law in, 139
  product strategies in, 334–335
  retailing in, 607
  selling telecommunications in, 596–597
  toy market in, 233
  trade restrictions with, 126–127
  U.S. investment in, 82, 83
  wholesalers in, 417
China Daily, 468
Christianity, 106
CIF quotes, 413, 533
Civil law, 137
Class groupings, 111
Climate, 75
Cluster analysis, 227–229
CNN, 469
Coaches, 657
Code law, 137
Codes of conduct, 136
Cold chain, 431
Commercial infrastructure, 78

Commercial News USA, 497
Commercial policy
  exchange control and, 45–46
  explanation of, 44
  nontariff barriers and, 46
  quotas and, 45
  tariffs and, 44–45
Common law, 137
Common markets, 53–54
Common territory, 111
Communications
  with distributors, 414
  market potential and, 77–78
Communications media
  distribution of, 80
  market potential and, 77
Comparative advantage
  explanation of, 40, 565
  service industries and, 592–594
  shifts in, 164
Comparative analysis
  advertising and, 472
  explanation of, 226
  for international planning, 639–640
Competition. *See also* Global competition
  advertising and, 450
  elements of global, 712, 713
  market entry and, 330
  marketing research and, 214–215
  pricing and, 522–524, 559, 564–566
  product line and, 320–321
  product policy and, 274
Competitive advantage
  achievement of, 160–161
  explanation of, 155–156
  service industries and, 594, 595
  sources of, 713–714
  strategies for, 156–157
Competitive audits, 330, 331
Competitive-parity approach, 471–472
Competitive risk, 536
Computer industry
  Apple and, 188–190
  globalization of, 186–188
  price-bundling for software and, 525–526
Computer-Readable Databases (Gale Research), 235
Conciliation, 142
Configuration, of value-added chain, 165–166
Confucianism, 105
Congo, 95
Consignment, 540
Consultation, 47
Consumer behavior
  cultural differences in, 220–221
  marketing research models and, 239
  need to understand, 110
  religiosity and, 242, 243
  types of, 222
Consumers. *See also* Customers
  age of, 720
  marketing to green, 718–720
  new-product development and, 298, 299
Continental Europe (Dunn & Bradstreet), 238
Contract manufacturing, 391–392
Control
  budget and, 663–664
  future outlook and, 717–718
  global networks and, 699–701
  information systems and, 664–666
  measurement techniques and, 663
  methods in, 662–663
  organization and, 663

steps in, 662
subsidiaries and, 664
Controllers, 657
Convention on Contracts for the International Sale of Goods, 132
Cooperation in exporting
  explanation of, 381
  export trading companies and, 382
  piggyback exporting and, 383–385
  Webb-Pomerene association and, 381–383
Cooperative advertising, 476–477
Copier industry, 306–309
Copyright laws, 267
Core competencies, 300, 301
Corporate goals
  choice of markets and, 178–179
  global marketing strategy and, 170–175
Counterpurchase, 571
Countertrade
  creativity in, 572–573
  explanation of, 503–505, 570–571
  forms of, 571–572
  implementation of, 573–574
  payment streams and, 574–575
Country managers, 657–659
Country of manufacture (COM), 240, 241
Country-of-origin effects
  explanation of, 240–241
  product standardization and, 255
Credit, promotional aspects of, 494–495
Credit-card market
  in Europe, 328–330
  overview of, 611–612
Cross-patrolling, 168
Cross-section comparison approach, 223, 224
Cuba, 38, 126
Cultural analysis, 90–91
Cultural differences
  bribery and, 721
  credit use and, 329
  international marketing and, 93–94
  marketing research and, 218–221, 240
  personal selling and, 485–486
  product adaptation and, 258
  product diffusion rate and, 228–229
  services and, 591–592
Culture
  aesthetics and, 98–100
  attitudes and values and, 108–110
  case examples, 115–117
  education and, 100–102
  elements of, 91
  explanation of, 90
  language and, 94–98
  material, 91–94
  religion and, 102–108
  social organization and, 110–113
Currency
  inconvertibility of, 561–562
  leasing and, 576–577
Customers. *See also* Consumers
  global, 169
  global linkages with, 681–684, 690–693
  identifying needs of, 4–5
  loyalty of, 274–275, 590
  satisfying global, 5
  sensory segmentation of, 301–302
Customer service level, 434
Customs unions, 53
Data Base Directory (Knowledge Industry Publications), 235
Database marketing, 678
Debit cards, 329–330